A SUPPLEMENTARY CATALOGUE
OF

SANSKRIT, PALI AND PRAKRIT BOOKS

IN THE

LIBRARY OF THE BRITISH MUSEUM

A SUPPLEMENTARY CATALOGUE
OF

SANSKRIT, PALI AND PRAKRIT BOOKS

IN THE

LIBRARY OF THE BRITISH MUSEUM

ACQUIRED DURING THE YEARS 1892-1906

COMPILED BY

L. D. BARNETT, M.A. LITT. D.
KEEPER OF THE DEPARTMENT OF ORIENTAL PRINTED BOOKS AND MSS.

GYAN

Published by

Gyan Publishing House
5, Ansari Road
Daryaganj, New Delhi-110002
Phone: 011-47034999, 9811692060
E-mail: books@gyanbooks.com

Distribution Network
gyanbooks.com
India, USA, Canada, UK, Australia, France

ISBN : 978-81-212-2269-3 (PB)
First Published, 1908

2nd Impression 2021

Printed at: Gyan Press, Delhi.

Sanskrit, Pali and Prakrit Books
in the
Library of the British Museum
Compiled by: L. D. Barnett

A SUPPLEMENTARY CATALOGUE
OF
SANSKRIT, PALI, AND PRAKRIT BOOKS
IN THE
LIBRARY
OF THE
BRITISH MUSEUM

ACQUIRED DURING THE YEARS 1892-1906.

COMPILED BY

L. D. BARNETT, M.A., LITT.D.

KEEPER OF THE DEPARTMENT OF ORIENTAL PRINTED BOOKS AND MSS.

PRINTED BY ORDER OF THE TRUSTEES OF THE BRITISH MUSEUM

London:

SOLD AT THE BRITISH MUSEUM;

AND BY

MESSRS. LONGMANS & CO., 39, PATERNOSTER ROW; BERNARD QUARITCH, 11, GRAFTON STREET, NEW BOND STREET; ASHER & CO., 13, BEDFORD STREET, COVENT GARDEN; AND HENRY FROWDE, OXFORD UNIVERSITY PRESS WAREHOUSE, AMEN CORNER.

1908

PREFACE.

As is implied by its title, the present volume is a supplement to the "Catalogue of Sanskrit, Pali, and Prakrit Books in the British Museum" compiled by the late Professor Bendall, and in essentials follows the principles observed in that work. In a few points, however, it has been found advisable to depart from them. Thus the reader will now find all the works of the Pali Canon arranged according to their places under the three headings *Abhidhammapiṭaka*, *Suttapiṭaka*, and *Vinayapiṭaka*, instead of being distributed into some twenty sometimes overlapping articles. Similarly the various recensions in which the grammars of Pāṇini and Kachchāyana are taught are here all brought together under the respective headings *Pāṇini* and *Kachchāyana*, in strict observance of the rules of the General Catalogue of the Museum Library.

Owing to the number of Burmese titles occurring in this Catalogue, it has been necessary to draw up a definitive scheme for the transliteration of Burmese vernacular sounds. As is well known, Burmese has undergone very great phonetic changes since the Pali language and alphabet were introduced. Thus *itthi*, *aṅga*, *vijjā*, *paṭichcha*, *samuppāda*, are now pronounced *eikti*, *inga*, *weikzā*, *padeiksa*, *thamôkpāda*. In the case of Pali words such phonetic eccentricities may be disregarded here. But in transliteration of vernacular words our guide must be the living pronunciation of educated society; and accordingly the following rules have been laid down for them, corresponding in the main to those formulated in the official "Tables for the Transliteration of Burmese into English" (Rangoon, 1896, 1898).

I. The representation of *open* vowels is as follows:—

အဲ	*è*	ေအာ	*aw*
အို	*o*	ေအာ်	*aw̱*

The other vowels are represented as in the case of Pali.

II. The representation of *consonants* is as follows :—

ခ	*hka*	ဌ	*hṭa*	ဘ	*hba*
င	*nga*	[ဎ	*hḍa*]	မှ	*hma*
စ	*sa*	ထ	*hta*	ရ	*ya*
ဆ	*hsa*	[ဓ	*hda*]	ရှ	*sha*
ဇ	*za*	နှ	*hna*	သ	*tha*
ဈ	*hza*	ဖ	*hpa*	လှ	*hla*

The remaining consonants are transliterated in the same manner as in Pali words.

III. The representation of *closed* vowels and the consonants immediately following them is according to the subjoined scheme :—

အက်	*et*	အစ်	*it*	အိန်, အိမ်	*ein*
အိုက်	*aik*	အည်	*i, in, aý*	အုန်, အုမ်	*ôn*
အောက်	*auk*	အတ်	*at*	ကွတ်, ကွပ်	*kût*
အင်	*in*	အိတ်, အိပ်	*eik*	ဝတ်, ဝပ်	*wût*
အိုင်	*aing*	အုတ်, အုပ်	*ôk*	ကွန်, ကွမ်	*kûn*
အောင်	*aung*	အန်	*an*	ဝန်, ဝမ်	*wûn*

In other cases the transliteration is as in Pali words.

IV. Whereas in actual pronunciation the tenues between vowels and after nasals are pronounced as soft, their transliteration follows the spelling; *e.g.* တောင်ပန် is written as it is spelt, *taung-pan*, though pronounced *taung-ban*.

For the transliteration of the various other characters used in this volume the reader is referred to the subjoined Table. Among them is included the Grantham, which hitherto, I believe, has never appeared in European books.

In conclusion I have to express my sincere thanks to Professor J. F. Blumhardt for much generous help in our common tasks.

L. D. BARNETT.

TABLE OF TRANSLITERATION.

NAGARI, GUJARATI, BENGALI, TAMIL, TELUGU, CANARESE, MALAYALAM, GRANTHAM, SINHALESE, AND BURMESE-PALI ALPHABETS.*

	Nag.	Guj.	Beng.	Tam.	Tel.	Can.	Mal.	Granth.	Sin.	Burm.-Pali.
a	अ	અ	অ	அ	అ	ಅ	അ	𑌅	අ	အ
ā	आ	આ	আ	ஆ	ఆ	ಆ	ആ	𑌆	ආ	အာ
i	इ	ઇ	ই	இ	ఇ	ಇ	ഇ	𑌇	ඉ	ဣ
ī	ई	ઈ	ঈ	ஈ	ఈ	ಈ	ഈ, ൗ	𑌈	ඊ	ဤ
u	उ	ઉ	উ	உ	ఉ	ಉ	ഉ	𑌉	උ	ဥ
ū	ऊ	ઊ	ঊ	ஊ	ఊ	ಊ	ഊ	𑌊	ඌ	ဦ
ṛi	ऋ	ઋ	ঋ	—	ఋ	ಋ	ഋ	𑌋	ඍ	—
e	ए	એ	এ	எ	ఎ	ಎ	എ	𑌏	එ	ဧ
ai	ऐ	ઐ	ঐ	ஐ	ఐ	ಐ	ഐ	𑌐	ඓ	—
o	ओ	ઓ	ও	ஒ	ఒ	ಒ	ഒ	𑌓	ඔ	ဩ
au	औ	ઔ	ঔ	ஔ	ఔ	ಔ	ഔ	𑌔	ඖ	—
ka	क	ક	ক	க	క	ಕ	ക	𑌕	ක	က
kha	ख	ખ	খ	—	ఖ	ಖ	ഖ	𑌖	ඛ	ခ
ga	ग	ગ	গ	—	గ	ಗ	ഗ	𑌗	ග	ဂ
gha	घ	ઘ	ঘ	—	ఘ	ಘ	ഘ	𑌘	ඝ	ဃ
ṅa	ङ	ઙ	ঙ	ங	ఙ	ಙ	ങ	𑌙	ඞ	င
cha	च	ચ	চ	(ச)	చ	ಚ	ച	𑌚	ච	စ
chha	छ	છ	ছ	—	ఛ	ಛ	ഛ	𑌛	ඡ	ဆ

* For transliteration of Burmese *vernacular* sounds see the Preface.

TABLE OF TRANSLITERATION.—(*Continued.*)

	NAG.	GUJ.	BENG.	TAM.	TEL.	CAN.	MAL.	GRANTH.	SIN.	BURM.-PALI.
ja	ज	જ	জ	—	జ	ಜ	ജ	𑌜	ජ	ဇ
jha	झ	ઝ	ঝ	—	ఝ	ಝ	ഝ	𑌝	ඣ	ဈ
ña	ञ	ઞ	ঞ	ஞ	ఞ	ಞ	ഞ	𑌞	ඤ	ဉ
ṭa	ट	ટ	ট	ட	ట	ಟ	ട	𑌟	ට	ဋ
ṭha	ठ	ઠ	ঠ	—	ఠ	ಠ	ഠ	𑌠	ඨ	ဌ
ḍa	ड	ડ	ড	—	డ	ಡ	ഡ	𑌡	ඩ	ဍ
ḍha	ढ	ઢ	ঢ	—	ఢ	ಢ	ഢ	𑌢	ඪ	ဎ
ṇa	ण	ણ	ণ	ண	ణ	ಣ	ണ	𑌣	ණ	ဏ
ta	त	ત	ত	த	త	ತ	ത	𑌤	ත	တ
tha	थ	થ	থ	—	థ	ಥ	ഥ	𑌥	ථ	ထ
da	द	દ	দ	—	ద	ದ	ദ	𑌦	ද	ဒ
dha	ध	ધ	ধ	—	ధ	ಧ	ധ	𑌧	ධ	ဓ
na	न	ન	ন	ந	న	ನ	ന	𑌨	න	န
pa	प	પ	প	ப	ప	ಪ	പ	𑌪	ප	ပ
pha	फ	ફ	ফ	—	ఫ	ಫ	ഫ	𑌫	ඵ	ဖ
ba	ब	બ	ব	—	బ	ಬ	ബ	𑌬	බ	ဗ
bha	भ	ભ	ভ	—	భ	ಭ	ഭ	𑌭	භ	ဘ
ma	म	મ	ম	ம	మ	ಮ	മ	𑌮	ම	မ
ya	य	ય	য (য়)	ய	య	ಯ	യ	𑌯	ය	ယ
ra	र	ર	র	ர	ర	ರ	ര	𑌰	ර	ရ
la	ल	લ	ল	ல	ల	ಲ	ല	𑌲	ල	လ
va	व	વ	ব	வ	వ	ವ	വ	𑌵	ව	ဝ
ṣa	श	શ	শ	ச	శ	ಶ	ശ	𑌶	ශ	—
sha	ष	ષ	ষ	ஷ	ష	ಷ	ഷ	𑌷	ෂ	—
sa	स	સ	স	—	స	ಸ	സ	𑌸	ස	သ
ha	ह	હ	হ	—	హ	ಹ	ഹ	𑌹	හ	ဟ
ḷa	ळ	ળ	—	ள	ళ	ಳ	ള	𑌳	ළ	ဠ

TABLE OF CONTENTS.

SUPPLEMENTARY CATALOGUE

OF

SANSKRIT, PALI, AND PRAKRIT BOOKS.

A. (S.) Notes . . . on the Sanskrit Entrance Course [of the University of Calcutta]. 1891-92. In the form of question and answer. Compiled . . . by S. A. pp. 60. *Calcutta,* 1891. 12°.
14085. b. 39.

ĀBĀJĪ VISHṆU KĀTHAVAṬE. Report on the Search for Sanskrit Manuscripts in the Bombay Presidency during the years 1891-2, 1892-3, 1893-4, 1894-5, *etc.* pp. i. 21, i. 121. *Bombay,* 1901. 8°.
14096. cc. 12.

ĀBDIKĀRĀDHANAVIDHI. అబ్దికారాధనవిధిః *etc.* [Ābdikārādhanavidhi. A manual for the periodical rites performed by Lingāyat Ṣaivas in honour of the dead.] pp. 28. ఒంగోలు [*Ongole,*] 1897. 8°.
14028. d. 59.(6.)

ABHAYACHANDRA SŪRI. *See* Ṣākaṭāyana. प्रक्रियासंग्रहसहितं शाकटायनव्याकरणम् The Grammar of Śākaṭāyana, with the Prakriyāsaṅgraha commentary of Abhayacandrasūri, *etc.* Vol. i. 1892. 8°.
14093. b. 30.

ABHAYADEVA SŪRI. [For the editions of the Prakrit hymn called Tijayapahutta which are included in the collection styled Navasmaraṇa:] *See* Navasmaraṇa.

ABHAYADEVA SŪRI, *the Navāṅgavṛittikṛit.* *See* Jñātādharmakathā. Specimen der Nâyâdhammakahâ. [Being Ṣrutaskandha I. i., with extracts from the commentary of Abhayadeva,] *etc.* 1881. 8°.
14100. c. 17.(1.)

ABHAYADEVA SŪRI, *the Navāṅgavṛittikṛit (continued).* जयतिहुयण स्तोत्र [Jayatihuaṇa-stotra.] *See* Jainastotraratnākara. जैनस्तोत्ररत्नाकर *etc.* [Jainastotraratnākara.] pp. 72-85. [1901.] 16°.
14100. a. 26.

ABHAYAVARDHANA (H. D.), *Appuhāmi.* *See* Suṣruta. Nidanasthana . . . Translated and edited by H. D. Abhayawardhane Appuhamy, *etc.* 1891. 8°.
14043. e. 25.

ABHIDHAMMAPIṬAKA. อภิธัมมปิฎก *etc.* [Abhidhammapiṭaka.] 11 vols. ๑๑๓ [*Bangkok,* 1894.] 8°.
14098. cc. 29-39.

Forms part of the King of Siam's edition of the Tipiṭaka.

See Hpo min, *Maung.* အဘိဓမ္မာဓာတ်ကျမ်း [Abhidhammā-dhāt-kyan. A Burmese treatise on *rūpa,* based on the Abhidhamma.] [1897.] 8°.
14300. d. 19.(7.)

—— [Second edition.] [1901.] 8°.
14300. d. 32.

See Paṇḍitaddhaja, known as Maingkaing Hsaya. ပိဋကဝိနိစ္ဆယကျမ်း *etc.* [Tipiṭakavinichchhaya-kyan.] 1900-1901. 8°.
14302. i. 19.

Selections.

အဘိဓမ္မာ ၇ ကျမ်း ရွတ် စဉ် *etc.* [Abhidhammā-hku-hnit-kyan-yût-sin. Seven chapters, extracted from the Dhammasaṅgaṇi and other books of the Abhidhamma. Compiled and edited by Shin

B

Dibba.] pp. 43, i. i. မန္တလေး [*Mandalay,*] 1901. 8°. **14098. d. 36.(2.)**

The Machchhachariya (Chariyāpiṭaka **X.**) *is appended.*

DHAMMASAṄGAṆI.

A Buddhist manual of Psychological Ethics of the fourth century B.C. Being a translation, now made for the first time, from the original Pali, of the first book in the Abhidhamma Piṭaka entitled Dhamma-sangaṇi, Compendium of States or Phenomena. With introductory essay and notes by Caroline A. F. Rhys Davids. pp. xcv. 393, i. 1900. *See* ACADEMIES, *etc.*—London.—*Oriental Translation Fund.* New Series V., vol. 12. 1891, *etc.* 8°. **14003. bb. (ser. 5, vol. 12.)**

မာတိကာ၊ဓါတုကထာအကောက် *etc.* [Mātikā-dhātukathā-akauk. The *mātikā* of the Dhammasaṅgaṇi, followed by an epitome of the Dhātukathā, with Burmese commentaries by Aggadhammālaṅkāra Thera and Guṇachāri Thera.] pp. ix. 125. ရန်ကုန် ၁၂၆၀ [*Rangoon,* 1898.] 8°. **14300. d. 5.(4.)**

မာတိကာဓာတုကထာအကော် *etc.* [The *mātikā* of the Dhammasaṅgaṇi and the Dhātukathā, with Burmese exegeses and dissertations thereupon by Tipiṭakālaṇkāra Siriddhaja as transmitted by Varateja, viz. Mātikā-akauk, M°-gaṇṭhi, Dhātukathā-akauk, and Dh°-gaṇṭhi; and followed by two treatises of the same author, viz. Yamaik-gaṇṭhi, upon the Yamaka, and Vithi-let-yo-hmat-pôn, on psychology. Edited by Ū Tissa and Ū Janinda.] pp. ii. 523. ရန်ကုန် ၁၂၆၂ [*Rangoon,* 1900.] 8°. **14098. dd. 23.**

အဘိဓမ္မာငါးစောင်တွဲးကျမ်း *etc.* [Abhidhammā-ngā-saung-twè-kyan. A collection of Burmese treatises, comprising (1) Mātikā-kye-môn, by Chandimā of Sagabin, upon the *mātikā* of the Dhammasaṅgaṇi, with Pali text of the latter; (2) Dhātukathā-hkyo and Dh°-ahpye, by the Dôk-lan Hsaya, treating of the Dhātukathā; (3) Dhātukathā-than-pauk, an epitome of the same, by the Kugyi Hsaya; (4) Tettiṃsama-puchchhāvisajjanā, 33 questions and answers on points suggested by the Abhidhammatthasaṅgaha, by the Salin Hsaya Ketumālābhiddhaja; (5) Devamanussachittaparivattavivādavinichchhaya, comprising the Pali text of the Daḷhadhammadhanuggahasutta (Saṃyuttanikāya, Nidānavagga ix.), with Burmese commentaries by the Sagu Hsaya Paṇḍavālankāra; and (6) Buddhanavamapūjārahavinichchhaya, a treatise on the offerings to the Nine Buddhas, by the Maungdaung Hsaya Paññāsāmi.] pp. xi. 419. မန္တလေး [*Mandalay,*] 1900. 8°. **14300. e. 14.**

See ACADEMIES, *etc.* — London. — *Pali Text Society.* BUDDHAGHOSA. The Atthasālinī, Buddhaghosa's commentary on the Dhammasaṅgaṇi, *etc.* 1897. 8°. **14098. b. 36.(1.)**

See BUDDHAGHOSA. [*Aṭṭhasālinī.*] အဋ္ဌသာလိနီ *etc.* [Aṭṭhasālinī.] [1901.] 8°. **14098. dd. 22.**

DHĀTUKATHĀ.

The Dhātu kathā pakaraṇa and its Commentary. Edited by Edmund Rowland Gooneratne. 1892. 8°. *See* ACADEMIES, *etc.*—London.—*Pali Text Society.* ABHIDHAMMAPIṬAKA. **14098. b. 29. (3.)**

ဓာတုကထာ *etc.* [Dhātukathā. With Burmese exegeses entitled Dh°-akauk and Dh°-gaṇṭhi, by Tipiṭakālaṅkāra Siriddhaja.] *See* above, DHAMMASAṄGAṆI. မာတိကာ *etc.* [The *mātikā* of the Dhammasaṅgaṇi, *etc.*] [1900.] 8°. **14098. dd. 23.**

ဓါတုကထာအကောက် [Dhātu-kathā-akauk. An epitome of the Dhātukathā, with Burmese commentary.] *See* above, DHAMMASAṄGAṆI. မာတိကာ၊ဓါတုကထာအကောက် *etc.* [Mātikā-dhātukathā-akauk.] pp. 97-125. [1898.] 8°. **14300. d. 5.(4.)**

KATHĀVATTHU.

Kathāvatthu. Edited by Arnold C. Taylor. 1894-1897. 8°. *See* ACADEMIES, *etc.*—London.—*Pali Text Society.* ABHIDHAMMAPIṬAKA. **14098. b. 32.(2.)**

Kathā Vatthu. [The heads of chapters of the Kathāvatthu, with translation and notes.] *See* DAVIDS (T. W. RHYS). Schools of Buddhist Belief, *etc.* 1892. 8°. [*Journal of the Royal Asiatic Society.*] **Ac. 8820/3 and 2098. a. b.**

ABHIDHAMMAPIṬAKA (*continued*).

PAṬṬHĀNA.

တိကပဋ္ဌာန်းပါဠိတော် [Tika-paṭṭhāna.] Pt. i., pp. 201. မော်လမြိုင် ၁၂၅၄ [*Maulmein*, 1893.] 8°. **14098. c. 67.**

Contains the portion corresponding to pp. 1—197 *in the edition of Bangkok*, 1894.

ပဋ္ဌာန်းသုံးချက်စု (ပဋ္ဌာန်းပစ္စည်းပြိုင်, ပဋ္ဌာန်းရာသီစု). Paṭṭhāna-thôn-hkyet-su, Paṭṭhāna-pachchaya-pyaing, and Paṭṭhāna-rāsi-su. Three Burmese dissertations on the Paṭṭhāna.] *See* KALYĀṆĀBHIVAṂSA, *Ū, of Chaungzon-ngay.* ပဋ္ဌာန်းညာဝါဂဏ္ဌိကျမ်း *etc.* [Paṭṭhāna-nya-wā-gaṇṭhi-kyan, *etc.*] 1898. 8°. **14300. e. 17.**

VIBHAṄGA.

See BUDDHAGHOSA. [*Sammohavinodanī.*] ဝိဘင်း . . . အဋ္ဌကထာ *etc.* [Sammohavinodanī. The commentary on the Vibhaṅga.] [1901.] 8°. **14098. dd. 25.**

See ÑĀNAKITTI. අභිධම්ම සම්මෝහවිනොදනී අත්ථයොජනා *etc.* (The Abhidhamma Sammohavinodani Atthayojana. [A gloss upon the Sammohavinodani,] *etc.*) [1893.] 8°. **14098. dd. 5.(2.)**

YAMAKA.

See NANDAMEDHA, *of the Bodhi Kyaung, Tantabin.* ယမိုက်ဆယ်ကျမ်းအရကောက် *etc.* [Yamaik-hsay-kyan-aya-kauk. A Burmese treatise on the Yamaka, illustrated from Pali texts.] 1900. 8°. **14300. e. 16.**

See ÑĀṆINDĀBHI KAVIDDHAJA. ယမကပဋ္ဌါနသာရာဓိပ္ပါယပကာသနီကျမ်း *etc.* [Yamakapaṭṭhānasārādhippāyappakāsanī. Burmese discourses on the Yamaka, *etc.*] 1896. 8°. **14300. d. 4.(2.)**

ABHINANDA, *son of Jayanta.* *See* YOGAVĀSISHṬHARĀMĀYAṆA. A translation of Yoga-Vâsishṭa Laghu—the smaller, *etc.* [Being an abridgment, ascribed to Abhinanda, of the Yogavāsishṭharāmāyaṇa.] 1896. 8°. **14048. cc. 5.**

ABHINANDA, *son of Jayanta* (*continued*). कादम्बरीकथासारः *etc.* [Kādambarīkathāsāra. With a commentary by Nandalāla Ṣarmā, son of Lakshmīnārāyaṇa. Edited by Achintyarāma Ṣarmā.] pp. 173. अमृतसर लवपुरे १९५७ [*Amritsar, Lahore* printed, 1900.] 8°. **14072. d. 44.**

ABHINAVAGUPTA. *See* ĀNANDAVARDHANA, *Rājānaka.* The Dhvanyâloka . . . With the commentary of Abhinavaguptâchârya, *etc.* 1891. 8°. [*Kâvyamâlâ.*] **14072. ccc. 12.(no. 25.)**

ABHINNA NĀYAKA. *See* KĀLIDĀSA.—*Supposititious Works.* କଟପାୟା *etc.* [Kaṭapāyā. Edited with Oriya translation *etc.* by Abhinna Nāyaka.] 1880. 12°. **14053. b. 17.(2.)**

ABHISAMBODHI - ALAṄKĀRA. අභිසම්බොධි අලඞ්කාරය *etc.* [Abhisambodhi-alaṅkāra. A Pali poem of 103 stanzas glorifying the Buddha, with a Sinhalese word-for-word interpretation, both traditionally ascribed to Veḷiviṭa Saranaṅkara.] pp. i. 34, i. [*Colombo*,] 1897. 8°. **14098. ccc. 2.(1.)**

ACADEMIES, *etc.*

ALLAHABAD.

University of Allahabad.

संस्कृत-शिक्षा-विवृतिः . . . Sanskrit-Siksha-Vivriti . . . A complete key to the Sanskrit Siksha, Sanskrit Entrance Course of the Allahabad University. [Comprising word-for-word grammatical analyses of (1) selections from the Hitopadeṣa, Bk. i., (2) selections from the Pañchatantra, (3) the Nītisārasaṅgraha of Chāṇakya, (4) the Hitopadeṣasārasaṅgraha, select stanzas from Hitopadeṣa i., (5) portions of the Ṣāntiparva of the Mahābhārata and of the Bālakāṇḍa of the Rāmāyaṇa. With Hindi and English translations of the texts, and as appendix an outline of rules of metre and a Liṅgānuṣāsana in Hindi, and a table of roots.] By Pandit Kanhaiya Lal Sastri. Third edition. pp. 405, xxii. *Allahabad*, 1899. 12°. **14085. b. 39.(2.)**

AMSTERDAM.

Koninklijke Akademie van Wetenschappen.

Verhandelingen . . . Afdeeling Letterkunde. *Amsterdam*, 1858, *etc.* 8°. **Ac. 944/3.**

New Series began in 1892.

ACADEMIES, *etc.* (*continued*).

BOMBAY.

Bombay Branch of the Royal Asiatic Society.

Catalogue of Manuscripts and Books belonging to the Bhau Daji Memorial [and now in the library of the Bombay Branch of the Royal Asiatic Society]. Prepared under the superintendence of . . . Vishvanáth Náráyan Mandlik and Ardaseer Framjee Moos. pp. i. 147, CLX. *Bombay*, 1882. 8°. **14096. cc. 11.**

BOSTON, *Mass.*

American Oriental Society.

Journal of the American Oriental Society, *etc. Boston, New York and London, New Haven*, 1849, *etc.* 8°. **Ac. 8824.**

CALCUTTA.

Asiatic Society of Bengal.

Journal, *etc. Calcutta*, 1832, *etc.* 8°. **Ac. 8826/11.**

In progress.

Bibliotheca Indica, *etc.* New Series. 1848, *etc.* 8°. **14002. a, b.**

Sanskrit works published in this series since 1892 *are to be found under the following headings :—*

Vol. 133. *Svayambhūpurāṇa.*
,, 134. *Brāhmanas.*—Aitareyabrāhmaṇa.
,, 136. *Jīmūtavāhana.*
,, 139. *Suṣruta.*
,, 140. *Nāgeṣa Bhaṭṭa.*
,, 141. *Khaṇḍadeva.*
,, 142. *Bhāskara Miṣra Bhaṭṭa.*
,, 143. *Merutuṅga Achārya.*
,, 144. *Siddharshi.*
Vol. 145. *Brāhmaṇas.*—Ṣatapathabrāhmaṇa.
,, 146. *Jaimini.*—Mīmāṃsāsūtra.
,, 147. *Gadādhara Rājaguru.*
,, 148. *Piṅgala.*
,, 149. *Govindānanda Kavikaṅkaṇa Bhaṭṭāchārya.*
,, 150. *Mahādeva Sarasvatī.*
,, 151. *Vidyākara Vājapeyi.*

Catalogue of Printed Books and Manuscripts in Sanskrit belonging to the Oriental Library of the Asiatic Society of Bengal. Compiled by Paṇḍit Kunja Vihāri Nyāyabhūṣaṇa under the supervision of Mahāmahopādhyāya Haraprasād Śhāstrī. *Calcutta*, 1899, *etc.* 4°. **14096. dd. 5.**

In progress. On page 259 *begins a catalogue of vernacular works in the same library.*

Report on the Search of Sanskrit [, Prakrit, Maithila, and Bengali] Manuscripts. 1895 to 1900. By . . . Haraprasad Shāstrī. pp. 25. *Calcutta*, 1901. 4°. **14096. dd. 6.**

ACADEMIES, *etc.*

CALCUTTA (*continued*).

Buddhist Text Society of India.

Journal of the Buddhist Text Society of India. Edited by Śarat Ćandra Dás. 1893, *etc.* 8°. **14003. b. 19.**

In progress. The title of this Society was in 1897 *altered to "Buddhist Text and Anthropological Society."*

Buddhist Texts of the Northern and Southern Schools, *etc. Calcutta*, 1894, *etc.* 8°. **14004. c.**

Calcutta Sanskrit College.

A Descriptive Catalogue of Sanskrit Manuscripts in the Library of the Calcutta Sanskrit College. Prepared under the orders of the Government of Bengal by Hṛishíkeśa Śástrí . . . and Śiva Chandra Gui. *Calcutta*, 1892, *etc.* 8°. **14096. cc. 10.**

In progress.

Mahābodhi Society.

Kaccayana's Pali Grammar. Edited in Devanagari character and translated into English [with introduction] by Satis Chandra Acharyya, Vidyabhusana. [With a proem by H. Dharmapāla.] (पालि-व्याकरणम्।) pp. ii. xliii. 383. *Calcutta*, 1901. 12°. **14098. a. 39.**

CAMBRIDGE, *Mass.*

Harvard University.

Harvard Oriental Series. Edited with the cooperation of various scholars by Charles Rockwell Lanman. *Boston, Leipsic*, 1891, *etc.* 8°. **14003. d. 1.**

In progress. The works issued in this series are catalogued under the headings :—

Vol. 1. *Ārya Śūra.*
,, 2. *Kapila.*
,, 3. *Warren (H. C.)*
,, 4. *Rājaśekhara.*

EUROPE.

International Congress of Orientalists.

Transactions of the Ninth International Congress of Orientalists, *etc.* 2 vols. *London*, 1893. 8°. **Ac. 8806. (Session 9.)**

Actes du Dixième Congrès International des Orientalistes. Session de Genève, 1894. 4 pts. *Leide*, 1895-1897. 8°. **Ac. 8806. (Session 10.)**

ACADEMIES, *etc.* (*continued*).

FLORENCE.

Società Asiatica Italiana.

Giornale, *etc.* *Firenze*, 1887, *etc.* 8°. **Ac. 8804.**

In progress.

GERMANY.

Deutsche Morgenlaendische Gesellschaft.

Abhandlungen für die Kunde des Morgenlandes, herausgegeben . . . unter der verantwortlichen Redaktion des Prof. Dr. H. Brockhaus, Bd. 1 (-4; des Prof. Dr. L. Krehl, Bd. 5; des Prof. Dr. O. Loth, Bd. 6; des Prof. Dr. E. Windisch, Bd. 7, *etc.*). *Leipzig*, 1859, *etc.* 8°. **753. f. 9-** .

In progress.

Zeitschrift . . . herausgegeben von den Geschäftsführern. (Herausgegeben unter der verantwortlichen Redaction des Prof. Dr. R. Anger, Bd. 5, 6; des Prof. Dr. H. Brockhaus, Bd. 7-19; des Prof. Dr. L. Krehl, Bd. 20-27; des Prof. Dr. O. Loth, Bd. 28-33; des Prof. Dr. E. Windisch, Bd. 34, *etc.*) *Leipzig*, 1846, *etc.* 8°. **Ac. 8815/2.**

In progress.

GOETTINGEN.

Academia Georgia Augusta.

See PRUSSIA. Verzeichniss der Handschriften im Preussischen Staate. I. Hannover. 3. Göttingen 3. (Sanskrit-Handschriften [in the Universitäts-Bibliothek], *etc.*) 1894. 8°. **011901. g.**

Nachrichten von der Georg-Augusts Universität und der Königl. Gesellschaft der Wissenschaften zu Göttingen. *Göttingen*, [1845, *etc.*] 8°. **P.P. 4672. a., 2097. a.**

In progress.

Koenigliche Gesellschaft der Wissenschaften.

Abhandlungen . . . Philologisch-historische Klasse. Neue Folge. *Göttingen*, *Berlin*, 1843, *etc.* 4°. **Ac. 670.**

In progress.

Festschrift zur Feier des hundertfünfzigjährigen Bestehens der königlichen Gesellschaft der Wissenschaften zu Göttingen. Abhandlungen der philologisch-historischen Klasse. 2 pts. *Berlin*, 1901. 4°. **Ac. 670.**

Nachrichten, *etc.* *See* above, ACADEMIA GEORGIA AUGUSTA. **P.P. 4672. a., 2097. a.**

THE HAGUE.

Koninklijk Instituut voor de Taal-, Land-, en Volkenkunde van Nederlandsch-Indië.

Bijdragen, *etc.* *'s Gravenhage*, 1853, *etc.* 8°. **Ac. 7519.**

In progress.

LEIPSIC.

Academia Lipsiensis.

Katalog der Sanskrit-Handschriften der Universitäts-Bibliothek zu Leipzig. Von Theodor Aufrecht. pp. vi. 493. *Leipzig*, 1901. 8°. **14096. ccc. 3.**

Forms Bd. i. *of the* Katalog der Handschriften der Universitäts-Bibliothek zu Leipzig.

Koeniglich Saechsische Gesellschaft der Wissenschaften.

Berichte über die Verhandlungen . . . Philologisch-historische Classe. *Leipzig*, 1848, *etc.* 8°. **Ac. 700/2.**

In progress.

LONDON.

Oriental Translation Fund.

New Series . . . published under the patronage of the Royal Asiatic Society. 1891, *etc.* 8°. **14003. bb.**

In progress. The Sanskrit and Pali works published in this series are catalogued under the following headings:—

New Ser. II. *Vol.* 6. *Kathākoṣa.*
" " " " 7. *Bāṇa.*
" " " " 8. *Bāṇa.*
" " *V.* " 12. *Abhidhammapiṭaka.*—Dhammasaṅgaṇi.

Pali Text Society.

Journal of the Pali Text Society . . . Edited by T. W. Rhys Davids. *London*, 1882, *etc.* 8°. **14098. b.**

In progress.

ABHIDHAMMAPIṬAKA. The Dhātu kathā pakaraṇa and its Commentary. Edited by Edmund Rowland Gooneratne. pp. i. i. 138. *London*, *Chilworth* [printed], 1892. 8°. **14098. b. 29.(3.)**

ACADEMIES, *etc.*

LONDON (*continued*).

Pali Text Society (*continued*).

ABHIDHAMMAPIṬAKA. Kathāvatthu. Edited by Arnold C. Taylor. 2 vols. *London*, 1894-1897. 8°. **14098. b. 32.(2.)**

BUDDHAGHOSA. The Atthasālinī, Buddhaghosa's commentary on the Dhammasaṅgaṇi. Edited by Edward Müller. pp. viii. 434, i. *London, Leipzig* [printed], 1897. 8°. **14098. b. 36.(1.)**

DHAMMAPĀLA. Dhammapāla's Paramattha-dīpanī, Part III. Being the commentary on the Petavatthu. Edited by Prof. E. Hardy. pp. x. 303. *London, Leipzig* [printed], 1894. 8°. **14098. b. 35.**

—— Dhammapāla's Paramattha-dīpanī, Part IV. Being the commentary on the Vimāna-vatthu. Edited by Prof. E. Hardy. pp. xv. 374. *London, Leipzig* [printed], 1901. 8°. **14098. b. 35.**

—— Paramattha Dīpanī by Dhammapāla of Kāñcipura. Part V. The commentary on the Therīgāthā. Edited by E. Müller. pp. xxviii. 319. *London, Chilworth* [printed], 1893. 8°. **14098. b. 35.**

KACHCHĀYANA. The Netti-pakaraṇa. With extracts from Dhammapāla's commentary. Edited by Prof. E. Hardy. pp. xli. 289. *London, Leipzig* [printed], 1902. 8°. **14098. b. 36.(2.)**

PAÑÑASĀMI. Sāsanavaṃsa (a History of Buddhism). Edited [with introductory dissertation, *etc.*,] by Mabel Bode. pp. iv. 60, 189, i. *London, Leipzig* [printed], 1897. 8°. **14098. b. 37.**

SUTTAPIṬAKA. The Aṅguttara-Nikāya. Part III. Edited by Prof. E. Hardy. Pañcaka-nipāta, and Chakka-nipāta. (Part IV. Edited by Prof. E. Hardy. Sattaka-nipāta, Aṭṭhaka-nipāta, and Navaka-nipāta. Part V. . . . Dasaka-nipāta, and Ekādasaka-nipāta.) 3 pts. *London, Leipzig* [printed], 1896-1900. 8°. **14098. b. 27.**

—— The Majjhima-Nikāya. Edited by Robert Chalmers. Vol. II. (Vol. III. . . . With indices . . . by Mabel Bode.) *London, Copenhagen* [printed], 1896-1902. 8°. **14098. b. 25.**

ACADEMIES, *etc.*

LONDON (*continued*).

Pali Text Society (*continued*).

UPATISSA. The Mahā-bodhi-vaṁsa. Edited by S. Arthur Strong. pp. xi. 182. *London, Chilworth*, 1891. 8°. **14098. b. 29.(2.)**

YOGĀVACHARA. The Yogāvacara's Manual of Indian Mysticism as practised by Buddhists [, in Sinhalese and Pali]. Edited [with introduction] by T. W. Rhys Davids. pp. xxxi. ii. 105, i. *London, Leipzig* [printed], 1896. 8°. **14098. b. 29.(4.)**

Royal Asiatic Society of Great Britain and Ireland.

The Journal of the Society, *etc.* *London*, 1834, *etc.* 8°. **Ac. 8820/3 and 2098. a.b.**

In progress.

MADRAS.

University of Madras.

The F.A. Sanskrit Text 1899, with critical, explanatory, and grammatical notes, translation, paraphrase &c. by T. Rajagopalachariar. [Comprising the Kishkindhākāṇḍa of Bhojarāja's Champūrāmāyaṇa, Bāṇa's Pārvatīpariṇaya, and Bhallaṭa's Ṣataka, followed by English notes on the first-named work and a translation thereof.] pp. 16, 51, 16, 27, 15. *Kumbhakonam, Anikara Chattram* [printed, 1898]. 8°. **14079. b. 34.(4.)**

The Sanskrit Text for the Matriculation Examination of the University of Madras, December 1900. [Comprising the Pañchatantra, Book I. xiv.-xxii., and the Rāmāyaṇa, Bālakāṇḍa, *sargas* i.-xi.] pp. ii. 66. *Madras*, 1899. 8°. **14060. c. 30.(3.)**

B.A. Sanskrit Text 1901. [Comprising the Kirātārjunīya, *sargas* i.-v., with Mallinātha's commentary and English notes, and Manu, *adhyāya* vii., with Kullūka's commentary and English notes and translation.] pp. 90, 36, 44, ii. 19, 22. *Madras*, 1900. 8°. **14060. c. 30.(4.)**

The authors of the English notes and translation, according to the List of Books Printed are T. R. Ratnam Aiyar, S. Vāsudevāchārya, and V. Saṅkara Ṣāstri.

Before the text of Manu has been bound up in this volume the first 12 pp. of an English commentary on the Uttararāmacharita.

ACADEMIES, *etc.*

MADRAS (*continued*).

University of Madras (*continued*).

Complete Sanskrit Text for the F.A. Examination, 1901. [Comprising the Raghuvaṃśa, *sargas* i.-v., and the Mālavikāgnimitra.] With full notes, translations, explanations, references, allusions, grammatical glosses, synonyms, paraphrase, &c., by T. V. Vaidyanatha Aiyar. pp. i. 34, 82, 202, 44, 80. *Madras*, 1900. 8°. **14072. ccc. 24.(2.)**

The pagination is imperfect, the notes on the Raghuvaṃśa occupying not 202 pages but 125.

B.A. Degree Examination 1901. The Sanskrit Text with an easy commentary, critical introductions and explanatory notes. Part I. [comprising Bhāravi's Kirātārjunīya, *sargas* i.-v., with commentary based on that of Mallinātha, and the Manusmṛiti, *adhyāya* vii., with Kullūka's commentary, together with English notes and translations of the texts.] By Subrahmanya Sastri . . . and P. S. Sundaram Ayyar, *etc.* pp. 82, 69, 34, 126, 20, 26. *Madras*, 1900. 8°. **14072. c. 50.(2.)**

MUNICH.

Koenigliche Akademie der Wissenschaften.

Abhandlungen der Philosophisch-philologischen Classe, *etc.* *München*, 1835, *etc.* 4°. **Ac. 713/6.**

In progress.

PARIS.

Académie des Inscriptions et Belles-Lettres.

Notices et Extraits des Manuscrits de la Bibliothèque du Roi, *etc.* (Notices . . . de la Bibliothèque Nationale.) *Paris*, 1787, *etc.* 4°. **R.R. Bar T.**

Bibliothèque Nationale.

Collection Orientale. Manuscrits inédits de la Bibliothèque Royale, *etc.* 1836, *etc.* Fol. **756. l.**

Musée Guimet.

Annales du Musée Guimet. *Paris*, 1880, *etc.* 4°. **7704. h. 21.**

In progress.

Annales du Musée Guimet. Bibliothèque d'Études. *Paris*, 1892, *etc.* 8°. **7704. i.**

In progress.

ACADEMIES, *etc.*

PARIS (*continued*).

Société Asiatique.

Journal Asiatique, ou recueil de mémoires, d'extraits et de notices relatifs à l'histoire, à la philosophie, aux langues, et à la littérature des peuples orientaux, *etc.* *Paris*, 1822, *etc.* 8°. **Ac. 8808. and 2098. d.**

In progress.

Société de Linguistique de Paris.

Mémoires, *etc.* Paris, 1868, *etc.* 8°. **Ac. 9810.**

In progress.

ST. PETERSBURG.

Academia Scientiarum Imperialis.

Bibliotheca Buddhica. [A series of Sanskrit and other Buddhist texts.] 1897, *etc.* 8°. **14003. dd.**

In progress.

For works published in this series see under the headings:—

1. *Śāntideva.*
2. *Rāshṭrapālaparipṛichchhā.*

TUEBINGEN.

Eberhard-Karls-Universitaet.

Verzeichniss der Doktoren welche die philosophische Fakultät . . . im Dekanatsjahre 1898—1899 ernannt hat. Beigefügt ist ein Verzeichniss der indischen Handschriften der Königlichen Universitäts-Bibliothek, Zuwachs der Jahre 1865-1889, von Richard Garbe. pp. i. 5, i. 114. *Tübingen*, 1899. 8°. **Ac. 730.**

VIENNA.

Kaiserliche Akademie der Wissenschaften.

Denkschriften . . . Philosophisch - historische Classe. *Wien*, 1850, *etc.* Fol. **Ac. 810/12.**

In progress.

Sitzungsberichte der Kaiserlichen Akademie der Wissenschaften. Philosophisch-historische Classe. *Wien*, 1849, *etc.* 8°. **Ac. 810/6.**

Sources of Sanskrit Lexicography. Edited by order of the Imperial Academy of Sciences of

Vienna. *Vienna, Bombay* [printed], 1893, *etc.* 4°. **14090. e. 23.**

In progress.

Works issued in this series since the publication of Professor Bendall's Catalogue are catalogued under the headings:—

Vol. 2, 4. *Hemachandra.*
,, 3. *Mañkha.*

ACHALA DVIVEDĪ, called VATSARĀJA, *Nāgara.* નિર્ણયદીપક *etc.* [Nirṇayadīpaka. A compendium of rules for religious observances. With a Gujarati translation by Kṛishṇājī Prahlāda-bhaṭṭajī Araṇke, composed under the supervision of Maṇilāla Nabhubhāī Dvivedī.] pp. xxxii. 651, xxxii. 492, lvi. નડિયાદ ૧૮૯૭ [*Nadiad*, 1897.] 8°. **14028. dd. 4.**

ĀCHĀRA, *Ū, Gaṇāchariya, of Talôkpin, Danubyu.* ကကြီးခခွေးဋီကာပါဠိဋီကာ *etc.* [Ka-kyī-hka-kwe-ṭīkā, or Akkharavaṇṇanāṭīkā. A Pali dissertation on the functions of the letters, with Burmese commentary. Preceded by the Namo-buddhāya-ṭīkā, a Pali dissertation on the phrase *namo buddhāya*, also with Burmese commentary, and followed by the Goṇamātikā-ovādakathā, a Burmese homily upon a series of Pali quotations.] pp. vi. 250. ရန်ကုန် ၁၂၆၀ [*Rangoon*, 1898.] 8°. **14098. ccc. 12.(4).**

ĀCHĀRĀṄGA. Â*k*ârâṅga Sûtra. [Translated, with notes *etc.*, by H. Jacobi.] 1884. *See* MUELLER (F. M.) The Sacred Books of the East, *etc.* Vol. xxii., pp. 1-214. 1879, *etc.* 8°. **2003. a. (vol. 22.)**

—— आचारंग प्रारंभ [Āchārāṅga. Śrutaskandha i., with Gujarati translation in supralinear glosses.] pp. 208, *lith.* मुंबई [*Bombay*, 1895.] *obl.* 8°. **14100. e. 4.**

ĀCHĀRYA (SATĪŚACHANDRA). *See* SATĪŚACHANDRA VIDYĀBHŪSHAṆA.

ĀCHĀRYA SVĀMĪ. *See* MADHUSŪDANA, *Āchārya of the Nigamāgama Maṇḍalī.*

ACHINTYARAMA ŚARMĀ, *of Amritsar.* *See* ABHINANDA, *son of Jayanta.* कादम्बरीकथासारः *etc.* [Kādambarīkathāsāra. With commentary. Edited by Achintyarāma.] [1900.] 8°. **14072. d. 44.**

ACHYUTA, *disciple of Raghūttama.* अच्युतकविविरचितमाकाशशतकं. [Ākāśaśataka. A religious-philosophical century.] *See* LAGHUKĀVYĀNI. लघुकाव्यानि . . . Miscellaneous Poetical Pieces, *etc.* pp. 215-221. 1888. [*Kāvyetihāsasaṅgraha, Vol.* X., *no.* 9.] **14072. d. 37. (vol. 10.)**

ACHYUTA KṚISHṆĀNANDA TĪRTHA, *disciple of Svayamprakāśānanda.* *See* APYAYA DĪKSHITA. The Siddhântaleśa . . . With extracts from the Śrîkṛishṇâlaṁkâra of Achyutakṛishṇânandatîrtha, *etc.* 1890. 8°. **14048. dd. 3. (vol. 1.)**

—— *See* APYAYA DĪKSHITA. ॥ सिद्धान्तलेशसङ्ग्रहः *etc.* [Siddhāntaleśasaṅgraha. With the Kṛishṇālaṅkāra.] 1894. 8°. [*Advaitamañjarī.*] **14048. e. 23.**

ACHYUTĀNANDA, *Commentator on the Ānandalaharī.* *See* ŚAṄKARA ĀCHĀRYA.—*Doubtful and Supposititious Works.* Ānanda Lahari. With . . . commentaries [based on those of Achyutānanda and others]. Translated into English, *etc.* 1899. 12°. **14048. b. 35.**

ACHYUTA ŚARMĀ MOḌAKA, *disciple of Nārāyaṇa Sūri.* भागीरथीचम्पूः। [Bhāgīrathīchampū. A mythological work in 7 *manorathas*, with footnotes.] pp. 144. [1889.] *See* PERIODICAL PUBLICATIONS.—*Bombay.* ग्रन्थरत्नमाला *etc.* (Granth Ratna Málá, *etc.*) Vol. II., no. 11, Vol. III., no. 4. 1887-[1892]. 8°. **14096. c. 8. (vol. 2, 3.)**

ADHYĀTMARĀMĀYAṆA. *See* PURĀṆAS.—*Brahmāṇḍapurāṇa.*

ĀDICHCHAVAṂSA, *Mahāthera.* *See* KAMMAVĀCHĀ. ဥပသမ္ပဒကမ္မဝါစာနိဿယ [Upasampadākammavāchā. With Burmese *nissaya* by Ādichchavaṃsa.] 1899. 8°. [*Vinayasamūhavinichchhaya.*] **14300. e. 15.**

—— ဋီကာကျော်ဂဏ္ဌိကျမ်း *etc.* [Ṭīkā-kyaw-ganṭhi-kyan. A Burmese dissertation upon the Ṭīkā-kyaw, by Ādichchavaṃsa. Followed by Dhammavilāsa's Paramatthasūra-kyan and Chakkindābhisiri's Vithichittappakāsanī and Bhummipuggalabheda-kyan, 3 psychological treatises in Burmese, Pali and Burmese, and Burmese respectively.] pp. v. 616, i. မန္တလေး ၁၂၆၃ [*Mandalay*, 1901.] 8°. **14300. d. 35.**

ĀDINĀRĀYAṆA PĀTRO, *P., of Palakonda.* The Hindu Law. Annotated and illustrated by Sanskrit texts[, viz. Manu and the writings of Devāṇḍa Bhaṭṭa, Jīmūtavāhana, Kamalākara Bhaṭṭa, Kuvera Upādhyāya, Mitra Miṣra, Nanda Paṇḍita, Nīlakaṇṭha Mīmāṃsakabhaṭṭa, Pratāparudra Deva, Vijñāneṣvara, Yājñavalkya, *etc.*,] and leading cases of all the High Courts and of the Privy Council. By P. Adinarayana Patro. pp. xv. 106, 482. *Madras*, 1899. 8°.
14039. c. 17.

ĀDITYARĀMA BHAṬṬĀCHĀRYA, *Mahāmahopādhyāya.* See ṢĀRṄGADHARA, *son of Dāmodara.* शान्तरसनिर्देश: *etc.* [Ṣāntarasanirdeṣa. With notes by Ādityarāma.] [1897.] 12°. **14070. b. 29.**

ADVAITĀNANDA SARASVATĪ, *disciple of Bhūmānanda and Rāmānanda.* See BĀDARĀYAṆA. ॥ ब्रह्मविद्याभरणम् *etc.* [Brahmasūtra. With the commentary Brahmavidyābharaṇa of Advaitānanda.] 1894. 8°. [*Advaitamañjarī.*] **14048. e. 23.**

AESOP. नीतिमाला . . . Nitimálá, or Æsop's Fables. Translated into easy Sanskrit with short notes [in Sanskrit] by Bhútanátha Vidyáratna. Second edition. pp. iv. 42. *Calcutta*, 1891. 12°. **14076. b. 28.(1.)**

ĀGAMAS. See NAÑJUṆḌA DĪKSHITA. శైవాగమ సారః॥ [Ṣaivāgamasāra. A collection of Ṣaiva rituals, compiled from the Āgamas, *etc.*] [1893.] 8°.
14028. d. 51.

—— See PĀRALIṄGA PRABHU AIYĀ. वीरशैवान्वय मूलतत्व प्रकाश *etc.* [Vīraṣaivānvayamūlatattvaprakāṣa. Compiled from Āgamik works.] [1893.] 12°.
14033. a. 29.

—— ஸ்ரீமத் ஸகலாகமஸார ஸங்க்ரஹம் *etc.* [Sakalāgamasārasaṅgraha. An epitome or digest of the Āgamas in their bearing upon everyday ritual. Edited with Tamil introduction by K. Shaṇmukhasundara Mudaliyār. Second edition.] pp. xlviii. 148. சென்னை சார்வரி [*Madras*, 1900.] 8°.
14033. aa. 11.

——[*Aṃṣumattantra.*] അംശുമത്തന്ത്രേ പടലഃ നിത്യപൂജാപ്രായശ്ചിത്തഃ [Nityapūjāprāyaṣchitta. A chapter on expiatory rites, forming *paṭala* 59 of the Aṃṣumattantra.] See AGHORA ṢIVĀCHĀRYA.

அகோரசிவாசாரியார் இயற்றிய . . . ப்ராயச்சித்தவிதி [Prāyaṣchittavidhi.] pp. 1-57. [1897.] 12°.
14028. b. 87.

—— [*Kāmikāgama.*] காமிகாகமம் *etc.* [Kāmikāgama. With Tamil commentary and glossary to every verse of the first volume.] 2 vols. சென்னை விளம்பி—விகாரி [*Madras*, 1898-1899.] 4°.
14033. d. 23.

In progress. Vol. i. has two title-pages; the first states that the printing was begun Nov. 1888 and ended Dec. 1898, while the second is dated Dec. 1889.

—— [*Kāraṇāgama.*] ஸ்ரீமத் பூர்வகாரணாகமம் *etc.* (உத்தர காரணாகமம்.) [Kāraṇāgama, (Pūrvakāraṇa and Uttarakāraṇa). Edited with Tamil introduction *etc.* by K. Shaṇmukhasundara Mudaliyār.] 2 vols. சென்னை விகாரி—ப்லவ [*Madras*, 1900-1902.] 8°. **14033. aa. 8.**

—— [*Mrigendrāgama.*] The Mrigendra Agama. [An *upāgama* of the Kāmika. Edited with English translation *etc.* by M. Nārāyaṇasvāmi Aiyar. Chap. 1-9.] 1900-1901. *See* PERIODICAL PUBLICATIONS.—*Madras.* The Light of Truth, or Siddhanta Deepika, *etc.* Vol. iv., no. 4-9. 1897, *etc.* 4°.
14170. fff. 4.(vol. 4.)

—— [*Siddhāgama.*] ದೇವಲಬ್ರಹ್ಮಬೋಧಕ ಸವೇಂ ಕಾತಾತ್ಪರ್ಯ ವೇದೋಕ್ತ ಮೂಲಸ್ತಂಭನ *etc.* [Devalabrahmabodhaka-vedokta-mūlastambhana. A chapter, partly anthological, on the divinity of the Muni Devāṅga or Devala and the origin of the Devāṅga caste of Brahman weavers. With the Devalopanishad and Devāṅgasaptāvatāranirṇaya. Edited with Canarese translations and commentaries by Ṣaṅkaraiya Devāṅga.] pp. ii. 100; 2 *plates.* ಮೈಸೂರು ೧೮೯೮ [*Mysore*, 1898.] 8°.
14058. b. 37.

—— [*Sūkshmāgama.*] सूक्ष्मागम *etc.* [Sūkshmāgama. With a Marathi translation by Tryambaka Gurunātha Kāḷe. Followed by an appendix of quotations from divers sources.] pp. xi. 128; 1 *plate.* सोलापूर १९०१ [*Solapur*, 1901.] 8°.
14033. aa. 20.

Forms no. 2 in the Vīraṣaiva-liṅgibrāhmaṇa-dharmagranthamālā *published by Rāu Sāhib Mallappā Basappā Vārad.*

—— [*Vātūlāgama.*] అనుభవసూత్రం [Anubhavasūtra, or Ṣivānubhavasūtra. Eight *adhikaraṇas* of the Vātūlottarāgama, on the *shaṭstha-*

lanirṇaya or exposition of the six rites of the Vīraṣaivas expressive of the supreme verities.] *See* ṢIVĀDVAITAPAÑCHAKA. శివాద్వైతపంచక *etc.* [Ṣivādvaitapañchaka.] pp. 40-68. [1897.] 8°.
14048. cc. 8.(4.)

—— —— వాతూలాగమే తత్త్వభేదపటలః (వర్ణ-భేదపటల్ *etc.*). [Vātūlāgama. Paṭalas 1-10 in the Sahasragranthasaṃhitā of the Vātūlottarāgama, expounding divers doctrines and rites of the Vīraṣaivas.] *See* ṢIVĀDVAITAPAÑCHAKA. శివాద్వైతపంచక *etc.* [Ṣivādvaitapañchaka.] pp. 175-212. [1897.] 8°. **14048. cc. 8.(4.)**

ĀGAMASĀRA. अथ महामारी कल्पः *etc.* [Mahāmārikalpa. A Tantric ritual to ensure safety from the plague, purporting to be from the Devīrahasya in the Āgamasāra. With a Hindi translation, styled Chandrikā, by Raghunātha Ṣarmā.] pp. 22. *Bankipore*, १९५८ [1901.] 8°.
14033. b. 42.(4.)
Pp. 17-20 *are wanting.*

AGASTYA. *See* PAÑCHADAṢĪMANTRA. ॥ श्रीविद्या दीपिका *etc.* [Ṣrīvidyādīpikā. A commentary, ascribed to Agastya, upon the Pañchadaṣīmantra.] 1902. 12°. [*Triśatī.*] **14033. a. 45.(1.)**

—— Agastimata. (Agastîyâ Ratnaparîkṣâ.) [Two tracts on the lapidary art, ascribed to Agastya. With French translation of the former.] *See* FINOT (L.) Les Lapidaires Indiens, *etc.* pp. 77-139, 179-193. 1896. 8°.
Ac. 8929. (fasc. 111.)

—— ॥ अथ अगस्त्यसंहिता प्रारम्भः ॥ [Agastyasaṃhitā. A poetical account of Rāma and his worship, in 34 *adhyāyas*, narrated by Agastya. Edited by Rāmanārāyaṇa Dāsa.] ff. 134, iv. *Lucknow*, 1898. *obl.* 8°. **14028. dd. 7.**

—— शब्दसंग्रहः ॥ [Ṣabdasaṅgraha. A vocabulary ascribed to the Ṛishi Agastya. With glosses, *etc.*] pp. 27. 1895-1896. *See* VEṄKAṬARAṄGANĀTHA SVĀMĪ, *Paravastu.* Grandha Pradarsani, *etc.* [No. 4.] 1895, *etc.* 8°. **14003. c. 2.(4.)**

AGGĀCHĀRA, *Mahāthera, of Piṭakanātha Kyaung, Ava.* *See* DHAMMASENĀPATI. ကာရိကာ *etc.* [Kārikā. With Burmese commentary by Aggāchāra.] [1899.] 8°. [*Saddā-ngay.*]
14098. ccc. 22.

AGGADHAMMĀLAṄKĀRA THERA. *See* ABHIDHAMMAPIṬAKA. — *Dhammasaṅgaṇi.* မာတိကာ၊ ဓါတုကထာအကောက် *etc.* [Mātikā-dhātukathā-akauk. With Burmese commentaries by Aggadhammālaṅkāra, *etc.*] [1898.] 8°.
14300. d. 5.(4.)

—— *See* KACHCHĀYANA. — *Kachchāyanappakaraṇa.* သဒ္ဒါကြီး *etc.* [Saddā-kyī. Kachchāyana's Pali grammar, with the Burmese commentary of Khemaraṃsi upon the Taddhitakappa and that of Aggadhammālaṅkāra on the other sections.] [1894-1896.] 8°. **14098. ccc. 13.**

—— *See* KACHCHĀYANA.—*Kachchāyanappakaraṇa.* ဗါးကရာမူ။ သဒ္ဒါကြီး *etc.* [Bā-ka-yā-mū Saddā-kyī. The aphorisms of Kachchāyana, with brief Burmese commentary based on that of Aggadhammālaṅkāra.] [1898.] 8°.
14098. ccc. 12.(1.)

—— ဓာတွတ္ထဒီပကပါဠိနိသျ *etc.* [Dhātvatthadīpaka. A treatise in Pali verse on the significations of Pali roots. With a Burmese commentary by Indāsabha of Pazun-hkyaung. Edited by Ū Vimalāchāra of Hpa-aung.] pp. iv. 226. ရန်ကုန် ၁၂၆၁ [*Rangoon*, 1899.] 8°.
14098. ccc. 29.(1.)

AGGAVAṂSA. *See* JINARATANA, *Hiṅgulvala.* Dhātwattha Dīpanī, *etc.* [A collection of Pali roots, based on the Mahāsaddanīti of Aggavaṃsa.] 1895. 8°. **14098. b. 19.**

—— သဒ္ဒနီတိပကိဏ်မည်သော။သဒ္ဒနီတိသုတ်နက် *etc.* [Saddanīti. A series of Pali aphorisms in 25 *parichchhedas* on Pali grammar. Followed by a Burmese translation and exposition thereof, styled Suttatthadīpaṇī or Saddanīti-thôk-net, by Chandimā.] pp. x. 361. ရန်ကုန် ၁၂၆၂ [*Rangoon*, 1900.] 8°. **14098. ccc. 29.(2.)**

—— သဒ္ဒနီတိပုဒ်ထုး [Saddanīti-pôk-htū. Selections from the Saddanīti.] *See* PAÑÑĀLAṄKĀRA, *of Maṅgalārāma.* နာမမာလာကျမ်း *etc.* [Nāmamālā.] pp. 262-268. 1895. 8°.
14098. ccc. 17.(1.)

AGHORANĀTHA VANDYOPĀDHYĀYA, *Vidyāratna.* *See* NĪLAKAṆṬHA, *son of Govinda.* भारतभावदीप: *etc.* [Bhāratabhāvadīpa. Edited by Aghoranātha.] [1900, *etc.*] 8°. **14068. b. 18.**

AGHORA ṢIVĀCHĀRYA. அகோரசிவாசாரியார் இயற்றிய க்ரியாக்ரம ஜ்யோதி த்வஜாரோஹண விதி [Dhvajārohaṇavidhi. A ritual for the annual hoisting of the flag in Ṣaiva temples, extracted from the Kriyākramadyotikā.] pp. 16, 100, i. 21. சென்னை விளம்பி [*Madras,* 1898.] 12°. **14028. b. 99.**

—— அகோரசிவாசாரியார் இயற்றிய க்ரியாக்ரம ஜ்யோதி ஆறும் பாகம் மஹோத்ஸவவிதி [Mahotsavavidhi. Rituals for the great Ṣaiva festivals, forming part 6 of the Kriyākramadyotikā. With Tamil preface by K. Shaṇmukhasundara Mudaliyār and a Tamil introduction.] pp. xxvi. 434. சென்னை ஹேவிளம்பி [*Madras,* 1897.] 12°. **14028. b. 89.**

—— அகோரசிவாசாரியார் இயற்றிய க்ரியாக்ரம ஜ்யோதி ஏழாம் பாகம் ப்ராயச்சித்தவிதி [Prāyaṣchittavidhi. Expiatory rituals, forming part 7 of the Kriyākramadyotikā. Preceded by the 59th *paṭala* of the Aṃṣumattantra, on the same theme.] pp. vi. 155. சென்னை ஹேவிளம்பி [*Madras,* 1897.] 12°. **14028. b. 87.**

—— அகோரசிவாசாரியார் இயற்றிய க்ரியாக்ரம ஜ்யோதி ஐந்தாம் பாகம் சுப்ரமண்ய ப்ரதிஷ்டாவிதி [Subrahmaṇyapratishṭhāvidhi. A ritual for consecration of images of Subrahmaṇya, forming part 5 of the Kriyākramadyotikā.] pp. i. 150. சென்னை ஹேவிளம்பி [*Madras,* 1898.] 12°. **14028. b. 88.**

AGNIVEṢA. [For the Charakasaṃhitā sometimes attributed to Agniveṣa:] *See* CHARAKA.

—— अञ्जननिदानम् *etc.* [Añjananidāna. A treatise on therapeutics ascribed to Agniveṣa. Edited with a Hindi translation styled Prabodhinī and notes by Rāmeṣvara Bhaṭṭa.] pp. iv. 89. कल्याण-मुंबई १८२० [*Kalyan,* 1898.] 8°. **14043. c. 45.(1.)**

—— श्रीमद्रामायणम् । [Ṣataṣlokī-rāmāyaṇa, or Rāmāyaṇasāra. A poetical epitome of the Rāmāyaṇa, ascribed to Agniveṣa.] pp. 18. [1890.] *See* PERIODICAL PUBLICATIONS.—*Bombay.* ग्रन्थरत्नमाला *etc.* (Granth Ratna Málá, *etc.*) Vol. iii., no. 9. 1887-[1892]. 8°. **14096. c. 8.(vol. 3.)**

AGNIVEṢA (*continued*). समयनिरूपणरामायण *etc.* [Samayanirūpaṇarāmāyaṇa. A series of excerpts from the Rāmāyaṇasāra or Rāmāyaṇasamayādarṣa of Agniveṣa, chronologically epitomising the Rāmāyaṇa. Extracted and edited with a Hindi version by Vrajaratna Bhaṭṭāchārya.] pp. 39. कल्याण-मुंबई १९५६ [*Kalyan,* 1900.] 12°. **14065. b. 21.**

ĀHNIKA. *See* NITYAKARMA.

AHOBALA, *son of Krishṇa Paṇḍita.* সঙ্গীতপারিজাতঃ। [Saṅgītapārijāta. A treatise on music.] pp. 18. [1891, *etc.*] *See* PERIODICAL PUBLICATIONS.—*Calcutta.* অরুণোদয় *etc.* [Aruṇodaya.] Pt. i., no. 24. [1890, *etc.*] 4°. **14133. g. 16. (pt. i. no. 24.)**

—— संगीतपारिजात: *etc.* [Saṅgītapārijāta.] pp. 134. पुण्याख्यपत्तन १८१९ [*Poona,* 1897.] 12°. **14053. b. 32.**

AHOBILĀCHĀRYA, *Vātsya, son of Rāghava.* *See* VARADĀCHĀRYA, *Vātsya,* called NAḌĀDŪR AMMĀḶ. ப்ரபன்னபாரிஜாதம் *etc.* [Prapannapārijāta, *etc.* Edited with Tamil interpretations and commentary by Ahobilāchārya.] [1895.] 8°. **14028. d. 55.**

AHOBILAM. తనయశ్లోకక్రమః (శ్రీమదహోబిలమఠీయ తనియశ్లోకాః) [Tanayaṣlokakrama. Metrical succession-lists of the pontiffs of the cult of Lakshmī-Nṛisiṃha at Ahobilam, in the Karnul district.] pp. 14. మహీశూర ౧౮౯౦ [*Mysore,* 1890.] 16°. **14058. a. 5.(2.)**

AIYAṄGĀR, *Chakravarti.* *See* CHAKRAVARTI AIYAṄGĀR.

AJITANĀTHA NYĀYARATNA, *Kavibhūshaṇa.* *See* KṚISHṆĀNANDA SARASVATĪ, *Vāchaspati.* अन्तर्व्याकरणनाट्यपरिशिष्टम् *etc.* [Antarvyākaraṇanāṭya-pariṣishṭa. Edited with a commentary styled Rājasaraṇī *etc.* by Ajitanātha.] [1894 ?—1899.] 8°. **14090. bb. 12.**

AJITASENA BHAṬṬĀRAKA. अलङ्कारचिन्तामणि: [Alaṅkārachintāmaṇi. A treatise on Poetics.] [1893-1894.] *See* PADMARĀJA PAṆḌITA, *son of Brahmasūri.* काव्याम्बुधि: *etc.* [Kāvyāmbudhi.] Pts. 1-6. [1893-1896.] 8°. **14028. c. 64.**

Not completed.

AJJHATTAJAYAMAṄGALAGĀTHĀ. *See* JAYAMAṄGALAGĀTHĀ.

AKALAṄKA KAVI. ಅಕಲಂಕಾಷ್ಟಕಮತ್ತು ವ್ರತಫಲವರ್ಣನೆ *etc.* [Akalaṅkāshṭaka and Vrataphala-varṇanā. Poems setting forth Jain doctrines. Edited with Canarese glosses and commentary by Padmarāja Paṇḍita.] pp. 22. ಬೆಂಗಳೂರು ೧೮೯೩ [*Bangalore*, 1893.] 8°. **14100. b. 3.(2.)**

AKHAṆḌĀNANDA, *disciple of Akhaṇḍānubhūti.* See PADMAPĀDA. The Pañchapâdikâ of Padmapâda. [A commentary on Ṣārīrakabhāshya, I. i. 1-4] *etc.* (Part II. The Pañchapâdikâvivaraṇa of Prakâśâtman. With extracts from the [supercommentaries] Tattvadîpana [of Akhaṇḍānanda], *etc.*) 1891-1892. 8°. **14048. dd. 3.(vol. 2.)**

—— तत्त्वदीपनम् । पञ्चपादिकाविवरणस्य व्याख्यानम् . . . Tattvadîpana, a commentary on Panchapâdikâvivaraṇa, [Prakāṣātmā's commentary on Padmapāda's Pañchapādikā, the latter being a commentary upon Ṣaṅkara's Bhāshya I. i. 1-4] . . . Edited by Râma Śâstrî Tailanga. 1901, *etc.* 8°. **14049. a. 3.**

In progress. Forms no. 57, *etc., of the* Benares Sanskrit Series.

AKHAṆḌĀNANDA VARṆĪ. अथ . . . श्रीपुरुषोत्तमकवचप्रारंभः॥ [Purushottamakavacha. A description of the mystic formula so styled, forming *parichchheda* i., *adhyāya* 42, in the Haricharitra of Akhaṇḍānanda. With Gujarati translation.] See BHAGAVATPRASĀDA ĀCHĀRYA. श्रीसारोपदेशः *etc.* [Sāropadeṣa, *etc.*] pp. 197-221. [1896.] 12°. **14028. b. 83.**

ĀKHYĀTA-VARANEGILLA. ආඛ්‍යාත රූපමාලා. [Ākhyāta-varanegilla, or °rūpamālā. A Pali tract on verbal conjugation, with Sinhalese translation and notes by K. Dhammārāma.] See PĀLI-NĀMA-VARANEGILLA. පාලි නාමවරනැගිලි *etc.* (Kaccayana Namika Rupamala, *etc.*) pp. 32-62. 1895. 8°. **14098. c. 42.(2.)**

ALAKA, *Rājānaka, son of Jayānaka.* See RATNĀKARA, *Rājānaka.* The Haravijaya . . . With the commentary of ... Alaka, *etc.* 1890. 8°. [*Kâvyamâlâ.*] **14072. ccc. 12.(no. 22.)**

ALAṢIṄGALA ĀCHĀRYA, *son of Tirumalai Āchārya, Pustakam.* ಚಾಣಿಕ್ಯ ತಂತ್ರ ಚಮತ್ಕಾರ *etc.* (Chanikya Tantra Chamatcara, *etc.*) [A summary, in 231 verses, of the plot of Viṣākhadatta's drama Mudrārākshasa. With Canarese version.] pp. 85. ಮೈಸೂರ್ [*Mysore,*] 1880. 16°. **14076. a. 21.**

ĀḶAVANDĀR. *See* YĀMUNA ĀCHĀRYA.

ALLAṬA. [For the portion of the Kāvyaprakāṣa added to it by this writer:] *See* MAMMAṬA ĀCHĀRYA.

ALMANACKS. *See* EPHEMERIDES.

ĀLOKĀBHIVARA SĀSANARAKKHA, called MYADAUNG HSAYA. ဝိပဿနာရှုနည်း *etc.* [Vipassanā-shu-naý, or °shuhbway-akyin. A Burmese guide to the attainment of spiritual insight, including a number of Pali texts and prayers.] pp. 24. *Rangoon,* 1880. 8°. **14300. d. 28.(2.)**

—— ဝိပဿနာရှုဘွယ် *etc.* [Vipassanā-shuhbway-akyin.] pp. 24. *Rangoon,* 1881. 8°. **14300. d. 22.(1.)**

—— ဝိပဿနာရှုဘွယ်အကျဉ်း [Vipassanā-shuhbway-akyin.] *See* PROME HSAYA. ဗြဟ္မဝိဟာရသင်္ဂဟကျမ်း *etc.* [Brahmavihārasaṅgaha, *etc.*] pp. 17-34. 1882. 8°. **14300. d. 9.(2.)**

ALWAR.—*Library of the Maharaja of Alwar.* Catalogue of the Sanskrit Manuscripts in the library of His Highness the Maharaja of Ulwar. By Peter Peterson. pp. ii. i. 101, 261. *Bombay,* 1892. 4°. **14096. dd. 4.**

ALWIS. *See* DE ALWIS.

AMALĀNANDA. *See* BĀDARĀYAṆA. The Vedânta-kalpataru of Amalânanda, *etc.* [Comprising the Brahmasūtra with the supercommentary of Amalānanda upon the Bhāmatī of Vāchaspati Miṣra.] 1895-1897. 8°. **14048. dd. 3.(vol. 11.)**

—— *See* BĀDARĀYAṆA. The Vedântakalpataruparimala, *etc.* [Comprising the Brahmasūtra with the gloss of Apyaya upon Amalānanda's supercommentary Vedāntakalpataru.] 1895-1898. 8°. **14048. dd. 3.(vol. 12.)**

AMARA, *disciple of Jinadatta Sūri.* *See* AMARACHANDRA SŪRI.

AMARACHANDRA SŪRI, *disciple of Jinadatta.* *See* ARISIṂHA, *son of Āsaḍa.* काव्यकल्पलता *etc.* [Kāvyakalpalatā. With the commentary Kaviśikshāvṛitti and supplements of Amarachandra. Translated into Marathi.] [1891.] 8°.
14140. b. 24.

—— The Bâlabhârata of Amarachandra Sûri. [A poem in 19 *parvas* on the legend of the Mahābhārata.] Edited [with biography of the poet] by Paṇḍit Śivadatta . . . and Kâśînâth Pâṇḍurang Parab. (बालभारतम् ।) pp. xvi. 491. 1894. *See* DURGĀPRASĀDA, *son of Vrajalāla*, and KĀŚĪNĀTHA PĀṆḌURAṄGA PARAB. Kâvyamâlâ. [No.] 45. 1886, *etc.* 8°. **14072. ccc. 12.(no. 45.)**

Appended is a praśasti of the poet.

AMARADĀSA, *Udāsīna Sādhu.* *See* SVĀRĀJYASIDDHI. ॥स्वाराज्यसिद्धि॰ [Svārājyasiddhi. With commentary. Edited by Amaradāsa.] *obl.* Fol.
14048. ee. 2.

AMARAJĪ HARISAṄKARA TRAVĀṚĪ and NATHU BHAGAVĀN DHOLKIĀ. ॥ प्रपन्न शिक्षामृत *etc.* [Prapannaśikshāmṛita. A collection of Vaishṇava poems of the Rāmānuji sect, with Gujarati translations, commentaries, and some metrical paraphrases. Compiled and edited by Amarajī Travāṛī and Nathu Dholkiā.] pp. xv. 127. અમદાવાદ ૧૮૯૭ [*Ahmadabad*, 1897.] 12°.
14028. bb. 9.

AMARASIṂHA. ଅମରକୋଷ *etc.* [Amarakoṣa.] pp. ii. 114. *Cuttack*, 1878. 8°.
14090. b. 39.

—— The Nâmalingânuśâsana [or Amarakoṣa] of Amarasiṃha. Edited by Paṇḍit Durgâprasâd, Kâśînâth Pâṇdurang Parab and Pandit Śivadatta. (नामलिङ्गानुशासनम् ।) pp. iv. 52. 1889. *See* DURGĀPRASĀDA, *son of Vrajalāla*, and others. The Abhidhâna-sangraha, *etc.* No. 1. 1889, *etc.* 8°.
14090. e. 20.(no. 1.)

—— അമരകൊശം *etc.* [Amarakoṣa. Edited with a Malayalam interpretation by Rāma Vāriyar.] pp. 339. തൃശ്ശിവപെരൂർ ൧൮൬൭ [*Trichur*, 1891.] 8°.
14090. bb. 8.

—— পাণ্ডিত্যম্ *etc.* (Panditya. The Imperial Lexicon of the Sanskrit Language, based on Amarkosh. Edited . . . by Bishnupada Mukhopadhyaya.) Pt. i., pp. 40. *Calcutta*, 1894. 8°.
14093. b. 37.

Apparently no more published.

—— ଅମରକୋଷ *etc.* [Amarakoṣa. With an Oriya translation and notes styled Bālabodhinī.] pp. 292. *Cuttack*, 1899. 12°.
14092. a. 23.(2.)

—— ସଟୀକ ଅମରକୋଷାଭିଧାନ ବା ଅମରାର୍ଥରତ୍ନମାଳିକା *etc.* Amarārtharatnamālikā. Being the Amarakoṣa with Oriya translation by Jaganmohana Siṃha Deva.] pp. i. ii. 473. *Cuttack*, 1899. 12°.
14092. a. 23.(1.)

—— నామలిఙ్గానుశాసనము అనునామాన్తరముగల అమరకోశము *etc.* [Nāmaliṅgānuśāsana. With analyses, introductions, and explanatory notes in Telugu. Edited by Daṇḍiguṇṭa Sūryanārāyaṇa Śāstrī.] pp. 394. మద్రాస్ [*Madras*,] 1899. 8°.
14090. bb. 14.

—— నామలిఙ్గానుశాసనము *etc.* [Nāmaliṅgānuśāsana. A detached copy of the first *kāṇḍa* of the preceding.] pp. 70. మద్రాస్ [*Madras*,] 1899. 8°.
14092. b. 42.

—— অমরকোষাভিধানম্ *etc.* [Amarakoṣa. With the commentary Chandrikā. Edited with indices by Chandramohana Tarkaratna.] pp. ii. lxxxv. 341. কলিকাতা ১৮২৩ [*Calcutta*, 1901.] 8°.
14090. bb. 17.

—— अमरकोश *etc.* [Amarakoṣa. Edited with a Nepali commentary and notes by Kulachandra Śarmā. Kāṇḍa 1.] pp. i. 113. काश्यां [*Benares*, 1901.] 8°.
14090. bb. 18.

—— अमरकोशादर्श ॥ [Amarakoṣādarśa. A Hindi glossary to the Amarakoṣa.] *See* KOṢAŚABDĀRTHASAṄGRAHA. कोष शब्दार्थसंग्रह *etc.* [Koṣaśabdārthasaṅgraha.] pp. 1-241. [1899.] 8°.
14160. c. 40.

AMAREṢA, *Bhāradvāja.* अथामरेशनिर्म्मिता वर्णरत्नप्रदीपिका शिक्षा *etc.* [Varṇaratnapradīpikā. A treatise of 227 stanzas on Vedic phonetics, based on Kātyāyana's Prātiṣākhya.] *See* YUGALAKIṢORA VYĀSA PĀṬHAKA. श्रीमच्छिक्षावल्क्यादि . . . शिक्षासङ्ग्रहः . . . A collection of Śikshás, *etc.* pp. 117-137. 1893. 8°.
14093. b. 31.

AMAREṢVARĀNANDA, *Svāmī Bhaṭṭāraka.* श्री मुक्तितत्त्वावलोकः *etc.* [Muktitattvāvaloka. A critical survey of the views of the various schools on the emancipation of the soul, in 2 parts. Followed by a poem in praise of Amareṣvarānanda.] pp. iii. 66. अमदावाद १९५७ [*Ahmadabad*, 1900.] 8°. **14048. cc. 15.**

AMARU. अमरुशतक *etc.* [Amaruṣataka. Edited with a Gujarati metrical paraphrase and commentary by Keṣava Harshada Dhruva.] pp. xii. 86, i. અમદાવાદ ૧૮૯૨ [*Ahmadabad*, 1892.] 8°. **14070. c. 48.**

—— Das Amaruçataka, in seinen Recensionen dargestellt, mit einer Einleitung und Auszügen aus den Commentatoren versehen, von Richard Simon. pp. i. i. 159. *Kiel, Bonn* [printed], 1893. 8°. **14072. d. 43.**

—— Amaruka Satakum. Translated . . . into [Malayalam in the style called] Manipravalam by Kerala Varma [, together with the original text in the Southern recension.] . . . With introduction and notes by Udaya Varma. pp. v. 88. *Calicut*, 1893. 8°. **14072. cc. 56.**

—— శృంగారామరుకకావ్యము *etc.* [Ṣriṅgārāmarukakāvya, *i.e.* Amaruṣataka. With the commentary Ṣriṅgāradīpikā of Vema Bhūpāla, and a Telugu commentary and Telugu metrical version by Sādhupalli Chandraṣekhara Ṣāstrī. Edited by Sāggera Ṣrīkaṇṭha Ṣāstrī.] pp. vii. 136. బెంగుళూరు [*Bangalore*,] 1898. 8°. **14076. c. 69.**

This volume forms the first āṣvāsa *in the collection called Ṣriṅgāralahari made by Chandraṣekhara Ṣāstrī.*

AMATHĀRĀMA LĪLĀDHARA VYĀSA. *See* SANDHYĀVANDANA. त्रिकाल संध्या *etc.* [Trikālasandhyā. Edited with Gujarati preface by Amathārāma.] [1900.] 12°. **14028. b. 104.(2.)**

AMBIKĀDATTA, *son of Durgādatta.* द्रव्यस्तोत्रम् *etc.* [Dravyastotra. A poem on wealth. With a Hindi translation by Rādhākṛishṇa Miṣra.] pp. 28. मुम्बय्याम् १८९३ [*Bombay*, 1893.] 16°. **14072. b. 4.(4.)**

AMBIKĀDATTA VYĀSA. ॥ अवतारमीमांसा ॥ अवतारकारिका-सहित *etc.* [Avatāramīmāṃsā. A Hindi treatise on Vishṇu's incarnations, illustrated from Sanskrit texts. Followed by Avatārakārikā or Avatāramīmāṃsāk°, a Sanskrit metrical summary of the same, in 261 stanzas.] pp. ix. 140; 2 *plates.* काशी १९५६ [*Benares*, 1899.] 8°. **14154. dd. 10.(1.)**

—— कथाकुसुमम् ∴ . Katha-kusuma. (An easy reader in idiomatic Sanskrit.) Second edition. pp. iii. 57, 52, v. *Bhagalpur*, 1890. 12°. **14085. b. 37.**

—— Practical Sanskrit. Part I. An elementary treatise on grammar and composition, *etc.* Second edition. pp. iii. ii. ii. 66, 14. *Bhagalpur.* 1890. 8°. **14092. a. 12.**

AMERICAN ORIENTAL SOCIETY. *See* ACADEMIES, *etc.*—*Boston, Mass.*

AMITĀYURDHYĀNASŪTRA. Amitâyur-Dhyâna-Sûtra, the Sûtra of the Meditation on Amitâyus. [Translated with notes *etc.* by J. Takakusu.] 1894. *See* MUELLER (F. M.). The Sacred Books of the East, *etc.* Vol. xlix. pt. 2. 1879, *etc.* 8°. **2003. b. (vol. 49.)**

AMMĀḶ. *See* VARADĀCHĀRYA, *Vātsya*, called NAḌĀDŪR AMMĀḶ.

AMOGHĀNANDINĪ ṢIKSHĀ. अयामोघानन्दिनी शिक्षा *etc.* [Amoghānandinī Ṣikshā. 130 stanzas of the Mādhyandina school on Vedic phonetics. Followed by the Laghu-Amoghānandinī Ṣikshā, in 17 stanzas.] *See* YUGALAKIṢORA VYĀSA PĀṬHAKA. श्रीमद्याज्ञवल्क्यादि . . . शिक्षासङ्ग्रहः . . . A collection of Śikshás, *etc.* pp. 93-108. **14093. b. 31.**

AMOGHAVARSHA, *son of Govinda III., Rāshṭrakūṭa King.* [For the Praṣnottararatnamālā sometimes ascribed to this king:] *See* VIMALACHANDRA SŪRI.

AMṚITALĀLA BHAṬṬĀCHĀRYA. *See* JAYADEVA, *son of Bhojadeva.* श्री गीतगोविंद° [Gītagovinda. With a Hindi translation by Amṛitalāla, *etc.* [1891.] 8°. **14072. d. 42.**

AMṚITĀNANDA, *Continuator of Aṣvaghosha.* [For this writer's supplement (Sargas xiv.-xvii.) to the Buddhacharita:] *See* AṢVAGHOSHA.

AMṚITARĀMA KARUṆĀṢAṄKARA ṬHĀKURA. *See* PURUSHOTTAMA ṢARMĀ, *son of Ṣārṅgadhara.* श्रीस्थल प्रकाशः *etc.* [Sthalaprakāṣa. Edited with Gujarati translation by Amṛitarāma.] [1898.] 8°. **14058. b. 38.**

ĀNANDA, *disciple of Vidyādhara.* *See* ĀNANDADHARA.

ĀNANDA BHAṬṬA, *descendant of Ananta Bhaṭṭa.* বল্লাল চরিতম্ *etc.* [Ballālacharita. A history of King Ballālasena, in which are incorporated portions of Bhaṭṭa Siṃha Giri's Vyāsapurāṇa and Śaraṇadatta's Ballālacharita. Edited with English introduction by Haraprasāda Śāstrī.] pp. xi. 110. কলিকাতা ১৮২৩ [*Calcutta,* 1901.] 12°.
14058. a. 18.(1.)

—— Vallala Charita in Sanskrit . . . Edited and translated [with introduction] . . . by . . . Haraprasad Sastri. pp. xi. 103. *Calcutta,* 1901. 12°. **14058. a. 18.(2.)**

Contains only the translation. The Sanskrit text to which the title refers is that contained in the preceding publication.

ĀNANDA BHAṬṬOPĀDHYĀYA, *son of Jataveda.* *See* UPANISHADS.—*Separate Upanishads.* ईशावास्योपनिषत् *etc.* ((1) Shri Íśávásyopanishad with the Bháshya of . . . Ánandabhattopádhyáya, *etc.*) [1888.] 8°. **14003. ccc. (no. 5.)**

—— *See* UPANISHADS.—*Separate Upanishads.* The Îśavâsyopanishad. Translated . . . with . . . notes from the Tika of . . . Anandabhatta. 1896. 8°. **14010. cc. 6.**

ĀNANDABODHA PARAMAHAṂSA, *Bhaṭṭārakāchārya.* न्यायमकरन्दः . . . Nyâya Makaranda, a treatise on Vedanta philosophy . . . with a commentary by Chitsukh Muni. Edited by . . . Swâmî Bâlarâm Udaseen Mándalíka. *Benares,* 1901, *etc.* 8°. **14004. a. 11.**

In progress. Forms nos. 38, etc., of the Chowkhambâ Sanskrit Series. *The title is from the wrapper.*

ĀNANDABODHENDRA SARASVATĪ, *disciple of Gaṅgādharendra.* *See* YOGAVĀSISHṬHARĀMĀYAṆA. বাশিষ্ঠমহারামায়ণম্ *etc.* [Yogavāsishṭharāmāyaṇa. With Ānandabodhendra's commentary Tātparyaprakāṣa, *etc.*] [1893, *etc.*] 8°. **14049. a. 2.**

ĀNANDACHANDRA BHAṬṬĀCHARYA VIDYĀBHŪSHAṆA. *See* RAGHUNANDANA BHAṬṬĀCHĀRYA. মহামহোপাধ্যায় . . . শ্রীরঘুনন্দন . . . বিরচিত তিথ্যদ্বাহতত্ত্বয়োঃ। আক্ষেপ-সমাধানম্ *etc.* [Ākshepasamādhāna. An interpretation by Ānandachandra of crucial passages in Raghunandana's Tithitattva and Udvāhatattva, with the text of those passages.] [1893.] 12°. **14033. a. 31.**

ANANDA CHARLU, *P.* *See* ĀNANDĀCHĀRYA VIDYĀVINODA.

ĀNANDĀCHĀRYA VIDYĀVINODA, *Rāi Bahādur P.* Virtue's Triumph, or, The Mahâ Bhârata [in an English epitome,] by . . . P. Ananda Charlu. pp. vii. 347, ii. *Madras,* 1894. 8°. **4505. de. 4.**

—— Love's Triumphs, orientally told. [A series of tales from the Mahābhārata, epitomised in English] by . . . P. Ananda Charlu, Vidya Vinoda. pp. i. i. 89. *Madras,* 1898. 12°.
14060. b. 16.(1.)

ĀNANDADHARA, *disciple of Vidyādhara.* The Mādhavânala-kathā . . . with a translation of the Prakrit passages. By Dr. P. E. Pavolini. 1893. *See* ACADEMIES, *etc.*—Europe.—*International Congress of Orientalists.* Transactions of the Ninth International Congress, *etc.* Vol. i., pp. 430-453. 1873, *etc.* 8°. **Ac. 8806. (Session 9.)**

ÁNANDADNYÁNA. *See* ĀNANDAGIRI.

ĀNANDAGIRI. *See* MAHĀBHĀRATA.—Bhagavadgītā.—*Sanskrit.* श्रीमद्भगवद्गीता *etc.* (Shrîmat Bhagavadgîta with the Bháshya by . . . Śankaráchárya, the commentary by Anadagiri [*sic*] on the same, *etc.*) [1896.] 8°. **14003. ccc. (no. 34.)**

—— *See* ŚAṄKARA ĀCHĀRYA.—*Two or more Works.* Śrí-Śankaráchárya's Miscellaneous Works, *etc.* [Vol. II., Śataślokī, with commentary ascribed to Ānandagiri, *etc.*] 1898-1899. 8°. [*Mysore Government Oriental Library Series: Bibliotheca Sanskrita.*] **14004. b. 10.(vol. 2.)**

—— *See* ŚAṄKARA ĀCHĀRYA. — *Doubtful and Supposititious Works.* शतश्लोकी° [Śataślokī, or Vedāntakesarī. With commentary of Ānandagiri.] [1885-1886.] 8°. [*Kāvyetihāsasaṅgraha.*] **14072. d. 37.(vol. 8, 9.)**

—— *See* SUREŚVARA ĀCHĀRYA. बृहदारण्यकोपनिषद्भाष्यवार्त्तिकम् *etc.* (Bṛihadáraṇyakopanishadbháshyavártika . . . With its commentary by . . . Ânandajnána[, styled Śāstraprakāśikā,] *etc.*) [1892-1894.] 8°. **14003. ccc. (no. 16.)**

—— *See* UPANISHADS. — *Separate Upanishads.* ईशावास्योपनिषत् *etc.* ((1) Shri Íśávásyopanishad with the Bháshya of . . . Śankaráchárya and Commentary by . . . Ánandadnyána, *etc.*) [1888.] 8°. **14003. ccc. (no. 5.)**

ĀNANDAGIRI (*continued*). *See* UPANISHADS.—*Separate Upanishads.* ईशोपनिषत् *etc.* (Isa-Upanishad. With the . . . Tika of Anandagiri, *etc.*) 1895. 8°. **14010. cc. 3.(1.)**

—— *See* UPANISHADS.—*Separate Upanishads.* The Īśavâsyopanishad. Translated . . . with . . . notes from the Tikas of Anandagiri, *etc.* 1896. 8°. **14010. cc. 6.**

—— *See* UPANISHADS.—*Separate Upanishads.* केनोपनिषत् *etc.* (The Kenopanishad with the . . . Bháshyás of . . . Śankarácharya and Commentary of . . . Ánandadnyána, *etc.*) [1888.] 8°. **14003. ccc. (no. 6.)**

—— *See* UPANISHADS.—*Separate Upanishads.* मुण्डकोपनिषत् *etc.* [Muṇḍakopanishad. With the commentary of Ṣaṅkara, the gloss of Ānandagiri, *etc.*] [1889.] 8°. **14003. ccc. (no. 9.)**

—— *See* UPANISHADS.—*Separate Upanishads.* प्रश्नोपनिषत् *etc.* (Śrí Praśnopanishad with the Bháshya of . . . Śankarácharya and its commentary by . . . Ánandajnyána, *etc.*) [1889.] 8°. **14003. ccc. (no. 8.)**

ĀNANDAJĪ KHETṢĪ. श्री जैनप्रबोध पुस्तक *etc.* [Jainaprabodha. A collection of Jain prayers, hymns, *etc.*, in Prakrit and Gujarati. Part i.] pp. ii. xxiv. 600; 8 *plates.* मुंबापुरी १९३९ [*Bombay*, 1883.] 12°. **14144. f. 17.**

ĀNANDAJÑĀNA. *See* ĀNANDAGIRI.

ANANDALVAR. *See* ANANTĀCHĀRYA, *Maṇḍayam A.*

ĀNANDANĀTHA. ज्ञानांगयोगमूलरहस्य अने . . . अष्टांगयोग मूलरहस्य *etc.* [Jñānāṅgayogamūlarahasya. A yogic commentary on the Gāyatrī, *etc.*, in Gujarati. Followed by Ashṭāṅgayogamūlarahasya, a work comprising select Sanskrit stanzas bearing on Yoga with Gujarati commentaries, *etc.* Edited by Moṭābhāī Motīlāl Deṣāī.] pp. 24. सुरत १९५३ [*Surat*, 1897.] 8°. **14048. cc. 10.**

ĀNANDANĀTHA KAVĪNDRAṢEKHARA. Chhandaḥsárahárávali, or A Garland of Sanskrit rhythms, *etc.* [Comprising stanzas illustrating the different metres, with commentary, in Sanskrit.] (छन्दःसारहारावली) pp. xii. 128, iv. *Calcutta*, 1890. 12°. **14053. b. 19.(2.)**

ĀNANDARĀYA MAKHĪ, *son of Nṛisiṃharāya.* The Jîvânandana of Ânandarâya Makhî. [A drama in seven acts.] Edited by Paṇdit Durgâprasâd and Kâśînâth Pâṇdurang Parab. (जीवानन्दनम्।) pp. 108. 1891. *See* DURGĀPRASĀDA, *son of Vrajalāla*, and KĀṢĪNĀTHA PĀṆDURAṄGA PARAB. Kâvyamâlâ. [No.] 27. 1886, *etc.* 8°. **14072. ccc. 12.(no. 27.)**

—— The Vidyâpariṇayana of Ânandarâya Makhî. [An allegorical play in 7 acts.] Edited by Paṇdit Śivadatta and Kâśînâth Pâṇdurang Parab. (विद्यापरिणयनम्।) pp. 88. 1893. *See* DURGĀPRASĀDA, *son of Vrajalāla*, and KĀṢĪNĀTHA PĀṆDURAṄGA PARAB. Kâvyamâlâ. [No.] 39. 1886, *etc.* 8°. **14072. ccc. 12.(no. 39.)**

ĀNANDĀṢRAMA SANSKRIT SERIES. The Ánandáśram Sanskrit Series. (आनन्दाश्रमसंस्कृतग्रन्थावलिः) [A series of Sanskrit works published at the Ānandāṣrama, an institution containing a library of manuscripts and a press, founded at Poona for the study and publication of Sanskrit literature under the direction of Mahādeva Chimnājī Āpṭe, and subsequently of Harinārāyaṇa Āpṭe.] *Poona*, 1888, *etc.* 8°. **14003. ccc.**

In progress.

Texts published in this series are to be found under the following headings. The titles of those that have been already described in Prof. Bendall's Catalogue, and hence are not reprinted in this Catalogue, are marked by an asterisk.

1. **Upanishads.* — Separate Upanishads.
2. **Vedas.* — Taittirīyasaṃhitā.
3. **Vedas.*—Rigveda.
4. **Yogaratnākara.*
5. *Upanishads.* — Separate Upanishads. [Iṣopanishad.]
6. *Upanishads.* — Separate Upanishads. [Kenopanishad.]
7. **Upanishads.* — Separate Upanishads.
8. *Upanishads.* — Separate Upanishads. [Praṣnopanishad.]
9. *Upanishads.* — Separate Upanishads. [Muṇḍakopanishad.]

10, 11, 12. **Upanishads.*—Separate Upanishads.

13. **Sureṣvara Āchārya*
14. **Upanishads.* — Separate Upanishads.
15. **Upanishads.* — Separate Upanishads.
16. *Sureṣvara Āchārya.*
17. **Upanishads* — Separate Upanishads.
18. **Purāṇas.*—Ādityapurāṇa.
19. **Vāgbhaṭa*, son of Siṃhagupta.
20. **Sāyaṇāchārya.* — Jīvanmuktiviveka.
21. **Bādarāyaṇa.*
22. **Sāyaṇāchārya* —Ṣaṅkaradigvijaya.
23. *Bādarāyaṇa.*
24. *Jaimini.*—Mīmāṃsāsūtra.
25. *Purāṇas.*—Skandapurāṇa. [Sūtasaṃhitā.]

Extra Number. *Purāṇas.* — Padmapurāṇa.

26. *Pālakāpya.*
27. *Vrinda.*
28. *Purāṇas.* — Brahmapurāṇa.
29. *Upanishads.* — General Collections.
30. *Upanishads.* — Separate Upanishads. [Nṛisiṃhatāpanīyopanishad.]
31. *Upanishads.* — Separate Upanishads. [Bṛihadāraṇyakopanishad.]
32. *Brāhmaṇas* — Aitareyabrāhmaṇa.
33. *Dhanvantari.*
34. *Mahābhārata.* — Bhagavadgītā.
35. *Ṣārṅgadeva.*
36. *Āraṇyakas.* [Taittirīyāraṇyaka.]
37. *Brāhmaṇas.* — Taittirīyabrāhmaṇa.
38. *Āraṇyakas.* [Aitāreyāraṇyaka.]
39. *Gopinātha Dikshita.*
40. *Kāṣīnātha Ṣāstri Āgāṣe.*
41. *Purāṇas.*—Agnipurāṇa.
42. *Vedas.*—Yajurveda.
43. *Bhaṭṭoji Dikshita.*

44, 45. *Mahābhārata.* — Bhagavadgītā.

ĀNANDATĪRTHA, surnamed **MADHVĀCHĀRYA**. [*Life.*] *See* GURURĀU RĀMACHANDRA. श्री मध्व पीठ गी वृक्ष [Genealogical tree of the pontifical successors of Ānandatīrtha,] *etc.* 1894. *s.s.* Fol.
14048. f. 24.

—— *See* KṚISHṆASVĀMI AIYAR, *C.N.* Madhwacharya . . . A short historic sketch. [1900.] 8°.
10604. bbb. 25.(5.)

—— *See* NĀRĀYAṆA PAṆḌITĀCHĀRYA, *son of Trivikrama.* मध्वविजय *etc.* [Madhvavijaya. A poem on the life of Ānandatīrtha.] [1895.] 16°.
14076. a. 26.

—— *See* BĀDARĀYAṆA. ॥ अथ ब्रह्मसूत्र भाष्य° [Brahmasūtra. With the commentary of Ānandatīrtha.] [1892.] *obl.* 16°.
14048. a. 16.

—— *See* BĀDARĀYAṆA. అథ శ్రీబ్రహ్మసూత్రభాష్యం *etc.* [Brahmasūtra. With the commentary of Ānandatīrtha.] [1898.] *obl.* 12°.
14048. b. 33.(3.)

—— *See* BĀDARĀYAṆA. श्रीमद्ब्रह्मसूत्राणि *etc.* [Brahmasūtra. With the *bhāshya* of Ānandatīrtha, and the Bhāshyadīpikā upon the latter by Jagannātha Yati. Followed by summaries of the *bhāshyas* of Ānandatīrtha, Ṣaṅkara, and Rāmānuja in catechetical form, *etc.*] [1900.] 8°.
14048. cc. 30.

—— *See* SANDHYĀVANDANA. யஜுர்வேத . . . ஸந்த்யாவந்தநம் *etc.* [Sandhyāvandana. Followed by the Purushasūkta, Ṣrīsūkta, *etc.* With extracts, in a Tamil translation, from the commentaries of Ānandatīrtha and others.] 1901. 8°.
14033. aa. 27.

—— सन्ध्याभाष्यम् *etc.* [Sandhyābhāshya, or Sandhyāmantravṛitti. A commentary upon the *sandhyā* prayers according to the Bahvṛicha school.] pp. 24. *See* SANDHYĀVANDANA. सन्ध्याभाष्यसमुच्चयः *etc.* [Sandhyābhāshyasamuchchaya.] [1899.] 8°. **14003. ccc. (no. 40.)**

—— శ్రీమధ్వదేవతార్చనవిధి [Madhvadevatārchanavidhi. A ritual for the worship of the Madhva sect.] pp. ii. 31. *Bezvada,* 1895. 12°.
14028. b. 61.(2.)

ĀNANDAVARDHANA, *Rājānaka, son of Noṇa.* The Dhvanyâloka of Ânandavardhanâchârya. [A treatise on the Ars Poetica, with special reference to *dhvani* or 'implication.'] With the commentary of Abhinavaguptâchârya. Edited by Paṇdit Durgâprasâd and Kâśînâth Pâṇdurang Parab. (ध्वन्यालोकः ।) pp. iii. ii. i. 246, ii. 1891. *See* DURGĀPRASĀDA, *son of Vrajalāla,* and KĀṢINĀTHA PĀṆḌURANGA PARAB. Kâvyamâlâ. [No.] 25. 1886, *etc.* 8°. **14072. ccc. 12.(no. 25.)**

—— Ānandavardhana's Dhvanyāloka. Übersetzt [with an introduction] von Hermann Jacobi. 1902-1903. *See* ACADEMIES, *etc.*—Germany.—*Deutsche Morgenlaendische Gesellschaft.* Zeitschrift, *etc.* Bd. 56, 57. 1846, *etc.* 8°.
Ac. 8815/2.(vol. 56, 57.)

ĀNANDAVIJAYAJĪ, also called ĀTMĀRĀMAJĪ. *See* ĀTMĀRĀMAJĪ ĀNANDAVIJAYAJĪ.

ANANTA BHAṬṬA, *the Grammarian.* *See* ANNAM BHAṬṬA.

ANANTA BHAṬṬA, *son of Nāga Bhaṭṭa.* *See* ANANTADEVA, *son of Nāgadeva.*

ANANTA BHAṬṬA, *the Poet.* Anantbhatt Kavi's Bharata Champû. With Antahpraveshikâ commentary by Gaanjan [*sic*] Chintaman Deo. (भारतचम्पूः) pp. 202. *Bombay,* १८२२ [1901.] 8°.
14072. ccc. 26.

ANANTĀCHĀRYA, *son of Nāga Bhaṭṭa.* *See* ANANTADEVA, *son of Nāgadeva.*

ANANTĀCHĀRYA, *Maṇḍayam A., Ṣeshārya, of Mysore.* शास्त्रारम्भसमर्थनम् (समासवादः, ब्रह्मलक्षणवादः, *etc.*) [Dissertations on the Viṣishṭādvaita philosophy, entitled (1) Ṣāstrārambhasamarthana, (2) Samāsavāda, (3) Brahmalakshaṇavāda, (4) Ṣarīravāda, (5) Ṣāstraikyavāda, (6) Jñānayāthārthyavāda, (7) Gurusāmānādhikaraṇavāda, (8) Laghusāmānādhikaraṇavāda, (9) Saṃvinnānātvasamarthana, (10) Vishayatāvāda, (11) Brahmapadaṣaktivāda, (12) Siddhāntasiddhāñjana, (13) Nirviṣeshapramāṇavyudāsavāda, (14) Vidhisudhākara, (15) Ākāṣādhikaraṇavichāra, (16) Pratijñāvāda, (17) Sudarṣanasuradruma, (18) Ṣrībhāshyabhāvāṅkura, (19) Īkshatyadhikaraṇavichāra, (20) Mokshakāraṇatāvāda. With a commentary upon nos. 1-5, styled Tātparyadīpikā, by T. E. S. Kuppan Aiyaṅgār.] [1898, *etc.*] *See* ANANTĀḶVĀR, *Maṇḍayam A.,* and NARASIṂHAIYAṄGĀR, *P. T.* वेदान्तवादावली *etc.* [Vedāntavādāvalī.] Nos. 1-20. [1898, *etc.*] 8°. **14048. cc. 18.**

ANANTĀCHĀRYA, *Prativādibhayaṅkara, of Conjevaram.* See VEDAS.—Ṛigveda.—*Single Hymns and Verses.* Purusha Suktha Bhashyam by P. B. Anantha chariar, *etc.* 1901. 8°. [*Śāstramuktāvalī.*] **14049. a. 1.(no. 9.)**

—— Nyayarathnavali, *etc.* [A series of logical works. Edited by Anantāchārya.] *Conjeeveram,* 1900, *etc.* 8°. **14048. e. 31.(1.)**

In progress.

For works published in this series see under the heading :— Gaṅgeśa Upādhyāya.

—— परतत्त्वनिर्णयः *etc.* [Paratattvanirṇaya. A lecture on the divinity of Nārāyaṇa as shown in ancient Sanskrit literature.] pp. 21. कल्याण-मुंबई १९५२ [*Kalyan,* 1896.] 12°. **14028. b. 71.(4.)**

—— शास्त्रमुक्तावली The Śasthramukthâvalî. A collection of Vedanta, Mimamsa and Nyaya works. Edited by P. B. Anantachariar. *Conjeeveram,* 1899, *etc.* 8°. **14049. a. 1.**

In progress.

The works published in this series are catalogued under the headings :—

No.	1.	*Vedas.*—Ṛigveda.	No.	7.	*Bādarāyaṇa.*
,,	2.	*Khaṇḍadeva.*	,,	8.	*Vimaladāsa.*
,,	3.	*Veṅkaṭanātha Vedāntāchārya.*	,,	9.	*Vedas.*—Ṛigveda.
,,	4.	*Gaṅgeśa Upādhyāya.*	,,	10.	*Yāmuna Āchārya.*
,,	5.	*Veṅkaṭanātha Vedāntāchārya.*	,,	11.	*Raghunātha Śiromaṇi.*
,,	6.	*Mahābhārata.*—Bhagavadgītā.	,,	12.	*Varadāchārya.*
			,,	13.	*Śrinivāsa Dikshita.*
			,,	14.	*Jaimini.*

—— వాధూలప్రవరచింతామణిః [Vādhūlapravarachintāmaṇi. A pamphlet on the genealogy of the Vādhūla tribe of Brahmans.] pp. 13. శ్రీకాంచీ [*Conjevaram,* 18]99. 8°. **14058. b. 32.(2.)**

ANANTĀCHĀRYA, *Seshārya, of Yadugirī.* ನ್ಯಾಯಭಾಸ್ಕರಾಖ್ಯಗ್ರಂಥಃ *etc.* [Nyāyabhāskara. A criticism, in twelve chapters, of the Laghuchandrikā of Brahmānanda Sarasvatī from a Rāmānujī standpoint.] pp. 173. ಮಹಿಶೂರು ೧೮೯೩ [*Mysore,* 1893.] 8°. **14048. bb. 47.**

ANANTADDHAJA, known as TAUNGBALU HSAYA. See NANDAMEDHA, *of the Bodhi Kyaung, Tantabin.* ယမိုက်ဆယ်ကျမ်းအရကောက် *etc.* [Yamaik-hsay-kyan-aya-kauk. A Burmese treatise on the 10 Yamakas, based on the work of Nandamedha as transmitted by Anantaddhaja, *etc.*] 1900. 8°. **14300. e. 16.**

ANANTADEVA, *son of Āpadeva.* कृष्णभक्तिचन्द्रिका। [Kṛishṇabhaktichandrikā. An allegorical religious play.] pp. 39. [1890.] See PERIODICAL PUBLICATIONS.—*Bombay.* ग्रन्थरत्नमाला *etc.* (Granth Ratna Málá, *etc.*) Vol. iv., no. 5, 6. 1887-[1892.] 8°. **14096. c. 8.(vol. 4.)**

—— सिद्धान्ततत्त्वं नाम वेदान्तप्रकरणम् *etc.* [Siddhāntatattva. A summary of Vedānta doctrine. Edited with introductions, *etc.*, by Rāma Śāstrī Mānavallī.] pp. 60, iii. vii. iv. v. 1900. See PERIODICAL PUBLICATIONS.—*Benares.* The Pandit, *etc.* New Series. Vol. xxii. 1876, *etc.* 8°. **14096. d. 6.(vol. 22.)**

ANANTADEVA, *son of Nāgadeva.* See KĀTYĀYANA. महर्षिकात्यायनप्रणीतम् . . . सर्वानुक्रमसूत्रम् . . . Kátyáyana's Sarvánukramasutras . . . with the commentary of Yájñikánantadeva, *etc.* 1893, *etc.* 8°. **14007. c. 25.**

—— See UPANISHADS. — *Separate Upanishads.* ईशावास्योपनिषत् *etc.* ((1) Shri Ísávásyopanishad with . . . (6) The Bhashyás of . . . Anantáchárya, *etc.*) [1888.] 8°. **14003. ccc.(no. 5.)**

—— See UPANISHADS. — *Separate Upanishads.* The Îśavâsyopanishad. Translated . . . with the commentaries of Sri Sankaracharya and Sri Anantacharya, *etc.* 1896. 8°. **14010. cc. 6.**

—— अथातोऽवसाननिर्णयं व्याख्यास्यामः ॥ [Avasānanirṇaya. A list of catchwords in the White Yajurveda.] See YUGALAKIŚORA VYĀSA PĀṬHAKA. श्रीमद्याज्ञवल्क्यादि . . . शिक्षासङ्ग्रहः . . . A collection of Śikshás, etc. pp. 166-171. 1893. 8°. **14093. b. 31.**

ANANTADEVA YĀJÑIKA. See ANANTADEVA, *son of Nāgadeva.*

ANANTAKṚISHṆA ŚĀSTRĪ, *R., of Adyar Library.* See BHĀSKARARĀYA DĪKSHITA BHĀRATĪ. Varivasyà Rahasya . . . Edited by R. Ananta Krishna Śâstri. 1901. 12°. **14048. a. 29.**

—— See MAHĀBHĀRATA.—*Anuśāsanaparva.* Śiva Sahasranâma Stotra, with . . . Nîlakantha's commentary. English translation, by R. Anantakrishna Sastri. 1902. 8°. **14016. dd. 1.**

—— See MAHĀBHĀRATA.—*Anuśāsanaparva.* The Vishnu Sahasranama, with Sri Sankaracharya's commentary, translated ... by R. Ananthakrishna Sastry. 1901. 8°. **14048. bb. 52.**

—— *See* Purāṇas.—*Brahmāṇḍapurāṇa.* [*Lalitā-sahasranāma.*] Lalita Sahasranama, with Bhaskararaya's commentary. Translated ... by R. Anantakrishna Sastri. 1899. 8°. **14016. c. 59.**

—— *See* Purāṇas.—*Brahmāṇḍapurāṇa.* [*Lalitā-triṣatī.*] Triśatî with ... Śankrâchârya's Bhâsya. Panchadaśî Mantra with Agastya's Bhâshya and Triśatî text. Edited by R. Ananta Krishna Sastry. 1902. 12°. **14033. a. 45.(1.)**

—— *See* Purāṇas.—*Skandapurāṇa.* അർദ്ധഗിരി മാഹാത്മ്യം Ardhagiri Mâhâtmya ... Edited by R. Anantakrishna Sastri. 1902. 8°.
14016. dd. 2.

—— *See* Saṅkara Āchārya.—*Doubtful and Supposititious Works.* Ananda Lahari. With yantras and commentaries. Translated ... by R. Anantakrishna Sastri. 1899. 12°. **14048. b. 35.**

—— *See* Upanishads.—*Separate Upanishads.* Gopala Tapani Upanishad. Part I. [Translated, with extracts from commentaries, by Anantakṛishṇa.] 1899. 8°. **P.P. 636. cm.(vol. 20.)**

—— *See* Upanishads.—*Separate Upanishads.* Kaivalyopanishad. [Translated by Anantakṛishṇa.] 1899. 4°. [*Siddhanta Deepika.*]
14170. fff. 4.(vol. 2.)

—— *See* Upanishads.—*Separate Upanishads.* Râja Yoga Bhâshya. Translated ... by Pandit R. Ananthakrishna Sastryar. 1896. 8°.
14048. c. 70.(2.)

ANANTĀNANDAGIRI, *Svāmī, disciple of Rāmagiri.* *See* Bādarāyaṇa. **श्री शारीरक मीमांसा भाष्य सारसंग्रहः** *etc.* [Brahmasūtra, or Ṣārīrakamīmāṃsā. With Ṣārīrakamīmāṃsābhāshyasārasaṅgraha, a compendious commentary in Sanskrit and Hindi by Anantānandagiri. Followed by Kāṣīmṛitimokshanirṇaya, an essay on the salvation gained by dying at Benares, by the latter.] [1900.] 8°.
14048. cc. 36.

ANANTAPRAPANNA ṢRĪNIVĀSADĀSA. *See* Amarajī Hariṣaṅkara Travāṛī.

ANANTARĀMA, *disciple of Keṣava Bhaṭṭa.* **वैष्णवधर्म्म मीमांसा** *etc.* [Vaishṇavadharmamīmāṃsā. An exposition of Vaishṇava doctrine according to the Nimbārka school. Edited by Dulāre-prasād Ṣarmā.] ff. 30. **श्रीवृन्दावन १९५८** [*Brindaban,* 1901.] 8°. **14028. dd. 3.(2.)**

ANANTĀṚVĀR, *of Mysore.* *See* Anantāchārya, *Maṇḍayam A.*

ANANTĀṚVĀR, *Maṇḍayam A.,* and **NARASIṂHAIYAṄGĀR,** *P. T.* **वेदान्तवादावली** *etc.* [Vedāntavādāvalī. A collection of treatises in exposition of Viṣishṭādvaita-Vedānta and the system of Rāmānuja. Published in monthly fascicules by M. A. Anantāṛvār and P. T. Narasiṃhaiyaṅgār. Series i., comprising works of M. A. Anantāchārya.] **कल्याणपुर १८९८** [*Bangalore,* 1898, *etc.*] 8°.
14048. cc. 18.
In progress.

ANANTĀRYA, *M.A., of Mysore.* *See* Anantāchārya, *Maṇḍayam A.*

ANANTENDRA YATI, *disciple of Mahādevendra, of Chidambaram.* അഥ വേദാന്തസാരസംഗ്രഹഃ *etc.* [Vedāntasārasaṅgraha. A popular summary of Vedānta philosophy in the form of a dialogue between a teacher and a disciple.] pp. 29. ஆணிக்காரச்சத்ரம் [*Anikkarachattram,* 1898.] 12°.
14048. b. 33.(2.)

ANANTHA CHARIAR. *See* Anantāchārya.

ANANTHAKRISHNA SASTRY. *See* Anantakṛishṇa Ṣāstrī.

ANDERSEN (Dines). *See* Rasavāhinī. Rasavāhinī ... i Udvalg med Indledning af Dines Andersen. 1891. 8°. **Ac. 9877/2.(vol. 1, no. 6.)**

—— *See* Suttapiṭaka.—*Khuddakanikāya.* [*Jātaka.*] The Jātaka, *etc.* (Vol. vii. Index to the Jātaka and its commentary ... By Dines Andersen.) 1877-1897. 8°. **14098. d. 23.(vol. 7.)**

AṄGIRAS. ॥ **अङ्गिरासंहिता** [*sic*] *etc.* [Aṅgirahṣaṃhitā, or Aṅgirodharmaṣāstra. A tract, in 72 stanzas, on expiatory rites. With Hindi version.] pp. 15. **कानपुर १८९९** [*Cawnpore,* 1899.] 8°.
14028. c. 85.(4.)

This tract is identical with the A°-smṛiti or A°-dharmaṣāstra published in Jīvānanda Vidyāsāgara's Dharmashastra Sangraha, *vol.* i. (1876), *but apparently differs considerably from the work generally known as A°-smṛiti.*

AṄGUTTARANIKĀYA. *See* Suttapiṭaka.

AṄKĀBHIDHĀNA. অথ অঙ্কাভিধান। [Aṅkābhidhāna. A list of words expressing numerals, in verse. With a Bengali translation.] *See* GOPĪRAMAṆA TARKARATNA. কোষচন্দ্রিকা *etc.* [Koṣachandrikā.] pp. 49-57. [1893.] 12°.
14090. b. 44.(1.)

ANNADĀCHARAṆA BHAṬṬĀCHĀRYA. তীর্থতত্ত্বপ্রদায়িনী *etc.* [Tīrthatattvapradāyinī, a work on pilgrimages. Compiled and edited with a Bengali translation by Annadācharaṇa.] pp. vi. 460. *Calcutta,* ১৩০১ [1894.] *obl.* 8°.
14033. c. 38.

ANNADĀCHARAṆA TARKACHŪḌĀMAṆI, *of Noakhali. See* DURGASIṂHA, *Commentator on the Kātantra.* নমস্কারবিবেকঃ *etc.* [Namaskāraviveka. The introductory stanza of Durgasiṃha's Kātantravṛitti and the parts of Trilochanadāsa's Pañjikā and Susheṇa's Kalāpachandra bearing on the latter. With a commentary upon the whole, called Kaumudī, by Annadācharaṇa.] [1900.] 12°.
14092. a. 24.(1.)

—— *See* RĀMACHANDRA NYĀYAVĀGĪṢA. Kabyachandrica . . . with notes by Annada Charan, *etc.* [1885.] 12°.
14053. b. 29.

—— महाप्रस्थानम् *etc.* [Mahāprasthāna. A poem in 22 *sargas* upon the Great Journey of the Pāṇḍava brethren.] pp. i. 288. नोयाखालिनगर्यां १३०८ [*Noakhali,* 1901.] 8°.
14072. ccc. 27.

—— सुमनोऽञ्जलिः *etc.* [Sumano'ñjali. Poems on various moral subjects, in 14 *añjalis.*] pp. 134. नोयाखालि १३०८ [*Noakhali,* 1901.] 8°.
14072. cc. 62.(4.)

ANNADĀPRASĀDA VASU, *of Chakdighi. See* KĀLIDĀSA.—*Meghadūta.* The Cloud Messenger . . . The Uttaramegha. Translated into English verse by Annadáprasád Basu. 1885. 12°.
14072. b. 10.(1.)

ANNAM BHAṬṬA, also called ANANTA BHAṬṬA. *See* PĀṆINI.—*Mitākshārā.* मिताक्षरा *etc.* (The Mitakshara. A commentary on Panini's grammatical aphorisms. By . . . Annambhatta, *etc.*) 1895. 8°.
14090. bb. 11.

—— *See* PĀṆINI. — *Mitākshārā.* मिताक्षरा *etc.* [Mitāksharā. The aphorisms of Pāṇini with Annam Bhaṭṭa's commentary.] 1896, *etc.* 8°. [*Grandha Pradarsani.*]
14003. c. 2.(15.)

ANNAM BHAṬṬA, also called ANANTA BHAṬṬA (*continued*). The Tarka Sangraha, or A system of Indian logic . . . Edited with a Siṇhalese translation, notes, and an introduction [in Sinhalese] by W. P. Ranesiṇghe . . . තර්කසංග්‍රහය *etc.* pp. iv. xxi. 42, i. කොළඹ [*Colombo,*] 1880. 8°.
14048. dd. 22.

—— तर्कसंग्रहप्रारम्भः Taraksangrah [*sic*]. Translated into Hindi [by Mādhavānanda Bhāratī, together with the Sanskrit text and the Sanskrit commentary of Chandraja Siṃha. Second edition.] pp. 56, *lith. Benares,* 1889. 8°. **14048. dd. 12.**

—— The Tarka-sangraha of Annambhaṭṭa, with the author's Dîpikâ, & Govardhana's Nyâya-Bodhinî and critical and explanatory notes by . . . Yaśavanta Vâsudev Âthalye . . . Revised . . . with a preface and introduction by Mahâdev Râjârâm Bodas. pp. ii. xx. lii. 380. *Bombay,* 1897. 8°. **14048. cc. 7.**

Forms vol. lv. *of the* Bombay Sanskrit Series.

—— तर्कसंग्रहः *etc.* [Tarkasaṅgraha.] pp. 24, *lith.* दिल्ली १९५५ [*Delhi,* 1898.] 12°. **14048. a. 26.**

—— The Tarka-sangraha of Annam Bhatta. [In the English version published in the Allahabad edition of 1851 and in part composed by Fitz-Edward Hall.] *See* MANMATHANĀTHA DATTA. Darshana, *etc.* pp. 101-123. 1897. 12°.
14048. a. 23.

AṆṆĀPPAṆGĀR. *See* VĪRARĀGHAVA, *son of Nṛisiṃha.*

AṆṆĀ ṢĀSTRI, *Govindapuram. See* MAHĀDEVA SŪRI, *Govindapuram.*

ANOMADASSI, *disciple of Hiṅgulvaḷa Jinaratana. See* MILINDA. මිලින්දපඤ්හා *etc.* [Milindapañha. Edited by Anomadassi.] Pt. i. 1896. 8°.
14098. c. 71.

ANTAKṚITADAṢĀ. श्री अंतगडदशा आठमुं अंग मूल अर्थ *etc.* [Antagaḍadasā, in Sanskrit Antakṛitadaṣā. The eighth *aṅga* of the Jain canon. With a supralinear Gujarati version.] pp. 143, *lith.* मुंबई १९५० [*Bombay,* 1893.] *obl.* 8°. **14100. d. 4**

ANUBHŪTIMĪMĀṂSĀ. அநுபூதிமீமாம்ஸா [Anubhūtimīmāṃsā, or Anubhūtisūtra. Aphorisms of Advaita-Vedānta philosophy, in 4 *adhyāyas.*

Edited by Pattamaḍai Appaya Dīkshita.] pp. 24. பாளையங்கோட்டை [*Tinnevelli,*] 1897. 12°.
14048. a. 24.(1.)

ANUBHŪTISVARŪPA ĀCHĀRYA. *See* SĀRASVATASŪTRA. श्रीसारस्वत° [Sārasvatavyākaraṇa. Comprising the Sārasvatasūtra with the Sarasvatīprakriyā or exposition by Anubhūtisvarūpa. Together with a gloss by Lokeṣvara.] [1890-1892.] 8°. **14093. d. 17.**

—— *See* SĀRASVATASŪTRA. सारस्वत *etc.* [Sārasvatavyākaraṇa. With Hindi commentary.] Pt. i. [1891.] 8°. **14090. bb. 6.**

—— *See* SĀRASVATASŪTRA. सारस्वतं व्याकरणम् *etc.* (Saraswata Vyakaranam. . . . [comprising the Sārasvatasūtra with the exposition] by Anubhuti Swarupacharya. With the commentary of Chandrakirti, *etc.*) Vol. ii. [1893.] 8°. **14093. b. 43.**

—— *See* SĀRASVATASŪTRA. सारस्वतं व्याकरणम् *etc.* [Sārasvatavyākaraṇa.] [1896.] 8°.
14090. c. 39.

—— *See* SĀRASVATASŪTRA. ॥ सारस्वत *etc.* [Sārasvatavyākaraṇa. Being the Sārasvatasūtra with a Gujaratī version of the Sarasvatīprakriyā.] Pt. i. [1899.] 12°. **14092. a. 20.**

—— *See* SĀRASVATASŪTRA. सारस्वतं व्याकरणम् *etc.* (The Saraswata Vyakarana . . . With the commentary of Vasudeva Bhatta. Part i.) [1901.] 8°.
14090. bb. 15.(2.)

ANUKŪLA CHANDRA GUPTA KĀVYATĪRTHA, *Kavirāja.* *See* SARVAVARMĀ. কলাপ-ব্যাকরণম্ *etc.* [Kalāpavyākaraṇa. Section i., with commentary of Durgasiṃha. Edited by Anukūla Chandra Gupta.] [1895.] 8°. **14090. bb. 13.(4.)**

ANUNDA CHARLU. *See* ĀNANDĀCHĀRYA VIDYĀVINODA.

ANUPAMAVAJRA. Ādikarmapradīpa. [A treatise on the esoteric rites of Northern Buddhism. With introduction, notes, *etc.*] *See* LA VALLÉE POUSSIN (L. DE). Bouddhisme. Études et Matériaux, *etc.* pp. 162-232. 1898. 4°. **14028. e. 32.**

ANŪP SINGH. *See* PURĀṆAS.—*Skandapurāṇa.* ਨਿੰਦਤ ਭ੍ਰਸ਼ਟਾਚਾਰ *etc.* [Nindita-bhrashṭāchāra. With Panjabi translation and verses by Anūp Singh.] [1902.] 12°. **14033. a. 33.(4.)**

ANURUDDHA. အဘိဓမ္မတ္ထသင်္ဂြိုဟ်ပါဠိနိသျှ။ ဘားဂရာပျှ။ [Abhidhammatthasaṅgaha. Followed by the same in a Burmese *nissaya* by Tipiṭakālaṅkāra Siriddhaja, Bagaya Hsaya.] pp. 248. ရန်ကုန် ၁၂၅၂ [*Rangoon,* 1890.] 8°.
14098. ccc. 10.(1.)

—— Abhidharmarthasangraha sanna. [Being the Abhidhammatthasaṅgaha with a word-for-word interpretation in Sinhalese.] Compiled by Sri Sariputra Sanagharaja [*sic*] . . . Edited by Rev. T. Pannamoli Tissa with the help of Rev. M. Dhammaratana Tissa. (අභිධර්මාර්ථසංග්‍රහ සන්නය) pp. v. 204. *Peliyagoda,* 1897. 8°.
14098. ccc. 6.

—— ဋီကာကျော်ပါဠိနိသျှဆင်တဲပု *etc.* [Abhidhammatthasaṅgaha. Followed by Sumaṅgalasāmi's Ṭīkā-kyaw̱ or Abhidhammatthavibhāvanī, in elucidation thereof, and lastly by a copious Burmese commentary on the Ṭīkā-kyaw̱ by Janindābhisiri of Sinde.] ရန်ကုန် ၁၂၆၀ [*Rangoon,* 1898.] 8°. **14098. ccc. 15.**

In progress?

The text of the Ṭīkā-kyaw̱ ends with Part iii. § 156 (= § 119 *of the other edition of Rangoon* 1898, *which continues to* § 389).

—— အဘိဓမ္မတ္ထသင်္ဂဟပါဠိ *etc.* [Abhidhammatthasaṅgaha. Followed by a Burmese exposition of the same entitled Thin-gyoh-than-pauk, mainly in catechetical form.] pp. 117. ရန်ကုန် ၁၂၆၀ [*Rangoon,* 1898.] 12°. **14098. a. 10.(2.)**

—— အဘိဓမ္မတ္ထသင်္ဂြိုဟ်ပါဠိ။ပါးကရာနိသျှ ပုမှန် [Abhidhammatthasaṅgaha. With the *nissaya* of the Bagaya Hsaya and an appendix by Puññasetṭha.] pp. xxix. 280. ရန်ကုန် ၁၂၆၀ [*Rangoon,* 1898.] 8°. **14098. ccc. 10.(2.)**

—— [Another edition.] pp. 248. ရန်ကုန် ၁၂၆၀ [*Rangoon,* 1899.] 8°. **14098. ccc. 10.(3.)**

—— အဘိဓမ္မတ္ထသင်္ဂြိုဟ် ချုပ် *etc.* [Abhidhammatthasaṅgaha. Followed by a Burmese *nissaya* abridged from that of Tipiṭakālaṅkāra, and some short Burmese poems on the same topics.] pp. 215. ပန္တလေး ၁၂၆၂ [*Mandalay*, 1901.] 8°. **14098. ccc. 35.**

—— *See* DHARMARATNA, *M.* අභිධර්මාර්ථ-සංග්‍රහශුද්ධිය *etc.* [Abhidharmārthasaṅgraha-ṣuddhiya. A criticism on H. Devamitta's edition of the Saṅgaha.] 1893. 8°. **14165. b. 21.(4.)**

—— *See* JĀGARĀBHIDDHAJA. အဘိ-ဓမ္မတ္ထသင်္ဂြိုဟ်ဂဏ္ဌိသစ် *etc.* [Abhidhammatthasaṅgahagaṇṭhi-thit. A dissertation on the Saṅgaha. With problems and memorial verses upon the same work, *etc.*] [1898.] 8°. **14300. e. 4.**

—— [Another edition.] [1901.] 8°. **14300. e. 18.**

—— *See* NĀGINDA, *of Ywa-gale.* သင်္ခေပဗျာကရဏကျမ်း။ [Saṅkhepavyākaraṇa. A Burmese epitome of Abhidhamma doctrine as codified in the Saṅgaha.] [1899.] 8°. **14300. d. 22.(11.)**

—— [For the Ṭīkā-kyaw or Abhidhammatthavibhāvanī, written to elucidate the Abhidhammatthasaṅgaha:] *See* SUMAṄGALASĀMI.

—— *See* SUNDARA, *of Vijitārāma.* မဏိ-မေဓဇောတကကျမ်း *etc.* [Maṇimedhajotaka-kyan. A Burmese treatise based upon the Saṅgaha.] 1882. 8°. **14300. d. 17.(2.)**

—— သရူပတ္ထဒီပနီကျမ်း။ [Sarūpatthadīpanī. A Burmese summary of the Saṅgaha, with commentary, *etc.*, by Ū Tin.] pp. 100. *Moulmein*, 1883. 8°. **14300. d. 4.(5.)**

—— අනුරුද්ධශතකය *etc.* [Anuruddhaṣataka. A century of Buddhist verses. Fourth edition.] pp. 39. *Colombo*, 1888. 8°. **14033. bb. 41.**

—— Anuruddha S'ataka. . . . With a [Sanskrit] commentary by the Rev. C. A. Seelakkhandha Thēra. pp. ii. 46. 1899. *See* ACADEMIES, *etc.*—Calcutta.—*Buddhist Text Society of India.* Buddhist Texts, *etc.* 1894, *etc.* 8°. **14004. c. (vol. 1, no. 5.)**

ANUTTARAUPAPĀTIKADAṢĀ. *End.* अणुत्तरोववाई-दसाओ नवमंअं सम्मत्तं [*sic*]. [Aṇuttarovavāidasāo, in Sanskrit Anuttaraupapātikadaṣā. The ninth *aṅga* of the Jain canon. With a supralinear Gujarati version.] pp. 51, *lith.* मुंबई १८४४ [*Bombay*, 1894.] *obl.* 8°. **14100. d. 5.**

No title-page.

AṆUTTAROVAVĀIDASĀO. *See* ANUTTARAUPAPĀTIKADAṢĀ.

ĀPADEVA, *son of Anantadeva.* मीमांसान्यायप्रकाशः *etc.* [Mīmāṃsānyāyaprakāṣa. An exposition of the principles of the Pūrvamīmāṃsā. Edited by Jīvānanda Vidyāsāgara.] pp. 82. कलिकाता १८९८ [*Calcutta*, 1898.] 8°. **14048. c. 79.(2.)**

_*The name of this author's father is often given wrongly as Ānanda.*

—— मीमांसा-न्यायप्रकाशः *etc.* [Mīmāṃsānyāyaprakāṣa. Edited with a commentary styled Arthadarṣanī by Krishṇanātha Nyāyapañchānana.] pp. 289. कलिकाता १८२३ [*Calcutta*, 1901.] 8°. **14048. dd. 34.(3.)**

APARĀDITYA. *See* APARĀRKA.

APARĀRKA. *See* KIRSTE (J.). Professor J. Kirstes Collation . . . der Yâjñavalkya-Smṛiti und Analyse der Citate in Aparârkas Commentare, *etc.* 1893. Fol. [*Denkschriften der Kais. Akademie der Wissenschaften zu Wien.*] **Ac. 810/12. (Bd. 42.)**

APAṢAṄKARA RĀMĀCHĀRYA, *Dharmaṣāstrī, of Kumbakonam.* *See* NĀRĀYAṆA PAṆḌITĀCHĀRYA, *son of Trivikrama.* मध्वविजयः *etc.* [Madhvavijaya. Edited by Apaṣaṅkara and Krishṇāchārya.] [1895.] 16°. **14076. a. 26.**

ĀPASTAMBA.

DHARMASŪTRA.

आपस्तम्बीयधर्मसूत्रम् । Aphorisms on the Sacred Law of the Hindus, by Apastamba. [Forming sections 28-29 of the Āpastambīya-Kalpasūtra.] Edited, with extracts from the commentary [of Haradatta], by Dr. George Bühler. Second edition. . . . Part i., containing the text, with critical notes, an index of the Sûtras, and the various readings of the Hiraṇyakeṣi-dharmasûtra. (Part ii., containing the extracts from the Sanskrit commentary of Haradatta, called Ujjvala, together with a verbal index to the Sûtras, by Dr. Th. Bloch.) 1892-1894. 8°. **14038. d. 34.**

Forms nos. xliv. *and* l. *of the* Bombay Sanskrit Series.

ĀPASTAMBA.

DHARMASŪTRA (*continued*).

The Dharma Sūtra, the Sacred Law of the Hindus, by Apastamba, with the commentary called Ujjvala of Haradatta Misra, and with 'bare text' separately added .... Edited ... by Pundit R. Halasyanatha Sastry of Malakudi. (श्रीमदापस्तम्बमहर्षिप्रणीतं ॥ धर्मसूत्रम् ॥) pp. xxxii. 70, i. 199. *Kumbakonam*, 1895. 8°. **14038. c. 45.**

ధర్మసూత్రమ్ *etc.* [Dharmasūtra. With the commentary Ujjvalā of Haradatta Miṣra. Edited by Dēvanaguḍi and Doḍḍabeli Nārāyaṇa Ṣāstrī.] pp. 272. బెంగుళూరు ౧౮౯౭ [*Bangalore*, 1897.] 8°. **14039. b. 24.**

आपस्तम्बधर्मसूत्रम् ... Ápastamba-Dharmasútra, with Haradatta's Ujjvalá. Edited [with an index of words] by A. Mahádeva Śástri ... and Pandita-ratnam K. Rangácharya. pp. iv. vii. ii. 374, lxxii. 1898. *See* MYSORE.—*Government of Mysore.* Government Oriental Library Series. Bibliotheca Sanskrita, *etc.* No. 15. 1893, *etc.* 8°. **14004. b. 9.**

Āpastamba, Aphorisms on the Sacred Law of the Hindus. [Translated, with introduction and notes, by Georg Bühler. Second edition.] 1897. *See* MUELLER (F. M.). The Sacred Books of the East, *etc.* Vol. ii., pp. ix.-xlviii., 1-172. 1879, *etc.* 8°. **2003. a. (vol. 2.)**

GṚIHYASŪTRA.

आपस्तम्बगृह्यसूत्रम् ... The Ápastamba-Gṛihya-Sútra, [the 27th *praṣna* of the Kalpasūtra,] with the commentary [styled Tātparyadarṣana or Gṛihya-tātparyadarṣana] of Sudarśanácharya. Edited by A. Mahádeva Śástri. pp. v. viii. ii. 314. 1893. *See* MYSORE.—*Government of Mysore.* Government Oriental Library Series. Bibliotheca Sanskrita, *etc.* No. 1. 1893, *etc.* 8°. **14004. b. 1.**

The Mantrapāṭha [or Mantrapraṣna], or The Prayer Book of the Āpastambins. [Comprising the formulae used in the rites of the Gṛihyasūtra, and forming *praṣnas* 25-26 of the Kalpasūtra.] Edited together with the commentary of Haradatta and translated by M. Winternitz ... First part. Introduction, Sanskrit text, varietas lectionis, and appendices. pp. xlix. i. 109. 1897. *See* OXFORD ANECDOTA. Anecdota Oxoniensia ... Aryan Series. Vol. i., pt. 8. 1881, *etc.* 4°. **12204. f. 8.(vol. 1, pt. 8.)**

See ṢIVARĀMAKṚISHṆA ṢĀSTRĪ, *Ā.* പ്രയോഗചിന്താമണിഃ *etc.* [Prayogachintāmaṇi. A manual of domestic ritual according to the school of Āpastamba.] 1901. 8°. **14033. aa. 22.**

See VEṄKAṬARĀMA ṢĀSTRĪ, *N.* ആപസ്തംബിനാം ഉപാകരണപ്രയോഗഃ *etc.* [Āpastambinām Upākaraṇaprayoga. A manual of the *upākaraṇa* rite according to the school of Āpastamba.] [1901.] 8°. **14039. b. 26.(2.)**

ആപസ്തംബഗൃഹ്യപ്രയോഗഃ സവ്യാഖ്യാനഃ *etc.* [Āpastambagṛihyaprayoga. A manual of domestic rites based on the Āpastambasūtra, and containing extracts therefrom, with *kārikā*. Edited by Īṣvara Yajvā and Rāmakṛishṇa Ṣāstrī of Kalpadi.] pp. 72. പാലക്കാട് വികാരി [*Palghat*, 1899.] 8°. **14028. c. 80.**

యజుశ్శాఖాధ్యాయినాముపనయనప్రయోగః *etc.* [Upanayanaprayoga. Being the sections of the Sūtra treating of the *upanayana* rite (viz. iv. 10-11) with a *prayoga* or practical guide to this ritual. Edited with Telugu interpretations of the rubrics, *etc.*, by A. Lakshmīnarasiṃha Somayājī.] pp. 54. *Vizagapatam*, 1901. 8°. **14033. c. 46.**

ṢRAUTASŪTRA.

॥ यज्ञपरिभाषासूत्रम् *etc.* [Yajñaparibhāshāsūtra, also called Sāmānyas° and Nyāyas°. Being a portion of the xxivth *praṣna* of the Ṣrautasūtra, and containing general rules for sacrifice. With the commentary of Dhūrtasvāmī and a Bengali translation by the editor, Satyavrata Sāmaṣramī.] pp. 105. 1891. *See* PERIODICAL PUBLICATIONS.—*Calcutta.* उषा *etc.* [Ushā.] Vol. i., nos. viii.-xii. [1889]-1893. 8°. **14010. c. 43.(vol. 1.)**

आपस्तम्बपरिभाषासूत्रम् ... The Ápastamba-Paribhāshá-Sútra, with the commentaries of Kapardisvámin and Haradattácharya. Edited by A. Mahádeva Śástri. pp. vii. vi. ii. 104. 1894. *See* MYSORE.—

Government of Mysore. Government Oriental Library Series. Bibliotheca Sanskrita, *etc.* No. 2. 1893, *etc.* 8°. **14004. b. 2.**

ఆధానపంచకము *etc.* [Ādhānapañchaka. Five chapters on the rites of the sacred fire, extracted from Āpastamba's Aphorisms, with a commentary. Edited by Vaṅgala Veṅkaiya.] pp. 78. కర్నూలు [*Karnul,*] 1898. 8°. **14028. d. 65.**

See Bhāskara Misra Bhaṭṭa. त्रिकाण्डमण्डनम्। Trikāṇḍa-maṇḍanam . . . an exposition of the Soma-yāga Aphorisms of Āpastamba, *etc.* 1898, *etc.* 8°. **14002. a. (vol. 142.)**

Ṣulbasūtra.

Das Āpastamba-Śulba-Sūtra, [the 30th *praṣna* of the Kalpasūtra,] herausgegeben, übersetzt und mit einer Einleitung versehen von Albert Bürk. 1901-1902. *See* Academies, *etc.*—Germany.—*Deutsche Morgenlaendische Gesellschaft.* Zeitschrift, *etc.* Bd. 55, pp. 543-591, Bd. 56, pp. 327-391. 1846, *etc.* 8°. **Ac. 8815/2. (vol. 55, 56.)**

ĀPODEVA. *See* Āpadeva.

APPADĪKSHITA, *son of Raṅgarāja.* *See* Apyaya Dīkshita.

APPAYADĪKṢITA, *son of Raṅgarāja.* *See* Apyaya Dīkshita.

APPAYA DĪKSHITA, *Pattamaḍai.* *See* Anubhūti-mīmāṃsā. அநுபூதிமீமாம்ஸா [Anubhūtimīmāṃsā. Edited by Appaya Dīkshita.] 1897. 12°. **14048. a. 24.(1.)**

—— *See* Gurujñānavāsishṭha. గురుజ్ఞానవాసిష్ఠ, జ్ఞానకాండః *etc.* [Gurujñānavāsishṭha. Vol. i., edited by Appaya.] [1882]-1897. 4°. **14048. e. 8.**

—— பாலபோதினி *etc.* [Bālabodhinī. A Tamil treatise of 6 *prakaraṇas*, in catechetical form, with copious Sanskrit quotations, forming a digest of Advaita-Vedānta teachings.] pp. 128, i. திருநெல்வேலி [*Tinnevelli,*] 1897. 8°. **14048. cc. 14.**

APTE (H. N.) *See* Hari Nārāyaṇa Āpṭe.

APTE (M. S.) *See* Mahādeva Ṣivarāma Āpṭe.

APTE (V. S.) *See* Vāmana Ṣivarāma Āpṭe.

APYAYA DĪKSHITA. चित्रमीमांसा *etc.* [Chitramīmāṃsā. A treatise on style. Edited by Rāma Ṣāstrī Mānavallī.] 1891. *See* Periodical Publications.—*Benares.* The Pandit, *etc.* New Series. Vol. xiii. 1876, *etc.* 8°. **14096. d. 6.(vol. 13.)**

—— The Chitramîmâmsâ of Appadîkshita. And the Chitramîmâmsâ-khaṇdana of Jagannâth Paṇdit [in refutation thereof, with a commentary extracted from the Rasagaṅgādharamarmaprakāṣa, Nāgeṣa's commentary on the Rasagaṅgādhara.] Edited by Paṇdit Śivadatta and Kâśînâth Pâṇdurang Parab. (चित्रमीमांसा . . . चित्रमीमांसाखण्डनं च।) pp. 104, 38. 1893. *See* Durgāprasāda, *son of Vrajalāla,* and Kāṣīnātha Pāṇḍuraṅga Parab. Kâvyamâlâ. [No.] 38. 1886, *etc.* 8°. **14072. ccc. 12.(no. 38.)**

—— Jívachintámaṇi. [An exposition of the principle of Life according to the Anubhavādvaita school. Translated by G. Kṛishṇa Ṣāstrī.] 1901. *See* Periodical Publications.—*Bombay.* The Theosophist, *etc.* Vol. xxii., Nos. x.-xi. 1879, *etc.* 8°. **P.P. 636. cm. (vol. 22.)**

—— Kuvalayananda . . . With the commentary called Rasika-ranjani of . . . Gangadhara Vajapeyin. Edited with copious notes [in Sanskrit] giving a succint [*sic*] view of other ancient rhetoricians where they differ from this work, as well as several readings of the text, and of [Jayadeva's] Chandraloka, its original, and published by . . . R. Halasyanatha Sastri, of Malakudi. (कुवलयानन्दः।) pp. xvi. 284. *Kumbhakonum,* 1892. 8°. **14053. cc. 64.**

—— பஞ்சரத்நஸ்துதி *etc.* [Pañcharatnastuti. A hymn to Ṣiva in 5 stanzas, with commentary. Edited by Vāsudeva Ṣāstrī. Second edition.] pp. 8. நடுக்காவேரி ஜெமலம்ப [*Nadukkaveri,* 1897.] 8°. **14028. d. 59.(8.)**

—— सविवरणम् श्रीरामायणभारतसारसंग्रहस्तोत्रद्वयम् *etc.* [Rāmāyaṇasārasaṅgrahastotra and Bhāratasārasaṅgrahastotra. Two hymns enunciating the supremacy of Ṣiva as the essence of the Rāmāyaṇa and Mahābhārata. With *vivaraṇas* by the author, and the Chakrāṅkitanigrahāshṭaka by the same. Edited with footnotes by Brahmānanda Tīrtha.] pp. ii. 90. प्रयाग १९५१ [*Allahabad,* 1895.] 8°. **14028. d. 54.**

APYAYA DĪKSHITA (*continued*). The Siddhântaleśa of Appayadîkshita. With extracts from the [commentary] Śrîkṛishṇâlaṁkâra of Achyutakṛishṇânandatîrtha. Edited [with preface] by Mahâmahopâdhyâya Gaṅgâdhara Śâstrî Mânavallî. Vol. i. Part i. Sanskrit text. (सिद्धान्तलेशसंग्रहः ।) pp. iv. i. viii. 116. 1890. 8°.
14048. dd. 3.(vol. 1.)

Forms vol. i. of the Vizianagram Sanskrit Series. *No more has been published in this series; the English translation appeared in the* Pandit.

—— ॥ सिद्धान्तलेशसंग्रहः *etc.* [Siddhāntaleṣasaṅgraha. With the commentary Kṛishṇālaṅkāra of Achyutakṛishṇānanda Tīrtha.] pp. ii. viii. ii. 472. 1894. *See* HARIHARA ṢĀSTRĪ, *Goshṭhīpuram*, and others. ॥ अद्वैतमञ्जरी *etc.* [Advaitamañjarī.] 1892-1895. 8°.
14048. e. 23.

—— सिद्धान्तलेशसंग्रहः *etc.* [Siddhāntaleṣasaṅgraha. Edited by Jīvānanda Vidyāsāgara, with a commentary compiled by the same. Second edition.] pp. ii. 744. कलिकाता १८९७ [*Calcutta*, 1897.] 8°.
14048. cc. 31.

—— The Siddhāntaleça of Appayadīkṣita. Translated by Arthur Venis. 1899, *etc.* *See* PERIODICAL PUBLICATIONS.—*Benares.* The Pandit, *etc.* New Series. Vol. xxi.- . 1876, *etc.* 8°.
14096. d. 6.(vol. 21- .)

In progress. This translation was originally intended for publication in the Vizianagram Sanskrit Series.

—— ॥ शिखरिणीमाला *etc.* [Ṣikhariṇīmālā. A religious-philosophical poem addressed to Ṣiva as supreme deity. With the author's commentary styled Ṣivatattvaviveka.] pp. 142. 1895. *See* HARIHARA ṢĀSTRĪ, *Goshṭhīpuram*, and others. ॥ अद्वैतमञ्जरी *etc.* [Advaitamañjarī.] 1892-1895. 8°.
14048. e. 23.

—— తాంత్రికమీమాంసా *etc.* [Tāntrikamīmāṃsā. A tract upon the religious and other studies appropriate to the higher castes.] pp. 24. చెన్నపురి ౧౮౯౪ [*Madras*, 1894.] 8°.
14033. a. 28.

—— ஶ்ரீவரதராஜஸ்தவ: . . . ம்ருத்யுஞ்ஜயமானஸிகபூஜாஸ்தோத்ரம் *etc.* [Varadarājastava. A hymn to Vishṇu. Followed by the Mṛityuṃjayamānasikapūjāstotra ascribed to Ṣaṅkara and the Naṭarājapādadhūlīpañchaka of Ṣrīnivāsa Ṣāstrī.] pp. 28. நடுக்காவேரி ஹேமலம்ப [*Nadukkaveri*, 1897.] 12°.
14076. a. 19.

APYAYA DĪKSHITA (*continued*). विधिरसायनम् *etc.* (Vidhi-rasayana[, a treatise on the *vidhis* of the Pūrva-Mīmāṃsā system, as expounded by Kumārila.] . . . Edited by Pandit Mukunda Shastri.) pp. ii. iii. 223. *Benares*, 1901. 8°.
14004. a. 13.

Forms nos. 42-43 *of the* Chowkhambâ Sanskrit Series. *The English title is from the wrapper.*

—— अथ वृत्तिवार्तिकम् । [Vṛittivārttika. A tract on the principles of literary composition. Chapters i. ii. Edited by Rāma Ṣāstrī Mānavallī.] 1890. *See* PERIODICAL PUBLICATIONS.—*Benares.* The Pandit, *etc.* New Series. Vol. xii. 1876, *etc.* 8°.
14096. d. 6.(vol. 12.)

—— The Vṛittivârtika of Appaya Dîkshita. Edited by Paṇdit Śivadatta and Kâśînâth Pâṇdurang Parab. (वृत्तिवार्त्तिकम् ।) pp. 27. 1893. *See* DURGĀPRASĀDA, *son of Vrajalāla*, and KĀṢĪNĀTHA PĀṆḌURAṄGA PARAB. Kâvyamâlâ. [No.] 36. 1886, *etc.* 8°.
14072. ccc. 12.(no. 36.)

—— *See* BĀDARĀYAṆA. The Vedântakalpataruparimala of Appayadîkshita. [Comprising the Brahmasūtra with the gloss of Apyaya upon Amalānanda's supercommentary Vedāntakalpataru,] *etc.* 1895-1898. 8°. **14048. dd. 3.(vol. 12.)**

—— *See* BĀDARĀYAṆA. శ్రీదక్షిణామూర్తిబ్రహ్మసంవాదాత్మకే . . . గురుజ్ఞానవాసిష్ఠే . . . బ్రహ్మమీమాంసా *etc.* [Brahmamīmāṃsā. Being the Brahmasūtra with the Jñānakāṇḍa of the Gurujñānavāsishṭha, Pāda II. i.-xvii. Together with the commentary Adhikaraṇakañchuka of Apyaya.] 1898. 12°.
14048. b. 32.

—— *See* BĀDARĀYAṆA. ஶ்ரீமச்சிவாசார்யவர்ய-ஶ்ரீகண்டப்ரணீத ப்ரஹ்மஸூத்ரபாஷ்யம் *etc.* [Brahmasūtra. With the exposition of Ṣrīkaṇṭha Ṣivāchārya, and footnotes based on Apyaya's commentary to the latter, styled Ṣivārkamaṇidīpikā.] [1899.] 8°.
14048. c. 72.(3.)

—— *See* GURUJÑĀNAVĀSISHṬHA. గురుజ్ఞానవాసిష్ఠే జ్ఞానకాండః *etc.* [Gurujñānavāsishṭha. Vol. i., including in Pāda II. i.-xvii. an exposition of the Brahmasūtra, with the commentary Adhikaraṇakañchuka of Apyaya.] [1882]-1897. 4°.
14048. e. 8.

APYAYA DĪKSHITA (*continued*). [For the Saṃskṛitachandrāloka, sometimes ascribed wrongly to Apyaya :] *See* JAYADEVA, *son of Mahādeva.*

—— *See* TRIVIKRAMA DEVA. प्राकृतमणिदीपः ॥ [Prākṛitamaṇidīpa. Trivikrama's aphorisms, with short notes ascribed to Apyaya.] 1895, *etc.* 8°. [*Grandha Pradarsani.*] **14003. c. 2.(8.)**

—— *See* UPANISHADS.—*Separate Upanishads.* Gopala Tapani Upanishad. Part i. [Translated, with extracts from the commentaries of Apyaya, *etc.*] 1899. 8°. [*The Theosophist.*] **P.P. 636. cm. (vol. 20.)**

ĀRĀDHYA VĪREṢVARA. *See* VĪREṢVARA ṢĀSTRĪ, *Ārādhya.*

ĀRAṆYAKAS.

AITAREYĀRAṆYAKA.

ऐतरेयारण्यकम् *etc.* [Aitareyāraṇyaka. With the commentary Vedārthaprakāṣa of Sāyaṇa. Edited by Bābā Ṣāstrī Phaḍke.] pp. i. 296. पुण्याख्यपत्तने १८९८ [*Poona*, 1898.] 8°. **14003. ccc. (no. 38.)**

Forms no. 38 *of the* Ānandāṣrama Sanskrit Series.

[For Bk. ii. 4-7 of this Āraṇyaka, forming the Aitareyopanishad :] *See* UPANISHADS.

KAUSHĪTAKYĀRAṆYAKA.

Der mahāvrata-Abschnitt des Çāṅkhāyana-Āraṇyaka herausgegeben, übersetzt und mit Anmerkungen versehen von Walter Friedlaender. pp. 81. *Berlin*, 1900. 8°. **14007. cc. 27.**

[For Ch. 3-6 of this Āraṇyaka, forming the Kaushītakyupanishad :] *See* UPANISHADS.

ṢĀṄKHĀYANĀRAṆYAKA.

See above, KAUSHĪTAKYĀRAṆYAKA.

TAITTIRĪYĀRAṆYAKA.

ஸ்ரீ8CC தைத்திரீயாரண்யவேதவேத ஸகாம்ஸகாரண்யமாவா *etc.* [Taittirīyāraṇyaka, or Āruṇaṣākhā. Followed by the Kāṭhaka, *i.e.* the Taittirīyabrāhmaṇa III. x.-xii. With notes giving the divergent text of the Dravidian recension, and accents. Edited by K. Veṅkaṭakṛishṇa Ṣāstrī and M. Deṣikāchārya.] pp. 244, iv. வெகுவடி [*Madras*,] 1894. 8°. **14010. cc. 1.**

In this recension the text of the Āraṇyaka is divided into 8 praṣnas *corresponding to the* 10 prapāṭhakas *of the Northern recension, the 8th* praṣna *containing* prapāṭhakas 7-9.

तैत्तिरीयारण्यकम् *etc.* [Taittirīyāraṇyaka. With Sāyaṇa's commentary. Edited by Bābā Ṣāstrī Phaḍke.] 2 vols. pp. ii. 909. पुण्याख्यपत्तने १८९७-१८९८ [*Poona*, 1897-1898.] 8°. **14003. ccc. (no. 36.)**

Forms no. 36 *of the* Ānandāṣrama Sanskrit Series.

CCதைத்திரீயாரண்யவ்யாக்யாவ்யாக்யா ப்ரதம ப்ரச்ந: [Āruṇa. Being Taittirīyāraṇyaka, *praṣna* i.] pp. 24. *See* BRĀHMAṆAS.—*Taittirīyabrāhmaṇa.* அஶ்வமேதம் ॥ [Aṣvamedha, *etc.*] [1900.] 8°. **14007. cc. 28.**

அயசு திரஸுபர்ணமந்த்ர: . . . பில்வோபநிஷத்ஸங்க்ரஹ: ॥ [Trisuparṇamantra. A lustratory ritual, extracted from the Nārāyaṇīyopanishad or Prapāṭhaka x. (Khilakāṇḍa) of this Āraṇyaka, with the commentary of Sāyaṇa. Followed by the Bilvopanishad, a fictitious Upanishad.] pp. 20. சிதம்பரம் [*Chidambaram*, 18]96. 16°. **14028. b. 80.(2.)**

This text (with the exception of two Vedic verses in the 3rd mantra) *corresponds to* x. 48-50, 64 *of the edition of the Taittirīyāraṇyaka published in the Bibliotheca Indica.*

त्रिसुपर्ण *etc.* [Trisuparṇamantra. With the commentary of Sāyaṇa. Edited with a Marathi introduction, notes, and translation and an English version by Gaṅgādhara Vāmana Lele.] pp. vii. 27, 4. पुणें १९०० [*Poona*, 1900.] 8°. **14028. d. 35.(2.)**

See KĀMEṢVARA AIYAR, *B. V.* The Sandhyavandanam of Rig, Yajus, and Sâma Vedins, *etc.* 1898. 12°. **14028. b. 97.(2.)**

See SANDHYĀVANDANA. संध्याभाष्यसमुच्चयः *etc.* [Sandhyābhāshyasamuchchaya. A collection of commentaries upon the *sandhyā* prayers.] [1899.] 8°. **14003. ccc. (no. 40.)**

See SCHROEDER (LEOPOLD VON). Die Tübinger Kaṭha-Handschriften und ihre Beziehung zum Taittirîya-Âraṇyaka, *etc.* 1897. 8°. [*Sitzungsberichte der Kais. Akademie der Wissenschaften zu Wien.*] **Ac. 810/6. (Bd. 137.)**

ĀRAṆYAKAS (*continued*).

See SUBRAHMAṆYA ṢĀSTRĪ, *K., of Uḍayārpālayam.* க்ருஷ்ணயஜு-ஸ்ஸம்ஹிதாப்ராஹ்மணாரண்யககா-டகாநாம் பஞ்சாசத-நுக்ரமணிகா *etc.* [Pañchāṣadanukramaṇikā. An index of catchwords for the Taittirīyasaṃhitā, its Brāhmaṇa, Āraṇyaka, and Kāṭhaka.] [1897.] 12°. **14028. b. 78.(2.)**

[For the Mahānārāyaṇopanishad of the Black Yajurveda (Bṛihann°, or Nārāyaṇīyā Yājñiki), forming the 10th *prapāṭhaka* of this Āraṇyaka, and for the Taittirīyopanishad, comprising *prapāṭhakas* vii.-ix. thereof:] *See* UPANISHADS.

ARAVINDĀNANDA YATI, *disciple of Charaṇadāsa.* *See* ṢAṄKARA ĀCHĀRYA.—*Philosophical Poems, etc.* विवेकचूडामणिः *etc.* [Vivekachūḍāmaṇi. With Hindi commentary, styled Advaitāmṛitabodhinī, by Aravindānanda.] [1902.] 8°. **14049. a. 6.**

ARDSHER FRĀMJĪ MŪS. *See* ACADEMIES, *etc.*—Bombay.—*Bombay Branch of the Royal Asiatic Society.* Catalogue of Manuscripts and Books belonging to the Bhau Daji Memorial. Prepared under the superintendence of ... Ardaseer ... Moos. 1882. 8°. **14096. cc. 11.**

ARISIMHA, *son of Āsaḍa.* काव्यकल्पलता वृत्तिसहित मूळग्रंथाचें मराठी भाषांतर *etc.* [Kāvyakalpalatā. Aphorisms of the Art of Poetry, with the commentary Kaviṣikshāvṛitti and supplements of Amarachandra disciple of Jinadatta Sūri. Translated into Marathi, but with the original Sanskrit stanzas and quotations retained, and edited with notes by Vāmana Ṣāstrī Islāmpurkar.] pp. xiv. 376. मुंबई १८९१ [*Bombay,* 1891.] 8°. **14140. b. 24.**

ĀRIYAN, *Pseud.* பேதவாத திரஸ்காரம் ... Bhêdavâda Tiraskaram, *etc.* [A series of texts, chiefly Sanskrit, in defence of monism, with Tamil dissertations and explanations, in refutation of the arguments of Ṣendinādaiyar.] pp. ii. 98, ii. சென்னை [*Madras,*] 1897. 8°. **14048. cc. 13.**

ARIYAVAMṢA. ဂန္ထာဘရဏ်သဋီက် [Ganthābharaṇa. A Pali poem in 93 stanzas on the use of particles and prepositions. With a *ṭīkā* or *vaṇṇanā* by Jāgara.] *See* SADDHAMMASIRI. သဒ္ဒတ္ထဘေဒစိန္တာ *etc.* [Saddatthabhedachintā, *etc.*] pp. 165-208. [1897.] 8°. **14098. ccc. 17.(2.)**

—— ဂန္ထာဘရဏ *etc.* [Ganthābharaṇa. With Burmese commentary by Tipiṭakālaṅkāra Siriddhaja.] [1898.] *See* SADDĀ-NGAY. သဒ္ဒါငယ် *etc.* [Saddā-ngay.] Vol. ii., pp. 135-154. [1898-1900.] 8°. **14098. ccc. 22.**

—— ဂန္ထာဘရဏပါဠိ။ [Ganthābharaṇa.] *See* SADDĀ-NGAY. သဒ္ဒါငယ် *etc.* [Saddā-ngay.] pp. 104-109. [1898.] 8°. **14098. ccc. 23.(1.)**

—— [Second edition.] pp. 105-111. [1899.] 8°. **14098. ccc. 24.(1.)**

ARIYAVAMṢA ĀDICHCHARAMṢI. ကမ္မဋ္ဌာနဒီပနီကျမ်း *etc.* [Kammaṭṭhānadīpanī. A treatise on the *kammaṭṭhāna* meditations. In Burmese, illustrated from Pali texts.] pp. 123. *Rangoon,* 1882. 8°. **14300. d. 25.(3.)**

—— သမန္တစက္ခုဒီပနီကျမ်း *etc.* [Samantachakkhudīpanī. A series of Responses to questions on divers points of Buddhist doctrine and tradition. In Burmese, illustrated from Pali texts.] pp. v. 420. ရန်ကုန် ၁၂၅၁ [*Rangoon,* 1889.] 8°. **14300. e. 13.**

ARJANSINGH. *See* ARJUNASIṂHA.

ARJUNA MIṢRA. *See* MAHĀBHĀRATA.—*Entire Work.* মহাভারতম্ *etc.* [Mahābhārata. With the commentary Bhāratārthadīpikā of Arjuna Miṣra, *etc.*] [1897, *etc.*] 8°. **14065. d. 38.**

ARJUNASIṂHA, *Bāvā, Editor of the "Arya Patrika," Lahore.* *See* DAYĀNANDA SARASVATĪ SVĀMĪ. Vedant Dhwanti Niwaran ... Translated into English by B. Arjansingh. [1900.] 12°. **14048. a. 24.(2.)**

ARNOLD (*Sir* EDWIN). *See* BILHAṆA. The Chaurapanchâsika ... Translated and illustrated by Sir Edwin Arnold. 1896. *obl.* 8°. **14072. b. 23.**

—— *See* HITOPADEṢA. The Book of Good Counsels. [Adapted] ... by Sir Edwin Arnold. ... New edition. 1893. 8°. **14076. c. 62.**

ARNOLD (*Sir* Edwin) (*continued*). *See* Hitopadeśa. The Book of Good Counsels. [Adapted] ... by Sir Edwin Arnold. Author's autograph edition. 1896. 8°. **14070. c. 52.**

ĀRŪḌHAŚĀSTRA. ஞானப்ரதீபிகை என்னும் ஆரூடசாஸ்திரம் *etc.* [Ārūḍhaṣāstra, or Jñānapradīpikā. An astrological treatise, here ascribed to Jaimini. With a Tamil commentary by K. Sorṇaṣāstri and V. R. Ṣrīnivāsāchārya, entitled Bhāvaprakāṣikā. Edited by Krishṇa Ṣāstrī of Devakota.] pp. 144. சென்னை விகாரி [*Madras*, 1899.] 8°. **14053. ccc. 27.**

ARUṆAGIRINĀTHA. सोमवल्लीयोगानन्दप्रहसनम्॥ [Somavallīyogānanda. A comedy of the *prahasana* form.] 1895. *See* Veṅkaṭaraṅganātha Svāmī, *Paravastu.* Grandha Pradarsani, *etc.* [No. 6.] 1895, *etc.* 8°. **14003. c. 2.(6.)**

Apparently this is the author called Diṇḍima in Taylor's Catalogue.

ĀRYA DEVA. The discovery of a work by Āryadēva in Sanskrit.—[Being the Sanskrit text of a Buddhist metrical treatise, published] by ... Haraprasād Shāstrī, *etc.* 1898. *See* Academies, *etc.*—Calcutta.—*Asiatic Society of Bengal.* Journal, *etc.* Vol. lxvii, pp. 175-184. 1832, *etc.* 8°. **Ac. 8826/11.(vol. 67.)**

ĀRYA MUNI, *of Ranchi.* *See* Bādarāyaṇa. वेदान्तार्य्यभाष्यम् ... The Vedantarya Bhashyam. [A Dvaita exposition of the Brahmasūtra.] ... By ... Arya Muni, *etc.* 1895. 8°. **14048. cc. 4.**

ĀRYA SAMĀJ. *See* Bhīmasena Ṣarmā. शास्त्रार्थ आगरा *etc.* [Ṣāstrārtha Āgrā. A correspondence between Bhīmasena and the Ārya Samāj, on the subject of *srāddhas.*] [1901.] 8°. **14033. bbb. 10.(3.)**

—— [For the expositions of the doctrine and practice of this Church as conveyed in the writings of its founder :] *See* Dayānanda Sarasvatī Svāmī.

—— *See* Mohanalāla Vishṇulāla Paṇḍyā. आर्य्यसिद्धान्त मार्तण्ड *etc.* [Āryasiddhāntamārtaṇḍa. An exposition of the principles of the Ārya Samāj.] [1890-1892.] 8°. **14154. c. 17.(1.)**

ĀRYA SAMĀJ (*continued*). *See* Mohanalāla Vishṇulāla Paṇḍyā. The Ten Commandments of the Arya Samajes, *etc.* 1897. 8°. **14154. c. 17.(2.)**

—— *See* Rāma, *Munshī, of Jalandhar.* آریہ سنگیت مالا الخ [Āryasaṅgītamālā. Hindi hymns for the liturgies of the Ārya Samāj. Followed by select Vedic *mantras.*] [1900.] 12°. **14154. cc. 7.**

—— *See* Rāmavilāsa and Vrajavilāsa. नित्यकर्म *etc.* [Nityakarma. A manual of the daily rites of the Ārya Samāj.] [1899.] 12°. **14028. b. 81.(3.)**

—— *See* Tulasīrāma, *Seth, of Moradabad,* and others. शास्त्रार्थ पत्र *etc.* [Ṣāstrārthapatra. A controversy between the Dharma Sabhā of Moradabad and the Ārya Samāj of Chandausi.] [1896.] 8°. **14028. d. 67.**

—— *See* Tulasīrāma Ṣarmā, *of Kuchesar.* शास्त्रार्थ खुर्जा *etc.* [Ṣāstrārtha Khurjā. A report of a controversy between the Ārya Samāj and Dharma Sabhā in Khurja.] [1890.] 8°. **14154. c. 16.(2.)**

—— —— [1894.] 8°. **14154. c. 16.(3.)**

—— आर्य्य सन्ध्या पद्धति *etc.* [Āryasandhyāpaddhati. Daily prayers of the Ārya Samāj. The *mantras* in Sanskrit, with Hindi introductions, rules for ritual, translations, and explanations by Pandit Rājārāma and Chhajjū Singh.] pp. 32. लाहौर [*Lahore*, 1897.] 12°. **14028. b. 96.(1.)**

—— سندھیا مترجم منظوم الخ [Sandhyā mutarjim manẕūm. The *sandhyā* prayers of the Ārya Samāj with a metrical version and notes in Urdu by Kevalakṛishṇa.] pp. 40, ii., *lith.* جالندھر ۱۹۰۲ [*Jalandhar*, 1902.] 12°. **14028. b. 96.(2.)**

—— ارتھ سہت سندھیا بمعہ ودھی [Sandhyā prayers. With Urdu transliteration and translation. Second edition.] pp. 20, *lith.* لاھور ۱۹۵۸ [*Lahore*, 1901.] 12°. **14028. b. 96.(3.)**

—— آریہ سنگیت پشپاولی الخ [Āryasaṅgītapushpāvalī. Devotional songs of the Ārya Samāj, in Hindi. Followed by a Sandhyāvidhi, with

Sanskrit *mantras*, transliterations thereof in the Persian script, and Hindi rubrics and notes.] pp. 12, 312, 58, *lith.* لاہور [*Lahore*, 1899.] 12°. **14154. cc. 4.**

ĀRYA ŚŪRA. The Jātaka-Mālā, or Bodhisattvāvadāna-Mālā. [A collection of Sanskrit Buddhist birth-stories] by Ārya-Çūra. Edited by Dr. Hendrik Kern. (जातकमाला) pp. xii. 254. 1891. *See* ACADEMIES, *etc.*—Cambridge, *Mass.*—*Harvard University.* Harvard Oriental Series, *etc.* Vol. i. 1891, *etc.* 8°. **14003. d. 1.(vol. 1.)**

—— Jâtakamalâ. Garland of Birth-Stories. Translated [into English] . . . by J. S. Speyer. 1893. *See* ACADEMIES, *etc.*—The Hague.—*Koninklijk Instituut voor de Taal-, Land- en Volkenkunde van Nederlandsch-Indië.* Bijdragen, *etc.* 5de Volgreeks, 8ste Deel, 2-4de Aflevering. 1853, *etc.* 8°. **Ac. 7519. (5de volgr., 8ste deel.)**

—— The *Gâtakamâlâ*, or Garland of Birth Stories . . . Translated from the Sanskrit by J. S. Speyer. pp. xxix. 350. 1895. *See* MUELLER (F. M.). The Sacred Books of the Buddhists, *etc.* Vol. i. 1895, *etc.* 8°. **14003. ccc. (vol. 1.)**

—— *See* OLDENBURG (S.). Буддійскій сборникъ „Гирлянда джатакъ“ *etc.* 1892. 8°. **4504. h. 15.**

—— *See* OLDENBURG (S.). Dr. Serge D'Oldenburg "On the Buddhist Jātakas," *etc.* (A detailed account of the Jātaka Mālā, *etc.*) 1893. 8°. [*Journal of the Royal Asiatic Society.*] **Ac. 8820/3 and 2098. a. b.**

ĀSABHA, Ū. အာဇီဝဋ္ဌမကာဒိသီလဝိနိစ္ဆယကျမ်း။ [Ājīvaṭṭhamakādisīlavinichchhaya. A series of Pali texts bearing on the rules of conduct, with Burmese commentary, *etc.* Followed by the Gôṇ-taw-payā-shi-hko and Buddhavandanā, two series of Pali devotional stanzas, with Burmese versions, *etc.*; the Dhāraṇaparitta, also with translation; and Lobhādivinichchhaya, a Burmese ethical tract.] pp. 115. ပဋ္ဌလေး [*Mandalay*, 1900.] 8°. **14300. d. 4.(3.)**

The pagination is irregular, the first page being numbered 11.

ASHṬĀVAKRA. अष्टावक्र सटीक *etc.* [Ashṭāvakrasaṃhitā, or Avadhūtānubhūti. With the commentary Adhyātmapradīpikā of Viṣveṣvara.] pp. 88. লক্ষনৌ ১৮৯৬ [*Lucknow*, 1896.] 8°. **14048. dd. 32.(3.)**

—— অষ্টাবক্র-সংহিতা। [Ashṭāvakrasaṃhitā. With a Bengali translation.] pp. 204. *See* PRASANNAKUMĀRA ŚĀSTRĪ BHAṬṬĀCHĀRYA. যোগাম্বুধি *etc.* [Yogāmbudhi.] [1896.] 16°. **14048. a. 19.**

—— Ashtabakra-samhita. A treatise on Vedanta philosophy, by Ashtabakra Muni. Edited . . . with a full commentary by Pandit-kulapati Shri Jibananda Vidyasagara. pp. 108. *Calcutta*, 1901. 8°. **14048. dd. 34.(2.)**

—— The Astabakra Sanhita. [Translated into English.] Edited by S. C. Mukhopadhaya [*sic*]. (The Light of the East. Publication Series. Vol. x., no. 7.) pp. 20. *Calcutta*, 1902. 8°. **P.P. 656. ba. (vol. x., no. 7.)**

Published as vol. x., *no.* 7 *of the periodical* Light of the East *for April* 1902. *Printed in* 1901.

ASHU BODHA. *See* ĀŚUBODHA.

ASHUTOSH. *See* ĀŚUTOSHA.

ASIATIC SOCIETY OF BENGAL. *See* ACADEMIES, *etc.*—*Calcutta.*

ASIATIC SOCIETY OF GREAT BRITAIN AND IRELAND. *See* ACADEMIES, *etc.*—*London.*

AŚOKA. *See* BUEHLER (J. G.). Beiträge zur Erklärung der Aśoka-Inschriften, *etc.* 1883-1894. 8°. [*Zeitschrift der Deutschen Morgenlaendischen Gesellschaft.*] **Ac. 8815/2. (Bd. 37-48.)**

ASSIER DE POMPIGNAN (R. H.). *See* MINAEV (I. P.). Recherches sur le Buddhisme . . . Traduit . . . par R. H. Assier de Pompignan. 1894. 8°. [*Annales du Musée Guimet: Bibliothèque d'Études.*] **7704. i. (tom. 4.)**

ĀŚUBODHA VIDYĀBHŪSHAṆA BHAṬṬĀCHĀRYA. *See* GOVINDADĀSA, *Kavirāja.* भैषज्यरत्नावली *etc.* (Bhaisajya Ratnavali . . . Edited . . . by . . . Ashu Bodha Vidyabhushana.) [1902.] 8°. **14043. cc. 24.**

—— *See* NARAHARI. राजनिघण्टुः *etc.* (Rajanighantu . . . Edited . . . with various modifications and notes . . . by Ashu Bodha . . . and Nitya Bodha, *etc.*) 1899. 8°. **14043. cc. 15.**

ĀṢUTOSHA ṢĀSTRĪ, *of the Sanskrit College, Calcutta.* *See* PURĀṆAS.—*Selections.* हिन्दूशास्त्र *etc.* [Ashṭādaṣa-purāṇa. Selections, with Bengali translations, *etc.* Compiled by Āṣutosha and Hṛishikeṣa.] [1897.] 8°. [*Hindu-ṣāstra.*]
14085. c. 45.(vol. 2.)

ĀṢUTOSHA SENA, *Kavirāja.* *See* UDAYACHANDRA DATTA. The Materia Medica of the Hindus . . . With additions and alterations by Kaviraj Binod Lall Sen and Kaviraj Athutosh[*sic*] Sen. 1900. 8°. **14043. c. 48.**

ĀṢUTOSHA TARKABHŪSHAṆA. *See* GOTAMA. ন্যায়দর্শন *etc.* [Nyāyadarṣana. The Aphorisms with a commentary by Harinātha and Āṣutosha.] [1894, *etc.*] 8°. **14048. dd. 21.**

ĀṢUTOSHA TARKATĪRTHA BHAṬṬĀCHĀRYA. *See* BHAṬṬI. ভট্টিকাব্যম্ *etc.* [Bhaṭṭikāvya. With Vidyāvinoda's gloss and Bharatasena's gloss. Edited with construing, paraphrases, notes, and Bengali translation by Āṣutosha.] [1902, *etc.*] 8°.
14070. dd. 24.

AṢVAGHOSHA. *See* WINDISCH (W. O. E.). Māra and Buddha, *etc.* [Illustrated by extracts and translations from the Buddhacharita, *etc.*] 1895. 4°. **759. e. 1.**

—— The Buddha-*k*arita of A*s*vaghosha. Edited, from three MSS., by E. B. Cowell. pp. xv. 175. 1893. *See* OXFORD ANECDOTA. Anecdota Oxoniensia . . . Aryan Series. Vol. i., pt. 7. 1881, *etc.* 4°. **12204. f. 8.(vol. i., pt. 7.)**

—— The Buddha-*k*arita of Asvaghosha. Translated from the Sanskrit [with notes, *etc.*,] by E. B. Cowell. pp. xiii. 206. 1894. *See* MUELLER (F. M.). The Sacred Books of the East, *etc.* Vol. xlix., pt. 1. 1879, *etc.* 8°.
2003. b. (vol. 49.)

—— Le Buddhacarita d'Açvaghoṣa, par M. Sylvain Lévi. [Comprising the text of Bk. i., with introduction and translation.] 1892. *See* ACADEMIES, *etc.*—Paris.—*Société Asiatique.* Journal Asiatique, *etc.* Ser. viii., tom. 19. pp. 201-236. 1822, *etc.* 8°. **Ac. 8808. (Ser. viii., tom. 19.)**

ĀṢVALĀYANA. আশ্বলায়ন-শ্রৌতসূত্রম্। (গৃহ্যসূত্রম্।) [Selections from the Ṣrautasūtra and Gṛihyasūtra. With Bengali translations and notes.] [1895.] *See* RAMEṢACHANDRA DATTA. हिन्दूशास्त्र *etc.* [Hindu-ṣāstra.] Pt. iii., pp. 15-19, 40-47. [1895-1897.] 8°. **14085. c. 45.(vol. 1.)**

—— ॥ अथ आश्वलायनगृह्यसूत्रं गृह्यपरिशिष्टं . . . कारिकाश्च *etc.* [Āṣvalāyana-Gṛihyasūtra. With the commentary of Nārāyaṇa son of Divākara. Followed by the Gṛihyapariṣishṭa and the Āṣvalāyana-Gṛihyakārikās of Kumārila. Edited by Dinakara Keṣava Gāḍgil.] ff. xx. 220. मोहमय्यां १८१७ [*Bombay*, 1895.] *obl.* 8°. **14010. dd. 6.**

—— ఆశ్వలాయనగృహ్యసూత్రములు. వి-వాహప్రకరణము. (మధుపర్క—8) [Gṛihyasūtra, i. 4-9 and 24. With glosses in Telugu.] pp. 16, 6. *See* NĀRĀYAṆA BHAṬṬA, *son of Rāmeṣvara.* The Vivahaprayoga, *etc.* 1891. 8°.
14033. b. 58.

—— *See* HARIVALLABHA ṢARMĀ. संस्कारमार्तण्डः *etc.* [Saṃskāramārtaṇḍa. Adapted from the Gṛihyasūtra of Āṣvalāyana, *etc.*] [1901.] 8°. **14033. bbb. 10.(1.)**

—— Études de Liturgie Védique. L'Agnishṭoma, d'après le Çrauta-Sûtra d'Âçvalâyana [Chapter v.], par M. P. Sabbathier. 1890. *See* ACADEMIES, *etc.*—Paris.—*Société Asiatique.* Journal Asiatique, *etc.* Ser. viii., tom. 15. pp. 5-101, 186-194. *Paris*, 1822, *etc.* 8°.
Ac. 8808. (Ser. viii., tom. 15.)

ATHALYE (Y. V.). *See* YAṢAVANTA VĀSUDEVA ĀṬHALYE.

ATIVĪRA RĀMA PĀṆḌIYAN. ॥ जयशक्तिकरम् . . . The Jayasakthikaram. [A Sanskrit version of the] Vetri Verkai [*i.e.* வெற்றிவேற்கை] of Athi Veera Rama Pandian. Translated . . . by Radhakrishna Sastriar. pp. 8. *See* RĀDHĀKṚISHṆA ṢĀSTRĪ, *of Pudukottai.* नीतिदशप्रबन्धौ . . . The Nitidasaprabandhi, *etc.* No. 6. 1894. 8°.
14085. c. 46.

ĀTMABODHENDRA SARASVATĪ, *disciple of Mahādevendra.* *See* SADĀṢIVA BRAHMENDRA. जगद्गुरुरत्नमालास्तवः [Jagadgururatnamālāstava. With the commentary Sushumā of Ātmabodhendra.] [1895.] 8°. **14048. bb. 51.(5.)**

—— புண்யஶ்லோகமஞ்ஜரீபரிஶிஷ்டு [Puṇyaṣlokamañjarīpariṣishṭa. A supplement to Sadāṣiva's Puṇyaṣlokamañjarī or epitaphs on the

Kāmakoṭi Pontiffs.] *See* SADĀŚIVA BRAHMENDRA. புண்யஶ்லோகமஞ்ஜரீ *etc.* [Puṇyaślokamañjarī, *etc.*] pp. 26-28. [1895.] 8°. **14048. bb. 42.(2.)**

ĀTMĀRĀMA, *Lālā.* *See* DAYĀNANDA SARASVATĪ SVĀMĪ. ਸਤਯਾਰਥਪ੍ਰਕਾਸ਼ *etc.* [Satyārthaprakāṣa. Translated into Panjabi by Ātmārāma.] [1899.] 8°. **14162. aaa. 1.**

ĀTMĀRĀMA, *Yogīndra.* *See* SVĀTMĀRĀMA.

ĀTMĀRĀMA, *Secretary of the "Punjab Vegetarian Society."* *See* UPANISHADS.—*Separate Upanishads.* माण्डूक्योपनिषत् *etc.* (Bhasha Translation of . . . Guru Datta M.A.'s English translation and exposition of Mandukyopanishat, by Atma Ram.) 1891. 12°. **14010. b. 8.**

ĀTMĀRĀMAJĪ. *See* DAYĀNANDA SARASVATĪ SVĀMĪ. ستیارتھ پرکاش الخ [Satyārthaprakāṣa. Translated into Urdu by Raimal Dasjī and Ātmārāmajī.] [1899.] 8°. **14106. a. 33.**

ĀTMĀRĀMAJĪ ĀNANDAVIJAYAJĪ, *disciple of Buddhivijaya.* अज्ञानतिमिरभास्कर *etc.* [Ajñānatimirabhāskara. An exposition of Jain doctrine, polemically set forth against other Hindu churches. In Hindi, illustrated from Sanskrit and Prakrit.] pp. ii. iv. 169, viii. मुंबइ १८८८ [*Bombay,* 1888.] 8°. **14154. i. 2.**

—— जैनतत्त्वादर्श ग्रंथ *etc.* [Jainatattvādarṣa. A Hindi work in 12 chapters on the principles, practice, and history of the Jain church, illustrated from Sanskrit and Prakrit texts. Edited with preface by Bhīmasiṃha Māṇaka.] pp. iv. xvi. 596; 2 *plates.* मुंबापुरी १८८४ [*Bombay,* 1884.] 8°. **14154. i. 4.**

—— श्री जैनतत्त्वादर्श *etc.* [Jainatattvādarṣa. Translated from the Hindi into Gujarati by Mūlchand Nathubhāī.] pp. xvi. 612. भावनगर मुंबई १८९९ [*Bhaunagar, Bombay* printed, 1899.] 8°. **14144. gg. 4.**

—— શ્રી જૈનતત્વાદર્શ ગ્રંથ *etc.* [Jainatattvādarṣa. Translated into Gujarati by Shāh Dīpchand Chhaganlāl.] Vol. i. અમદાવાદ વડોદરા ૧૮૯૯ [*Ahmadabad, Baroda,* 1899.] 8°. **14144. ggg. 11.**

ĀTMASVARŪPA UDĀSĪNA, *disciple of Bālarāma.* *See* PATAÑJALI.—*Philosophical Works.* पातञ्जलदर्शनप्रकाश *etc.* [Pātañjaladarṣanaprakāṣa. Edited with Hindi annotations by Ātmasvarūpa.] [1897.] 8°. **14048. d. 59.**

ATULAKṚISHṆA GOSVĀMĪ. *See* RŪPA GOSVĀMĪ. লঘুভাগবতামৃত *etc.* [Laghu-bhāgavatāmṛita. With commentary and Bengali translation. Edited by Balaichānd and Atulakṛishṇa.] [1897.] 8°. **14016. c. 58.**

AUFRECHT (THEODOR). *See* ACADEMIES, *etc.*—Leipsic.—*Academia Lipsiensis.* Katalog der Sanskrit-Handschriften der Universitäts-Bibliothek . . . Von Theodor Aufrecht. 1901. 8°. **14096. ccc. 3.**

—— *See* DHOYĪ. Nachahmungen des Meghaduta, *etc.* 1900. 8°. [*Zeitschrift der Deutschen Morgenlaendischen Gesellschaft.*] **Ac. 8815/2.(vol. 54.)**

—— Neue Erwerbungen aus Bombay, *etc.* [A list of rare printed books.] 1900. *See* ACADEMIES, *etc.*—Germany.—*Deutsche Morgenlaendische Gesellschaft.* Zeitschrift, *etc.* Bd. 54, pp. 83-96. 1846, *etc.* 8°. **Ac. 8815/2.(vol. 54.)**

AUPAPĀTIKASŪTRA. Das Aupapâtika Sûtra [or Uvavāī], erstes Upânga der Jaina. Einleitung mit Inhaltsangabe, Text, Anmerkungen und Glossar. I Theil, enthaltend Einleitung mit Inhaltsangabe und vom Texte §§1-38, der philosophischen Facultät der Universität Leipzig zur Erlangung der Doctorwürde vorgelegt von Ernst Leumann. pp. 50, i. *Leipzig,* 1882. 8°. **14100. b. 2.**

Identical with pp. 1-50 *of the same work published in the* Abhandlungen *of the Deutsche Morgenländische Gesellschaft,* 1883.

AUSHADHIKRIYĀ. औषधीक्रिया [Aushadhikriyā. A compilation of Sanskrit pharmacological prescriptions, with Marathi version and notes.] pp. ii. 60. मुंबई १९०० [*Bombay,* 1900.] 8°. **14043. c. 45.(2.)**

Forms no. 31 *of the* Āryabhishak Series.

AVADHŪTALAKSHAṆA. अवधूतलक्षणम् *etc.* [Avadhūtalakshaṇa. Ten stanzas on the condition of the ascetics called *avadhūta,* with a mystical acrostic on that term. With Hindi version by Hariṣaṅkara Ṣāstrī.] pp. 4. कानपूर १८९९ [*Cawnpore,* 1899.] 8°. **14028. c. 85.(3.)**

ĀVAṢYAKA. Die Āvaśyaka-Erzählungen. Herausgegeben von Ernst Leumann. 1897. *See* ACADEMIES, *etc.*—Germany.—*Deutsche Morgenlaendische Gesellschaft.* Abhandlungen, *etc.* Bd. 10, No. 2. 1859, *etc.* 8°. **753. f. 18.**

Incomplete, breaking off after p. 48.

AVINĀṢACHANDRA CHAKRAVARTĪ, *of Dhubri High School.* कविताकोरकम् *etc.* [Kavitākoraka. A collection of Sanskrit poems for educational purposes. With Bengali metrical translation.] pp. vi. 35, 44. कलिकाता १९०० [*Calcutta,* 1900.] 12°. **14076. b. 28.(3.)**

AVINĀṢACHANDRA KAVIRATNA, *Kavirāja. See* CHARAKA. Charaka-samhita. With the commentary of Chakrapani Datta. Edited by ... Avinasha Chandra Kaviratna, *etc.* Pt. vi. [1894.] 8°. **14043. dd. 1.**

—— *See* CHARAKA. Charaka-samhita. Translated ... Published by Avinash Chandra Kaviratna. 1892, *etc.* 8°. **14043. e. 26.**

AVVAIYĀR. ॥ मन्दारमाला ... The Mandara Mala. [A Sanskrit metrical version of the] Athisudi [*i.e.* Āttisūḍi] of Avvai. (॥ शम्याकमाला ... The Samyaka Mala ... [A version of the] Kondrai Vendan of Avvai. ॥ वागुल्लासः ... The ... Vagullasa. [A version of the] Vakkundam [or] Moodurai of Avvai ॥ तत्त्वपदवी ... The Thathvapadavee. [A version of the] Nulvali [*i.e.* Nalvaṛi] of Avvai.) Translated ... by Radhakrishna Sastriar. pp. 7, 6, 5, 11. *See* RĀDHĀKṚISHṆA ṢĀSTRĪ, *of Pudukottai.* नीतिदशप्रबन्धी ... The Nitidasaprabandhi, *etc.* No. 1, 2, 4, 7. 1894. 8°. **14085. c. 46.**

AYODHYĀNĀTHA, *Assistant Deputy Commissioner of Gonda.* श्रीभास्करमोक्षप्रकाश *etc.* [Bhāskaramokshaprakāṣa. A Hindi treatise on the worship of Ṣiva, with hymns, name-lists, and formulae in Sanskrit.] pp. 121. लखनऊ १९०१ [*Lucknow,* 1901.] 8°. **14154. ee. 13.(2.)**

AYODHYĀPRASĀDA BHAṬṬĀCHĀRYA. भक्तमनोरञ्जनी । [Ṣivastotra, or Ṣambhustotra. A hymn to Ṣiva, in 22 stanzas. With a commentary styled Bhaktamanorañjanī by Umādatta Tripāṭhī.] *See* UMĀDATTA TRIPĀṬHĪ. कूटपद्यव्याख्या *etc.* [Kūṭapadyavyākhyā.] pp. 70-85. [1899.] 12°. **14072. b. 24.**

BĀBĀ PADMANJĪ. संस्कृत-मराठी कोश. A Sanskrit-Marathi Dictionary, for the use of schools & families, *etc.* pp. xiii. 340. *Bombay,* 1891. 12°. **14090. a. 17.**

This work, according to the Preface, "includes all the Sanskrit words with almost all their significations used in the Marathi language."

BĀBĀ ṢĀSTRĪ PHADKE. *See* ĀRAṆYAKAS.—*Aitareyāraṇyaka.* ऐतरेयारण्यकम् *etc.* [Aitareyāraṇyaka. With commentary of Sāyaṇa. Edited by Bābā Phaḍke.] [1898.] 8°. **14003. ccc. (no. 38.)**

—— *See* ĀRAṆYAKAS. — *Taittirīyāraṇyaka.* तैत्तिरीयारण्यकम् *etc.* [Taittirīyāraṇyaka. With Sāyaṇa's commentary. Edited by Bābā Phaḍke.] [1897-1898.] 8°. **14003. ccc. (no. 36.)**

—— *See* GOPĪNĀTHA DĪKSHITA, *Bhaṭṭa.* संस्काररत्नमाला *etc.* [Saṃskāraratnamālā. Edited by Kāṣīnātha Āgāṣe and Bābā Phaḍke.] [1899.] 8°. **14003. ccc. (no. 39.)**

—— *See* MAHĀBHĀRATA.—Bhagavadgītā.—*Sanskrit.* श्रीमद्भगवद्गीता *etc.* [Bhagavadgītā. With the Paiṣāchabhāshya. Edited by Kāṣīnātha Āgāṣe and Bābā Phaḍke.] [1901.] 8°. **14003. ccc. (no. 44.)**

BĀBŪRĀU CHIMṆĀJĪ GONDHḶE. योगतत्त्वामृत *etc.* [Yogatattvāmṛita. An anthology of Sanskrit texts bearing on the Yoga. Compiled with copious metrical paraphrases in Marathi by Bābūrāu Gondhḷe.] pp. xv. 321. पुणे १८९७ [*Poona,* 1897.] 8°. **14048. cc. 12.**

BĀDARĀYAṆA. *See* KĀLĪVARA VEDĀNTAVĀGĪṢA. हिन्दूशास्त्र *etc.* [Shaḍdarṣana. A Bengali exposition of the six systems.] [1895.] 8°. [*Hinduṣāstra.*] **14085. c. 45.(vol. 1.)**

—— *See* PRABHUDAYĀLU, *Mu'āfīdār.* समीक्षाकर *etc.* [Samīkshākara. Select Aphorisms from the Vedānta and other systems, with a commentary.] [1898.] 8°. **14048. e. 22.(2.)**

—— வெயாஸகீ-ஶாரீரகமீமாம்ஸா [Vaiyāsakī Ṣārīrakamīmāṃsā, *i.e.* the Brahmasūtra.] *See* UPANISHADS.—*General Collections.* அஷ்டோத்தரஶதோபநிஷத: *etc.* [Ashṭottaraṣatopanishadaḥ, *etc.*] pp. 869-890. 1896. 8°. **14010. cc. 8.**

BĀDARĀYAṆA (*continued*). वेदान्तदर्शनम् *etc.* [Vedāntadarṣana, *i.e.* the Brahmasūtra. Edited by Rāmasvarūpa Ṣarmā.] pp. 23. १८९८ [*Moradabad*, 1898.] 8°. **14048. cc. 21.(6.)**

——— The Vedânta-Sûtras with the commentary by *S*aṅkarâ*k*ârya. Translated [with introduction] by George Thibaut. 2 vols. 1890-1896. *See* Mueller (F. M.). The Sacred Books of the East, *etc.* Vol. xxxiv., xxxviii. 1879, *etc.* 8°. **2003. b. (vol. 34, 38.)**

——— బ్రహ్మసూత్రార్థసంగ్రహము [Brahmasūtrārthasaṅgraha. Being the Aphorisms arranged in tabular form with Telugu paraphrases and synopses of the train of thought, according to Ṣaṅkara's Bhāshya, by Vallūri Jagannātha Rāu.] pp. ii. 113. *Vizagapatam*, ౧౮౯౪ [1894.] 8°. **14048. dd. 30.**

——— The Vedântakalpataru of Amalânanda. [Comprising the Brahmasūtra with the supercommentary of Amalānanda upon the Bhāmatī of Vāchaspati Miṣra in elucidation of Ṣaṅkara's Ṣārīrakabhāshya.] Edited by Râmaśâstrî Tailaṅga. (वेदान्तकल्पतरुः।) 2 vols. pp. xxi. ii. ii. i. 559, ii. v. ii. iv. xxiv. i. ii. *Benares*, 1895-1897. 8°. **14048. dd. 3.(vol. 11.)**

Forms vol. 11 *of the* Vizianagram Sanskrit Series.

——— The Vedântakalpataruparimala of Appayadikshita. [Comprising the Brahmasūtra with the gloss of Apyaya Dikshita upon Amalānanda's supercommentary Vedāntakalpataru.] Edited by Râmaśâstrî Tailaṅga. (वेदान्तकल्पतरुपरिमलः।) 3 vols. pp. ii. iv. 730, i. iii. ii. i. iv. ii. *Benares*, 1895-1898. 8°. **14048. dd. 3.(vol. 12.)**

Forms vol. 12 *of the* Vizianagram Sanskrit Series.

——— బ్రహ్మసూత్రార్థదీపికా *etc.* [Brahmasūtra. With a brief commentary based on that of Ṣaṅkara, styled Brahmasūtrārthadīpikā. Edited by Annavarōpa Veṅkaṭarāghava.] pp. iii. 110. నెల్లూరు హేమలంబి [*Nellore*, 1897.] 8°.

14048. cc. 8.(3.)

——— *See* Akhaṇḍānanda, *disciple of Akhaṇḍānubhūti.* तत्त्वदीपनम् . . . Tattvadîpana, a commentary on Panchapádikávivaraṇa, [Prakāṣātmā's commentary on Padmapāda's Pañchapādikā, the latter being a commentary upon Ṣaṅkara's Bhāshya I. i. 1-4] *etc.* 1901, *etc.* 8°. **14049. a. 3.**

——— *See* Padmapāda. The Pańchapâdikâ, *etc.* (Part II. The Pańchapâdikâvivaraṇa, *etc.*) 1891-1892. 8°.

14048. dd. 3.(vol. 2.)

——— *See* Padmapāda. The Pañcapādikā . . . Translated, *etc.* 1901, *etc.* 8°. [*The Pandit.*] **14096. d. 6.(vol. 23- .)**

——— *See* Rāmānanda Sarasvatī, *disciple of Govindānanda.* विवरणोपन्यासः . . . Vivaraṇopanyâsa, *etc.* 1901. 8°.

14048. cc. 37.

——— वैयासिकन्यायमाला। अथोत् वेदान्ताधिकरणन्यायमाला *etc.* (Vaiyásikanyáyamálá or Vedántádhikaraṇamálá. [An exposition of the Brahmasūtra] by S'rí Bháratitírthamuni. With sutras of each adhikaraṇa. Edited by Pandit S'ivadatta.) pp. iv. 164. पुण्याख्यपत्तने १८९१ [*Poona*, 1891.] 8°. **14003. ccc. (no. 23.)**

Forms no. 23 *of the* Ānandāṣrama Sanskrit Series. *The English title is taken from the cover.*

——— ॥ ब्रह्मविद्याभरणम् *etc.* [Brahmasūtra. With the commentary Brahmavidyābharaṇa of Advaitānanda Sarasvatī upon Ṣaṅkara's *bhāshya.*] pp. xvii. 819. 1894. *See* Harihara Ṣāstrī, *Goshṭhīpuram*, and others. ॥ अद्वैतमञ्जरी *etc.* [Advaitamañjarī.] 1892-1895. 8°. **14048. e. 23.**

——— The Vivaraṇaprameyasaṃgraha[, an exposition of Vedānta in the form of a commentary upon the Brahmasūtra, I. i. 1-4, ascribed to the authorship] of Mâdhavâchârya Vidyâraṇya. Edited by Râmaśâstrî Tailaṅga. (विवरणप्रमेयसंग्रहः।) pp. vii. i. xviii. 266. *Benares*, 1893. 8°.

14048. dd. 3.(vol. 5.)

Forms vol. 5 *of the* Vizianagram Sanskrit Series. *The authorship of this work is somewhat uncertain. Burnell* (Tanjore Catal., *p.* 88) *names* Bhāratītīrthavidyāraṇya. *Thus tradition wavers between Sāyaṇa and his master Bhāratītīrtha, and the evidence inclines towards the former.*

——— ॥ सूत्रवृत्तिः *etc.* [Brahmasūtra. With a commentary styled Sūtravṛitti and ascribed to a disciple of Ṣaṅkara.] pp. ii. ii. 133. 1894. *See* Harihara Ṣāstrī, *Goshṭhīpuram*, and others. ॥ अद्वैतमञ्जरी *etc.* [Advaitamañjarī.] 1892-1895. 8°. **14048. e. 23.**

BĀDARĀYAṆA (*continued*). బ్రహ్మామృతవర్షిణీనా-మాయంగ్రంథః *etc.* [Brahmasūtra. With the commentary Brahmāmṛitavarshiṇī or Brahmasūtraguruvṛitti of Rāmānanda Sarasvatī, here styled Dharma Bhaṭṭa. Edited by A. Veṅkaṭarāghava Ṣāstrī.] pp. 289. సింహపురి॥ [*Nellore*,] 1900. 8°. **14048. c. 77.**

—— The Brahma-Sutras [in English, with commentary translated from Nāgeṣa Bhaṭṭa's Vyāsasūtrenduṣekhara and notes, extending to Sūtra xxiii.]. 1900. *See* PERIODICAL PUBLICATIONS.—*Madras*. The Brahmavâdin. Vol. v., no. vii.–xii. 1895, *etc.* 8°. **14048. g. 1.(vol. 5.)**

—— श्री शारीरक मीमांसा भाष्य सारसंग्रहः *etc.* [Brahmasūtra, or Ṣārīrakamīmāṃsā. With Ṣārīrakamīmāṃsābhāshyasārasaṅgraha, a compendious commentary in Sanskrit and Hindi by Anantānandagiri. Followed by Kāṣīmṛitimokshanirṇaya, an essay on the salvation gained by dying at Benares, by the latter.] pp. ii. 180. काशी १९५७ [*Benares*, 1900.] 8°. **14048. cc. 36.**

—— ब्रह्मसूत्रभाष्यम् *etc.* (Brahma Sutra. With its commentary Viggyanamrita by Sri Viggyana Bhikshu. Edited by Pandit Mukundda Shastri.) pp. xi. ix. 628. *Benares*, 1901. 8°. **14004. a. 8.**

Forms nos. 30, 31, 34, 35, 37, *and* 40 *of the* Chowkhambâ Sanskrit Series.

—— ॥ अथ ब्रह्मसूत्रभाष्यप्रारंभः॥ [Brahmasūtra. With the commentary of Ānandatīrtha.] ff. 146. १८९२ [*Bombay*, 1892.] *obl.* 16°. **14048. a. 16.**

—— అథ శ్రీబ్రహ్మసూత్రభాష్యం ప్రారభ్యతే [Brahmasūtra. With the commentary of Ānandatīrtha. Edited by Ṣēḍambi Subrahmaṇya Ṣarmā.] pp. 208. చెన్నపురి ౧౮౯౮ [*Madras*, 1898.] *obl.* 12°. **14048. b. 33.(3.)**

—— श्रीमद्ब्रह्मसूत्राणि *etc.* [Brahmasūtra. With the *bhāshya* of Ānandatīrtha and the Bhāshyadīpikā upon the latter by Jagannātha Yati. Preceded by an introduction by Paḷḷe Cheñchala Rāu, tables, and indices; and followed by summaries of the *bhāshyas* of Ānandatīrtha, Ṣaṅkara, and Rāmānuja in catechetical form, composed by A. Mahādeva Ṣāstrī and K. Raṅgāchārya, indices, *etc.* Edited by Gopālakṛishṇa Āchārya.] pp. xxvi. xx. 1220. *Madras*, १९०० [1900.] 8°. **14048. cc. 30.**

—— ವಿಶಿಷ್ಟಾದ್ವೈತ ಬ್ರಹ್ಮಮೀಮಾಂಸಾ ಭಾಷ್ಯಂ *etc.* [Brahmasūtra. With the Ṣaiva-Viṣishṭādvaita commentary, commonly styled Ṣrikaṇṭhabhāshya or Ṣaivabhāshya, of Ṣrikaṇtha Ṣivāchārya, also called Nilakaṇṭha.] pp. x. 146, i. ಕಲ್ಯಾಣ-ಪುರಾಖ್ಯಂ ೧೮೯೦ [*Bangalore*, 1890.] 8°. **14048. e. 20.**

—— ஶைவவிஶிஷ்டாத்வைத-ஶ்ரீகண்ட-ஶிவாசார்யபாஷ்யம் *etc.* [Brahmasūtra. With the exposition of Ṣrīkaṇṭha Ṣivāchārya, and with footnotes based upon Apyaya Dīkshita's commentary to the latter, styled Ṣivārkamaṇidīpikā. Edited by Paṅgānāḍ Gaṇapati Ṣāstrī.] pp. 311. கும்பகோணம்॥ [*Kumbakonam*, 1899.] 8°. **14048. c. 72.(3.)**

The Ṣrīkaṇṭhabhāshya in this recension differs materially from the preceding edition.

—— The Vedánta-sútras with Śrikantha-bháshya. [Translated into English by A. Mahādeva Ṣāstrī.] 1897, *etc.* *See* PERIODICAL PUBLICATIONS.—*Madras*. The Light of Truth, or Siddhanta Deepika, *etc.* Vol. i., no. 1, *etc.* 1897, *etc.* 4°. **14170. fff. 4.(vol. 1- .)**

In progress.

—— శ్రీవేదాన్తసారసహితదీపః *etc.* [Brahmasūtra. With the commentaries of Rāmānuja entitled Vedāntasāra and Vedāntadīpa. Edited with notes and index by Tirumalāchārya and Vijayarāghavāchārya.] pp. 271, 44, lxx. xliv. చెన్నపురి॥ [*Madras*, 1890.] 8°. **14048. c. 73.**

—— வேதாந்தஸார: [Brahmasūtra. With the commentary Vedāntasāra of Rāmānuja.] pp. 110. கும்பகோணம்॥ [*Kumbakonam*,] 1894. 8°. **14048. bb. 48.**

—— The Vedānta-Sūtras with the Śrī-Bhāshya of Rāmānujāchārya. Translated into English [with introduction and notes] by M. Raṅgāchārya and M. B. Varadarāja Aiyangār. (Brahmavādin Series.) Vol. i. *Madras*, 1899. 8°. **14048. cc. 29.**

—— அதிகரணஸாராவளீ *etc.* [Brahmasūtra. With the Adhikaraṇasārāvalī, a metrical epitome of Rāmānuja's Ṣrībhāshya by Veṅkaṭanātha Vedāntāchārya, and a commentary upon the Adhikaraṇasārāvalī, styled Sahṛidayahṛidayaprakāṣikā, by Naḍādūr Sundararāja Āchārya.] கும்பகோணம் ॥ பராபவ—ஹுவ ॥ [*Kumbakonam*, 1900-1902.] 8°. **14048. e. 32.**

—— *See* ANANTĀRVĀR, *Maṇḍayam A.*, and NARASIṂHAIYAṄGĀR, *P. T.* वेदान्तवादावली *etc.* [Vedāntavādāvalī. A collection of treatises in exposition of Viṣishṭādvaita-Vedānta and the system of Rāmānuja.] [1898, *etc.*] 8°. **14048. cc. 18.**

—— *See* RAṄGARĀMĀNUJA, *disciple of Tātāchārya.* वेदान्त विषयवाक्यदीपिका *etc.* [Vishayavākyadīpikā. A treatise upon the scriptural passages quoted in the Ṣrībhāshya of Rāmānuja.] [1899.] 8°. **14048. e. 26.**

—— లక్ష్మీవిశిష్టాద్వైతభాష్యమితి ప్రసిద్ధమ్ . . . శ్రీనివాసదీక్షితీయం *etc.* [Brahmasūtra. With the Lakshmīviṣishṭādvaitabhāshya, a commentary of the Vaikhānasa-Viṣishṭādvaita school by Ṣrīnivāsa Dikshita, and the supercommentary called Nigamachūḍādarpaṇa by Sundararāja Bhaṭṭāchārya. Preceded by the Jñānakāṇḍa, or *paṭalas* 80-96, from the Vimānārchanakalpa of the Vaikhānasa, or Marīchipaṭala, an exposition of Viṣishṭādvaita theosophy ascribed in its present form to Marīchi and in its principles to Vikhanas. Edited by A. Ṣrīnivāsa Tātāchārya.] pp. ii. 15, 360, ii. చెన్నపురి ॥ [*Madras*,] 1896. 8°. **14048. dd. 29.(2.)**

—— ലക്ഷ്മീവിശിഷ്ടാദ്വൈതഭാഷ്യം *etc.* [Brahmasūtra. Sūtra i., or Jijñāsādhikaraṇa, with Ṣrīnivāsa's Lakshmīviṣishṭādvaitabhāshya and the Nigamachūḍādarpaṇa of Sundararāja. Preceded by the Jñānakāṇḍa from the Vimānārchanakalpa of the Vaikhānasa. Edited by A. Ṣrīnivāsa Tātāchārya.] pp. ii. 16, 48; 3 *plates.* ചെന്നപുരി ॥ [*Madras*,] 1896. 8°. **14048. dd. 29.(1.)**

—— Karyadhi karana vada. Part i. [Comprising the Aphorisms IV. iii. 6-15, with commentary] by Vidwan T. A. P. Sreeranga chariar, *etc.* (कार्याधिकरणवादः ।) pp. 62, iv. 1901. *See* ANANTĀCHĀRYA, *Prativādibhayaṅkara.* शास्त्रमुक्तावली. The Ŝasthramukthâvalî, *etc.* No. 7. 1899, *etc.* 8°. **14049. a. 1.(no. 7.)**

—— శ్రీదక్షిణామూర్తిబ్రహ్మసంవాదాత్మకే . . . తత్త్వసారాయణే . . . గురుజ్ఞానవాసిష్ఠే . . . బ్రహ్మమీమాంసాఖ్యగ్రన్థః [Brahmamīmāṃsā. Being the Brahmasūtra with the section from the Jñānakāṇḍa of the Gurujñānavāsishṭha (Pāda II. i.-xvii.) containing the exposition thereof. Together with the commentary Adhikaraṇakañchuka of Apyaya Dikshita.] pp. i. 290, iii. శ్రీకార్వేటినగర ॥ [*Karwaitnagar*,] 1898. 12°. **14048. b. 32.**

—— *See* GURUJÑĀNAVĀSISHṬHA. గురుజ్ఞానవాసిష్ఠే జ్ఞానకాండః *etc.* [Gurujñānavāsishṭha. Vol. i., including in Pāda II. i.-xvii. an exposition of the Brahmasūtra, with the commentary Adhikaraṇakañchuka of Apyaya Dīkshita, *etc.*] [1882]—1897. 4°. **14048. e. 8.**

—— శ్రీశుకభాష్యమ్ *etc.* [Brahmasūtra. With the commentary of Vātsya Ṣukāchārya, expounding the Aphorisms according to Bhāgavata doctrine, and a supercommentary called Chandrikā by Gārgya Kṛishṇam Āchārya. Edited by Tūppūl Veṅkaṭāchārya.] pp. iv. 13, 32, xviii. 344, 232. బెంగళూరు ౧౮౯౨ [*Bangalore*, 1892.] 8°. **14048. c. 76.**

—— বেদান্তদর্শন *etc.* [Vedāntadarṣana. Being the Brahmasūtra with the Govindabhāshya or Vaishṇava commentary of Baladeva Vidyābhūshaṇa, a gloss thereupon by the same, a Bengali translation by Ṣyāmalāla Gosvāmī of the *bhāshya*, and a Bengali commentary upon it. Edited by Kṛishṇagopāla Bhakta.] 5 pts. কলিকাতা ১৩০১ [*Calcutta*, 1894.] 8°. **14048. dd. 23.**

—— वेदान्तार्यभाष्यम् . . . The Vedantarya Bhashyam. [A Dvaita exposition of the Brahmasūtra, commencing with Sūtra II. i. 21.] . . . By Sri Pandit Arya Muni. With English & Hindi translations by Balkrishna Sahay, *etc.* Pt. i. *Ranchi*, 1895. 8°. **14048. cc. 4.**

Apparently no more has been published.

BADARĪDATTA ṢARMĀ. *See* UPANISHADS.—*Separate Upanishads.* **वाजसनेयोपनिषद्** *etc.* [Işopanishad. With Hindi translation and exposition by Badarīdatta.] [1901.] 8°. **14007. b. 4.(3.)**

—— *See* UPANISHADS.—*Separate Upanishads.* **तलवकारोपनिषद्** *etc.* [Kenopanishad. With Hindi translation and exposition by Badarīdatta.] [1901.] 8°. **14007. b. 4.(4.)**

BADARĪNĀTHA, *Pandit,* also called BADARĪLĀLA. *See* PṚITHUYAṢAS. **षट्पंचाशिका** *etc.* [Shaṭpañchāṣikā. With the Hindi paraphrase by Badarīnātha.] [1901.] 8°. **14053. ccc. 21.(2.)**

BADARĪNĀTHA KUDDĀLA, *son of Chhoṭilāl, of Jaipur.* *See* DHANAṂJAYA, *son of Vasudeva.* The Dvisandhâna ... With the commentary of Badarînâth. 1895. 8°. [*Kâvyamâlâ.*] **14072. ccc. 12.(no. 49.)**

BĀHAḌA. *See* VĀGBHAṬA.

BĀHIRAJAYAMAṄGALAGĀTHĀ. *See* JAYAMAṄGALAGĀTHĀ.

BAHUVALLABHA ṢĀSTRĪ. *See* NĀGEṢA BHAṬṬA. [*Mahābhāshyapradīpoddyota.*] Mahābhāṣya Pradīpoddyota ... Edited by Paṇḍita Bahuvallabha Çāstrī. 1901, *etc.* 8°. [*Bibliotheca Indica.*] **14002. a. (vol. 140.)**

BAL (B. G.). *See* BĀLAKṚISHṆA GOPĀLA BĀLA.

BĀLĀBHĀĪ JAMNĀDĀS VAIṢYA. પુનર્લગ્ન સશાસ્ત્ર છે? [Punarlagna saṣāstra chhe? A proof of the legality of the re-marriage of widows; being a compilation of Sanskrit texts bearing thereon, with Gujarati dissertations upon them.] pp. xviii. 56. અમદાવાદ ૧૮૯૭ [*Ahmadabad,* 1897.] 12°. **14144. b. 23.(1.)**

BĀLĀBHĀĪ TRIKAMLĀL. જૈનગુણ પ્રબોધ રત્નચિંતામણી *etc.* [Jaina-guṇaprabodharatnachintāmaṇi. A collection of Jain religious compositions, prose and verse, in Gujarati and Prakrit, by divers authors.] અમદાવાદ ૧૯૦૧ [*Ahmadabad,* 1901, *etc.*] 16°. **14144. c. 19.**

In progress?

BĀLACHANDRAṢEKHARA ṢĀSTRĪ, *Sādhupalli.* *See* CHANDRAṢEKHARA ṢĀSTRĪ, *Sādhupalli.*

BALADEVAPRASĀDA BHAṬṬA, *of Kuthar, Cawnpore.* *See* JĪVANĀTHA, *son of Ṣambhunātha.* **अथ दिनचर्यापञ्चस्वरोदाहरणम्** *etc.* [Dinacharyāpañchasvarodāharaṇa. Edited by Baladevaprasāda.] [1901.] *obl.* 8°. **14053. d. 60.**

BALADEVAPRASĀDA MISRA, *son of Sukhānanda, of Moradabad.* *See* NĀGA BHAṬṬA. ॥ **सिद्ध डाकिनी ... कामतन्त्र** *etc.* [Kāmaratna. With Hindi translation by Baladevaprasāda.] [1898.] 12°. **14033. a. 36.**

—— *See* PURĀṆAS.—*Kalkipurāṇa.* **कल्किपुराण** *etc.* (Kalki-purana [in Sanskrit and Hindi]. Translated [with Hindi commentary] by P. Baldew Prasad Mishra, *etc.*) [1897.] 8°. **14016. d. 52.**

—— *See* RUDRAJAPA. ॥ **अथ रुद्री** *etc.* [Rudrajapa. With Hindi translation and preface by Baladevaprasāda.] 1897. *obl.* 8°. **14028. dd. 3.(1.)**

—— *See* TANTRAS. [*Mahānirvāṇatantra.*] Mahanirvana-tantram ... Purva Kandam ... Translated [into Hindi] by P. Baldeo Prasad Misra, *etc.* 1896. 8°. **14033. aa. 2.**

—— *See* TANTRAS. [*Sarvavijayitantra.*] **सर्वविजयीतन्त्र** *etc.* [Sarvavijayitantra. With Hindi version by Baladevaprasāda.] [1898.] 12°. **14033. a. 35.(3.)**

—— *See* TANTRAS. [*Uḍḍīṣatantra.*] ॥ **उड्डीसतन्त्र** *etc.* [Uḍḍīṣatantra. With Hindi preface and translation by Baladevaprasāda.] 1898. 12°. **14033. a. 35.(2.)**

BALADEVA RATHA KAVISŪRYA, *Rāyaguru.* କିଶୋରଚନ୍ଦ୍ରାନନ୍ଦଚମ୍ପୂ *etc.* [Kiṣorachandrānanda. A *champū* composition on the sports of the youthful Krishṇa. With a metrical paraphrase in Oriya. Third edition.] pp. 31. *Cuttack,* 1901. 12°. **14076. a. 22.(3.)**

BALADEVA SIṂHA, *Raja of Kama.* A Vijayapatra of Digvijainie Victoria in Sanskrit and English, with the signatures of Pandits of Benares. [Being a series of stanzas in Sanskrit and Hindi upon the British rule, by Bechanrām; an English translation of the same; and a number of short panegyrics, historical notices,

&c., in Hindi, by Baladeva Siṃha. The whole compiled and edited] by Rájá Kámá Baldeva Sinh, *etc.* (चक्रवर्ती विक्टोरिया भारतवर्षे सम्वत ३२ । "विजयपत्र") *Benares*, 1889. 12°. **14058. a. 15.**

Each part has a separate pagination.

BALADEVA VIDYĀBHŪSHAṆA. *See* Bādarāyaṇa. বেদান্তদর্শন *etc.* [Vedāntadarṣana. Being the Brahmasūtra with the Govindabhāshya of Baladeva, a gloss thereupon by the same, a Bengali translation of the *bhāshya, etc.*] [1894.] 8°. **14048. dd. 23.**

—— *See* Rūpa Gosvāmī. লঘুভাগবতামৃত *etc.* [Laghu-bhāgavatāmṛita. With a Sanskrit commentary by Baladeva, *etc.*] [1897.] 8°. **14016. c. 58.**

—— *See* Upanishads.—*Separate Upanishads.* ईशोपनिषत् *etc.* (Isa-Upanishad. With the Bhasyas of Baladeva, *etc.*) 1895. 8°. **14010. cc. 3.(1.)**

—— The Sâhityakaumudî of Vidyâbhûshaṇa. [A treatise on stylistic, in 11 chapters.] With the Krishṇânandinî commentary. Edited [with a biographical preface] by ... Paṇḍit Śivadatta ... and Kâśinâth Pâṇdurang Parab. (साहित्यकौमुदी।) pp. vi. xxiii. 199, vii. 1897. *See* Durgāprasāda, *son of Vrajalāla*, and Kāśinātha Pāṇḍuraṅga Parab. Kâvyamâlâ. [No.] 63. 1886, *etc.* 8°. **14072. ccc. 12.(no. 63.)**

—— सिद्धान्तरत्नम् *etc.* [Siddhāntaratna. A Vedantic tractate by Vidyābhūshaṇa in confirmation of the same writer's Govindabhāshya, in exposition of the Chaitanya-Vaishṇava doctrine. With a commentary. Edited, with a Bengali translation, by Ṣyāmalāla Gosvāmī.] pp. ii. 333. কলিকাতা ১৩০৪ [*Calcutta*, 1897.] 8°. **14048. cc. 24.**

BĀLA GAṄGĀDHARA TILAKA. The Orion, or Researches into the antiquity of the Vedas, *etc.* [An English essay, illustrated from Sanskrit texts.] pp. vii. i. 227, i.; 2 *plates. Bombay*, 1893. 12°. **14053. b. 27.**

BĀLAGOPĀLENDRA. *See* Ṣaṅkara Āchārya.—*Doubtful and Supposititious Works.* अथ मनीषापञ्चकम् [Manīshāpañchaka. With the *ṭīkā* of Bālagopālendra.] [1891.] 8°. [*Vedāntagranthapañchaka.*] **14048. b. 15.(2.)**

BALAICHĀND GOSVĀMĪ. *See* Rūpa Gosvāmī. লঘুভাগবতামৃত *etc.* [Laghu-bhāgavatāmṛita. With commentary and Bengali translation. Edited by Balaichānd and Atulakṛishṇa.] [1897.] 8°. **14016. c. 58.**

BĀLĀJĪ HARI PHĀṬAK. A Guide to the Study of Dr. Bhandarkar's First Book of Sanskrit. pp. 72, i. *Ratnagiri*, 1898. 12°. **14085. b. 41.(2.)**

BĀLĀJĪ VIṬṬHALA GĀṆVASKAR. वेदोक्त संस्कार प्रकाश *etc.* [Vedokta-saṃskāraprakāṣa. A ritual for the chief domestic rites, based on the Gṛihyasūtras of Āṣvalāyana, Pāraskara, Gobhila, *etc.* With Gujarati rubrics, explanatory notes, translations, *etc.*] pp. iv. 178. મુંબઈ ૧૯૩૮ [*Bombay*, 1881.] 12°. **14144. b. 8.**

BĀLAKṚISHṆA, *Deṣamaṅgalam.* ஶ்ருங்காரமஞ்ஜரீமண்டநம்: [Ṣṛiṅgāramañjarīmaṇḍana. Studies in style, relative to the Ṣṛiṅgāramañjari of Mānavikrama.] *See* Mānavikrama, *Rājakumāra.* ஶ்ரீமாநவிக்ரமகவிராஜகுமாரேண ... க்ருதா: ஸம்ஸ்ருஷ்டா: *etc.* [Essays and poems.] [1890.] 8°. **14072. d. 35.**

BĀLAKṚISHṆA GAṆEṢA YOGĪ. *See* Pāṇini.—*Siddhāntakaumudī.* मध्यसिद्धान्तकौमुदी *etc.* [Madhyasiddhāntakaumudī. With notes by Bālakṛishṇa.] [1895.] 12°. **14090. b. 41.**

—— *See* Veṅkaṭārya Yajvā, *Ariṣānaphāla.* The Vishwaguṇâdarsh Champu ... Edited with commentary Padârthchandrikâ by Bâlkrishna Ganesh Yogi. 1899. 8°. **14076. c. 74.**

BĀLAKṚISHṆA GOPĀLA BĀLA. *See* Jagannātha Paṇḍitarāja. The Bhaminivilasa ... With a Sanskrit gloss Bhushana ... English translation, notes ... various readings and the poet's life, by B. G. Bal. 1895. 8°. **14070. c. 53.**

BĀLAKṚISHṆA GOSVĀMĪ. *See* Rāmānanda Rāya. श्रीजगन्नाथवल्लभनाटकम् *etc.* [Jagannāthavallabhanāṭaka. With Hindi translation by Bālakṛishṇa.] [1901.] 8°. **14079. d. 46.**

BĀLAKṚISHṆA SADĀSIVA GODṢE. अथ प्रातिशाख्यप्रदीपशिक्षा *etc.* [Prātiṣākhyapradīpaṣikshā. A treatise upon Kātyāyana's Prātiṣākhya of the

White Yajurveda.] *See* Yugalakiṣora Vyāsa Pāṭhaka. श्रीमद्याज्ञवल्क्यादि . . . शिक्षासङ्ग्रहः . . . A collection of Śikshás, *etc.* pp. 210-306. 1893. 8°. **14093. b. 31.**

BĀLAKRISHṆASAHĀYA, *Pleader, of Ranchi.* *See* Bādarāyaṇa. वेदान्तार्यभाष्यम् . . . The Vedantarya Bhashyam . . . With English & Hindi translations by Balkrishna Sahay, *etc.* 1895. 8°. **14048. cc. 4.**

BĀLAKRISHṆA ṢĀSTRĪ PAṬAVARDHANA. *See* Bhaṭṭojī Dīkshita. मनोरमा *etc.* [Manoramā. Edited by Bālakṛishṇa.] Pt. i. [1900.] 8°. **14093. d. 22.**

BĀLAMUKUNDA BHAṬṬA GAṆURKAR. *See* Pāraskara. पारस्करगृह्यसूत्रम् *etc.* [Pāraskaragṛihyasūtra. With commentaries, *etc.* Edited by Devanātha and Bālamukunda.] [1896.] 4°. **14010. f. 10.**

BALARĀMA MALLIKA. Krishna and Krishnaism. By Bulloram Mullick. pp. xii. 179. *Calcutta*, 1898. 12°. **14028. b. 98.**

BĀLARĀMA UDĀSĪNA MĀṆḌALĪKA, *Svāmī.* *See* Ānandabodha Paramahaṃsa. न्यायमकरन्दः . . . Nyâya Makaranda . . . with a commentary . . . edited by . . . Bâlarâm, *etc.* 1901, *etc.* 8°. **14004. a. 11.**

—— *See* Patañjali. — *Philosophical Works.* योगदर्शनम् *etc.* [Yogadarṣana. Being the Yogasūtra with the *bhāshya*, the supercommentary of Vāchaspati, and a gloss by the editor, Bālarāma.] [1890.] 8°. **14048. dd. 6.**

—— *See* Patañjali. — *Philosophical Works.* पातञ्जलदर्शनप्रकाश *etc.* [Pātañjaladarṣanaprakāṣa. With Hindi translation and commentary by Bālarāma.] [1897.] 8°. **14048. d. 59.**

BĀLA ṢĀSTRĪ ĀGĀṢE, *Mahāmahopādhyāya.* *See* Upanishads.—*Separate Upanishads.* ईशावास्योपनिषत् *etc.* ((1) Shri Isávásyopanishad with the Bháshya of . . . Śankaráchárya and Commentary by . . . Ânandadnyána. Edited by . . . Bāḷa Śástri Agáse, *etc.*) [1888.] 8°. **14003. ccc. (no. 5.)**

—— *See* Upanishads.—*Separate Upanishads.* केनोपनिषत् *etc.* (The Kenopanishad with the . . . Bháshyás of . . . Śankaráchárya and Commentary of . . . Ânandadnyána. Edited by . . . Báḷa Sástri Agáse, *etc.*) [1888.] 8°. **14003. ccc. (no. 6.)**

BĀLASUBRAHMAṆYA BRAHMASVĀMĪ, *Paramahaṃsa, of Madura.* *See* Mahābhārata.—Bhagavadgītā.—*Sanskrit and Vernaculars.* శ్రీభగవద్గీతా గూఢార్థదీపిక *etc.* [Bhagavadgītā. With Telugu interpretations and commentary styled Gūḍhārthadīpikā, by Bālasubrahmaṇya.] [1900.] 8°. **14065. c. 50.**

—— *See* Mahābhārata.—Bhagavadgītā.—*Sanskrit and Vernaculars.* பகவத்கீதா தாத்பரிய-தீபிகை, *etc.* [Bhagavadgītā. Edited with Tamil version by Bālasubrahmaṇya.] 1900. 32°. **14068. a. 10.**

—— *See* Mahābhārata.—Bhagavadgītā.—*Sanskrit and Vernaculars.* శ్రీభగవద్గీతారహస్యార్థ-బోధిని *etc.* [Bhagavadgītā. With Bhagavadgītārahasyārthabodhinī, a Telugu translation and exposition by Bālasubrahmaṇya.] 1900, *etc.* 16°. **14065. b. 22.**

—— *See* Upanishads. — *Separate Upanishads.* Isavasyopanishad. With [Tamil] commentaries [by] Sreemat Paramahamsa Bala Subrahmania Brahma Swamy. [1899.] 8°. **14010. b. 21.**

—— *See* Upanishads.—*Separate Upanishads.* கேனோபநிஷத்தீபிகை *etc.* [Kenopanishad. With the commentary Kenopanishaddīpikā of Bālasubrahmaṇya, in Tamil.] 1900. 12°. **14007. b. 13.**

—— *See* Upanishads.—*Separate Upanishads.* కేనోపనిషద్దీపిక *etc.* [Kenopanishad. With the commentary Kenopanishaddīpikā of Bālasubrahmaṇya, in Telugu.] [1900.] 8°. **14007. b. 12.(1.)**

—— శ్రీభగవద్గీతా శ్లోకానుక్రమణిక *etc.* [Bhagavadgītāṣlokānukramaṇikā. An index of the first words in the verses of the Gītā.] pp. 53. చెన్నపురి ౧౯౦౦ [*Madras*, 1900.] 8°. **14065. bbb. 5.**

BALAVANTA KHANḌŪJĪ PĀRAKH. *See* Mahābhārata. — *Anuṣāsanaparva.* अथ श्रीविष्णुसहस्रना-

मार्थमंजरी *etc.* [Vishṇusahasranāmārthamañjarī. Comprising the Vishnusahasranāma with a poetical explanation in Marathi by Balavanta Pārakh.] [1900.] *obl.* 8°. **14028. c. 84.**

BĀLĀVATĀRA. *See* KACHCHĀYANA.

BĀLCHAND HĪRĀCHAND CHĀNDVAḌKAR. *See* YAṢOVIJAYA. Dnyansar . . . Translated into Marâthi . . . by Balchand Hirachand. [1900.] 12°. **14100. b. 10.**

BALDEO. *See* BALADEVA.

BALDEW. *See* BALADEVA.

BALLĀLA. భోజమహారాజచరిత్రమ్ . . . Bhojamaharaja Charitram [or Bhojaprabandha. The story of king Bhoja.] With notes [in Telugu]. pp. ii. 147. *Madras,* 1890. 12°. **14058. a. 4.**

Forms part of "V. Venkataraya Sastry's Sanskrit Series."

—— శ్రీభోజచరిత్రం *etc.* [Bhojacharitra. Edited by Sāggera Ṣrīkaṇṭha Ṣāstrī.] pp. 66. *Bangalore,* 1898. 8°. **14076. c. 70.**

BALLĀLASENA, *King of Bengal.* [For the Ballālacharita or history of Ballāla :] *See* ĀNANDA BHAṬṬA, *descendant of Ananta Bhaṭṭa.*

BALLANTYNE (JAMES ROBERT). *See* SADĀNANDA YOGĪNDRA. The Vedanta-sara : translated by Dr. J. R. Ballantyne, *etc.* 1898. 8°. [*Sacred Books of the East Described and Examined.*] **14010. cc. 9.(vol. 2.)**

—— Dr. Ballantyne's English Primer. With translation in easy Sanskrit by Kṛishṇárám Páṭhak . . . बारम्भपुस्तकं *etc.* Second edition. pp. 12. *Benares,* 1890. 8°. **14085. d. 31.(1.)**

BĀṆA. हर्षचरितम् *etc.* (Harsha Charita, or Life of Rajah Harsha Bardhana, in prose, by Bana Bhatta. Edited with a full commentary and an epitome of the work by Pandit Jibananda Vidyasagara.) Second edition. pp. 54, 689. कलिकाता १८९२ [*Calcutta,* 1892.] 8°. **14070. dd. 16.**

English title taken from wrapper.

—— The Harṣa-carita of Bāṇa. Translated by E. B. Cowell . . . and F. W. Thomas. pp. xiv. 284. 1897. *See* ACADEMIES, *etc.*—London.—*Oriental Translation Fund.* New Series II., vol. 8. 1891, *etc.* 8°. **14003. bb. (ser. 2, vol. 8.)**

BĀṆA (*continued*). Harshacharita. A historical romance. Translated . . . by Pandit S. M. Natesa Sastri . . . Uchchhvasas i and ii. pp. i. 171. *Madras,* 1901. 12°. **14060. b. 16.(2.)**

—— *See* RĀUJĪ RĀMACHANDRA KĀḶE. Exhaustive Notes on Bana's Harshacharita. Chapters i, ii & iii, (iv), *etc.* 1892-1894. 12°. **14076. b. 30.**

—— कादम्बरी *etc.* (Kâdambarî. By Bânabhatta and his son. Edited with a full Sanskrit commentary, introductions in English and Sanskrit comprising an epitome of the work, and copious notes in English, by Moreshwar Ramachandra Kâle.) 2 pts. *Bombay,* १८१७ [1895]-1896. 8°. **14076. c. 65.**

—— Kâdambarîsâra : being an abridgment of Bána's Kádambari [in Sanskrit] ; with copious explanatory notes, a full glossary and an abstract of the tale [in English]. By Mahadev Shivram Apte. Second edition. pp. ii. 14, 208, liv. xxix. ii. *Poona,* 1891. 8°. **14076. c. 60.**

—— The Kādambarī of Bāṇa. Translated, with occasional omissions, and accompanied by a full abstract of the continuation of the romance by the author's son Bhūshaṇabhaṭṭa, by C. M. Ridding. pp. xxiv. 231. 1896. *See* ACADEMIES, *etc.*—London.—*Oriental Translation Fund.* New Series II., vol. 7. 1891, *etc.* 8°. **14003. bb. (ser. 2, vol. 7.)**

—— An English Translation of Kadambari. Second half. pp. i. 59. *Calcutta,* [1890]. 12°. **14072. b. 10.(2.)**

—— *See* ABHINANDA, *son of Jayanta.* कादम्बरीकथासारः *etc.* [Kādambarīkathāsāra. With commentary.] [1900.] 8°. **14072. d. 44.**

—— *See* ṢRĪKAṆṬHA KAVI, *Eḷandūr.* అభినవకాదంబరి *etc.* [Abhinavakādambarī. A *champū* on the story of the Kādambarī. With a preface summarising the plot.] [1892.] 8°. **14076. c. 72.**

—— Copious Notes on Kádambarî. Part ii. By a graduate of the Bombay University. pp. ii. 72, ii. *Bombay,* 1891. 8°. **14072. ccc. 24.**

BĀṆA (*continued*). The Pârvatîpariṇaya of Bâṇabhatta. Edited by Mangesh Râmkrishṇa Telang. (पार्वतीपरिणयम्) pp. i. 46, ii. *Bombay*, 1892. 8°.
14079. b. 29.(1.)

—— പാർവ്വതീപരിണയം ഭാഷാനാടകം *etc.* [Pārvatīpariṇaya. In the *maṇipravālam* style, the prose portions being given in Malayalam only and the stanzas furnished with Malayalam translations in footnotes. Edited with a Malayalam preface by Rājakumāra Mānavikrama.] pp. v. x. 67. കോഴിക്കോട് ൧൦൭൦ [*Calicut*, 1895.] 8°.
14079. c. 48.(3.)

—— The Parvati Parinaya of Banabhatta. With Sanskrit commentary, English notes & translation by T. R. Ratnam Aiyar. pp. xiii. 102, 74, 38. *Madras*, 1898. 8°. **14079. b. 34.(3.)**

No. 1 *of the* Madras Sanskrit Series.

—— पार्वतीपरिणयम् [Pārvatīpariṇaya.] pp. 51. *See* ACADEMIES, *etc.* — Madras. — *University of Madras.* The F. A. Sanskrit Text 1899, *etc.* [1898.] 8°. **14079. b. 34.(4.)**

—— [For the Ratnāvalī, conjecturally ascribed to Bāṇa:] *See* HARSHADEVA.

BANĀRASĪ DĀSA. *See* SOMAPRABHA ĀCHĀRYA. जय . . . सिंदूरप्रकर: *etc.* [Sindūraprakara. With a Gujarati metrical version by Banārasī Dāsa.] [1890.] 8°. [*Jainakathāratnakoṣa.*]
14144. gg. 1.(vol. 1.)

BANĀRASĪRĀMA ŞARMĀ, *son of Lālajī-Rāma, of Jalandhar.* शूद्र विवाह संस्कार पद्धति: *etc.* [Şūdravivāhasaṃskārapaddhati. A manual of the rites for the weddings of the fourth caste.] pp. 65. लहौर [*Lahore*, 1902.] 8°. **14033. aa. 23.(1.)**

—— उभयैकादशी व्रतोद्यापन विधि *etc.* [Ubhayaikādaşīvratodyāpanavidhi. A manual of the rites for the Ekādaşī.] pp. 29. लाहौर [*Lahore*, 1902.] 8°.
14033. aa. 23.(2.)

BÂNERJEE (B. N.). *See* VEṆĪNĀTHA VANDYOPĀDHYĀYA.

BANGA SENA. *See* VAṄGASENA.

BAṄKIMCHANDRA CHAṬṬOPĀDHYĀYA. *See* MAHĀBHĀRATA. — Bhagavadgītā. — *Sanskrit and Vernaculars.* হিন্দুশাস্ত্র *etc.* [Bhagavadgītā. With Bengali translation by Baṅkimchandra (Adh. i. ii.) and Dāmodara.] [1897.] 8°. [*Hindu-şāstra.*]
14085. c. 45.(vol. 2.)

BAPPA BHAṬṬI SŪRI, *Jain Poet.* *See* ḌĀHYĀBHĀI FATH-CHAND and MOTĪLĀL MAHĀSUKHBHĀI. शोभनस्तवनावली *etc.* [Şobhanastavanāvalī. Hymns by Bappa Bhaṭṭi and others.] [1897.] 12°.
14100. a. 17.

BĀPŪDEVA ŞĀSTRĪ. *See* BHĀSKARA ĀCHĀRYA. सिद्धान्तशिरोमणि: . . . The Siddhánta-şiromaṇi . . . Formerly edited by . . . Bápú Deva Śástri, *etc.* 1891. 8°. **14053. cc. 65.**

—— *See* EPHEMERIDES. पत्रा श्रीसंवत १९५६ *etc.* [Bāpūdeva Şāstrī's Almanack for Samvat 1956. Compiled by his pupils.] [1898.] *obl.* 8°.
14096. b. 10.(3.)

BARODA K. LAHERI. *See* VARADĀKĀNTA LAHIRI.

BARTH (AUGUSTE). Inscriptions sanscrites du Cambodge, *etc.* [With 17 facsimile plates.] 1879. *See* ACADEMIES, *etc.*—Paris.—*Académie des Inscriptions et Belles Lettres.* Notices et Extraits, *etc.* Tome xxvii., fasc. i. 1787, *etc.* 4°.
Bar T. u. (tome 27), 2060 f.

BASAVAPURĀṆA. ವಾಸ್ಸೆಂಕ್ತಬಸವಪುರಾಣಂ *etc.* [Basavapurāṇa. A Pauranic poem on the legends of the Vīraşaiva saint Basava.] [1895.] *See* PERIODICAL PUBLICATIONS.—*Mysore.* ವೀರಶೈವಮತಪ್ರಕಾಶಿಕೆ [Vīraşaivamataprakāşikā.] Vol. iv. [1892-1895.] 8°. **14028. d. 39.(vol. 4.)**

Incomplete, breaking off in the 20th canto.

BASTĪRĀM. *See* VASATIRĀMA.

BATUVANTUDAVE, *Pandit.* *See* DEVARAKKHITA (*Don* ANDRIS DE SILVA), *Baṭuvantuḍāvē.*

BAUDDHĀGAMACHAKRAVARTĪ. *See* RĀMACHANDRA BHĀRATĪ.

BAUDHĀYANA. ॥ पितृमेधसूत्राणि ॥ The Pitṛmedhasūtras of Baudhāyana, Hiraṇyakeśin, Gautama, *etc.* 1896. 8°. *See* CALAND (W.). [*Deutsche Morgenlaendische Gesellschaft ; Abhandlungen.*]
753. f. 18.

BAUDHĀYANA (*continued*). *See* CALAND (W.). Über das rituelle Sūtra des Baudhāyana. 1903. 8°. [*Deutsche Morgenlaendische Gesellschaft: Abhandlungen.*] **753. f. 20.**

—— —— [Another copy.] **14039. b. 26.(3.)**

—— *See* UDAKAṢĀNTI. ఉదకశాంతివిధిః *etc.* [Udakaṣāntividhi. A manual for the rite of *udakaṣānti* as prescribed by Baudhāyana.] [1900.] 8°. **14028. d. 35.(3.)**

—— 𑌬𑍋𑌧𑌾𑌯𑌨𑌗𑍃𑌹𑍍𑌯𑍋𑌕𑍍𑌤 𑌜𑌾𑌤𑌕𑌰𑍍𑌮𑌾𑌦𑌿 𑌪𑍍𑌰𑌯𑍋𑌗𑌃 ॥ [Bodhāyanagṛihyokta-jātakarmādi-prayoga. A manual of domestic ritual according to Baudhāyana, from the *jāta-karma* to the *tantrahoma*. With the *kārikā* or epitome of Gopāla and a gloss thereon by the editor, Rāmakṛishṇa Ṣāstrī of Kalpadi.] pp. 117. கல்பாத்தி வாயத்தூட் ௧௯௦௦ [*Kalpadi*, 1900.] 8°. **14038. c. 37.(2.)**

BAYNES (HERBERT). *See* KAMMAVĀCHĀ. A Collection of Kammavācās. [Texts with translation.] By Herbert Baynes. 1892. 8°. [*Journal of the Royal Asiatic Society.*] **Ac. 8820/3. and 2098. a.b.**

BEAMAN (GEORGE BURNHAM). On the Sources of the Dharma-śāstras of Manu and Yājñavalkya, *etc.* pp. iv. 47. *Leipzig*, 1895. 8°. **011850. k. 21.**

BECHANRĀM, *Pandit.* दिग्विजयिनी विक्टोरिया ॥ [Digvijayinī Victoria. A series of stanzas in Sanskrit & Hindi upon the British rule. Followed by an English translation.] pp. 12, 5. *See* BALADEVA SIṂHA, *Raja of Kama.* A Vijaya-patra of Digvijainie Victoria, *etc.* 1889. 12°. **14058. a. 15.**

BECHANRĀM TRIPĀṬHĪ. *See* CHANDRABHŪSHAṆA CHATURVEDA. जीवितवृत्तान्तः *etc.* [Jīvitavṛittānta. A metrical biography of Bechanrām.] [1890.] 8°. **14058. b. 26.**

BENARES.—*Sanskrit College.* List of Sanskrit, Jaina and Hindi Manuscripts purchased by order of Government and deposited in the Sanskrit College, Benares, during 1897, 1898, 1899, 1900 and 1901. pp. xl. ii. 241. *Allahabad*, 1902. 8°. **14096. ccc. 7.**

BENARES SANSKRIT SERIES. Benares Sanskrit Series; a collection of Sanskrit works edited by the Paṇḍits of the Benares Sanskrit College, under the superintendence of R. T. H. Griffith . . . & G. Thibaut.

Works of this Series issued since the publication of Prof. Bendall's Catalogue are to be found under the following headings. Those already catalogued are marked by a bracket.

No. 33, 37. [*Jagannātha Paṇḍitarāja.*]
,, 34, 36, 39. [*Jaimini.*]
,, 35, 40, 42, 44, 46. *Yugalakiṣora Vyāsa Pāṭhaka.*
,, 38, 41, 43. *Sureṣvara Āchārya.*
,, 45, 47, 49. *Kātyāyana.*
No. 48. *Ṣaunaka.*
,, 50. [*Kaṇāda.*] *Udayana Āchārya.*
,, 51–54. *Bhaṭṭoji Dīkshita.*
,, 55, 56. *Rāmānanda Sarasvati.*
,, 57 *etc.* *Akhaṇḍānanda.*

BENDALL (CECIL). *See* ṢĀNTIDEVA. Çikshāsamuccaya . . . Edited by C. Bendall. 1897, *etc.* 8°. [*Bibliotheca Buddhica.*] **14003. dd. 1.**

BERGAIGNE (ABEL). *See* VEDAS.—Rigveda.—*Selections.* Quarante Hymnes . . . traduits et commentés par Abel Bergaigne. 1892-1894. 8°. [*Mémoires de la Société de Linguistique de Paris.*] **Ac. 9810. (tom. 8.)**

—— Inscriptions sanscrites de Campā, *etc.* (Inscriptions sanscrites du Cambodge.) [With 28 facsimile plates.] 1893. *See* ACADEMIES, *etc.*—Paris.—*Académie des Inscriptions et Belles-Lettres.* Notices et Extraits, *etc.* Tome xxvii., fasc. ii. 1787, *etc.* 8°. **Bar T. u. (tome 27), 2060. f.**

BESANT (ANNIE), *Mrs.* *See* MAHĀBHĀRATA.—Bhagavadgītā.—*English.* The Bhagavad Gîtâ . . . Translated by Annie Besant. 1895. 16°. **14060. a. 14.**

BETTEI (VITTORIO). *See* VETĀLAPAÑCHAVIṂṢATI. Vetālapañcaviṃçatikā, *etc.* [Translated, with critical notes, by V. Bettei.] 1897, *etc.* 8°. [*Studi Italiani.*] **P.P. 4884. da. (vol. 1- .)**

—— *See* VETĀLAPAÑCHAVIṂṢATI. 6 Novelle Soprannumerarie alla Vetālapancaviçati. [Translated by V. Bettei.] 1894. 8°. [*Archivio per lo Studio delle Tradizioni Popolari.*] **P.P. 4168. d. (vol. 13.)**

BHADRABĀHU. [For the editions of the Uvasaggahara-stotra included in the collection styled Navasmaraṇa:] *See* NAVASMARAṆA.

—— *See* ṢAYYAMBHAVA. The Daśavaikālika-sūtra . . . and the Daśavaikālika-niryukti by Bhadrabāhu, *etc.* [1892.] 8°. **14100. c. 17.(2.)**

BHADRABĀHU (*continued*). The Kalpa Sûtra of Bhadrabâhu. [Translated, with notes, *etc.*, by H. Jacobi.] 1884. *See* MUELLER (F. M.). The Sacred Books of the East, *etc.* Vol. xxii., pp. 215-311. 1879, *etc.* 8°. **2003. a. (vol. 22.)**

BHADRĀDRIRĀMA ŞĀSTRĪ, *Şonthi*. శంబరాసు-రవిజయం *etc.* [Şambarāsuravijaya. A *champū* on the defeat of Şambara by Pradyumna, in 2 *ullāsas*.] pp. i. 76. కాకినాడ ౧౮౯౮ [*Cocanada*, 1898.] 12°. **14076. a. 22.(1.)**

BHĀGAVATĀCHĀRYA, *Svāmī*. *See* RĀMA ŞĀSTRĪ BHĀGAVATĀCHĀRYA.

BHAGAVATPRASĀDA ĀCHĀRYA, *Pontiff of the Uddhavīya school of the Svāmī-Nārāyaṇa sect, son of Raghuvīra*. *See* PURĀṆAS.—*Bhāgavatapurāṇa*. ॥ श्रीभागवत *etc.* [Bhāgavatapurāṇa. With the commentary Bhaktamanorañjanī or Bhaktarañjanī of Bhagavatprasāda.] [1897.] *obl.* Fol. **14018. cc. 2.**

—— श्रीसारोपदेश: *etc.* [Sāropadeşa. A metrical epitome of the tenets of the Svāmī-Nārāyaṇa sect, in 10 *adhyāyas*, with a Gujarati prose translation by Vihārilāla Āchārya. Followed by the Purushottamakavacha, *i.e.* *adhyāya* 42 of *parichchheda* i. of Akhaṇḍānanda Varṇī's Haricharitra, similarly translated.] pp. i. 224. मुंबई १९५२ [*Bombay*, 1896.] 12°. **14028. b. 83.**

BHAGAVATPRASĀDA TRIPĀṬHĪ, *son of Vişveşvara*. *See* PĀṆINI.—*Kāşikā*. काशिका ... Kashika ... with commentaries added by ... Bhagwatprasad, *etc.* 1890. 8°. **14090. bb. 7.**

BHAGULĀL BHĀUŞAṄKAR BHAṬṬA. *See* RUDRAJAPA. ॥ श्रीरुद्राभिषेकानुष्ठानपद्धति: *etc.* [Rudrābhishekānushṭhānapaddhati. With Gujarati introduction and notes by Bhagulāl Bhaṭṭa.] [1899.] 8°. **14028. c. 69.(2.)**

BHĀGYAVĀN VIDYĀLAṄKĀRA. *See* VIDYĀPATI ṬHĀKURA. শৈবসর্ব্বস্ব-সার *etc.* [Şaivasarvasvasāra. Edited with Bengali translations by Bhāgyavān.] [1897.] 8°. **14028. d. 57.(2.)**

BHAIRAVADATTA DVIVEDĪ, *son of Krishṇachandra*. धर्मप्रदीप: *etc.* [Dharmapradīpa. A treatise on the determination of the festival calendar, *etc.* Edited by Govinda Paraşurāma Rāverkar.] pp. xii. 204. मुंबय्यां १९०१ [*Bombay*, 1901.] 8°. **14033. aa. 24.**

BHAIRAVA MIŞRA. *See* NĀGEŞA BHAṬṬA. [*Paribhāshenduşekhara*.] परिभाषेन्दुशेखर: *etc.* (Paribhashendushekhara ... With the commentary of Bhairaba Mishra, *etc.*) [1892.] 8°. **14093. b. 42.(2.)**

—— *See* NĀGEŞA BHAṬṬA. [*Paribhāshenduşekhara*.] ॥ परिभाषेन्दुशेखर: *etc.* [Paribhāshenduşekhara. With commentary of Bhairava.] [1897.] 8°. **14090. c. 42.**

—— भैरवी कारकान्ता ... Karakanta-Bhairavi or commentary by the wellknown grammarian Pandit Bhairava Misra on Laghu Shabdaratna of ... Hari Dikshita. Revised by ... Damodar Shastri Sahasrabudhay. pp. 407. *Benares*, 1896. 8°. **14090. d. 32.**

BHAKTA (J. G.). *See* JAYAKRISHṆA GAṄGĀDĀSA BHAKTA. **14085. b. 36.(2.)**

BHALLAṬA. The Bhallata Satakam of Bhallata. [Stanzas on ethical topics.] With Sanskrit commentary[, English notes,] and translation. By S. Vasudeva Chariyar. pp. ii. 64, 18, 53. *Madras*, 1898. 8°. **14070. dd. 12.**

—— भल्लटशतकम् । [Bhallaṭaşataka.] pp. 16. *See* ACADEMIES, *etc.*—Madras.—*University of Madras*. The F. A. Sanskrit Text 1899, *etc.* [1898.] 8°. **14079. b. 34.(4.)**

BHĀMAHA. *See* VARARUCHI. प्राकृतप्रकाश: ... Prakrita Prakasha, [or rather, the commentary thereon, styled Prākṛitamanoramā,] by ... Bhamaha, with the sutras of Vararuchi, *etc.* 1899. 8°. **14093. b. 27.(3.)**

BHANAP (S. G.). *See* ŞRĪNIVĀSA GOVINDA BHĀNAP.

BHANDARKAR (R. G.). *See* RĀMAKRISHṆA GOPĀLA BHĀṆḌĀRKAR.

BHĀNU PAṆḌITA, *son of Vişvanātha*. सज्जनवल्लभ: ज्योति:शास्त्रम् । [Sajjanavallabha. A metrical manual of astrology, in 15 chapters. With annotations.] pp. 48. [1892.] *See* PERIODICAL PUBLICATIONS.—*Bombay*. ग्रन्थरत्नमाला *etc.* (Granth Ratna Málá, *etc.*) Vol. v., no. 7, 8. 1887-[1892.] 8°. **14096. c. 8.(vol. 5.)**

BHĀRADVĀJA. Bhâradvâjaçîkshâ. [A manual of phonetics for the distinction of words of

similar sound and form.] Cum versione latina, excerptis ex commentario, adnotationibus ... edidit Emil Sieg. pp. xvi. 64, i. *Berlin*, 1892. 8°.
14093. d. 16.(1.)

—— భారద్వాజరాఘవీయాఖ్య శిక్షావ్యాఖ్య [Bhāradvājaṣikshā. With the commentary Rāghavīya of Kaḷattūri Rāghavāchārya.] pp. ii. 68. చెన్నపురం [*Madras*,] 1893. 8°.
14092. a. 27.

—— భారద్వాజసూత్రము *etc.* [Bhāradvājasūtra. 45 aphorisms from a Pitṛimedhasūtra, on the rites of burial. With Telugu commentary. Edited by Iṅguva Veṅkaṭarāma Ṣāstrī.] pp. 24. ఒంగోలు [*Ongole*,] 1897. 8°. **14028. d. 59.(7.)**

BHĀRATACHANDRA RĀYA. The Poetical Works of Bharut Chunder Roy, [in Bengali, including some original stanzas in Sanskrit and the Sanskrit text of the Chorapañchāṣat or Chaurapañchāṣikā with Bhāratachandra's Bengali adaptation.] ... ভারতচন্দ্র রায় গুণাকরের গ্রন্থ সঙ্কলন *etc.* Second edition. pp. x. viii. 32, 580, 48. কলিকাতা ১২৭৫ [*Calcutta*, 1868.] 12°.
14129. a. 12.

—— —— [Another edition.] pp. viii. 616. কলিকাতা ১৩০৭ [*Calcutta*, 1901.] 12°.
14129. a. 53.

—— অন্নদামঙ্গল *etc.* [Annadāmaṅgala and other Bengali poems.] pp. vi. 391. কলিকাতা [*Calcutta*, 1870 ?] 12°.
14129. a. 11.

—— —— [Second edition.] pp. viii. 349. কলিকাতা ১২৮৭ [*Calcutta*, 1880.] 12°.
14129. a. 18.

—— কবিবর ভারতচন্দ্র রায় গুণাকরের গ্রন্থসঙ্কলন-পুস্তিকা *etc.* [Poems.] pp. viii. 50, 674. কলিকাতা ১২৮৫ [*Calcutta*, 1878.] 12°. **14129. b. 27.**

—— রায় গুণাকর ভারতচন্দ্রের গ্রন্থাবলী । [Poems.] কলিকাতা ১২৯৩ [*Calcutta*, 1886.] 12°.
14129. b. 32.

BHARAṬAKADVĀTRIṂṢIKĀ. Bharaṭakadvātriṃçikā. [Three stories from the collection of tales known by that name. Edited by P. E. Pavolini.] 1897. *See* PERIODICAL PUBLICATIONS.—*Florence.* Studi Italiani di Filologia Indo-Iranica, *etc.* Vol. i., pp. 51-57. 1897, *etc.* 8°.
P.P. 4884. da. (vol. 1.)

BHARATA MALLIKA. *See* BHARATASENA, *son of Gaurāṅga Mallika.*

BHARATA MUNI. The Nâtyaśâstra of Bharata Muni. Edited by Paṇdit Śivadatta . . . and Kâśînâth Pâṇdurang Parab. (नाट्यशास्त्रम् ।) pp. 447. 1894. *See* DURGĀPRASĀDA, *son of Vrajalāla*, and KĀŚĪNĀTHA PĀṆḌURAṄGA PARAB. Kâvyamâlâ. [No.] 42. 1886, *etc.* 8°. **14072. ccc. 12.(no. 42.)**

—— Bhāratīya-Nāṭya-Cāstram [*sic*]. Traité de Bharata sur le theatre. Texte sanskrit. Édition critique, avec une introduction, les variantes tirées de quatre manuscrits, une table analytique et des notes. Précédée d'une préface de M. Paul Regnaud . . . Par Joanny Grosset. (Annales de l'Université de Lyon, fasc. xl.). *Paris, Lyon* [printed], 1898, *etc.* 8°. **Ac. 365. (fasc. xl.)**
In progress.

—— La Métrique de Bharata. Texte sanscrit de deux chapitres du Nâṭya-çâstra, publié pour la première fois et suivi d'une interprétation française par M. Paul Regnaud. 1881. *See* ACADEMIES, *etc.*—Paris.—*Musée Guimet.* Annales, *etc.* Tom. ii., pp. 65-130. 1880, *etc.* 4°. **7704. h. 21.(tom. 2.)**

BHARATASENA, *son of Gaurāṅga Mallika.* *See* BHAṬṬI. ভট্টিকাব্যম্ *etc.* [Bhaṭṭikāvya. With Bharatasena's gloss, following the Mugdhabodha, *etc.*] [1902, *etc.*] 8°.
14070. dd. 24.

—— *See* BHAṬṬI. ভট্টিকাব্যম্ *etc.* [Bhaṭṭikāvya. Sargas i.-v., with the commentaries of Bharatasena, *etc.*] [1895-1896.] 8°. **14076. d. 49.**

—— চন্দ্রপ্রভা *etc.* [Chandraprabhā, or Vaidyakulapañjikā. An account in verse of the Vaidya caste. Edited by Vinodalāla Sena Gupta.] pp. i. ii. 450. কলিকাতা ১২৯৯ [*Calcutta*, 1893.] 8°.
14058. b. 29.

—— রত্নপ্রভা *etc.* [Ratnaprabhā, or Rāḍhīya-vaidyakulapañjikā. An account in verse of the Rāṛh Vaidya caste of Bengal, with the pedigrees of some of its families. Edited by Vinodalāla Sena Gupta.] pp. i. i. 106. কলিকাতা ১২৯৮ [*Calcutta*, 1892.] 8°.
14058. b. 34.

BHĀRATĪTĪRTHA. *See* BĀDARĀYAṆA. वैयासिकन्यायमाला *etc.* (Vaiyásikanyáyamálá or Vedántádhikaraṇamálá. [An exposition of the Brahmasūtra] by . . . Bháratitirthamuni, *etc.*) [1891.] 8°.
14003. ccc. (no. 23.)

BHĀRATĪTĪRTHA (*continued*). [For the Vivaraṇaprameyasaṅgraha, sometimes attributed to Bhāratītīrtha:] *See* BĀDARĀYAṆA.

BHĀRAVI. The Kirâtârjunîya of Bhâravi. With Ghantâpatha commentary of Mallinâtha. Edited by Pandit Hariher Datta. (**किरातार्जुनीयम् ।**) pp. ii. iii. 293. *Benares*, 1899. 8°. **14072. ccc. 25.**

—— కిరాతార్జునీయాఖ్యే ... కావ్యే ... ప్రథమాది నవమసర్గాంత మూలపూర్వార్ధం *etc.* [Kirātārjunīya. Sargas i.-ix.] pp. 40. మహీశూరు॥ వికృతి॥ [*Mysore*, 1891.] 8°. **14072. cc. 54.**

—— **किरातार्जुनीयम्** *etc.* [Kirātārjunīya. Sargas i.-v., with commentary based on that of Mallinātha and English notes and translation.] pp. 82, 69, 34. *See* ACADEMIES, *etc.*—Madras.—*University of Madras.* B.A. Degree Examination 1901, *etc.* 1900. 8°. **14072. c. 50.(2.)**

—— **किरातार्जुनीयम्** *etc.* [Kirātārjunīya. Sargas i.-v., with Mallinātha's commentary and English notes.] pp. 90, 36. *See* ACADEMIES, *etc.*—Madras.—*University of Madras.* B.A. Sanskrit Text 1901. 1900. 8°. **14060. c. 30.(4.)**

—— The Hunter and the Hero. [An abridgment of the Kirātārjunīya, in English verse.] *See* RAMESACHANDRA DATTA. Lays of Ancient India, *etc.* pp. 129-224. 1894. 8°. **2318. h. 9.**

BHARTṚIHARI, *the Poet.* The Nîtiśataka Śringâraśataka and Vairâgyaśataka of Bhartrihari. Edited with Hindi and English translation, copious critical and explanatory notes, parallel thoughts from numerous authors &c. &c. &c. by Purohit Gopi Nath. pp. lviii. 332, 80, viii. *Bombay*, 1896. 8°. **14072. c. 55.**

—— **अथ भर्तृहरिशतकम्** *etc.* [Bhartṛihariṣataka, *i.e.* the Nītiṣataka, Ṣṛingāraṣ°, and Vairāgyaṣ°. With Sanskrit commentary and Hindi paraphrases in prose and verse. Edited by Sītārāma Ṣrikṛishṇa Jāmbhekar. Second edition.] pp. ii. 212. **मुंबापुर्यां १९०२** [*Bombay*, 1902.] 8°. **14076. d. 53.**

—— The Nîtiśataka and Vairâgyaśataka of Bhartṛhari. Edited with [English introduction,] notes and an English translation by M. R. Kâle and M. B. Gurjar. pp. xii. 180, 4. *Bombay*, 1898. 8°. **14072. c. 56.**

BHARTṚIHARI, *the Poet* (*continued*). A Century of Indian Epigrams, chiefly from the Sanskrit of Bhartrihari. [Translated] by Paul Elmer More. pp. 124. *London, New York*, 1899. 12°. **14070. b. 27.**

—— ଭର୍ତ୍ତୃହରି ସୁଭାଷିତ ନୀତିଶତକ *etc.* [Nītiṣataka. With an Oriya commentary by Sūryanārāyaṇa Vishayī.] pp. 91, 2. *Parlakimedi*, 1896. 8°. **14072. cc. 14.(2.)**

—— An English translation of Bhartrihari's Niti-Shataka, by Vindhyeshwari Roy Sharma. pp. iv. 20. *Benares*, 1897. 8°. **14076. b. 36.(1.)**

—— Un Centinaio di Sentenze Morali di Bhartrhari [*scil.* the Nītiṣataka]. Versione rimata di E. Teza. (Dagli Atti e Memorie della R. Accademia di Padova.) pp. 45. *Padova*, 1897. 8°. **14070. dd. 13.(2.)**

—— Maharajah Bhartri's 100 Couplets on Renunciation. [Vairāgyaṣataka, translated into English.] pp. 24. [*Lahore*, 1892.] 16°. **14070. b. 20.**

—— Bhartrihari's Vidnyâna Ŝataka. Edited with introductions, tika and notes by K. B. Ghule. (**श्रीभर्तृहरिविरचितं विज्ञानशतकम् ।**) pp. xxvi. 44, xvii. *Nagpur*, 1897. 8°. **14072. d. 39.(2.)**

BHARTṚIHARI, *the Grammarian.* *See* JACOB (G. A.). **अनुक्रमणिका** [Index to the Vākyapadīya.] [1893?] 8°. **14093. b. 18.(2.)**

BHĀSAKA. *See* NĀRĀYAṆA ṢĀSTRĪ, *T. S.* Sriharsha the Dramatist. A dissertation on . . . the author of the Priyadarsika, the Ratnavali, and the Nagananda, [identifying him with Dhāvaka or Bhāsaka,] *etc.* [1902.] 8°. **14058. b. 40.(2.)**

BHĀSKARA, *son of Mudgala, of the Laugākshi Gotra.* **पूर्वमीमांसार्थसंग्रहः** *etc.* [Pūrvamīmāṃsārthasaṅgraha, or Arthasaṅgraha. With the commentary styled Ṭippaṇa. Edited by Kālīvara Vedāntavāgīṣa.] pp. 68. কলিকাতা ১৩০৪ [*Calcutta*, 1897.] 8°. **14048. b. 21.(2.)**

—— **॥ अर्थसङ्ग्रहः** *etc.* [Arthasaṅgraha. With the commentary Kaumudī of Rāmeṣvara Ṣivayogī. Edited by Gaṇeṣa Ṣāstrī Kshīrasāgara.] pp. 201. *Benares*, **१९५४** [1897.] 8°. **14048. cc. 20.**

BHĀSKARA, *son of Mudgala, of the Laugākshi Gotra (continued).* अर्थसंग्रहः . . . मीमांसाप्रकरणम् *etc.* [Arthasaṅgraha. Edited with a commentary styled Amalā by Pramathanātha Tarkabhūshaṇa.] pp. i. 110. कलिकाता १८९९ [*Calcutta*, 1899.] 8°.
14048. c. 79.(3.)

—— अर्थसंग्रहः *etc.* [Arthasaṅgraha. Edited with a commentary entitled Pratipādikā by Kṛishṇanātha Nyāyapañchānana Bhaṭṭāchārya.] pp. iii. 176. कलिकाता १८२१ [*Calcutta*, 1900.] 8°.
14048. c. 78.

BHĀSKARA ĀCHĀRYA, *son of Maheṣvara.* करणकुतूहलम् *etc.* [Karaṇakutūhala. With the commentary Gaṇakakumudakaumudī of Sumatiharsha. Edited by Mādhava Ṣāstrī Purohita.] pp. i. 156. बंबई १९५८ [*Bombay*, 1902.] 8°. **14053. ccc. 34.**

—— सिद्धान्तशिरोमणिः . . . The Siddhánta-śiromaṇi. A treatise on astronomy, by Bháskaráchárya, with his own exposition, the Vásanábháshya. Formerly edited by the late . . . Bápú Deva Śástri . . . Now revised and republised [*sic*] by Pandita Chandra Deva. pp. iv. ii. vi. ii. 400, xvi. *Benares*, 1891. 8°. **14053. cc. 65.**

—— সিদ্ধান্তশিরোমণিঃ গোলাধ্যায়ঃ বাসনাভাষ্যসহিতঃ। [Siddhāntaṣiromaṇi. The Golādhyāya, with the Vāsanābhāshya, Bengali translations of the text, and Bengali and English notes.] [1891, *etc.*] *See* PERIODICAL PUBLICATIONS.—*Calcutta.* অরুণোদয় *etc.* [Aruṇodaya.] Pt. i., no. 6. [1890, *etc.*] 4°.
14133. g. 16.(pt. i., no. 6.)
Imperfect, extending only over 28 pages.

BHĀSKARA MIṢRA BHAṬṬA. *See* SANDHYĀVANDANA. யஜுர்வேத . . . ஸந்த்யாவந்தநம் *etc.* [Sandhyāvandana, *etc.* With extracts, in a Tamil translation, from the commentaries of Bhāskara and others.] 1901. 8°. **14033. aa. 27.**

—— *See* UPANISHADS.—*Separate Upanishads.* तैत्तिरीयोपनिषत् [Taittirīyopanishad. With Bhāskara's commentary.] 1896, *etc.* 8°. [*Grandha Pradarsani.*] **14003. c. 2.(11.)**

—— *See* VEDAS.—Yajurveda.—*Taittirīyasaṃhitā.* तैत्तिरीयसंहिता . . . The Taittiríya Saṃhitá . . . with the commentary of Bhaṭṭabháskaramiśra [styled Jñānayajña], *etc.* 1894, *etc.* 8°. [*Mysore Government Oriental Library Series: Bibliotheca Sanskrita.*] **14004. b. 4.**

BHĀSKARA MIṢRA BHAṬṬA (*continued*). त्रिकाण्डमण्डनम्। Trikāṇḍa-maṇḍanam by Bhāskara-Miçra, Soma-yājī. Being an exposition of the Soma-yāga Aphorisms of Āpastamba [in the form of a *kārikā.*] With an anonymous commentary entitled Vivaraṇa. Edited by Mahāmahopādhyāya Candrakānta Tarkālaṃkāra. 1898, *etc. See* ACADEMIES, *etc.*—Calcutta.—*Asiatic Society of Bengal.* Bibliotheca Indica. New Series. [Vol. 142.] 1848, *etc.* 8°. **14002. a. (vol. 142.)**
In progress.

BHĀSKARĀNANDA SARASVATĪ, *disciple of Anantarāma.* *See* MAHĀDEVA ṢUKLA. स्वामी भास्करानन्द . . . जीवन चरितम् *etc.* [Bhāskarānanda-Sarasvatījīvanacharita. Verses on the life and teachings of Bhāskarānanda. [1891.] 8°. **14028. d. 48.**

—— *See* ṢIVAKUMĀRA MIṢRA. যতীন্দ্র-জীবন-চরিতম্ *etc.* [Yatīndrajīvanacharita. A poem on the history of Bhāskarānanda.] 1892. 8°.
14058. b. 26.(2.)

—— *See* SVĀRĀJYASIDDHI. स्वाराज्यसिद्धिः *etc.* [Svārājyasiddhi. With the commentary Kaivalyakalpadruma of Bhāskarānanda. [1896.] 8°.
14048. dd. 27.

—— *See* UPANISHADS.—*Small Collections.* उपनिषत्प्रसादः *etc.* [Upanishatprasāda. The Chāndogya and Bṛihadāraṇyaka Upanishads, with a brief commentary by Bhāskarānanda.] [1899.] 8°.
14010. dd. 15.

—— अनुभूतिविवरणादर्शः *etc.* [Anubhūtivivaraṇādarṣa. Comprising a Vedantic poem of 13 stanzas, styled Anubhūtivivaraṇa, and a commentary thereupon, both by Bhāskarānanda. Edited by Lakshmaṇarāma Ṣarmā.] pp. 14. काश्याम् १९५१ [*Benares*, 1894.] 12°.
14048. b. 15.(3.)

BHĀSKARA RĀMACHANDRA ARTE. *See* KĀLIDĀSA.—*Vikramorvaṣīya.* The Vikramorvaśīyam . . . Edited . . . by Shankar Pâṇḍurang Paṇḍit. Revised . . . by Bhâskar . . . Arte. 1901. 8°.
14080. c. 42.

BHĀSKARARĀYA DĪKSHITA BHĀRATĪ. *See* JAIMINI.—*Mīmāṃsāsūtra.* संकर्ष-काण्डम् . . . Saṃkarsha Káṇḍa, or the last four chapters of Jaimini, with the commentary called Bháṭṭa

Chandriká, of Bháskara, *etc.* [1894.] 8°. [*The Pandit.*] **14096. d. 6.(vol. 14, 15.)**

—— *See* PURĀṆAS.—*Brahmāṇḍapurāṇa.* [*Lalitāsahasranāma.*] శ్రీలలితాసహస్రనామస్తోత్రం [Lalitāsahasranāmastotra. With the commentary Saubhāgyabhāskara of Bhāskararāya.] 1892. 4°. **14016. e. 41.**

—— *See* PURĀṆAS.—*Brahmāṇḍapurāṇa.* [*Lalitāsahasranāma.*] Lalita Sahasranama, with Bhaskararaya's commentary. Translated into English, *etc.* 1899. 8°. **14016. c. 59.**

—— *See* UPANISHADS. — *Separate Upanishads.* भावनोपनिषत् *etc.* [Bhāvanopanishad. With commentary of Bhāskararāya.] 1896. 8°. [*Mysore Government Oriental Library Series: Bibliotheca Sanskrita.*] **14004. b. 8.**

—— अथ वैदिककोशः [Vaidikakoṣa. A metrical version of Yāska's Nighaṇṭu.] *See* YĀSKA. वैदिकनिघण्टु *etc.* [Vaidikanighaṇṭu.] pp. 1-32. [1898.] 12°. **14092. a. 21.(2.)**

—— Varivasyâ Rahasya. [A metrical treatise by Bhāskarāya on the mystic Ṣākta system styled Ṣrīvidyā.] With a commentary by Bhâskararâya. Edited by R. Ananta Krishna Śâstri. pp. iii. 94, i. *Bombay,* 1901. 12°. **14048. a. 29.**

BHĀSURĀNANDANĀTHA. *See* BHĀSKARARĀYA DĪKSHITA BHĀRATĪ.

BHAṬṬA BHĀSKARA. *See* BHĀSKARA MIṢRA BHAṬṬA.

BHAṬṬA BHĪMA. *See* BHĪMA, *Bhaṭṭa.*

BHAṬṬĀKALAṄKA DEVA. Bhaṭṭâkalaṅka Dêva's Karṇâṭaka Śabdânuśâsanaṃ; with its vṛitti or gloss, named Bhâshâ-Mañjarî, and vyâkhyâ or commentary thereon, called Mañjarî-Makarandaḥ: an exhaustive [Sanskrit] treatise on the grammar of the [Canarese] language, completed in 1604 A.D. . . ಕರ್ಣಾಟಕ ಶಬ್ದಾನುಶಾಸನಂ . . . Edited [with an introductory account of Canarese literature and translation of each aphorism] by B. Lewis Rice. pp. i. lviii. 291, i. xvi. 268, iii. xix. lxxxii. *Bangalore,* 1890. 4°. **14176. k. 7.**

Forms no. 2 of the Bibliotheca Carnatica. *The second part is a reprint in Canarese type of the text given in the first part.*

BHAṬṬA KALLAṬA. *See* KALLAṬA, *Bhaṭṭa.*

BHAṬṬA NĀRĀYAṆA, *author of the Veṇīsaṃhāra.* *See* NĀRĀYAṆA BHAṬṬA, called MṚIGARĀJALAKSHMĀ.

BHAṬṬI. The Bhaṭṭi-kâvya or Râvaṇavadha composed by Śri Bhaṭṭi . . . Edited with the commentary of Mallinâtha and with [introduction and] critical and explanatory notes [in English] by Kamalâśaṅkara Prâṇaśaṅkara Trivedî. (रावणवधं नाम भट्टिकाव्यम्) 2 vols. *Bombay,* 1898. 8°. **14072. c. 54.**

Forms nos. lvi. *and* lvii. *of the* Bombay Sanskrit Series. *Bhaṭṭi is also called* Bhaṭṭa Svāmī *and* Bhartṛisvâmī; *Vidyāvinoda styles him* Bhartṛihari son of Ṣrīdhara Svâmi.

—— ভট্টিকাব্যম্ *etc.* [Bhaṭṭikāvya. With Nārāyaṇa Vidyāvinoda's gloss, following the Saṅkshiptasāra grammar of Kramadīṣvara, and Bharatasena's gloss, following the Mugdhabodha of Vopadeva. Edited with construing, paraphrases, grammatical notes, and Bengali translation by Āṣutosha Tarkatīrtha.] কলিকাতা [*Calcutta,* 1902, *etc.*] 8°. **14070. dd. 24.**

In progress.

—— Bhatti . . . Cantos i, ii, iii, iv, v. Text with notes by Pundit Nobin Ch. Vidyaratna . . . With English and Bengali translations and model questions with model answers. Second edition. pp. 576, 84. *Calcutta,* [1894.] 8°. **14070. c. 57.(1.)**

—— ভট্টিকাব্যম্ *etc.* [Bhaṭṭikāvya. Sargas i.-v., with the commentaries of Jayamaṅgala, Bharatasena, and Nārāyaṇa Vidyāvinoda, analyses, and a Bengali translation by Tārāpada Kāvyatīrtha.] pp. i. iv. 312. কলিকাতা [*Calcutta,* 1895-1896.] 8°. **14076. d. 49.**

In 4 fascicules. No more seems to have been published.

BHAṬṬOJĪ DĪKSHITA. *See* PĀṆINI.—*Siddhāntakaumudī.* Balamanorama sahitha. Sidhantha Kowmuthi, *etc.* [Siddhāntakaumudī, with the commentary Bālamanoramā of Vāsudeva.] 1889-1901. 8°. **14092. b. 46.**

—— *See* PĀṆINI.—*Siddhāntakaumudī.* सिद्धान्तकौमुदी . . . Siddhanta Kaumudi . . . With . . . the "Tattwabodhini" of Jnanendra, *etc.* [1890-1892.] 8°. **14090. d. 29.**

—— *See* PĀṆINI.—*Siddhāntakaumudī.* The Siddhânta-kaumudî with the Tattvabodhinî Com-

mentary of Jnânendra Sarasvati and the Subodhinî Commentary of Jayakrishna, *etc.* 1899. 4°.
14092. c. 18.

—— *See* PĀṆINI.—*Siddhāntakaumudī.* मध्यसिद्धान्तकौमुदी *etc.* [Madhyasiddhāntakaumudī, or Madhyakaumudī. An abridgment of the Siddhāntakaumudī, by Varadarāja.] [1895.] 12°.
14090. b. 41.

—— *See* PĀṆINI.—*Siddhāntakaumudī.* मध्यकौमुदी . . . The Madhya Kaumudi, *etc.* 1899. 12°.
14092. a. 22.

—— मनोरमा *etc.* [Manoramā, or Prauḍhamanoramā. A commentary by Bhaṭṭojī on the Siddhāntakaumudī. With the supercommentary Ṣabdaratna of Hari Dīkshita. Edited by Bālakṛishṇa Ṣāstrī Paṭavardhana.] Part i. pp. 261. काश्यां १९५६ [*Benares,* 1900.] 8°. **14093. d. 22.**

—— *See* INDRADATTA UPĀDHYĀYA. फक्किकाप्रकाशः *etc.* [Phakkikāprakāṣa. A commentary on the Siddhāntakaumudī.] Pt. i. [1897.] 8°. **14090. c. 38.(4.)**

—— *See* JÑĀNENDRA SARASVATĪ. वैयाकरणसिद्धान्तकौमुदीव्याख्या तत्त्वबोधिनी *etc.* [Tattvabodhinī. A commentary on the Siddhāntakaumudī. Followed by the Subodhinī, Jayakṛishṇa's commentary upon the latter.] 1897. 8°. **14090. e. 25.**

—— *See* PĀṆINI.—*Appendix.* [*Liṅgānuṣāsana.*] अथ लिङ्गानुशासनम् [Liṅgānuṣāsana. In the forms ascribed to Bhaṭṭojī and Pāṇini.] 1899. 4°. [*Siddhāntakaumudī.*] **14092. c. 18.**

—— *See* PĀṆINI.—*Appendix.* [*Liṅgānuṣāsana.*] लिङ्गानुशासनम् [Liṅgānuṣāsana, in the form ascribed to Bhaṭṭojī. With Varadarāja's *vritti.*] 1899. 12°. [*Madhyakaumudī.*] **14092. a. 22.**

—— शब्दकौस्तुभः . . . Shabdakoustubha. By Pandit Bhattojee Deekshit. Edited and revised by Pandit Rama Krishna Shastri, alias Tatya Shastri Patwardhana. *Benares,* 1898, *etc.* 8°.
14004. a. 2.

In progress. Forms nos. 3-10, 13, 14, *etc., of the* Chowkhambâ Sanskrit Series.

BHAṬṬOJĪ DĪKSHITA (*continued*). तैत्तिरीयसंध्याभाष्यम् [Taittirīya-sandhyābhāshya. A commentary upon the *sandhyā* prayers according to the Taittirīyas.] pp. 8. *See* SANDHYĀVANDANA. संध्याभाष्यसमुच्चयः *etc.* [Sandhyābhāshyasamuchchaya.] [1899.] 8°.
14003. ccc. (no. 40.)

—— बृहत् वैयाकरणभूषणं पदार्थदीपिका च सहितम् . . . Brihat Vaiyâkaraṇa Bhûshaṇa, a treatise on Sanskrit grammar, [*scil.,* on the functions of the parts of speech, *etc.* In 15 chapters, comprising Bhaṭṭojī's Vaiyākaraṇasiddhāntakārikāḥ, 74 memorial couplets, with commentary styled Vaiyākaraṇabhūshaṇa] by Paṇḍit Kauṇḍa Bhaṭṭa: also Padârtha Dipikâ [or Nyāyapadārthadīpikā, an exposition of the Vaiṣeshika Categories,] by the same author [*scil.,* Kauṇḍa Bhaṭṭa]. Edited by Paṇḍit Ráma Krishṇa Śástrí, *etc.* pp. 325, 51. *Benares,* 1900. 8°. **14048. cc. 34.**

Forms nos. 51—54 *of the* Benares Sanskrit Series.

—— वैयाकरणसिद्धान्तकारिकाः *etc.* [Vaiyākaraṇasiddhāntakārikāḥ. With the Vaiyākaraṇabhūshaṇasāra of Kauṇḍa Bhaṭṭa, an abridgment of his Vaiyākaraṇabhūshaṇa.] pp. i. i. 64, ii. पुण्याख्यपत्तने १९०१ [*Poona,* 1901.] 8°.
14003. ccc. (no. 43.)

Forms no. 43 *of the* Ānandāṣrama Sanskrit Series.

BHAṬṬOTPALA. *See* UTPALA, *Bhaṭṭa.*

BHĀU DĀJĪ. *See* ACADEMIES, *etc.*—Bombay.—*Bombay Branch of the Royal Asiatic Society.* Catalogue of Manuscripts and Books belonging to the Bhau Daji Memorial, *etc.* 1882. 8°.
14096. cc. 11.

BHAUMA, *Bhaṭṭa.* *See* BHĪMA, *Bhaṭṭa.*

BHAUNAGAR.—*Archæological Department.* A Collection of Prakrit and Sanskrit Inscriptions. Published by the Bhavnagar Archæological Department, *etc.* [With a preface by P. Peterson.] pp. x. iii. ii. 233; 41 *plates. Bhavnagar,* [1895?] 4°. **14058. d. 6.**

BHAVABHŪTI. The Mahâvîracharita . . . With the commentary [Bhâvapradyotinî] of Vîrarâghava. Edited by T. R. Ratnam Aiyar . . . S. Rangachariar . . . and Kâśinâth Pândurang

Parab. (महावीरचरितम् ।) pp. 254, vi. i. *Bombay*, 1892. 8°. **14080. c. 32.**

——— The Mâlatîmâdhava of Bhavabhûti. With the commentaries of Tripurâri [on Acts i.-vii., of Nānyadeva on viii.-x.,] and [of] Jagaddhara. Edited by Mangesh Râmakrishṇa Telang. (मालतीमाधवम् ।) pp. ii. 267, 229, iv. v. *Bombay*, 1892. 8°. **14079. c. 61.**

——— Malati and Madhava; or The Stolen Marriage. A drama, translated . . . by H. H. Wilson. pp. viii. 133. 1901. *See* WILSON (H. H.). Hindu Dramatic Works, *etc.* 1901. 12°. **14080. b. 13.**

——— Malati und Madhava. Ein indisches Drama . . . Zum ersten Male und metrisch . . . übersetzt von Ludwig Fritze. pp. 125. *Leipzig*, [1884.] 12°. **012207. f. (no. 1844.)**

Forms no. 1844 *of Reclam's* Universal-Bibliothek.

——— ఉత్తరరామచరితనాటకమ్ *etc.* [Uttararāmacharita. With a commentary called Bhavabhūtibhāvatalasparṣinī or Talasparṣinī by Vīrarāghava. Edited by Kuṇḍaligiri Āchārya.] pp. viii. 248. బెంగుళూరు [*Bangalore*,] 1891. 8°. **14080. d. 21.**

——— ఉత్తరరామచరితనాటకమ్ . . . వాసంతికాపరిణయాఖ్యనాటకం *etc.* [Uttararāmacharita. With the commentary of Vīrarāghava. Followed by the Vāsantikāpariṇaya, a play by Ṣaṭhakopa Yati.] pp. vi. 284, iv. మహీశూరు॥ ౧౮౯౨ [*Mysore*, 1892.] 8°. **14080. d. 23.**

——— The Uttara Rama Charita . . . With Sanscrit commentary by Pandit Bhatji [Jayakrishṇa] Shastri Ghate . . . Together with a close English translation and notes . . . vocabulary of difficult words in the text and an introduction by Vinayak Sadashiv Patvardhan. (उत्तररामचरितं नाम नाटकं) pp. ii. i. xii. 192, 60, 51, viii. iii. *Nagpur*, 1895. 8°. **14080. d. 25.**

——— The Uttara-Râmacharita of Bhavabhûti. With the commentary of Vîrarâghava. Edited by T. R. Ratnam Aiyar . . . and Kâśînâth Pâṇdurang Parab. (उत्तररामचरितम् ।) pp. 174, iv. *Bombay*, 1899. 8°. **14080. c. 40.**

BHAVABHŪTI (*continued*). An English Translation of Uttararama Charita. By Krishna Kamal Bhattacharyya. pp. 142. *Calcutta*, 1891. 12°. **14080. b. 9.(2.)**

——— *See* KĀLĪKRISHṆA BHAṬṬĀCHĀRYA. Notes on Utter-charita, *etc.* [1893.] 12°. **14076. a. 14.**

BHĀVA MIŚRA. भावप्रकाश . . . सटीक *etc.* [Bhāvaprakāṣa. With Hindi translation by Kālīcharaṇa son of Gokulachandra.] 3 pts. लखनऊ १८९४ [*Lucknow*, 1894.] 4°. **14043. f. 4.**

——— भावप्रकाशः *etc.* (Bhavaprakasa. A medical work . . . Edited . . . by Pandit-kulapati Jibananda Vidyasagara.) Second edition. pp. 1242. *Calcutta*, १८९७ [1897.] 8°. **14043. cc. 10.**

The English title is taken from the cover. Pp. 277-300 *are missing.*

——— সানুবাদ-ভাবপ্রকাশঃ *etc.* [Bhāvaprakāṣa. Edited with a Bengali translation by Kālīprasanna Kaviṣekhara.] pp. i. lxxvi. 1000. *Calcutta*, [1901.] 8°. **14043. dd. 9.**

BHAVĀNANDA SIDDHĀNTAVĀGĪṢA. কারকচক্রম্ বা কারকাদ্যর্থনির্ণয়ঃ *etc.* [Kārakachakra, or Kārakādyarthanirṇaya. A treatise on the syntactic significance of the cases, from the author's Ṣabdārthasāramañjarī. With the commentaries of Rudra Tarkavāgīṣa and Mādhava Tarkālankāra, called Raudrī and Mādhavī respectively. Edited by Dvārakānātha Nyāyapañchānana and Gauragovinda Kāvyatīrtha.] pp. ii. 112. কলিকাতা ১৯০০ [*Calcutta*, 1900.] 8°. **14090. bb. 15.(1.)**

BHAVĀNRĀU PINGLE. Indian Music. By Bhavánráv A. Pingle. Second edition. pp. xvi. iii. 341, xxii.; 3 *plates*. *Bombay*, 1898. 8°. **14053. b. 33.**

BHAVAṢAṄKARA TANTRAVIṢĀRADA. সচিত্র দশমহাবিদ্যা *etc.* [Sachitra Daṣamahāvidyā. An illustrated account, in verse, of the nature and worship of the goddess Pārvatī in her 10 manifestations as Kālī, Tārā, Shoḍaṣī, Bhuvaneṣvarī, Bhairavī, Chhinnamastā, Dhūmāvatī, Vagalāmukhī, Mātaṅgī, and Kamalā. Compiled from tantric sources by Bhavaṣaṅkara, with Bengali preface, metrical introduction, notes, and other matter.] pp. xii. xiv. 84. *Calcutta*, ১৩০৭ [1901.] 12°. **14033. a. 41.(2.)**

Imperfect; pp. 85 ff., containing Bengali matter, are missing.

—— সর্ব্বসিদ্ধিপ্রদায়িনী মহাশক্তি তন্ত্র *etc.* [Mahāṣaktitantra. A compilation from magical works, chiefly in Sanskrit, but partly also in Bengali. Second edition.] pp. 132. *Gorokshobasini, Calcutta* [printed], ১৩০৭ [1901.] 12°. **14033. a. 10.(2.)**

BHĀVASENA, *Grammarian.* See SARVAVARMĀ. कातन्त्रव्याकरणम् *etc.* [Kātantra. With the commentary Kātantrarūpamālā of Bhāvasena.] [1895.] 8°. **14090. bb. 9.**

BHAVNAGAR. See BHAUNAGAR.

BHĪMA, *Bhaṭṭa*, also called BHAṬṬA BHAUMA. The Râvaṇârjunîya of Bhatta Bhîma. [A poem in 27 cantos upon the legend of the struggle between Kārtavīrya-Arjuna and Rāvaṇa, composed so as to illustrate the bulk of Pāṇini's Aphorisms i. 2—vi. 1, vi. 3—vii. 4, viii. 2-4, and with these Aphorisms included.] Edited by ... Paṇḍit Śivadatta ... and Kâshînâth Pâṇdurang Parab. (रावणार्जुनीयम् ।) pp. ii. ii. 208. 1900. See DURGĀPRASĀDA, *son of Vrajalāla*, and KĀŚINĀTHA PĀṆḌURAṄGA PARAB. Kâvyamâlâ. [No.] 68. 1886, *etc.* 8°. **14072. ccc. 12.(no. 68.)**

BHĪMĀCHĀRYA JHAḶKĪKAR, *Mahāmahopādhyāya.* Nyâyakośa, or Dictionary of the Technical Terms of the Nyâya Philosophy &c., by ... Bhîmâchârya Jhaḷakîkar. Second edition. (न्यायकोशः) pp. iv. iv. ii. i. xix. x. i. 1001, xxxvi. xiii. *Bombay*, 1893. 8°. **14048. dd. 11.**

Forms no. xlix. *of the* Bombay Sanskrit Series.

BHĪMADĀSA, *Oriya Poet.* See PURĀṆAS.—*Bhāgavatapurāṇa.* ଭକ୍ତିରତ୍ନାବଳୀ *etc.* [Bhaktiratnāvalī. With metrical paraphrase in Oriya by Bhīmadāsa.] 1900. 12°. **14016. b. 27.**

BHĪMASENA, *Grammarian.* See NĀRĀYAṆA BHAṬṬA, *Kerala.* ധാതുകാവ്യം *etc.* [Dhātukāvya. A poem to illustrate the accidence of the verbal roots as given in the Dhātupāṭha of Bhīmasena.] 1893. 8°. **14070. c. 50.**

—— See NĀRĀYAṆA BHAṬṬA, *Kerala.* ശ്രീ ... ധാതുകാവ്യം [Dhātukāvya, i.–ii. 32.] 1890. 8°. [*Essays and Poems.*] **14072. d. 35.**

BHĪMASENA ŚARMĀ, *disciple of Dayānanda Sarasvatī.* See MAHĀBHĀRATA.—Bhagavadgītā.—*Sanskrit and Vernaculars.* भगवद्गीताभाष्यम् *etc.* [Bhagavadgītā. With commentary in Sanskrit and Hindi by Bhīmasena. Edited by the latter.] [1897.] 8°. **14065. c. 46.**

—— See MANU.—*Dharmaśāstra.* मानवधर्मशास्त्रम् *etc.* [Dharmaśāstra. With Hindi introduction and commentary in Sanskrit and Hindi by Bhīmasena.] [1891-1896.] 8°. **14038. d. 33.**

—— See PĀṆINI.—*Ashṭādhyāyī.* अथ पाणिनीयाष्टकम् ... The Panini's Grammatical Aphorisms. Edited by Bhimsen Shurma, *etc.* 1892. 8°. **14093. b. 35.(2.)**

—— See PERIODICAL PUBLICATIONS.—*Allahabad.* आर्यसिद्धान्त [Āryasiddhānta. Vols. 3 and 4. Edited by Bhīmasena. Second edition.] [1895.] 8°. **14033. b. 49.**

—— See SĪTĀRĀMA ŚARMĀ, *son of Bālamukunda.* तीर्थनिन्दक मुखचपेटिका *etc.* [Tīrthanindakamukhachapeṭikā. A tract in answer to Bhīmasena's tract styled Tīrthavishaya.] [1891.] 8°. **14033. bb. 40.**

—— See UPANISHADS.—*Separate Upanishads.* अथ-ऋग्वेदीयैतरेयोपनिषद्भाष्यम् *etc.* [Aitareyopanishad. With commentary in Sanskrit and Hindi by Bhīmasena.] [1897.] 8°. **14010. cc. 7.(1.)**

—— —— [Second edition.] [1900.] 8°. **14010. cc. 3.(3.)**

—— —— वाजसनेयोपनिषद्भाष्यम् ... Vajasaneyopnishat[, *i.e.* Īṣopanishad]. With [Sanskrit and Hindi] commentary of Bhimsen Sharma. 1892. 8°. **14007. c. 26.(1.)**

—— —— अथ कठोपनिषद्भाष्यम् *etc.* [Kaṭhopanishad. With Sanskrit and Hindi commentary by Bhīmasena.] [1893.] 8°. **14007. c. 26.(3.)**

—— —— सामवेदीय ... केनोपनिषत् *etc.* [Kena or Talavakāra Upanishad. With commentary in Sanskrit and Hindi by Bhīmasena.] [1893.] 8°. **14007. c. 26.(2.)**

—— —— अथ माण्डूक्योपनिषद्भाष्यम् *etc.* [Māṇḍūkyopanishad. With commentary in Sanskrit and Hindi by Bhīmasena.] [1894.] 8°. **14007. c. 26.(4.)**

BHĪMASENA ŚARMĀ, *disciple of Dayānanda Sarasvatī (continued)*. *See* UPANISHADS.—*Separate Upanishads.* अथ मुण्डकोपनिषद्भाष्यम् *etc.* [Muṇḍakopanishad. With commentary in Sanskrit and Hindi by Bhīmasena.] [1894.] 8°.
14007. c. 26.(5.)

—— —— अथ प्रश्नोपनिषद्भाष्यम् *etc.* [Praśnopanishad. With commentary in Sanskrit and Hindi by Bhīmasena.] [1894.] 8°.
14007. c. 26.(6.)

—— —— अथ ... श्वेताश्वतरोपनिषद्-भाष्यम् ... Shwetashwataropanishat with [Sanskrit and Hindi] commentary of Bhimsen sharma. 1897. 8°.
14010. cc. 7.(2.)

—— —— अथ तैत्तिरीयोपनिषद्भाष्यम् *etc.* [Taittirīyopanishad. With commentary in Sanskrit and Hindi by Bhīmasena.] [1895.] 8°. **14007. c. 26.(7.)**

—— *See* VARDHAMĀNA, *disciple of Govinda.* गणरत्नमहोदधिः *etc.* [Gaṇaratnamahodadhi. Edited by Bhīmasena.] [1894.] 8°. **14090. d. 30.**

—— दर्शपौर्णमासपद्धतिः *etc.* [Darśapaurṇamāsapaddhati. A ritual for the celebration of the Full Moon and New Moon sacrifices. Compiled and edited with a Hindi commentary by Bhīmasena.] pp. iv. ii. 118, 16. इटावा [१८]९९ [*Etawah*, 1899.] 8°. **14028. dd. 6.(2.)**

—— इष्टिसंग्रहः *etc.* [Ishṭisaṅgraha. Rules for performing the rites of *ishṭi.* Compiled and edited with a Hindi version by Bhīmasena.] pp. 12, 12, 12, 32. इटावा [१८]९९ [*Etawah*, 1899.] 8°. **14033. c. 45.(3.)**

—— शास्त्रार्थ आगरा *etc.* [Śāstrārtha Āgrā. A correspondence in Hindi and Sanskrit between Bhīmasena and the Ārya Samāj of Agra, on the subject of *śrāddhas.*] pp. 57. मेरठ १९५८ [*Meerut*, 1901.] 8°. **14033. bbb. 10.(3.)**

—— अथ स्मार्तकर्मपद्धतिः *etc.* [Smārtakarmapaddhati. Liturgies for the rites of *svastipuṇyāhavāchana, maṇikāvadhāna, āvasathyādhāna, aupāsanahoma, pakshādikarma,* and the *pañchamahāyajña,* on the basis of Pāraskara's Gṛihyasūtra. Compiled, with a Hindi version, by Bhīmasena.] pp. iii. 37. इटावा १९०० [*Etawah*, 1900.] 8°. **14033. c. 45.(2.)**

—— अथ-उपनयनपद्धतिः *etc.* [Upanayanapaddhati. Directions for the investiture of young Brahmans with the sacred cord and rites connected therewith, on the basis of Pāraskara's Gṛihyasūtra. Compiled, edited, and furnished with a Hindi version by Bhīmasena.] pp. 56. इटावा १९०० [*Etawah*, 1900.] 8°. **14033. c. 45.(1.)**

BHĪMASIṂHA MĀṆAKA. जैनकथारत्नकोष *etc.* [Jainakathāratnakoṣa. A collection of Jain philosophical and devotional writings, stories, *etc.*, in prose and verse, in Sanskrit, Prakrit, Gujarati, and Hindi. Compiled and edited by Bhīmasiṃha.] 8 vols. मुंबापुरी १८९०-१८९३ [*Bombay*, 1890-1893.] 8°. **14144. gg. 1.**

BHOJADEVA. *See* BHOJARĀJA.

BHOJARĀJA, *King of Dhara.* [*Life.*] [For the Bhojacharitra or romantic biography of Bhoja :] *See* BALLĀLA.

—— The Champû-Râmâyaṇa [or Bhojachampū] of King Bhoja, 1—5 kâṇdas, and Lakshmaṇa Sûri, 6th kâṇda. With the commentary [Mañjūshikā] of Rāmachandra Budhendra. Edited by Kâshînâth Pâṇdurang Parab. (चम्पूरामायणम्) pp. 423, vii. *Bombay*, 1898. 8°. **14070. dd. 5.**

—— Champû Râmâyaṇa. Bâlakâṇḍa. With a choice commentary, English translation and copious notes by . . . M. C. Satakopachariar. pp. 80, 30, 36. *Kumbakonum*, [1896.] 8°.
14076. c. 67.(1.)

—— The Kishkindhakanda of Bhoja Champu, with an extract from the commentary of Ramachandra Budhendra. Edited, with English notes & translation, by S. Vasudevachariar. pp. 39, 46, 16. *Madras*, 1898. 8°. **14076. b. 36.(2.)**

—— भोजराज प्रणीत चम्पूरामायणे ॥ किष्किन्धाकाण्डप्रारंभः ॥ [Kishkindhākāṇḍa. Followed by English notes and translation.] pp. 16, 27, 15. *See* ACADEMIES, *etc.*—Madras.—*University of Madras.* The F. A. Sanskrit Text 1899, *etc.* [1898.] 8°.
14079. b. 34.(4.)

—— F. A. Examination of 1892. The Complete Sanskrit Text[, viz. Raghuvaṃśa iii.-xi. and the Sundarakāṇḍa of Bhoja's Champūrāmāyaṇa. Edited,] with . . . Sanskrit commentary . . . English notes, and . . . translation, by

S. Rangachariar ... and V. Srinivasa Aiyar. 1891. 8°. *See* KĀLIDĀSA.—*Raghuvaṃṣa.* **14076. c. 59.**

——— सरस्वतीकण्ठाभरणम् *etc.* [Sarasvatīkaṇṭhābharaṇa. With Ratneṣvara's commentary, entitled Darpaṇa, upon Sections i.-iii. Edited with a commentary upon Sections iv.-v. by Jīvānanda Vidyāsāgara. Second edition.] pp. 824. कलिकाता १८९४ [*Calcutta,* 1894.] 8°. **14053. cc. 68.**

——— *See* PATAÑJALI.—*Philosophical Works.* पातञ्जलदर्शनम् । [Pātañjaladarṣana. The Aphorisms with the *vritti* of Bhojarāja styled Rājamārtaṇḍa, *etc.*] [1891, *etc.*] 4°. [*Aruṇodaya.*] **14133. g. 16.(pt. i., no. 25.)**

BHRĀNTIRAHITASLOKA. భ్రాంతిరహితశ్లోకము *etc.* [Bhrāntirahitasloka. A religious-philosophical poem, in 14 stanzas. With Telugu glosses and version.] *See* PURĀṆAS.—*Skandapurāṇa.* సుజ్ఞానదీపము - గురుగీతలు *etc.* [Sujñānadīpa.] pp. 144-150. [1898.] 8°. **14016. c. 54.**

BHRIGU. ॥ अथ श्री भार्गवी संहिता *etc.* [Bhārgavī Saṃhitā, or Bhrigus°. A manual of astrology and magical science. Comprising a Jātakaprakaraṇa, a Santānopāyakhaṇḍa, and a Phalitakhaṇḍa, in Sanskrit and Hindi; with two Hindi appendices, viz. Kuṇḍalīsūchīpatra, astrological charts, and Pañchāṅgadarpaṇa, a series of calendars.] 5 pts. मेरठ १९५२-१९५७ [*Meerut,* 1895-1900.] *obl.* 4°. **14053. g. 16.**

The publisher in advertising this collection includes in it the Narapatijayacharyā and a Bhriguprasna. The work is lithographed, except in the Santānopāyakh° and Phalitakh°.

——— ॥ अथ भृगुसंहितान्तर्गतयोगावलिः प्रारभ्यते ॥ [Yogāvali. An account of the various forms of ascetic practices, extracted from the Bhrigusaṃhitā. Edited by Nandalāla Ṣāstrī.] ff. 8, 159. मुंबई १९५५ [*Bombay,* 1899.] *obl.* 4°. **14028. e. 33.(1.)**

BHŪDEVA ṢUKLA. धर्मविजयं नाटकम् । [Dharmavijaya. An allegorical drama in 5 acts.] pp. 68. [1889-1890.] *See* PERIODICAL PUBLICATIONS.—*Bombay.* ग्रन्थरत्नमाला *etc.* (Granth Ratna Málá, *etc.*) Vol. iii., no. 6, 7. 1887-[1892.] 8°. **14096. c. 8.(vol. 3.)**

BHŪDHARA CHAṬṬOPĀDHYĀYA. *See* MAHĀBHĀRATA.—*Entire Work.* মহাভারতম্ *etc.* [Mahābhārata. With the commentaries of Nīlakaṇṭha and Arjuna Miṣra. Edited by Bhūdhara Chaṭṭopādhyāya.] [1897, *etc.*] 8°. **14065. d. 38.**

——— धर्मानुष्ठान *etc.* [Dharmānushṭhāna. A manual for the performance of the *saṃskāras,* daily, monthly, annual, purificatory, and expiatory rites, *ṣrāddhas,* and divers other functions, consisting of Sanskrit texts with Bengali commentaries, translations, rubrics, *etc.*] pp. x. 604. কলিকাতা ১৩০২ [*Calcutta,* 1896.] 12°. **14028. bb. 1.**

——— ——— [Second edition.] pp. x. 588. কলিকাতা ১৩০৮ [*Calcutta,* 1901.] 12°. **14028. bb. 6.**

BHUKKAṆA. *See* BUKKAṆA.

BHŪPĀLA KAVI, *Jain Poet.* जिनचतुर्विंशतिका । [Jinachaturviṃṣatikā, or Bhūpālastotra. A hymn of 26 stanzas.] *See* JAINASTOTRASAṄGRAHA. जैनस्तोत्रसंग्रहः *etc.* [Jainastotrasaṅgraha.] pp. 35-40. [1890.] 12°. **14100. a. 13.**

——— सार्थ भूपालस्तोत्र [Jinachaturviṃṣatikā. With Marathi interpretation and notes.] pp. ii. 18. मुंबई १८९१ [*Bombay,* 1891.] 12°. **14028. b. 69.(1.)**

——— जिनचतुर्विंशतिका । [Jinachaturviṃṣatikā.] *See* JAINANITYAPĀṬHA. अथ जैननित्यपाठसंग्रहः [Jainanityapāṭhasaṅgraha.] pp. 107-117. [1901.] *obl.* 16°. **14100. a. 27.**

BHŪSHAṆA BĀṆA, also called BHŪSHAṆA BHAṬṬA, *son of Bāṇa.* [For the continuation of Bāṇa's Kādambarī by this writer:] *See* BĀṆA.

BHŪTA-CHHĀRĀN. ভূতছাড়ানপ্রকরণ । [Bhūtachhārān-prakaraṇa. A manual of magic. With Bengali translations, notes, *etc.* Followed by the Kumāratantra and extracts from other Tantric works.] pp. 18. [1894.] *See* PERIODICAL PUBLICATIONS.—*Calcutta.* অরুণোদয় *etc.* [Aruṇodaya.] Pt. i., no. 34. [1890, *etc.*] 4°. **14133. g. 16.(pt. i., no. 34.)**

BHŪTANĀTHA VIDYĀRATNA. *See* ÆSOP. नीतिमाला ... Nitimálá, or Æsop's Fables. Translated ... by Bhútanátha Vidyáratna. 1891. 12°. **14076. b. 28.**

BHUVANACHANDRA SIDDHĀNTACHŪḌĀMAṆI. *See* RAMĀNĀTHA CHAKRAVARTĪ. শব্দরত্নম্ *etc.* [Ṣabdaratna. Edited by Bhuvanachandra.] [1893.] 8°. **14093. b. 36.**

BHUVANAMOHANA BHAṬṬĀCHĀRYA, *of Murshidabad.* যোগেন্দ্র মাহাত্ম্য [Yogendramāhātmya. A poetical panegyric on Yogendra Nārāyaṇa Rāya. With a Bengali translation.] pp. i. 20. মুর্শিদাবাদ ১৮২২ [*Murshidabad,* 1901.] 12°. **14072. b. 25.(2.)**

BHUVANEṢVARA KAVICHANDRA. *See* ṢRĪNIVĀSA ĀCHĀRYA, *Astrologer.* ଶ୍ରୀ ଶ୍ରୀନିବାସଦୀପିକା *etc.* [Ṣrīnivāsadīpikā. With Oriya paraphrase and commentary by Bhuvaneṣvara.] 1900. 12°. **14053. a. 5.(2.)**

BIBLE.—NEW TESTAMENT.—*Selections.* ख्रिष्टधर्मनीति *etc.* [Khrishṭadharmanīti. Select passages from the New Testament, compiled and translated into Sanskrit and Gujarati by Nārāyaṇa Hemachandra.] pp. 18. મુંબઈ ૧૮૮૦ [*Bombay,* 1880.] 8°. **14006. c. 14.**

Forms no. 2 of a series styled Saddharmavachanasaṅgraha.

BIBLIOTHECA BUDDHICA. *See* ACADEMIES, *etc.*—Saint Petersburg.—*Academia Scientiarum Imperialis.*

BIBLIOTHECA INDICA. *See* ACADEMIES, *etc.*—Calcutta.—*Asiatic Society of Bengal.*

BIBLIOTHECA SANSKRITA. *See* MYSORE.—*Government of Mysore.*

BILHAṆA. [For the Chaurapañchāṣikā or Chorapañchāṣat as published together with Bhāratachandra Rāya's Bengali adaptation thereof in the various editions of the latter's works :] *See* BHĀRATACHANDRA RĀYA.

—— चौरपञ्चाशिका [Chaurapañchāṣikā. With footnotes.] pp. 11. [1889.] *See* PERIODICAL PUBLICATIONS.—*Bombay.* ग्रन्थरत्नमाला *etc.* (Granth Ratna Málá, *etc.*) Vol. ii., no. 9. 1887-[1892.] 8°. **14096. c. 8.(vol. 2.)**

—— चौर पंचाशिका सटीक *etc.* [Chaurapañchāṣikā. With Hindi version by Mahīdhara Ṣarmā.] pp. 30. *See* VIDYĀSUNDARA. विद्यासुन्दर *etc.* [Vidyāsundara, *etc.*] [1894.] 12°. **14070. b. 23.**

—— The Chaurapanchâsika, an Indian Love Lament. Translated and illustrated by Sir Edwin Arnold. [With the Sanskrit text.] pp. v. 52, *lith. London,* 1896. *obl.* 8°. **14072. b. 23.**

The Sanskrit text is that of von Bohlen.

BINOD. *See* VINODA.

BISHNU DATT VAIDIK. *See* VISHṆUDATTA, *Vaidika.*

BISHNUPADA. *See* VISHṆUPADA.

BISSESSUR NATH CHANDIK. *See* VIṢVEṢVARANĀTHA CHAṆḌIKA.

BLAU (AUGUST). Index zu Otto Böhtlingks Indischen Sprüchen, *etc.* pp. i. 109. 1893. *See* ACADEMIES, *etc.*—Germany.—*Deutsche Morgenlaendische Gesellschaft.* Abhandlungen, *etc.* Bd. 9, No. 4. 1859, *etc.* 8°. **753. f. 17.**

BLOCH (THEODOR). *See* ĀPASTAMBA.—*Dharmasūtra.* आपस्तम्बीयधर्मसूत्रम् । Aphorisms on the Sacred Law, *etc.* (Part ii., containing . . . a verbal index to the Sûtras, by Dr. Th. Bloch.) 1892-1894. 8°. **14038. d. 34.**

—— Über das Gṛhya- und Dharmasūtra der Vaikhānasa, *etc.* pp. 46. *Leipzig,* 1896. 8°. **14028. d. 53.**

BLOOMFIELD (MAURICE). *See* VEDAS.—*Atharvaveda.* Hymns of the Atharva-Veda, together with extracts from the ritual books and the commentaries. Translated by Maurice Bloomfield. 1897. 8°. [*Sacred Books of the East.*] **2003. b. (vol. 42.)**

—— *See* VEDAS.—*Atharvaveda.* The Kashmirian Atharvaveda . . . Reproduced by chromophotography from the manuscript in the University Library at Tübingen. Edited . . . by Maurice Bloomfield, *etc.* 1901. Fol. **14010. e. 15.**

BODAS (M. R.). *See* MAHĀDEVA RĀJĀRĀMA BODAS.

BODE (MABEL), *Mrs. See* ACADEMIES, *etc.*—London.—*Pali Text Society.* PAÑÑASĀMI. Sāsanavaṃsa. Edited [with introductory dissertation, *etc.,*] by Mabel Bode. 1897. 8°. **14098. b. 37.**

—— *See* ACADEMIES, *etc.*—London.—*Pali Text Society.* SUTTAPIṬAKA. The Majjhima-Nikāya, *etc.* (Vol. III. . . . With indices . . . by Mabel Bode.) 1896-1902. 8°. **14098. b. 25.**

—— *See* BUDDHAGHOSHA. [*Manorathapūraṇī.*] Women Leaders of the Buddhist Reformation. [Being an excerpt from the Manorathapūraṇī, with translation.] By Mabel Bode. 1893. 8°. [*Journal of the Royal Asiatic Society.*] **Ac. 8820/3. and 2098. a, b.**

BODE (Mabel), *Mrs.* (*continued*). Index to the Gandhavaṃsa [in Minaev's edition of 1886], *etc.* 1896. *See* Academies, *etc.*—London.—*Pali Text Society.* Journal . . . 1896, *etc.* pp. 53-101. 1882, *etc.* 8°. **14098. b.**

BODHĀYANA, *the Sūtrakāra.* *See* Baudhāyana.

BODHĀNANDA GIRI, *of Miani.* ਸਰਬ ਸ਼ਾਸਤ੍ਰ ਸਾਰਸੰਗ੍ਰਹ: [Sarvaṣāstrasārasaṅgraha. A Hindi treatise on the ordinary rites of the orthodox Vaishṇava faith, the holy places and their legends, the principles of Vedānta, *etc.*, copiously illustrated from Sanskrit texts.] pp. 340. ਲਾਹੌਰ १९५७ [*Lahore*, 1900.] 4°. **14154. gg. 3.**

—— [Second edition.] pp. 414. ਰਾਵਲ ਪਿੰਡੀ [*Rawalpindi*, 1902.] 4°. **14154. gg. 5.**

BOEHTLINGK (Otto von). *See* Blau (A.). Index zu Otto Böhtlingks Indischen Sprüchen, *etc.* 1893. 8°. [*Deutsche Morgenlaendische Gesellschaft : Abhandlungen.*] **753. f. 17.**

—— *See* Brāhmaṇas. — *Taittirīyabrāhmaṇa.* Probe einer rationellen Bearbeitung des Taittirîja-Brâhmaṇa. [Containing text of the first 6 *anuvākas*, edited with translation by O. von Böhtlingk.] 1892. 8°. [*Koeniglich Saechsische Gesellschaft der Wissenschaften : Berichte.*] **Ac. 700/2. (Bd. 44.)**

BOHRA (C. C.). *See* Chūnīlāl Bohrā.

BOMBAY.—*Library of Bhau Daji Memorial.* *See* Academies, *etc.*—Bombay.—*Bombay Branch of the Royal Asiatic Society.*

BOMBAY SANSKRIT SERIES. Bombay Sanskrit Series, *etc.* *Bombay*, 1868, *etc.* 8°.

The works that have appeared in this series since the publication of Prof. Bendall's Catalogue are to be found under the following headings :—

xxxvi., xli., xliii., lviii. *Vedas.*—Rigveda.
xlii. *Daṇḍi.*
xliv., l. *Āpastamba.*
xlv., li., liv. *Kalhaṇa.*
xlvi. *Patañjali.*
xlvii., xlviii., lix. *Parāṣara.*
xlix. *Bhīmāchārya Jhalkikar.*
lii. *Śūdraka.*
liii. *Padmagupta.*
lv. *Annam Bhaṭṭa.*
lvi., lvii. *Bhaṭṭi.*
lx. *Hemachandra.*
lxi.—lxii. *Euclid.*

BŌNĀLA KRISHṆA, *disciple of Polūr Veṅkaṭaramaṇa.* (మతతత్త్వప్రకాశినీ.) [Matatattvaprakāṣinī. An account of various Hindu sects, written from the standpoint of the Madhva school.] pp. 23. నెల్లూరు [*Nellore*, 1899.] *obl.* 8°. **14028. d. 50.(4.)**

BOPADEBA GOSWAMEE. *See* Vopadeva.

BOWER (Hamilton), *Lieut.-Colonel.* *See* India.—*Archæological Survey.* The Bower Manuscript, *etc.* 1893, *etc.* Fol. **14058. d. 5.**

BRAHMADEVA, *son of Chandradeva, of Mathura.* करणप्रकाशः *etc.* (Karaṇaprakâśa. [A compendium of astronomy, in 9 *adhikāras* and 225 stanzas.] . . . [Edited] with a commentary and theory of numbers . . . by Mahâmahopâdhyâya Sudhâkara Dvivadî.) pp. ii. 92. काश्याम् १८९९ [*Benares*, 1899.] 8°. **14004. a. 5.**

Forms no. 23 *of the* Chowkhambâ Sanskrit Series. *The English title is taken from the wrapper.*

BRAHMAGUPTA, *son of Jishṇu.* ब्राह्मस्फुटसिद्धान्तो ध्यानग्रहोपदेशाध्यायश्च . . . Brāhmasphuṭasiddhānta and Dhyānagrahopadeṣādhyāya. [Astronomical works] . . . edited with his own commentary by Mahāmahopādhyāya Sudhākara Dvivedin. pp. i. viii. 454. 1902. *See* Periodical Publications.—*Benares.* The Pandit, *etc.* New Series. Vol. xxiii., xxiv. 1876, *etc.* 8°. **14096. d. 6.(vol. 23, 24.)**

—— —— [A separate issue of the same.] p. i. viii. 454. *Benares*, 1902. 8°. **14053. ccc. 43.**

BRAHMĀNANDA, *Svāmī, Paramahaṃsa.* श्रीविचारदीपकः *etc.* [Vichāradīpaka. A Vedantic poem in 113 stanzas, with the author's commentary in Hindi. Followed by a few original hymns in Sanskrit and Hindi.] pp. ii. 270, xxxi.; 1 *plate.* मुंबय्यां १९४८ [*Bombay*, 1893.] 12°. **14048. b. 25.**

BRAHMĀNANDA, *disciple of Mauktikarāma.* *See* Devatīrtha Svāmī. Udásína Sádhu Stotra. [Translated, with extracts from the commentary of Brahmānanda.] 1898. 8°. [*The Theosophist.*] **P.P. 636. cm. (vol. 19.)**

BRAHMĀNANDA, *disciple of Meru Śāstrī.* *See* Svātmārāma. হঠযোগপ্রদীপিকা। [Haṭhayoga-pradīpikā. With the commentary Jyotsnā of Brahmānanda.] [1891, *etc.*] 4°. [*Aruṇodaya.*] **14133. g. 16.(pt. i. no. 21.)**

—— *See* Svātmārāma. हठयोगप्रदीपिका *etc.* (The Hatha-yoga Pradipika . . . with . . . its commentary [by Brahmānanda,] *etc.*) 1893. 12°. **14048. b. 30.**

BRAHMĀNANDA BHĀRATĪ, *disciple of Ānanda Bhāratītīrtha.* See ṢAṄKARA ĀCHĀRYA.—*Philosophical Poems, etc.* श्री . . . वाक्यसुधा *etc.* [Vākyasudhā. With commentary of Brahmānanda.] 1901. 8°. [*Vivaraṇopanyāsa.*] **14048. cc. 37.**

BRAHMĀNANDAGIRI TĪRTHA, *Avadhūta.* तारारहस्यम् *etc.* [Tārārahasya. A tantric treatise on the legends and cult of Tārā, in 4 *paṭalas.* Edited by Jīvānanda Vidyāsāgara. Second edition.] pp. 82. कलिकाता १८९६ [*Calcutta*, 1896.] 8°. **14033. aa. 6.(3.)**

BRAHMĀNANDA SARASVATĪ. *See* UPANISHADS. —*Separate Upanishads.* ईशावास्योपनिषत् *etc.* ((1) Shri Íśávásyopanishad with . . . (3) The Rahasya of . . . Brahmánanda, (4) The Rahasya Vivriti by Ramachandra Pandita, *etc.*) [1888.] 8°. **14003. ccc. (no. 5.)**

BRAHMĀNANDA SARASVATĪ, *disciple of Paramānanda.* *See* ṢAṄKARA ĀCHĀRYA.—*Philosophical Poems, etc.* ॥ सिद्धान्तबिन्दुः *etc.* [Daṣaṣlokī. With the commentary Siddhāntabindu of Madhusūdana Sarasvatī and the supercommentary Nyāyaratnāvalī or Ratnāvalī of Brahmānanda.] 1893. 8°. [*Advaitamañjarī.*] **14048. e. 23.**

—— ॥ लघुचन्द्रिका *etc.* [Laghuchandrikā. A commentary upon the Advaitasiddhi of Madhusūdana Sarasvatī.] pp. i. iv. iv. 643. 1893. *See* HARIHARA ṢĀSTRĪ, *Goshṭhīpuram,* and others. ॥ अद्वैतमञ्जरी *etc.* [Advaitamañjarī.] 1892-1895. 8°. **14048. e. 23.**

—— *See* ANANTĀCHĀRYA, *Ṣeshārya.* న్యాయభాస్కర॥ [Nyāyabhāskara. A criticism of the Laghuchandrikā.] [1893.] 8°. **14048. bb. 47.**

BRAHMĀNANDA TATTVADARṢĪ. *See* ṢASIBHŪSHAṆA MITRA MUSTAUPHĪ.

BRAHMĀNANDA TĪRTHA, *Draviḍasvāmī.* *See* APYAYA DĪKSHITA. सविवरणम् श्रीरामायणभारतसारसंग्रहस्तोत्रद्वयम् *etc.* [Rāmāyaṇasārasaṅgrahastotra and Bhāratasārasaṅgrahastotra. With *vivaraṇas, etc.* Edited with footnotes by Brahmānanda.] [1895.] 8°. **14028. d. 54.**

BRAHMĀNANDA TĪRTHA, *son of Ṣaṅkara.* तार्किकमोहप्रकाशः . . . तथा दयानन्दमोहप्रकाशश्च [Tārkikamohaprakāṣa. A modern controversial tract directed against the Nyāya school, with a Hindi version by Prakāṣānanda Purī. Followed by the Dayānandamohaprakāṣa, a polemic against Dayānanda Sarasvatī, likewise by Brahmananda, with Hindi version.] pp. viii. ii. 152. प्रयाग १९४९ [*Allahabad*, 1892.] 8°. **14048. dd. 8.**

BRĀHMAṆAS.

See MACDONALD (K. S.). The Brahmanas of the Vedas, *etc.* 1896. 8°. [*Sacred Books of the East Described and Examined.*] **14010. cc. 9.(vol. 1.)**

See PERIODICAL PUBLICATIONS.—*Calcutta.* उषा *etc.* [Ushā. A journal of Vedic and kindred studies.] [1889]-1893. 8°. **14010. c. 43.**

See SATYAVRATA SĀMASRAMĪ BHAṬṬĀCHĀRYA. ॥ त्रयीसङ्ग्रहः *etc.* [Trayīsaṅgraha. A digest of the matter of the Vedas, chiefly in the form of excerpts from them and their Brāhmaṇas, *etc.*] 1892-1893. 8°. [*Ushā.*] **14010. c. 43.(vol. 2.)**

The Science of the Rishis, illustrated from the Brahmanas of the Vedas. pp. 16. *Pokhuria,* [1895.] 8°. **14007. c. 9.(2.)**

AITAREYABRĀHMAṆA.

The Aitareya Bráhmaṇa of the Ṛg-Veda, with the commentary of Sáyaṇa Áchárya. Edited by Paṇḍit Satyavrata Sámaśramí. 1895, *etc.* *See* ACADEMIES, *etc.*—Calcutta.—*Asiatic Society of Bengal.* Bibliotheca Indica. New Series. [Vol. 134.] 1848, *etc.* 8°. **14002. a. (vol. 134.)**

In progress.

ऐतरेयब्राह्मणम् *etc.* (The Aitaréya Bráhmaṇam, with the Bháshya of S'rímat Sáyaṇáchárya . . . Edited by Pandit Kâśinâtha Sâstry Âgâśé.) 2 vols. pp. i. xiv. ix. 970, lv. पुण्याख्यपत्तने १८९६ [*Poona,* 1896.] 8°. **14003. ccc. (no. 32.)**

Forms no. 31 *of the* Ānandāṣrama Sanskrit Series. *The English title is taken from the cover.*

ĀRSHEYABRĀHMAṆA.

॥ आर्षेयब्राह्मणम् *etc.* [Ārsheyabrāhmaṇa. An index to the *sāmāni* of the Sāmaveda. With the commentary of Sāyaṇa. Edited by Satyavrata Sāmaṣramī.] pp. i. 191. 1891-1892. *See* PERIODICAL PUBLICATIONS.—*Calcutta.* उषा *etc.*

[Ushā.] Vol. I. no. xi.—vol. II. no. i. [1889]-1893. 8°. **14010. c. 43.(vol. 1, 2.)**

This tract is fourth in Sāyaṇa's list of Sāmaveda Brāhmaṇas. It also is found as the 5th book in the Talavakārabrāhmaṇa. The present editor classes it, with the Sāmavidhāna, Devatādhyāya, Saṃhitopanishad, and Vaṃśa, as an anubrāhmaṇa.

CHHĀNDOGYABRĀHMAṆA.

[For chap. 3-10 of this Brāhmaṇa, forming the Chhāndogyopanishad:] *See* UPANISHADS.

JAIMINĪYABRĀHMAṆA.

See below, TALAVAKĀRABRĀHMAṆA.

SĀMAVIDHĀNABRĀHMAṆA.

Das Sāmavidhānabrāhmaṇa. Ein altindisches Lehrbuch der Zauberei. Eingeleitet und übersetzt von Sten Konow. pp. vii. 82, i. *Halle*, 1893. 8°. **14007. c. 22.**

ṢATAPATHABRĀHMAṆA.

॥ शतपथब्राह्मणम् . . . The Çatapatha Brāhmaṇa of the White Yajurveda, with the commentary of Sāyaṇa Ācārya. Edited by Paṇḍit Satyavrata Sāmaçramī. 1900, *etc.* *See* ACADEMIES, *etc.*—Calcutta.—*Asiatic Society of Bengal.* Bibliotheca Indica. New Series. [Vol. 145.] 1848, *etc.* 8°. **14002. a. (vol. 145.)**

In progress.

—— यजुर्वेदीयमाध्यन्दिनीयम् शतपथब्राह्मणम् [Ṣatapathabrāhmaṇa. In the Mādhyandina recension.] pp. 748. अजमेर° १९५९ [*Ajmere*, 1902.] 8°. **14007. dd. 6.**

The Satapatha-Brâhmana, according to the text of the Mâdhyandina school. Translated [with introductions] by Julius Eggeling. 5 vols. 1882-1900. *See* MUELLER (F. M.). The Sacred Books of the East, *etc.* Vol. xi., xxvi., xli., xliii., xliv. 1879, *etc.* 8°. **2003. a, b.(vol. 11, 26, 41, 43, 44.)**

शतपथब्राह्मणम् *etc.* [Ṣatapathabrāhmaṇa. Kāṇḍa i. With notes giving references to passages cited.] pp. 144. अजमेर° १९५० [*Ajmere*, 1893.] 8°. **14007. cc. 23.**

Die Dîkshâ oder Weihe für das Somaopfer. [Being the Ṣatapathabrāhmaṇa III. i. 1—ii. 2, translated into German, with commentary.] Habilitationsschrift . . . [by] Dr. Bruno Lindner. pp. 47. *Leipzig*, 1878. 8°. **14010. d. 8.(2.)**

See REGNAUD (P.). Comment naissent les mythes . . . La légende hindoue du déluge.—Purūravas et Urvaçī, *etc.* 1897. 12°. **4503. dd. 13.**

SHAḌVIṂṢABRĀHMAṆA.

Das Ṣaḍviṃçabrāhmaṇa. Mit Proben aus Sāyaṇas Kommentar, nebst einer Übersetzung. Herausgegeben von Kurt Klemm. Prapāṭhaka 1. pp. i. iii. 94. *Gütersloh*, 1894. 8°. **14010. dd. 4.**

TAITTIRĪYABRĀHMAṆA.

॥ अथ कृष्णयजुर्वेदीयतैत्तिरीयब्राह्मणप्रारंभः ॥ [Taittirīyabrāhmaṇa.] ff. 60, 71, 102. मुंबय्यां १८१६ [*Bombay*, 1894.] *obl.* 8°. **14007. cc. 25.**

तैत्तिरीयब्राह्मणम् *etc.* [Taittirīyabrāhmaṇa. With the commentary Vedārthaprakāṣa of Sāyaṇa. Edited by Nārāyaṇa Bālakrishṇa Godbole.] 3 vols. pp. 1447. पुण्याख्यपत्तने १८१९ [*Poona*, 1898.] 8°. **14003. ccc. (no. 37.)**

Forms no. 37 of the Ānandāṣrama Sanskrit Series.

The Taittiriya Brahmana, with Swaram, in Telugu character, distinguishing the Mantra portion from the Brahmana, and noting the division of Vakyams, according to Sri Vidyaranya Swamy, together with the contents of the whole Sakha, including the Samhita and Aranyaka. [Edited by A. Lakshmīnarasiṃha Somayājī.] (తైత్తిరీయబ్రాహ్మణమ్, *etc.*). pp. iv. iv. ii. ix. 677. *Madras*, 1899. 8°. **14007. d. 21.**

Forms no. 2 of the Conjeeveram Oriental Literary Institution Series.

தைத்திரீயப்ராஹ்மணே ப்ரபாடகம் *etc.* (த்விதீயா ॥ த்ருதீயா ॥ *etc.*) [Taittirīyabrāhmaṇa. Edited, with accentuation, *etc.*, by Mullaṅguḍi Vaidyanātha Ṣāstrī and Mañjakuḍi Sāmbaṣiva Ghanapāṭhī.] கும்பகோணம் ॥ [*Kumbakonam*,] 1900, *etc.* 8°. **14007. cc. 30.**

In progress.

See SUBRAHMAṆYA ṢĀSTRĪ, *K., of Uḍayārpāḷayam.* க்ருஷ்ணயஜுர்வேத தைத்திரீயப்ராஹ்மணாரண்யககாண்டகாநாம் பஞ்சாஶதநுக்ரமணிகா *etc.* [Pañchāṣadanukramaṇikā.

An index of catchwords for the Taittirīya-saṃhitā, its Brāhmaṇa, Āraṇyaka, and Kāṭhaka.] [1897.] 12°. **14028. b. 78.(2.)**

See SANDHYĀVANDANA. संध्याभाष्यसमुच्चयः *etc.* [Sandhyābhāshyasamuchchaya. Commentaries upon the *sandhyā* prayers.] [1899.] 8°. **14003. ccc. (no. 40.)**

ஆப்ரஹ்ம [Ābrahman, viz. Taittirīyasaṃhitā VII. v. 18, Taitt.-br. III. viii. 13, T.-s. IV. v. 3, and T.-br. III. ix. 5.] *See* UPANISHADS.—*General Collections.* அஷ்டோத்தரஶதோபநிஷத: *etc.* [Ashṭottaraṣatopanishadaḥ, *etc.*] pp. 831-834. 1896. 8°. **14010. cc. 8.**

Probe einer rationellen Bearbeitung des Taittirîja-Brâhmaṇa. [Containing text of the first 6 *anuvākas*, edited with translation by O. von Böhtlingk.] 1892. *See* ACADEMIES, *etc.*—Leipsic. —*Koeniglich Saechsische Gesellschaft der Wissenschaften.* Berichte, *etc.* Bd. 44, pp. 199-226. 1848, *etc.* 8°. **Ac. 700/2. (Bd. 44.)**

அஶ்வமேதப்ராஹ்மணம் ஸஹித: தைத்திரீயோபநிஷச்ச *etc.* [Aṣvamedha, or section iii. 8 of the Taittirīyabrāhmaṇa; Āruṇa, or *praṣna* i. of the Taittirīyāraṇyaka; and the Taittirīyopanishad. Edited by Rāmakṛishṇa Ṣāstrī of Kalpadi.] pp. 20, 24, 34. பாலக்காட் [*Palghat*, 1900.] 8°. **14007. cc. 28.**

தைத்திரீயகாடகே . . . ப்ராஹ்மணம் [Kāṭhaka, *i.e.* the xth-xiith *prapāṭhakas* of the 3rd *ashṭaka* of this Brāhmaṇa. With accentuation.] *See* ĀRANYAKAS. — *Taittirīyāraṇyaka.* ஶ்ரீ . . . வகாரகாரண்யமாலா *etc.* [Taittirīyāraṇyaka, *etc.*] pp. 197-244. 1894. 8°. **14010. cc. 1.**

TALAVAKĀRABRĀHMAṆA.

The Jāiminīya or Talavakāra Upaniṣad Brāhmaṇa[, forming part 4 of the Talavakārabrāhmaṇa]: text, translation, and notes. By Hanns Oertel. 1894. *See* ACADEMIES, *etc.*—Boston, *Mass.*—*American Oriental Society.* Journal, *etc.* Vol. xvi., pp. 79-260. 1849, *etc.* 8°. **Ac. 8824. (vol. 16.)**

Extracts from the Jāiminīya-Brāhmaṇa and Upanishad-Brāhmaṇa, parallel to passages of the Çatapatha-Brāhmaṇa and Chāndogya-Upanishads. [Edited and translated] by Dr. Hanns Oertel. 1893. *See* ACADEMIES, *etc.*—Boston, *Mass.*—*American Oriental Society.* Journal, *etc.* Vol. xv., pp. 233-251. 1849, *etc.* 8°. **Ac. 8824. (vol. 15.)**

See OERTEL (HANNS). Contributions from the Jāiminīya Brāhmaṇa to the history of the Brāhmaṇa literature, *etc.* 1897-1898. 8°. [*Journal of the American Oriental Society.*] **Ac. 8824. (vol. 18, 19.)**

[For the Ārsheyabrāhmaṇa, forming the fifth book of this Brāhmaṇa:] *See* above, ĀRSHEYABRĀHMAṆA.

[For the Kenopanishad contained in the Upanishadbrāhmaṇa:] *See* UPANISHADS.

VAMṢABRĀHMAṆA.

॥ वंशब्राह्मणम् *etc.* [Vaṃṣabrāhmaṇa. A list of the teachers of the Sāmaveda. With Sāyaṇa's commentary. Edited with a Bengali translation by Satyavrata Sāmaṣramī.] pp. 12, 7. 1892. *See* PERIODICAL PUBLICATIONS.—*Calcutta.* उषा *etc.* [Ushā.] Vol. II., no. ii. [1889]-1893. 8°. **14010. c. 43. (vol. 2.)**

The editor regards this work as an anubrāhmaṇa, *of the same class as the Ārsheyabrāhmaṇa. It is eighth in Sāyaṇa's list.*

BRĀHMA-SAMĀJ. उपासना-पद्धतिः। [Upāsanāpaddhati. A Brahmist manual of devotions.] pp. 28. कलिकाता १९२२ [*Calcutta*, 1870.] 32°. **14028. a. 23.(1.)**

—— స్తోత్రపాఠపుస్తకములు [Stotrapāṭhapustakamulu. Hymns for the liturgies of the southern Brāhma-Samāj, in Sanskrit and Telugu. Second edition.] pp. 44. చెన్నపురి [*Madras.*] 1896. 12°. **14028. b. 73.(2.)**

—— Brahmo Marriage Ritual [in Sanskrit and English]. Published by the Southern India Brahma Samaj, Madras. pp. 20. *Madras*, 1902. 32°. **14028. a. 23.(2.)**

BRAHMASAMHITĀ. ব্রহ্মসংহিতা। [Brahmasaṃhitā. A work on Yoga. With Bengali translation.] pp. 31. *See* PRASANNAKUMĀRA ṢĀSTRĪ BHAṬṬĀCHĀRYA. যোগাম্বুধি *etc.* [Yogāmbudhi.] [1896.] 16°. **14048. a. 19.**

The work is said to be in 100 adhyāyas, *of which this contains only* 5.

BRAHMASŪRI, *Jain Poet.* ज्योतिःप्रभाकल्याणनाटकम् [Jyotiḥprabhākalyāṇa. A drama.] [1893-1894.] *See* PADMARĀJA PAṆḌITA, *son of Brahmasūri.* काव्याम्बुधिः *etc.* [Kāvyāmbudhi.] Pts. 1-6. [1893-1896.] 8°. **14028. c. 64.**

Not completed.

BRAJENDRANATH. *See* VRAJENDRANĀTHA.

BṚIHACH-CHHĀNTI. [For the editions of this devotional composition included in the collection styled Navasmaraṇa :] *See* NAVASMARAṆA.

BṚIHASPATI. ॥ बृहस्पतिसंहिता *etc.* [Bṛihaspati-saṃhitā. A modern tract, in 80 stanzas, on the modes of acquiring merit. With Hindi version.] pp. 18. कानपुर १८९९ [*Cawnpore,* 1899.] 8°. **14028. c. 85.(8.)**

BṚIHAT-SVARODAYATANTRA. *See* PAVANAVIJAYA.

BUCHCHAIYA PANTULU, *Mannava.* *See* UPANISHADS. — *Separate Upanishads.* Chhandogya Upanishad. Edited by M. B. Pantulu, *etc.* 1899. 8°. **14010. dd. 16.**

BUDDHA BHAṬṬA. Ratnaparîkṣâ de Buddhabhaṭṭa. [A treatise on the lapidary art, in 252 stanzas, sometimes alleged to be extracted from the Garuḍapurāṇa. With French translation.] *See* FINOT (L.). Les Lapidaires Indiens, *etc.* pp. 1-58. 1896. 8°. **Ac. 8929. (fasc. 111.)**

BUDDHAGHOSA. [*Life.*] *See* MAHĀMAṄGALA. Buddhaghosuppatti, or The Historical Romance . . . . of Buddhaghosa, *etc.* 1892. 8°. **14098. c. 59.**

—— [*Aṭṭhasālinī.*] The Atthasālinī, Buddhaghosa's commentary on the Dhammasaṅgaṇi. Edited by Edward Müller. 1897. 8°. *See* ACADEMIES, *etc.* — London. — *Pali Text Society.* BUDDHAGHOSA. **14098. b. 36.(1.)**

—— —— အဋ္ဌသာလိနီအဋ္ဌကထာ *etc.* [Aṭṭhasālinī.] pp. 463. ရန်ကုန် ၁၂၆၂ [*Rangoon,* 1901.] 8°. **14098. dd. 22.**

—— [*Dhammapadaṭṭhakathā.*] *See* SUTTAPIṬAKA.—*Khuddakanikāya.* [*Dhammapada.*] धम्मपदं । Dhammapadam. [With the commentary of Buddhaghosa,] *etc.* 1899. 8°. [*Buddhist Texts.*] **14004. c. (vol. 1, no. 4.)**

—— [*Manorathapūraṇī.*] මනොරථපූරණී, *etc.* [Manorathapūraṇī. The commentary on the Aṅguttaranikāya. Edited by K. Dhammārāma.] Pts. 1, 3-5. පෑලියගොඩ [*Peliyagoda,*] 1893-1896. 8°. **14098. c. 64.**

—— —— කම්මනිදානසුත්තට්ඨකථා [Kammanidānasuttaṭṭhakathā.] *See* SUTTAPIṬAKA.—*Aṅguttaranikāya.* කම්මනිදානසූත්‍රය *etc.* [Karmanidānasūtraya.] pp. 3-13. 1897. 8°. **14098. c. 73.(6.)**

—— —— සරභසුත්තට්ඨකථා [Sarabhasuttaṭṭhakathā. *See* SUTTAPIṬAKA.—*Aṅguttaranikāya.* සරභසූත්‍රය *etc.* [Sarabhasutta.] pp. 4-10. 1897. 8°. **14098. c. 73.(7.)**

—— —— Women Leaders of the Buddhist Reformation. [Being an excerpt from the Manorathapūraṇī on the Aṅguttaranikāya I. xiv., with translation.] By Mabel Bode. 1893. *See* ACADEMIES, *etc.*—London.—*Royal Asiatic Society of Great Britain and Ireland.* The Journal . . . 1893. pp. 517-566, 763-798. 1834, *etc.* 8°. **Ac. 8820/3 and 2098. a.b.**

—— —— The story of the merchant Ghosaka . . in its twofold Pāli form, [*scil.* as given in the Manorathapūraṇī and the Dhammapadaṭṭhakathā], with reference to other Indian parallels. By . . . E. Hardy. 1898. *See* ACADEMIES, *etc.*—London.—*Royal Asiatic Society of Great Britain and Ireland.* The Journal . . . 1898. pp. 741-794. 1834, *etc.* 8°. **Ac. 8820/3 and 2098. a.b.**

—— [*Papañchasūdanī.*] පපඤ්චසූදනී . . . මැඣිමසඞ්ගීතිඅටුවාව *etc.* [Papañchasūdanī. Being the commentary on the Majjhimanikāya. Edited by Giridhara Ratanajoti.] Pt. i. pp. 80. [*Colombo,*] 1898. 8°. **14098. ccc. 8.**

—— —— අච්ඡරියබ්භුතසුත්තට්ඨකථා. [Achchhariyabbhutasuttaṭṭhakathā.] *See* SUTTAPIṬAKA. — *Majjhimanikāya.* අච්ඡරියබ්භුතසූත්‍රය *etc.* [Achchhariyabbhutasutta.] 1897. 8°. **14098. ccc. 4.(3.)**

BUDDHAGHOSA. [*Papañchasūdanī.*] (*continued*). චෙතොඛිල සුත්තට්ඨ කථා. [Chetokhilasuttaṭṭhakathā.] *See* SUTTAPIṬAKA.—*Majjhimanikāya.* Chetokhila Sutraya, *etc.* pp. 22-25. 1897. 8°. **14098. c. 73.(1.)**

—— —— ඡඡක්ඛකථා [Chhachhakkasuttaṭṭhakathā.] *See* SUTTAPIṬAKA. — *Majjhimanikāya.* Chachakka Suttaraya, *etc.* pp. 7-8. 1896. 8°. **14098. c. 72.(3.)**

—— —— සංඛාරුප්පත්තිකථා [Saṅkhāruppattisuttaṭṭhakathā.] *See* SUTTAPIṬAKA.—*Majjhimanikāya.* Sankharuppatti Sutraya, *etc.* pp. 5-6. 1896. 8°. **14098. c. 72.(2.)**

—— —— Friendship between Bimbisāra and Pukkusāti King of Takshasila . . . Translated by . . . James Alwis, *etc.* [Followed by the Pali Text, in Nagari characters, edited by C. A. Sīlakkhandha.] 1894. *See* ACADEMIES, *etc.*—Calcutta. — *Buddhist Text Society of India.* Journal, *etc.* Vol. ii., pt. ii. pp. 22-32. 1893, *etc.* 8°. **14003. b. 19.(vol. 2.)**

—— [*Paramatthajotikā.*] *See* SUTTAPIṬAKA.—*Khuddakanikāya.* [*Suttanipāta.*] සුත්තනිපාතො *etc.* [Suttanipāta. With the commentary Paramatthajotikā of Buddhaghosa.] Pt. i. 1897. 8°. **14098. ccc. 5.**

—— —— ධම්මිකකථා. [Dhammikasuttaṭṭhakathā.] *See* SUTTAPIṬAKA. — *Khuddakanikāya.* [*Suttanipāta.*] ධම්මිකසූත්‍රය *etc.* [Dhammikasutta.] [1895.] 8°. **14098. c. 69.(5.)**

—— [*Samantapāsādikā.*] ဘိက္ခုဝိဘင်ပါဠိတော်အဋ္ဌကထာ ... ပါရာဇိကဏ်အဋ္ဌကထာပါဠိ။ [The *aṭṭhakathā* or commentary upon Part 1 of the Suttavibhaṅga, viz. the Pārājika, Saṅghādisesa, Aniyata, and Nissaggiya-pāchittiya.] pp. ii. ii. 760, iii. ရန်ကုန် ၁၂၆၄ [*Rangoon*, 1902.] 8°. **14098. dd. 26.**

—— [*Sammohavinodanī.*] ဝိဘင်းပါဠိတော်အဋ္ဌ ... သမ္မောဟဝိနောဒနီအဋ္ဌကထာပါဠိ။ [Sammohavinodanī. The commentary on the Vibhaṅga. In the recension of Tipiṭakālaṅkāra Siriddhaja.] pp. 525. ရန်ကုန် ၁၂၆၃ [*Rangoon*, 1901.] 8°. **14098. dd. 25.**

BUDDHAGHOSA. [*Sammohavinodanī.*] (*continued*).

—— *See* ÑĀNAKITTI. අභිධම්ම සම්මොහවිනොදනීඅත්ථයොජනා *etc.* (The Abhidhamma Sammohavinodani Atthayojana. [A gloss upon the Sammohavinodanī,] *etc.*) [1893.] 8°. **14098. dd. 5.(2.)**

—— [*Sāratthappakāsanī.*] පබ්බතූපම සුත්තට්ඨකථා [Pabbatūpamasuttaṭṭhakathā.] *See* SUTTAPIṬAKA.—*Saṃyuttanikāya.* පබ්බතූපම සූත්‍රය *etc.* [Pabbatūpamasutta.] pp. 4-5. 1897. 8°. **14098. c. 73.(5.)**

—— [*Sumaṅgalavilāsinī.*] Buddhagosha's [*sic*] Commentary on the Maha Satipa*tth*ana Sutta. 1894. *See* PERIODICAL PUBLICATIONS.—*Colombo.* The Buddhist, *etc.* Vol. vi., no. 5-13. 1888, *etc.* 8°. **P.P. 636. cn. (vol. 6.)**

—— [*Visuddhimagga.*] *See* WARREN (H. C.). Buddhism in Translations, *etc.* [Being select passages translated from the Visuddhimagga, *etc.*] 1896. 8°. [*Harvard Oriental Series.*] **14003. l. 3.(vol. 3.)**

—— —— विसुद्धिमग्गो । Visuddhi Maggo . . . Edited by Rev. Seelakkhanda Thera. 1896, *etc.* *See* ACADEMIES, *etc.* — Calcutta. — *Buddhist Text Society of India.* Buddhist Texts, *etc.* 1894, *etc.* 8°. **14004. c. (vol. 2, no. 1.)**

In progress.

—— —— The Visuddhimagga of Buddhaghosa Thera. [Translated by A. E. Buultjens.] 1894-1895. *See* PERIODICAL PUBLICATIONS.—*Colombo.* The Buddhist, *etc.* Vol. vi., no. 18-25, Vol. vii., no. 1-28. 1888, *etc.* 8°. **P.P. 636. cn. (vol. 6, 7.)**

Extends to the end of Book i.

—— —— Table of contents of Buddhaghosa's Visuddhi-magga. By Henry C. Warren. 1893. *See* ACADEMIES, *etc.*—London.—*Pali Text Society.* Journal . . . 1891-3, *etc.* pp. 76-164. 1882, *etc.* 8°. **14098. b.**

BUDDHAPPIYA. *See* DĪPAṄKARA, called BUDDHAPPIYA.

BUDDHARAKKHITA. Jinâlaṅkâra, or "Embellishments of Buddha" . . . Edited, with introduction, notes, and translation, by James Gray. pp. 112. *London*, 1894. 8°. **14098. c. 65.**

BUDDHIST MAHĀYĀNA TEXTS. Buddhist Mahâyâna Texts. Part I. The Buddha-*k*arita of Asvaghosha. Translated from the Sanskrit by E. B. Cowell. (Part II. The Larger Sukhâvatî-vyûha. The Smaller Sukhâvatî-vyûha. The Va*grakkh*edikâ. The Larger Pra*gñ*â-pâramitâ-h*r*idaya-sûtra. The Smaller Pra*gñ*â-pâramitâ-h*r*idaya-sûtra. Translated by F. Max Müller. The Amitâyur-dhyâna-sûtra. Translated by J. Takakusu.) pp. xiii. 206, xxvi. 208. 1894. *See* MUELLER (F. M.). The Sacred Books of the East, *etc.* Vol. xlix. 1879, *etc.* 8°. **2003. b. (vol. 49.)**

BUDDHIST TEXT SOCIETY OF INDIA. *See* ACADEMIES, *etc.*—*Calcutta.*

BUDHAKAUṢIKA. ॥ अथ रामरक्षादिस्तोत्राणि ॥ [Rāmarakshāstotra. Followed by the Ṣivapañchāksharastotra attributed to Ṣaṅkara Achārya, the Dvādaṣa-jyotirliṅganāmāni and the Vishṇor Ashṭāviṃṣatināmastotra.] ff. 16. देव्हारे [*Devhare*, 1890.] *obl.* 16°. **14028. a. 19.(3.)**

BUEHLER (JOHANN GEORG). *See* ĀPASTAMBA.—*Dharmasūtra.* आपस्तम्बीयधर्मसूत्रम् । Aphorisms on the Sacred Law . . . Edited . . . by Dr. George Bühler, *etc.* 1892-1894. 8°. **14038. d. 34.**

—— *See* JINAPRABHA SŪRI. A Legend of the Jaina Stūpa at Mathurā. By G. Bühler. 1897. 8°. [*Sitzungsberichte der Kais. Akademie der Wissenschaften zu Wien.*] **Ac. 810/6.(Bd. 137.)**

—— *See* KIRSTE (J.). Professor J. Kirstes Collation des Textes der Yâjñavalkya-smriti . . . herausgegeben von G. Bühler. 1893. Fol. [*Denkschriften der Kais. Akademie der Wissenschaften zu Wien.*] **Ac. 810/12.(Bd. 42.)**

—— Beiträge zur Erklärung der Aśoka-Inschriften, *etc.* 1883-1894. *See* ACADEMIES, *etc.* — Germany. — *Deutsche Morgenlaendische Gesellschaft.* Zeitschrift, *etc.* Bd. 37-48. 1846, *etc.* 8°. **Ac. 8815/2.(Bd. 37-48.)**

—— The Sacred Laws of the Âryas as taught in the schools of Âpastamba, Gautama, Vâsish*th*a, and Baudhâyana. Translated [with introductions] by Georg Bühler. Part i. Âpastamba and Gautama. Second edition. pp. lxii. 314. 1897. *See* MUELLER (F. M.). The Sacred Books of the East, *etc.* Vol. ii. 1879, *etc.* 8°. **2003. a. (vol. 2.)**

BUEHLER (JOHANN GEORG) and **KIRSTE** (JOHANN). Indian Studies. No. ii. Contributions to the History of the Mahâbhârata[, with especial reference to Kshemendra's Bhāratamañjarī,] *etc.* pp. 58. 1892. *See* ACADEMIES, *etc.*—Vienna.—*Kaiserliche Akademie der Wissenschaften.* Sitzungsberichte, *etc.* Band 127. 1849, *etc.* 8°. **Ac. 810/6.(Bd. 127.)**

BUERK (ALBERT). *See* ĀPASTAMBA.—*Ṣulbasūtra.* Das Āpastamba-Śulba-Sūtra, herausgegeben, übersetzt und mit einer Einleitung versehen von Albert Bürk. 1901-1902. 8°. [*Zeitschrift der Deutschen Morgenlaendischen Gesellschaft.*] **Ac. 8815/2.(vol. 55, 56.)**

BUKKAṆA, *Raja.* భామినీసుగుణమంజరి అను స్త్రీనీతిశాస్త్రము *etc.* [Bhāminīsuguṇamañjari. Thirty-one stanzas on the duties of women, purporting to be compiled by Bukkaṇa. With a Telugu translation. Edited by M. Viṣvanātha Ṣāstrī.] pp. 27. *Madras*, 1889. 12°. **14072. b. 20.(1.)**

The wrapper bears the date 1890.

BULLORAM MULLICK. *See* BALARĀMA MALLIKA.

BURGESS (JAMES). *See* DHANEṢVARA SŪRI. The Śatrunjaya Mâhâtmyam . . . Edited by James Burgess. 1901. 4°. [*Indian Antiquary.*] **14096. e. (vol. 30.)**

—— *See* INDIA.—*Archæological Survey.* Epigraphia Indica . . . Edited by J. Burgess, *etc.* 1892, *etc.* Fol. & 4°. **1710. b. 13, 14.**

BUULTJENS (A. E.). *See* BUDDHAGHOSA. The Visuddhimagga of Buddhaghosa Thera. [Translated by A. E. Buultjens.] 1894-1895. 8°. [*The Buddhist.*] **P.P. 636. cn. (vol. 6, 7.)**

—— *See* PERIODICAL PUBLICATIONS.—*Colombo.* The Buddhist . . . Edited by C. W. Leadbeater, vol. 1. (By A. E. Buultjens, vol. 2, *etc.*) 1888, *etc.* 8°. **P.P. 636. cn.**

—— *See* SUTTAPIṬAKA.—*Dīghanikāya.* Satipattana [*sic*] Sutta, *etc.* [With translation and notes by A. E. Buultjens.] 1893. 8°. [*The Buddhist.*] **P.P. 636. cn. (vol. 5.)**

ÇABARASVAMIN. *See* ṢABARASVĀMĪ.

ÇÂKAṬÂYANA. *See* ṢĀKAṬĀYANA.

CALAND (W.). *See* KAUṢIKA. Altindisches Zauberritual. Probe einer Uebersetzung der wichtigsten Theile des Kauśika Sūtra, *etc.* 1900. 8°. [*Verhandelingen der Koninklijke Akademie van Wetenschappen te Amsterdam.*]
14033. c. 40.

—— Ueber Totenverehrung bei einigen der indogermanischen Völker. pp. 81. 1888. *See* ACADEMIES, *etc.* — Amsterdam. — *Koninklijke Akademie van Wetenschappen.* Verhandelingen, *etc.* 17de Deel. [1858, *etc.*] 8°.
Ac. 944/3.(Deel 17.)

—— Altindischer Ahnencult. Das Çrāddha nach den verschiedenen Schulen mit Benutzung handschriftlicher Quellen dargestellt, *etc.* [With appendices containing extracts from divers texts.] pp. xii. 266. *Leiden,* 1893. 8°.
4503. ee. 29.

—— Die Altindischen Todten- und Bestattungsgebräuche. Mit Benützung handschriftlicher Quellen dargestellt von Dr. W. Caland. pp. xiv. 191. 1896. *See* ACADEMIES, *etc.*—Amsterdam.—*Koninklijke Akademie van Wetenschappen.* Verhandelingen, *etc.* Nieuwe Reeks. Deel i., No. 6. [1858, *etc.*] 8°. **Ac. 944/3.(Nieuwe Reeks, Deel 1.)**

—— ॥ पितृमेधसूत्राणि ॥ The Pitṛmedhasūtras of Baudhāyana, Hiraṇyakeśin, Gautama. Edited with critical notes and index of words by Dr. W. Caland. pp. xxiv. 132, i. 1896. *See* ACADEMIES, *etc.*—Germany.—*Deutsche Morgenlaendische Gesellschaft.* Abhandlungen, *etc.* Bd. 10, No. 3. 1859, *etc.* 8°. **753. f. 18.**

—— Zur Exegese und Kritik der rituellen Sūtras, *etc.* 1897, *etc.* *See* ACADEMIES, *etc.*—Germany. —*Deutsche Morgenlaendische Gesellschaft.* Zeitschrift, *etc.* Bd. 51, *etc.* 1846, *etc.* 8°. **Ac. 8815/2.(vol. 51, etc.)**
In progress.

—— Über das rituelle Sūtra des Baudhāyana. pp. viii. 65. 1903. *See* ACADEMIES, *etc.*—Germany.—*Deutsche Morgenlaendische Gesellschaft.* Abhandlungen, *etc.* Bd. 12, No. 1. 1859, *etc.* 8°.
753. f. 20.

—— —— [Another copy.] **14039. b. 26.(3.)**

CALCUTTA.—*Sanskrit College.* *See* ACADEMIES, *etc.*—*Calcutta.*

CALIDASA. *See* KĀLIDĀSA.

CANDRAGOMIN. *See* CHANDRA GOMĪ.

CANDRAKĀNTA. *See* CHANDRAKĀNTA.

ÇĀNTIDEVA. *See* ṢĀNTIDEVA.

ÇANTIPRABHA. *See* ṢĀNTIDEVA.

ÇARAT CHANDRA. *See* ṢARACHCHANDRA.

CARUS (PAUL). The Gospel of Buddha according to old records. Told by P. Carus. pp. xiv. 275. *New York,* 1894. 8°. **4503. b. 17.**

—— —— [Another copy, with a different title-page.] pp. xiv. 275. *London,* 1894 [1895.] 8°. **4503. b. 11.**

—— —— Cheaper edition. pp. xiv. 275. *London,* 1896. 8°. **4503. b. 23.**

ÇESAÇĀRṈGADHARA. *See* ṢESHAṢĀRṄGADHARA.

CHAITANYA. *See* KAVIKARṆAPŪRA. শ্রীচৈতন্য-চরিতামৃত° [Chaitanyacharitāmṛita. A poem on the life of Chaitanya.] [1885-1892.] 8°.
14058. b. 28.

—— *See* PRASANNAKUMĀRA VIDYĀRATNA. শ্রীগৌ-রাঙ্গ-তত্ত্ব *etc.* [Gaurāṅgacharita. A biography of Chaitanya. Preceded by Gaurāṅgatattva, an account of his doctrine.] [1899.] 8°.
14127. bb. 13.

—— *See* RĀMAPRASANNA GHOSHA. গৌরচন্দ্রোদয় *etc.* [Gaurachandrodaya. A Bengali anthological work on Chaitanya and his teaching.] [1901.] 8°. **14123. ff. 5.**

—— *See* ṢIṢIRAKUMĀRA GHOSHA. Lord Gauranga; or Salvation for All, *etc.* 1897-1898. 8°.
4506. df.

CHAITANYAKṚISHṆA NĀGA VARMĀ. Criticisms on Mr. Risley's articles on Brahmans, Kayasthas & Vaidyas as published in his "Tribes and Castes of Bengal," *etc.* [In English, illustrated by citations from Sanskrit texts.] Part 1. pp. iii. 76, i. *Calcutta,* 1893. 8°. **4503. b.**

CHAKKINDĀBHISIRI, *Saddhammaddhaja.* *See* SAṄGHARAKKHITA. ဆန်းနိဿျ *etc.* [Chhandonissaya, in Burmese Hsan-neikthaya. Being the Vuttodaya with Burmese translation and commentary by Chakkindābhisiri. Followed by the Hsan-linkā, *i.e.* Chhandālaṅkāra, a Burmese poem by the latter.] [1900.] 8°.
14098. c. 74.

—— *See* SUTTAPIṬAKA.—*Dīghanikāya.* မဟာသတိပဋ္ဌာနသုတ် *etc.* [Mahāsatipaṭṭhānasutta. With Burmese commentary by Chakkinda. Followed by the Chaturārakkhadhamma, with commentary by the same, *etc.*] [1895.] 8°.
14098. ccc. 9.(2.)

—— ဒါနဖလုပ္ပတ္တိကျမ်း *etc.* [Dānaphaluppatti. Homilies on the fruits of charity as determining rebirths. In Burmese, illustrated from Pali texts.] pp. ii. iv. 200. ရန်ကုန် ၁၂၅၂ [*Rangoon*, 1890.] 8°. **14300. d. 25.(5.)**

—— ဂိဟိဝိနယကျမ်းစာ *etc.* [Gihivinayakyan-sā. A short Pali poem on the duties of the Buddhist householder. With Burmese commentary. Followed by an anonymous Burmese treatise on spiritual exercises.] pp. 40. *Rangoon*, ၁၂၃၇ [1875.] 8°.
14098. ccc. 9.(1.)

—— လောကနီတိ *etc.* [Lokanīti. A Pali ethical poem. With Burmese version.] *See* KO SAUNG TWÈ. ကိုးစောင်တွဲ [Ko saung twè.] pp. 10-24, 57-100. 1881. 8°.
14098. ccc. 11.(5.)

—— လောကနီတိ *etc.* [Lokanīti. With Burmese paraphrase.] *See* HSAY SAUNG TWÈ. ဆယ်စောင်တွဲ [Hsay saung twè.] pp. 10-24, 57-100. 1882. 8°. **14098. ccc. 11.(6.)**

—— —— *See* HSAY SAUNG TWÈ. ၁၀ စောင်တွဲ [Hsay saung twè.] pp. 54-110. [1889.] 8°.
14098. ccc. 11.(7.)

—— လောကနီတိ *etc.* [Lokanīti. With Burmese version.] *See* HKYAUK SAUNG TWÈ. ခြောက်စောင်တွဲ [Hkyauk saung twè.] pp. 15-32, 71-120. 1883. 8°. **14098. ccc. 11.(2.)**

—— —— *See* HKYAUK SAUNG TWÈ. ခြောက်စောင်တွဲ [Hkyauk saung twè.] pp. 54-110. [1890.] 8°.
14098. ccc. 11.(3.)

—— —— *See* HKYAUK SAUNG TWÈ. The Chauk Saung Dwe, *etc.* pp. 15-32, 71-120. 1895. 8°.
14098. ccc. 11.(4.)

—— (လောကနီတိ) [Lokanīti. With Burmese interpretation.] *See* TA-HSÈ-HNIT SAUNG TWÈ. တဆဲ့နှစ်စောင်တွဲ [Ta-hsè-hnit saung twè.] pp. 51-104. [1899.] 8°. **14098. ccc. 39.**

—— —— *See* TA-HSÈ-THÔN SAUNG TWÈ. တဆဲ့သုံး စောင်တွဲ [Ta-hsè-thôn saung twè.] pp. 55-113. [1900.] 8°. **14098. ccc. 40.**

—— ဝီထိစိတ္တပကာသနီကျမ်း [Vithichittappakāsanī. A tract of 160 Pali stanzas upon Buddhist psychology, with Burmese interpretation appended.] *See* ĀDICHCHAVAṂSA. ဋီကာကျော်ဂဏ္ဌိကျမ်း *etc.* [Ṭīkā-kyaw-ganṭhi-kyan, *etc.*] pp. 558-605. [1901.] 8°.
14300. d. 35.

CHAKRADHARA, *son of Vāmana.* ॥ यंत्र चिन्तामणि *etc.* [Yantrachintāmaṇi. A compendium, in 25 stanzas, of astronomical mathematics. Edited with Hindi and Sanskrit commentaries, examples, and notes by Sundaradeva Ṣarmā.] pp. 72; 1 *plate.* मथुरा १८९८ [*Muttra*, 1898.] 8°.
14053. c. 56.(4.)

CHAKRA KAVI. చిత్రప్రశ్నోత్తర రత్నావళి *etc.* [Chitrapraṣnottararatnāvali. A series of riddling stanzas. Edited with Telugu commentaries and paraphrases by K. Ṣeshāchalam Nāyuḍu.] pp. 38. ౧౮౯౯ [*Madras*, 1899.] 8°. **14072. cc. 55.(2.)**

CHAKRAPĀṆIDATTA. *See* CHARAKA. Charakasamhita. With the commentary [Āyurvedadīpikā] of Chakrapani Datta, *etc.* Pt. vi. [1894.] 8° **14043. dd. 1.**

CHAKRAPĀṆIDATTA (*continued*). Chakradatta. චක්‍රදත්ත *etc.* [A work on pathology. With Sinhalese interpretation by Talavatugoḍa Jinaratana.] Pt. i. pp. 64. *Colombo*, 1893. 8°.
14043. d. 47.

—— চক্রদত্ত *etc.* [Chakradatta. With the commentary Tattvachandrikā of Śivadāsa Sena. Edited by Devendranātha Sena Gupta and Upendranātha Sena Gupta.] pp. ii. xi. 811. কলিকাতা [*Calcutta*, 1900.] 8°. **14043. cc. 17.**

—— দ্রব্যগুণঃ *etc.* [Dravyaguṇa, or Dravyaguṇasaṅgraha. A treatise on the properties of drugs. With the commentary of Śivadāsa Sena. Edited by Jīvānanda Vidyāsāgara. Second edition.] pp. 162. কলিকাতা ১৮৯৭ [*Calcutta*, 1897.] 8°.
14043. c. 37.(2.)

CHAKRAVARTI AIYAṄGĀR, *Dharmādhikārī, of Mysore*. *See* ŚRĪKAṆṬHA KAVI, *Eḷandūr*. అభినవకాదంబరి ॥ [Abhinavakādambarī. Edited by Chakravarti Aiyaṅgār.] [1892.] 8°.
14076. c. 72.

—— *See* ŚRĪKAṆṬHA ŚĀSTRĪ, *Sāggera*. శ్రీ . . . ధాతురూపప్రకాశికా *etc.* [Dhāturūpaprakāśikā. Edited by Chakravarti Aiyaṅgār.] [1898.] 8°.
14090. c. 41.

CHALMERS (ROBERT). *See* ACADEMIES, *etc.*—London.—*Pali Text Society*. SUTTAPIṬAKA. The Majjhima-Nikāya. Edited by Robert Chalmers. Vol. II. (Vol. III.) 1896-1902. 8°. **14098. b. 25.**

—— *See* SUTTAPIṬAKA. — *Khuddakanikāya*. [*Jātaka*.] The Jātaka . . . Vol. i., translated by Robert Chalmers. 1895, *etc.* 8°.
14098. dd. 8.(vol. 1.)

—— *See* SUTTAPIṬAKA.—*Majjhimanikāya*. The Nativity of the Buddha. By Robert Chalmers. 1895. 8°. [*Journal of the Royal Asiatic Society.*]
Ac. 8820/3 and 2098. a, b.

—— *See* SUTTAPIṬAKA.—*Majjhimanikāya*. The Madhura Sutta . . . [With translation.] By Robert Chalmers. 1894. 8°. [*Journal of the Royal Asiatic Society.*] **Ac. 8820/3 and 2098. a, b.**

—— The King of Siam's edition of the Pāli Tipiṭaka, *etc.* pp. 10. [*London*,] 1898. 8°.
14098. cc. 40.
From the Journal of the Royal Asiatic Society for Jan. 1898.

CHĀMANLĀL SĀKALCHAND MĀRPHATĪYĀ. *See* RATNAŚEKHARA SŪRI. શ્રી શ્રાદ્ધવિધિ° [Śrāddhavidhiprakaraṇa. With Gujarati translation of the Kaumudī by the editor, Chāmanlāl.] [1899.] 8°. **14100. d. 7.**

CHAMANRĀI ŚIVAŚAṄKARA, *Vaishṇava*. ઔષધિકોષ *etc.* [Aushadhikoṣa. A dictionary of the pharmacopœia. Part I, containing the Sanskrit names of the medicinal plants of India, with equivalents in Marathi, Gujarati, *etc.*] અમદાવાદ ૧૮૯૯ [*Ahmadabad*, 1899.] 4°.
14043. dd. 5.
In progress?

CHĀṆAKYA. [*Shorter Recension.*] ଚାଣକ୍ୟଶ୍ଳୋକ *etc.* [Chāṇakyaśloka. With an Oriya metrical version by Sudarśana Nanda. Third edition.] pp. 22. *Cuttack*, 1901. 12°. **14076. b. 26.(4.)**

—— —— Morals of Cháṇakya. Rendered into English verse by Rámchandra Ghosh Vidyávinoda. pp. 12. *Calcutta*, 1891. 12°.
14072. b. 10.(3.)

—— —— चाणक्यनीतिसारसंग्रहः [Chāṇakyanītisārasaṅgraha. Word-for-word grammatical analyses of Nītisārasaṅgraha. With English and Hindi translations.] *See* ACADEMIES, *etc.*—Allahabad. — *University of Allahabad*. संस्कृत-शिक्षा-विवृतिः . . . Sanskrit-Siksha-Vivriti, *etc.* pp. 270-327. 1899. 12°. **14085. b. 39.(2.)**

—— [*Longer Recension.*] ॥ चाणक्यनीतिदर्पणम् *etc.* [Chāṇakyanītidarpaṇa. With a Hindi translation.] pp. 98. *Lucknow*, 1897. 8°.
14070. dd. 14.

CHANDA, Ū, *Gaiṅ-ôk of Myobyingyi*. သမ္မောဟဆေဒနီကျမ်း *etc.* [Sammohachhedanī. An ethical discourse, in Burmese, illustrated from Pali texts.] pp. ii. 151, iv. မန္တလေး [*Mandalay*,] 1893. 8°. **14300. d. 25.(7.)**

CHAṆḌEŚVARA ŚŪLAPĀṆI. श्रीप्रत्यंगिरास्तोत्रप्रारम्भः [Pratyaṅgirāstotra. A mystic hymn to the Tantric goddess Pratyaṅgirā.] pp. 14. *See* SUDARŚANASAṂHITĀ. हनुमत्कवच *etc.* [Hanumatkavacha, *etc.*] [1897.] 8°. **14033. aa. 5.(1.)**

CHAṆḌEŚVARA ṬHAKKURA. Vivada-ratnakara of Chandesvara Thakkura. Portion dealing with

the law of partition and inheritance [and entitled Dāyabhāga. The Sanskrit text edited and] translated by Golápchandra Sarkár, Sástri, . . . and Digamvar Chattopádhyáya. pp. ii. ii. liii. ii. viii. 94, 61, xv. *Calcutta*, 1899. 8°.
14039. c. 18.

CHAṆḌĪCHARAṆA SMṚITIBHŪSHAṆA. *See* RAGHUNANDANA BHAṬṬĀCHĀRYA. মলমাসতত্ত্বম্ *etc.* [Malamāsatattva. With commentaries. Edited by Chaṇḍīcharaṇa.] [1900.] 8°. **14033. bbb. 5.**

—— —— তিথিতত্ত্বম্ *etc.* [Tithitattva. With commentary. Edited with annotations by Chaṇḍīcharaṇa.] [1901.] 8°. **14033. bb. 45.(3.)**

—— —— উদ্বাহতত্ত্বম্ *etc.* [Udvāhatattva. With commentary, *etc.* Edited by Chaṇḍīcharaṇa.] [1902.] 8°. **14033. bb. 45.(4.)**

—— *See* ŚRĪNIVĀSA ĀCHĀRYA. শুদ্ধিদীপিকা *etc.* [Śuddhidīpikā. With commentary. Edited with Bengali translation of the text by Chaṇḍīcharaṇa.] [1901.] 8°. **14053. ccc. 33.**

CHANDIK (B. N.). *See* VIŚVEŚVARANĀTHA CHAṆḌIKA.

CHANDIMĀ, *Thāvara*, called KYĀ-KOY. ဆက္ကပဉ္စာကျမ်းနှင့် ။ ယထာဘူတကမ္မဋ္ဌာန်း *etc.* [Chhakkapañhā-kyan. Six Responses, in Burmese. Followed by Jāgara's Ovādakathā, a Burmese homily; Puggalavisesāchariyavandanā, Pali stanzas upon Jāgara, with Burmese version; Chandimā's Yathābhūtakammaṭṭhān, a Burmese tract on devotional practices, and Hpo Ketu's Lakkhaṇā-ye-thôn-pā, a like work; Uyyojanīdīpaṇī, a Pali poem with Burmese version; Kāmādinavakathā, a passage from the Lalitavistara with Burmese commentary by Jāgara; an Ovādakathā, by the same; Dhammapānashubbway, philosophical Pali verses with Burmese commentary, by the same, *etc.*] pp. 385. ပန္တလေး [*Mandalay*,] 1898. 8°.
14300. d. 19.(9.)

CHANDIMĀ, *Ū, of Maṅgala-hbôn-kyaw Kyaung, Rangoon.* နဝကမ္မဝိနိစ္ဆယကျမ်း ။ ဗျာကရဏကျမ်း *etc.* [Navakammavinichchhaya-kyan. A treatise on the circumstances and influences of action. Followed by Vyākaraṇa-kyan, responses to 4 questions on the merit of certain religious actions. In Burmese, illustrated from Pali texts.] pp. 138. ရန်ကုန် ၁၂၆၁ [*Rangoon*, 1899.] 8°. **14300. d. 10.(3.)**

CHANDORKAR (D. T.). *See* DINAKARA TRYAMBAKA CHANDORKAR.

CHANDRA, *Kavi, of Mithila.* श्रीलक्ष्मीश्वरविलास: *etc.* [Lakshmīśvaravilāsa. A collection of Sanskrit and Maithili poems, religious and secular, *etc.* Compiled by Chandra Kavi.] Pt. i. pp. 18. दरभङ्गा १८७० [*Darbhangah*, 1888.] 8°.
14028. d. 56.(1.)

CHANDRABHŪSHAṆA CHATURVEDA. जीवितवृत्तान्त: *etc.* [Jīvitavṛittānta. A metrical biography of Pandit Bechanrām Tripāṭhī.] pp. 14. काशी १९४६ [*Benares*, 1890.] 8°. **14058. b. 26.**

CHANDRA DEVA, *disciple of Bāpū Deva.* *See* BHĀSKARA ĀCHĀRYA. सिद्धान्तशिरोमणि: . . . The Siddhánta-Śiromaṇi . . . Formerly edited by . . . Bápú Deva Śástri . . . revised . . . by Pandita Chandra Deva. 1891. 8°. **14053. cc. 65.**

CHANDRA GOMĪ. *See* LIEBICH (B.). Das Cāndra-vyākaraṇa. [A study of the various recensions,] *etc.* 1895. 8°. [*Nachrichten von der Georg-Augusts Universitaet zu Goettingen.*]
2097. a., P.P. 4672. a.

—— Cāndra-vyākaraṇa. Die Grammatik des Candragomin. Sūtra, Uṇādi, Dhātupāṭha. Herausgegeben von Bruno Liebich. pp. x. 47, 235. 1902. *See* ACADEMIES, *etc.*—Germany.—*Deutsche Morgenlaendische Gesellschaft.* Abhandlungen, *etc.* Bd. 11, No. 4. 1859, *etc.* 8°.
753. f. 19.

CHANDRAJA SIṂHA, *disciple of Gurudatta Siṃha.* *See* ANNAM BHAṬṬA. तर्कसंग्रहप्रारम्भ: Taraksangrah [*sic*]. [With the commentary of Chandraja Siṃha.] 1889. 8°. **14048. dd. 12.**

CHANDRAKĀNTA NYĀYĀLAṄKĀRA. *See* SARVAVARMĀ. কলাপ-ব্যাকরণম্ *etc.* [Kalāpavyākaraṇa. Section i., with notes and a Bengali translation by Chandrakānta. Third edition.] [1889.] 8°.
14090. c. 36.

—— —— [Fourth edition.] [1895.] 12°.
14090. b. 45.(3.)

CHANDRAKĀNTA TARKĀLAṄKĀRA BHAṬṬĀCHĀRYA, *Mahāmahopādhyāya.* See BHĀSKARA MIŚRA BHAṬṬA. त्रिकाण्डमण्डनम् । Trikāṇḍa-maṇḍanam . . . With . . . commentary entitled Vivaraṇa. Edited by . . . Candrakānta Tarkālaṇkāra. 1898, *etc.* 8°. [*Bibliotheca Indica.*]
14002. a. (vol. 142.)

—— *See* KHAṆḌADEVA. भाट्टदीपिका । Bhāṭṭa Dīpikā . . . Edited by . . . Candra Kānta Tarkālaṇkāra. 1899, *etc.* 8°. [*Bibliotheca Indica.*]
14002. a. (vol. 141.)

—— अलङ्कारसूत्रम् . . . Alankárasutram. Or The Rules of Rhetoric, *etc.* pp. vi. 285. *Calcutta*, 1899. 8°. **14053. ccc. 30.**

—— Chandrabansa. [A poem in 24 *sargas* on the Lunar Dynasty of India.] . . . चन्द्रवंशम् *etc.* pp. 334. *Calcutta*, 1892. 8°. **14072. cc. 59.**

—— कातन्त्रच्छन्दःप्रक्रिया . . . Kātantra Cchandah Prakriyā, *etc.* [A treatise on Vedic grammar, in the form of *sūtras* and a commentary, according to the Kātantra school of grammar.] pp. ii. iii. 247. *Calcutta*, 1896. 8°. **14090. bb. 10.**

—— उद्वाहचन्द्रालोकः . . . Udvāha-candrālokah. A treatise on the marriage rites of the Hindus. According to the Dharmahastras [*sic*], *etc.* pp. v. 6, 182. *Sherpur, Calcutta* [printed], 1897. 8°. **14028. d. 71.**

CHANDRAKĪRTI, *Āchārya.* See NĀGĀRJUNA. माध्यमिकावृत्ति । Mádhyamiká Vṛitti by Áchárya Chandra Kirtti, *etc.* 1894-1897. 8°. [*Buddhist Texts.*]
14004. c. (vol. 1, no. 1.)

—— *See* NĀGĀRJUNA. Caturāryasatyaparikṣā. Extraits du xxive chapitre de la Madhyamakavṛitti, *etc.* 1896. 4°. [*Mélanges Harlez.*]
12902. h. 22.

CHANDRAKĪRTI SŪRI, *of the Nagpur Tapāgachchha.* See SĀRASVATASŪTRA. सारस्वतं व्याकरणम् *etc.* (Saraswata Vyakaranam . . . [comprising the Sārasvatasūtra with the exposition] by Anubhuti Swarupacharya. With the commentary of Chandrakirti Suri, *etc.*) Vol. ii. [1893.] 8°.
14093. b. 43.

CHANDRAKIṢORA, *Nyāyaratna.* संस्कृतसोपान [Saṃskṛitasopāna. A first primer of Sanskrit, with passages of Hindi for translation into Sanskrit,] by Pandit Chandra Kishore, Nyayaratan. pp. 19. *Lahore*, 1898. 8°. **14085. c. 47.**

Forms no. 1 *of the* Sanskrit Series *of the 'Dayanand Anglo-Vedic College.'*

CHANDRAKUMĀRA KAVIBHŪSHAṆA. *See* GOVINDADĀSA, *Kavirāja.* ভৈষজ্য-রত্নাবলী *etc.* [Bhaishajyaratnāvalī. With Bengali translation by Chandrakumāra.] [1893.] 8°. **14043. e. 31.**

CHANDRAMAULI ṢARMĀ, *of Faizabad.* See SĀRASVATASŪTRA. सिद्धान्तचन्द्रिकोत्तरार्द्धः *etc.* [Sārasvatasūtra. With the Siddhāntachandrikā. Part II. With Hindi commentary by Chandramauli, based on the Subodhinī of Sadānanda.] [1900.] 4°.
14092. c. 20.

CHANDRAMOHANA GHOSHA. *See* PIṄGALA ĀCHĀRYA. Prákrita-paiṅgalam. With . . . commentaries . . . Edited . . . by Chandra Mohana Ghosha. 1902. 8°. [*Bibliotheca Indica.*]
14002. a. (vol. 148.)

CHANDRAMOHANA TARKARATNA BHAṬṬĀCHĀRYA. *See* AMARASIṂHA. অমরকোষাভিধানম্ *etc.* [Amarakoṣa. With commentary. Edited by Chandramohana.] [1901.] 8°.
14090. bb. 17.

CHANDRAṢEKHARA BARUWĀ. *See* PĀÑCHARĀTRA. শ্রীরাধিকা সহস্র নাম *etc.* [Rādhikāsahasranāma. Edited by Chandraṣekhara.] [1879.] 12°. **14028. c. 76.(1.)**

CHANDRAṢEKHARA ṢĀSTRĪ, *Sādhupalli, son of Veṅkaṭarāya.* See AMARU. శృంగారామరుకకావ్యము *etc.* [Sṛiṅgārāmarukakāvya, *i.e.* Amaruṣataka. With the commentary of Vema Bhūpāla and a Telugu commentary and Telugu metrical version by Chandraṣekhara.] 1898. 8°. **14076. c. 69.**

CHANDRAṢEKHARA SIṂHA, *Sāmanta.* Siddhánta-darpaṇa. A treatise on astronomy by Mahámahopádhyáya Sámanta Śrí Chandraśekhara Siṃha. Edited with an introduction by Jogeś Chandra Ráy. (सिद्धान्तदर्पणः) pp. 99, 344. *Calcutta*, 1899. 8°. **14053. ccc. 28.**

CHANDRASIṂHA SŪRI. *See* HARIBHADRA SŪRI. ॥ श्री षट् दर्शन समुचय *etc.* [Shaḍdarṣanasamuchchaya. With Gujarati prose version by Chandrasiṃha.] [1892.] 16°. **14048. a. 17.**

CHAṄGADĀSA. The Sambandhopadesa. Commonly called Changakarikas. [A tract in 63 stanzas, with commentary by the author, forming a supplement to the Kātantra.] . . . Edited by Pandit S. P. S. Jagannadhaswamy Ayyavaralugaru. (संबंधोपदेश:) pp. ii. 77. *Vizagapatam,* 1896. 12°. **14092. a. 10.(2.)**

The author was a Buddhist Kāyastha, presumably of Orissa, and sometimes styled Śriṅgadāsa.

CHARAKA. Charaka-samhita. With the commentary [Āyurvedadīpikā] of Chakrapani Datta. Edited by Kaviraj Avinasha Chandra Kaviratna . . . . चरकसंहिता *etc.* Pt. vi. कलिकाता [*Calcutta,* 1894.] 8°. **14043. dd. 1.**

—— सार्थ श्रीचरक संहिता. Shree Charaka Samhita. With translation & copious notes in Marathi. A quarterly journal. [Edited by Śaṅkara Dājī Śāstrī Pade.] Pts. i.-vi. मुंबई १८९७-१८९८ [*Bombay,* 1897-1898.] 8°. **14043. cc. 8.**

—— चरकसंहिता *etc.* [Charakasaṃhitā. Edited with Hindi paraphrase by Krishṇalāla.] 2 vols. मथुरा १८९८ [*Muttra,* 1898.] 8°. **14043. dd. 4.**

—— चरकसंहिता *etc.* [Charakasaṃhitā. With Hindi translation by Mihirachandra Miṣra.] pp. xxxv. 1480; 24 *plates.* मुम्बय्यां १८९८ [*Bombay,* 1898.] 8°. **14043. dd. 3.**

—— चरकसंहिता . . . सूत्रस्थान *etc.* (आर्षेयुर्वेदी चरकसंहिताका निदानस्थान *etc.*) [Charakasaṃhitā. With a Hindi version, styled Charakachandrodaya, by Dattarāma Chaube.] 8 pts. मथुरा मुंबई १९५७ [*Muttra, Bombay* printed, 1900.] 8°. **14043. dd. 6.**

—— Charaka-samhita. Translated into English . . . Edited and published by Avinash Chandra Kaviratna. *Calcutta,* 1902, *etc.* 8°. **14043. e. 26.**

In progress.

CHARAṆAVYŪHA. श्री . . . चरणव्यूहपरिशिष्टसूत्रम् *etc.* [Charaṇavyūha. With the commentary of Mahīdhara or Mahidāsa.] pp. 55. काश्याम् १९५८ [*Benares,* 1902.] 8°. **14093. d. 16.(2.)**

Apparently a new issue of the text which was appended to the edition of Kātyāyana's Prātiṣākhya in the Benares Sanskrit Series, 1883-8.

CHĀRITRAVARDHANA, *of the Kharatara-gachchha. See* KĀLIDĀSA.—*Raghuvaṃṣa.* The Raghuvanśa . . . with full extracts . . . from the commentaries of . . . Châritravardhana, *etc.* 1897. 8°. **14072. c. 53.**

CHARIYĀPIṬAKA. *See* SUTTAPIṬAKA.—*Khuddakanikāya.*

CHĀRUCHANDRA MUKHOPĀDHYĀYA. *See* PURĀṆAS.—*Mārkaṇḍeyapurāṇa.* The Márkandeya Puránam. Translated . . . by Charu Chandra Mukerjea. Pts. 1-3. 1893-1894. 8°. **14016. c. 44.**

CHATTERJEE (MOHINI M.). *See* MOHINĪMOHANA CHAṬṬOPĀDHYĀYA.

CHATTOPÁDHYÁYA (DIGAMVAR). *See* DIGAMBARA CHAṬṬOPĀDHYĀYA.

CHĀṬUDHĀRĀ. చాటుధారాచమత్కారసార ప్రారంభః [Chāṭudhārāchamatkārasāra. A series of miscellaneous epigrammatic stanzas, ascribed to various noted poets. With a commentary.] 1895-1897. *See* PERIODICAL PUBLICATIONS.—*Vizagapatam.* సకలవిద్యాభివర్ధని *etc.* [Sakalavidyābhivardhanī.] Vol. iii., pt. i.—vol. iv., pt. i. 1892-1897. 12° & 8°. **14174. g. 38.**

Not completed.

CHATURA KALLINĀTHA. *See* KALLINĀTHA, *Chatura.*

CHATURĀRAKKHADHAMMA. စတုရာရက္ခတရား လေးပါး [Chaturārakkhadhamma. A series of Pali stanzas on the observance of the 4 principles of *buddhānussati, mettā.°, asubhā.°,* and *maraṇā°.* With commentary and Burmese translation by Chakkindābhisiri.] *See* SUTTAPIṬAKA.—*Dīghanikāya.* မဟာသတိပဋ္ဌာန်သုတ် *etc.* [Mahāsatipaṭṭhānasutta, *etc.*] pp. 125-147. [1895.] 8°. **14098. ccc. 9.(2.)**

CHATURTHĪLĀLA, *Vaidya, son of Kastūrīchandra, of Ratnagarh. See* ŚRĀDDHA. पार्वणं श्राद्धम् *etc.* [Apātraka-pārvaṇa-ṣrāddha. Edited with a commentary styled Jyeshṭhānandī by Chaturthīlāla.] [1895.] 12°. **14010. b. 15.**

—— अथ अन्त्येष्टि श्राद्ध प्रकाश: *etc.* [Antyeshṭiṣrāddhaprakāṣa. A treatise on the ritual of funerals and *ṣrāddhas,* according to the usage of Gauḍa and Maithila Brahmans. With Hindi translation by the author. Second edition.] ff. 102, i. मुंबई [*Bombay*, 1898.] *obl.* 8°. **14028. dd. 2.(1.)**

—— नित्यकर्मप्रयोगमाला *etc.* [Nityakarmaprayogamālā. A compendium of the encyclical ritual according to the Mādhyandina school. Second edition.] pp. 192, *lith.* मुंबई १९५४ [*Bombay*, 1898.] 12°. **14028. b. 91.**

—— ॥ अथ शान्तिप्रकाशप्रारम्भः ॥ [Ṣāntiprakāṣa, or Chaturthilālabhāskara. A compendium of lustratory rites, in 3 *prakaraṇas*.] ff. ii. 107, iii. मंबई [*Bombay*, 1900.] *obl.* 4°. **14033. d. 24.**

The author enumerates as his chief sources the Pāraskarasūtra, Hariharabhāshya, Ṣāntiratna, Ṣāntisāra, Viṣrakarmaprakāṣa, Vasishṭhasaṃhitā. Kaṣyapas.°, Nāradas.°, Matsyapurāṇa, Dānachandrikā, Ṣāntimayūkha, and Saṃskārabhāskara.

CHAUDHURĪ (K.). अनुवादिनी [Anuvādinī] or Helps to Translation from English to Sanskrit . . . Revised and corrected by . . . Bidhu Bhushan Goswami. pp. xii. 119. *Calcutta*, 1895. 12°. **14085. b. 41.(1.)**

CHAUK SAUNG DWE. *See* HKYAUK SAUNG TWÈ.

CHAUTH MAL. *See* CHATURTHĪLĀLA.

CHEÑCHALA RĀU, *Palle.* *See* BĀDARĀYAṆA. श्रीमद्ब्रह्मसूत्राणि *etc.* [Brahmasūtra. With the *bhāshya* of Ānandatīrtha, *etc.* Preceded by an introduction by P. Chenchala Rāu, *etc.*] [1900.] 8°. **14048. cc. 30.**

—— *See* NĀRĀYAṆA BHAṬṬA, *son of Rāmeṣvara.* The Vivahaprayoga . . . with translation by P. Chentsal Ráo. 1891. 8°. **14033. b. 58.**

CHENTSAL RAO. *See* CHEÑCHALA RĀU.

CHERUÑÑAṬṬI DEVĪ, *Ghoshapura-Mahārājñī.* *See* NĪLAKAṆṬHA ṢARMĀ, *Punnacheri-nambi.* ॥ श्रीः . . . घोषपुरमहाराज्ञी-चरित्रम् *etc.* [Ghoshapuramahārājñīcharitra. A biography of Princess Cheruññaṭṭi Devī. Followed by verses upon her death.] [1902.] 8°. **14072. d. 45.(3.)**

CHHAJJŪ SINGH. *See* ĀRYA SAMĀJ. आर्य्य सन्ध्या पद्धति *etc.* [Āryasandhyāpaddhati. Daily prayers, with Hindi introductions, rules, translations, *etc.*, by Rājārāma and Chhajjū Singh.] [1897.] 12°. **14028. b. 96.(1.)**

CHHAJJŪ SINGH (*continued*). "What is the Arya Samaj ?" or, An [English] Exposition of the Principles of the Arya Samaj. Profusely illustrated with quotations [in Sanskrit and English] from the Vedas and other Shâstras. By Chhajju Singh. pp. 84. *Lahore*, [1890.] 12°. **14028. c. 61.**

CHHAVILĀLA SŪRI. Kushalavodaya Nataka. A Sanskrit drama [in 8 acts, on the fortunes of Rāma's sons,] with explanatory notes . . . by Chhubi Lal Soori. (कुशलवोदयं नाम नाटकम् ।) pp. i. 92. *Bombay*, 1897. 8°. **14079. b. 34.(2.)**

—— सुन्दरचरितं नाम नाटकम् *etc.* [Sundaracharita. A drama in seven acts, founded on the Sundarakāṇḍa of the Rāmāyaṇa.] pp. ii. 96. मुम्बापुर्यां १८१६ [*Bombay*, 1894.] 8°. **14079. b. 29.(2.)**

CHHOṬĀLĀL NARBHERĀM BHAṬṬA. *See* VĀGBHAṬA, *son of Siṃhagupta.* अष्टांगहृदय *etc.* [Ashṭāṅgahṛidaya. The Uttarasthāna, with Gujarati translation by Chhoṭālāl.] [1901.] 8°. **14043. cc. 22.**

CHHUBI LAL SOORI. *See* CHHAVILĀLA SŪRI.

CHIDGHANĀNANDA, *Paramahaṃsa Parivrājaka.* *See* ṢAÑKARA ĀCHĀRYA.—*Doubtful and Supposititious Works.* ॥ श्री हरिमीडे स्तोत्रम् *etc.* [Harim-īḍe-stuti. With a Gujarati commentary by Chidghanānanda, entitled Amṛitadhārā.] [1897.] 12°. **14033. a. 32.**

CHĪMANLĀL SĀKALCHAND MĀRPHATĪYĀ. *See* VIJAYALAKSHMĪ SŪRI. उपदेशप्रासाद *etc.* [Upadeṣaprāsāda. Translated into Gujarati. Edited by Chīmanlāl Mārphatīyā.] [1902, *etc.*] 8°. **14100. d. 10.**

CHINTĀMAṆI VINĀYAKA VAIDYA. *See* VĀLMĪKI.—Rāmāyaṇa.—*Abridgments and Selections.* संक्षिप्तवाल्मीकिरामायणम् । [Saṇkshipta-vālmīki-rāmāyaṇa. An abridgment of the Rāmāyaṇa, with glosses, by Chintāmaṇi Vaidya.] [1902.] 8°. **14065. c. 55.**

CHITSUKHA MUNI. *See* ĀNANDABODHA PARAMAHAṂSA. न्यायमकरन्दः . . . Nyâya Makaranda . . . with a commentary by Chitsukh Muni, *etc.* 1901, *etc.* 8°. **14004. a. 11.**

CHONKAR (R. M.). *See* RĀMAKṚISHṆA MĀDHAVARĀU CHONKAR.

CHOW HING-SZE. 梵語千字文 [Bongo Senjimon. The Sanskrit equivalents of words and phrases in Chow Hing-sze's Thousand-Character Classic. Edited with Japanese transliteration by Gishō.] [1773.] 8°. **16014. d. 2.**

CHOWKHAMBÂ SANSKRIT SERIES. Chowkhambâ Sanskrit Series. A collection of rare & extraordinary Sanskrit works. Under the superintendence of [the] Kashi Pandit Samaj. *Benares,* 1898, *etc.* 8°. **14004. a.**

In progress. Works published in this series are to be found catalogued under the headings:—

No. 1, 2. *Gopinātha Dikshita.*
,, 3-10, 13, 14. *Bhaṭṭoji Dikshita.*
,, 14. *Jayakrishṇa, son of Raghunātha.*
,, 11, 12, 15-21, 24. *Jaimini.—Mimāṃsāsūtra.*
,, 22, 26. *Lokāchārya Piḷḷai.*
,, 23. *Brahmadeva.*
,, 25, 27. *Visvesvara Bhaṭṭa.*
,, 28, 29. *Pārthasārathi Misra.*
,, 30, 31, 34, 35, 37, 40. *Bādarāyaṇa.*
No. 32, 33. *Hemachandra.*
,, 36. *Yāmuna Achārya.*
,, 38. *Anandabodha Paramahamsa.*
,, 39, 41, 44, 48, 54. *Giridhara Bhaṭṭāchārya.*
,, 42, 43. *Appaya Dikshita.*
,, 45, 46, 47, 49, 50, 52, 53, 55-57. *Jaimini.—Mīmāṃsāsūtra.*
,, 51. *Utpala Devāchārya.*
,, 58. *Ṣankara Bhaṭṭa.*

CHŪLANIDDESA. *See* SUTTAPIṬAKA.

CHULLAVAGGA. *See* VINAYAPIṬAKA.

CHŪNĪLĀL BOHRĀ, *of Bhaunagar.* *See* ṢAṄKARA ĀCHĀRYA.—*Philosophical Poems, etc.* Atma Bodha . . . [Translated] by Chunilal C. Bohra. 1901. 8°. [*The Brahmavâdin.*] **14048. g. 1.(vol. 6.)**

—— *See* ṢAṄKARA ĀCHĀRYA.—*Philosophical Poems, etc.* Vakya Vritti . . . [Translated] by Chunilal C. Bohra. 1901. 8°. [*The Brahmavâdin.*] **14048. g. 1.(vol. 6.)**

ÇIVADITYUS. *See* ṢIVĀDITYA MIṢRA.

COLEBROOKE (HENRY THOMAS). *See* ĪṢVARA KRISHṆA. Sankhya-karika. [In the English version of H. T. Colebrooke.] 1897. 12°. [*Darshana.*] **14048. a. 23.**

COLOMBO.—*Colombo Museum.* Catalogue of the Colombo Museum Library. Part i. Pali, Sinhalese, and Sanscrit Manuscripts. pp. 18. *Colombo,* 1892. 8°. **011901. ee.**

—— Catalogue of the Colombo Museum Library. List of Páli, Siŋhalese, and Sanscrit Manuscripts, *etc.* [Compiled by S. Guṇavardhana from the English catalogue.] pp. 5. 1894. 8°. **14096. c. 13.**

COLOMBO.—*Colombo Museum* (*continued*). Catalogue of Páli, Siŋhalese, and Sanskrit Manuscripts in the Colombo Museum Library. [Compiled by H. M. Guṇasekhara.] pp. xiv. 47. *Colombo,* 1901. 8°. **14098. ccc. 37.**

COOKE (JOSIAH PARSONS). *See* SUTTAPIṬAKA.—*Khuddakanikāya.* [*Dhammapada.*] Dhammapada . . . [A translation founded upon that of Max Müller.] . . . Together with . . . extracts . . . reflections and observations, spiritual and philosophical, by J. P. C(ooke). [1890.] 8°. **4503. bb. 23.(4.)**

COWELL (EDWARD BYLES). *See* AṢVAGHOSHA. The Buddha-*k*arita . . . Edited . . . by E. B. Cowell. 1893. 4°. [*Anecdota Oxoniensia.*] **12204. f. 8.(vol. 1, pt. 7.)**

—— *See* AṢVAGHOSHA. The Buddha-*k*arita . . . Translated . . . by E. B. Cowell. 1894. 8°. [*Sacred Books of the East.*] **2003. b. (vol. 49.)**

—— *See* BĀṆA. The Harṣa-carita . . . Translated by E. B. Cowell, *etc.* 1897. 8°. [*Oriental Translation Fund.*] **14003. bb. (ser. 2, vol. 8.)**

—— *See* SUTTAPIṬAKA.—*Khuddakanikāya.* [*Jātaka.*] The Jātaka . . . Translated . . . under the editorship of Professor E. B. Cowell, *etc.* 1895, *etc.* 8°. **14098. dd. 8.**

ÇRĪVARA. *See* ṢRĪVARA.

DADHIBHŪSHAṆA KAVIRATNA BHAṬṬĀCHĀRYA. टाकी-रायचतुर्धुरीण-वंशम् *etc.* [Ṭākī-Rāya-Chaturdhurīṇa-vaṃṣa. A poem in 9 *sargas*, giving an account of the Rāya-Chaturdhurīṇa or Rāi-Chaudhurī family of Kāyasthas in Taki. Accompanied by a Bengali prose translation, and followed by other short genealogical poems.] pp. viii. 85, 18. कलिकाता १८१८ [*Calcutta,* 1896.] 8°. **14076. c. 66.**

DĀHAVIDHI. अथ॥ ऋग्वेदस्य दाहविधिः॥ षट्पिंडः (संक्षिप्त दाहविधिः॥) [Ṛigvedasya Dāhavidhi. The ritual for burning the dead, according to the Ṛigveda liturgies. With Gujarati notes, rubrics, *etc.* Followed by a Saṅkshipta-dāhavidhi, or abbreviated ritual.] pp. iv. ii. 102, 19. मोहमयी १८९९ [*Bombay,* 1899.] *obl.* 12°. **14033. a. 42.**

DĀHAVIDHI (*continued*). **अथ ॥ सामवेदस्य दाहविधिः ॥ षट्पिंडः (संक्षिप्त दाहविधिः ॥)** [Sāmavedasya Dāhavidhi. The ritual for burning the dead, according to the Sāmaveda. With Gujarati notes, rubrics, *etc.* Followed by a Saṅkshipta-dāhavidhi.] pp. iv. 104, 22. **मोहमय्यां** १८९८ [*Bombay*, 1898.] *obl.* 12°. **14033. a. 43.**

—— **अथ ॥ यजुर्वेदस्य दाहविधिः ॥ षट्पिंडः (संक्षिप्त दाहविधिः ॥)** [Yajurvedasya Dāhavidhi. The ritual for burning the dead, according to the Yajurveda. With Gujarati notes, rubrics, *etc.* Followed by a Saṅkshipta-dāhavidhi.] pp. iv. 107, 22. **मोहमय्यां** १८९८ [*Bombay*, 1898.] *obl.* 12°. **14033. a. 44.**

DAHLMANN (JOSEPH). Das Mahābhārata als Epos und Rechtsbuch. Ein Problem aus Altindiens Cultur- und Literaturgeschichte, *etc.* pp. xx. 304. *Berlin*, 1895. 8°. **011824. k. 36.**

—— Nirvāṇa. Eine Studie zur Vorgeschichte des Buddhismus, *etc.* pp. xii. 197. *Berlin*, 1896. 8°. **4505. eee. 4.**

—— Buddha. Ein Culturbild des Ostens, *etc.* pp. ix. 223. *Berlin*, 1898. 8°. **4505. ccc. 6.**

—— Genesis des Mahābhārata. pp. xxxiv. 290. 1899. *See* below. Mahābhārata-Studien, *etc.* Vol. I. 1899, *etc.* 8°. **011852. k.**

—— Mahābhārata-Studien. Abhandlungen zur altindischen Literatur und Culturkunde, *etc.* *Berlin*, 1899, *etc.* 8°. **011852. k.**

In progress.

DĀHYĀBHĀI FATH-CHAND and MOTĪLĀL MAHĀSUKHBHĀI. **शोभनस्तवनावली** *etc.* [Ṣobhanastavanāvalī. Jain hymns in Sanskrit and Gujarati, the former being by Munisundara Sūri, Gaṇādhīṣa, Ṣobhana, Jinaprabha Sūri, Bappa Bhaṭṭi Sūri, and others.] pp. 112. અમદાવાદ ૧૮૯૭ [*Ahmadabad*, 1897.] 12°. **14100. a. 17.**

DAIVAJÑAMUKHAMAṆḌANA. දෛවඥමුඛමණ්ඩනය . . . නක්ෂත්‍ර නිඝණ්ටුව *etc.* [Daivajñamukhamaṇḍana. 162 stanzas on astrological divination. Followed by Kendra-liyana-kramaya, a Sinhalese astrological tract.] pp. 37. [*Colombo*,] 1895. 8°. **14053. ccc. 2.**

DĀJĪ NĀGEṢA DHARMĀDHIKĀRĪ. *See* ṢAṄKARA ĀCHĀRYA.—*Doubtful and Supposititious Works.* **मठाम्नायः** *etc.* [Maṭhāmnāya. Edited with a preface in Marathi by Dājī.] [1892.] 16°. **14048. a. 9.(3.)**

DAKSHIṆĀMŪRTI ṢĀSTRĪ, *of Bangalore.* *See* SĀYAṆA ĀCHĀRYA.—*Works on Philosophy, etc.* ಶಂಕರವಿಜಯವು *etc.* [Ṣaṅkaravijaya. Edited with a Canarese translation and commentary entitled Vāgvṛitti by Dakshiṇāmūrti Ṣāstrī.] [1898.] 8°. **14070. dd. 15.**

—— ವೈದಿಕಾರ್ಚನಚಂದ್ರಿಕೆ *etc.* [Vaidikārchanachandrikā. An *apologia* of the worship of Raṅganātha at Seringapatam.] Pt. i. pp. 80. ಬೆಂಗಳೂರು ೧೮೯೮ [*Bangalore*, 1898.] 8°. **14028. d. 60.**

DALAPATI RĀYA, *Vidyārthī.* The Sacred Books of India. No. I. The Upanishads. Vol. First. An introduction to their study, compiled and edited by Dalpat Rai, *etc.* pp. ii. 118. *Lahore*, 1897. 12°. **14010. b. 18.**

ḌALLAṆA MIṢRA. *See* SUṢRUTA. সুশ্রুত-সংহিতা *etc.* [Suṣrutasaṃhitā. With the commentary Nibandha of Ḍallaṇa.] [1898.] 8°. **14043. dd. 8.**

—— **निबन्धसंग्रहाख्या सुश्रुतसंहिताया व्याख्या** *etc.* (Nibandhasangraha. A commentary on the Sushruta-sanhita by Dallana Mishra. Edited . . . by Pandit Jibananda Vidyasagara . . . Third edition.) pp. 1377. *Calcutta*, 1891. 8°. **14043. d. 48.**

English title taken from wrapper.

DALPAT RAI. *See* DALAPATI RĀYA.

ḌALVAṆA ĀCHĀRYA. *See* ḌALLAṆA MIṢRA.

DĀMODARA, *son of Gaṅgādhara.* **॥ यन्त्रचिंतामणिः** *etc.* [Yantrachintāmaṇi. A treatise on the art of drawing magical figures. With a Hindi translation by Kanhaiyālāl Ṣarmā of Moradabad.] pp. 103. **मुरादाबाद** [*Moradabad*], *Cawnpore* [printed], 1902. 8°. **14033. bb. 7.(2.)**

DĀMODARA, *son of Lakshmīdhara,* called HARI BHAṬṬA. Dāmodara. [A critical edition of the Saṅgītadarpaṇa.] Von R. Simon. 1902. *See* SIMON (R.). Quellen zur indischen Musik, *etc.* 1902, *etc.* 8°. [*Zeitschrift der Deutschen Morgenlaendischen Gesellschaft.*] **Ac. 8815/2. (vol. 56.)**

DĀMODARA GOVINDĀCHĀRYA KĀNAḌE. *See* JINADATTA SŪRI. **विवेक-विलास** *etc.* [Vivekavilāsa. With Gujarati translation by Dāmodara.] [1898.] 8°. **14100. c. 20.**

—— *See* RATNAŚEKHARA SŪRI. **श्राद्धविधि** *etc.* [Śrāddhavidhi. With the Vidhikaumudī, translated into Gujarati by Dāmodara.] [1899.] 8°. **14100. e. 8.**

—— **श्रीमोहनचरितम्** *etc.* [Mohanacharita. A poetical biography, in 8 *sargas*, of the Jain religious teacher Mohanalāla or Muktikamala. With a Gujarati translation.] pp. ii. 192; 1 *plate.* મુંબઈ ૧૮૯૫ [*Bombay,* 1895.] 8°. **14070. d. 36.**

DĀMODARAGUPTA. Dāmodaragupta's Kuṭṭanimatam [or Śambhalīmata.] Lehren einer Kupplerin. Ins Deutsche übertragen von Johann Jacob Meyer. pp. iv. 156. [1903.] *See* SCHMIDT (R.). Altindische Schelmenbücher. No. ii. [1903, *etc.*] 8°. **14070. g. 2.**

DĀMODARALĀLA GOSVĀMĪ. *See* HEMACHANDRA. **स्याद्वादमञ्जरी** *etc.* (Syadwada Manjari . . . With a commentary . . . Edited by Sri Damodar Lal Goswami.) [1900.] 8°. **14004. a. 9.**

DĀMODARA MIŚRA, *of Dīrghaghosha Kula, Maithila.* The Vâṇîbhûshaṇa of Dâmodara Miśra. [A treatise on Sanskrit metres, with examples.] Edited by Paṇḍit Śivadatta . . . and Kâśînâth Pâṇḍurang Parab. (**वाणीभूषणम्।**) pp. iv. 53. 1895. *See* DURGĀPRASĀDA, *son of Vrajalāla,* and KĀŚINĀTHA PĀṆḌURAṄGA PARAB. Kâvyamâlâ. [No.] 53. 1886, *etc.* 8°. **14072. ccc. 12. (no. 53.)**

DĀMODARA ŚĀSTRĪ, *Vaidya, of Moradabad. See* PAÑCHATANTRA. **अथ-संस्कृतसागर** *etc.* [Saṃskṛitasāgara. Edited by Dāmodara.] [1899.] 8°. **14070. c. 63. (2.)**

DĀMODARA ŚĀSTRĪ SAHASRABUDDHI, *Bhāradvāja. See* BHAIRAVA MIŚRA. **भैरवी कारकान्ता** . . . Karakanta-Bhairavi . . . Revised by . . . Damodar Shastri, *etc.* 1896. 8°. **14090. d. 32.**

—— *See* PĀṆINI.—*Appendix.* [*Dhātupāṭha.*] **माधवीया धातुवृत्तिः** *etc.* [Dhātuvṛitti. Followed by the Nāmadhātuvṛitti. Edited by Dāmodara.] [1897.] 8°. **14093. b. 39.**

DĀMODARA ŚĀSTRĪ SAHASRABUDDHI, *Bhāradvāja (continued). See* RĀMĀNANDA SARASVATĪ, *disciple of Govindānanda.* **विवरणोपन्यासः** . . . Vivaraṇopanyâsa . . . Edited by . . . Dámodara Śástri, *etc.* 1901. 8°. **14048. cc. 37.**

—— *See* SĀYAṆA ĀCHĀRYA.—*Works on Grammar.* **॥ अथ . . . नामधातुवृत्तिः ॥** [Nāmadhātuvṛitti. Edited by Dāmodara.] 1897. 8°. [*The Pandit.*] **14096. d. 6. (vol. 19.)**

DĀMODARA VIDYĀNANDA. *See* RAMEŚACHANDRA DATTA. **হিন্দুশাস্ত্র** *etc.* [Hindu-śāstra. Pt. vii., compiled by Dāmodara. Pt. viii., with Bengali translation by Baṅkimchandra and Dāmodara.] [1895-1897.] 8°. **14085. c. 45. (vol. 2.)**

DAṆḌĪ. *See* MOREŚVARA RĀMACHANDRA KĀḶE. The Sâhityasârasangraha . . . based on the works of Dandin, *etc.* Pt. 1. 1891. 12°. **14053. a. 13.**

—— **॥ दशकुमारचरितं सटीकम् ॥** The Daśakumâracharita of Daṇḍin. Edited with critical and explanatory notes by Georg Bühler. Part I. [Books i.-iii.] (Part II. [Books iv.-viii.] Edited . . . by Peter Peterson.) 2 pts. *Bombay,* 1873-1891. 8°. **14076. c. 45.**

Forms nos. x. *and* xlii. *of the* Bombay Sanskrit Series.

—— Daçakumâracaritam. Die Abenteuer der zehn Prinzen. Nach dem Sanskrit-Originale des Daṇḍin übersetzt, eingeleitet und mit Anmerkungen versehen von Dr. M. Haberlandt. pp. i. 159, ii. *München, Wien* [printed], 1903. 8°. **14076. d. 38. (2.)**

DAṆḌĪDHAR ŚARMĀ, *of Jorhat.* **শ্লোকমালা-সংগ্ৰহ** *etc.* [Ślokamālāsaṅgraha. An anthology of simple verses for school reading, arranged in the order of their initial letters. Preceded by elementary reading lessons in Assamese, and followed by appendices on the numeral system.] pp. 34. কলিকাতা [*Calcutta,* 1901.] 12°. **14076. b. 26. (3.)**

DARŚANĀNANDA SARASVATĪ, *Svāmī, disciple of Anubhavānanda. See* KAPILA. **सांख्यदर्शनम्** *etc.* [Sāṅkhyadarśana. The Sāṅkhya Aphorisms, with Hindi paraphrase by Darśanānanda.] [1903.] 8°. **14049. b. 10.**

DAŚALAKSHAṆĪ. **दशलक्षण्यादि पूजनसंग्रह** *etc.* [Daśalakshaṇyādi-pūjanasaṅgraha. A manual of various rituals according to the use of the Mūlasaṅgha sect of Jains, in Sanskrit, Prakrit, and Gujarati. Comprising the Daṣalakshaṇī-pūjā, inclusive of Jinasena's Jinasahasranāma, and the Solā-kāraṇa-pūjā.] ff. 65. लखनऊ १८९९ [*Lucknow*, 1899.] *obl.* 8°. **14100. b. 7.**

DASAPAĪNNĀ. *See* PRAKĪRṆAKA.

DAṢAPRAKIRṆAKA. *See* PRAKĪRṆAKA.

DAṢAVAIKĀLIKASŪTRA. *See* ṢAYYAṂBHAVA.

DASAVEYĀLIYA. *See* ṢAYYAṂBHAVA.

DATTARĀMA CHAUBE, *son of Kanhaiyālāl, of Muttra.* *See* CHARAKA. चरकसंहिता *etc.* [Charaka-saṃhitā. With a Hindi version, styled Charaka-chandrodaya, by Dattarāma.] [1900.] 8°. **14043. dd. 6.**

—— अभिनवनिघंटु . . . Abhinavanighantu, or Hindu System of Medicine. Compiled and translated [into Hindi] from Sanskrit books . . . with the original texts, by Pandit Dattaram Chaube. pp. iv. xiv. xiv. xii. 265; 1 *plate.* मुंबय्यां १९५० [*sic*] [*Bombay*, 1893.] 8°. **14043. e. 27.**

—— [Second edition.] pp. iii. iii. xiii. xx. 269, 38. मुंबयां १९५६ [*Bombay*, 1900.] 8°. **14043. dd. 7.**

—— रसराजसुन्दर *etc.* [Rasarājasundara. A compilation treating of mineral substances and their medical application. With Hindi translations.] 4 pts., *lith.* मथुरा १८८८-१८९१ [*Muttra*, 1888-1891.] 8°. **14053. d. 48.**

DATTĀTREYA. अथ श्रीदत्तात्रेयावधूतगीता° [Avadhūtagītā. A poem of 8 *adhyāyas*, expounding Vedantic monism and ethics, and commonly ascribed to Dattātreya.] *See* GOVARDHANADĀSA LAKSHMĪDĀSA. बृहत्स्तोत्रसरित्सागर *etc.* [Bṛihat-stotrasaritsāgara.] Vol. i., pp. 409-435. [1892.] 12°. **14033. a. 27. (vol. 1.)**

—— ॥ अवधूतगीता *etc.* [Avadhūtagītā. With a Hindi version by Hariṣaṅkara Ṣāstrī.] pp. 79. कानपुर १८९९ [*Cawnpore*, 1899.] 8°. **14028. c. 85.(2.)**

DAULATRĀM NĀRĀYAṆA CHHĀṆIKAR, *of Baroda.* *See* PURĀṆAS.—*Padmapurāṇa.* श्रीगौडप्रकाश *etc.* [Gauḍaprakāṣa. With Gujarati translation, *etc.* Edited and translated by Daulatrām.] [1899.] 8°. **14058. b. 39.**

DAVIDS (CAROLINE AUGUSTA FOLEY RHYS), *Mrs.* *See* ABHIDHAMMAPIṬAKA. — *Dhammasaṅgaṇi.* A Buddhist manual of Psychological Ethics of the fourth century B.C. Being a translation . . . of the . . . Dhamma-sangaṇi . . . With introductory essay and notes by C. A. F. Rhys Davids. 1900. 8°. [*Oriental Translation Fund.*] **14003. bb. (series 5, vol. 12.)**

DAVIDS (THOMAS WILLIAM RHYS). *See* ACADEMIES, *etc.*—London.—*Pali Text Society.* YOGĀVACHARA. The Yogāvacara's Manual of Indian Mysticism . . . Edited by T. W. Rhys Davids. 1896. 8°. **14098. b. 29.(4.)**

—— *See* MILINDA. The Questions of King Milinda. Translated . . . by T. W. Rhys Davids. 1890-1894. 8°. [*Sacred Books of the East.*] **2003. b. (vol. 35, 36.)**

—— *See* SUTTAPIṬAKA.—*Dīghanikāya.* Dialogues of the Buddha. Translated from the Pâli by T. W. Rhys Davids. 1899. 8°. [*Sacred Books of the Buddhists.*] **14003. ccc. (vol. 2.)**

—— Schools of Buddhist Belief, *etc.* [Including the heads of chapters of the Kathāvatthu, with translation, *etc.*] 1892. *See* ACADEMIES, *etc.*—London.—*Royal Asiatic Society of Great Britain and Ireland.* The Journal . . . 1892. pp. 1-37. 1834, *etc.* 8°. **Ac. 8820/3 and 2098. a.b.**

DAYĀNANDA SARASVATĪ SVĀMĪ. [*Life.*] *See* SAMĀDDĀR (R. N.). Mahatma Dayananda Sarasvati. [1898.] 16°. **14058. a. 5.(3.)**

—— *See* HARIHARAPRASĀDA. सनातनधर्मविजय *etc.* [Sanātanadharmavijaya. A Hindi polemic against Dayānanda and his school.] [1902, *etc.*] 8°. **14154. c. 25.(2.)**

—— *See* TULASĪRĀMA SVĀMĪ. भास्करप्रकाश *etc.* (The Bhaskarprakasha. Or, Reply to Dayanand-timir-bhaskar[, Jvālāprasāda Miṣra's polemic against Dayānanda's Satyārthaprakāṣa.]) 1899. 8°. **14154. ee. 13.(1.)**

—— *See* VEDAS.—Ṛigveda.—*Entire Text.* ऋग्वेदभाष्यम् *etc.* [Ṛigveda. With commentaries in Sanskrit and Hindi by Dayānanda.] [1882-1899 ?] 8°. **14010. cc. 15.**

DAYĀNANDA SARASVATĪ SVĀMĪ (*continued*). *See* VEDAS. — *Selections.* ऋग्वेदादिभाष्यभूमिका *etc.* [Ṛigvedādibhāshyabhūmikā. A compilation by Dayānanda from the Vedic hymns, with Sanskrit and Hindi commentaries. Second edition.] [1893.] 8°. **14010. dd. 12.**

—— *See* YAMUNĀDĀSA ŚĀṆḌILYA. महताबदिवाकर *etc.* [Mahtāb-divākara. A refutation of Dayānanda, in Hindi.] [1895.] 8°. **14154. c. 20.**

—— The Five Great Duties of the Aryans. [Pañcha-Mahāyajñāḥ. The daily ritual of the Ārya-Samāj, being *mantras* compiled and expounded by Dayānanda.] . . . Englished and explained by Durga Prasad[, together with the Sanskrit text.] pp. iv. xvi. 75. *Lahore*, 1895. 16°. **14028. b. 76.**

—— পঞ্চ মহাযজ্ঞবিধিঃ *etc.* [Pañchamahāyajña-vidhi. With Bengali introduction and translations by Satyacharaṇa Rāya.] pp. xii. v. 122, ii. আজমীর কলিকাতা ১৮২০ [*Ajmere, Calcutta* printed, 1898.] 16°. **14028. a. 26.**

—— अथ संस्कारविधिः *etc.* [Saṃskāravidhi. A ritual for the 16 *saṃskāras* according to the Ārya Samāj. In Hindi, with the authorities and *mantras* quoted in Sanskrit and interpreted in Hindi. Fourth edition.] pp. i. 255, ii. अजमेर १९५६ [*Ajmere*, 1899.] 8°. **14028. d. 68.**

—— संस्कृतवाक्यप्रबोधः *etc.* [Saṃskṛitavākyaprabodha. Sanskrit-Hindi dialogues for the teaching of Sanskrit.] pp. 62. अजमेर १९५४ [*Ajmere*, 1897.] 8°. **14085. d. 31.(2.)**

—— अथ सत्यार्थप्रकाशः *etc.* [Satyārthaprakāṣa. A treatise on the true interpretation and teachings of the Vedas. In Hindi, illustrated by Sanskrit quotations. Fifth edition.] pp. iv. i. vii. 636. अजमेर १९५४ [*Ajmere*, 1898.] 8°. **14154. c. 22.**

—— ستیارتھ پرکاش الخ [Satyārthaprakāṣa. Translated into Urdu by Raimal Dāsjī and Ātmārāmajī.] pp. iv. iii. xx. viii. 751, *lith.* لکھنو ۱۸۹۹ [*Lucknow*, 1899.] 8°. **14106. a. 33.**

—— ਸਤਿਆਰਥਪ੍ਰਕਾਸ਼ *etc.* [Satyārthaprakāṣa. Translated into Panjabi by Lālā Ātmārāma.] pp. ii. 732. ਅੰਮ੍ਰਿਤਸਰ १९५६ [*Amritsar*, 1899.] 8°. **14162. aaa. 1.**

DAYĀNANDA SARASVATĪ SVĀMĪ (*continued*). সত্যার্থ প্রকাশ। [Satyārthaprakāṣa. Translated into Bengali.] pp. v. ix. 829. কলিকাতা ১৩০৮ [*Calcutta*, 1901.] 8°. **14123. gg. 1.**

—— Maharshi Swami Dayanand Saraswati on Indian religions. An English translation of the 11th chapter of the Satyartha prakasha, with a summary of his beliefs and a sketch of his life. By Durga Prasad, Preacher of Vedic Religion. pp. xvi. 300. *Lahore*, 1900. 12°. **14154. cc. 2.**

—— The Niyoga Doctrine of the Arya Samaj, being a literal translation of that portion of the Sattyarth Prakash which treats of the doctrine & practice of Niyoga. With some remarks by Ruchi Ram Sahni. pp. 40. *Lahore*, 1897. 12°. **14033. a. 33.(1.)**

—— शिक्षापत्रीध्वान्तनिवारणः अर्थात् स्वामी नारायणमत दोष दर्शनात्मकः *etc.* [Śikshāpattrīdhvāntanivāraṇa. A polemic against the Svāmī-Nārāyaṇa sect of Sahajānanda. With a Hindi translation.] pp. 17, 24. अजमेर १९५७ [*Ajmere*, 1900.] 12°. **14028. c. 25.(2.)**

—— वेदान्तिध्वान्तनिवारणम् *etc.* [Vedāntidhvāntanivāraṇa. A polemic against the modern Vedānta. In Hindi, with Sanskrit quotations.] pp. 17. मुंबई १९३२ [*Bombay*, 1875.] 8°. **14154. e. 7.**

—— [Second edition.] pp. 24. प्रयाग १९३९ [*Allahabad*, 1882.] 8°. **14154. c. 6.(2.)**

—— [Third edition.] pp. 28. प्रयाग १९४५ [*Allahabad*, 1889.] 8°. **14154. c. 9.(2.)**

—— [Fourth edition.] pp. 28. अजमेर १९३५ [*Ajmere*, 1896 ?] 8°. **14154. c. 16.(5.)**

—— Vedant Dhwanti Niwaran, or, Neo-Vedantism Refuted . . . Translated into English by B. Arjansingh. pp. 37. *Ajmere*, [1900.] 12°. **14048. a. 24.(2.)**

—— विवाहपद्धतिः *etc.* [Vivāhapaddhati. A manual of the rites of marriage, extracted from Dayānanda's Saṃskāravidhi. In Sanskrit and Hindi.] pp. 56. अजमेर १९५८ [*Ajmere*, 1901.] 8°. **14154. c. 26.**

—— व्यवहारभानुः *etc.* [Vyavahārabhānu. A catechetical treatise on ethics. In Hindi, illustrated from Sanskrit. Fifth edition.] pp. 50. अजमेर १९५७ [*Ajmere*, 1900.] 8°. **14028. d. 67.(2.)**

DE ALWIS (JAMES). *See* BUDDHAGHOSA. [*Papañchasūdanī.*] Friendship between Bimbisāra and Pukkusāti . . . Translated by J. Alwis, *etc.* 1894. 8°. [*Journal of the Buddhist Text Society of India.*] **14003. b. 19.(vol. 2.)**

—— *See* HATTHAVANAGALLA-VIHĀRA-VAṂSA. The Pali Text of the Attanagaluvansa and its ancient translation into Sinhalese; with notes . . . by . . . J. Alwis. Second edition. 1887. 8°. **14098. c. 66.**

DE ALWIS (W. B.). *See* VĀGBHAṬA, *son of Siṃhagupta.* Ashtanga Hridaya . . . Translated into Sinhalese by W. B. de Alwis, *etc.* Pt. i. 1893. 8°. **14043. d. 45.**

DE ALWIS GUṆATILAKA (*Don* ADIRIAN). බෞද්ධප්‍රතිපත්තිදීපනිය *etc.* [Bauddhapratipattidīpaniya. A compilation of short Pali texts with comments in Pali and Sinhalese, expounding the religious duties of Buddhists.] pp. 34. [*Colombo,*] 1889. 12°. **14098. a. 19.(2.)**

—— බෞද්ධප්‍රතිපත්තිදීපනිය *etc.* [Bauddhapratipattidīpaniya. Another edition, enlarged by the addition of the Mahāsatipaṭṭhānasutta, *etc.*] pp. ii. 76. [*Colombo,*] 1890. 12°. **14165. a. 58.(5.)**

—— [Another edition of the preceding.] pp. ii. 80. [*Colombo,*] 1895. 8°. **14098. a. 29.(2.)**

—— [Another edition, printed partly in larger type.] pp. i. ii. 122, iv. [*Colombo,*] 1897. 12°. **14098. a. 29.(3.)**

DEBI PRASAD. *See* DEVĪPRASĀDA.

DEṢAMAṄGALA BĀLAKṚISHṆA KAVI. *See* BĀLAKṚISHṆA, *Deṣamaṅgalam.*

DEṢIKĀCHĀRYA, *M.* *See* ĀRANYAKAS.—*Taittirīyāraṇyaka.* ஸ்ரீ . . . [illegible] *etc.* [Taittirīyāraṇyaka. Followed by the Kāṭhaka. Edited by Veṅkaṭakṛishṇa and Deṣikāchārya.] 1894. 8°. **14010. cc. 1.**

DE SILVA (W. A.). *See* VINAYAPIṬAKA. [*Mahāvagga.*] පටිච්චසමුප්පාදය *etc.* [Paṭichchasamuppādaya. Edited by W. De Silva.] 1895. 12°. **14098. b. 21.(2.)**

DEUSSEN (PAUL). *See* UPANISHADS.—*General Collections.* Sechzig Upanishad's des Veda . . . übersetzt und mit Einleitungen und Anmerkungen versehen von Dr. Paul Deussen. 1897. 8°. **14010. dd. 8.**

DEUTSCHE MORGENLAENDISCHE GESELLSCHAFT. *See* ACADEMIES, *etc.*—*Germany.*

DEVA, *Ārya.* *See* ĀRYA DEVA.

DEVADATTA ṢĀSTRĪ, *son of Ṣivadatta, of Cawnpore.* *See* KAṆĀDA. वैशेषिकदर्शनम् *etc.* [Vaiṣeshikadarṣana. With Sanskrit and Hindi commentaries by Devadatta.] [1898.] 8°. **14048. e. 22.(3.)**

DEVADATTA ṢĀSTRĪ, *Purohita to the Maharaja of Bilaspur.* रमलभैरवम् *etc.* [Ramal-bhairava, or Vijayachandra. A metrical treatise on the method of divination termed *ramal.*] pp. 131. काश्याम् १८९९ [*Benares,* 1899.] 8°. **14053. cc. 40.(2.)**

The compiler is termed in the colophon on p. 111 Devīdāsa.

DEVAMITTA, *Heyiyantuḍuvē.* *See* SUTTAPIṬAKA.—*Aṅguttara-Nikāya.* අඞ්ගුත්තරනිකායො *etc.* (Anguttara Nikaya. Collated and revised by H. Devamitta, *etc.*) Pt. i. [1893.] 8°. **14098. d. 41.**

—— *See* SUTTAPIṬAKA.—*Khuddakanikāya.* [*Dhammapada.*] ධම්මපදං . . . The Dhammapada . . . Revised by Rev. H. Dewamitta. [1886.] 8°. **14098. d. 44.**

DEVĀNANDA, *Hōkandara.* *See* SUTTAPIṬAKA.—*Khuddakanikāya.* [*Suttanipāta.*] මහාමඞ්ගලසූත්‍රය [Mahāmaṅgalasutta. With Sinhalese commentary. Edited by Devānanda.] 1894. 8°. **14098. d. 42.(3.)**

DEVANĀTHA ṢARMĀ, *Chāturmāsyayājī, Agnimūrti-Dviveda.* *See* PĀRASKARA. पारस्करगृह्यसूत्रम् *etc.* [Pāraskaragṛihyasūtra. With commentaries, *etc.* Edited by Devanātha and Bālamukunda.] [1896.] 4°. **14010. f. 10.**

DEVĀṆḌA BHAṬṬA. *See* ĀDINĀRĀYAṆA PĀTRO, *P.* The Hindu Law. Annotated and illustrated by Sanskrit texts[, viz. the writings of Devāṇḍa Bhaṭṭa and others,] *etc.* 1899. 8°. **14039. c. 17.**

DEVARĀJA YAJVĀ, *son of Yajñeṣvara*. *See* YĀSKA. The Nirukta. With commentaries, *etc.* [Vol. I, with the Nighaṇṭunirvachana of Devarāja.] 1882-1891. 8°. [*Bibliotheca Indica.*] **14002. a. (vol. 89.)**

DEVARAKKHITA (*Don* ANDRIS DE SILVA), *Baṭuvantuḍāvē*. *See* MĀDHAVA, *son of Indukara.* Madhavanidana . . . Translated [into Sinhalese] . . . by the late Pandit Batuvantudave, *etc.* Pt. i. 1893. 8°. **14043. d. 46.**

—— *See* MAHĀNĀMA. Maháwaṇsa Tiká . . . edited . . . by Pandit Baṭuwantuḍáwe and M. Ñáṇissara, *etc.* 1895. 8°. **14098. dd. 10.**

DEVATĪRTHA SVĀMĪ, *of Ramnagar, Purohita.* Udásina Sádhu Stotra. [A hymn to the Adepts, in 22 stanzas. Translated, with extracts from the commentary of Brahmānanda, by R. Sundararājam Aiyar.] 1898. *See* PERIODICAL PUBLICATIONS.—*Bombay.* The Theosophist, *etc.* Vol. XIX, no. vii. pp. 427-435. 1879, *etc.* 8°. **P.P. 636. cm. (vol. 19.)**

DEVAVIMALA GAṆĪ, *son of Ṣiva Sādhu and disciple of Sīhavimala Gaṇī.* The Hirasaubhâgya of Devavimalagaṇi[, a poem in 17 *sargas*, on the history of the Jain pontiff Hīravijaya Gaṇī,] with his own gloss. Edited by . . . Paṇḍit Śivadatta . . . and Kâshînâth Pâṇdurang Parab. (हीरसौभाग्यम् ।) pp. i. x. 918. 1900. *See* DURGĀPRASĀDA, *son of Vrajalāla*, and KĀṢĪNĀTHA PĀṆḌURAṄGA PARAB. Kâvyamâlâ. [No.] 67. 1886, *etc.* 8°. **14072. ccc. 12. (no. 67.)**

Appended is a praṣasti of the author and the line of teachers from Sripati. Hiravijaya was born 1583, and succeeded to the sūripada in 1610 Samvat.

DEVENDERNATH TAGORE. *See* DEVENDRANĀTHA ṬHĀKURA.

DEVENDRA GAṆĪ, *disciple of Amradeva*, also called NEMICHANDRA. चैत्यवंदन भाष्य. (गुरुवंदन भाष्य, पच्चक्खाण भाष्य, *etc.*) [Chaityavandana-bhāshya, Guruvandana-bhāshya, and Pachchakkhāṇa-bhāshya, three religious poems in Jain Prakrit, of respectively 63, 41, and 48 stanzas; and Dānakulaka, Ṣīlakulaka, Tapaḥkulaka, and Bhāvakulaka, likewise short religious poems in Prakrit. With Gujarati translation.] *See* HEMAṢAṄKARA LAKSHMĪṢAṄKARA VARDHAMĀNKAR. प्रकरण माला *etc.* [Prakaraṇamāla.] pp. 51-91, 149-165. [1901.] 8°. **14100. d. 11.**

DEVENDRA GAṆĪ, *disciple of Amradeva (continued).* Le Novelline Prācrite di Maṇḍiya e di Agaladatta. [An Italian translation by P. E. Pavolini of two stories taken from the commentaries on the Uttarādhyayana composed respectively by Devendra and Ṣānti Sūri and published as nos. 9 and 10*a* in Jacobi's "Ausgewählte Erzählungen in Mâhârâshṭrî."] pp. 11. *Roma*, 1892. 8°. **14100. c. 18.**

—— La Novella di Brahmadatta. [An Italian translation by P. E. Pavolini of the story from Devendra's commentary on the Uttarādhyayana published as no. 1 in Jacobi's "Ausgewählte Erzählungen."] 1892. *See* ACADEMIES, *etc.*—Florence.—*Società Asiatica Italiana.* Giornale, *etc.* Vol. vi., pp. 111-148. 1887, *etc.* 8°. **Ac. 8804. (vol. 6.)**

DEVENDRANĀTHA SENA GUPTA. *See* CHAKRAPĀṆIDATTA. चक्रदत्तः *etc.* [Chakradatta. Edited by Devendranātha, *etc.*] [1900.] 8°. **14043. cc. 17.**

DEVENDRANĀTHA ṬHĀKURA, *Maharshi.* The Offering of Srimat Maharshi Devendernath Tagore. [A Brahmo tract in English, with Sanskrit quotations.] Second edition. pp. ii. 52. *Madras*, 1898. 32°. **4504. de. 7.**

DEVÈZE (GÉRARD). *See* KRISHṆA MIṢRA, *Dramatist.* Le Lever de la Lune de la Connaissance . . . traduit [by G. Devèze,] *etc.* 1899-1902. 8°. [*Revue de Linguistique.*] **P.P. 4964. d. (tom. 32-35.)**

DEVĪDATTA JOṢĪ, *Assistant Interpreter, High Court, Allahabad.* *See* SANDHYĀVANDANA. सन्ध्यादर्पणः *etc.* [Sandhyādarpaṇa. Compiled by Devīdatta.] [1901.] 4°. **14033. bbb. 11.**

DEVĪDATTA PĀṆḌE, *of Almora.* *See* GUMĀNĪ PANTA. गुमानी कवि विरचित . . . काव्य *etc.* [Kāvyasaṅgraha. Edited with Hindi notes and translations by Devīdatta.] [1897.] 8°. **14070. dd. 6.**

DEVĪPAÑCHASTAVĪ. *See* DEVĪSTOTRAPAÑCHAKA.

DEVĪPRASĀDA, *Rāi*, called PŪRṆA. *See* KĀLIDĀSA.—*Meghadūta.* ॥ धाराधरधावन ॥ . . . Dhārā Dhara Dhāwana. Part ii., being a metrical Hindi translation of . . . Uttara Megha . . . by Rai Debi Prasad, "Poorna." [1902.] 8°. **14072. cc. 58 (2.)**

DEVĪSTOTRAPAÑCHAKA. देवीस्तोत्रपञ्चकम् [Devīstotrapañchaka. Five hymns—viz. Laghustuti, Charchāstava, Ghaṭastava, Ambāstava, and Sakalajananīstotra—addressed to Devī, and inspired by the Śrīvidyā form of the Śākta cult.] pp. 27. 1896. *See* MYSORE.—*Government of Mysore.* Government Oriental Library Series. Bibliotheca Sanskrita. No. 11. 1893, *etc.* 8°. **14004. b. 8.**

The Sakalajananīstotra is ascribed to Kālidāsa by Lakshmīdhara in his commentary to the Saundaryalaharī. See also the note to the edition in the Kāvyamālā, 1887.

DE ZOYSA (LOUIS). A Catalogue of Páli, Sinhalese, and Sanskrit Manuscripts in the Temple Libraries of Ceylon, *etc.* pp. iv. 31. *Colombo,* 1885. 4°. **14096. f. 7.**

DHAMMACHETĪ. The Kalyānī Inscriptions erected by King Dhammachetī at Pegu in 1476 A.D. Text and translation [by Taw Sein Ko, with a preface]. pp. vi. i. 105; 2 *plates.* *Rangoon,* 1892. 8°. **14098. dd. 9.**

—— A Preliminary Study of the Kalyani Inscriptions of Dhammacheti, 1476 A.D. [including the text and translation] by Taw Sein-Ko. pp. 60; 8 *plates.* *Bombay,* 1893. 4°. **14098. dd. 17.**

Reprinted from the Indian Antiquary.

—— Text of the Kalyani inscriptions. pp. 58. *See* TAW SEIN KO. Some Remarks on the Kalyani inscriptions, *etc.* 1894. 8°. **14098. dd. 24.**

DHAMMAKITTI, *Uḍugampola.* කුලධර්මදීපනිය *etc.* [Kuladharmadīpaniya. A Sinhalese ethical tract against imitation of foreign customs, illustrated by Sanskrit and Pali verses, *etc.*] pp. 26, ii. කොළඹ [*Colombo,*] 1897. 8°. **14165. f. 42.**

DHAMMAKITTI SAṄGHARĀJA. [For editions of the Bālāvatāra, traditionally ascribed to Dhammakitti:] *See* KACHCHĀYANA.—*Bālāvatāra.*

DHAMMĀLAṄKĀRA, *Yālagama.* *See* VISUDDHĀCHĀRA THERA. ධාත්වත්ථසඞ්ගහය *etc.* [Dhātvatthasaṅgaha. Edited by Dhammālaṅkāra.] 1897. 8°. **14098. a. 31.**

DHAMMĀNANDA, *Valāṇē, of Paramadhamma Cheti.* *See* SUTTAPIṬAKA.—*Khuddakanikāya.* [*Suttanipāta.*] සුත්තනිපාතය *etc.* [Suttanipāta. With commentary of Buddhaghosa. Edited by Dhammānanda.] Pt. 1. 1897. 8°. **14098. ccc. 5.**

DHAMMĀNANDA ĀCHARIYA, *of Tha-tôn.* ကစ္စာယနဘေဒ *etc.* [Kachchāyanabheda. A Pali treatise on the grammatical terminology of Kachchāyana. With Burmese commentary by Tipiṭakālaṅkāra Siriddhaja.] [1898.] *See* SADDĀ-NGAY. သဒ္ဒါငယ် *etc.* [Saddā-ngay.] Vol. ii., pp. 83-134. [1898-1900.] 8°. **14098. ccc. 22.**

—— ကစ္စာယနဘေဒပါဠိ။ [Kachchāyanabheda.] *See* SADDĀ-NGAY. သဒ္ဒါငယ် *etc.* [Saddā-ngay.] pp. 142-157. [1898.] 8°. **14098. ccc. 23.(1.)**

—— [Second edition.] pp. 145-156. [1899.] 8°. **14098. ccc. 24.(1.)**

—— කච්චායනසාරය *etc.* [Kachchāyanasāra. A summary of Kachchāyana's grammar. With a Sinhalese interpretation by Ñāṇatilaka Tissa.] pp. ii. 47. වැලිතොට 2436 [*Welitota,* 1892]. 12°. **14098. b. 18.(3.)**

—— ကစ္စာယနသာရ *etc.* [Kachchāyanasāra. With the Burmese commentary of Tipiṭakālaṅkāra Siriddhaja.] [1898.] *See* SADDĀ-NGAY. သဒ္ဒါငယ် [Saddā-ngay.] Vol. ii., pp. 118-151. [1898-1900.] 8°. **14098. ccc. 22.**

—— ကစ္စာယနသာရပါဠိ။ [Kachchāyanasāra.] *See* SADDĀ-NGAY. သဒ္ဒါငယ် *etc.* [Saddā-ngay.] pp. 26-30. [1898.] 8°. **14098. ccc. 23.(1.)**

—— [Second edition.] pp. 26-30. [1899.] 8°. **14098. ccc. 24.(1.)**

DHAMMAPADA. *See* SUTTAPIṬAKA. — *Khuddakanikāya.*

DHAMMAPĀLA. *See* ACADEMIES, *etc.*—London.—*Pali Text Society.* KACHCHĀYANA. The Nettipakarana. With extracts from Dhammapāla's commentary, *etc.* 1902. 8°. **14098. b. 36.(2.)**

—— Dhammapāla's Paramattha-dīpanī, Part III. Being the commentary on the Petavatthu. Edited by Prof. E. Hardy. 1894. 8°. *See* ACADEMIES, *etc.*—London.—*Pali Text Society.* DHAMMAPĀLA. **14098. b. 35.**

—— Dhammapāla's Paramattha-dīpanī, Part IV. Being the commentary on the Vimāna-vatthu.

Edited by Prof. E. Hardy. 1901. 8°. *See* ACADEMIES, *etc.* — London. — *Pali Text Society.* DHAMMAPĀLA. **14098. b. 35.**

—— Paramattha Dipanī by Dhammapāla of Kāñcipura. Part V. The commentary on the Therigāthā. Edited by E. Müller. 1893. 8°. *See* ACADEMIES, *etc.*—London.—*Pali Text Society.* DHAMMAPĀLA. **14098. b. 35.**

DHAMMAPĀLA, *disciple of Buddharakkhita Mahāthera.* ပါဠိဘာသာသံဂဟတ်စာအုပ် [Pāli-bhā-sā-saṅgabat-sā-ôk. A Pali-Burmese glossary.] pp. 72. *Rangoon,* 1895. 12°. **14098. a. 37.**

DHAMMARAKKHITA, *Levadora.* *See* SUTTAPIṬAKA. — *Majjhimanikāya.* චූලවෙදල්ලසූත්‍රය *etc.* [Chullavedallasutta. Edited with a Sinhalese word-for-word gloss and a translation by L. Dhammarakkhita.] [1897.] 8°. **14098. c. 73.(2.)**

DHAMMĀRĀMA, *Koḷaṁbapalāne, of Ratmalāna.* *See* BUDDHAGHOSA. [*Manorathapūraṇī.*] මනොරථපූරණී *etc.* [Manorathapūraṇī. Edited by Dhammārāma.] Pts. 1, 3-5. 1893-1896. 8°. **14098. c. 64.**

—— *See* PĀLI-NĀMA-VARANEGILLA. පාළි නාම වරනැගිල්ල *etc.* (Kaccayana Namika Rupamala and Akhyata Rupamala . . . Edited with notes and . . . translation by . . . Dharmarama.) 1895. 8°. **14098. c. 42.(2.)**

DHAMMARATANA, *Baddēgama.* *See* KACHCHĀYANA.—*Rūpasiddhi.* රූපසිද්ධි *etc.* [Rūpasiddhi. Edited with annotations by Sumaṅgala and Dhammaratana.] 1891-1897. 8°. **14098. d. 39.**

—— *See* THŪPAVAṂSA. ථූපවංසය *etc.* [Thūpavaṃsa. Edited by Dhammaratana.] 1896. 8°. **14098. d. 44.(2.)**

DHAMMARATANA TISSA, *Mīgamuvē.* *See* ANURUDDHA. Abhidharmarthasangraha sanna . . . Edited . . . with the help of . . . M. Dhammaratana Tissa. 1897. 8°. **14098. ccc. 6.**

DHAMMASAṄGAṆI. *See* ABHIDHAMMAPIṬAKA.

DHAMMASENĀPATI, *of Nandavihāra.* ကာရိကာ *etc.* [Kārikā. A metrical Pali treatise on grammar. With Burmese commentary by Aggāchāra Mahāthera.] [1899.] *See* SADDĀ-NGAY. သဒ္ဒါငယ် *etc.* [Saddā-ngay.] Vol. iv., pp. 1-160. [1898-1900.] 8°. **14098. ccc. 22.**

—— ကာရိကာပါဌ် [Kārikā.] *See* SADDĀ-NGAY. သဒ္ဒါငယ် *etc.* [Saddā-ngay.] pp. 158-191. [1898.] 8°. **14098. ccc. 23.(1.)**

—— [Second edition.] pp. 157-191. [1899.] 8°. **14098. ccc. 24.(1.)**

DHAMMASIRI, *Mahāsthavira.* Kudusika[, *i.e.* Khuddasikkhā.] By the Ven: Dharmasiri. . . . With paraphrase [in Sinhalese] by the Ven: Dimbulâgala Medhankara. Revised by the Rev: B. Sumedhankara . . . කුදුසික *etc.* pp. iv. 172. *Colombo,* 1894. 8°. **14098. d. 43.**

—— ခုဒ္ဒသိက္ခာ [Khuddasikkhā.] *See* WINI-NGAY. ဝိနည်းငယ် လေးစောင် *etc.* [Winingay le saung.] pp. 73-120. [1898.] 8°. **14098. ccc. 9.(4.)**

DHANAṂJAYA, *Jain writer.* विषापहारस्तोत्रम् [Vishāpahārastotra. A hymn of 40 stanzas.] *See* JAINASTOTRASAṄGRAHA. जैनस्तोत्रसंग्रहः *etc.* [Jainastotrasaṅgraha.] pp. 30-34. [1890.] 12°. **14100. a. 13.**

—— विषापहार *etc.* [Vishāpahāra. With a rendering in Hindi verse by Paramānanda of Narnaul. Edited by Bābū Jñānachandra.] pp. 18. लाहौर १९०० [*Lahore,* 1900.] 12°. **14100. a. 21.(2.)**

Forms no. 8 *of the editor's* Jain Religious Tracts Series.

—— विषापहारस्तोत्रम्। [Vishāpahārastotra.] *See* JAINANITYAPĀṬHA. अथ जैननित्यपाठसंग्रहः [Jainanityapāṭhasaṅgraha.] pp. 94-106. [1901.] *obl.* 16°. **14100. a. 27.**

DHANAṂJAYA, *son of Vasudeva.* The Dvisandhâna [or Rāghavapāṇḍavīya] of Dhananjaya. [A poem of 18 *sargas* that may be read either as a Rāmāyaṇa or as a Bhārata.] With the commentary of Badarînâth. Edited by Paṇḍit Sivadatta . . . and Kâśinâth Pâṇdurang Parab. (द्विसंधानम्।) pp. 226. 1895. *See* DURGĀPRASĀDA, *son of Vrajalāla,* and KĀŚINĀTHA PĀṆḌURAṄGA PARAB. Kâvyamâlâ. [No.] 49. 1886, *etc.* 8°. **14072. ccc. 12.(no. 49.)**

DHANAMJAYA, *son of Vishṇu.* *See* MOREṢVARA RĀMACHANDRA KĀḶE. The Sâhityasârasangraha . . . based on the works of . . . Dhananjaya, *etc.* Pt. 1. 1891. 12°. **14053. a. 13.**

DHANAMJAYA DEVA VARMĀ. *See* SĀRASVATA-SŪTRA. सूत्रमाला *etc.* [Sūtramālā. Comprising the Sārasvatasūtra and commentary. Edited by Dhanaṃjaya Deva.] Pt. i. [1894.] 12°. **14090. b. 42.**

DHANAPATI SŪRI, *son of Rāmakumāra.* *See* SĀYAṆA ĀCHĀRYA. — *Works on Philosophy, etc.* శ్రీశంకరవిజయము *etc.* [Ṣaṅkaravijaya. With the commentary Ṣaṅkaravijayaḍiṇḍima of Dhanapati.] [1894.] 8°. **14048. cc. 11.**

DHANEṢVARA SŪRI. The Śatrunjaya Mâhâtmyam. A contribution to the history of the Jainas by . . . Albert Weber. [Being an analysis of the work of Dhaneṣvara in English.] Edited by James Burgess. 1901. *See* PERIODICAL PUBLICATIONS.—*Bombay.* The Indian Antiquary, *etc.* Vol. xxx., pp. 239-251, 288-308. 1872, *etc.* 4°. **14096. e.(vol. 30.)**

DHANVANTARI. ధన్వంతరినిఘంటువు *etc.* [Dhanvantarinighaṇṭu. A metrical repertory of *materia medica.* Edited with Telugu interpretation by Siṅgarāju Kānū Ṣāstri and Piḍugu Veṅkaṭappā Rāu.] pp. xi. 302. *Madras,* ౧౮౯౨ [1892.] 8°. **14043. c. 40.**

—— राजनिघण्टुसहितो धन्वन्तरीयनिघण्टुः *etc.* (The Râjanighanta [of Narahari] and the Dhanvantarinighanta, two treatises on medicine[, the former supplementing and elucidating the latter]. Edited [with indices] by Vaidya Nárâyaṇa Shastri Purandare.) pp. iv. ii. i. 440, clxv. पुण्याख्यपत्तने १८९६ [*Poona,* 1896.] 8°. **14003. ccc.(no. 33.)**

Forms no. 33 *of the* Ānandāṣrama Sanskrit Series. *The English title is from the cover.*

DHĀRAṆĪ. *See* SHINGON. 眞言諸經 *etc.* [Shingon Shokiō Jōyōshiu. Comprising *dhāraṇīs, etc.*] [1851.] 8°. **16007. a. 5.**

—— *See* SHIUGEN. 修驗常用集 [Shiugen Jōyōshiu. Including *dhāraṇīs, etc.*] *n.d.* 8°. **16006. a. 7.**

—— *See* YOGA. 瑜伽課誦 [Yuga Kwaju. Including *dhāraṇīs, etc.*] [1718.] 8°. **16007. c. 11.**

DHĀRAṆĪ (*continued*). 大佛頂大陀羅尼 [Daibutsu Chōdai Darani, or "Great Dhāraṇī to Buddha." The Sanskrit text, with transliteration into Japanese characters and a Chinese version by Daikōchi.] *n.d.* 8°. **16007. c. 2.**

—— 大隨求陀羅尼 [Daizui-kiu Darani, "The Great Following-after-Salvation Dhāraṇī." The Sanskrit text, with transliteration into Japanese characters and a Chinese translation by Fukū.] [1760.] *obl.* 8°. **16006. d. 4.**

—— 佛頂尊勝陀羅尼 [Fuh ting tsun shing tŏ lo ne. "The honourable and excelling Dhāraṇī of Buddha's head." Sanskrit text, with transliteration in Japanese.] *n.d.* 12°. **15103. b. 12.**

DHARAṆĪDHARA, *Vipra.* *See* JAYADEVA, *son of Bhojadeva.* Gitagobinda, *etc.* [With metrical version in Oriya by Dharaṇīdhara.] 1878. 12°. **14076. b. 31.**

DHARAṆĪDHARA BHŪPA. *See* VEṄKAṬEṢA, *disciple of Nṛisiṃha.* The S'rînivâsavilâsa Champu . . . With the commentary of Dharanîdhara, *etc.* 1893. 8°. [*Kâvyamâlâ.*] **14072. ccc. 12.(no. 33.)**

DHĀREṢVARA. *See* BHOJARĀJA.

DHARMA BHAṬṬA. *See* RĀMĀNANDA SARASVATĪ, *son of Tirumalāchārya.*

DHARMAMERU. *See* KĀLIDĀSA. — *Raghuvaṃṣa.* The Raghuvanśa . . . with full extracts . . . from the commentaries of . . . Dharmameru, *etc.* 1897. 8°. **14072. c. 53.**

DHARMANIRṆAYA. अथ धर्मनिर्णयप्रारम्भः [Dharmanirṇaya. A religious poem containing an exposition of the teachings of the Rāmānuja sect of Vaishṇavas. With additional matter in Hindi prose and verse.] ff. 46. कल्याण १८१५ [*Kalyan,* 1894.] *obl.* 16°. **14028. b. 93.**

DHARMAPADDHATI. ॥ अथ वाटिकापूजनपद्धति प्रारम्भः ॥ [Vāṭikāpūjanapaddhati. A manual of rules and ceremonies for laying out gardens, *etc.*, extracted from the Dharmapaddhati.] ff. 20. *Lucknow,* १८९९ [1899.] *obl.* 8°. **14028. dd. 10.(1.)**

DHARMARĀJA BAṚUYĀ. Hastasar, or Bauddha Mahaparitran. A collection of Buddhist . . . Hymns, Precepts, Karmasthānas and Parittas in

Pali text with Bengali interpretations & translation in [Bengali] prose and poetry. By Dharma Raj Barhuya. (হুতুমাত্র) Pt. i. pp. iii. vi. ii. 342. *Calcutta*, 1893. 12°. **14098. a. 28.**

DHARMARĀJĀDHVARĪNDRA. *See* DHARMARĀJA DĪKSHITA.

DHARMARĀJA DĪKSHITA. వేదాన్తపరిభాషా [Vedāntaparibhāshā. A treatise on Vedantic terminology. With Telugu translation.] 1895, *etc.* 8°. *See* PERIODICAL PUBLICATIONS.—*Vizagapatam.* సకలవిద్యాభివర్ధని *etc.* [Sakalavidyābhivardhanī.] Vol. iii., pt. i., *etc.* 1892-1897. **14174. g. 38.**

Not completed.

——— वेदान्तपरिभाषा *etc.* [Vedāntaparibhāshā. With Hindi introduction and commentary by Svāmī Govindasiṃha of Benares.] pp. xii. ii. 144; 1 *plate. Bombay*, १९५७ [1901.] 8°. **14048. dd. 33.**

DHARMĀRĀMĀ, *K.* *See* DHAMMĀRĀMA, *K.*

DHARMARATNA, *M., Editor of the "Lakmiṇi Pahan."* *See* VINAYAPIṬAKA. [*Mahāvagga.*] Patichchha Samuppadaya, *etc.* [Edited by M. Dharmaratna.] [1896.] 8°. **14098. d. 45.(4.)**

——— අභිධර්මාර්ථසංග්‍රහශුද්ධිය *etc.* [Abhidharmārthasaṅgrahaṣuddhiya. A criticism on Heyiyantuḍuvē Devamitta's edition of Anuruddha's Abhidhammatthasaṅgaha, giving variants of the text.] pp. 18. කොළඹ [*Colombo*,] 1893. 8°. **14165. b. 21.(4.)**

DHARMASĀDHAKA, *Sāmi.* *See* KACHCHĀYANA.—*Chūlanirutti.* අභිනව චූලනිරුක්තිපකරණං [Abhinava-chūlanirutti. Edited by Dharmasādhaka.] 1896. 12°. **14098. a. 7.(3.)**

DHARMOTTARA ĀCHĀRYA. *See* NYĀYABINDU. The Nyayabindutika of Dharmottaracharya, *etc.* 1889. 8°. [*Bibliotheca Indica.*] **14002. a. (vol. 128.)**

DHĀTUKATHĀ. *See* ABHIDHAMMAPIṬAKA.

DHĀVAKA. *See* NĀRĀYAṆA ŞĀSTRĪ, *T. S.* Sriharsha the Dramatist. A dissertation on . . . the author of the Priyadarsika, the Ratnavali, and the Nagananda, [identifying him with Dhāvaka or Bhāsaka,] *etc.* [1902.] 8°. **14058. b. 40.(2.)**

DHĪRASIṂHA DEVA, *King of Mithila, son of Darpanārāyaṇa.* दुर्गाभक्तितरङ्गिणी [Durgābhaktitaraṅgiṇī. A manual for the ritual of Durgā. Composed ostensibly by Dhīrasiṃha Deva, with the assistance of Vidyāpati.] pp. 129, v. [*Calcutta*, 1900.] 8°. **14033. bbb. 7.**

The real author is probably Vidyāpati, who is casually mentioned once (v. 6 of the introduction).

DHĪRENDRANĀTHA PĀLA. Srikrishna; his life and teachings. [An English study, based upon the accounts given in the Mahābhārata and Vishṇupurāṇa,] *etc.* Second edition. 2 pts. pp. iv. xxix. 136, 177. *Calcutta*, 1901. 8°. **10606. c. 39.**

DHOLE (H.). *See* HĪRĀLĀL ḌHOL.

DHOLE (N.). *See* NANDALĀLA ḌHOL.

DHOYĪ. धोयी कवि का पवनदूत। [Pavanadūta. Select stanzas, with Hindi paraphrases, *etc.*] *See* RAJANĪKĀNTA GUPTA. जयदेवचरित *etc.* [Jayadevacharita.] pp. 66-80. [1901.] 8°. **14156. g. 75.**

——— Nachahmungen des Meghadūta. [Being extracts from the Pavanadūta of Dhoyī, *etc.*] Von Th. Aufrecht. 1900. *See* ACADEMIES, *etc.*—Germany.—*Deutsche Morgenlaendische Gesellschaft.* Zeitschrift, *etc.* Bd. 54. pp. 616-620. 1846, *etc.* 8°. **Ac. 8815/2.(vol. 54.)**

DHRUVA (H. H.). *See* HARILĀLA HARSHADARĀYA DHRUVA.

ḌHUṆḌHIRĀJA, *son of Nṛisiṃha.* जातकाभरण सटीक *etc.* [Jātakābharaṇa. A manual of astrology. With Hindi version by Sūryanārāyaṇa Siddhāntī.] pp. ii. 460. लखनऊ १९०० [*Lucknow*, 1900.] 8°. **14053. ccc. 32.**

DHŪRTASVĀMĪ. *See* ĀPASTAMBA.—*Şrautasūtra.* ॥ यज्ञपरिभाषासूत्रम् *etc.* [Yajñaparibhāshāsūtra. With the commentary of Dhūrtasvāmī.] 1891. 8°. [*Ushā.*] **14010. c. 43. (vol. 1.)**

DIBBA, *Shin, of Ngazinga.* *See* ABHIDHAMMAPIṬAKA.—*Selections.* အဘိဓမ္မာ ၇ ကျမ်း နှုတ်ဝဲ *etc.* [Abhidhammā-hku-hnit-kyan-yût-sin. Compiled and edited by Dibba.] 1901. 8°. **14098. d. 36.(2.)**

DIGAMBARA CHAṬṬOPĀDHYĀYA. *See* CHAṆḌEŚVARA ṬHAKKURA. Vivada-ratnakara . . . the law of partition and inheritance [entitled Dāyabhāga. The Sanskrit text edited and] translated by . . . Digamvar Chattopádhyáya. 1899. 8°. **14039. c. 18.**

DĪGHANIKĀYA. *See* SUTTAPIṬAKA.

DINACHARIYĀ. දිනචරියාව [Dinachariyā. A Pali tract on the daily observances of Buddhist devotees.] *See* HERAṆASIKA. හෙරණසික *etc.* [Heraṇasika, *etc.*] pp. 8-12. 1897. 12°. **14098. a. 30.**

DINAKARA BHAṬṬA, *son of Mahādeva Bhaṭṭa.* *See* VIŚVANĀTHA PAÑCHĀNANA BHAṬṬĀCHĀRYA. कारिकावली *etc.* [Kārikāvalī. With the Dinakarī or Muktāvalīprakāśa commenced by Mahādeva Bhaṭṭa and finished by Dinakara.] [1895.] 8°. **14048. dd. 25.**

—— [Another edition.] [1896.] 8°. **14048. dd. 26.**

DINAKARA KEŚAVA ŚĀSTRĪ GĀḌGIL. *See* PĀṆINI. —*Siddhāntakaumudī.* The Siddhânta-kaumudî . . . Edited by Dinkar . . . Gâdgil, *etc.* 1899. 4°. **14092. c. 18.**

DINAKARA MIŚRA, *son of Dharmāṅgada.* *See* KĀLIDĀSA.—*Raghuvaṃśa.* The Raghuvanśa . . . with full extracts . . . from the commentaries of . . . Dinakaramiśra, *etc.* 1897. 8°. **14072. c. 53.**

DINAKARA TRYAMBAKA CHANDORKAR. *See* MAMMAṬA ĀCHĀRYA. The Kâvya-prakâsh of Mammata, Ullâsa x. . . . Edited by Dinkar . . . Chandorkar . . . With notes and appendix. 1896. 8°. **14053. ccc. 6.**

DINĀLĀPANIKĀ-ŚUKASAPTATI. *See* ŚUKASAPTATI.

DĪNANĀTHA DEVA. *See* ŚAṄKARA ĀCHĀRYA.—*Doubtful and Supposititious Works.* The Mohamudgara . . . With its translation into English and Hindustani verse by Dina Nátha Deva. 1896. 8°. **14048. dd. 32.(2.)**

DĪNANĀTHA KAVIRATNA ŚĀSTRĪ. বৈদ্য রহস্য *etc.* [Vaidyarahasya, or Vaidyaviveka. A Bengali treatise, illustrated from Sanskrit texts, to prove that Vaidyas are of the *Śūdra* class.] pp. 118. কলিকাতা [*Calcutta,* 1899.] 8°. **14125. ee. 33.**

DIṆḌIMA, *Commentator on the Ānandalaharī.* *See* ŚAṄKARA ĀCHĀRYA.—*Doubtful and Supposititious Works.* Ānanda Lahari. With . . . commentaries [based on Diṇḍima, *etc.*] Translated into English, *etc.* 1899. 12°. **14048. b. 35.**

DINKAR. *See* DINAKARA.

DĪPA, *Mahāthera, of Salin.* နရုပဒေသကျမ်း *etc.* [Narupadesa-kyan. Burmese homilies, illustrated from Pali texts, on the doctrine and practice of Buddhism.] pp. iii. 193. မန္တလေး [*Mandalay,*] 1890. 8°. **14300. d. 21.(1.)**

DĪPĀLAṄKĀRA, known as NGAKON HSAYA, *disciple of Paññājotābhiddhaja.* *See* KACHCHĀYANA.—*Kachchāyanappakaraṇa.* သဒ္ဒါကြီးဂဏ္ဌိကျမ်း *etc.* [Saddā-kyī-ganthi, or Saddalakkhaṇavibhāvanī. Comprising Kachchāyana's aphorisms and Dīpālaṅkāra's Burmese commentary, *etc.*] 1900. 8°. **14098. dd. 21.**

DĪPAṄKARA, called BUDDHAPPIYA. *See* KACHCHĀYANA.—*Rūpasiddhi.* මහාරූපසිද්ධි *etc.* [Rūpasiddhi, or Mahārūpasiddhi. A grammar of Pali by Dīpaṅkara, based on Kachchāyana.] Pts. i., ii. 1891-1897. 8°. **14098. d. 39.**

—— *See* KACHCHĀYANA.—*Rūpasiddhi.* මහාරූපසිද්ධි *etc.* (Mahárúpasiddhi . . . [comprising the aphorisms of Kachchāyana with commentary] by . . . Buddhappiya, *etc.*) 1897. 8°. **14098. dd. 14.**

—— *See* KACHCHĀYANA. — *Rūpasiddhi.* ပဒရူပသိဒ္ဓိ *etc.* [Rūpasiddhi.] [1900.] 8°. **14098. dd. 20.**

—— *See* KACHCHĀYANA.—*Rūpasiddhi.* သဒ္ဒါရှစ်စောင်သုတ်နက်သစ် *etc.* [Saddā shitsaung thôk net thit. Kachchāyana's aphorisms with brief notes based on the Rūpasiddhi, *etc.*] 1901. 8°. **14098. dd. 19.**

—— *See* KACHCHĀYANA. — *Rūpasiddhi.* Das Sechste Kapitel der Rūpasiddhi, *etc.* 1883. 8°. **14098. b. 15.(2.)**

DĪPAVAṂSA. Dīpavaṁsa. Chapters I—IV. Based on a manuscript from the late Royal Library of Mandalay. (Chapters V—VII. Based on Burmese manuscripts.) Edited by James Gray. 2 vols. *Rangoon, Calcutta* [printed], 1900-1902. 12°. **14098. a. 35.**

—— Dīpavaṁsa. Chapters V—VII. (Translation and appendix [by J. Gray].) pp. 32, 19. *Calcutta*, 1902. 12°. **14098. a. 41.**

DĪPCHAND CHHAGANLĀL, *Shāh*. *See* ĀTMĀRĀMAJĪ ĀNANDAVIJAYAJĪ. શ્રી જૈનતત્ત્વાદર્શ ગ્રંથ *etc.* [Jainatattvādarṣa. Translated into Gujarati by Dīpchand.] Vol. i. [1899.] 8°. **14144. ggg. 11.**

—— *See* YAṢOVIJAYA. શ્રી જ્ઞાનસાર *etc.* [Jñānasāra. With Gujarati translation and commentary, *etc.*, by Dīpchand.] [1899.] 12°. **14100. b. 6.**

DIVĀKARA, *son of Nṛisiṃha*. मकरन्दविवरणम् । [Makarandavivaraṇa. An astrological tract by Divākara. Followed by Makarandopapatti, a tract by Gokulanātha, and Makarandodāharaṇa, by Divākara.] pp. 22. [1891.] *See* PERIODICAL PUBLICATIONS.—*Calcutta*. অরুণোদয় *etc.* [Aruṇodaya.] Pt. i., no. 15. [1890, *etc.*] 4°. **14133. g. 16.(pt. i., no. 15.)**

DIVĀKARA DĀJĪ SĀDHLE. ॥ अथ कृत्यदिवाकरः प्रारभ्यते ॥ [Kṛityadivākara. Rules for domestic rites, with *mantras*.] ff. iii. vi. 186, 3. मोहमय्यां° १८२० [*Bombay*, 1899.] *obl.* 8°. **14028. dd. 2.(2.)**

DIVYĀVADĀNA. *See* WINDISCH (W. O. E.). Māra und Buddha, *etc.* [Illustrated by extracts and translations from the Divyāvadāna, *etc.*] 1895. 4°. **759. e. 1.**

DOḌḌAYĀCHĀRYA. *See* RĀMĀNUJADĀSA, surnamed DOḌḌAYĀCHĀRYA.

DOLATRĀM. *See* DAULATRĀM.

DORASĀMAIYA, *Ōmandūru Vaidyam*. హిందూవివాహశాస్త్రసంగ్రహము *etc.* [Hinduvivāhaṣāstrasaṅgraha. A series of quotations from authoritative texts upon the rules regulating marriage.] pp. 12. చెన్నపట్టణము [*Madras*,] 1901. 8°. **14085. c. 28.(3.)**

—— పాతివ్రత్యలక్షణము. సత్పురుషలక్షణము *etc.* [Pātivratyalakshaṇa and Satpurushalakshaṇa. Two compilations of verses treating of wifely and manly virtues respectively. With Telugu translation and notes.] pp. 18. చెన్నపట్టణము [*Madras*,] 1901. 8°. **14085. c. 28.(4.)**

—— తత్త్వసారము *etc.* [Tattvasāra. An elementary catechism of philosophy and religion. With Telugu translation.] pp. 12. చెన్నపట్టణము [*Madras*, 1901.] 8°. **14085. c. 28.(2.)**

DORASVĀMI ṢĀSTRĪ, *Kārattūr*. *See* PURĀṆAS.—*Brahmāṇḍapurāṇa*. [*Ādipuramāhātmya*.] பேரூர் [*sic*] ஸ்தலபுராணம் *etc.* [Ādipuramāhātmya. Edited by Dorasvāmi and others.] [1902.] 8°. **14016. dd. 6.**

DRAVID (B. T.). *See* ṢESHĀDRI AIYAR.

DRAVID (S. T.). *See* ṢRĪNIVĀSA TRYAMBAKA DRAVIḌA.

DUBE (M. L.). The Maha-bharata. [An English epitome of the contents of the epic.] pp. iii. xxi. 114. *Agra*, 1894. 12°. **14065. b. 17.**

DULĀRE-PRASĀD TRIVEDĪ, *son of Chaṇḍikāprasāda*. *See* MĀDHAVAMUKUNDACHARAṆA. परपक्षगिरिवज्रः *etc.* [Parapakshagirivajra. Edited by Dulāreprasād.] [1902.] 8°. **14049. b. 6.**

DURGA ĀCHĀRYA. *See* YĀSKA. The Nirukta. With commentaries, *etc.* [Vol. II—IV, with the Ṛijvarthā of Durga.] 1882-1891. 8°. [*Bibliotheca Indica*.] **14002. a.(vol. 89.)**

DURGĀDĀSA VIDYĀVĀGĪṢA. *See* VOPADEVA. मुग्धबोधं *etc.* [Mugdhabodha. With commentary of Durgādāsa, *etc.*] [1891.] 8°. **14092. b. 44.**

—— *See* VOPADEVA. মুগ্ধবোধং *etc.* [Mugdhabodha. With Durgādāsa's commentary as far as the end of the *kṛidantādhyāya*.] [1894.] 8°. **14090. e. 24.**

—— *See* VOPADEVA. Kavikalpadruma . . . With the commentaries [called] Dhatudipika of Durgadas Vidyabagis, *etc.* 1897. 8°. **14090. c. 38.(2.)**

DURGĀMOHANA SMṚITITĪRTHA. *See* VIṢVADEVA ĀCHĀRYA. রাঘবদীপিকা *etc.* [Rāghavadīpikā. Edited with a translation and additional matter in Bengali by Durgāmohana.] [1892.] 8°. **14028. d. 48.(2.)**

DURGĀPRASĀDA, *Editor of the "Harbinger" and Manager of the Virajanand Press, Lahore.* *See*

DAYĀNANDA SARASVATĪ SVĀMĪ. The Five Great Duties of the Aryans . . . Englished and explained by Durga Prasad. 1895. 16°.
14028. b. 76.

—— *See* DAYĀNANDA SARASVATĪ SVĀMĪ. Maharshi Swami Dayanand Saraswati on Indian religions. An English translation of the 11th chapter of the Satyartha prakasha, with a summary of his beliefs and a sketch of his life. By Durga Prasad, *etc.* 1900. 12°.
14154. cc. 2.

—— *See* UPANISHADS. — *Separate Upanishads.* An English translation of the Kena Upanishat with exposition by Durga Prasad. 1898. 12°.
14010. b. 8.(3.)

—— *See* UPANISHADS. — *Separate Upanishads.* An English translation of the Prashnopanishat . . . By Durgaprasad, *etc.* 1899. 12°.
14048. a. 20.(2.)

—— The First (Second, Third, Fourth) Vedic Reader. **प्रथमं (द्वितीयं, तृतीयं, चतुर्थं) वेदपुस्तकं** By Durga Prasad. 4 vols. *Lahore,* 1894-1895. 12°.
14010. b. 11.

—— The Third Vedic Reader. **तृतीयं वेदपुस्तकं** *etc.* Second edition. pp. 34. *Lahore,* 1896. 12°.
14010. b. 17.

DURGĀPRASĀDA, *son of Vrajalāla.* [*Life.*] *See* DURGĀPRASĀDA DVIVEDĪ. Prasâdaśataka, *etc.* 1892. 8°.
14072. cc. 63.(1.)

—— *See* KALHAṆA. The Râjataraṅgiṇî . . . Edited by Durgâprasâda, *etc.* 1892-1896. 8°.
14058. b. 27.

DURGĀPRASĀDA, *son of Vrajalāla,* **and KĀŚĪNĀTHA PĀṆḌURAṄGA PARAB.** Kâvyamâlâ. A collection of old and rare Sanskrit Kâvyas, Nâtakas, Champûs, Bhâṇas, Prahasanas, Chhandas, Alankâras &c. . . . Edited by Paṇḍita Durgâprasâda [and after his death, from no. 36 onward, by Śivadatta son of Badarīnātha] and Kâshînâtha Pâṇḍuranga Paraba. **(काव्यमाला)** *Bombay,* 1886, *etc.* 8°.
14072. ccc. 11, 12.

The works issued in the separate series since the publication of Prof. Bendall's Catalogue are entered in this Catalogue under the headings :—

No. 23. Jagaddhara, *grandson of Gauradhara.*
,, 24. Govinda Ṭhakkura, *son of Keśava.*
,, 25. Ānandavardhana.
,, 26. Kshemendra.
,, 27. Ānandarāya Makhī.
,, 28. Subhaṭa.
,, 29. Harihara Upādhyāya.
,, 30. Vīranandī.
,, 31. Purushottama.
,, 32. Kṛishṇânanda.
,, 33. Veṅkaṭeśa.
,, 34. [Prāchīnalekhamālā.]
,, 35. Ruyyaka.
,, 36. Apyaya Dīkshita.
,, 37. Sadāśiva, *called* Yuvarāja Kavi.
,, 38. Apyaya Dikshita.
,, 39. Ānandarāya Makhī.
,, 40. Rāma Varmā.
,, 41. Piṅgala Āchārya.
,, 42. Bharata Muni.
,, 43. Vāgbhaṭa, *son of Nemikumāra.*
,, 44. Rāmabhadra Dīkshita.
,, 45. Amarachandra.
,, 46. Mathurādāsa.
,, 47. Pravarasena.
,, 48. Vāgbhaṭa, *son of Soma.*
,, 49. Dhanaṃjaya.
No. 50. Śauddhodani.
,, 51. Rāmabhadra Dīkshita.
,, 52. Kṛishṇa Śarmā, *disciple of Vāsudeva.*
,, 53. Dâmodara Miśra.
,, 54. Kāñchana Āchārya.
,, 55. Mahādeva Kavi.
,, 56. Vāgbhaṭa, *son of Soma.*
,, 57. Haradatta Sūri.
,, 58. Vāmana Bhaṭṭa Bāṇa.
,, 59. Gokulanātha Mahāmahopādhyāya.
,, 60. Vāsudeva, *disciple of Bhārata Guru.*
,, 61. Jayadratha, *Rājānaka.*
,, 62. Kavirāja Paṇḍita.
,, 63. Baladeva Vidyābhūshaṇa.
,, 64. [Prâchīnalekhamālā.]
,, 65. Kshemendra.
,, 66. Viśveśvara Paṇḍita.
,, 67. Devavimala Gaṇi.
,, 68. Bhīma, *Bhaṭṭa.*
,, 69. Kshemendra.
,, 70. Somadeva Sūri.
,, 71. Hemachandra.
,, 72. Śrīvara.
,, 73. Someśvara Deva.
,, 74. Viśvanātha Kavi, *nephew of Agastya.*

The chief works published in the Anthology of this series, with the names of their authors, are :—

1886. Jagannātha Paṇḍitarāja. — *Sudhālahari, Prāṇābharaṇa, Karuṇālahari, Lakshmilahari.*
Śambhu, *of Kashmir.*—*Rājendrakarṇapūra, Anyoktimuktālatā.*
Kshemendra. — *Kalāvilāsa, Auchityavichāracharchā, Suvrittatilaka, Sevyasevakopadeśa, Chārucharyā.*
Apyaya Dikshita.—*Vairāgyaśataka.*
Ratnākara, *son of Amṛitabhānu.*—*Vakroktipañchāśikā.*
Vishṇupādādikeśāntavarṇana [ascribed to Śaṅkara].
Gumāni Panta.—*Upadeśaśataka.*
Vikrama, *son of Sāṅgaṇa.*—*Nemidūta.*
Rudra Nyāyavāchaspati.—*Bhāvavilāsa.*
Madhusūdana Sarasvati.—*Ānandamandākinī.*
1887. Gokulanātha, *son of Pītāmbara Vidyānidhi.*—*Śivaśataka.*
Pañchastavī [*i.q.* Devistotrapañchaka].
Dāmodaragupta.—*Kuṭṭanīmata.*
Rudra Bhaṭṭa.—*Śriṅgāratilaka.*
Mādhava Bhaṭṭa.—*Dānalīlā.*
Bāṇa.—*Chaṇḍīśataka.*
Nāgarāja.—*Bhāvaśataka.*
Nārāyaṇa Bhaṭṭa, *Kerala.*—*Svāhāsudhākara.*
Kṛishṇa Bhaṭṭa, *son of Nārāyaṇa.*—*Tārāśaśāṅka.*
Rāmachandra, *son of Lakshmaṇa Bhaṭṭa.*—*Rasikarañjana.*
Kshemendra.—*Kavikaṇṭhābharaṇa.*
Bhallaṭa.—*Bhallaṭaśataka.*
Nīlakaṇṭha Dikshita.—*Sabhārañjanaśataka.*
1888. Mūka.—*Mūkapañchaśatī.*
Kshemendra.—*Chaturvargasaṅgraha.*
Vīreśvara Bhaṭṭa.—*Anyoktiśataka.*
Śivarāma Tripāṭhī.—*Nakshatramālā.*
Nīlakaṇṭha Dikshita.—*Kaliviḍambana.*
Somaprabha Āchārya.—*Śriṅgāravairāgyataraṅgiṇī.*
Nārāyaṇa Bhaṭṭa, *Kerala.*—*Koṭiviraha.*
1890. Śivapādādikeśāntavarṇana, Śivakeśādipādāntavarṇana [ascribed to Śaṅkara].
Nīlakaṇṭha Dikshita.—*Śāntivilāsa, Anyāpadeśaśataka.*
Loshṭadeva.—*Dīnākrandanastotra.*
Kṛishṇavallabha Bhaṭṭa.—*Kāvyabhūshaṇaśataka.*
Śrīnivāsa Āchārya.—*Jānakīcharaṇachāmara.*
Kshemendra.—*Darpadalana.*
Śivarāma Tripāṭhī.—*Rasaratnahāra.*
Mānatuṅga.—*Bhaktāmarastotra.*
Siddhasena Divākara.—*Kalyāṇamandirastotra.*
Vādirāja.—*Ekībhāvastotra.*
Dhanaṃjaya.—*Vishāpahārastotra.*
Bhūpāla Kavi.—*Jinachaturviṃśatikā.*
Devanandī.—*Siddhipriyastotra.*
Somaprabha Āchārya.—*Sūktimuktāvalī.*
Jambū Guru.—*Jinaśataka.*

Padmānanda.—*Vairāgyasataka.*
Jinaprabha Sūri.—*Siddhāntāgamastava.*
Dhanapāla.—*Ṛishabhapañchāsikā.*
Ṣobhana Muni.—*Chaturviṃsatijinastuti.*
1891. Kūranārāyaṇa.—*Sudarṣanaṣataka.*
Visvesvara Pāṇḍo.—*Kavindrakarṇābharaṇa, Romāvali-ṣataka.*
Prabodhasudhākara [ascribed to Ṣaṅkara].
Jalhaṇa.—*Mugdhopadeṣa.*
Veṅkaṭanātha Vedāntāchārya.—*Subhāshitanīvī.*
1893. Ānandavardhana.—*Devīṣataka.*
Avatāra Kavi.—*Isvaraṣataka.*
Madhusūdana, *son of Padmanābha, Maithila.*—*Anyāpadeṣa-ṣataka.*
Lakshmaṇa Veṇīmādhava Sāmaga.—*Chaṇḍīkuchapañchā-ṣikā.*
Vidyāvāgīṣa, *son of Mādhava.*—*Kaunteyavṛitta.*
Utprekshāvallabha.—*Sundarīsataka.*
Tripurasundarīmānasikopachārapūjā [ascribed to Ṣaṅkara].
Sundara Āchārya.—*Gītisataka.*
Sāmarāja Dīkshita.—*Tripurasundarīmānasapūjana.*
Chatuḥshashṭyupachāramānasapūjā [ascribed to Ṣaṅkara].
1894. Lalitāstavaratna [ascribed to Durvāsas].
Rāmabhadra Dīkshita.—*Rāmāshṭaprāsa.*
Vāsudeva, *Puruvanam.*—*Vāsudevavijaya.*
Nārāyaṇa Bhaṭṭa, *Kerala.*—*Dhātukāvya.*
1895. Tripurāmahimastotra [ascribed to Durvāsas].
Khaḍgasataka.
Dakshiṇāmūrti Sūri.—*Lokoktimuktāvalī.*
Nīlakaṇṭha Dīkshita.—*Ānandasāgarastava.*
Lolimbarāja.—*Harivilāsa.*
Janārdana Bhaṭṭa, *Gosvāmī.*—*Sṛiṅgāraṣataka.*
Sūrya Kavi.—*Rāmakṛishṇakāvya.*
1897. Rāmabhadra Dīkshita.—*Rāmachāpastava.*
,, ,, *Rāmabāṇastava.*
Narahari.—*Sṛiṅgāraṣataka.*
Utprekshāvallabha.—*Bhikshāṭanakāvya.*

In 1892 occurred the death of Pandit Durgāprasāda. An obituary notice was issued, and is bound with the Anthology, pt. 8.

—— The Prâchîna-lekha-mâlâ, or A Collection of Ancient Historical Records [*scil.* Sanskrit inscriptions] . . . Edited by . . . Paṇḍit Durgâprasâd (Vol. II, by . . . Paṇḍit Śivadatta) . . . and Kâśînâth Pâṇḍurang Parab. (प्राचीनलेखमाला ।) 1892, *etc.* *See* above. Kâvyamâlâ. [No.] 34, 64, *etc.* 1886, *etc.* 8°. **14072. ccc. 12. (no. 34, 64.)**

In progress.

DURGĀPRASĀDA, *son of Vrajalāla*, **and others.** The Abhidhâna-sangraha, or A Collection of Sanskrit Ancient Lexicons . . . Edited by Paṇḍit Durgâprasâd, Kâśînâth Pâṇḍurang Parab and Paṇḍit Śivadatta. (अभिधानसंग्रहः नाम संस्कृतप्राचीनकोशग्रन्थसमुच्चयः ।) *Bombay*, 1889, *etc.* 8°. **14090. e. 20.**

In progress? Durgāprasāda died before the publication of Vol. 2.

The works published in this collection are catalogued under the headings:—

1. Amarasiṃha.
2-5. Purushottama Deva.
6-10. Hemachandra.
11. Jinadeva Munisvara.

DURGĀPRASĀDA DVIVEDĪ. Prasâdaśataka, or The Life of Mahâmahopâdhyâya Pandit Durgâprasâd [in 115 Sanskrit stanzas], *etc.* (प्रसादशतकम्) pp. ii. 17. *Bombay*, 1892. 8°. **14072. cc. 63.(1.)**

DURGĀPRASĀDA ṢUKLA, *of Agra.* *See* YĀJÑAVALKYA. [*Dharmaṣāstra.*] मिताक्षर *etc.* [Yājñavalkyasmṛiti. Āchārādhyāya and Vyavahārādhyāya, with a translation and commentary by Durgāprasāda.] [1890.] 4°. **14038. f. 11.**

DURGASIṂHA, *Commentator on the Kātantra.* *See* SARVAVARMĀ. [Select Aphorisms of the Kātantra, with portions of Durgasiṃha's *vṛitti.*] [1902, *etc.*] 8°. [*Gāndharva-kalāpa vyākaraṇa.*] **14053. dd. 2.**

—— *See* SARVAVARMĀ. কলাপ-ব্যাকরণম্ *etc.* [Kalāpavyākaraṇa. Section i., with Durgasiṃha's *vṛitti.*] [1889.] 8°. **14090. c. 36.**

—— —— [1895.] 12°. **14090. b. 45.(3.)**

—— *See* SARVAVARMĀ. কলাপ-ব্যাকরণম্ *etc.* [Kalāpavyākaraṇa. Section i., with commentary of Durgasiṃha.] [1895.] 8°. **14090. bb. 13.(4.)**

—— *See* SARVAVARMĀ. কলাপ-ব্যাকরণম্ *etc.* [Kalāpavyākaraṇa. Section i., with commentary of Durgasiṃha.] [1900.] 8°. **14090. b. 32.(2.)**

—— *See* TRILOCHANADĀSA. কলাপ-ব্যাকরণম্ . . . চতুষ্টয়পঞ্জী *etc.* [Chatushṭayapañjī. A commentary on Durgasiṃha's Kātantravṛitti. Chapter ii.] 1893. 8°. **14090. bb. 13.(2.)**

—— কলাপ-ব্যাকরণম্ . . . চতুষ্টয়টীকা *etc.* [Chatushṭayaṭīkā, or Kātantravṛittiṭīkā. Being Durgasiṃha's longer commentary on the Kātantra. Chapter II, *pādas* i.–ii. Edited by Rasikachandra Vidyāratna.] pp. 102. *Dacca*, 1893. 8°. **14090. bb. 13.(1.)**

—— নমস্কারবিবেকঃ *etc.* [Namaskāraviveka. Comprising the introductory stanza of Durgasiṃha's Kātantravṛitti and the first part of Trilochanadāsa's Pañjikā commenting upon that verse and discussing the forms of religious address, and followed by the section of Susheṇa's Kalāpachandra bearing thereupon. Together with a commentary upon the whole, called Kaumudī, by Annadācharaṇa Tarkachūḍāmaṇi.] pp. i. 70. নোয়াখালী ১৩০৬ [*Noakhali*, 1900.] 12°. **14092. a. 24.(1.)**

DUTT (U. C.). *See* UDAYACHANDRA DATTA.

DUTT (R. C.). *See* RAMEṢACHANDRA DATTA.

DVĀRAKĀNĀTHA NYĀYABHŪSHAṆA, *of Midnapur.* See KRAMADĪṢVARA. लघुसंक्षिप्तसार° [Laghusaṅkshiptasāravyākaraṇa. A shorter recension of Kramadīṣvara's Saṅkshiptasāra. Abridged and edited with a commentary by Dvārakānātha.] 1890-1892. 8°. **14090. c. 37.**

—— अव्ययकोषः बृहदेकाक्षरकोषश्च *etc.* [Avyayakoṣa. A metrical vocabulary of indeclinable words. Followed by Bṛihad-ekāksharakoṣa, a similar work on monosyllables. With a metrical account of the author's family and literary work.] pp. 28. कलिकाता [*Calcutta,*] 1899. 8°. **14093. b. 20.(2.)**

DVĀRAKĀNĀTHA NYĀYAPAÑCHĀNANA. See BHAVĀNANDA SIDDHĀNTAVĀGĪṢA. কারকচক্রম্ *etc.* [Kārakachakra. With commentaries. Edited by Dvārakānātha and Gauragovinda.] [1900.] 8°. **14090. bb. 15.(1.)**

DYĀNATI RĀYA. समाधिमरण भाषा . . . तीर्थ वन्दना स्तोत्र [Samādhimaraṇa. A Jain religious poem, in a Hindi metrical version. Followed by the Tīrthavandanāstotra.] pp. 11. लखनऊ १९०१ [*Lucknow,* 1901.] 12°. **14100. a. 21.(3.)**

EAST. The Sacred Books of the East Described and Examined. Hindu Series. *London, Madras* [printed], 1895, *etc.* 8°. **14010. cc. 9.**

In progress? Works issued in this series are catalogued under the following headings:—

Vol. 1. Vedas. Macdonald (K. S.). ,, 2. Upanishads. Mahābhārata. — *Bhagavadgītā.* Sadānanda Yogīndra.	Vol. 2. Patañjali. Manu. ,, 3. Vālmīki. Murdoch (J.). Purāṇas. — *Vishṇupurāṇa.*

EDMUNDS (ALBERT J.). See SUTTAPIṬAKA. — *Khuddakanikāya.* [*Dhammapada.*] Hymns of the Faith. Dhammapada . . . Translated . . . by A. J. Edmunds. 1902. 8°. **14098. c. 74.**

EDWARD VII, *King of Great Britain and Ireland.* See ṢAURĪNDRAMOHANA ṬHĀKURA, *Sir.* The Coronation: being a compilation of the procedure as laid down in . . . classical works, with stanzas specially addressed to his . . . Majesty the Emperor of India, *etc.* 1903. 12°. **14053. ccc. 46.**

—— See ṢIVARĀMA PĀṆḌE. एडवर्ड राज्याभिषेक . . . Edward Rajyabhisbek. A . . . poem on the coronation of . . . Edward VII, *etc.* [1902.] 12°. **14072. b. 27.**

EGGELING (JULIUS). See BRĀHMAṆAS.—*Ṣatapathabrāhmaṇa.* The Satapatha-Brâhmana . . . Translated [with introductions] by J. Eggeling. 1882-1900. [*Sacred Books of the East.*] **2003. a, b. (vol. 11, 26, 41, 43, 44.)**

EKĀDAṢĪNIRṆAYA. अथैकादशीनिर्णयः [Ekādaṣīnirṇaya. A work on the determination of the Ekādaṣī festival.] See PURĀṆAS. — *Selections.* अथ . . . षड्विंशत्येकादशीमाहात्म्यं प्रा° [Ekādaṣīmāhātmya, *etc.*] ff. 1-3. [1899.] *obl.* 8°. **14016. d. 55.**

EKĀKSHARĪ-KOṢA. अथ एकाक्षरीकोशः *etc.* [Ekāksharī-koṣa. A metrical dictionary of monosyllabic words, in 38 stanzas.] See ṢABDARŪPĀVALI. एकाक्षरकोशसमेता शब्दरूपावलिः [Ṣabdarūpāvali, *etc.*] pp. 44-49. 1890. 12°. **14090. b. 38.(2.)**

EKĀMBARA ṢĀSTRĪ, *Komāṇḍūr.* See MAṬHĀMNĀYA. శ్రీమఠామ్నాయః *etc.* [Maṭhāmnāya, *etc.* Edited by Ekāmbara.] 1894. 8°. **14048. bb. 42.(3.)**

ELWELL (LEVI H.). See SUTTAPIṬAKA.—*Khuddakanikāya.* [*Jātaka.*] Nine Jatakas . . . with vocabulary by L. H. Elwell. 1886. 16°. **14098. a. 24.**

EPHEMERIDES. श्रीसंवत् १९४७ शकः १८१२ . . . तिथिपत्रं *etc.* [Almanack for Samvat 1947, A.D. 1890-91. Compiled by Sudhākara Dvivedī.] pp. 47. वाराणस्यां १८८९ [*Benares,* 1889.] *obl.* 8°. **14096. b. 10.(1.)**

—— श्रीमकरन्दीयपंचांगंश्रीसम्वत् १९४७ [Almanack for Samvat 1947, A.D. 1890-91.] pp. 31, *lith.* काशी १९४७ [*Benares,* 1890.] *obl.* 8°. **14096. b. 9.(1.)**

—— मु[*leg.* भु]शरनवेन्द्र १९५१ ब्दीयेनेपालदेशीयं पञ्चाङ्गम् [Almanack for Vikrama-Samvat 1951, Nepal-Samvat 1014-5, A.D. 1894-95. Compiled by Ratnamāna of Kathmandu.] ff. 18, *lith.* बनारस [*Benares,* 1893.] *obl.* 16°. **14096. a. 3.**

—— पत्रा श्रीसंवत १९५३ *etc.* [Almanack for Samvat 1953, A.D. 1896-97. Compiled by Sūryanārāyaṇa Siddhāntī.] pp. 40. लखनऊ १८९६ [*Lucknow,* 1896.] *obl.* 8°. **14096. b. 10.(2.)**

—— अजितप्रकाशपंचांगम् *etc.* [Ajitaprakāṣa-pañchāṅga. An almanack for Samvat 1954, A.D. 1897-98. Compiled by Kūrmall Ṣarmā.] pp. 42. अजमेर १८९७ [*Ajmere,* 1897.] *obl.* 8°. **14096. b. 11.**

EPHEMERIDES (*continued*). (**जोधपुरकेचंडूपंचांगग्रहगणितसहितसटीक**) [Chaṇḍū-pañchāṅga. An almanack for Samvat 1955, A.D. 1898-99, in Sanskrit and Hindi.] pp. 41. **मुंबई** [*Bombay*, 1897.] *obl.* 8°. **14096. b. 9.(2.)**

—— **पत्रा श्रीसंवत १९५६ श्रीबापूदेवशास्त्रीजीका** *etc.* [Bāpūdeva Ṣāstrī's Almanack for Samvat 1956, A.D. 1899-1900. Compiled by his pupils.] pp. 38. **काश्यां** [*Benares*, 1898.] *obl.* 8°. **14096. b. 10.(3.)**

ETTAN RAJA. *See* MĀNAVIKRAMA, *Rājakumāra.*

EUCLID. The Rekhâgaṇita, or Geometry in Sanskrit. Composed [*i.e.* translated from the Arabic version of Naṣīr al-Dīn Muḥammad ibn Muḥammad al-Ṭūsī] by Samrâḍ Jagannâtha. Volume I. Books I—VI. (Volume II. Books VII—XV.) Undertaken for publication by the late Harilâl Harshâdarâi Dhruva ... Edited ... with a critical preface, introduction, and notes in English by Kamalâśaṅkara Prâṇaśaṅkara Trivedî. (**रेखागणितम्**) 2 vols. *Bombay*, 1901-1902. 8°. **14053. ccc. 36.**

Forms nos. lxi.—lxii. *of the* Bombay Sanskrit Series.

—— **रेखागणितस्यैकादशद्वादशाध्यायौ** *etc.* [Rekhāgaṇita. A translation of the propositions of Euclid's Elements, by Sudhākara Dvivedī. Books xi.-xii. With a commentary styled Vāsanāmañjarī by Kṛishṇadatta Jhā.] pp. 36, *lith.* **वाराणस्यां १८९१** [*Benares*, 1891.] 8°. **14053. d. 53.**

FAUSBØLL (VIGGO). *See* GREAT BRITAIN AND IRELAND.—*India Office Library.* Catalogue of the Mandalay MSS. in the India Office Library ... By ... V. Fausböll. 1896. 8°. [*Journal of the Pali Text Society.*] **14098. b.**

—— *See* SUTTAPIṬAKA.—*Khuddakanikāya.* [*Dhammapada.*] The Dhammapada ... Edited a second time with a literal Latin translation and notes ... By V. Fausbøll. 1900. 8°. **14098. b. 23**

—— *See* SUTTAPIṬAKA.—*Khuddakanikāya.* [*Jātaka.*] The Jātaka ... with its commentary ... Edited ... by V. Fausbøll, *etc.* 1877-1897. 8°. **14098. d. 23.**

—— *See* SUTTAPIṬAKA.—*Khuddakanikāya.* [*Suttanipāta.*] The Sutta-nipâta ... Translated ... by V. Fausböll. 1898. 8°. [*Sacred Books of the East.*] **2003. a.(vol. 10.)**

FAUSBØLL (VIGGO) (*continued*). Indian Mythology according to the Mahābhārata, in outline by V. Fausbøll. (Luzac's Oriental Religions Series. Vol. I.) pp. xxxii. 206. *London, Copenhagen* [printed], 1903. 8°. **14003. l. 4.**

—— [Another copy.] **4506. f.**

FERNANDO (ABRAHAM), *S.* *See* SUṢRUTA. Susruta Sutra-sthana. 1st part. Translated [into Sinhalese] ... by S. A. Fernando. 1896. 8°. **14043. e. 32.**

FERNANDO (DANIEL), *H.*, called TAMBI-APPU GURUNNĀNSE. *See* NĀRĀYAṆA BHAṬṬA, *Astrologer.* චමත්කාරචින්තාමණී *etc.* [Chamatkārachintāmaṇi. With Sinhalese interpretation by Fernando.] 1891. 8°. **14053. cc. 63.(1.)**

—— *See* UḌUDĀYAPRADĪPA. උඩුදායප්‍රදීපය *etc.* [Uḍudāyapradīpa. With a Sinhalese interpretation by Fernando.] 1888. 8°. **14053. cc. 63.(3.)**

FINOT (LOUIS). *See* RĀSHṬRAPĀLAPARIPṚICHCHHĀ. **राष्ट्रपालपरिपृच्छा ।** Rāṣṭrapālaparipṛcchā ... Publié par L. Finot. 1901. 8°. [*Bibliotheca Buddhica.*] **14003. dd. 2.**

—— Les Lapidaires Indiens, *etc.* [Comprising a series of texts—viz. Buddha Bhaṭṭa's Ratnaparīkshā, Varāhamihira's Bṛihatsaṃhitā lxxx.-lxxxiii., the Agastimata and Ratnaparīkshā ascribed to Agastya, Nārāyaṇa Paṇḍita's Navaratnaparīkshā, Ratnasaṅgraha, Laghu-ratnaparīkshā, and Maṇimāhātmya or Maṇiparīkshā—with translation and introduction.] (Bibliothèque de l'École des Hautes Études ... Sciences philologiques et historiques. Cent-onzième fascicule.) pp. 280. *Paris, Chalon-sur-Saône* [printed], 1896. 8°. **Ac. 8929.(fasc. 111.)**

FIÓK (KÁROLY). *See* KĀLIDĀSA.—*Abhijñānaṣakuntala.* Sakuntala ... Forditotta Fiók Károly, *etc.* 1887. 8°. **Ac. 8983/23.**

FLECHIA (GIOVANNI). *See* KĀLIDĀSA.—*Meghadūta.* Meghaduta ... Tradotto da G. Flechia. 1897-1899. 8°. [*Studi Italiani.*] **P.P. 4884. da.(vol. 1-3.)**

—— [A separate issue of the preceding.] **14070. dd. 7.**

FLEET (JOHN FAITHFULL). *See* PERIODICAL PUBLICATIONS.—*Bombay*. The Indian Antiquary, *etc.* (Vol. xiv.-xx., edited by J. F. Fleet, *etc.*) 1872, *etc.* 4°. **14096. e.**

FORMICHI (CARLO). *See* KĀMANDAKI. Il Nîtisâra, *etc.* [Translated by C. Formichi.] 1899, *etc.* 8°. [*Giornale della Società Asiatica Italiana.*] **Ac. 8804. (vol. 12, *etc.*)**

—— *See* UPANISHADS.—*Separate Upanishads.* Il primo capitolo della Brahma-Upanishad, coll' annessovi commento di Nârâyaṇa, tradotto e . . . discusso dal Dr C. Formichi. 1897. 4°. **14010. ee. 2.**

FOUCAUX (PHILIPPE ÉDOUARD). *See* LALITAVISTARA. Le Lalita Vistara . . . Traduit . . . par Ph. Ed. Foucaux, *etc.* 1884, 1892. 4°. [*Annales du Musée Guimet.*] **7704. h. 21. (tom. 6, 19.)**

—— *See* MAHĀBHĀRATA. — *Ādiparva.* Vyasa. Sakountala. Traduction libre de P.-E. Foucaux, *etc.* 1894. 16°. **14060. a. 13.**

FOULKES (THOMAS). *See* PRATĀPARUDRA DEVA. The Hindu Law of Inheritance . . . translated . . . by . . . T. Foulkes. 1881. 8°. **14039. a. 16.**

FRANCIS (HENRY THOMAS). *See* SUTTAPIṬAKA.—*Khuddakanikāya.* [*Jātaka.*] The Jātaka, *etc.* (Vol. iii., translated by H. T. Francis . . . and R. A. Neil.) 1895, *etc.* 8°. **14098. dd. 8.**

FRANKE (R. OTTO). Die Indischen Genuslehren, mit dem Text der Liṅgânuçâsana's des Çâkaṭâyana, Harṣavardhana, Vararuci, nebst Auszügen aus den Commentaren des Yakṣavarman zu Ç. und des Çabarasvâmin zu H., und mit einem Anhang über die indischen Namen, *etc.* pp. 155, i. *Kiel, Bonn* [printed], 1890. 8°. **14093. d. 19.**

—— Pāli und Sanskrit in ihrem historischen und geographischen Verhältnis auf Grund der Inschriften und Münzen dargestellt, *etc.* pp. vi. 176. *Strassburg,* 1902. 8°. **759. c. 18.**

FRANKFURTER (O). Handbook of Pali. Being an elementary grammar, a chrestomathy, and a glossary. Compiled by O. Frankfurter. pp. xxi. 179; 4 *plates.* *London and Edinburgh, Hertford* [printed], 1883. 8°. **12906. cc. 20.**

FRIEDLAENDER (WALTER). *See* ĀRAṆYAKAS.—*Kaushītakyāraṇyaka.* Der mahāvrata-Abschnitt des Çāṅkhāyana-Āraṇyaka herausgegeben, übersetzt und mit Anmerkungen versehen von W. Friedlaender. 1900. 8°. **14007. cc. 27.**

FRITZE (LUDWIG). *See* BHAVABHŪTI. Malati und Madhava . . . übersetzt von L. Fritze. [1884.] 12°. **012207. f. (no. 1844.)**

—— *See* ŚŪDRAKA. Vasantasena . . . von E. Pohl. [Adapted from the version of L. Fritze.] 1893. 8°. **14079. b. 40.**

FUEHRER (ALOÏS ANTON). Classified List of the Samskrit, Prakrit, Pali, and Hindi Manuscripts in . . . the Provincial Museum, N.-W. Provinces and Oudh. Compiled by A. Führer. *See* LUCKNOW.—*Provincial Museum.* Catalogue, *etc.* pp. 157-169. 1892. 8°. **011900. ee. 15.**

FUMI (FAUSTO GHERARDO). *See* VETĀLAPAÑCHAVIṂŚATI. Novelle del Vetâla. Tradotte dal sanscrito [by F. G. Fumi.] 1892. 8°. [*Archivio per lo Studio delle Tradizioni Popolari.*] **P.P. 4168. d. (vol. 11.)**

GADĀDHARA BHAṬṬA, *son of Gaurīpati.* रसिकजीवनम् । [Rasikajīvana. A poetical anthology.] [1891.] *See* PERIODICAL PUBLICATIONS.—*Bombay.* ग्रन्थरत्नमाला *etc.* (Granth Ratna Málá, *etc.*) Vol. V, no. 3-6. 1887-[1892]. 8°. **14096. c. 8. (vol. 5.)**

Incomplete, wanting the end. Selected verses from this work have been published by P. Regnaud in the Annuaire de la Faculté des Lettres de Lyon, *Année* i.-iii. (1883-5).

GADĀDHARA BHAṬṬĀCHĀRYA, *the Logician.* *See* GAṄGEŚA UPĀDHYĀYA. హేత్వాభాససామాన్యనిరుక్తి *etc.* [Hetvābhāsasāmānyanirukti. With the Dīdhiti of Raghunātha. Followed by Gadādhara's Gādādharī upon the latter and Raghunātha Śāstrī Parvate's gloss upon Gadādhara.] [1893.] 8°. **14048. dd. 14.**

—— *See* GAṄGEŚA UPĀDHYĀYA. పక్షతా *etc.* [Pakshatā. With Raghunātha's Dīdhiti. Followed by the corresponding section of Gadādhara's Gādādharī upon the latter and Krishṇa Bhaṭṭa Ārḍe's gloss upon Gadādhara.] [1890.] 8°. **14048. e. 19.**

—— *See* GAṄGEŚA UPĀDHYĀYA. The Pramanyavadaha [*sic*] by . . . Gadadara . . . with Thathva

Chintamani by Gangasopadyaya and Didhithi by Raghunadha . . . Vol. 1. 1901. 8°. [*Śāstramuktāvali.*] **14049. a. 1. (no. 4.)**

—— *See* Gaṅgeṣa Upādhyāya. A Collection of Sadharana, Asadharana, Anupasambari, and Virodha, Grandhas. By . . . Gadadhara Bhattacharya. With [the corresponding passages from the] Mani and Didhithi of Gangesopadhyaya and Raghunatha, *etc.* 1900. 8°. [*Nyāyaratnāvalī.*] **14048. e. 31.(2.)**

—— *See* Gaṅgeṣa Upādhyāya. सत्प्रतिपक्ष° [Satpratipakshagrantha. The section on *satpratipaksha*, with the corresponding portions of the Dīdhiti and Gādādharī.] 1901. 8°. [*Nyāyaratnāvalī.*] **14048. e. 31.(3.)**

—— *See* Gaṅgeṣa Upādhyāya. Savyabhichara Samanyanirukthi . . . With [the corresponding passages from the] Mani and Didhithi of Gangesopadhyaya and Raghunatha, *etc.* 1900. 8°. [*Nyāyaratnāvalī.*] **14048. e. 31.(1.)**

—— *See* Gaṅgeṣa Upādhyāya. సిద్ధాన్తలక్షణమ్ *etc.* [Siddhāntalakshaṇa. With Raghunātha's Dīdhiti, and followed by the corresponding section of Gadādhara's commentary together with Kṛishṇa Bhaṭṭa Ārḍe's commentary upon Gadādhara.] [1893.] 8°. **14048. dd. 13.**

—— *See* Gaṅgeṣa Upādhyāya. व्याप्तिपञ्चकम् *etc.* [Vyāptipañchaka. With an extract from Raghunātha's commentary Ṣiromaṇi, and Gadādhara's gloss Gādādharī upon it, *etc.*] [1896.] 8°. **14048. e. 28.**

—— *See* Raghunātha Ṣiromaṇi. Avachedakata Nirukthi. By . . . Gadadhara . . . With Didhithi of Raghunadha, *etc.* 1901. 8°. [*Ṣāstramuktāvalī.*] **14049. a. 1. (no. 11.)**

—— *See* Udayana Āchārya. आत्मतत्त्वविवेकः *etc.* [Ātmatattvaviveka, or Bauddhadhikkāra. With portions of the gloss of Mathurānātha, the exposition by Raghunātha, and portions of the gloss upon the latter by Gadādhara, *etc.*] [1900, *etc.*] 8°. **14048. dd. 28.**

—— प्रतिबन्धकतावादः *etc.* [Pratibandhakatāvāda, or Viṣishṭavaiṣishṭyabodhavichāra.] pp. 37. काश्यां [*Benares*, 1892.] 8°. **14048. bb. 45.(3.)**

The second title is given in the colophon.

GADĀDHARA BHAṬṬĀCHĀRYA, *the Logician (continued).* शक्तिवादः *etc.* [Ṣaktivāda. With a commentary by Harinātha Tarkasiddhānta.] Pt. ii. pp. vii. 89-277. कलिकाता १८१२ [*Calcutta*, 1890.] 8°. **14048. bb. 43.**

Wanting Pt. 1, which contained the Sāmānyakāṇḍa.

—— ॥ व्युत्पत्तिवादः *etc.* [Vyutpattivāda. A discussion of logical denotation. Edited by Nārāyaṇa Ṣāstrī Paṭavardhana.] pp. 188. काश्यां १९५५ [*Benares*, 1899.] 8°. **14093. b. 27.(2.)**

—— ॥ व्युत्पत्तिवादः *etc.* [Vyutpattivāda. Edited by Karnāṭaka Kṛishṇa Ṣāstrī.] pp. 159. *Benares*, [1901.] 8°. **14049. a. 4.(1.)**

—— *See* Rākhāldās Nyāyaratna. शक्तिवाद-रहस्य-प्रकाशः [Ṣaktivādarahasyaprakāṣa. A dissertation on Gadādhara's Ṣaktivāda.] [1896.] 8°. **14048. bb. 50.(2.)**

—— *See* Viṣvanātha Pañchānana Bhaṭṭāchārya. शक्तिवाद . . . विवृतिः *etc.* [Ṣaktivādavivṛiti, Vyutpattivādavivṛiti, Jyeshṭhatvavādavivṛiti, Lakāravādavivṛiti, and Sādṛiṣyavādavivṛiti. Essays on dissertations of Gadādhara.] [1900.] 8°. **14049. a. 4.(2.)**

GADĀDHARA DĪKSHITA, *son of Vāmana. See* Kātyāyana. परिशिष्टकण्डिका [Pariṣishṭakaṇḍikā, Followed by the Ṣrāddhasūtra, with the *bhāshya* and Ṣrāddhasūtrapaddhati of Gadādhara, *etc.*] [1896.] 4°. [*Pāraskaragṛihyasūtra.*] **14010. f. 10.**

—— *See* Pāraskara. पारस्करगृह्यसूत्रम् *etc.* [Pāraskaragṛihyasūtra. With Gadādhara's Gṛihyasūtrabhāshya, *etc.*] [1896.] 4°. **14010. f. 10.**

GADĀDHARA RĀJAGURU. Gadādhara Paddhatau Kālasāra. By Gadādhara Rājaguru. Edited by Sadāçiva Miçra of Puri. 1900, *etc. See* Academies, *etc.*—Calcutta.—*Asiatic Society of Bengal.* Bibliotheca Indica. New Series. [Vol. 147.] 1848, *etc.* 8°. **14002. a. (vol. 147.)**

In progress.

GADĀDHARA TARKĀLAṄKĀRA. *See* Gadādhara Bhaṭṭāchārya, *the Logician.*

GADA SIṀHA. नानार्थमञ्जरी । [Nānārthamañjarī, or Anekārthamañjarī. A vocabulary of synonyms, with a Bengali translation.] *See* GOPĪRAMAṆA TARKARATNA. কোষচন্দ্রিকা *etc.* [Koṣachandrikā.] pp. 1-20. [1893.] 12°. **14090. b. 44.(1.)**

—— ऊष्मविवेकः *etc.* [Ūshmaviveka. A treatise in 112 stanzas on the orthography of words containing sibilants, with a commentary by Paramesvara Jhā of Tarauni. Followed by the Laghuratnakoṣa, a short lexicon attributed to Purushottama Deva.] pp. 27, 5. दरभङ्गा १८१२ [*Darbhangah,* 1890.] 8°. **14093. b. 17.(2.)**

GÂDGIL (D. K.). *See* DINAKARA KEṢAVA ṢĀSTRĪ GĀḌGIL.

GĀGĀ BHAṬṬA. *See* VIṢVEṢVARA BHAṬṬA, also called GĀGĀ BHAṬṬA.

GAJĀNANA CHINTĀMAṆI DEVA. *See* ANANTA BHAṬṬA, *the Poet.* Anantbhatt Kavi's Bharata Champû. With Antaḥpraveshikâ commentary by Gaanjan [*sic*] Chintaman Deo. [1901.] 8°. **14072. ccc. 26.**

GAJASĀRA, *disciple of Dhavalachandra.* अथ चोवीश दंडक [Chovīsa-daṇḍaka (Chaüvīsa-d.°), in Sanskrit Chaturviṃṣati-daṇḍaka. A Jain poem in 47 Prakrit stanzas upon the 24 phases of being. With Gujarati translation.] *See* HEMAṢAṄKARA LAKSHMĪṢAṄKARA VARDHAMĀNKAR. प्रकरण माला *etc.* [Prakaraṇamālā.] pp. 33-44. [1901.] 8°. **14100. d. 11.**

The author wrote under Jinahaṃsa, who died Samv. 1582.

GALADṚIKṢIKSHĀ. अथ गलदृक्शिक्षा *etc.* [Galadṛikṣikshā, or Luptarksaṅkhyā. A list of repeated passages in the text of the White Yajurveda.] *See* YUGALAKIṢORA VYĀSA PĀṬHAKA. श्रीमद्याज्ञवल्क्यादि . . . शिक्षासङ्ग्रहः . . . A collection of Śikshás, *etc.* pp. 181-184. 1893. 8°. **14093. b. 31.**

GAṆĀDHĪṢA, *Jain Poet.* *See* ḌĀHYĀBHĀI FATEHCHAND and MOTĪLĀL MAHĀSUKHBHĀI. शोभनस्तवनावली *etc.* [Ṣobhanastavanāvalī. Hymns by Gaṇādhīṣa and others.] [1897.] 12°. **14100. a. 17.**

GAṆAPATI, *son of Rāvala Hariṣaṅkara.* मुहूर्तगणपति *etc.* [Muhūrtagaṇapati. A manual of astrology. Edited with a Hindi version by Rāmasvarūpa Ṣarmā.] pp. xvii. 316. मुम्बई १८९८ [*Bombay,* 1898.] 8°. **14053. d. 57.**

GAṆAPATI ṢĀSTRĪ, *Paṅgānāḍ.* *See* BĀDARĀYAṆA. ശ്രീമദ്ബാദരായണപ്രണീതബ്രഹ്മസൂത്രശൈവഭാഷ്യം *etc.* [Brahmasūtra. With the exposition of Ṣrikaṇṭha, *etc.* Edited by Gaṇapati.] [1899.] 8°. **14048. c. 72.(3.)**

GAṆḌĀ SINGH, *Sādhu, disciple of Nihāl Singh.* *See* MAHĀDEVA SARASVATĪ. अथ तत्त्वानुसन्धान° [Tattvānusandhāna. With a gloss by Gaṇḍā Singh.] [1891.] *obl.* 4°. **14048. f. 23.**

GĀNDHARVARĀJAPRAYOGA. गांधर्वराज प्रयोग तथा लक्ष्मीस्तोत्र [Gāndharvarājaprayoga. A magic ritual for winning a bride. Followed by a Lakshmīstotra.] pp. 11. अमदावाद १८९० [*Ahmadabad,* 1890.] 12°. **14028. b. 78.(1.)**

GAṆEṢA, *son of Gopāla.* जातकालंकारः *etc.* [Jātakālaṅkāra. With the Sanskrit commentary of Harabhānu Ṣukla and a Hindi translation by Rāmanātha Ṣarmā. Edited by Sītārāma Ṣrīkrishṇa Jāmbhekar.] pp. 91. मुम्बापुर्यां १९०२ [*Bombay,* 1902.] 8°. **14053. ccc. 41.**

GAṆEṢA, *son of Keṣava, of Nandigram.* ग्रहलाघवम् *etc.* (Grahalaghava. By Pt. Ganesh Daivajna. With Hindi translation by Pandit Jiyá Rám Shástri. Corrected [with a preface] by Pt. Rameshwar Bhatt.) pp. vi. vi. 248, iii. *Kalyan-Bombay,* 1899. 8°. **14053. ccc. 26.**

GAṆEṢADATTA ṢĀSTRĪ, *of Forman Christian College, Lahore.* *See* PĀṆINI. — *Siddhāntakaumudī.* मध्यकौमुदी . . . The Madhya Kaumudi . . . Edited by . . . Ganesh Dutt, *etc.* 1899. 12°. **14092. a. 22.**

GAṆEṢA KĀṢĪNĀTHA KĀḶE. *See* PURĀṆAS.—*Bhavishyottarapurāṇa.* ॥ अथ . . . महालक्ष्मीव्रतकथा *etc.* [Mahālakshmīvratakathā. With Hindi translation by Gaṇeṣa Kāḷe.] [1900.] *obl.* 8°. **14016. d. 59.**

GAṆEṢA NĀRĀYAṆA KARVE, *of Gwalior.* श्रीदत्तात्रेयसर्वस्वं [Dattātreyasarvasva. A Pauranic poem in 44 *adhyāyas* upon the sage Dattātreya, Yoga, and various topics of metaphysics and myth.] pp. 308, iii. काश्यां १९५५ [*Benares,* 1899.] 8°. **14033. aa. 1.(2.)**

GAṆEṢA RAṄGANĀTHA LĀḶE, *of Kikwi, Poona.* *See* RAṄGANĀTHA SAKHĀRĀMA LĀḶE. आरोग्यसिंधु *etc.* [Ārogyasindhu. Edited by Gaṇeṣa Lāḷe.] [1900.] 8°. **14043. cc. 14.**

GAṆEṢA RAṄGANĀTHA LĀḶE, *of Kikwi, Poona (continued)*. मदनविलास. शृंगारसार. आरोग्यरक्षक etc. [Madanavilāsa, or Śriṅgārasāra. A medical Ars Amoris. Compiled from various sources. With Marathi translation, appendices, *etc.*] Vol. I—II. पुणें १९०० [*Poona*, 1900.] 8°. **14043. cc. 13.**

GAṆEṢA ŚĀSTRĪ KSHĪRASĀGARA. *See* BHĀSKARA, *son of Mudgala*. ॥ अर्थसङ्ग्रहः etc. [Arthasaṅgraha. With commentary. Edited by Gaṇeṣa Śāstrī.] [1897.] 8°. **14048. cc. 20.**

—— *See* NĀGEṢA BHAṬṬA. [*Paribhāshendusekhara.*] ॥ परिभाषेन्दुशेखरः *etc.* [Paribhāshendusekhara. With commentary of Bhairava Miṣra. Edited by Gaṇeṣa Śāstrī.] [1897.] 8°. **14090. c. 42.**

GANESH DUTT. *See* GAṆEṢADATTA.

GAṄGĀDĀSA, *disciple of Dharmachandra*. सम्मेदशिखरविधानसंस्कृतपूजनम् [Sammedaṣikharavidhānapūjana. Lyrics on the Sammedaṣikhara, a spot held sacred by the Jains.] *See* NEMICHANDRA NĀRĀYAṆA CHAVḌE. श्री सम्मेदशिखरजी विधान संगीत *etc.* [Sammedaṣikharajī-vidhānasaṅgīta, *etc.*] pp. 29-53. [1900.] 12°. **14100. a. 22.**

GAṄGĀDATTA, *Upretī*. लोक द्वयोपदेश Precepts for this world and the next . . . Translated [into English and Hindi, and compiled] from the Sanscrit [of Harivaṃṣa and others, with the original Sanskrit texts]. By Pandit Gangâ Datt Upreti, *etc.* pp. ii. 56. अल्मोड़ा [*Almora*,] 1892. 8°. **14085. d. 30.**

GAṄGĀDHARA, *Architect*. शिल्पदीपक *etc.* [Ṣilpadīpaka. A metrical treatise on architecture, in 5 *prakaraṇas*. Edited with Gujarati translation and notes by Govardhana Devarāma Tripāṭhī.] pp. 100; 6 *plates*. અમદાવાદ ૧૮૫૪ [*Ahmadabad*, 1898.] 8°. **14053. d. 54.**

GAṄGĀDHARA, *Vaidya*. *See* NĀḌĪVIJÑĀNA. नाड़ीविज्ञानम् *etc.* [Nāḍīvijñāna. With commentary by Gaṅgādhara.] [1902.] 12°. **14043. b. 10.(3.)**

GAṄGĀDHARA BHAṬṬĀCHĀRYA. *See* VYĀḌI. ॥ अथ विकृतिवल्ली ॥ [Vikṛitivallī. Chapter i., or Jaṭāpaṭala, with the commentary Vikṛitikaumudī of Gaṅgādhara.] [1889.] 8°. [*Ushā.*] **14010. c. 43.(vol. 1.)**

GAṄGĀDHARA SARASVATĪ. *See* SVĀRĀJYASIDDHI. ॥ स्वाराज्यसिद्धि° [Svārājyasiddhi. With commentary, called Kaivalyakalpadruma, by Gaṅgādhara.] [1891.] *obl.* Fol. **14048. ee. 2.**

GAṄGĀDHARA ŚĀSTRĪ DRAVIḌA. *See* SUDARṢANASAṂHITĀ. हनुमत कवच *etc.* [Hanumatkavacha, *etc.* Edited by Gaṅgādhara.] [1897.] 8°. **14033. aa. 5.(1.)**

—— *See* TANTRAS. [*Ḍāmaratantra.*] कार्तवीर्यकवचम् [*sic*] [Kārtavīryārjunakavacha. Edited by Gaṅgādhara.] [1897.] 8°. **14033. aa. 5.(3.)**

GAṄGĀDHARA ŚĀSTRĪ MĀNAVALLĪ, *Mahāmahopādhyāya*. *See* APYAYA DĪKSHITA. The Siddhântaleśa . . . Edited [with preface] by . . . Gaṅgâdhara, *etc.* 1890. 8°. **14048. dd. 3.(vol. 1.)**

—— *See* GOTAMA. The Nyâyamañjarî. . . . Edited by . . . Gaṅgâdhara, *etc.* 1895. 8°. **14048. dd. 3.(vol. 8.)**

—— *See* GOTAMA. The Nyâyasûtras with Vâtsyâyana's Bhâshya . . . Edited [with indexes] by . . . Gaṅgâdhara, *etc.* 1896. 8°. **14048. dd. 3.(vol. 9.)**

—— *See* PĀRTHASĀRATHI MIṢRA. न्यायरत्नमाला *etc.* (Nyâyaratnamâlâ . . . Edited by . . . Gangadhar, *etc.*) [1900.] 8°. **14004. a. 7.**

—— *See* RAGHUNĀTHA VARMĀ. लौकिकन्यायसंग्रहः . . . Laukikanyāyasaṃgraha. . . . Edited by . . . Gangādhara, *etc.* 1902. 8°. [*The Pandit.*] **14096. d. 6.(vol. 23, 24.)**

—— *See* VĀCHASPATI MIṢRA. [*Nyāyavārttikatātparyaṭīkā.*] The Nyâyavârttikatâtparyaṭîkâ . . . Edited by . . . Gaṅgâdhara, *etc.* 1898. 8°. **14048. dd. 3.(vol. 13.)**

—— *See* VĀCHASPATI MIṢRA. [*Tattvabindu.*] तत्त्वबिन्दुः । [Tattvabindu. Edited by Gaṅgādhara.] 1892. 8°. [*The Pandit.*] **14096. d. 6.(vol. 14.)**

GAṄGĀDHARA ŚĀSTRĪ TAILAṄGA. *See* GAṄGĀDHARA ŚĀSTRĪ MĀNAVALLĪ.

GAṄGĀDHARA VĀJAPEYĪ, *son of Devasiṃha and disciple of Viṣvarūpa*. *See* APYAYA DĪKSHITA. Kuvalayananda . . . With the commentary called Rasika-ranjani of . . . Gangadhara, *etc.* 1892. 8°. **14053. cc. 64.**

GAṄGĀDHARA VĀMANA LELE. *See* Āranyakas.—*Taittirīyāraṇyaka.* त्रिसुपर्णे *etc.* [Trisuparṇamantra. With commentary of Sāyana. Edited with a Marathi introduction, notes,and translation and an English version by Gaṅgādhara Lelc.] [1900.] 8°. **14028. d. 35.(2.)**

GAṄGĀDHARENDRA SARASVATĪ, *disciple of Rāmānanda.* *See* Ṣuka. शुकविरचितम् . . . निर्वाणाष्टकम् [Nirvāṇāshṭaka. With commentary by Gaṅgādharendra.] [1889.] 8°. [*Grantharatnamālā.*] **14096. c. 8.(vol. 2.)**

GAṄGĀJĪVANA ṢARMĀ PĀṬHAKA, *of Sohna.* आदि गौडप्रदीपिका *etc.* [Ādigauḍapradīpikā. A treatise in Hindi upon the geographical distribution of the early Hindus, notably of the Brahmans, and the religious quality of the early Gaur Brahmans. Illustrated by quotations from Manu, Puranic, and cognate literature. Edited by Keṣavānanda Vijñānendra Shaṭṣāstrī.] pp. 40, *lith.* इन्द्रप्रस्थे १९५६ [*Delhi,* 1899.] 12°. **14058. a. 14.(3.)**

GAṄGĀNĀTHA JHĀ, *of Darbhangah.* *See* Īṣvara Krishṇa. An English Translation, with the Sanskrit Text, of the Tattva-kaumudî . . . by Gangânâtha Jhâ. 1896. 8°. **14048. cc. 3.**

—— *See* Jaimini.—*Mīmāṃsāsūtra.* Çlokavārtika. Translated . . . with extracts from the commentaries of Sucarīta[*sic*] Miçra . . . and Pārthasārathi Miçra . . . by Gaṇgānātha Jhā. 1900, *etc.* 8°. [*Bibliotheca Indica.*] **14002. a. (vol. 146.)**

—— *See* Mammaṭa Āchārya. The Kāvya-prakāça . . . Translated . . . by Gaṅgānātha Jhā. 1898. 8°. [*The Pandit.*] **14096. d. 6.(vol. 18-21.)**

—— *See* Upanishads.—*Small Collections.* The Isa, Kena & Mundaka Upanishads, *etc.* (Vol. III, IV, The Chhándogya Upanishad and Sri Sankara's commentary, translated by Gangánath Jha'.). 1898, *etc.* 12°. **14010. b. 20.**

—— *See* Vijñānabhikshu. An English Translation . . . of the Yogasara-sangraha . . . by Gangânâtha Jha. 1894. 12°. **14048. b. 26.**

GAṄGĀPRASĀDA, *Professor at Meerut College.* The Constitution of Human Society. Being a philosophical exposition of the 9th Mantra of the Purusha Sukta [Ṛigveda X. xc. 12.] . . . By Gunga Prashad. pp. 16, ii. 1896. *See* Vedas. — Ṛigveda. — *Selections.* Vedic Texts. No. 1. 1896-1897. 8°. **14010. dd. 9.**

—— Septenary Composition of Solar Light. Being a scientific exposition of the 8th and 9th Mantrâs of the Sûrya Sûkta [Ṛigveda I. l.], *etc.* pp. 20, ii. 1897. *See* Vedas.—Ṛigveda.—*Single Hymns and Verses.* Vedic Texts. No. 2. 1896-1897. 8°. **14010. dd. 9.**

GAṄGĀPRASĀDA PĀṆḌEYA. आयुर्वेदशब्दार्णवः *etc.* [Āyurvedaṣabdārṇava. A glossary of Materia Medica, compiled from Sanskrit authorities and explained in Hindi.] pp. 212. प्रयाग १९५२ [*Allahabad,* 1895.] 8°. **14043. e. 29.**

GAṄGĀRĀMA DVIVEDĪ. भपरत्नद्योत *etc.* [Ratnadyota. A guide to good fortune by means of astrological and other like observations. With Hindi version. Second edition.] pp. iv. 110. *Lucknow,* १८९९ [1899.] 12°. **14053. b. 17.(6.)**

GAṄGĀSAHĀYA ṢARMĀ, *son of Rāmadhana, of Bundi.* *See* Purāṇas.—*Bhāgavatapurāṇa.* अथ . . . श्रीमद्भागवते प्रथमस्कन्धः *etc.* [Bhāgavatapurāṇa. With the commentary Anvitārthaprakāṣikā of Gaṅgāsahāya.] [1901.] *obl.* Fol. **14018. e. 3.**

GAṄGEṢA, styled Yakshavarmā, *Commentator upon Ṣākaṭāyana.* *See* Yakshavarmā.

GAṄGEṢA UPĀDHYĀYA. The Tattva-chintámaṇi . . . Part I, The Pratyaksha Khaṇḍa, with extracts from the commentaries of Mathuránátha Tarkavágíśa and of Jayadeva Miśra. (Part II, Anumána Khaṇḍa from Anumiti to Bádha from [*sic*] the commentaries of Mathuránátha Tarkavágíśa, Içvarānumāna with the commentary of Jayadeva Miçra. Part III, Upamāna Khaṇḍa, with the commentary of Krişṇakānta Vidyāvāgīça. Part IV, Çabda-khaṇḍa, from Vidhivāda to Pramāṇa-catuṣṭaya-prāmāṇyavāda, with the commentaries of Mathuranātha Tarkavāgīça and Jayadeva Miçra; and with the Ākhyātavāda and the Naṇvāda of . . . Raghunātha Çıromaṇi.) 4 vols. 1888-1901. *See* Academies, *etc.*—Calcutta.—*Asiatic Society of Bengal.* Bibliotheca Indica. New Series. [Vol. 98.] 1848, *etc.* 8°. **14002. a. (vol. 98.)**

GAṄGEṢA UPĀDHYĀYA (*continued*). హేత్వాభా-ససామాన్యనిరుక్తి *etc.* [Hetvābhāsasāmānya-nirukti. A paragraph from the section on Hetvābhāsa in the Anumānakhaṇḍa, with the Dīdhiti of Raghunātha. Followed by the corresponding section from Gadādhara's commentary Gādādharī upon the latter and Raghunātha Śāstrī Parvate's gloss Nyāyaratna upon Gadādhara. Edited by Koṇḍāpuram Kṛishṇārya.] pp. 212. మహీశూరు॥ ౧౮౯౩ [*Mysore*, 1893.] 8°.
14048. dd. 14.

—— केवलान्वयि अनुमानम् *etc.* [Kevalānvayyanumāna. Being the sections of °pūrvapaksha and °siddhānta from the Anumānakhaṇḍa of the Tattvachintāmaṇi. With excerpts from commentaries—viz. Raghunātha Śiromaṇi's Śiromaṇi, Jagadīśa Tarkavāgīśa's supercommentary thereon called Jāgadīśī Vivṛiti, and a gloss upon the last, called Jāgadīśīvādārtha, by the editor, Jīvānanda Vidyāsāgara. Second edition.] pp. 63. कलिकाता १८९७ [*Calcutta*, 1897.] 8°.
14048. bb. 45.(4.)

—— పక్షతా *etc.* [Pakshatā. Being the two paragraphs styled Pakshatāpūrvapaksha and Pakshatāsiddhānta in the Anumānakhaṇḍa, with Raghunātha's Dīdhiti. Followed by the corresponding section of Gadādhara's Gādādharī upon the latter and Kṛishṇa Bhaṭṭa Ārḍe's gloss upon Gadādhara. Edited by Kastūri Raṅgāchārya.] pp. 278. మహీశూరు॥ ౧౮౯౦ [*Mysore*, 1890.] 8°.
14048. e. 19.

—— पक्षता *etc.* [Pakshatā. With excerpts from commentaries—viz. the Śiromaṇi of Raghunātha, and its supercommentary, the Jāgadīśī Vivṛiti of Jagadīśa; the Māthurī of Mathurānātha Tarkavāgīśa; and the Jāgadīśīvādārtha, a gloss on Jagadīśa's work compiled by Jīvānanda Vidyāsāgara. Edited by the last-named. Second edition.] pp. 150. कलिकाता १८९७ [*Calcutta*, 1897.] 8°.
14048. bb. 45.(5.)

Pp. 77—78 are missing.

—— The Pramanyavadaha [*sic*] by Maha Mahopadyaya Sri Gadadara Bhattacharya, with [the corresponding part of the Pratyakshakhaṇḍa of the] Thathva Chinthamani by Gangasopadyaya and Didhithi by Raghunadha Siromani . . . Vol. 1 [comprising the Jñaptivāda.] (॥ ज्ञप्तिवादः ॥) pp. iv. 262. 1901. *See* ANANTĀCHĀRYA, *Prativādibhayaṅkara.* शास्त्रमुक्तावली. The Śasthramukthâvalî, *etc.* No. 4. 1899, *etc.* 8°.
14049. a. 1.(no. 4.)

—— A Collection of Sadharana, Asadharana, Anupasamhari, and Virodha, Grandhas. [Extracted from the Gādādharī, a commentary to Raghunātha's Dīdhiti upon Gaṅgeṣa's Tattvachintāmaṇi or Maṇi,] by . . . Gadadhara Bhattacharya. With [the corresponding passages from the] Mani and Didhithi of Gangesopadhyaya and Raghunatha Siromani. Edited by P. B. Anantha Chariar . . . సాధారణాసాధారణానుపసంహారి-విరోధగ్రంథా *etc.* pp. 90. 1900. *See* ANANTĀCHĀRYA, *Prativādibhayaṅkara.* Nyayarathnavali, *etc.* No. 2. 1900, *etc.* 8°. **14048. e. 31.(2.)**

—— सत्प्रतिपक्षग्रन्थः *etc.* [Satpratipakshagrantha. The section on *satpratipaksha* in the Anumānakhaṇḍa. With the corresponding portions of the Dīdhiti and the Gādādharī.] pp. 62. 1901. *See* ANANTĀCHĀRYA, *Prativādibhayaṅkara.* Nyayarathnavali, *etc.* No. 3. 1900, *etc.* 8°.
14048. e. 31.(3.)

—— Savyabhichara Samanyanirukthi. [An excerpt from the Gādādharī, a commentary to the Didhiti of Raghunātha upon Gaṅgeṣa's Tattvachintāmaṇi or Maṇi,] by . . . Gadadhara Bhattacharya. With [the corresponding passages from the] Mani and Didhithi of Gangesopadhyaya and Raghunatha Siromani. Edited by P. B. Ananthachariar . . . సవ్యభిచారసామా-న్యనిరుక్తి *etc.* pp. 77. 1900. *See* ANANTĀCHĀRYA, *Prativādibhayaṅkara.* Nyayarathnavali, *etc.* No. 1. 1900, *etc.* 8°. **14048. e. 31.(1.)**

—— గదాధరీయ సిద్ధాన్తలక్షణమ్ *etc.* [Siddhāntalakshaṇa. Being a paragraph from the Vyāptivāda of the Anumānakhaṇḍa, with Raghunātha's commentary Dīdhiti, and followed by the corresponding section of Gadādhara's commentary Gādādharī upon the latter, together with Kṛishṇa Bhaṭṭa Ārḍe's commentary upon Gadādhara. Edited by Lakshmīpuram Śrīnivāsāchārya.] pp. 190. మహీశూరు॥ ౧౮౯౩ [*Mysore*, 1893.] 8°.
14048. dd. 13.

GAṄGEṢA UPĀDHYĀYA (*continued*). सिद्धान्तलक्षणम् *etc.* (Siddhantalakshana ... With the commentaries[, respectively styled Ṣiromaṇi and Māthurī,] of Raghunatha Siromani, and Mathuranatha Tarkabagisha. With the gloss [upon the former] of Jagadisha Bhattacharya[, styled Jāgadīṣī]. Edited and published with questions and answers [entitled Phakkikāvivṛiti] by Pandit Jibananda Vidyasagara ... Second edition.) pp. 96. *Calcutta*, 1896. 8°. **14048. c. 79.(1.)**

English title taken from wrapper.

—— व्याप्तिपञ्चकम् *etc.* [Vyāptipañchaka. Five aphorisms from the Vyāptivāda of the Anumānakhaṇḍa. With an extract from Raghunātha's commentary Ṣiromaṇi; Mathurānātha's exegesis, styled Vyāptipañchakarahasya, from the Māthurī; Jagadīṣa's gloss Jāgadīṣī upon the former commentary; and Gadādhara's gloss Gādādharī upon the same. Edited, with notes styled Phakkikā upon Mathurānātha's commentary, by Jīvānanda Vidyāsāgara. Second edition.] pp. 32. कलिकाता १८९६ [*Calcutta*, 1896.] 8°. **14048. e. 28.**

—— व्याप्ति-पञ्चकम् *etc.* [Vyāptipañchaka. With the gloss of Mathurānātha and a commentary called Rahasyavivṛiti by Pramathanātha Tarkabhūshaṇa.] pp. 24. काश्यां १९५४ [*Benares*, 1897.] 8°. **14048. cc. 21.(1.)**

—— [For separately printed dissertations of Gadādhara upon Gaṅgesa's Logic:] *See* GADĀDHARA BHAṬṬĀCHĀRYA.

—— *See* RAGHUNĀTHA ṢIROMAṆI. Avachedakata Nirukthi ... With Didbithi of Raghunadha, *etc.* 1901. 8°. [*Ṣāstramuktāvalī.*] **14049. a. 1.(no. 11.)**

—— *See* RAGHUNĀTHA ṢIROMAṆI. जागदीशीव्यधिकरणधर्मावच्छिन्नाभावः [Vyadhikaraṇadharmāvachchhinnābhāva. Being the section from Raghunātha's commentary upon the chapter of that name in the Anumānakhaṇḍa. With Jagadīṣa's supercommentary Chaturdaṣalakshaṇī.] [1889.] *obl.* 4°. **14048. f. 21.**

—— *See* SAṄGAMEṢVARA ṢĀSTRĪ, *Gummalūri.* పంచలక్షణ్యపరి సంగమేశ్వరీయము *etc.* [Saṅgameṣvarīya. A commentary upon Mathurānātha's commentary to the Pañchalakshaṇī.] [1896.] 12°. **14048. b. 33.(1.)**

GAṄGULI (K. M.). *See* KIṢORĪMOHANA GAṄGOPĀDHYĀYA.

GAṆPAT-RĀU NĀRĀYAṆA KARVE. श्रीअनुसूयाचरित्र [Anusūyācharitra. A tract to propagate the worship of the goddess Devī-Anusūyā at the Anusūyākshetra and Atritīrtha, comprising a Sanskrit hymn to the goddess, a poetical Hindi *māhātmya*, and 15 Sanskrit stanzas describing the holy place.] pp. 15, 2. काशी [*Benares*, 1901.] 12°. **14154. d. 26.(3.)**

GAṆṬYAPPĀCHĀRI. *See* MŪLASTAMBHAPURĀṆA. ಮೂಲಸ್ತಂಭಮಹಾಪುರಾಣವು *etc.* [Mūlastambhapurāṇa. With Canarese translation by Gaṇṭyappāchāri and Ṣiddappāchāri.] 1893. 8°. **14028. c. 63.**

GARAḶAPURĪṢA ṢĀSTRĪ, *Sōsale.* ಚಮ್ಪೂರಾಮಾಯಣಯುದ್ಧಕಾಣ್ಡಃ *etc.* [Champūrāmāyaṇa. A *champū* on the story of the Rāmāyaṇa. Yuddhakāṇḍa, edited with a commentary called Madhumañjarī by Periyasvāmi Tirumalāchārya.] pp. 253. ಮೈಸೂರು ೧೮೯೧ [*Mysore*, 1891.] 8°. **14072. cc. 52.**

GARBE (RICHARD). *See* ĪṢVARA KṚISHṆA. Der Mondschein der Sâṃkhya-Wahrheit, Vâcaspatimiçra's Sâṃkhya-tattva-kaumudî, in deutscher Uebersetzung, nebst einer Einleitung ... von R. Garbe. 1892. 4°. [*Abhandlungen der Kgl. Bayerischen Akademie der Wissenschaften.*] **Ac. 713/6. (vol. 19.)**

—— *See* KAPILA. The Sāṁkhya-pravacana-bhāṣya ... Edited by R. Garbe. 1895. 8°. [*Harvard Oriental Series.*] **14003. l. 3.(vol. 2.)**

—— *See* VEDAS.—*Atharvaveda.* The Kashmirian Atharvaveda ... Reproduced by chromophotography from the manuscript in the University Library at Tübingen. Edited ... by ... R. Garbe, *etc.* 1901. Fol. **14010. e. 15.**

—— Die Sâṃkhya-Philosophie. Eine Darstellung des indischen Rationalismus nach den Quellen, *etc.* pp. viii. 347. *Leipzig*, 1894. 8°. **4503. bb. 43.**

—— Verzeichniss der Doktoren ... Beigefügt ist ein Verzeichniss der indischen Handschriften der . . . Universitäts-Bibliothek, Zuwachs der Jahre 1865-1899, von R. Garbe. 1899. 8°. *See* Academies, *etc.* — Tuebingen. — *Eberhard-Karls-Universitaet.* **Ac. 730.**

GARGA. ॥ अथ श्रीमद्गर्गसंहिता *etc.* [Gargasaṃhitā. A poetical account, in 9 cantos, of the life of Krishṇa. Prefaced by the Gargasaṃhitāmāhātmya, an excerpt from the Sammohanatantra. With Hindi translation by Vaṃṣīdhara. Edited by Kanhaiyālāl Vaṃṣīdhara.] 9 pts. [*Muttra*, 1898.] *obl.* 4°. **14028. e. 34.**

Wanting pp. 3-4 of preface and pp. 7-9 of pt. 6.

—— सामवेदीया लोमशीशिक्षा ॥ [Lomaṣī Ṣikshā. A Sāmavedī tract on Vedic phonetics, ascribed to Garga.] *See* Yugalakisora Vyāsa Pāṭhaka. श्रीमद्याज्ञवल्क्यादि . . . शिक्षासङ्ग्रहः . . . A collection of Śikshás, *etc.* pp. 456-462. 1893. 8°. **14093. b. 31.**

GĀRGYA GOPĀLA MISRA. *See* Gopāla Misra, *Gārgya.*

GAUḌAPĀDA ĀCHĀRYA. *See* Īṣvara Krishṇa. Sáṅkhya Káriká. With [a translation of] Gauḍapáda's scholia, *etc.* 1898. 8°. [*Sáṅkhya Philosophy.*] **14048. b. 34. (fasc. 1.)**

—— *See* Upanishads. — *Separate Upanishads.* The Mândûkyopanishad. With Gaudapâda's Kârikâs . . . Translated into English, *etc.* 1894. 8°. **14007. cc. 24.**

—— গৌড়পাদীয় আগম *etc.* [Āgamaṣāstra, or Māṇḍūkyopanishatkārikāḥ. Chapters ii. (Vaitathyaprakaraṇa), iii. (Mokshapr.° or Advaitapr.°), and iv. (Alātaṣāntipr.°). With a Bengali translation by Mahendranātha Ghoshāl.] pp. ii. 76. বারাণসী ১২৯৬ [*Benares,* 1890.] 8°. **14010. c. 52.(4.)**

—— கௌடபாதகாரிகா பாஷ்யம்: [Kārikāḥ. With the commentary of Ṣaṅkara in Tamil, Tamil glosses, *etc.*] *See* Upanishads.—*Small Collections.* தசோபநிஷத்த்ராவிடபாஷ்யம் *etc.* [Daṣopanishad-drāviḍabhāshya.] Pt. i., pp. 246-320. [1897-]1898. 8°. **14010. dd. 14.**

GAUḶĪṢĀSTRA. ഗൌളിശാസ്ത്രം. [Gauḷīṣāstra. A metrical tract on divination. With Malayalam version.] pp. 28. കൊച്ചി ൧൦൪൮ [*Cochin,* 1872.] 12°. **14053. b. 39.**

GAURAGOPĀLA ṢIROMAṆI. काकदूतम् *etc.* [Kākadūta. A poem in 94 stanzas on the Krishṇa-legend, modelled upon Kālidāsa's Meghadūta. With a commentary styled Ṣabdārthadarṣanī by the author.] pp. ii. 81, vi. কলিকাতা ১৮১২ [*Calcutta,* 1890.] 8°. **14072. cc. 62.(1.)**

GAURAGOVINDA KĀVYATĪRTHA. *See* Bhavānanda Siddhāntavāgīṣa. কারকচক্রম্ *etc.* [Kārakachakra. With commentaries. Edited by Dvārakānātha and Gauragovinda.] [1900.] 8°. **14090. bb. 15.(1.)**

GAURAGOVINDA RĀYA, *Upādhyāya of the Navavidhāna-maṇḍalī.* *See* Kesavachandra Sena. नवसंहिता *etc.* [Navasaṃhitā. A metrical Sanskrit version of the "New Samhita." Translated with Sanskrit commentary by Gauragovinda.] [1901.] 8°. **14033. aa. 15.**

—— *See* Purāṇas.—*Bhāgavatapurāṇa.* श्रीमद्गीताप्रपूर्तिः *etc.* [Gītāprapūrti. By Gauragovinda Rāya.] [1902.] 8°. **14016. e. 44.**

GAURĀṄGA. *See* Chaitanya.

GAURĪNĀTHA ṢARMĀ, *of Avam.* *See* Viṣuddhānanda Sarasvatī. यतीन्द्रविशुद्धानन्दोक्तिप्रकाशः *etc.* [Yatīndra-Viṣuddhānandoktiprakāṣa. Compiled and furnished with a commentary by Gaurīnātha.] [1891.] 8°. **14048. dd. 9.**

GAURĪṢAṄKARA LALU MEHTĀ. *See* Jayarāma, *Astrologer.* अथ श्री ग्रहगोचर *etc.* [Grahagochara. With Gujarati translation by Gaurīṣaṅkara.] [1892.] 12°. **14053. b. 17.(4.)**

GAURĪṢAṄKARA UDAYAṢAṄKARA OJHĀ, *'Āzam, C.S.I.* स्वरूपानुसन्धान *etc.* (Swarûpanusandhân, or Considerations on the nature of Atmá . . . and on the unity of Atmá with Paramátmá . . . Being an attempt to unfold some of the leading principles of the Vedánt philosophy, by Gowrishankar Udayshankar Ozá.) [Comprising a series of Sanskrit quotations with Gujarati exposition.] pp. vii. ii. i. 365, ii. ii. *Bombay,* 1884. 8°. **14144. d. 12.**

GAUTAMA. Gautama, Institutes of the Sacred Law. [Translated, with introduction and notes, by G. Bühler. Second edition.] 1897. *See* Mueller

(F. M.). The Sacred Books of the East, *etc.* Vol. II, pp. i.—xlix. 173-310. 1879, *etc.* 8°.
2003. a. (vol. 2.)

—— গৌতমীয়-ধর্ম্মসূত্রম্ । [Dharmasūtra. *Adhyāyas* iii., viii., xi., with Bengali translations and notes.] [1895.] *See* RAMEṢACHANDRA DATTA. হিন্দুশাস্ত্র *etc.* [Hindu-ṣāstra.] Pt. iii., pp. 48-58. [1895-1897.] 8°. **14085. c. 45. (vol. 1.)**

—— ॥ पितृमेधसूत्राणि ॥ The Pitṛmedhasūtras of Baudhāyana, Hiraṇyakeśin, Gautama, *etc.* 1896. 8°. *See* CALAND (W.). [*Deutsche Morgenlaendische Gesellschaft: Abhandlungen.*] **753. f. 18.**

—— सामवेदीया गौतमीशिक्षा ॥ [Gautamī Ṣikshā. A Sāmavedī tract on Vedic phonetics, ascribed to Gautama.] *See* YUGALAKIṢORA VYĀSA PĀṬHAKA. श्रीमद्याज्ञवल्क्यादि . . . शिक्षासङ्ग्रहः . . . A collection of Śikshás, *etc.* pp. 450-455. 1893. 8°.
14093. b. 31.

GAUTAMA, *the Gaṇadhara.* अथ . . . गौतमकुलक *etc.* [Gautamakulaka. 20 Prakrit stanzas on Jain ethics ascribed to Gautama. With copious Gujarati interpretation and commentary, illustrated by stories, by Padmavijaya.] pp. 392. 1891. *See* BHĪMASIṂHA MĀṆAKA. जैनकथारत्नकोष *etc.* [Jainakathāratnakoṣa.] Vol. VI. [1890-1893.] 8°.
14144. gg. 1. (vol. 6.)

GAUTAMAPṚICHCHHĀ. अथ . . . गौतमपृच्छा *etc.* [Gautamapṛichchhā, in Prakrit Goyamapuchchhā. Questions as to Jain principles asked by the Gaṇadhara Gautama and answered by the Tīrthaṅkara Mahāvīra, in Jain-Prakrit verse. With Gujarati commentary.] 1890. *See* BHĪMASIṂHA MĀṆAKA. जैनकथारत्नकोष *etc.* [Jainakathāratnakoṣa.] Vol. I, pp. 221-306. [1890-1893.] 8°.
14144. gg. 1. (vol. 1.)

GĀYATRĪ. *See* PĀÑCHARĀTRA. गायत्रीकवच [Gāyatrīkavacha. A tract on the formula based on the *gāyatrī.*] [1902.] *obl.* 12°.
14028. b. 73. (5.)

—— *See* UPANISHADS. — *Modern and Fictitious Upanishads.* गायत्र्युपनिषत् [Gāyatryupanishad. A tract on the *gāyatrī.*] [1902.] *obl.* 12°.
14028. b. 73. (4.)

—— अथचोवीसगायत्रीप्रा° [Chaturviṃṣati Gāyatryaḥ, or Chovīs Gāyatrī. Twenty-four modifications of the Gāyatrī to suit the worship of divers deities, *etc.*] ff. 30. मुंबई १९४६ [*Bombay*, 1890.] *obl.* 12°. **14028. b. 70. (2.)**

—— ॥ अथ श्रीचतुर्विंशति गायत्री° [Chaturviṃṣati Gāyatryaḥ. With Hindi version by Jvālāprasāda Miṣra.] ff. 23. मुंबय्यां १९५७ [*Bombay*, 1901.] *obl.* 8°. **14033. b. 33. (2.)**

GĀYATRĪRĀMĀYAṆA. [For the Gāyatrīrāmāyaṇa, an acrostic of 25 stanzas compiled from the Rāmāyaṇa, of which the initial letters spell the Gāyatrī, and which is sometimes prefixed to editions of the Rāmāyaṇa:] *See* VĀLMĪKI. — *Rāmāyaṇa.*

GEIGER (WILHELM). Dīpavaṃsa und Mahāvaṃsa, die beiden Chroniken der Insel Ceylon, *etc.* pp. 24. *Erlangen & Leipzig, Naumburg* [printed], 1901. 8°. **14098. ccc. 28.**

GELDNER (KARL F.). Sanskrit-Drucke. Eine Sammlung indischer Texte, begründet von Karl F. Geldner. *Greifswald*, 1900, *etc.* 8°.
14093. d. 21.

In progress?

GHĀSĪRĀM, *son of Wazīr-chand.* *See* RĀMADAYĀLU, *Jyotirvid, of Amritsar.* ॥ अथ . . . संकेतनिधिः *etc.* [Saṅketanidhi. A treatise on astrology, commenced by Ghāsīrām and completed by Rāmadayālu.] [1894.] *obl.* 4°. **14053. e. 30.**

GHELĀBHĀĪ LĪLĀDHARA. જૈન વિવેક વાણી યાને જૈન ધર્મ સાર સંગ્રહ. [Jainavivekavāṇī, or Jainadharmasārasaṅgraha. A collection of Jain devotional writings in Sanskrit, Prakrit, and Gujarati, including the Pratikramaṇasūtra, Navasmaraṇa, Tīrthamālā, lections, hymns, *etc.*] Part i. pp. ix. 343; 1 *plate.* મુંબઈ ૧૮૮૮ [*Bombay*, 1888.] 8°. **14144. g. 26.**

GHERAṆḌA. যোগশাস্ত্রঃ ঘেরণ্ডসংহিতা অন্যান্য প্রমাণসহ । [Yogaṣāstra. Being the Gheraṇḍasaṃhitā, with selections from other works on the Yoga and Bengali preface and paraphrases.] pp. 44. [1891, *etc.*] *See* PERIODICAL PUBLICATIONS. — *Calcutta.* অরুণোদয় *etc.* [Aruṇodaya.] Pt. i., no. 10. [1890, *etc.*] 4°.
14133. g. 16. (pt. i., no. 10.)

—— The Gheraṇḍa Sanhita. A treatise on Hatha Yoga. Translated . . . by Sris Chandra

Vasu. [With the Sanskrit text appended.] (हठयोगाम्नगीता घेरण्डसंहिता) pp. xxix. 53, i. iv. 47. *Bombay*, 1895. 12°. **14028. b. 75.**

—— ঘেরণ্ড-সংহিতা। [Gherandasamhitā. With a Bengali translation.] pp. 201. *See* PRASANNAKUMĀRA ŚĀSTRĪ BHAṬṬĀCHĀRYA. যোগাম্বুধি *etc.* [Yogāmbudhi.] [1896.] 16°. **14048. a. 19.**

—— घेरण्ड संहिता *etc.* [Gherandasamhitā. Edited with a Hindi translation by Jagannātha Śarmā.] pp. 136; 25 *plates.* प्रयाग १८९९ [*Allahabad*, 1899.] 8°. **14033. bb. 10.(2.)**

GHULĀM ḲĀDIR, *Paramayogī.* *See* ŚIVAŚAṄKARA ŚĀSTRĪ, *Kastūri.* గులాంఖాదరుచరిత్రము *etc.* [Ghulām-Ḳādir-charitra. A poem on Ghulām Ḳādir, a conciliator of Islam and Hinduism.] [1900.] 8°. **14058. b. 44.**

GHULE (K. B.). *See* KṚISHṆA BHĀŪ ŚĀSTRĪ GHULE.

GILMORE (D. C.). A Brief Vocabulary to the Pali Text of Jatakas I—XL, *etc.* pp. 63. *Rangoon*, 1895. 12°. **14098. a. 27.**

GIRIDARA RATANAJOTI. *See* RATANAJOTI, *Giridhara.*

GIRIDHARA BHAṬṬĀCHĀRYA, *son of Vāgīśa.* विभक्त्यर्थनिर्णयः *etc.* (Vibhaktyarthanirnaya, [a treatise on the logical significance of the cases.] . . . Edited by Sri Jivanatha Misra Nyayatirtha.) pp. ii. vii. vi. 477. *Benares*, १९०२ [1902.] 8°. **14004. a. 12.**

Forms nos. 39, 41, 44, 48, *and* 54 *of the* Chowkhambâ Sanskrit Series. The English title is from the wrapper.

GIRIDHARALĀLA AMṚITALĀLA NYĀYĀ. *See* PURĀṆAS.—*Bhāgavatapurāṇa.* ॥श्रीमद्भागवतसंहिता *etc.* [Bhāgavatapurāṇa. With Gujarati translation by Giridharalāla.] [1899.] *obl.* 4°. **14016. f. 13.**

GIRĪNDRANĀTHA DATTA, *Bābū.* *See* MAHĀDEVA SARASVATĪ. अद्वैतचिन्ताकौस्तुभः। [Tattvānusandhāna. With the author's commentary] Advaitacintā Kaustubha. Edited by . . . Girīndranātha Datta. 1901, *etc.* 8°. [*Bibliotheca Indica.*] **14002. a. (vol. 150.)**

GIRIPRASĀDA VARMĀ. *See* VEDAS.—Yajurveda.—*Vājasaneyisaṃhitā.* श्रीशुक्लयजुर्वेदे . . . वाजसनेयसंहिता *etc.* [Vājasaneyisaṃhitā. Edited with introduction and a commentary styled Vedārthapradīpa or Giridharabhāshya in Hindi by Giriprasāda.] [1874.] 4°. **14010. f. 9.**

GIRĪŚACHANDRA TARKĀLAṄKĀRA. *See* YĀJÑAVALKYA. [*Dharmaśāstra.*] Mitákshará. Vyávahára Adhyáy, Part III. Translated by Girish Chandra Tarkálankár. 1892. 8°. **14038. d. 35.**

GĪSHPATI RĀYA CHAUDHURĪ. সংস্কৃত-সাহিত্য-পরীক্ষা-দর্পণ *etc.* [Saṃskṛitasāhityaparīkshādarpaṇa. A collection of examination-papers in Sanskrit and in Bengali on Sanskrit literature, with Sanskrit notes.] pp. ii. iv. 118. *Calcutta*, 1893. 8°. **14070. c. 49.**

GĪTĀCHĀRYA, *Ketāṇḍapaṭṭī.* ಶ್ರೀಗೀತಾಚಾರ್ಯ . . . ವಿರಚಿತ ಶ್ರೀಕೃಷ್ಣರಾಜೋದಯ॥ [Śrikṛishṇarājodaya. A *champū* composition, in 7 *laharīs*, on the history of the rulers of Mysore down to the present Maharaja.] pp. iii. viii. 188. ೧೮೯೫ [*Mysore*, 1895.] 8°. **14058. b. 30.**

GOBHILA. গোভিল-গৃহ্যসূত্রম্। [Gṛihyasūtra. Extracts from Prap. ii. With Bengali translations and notes.] [1895.] *See* RAMEŚACHANDRA DATTA. হিন্দুশাস্ত্র *etc.* [Hindu-śāstra.] Pt. iii., pp. 20-39. [1895-1897.] 8°. **14085. c. 45.(vol. 1.)**

GOBHILAPUTRA. ॥ गृह्यासंग्रहः ॥ [Gṛihyāsaṅgraha. An epitome of rules for domestic rites, in two *prapāṭhakas*, forming a *pariśishṭa* to Gobhila's Sūtra.] pp. 22. 1891. *See* PERIODICAL PUBLICATIONS. — *Calcutta.* उषा *etc.* [Ushā.] Vol. I., no. x. [1889-]1893. 8°. **14010. c. 43.(vol. 1.)**

GODĀNAPADDHATI. गोदानपद्धतिः। [Godānapaddhati. The ritual for the presentation of a cow.] pp. 14. काश्याम् १९४७ [*Benares*, 1890.] 12°. **14028. b. 71.(3.)**

GODBOLE (N. B.). *See* NĀRĀYAṆA BĀLAKṚISHṆA GODBOLE.

GOETTINGEN, *University of.* *See* ACADEMIES, *etc.* —Goettingen.—*Academia Georgia Augusta.*

GOKULĀDHĪŚA, *son of Giridhara, Gosvāmī.* मुंबइस्थ . . . श्रीगोकुलाधीशजीकृतग्रंथाः। [Vallabhastutiratnāvalī and other poems on the doctrine of Vallabhāchārya.] *See* GOVARDHANADĀSA LAKSHMĪDĀSA. बृहत्स्तोत्रसरित्सागर *etc.* [Brihat-stotrasaritsāgara.] Vol. ii. [1892.] 12°. **14033. a. 27. (vol. 2.)**

GOKULANĀTHA, *Astrologer.* মকরন্দোপপত্তিঃ। [Makarandopapatti. An astrological tract.] *See* PERIODICAL PUBLICATIONS.—*Calcutta.* অরুণোদয় *etc.* [Aruṇodaya.] Pt. i., no. 15. pp. 4-11. [1890, *etc.*] 4°. **14133. g. 16. (pt. i., no. 15.)**

GOKULANĀTHA MAHĀMAHOPĀDHYĀYA, *Phandah, son of Pītāmbara.* The Amritodaya of Gokulanâtha. [An allegorical play, in five acts.] Edited by . . . Paṇḍit Śivadatta . . . and Kâśînâth Pâṇdurang Parab. (अमृतोदयम्।) pp. ii. 73. 1897. *See* DURGĀPRASĀDA, *son of Vrajalāla,* and KĀŚĪNĀTHA PĀṆḌURAṄGA PARAB. Kâvyamâlâ. [No.] 59. 1886, *etc.* 8°. **14072. ccc. 12. (no. 59.)**

GOLÁPCHANDRA. *See* GULĀB-CHANDRA.

GOLE (M. S.). *See* MAHĀDEVA ṢIVARĀMA GOLE.

GOONAWARDANA (S. F.). *See* GUṆAVARDHANA (S. F.).

GOONERATNE (E. R.). *See* GUṆARATNA (E. R.).

GOPĀLA, *Poet.* रासार्यागुच्छाः। [Rāsāryāguchchhāḥ. Five *guchchhas* of verses on the sports of Krishṇa.] pp. 18. [1890.] *See* PERIODICAL PUBLICATIONS.—*Bombay.* ग्रन्थरत्नमाला *etc.* (Granth Ratna Málá, *etc.*) Vol. IV., no. 1. 1887-[1892.] 8°. **14096. c. 8. (vol. 4.)**

GOPĀLA, *Paramahaṃsa Parivrājakāchārya.* *See* BAUDHĀYANA. போதாயனக்ருஹ்யோக்த . . . ப்ரயோக॥ [Bodhāyanagṛihyokta-jātakarmādi-prayoga. With the *kārikā* or epitome of Gopāla, *etc.*] [1900.] 8°. **14038. c. 37. (2.)**

GOPĀLA BHAṬṬA, *disciple of Prabodhānanda.* ଉପବାସ ତତ୍ତ୍ୱ *etc.* [Upavāsatattva. A treatise on fasts, consisting of select passages from the Haribhaktivilāsa of Gopāla Bhaṭṭa with explanations in Oriya by Yogendra Miṣra.] pp. 55. *Cuttack,* 1898. 12°. **14028. b. 84. (2.)**

GOPĀLACHANDRA CHAKRAVARTĪ, *Mahāmahopādhyāya.* *See* PURĀṆAS.—*Mārkaṇḍeyapurāṇa.* [*Devīmāhātmya.*] শ্রীশ্রীচণ্ডী *etc.* [Chaṇḍī. Accompanied by a commentary entitled Tattvaprakāṣikā by Gopālachandra, *etc.*] [1900.] 16°. **14028. a. 29.**

GOPĀLACHANDRA VIDYĀRATNA. A Companion to Sanskrit Grammar and Composition[, in Sanskrit, Bengali, and English,] *etc.* pp. ii. 76. *Calcutta,* 1891. 12°. **14092. a. 13. (1.)**

GOPĀLĀCHĀRLU, *S. E.* Sandhyâvandana, or The Daily Prayers of Brahmins. [An interpretation and exposition, in English,] by S. E. Gopâlâchârlu. pp. 90. *Bombay,* 1893. 12°. **4505. de. 2. (7.)**

—— [Second edition.] pp. 90. 1902. 12°. **14028. b. 104. (3.)**

GOPĀLĀCHĀRYA, *Dh.* *See* PĀÑCHARĀTRA. శ్రీపాంచరాత్రే . . . కపింజల సంహితా *etc.* [Kapiñjala-saṃhitā. Edited by Gopālāchārya, *etc.*] [1896.] 8°. **14028. d. 59. (5.)**

GOPĀLADĀSA, *Mahārāja, of Bauli.* वैष्णवधर्मरत्नाकर *etc.* [Vaishṇavadharmaratnākara. A metrical summary of the religious principles and practices of Rāmānujī Vaishṇavas, in 19 *adhyāyas.* With Hindi version and commentary by the author.] pp. ii. iv. 623. कल्याण-मुंबई १९५७ [*Kalyan,* 1901.] 8°. **14033. aa. 14.**

GOPĀLADĀSA MUKHOPĀDHYĀYA. *See* TANTRAS. [*Mahānirvāṇatantra.*] মহানির্ব্বাণ তন্ত্র *etc.* [Mahānirvāṇatantra. With Bengali translation by Gopāladāsa.] [1901.] 8°. **14033. aa. 17.**

GOPĀLAKRISHṆA, *Kavirāja.* रसेन्द्रसारसंग्रहः *etc.* [Rasendrasārasaṅgraha. A treatise on the therapeutic uses of mercury. Edited with notes by Jīvānanda Vidyāsāgara. Second edition.] pp. ii. 296. कलिकाता १८९६ [*Calcutta,* 1896.] 8°. **14043. cc. 12.**

GOPĀLAKRISHṆA ĀCHĀRYA, *Ṣrīmushṇam.* *See* BĀDARĀYAṆA. श्रीमद्ब्रह्मसूत्राणि *etc.* [Brahmasūtra. With the *bhāshya* of Ānandatīrtha, *etc.* Edited by Gopālakrishṇa.] [1900.] 8°. **14048. cc. 30.**

GOPĀLAKRISHṆA ĀCHĀRYA SOMAYĀJĪ, *Dhanvāḍa.* The Tiñantárṇavataraṇi, or Sanskrit Verbs Made Easy, *etc.* (श्रीतिङन्तार्णवतरणिः।) pp. ii. xxxiii. 578. *Benares,* 1897. 8°. **14093. b. 40.**

GOPĀLA MIṢRA, *Gārgya.* *See* VEDAS.—Yajurveda.—*Taittirīyasaṃhitā.* [*Prātiṣākhya.*] தைத்திரீய ப்ராதிஶாக்யம் *etc.* [Taittirīyaprātiṣākhya. With the commentary Vaidikābharaṇa of Gopāla.] 1901. 8°. **14090. e. 26.**

GOPĀLA RAGHUNĀTHA NANDARGIKAR. *See* Kālidāsa.—*Meghadūta.* The Meghadûta . . . With the commentary of Mallinâtha . . . Edited with . . . translation . . . notes . . . various readings, by Gopal . . . Nandargikar. 1894. 8°. **14076. c. 63.**

—— *See* Kālidāsa.—*Raghuvaṃṣa.* The Raghuvanśa . . . with the commentary of Mallinâtha, edited with a literal English translation, with copious notes in English . . . with various readings &c., &c., by Gopal . . . Nandargikar. Third edition. 1897. 8°. **14072. c. 53.**

GOPĀLA ṢĀSTRĪ, *of Chidambaram.* *See* Purāṇas.—*Skandapurāṇa.* പ്രണവകല്പ: *etc.* [Praṇavakalpa. Edited by Gopāla Ṣāstrī.] 1902. 8°. **14033. b. 55.(2.)**

GOPĀLAVALLABHA DĀSA. *See* Purāṇas.—*Bhāgavatapurāṇa.* ଭକ୍ତିରତ୍ନାବଳୀ *etc.* [Bhaktiratnâvalī. With commentary of Ṣrīdhara and metrical paraphrase in Oriya by Bhīmadāsa. Edited by Gopālavallabha Dāsa.] 1900. 12°. **14016. b. 27.**

GOPĀLA YAJVĀ, *Gārgya.* *See* Gopāla Miṣra, *Gārgya.*

GOPĀL-RĀU HARI ṢARMĀ. सुन्दरीसुधार। [Sundarīsudhāra. An anthology of verses on the duties of Hindu women and their social advancement. Compiled from the Ṣāstras, Epics, *etc.*, and furnished with an extensive Hindi commentary.] pp. 192. फ़र्रुखाबाद १८९५ [*Farukhabad,* 1895.] 8°. **14038. c. 47.**

GOPEE NATH BHATT OAK. *See* Gopīnātha Dīkshita, *Bhaṭṭa, son of Gaṇeṣa Dikshita Ok.*

GOPENDRA TIPPABHŪPĀLA. *See* Tippabhūpāla, *Gopendra.*

GOPĪNĀTHA, *Purohita, of Jaipur.* *See* Bhartṛihari. The Nîtiśataka Śringâraśataka and Vairâgyaśataka . . . Edited with Hindi and English translation, copious critical and explanatory notes . . . &c. by . . . Gopi Nath. 1896. 8°. **14072. c. 55.**

GOPĪNĀTHA DĪKSHITA, *Bhaṭṭa, son of Gaṇeṣa Dikshita Ok.* संस्काररत्नमाला। Sanskar Ratna Mala. [A digest of purificatory rites according to the tradition of the Hiraṇyakeṣī school.] By Shri Gopee Nath Bhatt Oak. Edited . . . by Pandit Rama Krishna Shastri, alias Tatya Shastri Patwardhana. *Benares,* 1898, *etc.* 8°. **14004. a. 1.**

Forms nos. 1, 2, *etc. of the* Chowkhambâ Sanskrit Series.

—— संस्काररत्नमाला *etc.* [Saṃskāraratnamālā. Edited by Kāṣīnātha Ṣāstrī Āgāṣe and Bābā Ṣāstrī Phaḍke.] 2 vols. pp. i. xxiii. 1203. पुण्याख्यपत्तने १८९९ [*Poona,* 1899.] 8°. **14003. ccc.(no. 39.)**

Forms no. 39 *of the* Ānandāṣrama Sanskrit Series.

GOPĪRAMAṆA TARKARATNA. কোষচন্দ্রিকা *etc.* [Koṣachandrikā. A collection of vocabularies, viz. Gadā Siṃha's Nānārthamañjarī; the Sārasvatābhidhāna; Purushottama Deva's Ekāksharakoṣa; a Rāṣikoṣa; a Nakshatrakoṣa; a Grahakoṣa; an Aṅkābhidhāna; and a Dvirūpakoṣa. Edited with Bengali translations by Gopīramaṇa.] pp. i. 60. ঢাকা ১৮৯৩ [*Dacca,* 1893.] 12°. **14090. b. 44.(1.)**

GORAKSHANĀTHA, *Yogīndra.* *See* Motīnāth, *Pandit.* आदेश शब्दार्थ आदि पञ्चामृत गुटका *etc.* [Ādeṣaṣabdārthādi - pañchāmṛitaguṭikā. Comprising the explanation of the salutation (*ādeṣa*) prescribed by Gorakshanātha, three metrical panegyrics on Gorakshanātha, *etc.*] [1898.] 12°. **14028. b. 101.(1.)**

—— कामशास्त्र *etc.* [Kāmaṣāstra. A work on divination and pharmacology as applied to sexual relations, in 8 *adhikāras,* ascribed to Gorakshanātha. Edited, expanded, and furnished with a Hindi version by Ṣaṅkaralāla son of Lālā Bhoja.] pp. iv. 87. मुरादाबाद १८९९ [*Moradabad,* 1899.] 8°. **14053. d. 61.**

GOSAINJĪ. *See* Viṭṭhaleṣvara, called Gosainjī.

GOTAMA, surnamed Akshapāda. ন্যায়-দর্শন *etc.* [Nyāyadarṣana. The Aphorisms with a commentary by Harinātha Tarkasiddhānta and Āṣutosha Tarkabhūshaṇa. With Bengali interpretation of the whole and notes by Sarveṣvara Sārvabhauma.] কলিকাতা ১৮১৬ [*Calcutta,* 1894, *etc.*] 8°. **14048. dd. 21.**

In progress?

—— न्यायतत्वबोधिनी . . . Nyayatatwa Bodhini [, *i.e.* the Nyāyasūtra with a Hindi commentary founded on that of Vātsyāyana] by Misra Shaligram Shastree. pp. ii. ii. 171. अजमेर १८९४ [*Ajmere*, 1894.] 8°. **14048. dd. 12.(3.)**

—— The Nyâyamañjarî of Jayanta Bhaṭṭa. [Comprising the Nyâyasūtra with commentary by Jayanta.] Edited by Mahâmahopâdhyâya Gangâdhara Śâstrî Tailaṅga. (न्यायमञ्जरी।) 2 pts. pp. v. ii. 659, x. iv. *Benares*, 1895. 8°. **14048. dd. 3.(vol. 8.)**

Forms vol. 8 *of the* Vizianagram Sanskrit Series.

—— The Nyâyasûtras with Vâtsyâyana's Bhâshya [called Nyāyabhāshya] and extracts from the Nyâyavârttika [of Uddyotakara] and the Tâtparyaṭîkâ [of Vāchaspati Miṣra, the Tātparyapariṣuddhi of Udayana Āchārya, and the Gautamasūtravṛitti, called also Nyāyasūtravṛitti, of Viṣvanātha Pañchānana]. Edited [with indexes] by Mahâmahopâdhyâya Gaṅgâdhara Śâstrî Tailaṅga. (न्यायभाष्यम्।) pp. iii. xi. 28, vii. 264. *Benares*, 1896. 8°. **14048. dd. 3.(vol. 9.)**

Forms vol. 9 *of the* Vizianagram Sanskrit Series.

—— न्यायसूत्रविवरणम्। [Nyāyasūtra. With the commentary Nyāyasūtravivaraṇa of Rādhāmohana. Edited by Surendralāla Gosvāmī.] 1901, *etc.* *See* Periodical Publications.—*Benares*. The Pandit, *etc.* New Series. Vol. XXIII., *etc.* 1876, *etc.* 8°. **14096. d. 6.(vol. 23, etc.)**

In progress.

—— The Naya [*sic*] Philosophy, or Hindu science of reasoning. [Comprising an abridgment of the Nyāyasūtra, preceded by an introduction to the subject, both in English. Translated and] edited by P. C. Sen. pp. i. 28. *Konnagar*, [1896.] 8°. **14048. c. 36.(2.)**

—— *See* Kālīvara Vedāntavāgīṣa. षड्दर्शन *etc.* [Shaḍdarṣana. A Bengali exposition of the six systems.] [1895.] 8°. [*Hindu-ṣāstra.*] **14085. c. 45.(vol. 1.)**

—— *See* Vāchaspati Miṣra. [*Nyāyavārttikatātparyaṭīkā.*] The Nyâyavârttikatâtparyaṭîkâ, *etc.* [A commentary upon Uddyotakara's commentary on the Nyāyasūtra.] 1898. 8°. **14048. dd. 3.(vol. 13.)**

GOTRĀVALĪ. गोत्रावली *etc.* [Gotrāvalī. A list of Brahman *gotras*, showing the Veda, *ṣākhā*, *sūtra*, *pravara*, *ṣikhā*, *pāda*, and deity of each. Fifth edition.] pp. 11. इलाहाबाद १९५१ [*Allahabad*, 1894.] 8°. **14058. b. 32.(1.)**

GOVARDHANADĀSA LAKSHMĪDĀSA. बृहत्स्तोत्रसरित्सागर प्रथमभाग: *etc.* (द्वितीयभाग:।) [Bṛihat-stotra-saritsāgara. A collection of religious poems, comprising in vol. 1 "Pañcharatnas" to 11 deities compiled from Tantric and Puranic literature, *etc.*, and in vol. 2 Vaishṇava works of the Pushṭimārga.] 2 vols. मुंबय्यां १८९२ [*Bombay*, 1892.] 12°. **14033. a. 27.**

GOVARDHANA DEVARĀMA TRIPĀṬHĪ, *Joṣī.* *See* Gaṅgādhara, *Architect.* शिल्पदीपक *etc.* [Ṣilpadīpaka. Edited with Gujarati translation, *etc.*, by Govardhana.] [1898.] 8°. **14053. d. 54.**

GOVARDHANA GHANAṢYĀMA GADDŪJĪ. ॥ अथ वेदांतचिंतामणि प्रारंभः ॥ [Vedāntachintāmaṇi. A metrical treatise in fifteen sections on the Vedānta as expounded in the school of Vallabhāchārya, with notes.] ff. 48. मुंबई १८७० [*Bombay*, 1870.] *obl.* 8°. **14048. e. 21.**

GOVARDHANA MIṢRA, *son of Balabhadra.* *See* Annam Bhaṭṭa. The Tarka-sangraha . . . with . . . Govardhana's Nyâya-Bodhinî, *etc.* 1897. 8°. **14048. cc. 7.**

—— *See* Keṣava Miṣra, *Logician.* The Tarka-bhâshâ . . . with the commentary of Govardhana, *etc.* 1894. 8°. **14048. dd. 18.**

GOVARDHANAM RAṄGĀCHĀRYA. *See* Raṅgāchārya, *Govardhanam.*

GOVINALĀLA VANDYOPĀDHYĀYA. *See* Hariṣchandra Bhaṭṭāchārya Kaviratna. जरावैराग्यम् *etc.* [Jarāvairāgya. Edited with metrical version in Bengali by Govinalāla.] [1898.] 12°. **14072. b. 20.(2.)**

GOVINDA, *Rhetorician.* *See* Govinda Ṭhakkura, *son of Keṣava.*

GOVINDA, *Parivrājaka Paramahaṃsa.* अद्वैतानुभूति *etc.* [Advaitānubhūti. A poem in 86 stanzas on Vedantic monism, ascribed to Govinda. With Hindi version.] pp. 20. कानपूर १८९९ [*Cawnpore*, 1899.] 8°. **14028. c. 85.(1.)**

The pages are numbered 26-45, *and bear the erroneous superscription* Avadhūtagītā. *The book begins with the same stanza as the MS. of the Vākyasudhā noticed by Rajendralal Mitra*, Notices, *No.* 1445.

GOVINDA ANTARVĀṆĪ, *son of Lakshmaṇa Sūri.* कविचित्तप्रमोदक: । [Kavichittapramodaka. A series of enigmatical stanzas, with a commentary.] [1892.] *See* PERIODICAL PUBLICATIONS.—*Bombay.* ग्रन्थरत्नमाला *etc.* (Granth Ratna Málá, *etc.*) Vol. V, no. 7, 8. 1887-[1892]. 8°.

14096. c. 8.(vol. 5.)

Incomplete, breaking off at iv. 3.

—— रुक्मिणीपाणिग्रहणं काव्यम् । [Rukmiṇīpāṇigrahaṇa. A poem on the bridals of Rukmiṇī and Krishṇa, in 9 *sargas.* With annotations.] pp. 210. [1891.] *See* PERIODICAL PUBLICATIONS.—*Bombay.* ग्रन्थरत्नमाला *etc.* (Granth Ratna Málá, *etc.*) Vol. IV, no. 9–Vol. V, no. 3. 1887-[1892]. 8°. **14096. c. 8.(vol. 4, 5).**

GOVINDACHANDRA MAHĀPĀTRA DEVA. ଉପଦେଶଗର୍ଭିତ ଅନ୍ୟାପଦେଶଶ୍ଳୋକଶତକଂ *etc.* [Anyāpadeṣaṣlokaṣataka. A century of stanzas conveying by implication various morals. Compiled with Oriya paraphrases and notes by Govindachandra.] pp. 42. *Cuttack,* 1902. 12°. **14072. b. 15.(2.)**

GOVINDACHANDRA VAIṢĀKHA. Caste system in Bengal, its baneful effects and their remedy. By Govinda Chandra Bysack. [An English essay, illustrated from Sanskrit texts.] pp. 37. *Mymensingh,* [1900.] 8°. **8022. cc. 17.(9.)**

GOVINDĀCHĀRYA, *A., of the Vedagriha, Mysore.* *See* MAHĀBHĀRATA. — Bhagavadgītā. — *English.* Ṣrī Bhagavad-gītā, with Ṣrī Rāmānujāchārya's Viṣishtādvaita-commentary. Translated into English by A. Govindāchārya. 1898. 8°.

14048. cc. 26.

GOVINDADĀSA, *Kavirāja.* ভৈষজ্য-রত্নাবলী *etc.* [Bhaishajyaratnāvalī. A treatise on therapeutics. With a Bengali translation by Chandrakumāra Kavibhūshaṇa.] pp. xvi. 772. কলিকাতা ১৩০০ [*Calcutta,* 1893.] 8°. **14043. e. 31.**

—— भैषज्यरत्नावली *etc.* (Bhaisajya Ratnavali. A treatise on Hindu medicine . . . Edited . . . by Pandit Ashu Bodha Vidyabhushana.) pp. 730; 1 *plate.* *Calcutta,* १९०२ [1902.] 8°.

14043. cc. 24.

The English title is taken from the cover.

GOVINDA KAULA, *Pandit, of Kashmir.* *See* JAYADRATHA, *Rājānaka.* The Haracharitachintâmaṇi, *etc.* [Followed by an index of the names of *tīrthas, etc.,* occurring in this poem, compiled and explained by Govinda Kaula.] 1897. 8°. [*Kāvyamālā.*] **14072. ccc. 12.(no. 61.)**

GOVINDA KAVI. *See* GOVINDĀNANDA KAVIKAṄKAṆA BHAṬṬĀCHĀRYA.

GOVINDĀNANDA KAVIKAṄKAṆA BHAṬṬĀCHĀRYA, *son of Gaṇapati Bhaṭṭa.* *See* ṢRĪNIVĀSA ĀCHĀRYA, *Astrologer.* দীপিকা *etc.* [Ṣuddhidīpikā. With commentaries of Govindānanda, *etc.*] [1901.] 8°. **14053. ccc. 23**

—— *See* ṢRĪNIVĀSA ĀCHĀRYA. শুদ্ধিদীপিকা *etc.* [Ṣuddhidīpikā. With commentary of Govindānanda.] [1901.] 8°. **14053. ccc. 33.**

—— *See* ṢŪLAPĀṆI, *Sāhuṛiyān.* प्रायश्चित्तविवेक: *etc.* [Prāyaṣchittaviveka. With the commentary, entitled Tattvārthakaumudī, of Govindānanda.] [1893.] 8°. **14028. c. 81.**

—— *See* ṢŪLAPĀṆI, *Sāhuṛiyān.* প্রায়শ্চিত্তবিবেকঃ *etc.* [Prāyaṣchittaviveka. With Govindānanda's commentary.] [1903.] 8°. **14033. aa. 31.**

—— Varṣa Kriyā Kaumudī. [A treatise on the annual cycle of religious celebrations] by Govindānanda Kavikaṇkanācāryya. Edited by Paṇḍitā Kamala Kṛṣṇa Smṛtibhūṣaṇa. (वर्षक्रियाकौमुदी ।) pp. vii. iii. 579, xlix. 1902. *See* ACADEMIES, *etc.*—Calcutta.—*Asiatic Society of Bengal.* Bibliotheca Indica. New Series. [Vol. 149.] 1848, *etc.* 8°. **14002. a. (vol. 149.)**

GOVINDA PARAṢURĀMA RĀVERKAR. *See* BHAIRAVADATTA DVIVEDĪ. धर्मप्रदीप: *etc.* [Dharmapradīpa. Edited by Govinda.] [1901.] 8°.

14033. aa. 24.

—— *See* KRISHṆĀNANDA SARASVATĪ. गीतासारोद्धार: *etc.* [Gītāsāroddhāra. With commentary in Marathi by Govinda.] [1892.] 8°.

14028. d. 50.(2.)

—— *See* PURĀṆAS.—*Bhavishyapurāṇa.* ॥ अथ श्रीभविष्यमहापुराणं *etc.* [Bhavishyapurāṇa. Edited by Govinda.] [1896-1897.] *obl.* Fol.

14018. cc. 1.

—— *See* PURĀṆAS.—*Brahmāṇḍapurāṇa.* [*Adhyātmabhāgavata.*] अथ ककारादिकृष्णाऽष्टोत्तरसहस्रनामस्तोत्रम्। [Kakārādi - Krishṇāshṭottarasahasranāmastotra. Edited by Govinda.] *obl.* 12°. **14016. b. 25.**

GOVINDA RATHA. ଶବ୍ଦମାଳା ଅଭିଧାନ *etc.* [Ṣabdamālā-abhidhāna. A metrical vocabulary of synonyms.] pp. 9. *Cuttack*, 1895. 12°. **14090. b. 44.(2.)**

GOVINDA ṢĀSTRĪ, *Bhāradvāja, Mahāmahopādhyāya.* See Nāgeṣa Bhaṭṭa. [*Paribhāshenduṣekhara.*] परिभाषेन्दुशेखरः। [Paribhāshenduṣekhara. With the commentary Laghu-jaṭājūṭa of Govinda.] 1892, *etc.* 8°. [*Vidyodaya.*]
14096. cc. (vol. 21, *etc.*)

—— लघुजटाजूटः। परिभाषेन्दुशेखरस्य क्रोडपत्रम् . . . Laghu Jatajoota. A gloss on Nagoji Bhatta's Paribhashendu Shekhar, *etc.* [Edited by Krishṇa Ṣāstrī and Narmadāṣaṅkara Bhaṭṭa.] pp. 235. *Benares*, 1899. 8°. **14092. b. 45.(1.)**

GOVINDA ṢĀSTRĪ, *son of Nīlakaṇṭha.* See Nārāyaṇa Tīrtha, *disciple of Ṣivarāma.*

GOVINDA SENA, *son of Krishṇavallabha, Kavirāja.* পরিভাষাপ্রদীপ *etc.* [Paribhāshāpradīpa. A metrical handbook of medical terminology, in four *khaṇḍas.* Edited with a Bengali paraphrase by Haralāla Gupta Kaviratna. Second edition.] pp. i. iv. 160. কলিকাতা ১৩০৭ [*Calcutta*, 1901.] 12°.
14043. b. 10.(2.)

GOVINDASIMHA SĀDHU, *Nirmala-Paṇḍita Svāmī, disciple of Ṭhākur Nihāl Singh, of Benares.* See Dharmarāja Dīkshita. वेदान्तपरिभाषा *etc.* [Vedāntaparibhāshā. With Hindi introduction and commentary by Govindasiṃha.] [1901.] 8°.
14048. dd. 33.

—— See Ṣaṅkara Āchārya.—*Doubtful and Supposititious Works.* लक्ष्मीनृसिंहस्तोत्रम् *etc.* [Lakshmīnṛisiṃhastotra. With Hindi translation by Govindasiṃha.] [1901.] 12°. **14028. b. 93.(6.)**

GOVINDA ṬHAKKURA, *son of Keṣava.* See Mammaṭa Āchārya. The Kâvyapradîpa of Govind. With the commentary [Prabhā] of Vaidyanâtha, *etc.* 1891. 8°. [*Kâvyamâlâ.*]
14072. ccc. 12. (no. 24.)

—— See Mammaṭa Āchārya. The Kâvyaprakâsh of Mammata, Ullâsa x. With the corresponding portions of the Kâvya-pradîpa of Gôvinda . . . With notes and appendix. 1896. 8°.
14053. ccc. 6.

GOWRISHANKAR UDAYSHANKAR OZÁ. See Gaurīṣaṅkara Udayaṣaṅkara Ojhā.

GOYAMA. See Gautama, *the Gaṇadhara.*

GOYAMAPUCHCHHĀ. See Gautamapṛichchhā.

GOYĪCHANDRA, *Autthāsanika.* See Kramadīṣvara. সংক্ষিপ্তসার° [Saṅkshiptasāravyākaraṇa. With the gloss Vivaraṇīṭikā of Goyīchandra.] [1901.] 8°.
14090. bb. 16.

GRAHAKOṢA. অথ গ্রহকোষ। [Grahakoṣa. A vocabulary of synonyms for the planets. With a Bengali translation.] See Gopīramaṇa Tarkaratna. কোষচন্দ্রিকা *etc.* [Koṣachandrikā.] pp. 46-48. [1893.] 12°. **14090. b. 44.(1.)**

GRANDJEAN (J M). See Ṣukarambhāsaṃvāda. Dialogue de Çuka et de Rambha . . . Publié [with French translation] par J.-M. Grandjean. 1887. 4°. [*Annales du Musée Guimet.*] **7704. h. 21. (tom. 10.)**

GRANT (*Sir* Alexander). Catalogue of Native Publications in the Bombay Presidency up to 31st December 1864. Prepared under orders of Government by Sir A. Grant . . . Second edition. pp. 35, 239. *Bombay*, 1867. 8°. **14096. ccc. 5.**
Continuation by J. B. Peile.

GRAY (James). See Buddharakkhita. Jinâlaṅkâra . . . Edited, with introduction, notes, and translation, by J. Gray. 1894. 8°.
14098. c. 65.

—— See Dīpavaṃsa. Dīpavaṁsa. Chapters I—IV. . . . (V—VII.) Edited by J. Gray. 1900-1902. 12°. **14098. a. 35.**

—— —— Dīpavaṁsa. Chapters V—VII. (Translation and appendix [by J. Gray].) 1902. 12°. **14098. a. 41.**

—— See Mahāmaṅgala. Buddhaghosuppatti . . . Edited [with English translation and introduction] by J. Gray. 1892. 8°. **14098. c. 59.**

—— See Suttapiṭaka.—*Khuddakanikāya.* [*Jātaka.*] Mahājanakajātakaṁ . . . Edited by J. Gray, *etc.* 1901. 12°. **14098. a. 40.**

—— —— Mahājanakajātakaṁ. Translation [by J. Gray]. 1901. 12°. **14098. a. 4.(3.)**

—— —— Temiyajātakaṁ . . . Edited by J. Gray. 1900. 12°. **14098. a. 38.**

GRAY (JAMES). *See* SUTTAPIṬAKA.—*Khuddakanikāya.* [*Jātaka*] (*continued*). Temiyajātakaṁ. Translation [by J. Gray]. 1900. 12°. **14098. a. 4.(2.)**

—— —— Two Jātakas: Temiya and Mahājanaka . . . Edited by J. Gray. 1903. 12°. **14098. a. 42.**

GREAT BRITAIN AND IRELAND.—*India Office.—Library.* Catalogue of the Mandalay [Pali] MSS. in the India Office Library, formerly part of the King's Library at Mandalay. By . . . V. Fausböll. 1896. *See* ACADEMIES, *etc.* — London.— *Pali Text Society.* Journal . . . 1896, *etc.* pp. 1-52. 1882, *etc.* 8°. **14098. b.**

—— —— Catalogue of Two Collections of Sanskrit Manuscripts preserved in the India Office Library. Compiled by Charles H. Tawney . . . and Frederick W. Thomas. pp. ii. 60. *London,* 1903. 8°. **14096. ccc. 8.**

GRIERSON (GEORGE ABRAHAM). *See* ĪṢVARA KAULA. The Kaçmīraçabdāmṛta . . . Edited with notes and additions by G. A. Grierson. 1898. 8°. **14164. h. 11.**

—— Curiosities of Indian Literature. Selected and translated by G. A. Grierson . . . Edited . . . by . . . Babu Ramadina Sinha. pp. 24. *Bankipore,* 1895. 12°. **14085. b. 45.(1.)**

GRIFFITH (RALPH THOMAS HOTCHKIN). *See* VĀLMĪKI. — Rāmāyaṇa. — *Abridgments and Selections.* The Light of India; or, Sita. Complied [*sic*] [chiefly from Griffith's translation of the Rāmāyaṇa] by Narayana Hemchandra. [1895.] 16°. **14065. a. 8.**

—— *See* VĀLMĪKI.—Rāmāyaṇa.—*Portions.* (The Ramayan.) [Bālakāṇḍa i.–ii., in Griffith's metrical version. Followed by Ragbuvaṃṣa xiv. 26–xv. 73, translated by the same.] [1891.] 12°. **14076. b. 24.(4.)**

—— *See* VEDAS.—*Atharvaveda.* The Hymns of the Atharva-veda. Translated with a popular commentary by Ralph T. H. Griffith. 1895-1896. 8°. [*The Pandit*] **14096. d. 6.(vol. 15-19, supplement.)**

—— —— [A separate issue of the preceding.] 1895-1896. 8°. **14010. dd. 7.**

GRIFFITH (RALPH THOMAS HOTCHKIN) (*continued*). *See* VEDAS. — *Atharvaveda.* The Atharvaveda Described; with a classified selection of hymns [in Griffith's version], *etc.* 1897. 8°. [*Sacred Books of the East Described and Examined.*] **14010. cc. 9.(vol. 1.)**

—— *See* VEDAS.—Ṛigveda.—*Entire Text.* The Hymns of the Rigveda. Translated with a popular commentary by Ralph T. H. Griffith. Second edition. 1896-1897. 8°. **14007. b. 7.**

—— *See* VEDAS.—Ṛigveda.—*Selections of Hymns and Verses.* An Account of the Vedas; with numerous extracts from the Rig-Veda [in Griffith's version]. 1897. 8°. [*Sacred Books of the East Described and Examined.*] **14010. cc. 9.(vol. 1.)**

—— *See* VEDAS.—*Sāmaveda.* The Hymns of the Sâmaveda. Translated with a . . . commentary by Ralph T. H. Griffith. 1893. 8°. **14010. dd. 3.**

—— *See* VEDAS.—Yajurveda.—*Vājasaneyisaṃhitā.* The Texts of the White Yajurveda. Translated with a popular commentary by Ralph T. H. Griffith. 1899. 8°. **14007. b. 8.**

GṚIHAVĀSTUPRADĪPA. गृहवास्तुप्रदीप *etc.* [Gṛihavāstupradīpa. Rules to be observed in building houses, *etc.* With Hindi translation.] pp. 87. *Lucknow,* 1901. 12°. **14033. a. 19.(4.)**

GROSSET (JOANNY). *See* BHARATA MUNI. Bhāratīya-Nāṭya-Cāstram [*sic*] . . . Édition critique . . . Par J. Grosset. 1898, *etc.* 8°. **Ac. 365. (fasc. xl.)**

GRUENWEDEL (ALBERT). *See* KACHCHĀYANA.— *Rūpasiddhi.* Das Sechste Kapitel der Rūpasiddhi . . . herausgegeben . . . von A. Grünwedel. 1883. 8°. **14098. b. 15.(2.)**

GUÉRINOT (A.). *See* KĀLIDĀSA. — *Meghadūta.* Meghadûta . . . Traduction française par A. Guérinot. 1902. 12°. **14080. b. 11.**

—— De Rhetorica Vedica. Thesim facultati litterarum in universitate lugdunensi proponebat A. Guérinot. pp. xi. 120. *Lutetiæ Parisiorum, Chalon-sur-Saône* [printed], 1900. 8°. **011852. h. 23.**

GUÉRINOT (A.) (*continued*). Recherches sur l'Origine de l'Idée de Dieu d'après le Rig-veda, *etc.* (Annales de l'Université de Lyon, nouvelle série II, fasc. iii.) pp. 356, i. *Paris, Lyon* [printed], 1900. 8°.
Ac. 365 (nouvelle série II, fasc. iii.)

GUIMET (ÉMILE). Annales du Musée Guimet. 1880, *etc.* 4°. *See* ACADEMIES, *etc.*—Paris.—*Musée Guimet.* **7704. h. 21.**

GUJJAR (K. BH.). *See* KALYĀṆADĀSA BHĀṆĀBHĀĪ GUJJAR.

GULĀB-CHANDRA SARKĀR, *Śāstrī.* *See* CHAṆḌEŚVARA ṬHAKKURA. Vivada-ratnakara . . . the law of partition and inheritance [entitled Dāyabhāga. The Sanskrit text edited and] translated by Golápchandra Sarkár, *etc.* 1899. 8°. **14039. c. 18.**

—— Hindu Law. With an appendix of Mahomedan Law of Inheritance. [With extracts from the law-books of Manu, Yājñavalkya, Nārada, and other Sanskrit texts.] pp. xviii. 307, 17, xi. *Calcutta,* 1897. 8°. **14038. c. 46.**

GULĀM KHĀDARU. *See* GHULĀM ḲĀDIR.

GUMĀNĪ PANTA. गुमानी कवि विरचित संस्कृत और भाषा काव्य *etc.* [Kāvyasaṅgraha. Collected poems of Gumānī, viz. Hitopadeśaśataka or Śatopadeśa, Durjanadūshaṇa, Jñānabhaishajyamañjarī, Pañchapañchāśikā, Vijñaptisāra, Gaṅgāryā, Bhaktivijñaptisāra, Sadrañjāshṭaka, Samasyāpūrti, *etc.*, together with some Hindi verses. Edited with Hindi notes and translations by Devīdatta Pāṇḍe.] pp. ii. 36, 8, 24, 16, 22, 6, 20, 14, 48, 5, 8, iv. इटावा [१८]६१ [*Etawah,* 1897.] 8°. **14070. dd. 6.**

—— गुमानी नीति *etc.* [Gumānī-nīti. An ethical poem of 61 stanzas. Edited with a Hindi prose translation by Revādhara Upretī.] pp. 14, i. *Almora,* 1894. 8°. **14076. d. 51.**

GUṆABHADRA ĀCHĀRYA. श्री आत्मानुशासनग्रन्थ *etc.* [Ātmānuśāsana. An ethical and philosophical poem, of the Digambara Jain sect, in 272 stanzas. Edited with a Hindi translation and commentary by Bābū Jñānachandra.] pp. ii. 344. लहौर १९५४ [*Lahore,* 1898.] *obl.* 8°. **14100. c. 19.**
Forms no. 2 of the 'Jain Religious Grantha Series.'

—— ಪಾರ್ಶ್ವನಾಥಸ್ವಾಮಿ ಪುರಾಣಂ *etc.* [Pārśvanāthasvāmipurāṇa. A poetical account of the Jain *tīrthaṅkara* Pārśvanātha, extracted from the Uttarapurāṇa or supplement by Guṇabhadra to the Mahāpurāṇa of Jinasena, *parvan* 73. Edited with Canarese version by Padmarāja Paṇḍita.] pp. 30. ಬೆಂಗಳೂರು ೧೮೯೩ [*Bangalore,* 1893.] 8°. **14100. b. 3.(1.)**

GUṆACHĀRI THERA. *See* ABHIDHAMMAPIṬAKA.—*Dhammasaṅgaṇi.* မာတိကာ၊ဓါတုကထာအ-ကောက် *etc.* [Mātikā-dhātukathā-akauk. With Burmese commentaries by Guṇachāri, *etc.*] [1898.] 8°. **14300. d. 5.(4.)**

GUṆARATANA, *Mulleriyāvē.* *See* KACHCHĀYANA.—*Rūpasiddhī.* රූපසිද්ධි *etc.* (Mahárúpasiddhi . . . Edited by . . . M. Gunaratana.) 1897. 8°. **14098. dd. 14.**

GUṆARATNA (EDMUND ROWLAND). *See* ACADEMIES, *etc.*—London.—*Pali Text Society.* ABHIDHAMMAPIṬAKA. The Dhātu kathā pakaraṇa and its Commentary. Edited by E. R. Gooneratne. 1892. 8°. **14098. b. 29.(3.)**

—— *See* SUTTAPIṬAKA.—*Aṅguttaranikāya.* Anguttara-Nikaya, *etc.* (Translated [from I. ii. onward] . . . by Mudaliyar E. R. Gooneratna.) 1891, 1896, *etc.* 8°. **P.P. 636. cn. (vol. 3, 8, *etc.*)**

GUNASEKERA. *See* GUṆASEKHARA.

GUṆASEKHARA (HENRY M.). *See* COLOMBO.—*Colombo Museum.* Catalogue of . . . Manuscripts in the Colombo Museum Library. [Compiled by H. M. Guṇasekhara.] 1901. 8°.
14098. ccc. 37.

GUṆAVĀBHILAṄKĀRA SADDHAMMADDHAJA. ပကိဏ္ဏကဝိသဇ္ဇနာကျမ်း *etc.* [Pakiṇṇakavisajjanā-kyan. A collection of Responsa in Burmese upon divers points arising from the Piṭakas and cognate literature.] 2 vols. ပန္တလေး [*Mandalay,*] 1900. 8°. **14300. e. 12.**

GUṆAVARDHANA (SIMON F.). *See* COLOMBO.—*Colombo Museum.* Catalogue of the Colombo Museum Library. List of . . . Manuscripts, *etc.* [Compiled by S. Guṇavardhana.] 1894. 8°.
14096. c. 13.

GUNGA PRASHAD. *See* GAṄGĀPRASĀDA.

GUṆINDA, Ū, *of Sagaing*. *See* SUTTAPIṬAKA.—*Dīghanikāya*. ဒသုတ္တရသုတ် *etc.* [Dasuttarasutta. With Burmese paraphrase by Guṇinda.] [1895.] 8°. **14098. ccc. 9.(3.)**

GURJAR (M. B.). *See* MUKUNDA BĀLAKṚISHṆA GURJARA.

GURUDATTA VIDYĀRTHĪ, *of Lahore Government College*. *See* UPANISHADS.—*Separate Upanishads*. The Mandukyopanishat . . . Translated and expounded by . . . Guru Datta Vidyarthi. 1893. 8°. **14010. dd. 5.(1.)**

—— *See* UPANISHADS. — *Separate Upanishads*. **माण्डूक्योपनिषत्** *etc.* (Bhasha Translation of . . . Guru Datta, M.A.'s English translation and exposition of Mandukyopanishat, *etc.*) 1891. 12°. **14010. b. 8.**

—— Works of late Pandit Guru Datta Vidyarthi. [Comprising English essays on Vedic subjects from the standpoint of Dayānanda Sarasvatī's doctrines, with reprints of some of the same author's "Vedic Texts," text of certain Upanishads with translation and exposition, *etc.*] . . . Revised and edited by Lala Jivan Das, *etc.* Part i. pp. 227. *Lahore*, 1897. 8°. **14010. dd. 11.**

—— [Another and enlarged edition, with biography.] 2 pts. *Lahore*, 1902. 8°. **759. c. 20.**

—— The Atmosphere, *etc.* [Comprising Ṛigveda I. ii. 1, with an English exposition construing the text to convey modern scientific theories of the atmosphere, in accordance with the principles of Dayānanda Sarasvati.] pp. 8. *See* VEDAS.—Ṛigveda.—*Single Hymns and Verses.* Vedic Texts. No. 1. 1888. 8°. **14007. d. 20.**

—— [Another edition.] pp. 6. *See* VEDAS.—Ṛigveda. — *Single Hymns and Verses.* Vedic Texts. No. 1. 1894. 12°. **14010. b. 16.**

—— The Composition of Water, *etc.* [Comprising Ṛigveda I. ii. 7, with an English exposition designed to deduce from this text a statement of the chemical composition of water.] pp. 4. *See* VEDAS.—Ṛigveda.—*Single Hymns and Verses.* Vedic Texts. No. 2. 1888. 8°. **14007. d. 20.**

—— **गृहस्थ.** Being a scientific exposition of Mantras Nos. 1, 2 & 3 of the xxx Sukta [*i.e.* Bk. I. l. 1-3] of the Rig Veda, bearing on the subject of household, *etc.* pp. 11. *See* VEDAS.—Ṛigveda. — *Single Hymns and Verses.* Vedic Texts. No. 3. 1894. 12°. **14010. b. 16.**

—— The Terminology of the Vedas and the European Scholars. Being a reprint from the Vedic Magzine [*sic*], *etc.* pp. 44. *Moradabad*, 1899. 8°. **4504. cc. 15.(2.)**

This essay was first reprinted in the author's "Works," Vol. I., 1897.

GURUJÑĀNAVĀSISHTHA. గురుజ్ఞానవాసిష్ఠ జ్ఞానకాండః *etc.* (ఉపాసనాకాణ్డః, కర్మకాణ్డః) [Gurujñānavāsishṭha, or Tattvasārāyaṇa. A metrical exposition of Anubhavādvaita theory and practice, including discussions on the Upanishads, in a dialogue between Śiva and Brahmā, communicated by Vasishṭha to Rāma. In 3 *kāṇḍas*, each containing 4 *pādas*, with 25 *adhyāyas* in each *pāda*. Vol. i., styled Jñānakāṇḍa, and including in Pāda II. i.–xvii. an exposition of the Brahmasūtra, with the commentary Adhikaraṇakañchuka of Apyaya Dikshita, edited by Pattamaḍai Appaya Dikshita; Vol. ii., styled Upāsanākāṇḍa, and including as Pāda II. i.–xviii. the Rāmagītā, an account of the mystic doctrine and *yoga* of the Anubhavādvaita school, as expounded by Rāma to Hanumān; Vol. iii., styled Karmakāṇḍa, and treating of religious offices.] చెన్నపురి [*Madras*,] *Karvetnagar*, ౧౮౮౨ [1882-]1897. 4°. **14048. e. 8.**

—— శ్రీదక్షిణామూర్తిబ్రహ్మసంవాదాత్మకే . . . గురుజ్ఞానవాసిష్ఠే . . . బ్రహ్మమీమాంసా॥ [Brahmamīmāṃsā. Being the Brahmasūtra with the section from the Jñānakāṇḍa (Pāda II. i.–xvii.) containing the exposition thereof. Together with the commentary Adhikaraṇakañchuka of Apyaya Dikshita.] 1898. 12°. *See* BĀDARĀYAṆA. **14048. b. 32.**

—— Śrî Râma Gîtâ. Forming part [viz. II. i.–xviii.] of 'Tattvasârâyana,' the Occult Philosophy taught by the great Sage Śrî Vasishtha. The Saṃskrita text, with an appendix containing the table of contents and the teachings in brief of the three Kândas of Tattvasârâyana. Edited by G. Krishna Śâstrî . . . श्रीवसिष्ठमहर्षिप्रोक्त तत्वसारा-

यथान्तगेता श्रीमद्रामगीता *etc.* (Átma Vidyá Series No. i.) pp. iv. i. iii. 103, xxxi. *Madras*, 1902. 8°. **14049. b. 2.**

—— Śrî Râma Gîtâ ... Translated into English by G. Krishna Śâstrî ... Reprinted from "The Theosophist," with an appendix. (Átma Vidyá Series No. ii.) pp. 135, xiv. *Madras*, 1902. 8°. **14049. b. 3.**

—— Ráma Gitá. [Translated, with introduction and notes, by G. Kṛishṇa Ṣāstrī.] 1901. *See* PERIODICAL PUBLICATIONS.—*Bombay*. The Theosophist, *etc.* Vol. XXII, no. v.—Vol. XXIII, no. ii. 1879, *etc.* 8°. **P.P. 636. cm. (vol. 22, 23.)**

GURULIṄGA ṢĀSTRĪ, *Nōri*. *See* HASTĀMALAKA ĀCHĀRYA. శ్రీ ... హస్తామలకభాష్యము *etc.* [Hastāmalakabhāshya. Edited with Telugu translation by Guruliṅga.] [1901.] 8°. **14049. a. 7.**

—— *See* JĪVANĀTHA, *son of Ṣambhunātha*. వాస్తురత్నావళి *etc.* [Vāsturatnāvali. Edited with Telugu version by Guruliṅga.] [1897.] 8°. **14053. ccc. 16.**

—— *See* NĀḌĪVIJÑĀNA. నాడీవిజ్ఞానము *etc.* [Nāḍīvijñāna. With Telugu paraphrase and notes by Guruliṅga.] [1901.] 8°. **14043. cc. 19.(1.)**

—— *See* NĀRĀYAṆA BHAṬṬA, *son of Ananta*. ముహూర్తమార్తండము *etc.* [Muhūrtamārtaṇḍa. With commentary. Edited with Telugu interpretation and commentary by Guruliṅga.] [1901.] 8°. **14053. ccc. 38.**

—— *See* PURĀṆAS.—*Brahmāṇḍapurāṇa*. [*Lalitāsahasranāma*.] శ్రీలలితారహస్యనామ॥ [Lalitārahasyanāmasāhasra. With a commentary in Telugu based upon that of Bhāskararāya, by Guruliṅga.] [1900.] 8°. **14016. c. 63.**

—— *See* ṢIVASVARODAYA. శివస్వరోదయము *etc.* [Ṣivasvarodaya. Edited with Telugu translation by Guruliṅga.] [1901.] 8°. **14033. aa. 28.(2.)**

—— *See* TANTRAS. [*Gāyatrītantra*.] శ్రీగాయత్రీతంత్రము *etc.* [Gāyatrītantra. Edited with Telugu translation by Guruliṅga.] [1901.] 8°. **14033. aa. 28.(1.)**

GURULIṄGA ṢĀSTRĪ, *Nōri* (*continued*). *See* VAIDYANĀTHA, *son of Veṅkaṭādri*. జాతకపారిజాతము *etc.* [Jātakapārijāta. With Telugu version by Guruliṅga.] [1897.] 8°. **14053. ccc. 9.**

—— *See* VIṢVAKARMĀ. విశ్వకర్మప్రకాశిక *etc.* [Viṣvakarmaprakāṣikā. With Telugu translation by Guruliṅga.] [1896.] 8°. **14053. ccc. 15.**

GURUNĀTHA VEṄKAṬEṢA KITTŪR. श्रीशङ्करविजयचूर्णिका *etc.* [Ṣaṅkaravijayachūrṇikā. Comprising an essay discussing the chronology of Ṣaṅkara's life and another summarising the data of history and legend attaching to him; Maṭhetivṛitta and Sampradāyachatushṭaya, two poems enumerating the *maṭhs* founded by him, their pontiffs, religious principles, *etc.*; a table giving a synopsis of the same, and another showing the succession from Maheṣvara to the 4 apostles of Ṣaṅkara.] pp. vi. i. 16, 53, 8, i. मुंबापुरी १८२० [*Bombay*, 1899.] 8°. **14058. b. 41.**

—— वाक्यदोषादर्शः *etc.* [Vākyadoshādarṣa. Examples of mistakes ordinarily made in Sanskrit composition, followed by corrections and explanations in Sanskrit and English.] pp. ii. 25. वेणुपत्तने १८१८ [*Belgaum*, 1896.] 12°. **14085. b. 42.**

GURUNĀTHA VIDYĀNIDHI KĀVYATĪRTHA. *See* SARVAVARMĀ. কলাপসূত্রম্ *etc.* [Kalāpasūtra. Edited by Gurunātha.] [1901.] 12°. **14092. a. 24.(2.)**

—— *See* ṢRĪNIVĀSA ĀCHĀRYA, *Astrologer*. দীপিকা *etc.* [Ṣuddhidīpikā. With commentaries and Bengali translation. Edited by Gurunātha.] [1901.] 8°. **14053. ccc. 23.**

—— নিত্য তন্ত্রম্ *etc.* [Nityatantra. A handbook of mystic rites, compiled from divers Tantras by Gurunātha. With Bengali translation.] pp. 158. *Calcutta*, 1891. 8°. **14028. c. 65.**

GURURĀU RĀMACHANDRA. श्री मध्व पील गी वृक्ष [Madhva-pīl-gī-vṛiksha. An oleograph pictorially representing the genealogical tree of the pontifical successors of Ānandatīrtha, or Madhvāchārya.] ... Edited by Gururao Ramchander. *Belgaum*, 1894. *s.sh.* Fol. **14048. f. 24.**

GURUSĀMI MUDALIYĀR, *C. Tāta.* *See* MANU.—*Dharmaṣāstra.* மநுதருமசாத்திரம் [Manudharmaṣāstra. Edited with Tamil translation by Gurusāmi Mudaliyār. Followed by the Vyavahārasārasaṅgraha, in Tamil, edited by the same.] 1896. 8°. **14039. b. 23.**

GURUṢARAṆA LĀLA, *Munshī Rāi.* अवधयात्रा *etc.* [Avadhayātrā. A Hindi manual for pilgrims visiting the holy places in Oudh, with appropriate Sanskrit quotations from Tantric and Puranic literature.] pp. iii. 50. लखनऊ १८६९ [*Lucknow*, 1869.] 8°. **14154. e. 2.(2.)**

GURUSTOTRA. (గురుస్తోత్రమ్) [Gurustotra. A panegyric on spiritual guides.] *See* UPANISHADS.—*Small Collections. Begin.* ఓమ్. శ్రీరామానుజ-సరస్వతీ ... నమః *etc.* [Kaivalya Upanishad, *etc.*] pp. 1-9. 1899. 32°. **14010. a. 6.**

HAAFNER (JACOB). Proeve van Indische Dichtkunde volgens den Ramaijon, naar het oorspronkelijke Sanscritisch gevolgd door Jacob Haafner ... in het licht gegeven door C. M. Haafner. pp. vi. 278. *Amsterdam*, 1823. 8°. **14065. c. 48.**

HABERLANDT (MICHAEL). *See* DAṆḌĪ. Daçakumâracaritam ... übersetzt, eingeleitet und mit Anmerkungen versehen von Dr. M. Haberlandt. 1903. 8°. **14076. d. 38.(2.)**

—— *See* ṢŪDRAKA. Vasantasenâ ... Frei wiedergegeben von M. Haberlandt. 1893. 16°. **14079. a. 9.**

HĀLĀSYANĀTHA ṢĀSTRĪ, *Malakuḍi.* *See* ĀPASTAMBA.—*Dharmasūtra.* The Dharma Sūtra ... with the commentary ... of Haradatta Misra ... Edited ... by Pundit R. Halasyanatha Sastry, *etc.* 1895. 8°. **14038. c. 45.**

—— *See* APYAYA DĪKSHITA. Kuvalayananda ... With the commentary ... of ... Gangadhara Vajapeyin. Edited with ... notes ... by ... Halasyanatha Sastri, *etc.* 1892. 8°. **14053. cc. 64.**

—— *See* PURĀṆAS.—*Nāradapurāṇa.* ഹരിഭക്തിസുധോദയഃ *etc.* [Haribhaktisudhodaya. With commentary of Ṣrīdhara Ṣvāmī. Edited by Hālāsyanātha Ṣāstrī and others.] 1892. 8°. **14016. c. 48.**

HALÂYUDHA BHAṬṬA, *Lexicographer.* కవిరహస్యము *etc.* [Kavirahasya.] pp. 28. *Vizagapatam*, 1891. 12°. **14090. b. 37.**

—— Halâyudha's Kavirahasya, in beiden Recensionen. Herausgegeben von Ludwig Heller. pp. viii. 101. 1900. *See* GELDNER (K. F.). Sanskrit-Drucke, *etc.* No. 1. 1900, *etc.* 8°. **14093. d. 21.(no. 1.)**

—— অথ কবি রহস্যং। [Kavirahasya.] *See* SARVAVARMĀ.—*Appendix.* গণতত্ত্ব-দীপিকা *etc.* [Gaṇatattvadīpikā, *etc.*] pp. 253-264. [1900.] 8°. **14093. b. 20.(3.)**

—— *See* HELLER (L.). Halâyudha's Kavirahasya. Inaugural-Dissertation ... von L. Heller, *etc.* 1894. 8°. **14093. b. 35.(1.)**

HALL (FITZ-EDWARD). *See* ANNAM BHAṬṬA. The Tarka-sangraha, *etc.* [In the English version published in the Allahabad edition of 1851 and in part composed by Hall.] 1897. 12°. [*Darshana.*] **14048. a. 23.**

HAṂSASVARŪPA, *Svāmī.* *See* SANDHYĀVANDANA. त्रिकुटीविलास॰ [Bṛihat-sandhyāvidhi. A compendium of *sandhyā* ritual by Haṃsasvarūpa, forming part 1 of his Trikuṭīvilāsa. With Hindi translations, *etc.*] [1902.] 12°. **14033. a. 51.**

HAṆMANTA KṚISHṆA ṢĀSTRĪ PĀDHYE. *See* VṚINDA. वृन्दमाधवापरनामा सिद्धयोगः *etc.* (The Vṛindamâdhava ... with its commentary 'Kusumávali' ... Edited by Pandita Hanmanta Śastrî Pâdhyé.) [1894.] 8°. **14003. ccc. (no. 27.)**

HANUMĀN. *See* MAHĀBHĀRATA.—Bhagavadgītā.—*Sanskrit.* श्रीमद्भगवद्गीता *etc.* [Bhagavadgītā. With the commentary, styled Paiṣāchabhāshya, ascribed to Hanumān.] [1901.] 8°. **14003. ccc. (no. 44.)**

—— महानाटकम् *etc.* (Mahanataka. A drama in 9 acts by Hanuman. Compiled by Madhusudana Mishra. Edited with a full commentary by

Pandit Jibananda Vidyasagara. . . . Second edition.) pp. 450. *Calcutta,* 1890. 8°. **14079. c. 70.**

English title taken from wrapper.

—— ମହାନାଟକ *etc.* [Mahānāṭaka. In Madhusūdana's recension.] pp. 147. *Cuttack,* 1899. 12°. **14079. a. 8.(2.)**

HANUMATSAMHITĀ. अथ श्रीहनुमत्संहिता प्रारम्भः। [Hanumatsaṃhitā. A poem in 6 *adhyāyas* on the dalliance of Rāma and Sītā by the Sarayū, narrated by Hanumān to Agastya. Edited by Rāmanārāyaṇa Dāsa and Rāmavallabhā Śaraṇa. Followed by Pañchadhā-bhaktirasa, a tract on the 5 religious emotions, by Rāmanārāyaṇa Dāsa, and a few small religious writings bearing on the cult of Rāma.] ff. 35. *Moradabad,* [1900.] *obl.* 8°. **14033. c. 44.(3.)**

HARABHĀNU ŚUKLA. *See* Gaṇeśa, *son of Gopāla.* जातकालंकारः *etc.* [Jātakālaṅkāra. With commentary of Harabhānu.] [1902.] 8°. **14053. ccc. 41.**

HARADATTA ĀCHĀRYA. *See* Sudarśana Āchārya, *Śāmbhavaśikhāmaṇi.*

HARADATTA MIŚRA. *See* Āpastamba.—*Dharmasūtra.* आपस्तम्बीयधर्मसूत्रम्। Aphorisms on the Sacred Law . . . with extracts from the commentary [of Haradatta], *etc.* 1892-1894. 8°. **14038. d. 34.**

—— *See* Āpastamba.—*Dharmasūtra.* The Dharma Sutra . . . with the commentary called Ujjvala of Haradatta Misra, *etc.* 1895. 8°. **14038. c. 45.**

—— *See* Āpastamba.—*Dharmasūtra.* ధర్మసూ-త్రమ్ *etc.* [Dharmasūtra. With commentary of Haradatta.] [1897.] 8°. **14039. b. 24.**

—— *See* Āpastamba.—*Dharmasūtra.* आपस्तम्बधर्मसूत्रम् . . . Ápastamba-Dharmasútra, with Haradatta's Ujjvalá, *etc.* 1898. 8°. [*Mysore Government Oriental Library Series : Bibliotheca Sanskrita.*] **14004. b. 9.**

—— *See* Āpastamba.—*Gṛihyasūtra.* The Mantrapāṭha . . . with the commentary of Haradatta, *etc.* 1897. 4°. [*Anecdota Oxoniensia.*] **12204. f. 8.(vol. 1, pt. 8.)**

—— *See* Āpastamba.—*Śrautasūtra.* आपस्तम्बपरिभाषासूत्रम् . . . The Ápastamba-Paribhâshá-Sútra, with the commentaries of . . . Haradattáchárya, *etc.* 1894. 8°. [*Mysore Government Oriental Library Series : Bibliotheca Sanskrita.*] **14004. b. 2.**

HARADATTA SŪRI, *son of Jayaśaṅkara.* The Râghava-naishadhîya of Haradattasûri. [A poem in 2 *sargas* which may be read as a history either of Rāma or of Nala.] With his own gloss. Edited by Paṇḍit Śivadatta . . . and Kâśînâth Pâṇdurang Parab. (राघवनैषधीयम् ।) pp. 68. 1896. *See* Durgāprasāda, *son of Vrajalāla,* and Kāśīnātha Pāṇḍuraṅga Parab. Kâvyamâlâ. [No.] 57. 1886, *etc.* 8°. **14072. ccc. 12.(no. 57.)**

HARADAYĀLU SVĀMĪ, *of Kambali, Gurgaon. See* Vasishṭha. धनुर्वेदसंहिता *etc.* [Vāsishṭhī Dhanurvedasaṃhitā. With a Hindi translation attributed on the title-page to Haradayālu.] [1902.] 8°. **14053. ccc. 35.**

HARADEVA ŚARMĀ, *of Jaliya, Ajmere. See* Jagannātha Paṇḍitarāja. अश्वधाटीकाव्यम् *etc.* [Aśvadhāṭīkāvya. With Hindi analyses and translation by Haradeva.] [1896.] 8°. **14048. cc. 8.(2.)**

HARAJĪVANA RĀICHAND SHĀH. *See* Siddhasena Divākara. कल्याणमंदिर॰ [Kalyāṇamandirastotra. Edited with prose translation, metrical version, notes, and biography of the poet in Gujarati by Harajīvana.] [1901.] 12°. **14100. b. 11.**

HARAKUMĀRA MUKHOPĀDHYĀYA, *of Dacca.* গুরু ও শিষ্য *etc.* [Guru o Śishya. A catechism of Vaishṇava religious philosophy for the use of the Nāgarbhāg Hari-sabhā. In Bengali, illustrated from Sanskrit texts.] pp. iv. i. 118. ঢাকা ১৮২৩ [*Dacca,* 1902.] 8°. **14123. e. 20.(2.)**

HARALĀLA GUPTA KAVIRATNA, *Kavirāja. See* Govinda Sena, *son of Krishṇavallabha.* পরিভাষাপ্রদীপ *etc.* [Paribhāshāpradīpa. Edited with Bengali paraphrase by Haralāla.] [1901.] 12°. **14043. b. 10.(2.)**

HĀRĀṆACHANDRA VANDYOPĀDHYĀYA. *See* Upanishads.—*Selections.* ॥ अथ शान्तिपाठः ॥ [Śāntipāṭha. With Bengali translation by Hārāṇachandra.] 1892. 8°. [*Ushā.*] **14010. c. 43.(vol. 2.)**

HARANĀMADATTA MIṢRA. *See* HARINĀMADATTA MIṢRA.

HARANĀRĀYAṆA. *See* HARINĀRĀYAṆA.

HARANĀTHA VIDYĀRATNA. সুগম-মুগ্ধবোধ-ব্যাকরণম্ [Sugama-mugdhabodha. The Mugdhabodha of Vopadeva versified and simplified.] pp. viii. 208. কলিকাতা ১৮৯১ [*Calcutta*, 1891.] 12°. **14092. a. 11.(2.)**

HARAPRASĀDA ŚĀSTRĪ, *Mahāmahopādhyāya.* *See* ACADEMIES, *etc.*—Calcutta.—*Asiatic Society of Bengal.* Report on the Search of Sanskrit Manuscripts. 1895 to 1900. By . . . Haraprasad Shāstrī. 1901. 4°. **14096. dd. 6.**

—— *See* ĀNANDA BHAṬṬA, *descendant of Ananta Bhaṭṭa.* বল্লাল চরিতম্ *etc.* [Ballālacharita. Edited with English introduction by Haraprasāda.] [1901.] 12°. **14058. a. 18.(1.)**

—— *See* ĀNANDA BHAṬṬA, *descendant of Ananta Bhaṭṭa.* Vallala Charita . . . translated . . . by . . . Haraprasad Sastri. 1901. 12°. **14058. a. 18.(2.)**

—— *See* ĀRYA DEVA. The discovery of a work by Āryadēva . . . [Being the text of a Buddhist treatise, published] by . . . Haraprasād Shāstrī, *etc.* 1898. 8°. [*Journal of the Asiatic Society of Bengal.*] **Ac. 8826/11.(vol. 67.)**

—— *See* PRAJÑĀPĀRAMITĀ. The Eleventh Chapter, *etc.* (Ashṭa Sahasrikā, Chapter xviii. . . . [Translated] by . . . Hara Prasad Çāstri.) 1894. 8°. [*Journal of the Buddhist Text Society.*] **14003. b. 19.(vol. 2.)**

—— *See* RĀJENDRALĀLA MITRA. Notices of Sanskrit MSS., *etc.* (Vol. X, by Haraprasád Shástri.) 1871-1892. 8°. **14096. cc.**

—— *See* RĀMACHANDRA BHĀRATĪ. Bhakti Sataka . . . Translated by . . . Hara Prasád Śástri. 1893. 8°. [*Journal of the Buddhist Text Society.*] **14003. b. 19.(vol. 1.)**

—— *See* SVAYAMBHŪPURĀṆA. The Vṛihat Svayambhú Puránam . . . Edited by . . . Haraprasád Śástri. 1894-1900. 8°. [*Bibliotheca Indica.*] **14002. a. (vol. 133.)**

HARAPRASĀDA ŚĀSTRĪ, *Mahāmahopādhyāya (continued).* Discovery of Living Buddhism in Bengal. By Haraprasád Śástri. pp. 31. *Calcutta*, 1897. 4°. **14123. k. 5.**

—— Notices of Sanskrit MSS. Second series . . . published under orders of the Government of Bengal. *Calcutta*, 1900, *etc.* 8°. **14096. cc.**

In progress. This series continues the Notices *of Rājendralāla Mitra* (1871-1892).

HARASUKHA RĀYA, *of Amritsar.* *See* NITYAKARMA. پتری ترپن الخ [Pitṛitarpaṇa. Compiled by Harasukha Rāya.] [1900.] 16°. **14028. a. 27.(2.)**

HARDY (EDMUND). *See* ACADEMIES, *etc.*—London.—*Pali Text Society.* DHAMMAPĀLA. Dhammapāla's Paramattha-dīpanī, Part III . . . Edited by Prof. E. Hardy. 1894. 8°. **14098. b. 35.**

—— *See* ACADEMIES, *etc.*—London.—*Pali Text Society.* DHAMMAPĀLA. Dhammapāla's Paramattha-dīpanī, Part IV . . . Edited by Prof. E. Hardy. 1901. 8°. **14098. b. 35.**

—— *See* ACADEMIES, *etc.*—London.—*Pali Text Society.* KACHCHĀYANA. The Netti-pakaraṇa. With extracts from Dhammapāla's commentary. Edited by Prof. E. Hardy. 1902. 8°. **14098. b. 36.(2.)**

—— *See* ACADEMIES, *etc.*—London.—*Pali Text Society.* SUTTAPIṬAKA. The Aṅguttara-Nikāya. Part III. Edited by . . . E. Hardy, *etc.* (Part IV., *etc.* Part V., *etc.*) 1896-1900. 8°. **14098. b. 27.**

—— *See* BUDDHAGHOSA. [*Manorathapūraṇī.*] The story of . . . Ghosaka . . . in its twofold Pāli form, with reference to other Indian parallels. By . . . E. Hardy. 1898. 8°. [*Journal of the Royal Asiatic Society.*] **Ac. 8820/3. and 2098. a, b.**

HARDYAL. *See* HARIDAYĀLU.

HARI, *disciple of Vajrasena.* অথ . . . কর্পূরপ্রকর° [Karpūraprakara. A series of stanzas on moral and philosophical topics of the Jain creed. Together with Gujarati interpretation and commentary.] 1891. *See* BHĪMASIṂHA MĀṆAKA. जैनकथारत्नकोष *etc.* [Jainakathāratnakoṣa.] Vol. v., pp. 1-168. [1890-1893.] 8°. **14144. gg. 1.(vol. 5.)**

The text comprises 128 stanzas, and an appendix contains 48 more.

—— कर्पूरप्रकर *etc.* [Karpūraprakara. With a gloss by Jinasāgara Sūri. Edited with Gujarati translation by Hariṣaṅkara Kālidāsa.] pp. i. 170. अमदावाद १९०१ [*Ahmadabad*, 1901.] 12°. **14100. b. 12.**

The stanzas which in the Jainakathāratnakoṣa form an appendix are here printed as part of the text, which thus comprises 179 verses.

HARIBHADRA SŪRI. *See* ṢAYYAMBHAVA. The Daśavaikālika-sūtra ... and the Daśavaikālika-niryukti ... with ... a list of all the tales ... in Haribhadra's Bṛhadvṛtti ... a shorted[*sic*] translation of most of the tales given in full by Haribhadra, *etc.* [1892.] 8°. **14100. c. 17.(2.)**

—— ॥ श्रीधर्मबिन्दु ॥ *etc.* [Dharmabindu. A compendium of the Jain doctrine, in 8 *adhyāyas*, comprising aphorisms by Haribhadra with a commentary styled Dharmabinduprakaraṇavṛitti by Munichandra, both in Sanskrit. With Gujarati translation of the text and commentary by Rāmachandra Dīnanātha.] ff. ii. xvii. 266. अमदावाद १९०४ [*Ahmadabad*, 1894.] *obl.* 4°. **14100. f. 13.**

—— लघु संग्रहणी. [Laghu-saṅgrahaṇī or Jambū-dvīpa-saṅgrahaṇī, in Prakrit Saṃghayaṇī. A Prakrit poem in 30 stanzas upon the geography of India. With Gujarati translation.] *See* HEMAṢAṄKARA LAKSHMĪṢAṄKARA VARDHAMĀNKAR. प्रकरण माला *etc.* [Prakaraṇamālā.] pp. 44-51. [1901.] 8°. **14100. d. 11.**

—— श्री लोकतत्त्व निर्णय ग्रंथ *etc.* [Lokatattvanirṇaya. A metrical Jain polemical work, chiefly in verse, and containing in all 145 stanzas. With Gujarati translation.] ff. 34. भावनगर अमदावाद १९५८ [*Bhaunagar, Ahmadabad* printed, 1902.] *obl.* 8°. **14100. d. 12.**

—— ॥ श्री षट् दर्शन समुच्चय *etc.* [Shaddarṣana-samuchchaya. A review of the 6 schools of philosophy. With Gujarati prose version by Chandrasiṃha Sūri.] pp. iv. 76. અમદાવાદ ૧૯૪૮ [*Ahmadabad*, 1892.] 16°. **14048. a. 17.**

HARICHARAṆA MAJUMDĀR, *of Gayhat.* ঘটপূজা *etc.* [Ghaṭapūjā, or Shashṭhi-suvachanī-pūjā. A ritual and lectionary for the ceremony of worshipping consecrated pots. With some appended matter in Bengali.] pp. iv. 68. গয়হাট। কলিকাতা ১৩০৯ [*Gayhat, Calcutta* printed, 1901.] *obl.* 8°. **14028. dd. 10.(3.)**

—— পুরোহিত-দর্পণ *etc.* [Purohitadarpaṇa. A manual for the use of priests in the performance of daily rites, with Bengali notes, rubrics, and translations. Edited by Kṛishṇanātha Nyāyaratna.] Pt. 1. pp. vi. 243. কলিকাতা ১৩০৬ [*Calcutta*, 1899.] 8°. **14028. d. 72.**

No more has been registered.

HARIDĀSA, *Gosvāmī.* *See* HARIRĀYAJĪ, *Gosvāmī.*

HARIDĀSA ṢĀSTRĪ, *Director of Public Instruction, Jaipur.* *See* KUMĀRADĀSA. Jánakíharaṇam ... Edited by ... Haridása Śástri, *etc.* 1893. 8°. **14072. cc. 57.**

—— तत्त्वसारविचारः ... Tattvasára Vichára. An examination of ... Paṇḍit Rákháldás Nyáyaratna's Tattvasára, *etc.* [With a preface in Bengali.] pp. viii. 31. *Calcutta*, 1891. 8°. **14048. bb. 51.(3.)**

HARIDAYĀLU ṢARMĀ, *of Meerut.* ॥ क्षत्रिय वर्ग कोषः ... Kshatria varga-kosh, part 1. [A reading-book for Kshatriyas, with vocabularies of Sanskrit words relating to their caste and other matters] translated in Hindi, by Pandit Hardyal Sarma for the good of Kshatrias. pp. 22. *Meerut*, 1895. 8°. **14160. c. 36.**

HARI DĪKSHITA, *grandson of Bhaṭṭoji.* *See* BHAIRAVA MIṢRA. भैरवी कारकान्ता ... Karakanta-Bhairavi or commentary ... on Laghu Shabdaratna of ... Hari Dikshita, *etc.* 1896. 8°. **14090. d. 32.**

—— *See* BHAṬṬOJĪ DĪKSHITA. मनोरमा *etc.* [Manoramā. With the supercommentary Ṣabdaratna of Hari Dikshita.] [1900.] 8°. **14093. d. 22.**

HARIHARA, *Agnihotrī.* *See* KĀTYĀYANA. परिशिष्टकण्डिका [Pariṣishṭakaṇḍikā, *etc.* Followed by the Snānasūtra, with Harihara's *vyākhyā* and Snānapaddhati, *etc.*] [1896.] 4°. [*Pāraskara-gṛihyasūtra.*] **14010. f. 10.**

HARIHARA, *Agnihotrī (continued)*. *See* PĀRASKARA. पारस्करगृह्यसूत्रम् *etc.* [Pāraskaragṛihyasūtra. With Harihara's *vyākhyā* and Prayogapaddhati, *etc.*] [1896.] 4°. **14010. f. 10.**

HARIHARA AIYAR, *J.* *See* ŚAṄKARA ĀCHĀRYA.—*Philosophical Poems, etc.* Svatmanirupanam ... Translated ... by J. Harihara Aiyar. 1900-1901. 8°. [*Brahmavâdin.*] **14048. g. 1.(vol. 6.)**

HARIHARA AIYAR, *Mullavasal S.* The South Indian Readers. Sanskrit. The Primer. बालशिक्षा [Bālaṣikshā], *etc.* pp. 46. *London, Madras* [printed], 1896. 8°. **14085. b. 40.**

Forms part of "Macmillan's Series of Text-books for Indian Schools."

HARIHARADATTA ŚĀSTRĪ TRIPĀṬHĪ. *See* BHĀRAVI. The Kirâtârjunîya ... With ... commentary of Mallinâtha. Edited by ... Hariher Datta. 1899. 8°. **14072. ccc. 25.**

HARIHARĀNANDA, *Sāṅkhyayogāchārya.* ॐ ... सांख्यतत्त्वालोकः तत्त्वनिदिध्यासनगाथा-महायोगेश्वरस्तोत्रादिसमेतः ... সানুবাদ সাংখ্যতত্ত্বালোক *etc.* [Sāṅkhyatattvāloka. A treatise on the Sāṅkhya philosophy. Followed by Tattvanididhyāsanagāthā and Mahāyogeṣvarastotra, short philosophical hymns, likewise by Hariharānanda. Edited with Bengali translation, notes, and appendices by Sachchidānanda Araṇya.] pp. 160; 1 *plate.* কলিকাতা ১৯০৩ [*Calcutta*, 1903.] 8°. **14049. b. 14.**

HARIHARAPRASĀDA, also called JĪTŪLĀL MUKHTĀR. सनातनधर्मविजय *etc.* [Sanātanadharmavijaya. A Hindi polemic against Dayānanda Sarasvatī and his school, including texts from Sanskrit and other authorities.] बांकीपुर १९०२ [*Bankipur*, 1902, *etc.*] 8°. **14154. c. 25.(2.)**

In progress.

HARIHARA RĀYA. *See* SĀYAṆA ĀCHĀRYA.—*Works on Philosophy, etc.* श्रीहरिगीता *etc.* [Pañchadaṣī. With a Marathi commentary in Ovī verse, styled Harigītā, by Harihara Rāya.] [1902, *etc.*] 8°. **14049. b. 1.**

HARIHARA ŚĀSTRĪ, *Goshṭhīpuram. See* PURĀṆAS.—*Nāradapurāṇa.* ஹரிபக்திஸுதோதய: *etc.* [Haribhaktisudhodaya. With the commentary of Ṣrīdhara Svāmī. Edited by Harihara and others.] 1892. 8°. **14016. c. 48.**

HARIHARA ŚĀSTRĪ, *Goshṭhīpuram (continued)*. *See* TYĀGARĀJA DĪKSHITA. ஸ்ரீத்யாகராஜஸ்தவ: *etc.* [Tyāgarājastava. Edited by Harihara.] [1894.] 8°. **14028. d. 58.(2.)**

HARIHARA ŚĀSTRĪ, *Goshṭhīpuram*, **and others.** ॥ अद्वैतमञ्जरी *etc.* [Advaitamañjarī. A series of works on the Advaita philosophy, published monthly.] *Kumbakonam*, 1892-1895. 8°. **14048. e. 23.**

HARIHARA UPĀDHYĀYA, *of Mithila.* The Bhartṛiharinirveda of Hariharopâdhyâya. [A drama in five acts.] Edited by Paṇdit Durgâprasâd and Kâśinâth Pâṇdurang Parab. (भर्तृहरिनिर्वेदम् ।) pp. 28. 1892. *See* DURGĀPRASĀDA, *son of Vrajalāla*, and KĀŚINĀTHA PĀṆḌURANGA PARAB. Kâvyamâlâ. [No.] 29. 1886, *etc.* 8°. **14072. ccc. 12.(no. 29.)**

HARI KAVI, *son of Nārāyaṇa Sūri*, also styled BHĀNUBHAṬṬA. Über das Haihayendracarita des Harikavi. [Comprising cantos i. and ii. of the Haihayendracharita, an epic poem by Hari, edited with German translation, notes, and introduction] von Th. von Schtscherbatskoi. (Mémoires de l'Académie Impériale des Sciences de St.-Pétersbourg. VIIIe série. Classe historico-philologique. Volume iv. No. 9.) pp. xi. 112. *St.-Pétersbourg*, 1900. 8°. **Ac. 1125/3.(classe hist.-phil., vol. iv., no. 9.)**

HARIKṚISHṆA VEṄKAṬARĀMA JYOTIRVID, *of Aurangabad.* अथ बृहज्ज्योतिषार्णवधर्मस्कंधान्तर्गत हनुमदुपासना *etc.* [Hanumadupāsanā. A ritual for the service of Hanumān, forming *adhyāya* 114 of the Upāsanāstabaka in the 8th *skandha* of the author's Bṛihajjyotishārṇava.] ff. ii. 242. मुम्बयी १९५५ [*Bombay*, 1899.] *obl.* 12°. **14028. b. 103.**

——. क्रीडाकौशल्यम् *etc.* [Krīḍākauṣalya. A work on various games of calculation, sports, *etc.*, forming the 20th *adhyāya* in the 6th *skandha* of the author's Bṛihajjyotishārṇava. With a Hindi version.] pp. viii. 258; 1 *plate.* मुम्बयी १९५७ [*Bombay*, 1901.] 8°. **14053. d. 62.**

HARILĀLA HARSHADARĀYA DHRUVA. *See* EUCLID. The Rekhâgaṇita ... Undertaken for publication by ... Harilâl ... Dhruva, *etc.* 1901-1902. 8°. **14053. ccc. 36.**

HARIMOHANA PRĀMĀṆIKA. কমলাকরুণাবিলাসো নাম শুভাঙ্কঃ *etc.* [Kamalākaruṇāvilāsa. An *aṅka* or drama in one act, with Bengali translation. Edited, with notes, by Yaṣodānanda Prāmāṇika.] pp. v. v. 96. কলিকাতা [*Calcutta*, 1899.] 8°.
14079. c. 42.(2.)

HARIMOHANA VIDYĀBHŪSHAṆA. *See* NĀGĀRJUNA. माध्यमिकावृत्ति । Mádhyamiká Vritti ... edited by ... Harimohan Vidyabhushaṇa, *etc.* 1894-1897. 8°. [*Buddhist Texts.*]
14004. c. (vol. 1, no. 1.)

—— *See* SAMĀDHIRĀJASŪTRA. समाधिराजसूत्रम् । Samādhirāja-sūtram ... edited by ... Harimohan Vidyābhūshaṇ, *etc.* 1896, *etc.* 8°. [*Buddhist Texts.*]
14004. c. (vol. 1, no. 2.)

HARINĀMADATTA MIṢRA, *Sārasvata, son of Haridhana. See* ṢAṄKARA ĀCHĀRYA.—*Philosophical Poems, etc.* ॥ अथ ... विवेकचूडामणि॰ [Viveka-chūḍāmaṇi. With the commentary Subodhinī of Harināmadatta.] [1901.] *obl.* 4°.
14048. e. 36.

HARINĀRĀYAṆA, *son of Lālā Amīr Chānd of Jalandhar. See* UPANISHADS.—*Separate Upanishads.* The Vedic Philosophy ... Mândukya Upanishad ... with ... translation and commentary ... by Har Nârâyana. 1895. 8°.
14010. cc. 2.

HARI NĀRĀYAṆA ĀPṬE. *See* ĀNANDĀṢRAMA SANSKRIT SERIES. The Ánandáśram Sanskrit Series. [Published under the direction of Hari Nārāyaṇa Āpṭe.] 1888, *etc.* 8°.
14003. ccc.

HARINĀRĀYAṆA JYOTĪRATNA. *See* SĀMUDRIKA. সানুবাদ বৃহৎ সামুদ্রিক *etc.* [Bṛihat-sāmudrika. With Bengali introduction, translation, *etc.* Edited by Harinārāyaṇa.] [1902.] 8°. **14053. ccc. 4.(4.)**

HARINĀRĀYAṆA ṢARMĀ, *of Jaipur. See* RATNĀKARA DĪKSHITA. जयसिंहकल्पद्रुमः *etc.* [Jayasiṃha-kalpadruma. Edited by Harinārāyaṇa.] [1903.] 8°. **14033. c. 47.**

HARINĀTHA TARKASIDDHĀNTA. *See* GADĀDHARA BHAṬṬĀCHĀRYA. शक्तिवादः *etc.* [Ṣaktivāda. With a commentary by Harinātha.] [1890.] 8°.
14048. bb. 43.

HARINĀTHA TARKASIDDHĀNTA (*continued*). *See* GOTAMA. ন্যায়-দর্শন *etc.* [Nyāyadarṣana. The Aphorisms, with a commentary by Harinātha and Āṣutosha.] [1894, *etc.*] 8°.
14048. dd. 21.

HARIPADA MUKHOPĀDHYĀYA. ধর্ম্ম ষোড়শকং নাম শ্রীশ্রীজামালপুরেশ্বর বুড়ারাজমাহাত্ম্যস্তোত্রম্। [Dharmashoḍaṣaka, or Jāmālpureṣvara-buṛārāja-māhātmyastotra. A poem of 16 stanzas in praise of Ṣiva, worshipped as a healing deity under the title of Buṛā-rāja or 'Venerable King' at Jamalpur. Preceded by a *maṅgalācharaṇa* of 8 stanzas, and accompanied by a commentary, with Bengali translations.] pp. i. 28. দাঁইহাট [*Daihat*, 1901.] *obl.* 12°. **14028. b. 68.(2.)**

HARIPRASĀDA, *Paṇḍitasvāmī, disciple of Ātmārāma and Jawāhir-dās.* मूर्तिपूजा *etc.* [Mūrtipūjā. A treatise on the worship of images and other symbols of deity.] pp. iv. 99, i. मुंबय्यां १९५८ [*Bombay*, 1902.] 8°. **14033. aa. 32.**

HARIRĀMA ṢĀSTRĪ, *Gūḍapalli. See* INDRAKAṆṬHAVALLABHA ĀCHĀRYA. ವೈದ್ಯಚಿಂತಾಮಣಿ *etc.* [Vaidyachintāmaṇi. Edited with Canarese translation by Harirāma.] 1897. 8°. **14043. c. 47.**

HARIRĀYAJĪ, *Gosvāmī.* गोस्वामी श्रीहरिरायजीकृत-ग्रंथाः । [Miscellaneous religious writings in verse on the doctrine of Vallabhāchārya.] pp. 242. *See* GOVARDHANADĀSA LAKSHMĪDĀSA. बृहत्स्तोत्र-सरित्सागर *etc.* [Bṛihat-stotrasaritsāgara.] Vol. ii. [1892.] 12°. **14033. a. 27.(vol. 2.)**

HARIṢAṄKARA KĀLIDĀSA. *See* HARI, *disciple of Vajrasena.* कर्पूरप्रकर *etc.* [Karpūraprakara. With gloss by Jinasāgara. Edited with Gujarati translation by Hariṣaṅkara.] [1901.] 12°.
14100. b. 12.

—— *See* JAYATILAKA SŪRI. ॥ अथ सुलसाचरितम् ॥ [Sulasācharita. With Gujarati version by Hariṣaṅkara.] [1899.] *obl.* 8°. **14100. d. 8.**

—— *See* MĀṆIKYASUNDARA SŪRI. ॥ गुणवर्मा चरित्र *etc.* [Guṇavarmacharitra. With Gujarati translation by Hariṣaṅkara.] [1901.] *obl.* 8°.
14100. c. 21.

HARIṢAṄKARA ṢĀSTRĪ, *of Hardwar, son of Kundanalāla. See* AVADHŪTALAKSHAṆA. अवधूत-

लक्षणम् etc. [Avadhūtalakshaṇa. With Hindi version by Hariṣaṅkara.] [1899.] 8°. 14028. c. 85.(3.)

—— See DATTĀTREYA. ॥ अवधूतगीता etc. [Avadhūtagītā. With Hindi version by Hariṣaṅkara.] [1899.] 8°. 14028. c. 85.(2.)

—— See PŪRṆĀNANDA GOSVĀMĪ, *disciple of Brahmānanda*. श्यामारहस्यतन्त्र etc. [Ṣyāmārahasya. With Hindi version by Hariṣaṅkara.] [1899.] 8°. 14033. c. 41.

—— See TANTRAS. [*Ḍāmaratantra*.] (डामरतन्त्रम्) [Ḍāmaratantra. With Hindi paraphrase by Hariṣaṅkara, *etc.*] [1898.] 8°. 14033. bbb. 4.(1.)

—— पांचसौपुस्तक [Pāṇch-sau Pustaka. A collection of 500 short writings, chiefly metrical, of devotional or ritual character, in Sanskrit and Hindi.] pp. 600. *Cawnpore*, १९५८ [1902.] 12°. 14033. a. 53.

HARIṢCHANDRA, *Jain Poet*. जीवन्धरचम्पू॰ [Jīvandharachampū. A Jain romance, in *champū* form, versified from the Ṣreṇikapraṣna.] [1893-1896.] See PADMARĀJA PAṆḌITA, *son of Brahmasūri*. काव्याम्बुधिः etc. [Kāvyāmbudhi.] Pts. 1-7. [1893-1896.] 8°. 14028. c. 64.

Not completed. Apparently this writer is the same as the Hariṣchandra son of Ardradeva who composed the Devaṣarmābhyudaya (Peterson, Second Report, *p. 77).*

HARIṢCHANDRA, *Bābū, son of Gopālachandra, of Benares*. श्री हरिश्चन्द्रकला etc. [Hariṣchandrakalā. The Hindi and Sanskrit works of Hariṣchandra, with biography. Compiled and edited by Rāmdīn Singh.] बांकीपुर १८८७ [*Bankipur*, 1887, *etc.*] 8° & 4°. 14158. g. 15.

In progress.

—— मानसोपायन etc. (The Intellectual Offering. Or A collection of poems in honour of the visit of His Royal Highness the Prince of Wales, to this country, written by several gentlemen in various languages [viz. Sanskrit, Persian, and various vernaculars]. Compiled by late Babu Harishchandra.) *Bankipur*, 1889. 8°. 14076. d. 52.

Separate pagination is given for each language. The English title is taken from the wrapper.

HARIṢCHANDRA, *son of Rāmadhana*. See KUMUDARAÑJANA VANDYOPĀDHYĀYA. হরিশ্চন্দ্র কুলদীপিকা [Hariṣchandra-kuladīpikā. A genealogy of Hariṣchandra.] [1891.] 32°. 14058. a. 6.

HARIṢCHANDRA BHAṬṬĀCHĀRYA KAVIRATNA. जरावैराग्यम् etc. [Jarāvairāgya. A poem in 77 stanzas on the disillusionment produced by age, with a commentary. Edited with a preface and metrical version in Bengali by Govinalāla Vandyopādhyāya.] pp. ii. i. 78. কলিকাতা ১৩০৫ [*Calcutta*, 1898.] 12°. 14072. b. 20.(2.)

HĀRĪTA. ഹാരീതധൎമ്മശാസ്ത്രം etc. [Hāritadharmaṣāstra. The shorter recension, in seven *adhyāyas*.] pp. 16. മദ്രാസ് ൧൮൯൪ [*Madras*, 1894.] 8°. 14038. c. 44.(2.)

—— हारीतसंहिता etc. [Hārītasaṃhitā. Edited by Jīvānanda Vidyāsāgara. Second edition.] pp. vii. 327. कलिकाता १८९४ [*Calcutta*, 1894.] 8°. 14033. aa. 6.(1.)

HARIVALLABHA KṚISHṆAVALLABHA. See SANDHYĀVANDANA. त्रिवर्णकर्मपद्धतिः etc. [Trivarṇakarmapaddhati. Edited with Hindi version, rubrics, and notes by Harivallabha.] [1899.] 12°. 14028. bb. 4.(2.)

HARIVALLABHA ṢARMĀ, also called ṬOPAṆLĀL KULACHANDRA. संस्कारमार्तण्डः etc. [Saṃskāramārtaṇḍa. Rules for the domestic lustratory rites, adapted from the Gṛihyasūtra of Pāraskara and Āṣvalāyana, *etc.*, for the use of the Priyatama-dharma-Sabhā of Shikarpur. With Hindi translation.] pp. iv. 180, 2. इटावा १९५७ [*Etawah*, 1901.] 8°. 14033. bbb. 10.(1.)

—— [A separate issue of pp. 1-50 of the Saṃskāramārtaṇḍa, under the title Garbhādhānādi-navasaṃskārapaddhati.] 14033. bbb. 10.(2.)

HARIVAṂṢA. See MAHĀBHĀRATA.

HARIVAṂṢA, *Brahman*. See GAṄGĀDATTA, *Upretī*. लोकद्वयोपदेश Precepts . . . Translated from the Sanscrit [of Harivaṃṣa and others,] *etc.* 1892. 8°. 14085. d. 30.

HARIVAṂṢA GOSVĀMĪ, called HITAPRABHUJĪ, *Founder of the Rādhā-vallabhī sect*. See MOHANALĀLA PRIYĀLĀLA, *Gosvāmī*. ॥ अथ श्री ॥ हितशिक्षा सार

etc. [Hitaṣikshāsāra. An exposition of Vaishṇava doctrines according to the teachings of Harivaṃṣa, *etc.*] [1897.] 8°. **14028. c. 75.**

HARLEZ (Charles de). *See* K'ang-he. Man-Han-Si Fan-tsyeh-yao, a Buddhist repertory in Sanscrit, Tibetan, Mandchu, Mongol & Chinese. [Translated by C. de Harlez.] 1887-1890. [*Babylonian & Oriental Record.*] **P.P. 3780. d. (vol. 2-4.)**

—— *See* K'ang-he. Vocabulaire Bouddhique Sanscrit-Chinois . . . Han-Fan Tsih-yao . . . [Edited and translated] par C. de Harlez. 1897. 8°. **11098. b. 37.**

—— *See* Vajrachchhedikā. Vajracchedikā Prajñâpâramitâ. Traduite . . . par M. C. de Harlez. 1891. 8°. [*Journal Asiatique.*] **Ac. 8808. (ser. viii., 18.)**

—— Mélanges Charles de Harlez. Recueil de travaux d'érudition offert à Mgr. Charles de Harlez à l'occasion du vingt-cinquième anniversaire de son professorat, *etc.* pp. xiv. 403. *Leyde*, 1896. 4°. **12902. h. 22.**

HĀṚPĀKĀ MADANASENA. *See* Madanasena, *Hāṛpākā.*

HARSHA, *author of the Naishadha. See* Ṣrīharsha, *son of Hīra Paṇḍita.*

HARSHADEVA, *King of Thanesar.* [For the Harshacharita, or romantic biography of this king :] *See* Bāṇa.

—— *See* Nārāyaṇa Ṣāstrī, *T.S.* Sriharsha the Dramatist. A dissertation on . . . the author of the Priyadarsika, the Ratnavali, and the Nagananda, [identifying him with Dhāvaka or Bhāsaka,] *etc.* [1902.] 8°. **14058. b. 40.(2.)**

—— Une Poésie Inconnue du Roi Harṣa Çîlâditya[, *scil.* the Ashṭamahāṣrīchaityastotra. Transliterated from the Chinese transcription of Fa-t'ien.] Par Sylvain Lévi. 1895-1897. *See* Academies, *etc.*—Europe.—*International Congress of Orientalists.* Actes du Dixième Congrès International, *etc.* Vol. II, Sect. i. pp. 187-203. 1873, *etc.* 8°. **Ac. 8806. (Session 10.)**

HARSHADEVA, *King of Thanesar (continued).* **नागानन्दं नाम नाटकम्** *etc.* (The Nâgânandam . . . Edited with copious Sanskrit and English notes by Shrînivâs Govind Bhânap.) pp. xviii. 91, 40. *Bombay*, 1892. 8°. **14080. c. 33.**

—— உ . . . நாகாநந்தம் நாம நாடகம் *etc.* [Nāgānanda. Edited by Ṣ. L. Ṣrīnivāsa Gopālāchārya.] pp. 52. [illegible] [*Tanjore*, 1897.] 8°. **14079. d. 44.**

—— **रत्नावली नाटिका** *etc.* (The Ratnávalí Nátiká of Sriharshdeva. Edited with Hindi translation by Pundit Rámeshwar Bhatt.) pp. iv. xxiv. ii. 115. *Bombay*, 1895. 8°. **14080. c. 35.**

This drama has been attributed with probability to Bāṇa (Weber, Akad. Vorlesungen, *2nd ed., pp.* 224, 333). *Native tradition ascribes it to Dhāvaka or his patron Harshadeva of Kashmir.*

—— **रत्नावली** *etc.* [Ratnāvalī. With commentary, entitled Vidyotanī, by Ṣivanātha Vidyāvāchaspati. Edited by Kṛishṇanātha Nyāyapañchānana.] pp. vi. 190. **कलिकाता १८२१** [*Calcutta*, 1900.] 8°. **14079. c. 65.(2.)**

—— The Ratnavali. A Sanskrit drama by Sriharsha. **रत्नावली । नाटिका** . . . Edited with English and Bengali translations, a Sanskrit commentary, and Anglo-Sanskrit notes by Sris Chandra Chakravarti, *etc.* 2 parts. *Dacca, Calcutta* [printed], 1902. 12°. **14080. b. 12.**

The title-page is in pt. 2.

—— Rathnavali. With Sanskrit commentary by Swetaranyam Narayana Sastriar. (F.A. Examination of 1903.) pp. 160. *Madras*, 1903. 8°. **14080. c. 45**

The English title is from the cover.

—— Ratnavali; or The Necklace. A drama, translated . . . by H. H. Wilson. pp. viii. 66. 1901. *See* Wilson (H. H.). Hindu Dramatic Works, *etc.* 1901. 12°. **14080. b. 13.**

HARSHAKĪRTI SŪRI, *disciple of Chandrakīrti, of Nagpur Tapā-gachchha. See* Somaprabha Āchārya. **अथ . . . सिंदूरप्रकरः** *etc.* [Sindūraprakara. With commentary by Harshakīrti.] 1890. 8°. [*Jainakathāratnakoṣa.*] **14144. gg. 1.(vol. 1.)**

—— **श्रीयोगचिन्तामणि** *etc.* [Yogachintāmaṇi. A treatise on therapeutics. With Gujarati version by Pūrṇachandra Ṣarmā. Edited by Mahādeva Rāmachandra Jāgushṭe.] pp. xv. 390. अमदावाद १९५४ [*Ahmadabad*, 1898.] 8°. **14053. ccc. 20.**

HARSHAVARDHANA, *King of Kanauj*. *See* HARSHADEVA.

HARSHAVARDHANA, *son of Ṣrīvardhana*. ॥ अथ . . . लिङ्गानुशासनम् ॥ [Liṅgānuṣāsana. With German translation and extracts from Ṣabarasvāmī's commentary.] *See* FRANKE (R. O.). Die Indischen Genuslehren, *etc.* pp. 83-117. 1890. 8°. **14093. d. 19.**

HARTMANN (FRANZ). *See* MAHĀBHĀRATA.—Bhagavadgītā.—*German*. Die Bhagavad Gita . . . ins Deutsche übertragen und mit . . . Anmerkungen und . . . Citaten . . . deutscher Mystiker versehen. Von Dr. F. Hartmann. 1892. 12°. **14060. b. 13.**

—— *See* MAHĀBHĀRATA.—Bhagavadgītā.—*German*. Die Bhagavad Gita . . . In poetischer Form nach Edwin Arnolds Sanskrit-Übersetzung . . . übertragen von F. Hartmann, *etc.* 1904. 12°. **14060. c. 34.**

—— *See* ṢAṄKARA ĀCHĀRYA.—*Philosophical Poems*, *etc.* Atma Bodha . . . Übersetzt von F. Hartmann. [1895.] 8°. **14048. bb. 9.(3.)**

—— *See* TATTVABODHA. Tattwa Bodha . . . übersetzt von F. Hartmann. [1895.] 8°. **14048. bb. 9.(2.)**

—— Die Erkenntnislehre der Bhagavad Gita im Lichte der Geheimlehre betrachtet. Ein Beitrag zum Studium derselben, *etc.* pp. 150. *Leipzig*, [1897.] 8°. **14048. b. 31.**

HARVARD ORIENTAL SERIES. *See* ACADEMIES, *etc.*—Cambridge, *Mass.*—*Harvard University*.

HASTĀMALAKA ĀCHĀRYA. वेदान्तसिद्धान्तः [Vedāntasiddhānta. Being the Hastāmalakastotra with the commentary Vedāntasiddhāntadīpikā.] *See* NITYĀNANDA SARASVATĪ. वेदान्तग्रन्थपञ्चकम् *etc.* [Vedāntagranthapañchaka.] pp. 48-78. [1891.] 12°. **14048. b. 15.(2.)**

—— హస్తామలక॥ [Hastāmalakaṣloka.] *See* ṢAṄKARA ĀCHĀRYA.—*Philosophical Poems*, *etc.* అయం సిద్ధాంతబిందుః *etc.* [Daṣaṣlokī, *etc.*] p. 36. [1892.] 8°. **14048. cc. 9.(1.)**

HASTĀMALAKA ĀCHĀRYA (*continued*). శ్రీ . . . హస్తామలకభాష్యము *etc.* [Hastāmalakabhāshya. The Hastāmalakastotra, with commentary ascribed to Ṣaṅkara. Edited with Telugu translation by N. Guruliṅga Ṣāstrī.] pp. 32. చెన్నపట్టణము ౧౯౦౧ [*Madras*, 1901.] 8°. **14049. a. 7.**

This commentary is not the Vedāntasiddhāntadīpikā, but is the same as that published by Maheṣachandra Pāla in the Vedântaratnâvali (*Calcutta*, 1883).

—— Hastamalakbhasyam . . . Translated [by Nandalāla Ḍhol,] *etc.* 1899. *See* PERIODICAL PUBLICATIONS.—*Calcutta*. The Oriental, *etc.* Vol. ii., no. 3. 1898, *etc.* 8°. **Ac. 8825. b.(vol. 2.)**

HATFIELD (JAMES TAFT). *See* VEDAS.—Atharvaveda.—*Pariṣishṭa*. The Auçanasādbhutāni, text & translation. By J. T. Hatfield. 1893. 8°. [*Journal of the American Oriental Society.*] **Ac. 8824.(vol. 15.)**

HATTHAVANAGALLA-VIHĀRA-VAṀSA. The Pali Text of the Attanagaluvansa and its ancient translation into Siṇhalese; with notes . . . by . . . James Alwis. (හත්වනගල්ලවිහාරවංශ) Second edition. pp. vii. 114. *Colombo*, 1887. 8°. **14098. c. 66.**

HBO. *See* HPO.

HBUYĀ. [For Burmese titles beginning with this word:] *See* PAYĀ.

HEDBERG (FRANS). *See* ṢŪDRAKA. Vasantasena . . . af Frans Hedberg. 1894. 12°. **11755. dd.**

HELLER (LUDWIG). *See* HALĀYUDHA BHAṬṬA. Halâyudha's Kavirahasya . . . Herausgegeben von L. Heller. 1900. 8°. [*Sanskrit-Drucke.*] **14093. d. 21.**

—— Halâyudha's Kavirahasya. Inaugural-Dissertation zur Erlangung der Doctorwürde . . . der Georg-Augusts-Universität zu Göttingen . . . von Ludwig Heller . . . Einleitung. pp. 56. *Göttingen*, 1894. 8°. **14093. b. 35.(1.)**

HEMACHANDRA, *disciple of Devachandra*. The Abhidhâna-chintâmaṇi, the Abhidhâna-chintâmaṇi-pariśishta, the Anekârtha-sangraha, the Nighaṇtu-śesha and the Lingânuśâsana of Hemachandra. And ... the Abhidhâna-chintâmaṇi-śilonchchha of Jinadeva Munîśvara. Edited by Paṇdit Śivadatta and Kâśînâth Pândurang Parab. (अभिधानचिन्तामणि - अभिधानचिन्तामणिपरिशिष्ट - अनेकार्थसंग्रह - निघण्टुशेष - लिङ्गानुशासनकोशाः ... अभिधानचिन्तामणिशिलोञ्छश्च ।) pp. vi. 58, 8, 69, 13, 10, 5, ii. 1896. *See* DURGĀPRASĀDA, *son of Vrajalāla*, and others. The Abhidhâna-sangraha, *etc.* No. 6-11. 1889, *etc.* 8°. **14090. e. 20.(no. 6-11.)**

—— अभिधानचिंतामणिः *etc.* [Abhidhānachintāmaṇi. With footnotes. Followed by the supplement called Ṣiloñchha by Jinadeva Munīṣvara; an alphabetical index; and the supplement styled Ṣeshanāmamālā. Edited by Narmadāṣaṅkara Dāmodara Ṣāstrī.] pp. 257, 19, 288, 26. मुम्बय्याम् १९५६ [*Bombay*, 1900.] 12°. **14090. b. 46.**

—— अथ श्रीहेमचन्द्रसूरिप्रणीतोनेकार्थसंग्रहः ॥ ... The Anekarthasamgraha of Hemachandra. Edited with extracts from the commentary [Anekārtha-kairavākarakaumudī] of Mahendra by Theodor Zachariæ. pp. xviii. 132, 206, 55. 1893. *See* ACADEMIES, *etc.*—Vienna.—*Kaiserliche Akademie der Wissenschaften.* Sources of Sanskrit Lexicography, *etc.* Vol. 1. 1893, *etc.* 4°. **14090. e. 23.(vol. 1.)**

—— ॥ अथ हैमधातुपारायणम् ॥ The Dhātupāṭha of Hemachandra, with the author's own commentary. Edited by Joh. Kirste. (Der Dhātupāṭha des Hemachandra, mit dem selbstverfassten Commentare des Autors.) pp. x. 288, cxxii. xxxiv. 1901. *See* ACADEMIES, *etc.*—Vienna.—*Kaiserliche Akademie der Wissenschaften.* Sources of Sanskrit Lexicography, *etc.* Vol. 4. 1893, *etc.* 4°. **14090. e. 23.(vol. 4.)**

—— हैमलघुप्रक्रियाख्यं व्याकरणम् *etc.* [Haima-laghu-prakriyā. An abridgement and rearrangement of the aphorisms of Hemachandra's Ṣabdānuṣā-sana, with an original commentary, by Vinaya-vijaya Gaṇī.] pp. viii. 194, ii. 222, i. मुंबा १९४९ [*Bombay*, 1892.] 12°. **14090. b. 40.**

—— The Kâvyânuśâsana of Hemachandra. [A treatise on the art of poetry.] With his own gloss. Edited by ... Paṇdit Śivadatta ... and Kâśînâth Pândurang Parab. (काव्यानुशासनम् । सटीकम् ।) pp. viii. 10, 341, xx. 1901. *See* DURGĀPRASĀDA, *son of Vrajalāla*, and KĀŚĪNĀTHA PĀṆḌURAṄGA PARAB. Kâvyamâlâ. [No.] 71. 1886, *etc.* 8°. **14072. ccc. 12.(no. 71.)**

—— The Kumârapâlacharita, Prâkṛita Dvyâśraya Kâvya, by Hemachandra. Being a Prâkṛita poem [in 8 *sargas*] intended to illustrate the eighth adhyâya ... of his own Siddha-hemachandra or grammar, with a commentary by Pûrṇakalaśagaṇi. [Followed by the text of the 8th *adhyāya* of the author's grammar, with his own commentary styled Prakāṣikā.] Edited by Shaṅkar Pâṇḍurang Paṇḍit. (कुमारपालचरित प्राकृत-द्व्याश्रयकाव्यम् *etc.*) pp. xxiv. xv. 298, xiv. ix. cxxiv. 209. *Bombay*, 1900. 8°. **14100. c. 23.**

Forms no. lx. *of the* Bombay Sanskrit Series.

—— Materialien zur Kenntnis des Apabhraṃśa. [Comprising the examples of this dialect in Hemachandra's grammar, iv. 329-446, with the Sanskrit translation of Udayasaubhāgya Gaṇī; in the Sarasvatīkaṇṭhābharaṇa; and in other sources.] Ein Nachtrag zur Grammatik der Prākrit-Sprachen. Von R. Pischel. pp. 86. 1902. *See* ACADEMIES, *etc.*—Goettingen.—*Koenigliche Gesellschaft der Wissenschaften.* Abhandlungen, *etc.* Band V, No. 4. 1843, *etc.* 4°. **Ac. 670. (Bd. 5, no. 4.)**

—— —— [Another copy.] **14093. d. 23.**

—— स्याद्वादमञ्जरी *etc.* (Syadwada Manjari. [A compendium of the logic of Jain metaphysics, in 32 stanzas.] By Mallishiena [or rather, by Hemachandra]. With a commentary of Hemchandra [or rather, of Mallisheṇa]. Edited by Sri Damodar Lal Goswami.) pp. viii. iii. 220. काश्याम् १९०० [*Benares*, 1900.] 8°. **14004. a. 9.**

Forms nos. 32-33 *of the* Chowkhambâ Sanskrit Series. *The English title is taken from the wrapper.*

—— अथ श्रीहेमचन्द्रसूरिविरचितमुणादिगणसूत्रं ... The Uṇâdigaṇasûtra of Hemachandra. With the author's own commentary. Edited by Johann Kirste, *etc.* (Das Unadiganasutra des Hemachandra. Mit dem selbstverfassten Commentare des Autors.) pp. ix. 241. 1895. *See* ACADEMIES, *etc.*—Vienna.—*Kaiserliche Akademie der Wissenschaften.* Sources of Sanskrit Lexicography, *etc.* Vol. 2. 1893, *etc.* 4°. **14090. e. 23.(vol. 2.)**

HEMACHANDRA, *disciple of Devachandra (continued).* वैद्यतत्त्व रत्नाकर *etc.* [Vaidyatattvaratnākara. A medical treatise said to be an abbreviated version of the Gudanigraha-grantha attributed to Hemachandra. Edited with Gujarati paraphrase and notes by Maganlāl Viśvanātha.] pp. vii. 287. अमदावाद १८९८ [*Ahmadabad,* 1898.] 8°. **14053. d. 56.**

—— ॥ अथ ... वीतराग स्तुतिः *etc.* [Vītarāgastuti. A Jain Sanskrit hymn in 20 *prakāśas,* with Gujarati explanation.] 1890. *See* BHĪMASIṂHA MĀṆAKA. जैनकथारत्नकोष *etc.* [Jainakathāratnakoṣa.] Vol. i., pp. 185-220. [1890-1893.] 8°. **14144. gg. 1.(vol. 1.)**

HEMACHANDRA VIDYĀRATNA. *See* MAHĀBHĀRATA.—Bhagavadgītā.—*Sanskrit and Vernaculars.* শ্রীমদ্ভগবদ্গীতা *etc.* [Bhagavadgītā. With a Bengali translation by Hemachandra.] [1895.] 16°. **14065. b. 15.**

HEMĀCHĀRYA SŪRI. अर्हन्नीतौ दायभागः *etc.* [Dāyabhāga. A Jain tract on inheritance, in 144 stanzas with explanations, extracted from a larger legal work styled Arhannīti.] pp. 36, *lith.* लखनऊ १८९१ [*Lucknow,* 1891.] 12°. **14038. b. 9.**

The editor of the Jinapūjāmahodadhi (Bombay, 1902) speaks, in his preface, of an Arhannīti by Jinadatta Sūri, *which is perhaps the book from which this Dāyabhāga is extracted. By Hemāchārya* Hemachandra *may be meant.*

HEMĀḌ PANTA. *See* HEMĀDRI.

HEMĀḌ PANTA. *See* NĀNĀBHĀĪ SADĀNANDAJĪ REḶE.

HEMĀDRI. [For the Kāmakautūhala ascribed to Hemādri:] *See* KĀMAKAUTŪHALA.

—— The Chaturvarga Chintámani ... Vol. I. Dánakhanda ... Revised and enlarged by Pandita Sadáshiva Ácharya Dikshita. (चतुर्वर्गचिन्तामणौ दानखण्डम् ।) *Benares,* 1902, *etc.* 8°. **14033. bbb. 16.**

In progress.

—— पुण्याहवाचन प्र. [Puṇyāhavāchanaprayoga. The ritual for the invocation of auspicious days. Extracted from the 3rd *adhyāya* of the Dānakhaṇḍa of the Chaturvargachintāmaṇi.] अमदावाद [*Ahmadabad,* 1899.] *obl.* 12°. **14028. b. 93.(3.)**

HEMĀDRI BHAṬṬA, *son of Īśvara Sūri.* *See* KĀLIDĀSA.—*Raghuvaṃṣa.* The Raghuvanśa ... with full extracts ... from the commentaries of Bhatta Hemâdri, *etc.* 1897. 8°. **14072. c. 53.**

HEMAṢAṄKARA LAKSHMĪṢAṄKARA VARDHAMĀNKAR. प्रकरण माला. भाषान्तर *etc.* [Prakaraṇamālā. A collection of poems, chiefly in Prakrit, upon the religious, philosophical, and ethical doctrines of the Jains, comprising the Jīvavichāra, Navatattva, Chaturviṃṣati-daṇḍaka, Jaṃbuddiva-saṃghayaṇī, Chaityavandana-bhāshya, Guruvandana-bhāshya, Pachchakkhāṇa-bhāshya, Indriyaparājaya-ṣataka, Vairāgyaṣataka, 8 *kulakas,* Samādhiṣataka, and Sajjanachittavallabha, *etc.* Edited with Gujarati translations by Hemaṣaṅkara.] pp. ii. 233, i. अमदावाद १९५८ [*Ahmadabad,* 1901.] 8°. **14100. d. 11.**

HENRY (VICTOR). *See* VEDAS.—*Atharvaveda.* Atharva-véda ... Le Livre VII (VIII et IX; X, XI, et XII; XIII) ... Traduit et commenté par V. Henry. 1891-1896. 8°. **14010. c. 53.**

—— *See* VEDAS.—Ṛigveda.—*Selections.* Quarante Hymnes ... traduits ... par A. Bergaigne. (Publiés par V. Henry.) 1892-1894. 8°. [*Mémoires de la Société de Linguistique de Paris.*] **Ac. 9810.(tom. 8.)**

—— *See* VEDAS.—Ṛigveda.—*Single Hymns and Verses.* Mudgala, ou l'Hymne du Marteau ... Par M. V. Henry. 1895. 8°. [*Journal Asiatique.*] **Ac. 8808.(ser. ix. 6.)**

—— La Magie dans l'Inde Antique. [With special reference to the Atharvaveda, Ṛigveda, and Kauṣikasūtra.] (Les Religions des Peuples Civilisés.) pp. xxxix. 286. *Paris, Chalon-sur-Saone* [printed], 1904. 12°. **08631. f. 35.**

HERAṆA-SIKA. හෙරණසික සහ දිනචරියාව [Heraṇa-sika. A Sinhalese tract on the rules for novices of the Buddhist clergy. Followed by the Dinachariyā, a tract on the daily observances of Buddhist devotees, in both the Sinhalese and the Pali version.] pp. 12. කොළඹ [*Colombo,*] 1897. 12°. **14098. a. 30.**

HEROLD (A. FERDINAND). *See* UPANISHADS.—*Separate Upanishads.* L'Upanishad du Grand Aranyaka, Brihadâranyakopanishad. Traduite ... par A.-F. Herold. 1894. 8°. **14007. c. 23.**

HERRERO (José J.). *See* Kālidāsa.—*Supposititious Works.* J. Herrero. Poetas del Amor. Kalidasa: Gringara [*sic*] Tilaka ... Versión Castellana. 1898. 12°. **14076. a. 18.**

HERTEL (Johannes). *See* Hitopadeśa. Zwei Erzählungen aus der Bonner Hitopadeśa-Hs. Ch., *etc.* 1901. 8°. [*Zeitschrift der Deutschen Morgenlaendischen Gesellschaft.*] **Ac. 8815/2. (vol. 55.)**

—— *See* Somadeva, *son of Rāma.* Bunte Geschichten vom Himalaja ... deutsch von J. Hertel. 1903. 8°. **14070. dd. 25.**

—— Kritische Bemerkungen zu Kosegartens Pañcatantra, *etc.* 1902. *See* Academies, *etc.*—Germany.—*Deutsche Morgenlaendische Gesellschaft.* Zeitschrift, *etc.* Bd. 56, pp. 293-326. 1846, *etc.* 8°. **Ac. 8815/2.(vol. 56.)**

HINDU TRIAD. History of the Hindu Triad, Brahma, Vishnu, and Siva, as described in the sacred books of the Hindus. pp. i. 60. *London, Madras* [printed], 1897. 8°. **14028. d. 61.**

HĪRĀCHAND KAKALBHĀĪ. *See* Navasmaraṇa. नव स्मरण *etc.* [Navasmaraṇa, *etc.* Edited by Hīrāchand.] [1900.] 16°. **14100. a. 24.**

HĪRĀCHAND NEMCHAND. *See* Samantabhadra Svāmī. रत्नकरंडश्रावकाचार *etc.* [Ratnakaraṇḍaśrāvakāchāra. Edited with Marathi and Hindi translations by Hīrāchand.] [1895.] 16°. **14028. b. 74.**

HĪRĀLĀL ḌHOL. *See* Sadānanda Yogīndra. সটীক ... বেদান্ত-সার *etc.* [Vedāntasāra. With commentary, *etc.* Edited by Hīrālāl Ḍhol.] [1903.] 12°. **14048. b. 41.**

HĪRĀLĀL GOPĀLA ŚARMĀ. शास्त्रार्थ *etc.* [Śāstrārtha. Responses of pandits, in Hindi and Marathi, on the right of Vaiśyas to perform Vedic rites, with citations from Sanskrit texts.] pp. 46. मुंबई १८८७ [*Bombay,* 1887.] 8°. **14154. e. 24.**

HIRAṆYAKEŚĪ. *See* Āpastamba.—*Dharmasūtra.* आपस्तम्बीयधर्मसूत्रम् । Aphorisms on the Sacred Law ... containing ... the various readings of the Hiraṇyakeśi-dharmasûtra. 1892-1894. 8°. **14038. d. 34.**

HIRAṆYAKEŚĪ (*continued*). க்ருஹ்யஸூத்ரம் [Gṛihyasūtra. Edited with a preface by K. Śrīnivāsa Dīkshita.] pp. v. iv. 95. நடுக்காவேரி [*Nadukkaveri,*] 1901. 12°. **14038. b. 10.(1.)**

—— ॥ पितृमेधसूत्राणि ॥ The Pitṛmedhasūtras of Baudhāyana, Hiraṇyakeśin, Gautama, *etc.* 1896. 8°. *See* Caland (W.). [*Deutsche Morgenlaendische Gesellschaft: Abhandlungen.*] **753. f. 18.**

—— *See* Śrīnivāsa Dīkshita, *K.* ஹிரண்யகேஶிமஹிமஸங்க்ரஹ: *etc.* [Hiraṇyakeṣimahimasaṅgraha. A poetical account of Hiraṇyakeṣī.] 1901. 16°. **14072. a. 1.(3.)**

—— ஶ்ரீஶுக்லயஜுஶ்ஶாகாய ... ஸத்யாஷாடஸூத்ரப்ரயோககாரிகா [Gṛihyakārikā. A metrical epitome of domestic ritual according to the Aphorisms of Hiraṇyakeṣī.] pp. 39. நடுக்காவேரி [*Nadukkaveri,*] 1901. 12°. **14038. b. 10.(2.)**

—— உபாகர்மப்ரயோக: [Upākarmaprayoga. A manual for the rites of *upākarma*, according to the Aphorisms of Hiraṇyakeṣī.] pp. 20. நடுக்காவேரி பிலவ [*Nadukkaveri,* 1901.] 8°. **14039. b. 26.(1.)**

Forms no. 3 *of the* Satyāshāḍhasūtraprayogasaṅgraha.

HIRZEL (A.). Der Rigveda und seine Sprache. Aus einem Vortrag über altindische Poesie, *etc.* pp. 19. *Aarau,* 1895. 8°. **012901. i. 2.(11.)**

HITAHARIVAṂŚA. *See* Harivaṃśa Gosvāmī.

HITAPRABHUJĪ. *See* Harivaṃśa Gosvāmī.

HITOPADEŚA. The Hitopadeśa of Nârâyaṇa Paṇdit. [With brief notes in Sanskrit.] (हितोपदेशः) pp. 139. *Bombay,* 1893. 8°. **14072. ccc. 28.**

—— A Popular Edition of the Hitopadesha [believed to be composed] by Bhatta Narayana. Containing a full glossary and a literal translation [into English] of the verses occurring in the text. Edited by Mahadev Shivaram Apte. pp. ii. 233. *Poona,* 1897. 12°. **14070. c. 61.**

—— The Book of Good Counsels. [Adapted] from the Sanskrit of the 'Hitopadeśa,' by Sir

Edwin Arnold ... New edition. With illustrations, *etc.* pp. 162. *London*, 1893. 8°.
14076. c. 62.

—— The Book of Good Counsels. [Adapted] ... by Sir Edwin Arnold. Author's autograph edition. pp. 162. *London*, 1896. 8°.
14070. c. 52.

—— English Translation of Hitopadesha, by B. T. Dravid, alias Sheshadri Iyar. pp. ii. 126. *Bombay*, 1896. 8°. **14070. c. 58.**

—— Lo Hitopadeça, o Buono Ammaestramento, di Nârâyana ... tradotto ... da Oreste Nazari. pp. i. 112. *Torino*, 1896. 8°.
14072. cc. 49.(2.)

—— *See* KIṢORĪMOHANA VIDYĀNIDHI. **वैयाकरण नीतिकौमुदी** *etc.* [Vaiyākaraṇa-nītikaumudī. Tales, with occasional verses from the Hitopadeṣa, *etc.*] [1898.] 12°. **14085. b. 43.**

—— ဟိတောပဒေသ *etc.* [Hitopadeṣa, viz. the stanzas of Book i, in Pali, with Burmese translation. Followed by the Sāmudrika, also in Pali and Burmese, and the Sāmudrikalakkhaṇakyan-linkā, a Burmese tract on palmistry. Edited and translated by Y̱an Hnin.] pp. iv. 96. *Rangoon*, ၁၂၄၄ [1882.] 8°. **14098. ccc. 19.(1.)**

—— **हितोपदेशः । आभाषः । (मित्रानुरागः)** [Hitopadeṣa, viz. part of the introduction and of Book i, here styled Mitrānurāga. With notes.] *See* NṚISIṂHARĀMA MUKHOPĀDHYĀYA. **साहित्य-रत्नाकरः** *etc.* [Sāhityaratnākara.] pp. 1-18. 1898. 12°.
14065. b. 18.

—— **हितोपदेशः (हितोपदेशसारसंग्रहः)** [Hitopadeṣa, viz. word-for-word grammatical analyses of selections from Bk. i., and likewise of the Hitopadeṣasārasaṅgraha, select stanzas from the same work. With English and Hindi translations.] *See* ACADEMIES, *etc.*—Allahabad.—*University of Allahabad.* **संस्कृत-शिक्षा-विवृतिः** ... Sanskrit-Siksha-Vivriti, *etc.* pp. 1-64, 328-355. 1899. 12°.
14085. b. 39.(2.)

—— Zwei Erzählungen aus der Bonner Hitopadeśa-Hs. Ch. [The stories of Ṣakuni and Ṣakaṭāra, sometimes included in the Hitopadeṣa.] Von Johannes Hertel. 1901. *See* ACADEMIES, *etc.*—Germany.—*Deutsche Morgenlaendische Gesellschaft.* Zeitschrift, *etc.* Bd. 55, pp. 487-494. 1846, *etc.* 8°. **Ac. 8815/2.(vol. 55.)**

HKY̱AUK SAUNG TWÈ. ခြောက်ဆောင်တွဲ *etc.* [Hky̱auk saung twè. Comprising the Maṅgalasutta, Bāhira and Ajjhatta Jayamaṅgala, Ratanapañjara, Namakāra, and Lokanīti. With Burmese versions and glossaries. Fourth edition.] pp. 227. *Rangoon*, 1883. 8°.
14098. ccc. 11.(2.)

—— The Chauk Saung Dwe. ခြောက်ဆောင်တွဲ *etc.* [Another edition of the preceding, with a different title-page.] pp. 227. *Rangoon*, 1895. 8°. **14098. ccc. 11.(4.)**

—— ခြောက်ဆောင်တွဲ [Hky̱auk saung twè.] pp. 110. ရန်ကုန် ၁၂၅၂ [*Rangoon*, 1890.] 8°.
14098. ccc. 11.(3.)

HNEGYO PONGYI. *See* SUTTAPIṬAKA.—*Selections.* သုတ်ကမ္မဋ္ဌာန်းအမျိုးမျိုး [Thôk-kammaṭṭhānamyo-myo. Thirteen *suttas* and other excerpts from the Suttapiṭaka, with Burmese version and notes by the Hnegyo Pongyi. Followed by the Sikkhāpadavinichchhaya-anuttānapadappakāsanī, a Burmese tract.] [1898.] 8°.
14098. ccc. 26.(5.)

—— သံမောဟဆေဒနီကျမ်း *etc.* [Sammohachhedanī. An ethical treatise, in Burmese, illustrated from Pali texts.] pp. 147. ရန်ကုန် ၁၂၅၈ [*Rangoon*, 1896.] 8°. **14300. d. 26.(4.)**

HODGSON (GERALDINE). *See* VĀLMĪKI.—Rāmāyaṇa.—*Appendix.* Rama & the Monkeys. Adapted ... by G. Hodgson, *etc.* 1903. 12°.
012200. e. 8.(no. 13.)

HOERNLE (AUGUST FRIEDRICH RUDOLF). *See* INDIA.—*Archaeological Survey.* The Bower Manuscript ... edited by A. F. R. Hoernle. 1893, *etc.* Fol. **14058. d. 5.**

—— *See* SUṢRUTA. **सुश्रुतसंहिता ।** The Suçrutasaṁhitā. ... Translated ... by Dr. A. F. R. Hoernle. 1897, *etc.* 8°. [*Bibliotheca Indica.*]
14002. a.(vol. 139.)

HOERNLE (August Friedrich Rudolf) (*continued*). Facsimile Reproduction of Weber MSS., Part ix, and Macartney MSS., Set i, with Roman transliteration and indexes. By A. F. Rudolf Hoernle. pp. i. 31, iv.; 25 and 17 *plates*. *Calcutta*, 1902. 4°. **759. k. 1.**

Reprinted from the Journal of the Asiatic Society of Bengal, vol. lxx., *Part I, extra No.* i.

HOLLER (P.). The Student's Manual of Indian Vedic-Sanskrit-Prakrut-Pali Literature. A system and review, with lists of commentaries, text-editions, translations, and expositions . . . a chronicle of Indian authors, *etc.* 2 pts.; 1 *plate*. *Rajahmundry*, 1901. 8°. **759. b.**

HOLME (T.). Sakuntala; or, The Fatal Ring: A drama. By Kalidasa, "The Shakespeare of India." To which is added Meghaduta; or, The Cloud Messenger, [and] the Bhagavad-gita, or Sacred Song. [In the translations of Sir W. Jones, H. H. Wilson, and Sir C. Wilkins respectively.] Edited, with an introduction, by T. Holme. pp. xviii. 240. *London, Newcastle-on-Tyne*, [1902.] 8°. **012208. ee. 117.**

Forms vol. 117 *of the* Scott Library.

HOLTZMANN (Adolf). Das Mahābhārata und seine Theile, *etc.* (Vol. 1, Zur Geschichte und Kritik des Mahābhārata. Vol. 2, Die neunzehn Bücher des Mahābhārata. Vol. 3, Das Mahābhārata nach der nordindischen Recension. Vol. 4, Das Mahābhārata im Osten und Westen.) 4 vols. *Kiel, Bonn* [printed], 1892-1895. 8°. **011840. l. 55.**

HOPKINS (Edward Washburn). The Mutual Relations of the Four Castes according to the Mānavadharmaçāstram. Inaugural-Dissertation for the Degree of Doctor of Philosophy at the University of Leipzig, *etc.* pp. vi. 115. *Leipzig*, 1881. 8°. **14039. b. 25.**

—— India Old and New. With a memorial address [in honour of E. E. Salisbury,] *etc.* (Yale Bicentennial Publications.) pp. viii. i. 342. *New York and London, Cambridge U.S.A.* [printed], 1901. 8°. **Ac. 2692. m./20.**

—— The Great Epic of India. Its character and origin, *etc.* (Yale Bicentennial Publications.) pp. xvi. 485. *New York and London, Cambridge U.S.A.* [printed], 1901. 8°. **Ac. 2692. m./2.**

HORILA ṢARMĀ. व्याकरण ॥ पूर्वपक्षावली ॥ [Pūrvapakshāvalī. A series of grammatical problems.] pp. 48. काश्याम् १९५९ [*Benares*, 1902.] 8°. **14090. bb. 21.(1.)**

—— व्याकरण ॥ उत्तरपक्षावली ॥ [Uttarapakshāvalī. Answers to the preceding problems, by various Pandits.] pp. 42. काश्याम् १९५९ [*Benares*, 1902.] 8°. **14090. bb. 21.(2.)**

HPO MIN, *Maung.* အဘိဓမ္မာဓာတ်ကျမ်း [Abhidhammā-dhāt-kyan. A Burmese treatise on the category of *rūpa* in its relation to physical science, based upon the Abhidhammapiṭaka, with quotations thence.] pp. 215. ရန်ကုန် ၁၂၅၉ [*Rangoon*, 1897.] 8°. **14300. d. 19.(7.)**

—— [Second edition.] pp. x. 232. ရန်ကုန် ၁၂၆၂ [*Rangoon*, 1901.] 8°. **14300. d. 32.**

HPO YAN. ဂုဏ်တော်ပွင့်ဘုရားရှိခိုး [Gôṇ-taw̱-hpwin-paya̱-shi-hko. Enumerations of the 9 *guṇas* of the Buddha, of the Dhamma, and of the Saṅgha, with copious Burmese commentary. Followed by 2 short prayers in Pali and Burmese; three Burmese compositions; and a tabular list of the 30 *saraṇaguṇas*, with Burmese commentary.] pp. 48, i. ရန်ကုန် ၁၂၆၁ [*Rangoon*, 1899.] 12°. **14098. a. 32.(2.)**

HPO YAN, *Hsaya Ū, of Toungoo.* *See* Vinaya-piṭaka. [*Chullavagga.*] သင်္ဂါယနာတင်ဝိနည်းကျမ်း *etc.* [Saṅgāyanā-tin-wini-kyan. With Burmese translation by Hpo Yan. Preceded by the Gôṇ-taw̱-hpwin, with Burmese version and commentary by the same.] [1900.] 8°. **14098. ccc. 26.(8.)**

HPO Y̱IN, *Ū.* မဟန္တဂုဏာနုဿရဏကျမ်း॥ အတုလဝန္ဒနာဘုရားရှိခိုး *etc.* [Mahantaguṇā-nussaraṇa-kyan. A series of Pali stanzas with Burmese commentaries, treating of the various qualities of the Buddha. Followed by the Atulavandanā-payā-shi-hko, a Burmese devotional treatise illustrated from Pali texts, on the same topic.] pp. 139, i. ii. iii. [*Mandalay*,] 1900. 8°. **14300. d. 32.(4.)**

HṚISHĪKEṢA ṢĀSTRĪ, *of the Sanskrit College, Calcutta.* See ACADEMIES, *etc.*—Calcutta.—*Calcutta Sanskrit College.* A Descriptive Catalogue of Sanskrit Manuscripts in the Library of the Calcutta Sanskrit College ... by Hṛishíkeśa Śástrí ... and Śiva Chandra Gui. 1892, *etc.* 8°.
14096. cc. 10.

—— See PURĀṆAS.—*Selections.* হিন্দুশাস্ত্র *etc.* [Ashṭādaṣa-purāṇa. Selections, with Bengali translations, *etc.* Compiled by Āṣutosha and Hṛishīkeṣa.] [1897.] 8°. [*Hindu-ṣástra.*]
14085. c. 45.(vol. 2.)

HṚISHĪKEṢA VIDYĀRATNA. See SARVAVARMĀ.—*Appendix.* গণতত্ত্ব-দীপিকা *etc.* [Gaṇatattvadīpikā. Edited by Hṛishīkeṣa, *etc.*] [1900.] 8°.
14093. b. 20.(3.)

HSAY SAUNG TWÈ. ဆယ်ဆောင်တွဲ [Hsay saung twè. Comprising the Maṅgalasutta, Bāhira and Ajjhatta Jayamaṅgala, Ratanapañjara, Namakāra, and Lokanīti, with Burmese versions; analyses and glosses of various words of the Pali texts; two Burmese grammatical works; and the Paritta, with Burmese paraphrase.] pp. 252. *Rangoon,* 1882. 8°. **14098. ccc. 11.(6.)**

—— ဆယ်ဆောင်တွဲ [Hsay saung twè.] pp. 248. ရန်ကုန် ၁၂၅၁ [*Rangoon,* 1889.] 8°.
14098. ccc. 11.(7.)

HUCHCHA-VĪRA ṢĀSTRĪ. *See* VIREṢVARA ṢĀSTRĪ, *Ārādhya.*

HULTZSCH (EUGEN). *See* INDIA.—*Archaeological Survey.* South-Indian Inscriptions ... Edited ... by E. Hultzsch. 1890, *etc.* Fol.
1710. b. 9, 10, 29, *etc.*

—— *See* INDIA.—*Archaeological Survey.* Epigraphia Indica, *etc.* (Vol. iv., *etc.*, edited by E. Hultzsch.) 1892, *etc.* Fol. & 4°.
1710. b. 13, 14.

ICHCHHĀRĀMA SŪRYARĀMA DEṢĀI. *See* PURĀṆAS.—*Bhāgavatapurāṇa.* ॥ अथ ... श्रीमद्भागवत *etc.* [Bhāgavatapurāṇa. With Gujarati translation and commentary by Ichchhārāma.] [1899.] *obl.* Fol.
14016. f. 14.

—— *See* SĀYAṆA ĀCHĀRYA.—*Works on Philosophy, etc.* The Panchadaśhî ... With Chandrakânta Vivaran and author's life [in Gujarati]. Translated into Gujarati by Ichhârâm ... Desâi. 1900. 4°.
14048. e. 34.

IMAÏZUMI (Y.). *See* SUKHĀVATĪVYŪHA. O-mi-to-king, ou Soukhavati-vyouha-soutra. ... Traduit du chinois par MM. Imaïzoumi et Yamata. 1881. 4°. [*Annales du Musée Guimet.*]
7704. h. 21.(tom. 2.)

INDĀSABHA, *of Pazun-hkyaung.* *See* AGGADHAMMĀLAṄKĀRA THERA. ဓာတွတ္ထဒီပကပါဠိနိဿယ *etc.* [Dhātvatthadīpaka. With Burmese commentary by Indāsabha.] [1899.] 8°. **14098. ccc. 29.(1.)**

INDIA.—*Archaeological Survey.* South-Indian Inscriptions, Tamil and Sanskrit ... Edited and translated by E. Hultzsch. *Madras,* 1890, *etc.* Fol. **1710. b. 9, 10, 29,** *etc.*

In progress. Forms vols. ix., x., xxix., &c., *of the* New Imperial Series *of the Archaeological Survey.*

—— —— Epigraphia Indica, and Record of the ... Survey ... Edited by J. Burgess, *etc.* (Vol. iii., *etc.*, published ... as a supplement to the "Indian Antiquary." Vol. iv., *etc.*, edited by E. Hultzsch.) 1892, *etc.* Fol. & 4°.
1710. b. 13, 14.

In progress.

—— —— The Bower Manuscript. Facsimile leaves, Nagari transcript, romanised transliteration and English translation with notes, edited by A. F. Rudolf Hoernle. pp. vii. 240; 54 *plates.* *Calcutta,* 1893, *etc.* Fol. **14058. d. 5.**

In progress. Part ii. 8, *containing the introduction and indices, has not yet appeared.*

—— —— [Another copy.]
1710. b. 22.(vol. 22.)

INDIA OFFICE LIBRARY. *See* GREAT BRITAIN AND IRELAND.—*India Office.—Library.*

INDRADATTA UPĀDHYĀYA. फक्किकाप्रकाशः *etc.* [Phakkikāprakāṣa, or Siddhāntakaumudīgūḍhaph°. A commentary on the Siddhāntakaumudī. Edited by Surendralāla Gosvāmī Tarkatīrtha.] Pt. i. pp. vi. 152. काश्याम् १९५४ [*Benares,* 1897.] 8°.
14090. c. 38.(4.)

Ends with the section on flectional endings (vibhakti).

INDRAJĀLA. ইন্দ্রজাল। [Indrajāla. A treatise on magic, with Bengali translation and appendix.]

pp. 26. [1891.] *See* PERIODICAL PUBLICATIONS.—*Calcutta.* অরুণোদয় *etc.* [Aruṇodaya.] Pt. i., no. 11. [1890, *etc.*] 4°. **14133. g. 16.(pt. i., no. 11.)**

—— इन्द्रजालम् [Indrajāla.] *See* INDRAJĀLAVIDYĀSAṄGRAHA. इन्द्रजालविद्यासंग्रहः *etc.* (Indrajalavidyasangraha.) pp. 1-22. [1891.] 8°. **14033. aa. 7.**

—— ഇന്ദ്രജാലം *etc.* [Indrajāla. With a Malayalam commentary.] pp. 36. പട്ടാമ്പി [*Pattambi,*] 1893. 16°. **14053. a. 11.(1.)**

Ascribed to Sadāṣiva, i.e. Ṣiva, and in a recension differing from that of the preceding edition.

INDRAJĀLAVIDYĀSAṄGRAHA. इन्द्रजालविद्यासंग्रहः। तत्र इन्द्रजालशास्त्रम्-कामरत्नम्-दत्तात्रेयतन्त्रम्-षट्कर्मदीपिका-सिद्धनागार्जुनकक्षपुटम्। (Indrajalavidyasangraha.) [A collection of treatises on sorcery, comprising the Indrajāla, Nāga Bhaṭṭa's Kāmaratna, the Dattātreyatantra, the Shaṭkarmadīpikā of Kṛishṇānanda, and Nāgārjuna's Kakshapuṭa. Edited by Jīvānanda Vidyāsāgara. Second edition.] pp. 385. कलिकाता १८९१ [*Calcutta,* 1891.] 8°. **14033. aa. 7.**

English title taken from wrapper.

INDRAKAṆṬHAVALLABHA ĀCHĀRYA, *son of Amareṣvara.* ವೈದ್ಯಚಿಂತಾಮಣಿ *etc.* [Vaidyachintāmaṇi. A treatise on Hindu therapeutics. Edited with a Canarese translation styled Bhāvabodhinī by Gūḍapalli Harirāma Ṣāstrī.] part i. pp. iv. xxxii. 823. *Bangalore,* 1897. 8°. **14043. c. 47.**

INDRĀKSHĪSTOTRA. अथ इन्द्राक्षीस्तोत्रं *etc.* [Indrākshīstotra. A hymn of 20 stanzas, with *nyāsas* and *dhyānas.*] ff. 12. कल्याण-मुंबई [*Kalyan,* 1901.] 16°. **14028. a. 19.(6.)**

INDRIYAPARĀJAYAṢATAKA. श्री इंद्रिय पराजय शतक [Indriyaparājayaṣataka. A century of Jain Prakrit verses on mortification of the flesh. With Gujarati translation.] *See* HEMAṢAṄKARA LAKSHMĪṢAṄKARA VARDHAMĀNKAR. प्रकरण माला *etc.* [Prakaraṇamālā.] pp. 92-114. [1901.] 8°. **14100. d. 11.**

IRATTINAVĒLU. *See* RATNAVĒLU.

ĪṢĀNACHANDRA VASU. આર્યધર્મનીતિ *etc.* [Āryadharmanīti. Moral stanzas compiled from Manu, the epics, Vishṇupurāṇa, Hitopadeṣa, *etc.* Edited with Gujarati translations by Nārāyaṇa Hemachandra. Second edition.] pp. ii. 167. અમદાવાદ ૧૮૯૫ [*Ahmadabad,* 1895.] 16°. **14085. a. 11.**

ĪṢVARACHANDRA VIDYĀSĀGARA. *See* RĀMASVĀMI RĀJU, *P. V.* श्रीमत्पण्डितराजतरङ्गिणी। Sreemat Pandita Rajatarangini. A brief account of the life and character of Pandit Iswara Chandra Vidyasagara, *etc.* 1893. 4°. **14076. f. 11.**

—— भूगोलखगोलवर्णनम् *etc.* [Bhūgola-khagolavarṇana. A description of heaven and earth in Sanskrit verse. Edited with annotations by Nārāyaṇachandra Vidyāratna. Second edition.] pp. vii. 51. *Calcutta,* 1893. 12°. **14053. b. 30.**

ĪṢVARA KAULA, *son of Gaṇeṣa.* The Kaçmīraçabdāmṛta. A Kāçmīrī grammar written in the Sanskrit language by Īçvara-Kaula. Edited with notes and additions by G. A. Grierson. pp. iii. 379, iii. ii. iii. *Calcutta,* 1898. 8°. **14164. h. 11.**

—— [Another copy.] **14164. h. 12.**

ĪṢVARA KṚISHṆA. An English Translation, with the Sanskrit Text, of the [Sāṅkhyakārikā with the commentary] Tattva-kaumudî . . . of Vâchaspati Miśra, by Gangânâtha Jhâ. (तत्त्वकौमुदी) pp. xxxii. 114, 2, 8, 82, 4. *Bombay,* 1896. 8°. **14048. cc. 3.**

—— সাংখ্যতত্ত্ব-কৌমুদী *etc.* [Sāṅkhyatattvakaumudī. Comprising the Sāṅkhyakārikā and the commentary of Vāchaspati Miṣra styled Sāṅkhyatattvakaumudī, with Sanskrit grammatical explanations and Bengali translations and notes by the editor, Pūrṇachandra Vedāntachuñchu.] pp. ii. iii. iii. 254, iii. সৈদাবাদ ১৯০১ [*Saidabad,* 1901.] 8°. **14048. dd. 34.(1.)**

—— Der Mondschein der Sâṃkhya-Wahrheit, Vâcaspatimiçra's Sâṃkhya-tattva-kaumudî, [including the Sāṅkhyakārikā,] in deutscher Uebersetzung, nebst einer Einleitung über das Alter und die Herkunft der Sâṃkhya-Philosophie, von Richard Garbe. 1892. *See* ACADEMIES, *etc.*—Munich.—*Koenigliche Akademie der Wissenschaften.* Abhandlungen, *etc.* Vol. xix., pp. 517-628. 1835, *etc.* 4°. **Ac. 713/6.(vol. 19.)**

ĪṢVARA KṚISHṆA (*continued*). Sáṅkhya Káriká. [Comprising introduction, text, translation, and notes.] With [a translation of] Gauḍapáda's scholia and Náráyaṇa's gloss [called Sāṅkhya-chandrikā]. pp. lvi. 300. 1898. *See* SATĪṢA-CHANDRA VANDYOPĀDHYĀYA. Sáṅkhya Philosophy. Fasciculus 1. 1898, *etc.* 8°.
14048. b. 34.(fasc. 1.)

—— सांख्यतत्त्वसुबोधिनी सटीक *etc.* [Sāṅkhyatattva-subodhinī. Being the Sāṅkhyakārikā, with Hindi glosses and commentary based on that of Gauḍapāda by Ẕālim Singh.] pp. 125. लखनऊ १८९९ [*Lucknow*, 1899.] 8°.
14048. d. 37.(2.)

—— সাংখ্যদীপনী ... শ্রীমদীশ্বরকৃষ্ণপ্রণীতসাংখ্যকারিকয়া সহিতা *etc.* [Sāṅkhyakārikā. With an exposition thereof styled Sāṅkhyadīpanī, by Kāmākhyanātha Tarkavāgīṣa. Edited by Āṣutosha Bhaṭṭāchārya.] pp. 48, iii. কলিকাতা ১৮২২ [*Calcutta*, 1901.] 12°.
14048. b. 16.(2.)

—— Sankhya-karika. [In the English version of H. T. Colebrooke.] *See* MANMATHANĀTHA DATTA. Darshana, *etc.* pp. 91-101. 1897. 12°.
14048. a. 23.

ĪṢVARĀNANDAGIRI, *Svāmī, disciple of Sarayūgiri.* *See* JAMBHA. जंभसंहिता *etc.* [Jambhasaṃhitā. Edited with Hindi paraphrases, *etc.*, by Īṣvarānandagiri.] [1899.] 8°.
14028. dd. 8.

ĪṢVARA YAJVĀ, *of Kalpadi.* *See* ĀPASTAMBA.—*Gṛihyasūtra.* ஆபஸ்தம்பக்ருஹ்யப்ரயோகா வ்யாக்யாஸஹிதः *etc.* [Āpastambagṛihyaprayoga. Edited by Īṣvara Yajvā and Rāmakṛishṇa.] [1899.] 8°.
14028. c. 80.

JACOB (GEORGE ADOLPHUS), *Colonel.* *See* RATNĀKARA, *Rājānaka.* The Haravijaya, *etc.* [With index of the verses by G. A. Jacob.] 1890. 8°. [*Kâvyamâlâ.*]
14072. ccc. 12.(no. 22.)

—— *See* SADĀNANDA YOGĪNDRA. The Vedântasâra ... with the commentaries of Nṛisiṃhasarasvatî and Râmatîrtha. Edited with notes and indices by ... G. A. Jacob. 1894. 8°.
14048. dd. 15.

—— अनुक्रमणिका. [Index to the edition of Bhartṛihari's Vākyapadīya in the Benares Sanskrit Series.] pp. 14. [*Bombay*, 1893 ?] 8°.
14093. b. 18.(2.)

JACOB (GEORGE ADOLPHUS), *Colonel* (*continued*). अनुक्रमणिका. [Index to Jolly's edition of the Mānavadharmaṣāstra.] pp. 51. [*Bombay*, 1894 ?] 8°.
2318. g. 22.(2.)

—— अनुक्रमणिका । [Index to Sureṣvara's Taittirīyopanishadbhāshyavārttika, as published in the Ānandāṣrama Series.] pp. 21. [*Bombay*, 1893?] 8°.
14003. ccc. (no. 13, pt. 2.)

—— लौकिकन्यायाञ्जलिः ॥ [Laukikanyāyāñjali.] A Handful of Popular Maxims current in Sanskrit Literature, collected by Colonel G. A. Jacob. pp. vi. 49, i. *Bombay*, 1900. 8°. **14070. dd. 18.**

—— Notes on Alaṅkāra Literature, *etc.* 1897-1898. *See* ACADEMIES, *etc.*—London.—*Royal Asiatic Society of Great Britain and Ireland.* The Journal . . . 1897 (1898). 1834, *etc.* 8°.
Ac. 8820/3. and 2098. a.b.

JACOBI (HERMANN GEORG). *See* ĀNANDAVARDHANA, *Rājānaka.* Ānandavardhana's Dhvanyāloka. Übersetzt [with an introduction] von H. Jacobi. 1902-1903. [*Zeitschrift der Deutschen Morgenlaendischen Gesellschaft.*]
Ac. 8815/2. (vol. 56, 57).

—— *See* SIDDHARSHI. Sacram Memoriam . . . Friderici Guilelmi III. . . . indicit Adolfus . . . Kamphausen. . . . Inest Upamitabhavaprapancae Kathae specimen, ab H. Iacobi editum. [1891.] 8°.
14070. e. 16.(2.)

—— *See* SIDDHARSHI. उपमितिभवप्रपञ्चा कथा . . . The Upamitibhavaprapancha Katha . . . (Originally) edited by (the late) P. Peterson (and continued by . . . H. Jacobi). 1899, *etc.* 8°. [*Bibliotheca Indica.*]
14002. a. (vol. 144).

—— *Gaina Sûtras.* Translated from Prâkrit [with introductions and notes] by Hermann Jacobi. Part I. The Âkârâṅga Sûtra. The Kalpa Sûtra. (Part II. The Uttarâdhyayana Sûtra. The Sûtrakritâṅga Sûtra.) 2 vols. 1884-1895. *See* MUELLER (F. M.). The Sacred Books of the East, *etc.* Vol. xxii., xlv. 1879, *etc.* 8°.
2003. a-b. (vol. 22, 45).

—— Das Râmâyaṇa. Geschichte und Inhalt, nebst Concordanz der gedruckten Recensionen, *etc.* pp. v. i. 256. *Bonn*, 1893. 8°.
14065. d. 35.

JACOBI (HERMANN GEORG) (*continued*). Ein Beitrag zur Rāmāyanakritik, *etc.* 1897. *See* ACADEMIES, *etc.*—Germany.—*Deutsche Morgenlaendische Gesellschaft.* Zeitschrift, *etc.* Bd. 51, no. 4. 1846, *etc.* 8°. **Ac. 8815/2. (vol. 51).**

—— Mahābhārata. Inhaltsangabe, Index und Concordanz der Calcuttaer und Bombayer Ausgaben. . . . Gedruckt mit Unterstützung der kaiserlichen Akademie der Wissenschaften zu Wien. pp. iv. 257. *Bonn, Leipzig* [printed], 1903. 8°. **14068. b. 19.**

JADUNATH MOZOOMDAR. *See* YADUNĀTHA MAJUMDĀR.

JAGADBANDHU TARKAVĀGĪSA. *See* RĀMACHANDRA NYĀYAVĀGĪSA. কাব্যচন্দ্রিকা *etc.* [Kāvyachandrikā. With a commentary entitled Subodhinī by Jagadbandhu.] [1896.] 8°. **14053. c. 65.**

JAGADDHARA, *son of Ratnadhara, Dharmādhikārī.* *See* BHAVABHŪTI. The Mâlatîmâdhava. . . . With the commentaries of Tripurâri and Jagaddhara, *etc.* 1892. 8°. **14079. c. 61.**

—— *See* NĀRĀYAṆA BHAṬṬA, called MṚIGARĀJALAKSHMĀ. The Venîsaṃhâra . . . With the commentary of Jagaddhara, *etc.* 1898. 8°. **14079. c. 67.**

JAGADDHARA, *grandson of Gauradhara, Kaṣmīrī.* The Stutikusumâñjali of Śrî Jagaddhara Bhatta. [Thirty-eight religious poems, with an account of the poet's family.] With the commentary [Laghupañchikā] of Râjânaka Ratnakaṇṭha. Edited by Paṇdit Durgâprasâd and Kâśînâth Pâṇdurang Parab. (स्तुतिकुसुमाञ्जलिः ।) pp. iii. ii. i. 456. 1891. *See* DURGĀPRASĀDA, *son of Vrajalāla,* and KĀṢĪNĀTHA PĀṆḌURAṄGA PARAB. Kâvyamâlâ. [No.] 23. 1886, *etc.* 8°. **14072. ccc. 12. (no. 23.)**

JAGADĪṢACHANDRA CHAṬṬOPĀDHYĀYA. *See* UPANISHADS.—*General Collections.* The Upanishads. Translated . . . with a preamble and arguments by G. R. S. Mead . . . and Jagadîsha Chandra Chaṭṭopâdhyâya, *etc.* 1896. *obl.* 8°. **14007. b. 5.**

JAGADĪṢAPRASĀDA TRIPĀṬHĪ, *of Narnaul.* *See* KEṢAVA, *son of Kamalākara.* केशवी जातक *etc.* [Keṣavī-jātaka. Edited with analyses, Hindi version, examples, and tables by Jagadīṣaprasāda.] [1900.] 8°. **14053. d. 63.**

JAGADĪṢA TARKĀLAṄKĀRA BHAṬṬĀCHĀRYA. *See* GAṄGEṢA UPĀDHYĀYA. केवलान्वयि अनुमानम् *etc.* [Kevalānvayyanumāna. With Raghunātha's Ṣiromaṇi, Jagadīṣa's supercommentary Jāgadīṣī, *etc.*] [1897.] 8°. **14048. bb. 45.(4.)**

—— *See* GAṄGEṢA UPĀDHYĀYA. पक्षता *etc.* [Pakshatā. With the Ṣiromaṇi of Raghunātha and its supercommentary, the Jāgadīṣī Vivṛiti of Jagadīṣa, *etc.*] [1897.] 8°. **14048. bb. 45.(5.)**

—— *See* GAṄGEṢA UPĀDHYĀYA. सिद्धान्तलक्षणम् *etc.* (Siddhantalakshana . . . With the commentaries of Raghunatha Siromani, and Mathuranatha Tarkabagisha. With the gloss [upon the former] of Jagadisha Bhattacharya[, styled Jāgadīṣī,] *etc.*) [1896.] 8°. **14048. c. 79.(1).**

—— *See* GAṄGEṢA UPĀDHYĀYA. व्याप्तिपञ्चकम् *etc.* [Vyāptipañchaka. With an extract from Raghunātha's commentary, Jagadīṣa's gloss Jāgadīṣī, *etc.*] [1896.] 8°. **14048. e. 28.**

—— *See* RAGHUNĀTHA ṢIROMAṆI. जागदीशी *etc.* [Vyadhikaraṇadharmāvachchhinnābhāva. Being the section from Raghunātha's commentary upon the chapter of that name in the Anumānakhaṇḍa. With Jagadīṣa's supercommentary Chaturdaṣalakshaṇī.] [1889.] *obl.* 4°. **14048. f. 21.**

JAGADĪṢVARA BHAṬṬĀCHĀRYA, *Dramatist.* हास्यार्णवप्रहसनम् *etc.* (Hasyarnaba. A [comic] drama in two acts . . . Edited [with a commentary] . . . by Pandit Shrinatha Vedantabagisha.) Second edition. pp. 98. कलिकाता १८९६ [*Calcutta,* 1896.] 8°. **14079. c. 53.(2.)**

The English title is taken from the wrapper.

JAGANMOHANA SIṂHA DEVA. *See* AMARASIṂHA. ଅମର ଅମରରେତାମାଳିକା *etc.* [Amarārtharatnamālikā. The Amarakoṣa with Oriya translation by Jaganmohana.] 1899. 12°. **14092. a. 23.(1.)**

JAGANMOHANA TARKĀLAṄKĀRA. *See* PARĀṢARA. [*Smṛiti.*] ପରାଶର-ସଂହିତା *etc.* [Parāṣarasaṃhitā. With an Oriya translation, from the Bengali version by Jaganmohana.] 1887. 8°. **14038. c. 44.(1.)**

JAGANMOHANA TARKĀLAṄKĀRA (*continued*). দশবিধসংস্কার-পদ্ধতি *etc.* [Daṣavidhasaṃskārapaddhati. A Tantric ritual for the Ten Purificatory Rites. Compiled by Jaganmohana, assisted by Chandrakānta Sena Gupta.] pp. ii. 75. কলিকাতা [*Calcutta*, 1897.] 8°. **14028. d. 59.(9.)**

JAGANNADHASVAMI AYYAVARALUGARU, *S.P.S.* *See* JAGANNĀTHA SVĀMĪ, *Paravastu Ṣrīnivāsa.*

JAGANNĀTHA, *Samrāṭ, Courtier of Savāi Jaisingh of Jaipur.* *See* EUCLID. The Rekhâgaṇita ... Composed [*i.e.* translated from the Arabic] by Samrâḍ Jagannâtha, *etc.* 1901-1902. 8°. **14053. ccc. 36.**

JAGANNĀTHA, *disciple of Kāmeṣvara, of Tanjore.* रतिमन्मथनाटकम् । [Ratimanmathanāṭaka. A mythological play in 5 acts.] pp. 101. [1890-1891.] *See* PERIODICAL PUBLICATIONS.—*Bombay.* ग्रन्थरत्नमाला *etc.* (Granth Ratna Málá, *etc.*) Vol. III, no. 10-Vol. V, no. 1. 1887-[1892]. 8°. **14096. c. 8.(vol. 3-5.)**

Apparently this Jagannātha is identical with the famous Jagannātha Paṇḍitarāja; see editor's note on the Prāṇābharaṇa in the Kâvyamâlâ, 1886.

JAGANNĀTHA ĀCHĀRYA, *son of Raṅgarāja, Kaḍāmbi.* *See* PĀÑCHARĀTRA. శ్రీపాఞ్చరాత్రే ... అష్టాధ్యాయీ *etc.* [Prapattiprapannavṛittisvarūpa. With the commentary Ṣrutārthadīpikā of Jagannātha.] [1894.] 8°. **14028. d. 62.**

JAGANNĀTHA BHAṬṬA, *son of Bhaṭṭabhaṭṭāraka Perubhaṭṭa.* *See* JAGANNĀTHA PAṆḌITARĀJA.

JAGANNĀTHA DĀSA, *the Oriya Poet.* *See* PURĀṆAS.—*Bhāgavatapurāṇa.* ସଚିତ୍ର ଏକାଦଶସ୍କନ୍ଧ *etc.* [Sachitra Ekādaṣa-skandha. Being selections from the 11th book of the Bhāgavata with the metrical Oriya paraphrase of the whole book by Jagannātha Dāsa.] 1901. 12°. **14016. b. 24.(1.)**

JAGANNĀTHA PAṆḌITARĀJA, *son of Bhaṭṭabhaṭṭāraka Perubhaṭṭa.* *See* MOREṢVARA RĀMACHANDRA KĀḶE. The Sâhityasârasangraha ... based on the works of ... Jagannatha, *etc.* 1891. 12°. **14053. a. 13.**

—— अश्वधाटीकाव्यम् *etc.* [Aṣvadhāṭīkāvya. A poem in 26 stanzas on the attainment of salvation through religion. With Hindi analyses and translation by Haradeva Ṣarmā.] pp. 36. कल्याण-मुम्बय्याम् १९५२ [*Kalyan*, 1896.] 8°. **14048. cc. 8.(2.)**

—— भामिनीविलासः । [Bhāminīvilāsa. With the commentary Bhāminīvilāsabhūshaṇa of Mahādeva Sūri Paṇḍitarāja.] pp. 122. [1890-1891.] *See* PERIODICAL PUBLICATIONS.—*Bombay.* ग्रन्थरत्नमाला *etc.* (Granth Ratna Málá, *etc.*) Vol. IV, no. 6-9. 1887-[1892.] 8°. **14096. c. 8.(vol. 4.)**

—— The Bhaminivilasa ... With a Sanskrit gloss Bhushana of Mahadeo Suri Dikshita Panditaja[*sic*], with English translation, notes ... various readings and the poet's life, by B. G. Bal. pp. v. vi. 122, 54. *Bombay*, 1895. 8°. **14070. c. 53.**

—— चित्रमीमांसाखण्डनम् *etc.* [Chitramīmāṃsākhaṇḍana. A refutation of Apyaya Dīkshita's Chitramīmāṃsā. With a commentary extracted from the Rasagaṅgādharamarmaprakāṣa, Nāgeṣa Bhaṭṭa's commentary on the Rasagaṅgādhara.] pp. 38. 1893. *See* DURGĀPRASĀDA, *son of Vrajalāla,* and KĀṢĪNĀTHA PĀṆḌURAṄGA PARAB. Kâvyamâlâ. [No.] 38. 1886, *etc.* 8°. **14072. ccc. 12.(no. 38.)**

—— अथ गङ्गालहरी प्रारम्भः [Gaṅgālaharī.] ff. 8. मुरादाबाद [*Moradabad*, 1898.] 12°. **14028. b. 93.(2.)**

—— శ్రీ ... పండితరాట్ శతకశ్లోకములు [Paṇḍitarāṭṣatakaṣloka. 14 centuries of verses, preceded by miscellaneous poems and followed by the Gaṅgālaharī. Edited by Paravastu Raṅgāchārya.] pp. vi. iii. 2, 2, 179, 4, 8. తుని నగరు [*Tuni*, 1899.] 12°. **14070. b. 28.**

—— శ్రీ ... పండితరాజశతకము *etc.* [338 stanzas of the Ṣatakas. With some translations into Telugu by Rāmānujāchārya Aiyar. Edited by Veṅkaṭarāmānuja Svāmī. Third edition.] pp. ii. 75. *Vizagapatam*, 1895. 12°. **14070. b. 22.**

JAGANNĀTHA RĀU, *Vallūri, Rāi Bahādur.* *See* BĀDARĀYAṆA. బ్రహ్మసూత్రార్థసంగ్రహము [Brahmasūtrārthasaṅgraha. The Aphorisms arranged in tabular form with Telugu paraphrases and synopses by Jagannātha Rāu.] [1894.] 8°. **14048. dd. 30.**

JAGANNĀTHA ṢARMĀ, *Rājavaidya.* *See* GHERAṆḌA. घेरण्ड संहिता *etc.* [Gheraṇḍasaṃhitā. Edited with Hindi translation by Jagannātha.] [1899.] 8°. **14033. bb. 10.(2.)**

JAGANNĀTHA SVĀMĪ, *Paravastu Ṣrīnivāsa, disciple of Veṅkaṭaraṅganātha.* *See* CHAṄGADĀSA. The Sambandhopadesa . . . Edited by . . . S. P. S. Jagannadhaswamy, *etc.* 1896. 12°. **14092. a. 10.(2.)**

—— *See* PĀṆINI.—*Mitāksharā.* मिताक्षरा *etc.* (The Mitakshara . . . Edited by . . . S. P. S. Jagannadhasvami, *etc.*) 1895. 8°. **14090. bb. 11.**

—— *See* PATAÑJALI. — *Philosophical Works.* యోగసారము [Yogasāra. With Telugu version by Jagannātha Svāmī.] 1892-1893. 12°. [*Sakalavidyābhivardhanī.*] **14174. g. 38.(vol. 1.)**

—— *See* SADĀNANDA YOGĪNDRA. అద్వైతవేదాంతసారః [Advaitavedāntasāra. With Telugu translation by Jagannātha Svāmī.] 1893-1894. 12°. [*Sakalavidyābhivardhanī.*] **14174. g. 38.(vol. 1, 2.)**

JAGANNĀTHA VIDYĀRṆAVA. *See* PURĀṆAS.—*Padmapurāṇa.* পদ্মপুরাণম্ *etc.* [Pātālakhaṇḍa. With Bengali translation by Jagannātha and others.] [1903.] 8°. **14018. b. 20.**

JAGANNĀTHA YATI, *disciple of Raghunātha Tīrtha.* *See* BĀDARĀYAṆA. श्रीमद्ब्रह्मसूत्राणि *etc.* [Brahmasūtra. With the *bhāshya* of Ānandatīrtha and the Bhāshyadīpikā upon the latter by Jagannātha, *etc.*] [1900.] 8°. **14048. cc. 30.**

JĀGARA, *of Kabyu.* *See* ARIYAVAṂSA. ဂန္ထာဘရဏသင်္ဂြိုဟ် [Ganthābharaṇa. With a *ṭīkā* or *vaṇṇanā* by Jāgara.] [1897.] 8°. [*Saddatthabhedachintā, etc.*] **14098. ccc. 17.(2.)**

JĀGARĀBHIDDHAJA, *Saddhammavaṃsa*, known as SHWEGYIN HSAYA. *See* LALITAVISTARA. ကာမာဒိနဝကထာ *etc.* [Kāmādinavakathā. A passage from the Lalitavistara. In Pali, with Burmese version by Jāgara.] 1894. 8°. **14098. c. 32.(3.)**

JĀGARĀBHIDDHAJA, *Saddhammavaṃsa (continued).* *See* LALITAVISTARA. ကာမာဒိနဝကထာ [Kāmādinavakathā.] 1898. 8°. [*Chhakkapañhā-kyan.*] **14300. d. 19.(9.)**

—— အဘိဓမ္မတ္ထသင်္ဂဟဂဏ္ဌိသစ် *etc.* [Abhidhammatthasaṅgahaganṭhi-thit. A Burmese dissertation on the Abhidhammatthasaṅgaha. With Puchchhāvisajjanā-kyan, problems, and Hmat-su-than-pauk, memorial verses, upon the same work, and Paṭṭhān-hkyet-su, three essays on the Paṭṭhāna. Edited by Ū Tissa and Ū Janinda.] pp. vii. 501, iii. မန္တလေး ၁၂၆၀ [*Mandalay*, 1898.] 8°. **14300. e. 4.**

—— [Another edition.] pp. vii. 520. မန္တလေး ရန်ကုန် [*Mandalay, Rangoon* printed, 1901.] 8°. **14300. e. 18.**

—— ဓမ္မပါန ရှုဗွယ်စာတမ်း။ [Dhammapāna-shuhbway-sā-tan. Moral and philosophical Pali stanzas, with Burmese version, by Jāgara.] *See* LALITAVISTARA. ကာမာဒိနဝကထာ *etc.* [Kāmādinavakathā, *etc.*] pp. 24-29. 1894. 8°. **14098. c. 32.(3.)**

—— ဓမ္မပါန ရှုဗွယ်စာတမ်း။ [Dhammapāna-shuhbway-sā-tan.] *See* CHANDIMĀ, *Thāvara*, called KYĀ-KOY. ဆက္ကပဉ္စာကျမ်း *etc.* [Chhakkapañhā-kyan, *etc.*] pp. 378-385. 1898. 8°. **14300. d. 19.(9.)**

—— ဂမ္ဘီရာဂမ္ဘီရမဟာနိဗ္ဗုတဒီပနီကျမ်း *etc.* [Gambhīrāgambhīramahānibbutadīpanī, a Burmese treatise on the significance of Nirvāṇa, *etc.*, with copious quotations from Pali texts. Preceded by the Chūlasissakovāda, religious exhortations addressed to disciples, in Burmese, and by the Mahāsissakovāda, a similar Pali treatise, with a Burmese explanation; and followed by the Vañchanādīpanī, a Pali-Burmese treatise based on the Netti-aṭṭhakathā and summarising in 10 *gāthās* the 36 forms of false impressions, and by the Vichitravandanā, a series of Pali devotional stanzas with Burmese version.] pp. iv. 33, 620, ii. မန္တလေး [*Mandalay*,] 1893. 8°. **14300. e. 5.**

JĀGARĀBHIDDHAJA, *Saddhammavaṃsa (continued)*. ကလျာဏမိတ္တ *etc.* [Kalyāṇamitta. A selection of brief extracts from Pali texts on cardinal points of Buddhism, with Burmese glosses.] pp. 28. *Rangoon*, ၁၂၃၆ [1874.] 8°. **14300. d. 27.**

—— ဝိစိတြဝန္ဒနာဘုရားရှိခိုး *etc.* [Vichitra-vandanā-payā-shi-hko. A series of devotional Pali stanzas with Burmese gloss, *etc.* Followed by the Paṭṭhāna-pachchaya, a Burmese treatise on the 24 *pachchayas*.] pp. 58. မန္တလေး [*Mandalay*,] 1893. 8°. **14098. ccc. 26.(3.)**

—— ဝိစိတြဝန္ဒနာဘုရားရှိခိုး *etc.* [Vichitra-vandanā and Paṭṭhāna-pachchaya. With Munindābhiddhaja's Buddha-thomanā, Burmese doxologies; Visuddhāchāra's Dāṭhādhātu-win-gāthā, devotional Pali stanzas based on the Dāṭhādhātu-vaṃsa, with Burmese gloss, and Visiṭṭhavandanā, a similar work, also in Pali and Burmese; and two Burmese works—Ū Ñāṇa's Sāsanā-hlyauk, on Buddhist chronology, and Visuddhāchāra's Buddhadāṭhā-thomanā, on the Tooth Relic in Ceylon.] pp. ii. 132. မန္တလေး [*Mandalay*,] 1900. 8°. **14098. ccc. 26.(7.)**

—— ဝိစိတြဝန္ဒနာဘုရားရှိခိုး *etc.* [Vichitra-vandanā, Paṭṭhānapachchaya, and Indriyovāda-kathā, the last a series of religious stanzas in Pali with Burmese explanation. With Munindā-bhiddhaja's Buddha-thomanā and Sīlavisodhana-kyan, and Visuddhāchāra's Dāṭhādhātu-win-gāthā and Visiṭṭhavandanā.] pp. 117. ရန်ကုန် ၁၂၆၂ [*Rangoon*, 1900.] 8°. **14098. ccc. 21.(2.)**

JAIMINI.

GṚIHYASŪTRA.

॥ जैमिनिगृह्यसूत्रम् *etc.* [Jaiminigṛihyasūtra. A code of domestic ritual ascribed to Jaimini. With the commentary Subodhinī of Śrīnivāsa Adhvarī. Edited by Kastūri Raṅgāchārya.] pp. i. i. ii. 93, ix. *Madras*, 1898. 8°. **14028. c. 74.**

JYOTISHASŪTRA.

जैमिनिसूत्रम् *etc.* [Jaiminisūtra. With the commentary Subodhinī of Nīlakaṇṭha. Edited by Rasikamohana Chaṭṭopādhyāya.] pp. 38. কলিকাতা ১২৯১ [*Calcutta*, 1884.] 8°. **14053. dd. 6.**

See ĀRŪḌHAŚĀSTRA. ஞானப்பிரதீபிகை *etc.* [Ārū-ḍhaśāstra, or Jñānapradīpikā. Here ascribed to Jaimini.] [1899.] 8°. **14053. ccc. 27.**

MĪMĀṂSĀSŪTRA.

जैमिनीयन्यायमाला । अथवा मीमांसाधिकरणन्यायमाला *etc.* (Jaiminîyanyâyamâlâ or Pûrvamîmânsâdhikarana-nyâyamâlâ by Śrî Mâdhavâchârya. With his own commentary and Jaiminî's Sûtràs of each Adhikaraṇa. Edited [with an index of the Sūtras] by Pandit Sivadatta.) pp. lviii. 704, xlii. xxiv. पुण्याख्यपत्तने १८१४ [*Poona*, 1892.] 8°. **14003. ccc.(no. 24.)**

Forms no. 24 of the Ānandāśrama Sanskrit Series. *The English title is taken from the cover.*

मीमांसाश्लोकवार्तिकम् *etc.* (The Mîmânsâ-śloka-vârtika of Kumârila Bhatta[, a commentary upon Śabara-svāmī's commentary on the Mīmāṃsāsūtra I. i.] With the commentary called Nyâyaratnâkara by Pârtha Sârathi Miśra. Edited by Râma Śâstrî Tailaṅga.) pp. vii. 956, xlviii. *Benares*, 1898-1899. 8°. **14004. a. 3.**

Forms nos. 11, 12, 15-21, *and* 24 *of the* Chowkhambâ Sanskrit Series. *The English title is from the wrapper.*

Kumārila's commentary on the Sūtras I. i. is styled Śloka-vārttika; on I. ii. ff. to the end of III. it bears the name Tantravārttika; for the remainder it is styled Ṭupṭīkā.

Çlokavārtika. Translated from the original Sanskrit with extracts from the commentaries of Sucarīta [*sic*] Miçra, the Kāçikā, and Pārtha-sārathi Miçra, the Nyāyaratnākara, by Gaṅgā-nātha Jhā. 1900, *etc.* *See* ACADEMIES, *etc.*—Calcutta.—*Asiatic Society of Bengal*. Bibliotheca Indica. New Series. [Vol. 146.] 1848, *etc.* 8°. **14002. a. (vol. 146.)**

In progress.

न्यायसुधा . . . Nyâyasudhâ, [also called Rāṇaka and Sarvopakāriṇī], a commentary on [Kumārila's] Tantravârtika. By Paṇḍit Sômeshwara Bhaṭṭa. [With the Mīmāṃsāsūtra.] Edited by Paṇḍit Mukunda Shâstri. *Benares*, 1901, *etc.* 8°. **14004. a. 14.**

In progress. Forms nos. 45, 46-7, 49, 50, 52-3, 55-7 *etc. of the* Chowkhambâ Sanskrit Series. *The title is from the wrapper.*

जैमिनिसूत्रवृत्तिः सुबोधिनीनामिका [Mīmāṃsāsūtra. With the commentary Subodhinī by Rāmeśvara Śivayogī, sometimes ascribed to Śitikaṇṭha Bhaṭṭa. Edited by Nityānanda Panta.] pp. 688, xxxiii. iii. vii. 1899. See PERIODICAL PUBLICATIONS.—*Benares.* The Pandit, *etc.* New Series. Vol. XVII-XXI. 1876, *etc.* 8°.
14096. d. 6.(vol. 17-21.)

—— [A separate issue of the above, reprinted from the "Pandit."] pp. 688, xxxiii. iii. vii. काश्याम् १९५६ [*Benares*, 1899.] 8°.
14033. aa. 10.

संकर्ष-काण्डम् . . . Saṁkarsha Káṇda, or the last four chapters of Jaimini, with the commentary called Bháṭṭa Chandriká, of Bháskara, edited with notes by Pandit Swámi Ráma Miśra Śástri. pp. xii. vii. 127. [1894.] See PERIODICAL PUBLICATIONS.—*Benares.* The Pandit, *etc.* New Series. Vol. XIV, XV. 1876, *etc.* 8°.
14096. d. 6.(vol. 14, 15.)

The commentary on these 4 chapters was added by Bhāskara to the Bhāṭṭadīpikā or commentary of Khaṇḍadeva upon ch. 1-12, and hence is often confused with the latter work.

The Meemamsa Kausthubha. Vol. -1 [*scil.* Adh. I. ii.]. A commentary on Jaimini Sutra. By Khanda Deva, *etc.* (मीमांसा कौस्तुभः) pp. 79, i. iii. 1902. See ANANTĀCHĀRYA, *Prativādibhayaṅkara.* शास्त्रमुक्तावली. The Śasthramukthâvalî, *etc.* No. 14. 1899, *etc.* 8°.
14049. a. 1.(no. 14.)

See ĀPADEVA. मीमांसान्यायप्रकाशः *etc.* [Mīmāṃsā-nyāyaprakāṣa. An exposition of Pūrva-mīmāṃsā.] [1898.] 8°.
14048. c. 79.(2.)

See APYAYA DĪKSHITA. विधिरसायनम् *etc.* (Vidhi-rasayana[, a treatise on *vidhis*, as expounded by Kumārila,] *etc.*) 1901. 8°.
14004. a. 13.

See KĀLĪVARA VEDĀNTAVĀGĪŚA. हिन्दुशास्त्र *etc.* [Shaḍdarṣana. A Bengali exposition of the six systems.] [1895.] 8°. [*Hindu-ṣāstra.*]
14085. c. 45.(vol. 1.)

See KHAṆḌADEVA. Bhatta Rahasyam, *etc.* [An introductory treatise upon Jaimini's Mīmāṃsā-sūtra. Parichchheda i.] 1900. 8°. [*Śāstra-muktāvalī.*]
14049. a. 1.(no. 2.)

See KIŚORĪLĀLA SARKĀR. The Introductory Lecture for Tagore Professorship, *etc.* [An English lecture on the principles of interpretation used in the Pūrva-mīmāṃsā school.] 1902. 8°.
14039. b. 27.

See NĀRĀYAṆA TĪRTHA, *disciple of Śivarāma.* भाट्टभाषाप्रकाशः *etc.* [Bhāṭṭabhāshāprakāṣa. A treatise on the terminology of the Mīmāṃsāsūtra.] [1900.] 8°.
14004. a. 4.(2.)

See ŚAṄKARA BHAṬṬA, *son of Nārāyaṇa.* ॥ मीमांसाबालप्रकाशः *etc.* (Mimânsâbâlaprakâsha, [a commentary on Jaimini's Mīmāṃsāsūtra,] *etc.*) 1902. 8°.
14004. a. 16.

See VIŚVEŚVARA BHAṬṬA, also called GĀGĀ BHAṬṬA. भाट्टचिन्तामणिः . . . Bhâṭṭa Chintâmani, *etc.* [A commentary on the Mīmāṃsāsūtra.] [1900, *etc.*] 8°.
14004. a. 6.

JAINAJÑĀNAPRAKĀṢA. जैन ज्ञान प्रकाश *etc.* [Jaina-jñānaprakāṣa. Comprising the Sūtrakṛidaṅga, I. vi. and II. vi.; Uttarādhyayana, I. i.; Gujarati translations and notes to the preceding; and Gujarati catechism, appendices on Jain doctrine, *etc.*] pt. i. pp. 155. અમદાવાદ ૧૮૯૮ [*Ahmadabad*, 1898.] 12°.
14100. a. 19.

JAINAKĀVYAPRAKĀṢA. જૈનકાવ્યપ્રકાશ *etc.* [Jainakāvyaprakāṣa. A collection of Jain devotional writings. Part i., comprising the Sāmāyikasūtra and Pachchakkhāṇas with Gujarati translation, followed by a series of Gujarati hymns.] pt. i. pp. xviii. 234. મુંબઈ ૧૮૯૪ [*Bombay*, 1894.] 16°.
14144. c. 9.

—— जैन काव्यप्रकाश *etc.* [Jainakāvyaprakāṣa.] pt. i. pp. xviii. 234. અમદાવાદ ૧૮૯૪ [*Ahmadabad*, 1894.] 16°.
14144. c. 10.

JAINA-KOHINŪR-SAṄGRAHA. શ્રી જૈન કોહિનુર સંગ્રહ [Jaina-kohinūr-saṅgraha. A Jain religious manual, comprising Sanskrit stanzas with Gujarati translations and Gujarati poems and appendices.] pp. viii. 56. અમદાવાદ ૧૮૯૮ [*Ahmadabad*, 1898.] 16°.
14144. c. 16.

JAINANITYAPĀṬHA. अथ जैननित्यपाठसंग्रहः [Jaina-nityapāṭhasaṅgraha. Devotional readings for Jains, comprising the Suprabhātastotra, Dṛishṭāshṭaka, Adyāshṭaka, the formula for salutation of Jinas, *etc.*, names of Jinas, Jinasena's Jinasahasranāma, Mānatuṅga's Bhaktāmarastotra, Siddhasena Divākara's Kalyāṇamandirast°., Vādirāja's Ekībhāvast°., Dhanaṃjaya's Vishāpahārast°., Bhūpāla Kavi's Jinachaturviṃṣatikā, the Tattvārthasūtra, a metrical Hindi paraphrase of the Sāmāyikasūtra by Mahāchandrajī, and Bhāgachandra's Mahāvīrāshṭaka.] pp. 180. १९०१ [*Bombay*, 1901.] *obl.* 16°. **14100. a. 27.**

JAINASTOTRARATNĀKARA. जैनस्तोत्ररत्नाकर *etc.* [Jainastotraratnākara. A collection of Jain hymns, including the Navasmaraṇa, Abhayadeva's Jayatihuaṇastotra, Kamalaprabha's Jinapañjarastotra, and the Grahaṣānti and Mantrādhirājastotra.] pp. ii. 112. मुंबई १९०१ [*Bombay*, 1901.] 16°. **14100. a. 26.**

JAINASTOTRASAṄGRAHA. जैनस्तोत्रसंग्रह: *etc.* [Jainastotrasaṅgraha, or Jinapañchastavī. 5 Jain devotional poems, viz. Mānatuṅga's Bhaktāmarastotra, Siddhasena's Kalyāṇamandirastotra, Vādirāja's Ekībhāvastotra, Dhanaṃjaya's Vishāpahārastotra, and Bhūpāla's Jinachaturviṃṣatikā. With biographical and explanatory notes.] pp. 40. मुम्बय्यां १९४७ [*Bombay*, 1890.] 12°. **14100. a. 13.**

JAMBHA. जंभसंहिता *etc.* [Jambhasaṃhitā. An anthological work on religious and moral topics, from Vedic texts, the Bhṛigusaṃhitā, and other sources, together with Hindi poems. Edited with Hindi paraphrases of the Sanskrit, notes, *etc.* by Īṣvarānandagiri.] pp. vi. iii. 263. प्रयाग १९५५ [*Allahabad*, 1899.] 8°. **14028. dd. 8.**

The devotee Jambha was a reputed incarnation of Vishṇu, born at Pipasar in Marwar, Samvat 1508.

JAMBUDDHAJA, *of Nyaunggan.* ရူပဘေဒပကာသနီ *etc.* [Rūpabhedappakāsanī. A Pali tract on stylistic discrimination between apparently synonymous terms. With a Burmese *nissaya.*] [1900.] *See* SADDĀ-NGAY. သဒ္ဒါငယ် *etc.* [Saddā-ngay.] Vol. v., pp. 140-182. [1898-1900.] 8°. **14098. ccc. 22.(vol. 5.)**

JĀMĪ. *See* ṢRĪVARA. Das Kathākautukam ... verglichen mit Dschāmī's Jusuf und Zuleikha, *etc.* 1893. 8°. **14070. d. 33.(1.)**

JĀMĪ (*continued*). [For editions of the Kathākautuka, Ṣrīvara's adaptation of Jāmī's romance "Yūsuf-Zulaikhā":] *See* ṢRĪVARA.

JAMMU.—*Raghunātha Temple Library.* Catalogue of the Sanskrit Manuscripts in the Raghunatha Temple Library of His Highness the Maharaja of Jammu and Kashmir. Prepared for the Kashmir State Council by M. A. Stein. pp. xvi. l. 423. *Bombay*, 1894. 4°. **14096. f. 8.**

JANINDA, *Ū, of Myinwunmin Kyaung, Mandalay.* *See* ABHIDHAMMAPIṬAKA.—*Dhammasaṅgaṇi.* မာတိကာ *etc.* [The *mātikā* of the Dhammaṅsagaṇi and the Dhātukathā, *etc.* Edited by Tissa and Janinda.] [1900.] 8°. **14098. dd. 23.**

—— *See* JĀGARĀBHIDDHAJA. အဘိဓမ္မတ္ထသင်္ဂြိုဟ်ဂဏ္ဌိသစ် *etc.* [Abhidhammatthasaṅgahagaṇṭhithit, *etc.* Edited by Tissa and Janinda.] [1898.] 8°. **14300. e. 4.**

—— —— [Another edition.] [1901.] 8°. **14300. e. 18.**

—— *See* PAṆḌITADDHAJA SĪLĀLAṄKĀRA. သဒ္ဒါပုဒ်စစ်။ အကျယ် *etc.* [Saddā-pôk-sit-akyay, *etc.* Edited by Tissa and Janinda.] [1896.] 8°. **14302. i. 15.**

—— *See* TISSA, *Ū*, and JANINDA, *Ū*. သမူဟနိယမဒီပနီကျမ်း *etc.* [Samūhaniyamadīpanī.] [1898.] 8°. **14302. i. 17.**

JANINDĀBHISIRI PARAMADDHAJA, *of Sinde.* *See* SUMAṄGALASĀMI. (ဋီကာကျော်နိဿယ) [Ṭīkā-kyaw-nissaya. Being sect. ii.-iv. of the Ṭīkā-kyaw, with Burmese *nissaya* by Janindābhisiri.] [1891.] 8°. **14098. ccc. 34.**

—— *See* SUMAṄGALASĀMI. ဋီကာကျော် *etc.* [Ṭīkā-kyaw. Parts i.-iii. (§§ 1-156). With Burmese *nissaya* by Janindābhisiri.] [1898.] 8°. [*Abhidhammatthasaṅgaha.*] **14098. ccc. 15.**

JĀTAKA. *See* SUTTAPIṬAKA.—*Khuddakanikāya.*

JAṬĀŞAṄKARA LĪLĀDHARA. *See* PURĀṆAS.—*Skandapurāṇa.* श्रीमालपुराण *etc.* [Ṣrīmālamāhātmya. With Gujarati translation, *etc.*, by Jaṭāṣaṅkara Lilādhara, *etc.*] [1899.] 8°. **14016. c. 62.**

JAVANA, *of Male.* *See* MINGUN-ALAY HSAYA. ပဉ္စစတ္တာလီသပုစ္ဆာ *etc.* [Pañchachattālīsa-puchchhāvisajjanā. 45 Burmese Questions by a Hsaya of Mingun-alay, with Responses by Javana. Followed by (1) Satapadika-puchchhāvisajjanā, 100 Questions by the latter answered by the former, (2) Samaṇapaṭirūpa, 9 *gāthās* from the Theragāthā, and Samaṇabhadrakathā, 8 *gāthās* from the Soṇajāṭaka, with Burmese commentary by Javana.] [1892.] 8°. **14300. d. 19.(4.)**

—— ဂတိဝိသောဓနကျမ်း ဒိဋ္ဌိဝိသောဓနဝဇိရဂ္ဂဒီပနီကျမ်း *etc.* [Gativisodhana-kyan and Diṭṭhivisodhana-vajiraggadīpanī. Buddhist homilies in Burmese, illustrated from Pali texts.] pp. i. ii. 110, 172. မန္တလေး [*Mandalay,*] 1896. 8°. **14300. d. 26.(3.)**

JAVANA, *of Min-ywa, Alon.* မနောဝါဒကထာ။ အသုဘကထာ။ဗုဒ္ဓဝန္ဒနာ။ ၃ ဝေါဟာရတွဲကျမ်း။ [Manovādakathā, Asubhakathā, and Buddhavandanā. Three Pali poems on topics of Buddhism, with Burmese translations. Followed by some Burmese glosses and notes on Pali vocables.] pp. 30. ရန်ကုန် ၁၂၅၉ [*Rangoon,* 1898.] 12°. **14098. a. 32.(1.)**

JAYACHANDRA, *of the Ārya Samāj, Lahore.* *See* VĀLMĪKI.—Rāmāyaṇa.—*Abridgments and Selections.* Selections from Ramayana . . . Compiled by Jai Chandra, *etc.* 1893. 8°. **14060. c. 32.(2.)**

JAYACHANDRA SĪTĀRĀMA ṢRĀVAṆE. *See* NEMICHANDRA BHAṆḌĀRĪ. उपदेशसिद्धान्तरत्नमाला *etc.* [Upadeṣasiddhāntaratnamālā. With Marathi translation and commentary by Jayachandra.] [1898.] 8°. **14100. b. 4.**

JAYADATTA ṢARMĀ, *Jyotirvid, of Almora.* धर्म्मनीति दर्पण *etc.* [Dharmanītidarpaṇa. An anthology from legendary and religious literature, for the moral and religious instruction of the young. With Hindi version.] pp. i. 50, ii. अल्मोड़ा १८९८ [*Almora,* 1898.] 8°. **14070. dd. 13.(1.)**

JAYADEVA, *son of Bhojadeva.* *See* RATIMAÑJARĪ. রতিমঞ্জরী *etc.* [Ratimañjarī. A manual of the Art of Love, based upon the works of Jayadeva and others.] [1901.] 12°. **14053. b. 41.(1.)**

—— गीतगुविन्दादर्स अर्थात् गीतगोविन्द संस्कृत और भाषा प्रतिबिंब [Gitagovindādarṣa. Being the Gitagovinda with an imitation in Hindi verse by Rāichand Nāgar.] pp. 80, *lith.* बनारस १८५८ [*Benares,* 1858.] 8°. **14076. c. 73.(1.)**

—— శ్రీ . . . గీతగోవిందనామాంకితంబుగ . . . యాంధ్రంబును *etc.* [Gītagovinda. With Telugu glosses of every word. Edited by Vaṅgīpuram Rāmakṛishṇam Āchārya and Sarasvatī Tiruveṅkaṭāchārya.] pp. 78. ౧౮౬౪ [*Madras,* 1864.] 8°. **14076. c. 73.(2.)**

Another issue of the edition of 1859.

—— Gitagobinda . . . ଗୀତଗୋବିନ୍ଦ *etc.* [With a metrical version in Oriya by Dharaṇīdhara.] *Cuttack,* 1878. 12°. **14076. b. 31.**

—— श्रीगीतगोविंदकाव्यं . . . राधाविनोद *etc.* [Gītagovinda. With the commentary of Nārāyaṇa Bhaṭṭa and a Hindi translation by Amṛitalāla Bhaṭṭāchārya. Followed by the Rādhāvinoda of Rāmachandra son of Janārdana, with the commentary of Nārāyaṇa.] pp. i. 186. मुम्बय्यां १९४८ [*Bombay,* 1891.] 8°. **14072. d. 42.**

—— ॥ गीतगोविन्दनामकाव्यम् *etc.* [Gītagovinda. Edited by Dāmodara Ṣāstrī.] ff. 42. काश्यां [*Benares,* 1897.] *obl.* 16°. **14070. a. 8.**

—— The Gita-govinda of Jayadeva. With the commentaries Rasikapriya of King Kumbha and Rasamanjari of Mahamahopadhyaya Shankara Mishra. Edited with various readings by Mangesh Ramkrishna Telang and Wasudev Laxuman Pansikar. [With a preface in Sanskrit by the senior editor, and at the end the Gaṅgāstavaprabandha of a Jayadeva.] (गीतगोविन्दकाव्यम् ।) pp. xxii. 176, ii. *Bombay,* 1899. 8°. **14070. dd. 3.**

—— শ্রীশ্রীগীতগোবিন্দম্ *etc.* [Gītagovinda. With an anonymous commentary styled Bālabodhinī

and a Bengali introduction and translation of the text.] pp. 390. *Calcutta*, [1901.] 16°.
14076. a. 27.

—— ବସନ୍ତରାସ *etc.* [Vasantarāsa. Being the Gitagovinda with paraphrases and expansions in Oriya verse by Ṣrichandana. Second edition.] pp. 128. *Cuttack*, 1902. 8°.
14070. dd. 21.(2.)

—— Le Gita-govinda. Pastorale de Jayadeva. Traduite par M. Gaston Courtillier . . . Avec une préface de M. Sylvain Lévi. pp. x. 83. i. *Paris*, 1904. 12°.
14070. b. 32.

Forms no. lxxviii. *of the* Bibliothèque Orientale Elzévirienne.

JAYADEVA, *son of Mahādeva.* चन्द्रालोकालङ्कारसमाख्या चन्द्रालोकव्याख्या *etc.* [Chandrāloka. A treatise on poetics, in 10 *mayūkhas*. With a commentary by Sūryabalirāma Chaube.] pp. 224. काश्याम् १९५२ [*Benares*, 1895.] 8°.
14053. c. 64.

—— The Andhra Chandraloka of Adidamu Soorakavi, with the Sanskrit Chandraloka [falsely supposed to be the work] of Appayya Deekshita. Edited . . . by Chevali Subrahmanyam. (సాంధ్ర-చంద్రాలోకము) pp. iv. 51, i. ii. *Vizagapatam*, 1898. 8°.
14053. c. 66.

This "Sanskrit Chandraloka" is incomplete, for it comprises only the bulk of vv. 11-178 *of the 5th* mayūkha, *according to Sūryabalirāma's edition* (*Benares*, 1895).

—— The Prasannarâghava . . . Edited by Kâśînâth Pâṇḍurang Parab. (प्रसन्नराघवम् ।) pp. 140, vi. *Bombay*, 1893. 8°.
14079. c. 60.(1.)

—— Prasanna Râghava . . . Edited with an introduction and notes, critical and explanatory, by Shivaram Mahadeo Paranjpe . . . and Narayan Sakharam Panse. pp. xvii. i. 209, 106, ii. *Poona*, 1894. 8°.
14079. c. 62.

—— Prasanna-raghava . . . With the Sanskrit commentary of Vyanketacharya Upadhye . . . and English notes, critical and explanatory, by Shivarama Raoji Khopakar. (प्रसन्नराघवम्) pp. iii. xvii. 277, vii. 84, 18, v. *Bombay*, 1894. 8°.
14080. d. 24.

JAYADEVA MIṢRA, called PAKSHADHARA, *disciple of Hari Miṣra.* *See* GAṄGEṢA UPĀDHYĀYA. The Tattva-chintámaṇi . . . with extracts from the commentaries of . . . Jayadeva, *etc.* 1888-1901. 8°. [*Bibliotheca Indica.*]
14002. a. (vol. 98.)

JAYĀDITYA, *the Grammarian.* *See* PĀṆINI.—*Kāṣikā.* काशिका . . . Kashika . . . [Begun] by Pandit Jayaditya [and completed by Vāmana,] *etc.* 1890. 8°.
14090. bb. 7.

—— *See* PĀṆINI.—*Kāṣikā.* The Ashṭádhyáyí . . . Translated into English, *etc.* [Being a translation of the Ashṭādhyāyī with a paraphrase of portions of the Kāṣikā.] 1891-1898. 8°.
14093. d. 18.

—— *See* PĀṆINI.—*Kāṣikā.* Zwei Kapitel der Kāçikā. Übersetzt . . . mit einer Einleitung . . . von Bruno Liebich. 1892. 8°.
14093. b. 34.

JAYADRATHA, *Rājānaka, son of Ṣriṅgāraratha.* The Haracharitachintâmaṇi of Râjânaka Jayaratha [*sic*]. [A cycle of Ṣaiva legends, in 32 *prakāṣas*.] Edited by . . . Paṇḍit Śivadatta . . . and Kâśînâth Pâṇḍurang Parab. [Followed by an index of the names of *tīrthas, etc.*, occurring in this poem, compiled and explained by Pandit Govinda Kaula, by order of Dr. M. A. Stein.] (हरचरितचिन्तामणिः ।) pp. 281, 10. 1897. *See* DURGĀPRASĀDA, *son of Vrajalāla*, and KĀṢĪNĀTHA PĀṆḌURAṄGA PARAB. Kâvyamâlâ, [No.] 61. 1886, *etc.* 8°.
14072. ccc. 12.(no. 61.)

The title-pages ascribe the work to Jayaratha, the colophons to Jayadratha.

JAYAKṚISHṆA, *son of Raghunātha, Maunī.* *See* PĀṆINI.—*Siddhāntakaumudī.* The Siddhântakaumudî with . . . the Subodhinî commentary of Jayakrishna, *etc.* 1899. 4°.
14092. c. 18.

—— अथ सुबोधिनी प्रारभ्यते ॥ [Subodhinī. A commentary upon the sections on accent and Vedic forms in the Siddhāntakaumudī.] pp. 98. *See* JÑĀNENDRA SARASVATĪ. वैयाकरणसिद्धान्तकौमुदीव्याख्या तत्त्वबोधिनी *etc.* [Tattvabodhinī, *etc.*] 1897. 8°.
14090. e. 25.

—— स्फोटचन्द्रिका *etc.* [Sphoṭachandrikā. A trea-

tise on the *sphoṭa* or eternal element in articulate speech.] pp. 12. *Benares,* 1899. 8°.
14004. a. 2.

Issued as appendix to ch. iii. 2 *of Bhaṭṭojī's* Ṣabdakaustubha *in fasc.* 14 *of the* Chowkhambâ Sanskrit Series.

JAYAKṚISHṆA, *son of Vidyānanda.* *See* PURUSHOTTAMA VIDYĀVĀGĪṢA BHAṬṬĀCHĀRYA. প্রয়োগরত্নমালা *etc.* [Prayogaratnamālā. With the commentary Prabhāprakāṣikā by Jayakṛishṇa.] [1890-1893.] 4°. **14090. e. 22.**

JAYAKṚISHṆA GAṄGĀDĀSA BHAKTA. Guide to [R. G. Bhāṇḍārkar's] Sanskrit Second Book. Part I. With rules, translations, copious notes, solutions of compounds, extracts from Kaumudi, etc., etc. ... By Jayakrishna Gangadas Bhakta. pp. vi. 168. *Surat,* [1900.] 12°.
14085. b. 36.(2.)

JAYAKṚISHṆA ṢRĪKṚISHṆA GHĀṬE, *Bhaṭṭa.* *See* BHAVABHŪTI. The Uttara Rama Charita ... With Sanscrit commentary by ... Bhatji Shastri Ghate, *etc.* 1895. 8°. **14080. d. 25.**

JAYAMAṄGALA, *the Commentator.* *See* BHAṬṬI. ভট্টিকাব্যম্ *etc.* [Bhaṭṭikāvya. Sargas i.-v., with the commentary of Jayamaṅgala, *etc.*] [1895-1896.] 8°. **14076. d. 49.**

JAYAMAṄGALAGĀTHĀ. ဇအောင်ခြင်းဂါထာ ... နမကာရ ... ရတနာပဥ္စရ ... ပရိတ်ကြီး *etc.* [Bāhira-jayamaṅgalagāthā, in Burmese Apyin-aung-hkyin. A Pali poem on the 8 'outward' victories of the Buddha. Followed by the Namakāra, Ratanapañjara, and Paritta. With Burmese translations and commentaries.] pp. 120. *Rangoon,* 1874. 8°. **14098. ccc. 26.(1.)**

—— ပြင်အောင်ခြင်းရှစ်ပါးနိသျ။ မဓုရဝါဒကထာကျမ်း *etc.* [Apyin-aung-hkyin. With Burmese version by Vimalālaṅkāra Kaviddhaja. Followed by Madhurovādakathā, a Burmese homily by the same, with illustrations from Pali texts, and a Burmese dissertation by Chakkindābhisiri.] pp. 56. မန္တလေး [*Mandalay,*] 1893. 8°. **14098. ccc. 26.(2.)**

—— [For popular Burmese collections of Pali-Burmese texts including editions of the Bāhira-jayamaṅgala and Ajjhatta-jayamaṅgala, see under the following headings :]

HKYAUK SAUNG TWÈ.
HSAY SAUNG TWÈ.
KO SAUNG TWÈ.
NGĀ SAUNG TWÈ.
TA-HSÈ-HNIT SAUNG TWÈ.
TA-HSÈ-THÔN SAUNG TWÈ.

JAYANTA BHAṬṬA, *son of Chandra.* *See* GOTAMA. The Nyâyamañjarî of Jayanta Bhaṭṭa, *etc.* [Comprising the Nyāyasūtra with commentary by Jayanta.] 1895. 8°. **14048. dd. 3.(vol. 8.)**

JAYANTA SVĀMĪ. *See* KĀTYĀYANA. अथ कात्यायनीशिक्षा *etc.* [Kātyāyanī Ṣikshā. With commentary by Jayanta.] 1893. 8°. [*Ṣikshāsaṅgraha.*]
14093. b. 31.

—— अथ स्वराङ्कुशशिक्षा *etc.* [Svarāṅkuṣaṣikshā. 25 stanzas on Vedic phonetics, of the Mādhyandina school.] *See* YUGALAKIṢORA VYĀSA PĀṬHAKA. श्रीमद्याज्ञवल्क्यादि ... शिक्षासंग्रहः ... A collection of Śikshás, *etc.* pp. 161-163. 1893. 8°.
14093. b. 31.

JAYANTĀBHIVAṂSA. သဒ္ဓမ္မပါလမေဓနီကျမ်း [Saddhammapālamedhanī. A general review of the Buddhist faith, in Burmese, illustrated from Pali writings. Preceded by a number of short excerpts from Pali texts with Burmese paraphrase, including the Gôn-taw, Rāhulasutta, Mettā-po, Sīvaligāthā, *etc.*] pp. 151. *Rangoon,* ၁၀၇၂ [1872.] 8°. **14300. d. 28.(1.)**

JAYĀPĪḌAKAVI, *author of the Kuṭṭanīmata.* *See* DĀMODARAGUPTA.

JAYARĀMA, *Astrologer.* अथ श्री ग्रहगोचर सटीक ज्योतिष ग्रंथ *etc.* [Grahagochara. An astrological work in verse, probably to be attributed to Jayarāma. With a Gujarati translation by Gaurīṣaṅkara Lalu Mehtā.] pp. 28. अमदावाद १९४८ [*Ahmadabad,* 1892.] 12°. **14053. b. 17.(4.)**

The attribution rests on Dr. Bühler's Cat. of Skt. MSS. in Gujarat, iv. 124, where a work of the same name and containing in all the same number of verses (54) is attributed to this writer.

JAYARĀMA, *Āchārya*. *See* PARASKARA. पारस्करगृह्यसूत्रम् *etc.* [Pāraskaragṛihyasūtra. With Jayarāma's Sajjanavallabhā, *etc.*] [1896.] 4°. **14010. f. 10.**

JAYARĀMA, *disciple of Viprarājendra*. श्रीविप्रराजेन्द्रदिग्विजयः *etc.* [Viprarājendradigvijaya. A poetical account in 33 *ullāsas* of the successes of Viprarājendra as a philosophical teacher, with a commentary apparently composed by the author.] pp. 79. काश्यां १९४७ [*Benares*, 1891.] 8°. **14048. dd. 5.(1.)**

JAYARĀMA RAGHUNĀTHA. *See* ŚANKARA ĀCHĀRYA.—*Two or More Works*. शंकराचार्य पंचरत्न *etc.* [Śaṅkarāchārya-pañcharatna. Edited with Gujarati translation by Jayarāma.] [1892.] 12°. **14098. b. 24.**

JAYARATHA, *son of Śriṅgāraratha*. *See* RUYYAKA. The Alankârasarvasva . . . With the commentary [Alaṅkāravimarṣinī] of Jayaratha, *etc.* 1893. 8°. [*Kâvyamâlâ*.] **14072. ccc. 12.(no. 35.)**

JAYATILAKA (D. B.). *See* PERIODICAL PUBLICATIONS.—*Colombo*. The Buddhist . . . Edited by C. W. Leadbeater, vol. 1. (By D. B. Jayatilaka, vol. 10, *etc.*) 1888, *etc.* 8°. **P.P. 636. cn.**

JAYATILAKA SŪRI, *Āgamika*. ॥ अथ श्रीसुलसाचरितम् ॥ [Sulasācharita, also styled Samyaktvasambhava. A Jain poem, in 8 *sargas*, upon the story of the chaste Sulasā. With Gujarati version by Hariṣaṅkara Kālidāsa.] ff. 112. मुंबइ १९५५ [*Bombay*, 1899.] *obl.* 8°. **14100. d. 8.**

JAYĪNĀRĀYAṆA DEVA. *See* PURĀṆAS.—*Bhāgavatapurāṇa*. ରାସପଞ୍ଚାଧ୍ୟାୟୀ *etc.* [Rāsapañchādhyāyī. With a prose Oriya translation by Jayīnārāyaṇa Deva.] 1901. 12°. **14016. b. 24.(2.)**

JENNINGS (JAMES G.), *Professor at Muir Central College, Allahabad*. Sakuntala. A play [based upon the drama of Kālidāsa,] *etc.* pp. i. 210. *Allahabad*, 1902. 12°. **11779. ff. 9.**

JĪMŪTAVĀHANA. *See* ĀDINĀRĀYAṆA PĀTRO. The Hindu Law. Annotated and illustrated by Sanskrit texts[, viz. the writings of Jīmūtavāhana and others,] *etc.* 1899. 8°. **14039. c. 17.**

JĪMŪTAVĀHANA (*continued*). दायभागः *etc.* [Dāyabhāga. With the commentary Dāyabhāgaprabodhanī of Krishṇa Tarkālaṅkāra. Edited by Jīvānanda Vidyāsāgara. Second edition.] pp. iv. 233. कलिकाता १८९३ [*Calcutta*, 1893.] 8°. **14038. c. 48.(1.)**

—— దాయభాగః *etc.* [Dāyabhāga. Edited by Ṣattanūru Kalyāṇasundara Ṣāstrī.] pp. 88. చెన్నపురి ౧౮౯౭ [*Madras*, 1897.] 8°. **14039. b. 22.**

—— জীমূতবাহনকৃত-দায়ভাগঃ। *etc.* [Dāyabhāga. With Krishṇa Tarkālaṅkāra's commentary and a Bengali translation of the text. Edited by Nīlakamala Vidyānidhi.] pp. i. 276. কলিকাতা ১৩০৪ [*Calcutta*, 1898.] 8°. **14038. c. 49.**

—— कालविवेकः। The Kāla-viveka. [A work on auspicious times for religious ceremonies.] Edited [with a commentary] by Paṇḍit Madhusūdana Smṛtiratna. 1897, *etc.* *See* ACADEMIES, *etc.*—Calcutta.—*Asiatic Society of Bengal*. Bibliotheca Indica. New Series. [Vol. 136.] 1848, *etc.* 8°. **14002. a. (vol. 136.)**
In progress.

JINABHADRA GAṆĪ, *Kshamāṣramaṇa*. Jinabhadra's Jîtakalpa, [a list of penances for Jain friars,] mit Auszügen aus Siddhasena's Cûrṇi. Von Ernst Leumann. (Sitzungsberichte der Königlich Preussischen Akademie der Wissenschaften zu Berlin . . . 22. December. 1892.) pp. 16. *Berlin*, 1892. 8°. **14100. d. 2.**

JINADATTA SŪRI, *disciple of Rāsila and Jīvadeva*. विवेक-विलास *etc.* [Vivekavilāsa. Jain precepts religious and ethical, in 12 *ullāsas*. With a Gujarati translation by Dāmodara Govindāchārya.] pp. iv. 256. अमदावाद १९५४ [*Ahmadabad*, 1898.] 8°. **14100. c. 20.**

JINADEVA MUNIṢVARA. The Abhidhâna-chintâmaṇi-śilonchchha of Jinadeva Munîśvara. [A supplement, in 139 stanzas, to Hemachandra's Abhidhānachintāmaṇi.] Edited by Pandit Ṣivadatta and Kâśînâth Pândurang Parab. (अभिधानचिन्तामणिशिलोञ्छः) pp. 5. 1896. *See* DURGĀPRASĀDA, *son of Vrajalāla*, and others. The Abhidhânasangraha, *etc.* No. 11. 1889, *etc.* 8°. **14090. e. 20.(no. 11.)**

JINADEVA MUNĪṢVARA (*continued*). शिलोञ्छः [Ṣiloñchha.] pp. 19. *See* HEMACHANDRA, *disciple of Devachandra.* अभिधानचिंतामणिः *etc.* [Abhidhānachintāmaṇi, *etc.*] [1900.] 12°. **14090. b. 46.**

JINAKĪRTI SŪRI, *disciple of Somasundara.* धन्ना-शालिभद्रनो रास *etc.* [Dhannā-Ṣālibhadra-no Rās. A Jain legend illustrating the virtue of charity. Translated into Gujarati by Jinavijaya Mahārāja, but with the Sanskrit stanzas of the original retained. Followed by Satā-satīo-nī Sajjhāya, 13 Prakrit stanzas on divers persons of the Jain hagiology, with Gujarati commentary. Edited by Kachrābhāī Gopāladāsa.] pp. iv. 212. અમદાવાદ ૧૮૯૪ [*Ahmadabad*, 1894.] 8°. **14144. f. 26.**

JINAPRABHA SŪRI. *See* ḌĀHYĀBHĀĪ FATH-CHAND and MOTĪLĀL MAHĀSUKHBHĀI. शोभनस्तवनावली *etc.* [Ṣobhanastavanāvalī. Hymns by Jinaprabha and others.] [1897.] 12°. **14100. a. 17.**

—— A Legend of the Jaina Stūpa at Mathurā [excerpted from Jinaprabha's Tīrthakalpa]. By G. Bühler. 1897. *See* ACADEMIES, *etc.*—Vienna.—*Kaiserliche Akademie der Wissenschaften.* Sitzungsberichte, *etc.* Band 137. 1849, *etc.* 8°. **Ac. 810/6.(Bd. 137.)**

JINAPŪJĀ. श्री जिन पूजा महोदधि *etc.* [Jinapūjāmahodadhi. A collection of Jain ritual poems, by various authors of the Kharatara Gachchha, in Hindi-Gujarati, Sanskrit, and Prakrit. Edited by Rāmalāla Gaṇī and others.] pp. x. 418. मुंबई १९५८ [*Bombay*, 1902.] 8°. **14144. gg. 5.**

JINARĀJADĀSA, *C.* *See* PERIODICAL PUBLICATIONS.—*Colombo.* The Buddhist . . . Edited by C. W. Leadbeater, vol. 1. (By C. Jinarājadāsa, vol. 11, no. 7-12.) 1888, *etc.* 8°. **P.P. 636. cn.**

JINARATANA, *Hiṅgulvala.* Dhātwattha Dīpanī. [A collection of Pali verbal roots cast into Pali verse, based on the Mahāsaddanīti of Aggavaṃsa. Followed by an alphabetical index in Sinhalese and Roman characters, with meanings in Sinhalese and English.] . . . ධාත්වත්ථදීපනී *etc.* pp. v. iii. 173, xiii. *Colombo*, 1895. 8°. **14098. b. 19.**

JINARATANA, *Talavatugoḍa.* *See* CHAKRAPĀṆIDATTA. Chakradatta, *etc.* [With Sinhalese interpretation by Jinaratana.] 1893. 8°. **14043. d. 47.**

JINASĀGARA SŪRI, *disciple of Jinachandra.* *See* HARI, *disciple of Vajrasena.* कर्पूरप्रकर *etc.* [Karpūraprakara. With gloss by Jinasāgara.] [1901.] 12°. **14100. b. 12.**

JINASENA ĀCHĀRYA. जिनसहस्रनाम स्तोत्र । [Jinasahasranāmastotra. A hymn containing the 1000 names of Jinas. Preceded by Yaṣonandi's Jinasnapana or stanzas on the washing of the statues of Jinas.] pp. 22. मुंबई १९५५ [*Bombay*, 1899.] 12°. **14076. a. 23.(3.)**

—— अथ सहस्रनामप्रारभ्यते [Jinasahasranāma.] *See* DAṢALAKSHAṆĪ. दशलक्षण्यादि पूजनसंग्रह *etc.* [Daṣalakshaṇyādi-pūjanasaṅgraha.] ff. 3-12. [1899.] *obl.* 8°. **14100. b. 7.**

—— श्रीजिनसहस्रनामस्तोत्रम्। [Jinasahasranāmastotra.] *See* JAINANITYAPĀṬHA. अथ जैननित्यपाठसंग्रहः [Jainanityapāṭhasaṅgraha.] pp. 17-48. [1901.] *obl.* 16°. **14100. a. 27.**

—— (ಸಹಸ್ರನಾಮಮಂತ್ರಾಃ) [Sahasranāmamantrāḥ. The 1000 names of the Jinas, arranged in the form of salutation.] pp. 41. [*Bangalore*, 1898.] 16°. **14100. a. 18.**

No title-page.

—— ॥ श्रीजिनसहस्रनामस्तोत्र ॥ [Jinasahasranāmastotra.] pp. 30. *See* UMĀSVĀTI. अथ तत्वार्थसूत्र° [Tattvārthasūtra, *etc.*] *obl.* 16°. **14100. a. 28.**

—— ಶ್ರೀಮದ್ಭಗವಜ್ಜಿನಸೇನಾಚಾರ್ಯಕೃತಮಹಾಪುರಾಣಂ *etc.* [Mahāpurāṇa, or Mahāpurāṇasaṅgraha. A poetical account of the Jain *tīrthaṅkara* Ṛishabha, *etc.* Edited with Canarese commentary by Padmarāja Paṇḍita.] ಬೆಂಗಳೂರು ೧೮೯೬ [*Bangalore*, 1896, *etc.*] 4°. **14100. e. 6.**

Contains only the first two parts; apparently no more has been published. The first portion of this work (Adipurāṇa) is for the most part the work of Jinasena; but the supplement (Uttarapurāṇa) is by his disciple Guṇabhadra.

—— *See* KĀLIDĀSA.—*Meghadūta.* The Meghadûta. As embodied [in the form of *samasyā*] in the Párśvábhyudaya [of Jinasena,] *etc.* 1894. 8°. **14076. b. 32.**

—— पार्श्वाभ्युदयकाव्यम् [Pārṣvābhyudaya. A poem on the *tīrthaṅkara* Pārṣvanātha, in which are incorporated line by line the verses of the Meghadūta of Kālidāsa. With a commentary.]

[1893.] *See* PADMARĀJA PAṆḌITA, *son of Brahmasūri.* काव्याम्बुधिः *etc.* [Kāvyāmbudhi.] pts. 1-4. [1893-1896.] 8°. **14028. c. 64.**

Not completed.

JINAVAṂSA PAÑÑĀSĀRA, *of Kosgoda.* *See* SUTTAPIṬAKA. — *Khuddakanikāya.* [*Petavatthu.*] පෙතවත්ථු *etc.* [Petavatthu. With Sinhalese commentary by Paññāsāra.] pts. 1, 3, 5. 1893-1896. 8°. **14098. c. 63.(2.)**

JINAVARAVAṂSA, *P. C., Prince of Siam.* *See* SUBHŪTI, *Vaskaḍuvē.* The Siam Standard Paritta. . . . Compiled by . . . W. Subhuti . . . assisted by . . . P. C. Jinavarawansa. 1897. 8°. **14098. b. 22.**

JINAVARDHANA SŪRI, *disciple of Jinarāja.* *See* VĀGBHAṬA, *son of Soma.* अलंकारशास्त्रम् । [Alaṅkāraśāstra. With commentary of Jinavardhana.] [1889-1890.] 8°. [*Grantharatnamālā.*] **14096. c. 8.(vol. 3.)**

JINAVIJAYA MAHĀRĀJA. *See* JINAKĪRTI SŪRI. धन्नाशालिभद्रनो रास *etc.* [Dhannā-Śālibhadra-no Rās. Translated into Gujarati by Jinavijaya.] [1894.] 8°. **14144. f. 26.**

JĪTŪLĀL MUKHTĀR. *See* HARIHARAPRASĀDA.

JĪVA GOSVĀMĪ. *See* RŪPA GOSVĀMĪ. সটীক . . . শ্রীস্তবপুষ্পাঞ্জলিঃ *etc.* [Stavapushpāñjali. A series of lyrics compiled from the Stavamālā of Rūpa, as arranged by Jīva, *etc.*] [1902.] 8°. **14072. ccc. 34.**

—— *See* RŪPA GOSVĀMĪ. উজ্জ্বলনীলমণিঃ *etc.* [Ujjvalanīlamaṇi. With the commentary Lochanarochanī by Jīva, *etc.*] [1889.] 8°. **14053. d. 49.**

—— ষট্‌সন্দর্ভাপরনামা শ্রীভাগবতসন্দর্ভঃ *etc.* [Shaṭsandarbha, or Bhāgavatasandarbha. A commentary upon the Bhāgavatapurāṇa, supplementing the work of Śrīdhara. In 6 books, entitled Tattvasandarbha, Bhagavatsandarbha, Paramātmas°., Śrīkṛishnas°., Bhaktis°., and Prītis°., with annotations upon the Tattvasandarbha by Baladeva Vidyābhūshaṇa. Edited by Śyāmalāla Gosvāmī.] pp. 895. কলিকাতা ১৩০৮ [*Calcutta,* 1899-1901.] 8°. **14016. d. 62.**

JĪVANĀCHĀRYA VALLABHA, *Gosvāmī.* ॥ शुक्लयजुर्वेदीय ॥ ॥ वैष्णवद्विजाह्निकम् *etc.* [Vaishṇavadvijāhnika. A manual of the encyclical rites for Brahmans, Kshatriyas, and Vaiśyas of the sect of Vallabhāchārya, according to the Vājasaneyisaṃhitā. In Hindi, with the texts and numerous quotations in Sanskrit.] pp. ii. ii. ii. 99. मुंबई १९५७ [*Bombay,* 1901.] 8°. **14154. ee. 12.**

JĪVANADĀSA, *Lālā, of Lahore.* *See* GURUDATTA VIDYĀRTHĪ. Works of . . . Guru Datta Vidyarthi . . . Revised and edited by Lala Jivan Das, *etc.* 1897. 8°. **14010. dd. 11.**

—— —— [Another edition, with biography.] 1902. 8°. **759. c. 20.**

JĪVANAJĪ, *son of Gokulotsava, Gosvāmī.* मुंबइस्थ . . . श्रीजीवनजीकृतग्रंथाः । [Miscellaneous writings in verse on the doctrine of Vallabhāchārya.] *See* GOVARDHANADĀSA LAKSHMĪDĀSA. बृहत्स्तोत्रसरित्सागर *etc.* [Bṛihat-stotrasaritsāgara.] Vol. ii. [1892.] 12°. **14033. a. 27.(vol. 2.)**

JĪVĀNANDA VIDYĀSĀGARA BHAṬṬĀCHĀRYA.

Works registered in this Catalogue that have been edited or prepared for press by this Pandit are to be found under the following headings:—

Āpadeva.
Bhāva Miśra.
Brahmānandagiri Tīrtha.
Chakrapāṇidatta.
Dallaṇa Miśra.
Hārita.
Indrajālavidyāsaṅgraha.
Jīmūtavāhana.
Kramadīśvara.
Mahīdhara, *son of Rāmabhakta.*
Nāgeśa Bhaṭṭa.
Pūrṇānanda Gosvāmī.
Raghunandana Bhaṭṭāchārya.
Sārasvatasūtra.
Śūlapāṇi, *Sāhuṛiyān.*
Tantras.
Tārānātha Tarkavāchaspati.
Vaṅgasena.
Vedas.—*Sāmaveda.*
Vopadeva.

—— *See* APYAYA DĪKSHITA. सिद्धान्तलेशसंग्रहः *etc.* [Siddhāntaleśasaṅgraha. Edited by Jīvānanda, with a commentary compiled by the same.] [1897.] 8°. **14048. cc. 31.**

—— *See* ASHṬĀVAKRA. Ashtabakra-samhita . . . Edited . . . with a full commentary by . . . Jibananda Vidyasagara. 1901. 8°. **14048. dd. 34.(2.)**

—— *See* BĀṆA. हर्षचरितम् *etc.* (Harsha Charita . . . Edited with a full commentary and an epitome of the work by . . . Jibananda Vidyasagara.) [1892.] 8°. **14070. dd. 16.**

—— *See* BHOJARĀJA. सरस्वतीकण्ठाभरणम् *etc.* [Sarasvatīkaṇṭhābharaṇa. With Ratneśvara's commentary. Edited with a commentary upon Sections iv.-v. by Jīvānanda.] [1894.] 8°. **14053. cc. 68.**

JĪVĀNANDA VIDYĀSĀGARA BHAṬṬĀCHĀRYA (*continued*). *See* GAṄGEṢA UPĀDHYĀYA. **केवलान्वयि अनुमानम्** *etc.* [Kevalānvayyanumāna. With Raghunātha's Śiromaṇi, Jagadīṣa's Jāgadīṣī, and a gloss upon the last, called Jāgadīṣīvādārtha, by the editor, Jīvānanda.] [1897.] 8°. **14048. bb. 45.(4.)**

—— *See* GAṄGEṢA UPĀDHYĀYA. **पक्षता** *etc.* [Pakshatā. With commentaries of Raghunātha, Jagadīṣa, and Mathurānātha, and the Jāgadīṣīvādārtha, a gloss on Jagadīṣa by Jīvānanda. Edited by the last.] [1897.] 8°. **14048. bb. 45.(5.)**

—— *See* GAṄGEṢA UPĀDHYĀYA. **सिद्धान्तलक्षणम्** *etc.* (Siddhantalakshana . . . With . . . commentaries . . . Edited and published with questions and answers [entitled Phakkikāvivṛiti] by . . . Jibananda Vidyasagara, *etc.*) [1896.] 8°. **14048. c. 79.(1.)**

—— *See* GAṄGEṢA UPĀDHYĀYA. **व्याप्तिपञ्चकम्** *etc.* [Vyāptipañchaka, *etc.* Edited, with notes styled Phakkikā upon Mathurānātha's commentary, by Jīvānanda.] [1896.] 8°. **14048. e. 28.**

—— *See* GOPĀLAKṚISHṆA, *Kavirāja.* **रसेन्द्रसारसंग्रहः** *etc.* [Rasendrasārasaṅgraha. Edited with notes by Jīvānanda.] [1896.] 8°. **14043. cc. 12.**

—— *See* HANUMĀN. **महानाटकम्** *etc.* (Mahanataka . . . Edited with a full commentary by . . . Jibananda, *etc.*) [1890.] 8°. **14079. c. 70.**

—— *See* NĀḌĪVIJÑĀNA. **नाडीविज्ञानम्** [Nāḍīvijñāna. Edited with a commentary by Jīvānanda.] [1897.] 8°. **14043. c. 37.(3.)**

JĪVANARĀMA KĀLIDĀSA GONDLEKAR. *See* PURĀṆAS.—*Varāhapurāṇa.* **अथ श्रीमद्वाराहमहापुराणं** *etc.* [Varāhapurāṇa. With index by Jīvanarāma.] [1903.] Fol. **14016. f. 16.**

JĪVANA ṢARMĀ, *son of Vanamālī Jhā, of Haripur, Darbhangah.* **शृङ्गारसागरः** *etc.* [Śṛiṅgārasāgara. A metrical treatise, in 7 *taraṅgas*, upon the literary expression of amorous emotion.] pp. 21. **वाराणस्यां १९०२** [*Benares,* 1902.] 8°. **14053. cc. 17.(2.)**

JĪVANĀTHA, *son of Ṣambhunātha, Maithila.* භාවකුතූහලය *etc.* [Bhāvakutūhala. A metrical manual of astrology. Edited with a Sinhalese word-for-word gloss and notes by B. L. Sarnēlis.] pt. 1. [*Colombo,*] 1897. 8°. **14053. ccc. 4.**

Breaks off at vii. 47.

—— **अथ दिनचर्यापञ्चस्वरोदाहरणम् । प्रारभ्यते ॥** [Dinacharyāpañchasvarodāharaṇa. A treatise on the magic values of the vowels. Edited by Baladevaprasāda Bhaṭṭa.] ff. 21. *Benares,* [1901.] *obl.* 8°. **14053. d. 60.**

—— వనమాలా సటీకా *etc.* [Vanamālā. A tract on divination, in 5 *adhyāyas.* With Telugu translation.] pp. 30. చెన్నపురి ౧౮౯౩ [*Madras,* 1893.] 12°. **14053. b. 31.(2.)**

—— వాస్తురత్నావళి *etc.* [Vāsturatnāvali. A collection of rules for the religious rites, *etc.*, connected with building. Edited with a Telugu version by N. Guruliṅga Ṣāstrī.] pp. ii. 91. చెన్నపురి ౧౮౯౭ [*Madras,* 1897.] 8°. **14053. ccc. 16.**

JĪVANĀTHA MIṢRA NYĀYATĪRTHA. *See* GIRIDHARA BHAṬṬĀCHĀRYA. **विभक्त्यर्थनिर्णयः** *etc.* (Vibhaktyarthanirnaya . . . Edited by . . . Jivanatha, *etc.*) [1902.] 8°. **14004. a. 12.**

JĪVARĀMA LALLURĀM RAIKVĀL. *See* PĀṆINI.—*Siddhāntakaumudī.* **मध्यसिद्धान्तकौमुदी** *etc.* [Madhyasiddhāntakaumudī. Edited by Jīvarāma.] [1895.] 12°. **14090. b. 41.**

—— *See* SARVAVARMĀ. **कातन्त्रव्याकरणम्** *etc.* [Kātantra. With commentary of Bhāvasena. Edited by Jīvarāma.] [1895.] 8°. **14090. bb. 9.**

JĪVEṢVARA BHAṬṬĀCHĀRYA. *See* PURUSHOTTAMA VIDYĀVĀGĪṢA BHAṬṬĀCHĀRYA. প্রয়োগরত্নমালা *etc.* [Prayogaratnamālā. With the Pañjikā of Jīveṣvara.] [1890-1893.] 4°. **14090. e. 22.**

JIYĀRĀM ṢĀSTRĪ, *son of Ravidatta, of Beri, Rohtak.* *See* GAṆEṢA, *son of Keṣava.* **ग्रहलाघवम्** *etc.* (Grahalaghava . . . With Hindi translation by . . . Jiyá Rám Shástri, *etc.*) 1899. 8°. **14053. ccc. 26.**

JÑĀNACHANDRA, *Bābū, of Lahore.* *See* DHANAMJAYA, *Jain writer.* **विषापहार** *etc.* [Vishāpahāra. Edited by Jñānachandra.] [1900.] 12°. **14100. a. 21.(2.)**

JÑĀNACHANDRA, *Bābū, of Lahore (continued)*. *See* GUṆABHADRA ĀCHĀRYA. श्री आत्मानुशासनग्रन्थ *etc.* [Ātmānuṣāsana. Edited with Hindi translation and commentary by Jñānachandra.] [1898.] *obl.* 8°. **14100. c. 19.**

—— जैनबालगुटका [Jaina-bālaguṭikā. Comprising formulas and lists of the persons who are the subjects of Jain worship, also of other matters and forms connected with the cult. With Hindi notes.] pp. 16. लाहौर १९०० [*Lahore*, 1900.] 12°. **14100. a. 6.(3.)**

Forms no. 2 of the compiler's Jain Religious Tracts Series.

JÑĀNACHANDRA CHAUDHURĪ. সমস্যাকল্পলতা *etc.* [Samasyākalpalatā. A collection of impromptu verses composed on various occasions by Premachandra Tarkavāgīṣa and other scholars. Edited with Bengali preface by Jñānachandra.] pp. v. 112, 9. কলিকাতা ১৩০৭ [*Calcutta*, 1900.] 8°. **14079. c. 72.**

JÑĀNADEVA, called JÑĀNOBĀ. *See* MAHĀBHĀRATA.—Bhagavadgītā.—*Sanskrit and Vernaculars.* ज्ञानेश्वरी *etc.* [Bhagavadgītā. With the Jñāneṣvarī or Bhāvārthadīpikā, a Marathi paraphrase by Jñānadeva.] [1897.] 12°. **14060. b. 15.**

JÑĀNĀNANDA DEVA, *Yogāchārya, Avadhūta.* সিদ্ধান্তদর্শন *etc.* [Siddhāntadarṣana. Bengali essays reconciling monism and dualism by examination of passages from Sanskrit authors, notably Ṣaṅkara and Ashṭāvakra. Preceded by the Ānandalaharī.] pp. i. ii. xx. 275. নবদ্বীপ কলিকাতা ১৩০৪ [*Nadiya, Calcutta* printed, 1898.] 12°. **14048. b. 33.(5.)**

JÑĀNAPŪRṆA, *disciple of Vishṇu Svāmī.* *See* VARADARĀJA, *Logician.* तार्किकरक्षा *etc.* (The Tārkikarakṣā and Sārasaṃgraha . . . With the glosses Niṣkaṇṭakā of Mallinātha Kolācala and Laghudīpikā of Jñānapūrṇa.) 1903. 8°. [*The Pandit.*] **14096. d. 6. (vol. 21-25.)**

JÑĀNENDRANĀTHA TANTRARATNA BHAṬṬĀCHĀRYA. রহস্যপূজা-পদ্ধতি *etc.* [Rahasyapūjāpaddhati. A supplementary mystic ritual. With Bengali introductions, rubrics, and notes, and an appendix of Sanskrit and Bengali hymns.] pp. i. iv. xxxvii. 78. কলিকাতা ১৩০৮ [*Calcutta*, 1901.] 8°. **14033. bb. 42.(3.)**

JÑĀNENDRA SARASVATĪ. *See* PĀṆINI.—*Siddhāntakaumudī.* सिद्धान्तकौमुदी . . . Siddhanta Kaumudi. With . . . the "Tattwabodhini" by Jnanendra, *etc.* [1890-1892.] 8°. **14090. d. 29.**

—— *See* PĀṆINI.—*Siddhāntakaumudī.* The Siddhânta-kaumudî with the Tattvabodhinî commentary of Jnânendra, *etc.* 1899. 4°. **14092. c. 18.**

—— वैयाकरणसिद्धान्तकौमुदीव्याख्या तत्त्वबोधिनी *etc.* [Tattvabodhinī. A commentary on the Siddhāntakaumudī. Followed by the Subodhinī of Jayakrishṇa, a commentary upon the sections on accent and Vedic forms in the Siddhāntakaumudī. Edited by Nārāyaṇa Ṣāstrī Paṭavardhana.] pp. 438, 315, 98. काश्यां [*Benares*,] 1897. 8°. **14090. e. 25.**

JÑĀNOTTAMA MIṢRA. *See* SUREṢVARA ĀCHĀRYA. नैष्कर्म्यसिद्धिनाम वेदान्तप्रकरणम् . . . Naishkarmyasiddhi . . . with a commentary called Chandriká by Jńánottama Miśra, *etc.* 1890, *etc.* 8°. **14048. dd. 7.**

JÑĀTĀDHARMAKATHĀ. Specimen der Nâyâdhammakahâ. [Being Ṣrutaskandha I. i., with extracts from the commentary of Abhayadeva, notes, and a Prakrit-Sanskrit glossary.] Inaugural Dissertation zur Erlangung der philosophischen Doctorwürde an der Königlichen Akademie zu Münster, von P. Steinthal. pp. 84. *Leipzig*, 1881. 8°. **14100. c. 17.(1.)**

The Jñātādharmakathā forms the 6th aṅga *in the Jain Canon.*

JOGES CHANDRA RAY. *See* YOGEṢACHANDRA RĀYA.

JOGESH CHUNDER DUTT. *See* YOGEṢACHANDRA DATTA.

JOGINDRANATH. *See* YOGĪNDRANĀTHA.

JOHNSTON (CHARLES), *sometime of the Bengal Civil Service.* *See* ṢAṄKARA ĀCHĀRYA.—*Philosophical Poems, etc.* The Awakening to the Self. Translated . . . by C. Johnston. 1897. *obl.* 12°. **14048. a. 18.**

—— *See* UPANISHADS.—*Selections.* From the Upanishads. [Translated] by C. Johnston. 1896. 12°. **14010. b. 10.**

JOHNSTONE (Pierce de Lacy). *See* Kālidāsa.—*Raghuvaṃṣa.* The Raghuvança . . . Translated [into verse] by P. de Lacy Johnstone. 1902. 8°. **14072. c. 57.**

JOLLY (Julius Ernst). Beiträge zur indischen Rechtsgeschichte, *etc.* 1890-1896. *See* Academies, *etc.*—Germany.—*Deutsche Morgenlaendische Gesellschaft.* Zeitschrift, *etc.* Bd. 44-50. 1846, *etc.* 8°. **Ac. 8815/2. (Bd. 44-50.)**

JONARĀJA. द्वितीया राजतरङ्गिणी । [Dvitīyā Rājataraṅgiṇī. The first supplement to Kalhaṇa's history.] 1896. *See* Kalhaṇa. The Râjataraṅgiṇî, *etc.* Vol. iii., pp. 1-116. 1892-1896. 8°. **14058. b. 27.**

—— Kings of Kashmíra: being a translation of the Sanskṛita works of Jonarāja . . . by Jogesh Chunder Dutt. *See* Kalhaṇa. Kings of Káshmíra, *etc.* Vol. iii. 1879-1898. 12°. **14070. b. 13.**

JONES (*Sir* William). *See* Kālidāsa.—*Collected Works.* Works of Kalidasa . . . 1. Shakuntala [in the translation of Jones], *etc.* 1901. 12°. **14080. b. 10.**

—— —— [Another copy.] **14070. b. 30.**

—— *See* Kālidāsa.—*Abhijñānaṣakuntala.* Shakuntala, or The Fatal Ring . . . Reprinted from the translation of Sir William Jones. 1899. 12°. **14079. a. 8.(3.)**

—— *See* Kālidāsa.—*Abhijñānaṣakuntala.* Kalidasa's Sakuntala, *etc.* [In the translation of Jones.] [1902.] 8°. **012208. ee. 117.**

—— *See* Manu.—*Dharmaṣāstra.* The Laws of Manu . . . Abridged English translation [based on that of Jones], *etc.* 1898. 8°. [*Sacred Books of the East Described and Examined.*] **14010. cc. 9.(vol. 2.)**

JOTIKA, *Ū*, *Pongyi.* *See* Kachchāyana.—*Kachchāyanappakaraṇa.* သဒ္ဒါရှစ်ဆောင်သုတ်နက် [Saddā-shitsaung-thôk-net. The aphorisms of Kachchāyana, with brief Burmese commentary by Jotika. Second edition.] [1897.] 8°. **14098. ccc. 12.(2.)**

—— —— [Third edition.] [1899.] 8°. **14098. ccc. 12.(3.)**

JUMARANANDĪ. *See* Kramadīṣvara. संक्षिप्तसार॰ [Saṅkshiptasāravyākaraṇa. With the commentary Rasavatī in the recension of Jumaranandī, *etc.*] [1901.] 8°. **14090. bb. 16.**

—— *See* Kramadīṣvara. संक्षिप्तसार॰ [Saṅkshiptasāravyākaraṇa. Abridged with selections from the commentary Rasavatī.] pt. i. 1891. 8°. **14090. c. 38.**

JVĀLĀDATTA ṢARMĀ, *of the Baladevārya Sanskrit School, Moradabad.* ॥ विद्यामार्त्तण्ड *etc.* [Vidyāmārtaṇḍa. A series of texts with Hindi translations, *etc.*, published in monthly parts. Compiled and edited by Jvālādatta.] Vol. i., pts. 1-3. इलाहाबाद १९४५ [*Allahabad,* 1889.] 8°. **14096. c. 9.**

The contents are catalogued under the heading:— Pāṇini.—*Ashṭādhyāyī.*

—— विद्यामार्त्तण्ड *etc.* [Vidyāmārtaṇḍa. A new issue.] Vol. i., 1-3. इटावा १९००-१९०१ [*Etawah,* 1900-1901.] 8°. **14096. c. 9.***

In progress?

—— —— [Another issue.] Vol. i., 1. मुरादाबाद १९५७ [*Moradabad,* 1900.] 8°. **14096. c. 9.****

JVĀLĀPRASĀDA MIṢRA, *son of Sukhānanda, of Moradabad.* *See* Gāyatrī. ॥ अथ चतुर्विंशति गायत्र्यो॰ [Chaturviṃṣati Gāyatryaḥ. With Hindi version by Jvālāprasāda.] [1901.] *obl.* 8°. **14033. b. 33.(2.)**

—— *See* Nāga Bhaṭṭa. कामरत्नम् *etc.* [Kāmaratna. With Hindi translation by Jvālāprasāda, and an appendix treating of magic diagrams, *etc.*] [1899.] 8°. **14033. aa. 4.**

—— *See* Pañchatantra. Pancha Tantra . . . With a [Hindi] commentary [styled Nītisarvasva] by . . . Jwala Prasad Misra. 1898. 8°. **14070. c. 62.**

—— *See* Purāṇas.—*Devībhāgavatapurāṇa.* सावित्र्युपाख्यान *etc.* [Sāvitryupākhyāna. With Hindi translation by Jvālāprasāda.] [1902.] 12°. **14016. b. 28.**

—— *See* Rūpa Gosvāmī. श्रीलघुभागवतामृतम् *etc.* [Laghu-bhāgavatāmṛita. With commentary, *etc.* Edited by Jvālāprasāda.] [1903.] 8°. **14076. d. 55.**

JVĀLĀPRASĀDA MIŚRA, *son of Sukhānanda, of Moradabad (continued).* See TANTRAS. [*Mahānirvāṇatantra.*] Mahanirvana-tantram ... Purva Kandam. Corrected by ... Jwala Prasad Misra, *etc.* 1896. 8°. **14033. aa. 2.**

—— See TULASĪRĀMA SVĀMĪ. भास्करप्रकाश *etc.* (The Bhaskarprakasha. Or, Reply to Dayanand-timir-bhaskar[, Jvālāprasāda's polemic against Dayānanda's Satyārthaprakāśa.]) 1899. 8°. **14154. ee. 13.(1.)**

—— See VEDAS.—Yajurveda.—*Vājasaneyisaṃhitā.* वाजसनेयि ... संहिता *etc.* [Vājasaneyisaṃhitā. With interpretation and commentary in Hindi, *etc.*, by Jvālāprasāda.] [1903.] 8°. **14007. f. 4.**

—— जातिनिर्णयः *etc.* [Jātinirṇaya. An anthology of passages bearing upon the functions, *etc.*, of the castes, with Hindi translation and notes.] pp. 93. कल्याण-मुंबई १९५७ [*Kalyan,* 1900.] 8°. **14058. b. 43.**

JVĀLĀPRASĀDA MIŚRA, *of Garhi Khiri, Parshadepur.* See TANTRAS. [*Dattātreyatantra.*] दत्तात्रेयतन्त्रम् *etc.* [Dattātreyatantra. Edited with Hindi translation by Jvālāprasāda.] [1902.] 12°. **14033. aa. 29.**

JVĀLĀPRASĀDA ŚARMĀ, *son of Nāthūrām, Bhārgava.* See VEDAS.—*Sāmaveda.* श्रीसामवेदस्य संहिता *etc.* [Sāmaveda. Edited with interpretation and commentary in Hindi by Jvālāprasāda.] [1890-1891.] 8°. **14010. d. 30.**

JWALA PRASAD MISRA. See JVĀLĀPRASĀDA MIŚRA.

K ... CHAUDHURI. See CHAUDHURĪ (K.).

KABIBHUSHAN (R. K.). See KAVIBHŪSHAṆA (R. K.).

KABĪR. See TANTRAS. [*Brahmayāmalatantra.*] कबीरशतक *etc.* [Kabīr-śataka. A century on the significance of the name and attributes of Kabīr.] [1901.] 8°. **14033. bbb. 15.(1.)**

KACHCHĀYANA.

KACHCHĀYANAPPAKARAṆA.

කාච්චායන සූත්‍රපාඨය *etc.* [Sūtrapāṭha.] pp. i. 10, i. කොළඹ [*Colombo,*] 1895. 8°. **14098. c. 42.(4.)**

KACHCHĀYANA (*continued*).

Kachchayana's Pali Grammar. Edited in Devanagari character and translated ... [with introduction] by Satis Chandra Acharyya, *etc.* pp. ii. xliii. 383. 1901. *See* ACADEMIES, *etc.*—Calcutta.—*Mahābodhi Society.* **14098. a. 39.**

သဒ္ဒါကြီးဥဒေါင်နှိသျှန်းကျောင်းပု [Saddā-kyī. Being the aphorisms of Kachchāyana's Pali grammar and the *vārttikas* thereupon, together with the Burmese commentary of Khemaraṃsi upon the Taddhitakappa and that of Aggadhammālaṅkāra on the other sections.] 2 vols. ရန်ကုန် ၁၂၅၅–၁၂၅၇ [*Rangoon,* 1894-1896.] 8°. **14098. ccc. 13.**

သဒ္ဒါရှစ်စောင်သုတ်နက် [Saddā-shitsaung-thôk-net. The aphorisms of Kachchāyana without *vārttikas,* and with a brief Burmese commentary by Ū Jotika. Edited by Vimalālaṅkāra Kaviddhaja. Second edition.] pp. 151. ရန်ကုန် ၁၂၅၉ [*Rangoon,* 1897.] 8°. **14098. ccc. 12.(2.)**

—— [Third edition.] pp. 197. ရန်ကုန် ၁၂၆၀ [*Rangoon,* 1899.] 8°. **14098. ccc. 12.(3.)**

ဗါးကရာမူ။သဒ္ဒါကြီး *etc.* [Bā-ka-ya-mū Saddā-kyī. A version of the Saddā-kyī, containing the aphorisms of Kachchāyana without *vārttikas,* and with a brief Burmese commentary based upon that of Aggadhammālaṅkāra, by Tipiṭakālaṅkāra. To which are appended 3 Burmese dissertations entitled Sā-sat-hso-yo, Gaṇabhedadīpanī, and Samāsagaṇṭhi.] pp. 295. ရန်ကုန် ၁၂၅၉ [*Rangoon,* 1898.] 8°. **14098. ccc. 12.(1.)**

သဒ္ဒါကြီးဂဏ္ဌိကျမ်း *etc.* [Saddā-kyī-gaṇṭhi, or Saddalakkhaṇavibhāvanī. Comprising Kachchāyana's aphorisms and Dīpālaṅkāra's Burmese commentary. Followed by the Saddā-lûn, containing the aphorisms with Obhāsālaṅkāra's Burmese commentary, and Jāgarābhiddhaja's Saddamedhanī, a Burmese essay on terms of Pali grammar.] pp. ii. 13, 583, viii. မန္တလေး [*Mandalay,*] 1900. 8°. **14098. dd. 21.**

KACHCHĀYANA (*continued*).

သဒ္ဒါလွန် နယရွှေသိမ်းသောင်း *etc.* [Saddā-lûn. A Burmese grammar of the Pali language based upon and containing Kachchāyana's aphorisms. Followed by Naya-shwe-thein-thaung, a Burmese treatise on Pali semasiology and syntax by the Saṅgharāja of the Shwe-kyaung, and Saddatthamedhajotaka-kyan, a Burmese dissertation on Pali grammatical terms illustrating Kachchāyana.] pp. 235. ရန်ကုန် ၁၂၆၂ [*Rangoon*, 1900.] 8°. **14098. ccc. 32.**

သဒ္ဒဝိဝိဓဝိနိစ္ဆယကျမ်း *etc.* [Saddavividhavinichchhaya-kyan, also styled Saddā-kyan-tet. A grammar of the Pali language, consisting of Kachchāyana's aphorisms with Burmese commentaries and dissertations.] pp. 328. မန္တလေး [*Mandalay*,] 1900. 8°. **14098. ccc. 30.(1.)**

မှန်ပြသုတ်စဉ် [Hman-pya-thôk-sin. A table of the aphorisms of the Nāmakappa.] *See* PAÑÑĀLAṄKĀRA, *of Maṅgalārāma.* နာမမာလာကျမ်း *etc.* [Nāmamālā.] pp. 256-261. 1895. 8°. **14098. ccc. 17.(1.)**

See PAṆḌITADDHAJA SĪLĀLAṄKĀRA. သဒ္ဒါပုဒ်စိတ်။ အကျယ် *etc.* [Saddā-pôk-sit-akyay. A Burmese supercommentary on Kachchāyana, based on Ñāṇābhidhammālaṅkāra's commentary on the Mukhamattadīpanī, *etc.*] [1896.] 8°. **14302. i. 15.**

See SADDĀ-NGAY. သဒ္ဒာငယ် *etc.* [Saddā-ngay. A collection of grammatical works based on Kachchāyana.] [1898-1900.] 8°. **14098. ccc. 22.**

See SADDĀ-NGAY. သဒ္ဒါငယ် *etc.* [Saddā-ngay.] [1898.] 8°. **14098. ccc. 23.(1.)**

—— —— [Second edition.] [1899.] 8°. **14098. ccc. 24.(1.)**

See THA TO AUNG. A Grammar of the Pali Language after Kaccâyana, *etc.* 1899-1902. 8°. **14098. dd. 18.**

KACHCHĀYANA (*continued*).

BĀLĀVATĀRA.

Bálávatára. Pali grammar [traditionally said to have been composed] by ... Dhammakitti Sangharája Thera. With a commentary [in Pali, and an introduction in English and in Pali], by the Venerable H. Sumangala. (බාලාවතාරෙය) pp. vii. 8, ii. 327, iii. *Colombo*, 1892. 8°. **14098. c. 60.**

ဗာလာဝတာရဋီကာပါဠိ *etc.* [Bālāvatāra. With the commentary of H. Sumaṅgala. Edited by Paṇḍava Mahāthera.] pp. iv. 468. ရန်ကုန် ၁၂၆၁ [*Rangoon*, 1900.] 8°. **14098. ccc. 27.(2.)**

CHŪLANIRUTTI.

අභිනව චූලනිරුත්තිපකරණං *etc.* [Abhinava-chūlanirutti. A new recension of the Chūlanirutti, compiled by Saddhammālaṅkara. Edited by Dharmasādhaka Sāmi.] pp. 36. කොළඹ [*Colombo*,] 1896. 12°. **14098. a. 7.(3.)**

RŪPASIDDHI.

මහාරූපසිද්ධි සන්නය *etc.* [Rūpasiddhi, or Mahārūpasiddhi. A grammar of the Pali language by Dīpaṅkara, based on Kachchāyana's Aphorisms. Edited with annotations in Pali and Sinhalese by M. Sumaṅgala and B. Dhammaratana.] pts. i. ii. pp. i. 137. කොළඹ [*Colombo*,] 1891-1897. 8°. **14098. d. 39.**

මහාරූපසිද්ධි *etc.* (Mahárúpasiddhi, or A superior grammar of Páli [comprising the aphorisms of Kachchāyana with commentary] by the Venerable Buddhappiya, Maha Thera. Edited by the Reverend M. Gunaratana.) pp. 279. *Brandiawatta*, 1897. 8°. **14098. dd. 14.**

ပဟာရူပသိဒ္ဓိပါဠိ *etc.* [Rūpasiddhi.] pp. xxviii. 321. ရန်ကုန် ၁၂၆၂ [*Rangoon*, 1900.] 8°. **14098. dd. 20.**

သဒ္ဒါရှစ်စောင်သုတ်နက်သစ် *etc.* [Saddā-shit-saung-thôk-net-thit. Comprising Kachchāyana's aphorisms together with brief Pali notes based on the Rūpasiddhi, *etc.*, and a Burmese commentary by Ū Nāga.] pp. 284, ix. ပဒ္ဒေလး ၁၂၆၂ [*Mandalay*, 1901.] 8°. **14098. dd. 19.**

Das Sechste Kapitel der Rūpasiddhi, nach drei singhalesischen Pâli-Handschriften herausgegeben. Inaugural-Dissertation der philosophischen Fakultät zu München . . . von Albert Grünwedel. pp. viii. 72. *Berlin*, 1883. 8°.
14098. b. 15.(2.)

NETTIPPAKARAṆA.

The Netti-pakaraṇa. With extracts from Dhammapāla's commentary. Edited by Prof. E. Hardy. 1902. 8°. *See* ACADEMIES, *etc.*—London.—*Pali Text Society*. KACHCHĀYANA. **14098. b. 36.(2.)**

KACHRĀBHĀĪ GOPĀLADĀSA. *See* JINAKĪRTI SŪRI. धन्नाशालिभद्रनो रास *etc.* [Dhannā-Śālibhadra-no Rās. Edited by Kachrābhāī.] [1894.] 8°.
14144. f. 26.

—— *See* SŪTRAKṚIDAṄGA. महावीरस्तुति *etc.* [Mahāvīrastuti. With Gujarati interpretation. Edited by Kachrābhāī.] [1892.] 12°. **14100. a. 14.**

KAHĀNJĪ DHARMASIṂHA. *See* PARĀŚARA. [*Smṛiti.*] श्रीपराशरसंहिता *etc.* [Parāśarasaṃhitā. With Gujarati translation. Edited by Kahānjī.] [1899.] 8°. **14038. c. 48.(2.)**

KAHLANA. *See* KALHAṆA.

KAILĀSA ŚĀSTRĪ, *Brahmaśrī, of Trichinopoly.* ஸ்துதிரத்நாகரம் *etc.* [Stutiratnākara. A collection of songs on moral and religious subjects, compiled and in part composed by Kailāsa Śāstrī, for the use of the schools of the Trichinopoly Hindu Religious Union.] pp. i. 35. கும்பகோணம் [*Kumbakonam*, 1902.] 8°.
14076. a. 23.(4.)

KAIVALYĀŚRAMA, *Commentator on the Ānandalaharī.* *See* ŚAṄKARA ĀCHĀRYA.—*Doubtful and Supposititious Works.* Ānanda Lahari. With . . . commentaries [based on the Saubhāgyavardhinī of Kaivalyāśrama, *etc.*] Translated into English, *etc.* 1899. 12°. **14048. b. 35.**

KAIYYAṬA. *See* NĀGEŚA BHAṬṬA. [*Mahābhāshyapradīpoddyota.*] Mahābhāṣya Pradīpoddyota[, a commentary on Kaiyyaṭa's Mahābhāshyapradīpa,] *etc.* 1901, *etc.* 8°. [*Bibliotheca Indica.*]
14002. a. (vol. 140.)

KĀLĀMṚITA. ಕಾಲಾಮೃತಗ್ರಂಥವು *etc.* [Kālāmṛita. With the Sanskrit commentary of Veṅkaṭa Yajvā, and a Canarese paraphrase by S. Veṅkaṭeśa Śāstrī.] pp. vi. 296. *Bangalore*, 1891. 8°.
14053. cc. 61.

KĀLATATTVAVIVEKAVALLARI. ಶ್ರೀ . . . ಸ್ವಪ್ನಮಂಜರಿಯು *etc.* [Svapnamañjari. A tract on dream-interpretation, extracted from the Kālatattvavivekavallari. Edited with Canarese translation by Doḍḍabeli Nārāyaṇa Śāstrī.] pp. 179. ಬೆಂಗಳೂರು ೧೮೯೬ [*Bangalore*, 1896.] 8°.
14053. ccc. 10.

KALE (M. R.). *See* MOREŚVARA RĀMACHANDRA KĀḶE.

KALE (R. R.). *See* RĀUJĪ RĀMACHANDRA KĀḶE.

KALHAṆA. Kalhaṇa's Râjataraṅgiṇî, or Chronicle of the Kings of Kashmir. Edited by M. A. Stein . . . Vol. I. Sanskrit text with critical notes. pp. xix. 296. *Bombay*, 1892. 4°.
14058. d. 4.

—— The Râjataraṅgiṇî of Kalhaṇa. Edited by Durgâprasâda, son of Vrajalâla. Vol. I. Tarangas I-VII. (Vol. II, Taranga VIII. Vol. III, containing the supplements to the work of Jonarâja, Srîvara and Prâjyabhaṭṭa. Edited by P. Peterson.) (राजतरङ्गिणी ।) 3 vols. *Bombay*, 1892-1896. 8°. **14058. b. 27.**

Forming nos. xlv., li., *and* liv. *of the* Bombay Sanskrit Series.

—— Kings of Káshmíra: being a translation of the Sanskrita work Rájataranggini of Kahlana Pandita. By Jogesh Chunder Dutt. (Vol. iii. Kings of Kashmíra: being a translation of the Sanskrita works of Jonarāja, Shrīvara, and of Prājyabhaṭṭa and Shuka.) 3 vols. *Calcutta*, 1879-1898. 12°. **14070. b. 13.**

—— Kalhaṇa's Rājataraṅgiṇī, a chronicle of the kings of Kaśmīr. Translated, with an introduction, commentary, and appendices, by M. A. Stein. Vol. I. Introduction. Books i.-vii. (Vol. II. Book viii. Notes. Geographical Memoir. Index. Maps.) 2 vols. *Westminster*, 1900. 4°.
14058. c. 9.

KĀLĪCHARAṆA MITRA. *See* UTPALA DEVĀCHĀRYA. शिवस्तोत्रावली . . . Sivastotrâvalî . . . with the commentary of Kshemarâja. Edited by . . . Pramadâdâsa Mittra . . . and . . . Kâlîcharaṇa Mittra. 1902, *etc.* 8°. **14004. a. 15.**

KĀLĪCHARAṆA ŚARMĀ, *son of Gokulachandra, of Agra. See* BHĀVA MIŚRA. भावप्रकाश *etc.* [Bhāvaprakāśa. With Hindi translation by Kālīcharaṇa.] [1894.] 4°. **14043. f. 4.**

—— *See* MĀGHA. शिशुपालवध *etc.* [Śiśupālavadha. With Hindi translation by Kālīcharaṇa.] [1891.] 8°. **14076. d. 47.**

—— *See* PURĀṆAS.—*Matsyapurāṇa.* मत्स्यपुराण *etc.* [Matsyapurāṇa. Edited by Vasatirāma and Kālīcharaṇa.] [1892.] 4°. **14018. c. 31.**

KĀLIDĀSA. [*Life.*] *See* KRISHṆAMŪRTI KAVIRĀJA, *Śrīpāda.* కాళిదాసవిలాసము *etc.* [Kālidāsavilāsa. A romantic account of Kālidāsa's career, in Telugu, interspersed with Sanskrit stanzas.] [1899.] 8°. **14174. g. 51.**

COLLECTED WORKS.

মহাকবি কালিদাসের গ্রন্থাবলী *etc.* [Granthāvalī. Comprising the Raghuvaṃśa and Meghadūta, with commentaries of Mallinātha; Ṛitusaṃhāra, with gloss of Maṇirāma; Dvātriṃśatputtalikā, or Vikramārkacharita; Pushpabāṇavilāsa, with commentary of Veṅkaṭa; Nalodaya, with commentary of Prajñākara; Kumārasambhava, with that of Mallinātha on i.-vii., and that of Rohiṇīnandana Sarkār on viii.-xvii.; Mālavikāgnimitra, with commentary; Abhijñānaśakuntala and Vikramorvaśīya, with gloss by Tejaśchandra Vidyānanda; and Śrutabodha, Śṛiṅgāratilaka, and Śṛiṅgārarasāshṭaka, with gloss of Kālīpada Vidyāratna. With analyses and Bengali translations. Edited by Kālīpada Vidyāratna.] pp. 2375, 390, 217, 21, 15, 6. কলিকাতা ১৩০২ [*Calcutta,* 1895.] 8°. **14070. d. 34.**

মহাকবি কালিদাসের গ্রন্থাবলি [Granthāvali. Comprising the Raghuvaṃśa, Kumārasambhava, Abhijñānaśakuntala, Meghadūta, and Ṛitusaṃhāra.] pp. 141, 103, 120, 21, 20. কলিকাতা ১৩০৬ [*Calcutta,* 1899.] 12°. **14076. a. 25.**

KĀLIDĀSA. COLLECTED WORKS (*continued*).

Works of Kalidasa. Translaed [*sic*] from original Sanskrit into English. 1. Shakuntala [in the translation of Sir W. Jones], 2. Vikrama-urvashi [translated by H. H. Wilson], 3. Kumarasambhavam, 4. Megha-duta [translated by H. H. Wilson], 5. Ritu-samhara, 6. Raghuvamsha. 6 pts. *Calcutta,* 1901. 12°. **14080. b. 10.**

—— [Another copy.] **14070. b. 30.**

SELECTIONS.

See KRISHṆAM ĀCHĀRYA, *Maṅgāḍu.* Portraits from Indian Classics, *etc.* 1901. 12°. **14070. b. 31.**

कालिदास-सूक्तय: Kalidas's Apothegms [*sic*]. [Selected, with English and Bengali paraphrases,] by Rai Radhanath Rai Bahadur . . . Bengal-edition. pp. iii. i. 102. *Calcutta,* [1903.] 12°. **14085. b. 23.(2.)**

—— Indian edition [in Sanskrit and English only]. pp. iii. 71. *Calcutta,* [1903.] 12°. **14085. b. 23.(3.)**

ABHIJÑĀNAŚAKUNTALA.

The Abhijnánaśakuntala of Kálidása. With the commentary styled 'Arthadyotanika of Rághavabhatta. Edited with an English translation, critical and explanatory notes, and various readings, by M. R. Kále. (अभिज्ञानशकुन्तलम्) pp. xxxii. x. ii. 214, iii. 15, 92, 131. *Bombay,* 1898. 8°. **14080. c. 37.**

अभिज्ञानशकुन्तलम् *etc.* (Kalidasa's Abhijnana Sakuntalam. Edited with an introduction, glossary, English and Bengali translations, various readings, &&&. [*sic*] and the commentary Sarala by Pandit Nabin Chandra Vidyaratna . . . New edition.) pp. ix. xii. 418, 352, viii. कलिकाताया १८२२ [*Calcutta,* 1901.] 8°. **14080. c. 41.**

English title taken from wrapper.

The Abhijnânaśakuntala of Kalidasa. The purer Devanagari text. Edited with a literal English translation, various readings, a preface principally treating of the relative value of the several recensions, full notes and useful appendices. By P. N. Patankar. Second edition. pp. xix. ii. 223, 89, vi. xvi. iii. *Poona,* 1902. 8°.

14080. d. 26.

Śakoontalá, or The Lost Ring. An Indian drama. Translated into English prose and verse . . . by Sir Monier Monier-Williams. pp. xl. 240. *London, Edinburgh* [printed], 1894. 8°.

012207. l. 81.

A Literal English Translation of Abhijnana Sakuntala, together with an introduction, by T. R. Ratnam Aiyar. Second edition. pp. viii. 84. *Madras,* 1896. 8°. **14079. b. 23.(2.)**

Shakuntala, or The Fatal Ring. An Indian drama by Calidasa. Reprinted from the translation of Sir William Jones. pp. iv. ii. 74. *Calcutta,* 1899. 12°. **14079. a. 8.(3.)**

Kalidasa's Sakuntala; or The Fatal Ring. [In the translation of Sir W. Jones, slightly abridged.] *See* Holme (T.). Sakuntala, *etc.* pp. 1-127. [1902.] 8°. **012208. ee. 117.**

Sakuntala. Indisches Schauspiel von Kalidasa. Frei bearbeitet von Gustav Schmilinsky. pp. 106. *Leipzig, Dresden* [printed], 1900. 8°.

14079. b. 40.(2.)

Sakuntala. Ein indisches Spiel des Königs [*sic*] Kalidasa. In deutscher Bühnenfassung von Marx Möller. pp. i. 117. *Berlin,* [1902?] 8°.

14080. c. 43.

Sakuntala. Hindu dráma. Irta Kálidász. Fordidotta Fiók Károly. Kiadja a Kisfaludy-Társaság. pp. 268. *Budapest,* 1887. 8°.

Ac. 8983/23.

See Jennings (J. G.). Sakuntala. A play [based upon the drama of Kālidāsa,] *etc.* 1902. 12°. **11779. ff. 9.**

See Kālīpada Mukhopādhyāya. Notes on Sakuntala, *etc.* 1895. 12°.

14072. b. 22.

See Naṭeṣa Ṣāstrī. A Review of Sakuntala, *etc.* 1897. 8°. **14079. b. 41.**

KĀLIDĀSA. Abhijñānaṣakuntala (*continued*).

See Ṣrīnivāsa Dīkshita, *K.* శ్రీ . . . కృత్యయోరిత్యాదేః శ్లోకస్య తా॥ [An essay upon the interpretation of stanza 51 (beginning *Kṛityayor bhinnadeṣatvād*) of the Abhijñānaṣakuntala.] [1902.] 16°.

14076. a. 16.(5.)

Kumārasambhava.

Kumarasambhabam. As fixed for the B.A. Course,—Cantos I, II, III, IV, V, VI, VII. Text with notes by Pundit Nobin Ch. Vidyaratna . . . with English and Bengali translations and model questions with model answers. pp. 764. *Calcutta,* [1894.] 12°. **14070. c. 57.(2.)**

कुमारसंभवम् [Kumārasambhava. With short notes in Sanskrit and English.] *See* Periodical Publications.—*Poona.* The Kavi, *etc.* Vol. i., pts. 8, 9. 1895. 8°. **14070. c. 56.**

Incomplete, breaking off after Canto IV, 31.

ಕುಮಾರಸಂಭವ ಕಾವ್ಯ ಪ್ರಾರಂಭಃ [Kumārasambhava. With the commentary of Mallinātha, Canarese notes, and Canarese paraphrase.] *See* Periodical Publications.—*Bangalore.* Kâvyakalpadrumam, *etc.* Vol. I, pt. 1. 1897. 8°.

14076. cc. 1.

Incomplete, extending only to the 7th stanza.

Mālavikāgnimitra.

The Mâlavikâgnimitra . . . With the commentary [Kumāragirirājīya] of Kâṭayavema. Edited with notes by Shankar Pâṇḍurang Pandit. Second edition. pp. xxxv. 230, i. *Bombay,* 1889. 8°.

14080. c. 31.

Forms no. vi. of the Bombay Sanskrit Series.

The Mâlavikâgnimitram . . . Edited with a close English translation chiefly collected from the notes given in class by the late Mr. V. S. Apte . . . and copious English notes by Sadâsiv Bhimrâo Bhâgwat . . . under the general supervision of Nârâyan Bâlkrishna Godabole. (मालविकाग्निमित्रं नाम नाटकम्) pp. i. 124, ii. *Poona,* 1897. 8°.

14079. c. 66.

KĀLIDĀSA. Mālavikāgnimitra (*continued*).

The Mâlavikâgnimitra ... With the commentary of Kátayavêma and several others embodied therein, edited with critical notes and translation [in English] ... by Ṣ. Ṣêshâdri Ayyar. (मालविकाग्निमित्रं नाटकम्) pp. xvii. 158, 124. *Poona*, 1896. 8°. **14080. c. 36.**

मालविकाग्निमित्रम् [Mālavikāgnimitra. With English notes and translation by T. V. Vaidyanātha Aiyar.] pp. 82, 44, 80. *See* Academies, *etc.*—Madras.—*University of Madras.* Complete Sanskrit Text for the F. A. Examination, 1901, *etc.* 1900. 8°. **14072. ccc. 24.(2.)**

The Malavikágnimitra ... Literally translated into English prose by C. H. Tawney. Second edition. pp. xvi. 96. *Calcutta*, 1891. 12°. **14080. b. 9.(1.)**

Malavikagnimitra ... literally translated into English, together with an introduction. By T. R. Ratnam Aiyer. Second edition. pp. i. i. xii. i. 69. *Trichinopoly*, 1891. 8°. **14079. c. 58.**

Meghadūta.

॥ श्री ... मेघधूत [*sic*], *etc.* [Meghadūta. With an *avachūrṇi* by Kanakakīrti Gaṇī.] ff. 28, *lith.* काशी १९२४ [*Benares*, 1867.] *obl.* 4°. **14072. e. 3.**

The Meghadûta ... With the commentary of Mallinâtha ... Edited with a literal English translation, with copious notes in English, and with various readings, by Gopal Raghunatha Nandargikar. pp. viii. lxxxiv. 100, 118. *Bombay*, 1894. 8°. **14076. c. 63.**

The Meghadûta. As embodied [in the form of *samasyā*] in the Párśvábhyudaya [of Jinasena Āchārya] with the commentary of Mallinátha ... and a literal English translation, various readings, critical notes, and an introductory essay, determining the date of Kâlidâsa ... Edited by Kashinath Bapu Pathak. pp. xvi. iv. 106, i. xxvi. *Poona*, 1894. 8°. **14076. b. 32.**

KĀLIDĀSA. Meghadūta (*continued*).

मेघदूतम् ... The Meghadúta ... With the commentary of Mallinátha and ... extracts from the ... commentaries of Bharata, Sanátana, Makaranda, Kalyánmalla, and nine others. Edited by Lálmohan Vidyánidhi Bhattácharya. pp. iii. 102. *Hooghly*, 1894. 8°. **14072. cc. 58.(1.)**

Exhaustive Notes on the Meghaduta ... Comprising various readings, the text with the commentary of Mallinath, literal translation in English, life of Kalidas, &c., &c. pp. 114, xi. 112. *Bombay*, 1894. 12°. **14076. a. 15.**

मेघदूतम् । [Meghadūta. With short notes in Sanskrit and English.] *See* Periodical Publications.—*Poona.* The Kavi, *etc.* Vol. i., pts. 7, 8. 1895. 8°. **14070. c. 56.**

मेघदूतकाव्याचें समवृत्त मराठी भाषांतर *etc.* [Meghadūta. Edited with a metrical Marathi version and notes by Lakshmaṇa Gaṇeṣa Ṣāstrī Lele.] pp. viii. 68. पुणें १९०१ [*Poona*, 1901.] 8°. **14070. dd. 20.**

Kalidasa's Meghadutam [I. 1-38]. Containing ... Mallinatha's commentary ... Bengali and English translations, Anglosanskrit notes ... with ... grammatical, rhetorical, and explanatory notes ... by Pandit Nabin Chandra Vidyaratna. New edition. pp. 168. *Calcutta*, [1901.] 8°. **14085. c. 49.(1.)**

यक्षसंदेश अर्थात् मेघदूताचें समवृत्त व समश्लोकी मराठी भाषांतर *etc.* [Yakshasandeṣa. Being the Meghadūta with a metrical Marathi version by Bhālachandra Ṣaṅkara Devasthaḷī.] pp. ii. 64. मुंबई १९०२ [*Bombay*, 1902.] 16°. **14076. a. 20.(2.)**

॥ धाराधरधावन ॥ ... Dhārā Dhara Dhāwana. Part ii., being a metrical Hindi translation of Kali Das' Uttara Megha or second part of Meghaduta, by Rai Debi Prasad, "Poorna." [With the Sanskrit text.] pp. iv. 39, ix. कानपुर १९०२ [*Cawnpore*, 1902.] 8°. **14072. cc. 58.(2.)**

The Cloud Messenger of Kálidása. The Uttaramegha. Translated into English verse by Annadáprasád Basu. pp. 24. *Calcutta*, 1885. 12°. **14072. b. 10.(1.)**

KĀLIDĀSA. Meghadūta (*continued*).

The Meghadûta, or Cloud Messenger. A poem in the Sanskrit language . . . Translated into English verse, with notes and illustrations, by H. H. Wilson . . . Edited by Lal Mohan Vidyanidhi. pp. 93. *Calcutta*, 1901. 8°.
14070. dd. 22.

The Meghaduta; or, Cloud Messenger. [In the version of H. H. Wilson.] *See* Holme (T.). Sakuntala, *etc.* pp. 131-155. [1902] 8°.
012208. ee. 117.

Meghadûta. Le Nuage Messager . . . Traduction française par A. Guérinot. pp. ix. 95. *Paris, Le Puy-en-Velay* [printed], 1902. 12°. **14080. b. 11.**

Forms no. lxxx. *of the* Bibliothèque Orientale Elzévirienne.

Meghadūta o la Nube Messaggera. Tradotto da Giovanni Flechia. [With a note on the geography of the poem, by F. L. Pullé.] pp. 152. 1897-1899. *See* Periodical Publications. — *Florence.* Studi Italiani di Filologia Indo-Iranica, *etc.* Vol. I—III. 1897, *etc.* 8°. **P.P. 4884. da. (vol. 1-3.)**

—— [A separate issue of the preceding.]
14070. dd. 7.

See Dhoyī. Nachahmungen des Meghadūta, *etc.* 1900. 8°. [*Zeitschrift der Deutschen Morgenlaendischen Gesellschaft.*]
Ac. 8815/2. (vol. 54.)

See Jinasena Āchārya. पार्श्वाभ्युदय° [Pārṣvābhyudaya. A poem in which are incorporated the verses of the Meghadūta.] [1893.] 8°. [*Kāvyāmbudhi.*] **14028. c. 64.**

See Vikrama, *son of Sāṅgaṇa.* नेमिदूतकाव्य *etc.* [Nemidūta, or Nemicharita. A Jain poem, containing a line of Kālidāsa's Meghadūta interwoven in every stanza.] [1892.] 12°. **14028. b. 69. (3.)**

Raghuvaṃṣa.

॥ रघुवंशम् ॥ [Raghuvaṃṣa. With short notes in Sanskrit and English.] *See* Periodical Publications.—*Poona.* The Kavi, *etc.* Vol. i., pts. 1-7. 1895. 8°. **14070. c. 56.**

The Raghuvanśa of Kâlidâsa . . . with the commentary of Mallinâtha, edited with a literal English translation, with copious notes in English intermixed with full extracts . . . from the commentaries of Bhatta Hemâdri, Châritravardhana, Vallabha, Dinakaramiśra, Sumativijaya, Vijayagani, Vijayânandasûriśvaracharanasevaka and Dharmameru, with various readings &c., &c., by Gopal Raghunath Nandargikar. Third edition. Revised and enlarged. pp. i. x. xviii. 202, 600, ccclxxiv. xi. *Poona*, 1897. 8°. **14072. c. 53.**

రఘువంశాఖ్యమహాకావ్యే ఏకాదిదశసర్గాన్త-ర్గ్రన్థః *etc.* [Raghuvaṃṣa, i.–x.] pp. 96. మహీ-శూరు॥ ౧౮౯౦ [*Mysore*, 1890.] 12°.
14072. b. 19.

Raghuvanśam, Cantos i.–v. (vi., vii.), literally translated into English, with notes, elucidatory, critical, and grammatical, followed by a glossary, by Kunja Lál Nág. 3 pts. *Calcutta*, 1893-1897. 8°. **14072. ccc. 19. (2.)**

Raghubamsam. Cantos i.—vi. Containing prose version, paraphrase . . . Sanjivani . . . Bengali and English translations of all the slokas, grammatical and explanatory notes both in English and Sanskrit . . . &c. &c. &c. . . . Edited by Pandit Nabin Chandra Vidyaratna. Thoroughly revised and enlarged edition. 2 pts. *Calcutta*, 1901. 8°.
14085. c. 50.

Contains only Cantos i. *and* ii.

रघुवंशम् [Raghuvaṃṣa, i.–v. With notes and translation by T. V. Vaidyanātha Aiyar.] pp. 34, 202. *See* Academies, *etc.*—Madras.—*University of Madras.* Complete Sanskrit Text for the F.A. Examination, 1901, *etc.* 1900. 8°. **14072. ccc. 24. (2.)**

F.A. Examination of 1892. The Complete Sanskrit Text[, viz. Raghuvaṃṣa iii.–xi. and the Sundarakāṇḍa of Bhoja's Champūrāmāyaṇa. Edited,] with exaustive [*sic*] Sanskrit commentary, copious English notes, and . . . translation, by S. Rangachariar . . . and V. Srinivasa Aiyar. 5 pts. *Tanjore*, 1891. 8°. **14076. c. 59.**

Il Laménto dél Ré Àgia sópra Indumatî súa mòglie di Kâlidâsa [*i.e.* Sarga 8]. Côi comménti di Mallinâṫa. Recàto di sàmskṛito a comúne volgàre pér cúra di Giusèppe Turríni. *Bologna*, 1899, *etc.* 4°.
14070. e. 20.

In progress?

KĀLIDĀSA. RAGHUVAṂṢA (*continued*).

రఘువంశాఖ్యమహాకావ్యే ఏకాదశాద్యేకోనవింశసర్గాంతసమగ్రగ్రంథః *etc.* [Raghuvaṃṣa, xi.–xxi. With the commentary of Mallinātha.] pp. 260. మహీశూరు ౧౮౯౦ [*Mysore*, 1890.] 8°. **14072. cc. 53.**

The Raghuvança. The story of Raghu's line ... Translated [into verse] by P. de Lacy Johnstone. pp. xlviii. 200. *London*, 1902. 8°. **14072. c. 57.**

Raghuvansa. Ein indisches Gedicht ... In deutscher Nachbildung von Adolf Friedrich Graf von Schack. (Orient and Occident. III.) pp. vi. 167. *Stuttgart*, 1890. 8°. **12205. e. 12.(no. 3.)**

ṚITUSAṂHĀRA.

The Ritusanhara of Kalidasa, with notes and English translation, by C. S. Sitaram Ayyar. (ऋतुसंहारम्) pp. iv. 20, 43. *Bombay*, 1897. 8°. **14070. c. 60.**

ऋतुसंहारः *etc.* [Ṛitusaṃhāra. With the commentary Chandrikā of Maṇirāma, and a Hindi translation by Vrajaratna Bhaṭṭāchārya.] pp. ii. ii. 94. कल्याण-मुंबई १९५७ [*Kalyan*, 1901.] 8°. **14070. dd. 21.(1.)**

ṢĀKUNTALA.

See above, ABHIJÑĀNAṢAKUNTALA.

VIKRAMORVAṢĪYA.

Vikramorvaśiyam, with Sanskrit text, English translation, copious notes, and an elaborate introduction, by Keshav Balkrishna Paranjpe. pp. i. xli. 149, xx. xviii. xiii. xi. xi. *Bombay*, 1898. 8°. **14080. c. 38.**

The Vikramorvaśîyam ... Edited with English notes, containing extracts from two commentaries, [*scil.* of Kāṭayavema and Raṅganātha,] by Shankar Pâṇḍurang Paṇḍit. Revised and improved, by Bhâskar Râmchandra Arte. Third edition. pp. x. ii. 1—171, 108A—136A, 1—177. *Bombay*, 1901. 8°. **14080. c. 42.**

Forms no. xvi. *of the* Bombay Sanskrit Series.

—— [Another copy.] **14080. c. 42.***

KĀLIDĀSA (*continued*).

SUPPOSITITIOUS WORKS.

କଟପାୟା *etc.* [Kaṭapāyā. 28 stanzas on the asterisms. Edited with an Oriya metrical version and further matter in Oriya by Abhinna Nāyaka.] pp. 12. *Cuttack*, 1880. 12°. **14053. b. 17.(2.)**

राक्षसकाव्यम् *etc.* [Rākshasakāvya. A poem in 20 stanzas ascribed to Kālidāsa. With a Sanskrit commentary and Hindi prose translation.] pp. 31. मुंबय्यां १८१६ [*Bombay*, 1895.] 12°. **14076. a. 23.(2.)**

শৃঙ্গারতিলকম্। (শৃঙ্গাররসাষ্টকম্।) [Ṣṛiṅgāratilaka. Followed by the Ṣṛiṅgārarasāshṭaka, another erotic poem also ascribed to Kālidāsa. With gloss by Kālīpada Vidyāratna and Bengali translation.] pp. 15, 6. *See* above, COLLECTED WORKS. মহাকবি কালিদাসের গ্রন্থাবলী *etc.* [Granthāvalī.] [Vol. 4.] [1895.] 8°. **14070. d. 34.(vol. 4.)**

J. Herrero. Poetas del Amor. Kalidasa: Gringara [*sic*] Tilaka [*i.e.* Ṣṛiṅgāratilaka.] Heine: Intermezzo. Versión Castellana. pp. xxiv. 146. *Madrid*, 1898. 12°. **14076. a. 18.**

श्रुतबोधः *etc.* [Ṣrutabodha. A compendium of metres, popularly ascribed to Kālidāsa.] pp. 6. कलिकाता १८९२ [*Calcutta*, 1892.] 8°. **14053. cc. 57.(2.)**

See Peterson, Third Report, *Appendix*, *p.* 225.

শ্রুতবোধঃ। [Ṣrutabodha. With a gloss by Kālīpada Vidyāratna and Bengali translation.] pp. 21. *See* above, COLLECTED WORKS. মহাকবি কালিদাসের গ্রন্থাবলী *etc.* [Granthāvalī.] [Vol. 4.] [1895.] 8°. **14070. d. 34.(vol. 4.)**

কালিদাসের কবিতা *etc.* [Kālidāser Kavitā. A cycle of stanzas entitled Kavitā, ascribed to Kālidāsa, with Bengali translations and notes, preceded by a biography and critique in Bengali. To which is added a selection of Sanskrit stanzas by various authors and some Hindi *dohās* by Tulasīdāsa, with Bengali translations. Compiled and edited by Vaishṇavacharaṇa Basāk.] pp. 132, 46. কলিকাতা ১৩০৩ [*Calcutta*, 1897.] 12°. **14127. aa. 14.(1.)**

কালিদাসের কবিতা *etc.* [Kālidāser Kavitā. Two series of stanzas, the first being entitled Vividha-

kavitā, or miscellaneous verses, and the second being the cycle known as Kavitā. Compiled and edited with a Bengali translation and romantic biography of the poet by Ṣaratkumāra Sena.] pp. 178. কলিকাতা ১৩০৮ [*Calcutta*, 1901.] 12°.
14076. b. 26.(2.)

চতুর্থ অধ্যায়। [Miscellaneous stanzas, purporting to be by Kālidāsa and other poets. With Bengali translation and additional matter.] *See* Nīlamaṇi Vidyālaṅkāra Bhaṭṭāchārya. উদ্ভট কবিতা-কৌমুদী *etc.* [Udbhaṭakavitākaumudī.] pt. i., pp. 42—70. [1890.] 8°.
14085. c. 43.

KĀLIDĀSA, called Veṅkaṭeṣvara. అథ...లమ్బో-దరప్రహసనాఖ్యరూపకః॥ [Lambodaraprahasana. A farce on the legend of Gaṇeṣa.] pp. 30. *See* Rāmachandra, *Veḷḷala.* శ్రీ . . . శ్రీకృష్ణవిజయము॥ [Kṛishṇavijaya, *etc.*] [1890.] 8°.
14080. d. 22.(1.)

KĀLIDĀSA, *Pseud., author of the Nalodaya.* নলোদয়ঃ। [Nalodaya. With the commentary Subodhinī of Prajñākara Miṣra and a Bengali version.] *See* Kālidāsa.—*Collected Works.* মহাকবি কালিদাসের গ্রন্থাবলী *etc.* [Granthāvalī.] [Vol. 2.] pp. 1273—1402. [1895.] 8°.
14070. d. 34.(vol. 2.)

—— नलोदयकाव्यम् *etc.* [Nalodaya. With Prajñākara's commentary Subodhinī. Edited by Nandalāla Ṣāstrī.] pp. i. 150. मुम्बय्यां १९५५ [*Bombay*, 1899.] 8°.
14070. dd. 11.

—— ॥ नलोदयकाव्यम् *etc.* [Nalodaya. With Prajñākara's Subodhini and a gloss by Bhāskarānanda Sarasvatī.] pp. 345. काश्यां १९५९ [*Benares*, 1902.] 8°.
14076. d. 54.

KĀLIDĀSA, *Pseud.*, [*i.e.* Kālidāsa Sārvabhauma Bhaṭṭāchārya.] পুষ্পবাণবিলাসঃ। [Pushpabāṇavilāsa. A poem in 26 stanzas on Kṛishṇa's amours. With commentary of Veṅkaṭa Sārvabhauma and Bengali translation.] *See* Kālidāsa.—*Collected Works.* মহাকবি কালিদাসের গ্রন্থাবলী *etc.* [Granthāvalī.] [Vol. 2.] pp. 1227—1272. [1895.] 8°.
14070. d. 34.(vol. 2.)

—— पुष्पबाणविलासम् *etc.* [Pushpabāṇavilāsa. With commentary of Veṅkaṭa Sārvabhauma. Edited by Kāṣīnātha Pāṇḍuraṅga Parab.] pp. 33. मुम्बय्याम् १९०१ [*Bombay*, 1901.] 8°.
14072. cc. 62.(3.)

KĀLIDĀSA GOVINDAJĪ, *Ṣāstri, of Jamnagar.* *See* Kamalākara Bhaṭṭa, *son of Rāmakṛishṇa.* निर्णयसिंधु *etc.* [Nirṇayasindhu. With Gujarati translation by Kālidāsa.] [1901.] 4°.
14028. dd. 11.

KĀLIKĀNANDA AVADHŪTA, *Kaula.* गंधोत्तमानिर्णय: [Gandhottamānirṇaya. A guide to salvation, based chiefly on tantric sources.] pp. 49. कानपुर १९०० [*Cawnpore*, 1900.] 8°.
14033. aa. 13.

KĀLĪKṚISHṆA BHAṬṬĀCHĀRYA. Notes on Utter-charita. B.A. Course for 1893 & 94. In the form of questions and answers, *etc.* pp. x. 158. *Calcutta*, [1893.] 12°.
14076. a. 14.

KĀLĪMOHANA BHAṬṬĀCHĀRYA. *See* Tantras. [*Yoginītantra.*] সানুবাদ যোগিনীতন্ত্রম্ *etc.* [Yoginītantra. Edited by Kālīmohana.] [1894.] 8°.
14033. aa. 12.

KĀLĪPADA MUKHOPĀDHYĀYA. Notes on Sakuntala [in Sanskrit, Bengali, and English] . . . With 1. Notes . . . 2. Translation. 3. Important appendices containing criticism of the important characters and University questions. pp. 323. *Calcutta*, 1895. 12°.
14072. b. 22.

KĀLĪPADA VIDYĀRATNA, *of Bhatpalli.* *See* Kālidāsa.—*Collected Works.* মহাকবি কালিদাসের গ্রন্থাবলী *etc.* [Granthāvalī. Comprising the Ṣrutabodha, Ṣriṅgāratilaka, and Ṣriṅgārarasāshṭaka, with gloss of Kālīpada, *etc.* Edited by Kālīpada.] [1895.] 8°.
14070. d. 34.

—— *See* Purāṇas.—*Mārkaṇḍeyapurāṇa.* [*Devīmāhātmya.*] শ্রীশ্রীচণ্ডী *etc.* [Chaṇḍī. Edited by Kālīpada.] [1900.] 16°.
14028. a. 29.

—— *See* Ṣātātapa. শাতাতপীয়-কর্ম্মবিপাকঃ *etc.* [Ṣātātapīya-karmavipāka. Edited by Kālīpada.] [1902.] 8°.
14033. aa. 28.(3.)

KĀLĪPRASANNA KAVIṢEKHARA, *Kavirāja.* *See* Bhāva Miṣra. সানুবাদ-ভাবপ্রকাশঃ *etc.* [Bhāvaprakāṣa. Edited with Bengali translation by Kālīprasanna.] [1901.] 8°.
14043. dd. 9.

—— *See* Suṣruta. সুশ্রুত-সংহিতা *etc.* [Suṣruta-saṃhitā. With commentary of Ḍallaṇa. Edited with Bengali translation by Kālīprasanna.] [1898.]. 8°.
14043. dd. 8.

KĀLĪPRASANNA KAVIṢEKHARA, *Kavirāja (continued)*. রত্নপ্রভা *etc.* [Ratnaprabhā. A metrical compilation upon Materia Medica, in 18 *adhyāyas*. With Bengali translation and notes.] pp. i. xvi. 268. *Calcutta*, [1901.] 8°. **14043. cc. 21.**

KĀLĪPRASANNA VIDYĀRATNA BHAṬṬĀCHĀRYA, *of Mallikpur, Jessore.* See NĀGA BHAṬṬA. কামরত্ন *etc.* [Kāmaratna. Edited with Bengali translation by Kālīprasanna.] [1894.] 8°. **14033. bb. 43.**

—— See PARĀṢARA. [*Smṛiti.*] সানুবাদ পরাশর-সংহিতা *etc.* [Parāṣarasaṃhitā. Edited with Bengali translation by Kālīprasanna.] [1903.] 8°. **14039. b. 15.(3.)**

—— See PAVANAVIJAYA. পবনবিজয় স্বরোদয়ঃ *etc.* [Pavanavijaya-svarodaya. Edited by Kālīprasanna.] [1892.] 12°. **14028. b. 72.(2.)**

—— See PURĀṆAS.—*Kalkipurāṇa.* কল্কিপুরাণম্ *etc.* [Kalkipurāṇa. With Bengali translation by Kālīprasanna.] [1899.] 8°. **14016. d. 36.(2.)**

—— See RATIMAÑJARĪ. রতিমঞ্জরী *etc.* [Ratimañjarī. Edited by Kālīprasanna.] [1901.] 12°. **14053. b. 41.(1.)**

—— See RATIṢĀSTRA. রতি-শাস্ত্র *etc.* [Ratiṣāstra. With Bengali translation by Kālīprasanna.] [1895.] 12°. **14053. b. 28.**

—— See SĀMUDRIKA. বৃহৎসামুদ্রিক *etc.* [Sāmudrika. Enlarged and edited with Bengali translation by Kālīprasanna.] [1892.] 8°. **14053. cc. 66.**

—— See ṢAṄKARA ĀCHĀRYA. — *Two or More Works.* শঙ্করাচার্য্যের গ্রন্থমালা *etc.* [Ṣaṅkarāchāryer Granthamālā. With Bengali translations by Kālīprasanna.] [1903.] 8°. **14033. aa. 30.**

—— হিন্দু-তীর্থ তরঙ্গিণী। যাবতীয় তীর্থকৃত্যসম্বলিত *etc.* [Hindutīrthataraṅgiṇī. A handbook for pilgrims visiting the holy places, comprising Sanskrit texts on the various legends and rites with Bengali translations, notes, and ritual rules.] pp. ii. iv. 184. কলিকাতা ১৩১০ [*Calcutta*, 1903.] 8°. **14039. b. 15.(4.)**

—— কবির ঝঙ্কার। বিচিত্র বিচিত্র উদ্ভট শ্লোকাবলী *etc.* [Kavir Jhaṅkāra. 717 miscellaneous stanzas, compiled from various sources, with Bengali translation and notes.] pp. xvii. 306. কলিকাতা ১৩০৯ [*Calcutta*, 1902.] 12°. **14076. a. 28.**

—— নিত্যতন্ত্রম্ *etc.* [Nityatantra. A work on tantric practices of religion, with Bengali version. Compiled by Kālīprasanna.] pp. ii. 140. *Calcutta*, 1900. 8°. **14033. aa. 18.**

—— যোগাঙ্কুর অর্থাৎ যোগশিক্ষার সহজ উপায় *etc.* [Yogāṅkura. A collection of tracts on the Yoga, comprising the Shaṭchakra of Pūrṇānanda Gosvāmī, the Kshurikopanishad, the Rāmagītā from the Adhyātmarāmāyaṇa, and the Pañcharatnastotra from the Muṇḍamālātantra. With commentaries and Bengali translations.] pp. ii. 159. কলিকাতা ১৩০০ [*Calcutta*, 1894.] 12°. **14048. b. 28.(2.)**

KĀLĪVARA VEDĀNTAVĀGĪṢA. See BHĀSKARA, *son of Mudgala.* পূর্ব্বমীমাংসার্থসংগ্রহঃ *etc.* [Arthasaṅgraha. With commentary. Edited by Kālīvara.] [1897.] 8°. **14048. b. 21.(2.)**

—— See SADĀNANDA YOGĪNDRA. সটীক . . . বেদান্তসার *etc.* [Vedāntasāra. With Bengali translation by Kālīvara.] [1903.] 12°. **14048. b. 41.**

—— See YOGAVĀSISHṬHARĀMĀYAṆA. বাশিষ্ঠমহারামায়ণম্ *etc.* [Yogavāsishṭharāmāyaṇa. With Ānandabodhendra's commentary. Edited with Bengali translation and notes by Kālīvara.] [1893, *etc.*] 8°. **14049. a. 2.**

—— হিন্দুশাস্ত্র . . . ষড়্‌দর্শন। [Shaḍdarṣana. A Bengali exposition of the six great philosophical systems, illustrated by quotations. Followed by the Vedāntasāra, with Bengali translation.] pp. i. 205. [1895.] See RAMEṢACHANDRA DATTA. হিন্দুশাস্ত্র *etc.* [Hindu-ṣāstra.] pt. v. [1895-1897.] 8°. **14085. c. 45.(vol. 1.)**

KALLAṬA, *Bhaṭṭa, disciple of Vasugupta.* The Spandapradîpikâ of Utpalâchârya, a commentary on the Spandakârikâ [of Kallaṭa, together with the text of the latter work, summarising the Tantric-Ṣaiva system of philosophy called Spanda.] Edited by Pandit Vâman Śâstrî Islâmpurkar of Bombay. pp. i. ii. 55. *Benares*, 1898. 8°. **14048. dd. 3.(vol. 14.)**

Forming vol. 14 *of the* Vizianagram Sanskrit Series.

KALLINĀTHA, *Chatura, son of Lakshmaṇa.* See Ṣārṅgadeva, *Niḥṣaṅka, son of Soḍhala.* संगीतरत्नाकरः *etc.* (The Sangîta Ratnâkara . . . with its commentary [called Kalānidhi] by Chatura Kallinâtha, *etc.*) [1896-1897.] 8°.
14003. ccc.(no. 35.)

KALPAMAÑJARĪ. கல்பமஞ்சரீ [Kalpamañjarī. A manual for the ritual of divers deities. Edited by Chokkanāthapuram Ṣrīnivāsa Ṣāstrī.] pt. 1. pp. 48. கும்பகோணம் ॥ க௯00 [*Kumbakonam,* 1900.] 16°. **14028. b. 105.(2.)**

KALYĀṆĀBHIVAMSA, *Ū. of Chaungzon-ngay, Pagan.* ပဋ္ဌာန်းညွှန်ဝါဂဏ္ဌိကျမ်း *etc.* [Paṭṭhāna-nya-wā-gaṇṭhi-kyan. Comprising Paṭṭhāna-thôn-hkyet-su-gaṇṭhi, Paṭṭhāna-pachchaya-pyaing-gaṇṭhi, and Paṭṭhāna-rāsi-su, Burmese dissertations upon the Paṭṭhāna illustrated from Pali texts, by Kalyāṇābhivaṃsa. Followed by Mātikāgaṇṭhi, Dhātukathāgaṇṭhi, and Yamaikgaṇṭhi, similar treatises upon the *mātikā* of the Dhammasaṅgaṇi, the Dhātukathā, and the Yamaka, by Ñāṇābhidhammālaṅkāra of Taungdwin.] pp. ii. viii. 372, iv. ပုဂ္ဂလေး [*Mandalay,*] 1898. 8°. **14300. e. 17.**

KALYĀṆADĀSA BHĀṆĀBHĀĪ GUJJAR. See Kalyāṇa Ṣivanārāyaṇa. ॥ शिल्पशास्त्र सार संग्रह *etc.* [Ṣilpaṣāstrasārasaṅgraha. With Gujarati translation by Kalyāṇadāsa.] [1898.] 8°.
14053. d. 55.

—— (શિલ્પ સાર સંગ્રહ નામનો ગ્રંથ) [Ṣilpasārasaṅgraha. A compilation treating of the legends of the divine architect Viṣvakarmā and his teachings and cult, and comprising (1) 167 stanzas from the Viṣvakarmajñānabodhakapurāṇa, with Gujarati translation, (2) some chapters in Gujarati, (3) several Sanskrit rituals and hymns.] pp. 28, 8; 1 *plate.* [*Ahmadabad,* 1898.] 8°.
14028. dd. 6.

Wanting title-page. According to the official Register (1898, 3rd *quarter, p.* 40), *the title of the work is* Viṣvakarmacharitrāṇi Pūjāsametāni.

KALYĀṆAJĪ RAṆACHHODAJĪ VYĀSA. See Purāṇas.—*Bhavishyottarapurāṇa.* ऋषिपंचमी व्रत कथा [Ṛishipañchamīvratakathā. With Gujarati translation by Kalyāṇajī.] [1899.] 12°.
14028. b. 78.(3.)

KALYĀṆAKITTIDDHAJA. See Kaviñāṇaddhaja.

KALYĀṆARĀMA ṢĀSTRĪ, *P. K.* See Krishṇa Ṣāstrī, *Parittiyūr.* Kaumudi Sómam . . . Edited by P.K. Kalyana Rama Sastri. 1896. 8°.
14079. c. 69.

—— See Ṣrīharsha, *son of Hīra Paṇḍita.* Nîshadha Charita. [Cantos x.-xii.] With the commentary . . . of Narayanabhatta. With an introduction and notes . . . by . . . Kalyanarama Sastri. 1903. 8°. **14072. ccc. 36.**

KALYĀṆASAUGANDHIKA. വടക്കൻ കല്യാണസൗഗന്ധികം *etc.* [Vaḍakkan Kalyāṇasaugandhikaṃ. A composition on the legend of Rāma, in Sanskrit verses and Malayalam prose. Edited, with Malayalam glossary, *etc.,* by Māṭavil Rāmuṇṇi Vaidyar.] pp. 19, 60. തലശ്ശേരി [*Tellicherri,*] 1895. 8°. **14072. cc. 60.(2.)**

—— See Nārāyaṇa Gupta. कल्याणसौगन्धिकपद्यार्थनिर्णयः *etc.* [Kalyāṇasaugandhikapadyārthanirṇaya. A lecture upon some passages in the Kalyāṇasaugandhika.] [1902.] 8°. **14072. ccc. 20.(2.)**

KALYĀṆA ṢIVANĀRĀYAṆA, *of Surat.* ॥ शिल्पशास्त्र सार संग्रह *etc.* [Ṣilpaṣāstrasārasaṅgraha. A manual of architecture. Pt. I, *adhyāyas* iii.-viii. of the *madhyabhāga*; pt. II, *adhyāyas* ix.-xii. of the *antabhāga.* With a Gujarati translation by Kalyāṇadāsa Bhāṇābhāī Gujjar.] pp. iv. 80, 64, iv.; 12 *plates.* राजनगरे १९५४ [*Rajnagar,* 1898.] 8°.
14053. d. 55.

KALYĀṆASUNDARA ṢĀSTRĪ, *Ṣāttanūru.* See Jīmūtavāhana. దాయభాగః *etc.* [Dāyabhāga. Edited by Kalyāṇasundara.] [1897.] 8°.
14039. b. 22.

—— See Sāyaṇa Āchārya.—*Works on Smṛiti.* శ్రీ . . . వ్యవహారకాండః *etc.* [Mādhavīya-vyavahārakāṇḍa. Edited by Kalyāṇasundara.] [1898.] 8°. **14039. c. 16.**

KALYĀṆCHANDJĪ JAICHANDJĪ. See Pratikramaṇasūtra. લોંકાગચ્છીય . . . પ્રતિક્રમણસૂત્ર *etc.* [Pañcha-pratikramaṇasūtra, *etc.* Edited by Kalyāṇchandjī.] [1883.] 8°. **14144. g. 18.**

KĀMADEVA DĪKSHITA, *son of Viṣvāmitra.* See Kātyāyana. परिशिष्टकण्डिका [Pariṣishṭakaṇḍikā.

With the Gṛihyapariṣishṭabhāshya and °prayoga-paddhati of Kāmadeva, etc.] [1896.] 4°.
14010. f. 10.

KĀMAKAUTŪHALA. कामकौतूहल वैद्यकग्रन्थ *etc.* [Kāmakautūhala. A metrical compendium of sexual therapy, ascribed to Hemādri. With a Hindi translation by Ṣālagrāma Vaiṣya.] pp. ii. 52. बंबई १९५८ [*Bombay*, 1902.] 8°.
14043. cc. 19.(2.)
The author in his introduction terms himself mehanāthaka.

KĀMĀKHYANĀTHA TARKAVĀGĪṢA. *See* Īṣvara Kṛishṇa. সাংখ্যদীপনী *etc.* [Sāṅkhyakārikā. With an exposition styled Sāṅkhyadīpanī, by Kāmākhyanātha.] [1901.] 12°.
14048. b. 16.(2.)

KAMALĀKARA BHAṬṬA, *son of Rāmakrishṇa.* निर्णयसिंधु *etc.* [Nirṇayasindhu. With Gujarati translation by Kālidāsa Govindajī.] pp. ii. xl. 971. મુંબઈ ૧૯૦૧ [*Bombay*, 1901.] 4°.
14028. dd. 11.

—— निर्णयसिन्धु *etc.* [Nirṇayasindhu. Edited with a Hindi translation by Vrajaratna Bhaṭṭāchārya.] pp. iv. viii. 1076. बंबई १९५८ [*Bombay*, 1901.] 8°.
14028. dd. 12.

—— శాంతికమలాకరనామకగ్రంథ *etc.* [Ṣānti-kamalākara. A treatise on expiatory rituals, forming part iv. of the Dharmatattva.] pp. iv. 557; 32 *plates.* చెన్నపురాజధాన్యాం [*Madras*,] 1900. 8°.
14033. aa. 21.

—— ஶூத்ரகமலாகரவ்யாஶூத்ரஸர்வ-ஸ்வவ்யாக்யானம்: [Ṣūdrakamalākara, or Ṣūdra-dharmatattva. Part ix. of the Dharmatattva, treating of the religious duties of the fourth caste. Edited with a commentary called Ṣūdrasarvasva and Tamil translation by Ṣrīnivāsa Dikshita.] 1901, *etc.* *See* Periodical Publications.—*Chidambaram.* ப்ரஹ்மவித்யா *etc.* [Brahma-vidyā.] Vol. xv., no. 1, *etc.* 1886, *etc.* 4°.
14096. dd. 3.(vol. 15, etc.)
In progress.

KAMALAKRISHṆA SMṚITIBHŪSHAṆA. *See* Govindānanda Kavikaṅkaṇa Bhaṭṭāchārya. Varṣa Kriyā Kaumudī . . . Edited by . . . Kamala Kṛṣṇa Smṛtibhūṣaṇa. 1902. 8°. [*Bibliotheca Indica.*]
14002. a. (vol. 149.)

KAMALĀNANDA SIṂHA, *Sāmba, Prince, of Srinagar.* *See* Ṣrīkānta Miṣra. ॥ साम्बकमलानन्दकुलरत्नं *etc.* [Sāmbakamalānandakularatna. A historical poem, in panegyric of Kamalānanda Siṃha and his family.] [1901.] 4°.
14058. cc. 5.

KAMALAPRABHA ĀCHĀRYA, *disciple of Devaprabha, of Rudrapallīya-gachchha.* जिनपञ्जरस्तोत्रं *etc.* [Jinapañjarastotra. A Jain hymn.] *See* Jainastotraratnākara. जैनस्तोत्ररत्नाकर *etc.* [Jainastotraratnākara.] pp. 86-92. [1901.] 16°.
14100. a. 26.

KAMALĀṢAṄKARA PRĀṆAṢAṄKARA TRIVEDĪ. *See* Bhaṭṭi. The Bhaṭṭi-kâvya . . . Edited with the commentary of Mallinâtha and with . . . notes by Kamalâśaṅkara . . . Trivedî. 1898. 8°.
14072. c. 54.

—— *See* Euclid. The Rekhâgaṇita . . . Edited . . . with . . . preface, introduction, and notes in English by Kamalâśaṅkara . . . Trivedî. 1901-1902. 8°.
14053. ccc. 36.

KĀMANDAKI. Kámandakíya Nítisára. With full notes . . . translation . . . &c. by S. Venkatarama Sastry. pp. 240. *Madras*, 1895. 8°.
14070. c. 55.

—— Kamandakiya Nitisara, or The Elements of Polity, in English. Edited . . . by Manmatha Nath Dutt. pp. vi. 254, ii. 1896. *See* Manmathanātha Datta. The Wealth of India, *etc.* Vol. iv. 1892, *etc.* 8°.
14085. d. 32.(vol. 4.)

—— Il Nîtisâra di Kâmandaki. [Translated into Italian by C. Formichi.] 1899, *etc.* *See* Academies, *etc.* — Florence. — *Società Asiatica Italiana.* Giornale, *etc.* Vol. xii., *etc.* 1887, *etc.* 8°.
Ac. 8804.(vol. 12, etc.)

KĀMAṢĀSTRĪ, *Kollūr, of Vizianagram.* *See* Veṅkaṭanārāyaṇa Rāya, *son of Vemulakoṇḍa Konaya.* शशिकला *etc.* [Ṣaśikalā. Edited by Kāmaṣāstrī.] 1898. 8°.
14076. b. 33.

KĀMAṢĀSTRĪ, *Susurla.* గిరికాకల్యాణ నాటకము *etc.* [Girikākalyāṇa. A poetical drama in 5 acts upon the loves of Vasu and Girikā.] pp. ii. v. 42. *Madras*, 1901. 8°.
14076. c. 67.(2.)

KĀMEṢVARA AIYAR, *B. V., of Pudukottai.* *See* Periodical Publications. — *Kumbakonam.* The

Sanskrit Journal ... Edited by ... B. V. Kamesvara Aiyar, *etc.* 1896, *etc.* 8°. **14096. ccc. 1.**

—— *See* SANDHYĀVANDANA. The Sandhyavandanam of Rig, Yajus, and Sâma Vedins. With ... translation, ... paraphrase & commentary in English. By B. V. Kamesvara Aiyar. 1898. 12°. **14028. b. 97.(2.)**

—— *See* SVĀMI ṢĀSTRĪ, *P.K.*, and KĀMEṢVARA AIYAR, *B.V.* Matriculation Examination, 1891. The Sanskrit Text Examiner, *etc.* 1891. 12°. **14072. b. 18.**

—— *See* VEDAS.—Ṛigveda.—*Single Hymns and Verses.* The Purusha Sukta. Translated and explained by B. V. Kamesvara Aiyar. 1898. 12°. **14028. b. 97.(1.)**

KAMMAVĀCHĀ. A Collection of Kammavācās. [Texts with translation.] By Herbert Baynes. 1892. *See* ACADEMIES, *etc.*—London.—*Royal Asiatic Society of Great Britain and Ireland.* The Journal ... 1892. pp. 53—75. 1834, *etc.* 8°. **Ac. 8820/3 and 2098. a., b**

—— ဥပသမ္ပဒဩဝါဒခဏ္ဍကအနုသာသနကထာ။ [Upasampadā-ovāda-khaṇḍaka-anusāsana-kathā. The first three sections of the Kammavāchā liturgy. With introductory and explanatory matter in Burmese.] pp. 10. ရန်ကုန် ၁၂၅၄ [*Rangoon*, 1892.] *obl.* Fol. **14098. a. 23.**

—— ဥပသမ္ပဒကမ္မဝါစာနိသျ [Upasampadā-kammavāchā. Being the first section of the Kammavāchā, with a Burmese *nissaya* by Ādichchavaṃsa.] 1899. *See* VINAYAPIṬAKA.—*Appendix.* ဝိနယသမူဟဝိနိစ္ဆယကျမ်း *etc.* [Vinayasamūha-vinichchhaya-kyan.] Vol. I, pp. 477-495. 1899, *etc.* 8°. **14300. e. 15.(vol. 1.)**

—— မူလာယပဋိကဿနကမ္မဝါ [Mūlāya-paṭikassana-kammavāchā. With Burmese translation and commentary.] *See* PAṆḌITADDHAJA, known as MAINGKAING HSAYA. တိပေဋကဝိနိစ္ဆယကျမ်း *etc.* [Tipiṭakavinichchhaya-kyan.] Vol. I, pp. 253-292. . 1900-1901. 8°. **14302. i. 19.(vol. 1.)**

KAṆĀDA. *See* KĀLĪVARA VEDĀNTAVĀGĪṢA. हिन्दूशास्त्र *etc.* [Shaḍdarṣana. A Bengali exposition of the 6 systems.] [1895.] 8°. [*Hindu-ṣāstra.*] **14085. c. 45.(vol. 1.)**

—— [For the Nāḍīvijñāna popularly attributed to Kaṇāda:] *See* NĀḌĪVIJÑĀNA.

—— *See* PRABHUDAYĀLU, *Mu'āfīdār.* समीक्षाकर *etc.* [Samīkshākara. Select Aphorisms from the Vaiṣeshika and other systems, with a commentary.] [1898.] 8°. **14048. e. 22.(2.)**

—— *See* PRAṢASTAPĀDA. The Bhāshya of Praśastapâda [upon the Vaiṣeshika Aphorisms], *etc.* 1895. 8°. **14048. dd. 3.(vol. 4.)**

—— *See* ṢIVĀDITYA MIṢRA. The Saptapadârthî, [a manual] of the Vaiśeshika system, *etc.* 1893. 8°. **14048. dd. 3.(vol. 6.)**

—— वैशेषिकदर्शनम् *etc.* [Vaiṣeshikadarṣana. The Aphorisms of Kaṇāda, with Sanskrit and Hindi commentaries by Devadatta Ṣāstrī, son of Ṣivadatta.] pp. iii. iv. 135. मुरादाबाद १८९८ [*Moradabad*, 1898.] 8°. **14048. e. 22.(3.)**

—— وشيشك درشن لغ [Vaiṣeshikadarṣana. The Vaiṣeshika Aphorisms, with Hindustani translation and commentary by Darṣanānanda Sarasvatī.] pp. 284, *lith.* بلندشهر [*Bulandshahr*, 1902.] 8°. **14049. b. 18.**

KANAKAKĪRTI GAṆĪ, *disciple of Jayamandira.* *See* KĀLIDÀSA.—*Meghadūta.* ॥ अथ ... मेघदुत [*sic*], *etc.* [Meghadūta. With *avachūrṇi* by Kanakakīrti.] [1867.] *obl.* 4°. **14072. e. 3.**

KĀÑCHANA ĀCHĀRYA, *son of Nārāyaṇa Vādīṣvara.* The Dhanañjayavijaya of Kâñchanâchârya. [A drama of the *vyāyoga* class.] Edited by Paṇḍit Śivadatta ... and Kâśînâth Pâṇḍurang Parab. (धनंजयविजयः।) pp. 20. 1895. *See* DURGĀPRASĀDA, *son of Vrajalāla*, and KĀṢĪNĀTHA PĀṆḌURAṄGA PARAB. Kâvyamâlâ. [No.] 54. 1886, *etc.* 8°. **14072. ccc. 12.(no. 54.)**

K'ANG-HE, *Emperor of China.* Man-Han-Si Fan-tsyeh-yao, a Buddhist repertory, in Sanscrit, Tibetan, Mandchu, Mongol & Chinese. [Translated by C. de Harlez.] 1887-1890. *See* PERIODICAL PUBLICATIONS.—*London.* The Babylonian & Oriental Record, *etc.* Vols. 2-4. 1886, *etc.* 8°. **P.P. 3780. d. (vol. 2-4.)**

K'ANG-HE, *Emperor of China (continued)*. Vocabulaire Bouddhique Sanscrit-Chinois. 漢梵集要 Han-Fan Tsih-yao. Précis de Doctrine Bouddhique. [Edited and translated] par C. de Harlez. pp. 66. *Leide*, 1897. 8°. **11098. b. 37.**

A reprint from the T'oung-pao, vii. 4, viii. 2.

KANHAIYĀLĀL MIṢRA, *son of Sukhānanda, of Moradabad. See* Nāgārjuna. सिद्धविनोद *etc.* [Siddhavinoda, or Ratiṣāstra. Edited with a Hindi version by Kanhaiyālāl.] [1899.] 8°. **14053. d. 59.**

—— *See* Tantras. [*Kālītantra.*] कालीतन्त्र । [Kālītantra. With Hindi translation by Kanhaiyālāl.] [1902.] 8°. **14033. bbb. 15.(3.)**

—— *See* Tantras. [*Yoginītantra.*] ॥ श्रीः . . . योगिनीतन्त्र *etc.* [Yoginītantra. Edited with Hindi translation by Kanhaiyālāl.] [1903.] 8°. **14033. aa. 34.**

—— ॥ ज्योतिषतत्वविचार *etc.* [Jyotishatattvavichāra. A treatise on astrology, compiled from various sources. With Hindi version and notes.] pp. 224. कानपुर १९५६ [*Cawnpore*, 1899.] 12°. **14053. b. 35.**

KANHAIYĀLĀL ṢARMĀ, *son of Bhagavāndāsa, of Reti, Moradabad. See* Upanishads.—*Separate Upanishads.* अथर्ववेदान्तर्गत-गोपालतापनीउपनिषत् *etc.* [Gopālatāpanyupanishad. With gloss. Edited with Hindi version by Kanhaiyālāl.] [1898.] **14010. c. 51.(4.)**

KANHAIYĀLĀL ṢARMĀ, *son of Jagannātha, of Moradabad. See* Dāmodara, *son of Gaṅgādhara.* ॥ यन्त्रचिंतामणिः *etc.* [Yantrachintāmaṇi. With Hindi translation by Kanhaiyālāl.] 1902. 8°. **14033. bb. 7.(2.)**

—— *See* Tantras. [*Siddhaṣaṅkaratantra.*] सिद्धशङ्करतंत्रम् *etc.* [Siddhaṣaṅkaratantra. With Hindi version by Ṣyāmasundaralāla and Kanhaiyālāl.] [1899.] 8°. **14033. bbb. 6.**

—— *See* Vaidyanātha Ṣāstrī Tivārī, *of Jalalabad*, and others. [Miscellaneous tracts. With Hindi versions of the Sanskrit texts by Kanhaiyālāl and others.] [1899.] 12°. **14033. a. 37.**

—— कामकुतूहल. अथवा नपुंसकानंदमंदार *etc.* [Kāmakutūhala, or Napuṃsakānandamandāra. A treatise on impotence. Compiled from various sources, with Hindi preface and translation, by Kanhaiyālāl.] pt. 1. pp. iv. 59. मुरादाबाद १९०० [*Moradabad*, 1900.] 12°. **14053. b. 36.**

In progress?

KANHAIYĀLĀL ṢĀSTRĪ, *Examiner, Calcutta University. See* Academies, *etc.*—Allahabad.—*University of Allahabad.* संस्कृत-शिक्षा-विवृतिः . . . Sanskrit-Siksha-Vivriti . . . By . . . Kanhaiya Lal Sastri. 1899. 12°. **14039. b. 39.(2.)**

KANHAIYĀLĀL TANTRAVAIDYA. *See* Kanhaiyālāl Ṣarmā, *son of Jagannātha.*

KANHAIYĀLĀL VAMṢĪDHARA, *Bhārgava, of Muttra. See* Garga. ॥ अथ श्रीमद्गर्गसंहिता *etc.* [Gargasaṃhitā. Edited by Kanhaiyālāl.] [1898.] *obl.* 4°. **14028. e. 34.**

KANNAN AIYA, *Tirukuḍandai Purohita Ṣendāmarai.* తిరువారాధనక్రమసంగ్రహము *etc.* [Tiruvārādhanakramasaṅgraham. A book of hymns and offices for the liturgies of the Rāmānujī Vaishṇavas, in Sanskrit, Telugu, and Tamil.] pp. ii. 96; 1 *plate.* చెన్నపట్టణము [*Madras*,] 1902. 12°. **14033. a. 46.**

KAPARDISVĀMĪ. *See* Āpastamba.—*Ṣrautasūtra.* आपस्तम्बपरिभाषासूत्रम् . . . The Ápastamba-Paribháshá-Sútra, with the commentaries of Kapardisvámin, *etc.* 1894. 8°. [*Mysore Government Oriental Library Series: Bibliotheca Sanskrita.*] **14004. b. 2.**

KAPILA. ॥ सांख्यदर्शनम् *etc.* [Sāṅkhyadarṣana. The Sāṅkhya Aphorisms, falsely ascribed to Kapila. Edited by Rāmasvarūpa Ṣarmā of Moradabad.] pp. 25. १८९७ [*Moradabad*, 1897.] 8°. **14048. cc. 21.(4.)**

—— ॥ सांख्यसूत्रम् *etc.* [Sāṅkhyasūtra.] pp. 25. मुरादाबाद १८९७ [*Moradabad*, 1897.] 8°. **14048. cc. 21.(5.)**

—— सांख्य-दर्शन *etc.* (Sankhya-Philosophy. Edited by Maharshi Kapil. Translated into Hindi [*i.e.* edited in Sanskrit with a Hindi paraphrase and explanations] by Kshetra Pall Sarma.) pp. ii. 216. *Calcutta*, 1891. 8°. **14048. bb. 44.**

The English title is from the wrapper.

—— The Sāṁkhya-pravacana-bhāṣya, or Commentary on the Exposition of the Sāṅkhya

Philosophy, by Vijñānabhikṣu. [Including the text of the Sāṅkhya Aphorisms.] Edited by Richard Garbe. pp. xiv. 196. 1895. *See* ACADEMIES, *etc.* — Cambridge, *Mass.* — *Harvard University.* Harvard Oriental Series, *etc.* Vol. ii. 1891, *etc.* 8°. **14003. l. 3.(vol. 2.)**

—— साङ्ख्यदर्शनम् । महर्षिकपिलप्रणीतम् *etc.* [Sāṅkhyadarṣana. The Sāṅkhya Aphorisms, with copious Hindi paraphrase by Darṣanānanda Sarasvatī. Second edition.] pp. 108. अजमेर० १९०३ [*Ajmere,* 1903.] 8°. **14049. b. 10.**

—— *See* GARBE (R.). Die Sâṃkhya-Philosophie, *etc.* 1894. 8°. **4503. bb. 43.**

—— *See* HARIHARĀNANDA. ॐ . . . साङ्ख्यतत्त्वालोकः *etc.* [Sāṅkhyatattvāloka. A treatise on the Sāṅkhya.] [1903.] 8°. **14049. b. 14.**

—— *See* KĀLĪVARA VEDĀNTAVĀGĪṢA. हिन्दुशास्त्र *etc.* [Shaḍdarṣana. A Bengali exposition of the six systems.] [1895.] 8°. [*Hindu-ṣāstra.*] **14085. c. 45.(vol. 1.)**

—— *See* PRABHUDAYĀLU, *Mu'āfidār.* समीक्षाकर *etc.* [Samīkshākara. Select Aphorisms from the Sāṅkhya and other systems, with a commentary.] [1898.] 8°. **14048. e. 22.(2.)**

KAPILEṢVARA VIDYĀBHŪSHAṆA. *See* RŪPA GOSVĀMĪ. ହଂସଦୂତ *etc.* [Haṃsadūta. With metrical translation in Oriya by Kapileṣvara.] 1894. 12°. **14070. b. 24.**

—— *See* SVAPNĀDHYĀYA. ସ୍ୱପ୍ନାଧ୍ୟାୟ *etc.* [Svapnādhyāya. Edited with Oriya metrical version by Kapileṣvara.] 1880. 12°. **14053. b. 17.(3.)**

—— ଅଷ୍ଟକମାଳା *etc.* [Ashṭakamālā. A collection of hymns in praise of several deities. Compiled, with a metrical Oriya version, by Kapileṣvara.] pp. 13. *Cuttack,* 1880. 12°. **14033. a. 26.(2.)**

KARIBASAVA ṢĀSTRĪ, *N. R.* *See* VĪRAṢAIVA. ಸಟೀಕ ವೀರಶೈವ ದೀಕ್ಷಾವಿಧಿಯು [Vīraṣaivadīkshāvidhi. Edited, with Canarese commentary, by Karibasava.] 1897. 8°. **14028. d. 64.**

KARKA UPĀDHYĀYA. *See* KĀTYĀYANA. परिशिष्टकण्डिका [Pariṣishṭakaṇḍikā, *etc.* Followed by the Ṣrāddhasūtra, with Karka's *vyākhyā, etc.*] 1896. 4°. [*Pāraskaragrihyasūtra.*] **14010. f. 10.**

—— *See* PĀRASKARA. पारस्करगृह्यसूत्रम् *etc.* [Pāraskaragṛihyasūtra. With Karka's Gṛihyabhāshya, *etc.*] [1896.] 4°. **14010. f. 10.**

KARNĀṬAKA KṚISHṆA ṢĀSTRĪ. *See* GADĀDHARA BHAṬṬĀCHĀRYA. ॥ व्युत्पत्तिवादः *etc.* [Vyutpattivāda. Edited by Karnāṭaka Kṛishṇa.] [1901.] 8°. **14049. a. 4.(1.)**

—— *See* NĀGEṢA BHAṬṬA. [*Ṣabdenduṣekhara.*] ॥ लघुशब्देन्दुशेखरः *etc.* [Laghu-ṣabdenduṣekhara. Edited by Karnāṭaka Kṛishṇa.] 1901, *etc.* 8°. **14090. bb. 20.**

KARUṆĀPUṆḌARĪKA. करुणा-पुण्डरीकम् । Karuṇāpuṇḍarīkam. [A sūtra of the Mahāyāna.] For the first time edited by Rai Çarat Chandra Dās . . . and Paṇḍit Çarat Chandra Çāstrī. pp. 129. 1898. *See* ACADEMIES, *etc.*—Calcutta.—*Buddhist Text Society of India.* Buddhist Texts, *etc.* 1894, *etc.* 8°. **14004. c. (vol. 1, no. 3.)**

KASHINATH. *See* KĀṢĪNĀTHA.

KASHMIR.—JAMMU.—*Raghunātha Temple Library.* *See* JAMMU.

KĀṢICHINTĀMAṆI BHAṬṬA. *See* VEDAS.—Yajurveda.—*Vājasaneyisaṃhitā.* வாஜஸநேயா-ஷ்கா . . . ஸ-ஹய-வெஷ-ஸம்ஹிதா *etc.* [Vājasaneyisaṃhitā. With commentary. Edited by Kāṣichintāmaṇi Bhaṭṭa.] 1901, *etc.* 8°. **14007. cc. 29.**

KĀṢĪDĀSA MUSTAUPHĪ. শান্তিগীতা *etc.* [Ṣāntigītā. A poem on resignation and the supreme truths of religion. With a copious Bengali commentary by the author's nephew Ṣaṣibhūshaṇa Mitra Mustauphī, also known as Brahmānanda Tattvadarṣī.] pp. viii. 215. *Calcutta,* 1897. 8°. **14076. b. 41.**

Contains also a pedigree of the author.

KĀṢĪNĀTHA BĀLA ṢĀSTRĪ ĀGĀṢE. *See* BRĀHMAṆAS.—*Aitareyabrāhmaṇa.* ऐतरेयब्राह्मणम् *etc.* (The Aitaréya Bráhmaṇam, with the Bháshya of . . . Sáyaṇáchárya . . . Edited by . . . Kâśînâtha Sâstry Âgâśé.) [1896.] 8°.

14003. ccc. (no. 32.)

KĀṢĪNĀTHA BĀLA ṢĀSTRĪ ĀGĀṢE (*continued*). *See* GOPĪNĀTHA DĪKSHITA, *Bhaṭṭa.* संस्काररत्नमाला *etc.* [Saṃskāraratnamālā. Edited by Kāṣīnātha Āgāṣe, *etc.*] [1899.] 8°.
14003. ccc. (no. 39.)

—— *See* MAHĀBHĀRATA.—Bhagavadgītā.—*Sanskrit.* श्रीमद्भगवद्गीता *etc.* (Shrîmat Bhagavadgîta with the Bháshya by . . . Śankarácbárya, the commentary by Anadagiri [*sic*] on the same, index . . . Edited by . . . Kâśînâtha Śâstrî Âgâśé.) 1897. 8°. **14003. ccc. (no. 34.)**

—— *See* MAHĀBHĀRATA. — Bhagavadgītā. — *Sanskrit.* श्रीमद्भगवद्गीता *etc.* [Bhagavadgītā. With the Paiṣāchabhāshya. Edited by Kāṣīnātha Āgāṣe, *etc.*] [1901.] 8°.
14003. ccc. (no. 44.)

—— *See* MAHĀBHĀRATA. — Bhagavadgītā. — *Sanskrit.* श्रीमद्भगवद्गीता *etc.* [Bhagavadgītā. With commentaries of Madhusūdana and Ṣrīdhara. Edited by Kāṣīnātha Āgāṣe.] [1901.] 8°.
14003. ccc. (no. 45.)

—— *See* SANDHYĀVANDANA. सन्ध्याभाष्यसमुच्चयः *etc.* [Sandhyābhāshyasamuchchaya. Edited by Kāṣīnātha Āgāṣe.] [1899.] 8°.
14003. ccc. (no. 40.)

—— *See* SUREṢVARA ĀCHĀRYA. बृहदारण्यकोपनिषद्भाष्यवार्त्तिकम् *etc.* (Bṛihadáraṇyakopanishadbháshyavártika . . . With its commentary . . . and an index . . . Edited by . . . Káśînátha Śástri Âgáśe, *etc.*) [1892]-1894. 8°.
14003. ccc. (no. 16.)

—— *See* UPANISHADS.—*Separate Upanishads.* बृहदारण्यकोपनिषन्मिताक्षरा *etc.* [Bṛihadāraṇyakopanishad. With commentary. Edited by Kāṣīnātha Āgāṣe.] [1896.] 8°.
14003. ccc. (no. 31.)

—— *See* VEDAS. — Yajurveda. — *Taittirīyasaṃhitā.* कृष्णयजुर्वेदीयतैत्तिरीयसंहिता *etc.* [Taittirīyasaṃhitā. With commentary. Edited by Kāṣīnātha.] [1900, *etc.*] 8°.
14003. ccc. (no. 42.)

KĀṢĪNĀTHA BĀPŪ PĀṬHAKA. *See* KĀLIDĀSA.—*Meghadûta.* The Meghadûta . . . with the commentary of Mallinátha . . . and . . . translation, various readings, critical notes, and an introductory essay . . . Edited by Kashinath . . . Pathak. 1894. 8°. **14076. b. 32.**

KĀṢĪNĀTHA PĀṆḌURAṄGA PARAB. *See* BHAVABHŪTI. The Mahâvîracharita . . . With the commentary of Vîrarâghava. Edited by T. R. Ratnam Aiyar . . . and Kâśînâth . . . Parab. 1892. 8°. **14080. c. 32.**

—— *See* BHAVABHŪTI. The Uttara-Râmacharita . . . With the commentary of Vîrarâghava. Edited by T. R. Ratnam Aiyar . . . and Kâśînâth . . . Parab. 1899. 8°. **14080. c. 40.**

—— *See* BHOJARĀJA. The Champû-Râmâyaṇa . . . With the commentary of Râmachandra . . . Edited by Kâshînâth . . . Parab. 1898. 8°.
14070. dd. 5.

—— *See* DURGĀPRASĀDA, *son of Vrajalāla*, and others. The Abhidhâna-sangraha . . . Edited by . . . Durgâprasâd, Kâśînâth . . . Parab, *etc.* 1889, *etc.* 8°. **14090. e. 20.**

—— *See* JAYADEVA, *son of Mahādeva.* The Prasannarâghava . . . Edited by Kâśînâth . . . Parab. 1893. 8°. **14079. c. 60.(1.)**

—— *See* KĀLIDĀSA, *Pseud.*, [*i.e.* KĀLIDĀSA SĀRVABHAUMA BHAṬṬĀCHĀRYA.] पुष्पबाणविलासम् *etc.* [Pushpabāṇavilāsa. With commentary of Veṅkaṭa. Edited by Kāṣīnātha Parab.] [1901.] 8°. **14072. cc. 62.(3.)**

—— *See* NĀRĀYAṆA BHAṬṬA, called MṚIGARĀJALAKSHMĀ. The Veṇîsaṃbâra . . . With the commentary of Jagaddhara . . . Edited by Kâśînâth . . . . Parab, *etc.* 1898. 8°.
14079. c. 67.

—— *See* PAÑCHATANTRA. The Pañchatantraka . . . Edited by Kâśînâth . . . Parab. 1896. 8°. **14070. c. 59.**

—— *See* ṢŪDRAKA. The Mṛichchhakaṭika . . . with the commentary of Pṛithvîdhara. Edited by Kâshinâth . . . Parab. 1900. 8°.
14079. c. 60.(2.)

KĀṢĪNĀTHA PĀṬHAKA, *son of Viṣveṣvara. See* PURĀṆAS.—*Selections.* ॥ शाकद्वीपीय कुलभास्करः *etc.* [Ṣākadvīpīya-kulabhāskara. Compiled by Kāṣīnātha.] [1901.] 8°. **14058. b. 45.**

KĀṢĪNĀTHA ṢĀSTRĪ ĀGĀṢE. *See* KĀṢĪNĀTHA BĀLA ṢĀSTRĪ ĀGĀṢE.

KĀṢĪNĀTHA TRYAMBAKA TELANG. *See* MAHĀBHĀRATA.—*Abridgments and Selections.* The Bhagavadgîtâ with the Sanatsugâtîya and the Anugîtâ. Translated by . . . Kâshinâth . . . Telang. 1898. 8°. [*Sacred Books of the East.*]
2003. a. (vol. 8.)

KĀṢĪNĀTHA UPĀDHYĀYA, *son of Ananta.* धर्मसिंधु *etc.* [Dharmasindhu. With Hindi translation by Ravidatta Ṣāstrī.] pp. iii. xvi. 770; 2 *plates.* मुंबई १९४८ [*Bombay,* 1891.] 8°.
14033. bb. 39.

—— ಧರ್ಮಾಬ್ಧಿಸಾರವು [Dharmābdhisāra, or Dharmasindhusāra. Sections i.-iii.] pp. 126. ಬೆಂಗಳೂರು ೧೮೯೨ [*Bangalore,* 1892.] 8°.
14028. d. 46.

Imperfect at the end.

——. वर्णविवेकचन्द्रिका *etc.* [Varṇavivekachandrikā. A tract on Hindu castes, in 96 stanzas.] pp. 23. [*Bombay,*] 1891. 8°. **14058. a. 12.**

KĀṢIRĀMA VĀCHASPATI. *See* RAGHUNANDANA BHAṬṬĀCHĀRYA. मलमासतत्त्वम् *etc.* [Malamāsatattva. With commentary of Kāṣirāma, *etc.*] [1900.] 8°. **14033. bbb. 5.**

—— *See* RAGHUNANDANA BHAṬṬĀCHĀRYA. तिथितत्त्वम् *etc.* [Tithitattva. With commentary of Kāṣirāma.] [1901.] 8°. **14033. bb. 45.(3.)**

—— *See* RAGHUNANDANA BHAṬṬĀCHĀRYA. उद्वाहतत्त्वं *etc.* [Udvāhatattva. With commentary of Kāṣirāma.] [1896.] 8°. **14033. bb. 42.**

—— *See* RAGHUNANDANA BHAṬṬĀCHĀRYA. उद्वाहतत्त्वम् *etc.* [Udvāhatattva. With commentary of Kāṣirāma, *etc.*] [1902.] 8°.
14033. bb. 45.(4.)

KASTŪRIRAṄGA AIYAṄGĀR, *G.* *See* VEṄKAṬANĀTHA VEDĀNTĀCHĀRYA. श्रीः . . . हंससन्देशः° (Hamsa Sandesa . . . With an [English] introduction . . . notes and translation [by Deṣikāchārya and Kastūriraṅga,] *etc.*) 1903. 12°. **14060. b. 19.**

KĀṬAYAVEMA SŪRI. *See* KĀLIDĀSA.—*Mālavikāgnimitra.* The Mâlavikâgnimitra . . . With the commentary [Kumāragirirājīya] of Kâṭayavema, *etc.* 1889. 8°. **14080. c. 31.**

KĀṬAYAVEMA SŪRI (*continued*). *See* KĀLIDĀSA.—*Mālavikāgnimitra.* The Mâlavikâgnimitra . . . With the commentary of Kátayavêma, *etc.* 1896. 8°.
14080. c. 36.

—— *See* KĀLIDĀSA. — *Vikramorvaṣīya.* The Vikramorvaśîyam . . . with English notes, containing extracts from two commentaries, [*scil.,* of Kāṭayavema and Raṅganātha,] *etc.* 1901. 8°.
14080. c. 42.

KATHĀKOṢA. The Kathákoça; or, Treasury of Stories. Translated from Sanskrit manuscripts by C. H. Tawney . . . With appendix, containing notes, by . . . Ernst Leumann. pp. xxiii. 260. 1895. *See* ACADEMIES, *etc.*—London.—*Oriental Translation Fund.* New Series II, vol. 2. 1891, *etc.* 8°. **14003. bb. (ser. 2, vol. 2.)**

KATHAVATE (A. V.). *See* ĀBĀJĪ VISHṆU KATHAVAṬE.

KATHĀVATTHU. *See* ABHIDHAMMAPIṬAKA.

KĀTYĀYANA. परिशिष्टकण्डिका (परिशिष्टशौचसूत्रम् *etc.*) [Pariṣishṭakaṇḍikā. With the Gṛihyapariṣishṭabhāshya and °prayogapaddhati of Kāmadeva Dīkshita. Followed by other *sūtras* ascribed to Kātyāyana,—viz. the Pariṣishṭaṣauchasūtra; the Snānasūtra, with Harihara's *vyākhyā* and Snānapaddhati; the Ṣrāddhasūtra, with Karka's *vyākhyā* and the *bhāshya* and Ṣrāddhasūtrapaddhati of Gadādhara Dikshita; and the Bhojanasūtra.] *See* PĀRASKARA. पारस्करगृह्यसूत्रम् *etc.* [Pāraskaragṛihyasūtra, *etc.*] pp. 547-639. [1896.] 4°.
14010. f. 10.

—— अथ कातीयतर्पणप्रयोगः *etc.* [Kātīya-tarpaṇaprayoga. A ritual for the ceremonial entertainment of gods, saints, and ancestors, based on the Sūtra of Kātyāyana. Edited with Hindi translations and rubrics by Bhīmasena Ṣarmā.] pp. 12, 24. इटावा [१९]०२ [*Etawah,* 1902.] *obl.* 12°. **14028. bb. 4.(4.)**

—— अथानुवाकसूत्राध्यायः। (अथ सर्वानुक्रमणी।) [Anuvākasūtrādhyāya. An index to the catchwords of the *anuvākas* in the Vājasaneyisaṃhitā. Followed by the Sarvānukramaṇī.] *See* VEDAS.—Yajurveda. — *Vājasaneyisaṃhitā.* वाजसनेयि . . . संहिता *etc.* [Vājasaneyisaṃhitā.] Vol. ii. [1903.] 8°. **14007. f. 4.(vol. 2.)**

KĀTYĀYANA (*continued*). महर्षिकात्यायनप्रणीतम् शुक्लयजुःसर्वानुक्रमसूत्रम् . . . Kátyáyana's Sarvánukramasutras of the White Yajurveda, with the commentary of Yájñikánantadeva. Edited and annotated by Pandit Yugalakiśora Páthaka. *Benares*, 1893, *etc.* 8°. **14007. c. 25.**

In progress? Forms nos. 45, 47, 49 *of the* Benares Sanskrit Series.

—— *See* Bālakrishna Sadāśiva Godse. अथ प्रातिशाख्यप्रदीपशिक्षा *etc.* [Prātiśākhyapradīpaśikshā. A treatise upon Kātyāyana's Prātiśākhya.] 1893. 8°. [*Śikshāsaṅgraha.*] **14093. b. 31.**

—— अथ कात्यायनीशिक्षा *etc.* (अथ . . . स्वरभक्तिलक्षणपरिशिष्टशिक्षा) [Kātyāyanī Śikshā and Svarabhaktilakshaṇa-pariśishṭaśikshā. Two tracts of the Mādhyandina school, of 13 and 42 stanzas respectively, the former on the accentuation of the White Yajurveda, the latter on vocalic 'glides.' With commentary on the former by Jayanta Svāmī.] *See* Yugalakiśora Vyāsa Pāṭhaka. श्रीमद्याज्ञवल्क्यादि . . . शिक्षासङ्ग्रहः . . . A collection of Śikshás, *etc.* pp. 46-51, 172-175. 1893. 8°. **14093. b. 31.**

—— [For the *vārttikas* of Kātyāyana upon the aphorisms of Pāṇini :] *See* Pāṇini.

—— [For the Kritprakaraṇa ascribed to Kātyāyana and incorporated in the Kātantra :] *See* Sarvavarmā.

KĀTYĀYANĪ ŚĀNTI. ॥ अथ कात्यायनी शान्ती ॥ [Kātyāyanī Śānti. A collection of charms, *etc.*] pp. 40. लाहौर [*Lahore*, 1900.] *obl.* 12°. **14028. b. 101.(2.)**

KAUṆḌA BHAṬṬA, *son of Raṅgojī. See* Bhaṭṭojī Dīkshita. बृहत् वैयाकरणभूषणं . . . Brihat Vaiyâkaraṇa Bhûshaṇa, a treatise on Sanskrit grammar, [comprising Bhaṭṭoji's Vaiyākaraṇasiddhāntakārikāḥ with commentary styled Vaiyākaraṇabhūshaṇa] by . . . Kauṇḍa Bhaṭṭa : also Padârtha Dîpikâ [or Nyāyapadārthadīpikā, an exposition of the Vaiśeshika Categories,] by the same author [*scil.*, Kauṇḍa Bhaṭṭa] *etc.* 1900. 8°. **14048. cc. 34.**

—— *See* Bhaṭṭojī Dīkshita. वैयाकरणसिद्धान्तकारिकाः *etc.* [Vaiyākaraṇasiddhāntakārikāḥ. With the Vaiyākaraṇabhūshaṇasāra of Kauṇḍa Bhaṭṭa, an abridgment of his Vaiyākaraṇabhūshaṇa.] [1901.] 8°. **14003. ccc. (no. 43.)**

KAUŚIKA. *See* Caland (W.). Zur Exegese und Kritik der rituellen Sūtras, *etc.* 1897, *etc.* 8°. [*Zeitschrift der Deutschen Morgenlaendischen Gesellschaft.*] **Ac. 8815/2.(vol. 51, etc.)**

—— *See* Henry (V.). La Magie dans l'Inde Antique. [With special reference to the Kauśikasūtra.] 1904. 12°. **08631. f. 35.**

—— Altindisches Zauberritual. Probe einer Uebersetzung der wichtigsten Theile des Kauśika Sūtra von Dr. W. Caland. 1900. *See* Academies, *etc.* — Amsterdam. — *Koninklijke Akademie van Wetenschappen.* Verhandelingen, *etc.* Nieuwe Reeks. Deel iii., No. 2. [1858, *etc.*] 8°. **Ac. 944/3. (Nieuwe Reeks, Deel 3.)**

—— [Another copy.] **14033. c. 40.**

KAVIBHŪSHAṆA (R. K.). Kayastha-tattvam. [An anthological work in 208 stanzas, to prove the descent of the Kāyastha caste from the Kshatriyas. With Bengali notes and translations.] pp. iii. 56. কুমারখালী ১৩০৬ [*Kumarkhali*, 1899.] 12°. **14058. a. 13.(3.)**

Forms no. 1 *of the* Tattvāmbudhi *series.*

KAVIBHŪSHAṆA KUMĀRA TĀTĀRYA. *See* Kumāra Tātārya, *Kavibhūshaṇa.*

KAVIKARṆAPŪRA, *son of Śivānandasena.* অলঙ্কারকৌস্তুভঃ *etc.* [Alaṅkārakaustubha. A treatise on stylistic, in 10 *kiraṇas.* With the commentary Subodhanī of Viśvanātha Chakravartī. Edited with a Bengali version by Rāmanārāyaṇa Vidyāratna.] pp. i. 834, xx. মুর্শিদাবাদ ১৩০৫ [*Murshidabad*, 1899.] 8°. **14053. ccc. 25.**

—— आनन्दवृन्दावनचम्पूः *etc.* [Ānandavrindāvanachampū. A poem on Krishṇa's life in Brindaban. With the commentary Sukhavartinī. Edited by Mukundadeva Śāstrī.] pp. 622 ; 4 *plates.* मथुरा १९५५ [*Muttra*, 1898.] 8°. **14070. dd. 8.**

—— শ্রী চৈতন্যচরিতামৃত মহাকাব্যং *etc.* [Chaitanyacharitāmrita. A poem in 20 *sargas* on the life of Chaitanya. Edited with a Bengali translation by Rāmanārāyaṇa Vidyāratna.] pp. i. 704, ii. মুর্শিদাবাদ ১২৯২-১২৯৮ [*Murshidabad*, 1885-1892.] 8°. **14058. b. 28.**

KAVIÑĀṆADDHAJA, known as TAUNGLELÔN HSAYA. *See* SUTTAPIṬAKA.—*Khuddakanikāya.* [*Chariyā-piṭaka.*] စရိယာပိဋကတ် *etc.* [Chariyāpiṭaka. With Burmese commentary by Kaviñāṇaddhaja.] 1899. 8°. **14098. c. 29.(2.)**

KAVĪNDRA VIṢVĀSA. *See* NARAHARI DĀSA GUPTA.

KAVIRĀJA PAṆḌITA, *Courtier of Kāmadeva Kādamba of Hangal.* राघवपाण्डवीयम् *etc.* [Rāghava-pāṇḍavīya. A poem in 13 *sargas* that may be read alike as a Rāmāyaṇa or as a Bhārata. With the commentary Sārachandrikā of Lakshmaṇa Paṇḍita.] pp. 205. [1890.] *See* PERIODICAL PUBLICATIONS.—*Bombay.* ग्रन्थरत्नमाला *etc.* (Granth Ratna Málá, *etc.*) Vol. III, no. 9—Vol. IV, no. 3. 1887-[1892.] 8°. **14096. c. 8.(vol. 3, 4.)**

—— The Râghavapâṇḍavîya of Kavirâja. With the commentary [Rāghavapāṇḍavīyaprakāṣa] of Śaśadhara. Edited by . . . Paṇḍit Śivadatta . . . and Kâśînâth Pâṇdurang Parab. (राघवपाण्डवीयम् ।). pp. 200, xi. 1897. *See* DURGĀPRASĀDA, *son of Vrajalāla*, and KĀṢĪNĀTHA PĀṆḌURAṄGA PARAB. Kâvyamâlâ. [No.] 62. 1886, *etc.* 8°. **14072. ccc. 12.(no. 62.)**

KAVIRĀKSHASĪYA. కవిరాక్షసీయము . . . ద్వ్యర్థి కావ్యము *etc.* [Kavirākshasīya. A series of 105 stanzas, each of which can be construed so as to yield two different meanings, on themes of poetry, ethics, *etc.* With Telugu analyses and commentary by Ṣrīnivāsapuram Lokanātha Kavi.] pp. i. 70. మద్రాసు [*Madras*,] 1902. 8°. **14072. d. 38.(3.)**

KEDĀRAKALPA. ॥ अथ श्रीकेदार कल्प प्रारम्भः ॥ [Kedārakalpa. A Ṣaiva Pauranic work, giving an account of various mythological regions and spheres, aspects of the Deity, *etc.*, with rituals for its study.] ff. 92. बनारस [*Benares*, 1894.] *obl.* 8°. **14053. ccc. 5.**

KEDĀRANĀTHA, *Zamindar.* গ্রহবিপ্র *etc.* [Graha-vipra. A Bengali tract on the functions of astrologers, illustrated by Sanskrit quotations.] pp. 8. উলুবেড়িয়া ১২৯৯ [*Ulubaria*, 1893.] 8°. **14053. c. 56.(3.)**

KEDĀRANĀTHA DATTA. দত্তবংশমালা *etc.* [Datta-vaṃṣamālā. Comprising genealogical tables of the Datta family and a poem in 6 cantos styled Dattavaṃṣa and treating of the same topic. Second edition.] pp. iv. 232. কলিকাতা ১৩০৬ [*Calcutta*, 1900.] 16°. **14053. a. 16.**

KELĀSA, Ū. *See* SUMAṄGALASĀMI. ဋီကာကျော် *etc.* [Ṭīkā-kyaw. With Burmese *nissaya* by Kelāsa.] 1903. 8°. **14099. b. 2.**

KERALA VARMĀ, *Valiya-kōyil Tamburān, of Travancore.* *See* AMARU. Amaruka Satakum. Translated . . . into Manipravalam by Kerala Varma, *etc.* 1893. 8°. **14072. cc. 56.**

—— ശ്രീ വിക്ടോറിയാ ചരിതസംഗ്രഹം *etc.* [Victoria-charitasaṅgraha. A brief poetical history of Queen Victoria in 108 stanzas, with explanation in Malayalam.] pp. 61, ii. കൊട്ടയം പ്രവൃത്തി [*Kottayam*, 1889.] 8°. **14076. cc. 2.(2.)**

KERN (JOHAN CASPAR HENDRIK). *See* ĀRYA ŚŪRA. The Jātaka-Mālā . . . Edited by Dr. H. Kern. 1891. 8°. [*Harvard Oriental Series.*] **14003. l. 3.(vol. 1.)**

KEṢAVA, *son of Kamalākara, of Nandigram.* केशवी जातक *etc.* [Keṣavī-jātaka, or Keṣavajātaka-paddhati. A manual of horoscopy. Edited with analyses, Hindi version, examples, and tables by Jagadiṣaprasāda Tripāṭhī.] pp. vi. 232, *lith.* मुंबई १९५६ [*Bombay*, 1900.] 8°. **14053. d. 63.**

KEṢAVA BĀLAKṚISHṆA PARĀÑJPYE. *See* KĀLIDĀSA.—*Vikramorvaṣīya.* Vikramorvaśíyam, with . . . English translation . . . notes, and . . . introduction, by Keshav . . . Paranjpe. 1898. 8°. **14080. c. 38.**

KEṢAVACHANDRA SENA. नवसंहिता *etc.* [Nava-saṃhitā. A metrical Sanskrit version of the "New Samhita," a series of ethical writings in English by Keṣavachandra. Translated with Sanskrit commentary by Gauragovinda Rāya Upādhyāya.] pp. i. 208. कलिकातायां १८२२ [*Calcutta*, 1901.] 8°. **14033. aa. 15.**

***The name of the translator is taken from the Catalogue of Books Registered, Calcutta, March* 1901.**

KEṢAVA DAIVAJÑA, *son of Gokulachandra.* अथ केशवदैवज्ञविरचिता नवसूत्रात्मिका *etc.* [Mādhyandinīya-vedaparibhāshāṅkasūtra. 9 aphorisms on Vedic phonetics, sometimes ascribed to Kātyāyana, but here attributed to Keṣava, with a commentary by Keṣava, the whole being entitled Keṣavī Ṣikshā and claiming the authority of the Prati-jñāsūtra. Followed by a *kārikā* to the same by Keṣava, styled Kārikāvalī or Padyātmikā Ṣikshā.] *See* YUGALAKIṢORA VYĀSA PĀṬHAKA. श्रीमद्याज्ञवल्क्यादि . . . शिक्षासंग्रहः . . . A collection of Śikshás, *etc.* pp. 138-152. 1893. 8°. **14093. b. 31.**

KEṢAVA HARSHADA DHRUVA. *See* AMARU. अमरुशतक *etc.* [Amaruṣataka. Edited with Gujarati metrical paraphrase and commentary by Keṣava Dhruva.] [1892.] 8°. **14070. c. 48.**

KEṢAVAJĪ VIṢVANĀTHA. *See* PURĀṆAS.—*Skanda-purāṇa.* श्रीमालपुराण *etc.* [Ṣrīmālamāhātmya. With Gujarati translation by Keṣavajī, *etc.*] [1899.] 8°. **14016. c. 62.**

KEṢAVA KAVI, *Vedādhinātha Bhaṭṭāchārya.* ஸ்ரீ கோதாபரிணய சம்பூ காவ்யம் *etc.* [Godāpariṇaya. A *champū* composition on the union of the river-goddess Godā or Āṇḍāḷ with Raṅganātha. With the commentary Sumano-rañjanī of Elattūr Sundararāja.] pp. 106. தென்காசி [*Tenkasi,*] 1896. 8°. **14070. dd. 9.(1.)**

KEṢAVALĀLA ṢIVARĀMA. जैनबालज्ञानसुबोध *etc.* [Jaina-bālajñānasubodha. A Jain primer of religious instruction and devotion. Part i., comprising Gujarati hymns, lists and explanations of technical terms, and the Sāmāyikasūtra with Gujarati translations, *etc.*] pp. 48. અમદાવાદ ૧૮૮૮ [*Ahmadabad,* 1888.] 12°. **14144. f. 30.(2.)**

KEṢAVA MIṢRA, *Logician.* The Tarkabhâshâ of Kes'avamis'ra, [a treatise on logic,] with the commentary of Govardhana. Edited with an introduction and notes, critical and explanatory, by Shivaram Mahadeo Paranjape. pp. i. vi. 113, iii. 86, ii. iv. *Poona,* 1894. 8°. **14048. dd. 18.**

—— तर्कभाषा . . . The Tarkabhāṣā of Keçava-miçra. With the commentary Nyāyapradīpa of Viçwakarman. Edited by Surendralāla Gosvāmin. pp. 185, vii. xii. iv. v. ii. 1901. *See* PERIODICAL PUBLICATIONS.—*Benares.* The Pandit, *etc.* New Series. Vol. XXII–XXIII. 1876, *etc.* 8°. **14096. d. 6.(vol. 22-23.)**

—— [A separate issue of the same.] **14049. a. 5.**

KEṢAVA MIṢRA, *Rhetorician.* *See* ṢAUDDHODANI. The Alankâraśekhara of Keśavamiśra[, comprising the aphorisms ascribed to Ṣauddhodani with the commentary of Keṣava,] *etc.* 1895. 8°. [*Kâvyamâlâ.*] **14072. ccc. 12.(no. 50.)**

KEṢAVĀNANDA SVĀMĪ. Anubhavānanda Lahari of Kesavánanda Swami. [A Vedantic poem in 54 stanzas. In an English prose version.] 1898. *See* PERIODICAL PUBLICATIONS.—*Bombay.* The Theosophist, *etc.* Vol. XX, nos. iii., vi., xii., Vol. XXI, no. ix. 1879, *etc.* 8°. **P.P. 636. cm. (vol. 20.)**

KEṢAVĀNANDA SVĀMĪ, *Udāsīna Paramahaṃsa, disciple of Gauradeva.* *See* NĀNAK. श्रीमद्गुरुनानकगीता *etc.* [Nānakagītā. With the commentary Kaiṣavapada of Keṣavānanda.] [1901.] 8°. **14049. b. 4.**

—— *See* NĀNAK. अथ निराकारमीमांसादर्शनम् *etc.* [Nirākāramīmāṃsādarṣana. With exposition by Keṣavānanda.] [1903.] 8°. **14049. bb. 3.**

KEṢAVA NĀRĀYAṆA DĀMLE. परमार्थदर्शनम् *etc.* [Paramārthadarṣana. A treatise in 1891 stanzas on metaphysics, notably the Sāṅkhya, Yoga, and Vedānta systems. In 3 parts of graduated difficulty, termed Bāladhikāra, Taruṇādhikāra, and Prauḍhādhikāra.] pp. ii. 151. पुण्यपत्तने १८२१ [*Poona,* 1900.] 12°. **14048. b. 37.**

KEṢAVAPRASĀDA ṢARMĀ, *son of Paramasukha.* *See* MANU.—*Dharmaṣāstra.* श्रीमनुस्मृति *etc.* [Manusmṛiti. With Hindi paraphrase by Keṣavaprasāda.] [1891.] 8°. **14038. d. 32.**

KEṢAVA ṢĀSTRĪ, *of the Sanskrit College, Benares.* *See* RĀMA MIṢRA ṢĀSTRĪ. स्नेहपूर्तिपरीक्षा। [Snehapūrtiparikshā. Edited by Keṣava Ṣāstrī.] 1895-1896. 8°. [*The Pandit.*] **14096. d. 6.(vol. 17, 18.)**

KESHAV. *See* KEṢAVA.

KESINDA, Ū. *See* SĀDHUNARADHAMMA-SĀ-TAN. သာဓုနရဓမ္မစာတမ်း [Sādhunaradhamma-sā-tan. Edited by Kesinda.] [1897.] 8°.
14098. ccc. 26.(4.)

KEVALAKRISHṆA, called 'URF. *See* ĀRYA SAMĀJ. سندهیا مترجم منظوم [Sandhyā mutarjim manẓūm. The *sandhyā* prayers with metrical version in Urdu by Kevalakṛishṇa.] [1902.] 12°.
14028. b. 96.(2.)

KEVAL KISHAN. *See* KEVALAKṚISHṆA.

KHAGENDRANĀTHA ŚĀSTRĪ, *of Bhawanipur.* *See* PURĀṆAS.—*Brahmāṇḍapurāṇa.* [*Adhyātma-rāmāyaṇa.*] অধ্যাত্মরামায়ণম্ *etc.* [Adhyātma-rāmāyaṇa. With commentary of Rāma Varmā. Edited with analyses and Bengali translations, *etc.*, by Khagendranātha.] [1901, *etc.*] 8°.
14016. d. 61.

KHAṆḌADEVA, *son of Rudradeva.* *See* JAIMINI.—*Mīmāṃsāsūtra.* The Meemamsa Kausthubha. Vol. -1 [*scil.* Adh. I. ii.]. A commentary on Jaimini Sutra. By Khanda Deva, *etc.* 1902. 8°. [*Śāstramuktāvalī.*] **14049. a. 1.(no. 14.)**

—— भाट्टदीपिका । Bhāṭṭa Dīpikā, a work belonging to the Pūrvva Mīmāṃsā school of Hindu philosophy, by Khaṇḍa Deva. Edited by . . . Candra Kānta Tarkālaṅkāra. 1899, *etc.* *See* ACADEMIES, *etc.*—Calcutta.—*Asiatic Society of Bengal.* Bibliotheca Indica. New Series. [Vol. 141.] 1848, *etc.* 8°. **14002. a. (vol. 141.)**
In progress.

—— Bhatta Rahasyam, *etc.* [An introductory treatise upon Jaimini's Mīmāṃsāsūtra. Parichchheda i.] (भाट्टरहस्यम् ॥) pp. iv. 128. 1900. *See* ANANTĀCHĀRYA, *Prativādibhayaṅkara.* शास्त्रमुक्तावली. The Ŝasthramukthâvalî, *etc.* No. 2. 1899, *etc.* 8°.
14049. a. 1.(no. 2.)

KHAṆḌARĀJA DĪKSHITA. *See* SANDHYĀVANDANA. सन्ध्याभाष्यसमुच्चयः *etc.* [Sandhyābhāshyasamuchchaya. A collection of commentaries upon the *sandhyā* prayers, including Khaṇḍarāja's Bahvṛichasandhyāmantrārthadīpikā, with his gloss Prabhā, *etc.*] [1899.] 8°. **14003. ccc. (no. 40.)**

KHĀN-KHĀNĀ-NAWĀB. *See* NAWĀB-KHĀN-KHĀNĀN.

KHEMARAṂSI, *of Payaba, Kugan.* *See* KACHCHĀYANA.—*Kachchāyanappakaraṇa.* သဒ္ဒါကြီး *etc.* [Saddā-kyī. Kachchāyana's Pali grammar, with the Burmese commentary of Khemaraṃsi upon the Taddhitakappa, *etc.*] [1894-1896.] 8°.
14098. ccc. 13.

KHUDDAKANIKĀYA. *See* SUTTAPIṬAKA.

KHUDDĪ JHĀ, *son of Umādatta, Maithila, of Benares.* नागेशोक्तिप्रकाश . . . Nágeśokti-prakáśa. Notes on the Laghu-śabdendu Śekhara . . . Vol. i. Corrected by Ramánanda Jhá. pp. 184. *Benares,* 1899. 8°. **14093. d. 20.**

KIELHORN (FRANZ). *See* PATAÑJALI.—*Grammatical Works.* The Vyâkaraṇa-mahâbhâshya . . . Edited by F. Kielhorn. 1892, *etc.* 8°.
14090. d. 28.

—— *See* PRUSSIA. Verzeichniss der Handschriften im Preussischen Staate. I. Hannover. 3. Göttingen 3. (Sanskrit-Handschriften. Beschrieben von . . . F. Kielhorn.) 1894. 8°.
011901. g.

—— *See* SOMADEVA, *Courtier of Vigraharāja.* Sanskrit Plays, partly preserved as inscriptions at Ajmere. [Edited] by . . . F. Kielhorn. 1891. 4°. [*Indian Antiquary.*] **14096. e. (vol. 20.)**

—— *See* SOMADEVA, *Courtier of Vigraharāja.* Bruchstücke des Lalita-vigraharâja Nâṭaka. Von F. Kielhorn. 1893. 8°. [*Nachrichten von der Georg-Augusts Universitaet zu Goettingen.*]
2097. a.

—— *See* SOMADEVA, *Courtier of Vigraharāja.* Bruchstücke indischer Schauspiele in Inschriften zu Ajmere. Von F. Kielhorn. 1901. 4°. [*Koenigliche Gesellschaft der Wissenschaften zu Goettingen: Festschrift.*] **Ac. 670.**

KING (GEORGE). A glossary of Indian plants mentioned in Sanskrit medical works with Bengali, Hindi, and Latin synonyms. *See* UDAYACHANDRA DATTA. The Materia Medica of the Hindus, *etc.* pp. 289-324. 1900. 8°.
14043. c. 48.

KIRSTE (JOHANN). *See* BUEHLER (J. G.) and KIRSTE (J.). Indian Studies. No. ii., *etc.* 1892. 8°. [*Sitzungsberichte der Kaiserlichen Akademie der Wissenschaften, Wien.*] **Ac. 810/6. (Bd. 127.)**

KIRSTE (JOHANN) (*continued*). *See* HEMACHANDRA, *disciple of Devachandra.* ॥ अथ हैमधातुपारायणम् ॥ The Dhātupāṭha . . . with . . . commentary. Edited by Joh. Kirste. 1901. 4°. [*Sources of Sanskrit Lexicography.*] **14090. e. 23.(vol. 4.)**

—— *See* HEMACHANDRA, *disciple of Devachandra.* अथ श्रीहेमचन्द्रसूरिविरचितमुणादिगणसूत्रं . . . The Uṇâdigaṇasûtra . . . With . . . commentary. Edited by J. Kirste, *etc.* 1895. 8°. [*Sources of Sanskrit Lexicography.*] **14090. e. 23.(vol. 2.)**

—— Professor J. Kirstes Collation des Textes der Yâjñavalkya-smṛiti und Analyse der Citate in Aparârkas Commentare, herausgegeben von G. Bühler. pp. 11. 1893. *See* ACADEMIES, *etc.*—Vienna.—*Kaiserliche Akademie der Wissenschaften.* Denkschriften, *etc.* Band xlii., Abhandl. 5. 1850, *etc.* Fol. **Ac. 810/12.(Bd. 42.)**

KISHORY LAL SARKAR. *See* KIṢORĪLĀLA SARKĀR.

KIṢORADĀSA, *of Brindaban.* *See* NIMBĀRKA. श्री . . . वेदान्तकामधेनु *etc.* [Vedāntakāmadhenu. Edited with a Hindi commentary styled Sārārthadarṣikā by Kiṣoradāsa.] [1903.] 8°. **14049. a. 7.(2.)**

KIṢORĪLĀLA SARKĀR. The Hindu System of Religious Science & Art, or The Revelations of Rationalism and Emotionalism, *etc.* [In English, illustrated from Sanskrit texts.] pp. iv. 159. *Calcutta,* 1898. 12°. **14033. a. 34.**

—— The Introductory Lecture for Tagore Professorship, *etc.* [An English lecture on the principles of interpretation used in the Pūrvamīmāṃsā school.] pp. 32. *Calcutta,* 1902. 8°. **14039. b. 27.**

KIṢORĪLĀLA ṢARMĀ, *of Hapur, Meerut.* मृत्युपरीक्षा *etc.* [Mṛityuparīkshā. An account of the circumstances and symptoms of death, compiled from various Sanskrit writers, with Hindi translation.] pp. iv. 96. मेरठ १९५९ [*Meerut,* 1902.] 12°. **14043. a. 5.**

KIṢORĪMOHANA DĀSA. ସଙ୍ଗୀତଶିକ୍ଷା । *etc.* [Saṅgītaṣikshā. An Oriya treatise on Hindu music, illustrated from Sanskrit texts.] pt. 1. pp. ii. viii. 181. *Cuttack,* 1899. 12°. **14121. c. 14.**

KIṢORĪMOHANA GAṄGOPĀDHYĀYA. *See* MAHĀBHĀRATA.—*Entire Work.* The Mahabharata . . . Translated into English prose [by Kiṣorīmohana,] *etc.* 1883-1896. 8°. **14065. bb. 2.**

KIṢORĪMOHANA VIDYĀNIDHI, *Kāvyatīrtha.* वैयाकरण नीतिकौमुदी *etc.* [Vaiyākaraṇa-nītikaumudī. A series of moral tales, with occasional verses extracted from the Hitopadeṣa and Pañchatantra, constructed so as to illustrate the grammatical rules for case-inflection according to the Kālāpa school.] pp. i. i. i. 69. कलिकाता १३०४ [*Calcutta,* 1898.] 12°. **14085. b. 43.**

KITTUR (G. V.). *See* GURUNĀTHA VEṄKAṬEṢA KITTŪR.

KLATT (JOHANNES). Specimen of a Literary-bibliographical Jaina-Onomasticon. pp. iv. 55. *Leipzig, Berlin* [printed], 1892. 8°. **11900. f. 34.**

KLEMM (KURT). *See* BRĀHMAṆAS.—*Shaḍviṃṣabrāhmaṇa.* Das Ṣaḍviṃçabrāhmaṇa. Mit Proben aus Sāyaṇas Kommentar, nebst einer Übersetzung. Herausgegeben von K. Klemm. Prapāṭhaka 1. 1894. 8°. **14010. dd. 4.**

KNAUER (FRIEDRICH). *See* MANU.—*Gṛihyasūtra.* ॥ मानवगृह्यसूत्रम् ॥ Das Mānava-gṛhya-sūtra, nebst Commentar . . . Herausgegeben von Dr. F. Knauer. 1897. 4°. **14010. ee. 3.**

—— *See* MANU.—*Ṣrautasūtra.* ॥ मानवश्रौतसूत्रम् ॥ Das Mānava-çrauta-sūtra. Herausgegeben von Dr. F. Knauer. 1900, *etc.* 4°. **14028. e. 35.**

KO AUNG MIN, *Hsaya.* *See* VINAYAPIṬAKA. ဝိနည်း *etc.* [Vinayapiṭaka. The text with Burmese interpretation. Edited by Hbi, Ko Aung Min, and Ko Kyaw.] 1903-1904. 8°. **14099. aa.**

KODAṆḌAMAṆḌANA. बाण विद्या (कोदण्डमण्डन) । [Kodaṇḍamaṇḍana, or Bāṇavidyā. A metrical treatise on archery, in 22 *adhyāyas.* With Hindi translation.] pp. 76. *Moradabad,* १९०१ [1901.] 8°. **14053. ccc. 40.**

Stated on the title-page to form the second volume of the Dhanurveda.

KOENIGLICH SAECHSISCHE GESELLSCHAFT DER WISSENSCHAFTEN. *See* ACADEMIES, *etc.*—*Leipsic.*

KOKILEṢVARA BHAṬṬĀCHĀRYA VIDYĀRATNA. *See* ṢRĪṢVARA VIDYĀLAṄKĀRA BHAṬṬĀCHĀRYA. Vijayiní-kávyam . . . Edited with . . . notes by Kokileswar Bhattacharyya, *etc.* 1902. 8°. **14058. b. 48.**

—— *See* ṢRĪṢVARA VIDYĀLAṄKĀRA BHAṬṬĀCHĀRYA. Dilli-mahotsava-kavyam . . . Edited with . . . notes . . . by Kokilesvar Bhattacharyya, *etc.* 1903. 8°. **14076. d. 56.**

KO KYAW, *Hsaya.* *See* VINAYAPIṬAKA. ဝိနည်း *etc.* [Vinayapiṭaka. The text with Burmese interpretation. Edited by Hbi, Ko Aung Min, and Ko Kyaw.] 1903-1904. 8°. **14099. aa.**

KOṆḌA BHAṬṬA. *See* KAUṆḌA BHAṬṬA.

KOṆḌAMĀCHĀRYA, *D.* ಸಾತ್ವಿಕಶ್ರೀವೈಷ್ಣವಮತಸಾರಸಂಗ್ರಹಃ [Sāttvika-ṣrīvaishṇavamatasāra-saṅgraha. A compilation treating of the religious and philosophic dogmas and the social divisions of the Ṣrīvaishṇavas, consisting chiefly of excerpts from Sanskrit authorities with Canarese translations and expositions.] pt. 1. pp. ii. iv. 146, vi. ಬೆಂಗಳೂರು [*Bangalore*,] 1901. 8°. **14033. bbb. 12.**
In progress?

KONOW (STEN). *See* BRĀHMAṆAS.—*Sāmavidhāna-brāhmaṇa.* Das Sāmavidhānabrāhmaṇa . . . Eingeleitet und übersetzt von S. Konow. 1893. 8°. **14007. c. 22.**

—— *See* RĀJAṢEKHARA, *son of Durduka.* Rājaçekhara's Karpūra-mañjarī . . . edited . . . with . . . index, and an essay on the life and writings of the poet, by S. Konow, *etc.* 1901. 8°. [*Harvard Oriental Series.*] **14003. l. 3.(vol. 4.)**

KOṢARATNĀKARA. कोशरत्नाकर *etc.* [Koṣaratnākara. A Sanskrit-Hindi dictionary. Edited by Sadāsukha Lāla.] pp. iv. 459, xlv., *lith.* इलाहाबाद १९३२ [*Allahabad*, 1876.] 8°. **14160. c. 37.**

KOṢAṢABDĀRTHASAṄGRAHA. कोष शब्दार्थसंग्रह *etc.* [Koṣaṣabdārthasaṅgraha. Comprising (1) Amarakoṣādarṣa, a Hindi glossary to the Amarakoṣa, (2) Vaidyakakoṣa, a similar glossary of medical terms, and (3) Ṣabdasaṅgraha, another glossary.] pp. 368. लखनऊ १८९९ [*Lucknow*, 1899.] 8°. **14160. c. 40.**

KO SAUNG TWÈ. ကိုးဆောင်တွဲ [Ko saung twè. Comprising the Maṅgalasutta, Bāhira-jayamaṅgalagāthā and Ajjhatta-j°., Ratanapañjara, Namakāra, and Lokanīti, all with Burmese versions; a series of glosses on Pali words; and two Burmese grammatical works.] pp. 168. *Rangoon*, 1881. 8°. **14098. ccc. 11.(5.)**

KOSEGARTEN (JOHANN GOTTFRIED LUDWIG). *See* HERTEL (J.). Kritische Bemerkungen zu Kosegartens Pañcatantra, *etc.* 1902. 8°. [*Zeitschrift der Deutschen Morgenlaendischen Gesellschaft.*] **Ac. 8815/2.(vol. 56.)**

KOUMARAJIVA. *See* KUMĀRAJĪVA.

KŌVILAGATTA UṆṆIKIḌAN, *Maṅgaḍa.* *See* ṢRĪVALLABHA, *Tamburān.*

KRAMADĪṢVARA. সংক্ষিপ্তসারব্যাকরণম্ *etc.* [Saṅkshiptasāravyākaraṇa. With the commentary Rasavatī in the recension of Jumaranandī, and the gloss Vivaraṇiṭīkā of Goyīchandra. Edited by Jīvānanda Vidyāsāgara.] pp. xviii. 1455. কলিকাতা° ১৯০১ [*Calcutta*, 1901.] 8°. **14090. bb. 16.**

—— সংক্ষিপ্তসারব্যাকরণ *etc.* [Saṅkshiptasāravyākaraṇa. Abridged and edited, with selections from the commentary Rasavatī and a Bengali translation, by Upendranātha Chakravartī.] pt. 1. pp. i. 28. কলিকাতা [*Calcutta*,] 1891. 8°. **14090. c. 38.**

—— লঘুসংক্ষিপ্তসারব্যাকরণম্ *etc.* [Laghu-saṅkshiptasāravyākaraṇa. A shorter recension of Kramadīṣvara's Saṅkshiptasāra. Abridged and edited with a commentary by Dvārakānātha Nyāyabhūshaṇa.] 7 pts. *Suoyadighi, Calcutta* [printed], 1890-1892. 8°. **14090. c. 37.**

KRAMASANDHĀNA. अथ क्रमसन्धानशिक्षा *etc.* [Kramasandhānaṣikshā. A list of 115 *kramasandhānas* in the recitation of the White Yajurveda.] *See* YUGALAKIṢORA VYĀSA PĀṬHAKA. श्रीमद्याज्ञवल्क्यादि . . . शिक्षासङ्ग्रहः . . . A collection of Śikshás, *etc.* pp. 176-180. 1893. 8°. **14093. b. 31.**

KṚIKALĀSADĪPIKĀ. বিবিধসাধন। কৃকলাসদীপিকা। [Kṛikalāsadīpikā. A work on Tantric magic. With Bengali translation.] pp. 20. [1893, *etc.*] *See* PERIODICAL PUBLICATIONS.—*Calcutta.* অরুণোদয় *etc.* [Aruṇodaya.] pt. i., no. 31. [1890, *etc.*] 4°. **14133. g. 16.(pt. i., no. 31.)**

KṚIPĀNĀTHA ŚARMĀ VIŚVĀSA. অকলঙ্ক যোগ etc. [Akalaṅka Yoga. Miscellaneous Bengali writings in prose and verse, with occasional Sanskrit stanzas.] pp. ii. i. iii. 276. কলিকাতা ১৩১০ [*Calcutta*, 1903.] 12°. **14131. d. 45.**

KṚIPĀRĀMA, *of Bulandshahr. See* UPANISHADS.—*Separate Upanishads.* ایش اوپنشد الخ [Īśopanishad. With Urdu translation and commentary by Kṛipārāma.] [1899.] 8°. **14007. dd. 5.**

KṚISHṆA, *Grammarian. See* PIṄGALA ĀCHĀRYA. Prákrita-paiṅgalam. With the commentaries of . . . Krishṇa, *etc.* 1902. 8°. [*Bibliotheca Indica.*] **14002. a. (vol. 148.)**

KṚISHṆA AVADHŪTA, styled GHAṬIKĀŚATAMAHĀKAVI. సర్వవినోదనాటకమ్ . . . ఈహామృగీతి గర్భరూపకం *etc.* [Īhāmṛigī, or Sarvavinoda. A play (*garbharūpaka*) of the *īhāmṛigī* type, in 4 acts illustrating the emotions respectively of *śriṅgāra*, *bībhatsa*, *hāsya*, and *vairāgya*. With annotations.] pp. 64. బళ్లారి ౧౮౯౫ [*Bellary*, 1895.] 12°. **14079. b. 43.**

KṚISHṆA BALADEVA VARMĀ. भर्तृहरिराजत्याग नाटक *etc.* [Bhartṛiharirājatyāga. A drama on the legend of Bhartṛihari's abdication of his kingdom and entrance upon the religious life. In Hindi, interspersed with Sanskrit verses.] pp. viii. xi. 428. लखनऊ [*Lucknow*, 1898.] 12°. **14158. a. 16.**

KṚISHṆA BHAṬṬA, *son of Raghunātha, Maunī. See* JAYAKṚISHṆA, *son of Raghunātha.*

KṚISHṆA BHAṬṬA ĀRDE. *See* GAṄGEŚA UPĀDHYĀYA. పక్షతా *etc.* [Pakshatā. Followed by Gadādhara's Gādādharī and Kṛishṇa Bhaṭṭa's gloss upon Gadādhara.] [1890.] 8°. **14048. e. 19.**

—— *See* GAṄGEŚA UPĀDHYĀYA. గాదాధరీయమైన సిద్ధాన్తలక్షణమ్ *etc.* [Siddhāntalakshaṇa. With Gadādhara's Gādādharī, together with Kṛishṇa Bhaṭṭa's commentary upon Gadādhara.] [1893.] 8°. **14048. dd. 13.**

KṚISHṆA BHĀŪ ŚĀSTRĪ GHULE. *See* BHARTṚIHARI. Bhartrihari's Vidnyâna Śataka. Edited with introductions, tika and notes by K. B. Ghule. 1897. 8°. **14072. d. 39.(2.)**

KṚISHṆACHANDRA, *of Benares.* Preeti Kusumanjali, or, An Offering of a Handful of Flowers of Joy. [Poems in Sanskrit and Hindi] compiled by the Pandits of Benares to commemorate the Diamond Jubilee of Her Most Gracious Majesty Victoria . . . Offered by Krishna Chandra, *etc.* (प्रीतिकुसुमाञ्जलिः) pp. ii. 44. *Benares*, 1897. 12°. **14072. b. 27.(3.)**

KṚISHṆĀCHĀRLU, *B. See* BONĀLA KṚISHṆA.

KṚISHṆĀCHĀRYA, *Sārvabhauma.* अथ श्रीराघवेन्द्रगुरोस्तारहारः प्रार्थनावलीच [Rāghavendratārahāra and Rāghavendraprārthanāvalī. Short poems in praise of Rāghavendra Guru, a religious preceptor of the Mādhva sect.] ff. 12. मुंबय्यां १८१४ [*Bombay*, 1892.] *obl.* 16°. **14028. b. 80.(1.)**

KṚISHṆĀCHĀRYA, *T. R., of Kumbakonam. See* NĀRĀYAṆA PAṆḌITĀCHĀRYA, *son of Trivikrama.* मध्वविजयः *etc.* [Madhvavijaya. Edited by Apaśaṅkara and Kṛishṇāchārya.] [1895.] 16°. **14076. a. 26.**

—— ॥ कन्नडभाषान्तरमाला *etc.* [Kannaḍabhāshāntaramālā. A collection of Sanskrit texts, edited with Canarese version and commentary by Kṛishṇāchārya.] pt. 1. कुंभघोणद्रङ्ग १८१८ [*Kumbhakonam*, 1898.] 8°. **14007. b. 14.**

Part 1, which apparently is all that has been published, contains the Īśa, Kena, and part of the Māṇḍūkya Upanishads. The Canarese is printed in the Nagari character.

KṚISHṆĀCHĀRYA, *Bonāla. See* BONĀLA KṚISHṆA.

KṚISHṆĀCHĀRYA PURĀṆIKA MULGUNDKAR. देवांगसन्मार्गदर्शिका *etc.* [Devāṅgasanmārgadarśikā. A treatise on the duties of the Devāṅga caste. Compiled by Kṛishṇāchārya.] pp. 12. धारवाड [*Dharwar*,] 1895. *obl.* 12°. **14058. a. 13.(1.)**

—— ದೇವಾಂಗಸನ್ಮಾರ್ಗದರ್ಶಿಕಾ *etc.* [Devāṅgasanmārgadarśikā. The same work, in the Canarese character.] pp. 16. ಧಾರವಾಡ ೧೮೯೫ [*Dharwar*, 1895.] *obl.* 12°. **14058. a. 13.(2.)**

KṚISHṆADĀSA KAVIRĀJA, *Gosvāmī.* শ্রীশ্রীচৈতন্যচরিতামৃত *etc.* [Chaitanyacharitāmṛita. Bengali text, edited with Sanskrit commentary and copious notes by Madanagopāla Gosvāmī.] pts. 1-12, 14-19, 23, 24. কাল্না ১৮১৩ [*Kalna*, 1891, *etc.*] 4°. **14123. i. 8.**

Illustrated with full-page plates.

KṚISHṆADATTA, *disciple of Gopālānanda Svāmī.* ॥ एकत्वखण्डनारम्भः ॥ [Ekatvakhaṇḍana. A refutation of monism, from the Vaishṇava standpoint. Followed by two hymns styled Karāvalambāshṭaka and Harikṛishṇanandanavandana. Edited by Rāmachandra Dīnānātha Ṣāstrī.] ff. 12. अमदाबाद १९४९ [*Ahmadabad*, 1892.] *obl.* 8°.
14028. d. 50.(3.)

KṚISHṆADATTA JHĀ. *See* EUCLID. रेखागणितस्येकादशद्वादशाध्यायौ *etc.* [Rekhāgaṇita. A translation of the propositions of Euclid's Elements. Books xi.-xii. With a commentary styled Vāsanāmañjarī by Kṛishṇadatta.] [1891.] 8°.
14053. d. 53.

KṚISHṆADATTA ṢARMĀ, *son of Bhānudatta.* *See* RĀKHĀLDĀS VIDYĀRATNA. अनुवादभानु [Anuvādabhānu.] . . . Hindi translation [of the rules] by . . . Krishna Datta. 1902. 12°.
14160. a. 43.

KṚISHṆAGOPĀLA BHAKTA. *See* BĀDARĀYAṆA. বেদান্তদর্শন *etc.* [Vedāntadarṣana. Being the Brahmasūtra with the Govindabhāshya, *etc.* Edited by Kṛishṇagopāla.] [1894.] 8°.
14048. dd. 23.

—— *See* RĀDHĀKĀNTA DEVA. শব্দকল্পদ্রুমঃ *etc.* [Ṣabdakalpadruma. Edited by Kṛishṇagopāla Bhakta.] [1903, *etc.*] 4°. **14092. cc. 2.**

KṚISHṆAIYAṄGĀR, *Belūr.* ವಜ್ರಮುಕುಟೀಮಹೋತ್ಸವವರ್ಣನ *etc.* [Vajramukuṭīmahotsavavarṇana. A *champū* composition describing the annual Vairamuḍi festival at Melukote. Edited by Tirunārāyaṇa Perumāl Svāmi.] pp. 24. ಮೈಸೂರು ೧೯೦೦ [*Mysore*, 1900.] 16°.
14076. a. 16.(4.)

KṚISHṆĀJĪ GOVINDA OK. Companion to Sanskrit Grammar, *etc.* pp. i. vi. 368. *Poona*, 1895. 12°. **14092. a. 18.**

KṚISHṆĀJĪ NĀRĀYAṆA JOṢĪ. *See* VIKRAMA, *son of Sāṅgaṇa.* नेमिदूतकाव्य *etc.* [Nemidūta. With Marathi translation by Kṛishṇājī.] [1892.] 12°. **14028. b. 69.(3.)**

KṚISHṆĀJĪ PRAHLĀDABHAṬṬAJĪ ARANKE. *See* ACHALA DVIVEDĪ. નિર્ણયદીપક *etc.* [Nirṇayadīpaka. With Gujarati translation by Kṛishṇājī.] [1897.] 8°. **14028. dd. 4.**

KṚISHṆAKAMALA BHAṬṬĀCHĀRYA. *See* BHAVABHŪTI. An English Translation of Uttararama Charita. By Krishna Kamal Bhattacharyya. 1891. 12°. **14080. b. 9.(2.)**

—— *See* MANU.—*Dharmaṣāstra.* হিন্দুশাস্ত্র *etc.* [Selections from the Dharmaṣāstra, *etc.* With Bengali translations and introduction. Edited by Kṛishṇakamala.] [1895.] 8°. [*Hindu-ṣāstra.*]
14085. c. 45.(vol. 1.)

KṚISHṆAKĀNTA VIDYĀVĀGĪṢA. *See* GAṄGEṢA UPĀDHYĀYA. The Tattva-chintámaṇi, *etc.* (Part III. Upamāna Khaṇḍa, with the commentary of Kriṣṇakānta, *etc.*) 1888-1901. 8°. [*Bibliotheca Indica.*] **14002. a. (vol. 98.)**

KṚISHṆALĀLA, *of Muttra.* *See* CHARAKA. चरकसंहिता *etc.* [Charakasaṃhitā. Edited with Hindi paraphrase by Kṛishṇalāla.] [1898.] 8°.
14043. dd. 4.

—— *See* SUṢRUTA. श्रीसुश्रुताचार्य्यविरचिता सुश्रुतसंहिता . . . Sushrut Sanhita . . . With the Hindi commentary of Shri Krishna Lal. 1895. 8°. **14043. dd. 2.**

—— *See* TRIMALLA BHAṬṬA, *son of Vallabha.* शतश्लोकी *etc.* [Ṣataṣlokī. With Hindi translation by Kṛishṇalāla.] [1894.] 8°.
14043. e. 28.

KṚISHṆALĀLA GOVINDARĀMA DEVĀṢRAYĪ. *See* SĀYAṆA ĀCHARYA.—*Works on Philosophy, etc.* The Saṅkshepaṡaṁkarajaya . . . with Gujarâtî translation. Edited with notes and criticised [*sic*] essay on the date of Śaṁkarâchârya by Kṛishṇalâla, *etc.* 1899. 8°. **14048. cc. 35.**

—— શ્રીમચ્છંકરાચાર્યનો સમય *etc.* [Ṣaṅkarāchārya-no Samaya. A Gujarati dissertation on the chronology of Ṣaṅkara's life, illustrated from Sanskrit. With an abstract of the Saṅkshepa-ṣaṅkarajaya.] pp. 88, 34. મુંબાઈ ૧૮૯૮ [*Bombay*, 1898.] 8°. **14146. gg. 4.**

Identical with the essay prefixed to the author's edition of the Saṅkshepa-ṣaṅkarajaya.

KṚISHṆAM ĀCHĀRYA, *Gārgya.* *See* BĀDARĀYAṆA. శ్రీశుకభాష్యమ్ *etc.* [Brahmasūtra. With commentary of Ṣukāchārya and supercommentary called Chandrikā by Kṛishṇam.] [1892.] 8°.
14048. c. 76.

KṚISHṆAM ĀCHĀRYA, *Maṅgāḍu.* Portraits from Indian Classics. Being sketches of men and women selected from the best Sanskrit poets, with English renderings and full critical and explanatory notices, *etc.* pp. viii. ii. 109, i. *Madras,* 1901. 12°. **14070. b. 31.**

Forms no. 4 of the Vidvan Mano Ranjani Series.

KṚISHṆAM ĀCHĀRYA, *Paravastu, of Pudukottai.* *See* PERIODICAL PUBLICATIONS.—*Kumbakonam.* The Sanskrit Journal. . . . . Edited by R. Krishnamachariar, *etc.* 1896, *etc.* 8°. **14096. ccc. 1.**

—— *See* SHAKSPERE (W.). Vasantikaswapnam, an adaptation of Shakespeare's Midsummer-Night's Dream . . . by R. Krishnamachari. 1892. 8°. **14080. c. 34.**

KṚISHṆA MIṢRA, *Astrologer.* കൃഷ്ണീയാഖ്യം ജ്യോതിശ്ശാസ്ത്രരത്നം *etc.* [Kṛishṇīya-jyotiḥṣāstra-ratna. An astrological tract.] pp. 29. ശ്രീമച്ഛാരദാപത്തനം ചരം [*Palghat,* 1891.] 8°. **14053. cc. 62.(1.)**

KṚISHṆA MIṢRA, *Dramatist.* प्रबोधचन्द्रोदयम् *etc.* [Prabodhachandrodaya. With the commentary Chandrikā of Nāṇḍillagopa and the gloss called Prakāṣa by Rāmadāsa Dīkshita. Edited by Vāsudeva Lakshmaṇa Paṇṣīkar.] pp. ii. 245, iv. मुंबय्यां १८९८ [*Bombay,* 1898.] 8°. **14080. c. 39.**

Nāṇḍillagopa wrote in the 16th century, as Kṛishṇarāya of Vijayanagar, whose minister was Sālvatimma the uncle of Nāṇḍillagopa, reigned 1508-30.

—— Le Lever de la Lune de la Connaissance, Prabōdhacandrōdaya. Drame en 6 actes, traduit pour la première fois en français du sanskrit et du prâkrit [by G. Devèze]. 1899-1902. *See* PERIODICAL PUBLICATIONS. — *Paris.* Revue de Linguistique et de Philologie Comparée, *etc.* Tom. xxxii., pt. 3—tom. xxxv., pt. 3. 1867, *etc.* 8°. **P.P. 4964. d. (tom. 32-35.)**

KṚISHṆAMŪRTI KAVIRĀJA, *Śrīpāda.* కాళిదాస-విలాసము *etc.* [Kālidāsavilāsa. A romantic account of Kālidāsa's career, in Telugu, interspersed with Sanskrit stanzas.] pp. 86, ii. చెన్నపట్టణము ౧౮౯౯ [*Madras,* 1899.] 8°. **14174. g. 51.**

KṚISHṆĀNANDA, *Brahmachārī, son of Kālīcharaṇa.* गङ्गास्थितिः निर्णयः *etc.* [Gaṅgāsthitinirṇaya. A proof, supported by texts, of the permanence of the Ganges. With Hindi version.] pp. 36. कानपुर॰ [*Cawnpore,* 1899.] 12°. **14028. bb. 4.(1.)**

KṚISHṆĀNANDA, *Sāndhivigrahika.* The Sahṛidayânanda [or Nalacharita] of Kṛishṇânanda. [A poem in 15 *sargas.*] Edited by . . . Paṇdit Durgâprasâd and Kâśinâth Pândurang Parab. (सहृदयानन्दम् ।) pp. ii. 87, ii. 1892. *See* DURGĀPRASĀDA, *son of Vrajalāla,* and KĀṢINĀTHA PĀṆḌURAṄGA PARAB. Kâvyamâlâ. [No. 32.] 1886, *etc.* 8°. **14072. ccc. 12.(no. 32.)**

KṚISHṆĀNANDA SARASVATĪ, *disciple of Sachchidānanda, of the Kaivalyadhāma.* ॥ अथाद्वैतसाम्राज्यप्रारंभः ॥ [Advaitasāmrājya. A Vedantic tract.] ff. 32. मुंबय्यां १८१३ [*Bombay,* 1891.] *obl.* 8°. **14048. dd. 4.**

—— ब्राह्मणसर्वस्वं *etc.* [Brāhmaṇasarvasva. A critique of the Turīyamīmāṃsā of Rāma Miṣra Ṣāstrī, on the caste-divisions of Hinduism.] pp. 36. श्रीकाश्यां १८१२ [*Benares,* 1902.] 8°. **14039. b. 21.(2.)**

—— गीतासारोद्धारः *etc.* [Gītāsāroddhāra. 62 stanzas forming an epitome of the Bhagavadgītā. With a commentary in Marathi by Govinda Paraṣurāma Rāverkar.] pp. 48. मुंबय्यां १८९२ [*Bombay,* 1892.] 8°. **14028. d. 50.(2.)**

—— अथ कैवल्यगाथा प्रारंभः [Kaivalyagāthā. A metrical summary of the Vaishṇava Vedānta, in 18 chapters. Followed by Saṅgatisūtra, an epitome of the religious philosophy of the Bhagavadgītā, with especial reference to xviii. 66.] ff. 102, 6. काश्यां १९५९ [*Benares,* 1903.] *obl.* 12°. **14048. b. 42.**

KṚISHṆĀNANDA SARASVATĪ, *Vāchaspati.* अन्तर्व्याकरणनाट्यपरिशिष्टम् *etc.* [Antarvyākaraṇanāṭya-pariṣishṭa. A grammatical work in the form of a drama, in which the verses are to be read both as rules of grammar and as moral and philosophical precepts. Edited with a commentary styled Rājasaraṇī, *etc.*, by Ajitanātha Nyāyaratna. With a Bengali biography of the author by Rājakiṣora Maṇḍala.] 4 pts. कलिकाता १९५६ [*Calcutta,* 1894?-1899.] 8°. **14090. bb. 12.**

KṚISHṆĀNANDA VĀGĪṢA BHAṬṬĀCHĀRYA. বৃহৎ তন্ত্রসার *etc.* [Bṛihat-tantrasāra. An epitome of the Tantras. With a Bengali translation by Prasannakumāra Ṣāstrī.] pp. vi. 374, 198; 17 *plates.* কলিকাতা ১৩০৩ [*Calcutta*, 1896.] 4°. **14033. c. 39.**

—— ষট্‌কর্ম্মদীপিকা । [Shaṭkarmadīpikā. A work on magic. With Bengali version.] pp. 40. [1890, *etc.*] *See* Periodical Publications. — *Calcutta.* অরুণোদয় *etc.* [Aruṇodaya.] pt. i., no. 2. [1890, *etc.*] 4°. **14133. g. 16.(pt. i., no. 2.)**

—— षट्कर्मदीपिका [Shaṭkarmadīpikā.] *See* Indrajālavidyāsaṅgraha. इन्द्रजालविद्यासंग्रहः *etc.* (Indrajalavidyasangraha.) pp. 183-264. [1891.] 8°. **14033. aa. 7.**

KṚISHṆANĀTHA NYĀYAPAÑCHĀNANA BHAṬṬĀCHĀRYA, *Mahāmahopādhyāya, of Purvasthali, Bardwan.* *See* Āpadeva, *son of Anantadeva.* मीमांसान्यायप्रकाशः *etc.* [Mīmāṃsānyāyaprakāṣa. Edited with a commentary styled Arthadarṣanī by Kṛishṇanātha.] [1901.] 8°. **14048. dd. 34.(3.)**

—— *See* Bhāskara, *son of Mudgala.* अर्थसंग्रहः *etc.* [Arthasaṅgraha. Edited with a commentary entitled Pratipādikā by Kṛishṇanātha.] [1900.] 8°. **14048. c. 78.**

—— *See* Harshadeva. रत्नावली *etc.* [Ratnāvalī. With commentary. Edited by Kṛishṇanātha.] [1900.] 8°. **14079. c. 65.(2.)**

—— *See* Vopadeva. বৃহন্মুগ্ধবোধব্যাকরণম্ *etc.* [Bṛihan-mugdhabodhavyākaraṇa. The Mugdhabodha with additions by Kṛishṇanātha. Edited by the latter.] [1898.] 8°. **14093. b. 41.(1.)**

—— वातदूतम् । सटीकम् *etc.* [Vātadūta. A poem of 100 stanzas on the subject of Sītā's separation from Rāma, in imitation of Kālidāsa's Meghadūta. With commentary.] pp. ii. 76. कलिकाता० १८२२ [*Calcutta*, 1901.] 8°. **14072. d. 38.(2.)**

KṚISHṆANĀTHA NYĀYARATNA. *See* Haricharaṇa Majumdār. পুরোহিত-দর্পণ *etc.* [Purohitadarpaṇa. Edited by Kṛishṇanātha.] [1899.] 8°. **14028. d. 72.**

KṚISHṆANĀTHA RAGHUNĀTHAJĪ. *See* Nārāyaṇa Bhaṭṭa, *Astrologer.* Chamatkar Chintamani, *etc.* [Translated, with additions, by Kṛishṇanātha.] 1894. 12°. **14053. b. 31.(1.)**

KṚISHṆANJĪ DAVE, *Brahmaṣrī.* *See* Purāṇas.—*Padmapurāṇa.* *Begin.* శ్రీమాఘమాహాత్మ్యసారమ్. [Māghamāhātmyasāra. Compiled by Kṛishṇanjī Dave.] 1897. 12°. **14016. b. 20.**

KṚISHṆA PAṆḌITA, *son of Rāma Bhaṭṭa.* *See* Sandhyāvandana. सन्ध्याभाष्यसमुच्चयः *etc.* [Sandhyābhāshyasamuchchaya. A collection of commentaries upon the *sandhyā* prayers, including Kṛishṇa's Taittirīyasandhyābhāshya, *etc.*] [1899.] 8°. **14003. ccc. (no. 40.)**

KṚISHṆARĀJA OḌEYAR, *Añjarāja Mummaḍī, Maharaja of Mysore.* श्रीतत्त्वनिधिः *etc.* [Tattvanidhi. An encyclopaedia of Hindu mythology and sports, in 9 *nidhis.* With Canarese commentary upon the 9th *nidhi.*] pp. xii. xliv. 416. मुम्बय्यां १९५८ [*Bombay*, 1902.] 8°. **14033. c. 43.**

Preceded by a full genealogy of the Maharajas of Mysore.

KṚISHṆA RĀMACHANDRA MĀḌGĀVKAR. *See* Nārāyaṇa Bhaṭṭa, called Mṛigarājalakshmā. The Veṇîsaṃhâra ... With the commentary of Jagaddhara ... Edited by Kâṡînâth ... Parab and Kṛishṇa ... Mâḍgâvkar. 1898. 8°. **14079. c. 67.**

KṚISHṆARĀMA KUNDANARĀMA VYĀSA, *Rājavaidyabhaṭṭa, of Jaipur.* सिद्धभेषजमणिमाला *etc.* [Siddhabheshajamaṇimālā. A metrical treatise, in 5 *guchchhas,* on Hindu pharmacology. With introductory stanzas and annotations by Lakshmīrāma, of the Royal Sanskrit College, Jaipur, and a preface by the author's son Gaṅgādhara Kṛishṇarāma.] pp. i. ii. ii. 236. मुंबई १९५६ [*Bombay*, 1900.] 8°. **14043. cc. 16.**

KṚISHṆĀRĀMA PĀṬHAKA. *See* Ballantyne (J. R.). Dr. Ballantyne's English Primer. With translation in easy Sanskrit by Kṛishṇárám Páṭhak, *etc.* 1890. 8°. **14085. d. 31.(1.)**

KṚISHṆARĀU ARJUNA KEḶŪSKAR. *See* Mahābhārata.—Bhagavadgītā.—*Sanskrit and Vernaculars.* श्रीमद्भगवद्गीता *etc.* [Bhagavadgītā. With glosses, translation, exposition, and metrical versions, in Marathi. Compiled and edited by Kṛishṇarāu Keḷūskar.] [1902.] 8°. **14065. bbb. 10.**

KṚISHṆĀRYA, *Koṇḍāpuram*. *See* GAṄGEŚA UPĀDHYĀYA. హేత్వాభాససామాన్యనిరుక్తి etc. [Hetvābhāsasāmānyanirukti. Followed by commentary and gloss. Edited by Kṛishṇārya.] [1893.] 8°. **14048. dd. 14.**

KṚISHṆA ŚARMĀ, *disciple of Vāsudeva*. The Mandâramaranda-champû of Srîkṛishṇa Kavi. [A metrical treatise on Poetics.] With a commentary [entitled Mādhuryarañjanī]. (मन्दारमरन्दचम्पूः ।) pp. xviii. 196. 1895. *See* DURGĀPRASĀDA, *son of Vrajalāla*, and KĀŚĪNĀTHA PĀṆḌURAṄGA PARAB. Kâvyamâlâ. [No.] 52. 1886, *etc.* 8°. **14072. ccc. 12.(no. 52.)**

KṚISHṆA ŚARMĀ, *of Karuppatur, also called* VEṄKAṬARĀMA. *See* VEDAS.—Yajurveda.—*Ātreyisaṃhitā*. உபோ காண்டாநுக்ரமணிகா *etc.* [Kāṇḍānukramaṇikā. With metrical epitome. Together with a commentary by Kṛishṇa.] [1900.] 8°. **14010. b. 14.(2.)**

KṚISHṆA ŚĀSTRĪ, *Bhāradvāja*. *See* GOVINDA ŚĀSTRĪ, *Bhāradvāja*. लघुजटाजूटः . . . Laghu Jatajoota, *etc.* [Edited by Kṛishṇa, *etc.*] 1899. 8°. **14092. b. 45.(1.)**

KṚISHṆA ŚĀSTRĪ, *of Devakota*. *See* ĀRŪḌHAŚĀSTRA. ஞானப்ரதீபிகை *etc.* [Ārūḍhaśāstra. With Tamil commentary. Edited by Kṛishṇa Śāstrī.] [1899.] 8°. **14053. ccc. 27.**

KṚISHṆA ŚĀSTRĪ, *G., of Adyar Library*. *See* APYAYA DĪKSHITA. Jívachintámaṇi. [Translated by Kṛishṇa Śāstrī.] 1901. 8°. [*The Theosophist.*] **P.P. 636. cm. (vol. 22.)**

—— *See* GURUJÑĀNAVĀSISHṬHA. Śrî Râma Gîtâ . . . Edited by G. Krishna Śâstrî, *etc.* 1902. 8°. **14049. b. 2.**

—— *See* GURUJÑĀNAVĀSISHṬHA. Śrî Râma Gîtâ . . . Translated . . . by G. Krishna Śâstrî, *etc.* 1902. 8°. **14049. b. 3.**

—— *See* GURUJÑĀNAVĀSISHṬHA. Ráma Gitá. [Translated, with introduction and notes, by Kṛishṇa Śāstrī.] 1901. 8°. [*The Theosophist.*] **P.P. 636. cm. (vol. 22, 23.)**

KṚISHṆA ŚĀSTRĪ, *Karṇāṭaka*. *See* KARṆĀṬAKA KṚISHṆA ŚĀSTRĪ.

KṚISHṆA ŚĀSTRĪ, *Nallepuḷi, of Chitpur*. *See* PURĀṆAS. — *Brahmāṇḍapurāṇa*. [*Ādipuramāhātmya.*] ஆதிபுர[sic]ஸ்தலபுராணம் *etc.* [Ādipuramāhātmya. Edited by Kṛishṇa Śāstrī and others.] [1902.] 8°. **14016. dd. 6.**

KṚISHṆA ŚĀSTRĪ, *Parittiyūr Rāmasvāmi*. Kaumudí Sómam. An original Sanskrit drama in five acts by Brahmasri Parithiyur Krishna Sastri, the celebrated Puranist. Edited by P. K. Kalyana Rama Sastri. (కౌముదీ సోమమ్) pp. ii. iv. 104, ii. *Madras*, 1896. 8°. **14079. c. 69.**

KṚISHṆA SŪRI. *See* PERIYAVĀCHĀN PIḶḶAI, called KṚISHṆA SŪRI.

KṚISHṆA SŪRI, *Addepalli, son of Sadāśiva*. *See* RĀMA SUDHĪVARA, *Chāvali*. అలంకారముక్తావళీ [Alaṅkāramuktāvalī. With the commentary Ratnaśobhākara of Kṛishṇa.] 1898. 8°. **14053. ccc. 24.**

KṚISHṆASVĀMI AIYAR, *C.N.* Madhwacharya, the Founder of the Dwaita System of Philosophy. A short historic sketch. pp. 32, ii. *Coimbatore*, [1900.] 8°. **10604. bbb. 25.(5.)**

KṚISHṆA TARKĀLAṄKĀRA. *See* JĪMŪTAVĀHANA. दायभागः *etc.* [Dāyabhāga. With the commentary Dāyabhāgaprabodhanī of Kṛishṇa.] [1893.] 8°. **14038. c. 48.(1.)**

—— *See* JĪMŪTAVĀHANA. জীমূতবাহনকৃত-দায়ভাগঃ *etc.* [Dāyabhāga. With Kṛishṇa's commentary, *etc.*] [1898.] 8°. **14038. c. 49.**

KṚISHṆA VĀSUDEVA BHAṬṬA, *of Sachchidānanda Press, Basrur*. कृष्णाष्टमीविचारः *etc.* [Kṛishṇāshṭamīvichāra. A Canarese polemical treatise on the date of the celebration of Kṛishṇa's birth in the Vikāri year, copiously illustrated from Sanskrit texts. Followed by another polemic on the same theme, styled Chapeṭikāpratikriyā.] pp. 44. *Basrur*, १८२१ [1900.] 8°. **14176. b. 51.**

KṚITTIVĀSAS. ବାଲୁଙ୍କେଶ୍ୱରଙ୍କ ଜଣାଣ . . . ଦାରିଦ୍ର୍ୟଭଞ୍ଜନାଷ୍ଟକ । [Bāluṅkeśvaraṅka Jaṇāṇ. An Oriya religious poem. Followed by the Dāridryabhañjanāshṭaka ascribed to Śankara.] pp. 12. *Cuttack*, 1901. 16°. **14028. a. 19.(4.)**

KRIYĀPUSTAKA. ಕ್ರಿಯಾಪುಸ್ತಕ *etc.* [Kriyāpustaka. Sanskrit and Prakrit hymns, *etc.*, for

Jain ritual. Edited by Padmarāja Paṇḍita.] pp. 34. ಬೆಂಗಳೂರು ೧೮೯೬ [*Bangalore*, 1896.] 8°. **14100. b. 3.(5.)**

KṢEMENDRA. *See* KSHEMENDRA.

KSHAURANIRṆAYA. अथ गृहस्थानां क्षौरनिर्णयः *etc.* [Gṛihasthānāṃ Kshauranirṇaya. Rules for the shaving of householders. With Hindi translation by Rāmapratāpa Ṣarmā, or, according to the title-page, Nandalāla Ṣarmā.] pp. 14. बम्बई १९५९ [*Bombay*, 1902.] 12°. **14033. a. 33.(3.)**

KSHEMĀNANDA BRAHMACHĀRĪ. সচিত্র সম্ভোগরত্নাকর ও ঐন্দ্রজালিকবশীকরণ বিদ্যা। কামরত্নসমুচ্চয়ঃ *etc.* [Sambhogaratnākara o Aindrajālika-vaṣikaraṇavidyā, or Kāmaratnasamuchchaya. A treatise on the psychology and physiology of love, chiefly in Sanskrit verses compiled from divers sources, with metrical Bengali paraphrases.] pp. i. 224. *Calcutta*, 1902. 12°. **14053. b. 41.(2.)**

—— সচিত্র লজ্জতন্নেছা *etc.* [Another issue of the preceding work, under the title of Lazzat al-nisā, with an appended chapter in Bengali.] pp. i. 229. *Calcutta*, 1902. 12°. **14053. b. 41.(3.)**

KSHEMARĀJA, *Rājānaka, disciple of Abhinavagupta.* *See* UTPALA DEVĀCHĀRYA. शिवस्तोत्रावली . . . Sivastotrâvalî . . . with the commentary of Kshemarâja, *etc.* 1902, *etc.* 8°. **14004. a. 15.**

KSHEMENDRA, *son of Prakāṣendra,* called VYĀSADĀSA. The Bhâratamañjarî of Kshemendra. [A poetical summary of the Mahābhārata.] Edited by . . . Paṇḍit Śivadatta . . . and Kâśînâth Pâṇdurang Parab. (भारतमञ्जरी।) pp. viii. 851. 1898. *See* DURGĀPRASĀDA, *son of Vrajalāla,* and KĀṢĪNĀTHA PĀṆḌURAṄGA PARAB. Kâvyamâlâ. [No.] 65. 1886, *etc.* 8°. **14072. ccc. 12.(no. 65.)**

—— *See* BUEHLER (J. G.) and KIRSTE (J.). Indian Studies. No. ii. Contributions to the History of the Mahâbhârata[, with especial reference to Kshemendra's Bhāratamañjarī,] *etc.* 1892. 8°. [*Sitzungsberichte der Kaiserlichen Akademie der Wissenschaften, Wien.*] **Ac. 810/6.(Bd. 127.)**

—— The Bṛihatkathâmañjarî of Kshemendra. Edited [with indices] by . . . Paṇḍit Śivadatta . . . and Kâshînâth Pâṇdurang Parab. (बृहत्कथामञ्जरी।) pp. v. 620, v. 7. 1901. *See* DURGĀPRASĀDA, *son of Vrajalāla,* and KĀṢĪNĀTHA PĀṆḌURAṄGA PARAB. Kâvyamâlâ. [No.] 69. 1886, *etc.* 8°. **14072. ccc. 12.(no. 69.)**

—— Der Auszug aus dem Pañcatantra in Kshemendra's Bṛihatkathâmañjarî. Einleitung, Text, Uebersetzung und Anmerkungen von Leo von Mańkowski. (पञ्चतन्त्रसारः) pp. i. lv. 32, 80. *Leipzig*, 1892. 8°. **14072. d. 41.**

—— The Daśâvatâracharita of Kshemendra. Edited by Paṇdit Durgâprasâd and Kâśînâth Pâṇdurang Parab. (दशावतारचरितम्।) pp. 164. 1891. *See* DURGĀPRASĀDA, *son of Vrajalāla,* and KĀṢĪNĀTHA PĀṆḌURAṄGA PARAB. Kâvyamâlâ. [No.] 26. 1886, *etc.* 8°. **14072. ccc. 12.(no. 26.)**

—— [Chapters from the Bodhisattvāvadānakalpalatā, with translations by various scholars.] *See* ACADEMIES, *etc.* — Calcutta. — *Buddhist Text Society of India.* Journal, *etc.* 1893, *etc.* 8°. **14003. b. 19.**

—— Legends and Miracles of Buddha, Sakya Sinha. Part 1. Translated from the Avadan Kalpalata of Bodhi-satwas of . . . Kshemendra by Nobin Chandra Das. pp. xvi. 59. *Calcutta*, 1895. 8°. **14076. c. 64.**

—— ज्योतिष्कावदानम्। [Jyotishkāvadāna.] pp. 10. *See* ACADEMIES, *etc.* — Calcutta. — *Buddhist Text Society of India.* Buddhist Texts, *etc.* 1894, *etc.* 8°. **14004. c.(vol. 1, no. 8.)**

—— Kṣemendra's Samayamatrika. Das Zauberbuch der Hetären. Ins Deutsche übertragen von Johann Jacob Meyer. pp. lviii. 108. [1903.] *See* SCHMIDT (R.). Altindische Schelmenbücher. No. i. [1903, *etc.*] 8°. **14070. g. 1.**

KSHETRAPĀLA ṢARMĀ, *of Calcutta.* *See* KAPILA. सांख्य-दर्शन *etc.* (Sankhya-Philosophy . . . Translated into Hindi by Kshetra Pall Sarma.) 1891. 8°. **14048. bb. 44.**

KSHITĪNDRANĀTHA ṬHĀKURA. *See* MAHĀBHĀRATA.—Bhagavadgītā.—*Sanskrit and Vernaculars.* শ্রীমদ্ভগবদ্গীতা *etc.* [Bhagavadgītā. With commentary and Bengali translation. Edited with a Bengali introduction by Kshitīndranātha.] [1895.] 16°. **14065. b. 15.**

KUEHNAU ( ). *See* STENZLER (A. F.). Metrische Sammlungen . . . Veröffentlicht von Dr.

Kühnau. 1890. 8°. [*Zeitschrift der Deutschen Morgenlaendischen Gesellschaft.*]
Ac. 8815/2.(Bd. 44.)

KULACHANDRA DE DĀSA. *See* VIPINAVIHĀRĪ VANDYOPĀDHYĀYA and KULACHANDRA DE DĀSA. হুঁকাপুরাণ মাহাত্ম্য etc. [Huṇkāpurāṇamāhātmya.] [1892.] 8°. **14072. b. 21.**

KULACHANDRA ŚARMĀ, *Gotama.* *See* AMARASIṂHA. अमरकोश etc. [Amarakoṣa. Edited with Nepali commentary, *etc.*, by Kulachandra.] [1901.] 8°. **14090. bb. 18.**

—— शोकमहोर्मिः etc. [Śokamahormi. A dialogue in prose and verse on the death of Queen Victoria.] pp. 12. श्रीकाश्यां १९५७ [*Benares,* 1901.] 8°. **14072. ccc. 33.**

KULAKA. ॥ अथ अभव्य कुलकम् ॥ (पुण्यकु॰, पुण्यपाप कु॰, *etc.*) [Abhavyakulaka, Puṇyakulaka, and Puṇyapāpakulaka. Short philosophical poems in Jain Prakrit. With Gujarati translation.] *See* HEMAŚAṄKARA LAKSHMĪŚAṄKARA VARDHAMĀNKAR. प्रकरणमाला etc. [Prakaraṇamālā.] pp. 137-148. [1901.] 8°. **14100. d. 11.**

KULANIDHI ŚARMĀ, *of Nepal.* *See* NITYAKARMA. The Nityakarmaprakáshiká . . . By . . . Kulanidhi Sharma, *etc.* 1902. 8°.
14033. bbb. 15.(2.)

KULAŚEKHARA, *Raja of Kerala.* ముకుంద-మాలా॥ [Mukundamālā.] *See* SAHASRANĀMASTABAKA. శ్రీసహస్రనామస్తబకమ్. [Sahasranāmastabaka.] pp. 302-315. [1902.] *obl.* 16°.
14033. a. 52.

—— Garland of Hymns to Sri Krishna, *etc.* [Mukundamālā, in English.] 1901. *See* PERIODICAL PUBLICATIONS.—*Madras.* The Brahmavâdin, *etc.* Vol. vii., no. 2. pp. 100-106. 1895, *etc.* 8°. **14048. g. 1.(vol. 7.)**

KULAYAŚASVI ŚĀSTRĪ. योगमकरन्दः (योगमञ्जरी ।) [Yogamakaranda. A metrical summary of the Yoga philosophy in 4 chapters, with the author's commentary styled Yogamañjarī.] pp. ii. 122, v. वाराणस्यां १९४५ [*Benares,* 1889.] 12°.
14048. bb. 12.(2.)

KULLŪKA BHAṬṬA. *See* MANU.—*Dharmaśāstra.* अथ मनुस्मृतिः etc. [Manusmṛiti. Book vii., with Kullūka's commentary, *etc.*] 1900. 8°. [*University of Madras : B.A. Sanskrit Text* 1901.]
14060. c. 30.(4.)

—— *See* MANU.—*Dharmaśāstra.* मनुस्मृतिः *etc.* [Manusmriti. Book vii., with Kullūka's commentary, *etc.*] 1900. 8°. [*University of Madras : B.A. Degree Examination* 1901.]
14072. c. 50.(2.)

KUMĀRADĀSA. *See* THOMAS (F. W.). The Jānakīharaṇa, *etc.* 1901. 8°. [*Journal of the Royal Asiatic Society.*]
Ac. 8820/3 and 2098. a., b.

—— Jánakíharaṇam, by Kumáradása. Edited by . . . Paṇḍit Haridása Śástrí . . . जानकीहरणम् *etc.* pp. vii. 214. *Calcutta,* 1893. 8°.
14072. cc. 57.

KUMARAGURUPARA, *Tambirān.* ॥ नीतिमार्गप्रदीपिका . . . The Neethimargapradipika. [A Sanskrit version of the] Neethineri Vilakkam [*i.e.* நீதிநெறிவிளக்கம்] of Kumaraguruparadasikar. Translated . . . by Radhakrishna Sastriar. pp. 28. *See* RĀDHĀKṚISHṆA ŚĀSTRĪ, *of Pudukottai.* नीतिदशप्रबन्धी . . . The Nitidasaprabandhi, *etc.* No. 10. 1894. 8°. **14085. c. 46.**

KUMĀRAJĪVA. *See* SUKHĀVATĪVYŪHA. O-mi-to-king, ou Soukhavati-vyouha-soutra. D'après la version chinoise de Koumarajiva, *etc.* 1881. 4°. [*Annales du Musée Guimet.*]
7704. h. 21.(tom. 2.)

KUMĀRA TĀTĀRYA, *Kavibhūshaṇa, son of Lakshmīnṛisiṃha.* पादुकास्तुतिः etc. [Pādukāstuti. A poem of 108 stanzas, celebrating the slippers of Vishṇu-Raṅganātha.] pp. ii. 20. पट्टाम्बि १९०० [*Pattambi,* 1900.] 8°. **14072. ccc. 22.(2.)**

—— సదాచారసారః *etc.* [Sadāchārasāra. A treatise on Vaishṇava practices.] pp. 39. *Madras,* 1901. 12°. **14033. a. 33.(2.)**

KUMĀRILA BHAṬṬA. *See* APYAYA DĪKSHITA. विधिरसायनम् *etc.* (Vidhi-rasayana[, a treatise on *vidhis,* as expounded by Kumārila] *etc.*) 1901. 8°. **14004. a. 13.**

—— *See* JAIMINI.—*Mīmāṃsāsūtra.* मीमांसाश्लोकवार्तिकम् *etc.* (The Mîmânsâ-śloka-vârtika of Kumârila Bhatta[, a commentary upon Śabarasvāmī's commentary on the Mīmāṃsāsūtra I. i.] With the commentary . . . by Pârtha Sârathi Miśra, *etc.*) 1898-1899. 8°. **14004. a. 3.**

—— *See* JAIMINI.—*Mīmāṃsāsūtra.* Çlokavārtika. Translated . . . with extracts from the commentaries of Sucarīta [*sic*] Miçra . . . and Pārthasārathi Miçra, *etc.* 1900, *etc.* 8°. [*Bibliotheca Indica.*] **14002. a. (vol. 146.)**

—— *See* JAIMINI.—*Mīmāṃsāsūtra.* **न्यायसुधा** . . . Nyâyasudhâ, a commentary on Tantravârtika. By . . . Sômeshwara Bhaṭṭa, *etc.* 1901, *etc.* 8°. **14004. a. 14.**

—— ॥ **अथ . . . आश्वलायनगृह्यकारिकाः** ॥ [Âṣvalāyana-Gṛihyakārikāḥ. An epitome of Āṣvalāyana's Gṛihyasūtra.] *See* ĀṢVALĀYANA. ॥ **अथ . . . गृह्यसूत्रं** *etc.* [Āṣvalāyana-Gṛihyasūtra, *etc.*] ff. 173-220. [1895.] *obl.* 8°. **14010. dd. 6.**

KUMBAKONAM. — *Yāgaṣālāvīthikā.* **श्रीकुम्भघोणे यागशालावीथिकायां श्रीलक्ष्मीनारायणस्य ६३तमे आविर्भावोत्सवे . . . विद्वज्जनैर्वर्णितनिर्णीतविषयको ग्रन्थः** । [Report of answers given by Pandits to twenty briefly specified questions on points of religion and philosophy, at a festival in the Yāgaṣālāvīthikā, a sanctuary at Kumbakonam.] pp. 37. **कुम्भघोणे** १८९३ [*Kumbakonam*, 1893.] 8°. **14048. bb. 51.(2.)**

KUMBHA, *Raja.* *See* KUMBHAKARṆA MAHENDRA.

KUMBHAKARṆA MAHENDRA, *Raja of Mewar.* *See* JAYADEVA, *son of Bhojadeva.* The Gitagovinda . . . With the commentaries Rasikapriya of King Kumbha and Rasamanjari of . . . Shankara Mishra, *etc.* 1899. 8°. **14070. dd. 3.**

KUMUDACHANDRA. *See* SIDDHASENA DIVĀKARA.

KUMUDARAÑJANA VANDYOPĀDHYĀYA. হরিশ্চন্দ্র কুলদীপিকা [Hariṣchandrakuladīpikā. A genealogy, in prose and verse, of Hariṣchandra, son of Rāmadhana.] pp. 13. হুগলী ১২৯৮ [*Hugli*, 1891.] 32°. **14058. a. 6.**

KUNDAKUNDA ĀCHĀRYA. Il Compendio dei Cinque Elementi, Pañcatthiyasaṃgahasuttaṃ [or Pañchāstikasaṅgraha. A metrical Jain treatise, in 173 Prakrit stanzas, on the principles of existence. Edited by P. E. Pavolini]. 1901. *See* ACADEMIES, *etc.*—Florence.—*Società Asiatica Italiana.* Giornale, *etc.* Vol. xiv., pp. 1-40. 1887, *etc.* 8°. **Ac. 8804.(vol. 14.)**

KUṆḌALAGIRI ĀCHĀRYA, *V.* *See* MAHĀBHĀRATA.—*Vanaparva.* University of Madras . . . Notes on the Mahabharata [and Pañchatantra,] with English translation, by C. Raghavendra Rao . . . and Kundalagiriyachar. 1891. 8°. **14060. c. 30.(2.)**

KUÑJALĀLA NĀGA. *See* KĀLIDĀSA.—*Raghuvaṃṣa.* Raghuvanśam, Cantos i.-v. (vi., vii.), literally translated . . . with notes . . . by Kunja Lál Nág. 1893-1897. 8°. **14072. ccc. 19.(2.)**

KUÑJAVIHĀRĪ NYĀYABHŪSHAṆA. *See* ACADEMIES, *etc.*—Calcutta.—*Asiatic Society of Bengal.* Catalogue of Printed Books and Manuscripts in Sanskrit belonging to the Oriental Library of the Asiatic Society of Bengal. Compiled by Paṇḍit Kunja Vihāri Nyāyabhūṣaṇa, *etc.* 1899, *etc.* 4°. **14096. dd. 5.**

KUPPAN AIYAṄGĀR, *T. E. S., of Yadugiri.* *See* ANANTĀCHĀRYA, *Maṇḍayam A.* **शास्त्रारम्भसमर्थनम्** *etc.* [Dissertations on the Viṣishṭādvaita. With a commentary upon nos. 1-5, styled Tātparyadīpikā, by Kuppan Aiyaṅgār.] [1898, *etc.*] 8°. [*Vedāntavādāvalī.*] **14048. cc. 18.**

KUPPU ṢĀSTRI, *Ādanūr N.* *See* VEṄKAṬĀCHALA ṢARMĀ, *Ādanūr N.*

KUPPUSVĀMI AIYAR, *Villavarambal.* *See* UPANISHADS.—*Small Collections.* 𑌪𑌂𑌚𑌦𑌶𑍋𑌪𑌨𑌿𑌷𑌦𑌃 *etc.* [Pañchadaṣopanishadaḥ. Edited with Tamil introduction and translation by Kuppusvāmi.] [1898.] 8°. **14010. cc. 12.**

—— *See* VĀSUDEVA YATI. 𑌵𑌾𑌸𑍁𑌦𑌵𑌮𑌨𑌨 ॥ [Vāsudevamanana. With Tamil version by Kuppusvāmi.] [1895.] 8°. **14048. dd. 19.**

—— The Aryamatasiddhanta Sangraha, *etc.* [A digest, in dialogue form, of the principles of the Dvaita, Advaita, Viṣishṭādvaita, and Ṣaiva philosophies. In Tamil, copiously illustrated from Sanskrit texts.] (॥ **आर्यमतसिद्धान्ताख्य ग्रन्थः** ॥ 𑌆𑌰𑍍𑌯𑌮𑌤𑌸𑌿𑌦𑍍𑌧𑌾𑌨𑍍𑌤𑌾𑌖𑍍𑌯𑌗𑍍𑌰𑌨𑍍𑌥𑌃 . . . ஆரியமதஸித்தாந்தஸங்கிரகம்) pp. 32, 566, 138. *Kumbakonam*, 1902. 8°. **14170. ee. 49.**

The Sanskrit extracts are printed in Nagari characters at the foot of the page, and reprinted in Grantham type in an appendix.

KUPPUSVĀMI RĀJU, *V.* *See* SVĀTMĀRĀMA. ஹட-யோகப்பிரதீபிகை *etc.* [Haṭhayogapradīpikā. Edited with Tamil translation and commentary by Kuppusvāmi.] [1897.] 8°. **14048. cc. 16.**

KUPPUSVĀMI ŚĀSTRI, *T. S.* *See* RĀMABHADRA DĪKSHITA, *Kaṇḍaramāṇikkam.* The Śṛingâra-tilaka Bhâṇa, *etc.* [With a biography of the poet and an account of contemporary writers by Kuppusvāmi.] 1894. 8°. [*Kâvyamâlâ.*] **14072. ccc. 12.(no. 44.)**

—— *See* VĀDĪBHASIṂHA SŪRI. The Gadya-chintâmani . . . [Edited with preface] by T. S. Kuppuswami Sastri . . . and S. Subrahmanya Sastri. 1902. 8°. **14070. dd. 23.**

KŪṢMĀṆḌAHOMA. கூஷ்மாண்டஹோமம் கணஹோமம் வைஶ்வதேவம் *etc.* [Kūṣmāṇḍa-homa, Gaṇahoma, and Vaiṣvadeva. Rituals of the Vedic lustratory sacrifices known by these names.] pp. 32. கல்பாடி [*Kalpadi,* 1900.] 16°. **14028. b. 80.(3.)**

KUVERA UPĀDHYĀYA. *See* ĀDINĀRĀYAṆA PĀTRO. The Hindu Law. Annotated and illustrated by Sanskrit texts[, viz. the writings of Kuvera and others,] *etc.* 1899. 8°. **14039. c. 17.**

KYAW-AUNG-SAN-TĀ HSAYA. *See* MOGGALLĀNA. အဘိဓာန်နိဿယ *etc.* [Abhidhānappadīpikā. With Burmese *nissaya* by the Kyaw-aung-san-tā Hsaya.] [1900.] 8°. **14098. ccc. 30.(2.)**

KYAW ZAN Ū, *Maung.* *See* ZIN-PYU-MYA-SHIN. ကိုးဆောင်ချုပ်ဓမ္မသတ် *etc.* [Ko saung hkyôk dhamma-that, or Navadhammasattha. Section viii. Edited, with Burmese translations, by Kyaw Zan Ū, *etc.*] [1894.] 8°. **14098. ccc. 20.**

LĀDILĪ CHANDRA. सिद्धिसाधन . . . ब्रह्मस्तव *etc.* [Brahmastava. A mystical poem of the Advaita school in 49 stanzas upon the Supreme Being. With a Hindi prose translation and commentary, styled Siddhisādhana, by Rasamaya Siddha.] pp. 33. लखनऊ १८९० [*Lucknow,* 1890.] 8°. **14048. e. 22.(1.)**

LAGADHA. ॥ अथ ज्योतिष° [Jyotisha.] ff. 3. *See* VEDAS.—*Appendix.* ॥ अथ . . . षडङ्ग° [Shadaṅga.] pt. 2. [1892]. *obl.* 8°. **14007. c. 27.**

LAGHUKĀVYĀNI. लघुकाव्यानि अनेककविप्रणीतानि . . . Miscellaneous Poetical Pieces by various Sanskrit authors, *etc.* [Comprising Sadāṣiva Yuvarāja's Sādāṣivī or Sphuṭaṣlokaprakaraṇa, Muraripustotra, Hetvābhāsodāharaṇaṣlokāḥ, Sudhānandalaharīstotra, Tripuradahanacharita, *etc.*; various minor works ascribed to Ṣaṅkara Āchārya; minor poems of Moropanta; Trivikrama's Vyājokti; the Suvarṇamuktāsaṃvāda; Viṭhobā Aṇṇā's Ṣivagītimālā and Kaṭāva; Achyuta's Ākāṣaṣataka; Nīlakaṇṭha's Kaliviḍambana, *etc.*] pp. 238. 1888. *See* PERIODICAL PUBLICATIONS.—*Poona.* काव्येतिहास-संग्रह [Kāvyetihāsasaṅgraha.] Vol. iv., no. 3; v., no. 7—vi., no. 5; ix., no. 11—x., no. 12. [1878-1888.] 8°. **14072. d. 37.(vol. 4-10.)**

LAHERI (BARODA K.). *See* VARADĀKĀNTA LAHIRĪ.

LAKSHMĀJĪ PAṆḌIT, *Liṅgam.* A Lecture on Religion, by the light of the Ashstádhyáyí [*sic*], *etc.* pp. 25. *Madras,* 1890. 8°. **4503. c. 24.(7.)**

LAKSHMAṆADĀSA, *disciple of Lakshmaṇa Āchārya, of Brindaban.* *See* RAṄGARĀMĀNUJA, *disciple of Tātāchārya.* वेदान्त विषयवाक्यदीपिका *etc.* [Vishayavākyadīpikā. With footnotes by Lakshmaṇadāsa.] [1899.] 8°. **14048. e. 26.**

LAKSHMAṆA GAṆEṢA ṢĀSTRĪ LELE, *of Nasik.* *See* KĀLIDĀSA.—*Meghadūta.* मेघदूतकाव्याचें . . . भाषांतर *etc.* [Meghadūta. Edited with metrical Marathi version and notes by Lakshmaṇa Lele.] [1901.] 8°. **14070. dd. 20.**

LAKSHMAṆĀNANDA, *Svāmī, disciple of Dayānanda Sarasvatī.* ध्यानयोगप्रकाश: *etc.* [Dhyānayogaprakāṣa. A treatise on Yogic meditations, comprising series of Sanskrit formulae and quotations with Hindi exposition, *etc.*] pp. 370. मेरठ १९५८ [*Meerut,* 1901.] 8°. **14154. dd. 10.(2.)**

LAKSHMAṆA PAṆḌITA, *son of Ṣrīdatta Sūri, Brahmajñānī.* *See* KAVIRĀJA PAṆḌITA, *Courtier of Kāmadeva.* राघवपाण्डवीयम् *etc.* [Rāghavapāṇḍavīya. With the commentary Sārachandrikā of Lakshmaṇa.] [1890.] 8°. [*Grantharatnamālā.*] **14096. c. 8.(vol. 3, 4.)**

LAKSHMAṆA ṢĀSTRĪ, *Mallādi.* *See* LAKSHMAṆA SŪRI.

LAKSHMAṆA ṢRAUTĪ, *son of Krishṇasvāmī, of Tiruvadi.* See VEDAS.—*Sāmaveda.* தசராத்ர-ஸாமானி ... உ ஸாமா ॥ [Daṣarātra. Edited by Lakshmaṇa.] [1902.] 8°. **14007. b. 18.**

LAKSHMAṆA SŪRI. श्री . . . भारतसंग्रहे आदितः पर्वपञ्चकम् Bharata Sangraha. [An epitome of the Mahābhārata.] Part I. [comprising Bks. i.-v.] pp. 60. तञ्जानगरे १९०२ [*Tanjore*, 1902.] 8°. **14072. ccc. 37.**

LAKSHMAṆA SŪRI, *son of Gaṅgādhara, of Ṣanagaram.* युद्धकाण्डम् [Yuddhakāṇḍa. An epilogue to the Champūrāmāyaṇa of Bhojarāja. With the commentary of Rāmachandra Budhendra.] See BHOJARĀJA. The Champû-Râmâyaṇa of King Bhoja, *etc.* pp. 330-423. [1898.] 8°. **14070. dd. 5.**

LAKSHMAṆA SŪRI, *Mallādi.* See MAMMAṬA ĀCHĀRYA. కావ్యప్రకాశః *etc.* [Kāvyaprakāṣa. With the commentary Budhamanorañjanī by Lakshmaṇa.] [1891.] 8°. **14053. cc. 60.**

LAKSHMAṆA SŪRI, *Punalveli Muddusubba.* See MURĀRI MIṢRA. अनर्घराघवम् *etc.* [Anargharāghava. With the commentary Ākara of Lakshmaṇa.] [1900.] 8°. **14079. c. 71.**

—— See MURĀRI MIṢRA. अनर्घराघवम् *etc.* [Anargharāghava. With the commentary of Lakshmaṇa. Acts i.-v.] [1898.] 8°. **14079. d. 45.**

LAKSHMĪDĀSA KAVI, *of Kerala.* ശ്രീ ... ശുകസന്ദേശം ... *etc.* [Ṣukasandeṣa. A romantic poem in 2 *sargas*, modelled on the Meghadūta. With a commentary styled Vilāsinī by Rājakumāra Mānaveda.] pp. 146. ... ॥ [*Palghat*, 1891.] 8°. **14076. c. 61.**

LAKSHMĪDHARA, *disciple of Kaivalyānanda.* శ్రీ ... అద్వైతమకరన్దాఖ్యగ్రన్థః ... అద్వైతతారావళిః *etc.* [Advaitamakaranda. With the commentary Rasābhivyakti of Svayamprakāṣa. Followed by Sadāṣiva Brahmendra's Advaitatārâvali, a philosophical poem.] pp. 24. *Madras*, 1891. 8°. **14048. bb. 39.(4.)**

LAKSHMĪDHARA DEṢIKA, *son of Viṣvanātha.* See ṢAṄKARA ĀCHĀRYA. — *Doubtful and Supposititious Works.* శ్రీ ... శ్రీసౌందర్యలహరీ *etc.* [Saundaryalaharī. With the commentary Lakshmīdharā of Lakshmīdhara.] 1892. 8°. **14028. c. 67.**

—— See ṢAṄKARA ĀCHĀRYA. — *Doubtful and Supposititious Works.* Saundaryalaharí of Śrí Śankaráchárya with Lakshmídhara's commentary, *etc.* 1896. 8°. [*Mysore Government Oriental Library Series: Bibliotheca Sanskrita.*] **14004. b. 8.**

—— See ṢAṄKARA ĀCHĀRYA.—*Doubtful and Supposititious Works.* Ānanda Lahari. With ... commentaries [based on the commentaries of Lakshmīdhara and others.] Translated into English, *etc.* 1899. 12°. **14048. b. 35.**

LAKSHMĪNARASIṂHA SOMAYĀJĪ, *Ātmūri.* See ĀPASTAMBA.—*Grihyasūtra.* యజుశ్శాఖాధ్యాయి-నాముపనయనప్రయోగః *etc.* [Upanayanaprayoga. Edited with Telugu interpretations of the rubrics, *etc.*, by Lakshmīnarasiṃha.] 1901. 8°. **14033. c. 46.**

—— See BRĀHMAṆAS.—*Taittirīyabrāhmaṇa.* The Taittiriya Brahmana, *etc.* [Edited by Lakshmīnarasiṃha.] 1899. 8°. **14007. d. 21.**

—— Pasu Vatba Khandanam; or A Protest against the Torture of Animals at Religious Sacrifices ... By A. Lakshmi Narasimha Somayajulu. pp. 22. *Madras*, [1900.] 8°. **4504. cc. 14.(3.)**

LAKSHMĪNĀRĀYAṆA, *Astrologer.* ॥ अथ लघुसंग्रह मूल प्रारम्भः ॥ [Laghusaṅgraha. A compendium of astrology.] ff. 44. *Lucknow*, १९०२ [1902.] *obl.* 8°. **14053. ccc. 45.**

LAKSHMĪNĀRĀYAṆA, *Retired Deputy-Collector, of Agra.* See MAHĀBHĀRATA.—Bhagavadgītā.—*Sanskrit and Vernaculars.* लक्ष्मीनारायन सरोवर *etc.* [Lakshmīnārāyaṇa-sarovara. The Bhagavadgītā, with Hindi translation and commentaries in Persian and Hindi by Lakshmīnārāyaṇa.] [1898.] 8°. **14065. d. 39.**

LAKSHMĪNĀRĀYAṆA ṢARMĀ, *of Benares.* मदनमुखचपेटिका *etc.* [Madanamukhachapeṭikā. A poem in 121 stanzas, setting forth in dialogue form the counter-claims of love and morality. With a Hindi prose translation by Sarayūprasāda Vājapeyī.] pp. 74. मुंबई १८१६ [*Bombay*, 1894.] 12°. **14076. b. 34.**

Apparently this writer is identical with Lakshmīnārāyaṇa Ṣarmā disciple of Ṭhākuradatta.

LAKSHMĪNĀRĀYAṆA ṢARMĀ, *disciple of Ṭhākuradatta, Kauṣalya Sārasvata.* कवीन्द्रलक्ष्मीनारायणजीका जीवनचरित्र *etc.* [Kavīndra-Lakshmīnārāyaṇa-jī-kā Jīvanacharitra. A brief biography of Lakshmīnārāyaṇa in Hindi, followed by four of his Sanskrit works, viz. (1) Victoria-daṣaka, two decads of verses to Queen Victoria, (2) a commentary called Ṣivatāṇḍavachandrikā upon the Ṣivatāṇḍavastotra, and (3) Gaṅgālaharī-ṣataka, a century of verses to the Ganges.] pp. 37. लखनऊ १९०२ [*Lucknow*, 1902.] 8°. **14072. d. 46.**

LAKSHMĪNĀRĀYAṆA ṢĀSTRĪ, *Bhāgavata, son of Bhāgavata Veṅkaṭa Ṣāstrī, of Vizianagram.* Śrî Râmavijaya. A Sanskrit drama [of the *vyāyoga* type, upon the story of Rāma's victory,] by Bhâgavatula Lakshmînârâyana Shâstri, [preceded by a review of the play, in English, by G. V. Appārāu.] (श्रीरामविजयः ।) pp. i. ix. 53. *Bombay*, 1901. 8°. **14080. d. 27.**

—— संक्षिप्तरामचरितम् *etc.* [Saṅkshipta-rāmacharita. A poetical summary of the Rāmāyaṇa. Part ii., comprising the Ayodhyākāṇḍa, Araṇyak°., and Kishkindhāk°., and illustrating the rules in the first 15 lessons of Bhāṇḍārkar's Second Book of Sanskrit. With notes appended.] pp. i. 23, vi. मुंबापुर्याम् १९०० [*Bombay*, 1900.] 8°. **14072. cc. 61.**

LAKSHMĪNĀRĀYAṆA ṢĀSTRĪ, *son of Lakshmaṇa, of Kottapattanam. See* SĀYAṆA ĀCHĀRYA.—*Works on Philosophy, etc.* శ్రీ . . . శ్రీ వేదాంతపంచదశి ॥ [Pañchadaṣī. With interpretation and commentary in Telugu by Lakshmīnārāyaṇa.] 1895-1898. 8°. **14048. dd. 24.**

LAKSHMĪNĀTHA BHAṬṬA, *son of Rāya Bhaṭṭa. See* PIṄGALA ĀCHĀRYA. The Prâkṛita-piṅgala-sûtras. With the commentary [Piṅgalapradīpa] of Lakshmīnātha, *etc.* 1894. 8°. [*Kâvyamâlâ.*] **14072. ccc. 12.(no. 41.)**

LAKSHMĪNṚISIṂHA ṢĀSTRĪ, *Challā-nāgaliṅga, of Masulipatam.* పురాణోక్తకర్మప్రకాశిక *etc.* [Purāṇokta-karmaprakāṣika. A collection of rules for divers rites, compiled from Purāṇas and Dharmaṣāstras. Edited by Narasiṃha Ṣāstrī.] pp. viii. 188, viii. చెన్నపట్టణం ౧౮౯౯ [*Madras*, 1899.] 8°. **14028. c. 79.**

LAKSHMĪRĀMA, *Professor of Medicine at the Royal Sanskrit College, Jaipur. See* KṚISHṆA-RĀMA KUNDANARĀMA VYĀSA. सिद्धभेषजमणिमाला *etc.* [Siddhabheshajamaṇimālā. With introductory stanzas and annotations by Lakshmīrāma.] [1900.] 8°. **14043. cc. 16.**

LAKSHMĪ SŪRI. *See* VIJAYALAKSHMĪ SŪRI.

LĀLACHANDRA ṢARMĀ, *of Jodhpur.* ॥ पद्यप्राकृतव्याकरणम् *etc.* [Padyaprākṛitavyākaraṇa. A Prakrit grammar in 76 Sanskrit stanzas, with Hindi commentary. Edited with preface by Ṣivadāna Malla.] pp. viii. 40. काशी १९५७ [*Benares*, 1901.] 8°. **14093. b. 6.(2.)**

LĀLAMAṆI ṢĀSTRĪ. *See* TANTRAS. [*Ḍāmara-tantra.*] (डामरतन्त्रम्) [Ḍāmaratantra. With Hindi paraphrase by Hariṣaṅkara and Lālamaṇi.] [1898.] 8°. **14033. bbb. 4.(1.)**

LĀLAMOHANA VIDYĀNIDHI BHAṬṬĀCHĀRYA. *See* KĀLIDĀSA.—*Meghadūta.* मेघदूतम् . . . The Meghadúta . . . With the commentary of Mallinátha . . . Edited by Lálmohan, *etc.* 1894. 8°. **14072. cc. 58.(1.)**

—— *See* KĀLIDĀSA.—*Meghadūta.* The Meghadúta . . . Translated . . . by H. H. Wilson . . . Edited by Lal Mohan Vidyanidhi. 1901. 8°. **14070. dd. 22.**

LALITAMOHANA SARKĀR. *See* PAÑCHATANTRA. Provesika. Translated . . . by Lalit Mohan Sarkar, *etc.* 1890. 12°. **14070. b. 19.**

LALITAVISTARA. *See* WINDISCH (W. O. E.). Māra und Buddha, *etc.* [Illustrated by extracts and translations from the Lalitavistara, *etc.*] 1895. 4°. **759. e. 1.**

—— Lalita Vistara. Leben und Lehre des Çâkya-Buddha. Textausgabe, mit Varianten-, Metren- und Wörterverzeichnis, von Dr. S. Lefmann. (Erster Teil: Text.) *Halle a. S.*, 1902, *etc.* 8°. **14070. dd. 19.**

In progress.

LALITAVISTARA (*continued*). Le Lalita Vistara—Développement des Jeux—contenant l'histoire du Bouddha Çakya-Mouni depuis sa naissance jusqu'à sa predication. Traduit du sanskrit ... par Ph. Ed. Foucaux ... Première partie. Traduction française. (Seconde partie. Notes, variantes et index.) 2 vols. 1884, 1892. *See* ACADEMIES, *etc.*—Paris.—*Musée Guimet.* Annales, *etc.* Tom. vi., xix. 1880, *etc.* 4°.
7704. h. 21.(tom. 6, 19.)

—— Die Buddhalegende in den Skulpturen des Tempels von Bôrô-Budur [elucidated by a summary of the Lalitavistara] von C. M. Pleyte. (Lalitavistara. Erzählung von dem Leben des Çâkya Sinha.) pp. xvi. 183, i. *Amsterdam,* 1901. 4°.
14070. f. 7.

—— ကာမာဒီနဝကထာ *etc.* [Kāmādinavakathā. A passage from the Lalitavistara, *adhyāya* xv. (pp. 252 f. ed. Bibliotheca Indica), in disparagement of feminine charms. In Pali, with Burmese version by Jāgara. Followed by 3 works of Jāgara, viz. an Ovādakathā or Burmese homily; Dhammapāna-shuhbway, Pali verses with Burmese version; and Upāsakovāda-shuhbway, Burmese homilies.] pp. i. 88. မန္တလေး [*Mandalay,*] 1894. 8°.
14098. c. 32.(3.)

—— ကာမာဒီနဝကထာ [Kāmādinavakathā.] *See* CHANDIMĀ, *Thāvara,* called KYĀ-KOY. ဆက္က-ပဉှာကျမ်း *etc.* [Chhakkapañhā-kyan, *etc.*] pp. 353-366. 1898. 8°.
14300. d. 19.(9.)

LALLĀ DĪKSHITA, *son of Lakshmaṇa.* *See* ŚŪDRAKA. The Mṛichchhakaṭika ... Containing ... the Suvarṇâlaṃkaraṇa of Lalla Dîkshita, *etc.* 1896, *etc.* 8°.
14079. c. 63.

LANMAN (CHARLES ROCKWELL). *See* ACADEMIES, *etc.*—Cambridge, *Mass.*—*Harvard University.* Harvard Oriental Series. Edited ... by C. R. Lanman. 1891, *etc.* 8°.
14003. l. 3.

—— *See* RĀJAŚEKHARA, *son of Durduka.* Rājaçekhara's Karpūra-mañjarī ... translated ... with notes by ... C. R. Lanman. 1901. 8°. [*Harvard Oriental Series.*]
14003. l. 3.(vol. 4.)

LA VALLÉE POUSSIN (LOUIS DE). *See* NĀGĀRJUNA. Caturāryasatyaparīkṣā. Extraits ... de la Madhyamakavṛtti. Par L. de la Vallée Poussin. 1896. 4°. [*Mélanges Harlez.*]
12902. h. 22.

—— *See* NĀGĀRJUNA. Études et Textes Tantriques. Pañcakrama[, with the gloss of Parahitarakshita. Edited with introduction] par L. de la Vallée Poussin. 1896. 8°.
Ac. 2647/3.(fasc. 16.)

—— *See* ŚĀNTIDEVA. Bodhicaryâvatâra ... Chapitres i. ii. iii. iv. (v.) et x. Texte et traduction [with introduction, by L. de la Vallée Poussin]. 1891-1896. 8°. [*Muséon.*]
P.P. 4453.(tom. 11, 15.)

—— *See* SĀYAṆA ĀCHĀRYA.—*Works on Philosophy, etc.* Le Bouddhisme d'après les sources brahmaniques. I. Sarvadarçanasaṁgraha[, translated with notes by] L. de la Vallée Poussin. II. Sarvasiddhāntasaṁgraha[, edited by] F. W. Thomas et L. de la Vallée Poussin. 1902. 8°.
14048. e. 35.

—— *See* SVAYAMBHŪPURĀṆA. Svayambhūpurāṇa. Dixième chapitre. [Edited] par L. de la Vallée Poussin. 1893. 8°. **Ac. 2647/3.(fasc. 9.)**

—— *See* SVAYAMBHŪPURĀṆA. Maṇicūḍâvadāna ... [An epitome, in French.] By L. de la Vallée Poussin. 1894. 8°. [*Journal of the Royal Asiatic Society.*] **Ac. 8820/3., 2098. a., b.**

—— Bouddhisme. Études et Matériaux. Ādikarmapradīpa[, a treatise on esoteric rites of Northern Buddhism, by Anupamavajra.] Bodhicaryāvatāraṭīkā[, being Book ix. of Śāntideva's Bodhicharyāvatāra with the commentary of Prajñākaramati Śrījñāna.] Par Louis de la Vallée Poussin. pp. iv. 417. *London, Bruxelles* [printed], 1898. 4°.
14028. e. 32.

"*Extrait du tome LV. des* Mémoires couronnés et Mémoires des savants étrangers, *publiés par l'Académie royale des sciences, des lettres, et des beaux-arts de Belgique.*—1898."

—— [Another copy, included in the Mémoires of the Académie Royale des Sciences et des Beaux-Arts de Belgique.] *Bruxelles,* 1896-1898. 4°.
Ac. 985/6.(tom. 55.)

LEADBEATER (C. W.). *See* PERIODICAL PUBLICATIONS.—*Colombo.* The Buddhist ... Edited by C. W. Leadbeater, vol. 1. 1888, *etc.* 8°.
P.P. 636. cn.

LECOUTERE (C.). *See* MAHĀBHĀRATA.—*Vanaparva.* Sâvitrî ... vertaald ... door C. Lecoutere. 1893. 8°. **14065. d. 25.(2.)**

LEFMANN (SALOMON). *See* LALITAVISTARA. Lalita Vistara ... Textausgabe, mit Varianten-, Metren- und Wörterverzeichnis, von Dr. S. Lefmann. 1902, *etc.* 8°. **14070. dd. 19.**

LEIPZIG, *University of.* *See* ACADEMIES, *etc.*—*Leipsic.*

LELE (G. V.). *See* GAṄGĀDHARA VĀMANA LELE.

LELE (L. G.). *See* LAKSHMAṆA GAṆEṢA ṢĀSTRĪ LELE.

LEUMANN (ERNST). *See* AUPAPĀTIKASŪTRA. Das Aupapâtika Sûtra ... Einleitung mit Inhaltsangabe ... und vom Texte §§ 1-38, der philosophischen Facultät der Universität Leipzig ... vorgelegt von E. Leumann. 1882. 8°.
14100. b. 2.

—— *See* ĀVAṢYAKA. Die Âvaśyaka-Erzählungen. Herausgegeben von E. Leumann. 1897, *etc.* 8°. [*Deutsche Morgenlaendische Gesellschaft: Abhandlungen.*] **753. f. 18.**

—— *See* JINABHADRA GAṆĪ, *Kshamāṣramaṇa.* Jinabhadra's Jîtakalpa, mit Auszügen aus Siddhasena's Cûrṇi. Von E. Leumann. 1892. 8°.
14100. d. 2.

—— *See* KATHĀKOṢA. The Kathâkoça ... With appendix ... by ... E. Leumann. 1895. 8°. [*Oriental Translation Fund.*]
14003. bb. (ser. 2, vol. 2.)

—— *See* ṢAYYAṂBHAVA. The Daśavaikālika-sūtra ... and the Daśavaikālika-niryukti ... Published [by E. Leumann] ... with a German introduction, *etc.* [1892.] 8°. **14100. c. 17.(2.)**

—— Liste von transcribirten Abschriften und Auszügen vorwiegend aus den Jaina-Literatur, *etc.* 1891-1893. *See* ACADEMIES, *etc.*—Germany.—*Deutsche Morgenlaendische Gesellschaft.* Zeitschrift, *etc.* Bd. 45, 47. 1846, *etc.* 8°.
Ac. 8815/2. (Bd. 45, 47.)

LÉVI (SYLVAIN). *See* AṢVAGHOSHA. Le Buddhacarita d'Açvaghoṣa, par M. S. Lévi. [The text of Bk. I., with introduction and translation.] 1892. 8°. [*Journal Asiatique.*]
Ac. 8808. (Ser. viii., tom. 19.)

—— *See* HARSHADEVA. Une Poésie Inconnue du Roi Harṣa ... Par S. Lévi. 1895-1897. 8°. [*Actes du Dixième Congrès International des Orientalistes.*] **Ac. 8806. (Session 10.)**

—— *See* JAYADEVA, *son of Bhojadeva.* Le Gîtagovinda ... Traduite ... Avec une préface de M. S. Lévi. 1904. 12°. **14070. b. 32.**

—— La Doctrine du Sacrifice dans les Brâhmaṇas, *etc.* (Bibliothèque de l'École des Hautes Études. Sciences Religieuses. Onzième Volume.) pp. i. 182, i. *Paris, Le Puy* [printed], 1898. 8°.
Ac. 8929/7. (vol. 11.)

LIEBICH (BRUNO). *See* CHANDRA GOMĪ. Cāndra-vyākaraṇa ... Herausgegeben von B. Liebich. 1902. 8°. [*Deutsche Morgenlaendische Gesellschaft: Abhandlungen.*] **753. f. 19.**

—— *See* PĀṆINI.—*Kāṣikā.* Zwei Kapitel der Kāçikā. Übersetzt ... mit einer Einleitung ... von B. Liebich. 1892. 8°. **14093. b. 34.**

—— Das Cāndra-vyākaraṇa. [A study of the various recensions,] von Bruno Liebich. 1895. *See* ACADEMIES, *etc.* — Goettingen. — *Academia Georgia Augusta.* Nachrichten ... Aus dem Jahre 1895. pp. 272-321. [1845, *etc.*] 8°.
2097. a., P.P. 4672. a.

LINDNER (BRUNO). *See* BRĀHMAṆAS.—*Ṣatapatha-brāhmaṇa.* Die Dikshâ oder Weihe für das Somaopfer. [Translated into German, with commentary.] Habilitationsschrift ... [by] Dr. B. Lindner. 1878. 8°. **14010. d. 8.(2.)**

LIṄGĀSHṬAKA. শ্রীবিশ্বেশ্বরের ধ্যান *etc.* [Liṅgāshṭaka. Eight stanzas in praise of Ṣiva-Viṣveṣvara, purporting to be extracted from the Bṛihad-dharmapurāṇa. With a lithographed picture of the god's temple at Benares.] pp. 4; 1 *folding plate.* কাশী [*Benares,* 1891.] 12°.
14003. e. 2.(21.)

LITTLE (CHARLES EDGAR). A Grammatical Index to the Chāndogya-upaniṣad, *etc.* pp. x. 192, i. *New York, Cincinnati, Chicago*, [1900 ?]. 12°. **14003. m. 2.**

Forms part of the Vanderbilt Oriental Series.

LOKĀCHĀRYA PIḶḶAI. तत्त्वत्रयम् *etc.* (The Vedânta-tattvatraya of Srî Lokâchâryya Svâmî, with a commentary [by Maṇavāḷa Māmuni.] Edited [with preface] by Swâmî Bhâgavatâchâryya. pp. ii. 144. *Benares*, 1900. 8°. **14004. a. 4.**

Forms no. 22 *and part of no.* 26 *of the* Chowkhambâ Sanskrit Series.

The English title is taken from the wrapper.

—— Tattva-traya or Aphorisms on the Three Verities, Soul, Matter and God, by Sri Pillai Lokáchárya, translated [with annotations based chiefly on the commentary of Maṇavāḷa Māmuni] by Sri-Párthasárathy Aiyangar. pp. viii. 237. *Madras*, 1900. 8°. **14170. ee. 17.**

LOKANĀTHA KAVI, *Śrīnivāsapuram.* *See* KAVIRĀKSHASĪYA. కవిరాక్షసీయము *etc.* [Kavirākshasīya. With Telugu analyses and commentary by Lokanātha.] 1902. 8°. **14072. d. 38.(3.)**

—— *See* SANATKUMĀRA. ಗೃಹವಾಸ್ತುದರ್ಪಣ. [Gṛihavāstudarpaṇa. Edited with Canarese paraphrase by Lokanātha.] 1894. 8°. **14053. ccc. 17.**

LOKANĀTHA UPĀDHYĀYA, *of Gangauli.* *See* UDAYANA ĀCHĀRYA. ॥ लक्षणावली *etc.* [Lakshaṇāvalī. With commentary. Edited by Lokanātha.] [1901.] 8°. **14049. a. 4.(3.)**

LOKEṢVARA ṢUKLA, *of Bajiganj.* *See* SĀRASVATASŪTRA. श्रीसारस्वत° [Sārasvatavyākaraṇa. Together with a gloss by Lokeṣvara.] [1890-1892.] 8°. **14093. d. 17.**

LOMAṢA. लोमशसंहितास्थित: भावफलाध्याय: *etc.* [Bhāvaphalādhyāya. A chapter on the influence of planets, excerpted from the Lomaṣasaṃhitā. Edited by Dulāre Tivāṛī.] pp. 14. कल्याण-मुंबई १९५६ [*Kalyan*, 1900.] 12°. **14053. b. 17.(5.)**

LUCKNOW.—*Provincial Museum.* Catalogue of the Reference Library of the Provincial Museum, N.-W.P. and Oudh (Appendix III. Classified List of the Samskrit, Prakrit, Pali, and Hindi Manuscripts ... Compiled by A. Führer.) pp. xxiii. 169. *Allahabad*, 1892. 8°. **011900. ee. 15.**

LUEDERS (HEINRICH). *See* MAHĀBHĀRATA.—*Abridgments and Selections.* Über die Grantharecension des Mahābhārata. Epische Studien I. Von H. Lüders. 1901. 4°. [*Abhandlungen der Koenigl. Gesellschaft der Wissenschaften zu Goettingen.*] **14065. e. 29, Ac. 670.**

—— *See* MAHĀBHĀRATA.—*Vanaparva.* Zur Sage von Ṛsyaśṛṅga. [Text in the Southern recension, critically examined,] von H. Lüders. 1901. 8°. [*Nachrichten von der Georg-Augusts Universitaet zu Goettingen.*] **2097. a., P.P. 4672. a.**

—— Die Sage von Ṛsyaśṛṅga [in the Vanaparva, critically examined,] von H. Lüders. 1897. *See* ACADEMIES, *etc.* — Goettingen. — *Academia Georgia Augusta.* Nachrichten ... Aus dem Jahre 1897. pp. 87-135. [1845, *etc.*] 8°. **2097. a., P.P. 4672. a.**

—— Die Vyâsa-Çikshâ, besonders in ihrem Verhältnis zum Taittirîya-Prâtiçâkhya ... Von der philosophischen Fakultät der Universität Göttingen gekrönte Preisschrift. pp. 118. *Kiel*, 1895. 8°. **011840. m. 55.**

LUPTON (WALTER). *See* SUTTAPIṬAKA.—*Majjhimanikāya.* The Raṭṭhapāla Sutta. [With translation.] By W. Lupton. 1894. 8°. [*Journal of the Royal Asiatic Society.*] **Ac. 8820/3., 2098. a.,b.**

M ... L ... DUBE. *See* DUBE (M. L.).

MACARTNEY (GEORGE). *See* HOERNLE (A. F. R.). Facsimile Reproduction of ... Macartney MSS., Set i, *etc.* 1902. 4°. **759. k. 1.**

MACDONALD (K. S.). The Brahmanas of the Vedas, *etc.* pp. vii. 211. 1896. *See* EAST. The Sacred Books of the East Described and Examined. Hindu Series. Vol. I, pt. 3. 1895, *etc.* 8°. **14010. cc. 9.(vol. 1.)**

MACDONELL (ARTHUR ANTHONY). A History of Sanskrit Literature, *etc.* pp. viii. 472. *London*, 1900. **2312. a. 10.**

Forms no. ix. *in the series* Short Histories of the Literatures of the World.

MADANAGOPĀLA GOSVĀMĪ. *See* KRISHṆADĀSA KAVIRĀJA, *Gosvāmī*. শ্রীশ্রীচৈতন্যচরিতামৃত *etc.* [Chaitanyacharitāmṛita. Edited with a Sanskrit commentary and notes by Madanagopāla.] [1891, *etc.*] 4°. **14123. i. 8.**

—— *See* RŪPA GOSVĀMĪ. লঘুভাগবতামৃত *etc.* [Laghu-bhāgavatāmṛita. With Bengali translation and notes by Madanagopāla.] [1897.] 8°. **14016. c. 58.**

MADANASENA, *Hārpākā*. *See* MOHINĪMOHANA SENA GUPTA. "হাড়পাকা" মদনসেনস্য বংশপঞ্জিকা *etc.* [Hāṛpākā-Madanasenasya Vaṃsapañjikā. A pedigree of the family of Madanasena.] [1896.] 16°. **14058. a. 11.**

MÂḌGÂVKAR (K. R.). *See* KRISHṆA RĀMACHANDRA MĀḌGĀVKAR.

MĀDHAVA, *son of Indukara*. Nidana. A Sanskrit system of pathology. An English translation, with Sanskrit passages, by Kaviraj Russick Lal Gupta. pp. v. 270. *Calcutta*, 1892. 8°. **14043. cc. 6.**

The text is given without the introduction, and in other respects also is somewhat imperfect; the English translation includes additional matter from various sources.

—— Madhavanidana. Translated [into Sinhalese] out of the Sanskrit by the late Pandit Batuvantudave[, together with the original text]. මාධවනිදානය, *etc.* Third edition. pt. i. pp. xii. 88. *Colombo*, 1893. 8°. **14043. d. 46.**

—— সটীক-নিদান *etc.* [Nidāna. With the commentary Vyākhyāmadhukoṣa composed by Vijayarakshita (as far as the end of the Aṣmarīnidāna) and Ṣrīkaṇṭhadatta (from the Prameha-madhumeha-piḍakā-nidāna to the end). Edited by Sāradācharaṇa Sena Kaviratna.] pp. xii. 538. কলিকাতা ১৯৫৭ [*Calcutta*, 1901.] 8°. **14043. c. 44.**

MĀDHAVACHANDRA TARKACHŪḌĀMAṆI. *See* SUSHEṆA, *Kavirāja*. আখ্যাত-কবিরাজঃ *etc.* [Ākhyāta-kavirāja. Edited by Mādhavachandra.] [1895.] 8°. **14093. b. 36.(2.)**

—— শ্রীশ্রীগৌরগোপীবল্লভার্চ্চন চন্দ্রিকা *etc.* [Gauragopīvallabhārchanachandrikā. A manual of devotions for worshippers of Kṛishṇa. With Bengali translations, *etc.* Third edition.] pp. 39. ঢাকা ১২৯৯ [*Dacca*, 1892.] 8°. **14028. d. 59.(2.)**

MĀDHAVĀCHĀRYA. *See* SĀYAṆA ĀCHĀRYA.

MĀDHAVAJĪ GOPĀLAJĪ VAIDYA. *See* VALLABHĀCHĀRYA. ષોડશ ગ્રંથ *etc.* [Shoḍaṣa-grantha. Edited with Gujarati translations and explanations by Mādhavajī Vaidya.] [1896.] 8°. **14028. c. 70.**

MĀDHAVA KARA. *See* MĀDHAVA, *son of Indukara*.

MĀDHAVA MISRA. *See* ṢATĀNANDA, *son of Ṣaṅkara*. भास्वतीउदाहरणम् । [Bhāsvatyudāharaṇa. With the commentary Bhāsvatīvivaraṇa of Mādhava.] [1891, *etc.*] 4°. [*Aruṇodaya.*] **14133. g. 16.(pt. i., no. 19.)**

MĀDHAVAMUKUNDACHARAṆA, *of Aruṇaghaṭā*. परपक्षगिरिवज्रः *etc.* [Parapakshagirivajra, or Adhyāsagirivajra. A polemical exposition of the Brahmasūtra and Vedānta, according to the Nimbārka school. Edited by Dulāre-prasād Trivedī.] pp. ii. 638, ii. श्रीवृन्दावन° १९५९ [*Brindaban*, 1902.] 8°. **14049. b. 6.**

MĀDHAVĀNANDA BHĀRATĪ, *disciple of Īṣvarānanda*. *See* ANNAM BHAṬṬA. तर्कसंग्रहप्रारम्भः Taraksangrah [*sic*]. Translated into Hindi [by Mādhavānanda, *etc.*] 1889. 8°. **14048. dd. 12.**

—— *See* SADĀNANDA YOGĪNDRA. ॥ वेदान्तसार भाषाटीका । [Vedāntasāra, with Hindi commentary by Mādhavānanda.] 1889. 8°. **14154. e. 27.(3.)**

MĀDHAVA SARASVATĪ. *See* ṢIVĀDITYA MIṢRA. The Saptapadârthî ... with its commentary the Mitabhâshiṇî of Mâdhava, *etc.* 1893. 8°. **14048. dd. 3.(vol. 6.)**

MĀDHAVA ṢĀSTRĪ PUROHITA. *See* BHĀSKARA ĀCHĀRYA. करणकुतूहलम् *etc.* [Karaṇakutūhala. With commentary. Edited by Mādhava Ṣāstrī.] [1902.] 8°. **14053. ccc. 34.**

MĀDHAVASVARŪPĀNANDA BHĀRATĪ. *See* MĀDHAVĀNANDA BHĀRATĪ.

MĀDHAVA TARKĀLAṄKĀRA. *See* BHAVĀNANDA SIDDHĀNTAVĀGĪṢA. কারকচক্রম্ *etc.* [Kārakachakra. With the commentaries of Mādhava called Mādhavī, *etc.*] [1900.] 8°. **14090. bb. 15.(1.)**

MADHURA KAVI, *of Mandarpur.* अर्चावतारस्थलवैभवदर्पणम् दिव्यदेशतीर्थयात्रा *etc.* [Archāvatārasthalavaibhavadarpaṇa or Divyadeṣatīrthayātrā. A metrical description of the most celebrated Vaishṇava places of pilgrimage in India, illustrated from epic and Pauranic texts. With hymns, rituals of worship, and a Hindi commentary.] pp. i. v. 301, ii. कल्याण-मुंबई १८१९ [*Kalyan*, 1897.] 8°. **14058. b. 36.**

MADHUSŪDANA, *Āchārya of the Nigamāgama-Maṇḍalī, Muttra.* Sri Madhusudana Sanhitá. A key to understand the system of Hinduism the universal religion. [Sanskrit text, with a Bengali translation and notes.] (শ্রীশ্রীমধুসূদন সংহিতা) pp. iv. 6, iv. iii. 305. *Calcutta*, [1899.] 8°. **14028. d. 73.**

—— सद्धर्मानुशासनं नाम । श्रीश्रीमधुसूदनसंहिता *etc.* [Madhusūdanasaṃhitā, or Saddharmānuṣāsana. With Sanskrit notes.] pp. 218. मुम्बय्यां १९०१ [*Bombay*, 1901.] 8°. **14033. aa. 19.**

MADHUSŪDANA, *son of Būṛhana, of Hati, Darbhangah.* जानकीपरिणय नाटक । [Jānakīpariṇaya. A short dramatic poem, in 4 acts, on the bridal of Sītā and Rāma.] pp. 22. दरभङ्गा १८१६ [*Darbhangah*, 1894.] 8°. **14079. c. 57.(4.)**

The colophon ascribes the work to Devakīnandana Miṣra; the text explicitly mentions Madhusūdana as author. The date given is pushkara-nāga-vāji-vidhu (1783) *Ṣaka.*

MADHUSŪDANA DATTA (MICHAEL). *See* VASANTAKUMĀRA BHAṬṬĀCHĀRYA. माइकेलचरितम् . . . Life of Micheal [*sic*] Madhushudana, *etc.* 1890. 12°. **14058. a. 7.**

MADHUSŪDANA MIṢRA. [For editions of Madhusūdana's recension of the Mahānāṭaka:] *See* HANUMĀN.

MADHUSŪDANA SARASVATĪ, *disciple of Viṣveṣvara.* *See* MAHĀBHĀRATA. — Bhagavadgītā. — *Sanskrit.* ॥ अथ . . . भगवद्गीता° [Bhagavadgītā. With the commentary Gūḍhārthadīpikā of Madhusūdana.] [1901.] *obl.* 8°. **14048. cc. 38.**

—— *See* MAHĀBHĀRATA.—Bhagavadgītā.—*Sanskrit.* श्रीमद्भगवद्गीता *etc.* [Bhagavadgītā. With the Gūḍhārthadīpikā of Madhusūdana.] [1901.] 8°. **14003. ccc. (no. 45.)**

—— *See* ṢAṄKARA ĀCHĀRYA.—*Two or More Works.* Śrī-Śankaráchárya's Miscellaneous Works, *etc.* [Vol. II, Daṣaṣlokī, with commentaries of Madhusūdana, *etc.*] 1898-1899. 8°. [*Mysore Government Oriental Library Series: Bibliotheca Sanskrita.*] **14004. b. 10.(vol. 2.)**

—— *See* ṢAṄKARA ĀCHĀRYA. — *Philosophical Poems, etc.* అయం సిద్ధాంతబిందుః *etc.* [Daṣaṣlokī. With the commentary Siddhāntabindu or Siddhāntatattvab°. of Madhusūdana.] [1892.] 8°. **14048. cc. 9.(1.)**

—— *See* ṢAṄKARA ĀCHĀRYA.—*Philosophical Poems, etc.* ॥ सिद्धान्तबिन्दुः *etc.* [Daṣaṣlokī. With the commentary Siddhāntabindu of Madhusūdana and the supercommentary Nyāyaratnāvalī of Brahmānanda.] 1893. 8°. [*Advaitamañjarī.*] **14048. e. 23.**

—— ॥ अद्वैतसिद्धिः *etc.* [Advaitasiddhi. An exposition of monist philosophy.] pp. i. iv. iv. 343. 1893. *See* HARIHARA ṢĀSTRĪ, *Goshṭhīpuram*, and others. ॥ अद्वैतमञ्जरी *etc.* [Advaitamañjarī.] 1892-1895. 8°. **14048. e. 23.**

—— *See* BRAHMĀNANDA SARASVATĪ, *disciple of Paramānanda.* ॥ लघुचन्द्रिका *etc.* [Laghuchandrikā. A commentary upon the Advaitasiddhi.] 1893. 8°. [*Advaitamañjarī.*] **14048. e. 23.**

MADHUSŪDANA SMṚITIRATNA. *See* JĪMŪTAVĀHANA. कालविवेकः । The Kāla-viveka. Edited [with commentary] by . . . Madhusūdana Smṛtiratna. 1897, *etc.* 8°. [*Bibliotheca Indica.*] **14002. a. (vol. 136.)**

MADHVĀCHĀRYA. *See* ĀNANDATĪRTHA.

MĀDHYANDINA. *See* ṢRĀDDHA. श्री . . . पार्वणं श्राद्धम् *etc.* [Apātrika-pārvaṇa-ṣrāddha. According to the Mādhyandina school.] [1895]. 12°. **14010. b. 15.**

—— अथ माध्यन्दिनमहर्षिप्रणीता शिक्षा *etc.* [Mādhyandinīya-ṣikshā. A tract on Vedic phonetics. Followed by the Laghu-mādhyandinīya-ṣikshā.] *See* YUGALAKIṢORA VYĀSA PĀṬHAKA. श्रीमद्याज्ञवल्क्यादि . . . शिक्षासङ्ग्रहः . . . A collection of Śikshás, *etc.* pp. 109-116. 1893. 8°. **14093. b. 31.**

MADIRĀVATĪKATHĀNAKA. La Novellina Jainica di Madirāvatī. [A poetical version of the Kanaka-

rathakathānaka in the Kathākoṣa. Edited with a translation by E. L. de Stefani.] 1900. *See* Academies, *etc.*—Florence.—*Società Asiatica Italiana.* Giornale, *etc.* Vol. xiii. pp. 1-26. 1887, *etc.* 8°.
Ac. 8804.(vol. 13.)

MADRAS.—*Government Oriental Manuscripts Library.* Alphabetical Index of Manuscripts in the Government Oriental MSS. Library, *etc.* 10 pts. *Madras,* 1893. Fol. **14096. f. 9.**

—— —— A Descriptive Catalogue of the Sanskrit Manuscripts of the Government Oriental Manuscripts Library, Madras. By the late M. Seshagiri Sastri (and M. Rangacharya) . . . Vol. i. —Vedic Literature. *Madras,* 1901, *etc.* 8°.
14096. ccc. 4.

In progress.

MAGANLĀL DALPATRĀM KHAKKHAR. *See* Sarvānanda Sūri. જગડૂ ચરિત *etc.* [Jagaḍūcharita. Preceded by introduction, translation, *etc.*, in Gujarati, by Maganlāl.] [1896.] 12°.
14100. b. 9.

MAGANLĀL VIṢVANĀTHA, *of Wasna.* *See* Hemachandra, *disciple of Devachandra.* वैद्यतत्त्वरत्नाकर *etc.* [Vaidyatattvaratnākara. Edited with Gujarati paraphrase and notes by Maganlāl.] [1898.] 8°. **14053. d. 56.**

MĀGHA. शिशुपालवध *etc.* [Śiṣupālavadha. With Hindi translation by Kālīcharaṇa Ṣarmā.] pp. ii. 615. लखनऊ १८९१ [*Lucknow,* 1891.] 8°.
14076. d. 47.

—— Magha's Shishupal badham. [Sarga i.] Containing an introduction in English . . . paraphrase . . . Mallinatha's Sarbankasa, Bengali & English translations, anglosanskrit notes . . . grammatical notes . . . &c. &c. . . . by Pandit Nabin Chandra Vidyaratna. New edition. pp. iv. 236. *Calcutta,* [1901.] 8°.
14085. c. 49.(2.)

—— Some Important Notes and Questions [in English, Sanskrit, and Bengali] on Sisupal Badha. With an English translation thereof. Cantos i. & ii. pp. 56. *Calcutta,* [1891?] 12°.
14076. b. 24.(3.)

MAHĀBHĀRATA.

Entire Work.

ശ്രീമഹാഭാരതം *etc.* [Mahābhārata. With a Malayalam translation.] pts. 1-24. കോഴി-ക്കോട പവ്യൻ്റ [*Calicut,* 1891, *etc.*] 8°.
14060. c. 33.

Breaks off at Aranyoparva xxxi. *Apparently no more has been published.*

মহাভারতম্ *etc.* [Mahābhārata. With the commentaries Bhāratabhāvadīpa of Nīlakaṇṭha and Bhāratārthadīpikā of Arjuna Miṣra. Edited by Bhūdhara Chaṭṭopādhyāya.] কলিকাতা ১৮১৯ [*Calcutta,* 1897, *etc.*] 8°. **14065. d. 38.**

In progress.

॥ महाभारतम् *etc.* [Mahābhārata. With the commentary Lakshālaṅkāra of Vādirāja.] आणिक्कारसत्रे १८९८ [*Anikkaran Chattram,* 1898, *etc.*] 4°.
14065. f. 4.

In progress?

महाभारत . . . श्रीवेदव्यास रचित संस्कृत मूल और हिन्दी अंग्रेजी अनुवाद सहित ॥ The Mahabharat . . . The Sanskrit text of Maharshi Vyas with complete English and Hindi translations. *Moradabad,* 1902, *etc.* 8°. **14068. c. 16.**

In progress.

The Mahabharata of Krishna-Dwaipayana Vyasa. Translated into English prose [by Kiṣorīmohana Gaṅgopādhyāya, assisted by Chāruchandra Mukhopādhyāya and Kṛishṇakamala Bhaṭṭāchārya]. Published . . . by Protap Chandra Roy. *Calcutta,* 1883-1896. 8°. **14065. bb. 2.**

A Prose English Translation of the Mahabharata. Translated literally from the original . . . text. Edited and published by Manmatha Nath Dutt. *Calcutta,* 1895, *etc.* 8°. **14068. b. 17.**

In progress.

The Mahabharata of Krishna-Dwaipayana Veda Vyas. Translated into English prose with esoteric commentary. Edited by S. C. Mukhopadhaya. *Calcutta,* 1899, *etc.* 8°.
14065. e. 28.

In progress.

See Nīlakaṇṭha, *son of Govinda.* भारतभावदीपः *etc.* [Bhāratabhāvadīpa. Nīlakaṇṭha's commentary on the Mahābhārata.] [1900, *etc.*] 8°. **14068. b. 18.**

MAHĀBHĀRATA (*continued*).

ABRIDGMENTS AND SELECTIONS.

Mahabharata. Abridged by C. V. Vaidya. (संक्षिप्तमहाभारत.) pp. ii. 522, iii. *Bombay*, 1902. 8°. **14065. bbb. 11.**

Miscellaneous Extracts, metrically and freely translated, or paraphrased, from the Mahābhārata. Third series. By John Muir. pp. 32. *For private circulation : Edinburgh*, 1877. 12°. **14065. b. 14.(1.)**

Fourth Set of Metrical Translations from the Sanskrit [viz. the Mahābhārata and Rāmāyaṇa]. By J. Muir. pp. 29. *For private circulation : Edinburgh*, 1878. 12°. **14065. b. 14.(2.)**

Further Metrical Translations from the Mahabharata . . . and two short . . . translations from the Greek. By J. Muir. pp. i. 50. [*Edinburgh*, 1880 ?] 12°. **14065. b. 14.(3.)**

A reprint. For private circulation ?

श्रीमद्भगवद्गीता पञ्चरत्न तथा ईश, केन, मुण्डक अने ऐतरेयोपनिषद् *etc.* [Pañcharatna. Comprising the Bhagavadgītā; the Vishṇusahasranāmastotra, from the Anuṣāsanaparva; the Bhīshmastavarāja, from the Ṣāntiparva; the Anusmṛiti; and the Gajendramoksha, from the Ṣāntiparva. Preceded by the Gītāmāhātmya from the Varāhapurāṇa, *dhyānas*, *nyāsas*, *etc.*; and followed by the Īṣa, Kena, Muṇḍaka, and Aitareya Upanishads. Edited with analyses, indices, and Gujarati translations and commentaries by Raṇachhoḍajī Uddhavajī Ṣāstrī. Second edition.] pp. xxiv. 545, 103; 7 *plates*. मुंबई १८९६ [*Bombay*, 1896.] 8°. **14060. d. 15.**

अथ श्रीमद्भगवद्गीता ॥ पञ्चरत्न ॥ [Pañcharatna. Preceded by the Gītāmāhātmya from the Varāhapurāṇa, *nyāsas*, and *dhyānas*.] pp. 528; 8 *plates*. लखनऊ १८९९ [*Lucknow*, 1899.] *obl.* 12°. **14065. b. 23.**

अथ . . . श्रीमहाविष्णुपंचरत्न° [Pañcharatna.] *See* GOVARDHANADĀSA LAKSHMĪDĀSA. बृहत्स्तोत्रसरित्सागर *etc.* [Bṛihat-stotrasaritsāgara.] Vol. i., pp. 95-192. [1892.] 12°. **14033. a. 27.(vol. 1.)**

अथ पाण्डवगीता प्रारंभः [Pāṇḍavagītā. A cento of eighty stanzas from the Mahābhārata in praise of Vishṇu. Followed by a Prātaḥsmaraṇa.] pp. 24. [*Benares*, 1890.] *obl.* 12°. **14028. b. 81.(1.)**

হিন্দুশাস্ত্র . . . মহাভারত। [Selections from the Ādi, Sabhā, Āraṇya, Virāṭa, Udyoga, Bhīshma, Droṇa, Karṇa, Ṣalya, and Sauptika *parvas*. Edited with Bengali epitomes, *etc.*, by Dāmodara Vidyānanda.] pp. i. 157. [1897.] *See* RAMEṢACHANDRA DATTA. হিন্দুশাস্ত্র *etc.* [Hindu-ṣāstra.] Pt. vii. [1895-1897.] 8°. **14085. c. 45. (vol. 2.)**

The Bhagavadgîtâ with the Sanatsugâtîya and the Anugîtâ. Translated by the late Kâshinâth Trimbak Telang. Second edition. pp. 446. 1898. *See* MUELLER (F. M.). The Sacred Books of the East, *etc.* Vol. viii. 1879, *etc.* 8°. **2003. a. (vol. 8.)**

पतिव्रतादर्पण *etc.* [Pativratādarpaṇa. An anthology from the Mahābhārata, *etc.*, on wifely virtues.] [1899.] 16°. *See* SATYĀNANDA AGNIHOTRĪ. **14076. a. 24.**

Légendes Morales de l'Inde, empruntées au Bhagavata Purana et au Mahabharata. Traduites . . . par A. Roussel. 1900-1901. 12°. *See* PURĀṆAS.—*Bhāgavatapurāṇa.* **14065. b. 20.**

Über die Grantharecension des Mahābhārata. [Comprising specimens of the Southern recension from the Virāṭaparva, Sauptikap.°, Aishikap.°, Strīp.°, and Ṣāntip.°] Epische Studien I. Von Heinrich Lüders. pp. 91. 1901. *See* ACADEMIES, *etc.* — Goettingen. — *Koenigliche Gesellschaft der Wissenschaften.* Abhandlungen . . . Philologisch-historische Klasse. Neue Folge, Band IV. Nro. 6. 1843, *etc.* 4°. **14065. e. 29.**

ĀDIPARVA.

On the South-Indian Recension of the Mahabharata. [Comprising specimens from the Ādiparva.] By M. Winternitz. 1898. *See* PERIODICAL PUBLICATIONS.—*Bombay.* The Indian Antiquary, *etc.* Vol. xxvii., pp. 67-81, 92-104, 122-136. 1872, *etc.* 4°. **14096. e. (vol. 27.)**

Vyasa. Sakountala. Traduction libre de P.-E. Foucaux, *etc.* pp. 137, i.; 7 *plates*. *Paris*, 1894. 16°. **14060. a. 13.**

Forms part of the Petite Collection Guillaume.

MAHĀBHĀRATA (*continued*).

ANUŚĀSANAPARVA.

॥ भारतीश्लोकत्रिशती ॥ [Bhāratī Ślokatriśatī. 300 moral stanzas. Followed by a few verses from other parts of the Mahābhārata.] *See* VEṄKAṬARĀMA ŚĀSTRĪ, *of Mysore*. कथाशतकम् "Kathasataka," *etc*. pp. 135-169. 1898. 8°.
14070. c. 63.(1.)

Śiva Sahasranâma Stotra, with Śrî Nîlakantha's commentary. English translation, by R. Anantakrishna Sastri. [With the Sanskrit text of the hymn appended.] pp. iv. 67, 15. *Madras*, 1902. 8°.
14016. dd. 1.

भगवद्गुणदर्पणाख्यभाष्य-निर्वचन-निरुक्तिख्याख्या-त्रयोपेतम् श्रीविष्णोर्नामसहस्रम् *etc*. [Vishṇusahasranāma. With Parāśara Bhaṭṭa's commentary Bhagavadguṇadarpaṇa; the grammatical supercommentary Bhagavannāmasahasranirvachana or Vishṇun.° by Varadāchārya Sūri; and another commentary in memorial verses styled Vishṇusahasranāmanirukti or Bhagavats.° Preceded by 2 indices, one giving the names alphabetically, the other comprising 107 stanzas with notes showing the occurrence of the names by their final letters; and containing critical notes, supplements, *etc*.] pp. iii. ii. xvi. i. ii. xii. 837, viii. कल्याण १९५० [*Kalyan*, 1894.] 8°.
14065. e. 27.

श्रीविष्णुसहस्रनामस्तोत्रम् *etc*. [Vishṇusahasranāma. With commentary of Śaṅkara.] 1898. *See* ŚAṄKARA ĀCHĀRYA.—*Two or More Works*. Śrí-Śankaráchárya's Miscellaneous Works, *etc*. Vol. i., pp. 1-128. 1898-1899. 8°. [*Mysore Government Oriental Library Series: Bibliotheca Sanskrita*.]
14004. b. 10.(vol. 1.)

अथ श्रीविष्णुसहस्रनामार्थमंजरी प्रारभ्यते ॥ [Vishṇusahasranāmārthamañjarī. Comprising the Vishṇusahasranāma, together with a poetical explanation of the latter in Marathi by Balavanta Khaṇḍūjī Pārakh.] ff. i. 60. मुंबई १९०० [*Bombay*, 1900.] *obl*. 8°.
14028. c. 84.

ಶ್ರೀವಿಷ್ಣುಸಹಸ್ರನಾಮಸ್ತೋತ್ರಂ *etc*. [Vishṇusahasranāma. Followed by the 1000 names in *mantra* form.] pp. 155. *Mysore*, [1901.] 32°.
14068. a. 8.

The Vishnu Sahasranama, with Sri Sankaracharya's commentary, translated into English by R. Ananthakrishna Sastry. [With the Sanskrit text of the Vishṇusahasranāma appended.] pp. iii. 126, 12. *Madras*, 1901. 8°.
14048. bb. 52.

శ్రీవిష్ణుసహస్రనామస్తోత్రమ్. [Vishṇusahasranāma.] *See* SAHASRANĀMASTABAKA. శ్రీసహస్రనామస్తబకమ్. [Sahasranāmastabaka.] pp. 1-32. [1902.] *obl*. 16°.
14033. a. 52.

[For editions of the Vishṇusahasranāma printed in the collection styled Pañcharatna:] *See above*, ABRIDGMENTS AND SELECTIONS.

ĀRAṆYAPARVA.

See VANAPARVA.

AŚVAMEDHAPARVA.

Anugîtâ. [Translated, with introduction, by Kāśīnātha Tryambaka Telang. Second edition.] 1898. *See* MUELLER (F. M.). The Sacred Books of the East, *etc*. Vol. viii., pp. 195-394. 1879, *etc*. 8°.
2003. a.(vol. 8.)

BHAGAVADGĪTĀ.

Sanskrit.

श्रीमद्भगवद्गीता . . . The Bhagavad-gítá, with the commentary of Śrí Śankaráchárya. Edited by A. Mahádeva Śástri . . . and Panditaratnam K. Rangácharya. pp. iv. xiv. 446, ii. 1895. *See* MYSORE.—*Government of Mysore*. Government Oriental Library Series. Bibliotheca Sanskrita, *etc*. No. 8. 1893, *etc*. 8°.
14004. b. 6.

श्रीमद्भगवद्गीता *etc*. (Shrîmat Bhagavadgîta with the Bháshya by . . . Śankaráchárya, the commentary by Anadagiri [*sic*] on the same, index to all the words in the text, index to all the sloks &c., &c., &c. Edited by Pandit Kâśînâtha Śâstrî Âgâsé.) pp. xii. 545, vii. xli. viii. *Poona*, 1897. 8°.
14003. ccc. (no. 34.)

Forms no. 34 of the Ānandāśrama Sanskrit Series. *The English title is taken from the wrapper, which gives the date as* 1897, *while it appears on the Sanskrit title as* 1896.

श्रीमद्भगवद्गीता *etc*. [Bhagavadgītā. With the commentary Krishṇatoshiṇī of Yādavendra.] pp. 159. कुम्भघोणे १८९९ [*Kumbakonam*, 1899.] 8°.
14065. c. 51.

॥ अथ श्रीमधुसूदनटीकायुतभगवद्गीताप्रारंभः ॥ [Bhagavadgītā. With the commentary Gūḍhārthadīpikā of

Madhusūdana Sarasvatī.] ff. i. 190; 1 *plate.* मुंबय्याख्यां राजधान्यां १८२३ [*Bombay*, 1901.] *obl.* 8°.
14048. cc. 38.

श्रीमद्भगवद्गीता *etc.* [Bhagavadgītā. With the commentaries Gūḍhārthadīpikā of Madhusūdana Sarasvatī and Subodhinī of Śrīdhara Svāmī. Edited by Kāśinātha Śāstrī Āgāśe.] pp. ii. 519. पुण्याख्यपत्तने १९०१ [*Poona*, 1901.] 8°.
14003. ccc. (no. 45.)

Forms no. 45 *of the* Ānandāśrama Sanskrit Series.

श्रीमद्भगवद्गीता *etc.* [Bhagavadgītā. With the commentary, styled Paiśāchabhāshya, ascribed to Hanumān. Edited by Kāśinātha Śāstrī Āgāśe and Bābā Śāstrī Phaḍke.] pp. i. 146. पुण्याख्यपत्तने १९०१ [*Poona*, 1901.] 8°.
14003. ccc. (no. 44.)

Forms no. 44 *of the* Ānandāśrama Sanskrit Series.

Sri Bhagavad Githa. With Githartha Sangraha, a [prose] commentary [purporting to be] by Srimad Yamuna charya, *etc.* (॥ श्री भगवद्गीता ॥) pp. 182. 1901. *See* Anantāchārya, *Prativādibhayaṅkara.* शास्त्रमुक्तावली. The Śasthramukthâvalî, *etc.* No. 6. 1899, *etc.* 8°.
14049. a. 1.(no. 6.).

The editor suggests that this work may be by Yāmuna the father of Krishṇa Guru and author of the Chaturviṃśatisāhasrī on the Sahasragīti, but admits that he is not known to have written a book of this name.

[For editions of the Bhagavadgītā printed in the collection styled Pañcharatna:] *See* above, Abridgments and Selections.

Sanskrit and Vernaculars.

यथार्थदीपिका. [Bhagavadgītā. With the poetical Marathi commentary, styled Yathārthadīpikā, of Vāmana.] pp. 1279. [1889-1891.] *See* Vāmana Paṇḍita, *the Marathi Poet.* वामनी ग्रंथ *etc.* [Vāmanī Grantha.] Vol. 1, 2. [1889-1891.] 8°.
14140. b. 23.(vol. 1, 2.)

The Yathârthadîpikâ, a commentary on the Bhagavadgîtâ, of Vamana Pandita, the great Marathi poet of the Mahârâshtra. [With the Sanskrit text of the Bhagavadgītā.] . . . Edited . . . by Vâman Dâjî Ok. (यथार्थदीपिका.) *Bombay*, 1896, *etc.* 8°.
14140. aa. 16.

In progress. Forms no. 28, *etc., of the* Kâvyasangraha.

श्रीमद्भगवद्गीता समश्लोकी. [Bhagavadgītā. With the Marathi *samaślokī* version of Vāmana.] [1891.] *See* Vāmana Paṇḍita, *the Marathi Poet.* वामनी ग्रंथ *etc.* [Vāmanī Grantha.] Vol. 4. pp. 1-178. [1889-1891.] 8°.
14140. b. 23.(vol. 4.)

শ্রীমদ্ভগবদ্গীতা *etc.* [Bhagavadgītā. With Śrīdhara Svāmī's commentary and a Bengali translation by Hemachandra Vidyāratna. Edited with a Bengali introduction by Kshitīndranātha Ṭhākura.] pp. i. iv. xv. 143, 574. কলিকাতা ১৮১৬ [*Calcutta*, 1895.] 16°.
14065. b. 15.

ज्ञानेश्वरी किंवा भावार्थदीपिका *etc.* [Bhagavadgītā. With the Jñāneśvarī or Bhāvārthadīpikā, a Marathi amplificative paraphrase by Jñānadeva. Edited with glosses in Marathi by Tukārām Tātyā.] pp. 16, 496. मुंबई १८१९ [*Bombay*, 1897.] 12°.
14060. b. 15.

॥ श्रीमद्भगवद्गीतेवरील अभंग ॥ [Bhagavadgītā. With the Marathi metrical version of Ṭhākuradāsa.] *See* Ṭhākuradāsa, *the Marathi Poet.* ठाकुरदास बावांचें उपलब्ध ग्रंथ. [Ṭhākuradāsa-Bāvāṇchen Upalabdha Grantha.] pp. 16-133. [1897.] 8°.
14140. b. 28.

হিন্দুশাস্ত্র · · · শ্রীমদ্ভগবদ্গীতা। [Bhagavadgītā. With a Bengali translation by Baṅkimchandra Chaṭṭopādhyāya (Adh. i. ii.) and Dāmodara Vidyānanda (iii.–xviii.).] pp. i. 121. [1897.] *See* Rameśachandra Datta. হিন্দুশাস্ত্র *etc.* [Hinduśāstra.] Pt. viii. [1895-1897.] 8°.
14085. c. 45.(vol. 2.)

भगवद्गीताभाष्यम् *etc.* [Bhagavadgītā. With commentary in Sanskrit and Hindi by Bhīmasena Śarmā. Edited by the latter, assisted by Rāmadayālu Śarmā.] pp. 566, ii. इटावा [१८]९७ [*Etawah*, 1897.] 8°.
14065. c. 46.

भगवद्गीता [Bhagavadgītā. Edited with a Hindi translation by Rāmasvarūpa Śarmā.] pp. i. 120, ii. मुरादाबाद १९५४ [*Moradabad*, 1897.] 8°.
14065. c. 49.

लक्ष्मीनारायन सरोवर . . . لکشمی نارایں سرؤور . . . *etc.* [Lakshmīnārāyaṇa-sarovara. The Bhagavadgītā, with Hindi translation and commentaries in Persian and in Hindi in the Persian character by Lakshmīnārāyaṇa of Agra.] pp. iv. 506, *lith.* आगरा १८९८ [*Agra*, 1898.] 8°.
14065. d. 39.

MAHĀBHĀRATA.—BHAGAVADGĪTĀ.—*Sanskrit and Vernaculars (continued).*

ଶ୍ରୀମଦ୍ଭଗବଦ୍ଗୀତା *etc.* [Bhagavadgītā. With an Oriya translation by Rāmaṣaṅkara Rāya. Third edition.] pp. i. 98. *Cuttack,* 1898. 8°. **14065. c. 14.(1.)**

ಶ್ರೀಗೀತಾರ್ಥಸಾರವು *etc.* [Gītārthasāra. Being the Bhagavadgītā with explanatory notes and a compendium of the leading commentaries of the Dvaita, Advaita, and Viṣishṭādvaita schools, in Canarese, edited by Tūppūl Veṅkaṭāchārya.] 3 vols. *Bangalore,* 1898-1901. 8°. **14048. cc. 19.**

ஸ்ரீபகவத்கீதை *etc.* [Bhagavadgītā. With Tamil glosses and translations. Preceded by the Kṛishṇāshṭottaraṣatanāmastotra, a short metrical prayer, the Bhagavadgītāmāhātmya, and *nyāsas*; and followed by Yāmuna Āchārya's Gītārthasaṅgraha, with Tamil version, and the Kṛishṇāshṭaka. Edited and translated by A. Ṣrīnivāsa Tātāchārya and K. Rāmasvāmi Nāyuḍu.] pp. 12, ii. 714, xxii.; 1 *plate.* சென்னை விகாரி [*Madras,* 1899.] 16°. **14065. b. 19.**

The Sanskrit text is printed in both the Grantham and the Tamil character.

శ్రీభగవద్గీతా గూఢార్థదీపిక *etc.* [Bhagavadgītā. With Telugu interpretations of each word and a Telugu commentary based on that of Ṣaṅkara, and styled Gūḍhārthadīpikā, by Bālasubrahmaṇya Brahmasvāmī. Second edition.] pp. vi. 809. చెన్నపురి ౧౯౦౦ [*Madras,* 1900.] 8°. **14065. c. 50.**

பகவத்கீதா தாத்பரிய தீபிகை *etc.* [Bhagavadgītā. In the Tamil character, edited with a Tamil version styled Bhagavadgītātātparyadīpikā by Bālasubrahmaṇya Brahmasvāmī.] pp. 494. சென்னை [*Madras,*] 1900. 32°. **14068. a. 10.**

శ్రీభగవద్గీతారహస్యార్థబోధిని *etc.* [Bhagavadgītā. With Bhagavadgītārahasyārthabodhinī, a Telugu translation and exposition by Bālasubrahmaṇya Brahmasvāmī.] చెన్నపురి [*Madras,*] 1900, *etc.* 16°. **14065. b. 22.**

In progress?

भगवद्गीता सटीका *etc.* [Bhagavadgītā. With grammatical analyses and Hindi word-for-word interpretations and general expositions by Ẓālim Singh. With an appendix of hymns.] 2 vols. pp. viii. iv. 520, 425. लखनऊ १९०१ [*Lucknow,* 1901.] 8°. **14065. c. 54.**

శ్రీభగవద్గీతార్థబోధిని *etc.* [Bhagavadgītā. With a Telugu paraphrase, styled Bhagavadgītārthabodhini, by Veṅkaṭaprasannābhi Svāmī. Preceded by the Bhagavadgītāmāhātmya as given in the Varāhapurāṇa and Skandapurāṇa, and other prefatory matter.] pp. xxiv. 773. *Madras,* 1901. 12°. **14065. b. 27.**

श्रीमद्भगवद्गीता सान्वयपदबोध, सार्थ साथि सटीक *etc.* [Bhagavadgītā. With word-for-word glosses, translation, exposition, and metrical versions of divers metres, in Marathi. Compiled and edited by Kṛishṇarāu Arjuna Keḷūskar.] pp. i. ii. 1117. मुंबई १९०२ [*Bombay,* 1902.] 8°. **14065. bbb. 10.**

અથ સપ્તશ્લોકી ગીતા [Saptaṣlokī Gītā. Seven stanzas from the Gītā, regarded as its epitome. With Gujarati translation.] *See* PURĀṆAS.—*Skandapurāṇa.* श्रीसुदाममहात्म्य *etc.* [Sudāmamāhātmya, *etc.*] pp. 84-89. [1898.] 16°. **14016. a. 30.**

Sanskrit and English.

The Bhagabat Gita [in Sanskrit and English] with [English translation of] the commentary by Shri Shankaracharya ... Edited by S. C. Mukhopadhaya [*sic*]. pp. 32, 402. *Calcutta,* 1902. 8°. **14065. c. 52.**

Bhagavad Gita Sara Bodhini. The essential teachings of the Bhagavad Gita. Containing the grand truths of Hinduism treasured up in the most excellent Sanskrit stanzas selected from the Bhagavad Gita, with English translations and exaplanations [*sic*]. Edited by Brahmasri Satchidananda Yogi R. Sivasankara Pandiyaji. Second edition. pp. vi. xii. 12, 36. *Madras,* 1897. 12°. **14003. c.**

Forms no. xv. of the editor's Hindu Excelsior Series. *The text is printed first in Devanagari in the 2nd folio; in the 3rd folio each stanza is printed first in Telugu and again in Grantham, and is followed by its English translation.*

English.

The Bhagavad Gîtâ, or The Lord's Song. Translated by Annie Besant. pp. 168. *London,* 1895. 16°. **14060. a. 14.**

Forms no. 2 of the series Lotus Leaves.

MAHĀBHĀRATA.—Bhagavadgītā.—*English (continued).*

Gita. A prose English translation ... The teachings of Srikrishna on the field of Kurukshetra. ... Edited ... by Manmatha Nath Dutt. Second edition. pp. i. 66. *Calcutta*, 1895. 12°. **14065. a. 6.**

Forms part of Dutt's Cheap Sanskrit Translation Series.

The Bhagavad Gita: with an English translation [based on that of Wilkins], explanatory notes, and an examination of its doctrines. Compiled from various writers. pp. vi. 90. 1895. *See* East. The Sacred Books of the East Described and Examined. Hindu Series. Vol. II, pt. 2. 1895, *etc.* 8°. **14010. cc. 9.(vol. 2.)**

The Bhagavad Gîtâ, or The Divine Ode. Translated by Pramadâdâsa Mitra. pp. xxiii. 192, i. *Benares*, 1896. 16°. **14060. a. 15.**

The Bhagavad-gîtâ, with the commentary of Shrî Shankarâchârya [and footnotes, derived in part from the gloss of Ânandagiri]. Translated by A. Mahâdeva Śâstri. Part i. pp. xvi. 360. *Madras*, 1897. 8°. **14048. cc. 25.**

This volume is no. i. of the Vedic Religion Series, *and contains the whole text of the Gītā and the commentary in translation.*

Ṣrī Bhagavad-gītā, with Ṣrī Rāmānujāchārya's Viṣishtādvaita-commentary. Translated into English [and annotated] by A. Govindāchārya. pp. xxii. 582. *Madras*, 1898. 8°. **14048. cc. 26.**

Bhagavadgîtâ. [Translated, with an introduction, by Kāṣīnātha Tryambaka Telang. Second edition.] 1898. *See* Mueller (F. M.). The Sacred Books of the East, *etc.* Vol. viii. pp. 1-131. 1879, *etc.* 8°. **2003. a. (vol. 8.)**

The Young Men's Gítá. An English translation with introduction, notes, index and glossary. Edited by Jogindranath Mukharji. pp. ii. ii. xlii. 179. *Calcutta*, 1900. 12°. **14065. a. 6.(2.)**

The Bhagavad-gita; or, Sacred Song. [In the version of Sir C. Wilkins.] *See* Holme (T.). Sakuntala, *etc.* pp. 159-240. [1902.] 8°. **012208. ee. 117.**

German.

Die Bhagavad Gita. Das Lied von der Gottheit, oder die Lehre vom göttlichen Sein ... ins Deutsche übertragen und mit erläuternden Anmerkungen und ... Citaten hervorragender deutscher Mystiker versehen. Von Dr. Franz Hartmann. pp. v. 162. *Braunschweig*, 1892. 12°. **14060. b. 13.**

Die Bhagavad Gita, oder Das Hohe Lied, enthaltend die Lehre der Unsterblichkeit. In poetischer Form nach Edwin Arnolds Sanskrit-Übersetzung ins Deutsche übertragen von Franz Hartmann. Zweite Auflage. pp. 126. *Leipzig, Ellrich a. Harz* [printed], 1904. 12°. **14060. c. 34.**

Bhagavadgītā.—*Appendix.*

See Bālasubrahmaṇya Brahmasvāmī, *Paramahaṃsa.* శ్రీభగవద్గీతా శ్లోకానుక్రమణిక, *etc.* [Bhagavadgītāṣlokānukramaṇikā. An index of the catchwords of the Gītā.] [1900.] 8°. **14065. bbb. 5.**

See Hartmann (F.). Die Erkenntnislehre der Bhagavad Gita, *etc.* [1897.] 8°. **14048. b. 31.**

See Kṛishṇānanda Sarasvatī, *disciple of Sachchidānanda.* गीतासारोद्धारः *etc.* [Gītāsāroddhāra. 62 stanzas, forming an epitome of the Bhagavadgītā.] [1892.] 8°. **14028. d. 50.(2.)**

See Kṛishṇānanda Sarasvatī, *disciple of Sachchidānanda.* अथ कैवल्यगाथा° [Kaivalyagāthā. Followed by Saṅgatisūtra, an epitome of the philosophy of the Bhagavadgītā.] [1903.] *obl.* 12°. **14048. b. 42.**

See Nārāyaṇa Gajapati Rāya, *Goḍē.* భగవద్గీతా-పాదసూచిక *etc.* [Bhagavadgītāpādasūchikā. An index to the Bhagavadgītā.] 1896. 8°. **14065. bbb. 4.**

—— [Another copy.] **14174. g. 38.(vol. 3.)**

See Purāṇas.—*Bhāgavatapurāṇa.* श्रीमद्गीताप्रपूर्तिः *etc.* [Gītāprapūrti. A series of extracts compiled from the Bhāgavatapurāṇa so as to form a supplement of the Bhagavadgītā.] [1902.] 8°. **14016. e. 44.**

[For editions of the Gītārthasaṅgraha, or metrical summary of the Gītā:] *See* Yāmuna Āchārya.

MAHĀBHĀRATA (*continued*).

BHĪSHMAPARVA.

[For the Bhagavadgītā contained in this section:] *See* above, BHAGAVADGĪTĀ.

HARIVAṂSA.

A Prose English Translation of Harivamsha. Translated literally into English prose. Edited and published by Manmatha Nath Dutt. pp. vii. iv. 951. 1897. *See* MANMATHANĀTHA DATTA. The Wealth of India, *etc.* Vol. vi. 1892, *etc.* 8°. **14085. d. 32.(vol. 6.)**

ṢĀNTIPARVA.

శ్రీమన్మహాభారతము శాన్తిపర్వము *etc.* [Ṣāntiparva. Edited with interpretations and expositions in Telugu by Dubbāka Veṅkaṭāchala Ṣāstrī.] Vol. i.-ii. 16. కడప ౧౮౯౧-౧౮౯౩ [*Cuddapah*, 1891-1893.] 8°. **14060. d. 14.**

Breaks off at ch. lxxiii. 7.

మోక్షధర్మము *etc.* [Mokshadharma. Being chap. clxxiv.-ccclxv. of the Ṣāntiparva. With the Advaita commentary of Nīlakaṇṭha and the Viṣishtādvaita commentary styled Vyāsahṛidaya, and likewise a Telugu translation of the text. Edited by Paravastu Veṅkaṭaraṅganātha Āchārya.] *Vizagapatam*, 1887, *etc.* 8°. **14065. bbb. 8.**

In progress?

[For the Anusmṛiti, or Vishṇor Divyānusmṛiti, commonly ascribed to this *Parva*, and printed in the collection styled Pañcharatna:] *See* above, ABRIDGMENTS AND SELECTIONS.

[For editions of the Bhīshmastavarāja printed in the collection styled Pañcharatna:] *See* above, ABRIDGMENTS AND SELECTIONS.

[For editions of the Gajendramoksha printed in the collection styled Pañcharatna:] *See* above, ABRIDGMENTS AND SELECTIONS.

UDYOGAPARVA.

సనత్సుజాతపర్వము [Sanatsujātaparva. With Telugu commentary.] pp. 104. 1895-1896. 8°. *See* PERIODICAL PUBLICATIONS.—*Vizagapatam.* సక-లవిద్యాభివర్ధని *etc.* [Sakalavidyābhivardhanī.] Vol. III, pt. i.-iv. 1892-1897. 12°. & 8°. **14174. g. 38.(vol. 3.)**

सनत्सुजातीयभाष्यम् [Sanatsujātīya. With commentary of Ṣaṅkara.] 1898. *See* ṢAṄKARA ĀCHĀRYA.—*Two or More Works.* Śrí-Śankaráchárya's Miscellaneous Works, *etc.* Vol. i., pp. 129-245. 1893, *etc.* 8°. [*Mysore Government Oriental Library Series: Bibliotheca Sanskrita.*] **14004. b. 10.(vol. 1.)**

Sanatsugâtîya. [Translated, with introduction, by Kāṣīnātha Tryambaka Telang. Second edition.] 1898. *See* MUELLER (F. M.). The Sacred Books of the East, *etc.* Vol. viii., pp. 133-194. 1879, *etc.* 8°. **2003. a. (vol. 8.)**

विदुरनीतिः *etc.* [Viduranīti. Being Udyogaparva xxxiii.-xl. With brief notes.] pp. 86. प्रयाग १९४९ [*Allahabad*, 1892.] 12°. **14060. b. 14.**

VANAPARVA.

மகாபாரதம். திரௌபதிசத்தியபாமாசம்வாதம். [Draupadīsatyabhāmāsaṃvāda. The dialogue of Draupadī and Satyabhāmā on wifely duty (Mārkaṇḍeyasamasyāparva, ch. ccxxxii.-iii.). With Tamil glosses and commentary.] *See* SUNDARARĀJA ṢARMĀ, *D.* வியாஸ வாத்ஸ்யாயந . . . பார்யாதருமம் *etc.* (Vyasa and Vatsyayana's Bharyadharmam, *etc.*) pp. 96-178. 1901. 12°. **14085. b. 44.**

Nal og Damajanti. Fornindversk saga. Í íslenzkri þýðingu eptir Steingrim Thorsteinson. pp. 92. *Reykjavik*, 1895. 12°. **14065. b. 16.**

ಮಹಾಭಾರತದಲ್ಲಿನ ಋಷ್ಯಶೃಂಗೋಪಾಖ್ಯಾನವು. [Ṛishyaṣṛiṅgopākhyāna. The tale of Ṛishya Ṣṛiṅga, as told in the Tīrthayātrāparva of the Vanaparva, chap. cx.-cxiii. With Canarese translation.] *See* PAṬṬĀBHIRĀMA ṢĀSTRĪ. ಶ್ರೀ-ಋಷ್ಯಶೃಂಗೋಪಾಖ್ಯಾನವು *etc.* [Ṛishyaṣṛiṅgopākhyāna.] pp. 172-208. [1891.] 8°. **14016. c. 45**

The story of Rishya Śriṅga, *etc.* [In English and Sanskrit, the former from the edition of Pratāpachandra Rāya.] 1893. *See* ACADEMIES, *etc.*—

Calcutta.—*Buddhist Text Society of India.* Journal, *etc.* Vol. I, pt. ii. 1893, *etc.* 8°.
14003. b. 19.(vol. 1.)

Zur Sage von Ṛsyaśṛnga. [Text in the Southern recension, critically examined] von Heinrich Lüders. 1901. *See* ACADEMIES, *etc.*—Goettingen.—*Academia Georgia Augusta.* Nachrichten ... Aus dem Jahre 1901. pp. 28-56. [1845, *etc.*] 8°.
2097. a., P.P. 4672. a.

See LUEDERS (H.). Die Sage von Ṛsyaśṛnga [critically examined,] *etc.* 1897. 8°. [*Nachrichten von der Georg-Augusts Universitaet zu Goettingen.*]
2097. a., P.P. 4672. a.

The Story of Savitri. Freely translated, *etc.* *See* above, ABRIDGMENTS AND SELECTIONS. Further Metrical Translations ... By J. Muir. pp. 26-48. [1880 ?] 8°.
14065. b. 14.(3.)

Sâvitrî. Eene episode uit het Mahâbhârata. Uit het Sanskrit vertaald en toegelicht door C. Lecoutere. pp. 45, i. *Gent,* 1893. 8°.
14065. d. 25.(2.)

Reprinted from Het Belfort.

యక్షప్రశ్నలు *etc.* [Yakshapraṣna. Being the questions of a Yaksha and the replies of Yudhishṭhira forming chap. cccxii. 43-131 of this section. Edited with Telugu paraphrase, *etc.*, by T. K. Rāmānujāchārya.] pp. viii. 22. *Madras,* 1901. 8°.
14065. c. 53.

University of Madras. Matriculation Examination of 1891. Full Notes on the Sanskrit text. Notes on the Mahabharata [Vanaparva, xxiii.-xxxii., and on the Pañchatantra, I. 6-13] with English translation, by C. Raghavendra Rao ... and Kundalagiriyachar. 4 pts. *Bangalore,* 1891. 8°.
14060. c. 30.(2.)

See SVĀMI ṢĀSTRĪ, *P. K.*, and KĀMEṢVARA AIYAR, *B. V.* Matriculation Examination, 1891. The Sanskrit Text Examiner [upon Pañchatantra I. 6-13 and Mahābhārata, Vanaparva, xxiii.-xxxii.], *etc.* 1891. 12°.
14072. b. 18.

Mahabhárata und Wate. Ein indogermanische Studie von ... W. Sauer[, comprising translations in verse and prose from the Vanaparva cclxi.-cclxxii., with corresponding Germanic legends]. pp. i. i. 74. *Stuttgart,* 1893. 4°.
11840. m. 39.(6.)

APPENDIX.

See ĀNANDĀCHĀRYA VIDYĀVINODA. Virtue's Triumph, or, The Mahâ Bhârata [in an English epitome,] *etc.* 1894. 8°.
4505. de. 4.

See ĀNANDĀCHĀRYA VIDYĀVINODA. Love's Triumphs, *etc.* [A series of tales from the Mahābhārata, epitomised in English.] 1898. 12°.
14060. b. 16.(1.)

See APYAYA DĪKSHITA. सविवरणम् श्रीरामायणभारतसारसंग्रहस्तोत्रद्वयम् *etc.* [Rāmāyaṇasārasangrahastotra and Bhāratasārasangrahastotra. Two hymns enunciating the supremacy of Ṣiva as the essence of the Rāmāyaṇa and Mahābhārata.] [1895.] 8°.
14028. d. 54.

See BUEHLER (J. G.) and KIRSTE (J.). Indian Studies. No. ii. Contributions to the History of the Mahâbhârata, *etc.* 1892. 8°. [*Sitzungsberichte der Kaiserlichen Akademie der Wissenschaften, Wien.*]
Ac. 810/6.(Bd. 127.)

See DAHLMANN (J.). Das Mahābhārata als Epos und Rechtsbuch, *etc.* 1895. 8°. **011824. k. 36.**

See DAHLMANN (J.). Mahābhārata-Studien, *etc.* 1899, *etc.* 8°.
011852. k.

See DHĪRENDRANĀTHA PĀLA. Srikrishna; his life and teachings. [An English study, based on the Mahābhārata and Vishṇupurāṇa,] *etc.* 1901. 8°.
10606. c. 39.

See DUBE (M. L.). The Maha-bharata. [An English epitome.] 1894. 12°. **14065. b. 17.**

See FAUSBØLL (V.). Indian Mythology according to the Mahābhārata, *etc.* 1903. 8°. **14003. l. 4.**

—— [Another copy.] **4506. f.**

See HOLTZMANN (A.). Das Mahābhārata und seine Theile, *etc.* 1892-1895. 8°. **011840. l. 55.**

See HOPKINS (E. W.). The Great Epic of India. Its character and origin, *etc.* 1901. 8°.
Ac. 2692. m./2.

MAHĀBHĀRATA.—APPENDIX (*continued*).

See JACOBI (H. G.). Mahābhārata. Inhaltsangabe, Index und Concordanz der Calcuttaer und Bombayer Ausgaben, *etc.* 1903. 8°. **14068. b. 19.**

See KSHEMENDRA. The Bhâratamañjarî, *etc.* [A poetical summary of the Mahābhārata.] 1898. 8°. [*Kâvyamâlâ.*] **14072. ccc. 12.(no. 65.)**

See LAKSHMAṆA SŪRI. श्री . . . भारतसंग्रहे आदितः पर्वपञ्चकम् Bharata Sangraha. [An epitome of the Mahābhārata.] [1902.] 8°. **14072. ccc. 37.**

See MURALĪDHARA RĀYA. Sree Krishna. [An epitome of the *līlās* of Kṛishṇa as narrated in the Mahābhārata and Bhāgavata,] *etc.* 1901. 8°. **4503. df. 5.**

See MURDOCH (J.). The Mahabharata: an English abridgment, with introduction, notes, and review, *etc.* 1898. 8°. [*Sacred Books of the East Described and Examined.*] **14010. cc. 9.(vol. 3.)**

See OMAN (J. C.). Struggles in the Dawn. The stories of . . . the Ramayana and Mahabharata, *etc.* 1893. 8°. **11824. ccc. 43.**

See OMAN (J. C.). The Great Indian Epics. The stories of the Ramayana and the Mahabharata, *etc.* 1894. 8°. **011850. g. 39.**

—— [Second edition.] 1899. 8°. **2504. k. 18.**

See SÖRENSEN (S.). An Index to the Names in the Mahabharata, *etc.* 1904, *etc.* 4°. **14065. f. 5.**

[For the Uttaragītā, commonly alleged to form part of one or another of the books of the Mahābhārata:] *See* UTTARAGĪTĀ.

Maha-Bharata. The epic of ancient India. Condensed into English verse by Romesh Dutt, C.I.E. With an introduction by the Right Hon. F. Max Müller. Twelve photogravures from original illustrations designed from Indian sources by E. Stuart Hardy. pp. xii. ii. 188. *London*, 1899. 8°. **14065. c. 45.**

MAHĀBODHI SOCIETY. *See* ACADEMIES, *etc.*—*Calcutta.*

MAHĀCHĀRYA. *See* RĀMĀNUJADĀSA, surnamed DOḌḌAYĀCHĀRYA.

MAHADEVA AIYAR, *Alladi.* *See* MAHĀDEVA ŚĀSTRĪ, *Allādi.*

MAHĀDEVA BHAṬṬA, *son of Bālakṛishṇa.* *See* VIŚVANĀTHA PAÑCHĀNANA BHAṬṬĀCHĀRYA. कारिकावली *etc.* [Kārikāvalī. With the Dinakarī or Muktāvalīprakāśa commenced by Mahādeva and finished by Dinakara Bhaṭṭa, *etc.*] [1895.] 8°. **14048. dd. 25.**

—— —— [Another edition.] [1896.] 8°. **14048. dd. 26.**

MAHĀDEVA KAVI, *disciple of Bālakṛishṇa, of Palmaner.* The Adbhutadarpaṇa of Mahâdeva. [A drama in 10 acts, on an episode of the Rāmāyaṇa.] Edited by Paṇḍita Śivadatta . . . and Kâśinâtha Pâṇḍurang Parab. (अद्भुतदर्पणम् ।) pp. 124, iv. 1896. *See* DURGĀPRASĀDA, *son of Vrajalāla,* and KĀŚĪNĀTHA PĀṆḌURAṄGA PARAB. Kâvyamâlâ. [No.] 55. 1886, *etc.* 8°. **14072. ccc. 12.(no. 55.)**

MAHĀDEVĀNANDA SARASVATĪ. *See* MAHĀDEVA SARASVATĪ.

MAHĀDEVA RĀJĀRĀMA BODAS. *See* ANNAM BHAṬṬA. The Tarka-sangraha . . . Revised . . . with a preface and introduction by Mahâdev . . . Bodas. 1897. 8°. **14048. cc. 7.**

MAHĀDEVA SARASVATĪ, *disciple of Svayamprakāśa.* अथ तत्त्वानुसन्धानमद्वैतकौस्तुभटीकोपेतंप्रारभ्यते ॥ [Tattvānusandhāna. A digest and exposition of texts in favour of Vedānta. With the author's commentary Advaitakaustubha, and a gloss by Gaṇḍā Singh.] ff. 109, *lith.* काश्यां १९४८ [*Benares*, 1891.] *obl.* 4°. **14048. f. 23.**

—— अद्वैतचिन्ताकौस्तुभः। [Tattvānusandhāna. With the author's commentary styled] Advaitacintā Kaustubha. Edited by Babu Girīndranātha Datta. 1901, *etc.* *See* ACADEMIES, *etc.* — Calcutta.—*Asiatic Society of Bengal.* Bibliotheca Indica. New Series. [Vol. 150.] 1848, *etc.* 8°. **14002. a. (vol. 150.)**

In progress.

MAHĀDEVA ŚĀSTRĪ, *of Trichengode.* ஸ்ரீஞாந-ஸம்பந்தசரித்ரம் [Jñānasambandhacharitra.

60 verses on the history of the Ṣaiva saint Ñānasambandhar.] *See* PURĀṆAS.—*Skandapurāṇa.* ஸ்ரீ ... நாககிரிமாஹாத்ம்யம் *etc.* [Nāgagiri-māhātmya.] pp. 56-61. 1903. 8°.
14016. dd. 2.(2.)

MAHĀDEVA ṢĀSTRĪ, *Allādi,* known also as MAHĀDEVA AIYAR, *Curator of Mysore Government Oriental Library.* *See* BĀDARĀYAṆA. The Vedánta-sútras with Śríkantha-bháshya. [Translated by Mahādeva Ṣāstrī.] 1897, *etc.* 4°. [*Siddhanta Deepika.*]
14170. fff. 4.

—— *See* MAHĀBHĀRATA. — Bhagavadgītā. — *English.* The Bhagavad-gîtâ, with the commentary of Shrî Shankarâchârya. Translated by A. Mahâdeva Śâstri. Part i. 1897. 8°.
14048. cc. 25.

—— *See* MYSORE. — *Government of Mysore.* Government Oriental Library Series. Bibliotheca Sanskrita ... Edited by A. Mahádeva Śástri, *etc.* 1893, *etc.* 8°.
14004. b.

—— *See* ṢAṄKARA ĀCHĀRYA. — *Doubtful and Supposititious Works.* The Vedânta Doctrine of Śrí Sankarâchârya. [Comprising Ṣaṅkara's Dakshiṇāmūrtistotra with Sureṣvara's Mānasollāsa, the Praṇavavārttika of the latter, and the Dakshiṇāmūrtyupanishad, translated and annotated, with preface and introduction,] by A. Mahâdeva Śâstri. 1899. 12°. **14048. b. 36.**

—— *See* UPANISHADS.—*Small Collections.* Amritabindu and Kaivalya Upanishads. With commentaries. Translated ... by A. Mahadeva Sastri. 1898. 12°. **14010. b. 19.**

MAHĀDEVA ṢIVARĀMA ĀPṬE. *See* BĀṆA. Kâdambarîsâra: being an abridgment of Bána's Kádambari; with ... notes ... glossary and ... abstract. By Mahadev ... Apte. 1891. 8°.
14076. c. 60.

—— *See* HITOPADEṢA. A Popular Edition of the Hitopadesha ... Containing ... glossary and ... translation of the verses ... Edited by Mahadev ... Apte. 1897. 12°. **14070. c. 61.**

—— *See* PAÑCHATANTRA. A Popular Edition of the First (Second and Third, Fourth and Fifth) Tantra of Vishnuśarman. Containing ... glossary and ... translation of the verses ... By Mahadeva ... Âpte. 1893-1894. 12°. **14070. b. 21.**

—— *See* VĀMANA ṢIVARĀMA ĀPṬE. Kusumamala ... No. I ... 2nd edition ... revised by M. S. Apte. 1894. 12°. **14085. c. 44.**

—— —— Kusumamâlâ ... No. II ... Fourth edition. Revised ... by M. S. Apte. 1902. 8°.
14085. c. 51.

—— *See* VĀMANA ṢIVARĀMA ĀPṬE. The Students' Hand-book ... revised by M. S. Apte. 1894-1899. 12°. **14092. a. 14.**

MAHĀDEVA ṢIVARĀMA GOLE. First Sanskrit Course. By Mahadev Shivram Gole. pp. x. 200. *Bombay,* 1895. 12°. **14092. a. 15.**
Part of The New Sanskrit Reader Series.

—— Second Sanskrit Course. Intended for Anglo-Vernacular Standard V. By Mahadev Shivram Gole. pp. iii. i. 229. *Poona,* 1896. 8°.
14092. a. 19.
Part of The New Sanskrit Reader Series.

MAHĀDEVA ṢUKLA, *son of Sūryaprasāda.* स्वामी भास्करानन्द सरस्वती जीवनचरितम् *etc.* [Bhāskarānanda-Sarasvatī-jīvanacharita. A century of verses on the life and teachings of Bhāskarānanda. With a Hindi prose version and occasional poems.] pp. ii. 115. काशी १९४८ [*Benares,* 1891.] 8°.
14028. d. 48.

MAHĀDEVA SŪRI, *Govindapuram, son of Dharmarāja Sūri,* also called AṆṆĀ ṢĀSTRI. ॥ वृत्तिविग्रहसंग्रहः *etc.* (Vrithi Vigraha Sangraha. [A treatise on the formation of compounds, on the basis of the Paninian doctrine of *vṛittis* and *vigrahas.*] ... With English translation.) pp. vi. ii. 153. *Kumbakonum,* 1891. 8°. **14093. b. 33.**

MAHĀDEVA SŪRI, *Paṇḍitarāja, son of Mādhava Dīkshita.* *See* JAGANNĀTHA PAṆḌITARĀJA. भामिनीविलासः । [Bhāminīvilāsa. With the commentary Bhāminīvilāsabhūshaṇa of Mahādeva.] [1890-1891.] 8°. [*Grantharatnamālā.*]
14096. c. 8.(vol. 4.)

—— *See* JAGANNĀTHA PAṆḌITARĀJA. The Bhaminivilasa ... With a Sanskrit gloss Bhushana of Mahadeo Suri, *etc.* 1895. 8°. **14070. c. 53.**

MAHĀDEVENDRA SARASVATĪ, also called SUDARṢANENDRA. శ్రీజగద్గురుపరంపరాస్తుతి etc. [Jagadguruparamparāstuti. A poem in 55 stanzas, on the pontifical succession from Ṣaṅkara in the Kāmakoṭi *pīṭha* of the Ṣāradā monastery at Conjevaram.] *See* MAṬHĀMNĀYA. శ్రీమఠామ్నాయః *etc.* [Maṭhāmnāya, *etc.*] pp. 5-8. 1894. 8°. **14048. bb. 42.(3.)**

—— जगद्गुरुपरम्परास्तवः [Jagadguruparamparāstava.] *See* SVĀMINĀTHA ṢRAUTĪ, *Brahmadeṣam.* ॥ वेदान्तपञ्चप्रकरणी *etc.* [Vedāntapañchaprakaraṇī.] [1895.] 8°. **14048. bb. 51.(5.)**

—— ஜகத்குருபரம்பராஸ்தவ: [Jagadguruparamparāstava.] *See* SADĀṢIVA BRAHMENDRA. புண்யஶ்லோகமஞ்ஜரீ *etc.* [Puṇyaṣlokamañjarī, *etc.*] pp. 29-32. [1895.] 8°. **14048. bb. 42.(2.)**

MAHĀDHAMMASENĀPATINĀGA. *See* SADDHAMMAKITTI.

MAHĀMAṄGALA. Buddhaghosuppatti, or The Historical Romance of the Rise and Career of Buddhaghosa. Edited [with an English translation and introduction] by James Gray. 2 pts. pp. 75, 36. *London*, 1892. 8°. **14098. c. 59.**

MAHĀMUDGALA ĀCHĀRYA. *See* MUDGALA BHAṬṬA.

MAHĀNĀMA. *See* GEIGER (W.). Dīpavaṃsa und Mahāvaṃsa, *etc.* 1901. 8°. **14098. ccc. 28.**

—— *See* SNYDER (E. N.). Der Commentar und die Textüberlieferung des Mahāvaṃsa, *etc.* 1891. 8°. **14098. d. 22.(2.)**

—— Maháwaṇsa Tíká, or Waṇsatthappakásiní. With Maháwaṇsa Páli [*i.e.* the text of the Mahāvaṃsa]. Revised and edited, under order of the Ceylon Government, by Pandit Baṭuwantuḍáwe and M. Ñáṇissara Bhikshu . . . වංසත්ථප්පකාසිනී මහාවංස ටීකා *etc.* pp. iv. 504. *Colombo*, 1895. 8°. **14098. dd. 10.**

—— An account of the Three Convocations in connection with the Three Piṭakas . . . From Mahāvaṁça and other ancient scriptures. 1898. *See* ACADEMIES, *etc.*—Calcutta.—*Buddhist Text Society of India.* Journal, *etc.* Vol. VI, pts. i.-ii., pp. 1-18. 1893, *etc.* 8°. **14003. b. 19.(vol. 6.)**

MAHĀNIDDESA. *See* SUTTAPIṬAKA.—*Khuddakanikāya.*

MAHARĀJDĪN, *Brahma-bhaṭṭa.* ॥ भट्टोपाख्यान *etc.* [Bhaṭṭopākhyāna. A short metrical tract, with translation and other matter in Hindi, upon the origin and duties of the Bhaṭṭa Brahmans.] pp. 19. कानपुर १९४७ [*Cawnpore*, 1890.] 8°. **14028. c. 42.(2.)**

MAHĀVAGGA. *See* VINAYAPIṬAKA.

MAHĀVIBHAṄGA. *See* VINAYAPIṬAKA.

MAHĀVĪRAPRASĀDA NĀRĀYAṆA SIṂHA. *See* RĀMĀNUJA.—*Original Works.* ॥ वेदान्त तत्वसार: *etc.* [Vedāntatattvasāra. With Hindi translation by Mahāvīraprasāda.] [1893.] 8°. **14048. dd. 12.(2.)**

MAHĀVYUTPATTI. Buddhistische Triglotte, d. h. Sanskrit-Tibetisch-Mongolisches Wörterverzeichniss. Gedruckt mit den aus dem Nachlass des Barons Schilling von Canstadt stammenden Holztafeln und mit einem kurzen Vorwort versehen von A. Schiefner. ff. 37. *St. Petersburg*, 1859. *obl.* Fol. **761. l.**

MAHĀYASA THERA. [For the Kachchāyanabheda and Kachchāyanasāra current under the name of Mahāyasa:] *See* DHAMMĀNANDA ĀCHARIYA.

MAHENDRA DEVA, *Maharaja of Athmallik.* *See* PAṆḌITASARVASVA. ପଣ୍ଡିତସର୍ବ୍ବସ୍ୱ *etc.* [Paṇḍitasarvasva. Edited, with Oriya translation, by Mahendra Deva.] 1897. 8°. **14038. d. 36.**

MAHENDRALĀLA DĀSA. *See* RATNAMĀLĀ. The Merchant's Wife. Translated . . . by . . . Mahendra Lal Das. 1894. 8°. [*Journal of the Buddhist Text Society of India.*] **14003. b. 19.(vol. 2.)**

MAHENDRANĀTHA BHAṬṬĀCHĀRYA. *See* SARVAVARMĀ. কলাপ-ব্যাকরণম্ *etc.* [Kalāpavyākaraṇa. Section i., with commentary of Durgasiṃha, and Bengali translation and notes by Mahendranātha.] [1900.] 8°. **14090. b. 32.(2.)**

—— *See* SARVAVARMĀ.—*Appendix.* গণতত্ত্ব-দীপিকা *etc.* [Gaṇatattvadīpikā. Edited by Mahendranātha, *etc.*] [1900.] 8°. **14093. b. 20.(3.)**

MAHENDRANĀTHA CHAṬṬOPĀDHYĀYA. See ṢIHLAṆA MIṢRA. The Çántiçatakam . . . translated and edited . . . by Mohendranath Chatterjee, with notes and original text. 1896. 12°. **14070. b. 25.**

MAHENDRANĀTHA GHOSHĀL. *See* GAUḌAPĀDA ĀCHĀRYA. গৌড়পাদীয় আগম *etc.* [Āgamaṣāstra. Chapters ii., iii., iv. With Bengali translation by Mahendranātha.] [1890.] 8°. **14010. c. 52.(4.)**

MAHENDRANĀTHA KAVIRATNA. भूदेव निर्वाणम् *etc.* [Bhūdevanirvāṇa. A poem in 8 *sargas* on the death and beatification of Bhūdeva Mukhopādhyāya.] pp. 100. हुगली १८२० [*Hugli*, 1899.] 12°. **14076. b. 28.(2.)**

MAHENDRA SŪRI, *disciple of Hemachandra. See* HEMACHANDRA, *disciple of Devachandra.* अथश्रीहेमचन्द्रसूरिप्रणीतोनेकार्थसंग्रहः॥ . . . The Anekarthasamgraha . . . with extracts from the commentary [Anekārthakairavākarakaumudī] of Mahendra, *etc.* 1893. 4°. [*Sources of Sanskrit Lexicography.*] **14090. e. 23.(vol. 1.)**

MAHENDRA UPĀDHYĀYA. *See* PURUSHOTTAMA VIDYĀVĀGĪṢA BHAṬṬĀCHĀRYA. প্রয়োগরত্নমালা *etc.* [Prayogaratnamālā. With the Kṛitpradīpikā of Mahendra.] [1890-1893.] 4°. **14090. e. 22.**

MAHEṢACHANDRA CHŪḌĀMAṆI. *See* PIṄGALA ĀCHĀRYA. प्राकृत पिङ्गलच्छन्दःशास्त्रम् । [Prākritachchhandaḥṣāstra. With the commentary Rahasyākhyāyinī of Maheṣachandra.] 1900, *etc.* 8°. [*Vidyodaya.*] **14096. cc. (vol. 29, etc.)**

MAHEṢACHANDRA KĀVYATĪRTHA. *See* MOHINĪMOHANA SENA GUPTA. "হাড়পাকা" মদনসেনস্য বংশপঞ্জিকা *etc.* [Hārpākā-Madanasenasya Vaṃṣapañjikā. Edited by Maheṣachandra.] [1896.] 16°. **14058. a. 11.**

MAHEṢACHANDRA TARKACHŪḌĀMAṆI. A History of the Dinájpur Ráj Family. An epic poem in Sanskrit, with short notes. Part I. To the end of the Mahomedan rule, *etc.* (दिनाजपुर-राजवंशम्) pp. xxix. i. i. i. 3, 228. *Calcutta*, 1895. 8°. **14058. b. 33.**

—— The Cabinet of Poesy, or A series of detatched [*sic*] Sanskrit stanzas each giving in itself a pithy saying and a complete poetical idea. [With commentary and Bengali metrical version.] . . . Third edition. Composed by Mahesh Chandra Tarkachurhamani. (काव्यपेटिका) pt. i. pp. xxii. 211, iv. *Chinsurah*, [1902, *etc.*] 8°. **14072. ccc. 35.**

In progress.

MAHEṢADATTA SUKULA, *of Dhanauli. See* VĀLMĪKI.—Rāmāyaṇa.—*Entire Text.* ॥ अथ . . . रामायणम् ॥ [Rāmāyaṇa. With Hindi translation by Maheṣadatta.] [1902.] Fol. **14068. d. 11.**

MAHEṢA ṢARMĀ, *of Srinagar, courtier of Shāh Bahādur.* सुवर्णमुक्तासंवादः [Suvarṇamuktāsaṃvāda. A poetical controversy between Gold and Pearl.] 1888. *See* LAGHUKĀVYĀNI. लघुकाव्यानि . . . Miscellaneous Poetical Pieces, *etc.* pp. 171-179. 1888. 8°. [*Kāvyetihāsasaṅgraha, Vol. X, no.* 6.] **14072. d. 37.(vol. 10.)**

MAHESH CHANDRA TARKACHURHAMANI. *See* MAHEṢACHANDRA TARKACHŪḌĀMAṆI.

MAHEṢVARA. *See* MUDGALA BHAṬṬA. मुद्गलाचार्य . . . आर्याः [Āryāḥ. With commentary by Maheṣvara.] [1889.] 8°. [*Grantharatnamālā.*] **14096. c. 8.(vol. 2, 3.)**

MAHEṢVARA, *Vaishṇava Poet.* लक्ष्मीविलासः । [Lakshmīvilāsa. A poem in 4 *sargas*, describing the attainment and quality of heavenly bliss and the incarnations of Vishṇu. With notes.] pp. 20. [1891.] *See* PERIODICAL PUBLICATIONS.—*Bombay.* ग्रन्थरत्नमाला *etc.* (Granth Ratna Málá, *etc.*) Vol. V, no. 6. 1887-[1892.] 8°. **14096. c. 8.(vol. 5.)**

MAHEṢVARA RĀMACHANDRA SUKHṬHĀṄKAR. *See* RAGHUNĀTHA DAIVAJÑA, *son of Nrisiṃha.* मुहूर्तमाला *etc.* [Muhūrtamālā. With the commentary Saundaryabodhinī by Maheṣvara.] [1892.] 8°. **14053. c. 62.**

MAHEṢVAR-BAKHSH SINGH, *Ṭhākura, Raja of Rampur, Mathura.* महेश्वरस्मृति सटीक *etc.* [Maheṣvarasmṛiti. A collection of codes of law. Compiled with metrical Hindi paraphrases, *etc.*, by Maheṣvar-bakhsh Singh.] लखनऊ कानपुर १८९९ [*Lucknow, Cawnpore*, 1899, *etc.*] 8°. **14039. a. 17.**

In progress? The collection down to the present comprises the codes of Manu (vol. 1) and Yājñavalkya (vol. 2). In vol. 1 the general series-title Maheṣvarasmṛiti *is given to the Manusmṛiti.*

MAHIDĀSA. *See* MAHĪDHARA.

MAHĪDHARA, *son of Rāmabhakta*, also called MAHIDĀSA. *See* CHARAṆAVYŪHA. श्री . . . चरणव्यूह° [Charaṇavyūha. With commentary of Mahīdhara.] [1902.] 8°. **14093. d. 16.(2.)**

—— *See* PURUSHOTTAMA, *son of Vishṇu.* The Vishṇubhaktikalpalatâ . . . With the commentary of Mahîdhara. 1892. 8°. [*Kâvyamâlâ.*] **14072. occ. 12.(no. 31.)**

—— मन्त्रमहोदधिः। नौकाख्यटीकासमलङ्कृतः *etc.* (Mantramahodadhi. A treatise on Tantra Sastra. With the commentary [Naukā] of Mahidhara. Edited . . . by Pandit Jibananda Vidyasagara . . . Second edition.) pp. 399. *Calcutta,* 1892. 8°. **14033. bbb. 18.**

The English title is from the wrapper.

MAHĪDHARA ṢARMĀ, *of Tihari.* *See* VIDYĀSUNDARA. विद्यासुन्दर *etc.* [Vidyāsundara. Followed by Chaurapañchāṣikā. With Hindi translation of both by Mahīdhara.] [1894.] 12°. **14070. b. 23.**

MAHTĀB-SINGH, *Ūmaṭ, Raja of Narsinghgarh.* *See* YAMUNĀDĀSA ṢĀṆḌILYA. महताबदिवाकर *etc.* [Mahtāb-divākara. Preceded by verses panegyrising Raja Mahtāb-singh; and followed by a poem upon the history of Narsinghgarh.] [1895.] 8°. **14154. c. 20.**

MAJJHIMANIKĀYA. *See* SUTTAPIṬAKA.

MALLĀCHĀRYA, *son of Mādhava, Ṣâkalla.* उदारराघवः। [Udārarāghava. A mythological poem in 9 *sargas*, with notes.] pp. 136. [1891.] *See* PERIODICAL PUBLICATIONS.—*Bombay.* ग्रन्थरत्नमाला *etc.* (Granth Ratna Málá, *etc.*) Vol. IV, no. 8—Vol. V, no. 4. 1887-[1892.] 8°. **14096. c. 8.(vol. 4, 5.)**

MALLAMALLA. *See* MALLĀCHĀRYA, *son of Mādhava.*

MALLANĀGA. *See* VĀTSYĀYANA.

MALLA ṢARMĀ, *son of Khagapati, of Ghatampur.* अथ मल्लशर्म्मकृता शिक्षा *etc.* [Svaraprakriyā. 65 stanzas of the Mādhyandina school on Vedic accentuation.] *See* YUGALAKIṢORA VYĀSA PĀṬHAKA. श्रीमद्याज्ञवल्क्यादि . . . शिक्षासङ्ग्रहः . . . A collection of Śikshás, *etc.* pp. 153-160. 1893. 8°. **14093. b. 31.**

MALLIKĀRJUNA ṢĀSTRĪ, *Mallampalli.* *See* ṢIVĀDVAITAPAÑCHAKA. శివాద్వైతపంచక *etc.* [Ṣivādvaitapañchaka. Edited by Mallikārjuna.] [1897.] 8°. **14048. cc. 8.(4.)**

MALLINĀTHA, *Kolāchala.* *See* BHĀRAVI. The Kirâtârjunîya . . . With Ghantâpatha commentary of Mallinâtha, *etc.* 1899. 8°. **14072. ccc. 25.**

—— *See* BHĀRAVI. किरातार्जुनीयम् *etc.* [Kirātārjunīya. Sargas i.-v., with Mallinātha's commentary.] 1900. 8°. [*University of Madras: B.A. Sanskrit Text* 1901.] **14060. c. 30.(4.)**

—— *See* BHĀRAVI. किरातार्जुनीयम् *etc.* [Kirātārjunīya. Sargas i.-v., with Mallinātha's commentary, *etc.*] 1900. 8°. [*University of Madras: B.A. Sanskrit Text* 1901.] **14060. c. 30.(4.)**

—— *See* BHAṬṬI. The Bhaṭṭi-kâvya . . . with the commentary of Mallinâtha, *etc.* 1898. 8°. **14072. c. 54.**

—— *See* KĀLIDĀSA.—*Collected Works.* মহাকবি কালিদাসের গ্রন্থাবলী *etc.* [Granthāvalī. Comprising the Raghuvaṃṣa and Meghadūta, with commentaries of Mallinātha; Kumārasambhava, with that of Mallinātha on i.-vii., *etc.*] [1895.] 8°. **14070. d. 34.(vol. 1-3.)**

—— *See* KĀLIDĀSA.—*Meghadūta.* The Meghadûta . . . With the commentary of Mallinâtha, *etc.* 1894. 8°. **14076. c. 63.**

—— *See* KĀLIDĀSA.—*Meghadūta.* The Meghadûta . . . with the commentary of Mallinátha, *etc.* 1894. 8°. **14076. b. 32.**

—— *See* KĀLIDĀSA.—*Meghadūta.* मेघदूतम् . . . The Meghadúta . . . With the commentary of Mallinátha, *etc.* 1894. 8°. **14072. cc. 58.(1.)**

—— *See* KĀLIDĀSA.—*Meghadūta.* Exhaustive Notes on the Meghaduta . . . text with the commentary of Mallinath, *etc.* 1894. 12°. **14076. a. 15.**

—— *See* KĀLIDĀSA.—*Meghadūta.* Kalidasa's Meghaduta [I. 1-38]. Containing . . . Mallinatha's commentary, *etc.* [1901.] 8°. **14085. c. 49.(1.)**

—— *See* KĀLIDĀSA.—*Raghuvaṃṣa.* The Raghuvanśa . . . with the commentary of Mallinâtha, *etc.* 1897. 8°. **14072. c. 53.**

MALLINĀTHA, *Kolāchala (continued)*. *See* KĀLIDĀSA.—*Raghuvaṃṣa*. Raghubamsam. Cantos I-VI. Containing . . . Sanjivani, *etc.* 1901. 8°. **14085. c. 50.**

—— *See* KĀLIDĀSA.—*Raghuvaṃṣa*. Il Laménto dél Ré Àgia . . . Côi comménti di Mallinâťa, *etc.* 1899, *etc.* 4°. **14070. e. 20.**

—— *See* KĀLIDĀSA.—*Raghuvaṃṣa*. రఘువంశం॥ [Raghuvaṃṣa, xi.-xxi. With the commentary of Mallinātha.] [1890.] 8°. **14072. cc. 53.**

—— *See* MĀGHA. Magha's Shishupal badham. [Sarga i.] Containing . . . Mallinatha's Sarbankasa, *etc.* [1901.] 8°. **14085. c. 49.(2.)**

—— *See* VARADARĀJA, *Logician*. तार्किकरक्षा *etc.* (The Tārkikarakṣā and Sārasaṃgraha . . . With the glosses Niṣkaṇṭakā of Mallinātha Kolācala, *etc.*) 1903. 8°. [*The Pandit.*] **14096. d. 6.(vol. 21-25.)**

MALLISHEṆA SŪRI, *of the Nāgendra-gachchha*. *See* HEMACHANDRA. स्याद्वादमञ्जरी *etc.* (Syadwada Manjari. By Mallishiena [or rather, by Hemachandra]. With a commentary of Hemchandra [or rather, of Mallisheṇa] *etc.*) [1900.] 8°. **14004. a. 9.**

—— सज्जनचित्तवल्लभ *etc.* [Sajjanachittavallabha. A Jain religious poem in 25 stanzas. Edited, with grammatical explanations in Sanskrit and Hindi and Hindi translations in prose and verse, by Mihrchand Dās.] pp. 68, *lith.* दिल्ली १९४९ [*Delhi*, 1893.] 8°. **14076. d. 48.**

—— ॥ अथ सज्जनचित्तवल्लभ ॥ [Sajjanachittavallabha. With Gujarati translation.] *See* HEMAṢAṄKARA LAKSHMĪṢAṄKARA VARDHAMĀNKAR. प्रकरण माला *etc.* [Prakaraṇamālā.] pp. 217-226. [1901.] 8°. **14100. d. 11.**

MAMMAṬA ĀCHĀRYA. కావ్యప్రకాశః *etc.* [Kāvyaprakāṣa. With the commentary Budhamanorañjanī by Mallādi Lakshmaṇa Sūri.] pp. 410. *Madras*, ౧౮౯౧ [1891.] 8°. **14053. cc. 60.**

The Kāvyaprakāṣa, according to the view now generally accepted, is the work of Mammaṭa as far as the paragraph on parikara *in Bk.* x.; *the rest is by Allaṭa. See Peterson,* First Report, *pp.* 21 ff., Second Report, *pp.* 13 ff., *Stein,* Jammu Catalogue, *pp.* xxiii. ff.

—— The Kâvyapradîpa of Govind [with the aphorisms of the Kāvyaprakāṣa]. With the commentary [Prabhā] of Vaidyanâtha Tatsat. Edited by Paṇdit Durgâprasâd and Kâśînâth Pâṇdurang Parab. (काव्यप्रदीपः ।) pp. ii. vi. 472, xi. i. 1891. *See* DURGĀPRASĀDA, *son of Vrajalāla*, and KĀṢĪNĀTHA PĀṆḌURAṄGA PARAB. Kâvyamâlâ. [No.] 24. 1886, *etc.* 8°. **14072. ccc. 12.(no. 24)**

—— The Kâvya-prakâsh of Mammata, Ullâsa x. With the corresponding portions of the Kâvyapradîpa of Gôvinda and the Udyôta of Nâgôjî-Bhatta. Edited by Dinkar Trimbak Chandorkar . . . With notes and appendix. pp. i. iii. i. iii. iv. iii. 167, 182, xxv. iii. *Poona*, 1896. 8°. **14053. ccc. 6.**

—— The Kāvya-prakāça of Mammata. A treatise on rhetoric. Translated into English by Gaṅgānātha Jhā. pp. 290, xx. 1898. *See* PERIODICAL PUBLICATIONS.—*Benares*. The Pandit, *etc.* New Series. Vol. XVIII-XXI. 1876, *etc.* 8°. **14096. d. 6.(vol. 18-21.)**

—— *See* MOREṢVARA RĀMACHANDRA KĀḶE. The Sâhityasârasangraha . . . based on the works of . . . Mammata, *etc.* Pt. 1. 1891. 12°. **14053. a. 13.**

MĀNATUṄGA ĀCHĀRYA. भक्तामरस्तोत्रम् [Bhaktāmarastotra. A hymn of 44 stanzas.] *See* JAINASTOTRASAṄGRAHA. जैनस्तोत्रसंग्रहः *etc.* [Jainastotrasaṅgraha.] pp. 1-13. [1890.] 12°. **14100. a. 13.**

—— भक्तामर स्तोत्र *etc.* [Bhaktāmarastotra. With Gujarati translation and metrical paraphrase.] *See* MANGROL.—*Jaina Saṅgīta-Maṇḍalī*. શ્રી જૈન સંગીત-રાગમાળા *etc.* [Jainasaṅgītarāgamālā.] pp. 57-122. [1895.] 8°. **14144. ggg. 4.**

—— भक्तामरस्तोत्रम् । [Bhaktāmarastotra.] *See* JAINANITYAPĀṬHA. अथ जैननित्यपाठसंग्रहः [Jainanityapāṭhasaṅgraha.] pp. 49-66. [1901.] *obl.* 16°. **14100. a. 27.**

—— [For the editions of the Bhaktāmarastotra and Bhayaharastotra (also called Mahābhayahara and Namiūṇa-stotra) included in the collection styled Navasmaraṇa :] *See* NAVASMARAṆA.

MĀNAVAGṚIHYASŪTRA. *See* MANU.—*Gṛihyasūtra.*

MAṆAVĀḶA MĀMUNI, called VARAYOGI. *See* LOKĀCHĀRYA PIḶḶAI. तत्त्वत्रयम् *etc.* (The Vedânta-tattwatraya . . . with a commentary [by Maṇavāḷa Māmuni], *etc.*) 1900. 8°. **14004. a. 4.**

—— *See* LOKĀCHĀRYA PIḶḶAI. Tattva-traya . . . translated [with annotations based chiefly on the commentary of Maṇavāḷa], *etc.* 1900. 8°. **14170. ee. 17.**

MĀNAVAṢRAUTASŪTRA. *See* MANU.—*Ṣrauta-sūtra.*

MĀNAVEDA, *Rājakumāra, son of Mānavikrama, Zamorin of Calicut.* *See* LAKSHMĪDĀSA KAVI, *of Kerala.* ശ്രീ . . . ശുകസന്ദേശം॥ [Ṣukasandeṣa. With commentary styled Vilāsinī by Mānaveda.] [1891.] 8°. **14076. c. 61.**

—— ശ്രീമാനവേദ ചമ്പൂഭാരതേ ഷഷ്ഠസ്തബകഃ [Champūbhārata. A work in prose and verse on the subject of the Mahābhārata. Stabaka vi. With an account of the author by Mānavikrama.] *See* MĀNAVIKRAMA, *Rājakumāra.* ശ്രീമാനവിക്രമകവിരാജകൃതാ . . . ഗ്രന്ഥാഃ സംഗൃഹീതാഃ *etc.* [Essays and poems.] [1890.] 8°. **14072. d. 35.**

MĀNAVIKRAMA, *Rājakumāra, of Calicut.* *See* BĀṆA. പാർവ്വതീപരിണയം *etc.* [Pārvatīpariṇaya. The prose portions in Malayalam only, and the stanzas furnished with Malayalam translations. Edited by Mānavikrama.] [1895.] 8°. **14079. c. 48.(3.)**

—— *See* NĪLAKAṆṬHA ṢARMĀ, *Punnacheri-nambi.* ॥ श्रीः . . . घोषपुरमहाराज्ञी-चरित्रम् *etc.* [Ghoshapura-mahārājñīcharitra. A biography of the mother of Mānavikrama. Followed by verses upon her death, by the latter and other poets.] [1902.] 8°. **14072. d. 45.(3.)**

—— *See* NĪLAKAṆṬHA ṢARMĀ, *Punnacheri-nambi*, and VĀSUDEVA ṢARMĀ, *V.* തൃതീയസഹൃദയസമാഗമഃ *etc.* [Tṛitīya-sahṛidayasamāgama. Stanzas composed at the third Congress of Wits held under the presidency of Mānavikrama in 1897.] 1899. 8°. **14070. dd. 9.(2.)**

—— —— तुरीयसहृदयसमागमः *etc.* [Turīya-sahṛidayasamāgama. Stanzas composed at the fourth Congress of Wits held under the presidency of Mānavikrama in 1900.] [1900.] 8°. **14072. d. 45.**

MĀNAVIKRAMA, *Rājakumāra, of Calicut (continued).* ശ്രീമാനവിക്രമകവിരാജകൃതാ . . . ഗ്രന്ഥാഃ സംഗൃഹീതാഃ . . . ശൃംഗാരമഞ്ജരീമണ്ഡനം . . . രണസിംഹചരിതം . . . രാമസ്തവരത്നത്രയീ . . . രാമഭക്തിസേവാസ്തവഃ . . . ധന്യാധന്യവിവേചിനീ . . . കേരളവിലാസഃ . . . ധാതുകാവ്യം . . . ജ്ഞാനപ്രദീപികാ . . . ചമ്പൂഭാരതം *etc.* [Essays and poems collected and edited by Mānavikrama, viz. (1) Ṣriṅgāramañjarīmaṇḍana, by the editor, studies in style relative to criticisms on his Ṣriṅgāramañjarī; (2) the Maṇḍana of Punnacheri-nambi Nīlakaṇṭha, on the same topic; (3) the Maṇḍana of Deṣamaṅgalam Bālakṛishṇa, on the same topic; (4) Raṇaṣiṅgurājacharita, an incomplete heroic poem, by the editor; (5) Pratiṣrutadaṣaka, Kṛishṇastavanavaratnamālikā, Rāmastavaratnatrayī or Rāmabhaktisevāstava, and Dhanyādhanyavivechinī, short religious-philosophical poems by the editor; (6) Keralavilāsa, a poem on the legends of Malabar, by the editor, canto i.; (7) Bhikshugītāstava, a religious poem by the editor, with an account of the latter; (8) Dhātukāvya, a poem on Kṛishṇa illustrating the use of verbal roots, by Nārāyaṇa Bhaṭṭa, cantos i.-ii. 32, with an account of the author; (9) Jñānapradīpikā, a poem ascribed to Ṣaṅkara; (10) Champūbhārata, a prose and verse composition on the Mahābhārata, by Mānaveda, canto vi., with an account of the author, *etc.*] pp. ii. iv. ii. 60, 42, 18, 9. ൧൦൬൫ [*Calicut*, 1890.] 8°. **14072. d. 35.**

—— केरळविलासः *etc.* [Keralavilāsa. Ullāsa i.] pp. 20. [*Pattambi*, 1893.] 16°. **14076. a. 16.**

MAṆḌANA, *son of Kshetra, of Chittor.* राजवल्लभ अथवा शिल्पशास्त्र *etc.* [Rājavallabha. A metrical treatise on architecture, in 14 *adhyāyas.* Edited with a Gujarati translation and over 100 plates and diagrams by Nārāyaṇa-Bhāratī Yaṣavanta-Bhāratī.] pp. iv. i. x. iv. 240, ix. बडोदर १८९१ [*Baroda*, 1891.] 8°. **14053. d. 47.**

Stated to have been composed at Udaipur in Samv. 1480.

MĀṆḌAVYA. अथ माण्डव्यमहर्षिप्रणीता शिक्षा *etc.* [Māṇḍavī Ṣikshā. A list of memorial-words of the White Yajurveda containing labial sounds, ascribed to Māṇḍavya, and belonging to the Mādhyandina school.] *See* YUGALAKIṢORA VYĀSA

PĀṬHAKA. श्रीमद्याज्ञवल्क्यादि ... शिक्षासङ्ग्रहः ... A collection of Śikshás, *etc.* pp. 72-92. 1893. 8°. **14093. b. 31.**

MANDLIK (V. N.). *See* VIṢVANĀTHA NĀRĀYAṆA MAṆḌALĪKA.

MAṆḌŪKA. अथर्ववेदीया माण्डूकी शिक्षा ॥ [Māṇḍūkī Śikshā. An Atharvavedī tract in 179 stanzas on Vedic phonetics.] *See* YUGALAKIṢORA VYĀSA PĀṬHAKA. श्रीमद्याज्ञवल्क्यादि ... शिक्षासङ्ग्रहः ... A collection of Śikshás, *etc.* pp. 463-478. 1893. 8°. **14093. b. 31.**

MAṄGALA, *author of the Buddhaghosuppatti. See* MAHĀMAṄGALA.

MAṄGALADĀSA, *Mahanta.* निम्बार्क स्तोत्रम् *etc.* [Nimbārkastotra. Nine stanzas in adoration of the Vaishṇava sage Nimbārka. Followed by the Pañchadhāṭīstotra of Viṣva Āchārya and a Dvaitādvaitavivaraṇa or short account in verse of the fundamental differences between the monist and dualist schools. Edited by Dulāre-prasād Ṣarmā.] ff. 3. मथुरा [*Muttra*, 1901.] *obl.* 12°. **14033. a. 19.(6.)**

The Nimbārkastotra is here ascribed to an Audumbara Ṛishi: but in a MS. of the Leipzig University the author's name is apparently given as Maṅgaladāsa. See Aufrecht's Leipzig Catalogue, p. 245.

MAṄGALA THERA, *of Ayadi.* (ဂန္ထဋ္ဌိပကရဏ်) [Ganthaṭṭhippakaraṇa. A Pali lexicographical treatise.] *See* SADDĀ-NGAY. သဒ္ဒါငယ် *etc.* [Saddā-ngay.] pp. 110-123. [1898.] 8°. **14098. ccc. 23.(1.)**

—— —— pp. 112-125. [1899.] 8°. **14098. ccc. 24.(1.)**

MAṄGEṢA RĀMAKṚISHṆA TELANG. *See* BĀṆA. The Pârvatîpariṇaya ... Edited by Mangesh ... Telang. 1892. 8°. **14079. b. 29.(1.)**

—— *See* BHAVABHŪTI. The Mâlatîmâdhava ... With ... commentaries ... Edited by Mangesh ... Telang. 1892. 8°. **14079. c. 61.**

—— *See* JAYADEVA, *son of Bhojadeva.* The Gita-govinda ... With ... commentaries ... Edited ... by Mangesh ... Telang and Wasudev ... Pansikar. 1899. 8°. **14070. dd. 3.**

—— *See* ṢĀRṄGADEVA, *Niḥṣaṅka, son of Soḍhala.* संगीतरत्नाकरः *etc.* (The Sangîta Ratnâkara ... with its commentary by ... Kallinâtha ... Edited by ... Mangesh ... Telang.) [1896-1897.] 8°. **14003. ccc. (no. 35.)**

MANGROL. — *Jaina Saṅgīta-Maṇḍalī.* શ્રી જૈન સંગીત-રાગમાળા *etc.* [Jainasaṅgītarāgamālā. A collection of Jain devotional songs in Gujarati, with which is incorporated a series of Sanskrit hymns with Gujarati translations, *etc.*, viz. Mānatuṅga's Bhaktāmarastotra, Muni Haṃsavijaya's Chaturviṃṣatijinastuti, and various short hymns.] pp. ii. xxiv. ii. vii. 269. મુંબઈ ૧૮૯૫ [*Bombay*, 1895.] 8°. **14144. ggg. 4.**

MĀṆIKYASUNDARA SŪRI, *of the Añchala-gachchha.* ॥ गुणवर्मा चरित्र *etc.* [Guṇavarmacharitra. A series of Jain stories in verse, illustrating the rewards of the various kinds of worship. With a Gujarati translation by Hariṣaṅkara Kālidāsa.] ff. i. 119. अमदावाद १९५८ [*Ahmadabad*, 1901.] *obl.* 8°. **14100. c. 21.**

Composed in Samvat 1484. The author also wrote a Ṣukarājakathā and Prithvīchandracharitra.

MĀṆIKYA SŪRI, *of Añchala-gachchha. See* MĀṆIKYASUNDARA SŪRI.

MAṆILĀLA NABHUBHĀĪ DVIVEDĪ. *See* PATAÑJALI. — *Philosophical Works.* The Yoga-sutra of Patanjali. Translation, with introduction, appendix, and notes ... By Manilal ... Dvivedi, *etc.* [1890 ?] 8°. **14048. cc. 33.**

—— —— [1904 ?] 8°. **14049. b. 22.**

—— *See* SAMĀDHIṢATAKA. श्री ... श्रीसमाधिशतकं *etc.* (The Samâdhi-śataka ... Translated ... with notes, by Manilal N. Dvivedi.) 1895. 12°. **14048. b. 29.**

—— *See* ṢAṄKARA ĀCHĀRYA. — *Two or More Works.* A Compendium of the Raja Yoga Philosophy, *etc.*[*scil.* the Aparokshānubhūti and Vākyasudhā, in Sanskrit, with translation by Maṇilāla Dvivedī, *etc.*] 1901. 8°. **14048. bb. 53.**

—— *See* SĀYAṆA ĀCHĀRYA.—*Works on Philosophy, etc.* The Jivanmuktiviveka ... Rendered into English by Manilal N. Dvivedi. 1897. 8°. **14048. cc. 6.**

—— *See* UPANISHADS. — *Separate Upanishads.* The Mândûkyopanishad. With Gaudapâda's Kârikâs and the Bhâshya of Śankara. Translated ... by Manilal N. Dvivedi. 1894. 8°. **14007. cc. 24.**

MAṆILĀLA NABHUBHĀĪ DVIVEDĪ (*continued*). The Imitation of Śankara. Being a collection of several texts bearing on the Advaita [compiled from the Upanishads, Ṣaṅkara's works, *etc.*, with English translation,] by Manilal N. Dvivedi. pp. i. xxvi. i. 235. *Bombay,* 1895. 8°. **14048. cc. 1.**

MAṆIMĀHĀTMYA. Maṇimâhâtmya [or Maṇiparīkṣā. A tract on the properties of precious stones, in 58 stanzas.] *See* FINOT (L.). Les Lapidaires Indiens, *etc.* pp. 203-207. 1896. 8°. **Ac. 8929. (fasc. 111.)**

MAṆĪNDRALĀLA GHOSHA. *See* PURĀṆAS.—*Padmapurāṇa.* সচিত্র রতিশাস্ত্র *etc.* [Ratiṣāstra. Edited and translated into Bengali by Maṇīndralāla.] [1901.] 12°. **14053. b. 42.**

MAṆIPARĪKSHĀ. *See* MAṆIMĀHĀTMYA.

MAṆIRĀMA, *son of Nīlakaṇṭha, Bhāradvāja.* *See* KĀLIDĀSA.—*Collected Works.* মহাকবি কালিদাসের গ্রন্থাবলী *etc.* [Granthâvalī. Comprising the Ṛitusaṃhāra, with gloss of Maṇirāma, *etc.*] [1895.] 8°. **14070. d. 34.(vol. 2.)**

—— *See* KĀLIDĀSA.—*Ṛitusaṃhāra.* ऋतुसंहारः *etc.* [Ṛitusaṃhāra. With the commentary Chandrikā of Maṇirāma.] [1901.] 8°. **14070. dd. 21.(1.)**

MAṆIRATNA SŪRI. [For the Navatattva, said to have been compiled in its first form by Maṇiratna] *See* NAVATATTVA.

MAṆIṢAṄKARA MAGANLĀL, *Ayāchī.* ॥ ज्ञानमणिप्रकाश *etc.* [Jñānamaṇiprakāṣa. A compilation of verses on Vedantic themes. With Gujarati paraphrase.] pp. viii. 263. अमदावाद १८९३ [*Ahmadabad,* 1893.] 8°. **14048. b. 27.**

MAÑJUṢRĪ. ॥आर्यमञ्जुश्रीनामसङ्गीतिविहरतिस्म। ༄|| ཨཱརྱ་མ་ཛྙུ་ཤྲཱི་ན་མ་སཾ་གཱི་ཏི་བི་ཧ་ར་ཏི་སྨ། ༄། འཕགས་པ་འཇམ་དཔལ་གྱི་མཚན་ཡང་དག་པར་བརྗོད་པ་བཞུགསོ || [Ārya-mañjuṣrī-nāmasaṅgīti, in Tibetan 'Phags pa 'jam dpal gyi mtshan yang dag par brjod pa. A metrical list of epithets and hymns of the god Mañjuṣrī, in Sanskrit and Tibetan.] ff. 39. [*Peking?*] *n. d.* *obl.* Fol. **Tib. 62.(1.)**

The Sanskrit text is written in both Lantsa and Tibetan characters.

MAṄKHA. अथ श्रीमङ्खकोशष्टीकासारसहितः॥ The Maṅkhakośa. Edited, together with extracts from the commentary, and three indexes, by Theodor Zachariæ. (Der Maṅkhakośa . . . mit Auszügen aus dem Commentare und drei Indices.) pp. vii. 73, 160. 1897. *See* ACADEMIES, *etc.*—Vienna.—*Kaiserliche Akademie der Wissenschaften.* Sources of Sanskrit Lexicography, *etc.* Vol. 3. 1893, *etc.* 4°. **14090. e. 23.(vol. 3.)**

MAṄKOWSKI (LEO VON). *See* KSHEMENDRA. Der Auszug aus dem Pañcatantra in Kshemendra's Bṛihatkathâmañjarî. Einleitung, Text, Uebersetzung . . . von L. von Maṅkowski. 1892. 8°. **14072. d. 41.**

MANMATHANĀTHA DATTA. *See* MAHĀBHĀRATA.—*Entire Work.* A Prose English Translation of the Mahabharata . . . Edited . . . by Manmatha Nath Dutt. 1895, *etc.* 8°. **14068. b. 17**

—— *See* MAHĀBHĀRATA. — Bhagavadgītā. — *English.* Gita. A prose English translation . . . Edited . . . by Manmatha Nath Dutt. 1895. 12°. **14065. a. 6.**

—— *See* VĀLMĪKI. — *Rāmāyaṇa.* The Ramayana. Translated . . . Edited by Manmatha Nath Dutt. 1892-1894. 8°. **14065. bbb. 3.**

—— The Wealth of India. A monthly magazine solely devoted to the English translation of the best Sanskrit works. Edited and published by Manmatha Nath Dutt. *Calcutta,* 1892, *etc.* 8°. **14085. d. 32.**

In progress. The texts translated appear under the following headings:—

Vol. 1.	Purāṇas.—*Vishṇupurāṇa.*
,, 2, 3.	,, *Bhāgavatapurāṇa.*
,, 4.	Kāmandaki.
,, 5.	Purāṇas.—*Mārkaṇḍeyapurāṇa.*
,, 6.	Mahābhārata.—*Harivaṃṣa.*
,, 7.	Tantras. [*Mahānirvāṇatantra.*]
,, 8.	Purāṇas.—*Agnipurāṇa.*
,, 9.	,, *Garuḍapurāṇa.*

—— Darshana, or Six Systems of Hindu Philosophy. [To which are appended Īṣvara Kṛishṇa's Sāṅkhyakārikā in Colebrooke's translation and Annam Bhaṭṭa's Tarkasaṅgraha in the version published in the Allahabad edition of 1851 and in part composed by Fitz-Edward Hall.] pp. i. i. 123. *Calcutta,* 1897. 12°. **14048. a. 23.**

—— Buddha: his Life, his Teachings, his Order. Together with the history of the Buddhism. [A compilation, in English, from Buddhist literature and modern writings] by Manmatha Nath Shastri. pp. ii. xi. lviii. 279. *Calcutta,* 1901. 8°. **4505. cc. 27.**

MANMATHANĀTHA VIDYĀRATNA BHAṬṬĀCHĀRYA. কামরূপ তন্ত্রমন্ত্র *etc.* [Kāmarūpa-tantramantra. A collection of magic charms, compiled with a Bengali translation by Manmathanātha.] pp. ii. 56. কলিকাতা ১৩০৯ [*Calcutta*, 1902.] 8°. **14028. c. 52.(2.)**

MANMATHA NATH SHASTRI. *See* MANMATHANĀTHA DATTA.

MANU.

DHARMAŚĀSTRA.

See ĀDINĀRĀYAṆA PĀTRO. The Hindu Law. Annotated and illustrated by Sanskrit texts[, viz. Manu and other writings,] and leading cases, *etc.* 1899. 8°. **14039. c. 17.**

See GULĀB-CHANDRA SARKĀR. Hindu Law, *etc.* [With extracts from the law-books of Manu and others.] 1897. 8°. **14038. c. 46.**

See PRĀṆAJĪVANA HARIHARA. માનવ ધર્મમાલા *etc.* [Mānavadharmamālā. An anthology, chiefly from the Manusmṛiti.] [1903.] 12°. **14072. b. 29.**

मनुस्मृति सटीक *etc.* [Manusmṛiti. Edited with analyses, Sanskrit and Hindi paraphrases, and Hindi commentary by Mihirachandra Miṣra.] pp. ii. xxi. 848, xi. लखनऊ १८९० [*Lucknow*, 1890.] 4°. **14039. e. 3.**

श्रीमनुस्मृति *etc.* [Manusmṛiti. With a Hindi paraphrase founded on the commentary of Kullūka, by Keṣavaprasāda Ṣarmā.] pp. xxxvi. 456. मुंबई १८९१ [*Bombay*, 1891.] 8°. **14038. d. 32.**

मानवधर्मशास्त्रम् *etc.* [Dharmaṣāstra. With a Hindi introduction and a commentary in Sanskrit and Hindi by Bhīmasena Ṣarmā.] Vol. i.-iii., 6. प्रयाग इटावा १८९१-१८९६ [*Allahabad, Etawah*, 1891-1896.] 8°. **14038. d. 33.**

Incomplete, breaking off with chap. iii. 131.

மநுதருமசாத்திரம். [Manudharmaṣāstra. Edited with Tamil translation by C. Tāta Gurusāmi Mudaliyār. Followed by the Vyavahārasārasaṅgraha, a summary of law according to the school of Manu, in Tamil, edited by the same. Third edition.] pp. i. xiv. 559, xvi. lviii. 121, 6. *Madras*, 1896. 8°. **14039. b. 23.**

The text is printed in Telugu letters.

अथमहेश्वरस्मृति अर्थात् ॥ मनुस्मृतिभाषा॰ [Maheṣvarasmṛiti. Being the Manusmṛiti with metrical Hindi paraphrases, *etc.*, by Maheṣvar-bakhsh Singh, Raja of Rampur.] pp. viii. xv. 615. [1899.] *See* MAHEṢVAR-BAKHSH SINGH. महेश्वरस्मृति *etc.* [Maheṣvarasmṛiti.] Vol. 1. [1899, *etc.*] 8°. **14039. a. 17.(vol. 1.)**

The title "Maheṣvarasmṛiti" here given to the Manusmṛiti is in the later volumes extended to the whole series.

मनुस्मृति मानवधर्मशास्त्र-मनुसंहिता *etc.* [Manusmṛiti. With a Hindi translation styled Kīrtivardhinī by Rāmasvarūpa Ṣarmā.] pp. iv. 337. *Moradabad*, १९५९ [1902.] 8°. **14039. c. 19.**

—— [Another copy.] **14039. c. 21.**

The Laws of Manu: or, Manava Dharma-Sastra. Abridged English translation [based on that of Sir W. Jones]; with notices of other Dharma-Sastras. Compiled by John Murdoch. pp. xvii. 66. 1898. *See* EAST. The Sacred Books of the East Described and Examined. Hindu Series. Vol. II, pt. 5. 1895, *etc.* 8°. **14010. cc. 9.(vol. 2.)**

Mânava Dharma Çâstra. Les Lois de Manou. Traduites . . . par G. Strehly. pp. xxiii. i. 402. 1893. *See* ACADEMIES, *etc.*—Paris.—*Musée Guimet.* Annales . . . Bibliothèque d'Études. Tome ii., 1892, *etc.* 8°. **7704. i. (tom. 2.)**

See BEAMAN (G. B.). On the Sources of ... Manu, *etc.* 1895. 8°. **011850. k. 21.**

See HOPKINS (E. W.). The Mutual Relations of the Four Castes according to the Mānavadharmaçāstram, *etc.* 1881. 8°. **14039. b. 25.**

See JACOB (G. A.). अनुक्रमणिका. [Index to Jolly's edition of the Mānavadharmaṣāstra.] [1894 ?] 8°. **2318. g. 22.(2.)**

हिन्दुशास्त्र . . . धर्मशास्त्र। [Selections from the Dharmaṣāstra of Manu. Followed by extracts from other Dharmaṣāstras. With Bengali translations, *etc.* Edited by Kṛishṇakamala Bhaṭṭāchārya.] pp. i. 95. [1895.] *See* RAMEṢACHANDRA DATTA. हिन्दुशास्त्र *etc.* [Hindu-ṣāstra.] Pt. iv. [1895-1897.] 8°. **14085. c. 45.(vol. 1.)**

अथ मनुस्मृतिः *etc.* [Manusmṛiti. Book vii., with Kullūka's commentary and English notes and translation.] pp. 44, ii. 19, 22. *See* ACADEMIES, *etc.*—Madras.—*University of Madras.* B.A. Sanskrit Text 1901. 1900. 8°. **14060. c. 30.(4.)**

मनुस्मृतिः *etc.* [Manusmṛiti. Book vii., with Kullūka's commentary and English notes and translation.] pp. 126, 20, 26. *See* ACADEMIES, *etc.* — Madras. — *University of Madras.* B.A. Degree Examination 1901, *etc.* 1900. 8°. **14072. c. 50.(2.)**

GṚIHYASŪTRA.

॥ मानवगृह्यसूत्रम् ॥ Das Mānava-gṛbya-sūtra, nebst Commentar in kurzer Fassung [probably based on the commentaries of Ashṭāvakra and Ṣrīkumāra.] Herausgegeben von Dr. Friedrich Knauer. pp. viii. liv. 191. *St. Petersburg,* 1897. 4°. **14010. ee. 3.**

ṢRAUTASŪTRA.

॥ मानवश्रौतसूत्रम् ॥ Das Mānava-çrauta-sūtra. Herausgegeben von Dr. Friedrich Knauer. *St. Petersburg,* 1900, *etc.* 4°. **14028. e. 35.**
In progress.

MANU, *son of Lakshmaṇa.* वैद्यकसर्वस्वम् *etc.* [Vaidyakasarvasva. A collection of 117 medical prescriptions. With Hindi translation by Vasatirāma son of Ṣālagrāma. Edited by Raghuvamṣa Ṣarmā.] pp. i. iv. 55. मुंबई १८९६ [*Bombay,* 1896.] 12°. **14043. b. 9.(2.)**

MARĪCHI. అథమరీచిపటలే జ్ఞానకాణ్డప్రారమ్భః [Jñānakāṇḍa, or Paṭalas 80-96, from the Vimānārchanakalpa of the Vaikhānasa, or Marīchipaṭala, an exposition of Viṣishṭādvaita theosophy ascribed in its present form to Marīchi and in its principles to Vikhanas.] pp. 15. *See* BĀDARĀYAṆA. లక్ష్మీవిశిష్టాద్వైతభాష్య ॥ [Brahmasūtra. With Lakshmīviṣishṭādvaitabhāshya, *etc.*] 1896. 8°. **14048. dd. 29.(2.)**

—— அத மரீசிபடலே ஜ்ஞாநகாண்டப்ராரம்ப: [Jñānakāṇḍa of the Vaikhānasa.] pp. 16. *See* BĀDARĀYAṆA. லக்ஷ்மீவிஶிஷ்டாத்வைதபாஷ்யம் *etc.* [Brahmasūtra. Sūtra i., with Lakshmīviṣishṭādvaitabhāshya, *etc.*] 1896. 8°. **14048. dd. 29.(1.)**

MĀRKAṆḌEYA ṢĀSTRĪ, *Dhārā.* Orgamathabodhini [*sic*]. ఆర్యమతబోధిని *etc.* [Āryamatabodhini. A tract on the Hindu religion under the heads of *advaita* and *bhakti,* comprising select Sanskrit stanzas with Telugu translations and expositions, *etc.*] pp. 28. *Ongole,* 1895. 8°. **14028. c. 73.**

MAṬHĀMNĀYA. శ్రీమఠామ్నాయః, శ్రీజగద్గురుపరంపరాస్తుతిః, జగద్గురునామమాలా, మఠామ్నాయసేతుశ్చేతి గ్రన్థచతుష్టయమ్ *etc.* [Maṭhāmnāya. A tract on the pontifical succession from Ṣaṅkara, in 55 stanzas. Followed by Mahādevendra Sarasvatī's Jagadguruparamparāstuti and Rāma Brahmendra's Jagadguruparamparānāmamālā, on the pontifical succession at the Kāmakoṭi *pīṭha* of Conjevaram, and by the Āmnāyavistara, from the Maṭhāmnāyasetu, a work on clerical discipline ascribed to Ṣaṅkara. Edited by K. Ekāmra Ṣāstrī.] pp. 16. చెన్నపుర [*Madras,*] 1894. 8°. **14048. bb. 42.(3.)**

MATHURĀDĀSA, *Kāyastha, of Suvarṇaṣekharanagara.* The Vṛishabhânujâ Nâtikâ of Mathurâdâsa. [A mythological play in 4 acts.] Edited by Paṇḍit Śivadatta . . . and Kâśînâth Pâṇḍurang Parab. (वृषभानुजा ।) pp. 60. 1895. *See* DURGĀPRASĀDA, *son of Vrajalāla,* and KĀṢINĀTHA PĀṆḌURAṄGA PARAB. Kâvyamâlâ. [No.] 46. 1886, *etc.* 8°. **14072. ccc. 12.(no. 46.)**

MATHURĀNĀTHA TARKAVĀGĪṢA. *See* GAṄGEṢA UPĀDHYĀYA. The Tattva-chintámaṇi . . . with extracts from the commentaries of Mathuránátha, *etc.* 1888-1901. 8°. [*Bibliotheca Indica.*] **14002. a. (vol. 98.)**

—— *See* GAṄGEṢA UPĀDHYĀYA. पक्षता *etc.* [Pakshatā. With the Māthurī of Mathurānātha, *etc.*] [1897.] 8°. **14048. bb. 45.(5.)**

—— *See* GAṄGEṢA UPĀDHYĀYA. सिद्धान्तलक्षणम् *etc.* (Siddhantalakshana . . . With the commentaries of Mathuranatha, *etc.*) [1896.] 8°. **14048. c. 79.(1.)**

—— *See* GAṄGEṢA UPĀDHYĀYA. व्याप्तिपञ्चकम् *etc.* [Vyāptipañchaka. With Mathurānātha's exegesis, styled Vyāptipañchakarahasya, from the Māthurī, *etc.*] [1896.] 8°. **14048. e. 28.**

—— *See* GAṄGEṢA UPĀDHYĀYA. व्याप्ति-पञ्चकम् *etc.* [Vyāptipañchaka. With gloss of Mathurānātha, *etc.*] [1897.] 8°. **14048. cc. 21.(1.)**

MATHURĀNĀTHA TARKAVĀGĪṢA (*continued*). *See* SAṄGAMEṢVARA ṢĀSTRĪ, *Gummalūri*. పంచ-లక్షణ్యుపరి సంగమేశ్వరీయ ॥ [Saṅgameṣvarīya. A commentary upon Mathurānātha's commentary to the Pañchalakshaṇī.] [1896.] 12°. **14048. b. 33.(1.)**

—— *See* UDAYANA ĀCHĀRYA. आत्मतत्त्वविवेकः *etc.* [Ātmatattvaviveka, or Bauddhadhikkāra. With portions of the gloss Bauddhadhikkārarahasya of Mathurānātha, *etc.*] [1900, *etc.*] 8°. **14048. dd. 28.**

MAUKTIKANĀTHA. *See* MOTĪNĀTH, *Pandit*.

MAUNAPPA, *of Keladi*. ಶ್ರೀ ... ವೀರಶೈವಾಚಾರ-ಕೌಸ್ತುಭಾಂತರ್ಗತಾಃ ಗರ್ಭಾಧಾನಾದಿವಿಧಯಃ *etc.* [Vīraṣaiva-garbhādhānādi-vidhayaḥ. Rituals of the Vīraṣaiva sect for the ceremonies connected with birth, extracted from Maunappa's Vīraṣaivāchārakaustubha. Edited by Nañjuṇḍa Svāmi.] pp. ii. 64. ಬೆಂಗಳೂರು [*Bangalore*,] 1902. 8°. **14033. bbb. 19.**

MAYŪRA, *Rāmanandana-Satkavi*. *See* MOROPANTA.

MEAD (GEORGE ROBERT STOW). *See* UPANISHADS.—*General Collections*. The Upanishads. Translated ... with a preamble and arguments by G. R. S. Mead ... and Jagadîsha Chandra Chaṭṭopâdhyâya, *etc.* 1896. *obl.* 8°. **14007. b. 5.**

MEDHĀNANDA, *Māgammana*. *See* SUTTAPIṬAKA.—*Majjhimanikāya*. Weranjasutraya ... වෙරඤ්ජ-සූත්‍රය *etc.* [Verañjasutta. Followed by a Sinhalese interpretation. Edited by Medhānanda.] 1893. 8°. **14099. c. 69.(3.)**

MEDHAṄKARA, *Dimbulāgala*. *See* DHAMMASIRI. Kudusika ... With paraphrase [in Sinhalese] by ... Medhankara, *etc.* 1894. 8°. **14098. d. 43.**

MEDHIYADDHAJA, *Thera, of the Bodhodadhi Kyaung*. *See* SAṄGHARAKKHITA. သမ္ဗန္ဓစိန္တာ *etc.* [Sambandhachintā. With Burmese *nissaya* by Medhiyaddhaja.] [1898.] 8°. [*Saddā-ngay.*] **14098. ccc. 22.**

MERUTUṄGA ĀCHĀRYA. प्रबन्धचिन्तामणिः *etc.* [Prabandhachintāmaṇi. A romantic history of several Jain and other sovereigns. Edited with various readings, index, *etc.*, by Rāmachandra Dīnānātha.] pp. iv. xvi. 342, xxxviii. मुम्बापुर्यां १८८८ [*Bombay*, 1888.] 8°. **14058. b. 31.**

—— The Prabandhacintāmaṇi or Wishing-stone of Narratives ... Translated from the original Sanskrit by C. H. Tawney. pp. xx. 236. 1901. *See* ACADEMIES, *etc.*—Calcutta.—*Asiatic Society of Bengal*. Bibliotheca Indica. New Series. [Vol. 143.] 1848, *etc.* 8°. **14002. a. (vol. 143.)**

MEYER (JOHANN JACOB). *See* DĀMODARAGUPTA. Dāmodaragupta's Kuṭṭanimatam ... Ins Deutsche übertragen von J. J. Meyer. [1903.] 8°. [*Altindische Schelmenbücher.*] **14070. g. 2.**

—— *See* KSHEMENDRA. Kṣemendra's Samayamatrika ... Ins Deutsche übertragen von J. J. Meyer. [1903.] 8°. [*Altindische Schelmenbücher.*] **14070. g. 1.**

—— Kāvyasaṃgraha. Erotische und esoterische Lieder. Metrische Übersetzungen aus indischen und anderen Sprachen, *etc.* pp. i. i. 221, i. *Leipzig*, [1903.] 8°. **14070. dd. 26.**

MIHIRACHANDRA MIṢRA, *son of Harisahāya, of Lankh, Muzaffarnagar*. *See* CHARAKA. चरकसंहिता *etc.* [Charakasaṃhitā. With Hindi translation by Mihirachandra.] [1898.] 8°. **14043. dd. 3.**

—— *See* MANU.—*Dharmaṣāstra*. मनुस्मृति *etc.* [Manusmṛiti. Edited with analyses, Sanskrit and Hindi paraphrases, and Hindi commentary by Mihirachandra.] [1890.] 4°. **14039. e. 3.**

—— *See* VIṢVAKARMĀ. ॥ अथ विश्वकर्मप्रकाशो भाषाटीकायुतः *etc.* [Viṣvakarmaprakāṣa. With Hindi translation by Mihirachandra.] [1896.] *obl.* 4°. **14053. e. 31.**

MIHRCHAND DĀS, *of Sonpat*. *See* MALLISHEṆA SŪRI. सज्जनचित्तवल्लभ *etc.* [Sajjanachittavallabha. Edited with grammatical explanations in Sanskrit and Hindi and translations in prose and verse by Mihrchand Dās.] [1893.] 8°. **14076. d. 48.**

MILINDA. *See* WARREN (H. C.). Buddhism in Translations. [Being select passages translated from the Milindapañha,] *etc.* 1896. 8°. [*Harvard Oriental Series.*] **14003. l. 3.(vol. 3.)**

MILINDA (*continued*). මිලින්දප්‍රශ්නය *etc.* [Milindapañha. Edited by Anomadassi.] pt. i. pp. 80. [*Colombo,*] 1896. 8°. **14098. c. 71.**

—— The Questions of King Milinda. Translated from the Pâli [with introduction] by T. W. Rhys Davids. 2 vols. 1890-1894. *See* MUELLER (F. M.). The Sacred Books of the East, *etc.* Vol. xxxv., xxxvi. 1879, *etc.* 8°. **2003. b. (vol. 35, 36.)**

MILLOUÉ (LÉON DE). *See* SUKHĀVATĪVYŪHA. Textes Sanscrits découverts au Japon . . . par M. F. Max Müller . . . Traduit par M. de Milloué, *etc.* 1881. 4°. [*Annales du Musée Guimet.*] **7704. h. 21.(tom. 2.)**

MĪMĀṂSĀVALLABHA VARADĀRYA. *See* VARADĀCHĀRYA, *Mīmāṃsāvallabha Vātsya.*

MINAEV (IVAN PAVLOVICH). Recherches sur le Bouddhisme . . . Traduit du russe par R. H. Assier de Pompignan. [With preface by E. Senart.] pp. v. xv. 315, i. 1894. *See* ACADEMIES, *etc.*—Paris.—*Musée Guimet.* Annales . . . Bibliothèque d'Etudes. Tome iv. 1892, *etc.* 8°. **7704. i. (tom. 4.)**

MINAYEFF. *See* MINAEV.

MINGUN-ALAY HSAYA. ပဉ္စစတ္တာလီသပုစ္ဆာ . . . သတပဒိကပုစ္ဆာ *etc.* [Pañchachattālīsapuchchhāvisajjanā. 45 Burmese questions on knotty points in the Nikāyas propounded by a Hsaya of the Mingun-alay *kyaung,* with responses by Javana of Male. Followed by (1) Satapadikapuchchhāvisajjanā, 100 questions as to material and transcendental existence propounded by the latter and answered by the former, likewise in Burmese, (2) Samaṇapaṭirūpa, consisting of 9 Pali *gāthās* from the Theragāthā, Nipāta x., and Samaṇabhadrakathā, 8 *gāthās* from the Soṇajātaka, Nipāta lx., with Burmese commentaries upon both by Javana. Edited by Ū Pañchaṅga and Ū Vilāsa.] pp. 162, iv. 41. ပဋကလေး ၁၂၅၄ [*Mandalay,* 1892.] 8°. **14300. d. 19.(4.)**

MIṢRĪLĀLA MIṢRA, *Jyotishī.* ज्योतिषनवरत्न *etc.* [Jyotishanavaratna. Chapters on topics of astrology in Sanskrit and Hindi.] 10 pts. मुरादाबाद [*Moradabad,* 1899.] 12°. **14053. b. 34.**

Each chapter has a pagination and title-page of its own.

MITRA MIṢRA. *See* ĀDINĀRĀYAṆA PĀTRO. The Hindu Law. Annotated and illustrated by Sanskrit texts[, viz. the writings of Mitra Miṣra and others], *etc.* 1899. 8°. **14039. c. 17.**

MOELLER (MARX). *See* KĀLIDĀSA.—*Abhijñānaṣakuntala.* Sakuntala . . . In deutscher Bühnenfassung von M. Möller. [1902 ?] 8°. **14080. c. 43.**

MOGGALIPUTTA TISSA. [For the Kathāvatthu, traditionally ascribed to Moggaliputta:] *See* ABHIDHAMMAPIṬAKA.

MOGGALLĀNA. *See* SAṄGHARAKKHITA. ဉာဒိမောဂ္ဂလာန်ပါဠိနိဿယ *etc.* [Ṇvādi-moggallāna. A treatise on gender, based on the grammar of Moggallāna.] [1900.] 8°. **14098. ccc. 29.(3.)**

—— *See* SUBHŪTI, *V.* A Complete Index to the Abhidhánappadípiká, *etc.* 1893. 8°. **14098. c. 62.**

—— Sinhalese Translation[, or rather, a *sannaya* or word-for-word gloss with the original text] of Abhidhanapradipika or Pali Vocabulary. Edited by Totagamuwe Pannamolitissa Unnanse, *etc.* (අභිධානප්‍රදීපිකා සන්නය ගෙවත් පාළිනිඝණ්ඩු සන්නය.) pp. ii. 161, iii. [*Colombo,*] 1895. 8°. **14098. ccc. 1.**

The Gandhavaṃsa (§ ii.) distinguishes between Moggallāna the author of this Abhidhānappadipikā and the Moggallāna of the Vyākaraṇa.

—— အဘိဓာနက္ခရာဝလီကျမ်း *etc.* [Abhidhānakkharāvalī. A compilation by Paññālaṅkāra, comprising a general index to the Abhidhānappadīpikā with Burmese glosses and notes; together with lists of homonyms and indeclinable words, and likewise the glosses of the Abhidhānappadīpikā relating thereto, their reference-numbers, and Burmese translations. Followed by the Abhidhānappadīpikā in Pali, with grammatical notes.] pp. vi. 449. ပဋကလေး [*Mandalay,*] 1896. 8°. **14098. ccc. 25.**

—— အဘိဓာန်၊ အလင်္ကာ၊ ဆန်း *etc.* [Abhidhānappadīpikā. Followed by Saṅgharakkhita's Subodhālaṅkāra and Vuttodaya, and a Burmese dissertation on the introductory stanzas of divers works.] pp. iv. 165. ရန်ကုန် ၁၂၆၀ [*Rangoon,* 1898.] 8°. **14098. ccc. 23.(2.)**

MOGGALLĀNA (*continued*). [Second edition.] pp. iv. 165. ရန်ကုန် ၁၂၆၁ [*Rangoon*, 1899.] 8°. **14098. ccc. 24.(2.)**

—— အဘိဓာန်နိသျ *etc.* [Abhidhānappadīpikā. With Burmese *nissaya* by the Kyaw-aung-san-tā Hsaya.] pp. 446. ရန်ကုန် ၁၂၆၂ [*Rangoon*, 1900.] 8°. **14098. ccc. 30.(2.)**

—— အဘိဓာန်ပါဠိ။ [Abhidhānappadīpikā.] *See* SADDHAMMASIRI. သဒ္ဒတ္ထဘေဒစိန္တာ *etc.* [Saddatthabhedachintā, *etc.*] pp. 41-118. 1903. 8°. **14099. bb. 2.**

MOHANALĀLA, *son of Badar Mall.* *See* MUKTIKAMALA MUNI.

MOHANALĀLA PRIYĀLĀLA, *Gosvāmi, of Brindaban.* ॥ अथ श्री ॥ हितशिक्षा सार ॥ नित्य नियम पाठ सहित *etc.* [Hitaṣikshāsāra. An anthological exposition, in 79 stanzas, of Vaishṇava (Rādhāvallabhī) doctrines according to the teachings of Harivaṃṣa Gosvāmī. Followed by divers religious poems and extracts from Sanskrit authors—viz. Kṛishṇachandra Gosvāmī, Prabodhānanda Sarasvatī, Ṣivaprasāda, Mohanachandra Gosvāmī, Harivaṃṣa, and the Brahmāṇḍapurāṇa—likewise from Hindi and Gujarati works. With Gujarati paraphrases of the Sanskrit, notes, *etc.*] pp. vi. 162, ii. અમદાવાદ ૧૮૯૭ [*Ahmadabad*, 1897.] 8°. **14028. c. 75.**

MOHANALĀLA VISHṆULĀLA PAṆḌYĀ. आर्यसिद्धान्त मार्तण्ड *etc.* [Āryasiddhāntamārtaṇḍa. An exposition of the principles of the Ārya Samāj, in Hindi, illustrated from Sanskrit texts.] pts. 1, 2. अजमेर १८९०-१८९२ [*Ajmere*, 1890-1892.] 8°. **14154. c. 17.(1.)**

—— The Ten Commandments of the Arya Samajes of Aryavarta, with English translations & Arya-bhasha commentary [with illustrations from Sanskrit texts] . . . आर्यावर्त्तान्तर्गत आर्यसमाजों के . . . दश नियम *etc.* pp. viii. 72. *Ajmere*, 1897. 8°. **14154. c. 17.(2.)**

MOHAN SINGH VAIDYA, *Bhāī.* *See* PURĀṆAS.—*Skandapurāṇa.* ਨਿੰਦਤ ਭ੍ਰਸ਼ਟਾਚਾਰ *etc.* [Ninditabhrashṭāchāra. With Panjabi translation *etc.* by Mohan Singh.] [1902.] 12°. **14033. a. 33.(5.)**

MOHENDRANATH CHATTERJEE. *See* MAHENDRANĀTHA CHAṬṬOPĀDHYĀYA.

MOHINEE M. CHATTERJEE. *See* MOHINĪMOHANA CHAṬṬOPĀDHYĀYA.

MOHINĪMOHANA CHAṬṬOPĀDHYĀYA. *See* ṢAṄKARA ĀCHĀRYA.—*Philosophical Poems, etc.* Das Palladium der Weisheit . . . übersetzt von Mohini Chatterji. [1895.] 8°. **14048. bb. 9.(4.)**

—— *See* ṢAṄKARA ĀCHĀRYA.—*Two or More Works.* A Compendium of the Raja Yoga Philosophy, *etc.* [*scil.* the Ātmaviveka and Vivekachūḍāmaṇi, translated by M. Chaṭṭopādhyāya, *etc.*] 1901. 8°. **14048. bb. 53.**

MOHINĪMOHANA SENA GUPTA. "হাড়পাকা" মদনসেনস্য বংশপঞ্জিকা *etc.* [Hāṛpākā-Madanasenasya Vaṃṣapañjikā. A metrical pedigree of the family of Hāṛpākā Madanasena, with an account of the Vaidya caste. Edited by Maheṣachandra Kāvyatīrtha.] pp. 50; 1 *plate*. সিরাজগঞ্জ ১৮১৭ [*Sirajganj*, 1896.] 16°. **14058. a. 11.**

MORE (PAUL ELMER). *See* BHARTṚIHARI. A Century of Indian Epigrams, . . . [Translated] by P. E. More. 1899. 12°. **14070. b. 27.**

MOREṢVARA RĀMACHANDRA KĀḶE. *See* BĀṆA. कादम्बरी *etc.* (Kâdambarî . . . Edited with . . . Sanskrit commentary, introductions in English and Sanskrit . . . and . . . notes in English, by Moreshwar . . . Kâle.) [1895]-1896. 8°. **14076. c. 65.**

—— *See* BHARTṚIHARI. The Nîtiśataka and Vairâgyaśataka . . . Edited with [introduction,] notes and . . . translation by M. R. Kâle and M. B. Gurjar. 1898. 8°. **14072. c. 56.**

—— *See* KĀLIDĀSA.—*Abhijñānaṣakuntala.* The Abhijnánaśakuntala . . . With the commentary . . . of Rághavabhatta. Edited with . . . translation, . . . notes, and various readings, by M. R. Kále. 1898. 8°. **14080. c. 37.**

—— The Sâhityasârasangraha. Being a treatise [in English] on Indian Poetics based[, with numerous quotations,] on the works of Dandin, Dhananjaya, Mammata, Vishwanatha, Jagannatha &c. . . . For the use of College students. By Moreshwara Râmachandra Kâle. Part i. pp. iii. ii. 84. *Bombay*, 1891. 12°. **14053. a. 13.**

MOROPANTA. The Miscellaneous Poems of Moropanta, the great Marâthî poet of the Mahârâshtra. [Including in vol. 1 divers Sanskrit religious poems, viz. Gaṅgāvijñapti, 4 Pāṇḍuraṅgastotras, Ṣivāryāṣataka, Ṣaṅkarastava, Rāmastuti, Muktāmālā, Amlānapaṅkajamālābandha, Kṛishṇastavarāja, Harisambodhanastotra, *padas*, *ārtīs*, *etc.*] . . . Edited . . . by Vâman Dâjî Oka. (स्फुटकाव्ये) *Bombay*, 1896, *etc.* 8°.
14140. aa. 17.

In progress. Forms no. 29 etc. of the Kâvyasangraha.

——— रामस्तवः *etc.* (शंकरस्त°, अम्लानपंकजमालाबंधपंचकं *etc.*) [Rāmastava, Ṣaṅkarastava, Amlānapaṅkajamālābandha, 4 Pāṇḍuraṅgastotras, Gaṅgāvijñapti, Harisambodhanastotra, Daṣamaskandhagīti, Muktāmālā, and other religious poems.] 1888. *See* LAGHUKĀVYĀNI. लघुकाव्यानि . . . Miscellaneous Poetical Pieces, *etc.* pp. 118-158. 1888. 8°. [*Kāvyetihāsasaṅgraha, Vol.* X, *no.* 2-5.]
14072. d. 37.(vol. 10.)

——— The Râmâyaṇs of Moropant, the great Marâthî poet of the Mahârâshtra. [Containing as no. 42 a Mantrarāmāyaṇa in Sanskrit.] . . . Edited . . . by the editors of the 'Kâvyasangraha' (Vâmana Dâjî Oka . . . and Śivarâma Tânbâ Dube.) (रामायणे) 4 pts. *Bombay*, 1891-1896. 8°.
14140. aa. 2.

Forms nos. 4, 12, 15, *and* 18 *of the* Kâvyasangraha.

MOṬĀBHĀĪ MOTĪLĀL DEṢĀĪ. *See* ĀNANDANĀTHA. ज्ञानांगयोगमूलरहस्य *etc.* [Jñānāṅgayogamūlarahasya, *etc.* Edited by Moṭābhāī Deṣāī.] [1897.] 8°.
14048. cc. 10.

MOTĪCHAND KAPURCHAND GĀNDHĪ. *See* PURĀṆAS. — *Skandapurāṇa.* श्रीसुदाममहात्म्य *etc.* [Sudāmamāhātmya, *etc.* Edited with Gujarati paraphrases of the Sanskrit by Motīchand.] [1898.] 16°.
14016. a. 30.

MOTĪLĀL MAHĀSUKHBHĀI. *See* ḌĀHYĀBHĀĪ FATḤ-CHAND and MOTĪLĀL MAHĀSUKHBHĀI. शोभनस्तवनावली *etc.* [Ṣobhanastavanāvalī.] [1897.] 12°.
14100. a. 17.

MOTĪNĀTH, *Pandit.* आदेश शब्दार्थ आदि पंचामृत गुटका *etc.* [Ādeṣaṣabdārthādi-pañchāmṛitaguṭikā. Comprising the Ādeṣaṣabdārthanirṇaya or explanation of the salutation (*ādeṣa*) prescribed for Yogīs by Gorakshanātha, three metrical panegyrics styled Gorakshanāthāshṭaka, Gorakshanāthagītā Saptaṣlokī, and Mastanāthāshṭaka, on Gorakshanātha and his incarnation Mastanātha, and a Hindi *ārtī*, likewise in honour of Gorakshanātha. With Hindi translations of the Sanskrit, also by Motīnāth.] pp. 80, *lith.* दिल्ली १९५५ [*Delhi*, 1898.] 12°.
14028. b. 101.(1.)

MUDALIYĀNDĀN DĀSAR, *disciple of Bhaṭṭar-birān Rāmānuja-Jīyar-svāmi.* வேதாந்தஸாரஸங்க்ரஹம் *etc.* [Vedāntasārasaṅgraha. A digest of texts supporting Viṣishṭādvaita philosophy, with Tamil introduction and translations, *etc.*] pp. xvi. 170. சென்னை ஸ்ரீபாரங்குசார் திருவவதார ௵ 5000. [*Madras*, 1898.] 8°. **14048. cc. 17.**

Each Sanskrit quotation is printed in both Grantham and Telugu script.

MUDGALA BHAṬṬA. मुद्गलाचार्यविरचिताः । आर्याः [Āryāḥ, or Rāmāryāḥ. 108 verses in praise of Rāma. With a commentary by Maheṣvara.] pp. 64. [1889.] *See* PERIODICAL PUBLICATIONS.—*Bombay.* ग्रन्थरत्नमाला *etc.* (Granth Ratna Málá, *etc.*) Vol. II, no. 10—Vol. III, no. 2. 1887-[1892.] 8°.
14096. c. 8.(vol. 2, 3.)

MUELLER (EDUARD). *See* ACADEMIES, *etc.*—London.—*Pali Text Society.* BUDDHAGHOSA. The Atthasālinī . . . Edited by E. Müller. 1897. 8°.
14098. b. 36.(1.)

——— *See* ACADEMIES, *etc.*—London.—*Pali Text Society.* DHAMMAPĀLA. Paramattha Dīpanī . . . Part V. . . Edited by E. Müller. 1893. 8°.
14098. b. 35.

MUELLER (*Right Hon.* FRIEDRICH MAX). *See* BUDDHIST MAHĀYĀNA TEXTS. Buddhist Mahâyâna Texts, *etc.* (Part II. The Larger Sukhâvatî-vyûha. The Smaller Sukhâvatî-vyûha. The Vagra*kkh*edikâ. The Larger Pra*gñ*â-pâramitâ-*h*ridaya-Sûtra. The Smaller Pra*gñ*â-pâramitâ-*h*ridaya-Sûtra. Translated by F. Max Müller, *etc.*) 1894. 8°. [*Sacred Books of the East.*]
2003. b. (vol. 49.)

——— *See* SUKHĀVATĪVYŪHA. Textes Sanscrits découverts au Japon . . . par M. F. Max Müller, *etc.* 1881. 4°. [*Annales du Musée Guimet.*]
7704. h. 21.(tom. 2.)

——— *See* SUTTAPIṬAKA.—*Khuddakanikāya.* [*Dhammapada.*] The Dhammapada . . . Translated . . . by F. Max Müller. Second edition. 1898. 8°. [*Sacred Books of the East.*] **2003. a. (vol. 10.)**

MUELLER (*Right Hon.* FRIEDRICH MAX) (*continued*). *See* SUTTAPIṬAKA.—*Khuddakanikāya.* [*Dhammapada.*] Dhammapada: being Footprints in the Way of Life . . . [A translation founded upon that of Max Müller] *etc.* [1890.] 8°.
4503. bb. 23.(4.)

—— *See* VEDAS.—Ṛigveda.—*Selections of Hymns and Verses.* Vedic Hymns. Translated by F. Max Müller. Part i., *etc.* 1891. 8°. [*Sacred Books of the East.*]
2003. b. (vol. 32.)

—— *See* VIKRAMASIṂHA (*Don* M. DE Z.). Catalogue of . . . Professor Fr. Max Müller's Sanskrit Manuscripts, *etc.* 1902. 8°. [*Journal of the Royal Asiatic Society.*] **Ac. 8820/3 and 2098 a,b.**

—— The Sacred Books of the East, translated by various oriental scholars and edited by F. Max Müller. *Oxford,* 1879, *etc.* 8°. **2003. a, b.**

Sanskrit and Pali works that have appeared in this series since 1892 *are catalogued under the following headings :—*

- Vol. 2. Buehler (J. G.).
- ,, 8. Mahābhārata.—*Abridgments and Selections.*
- ,, 10. Suttapitaka —*Khuddakanikāya.*
- ,, 11, 26, 41, 43, 44. Brāhmaṇas.
- ,, 22, 45. Jacobi (H. G.).
- ,, 32, 46. Vedas.—*Rigveda.*
- ,, 34, 38. Bādarāyaṇa.
- ,, 35, 36. Milinda.
- ,, 42. Vedas.—*Atharvaveda.*
- ,, 49. Buddhist Mahāyāna Texts.

—— The Sacred Books of the Buddhists. Translated by various oriental scholars and edited by F. Max Müller. *London,* 1895, *etc.* 8°.
14003. ccc.

The works in this series are catalogued under the following headings :—

1. Ārya Śūra.
2. Suttapiṭaka.—*Dīghanikāya.*

MŪGĀRĀM ŚARMĀ, *of Rachher, Gwalior.* राजरूपसिंह करुणामञ्जरी । [Rāja-Rūpasiṃha-karuṇāmañjarī. A poetical eulogy on the late Raja Rūpa Siṃha of Rachher.] pp. 14. रछेड़ कलकत्ता १८९९ [*Rachher, Calcutta* printed, 1899.] 8°. **14072. ccc. 22.**

MUHŪRTAPADAVĪ. സഭാഷാ മുഹൂർത്തപദവീ *etc.* [Muhūrtapadavī. Thirty-six stanzas on the determination of auspicious times. With Malayalam commentary. Edited by Veṅkaṭāchala Śāstrī of Kalpadi.] pp. 56. ശ്രീമച്ഛാരദ-പത്തന മുദ്രിതം [*Palghat,* 1897.] 8°.
14053. ccc. 11.

The author is described on the title-page as a Malabari Brahman. The Catalogue of Books Registered (1897, i., *p.* 28) *mentions Namburi, apparently as the traditional author.*

MUIR (JOHN). *See* MAHĀBHĀRATA.—*Abridgments and Selections.* Miscellaneous Extracts . . . translated . . . By J. Muir. 1877. 12°.
14065. b. 14.(1.)

—— *See* MAHĀBHĀRATA. — *Abridgments and Selections.* Fourth Set of Metrical Translations . . . By J. Muir. 1878. 12°. **14065. b. 14.(2.)**

—— *See* MAHĀBHĀRATA. — *Abridgments and Selections.* Further Metrical Translations . . . By J. Muir. [1880 ?] 12°. **14065. b. 14.(3.)**

MUKHOPADHAYA (S. C.). *See* ŚARACHCHANDRA MUKHOPĀDHYĀYA.

MUKTIKAMALA MUNI, previously called MOHANALĀLA. [*Life.*] *See* DĀMODARA GOVINDĀCHĀRYA KĀNAḌE. श्रीमोहनचरितम् *etc.* [Mohanacharita. A biography of Mohanalāla.] [1895.] 8°.
14070. d. 36.

—— रत्नसागर *etc.* [Ratnasāgara, or Mohanaguṇamālā. A collection comprising grammatical rules, Jain devotional lections, hymns, offices, *etc.*, in Sanskrit, Prakrit, and Hindi, followed by a brief history of the Jain Church, in Hindi. Second edition.] 2 vols. मुंबई १९४६-१९४८ [*Bombay,* 1889-1891.] 8°. **14100. c. 16.**

—— रत्नसागर *etc.* [Ratnasāgara. Third and enlarged edition.] Vol. 1. pp. xxvii. 832. मुंबई १९०३ [*Bombay,* 1903.] 4°. **14100. e. 9.**

MUKUNDA BĀLAKṚISHṆA GURJARA. *See* BHARTṚIHARI. The Nītiśataka and Vairâgyaśataka . . . Edited with notes and . . . translation by M. R. Kâle and M. B. Gurjar. 1898. 8°.
14072. c. 56.

MUKUNDADAYĀLU VASU. *See* PĀṆINI.—*Appendix.* [*Liṅgānuśāsana.*] लिङ्गानुशासनम् *etc.* [Liṅgānuśāsana. Edited with Bengali notes by Mukundadayālu Vasu.] [1894.] 12°.
14090. b. 43.(2.)

—— *See* UṆĀDISŪTRA. उणादिसूत्रम् । [Uṇādisūtra. Selections, with commentary in Sanskrit and Bengali by Mukundadayālu.] [1893.] 12°.
14092. a. 17.(2.)

MUKUNDADEVA ŚĀSTRĪ, *son of Udayaprakāśadeva.* *See* KAVIKARṆAPŪRA. आनन्दवृन्दावनचम्पूः *etc.* [Ānandavṛindāvanachampū. With commentary. Edited by Mukundadeva.] [1898.] 8°.
14070. dd. 8.

MUKUNDARĀMA MIṢRA, *son of Ṣobhārāma.* See NĀRĀYAṆAPRASĀDA MIṢRA and MUKUNDARĀMA MIṢRA. विनयपंचाशिका *etc.* [Vinayapañchāṣikā.] [1899.] 8°. **14028. c. 44.(2.)**

—— —— विज्ञप्तिशतकम् *etc.* [Vijñaptiṣataka.] [1902.] 8°. **14028. c. 44.(3.)**

—— See TANTRAS. [*Māheṣvaratantra.*] माहेश्वर तंत्रम् *etc.* [Māheṣvaratantra. Edited with Hindi translation by Nārāyaṇaprasāda and Mukundarāma.] [1902.] 12°. **14033. a. 45.(5.)**

MUKUNDA ṢĀSTRĪ ADKAR. See APYAYA DĪKSHITA. विधिरसायनम् *etc.* (Vidhi-rasayana . . . Edited by . . . Mukunda Shastri.) 1901. 8°. **14004. a. 13.**

—— See BĀDARĀYAṆA. ब्रह्मसूत्रभाष्यम् *etc.* (Brahma Sutra. With its commentary . . . by Sri Viggyana Bhikshu. Edited by . . . Mukundda Shastri.) 1901. 8°. **14004. a. 8.**

—— See JAIMINI.—*Mīmāṃsāsūtra.* न्यायसुधा . . . Nyâyasudhâ . . . Edited by . . . Mukunda Shâstri. 1901, *etc.* 8°. **14004. a. 14.**

—— See ṢAṄKARA BHAṬṬA, *son of Nārāyaṇa.* ॥ मीमांसाबालप्रकाशः *etc.* (Mimânsâbâlaprakâsha . . . Edited by . . . Mukunda Shâstri.) 1902. 8°. **14004. a. 16.**

MŪLAṢAṄKARA JAYĀNANDA, *Ṣrīmālī, Ojhā.* साठी *etc.* [Sāṭhī. A series of 60 stanzas treating of the various *lagnas* or auspicious moments. Followed by two other sets of verses.] pp. 21. सुरत १९५७ [*Surat,* 1901.] 8°. **14053. b. 37.**

MŪLASIKKHĀ. မူလသိက္ခာ [Mūlasikkhā.] See WINI-NGAY. ဝိနည်းငယ်လေးစောင် *etc.* [Wini-ngay le saung.] pp. 121-132. [1898.] 8°. **14098. ccc. 9.(4.)**

—— မူလသိက္ခာပါဠိ॥ [Mūlasikkhā.] See WINI-NGAY. ဝိနည်းငယ် *etc.* [Wini-ngay le saung.] pp. 122-133. 1903. 8°. **14099. bb. 1.**

MŪLASTAMBHAPURĀṆA. ಮೂಲಸ್ತಂಭಪುರಾಣವು *etc.* [Mūlastambhapurāṇa. A Paurāṇik poem, in 18 *adhyāyas,* on the legends and cult of the deity Viṣvakarmā according to the tradition of the caste claiming descent from him. With a Canarese translation by Gaṇṭyappāchāri and Ṣiddappāchāri. Second edition.] pp. xxiii. 183. ಬೆಂಗಳೂರು [*Bangalore,*] 1893. 8°. **14028. c. 63.**

MŪLCHAND NATHUBHĀĪ, *of Bhaunagar.* See ĀTMĀRĀMAJĪ ĀNANDAVIJAYAJĪ. श्री जैनतत्त्वादर्श *etc.* [Jainatattvādarṣa. Translated into Gujarati by Mūlchand.] [1899.] 8°. **14144. gg. 4.**

MUNICHANDRA SŪRI, *disciple of Vinayachandra.* See HARIBHADRA SŪRI. ॥ धर्मबिन्दु ॥ *etc.* [Dharmabindu. With a commentary styled Dharmabinduprakaraṇavṛitti by Munichandra.] [1894.] *obl.* 4°. **14100. f. 13.**

MUNINDĀBHIDDHAJA, *Kyi-thè Hsaya, of Shwedaung.* ဇိနတ္ထပကာသနီကျမ်း *etc.* [Jinatthappakāsanī. A legendary account of the Buddha in Burmese, illustrated from Pali texts.] pp. ix. ii. 776. ရန်ကုန် ၁၂၄၅ [*Rangoon,* 1883.] 8°. **14300. e. 10.**

—— [Another edition.] pp. xiv. 776. ရန်ကုန် ၁၂၅၂ [*Rangoon,* 1890.] 8°. **14300. e. 7.**

—— [Another edition.] pp. ix. i. 781. *Ragoon* [*sic*], 1893. 8°. **14300. e. 9.**

MUNISUNDARA SŪRI, *disciple of Somasundara.* See ḌAHYĀBHĀI FATH-CHAND and MOTĪLĀL MAHĀSUKHBHĀI. शोभनस्तवनावली *etc.* [Ṣobhanastavanāvalī. Hymns by Munisundara and others.] [1897.] 12°. **14100. a. 17.**

—— [For the editions of the Santikarastotra included in the collection styled Navasmaraṇa :] See NAVASMARAṆA.

MUNĪṢVARA ṢARMĀ, *of Jagraon.* See PATAÑJALI.—*Philosophical Works.* The Aphorisms of Patanjali. With . . . commentaries . . . Edited by Munishwar Sharma, *etc.* [1899.] 8°. **14048. c. 75.(2.)**

MUNNĀLĀL ṢARMĀ, *of Chandausi.* See UPANISHADS.—*Modern and Fictitious Upanishads.* कालिकोपनिषत् *etc.* [Kālikopanishad. With Hindi version by Munnālāl.] [1899.] 8°. **14028. c. 85.(5.)**

—— See YOGABĪJA. योगबीजम् *etc.* [Yogabīja. With Hindi version by Munnālāl.] [1899.] 8°. **14028. c. 85.(6.)**

MURALĪDHARA, *of Bhagalpur*. *See* ṢIVATĀṆḌAVA. अथ ताण्डव प्रतिबिम्ब *etc*. [Ṣivatāṇḍavastotra. With Hindi metrical version, *etc*., by Muralīdhara.] 1900. 12°. **14028. b. 66.(2.)**

MURALĪDHARA JHĀ, *of Benares Sanskrit College*. *See* NITYAKARMA. The Nityakarmaprakáśbiká . . . Corrected and enlarged by . . . Murali Dhara Jhá. 1902. 8°. **14033. bbb. 15.(2.)**

—— *See* PRATĀPASIṂHA, *Shāh Bahādur*. Puraścharyarṅava . . . Edited by . . . Murali Dhara Jha. 1901, *etc*. 8°. **14033. bbb. 14.**

—— *See* PURĀṆAS.—*Skandapurāṇa*. Nepal Mâhâtmya . . . Edited by . . . Murali Dhara Jha. 1901. 8°. **14016. dd. 3.**

MURALĪDHARA RĀYA. Sree Krishna. [An epitome, in English, of the *līlās* of Kṛishṇa as narrated in the Mahābhārata and Bhāgavata.] By Muralidhur Roy. pp. xiii. i. vi. 393. *Calcutta*, 1901. 8°. **4503. df. 5.**

MURĀRIDĀNA, *Kavirāja*. ॥ जसवन्तजसोभूषणग्रन्थः *etc*. [Yaṣavantayaṣobhūshaṇa (Jaswant-jasobhūshaṇ). A Hindi treatise upon the Art of Poetry, with extracts from Sanskrit authorities, preceded by a Rājavaṃṣavarṇana, or metrical history of the Rathor rulers of Rajputana. Composed under the patronage of Maharaja Jaswant Singh of Marwar. Edited by Pandit Rāmakarṇa.] pp. iv. viii. xxiv. 852, 8, iii. xi. जोधपुर १९५४ [*Jodhpur*, 1897.] 4°. **14156. ff. 1.**

—— ॥ यशवन्तयशोभूषणग्रन्थः *etc*. [Yaṣavantayaṣobhūshaṇa. Translated into Sanskrit by Subrahmaṇya Ṣāstrī. Edited by Pandit Rāmakarṇa.] pp. iii. iii. xxiv. 670, xxv. iii. xix. योधपुरम् १९५८ [*Jodhpur*, 1901.] 4°. **14053. g. 17.**

MURĀRI MIṢRA. अनर्घराघवम् *etc*. [Anargharāghava. A drama on the legend of Rāma. With the commentary Ākara of Lakshmaṇa Sūri.] pp. 335. श्रीमत्तञ्जानगरे १९०० [*Tanjore*, 1900.] 8°. **14079. c. 71.**

—— अनर्घराघवम् *etc*. [Anargharāghava. With the commentary of Lakshmaṇa Sūri. Acts i.-v.] pp. 222. तञ्जानगरे १८९८ [*Tanjore*, 1898.] 8°. **14079. d. 45.**

MURDOCH (JOHN). *See* MANU.—*Dharmaṣāstra*. The Laws of Manu . . . Abridged English translation; with notices of other Dharma-Sastras. Compiled by J. Murdoch. 1898. 8°. [*Sacred Books of the East Described and Examined*.] **14010. cc. 9.(vol. 2.)**

—— The Mahabharata: an English abridgment, with introduction, notes, and review . . . Compiled by John Murdoch. pp. iv. 160. 1898. *See* EAST. The Sacred Books of the East Described and Examined. Hindu Series. Vol. III, pt. 2. 1895, *etc*. 8°. **14010. cc. 9.(vol. 3.)**

MUSADDĪ-RĀM ṢARMĀ, *Preacher of the Ārya Samāj*. *See* ṢIHLAṆA MIṢRA. शान्तिशतक° [Ṣāntiṣataka-ṣlokaratnamālā. With Hindi translation by Musaddī-rām.] [1904.] 8°. **14070. c. 63.(3.)**

—— यथार्थशान्तिनिरूपणम् *etc*. [Yathārthaṣāntinirūpaṇa. Sanskrit selections, treating of moral peace, with Hindi commentary and paraphrase. Followed by Yathārthasukhāptivarṇana, another anthology on spiritual beatitude, also in Sanskrit and Hindi, and Sandhyopāsanamīmāṃsā, a Hindi exposition of the *sandhyāvandana* according to the Ārya Samāj, with texts *etc*. in Sanskrit. Second edition.] (यथार्थसुखाप्तिवर्णनम् ।) pp. 150. अजमेर [*Ajmere*, 1904.] 12°. **14072. b. 26.(2.)**

—— यथार्थसुखाप्तिवर्णनम् *etc*. [Yathārthasukhāptivarṇana.] pp. 40. मेरठ १९०१ [*Meerut*, 1901.] 12°. **14154. d. 26.(2.)**

MYSORE.—*Government of Mysore*. Government Oriental Library Series. Bibliotheca Sanskrita . . . Edited by A. Mahádeva Śástri (and Panditaratnam K. Rangácharya). *Mysore*, 1893, *etc*. 8°. **14004. b.**

In progress. Works published in this series are to be found under the following headings :—

No. 1. Āpastamba.—*Gṛihyasūtra*.
,, 2. ,, —*Ṣrautasūtra*.
,, 3, 23, 24, 31. Pāṇini.—*Appendix*.
,, 4, 5, 7, 9, 12-14, 16-18. Vedas.—*Yajurveda*.
,, 6, 11. Ṣaṅkara Āchārya.—*Doubtful and Supposititious Works*.
No. 8. Mahābbārata.—*Bhagavadgītā*.
,, 10. Upanishads.—*Separate Upanishads*.
,, 15. Āpastamba.—*Dharmasūtra*.
,, 19-22. Ṣaṅkara Āchārya.—*Two or More Works*.

—— Epigraphia Carnataca. [Sanskrit and vernacular] inscriptions . . . Published . . . by B. Lewis Rice. *Bangalore*, 1886, *etc*. 4°. **14058. c. 8.**

In progress.

NABIN CHANDRA VIDYARATNA. *See* NAVĪNACHANDRA VIDYĀRATNA.

NAḌĀDŪR AMMĀḶ. *See* VARADĀCHĀRYA, *Vātsya*, called NAḌĀDŪR AMMĀḶ.

NĀḌĪJÑĀNA. నాడిజ్ఞానము *etc.* [Nāḍījñāna. A treatise on the pulse. With Telugu paraphrase.] pp. xi. 46. *Madras*, ౧౮౯౫ [1895.] 12°. **14043. b. 6.(2.)**

NĀḌĪVIJÑĀNA. नाडीविज्ञानम् *etc.* [Nāḍīvijñāna. A treatise on the pulse in 105 stanzas, ascribed to Kaṇāda. Edited with a commentary by Jīvānanda Vidyāsāgara. Second edition.] pp. 44. कलिकाता १८१९ [*Calcutta*, 1897.] 8°. **14043. c. 37.(3.)**

—— నాడీవిజ్ఞానము *etc.* [Nāḍīvijñāna. With Telugu paraphrase and notes by N. Guruliṅga Ṣāstrī.] pp. 54. చెన్నపురి ౧౯౦౧ [*Madras*, 1901.] 8°. **14043. cc. 19.(1.)**

—— नाड़ीविज्ञानम् *etc.* [Nāḍīvijñāna, or Nāḍīparīkshā. Another treatise on the subject, in 32 stanzas, also ascribed to Kaṇāda. With a commentary by Vaidya Gaṅgādhara.] pp. 44. कलिकाता १८२३ [*Calcutta*, 1902.] 12°. **14043. b. 10.(3.)**

NĀGA, *Ū*, *of Thabyebin Kyaung*. *See* KACHCHĀYANA.—*Rūpasiddhi.* သဒ္ဒါရှစ်ဆောင်သုတ်နက်သစ် *etc.* [Saddā-shitsaung-thôk-net-thit. Kachchāyana's aphorisms with Pali notes and Burmese commentary by Nāga.] [1901.] 8°. **14098. dd. 19.**

NĀGA BHAṬṬA, *Sādhu*. कामरत्नम् [Kāmaratna. A work on magic.] *See* INDRAJĀLAVIDYĀSAṄGRAHA. इन्द्रजालविद्यासंग्रहः *etc.* (Indrajalavidyasangraha.) pp. 22-134. [1891.] 8°. **14033. aa. 7.**

—— কামরত্নম্। [Kāmaratna. With Bengali translation.] pp. 70. [1891, *etc.*] *See* PERIODICAL PUBLICATIONS.—*Calcutta.* অরুণোদয় *etc.* [Aruṇodaya.] Pt. i., no. 18. [1890, *etc.*] 4°. **14133. g. 16.(pt. i., no. 18.)**

—— কামরত্ন বা বশীকরণ তন্ত্র *etc.* [Kāmaratna. Edited with Bengali translation by Kālīprasanna Vidyāratna.] pp. i. 116. কলিকাতা ১৩০১ [*Calcutta*, 1894.] 8°. **14033. bb. 43.**

NĀGA BHAṬṬA, *Sādhu* (*continued*). ॥ सिद्ध डाकिनी ॥ अथोत् ॥ कामरत्न तन्त्र *etc.* [Kāmaratna, here styled also Siddhaḍākinītantra. With Hindi translation by Ṣyāmasundara Tripāṭhī.] pp. ii. 173. कानपुर १८१९ [*Cawnpore*, 1897.] 12°. **14028. b. 71.(5.)**

The editor states that there are two works styled Kāmaratna, the present book by Nāga Bhaṭṭa and a different work by Nityanātha.

—— ॥ सिद्ध डाकिनी ॥ उपनाम ॥ कामतन्त्र *etc.* [Kāmaratna. With Hindi translation by Baladevaprasāda Miṣra.] pp. 176. कानपुर १८२० [*Cawnpore*, 1898.] 12°. **14033. a. 36.**

—— कामरत्नम् *etc.* [Kāmaratna. With a Hindi translation by Jvālāprasāda Miṣra, and an appendix in Hindi treating of magic diagrams, *etc.*] pp. xii. 316, 27. मुम्बयी १९५६ [*Bombay*, 1899.] 8°. **14033. aa. 4.**

The work is here ascribed to Nityanātha Yogeṣvara. The last 27 pages are lithographed.

NĀGA BHAṬṬA, *Jammaṭige*. *See* RĀMAKṚISHṆA PAṆḌITA, *Writer on Dharma.* ನಿತ್ಯಕರ್ಮ ಚಂದ್ರಿಕೆ *etc.* [Nityakarmachandrike. Edited by Nāga Bhaṭṭa.] [1901, *etc.*] 8°. **14033. aa. 33.**

NĀGARARĀMA ṢARMĀ, *son of Ṣivalāla*. कर्मदर्पणम् *etc.* [Karmadarpaṇa. A manual of domestic rites and observances, with Hindi footnotes. Edited by Rāmachandra Ṣāstrī of Lahore.] pp. viii. 56, ii., *lith.* अमृतसर १९५५ [*Amritsar*, 1899.] 8°. **14028. d. 56.(3.)**

NĀGĀRJUNA, *Siddha*. सिद्धनागार्ज्जुनकक्षपुटम्। [Kakshapuṭa. A manual of the black art. With Bengali translation.] pp. 71. [1891, *etc.*] *See* PERIODICAL PUBLICATIONS.—*Calcutta.* অরুণোদয় *etc.* [Aruṇodaya.] Pt. i., no. 16. [1890, *etc.*] 4°. **14133. g. 16.(pt. i., no. 16.)**

—— सिद्धनागार्जुनकक्षपुटम्। [Kakshapuṭa.] *See* INDRAJĀLAVIDYĀSAṄGRAHA. इन्द्रजालविद्यासंग्रहः *etc.* (Indrajalavidyasangraha.) pp. 265-385. [1891.] 8°. **14033. aa. 7.**

—— माध्यमिकावृत्ति। Mádhyamiká Vṛitti[, comprising the Mādhyamikasūtra of Nāgārjuna and a commentary] by Ácharya Chandra Kirtti . . . For the first time edited by . . . Çrí Çarat Chandra Dás . . . Pandit Harimohan Vidyabhushaṇa (and Paṇḍit Çarat Chandra Çāstri).

pp. 224. 1894-1897. *See* ACADEMIES, *etc.*—Calcutta.—*Buddhist Text Society of India.* Buddhist Texts, *etc.* 1894, *etc.* 8°.

14004. c.(vol. 1, no. 1.)

—— The Mādhyamika School of the Buddhist Philosopyh [*sic*]. By Çri Satīç Chandra Vidyā Bhushan, *etc.* (The Mādhyamika Aphorisms.) 1895-1898. *See* ACADEMIES, *etc.*—Calcutta.—*Buddhist Text Society of India.* Journal, *etc.* Vol. iii.-vi. 1893, *etc.* 8°.

14003. b. 19.(vol. 3-6.)

—— Caturāryasatyaparīkṣā. Extraits du xxive chapitre de la Madhyamakavṛtti. Par L. de la Vallée Poussin. *See* HARLEZ (C. DE). Mélanges, *etc.* pp. 313-320. 1896. 4°. **12902. h. 22.**

—— Études et Textes Tantriques. Pañcakrama[, a Tantric text attributed to Nāgārjuna, with the gloss of Parahitarakshita. Edited with an introduction] par L. de la Vallée Poussin. (Université de Gand. Recueil de travaux publiés par la faculté de philosophie et lettres. 16me fascicule.) pp. xv. 56. *Gand*, 1896. 8°.

Ac. 2647/3.(fasc. 16.)

—— सिद्धविनोद अर्थात् . . . रतिशास्त्र *etc.* [Siddhavinoda, or Ratiṣāstra. A manual of divination from sexual affairs, in 11 *pādas*, ascribed to Nāgārjuna. Edited with a Hindi version by Kanhaiyālāl Miṣra.] pp. ii. 84. मुरादाबाद १८९९ [*Moradabad*, 1899.] 8°. **14053. d. 59.**

NAGASWARAM, *K. D.* *See* NĀGEṢVARAM, *K. D.*

NĀGA VARMĀ. Nâga Varmmâ's Karṇâṭaka Bhâshâ-Bhûshaṇa. The oldest grammar extant of the [Canarese] language[, comprising aphorisms and *vṛitti* in Sanskrit with examples and explanations in Canarese] . . . ಕರ್ಣಾಟಕ ಭಾಷಾಭೂಷಣ. Edited, with an introduction [upon the author and the Canarese language and literature, and a translation of the aphorisms], by Lewis Rice. pp. i. xliv. 96, 22. *Bangalore*, 1884. 8°.

14176. k. 9.

Forms no. 1 *of the* Bibliotheca Carnatica. *The aphorisms, vṛitti, and examples are given in both Roman and Canarese characters.*

NAGENDRANĀTHA VASU. *See* PURĀṆAS.—*Brahmāṇḍapurāṇa.* ব্রহ্মাণ্ড-পুরাণম্ *etc.* [Brahmāṇḍapurāṇa. Edited with Bengali notes and translation by Nagendranātha.] [1891-1894.] 8°.

14016. c. 46.

—— Kāyastha Ethnology . . . কায়স্থের বর্ণ-নির্ণয় *etc.* [Kāyasther Varṇanirṇaya. A Bengali treatise, quoting Sanskrit authorities.] pp. iii. ii. 146. *Calcutta*, [1901.] 8°. **14125. ee. 35.**

NĀGEṢA BHAṬṬA, also called NĀGOJĪ BHAṬṬA. [*Kāvyaprakāṣoddyota.*] *See* MAMMAṬA ĀCHĀRYA. The Kâvya-prakâsh of Mammata, Ullâsa x. With the corresponding portion of the . . . Udyôta of Nâgôjî-Bhatta, *etc.* 1896. 8°. **14053. ccc. 6.**

—— [*Mahābhāshyapradīpoddyota.*] Mahābhāṣya Pradīpoddyota[, a commentary on the Mahābhāshyapradīpa, Kaiyyaṭa's commentary to the Mahābhāshya.] . . . Edited by Paṇḍita Bahuvallabha Çāstrī. (महाभाष्यप्रदीपोद्द्योतः ।). 1901, *etc.* *See* ACADEMIES, *etc.*—Calcutta.—*Asiatic Society of Bengal.* Bibliotheca Indica. New Series. [Vol. 140.] 1848, *etc.* 8°. **14002. a.(vol. 140.)**

In progress.

—— [*Paribhāshenduṣekhara.*] परिभाषेन्दुशेखरः *etc.* (Paribhashendushekhara . . . With the commentary of Bhairaba Mishra. Edited . . . by Pandit Jibananda Vidyasagara . . . Second edition.) pp. 281. *Calcutta*, 1892. 8°.

14093. b. 42.(2.)

The English title is taken from the wrapper.

—— —— परिभाषेन्दुशेखरः । [Paribhāshenduṣekhara. With the commentary Laghu-jaṭājūṭa of Govinda Ṣāstrī Bhāradvāja.] 1892, *etc.* *See* PERIODICAL PUBLICATIONS.—*Calcutta.* विद्योदयः *etc.* [Vidyodaya.] Vol. xxi., *etc.* 1874, *etc.* 8°.

14096. cc.(vol. 21, etc.)

—— —— ॥ परिभाषेन्दुशेखरः *etc.* [Paribhāshenduṣekhara. With the commentary of Bhairava Miṣra. Edited by Gaṇeṣa Ṣāstrī Kshīrasāgara.] pp. 281. काश्यां १८९७ [*Benares*, 1897.] 8°.

14090. c. 42.

—— —— परिभाषेन्दुशेखरः *etc.* [Paribhāshenduṣekhara. With a commentary entitled Bhūti by Rāmakṛishṇa Ṣāstrī Paṭavardhana. Edited by Nārāyaṇa Ṣāstrī Paṭavardhana.] pp. 320. काश्यां १९५४ [*Benares*, 1897.] 8°. **14090. d. 33.**

NĀGEŚA BHAṬṬA, also called NĀGOJĪ BHAṬṬA (*continued*).

—— *See* GOVINDA ŚĀSTRĪ, *Bhāradvāja*. लघुजटाजूटः . . . Laghu Jatajoota. A gloss on . . . Paribhashendu Shekhar, *etc.* 1899. 8°. **14092. b. 45.(1.)**

—— [*Rasagaṅgādharamarmaprakāśa.*] *See* JAGANNĀTHA PAṆḌITARĀJA. चित्रमीमांसाखण्डनम् *etc.* [Chitramīmāṃsākhaṇḍana. With a commentary extracted from Nāgeśa's commentary on the Rasagaṅgādhara.] 1893. 8°. [*Kâvyamâlâ.*] **14072. ccc. 12.(no. 38.)**

—— [*Śabdenduśekhara.*] ॥ लघुशब्देन्दुशेखरः *etc.* [Laghu-śabdenduśekhara. An abridged commentary on the Siddhāntakaumudī. Edited by Karnāṭaka Kṛishṇa Śāstrī.] काश्याम् [*Benares,*] 1901, *etc.* 8°. **14090. bb. 20.**

In progress.

—— *See* KHUDDĪ JHĀ. नागेशोक्तिप्रकाश . . . Nágeśokti-prakáśa. Notes on the Laghu-śabdendu Śekhara, *etc.* 1899. 8°. **14093. d. 20.**

—— [*Vyāsasūtrenduśekhara.*] *See* BĀDARĀYAṆA. The Brahma-Sutras [in English, with commentary translated from Nāgeśa's Vyāsasūtrenduśekhara, *etc.*, extending to Sūtra xxiii.] 1900. 8°. [*Brahmavâdin.*] **14048. g. 1.(vol. 5.)**

NĀGEŚA DAIVAJÑA, *son of Śiva. Begin.* अथ ग्रहप्रबोधप्रारंभः [Grahaprabodha. A short astrological tract on the planets.] 3 pts., *lith.* [*Bombay ?* 1833 ?] 4°. **Add. 14,357. III.**

The tract is preceded by a few stanzas on the same subject by an author describing himself as the "son of Govinda," and is followed by several sheets of calculations with MS. notes. The appearance of the lithography resembles that of the tract of Lagadha, a copy of which is found in the same collection of MSS. See Add. 14,354, *sub fin.*

—— [Another copy.] **Add. 14,365. II.**

NĀGEŚVARAM, *K. D. See* RĀMACHANDRA, *Korāḍa.* శృంగారసుధార్ణవః . . . Srungara Sudarnava . . . Edited by K. D. Nagaswaram. 1899. 8°. **14079. c. 54.(2.)**

NĀGINDA, *Ū, Mahāthera, of Ywagale Kyaung.* သင်္ခေပဗျာကရဏကျမ်း။ [Saṅkhepavyākaraṇa. A Burmese epitome of Abhidhamma doctrine as codified in the Abhidhammatthasaṅgaha, illustrated from Pali texts.] pp. 50. ရန်ကုန် ၁၂၆၀ [*Rangoon,* 1899.] 8°. **14300. d. 22.(11.)**

NĀGITA. သဒ္ဒသာရတ္ထဇာလိနီ *etc.* [Saddasāratthajālinī. A Pali treatise on the principles of grammar and stylistic. With Burmese commentary by Sīlāchāra.] [1898.] *See* SADDĀ-NGAY. သဒ္ဒါငယ် *etc.* [Saddā-ngay.] Vol. iii., pp. 1-110. [1898-1900.] 8°. **14098. ccc. 22.**

—— သဒ္ဒသာရတ္ထဇာလိနီပါဌ်။ [Saddasāratthajālinī.] *See* SADDĀ-NGAY. သဒ္ဒါငယ် *etc.* [Saddā-ngay.] pp. 49-80. [1898.] 8°. **14098. ccc. 23.(1.)**

—— [Second edition.] pp. 49-81. [1899.] 8°. **14098. ccc. 24.(1.)**

NĀGOJĪ BHAṬṬA. *See* NĀGEŚA BHAṬṬA.

NĀHNIDATTA. नाह्निदत्तपञ्चविंशतिका [Nāhnidatta-pañchaviṃśatikā. 25 stanzas on astrology. Edited by Muralīdhara Jhā.] pp. 25. वाराणस्यां [*Benares,* 1902.] *obl.* 16°. **14053. a. 11.(2.)**

NAKSHATRAKOŚA. অথ নক্ষত্রকোষ । [Nakshatrakośa. A list of synonyms for the lunar mansions, with Bengali translation.] *See* GOPĪRAMAṆA TARKARATNA. কোষচন্দ্রিকা *etc.* [Kośachandrikā.] pp. 40-45. [1893.] 12°. **14090. b. 44.(1.)**

NALINĪMOHANA DEVA ŚARMĀ. সঞ্জয়রায়-বংশম্ *etc.* [Sañjaya-Rāya-vaṃśa. A metrical genealogy of the chief descendants of Sañjaya Rāya, a *mansab-dār* under the Emperor Akbar.] pp. 40. ঢাকা ১৩০০ [*Dacca,* 1893.] 12°. **14058. a. 10.**

NAMAKĀRA. [For Burmese collections of Pali-Burmese texts including editions of the devotional Pali poem styled Namakāra, with its Burmese translation, see under the following headings:]

HKYAUK SAUNG TWÈ.
HSAY SAUNG TWÈ.
JAYAMAṄGALAGĀTHĀ.
KO SAUNG TWÈ.
NGĀ SAUNG TWÈ.
TA-HSÈ-HNIT SAUNG TWÈ.
TA-HSÈ-THÔN SAUNG TWÈ.

NĀMA-VARANEGILLA. *See* PĀLI-NĀMA-VARANEGILLA.

NĀNĀBHĀĪ SADĀNANDAJĪ REḶE, also called HEMĀḌ PANTA. See PATAÑJALI.—*Philosophical Works.* पातञ्जलयोगशास्त्राचा अभिप्राय *etc.* [Pātañjala-yogaṣāstrā-chā Abhiprāya. The Aphorisms with Marathi translation and commentary by Nānābhāī Reḷe.] [1897.] 8°. **14048. dd. 31.(1.)**

—— See PATAÑJALI.—*Philosophical Works.* पातञ्जलयोगशास्त्रम् *etc.* [Yogaṣāstra. With the *bhāshya* and a Marathi translation of the whole by Nānābhāī Reḷe.] [1897.] 8°. **14048. dd. 31.(2.)**

ÑĀṆĀBHIDHAMMĀLAṄKĀRA, *of Taungdwin.* မာတိကာဂဏ္ဌိ *etc.* [Mātikā-ganṭhi, Dhātukathā-ganṭhi, and Yamaik-ganṭhi. Burmese treatises on the Dhammasaṅgaṇi *mātikā*, Dhātukathā, and Yamaka, illustrated from Pali texts.] See KALYĀṆĀBHIVAṂṢA, *Ū, of Chaungzon-ngay.* ပဋ္ဌာန်း ညွှဝါဂဏ္ဌိကျမ်း *etc.* [Paṭṭhāna-nya-wā-ganṭhi-kyan, *etc.*] pp. 299-370. 1898. 8°. **14300. e. 17.**

NĀNAK, *Bābā.* ਸ੍ਰੀ . . . ਸਲੋਕ ਸਹੰਸਕ੍ਰਿਤੀ *etc.* [Ṣloka Saṃskritī. Sanskrit stanzas from the Ādi-Granth.] pp. 48, *lith.* ਅੰਮ੍ਰਿਤਸਰ [*Amritsar,* 1891.] *obl.* 12°. **14028. a. 24.**

—— ਸ੍ਰੀ . . . ਸਹਸਕ੍ਰਿਤੀ ਸਲੋਕ ਭਾਵਪ੍ਰਕਾਸ਼ਨੀਟੀਕਾ ਸਹਿਤ [Saṃskritī Ṣloka. The same verses, with Panjabi translation and commentary.] pp. 144. ਅੰਮ੍ਰਿਤਸਰ ੧੯੦੩ [*Amritsar,* 1903.] 12°. **14028. bb. 13.**

—— श्रीमद्गुरुनानकगीता अद्भुतगीता। कैशवपदभाष्यभूषिता *etc.* [Nānakagītā, or Adbhuṭagītā. A poem in 8 *adhyāyas*, purporting to be originally by Nānak, and to give his teachings on philosophy and religion. With the commentary Kaiṣavapada of Keṣavānanda Svāmī, notes, and a Hindi version by Ṣaṅkarānanda Avadhūta.] pp. iii. 129. मुरादाबाद० १९५८ [*Moradabad,* 1901.] 8°. **14049. b. 4.**

—— अथ निराकारमीमांसादर्शनम् . . . कैशवभाष्येण . . . संस्कृतव्याख्यया . . . भाषाभावार्थ दीपिकया च भूषितेनभूषितम्। [Nirākāramīmāṃsādarṣana. Three chapters, containing respectively 40, 40, and 25 aphorisms, ascribed to Nānak and formulating his philosophic doctrine of a formless Supreme Being. With an exposition (*bhāshya*) by Keṣavānanda Svāmī, a supercommentary styled Svarūpadīpikā by Svarūpa Sūri, and a Hindi translation of Keṣavānanda's *bhāshya* by Ṣaṅkarānanda Avadhūta.] pp. ii. iv. 498, 26. मुरादाबाद० १९५९ [*Moradabad,* 1903.] 8°. **14049. bb. 3.**

ÑĀṆAKITTI. අභිධම්ම සම්මොහවිනොදනී-අත්ථයොජනා *etc.* (The Abbidhamma Sammohavinodani Atthayojana. [A gloss upon the Sammohavinodanī, Buddhaghosa's commentary on the Vibhaṅga.] Composed by Nanakitti Thera. Presented by His Supreme Majesty the King of Siam Culalankara . . . Edited by Kodagoda Pannasekhara Thera.) pp. xviii. i. 264, ii. i. *Kataluwa,* 2436 [1893.] 8°. **14098. dd. 5.(2.)**

NĀNĀLĀL MAGANLĀL. સુંદર શૃંગાર [Sundara-ṣriṅgāra. A collection of erotic verses, with Gujarati prose translations.] pp. 48. अमदावाद १९५२ [*Ahmadabad,* 1896.] 16°. **14076. a. 20.(1.)**

ÑĀṆĀLAṄKĀRA, *Mahāthera, of Môn-ywa.* See SUTTAPIṬAKA.—*Khuddakanikāya.* [*Suttanipāta.*] ပဓာနသုတ် *etc.* [Padhānasutta. With Burmese version by Ñāṇālaṅkāra.] [1899.] 8°. [*Ariya-maggadīpanī.*] **14300. d. 28.(4.)**

ÑĀṆĀLAṄKĀRĀBHI SADDHAMMA, *of Amarapura.* သရဏာဒိဝိနိစ္ဆယ *etc.* [Saraṇādivinichchhaya. A Burmese treatise illustrated from Pali, on the 3 *saraṇas* and other topics of the Buddhist creed and practice. Followed by two similar Burmese works, viz. the Kammavinichchhaya of Sāgara-vaṃsābhiddhaja, on *karma*, and the Vipassanā-nayadīpanī of Paññāsāmi, a work on spiritual insight, based on the Visuddhimagga.] pp. 268. *Rangoon,* 1882. 8°. **14300. d. 19.(1.)**

ÑĀṆATILAKA TISSA. See DHAMMĀNANDA ĀCHARIYA. කච්චායනසාරය *etc.* [Kachchāyanasāra. With Sinhalese interpretation by Ñāṇatilaka.] [1892.] 12°. **14098. b. 18.(3.)**

ÑĀṆAVAṂSADDHAJA, *Mahādhammarājādhirāja-guru.* See ÑĀṆINDĀBHI KAVIDDHAJA.

ÑĀṆAVIMALA TISSA, *Taṅgallē.* See SUTTAPIṬAKA.—*Aṅguttaranikāya.* The Maithunasanyoga Sutraya. With [Sinhalese] paraphrase by . . . Nanawimala Tissa, *etc.* [1897.] 8°. **14098. c. 72.(4.)**

NANDADDHAJA, *Ū, of Min Kyaung, Dabein, Pegu.* အကုသလစ္ဆေဒမေဓနီကျမ်း *etc.* [Akusalachchhedamedhanī. A Burmese discourse on the ways to rebirth in higher spheres, illustrated from Pali texts.] pp. 265. ရန်ကုန် ၁၂၅၉ [*Rangoon*, 1897.] 8°. **14300. d. 5.(3.)**

NANDAGOPĀLA VANDYOPĀDHYĀYA, calling himself VISHṆUPADA ŚARMĀ. काव्य-रहस्य। [Kāvya-rahasya. A century of verses.] pp. 16. कलिकाता [*Calcutta*, 1892.] 8°. **14072. cc. 55.(1.)**

NANDAKIŚORA, *son of Rameśa.* दीपावली निर्णयः *etc.* [Dīpāvalīnirṇaya. A tract on the determination of the Dīpāvalī festival.] pp. 20. मथुरायाम् [*Muttra*, 1900.] 8°. **14028. c. 25.(3.)**

NANDALĀLA ḌHOL. *See* HASTĀMALAKA ĀCHĀRYA. Hastamalak bhasyam . . . Translated [by N. Ḍhol,] *etc.* 1899. 8°. [*The Oriental.*] **Ac. 8825. b.(vol. 2.)**

—— *See* ŚAṄKARA ĀCHĀRYA. — *Philosophical Poems, etc.* Atmabodha . . . Translated . . . by . . . N. Dhole. 1899. 8°. [*The Oriental.*] **Ac. 8825. b.(vol. 1.)**

—— *See* ŚAṄKARA ĀCHĀRYA.—*Doubtful and Supposititious Works.* Parmarthasara . . . Translated . . . by N. D. 1899. 8°. [*The Oriental.*] **Ac. 8825. b. (vol. 1.)**

—— *See* SĀYAṆA ĀCHĀRYA.—*Works on Philosophy, etc.* A Hand-book of Hindu Pantheism. The Panchadasi . . . Translated . . . by Nandalal Dhole. 1899-1900. 8°. **14048. cc. 32.**

NANDALĀLA ŚARMĀ, *of Muhammadpur.* *See* PURĀṆAS. — *Brahmapurāṇa.* कर्मविपाकसंहिता *etc.* [Karmavipākasaṃhitā. Edited with Hindi translation by Nandalāla.] [1902.] 8°. **14053. ccc. 42.**

NANDALĀLA ŚARMĀ, *son of Lakshmīnārāyaṇa, Paushkaravaṃśya, of Amritsar.* *See* ABHINANDA, *son of Jayanta.* कादम्बरीकथासारः *etc.* [Kādambarīkathāsāra. With commentary by Nandalāla.] [1900.] 8°. **14072. d. 44.**

NANDALĀLA ŚĀSTRĪ, *of Mazra.* *See* KĀLIDĀSA, *Pseud., author of the Nalodaya.* नलोदयकाव्यम् *etc.* [Nalodaya. With commentary. Edited by Nandalāla.] [1899.] 8°. **14070. dd. 11.**

NANDAMEDHA, *of the Bodhi Kyaung, Tantabin.* ယမိုက်ဆယ်ကျမ်းအရကောက် *etc.* [Yamaik-hsay-kyan-aya-kauk. A Burmese treatise, illustrated from Pali texts, upon the Yamaka, based on the work of Nandamedha as transmitted by Anantaddhaja of Taungbalu. Followed by Yamaik-gaṇṭhi, a dissertation on the same subject by Ñāṇābhidhammālaṅkāra. Edited by Nandavaṃsa, Atwin-wûn of Pagan.] pp. v. 657, ii. မန္တလေး [*Mandalay*,] 1900. 8°. **14300. e. 16.**

NANDA PAṆḌITA, *son of Rāma Paṇḍita.* *See* ĀDINĀRĀYAṆA PĀTRO. The Hindu Law. Annotated and illustrated by Sanskrit texts[, viz. the writings of Nanda and others,] *etc.* 1899. 8°. **14039. c. 17.**

NANDAPAÑÑĀCHARIYA. *See* BODE (M.). Index to the Gandhavaṁsa, *etc.* 1896. 8°. [*Journal of the Pali Text Society.*] **14098. b.**

NANDARGIKAR (G. R.). *See* GOPĀLA RAGHUNĀTHA NANDARGIKAR.

NANDAVAṂSA, *Mahāthera, Atwin-wûn of Pagan.* *See* NANDAMEDHA, *of the Bodhi Kyaung, Tantabin.* ယမိုက်ဆယ်ကျမ်းအရကောက် *etc.* [Yamaik-hsay-kyan-aya-kauk. Edited by Nandavaṃsa.] 1900. 8°. **14300. e. 16.**

NANDIKEŚVARA, *son of Śilāda Muni.* [For editions of the Yogatārāvalī, sometimes ascribed to Nandikeśvara :] *See* ŚAṄKARA ĀCHĀRYA.—*Doubtful and Supposititious Works.*

—— శ్రీనందికేశ్వరకృతా శ్రీమదాదిసూత్రకాశికా *etc.* [Nandikeśvara-kāśikā, or Ādisūtra-kāśikā. 27 stanzas, with a *vritti*, mystically interpreting the Śivasūtra or aphorisms on the alphabet which are prefixed to Pāṇini's grammar. With the commentary Tattvavimarśinī ascribed to Upamanyu.] pp. 12. నడుక్కావేరి ౧౯౦౨ [*Nadukkaveri*, 1902.] 12°. **14033. a. 26.(3.)**

NĀṆḌILLAGOPA MANTRĪ, *nephew of Sālvatimma and son of Timmaya.* *See* KṚISHṆA MIŚRA, *Dramatist.* प्रबोधचन्द्रोदयम् *etc.* [Prabodhachandrodaya. With the commentary Chandrikā of Nāṇḍillagopa, *etc.*] [1898.] 8°. **14080. c. 39.**

NANDISHEṆA. [For the editions of the Ajitaśāntistava included in the collection styled Navasmaraṇa :] *See* NAVASMARAṆA.

ÑĀṆINDĀBHI KAVIDDHAJA, known as SHWEPYI HSAYA. *See* SAṄGHARAKKHITA. ဆန္ဒသာရတ္ထိပ္ပါယပကာသနီကျမ်း *etc.* [Vuttodaya. Preceded by Chhandasārādhippāyappakāsanī, a Burmese commentary by Ñāṇindābhi.] 1897. 8°.
14098. ccc. 27.(1.)

—— ယမကပဋ္ဌာနသာရတ္ထိပ္ပါယပကာသနီကျမ်း *etc.* [Yamakapaṭṭhānasārādhippāyappakāsanī. Discourses on the Yamaka and Paṭṭhāna, in Burmese, illustrated by Pali quotations. Followed by other cognate essays.] pp. iv. iii. 128. မန္တလေး [*Mandalay,*] 1896. 8°.
14300. d. 4.(2.)

ÑĀṆISSARA, *Mahagoḍa.* *See* MAHĀNĀMA. Mahá-waṇsa Tiká . . . edited . . . by Pandit Baṭu-wantuḍáwe and M. Ñáṇissara, *etc.* 1895. 8°.
14098. dd. 10.

—— *See* SAṄGHĀNANDA, *Kaṁburugamuvē.* පදවීතිහාරානිසංසය *etc.* [Padavītihārānisaṃsaya. Edited by Ñāṇissara.] [1894.] 12°.
14098. a. 29.(1.)

—— *See* SUŚRUTA. Susruta Sutra-sthana. 1st part. Translated under the instruction of . . . M. Nanissara, *etc.* 1896. 8°. **14043. e. 32.**

—— *See* VĀGBHAṬA, *son of Siṃhagupta.* Ashtanga Hridaya . . . Translated . . . by W. B. de Alwis . . . Revised by M. Nanissara, *etc.* 1893. 8°. **14043. d. 45.**

NAÑJUṆḌA DĪKSHITA, *of Devanḍapalle.* ಶೈವಾಗಮಸಾರಾಖ್ಯಯಂ ಗ್ರಂಥಃ *etc.* [Ṣaivāgamasāra. A collection of Ṣaiva rituals, compiled from the Āgamas and Āgamik literature.] pp. 293, iii. ಬೆಂಗಳೂರು ೧೮೯೩ [*Bangalore,* 1893.] 8°.
14028. d. 51.

NAÑJUṆḌA SVĀMI, *of Bangalore.* *See* MAUNAPPA. ಶ್ರೀ . . . ಗರ್ಭಾಧಾನಾದಿವಿಧಯಃ *etc.* [Vīraṣaiva-garbhādhānādi-vidhayaḥ. Edited by Nañjuṇḍa.] 1902. 8°. **14033. bbb. 19.**

NĀNYADEVA, *son of Harichandra.* *See* BHAVABHŪTI. The Mâlatîmâdhava . . . With the commentaries of Tripurâri [on Acts i.-vii., of Nānyadeva on viii.-x.,] *etc.* 1892. 8°. **14079. c. 61.**

NĀRADA. [*Ṣikshā.*] ॥ अथ नारदीया शिक्षा ॥ [Nāradaṣikshā. A Sāmavedī metrical tract on Vedic phonetics, in 2 *prapaṭhakas*, ascribed to Nārada. Edited by Satyavrata Sāmaṣramī.] pp. 26. 1890. *See* PERIODICAL PUBLICATIONS.—*Calcutta.* उषा *etc.* [Ushā.] Vol. I, nos. vi.-vii. [1889]-1893. 8°.
14010. c. 43.(vol. 1.)

—— —— सटीका नारदीशिक्षा ॥ [Nāradaṣikshā. With commentary by Ṣobhākara Bhaṭṭa.] *See* YUGALAKIṢORA VYĀSA PĀṬHAKA. श्रीमद्याज्ञवल्क्यादि . . . शिक्षासंग्रहः . . . A collection of Śikshás, *etc.* pp 394-449. 1893. 8°. **14093. b. 31.**

—— [*Smṛiti.*] *See* GULĀB-CHANDRA SARKĀR. Hindu Law, *etc.* [With extracts from the law-books of Nārada and others.] 1897. 8°.
14038. c. 46.

—— [*Sūtra.*] [For editions of the Nāradasūtra or Bhaktisūtra :] *See* ṢĀṆḌILYA.

NĀRADA-PĀÑCHARĀTRA. *See* PĀÑCHARĀTRA.

NARAHARI, *Commentator on Vedāntasāra.* *See* NṚISIṂHA SARASVATĪ.

NARAHARI, *son of Īṣvara Sūri.* राजनिघण्टुसहितो धन्वन्तरीयनिघण्टुः *etc.* (The Râjanighanta [of Narahari] and the Dhanvantarinighanta, two treatises on medicine[, the former supplementing and elucidating the latter]. Edited [with indices] by Vaidya Náráyaṇa Shastri Purandare.) [1896.] 8°. *See* DHANVANTARI. **14003. ccc. (no. 33.)**

—— राजनिघण्टुः *etc.* (Rajanighantu. A popular dictionary of medical terms . . . Edited and published with various modifications and notes critical and explanatory by Ashu Bodha Bhattacharjya and Nitya Bodha Bhattacharjya.) pp. xx. ii. 476. *Calcutta,* 1899. 8°. **14043. cc. 15.**

The English title is from the wrapper.

NARAHARI BHAṬṬA, called SAPTARSHI. अथ सप्तर्ष्युपाख्यनरहरिभट्टविरचितसंस्कारनृसिंहः *etc.* [Saṃskāra-nṛisiṃha. A work on ritual purification.] ff. v. 102. काश्याम् १९५० [*Benares,* 1894.] *obl.* 8°.
14033. bbb. 1.

NARAHARI DĀSA GUPTA, *son of Dāmodara Dāsa,* called KAVĪNDRA VIṢVĀSA. *দুর্গাপূজা পদ্ধতি *etc.* [Durgāpūjāpaddhati. A ritual of Durgā, based on the Kālikāpurāṇa. Edited, with a Bengali biography of the author, by Tārakanātha Dāsa Gupta.] pp. vi. 122, i. বরিশাল ১৩০৮ [*Barisal*, 1901.] 8°. **14033. bb. 42.(2.)**

NARAPATI, *son of Āmradeva.* ॥ अथ नरपत जय चरिया प्रारभ्यते ॥ [Narapatijayacharyā. A manual for the attainment of magical powers and knowledge.] pp. 112, *lith.* मेरठ [*Meerut*, 1900.] *obl.* 4°. **14053. g. 15.**

NARASIMHA, *disciple of Tātārya.* *See* NṚISIṂHA ŚĀSTRĪ, *Kānkānphallī.*

NARASIMHĀCHĀRYA, *Tirumaṅgalam Naḍādur.* *See* RĀMĀNUJĀCHĀRYA, *Kandāḍai Varadārya.* श्रीमद्वेदपादरामायणम् *etc.* [Vedapāda-rāmāyaṇa. Edited by Narasiṃhāchārya.] 1902. 8°. **14072. b. 31.**

—— *See* VARADĀCHĀRYA, *Mīmāṃsāvallabha Vātsya.* வரதமேசிகவைபவப்ரகாசிகா *etc.* [Varadadeṣikavaibhavaprakāṣikā, *etc.* Edited with prefaces by Narasiṃhāchārya, *etc.*] 1897. 8°. **14076. d. 50.**

—— ஸ்ரீநிவாஸமுநிபஞ்சாசத் தேசிகதசகம் [Ṣrīnivāsa-Muni-pañchāṣat. A poem in 56 stanzas on Ṣrīnivāsa Deṣika of Srirangam. Followed by Deṣikadaṣaka, 12 stanzas on the Vedāntadeṣika.] pp. 12. கஅகூக [*Madras*, 1891.] 12°. **14048. b. 23.(2.)**

NARASIMHADATTA, *disciple of Umādatta.* *See* YAJÑADATTA TRIPĀṬHĪ. नारसिंही । [Nārasiṃhī. A stanza by Yajñadatta, with commentary by Narasiṃhadatta.] [1899.] 12°. [*Kūṭapadyavyākhyā.*] **14072. b. 24.**

—— याज्ञी । [Yājñī. A stanza by Narasiṃhadatta, which as exoterically interpreted refers to the loss of a father. With commentary by Yajñadatta.] *See* UMĀDATTA TRIPĀṬHĪ. कूटपद्यव्याख्या *etc.* [Kūṭapadyavyākhyā.] pp. 86-94. [1899.] 12°. **14072. b. 24.**

NARASIMHAIYĀ, *Basavapatna.* *See* ŚAṄKARA ĀCHĀRYA.—*Two or More Works.* A Compendium of the Raja Yoga Philosophy, *etc.* [*scil.* the Ātmabodha, translated by B. Narasiṃhaiyā, *etc.*] 1901. 8°. **14048. bb. 53.**

NARASIMHAM, *Guḍimella, of Gudivada.* మంత్రశాస్త్రము *etc.* [Mantra-ṣāstra. A collection of magical recipes and incantations, in Sanskrit and Telugu.] pp. 4, 106. బెజవాడ [*Bezwada*,] 1895. 12°. **14174. e. 21.**

NARASIMHA ṢĀSTRĪ, *son of Ṣishṭā Sītārāma, of Masulipatam.* *See* LAKSHMĪNṚISIṂHA ṢĀSTRĪ. పురాణోక్తకర్మప్రకాశిక *etc.* [Purāṇokta-karmaprakāṣika. Edited by Narasiṃha.] [1899.] 8°. **14028. c. 79.**

NARASIMHA SOMAYĀJĪ, *A. L.* *See* LAKSHMĪNARASIṂHA SOMAYĀJĪ, *A.*

NARASIMHA YOGĪ, *Commentator on Vedāntasāra.* *See* NṚISIṂHA SARASVATĪ.

NARASIMMALU NĀYUḌU, *Sēlam Pagaḍāla.* *See* SANDHYĀVANDANA. ஆரியர் சந்தியாவந்தநம் *etc.* [Āryar-sandhyāvandanam. With Tamil version, *etc.*, by Narasimmalu.] 1898. 8°. **14170. e. 47.(8.)**

—— *See* UPANISHADS.—*Selections.* இந்து பைபில் *etc.* (The Hindu Holy Bible . . . Compiled by S. P. Narasimmalu Nayudu.) 1898. 8°. **14170. ee. 15.**

NARASIMMIAH, *B. P.* *See* NARASIṂHAIYĀ, *Basavapatna.*

NĀRĀYAṆA, *son of Ananta.* *See* NĀRĀYAṆA BHAṬṬA, *son of Ananta.*

NĀRĀYAṆA, *son of Bhābhalla.* *See* VṚINDA. वृन्दमाधवापरनामा सिद्धयोगः *etc.* (The Vṛindamâdhava . . . with its commentary 'Kusumávali' [commenced] by Śrî kanthadutta [and completed by Nārāyaṇa,] *etc.*) [1894.] 8°. **14003. ccc. (no. 27.)**

NĀRĀYAṆA, *son of Divākara.* *See* ĀṢVALĀYANA. ॥ अथ . . . गृह्यसूत्रं *etc.* [Āṣvalāyanagṛihyasūtra. With commentary of Nārāyaṇa, *etc.*] [1895.] *obl.* 8°. **14010. dd. 6.**

NĀRĀYAṆA, *son of Ṣrīratnākara.* *See* UPANISHADS.—*General Collections.* उपनिषदां समुच्चयः *etc.* (Thirty two Upaniśads. With Dîpikâs by . . . Nârâyaṇa, *etc.*) [1895.] 8°. **14003. ccc. (no. 29.)**

—— *See* UPANISHADS.—*Small Collections.* उपनिषदावली *etc.* [Upanishadāvalī. Ten Upanishads, including the Garbhop°., Brahmop°., Sarvop°., Kaivalyop°., Brahmabindūp°., Rāmop°., and Nādabindūp°., with the commentaries of Nārāyaṇa.] [1896.] 12°. **14010. b. 12.**

—— *See* UPANISHADS.—*Small Collections.* Amritabindu and Kaivalya Upanishads. With commentaries [in English, compiled from the works of Nārāyaṇa and others]. Translated . . . by A. Mahadeva Sastri. 1898. 12°. **14010. b. 19.**

—— *See* UPANISHADS. — *Separate Upanishads.* Il primo capitolo della Brahma-Upanishad, coll' annessovi commento di Nârâyaṇa, *etc.* 1897. 4°. **14010. ee. 2.**

—— *See* UPANISHADS.—*Separate Upanishads.* Gopala Tapani Upanishad. Part i. [Translated, with extracts from the commentaries of Nārāyaṇa, *etc.*] 1899. 8°. [*The Theosophist.*] **P.P. 636. cm. (vol. 20.)**

—— *See* UPANISHADS.—*Separate Upanishads.* केनोपनिषत् *etc.* (The Kenopanishad . . . And the Dípikás of the same by . . . Náráyaṇa, *etc.*) [1888.] 8°. **14003. ccc. (no. 6.)**

—— *See* UPANISHADS.—*Separate Upanishads.* मुण्डकोपनिषत् *etc.* [Muṇḍakopanishad. With the Dīpikā of Nārāyaṇa, *etc.*] [1889.] 8°. **14003. ccc. (no. 9.)**

NĀRĀYAṆA, *son of Vāsudeva.* *See* VĀSUDEVA BHAṬṬĀCHĀRYA. ஆஹ்நிகாம்ருதம் [Āhnikāmṛita. With commentary by Nārāyaṇa.] 1900. 8°. [*Pāramātmikopanishad.*] **14033. bbb. 13.**

NĀRĀYAṆA ADHVARĪ. *See* NĀRĀYAṆA SOMAYĀJĪ, *Kalvakūrtipalli.*

NĀRĀYAṆA AIYAṄGĀR, *Retired Assistant-Commissioner.* *See* VEDAS.—Ṛigveda.—*Single Hymns and Verses.* An Essay on the Vrishâkapi Hymn, *etc.* 1899. 8°. **14010. c. 35.(2.)**

—— Essays on Indo-Aryan Mythology, *etc.* *Bangalore, Madras,* 1898, *etc.* 8°. **14028. c. 72.**

In progress.

NĀRĀYAṆA BĀLAKṚISHṆA GOḌBOLE. *See* BRĀHMAṆAS.—*Taittirīyabrāhmaṇa.* तैत्तिरीयब्राह्मणम् *etc.* [Taittirīyabrāhmaṇa. With commentary of Sāyaṇa. Edited by Nārāyaṇa Goḍbole.] [1898.] 8°. **14003. ccc. (no. 37.)**

—— *See* KĀLIDĀSA.—*Mālavikāgnimitra.* The Mâlavikâgnimitram . . . Edited . . . under the general supervision of Nârâyan Bâlkrishna Godabole. 1897. 8°. **14079. c. 66.**

—— *See* ŚŪDRAKA. The Mṛichchhakaṭika . . . Vol. I. Containing two commentaries . . . Edited by Nârâyaṇa . . . Goḍabole. 1896, *etc.* 8°. **14079. c. 63.**

NĀRĀYAṆA-BHĀRATĪ YAŚVANTA-BHĀRATĪ, *Gosāin.* *See* MAṆḌANA. राजवल्लभ *etc.* [Rājavallabha. Edited with Gujarati translation by Nārāyaṇa-Bhāratī.] [1891.] 8°. **14053. d. 47.**

NĀRĀYAṆA BHAṬṬA. सुभद्राहरणचम्पुकाव्यम् *etc.* [Subhadrāharaṇa. A composition in mixed prose and verse on the rape of Subhadrā by Arjuna. Edited with glosses and notes by Punnacheri Nīlakaṇṭha Śarmā and Vāsudeva Śarmā.] pp. 53. पट्टाम्बि १८९७ [*Pattambi,* 1897.] 8°. **14072. cc. 60.(3.)**

This volume apparently forms part of a series entitled Sāhityaratnāvali.

NĀRĀYAṆA BHAṬṬA, *Kerala.* ധാതുകാവ്യം *etc.* [Dhātukāvya. A poem in 3 *sargas*, treating of the legends of Kṛishṇa so as to illustrate the accidence of the verbal roots as given in the Dhātupāṭha of Bhīmasena. With a commentary.] pp. 192. [*Pattambi,*] 1893. 8°. **14070. c. 50.**

This work was written to form a supplement to the Vāsudevavijaya of Puruvanam Vāsudeva, published in the Kâvyamâlâ (*Anthology*), *pt.* x., 1894. *Nārāyaṇa was a Brahman of Meppatūr or Meppunnār, a disciple of Achyuta, and a contemporary of Bhaṭṭojī Dīkshita, according to tradition.*

—— ശ്രീകേരളനാരായണഭട്ടകൃത ധാതുകാവ്യം [Dhātukāvya, i.-ii. 32. With notes. Followed by an account of the author.] *See* MĀNAVIKRAMA, *Rājakumāra.* ശ്രീമാനവിക്രമ-കവിരാജകുമാരേണ . . . കൃതാഃ സംഗൃഹീതാഃ *etc.* [Essays and poems.] [1890.] 8°. **14072. d. 35.**

NĀRĀYAṆA BHAṬṬA, *courtier of Dhavalachandra.* [For the Hitopadeṣa ascribed to Nārāyaṇa:] *See* HITOPADEṢA.

NĀRĀYAṆA BHAṬṬA, *Astrologer.* චමත්කාරචින්තාමණී *etc.* [Chamatkārachintāmaṇi. With a Sinhalese interpretation by H. D. Fernando Tambi-Appu Gurunnānse.] pp. 49. [*Colombo,*] 1891. 8°. **14053. cc. 63.(1.)**

NĀRĀYAṆA BHAṬṬA, *Astrologer* (*continued*). Chamatkar Chintamani, or The Gem of Astrology, *etc.* [Translated, with some additions from other sources, by Kṛishṇanātha Raghunāthajī.] pp. 47. *Bombay*, 1894. 12°. **14053. b. 31.(1.)**

NĀRĀYAṆA BHAṬṬA, called MṚIGARĀJALAKSHMĀ. The Venisamhâra ... Edited [with introduction and notes in English] by B. T. Dravid alias Sheshadri Iyer and S. T. Dravid. (वेणीसंहारनाटकम्) pp. xxv. ii. 117, 92, xxxiv. ii. *Poona*, 1896. 8°. **14079. c. 65.(1.)**

—— The Veṇîsaṃhâra ... With the commentary of Jagaddhara, and various readings. Edited by Kâśînâth Pâṇḍurang Parab and Kṛishṇa Râmchandra Mâḍgâvkar. (वेणीसंहारम् ।) pp. 213, iii. *Bombay*, 1898. 8°. **14079. c. 67.**

—— வெணீ ஸம்ஹார நாடகம் *etc.* [Veṇīsaṃhāra. Edited by Nallicheri V. S. Veṅkaṭarāma Ṣāstrī.] pp. 110. நடுக்காவேரி [*Nadukkaveri,*] 1902. 8°. **14080. c. 44.**

—— Stanzas from Veṇi Samhára Nátaka [in Sanskrit and English], set to music [in European notation] by Raja Sir Sourindro Mohun Tagore. pp. 32. *Calcutta*, 1893. 8°. **14080. c. 17.(2.)**

NĀRĀYAṆA BHAṬṬA, *son of Ananta.* ముహూర్త-మార్తండము మార్తండవల్లభా ... సహితము *etc.* [Muhūrtamārtaṇḍa. A work on auspicious times. With the commentary Mārtaṇḍavallabhā. Edited with Telugu interpretation and commentary by N. Guruliṅga Ṣāstrī.] pp. vii. 450. చెన్నపురి ౧౯౦౧ [*Madras*, 1901.] 8°. **14053. ccc. 38.**

NĀRĀYAṆA BHAṬṬA, *son of Rāmeṣvara.* The Vivahaprayoga or Marriage Ritual prescribed for Brahmans of Riksakha, with translation[, *scil.* a literal Telugu version and a free English paraphrase,] by P. Chentsal Ráo. [Followed by extracts from Āṣvalāyana's Gṛihyasūtra, *etc.*] (వివాహప్రయోగః) pp. 70, x. 247, ix. 16, 6, 5, 2, i. iii. *Bangalore*, 1891. 8°. **14033. b. 58.**

NĀRĀYAṆA BHAṬṬA, *son of Raṅganātha.* See JAYADEVA, *son of Bhojadeva.* श्रीगीतगोविंद° [Gitagovinda. With commentary of Nārāyaṇa, *etc.*] [1891.] 8°. **14072. d. 42.**

NĀRĀYAṆA BHAṬṬA, *son of Raṅganātha* (*continued*). *See* RĀMACHANDRA, *son of Janārdana.* राधाविनोदः । [Rādhāvinoda. With the commentary Prakāṣa of Nārāyaṇa.] [1890.] 8°. [*Grantharatnamālā.*] **14096. c. 8.(vol. 4.)**

—— *See* RĀMACHANDRA, *son of Janārdana.* राधाविनोद° [Rādhāvinoda. With commentary of Nārāyaṇa.] [1891.] 8°. [*Gītagovinda.*] **14072. d. 42.**

NĀRĀYAṆA BHAṬṬĀCHĀRYA, *son of Gopālakṛishṇa, of Karupur, Tiruvadi.* See VIKHANAS. ஸ்ரீவைகானஸஸூத்ரப்ரயோகம் [Vaikhānasasūtraprayoga. Edited by Nārāyaṇa, *etc.*] [1897.] 12°. **14028. b. 86.**

NĀRĀYAṆACHANDRA VIDYĀRATNA. *See* ĪṢVARACHANDRA VIDYĀSĀGARA. भूगोलखगोलवर्णनम् *etc.* [Bhūgola-khagola-varṇana. Edited by Nārāyaṇachandra.] 1893. 12°. **14053. b. 30.**

NĀRĀYAṆADĀSA KAVIRĀJA. [For editions of the work styled Rājavallabha, Rājavallabhīyadravyaguṇa, Dravyaguṇa, or Rājavallabhanighaṇṭu, in the redaction of Nārāyaṇadāsa :] *See* RĀJAVALLABHA.

NĀRĀYAṆA GAJAPATI RĀYA, *Goḍē.* భగవద్గీతా-పాదసూచిక *etc.* [Bhagavadgītāpādasūchikā. An index to the stanzas of the Bhagavadgītā.] pp. 48. *Vizagapatam*, 1896. 8°. **14065. bbb. 4.**

—— [Another copy, without title-page.] *See* PERIODICAL PUBLICATIONS.—*Vizagapatam.* సకల-విద్యాభివర్ధని *etc.* [Sakalavidyābhivardhanī.] Vol. III, pt. v. 1892-1897. 12° & 8°. **14174. g. 38.(vol. 3.)**

NĀRĀYAṆA GUPTA, *C. K.* कल्याणसौगन्धिकपद्यार्थ-निर्णयः *etc.* [Kalyāṇasaugandhikapadyārthanirṇaya. A lecture upon some passages in the Kalyāṇasaugandhika.] pp. 11. पट्टांबि १९०२ [*Pattambi*, 1902.] 8°. **14072. ccc. 20.(2.)**

NĀRĀYAṆA HEMACHANDRA. *See* BIBLE. ख्रिष्टधर्मनीति *etc.* [Khrishṭadharmanīti. Compiled by Nārāyaṇa.] [1880.] 8°. **14006. c. 14.**

—— *See* ĪṢĀNACHANDRA VASU. આર્યધર્મનીતિ *etc.* [Āryadharmanīti. Edited with Gujarati translations by Nārāyaṇa Hemachandra.] [1895.] 16°. **14085. a. 11.**

NĀRĀYAṆA HEMACHANDRA (*continued*). *See* VĀLMĪKI.—Rāmāyaṇa.—*Abridgments and Selections.* The Light of India . . . Complied [*sic*] by Narayana Hemchandra. [1895.] 16°. **14065. a. 8.**

—— Sayings of Sages from Hindu Sacred Books[, *scil.* the Ṣruti, Smṛiti, epic, and Puranic literature, *etc.*, translated into English.] Introduction by Narsingrao Bholanath Divatia, B.A. Compiler [and translator] Narayana Hemchandra. pp. xiv. 90, 118, xx. *Ahmedabad*, 1895. 16°. **14085. a. 10.**

NĀRĀYAṆA NARASIṂHA BEDARKAR. *See* ṢRĪHARSHA, *son of Hīra Paṇḍita.* Śrîharsha's Naishadhîyacharita, with the commentary Naishadhîyaprakâśa of Nârâyaṇa, *etc.* 1894. 8°. **14070. d. 35.**

—— *See* ṢRĪHARSHA, *son of Hīra Paṇḍita.* Nîshadha Charita. [Cantos x.-xii.] With the commentary, Nishada Prakasa of Narayanabhatta, *etc.* 1903. 8°. **14072. ccc. 36.**

NĀRĀYAṆA PAṆḌITA, *Smārta.* [For the Navaratnaparīkshā, sometimes alleged to form part of this writer's Smṛitisāroddhāra :] *See* RATNAPARĪKSHĀ.

NĀRĀYAṆA PAṆḌITĀCHĀRYA, *son of Trivikrama.* मध्वविजयः *etc.* [Madhvavijaya. A poem in 16 *sargas*, on the life of Ânandatîrtha. Edited by Apaṣaṅkara Rāmāchārya and T. R. Kṛishṇāchārya.] pp. 184. मुंबय्यां १८१६ [*Bombay*, 1895.] 16°. **14076. a. 26.**

—— अथ मणिमंजरी [Maṇimañjarī. Verses on mythological subjects.] ff. 43. आनिक्कारत्सत्रे [१८]९८ [*Anikkarachatram*, 1898.] *obl.* 16°. **14072. a. 2.**

—— श्रीमत्सटीकपारिजातापहरणमारंभः [Pārijātāpaharaṇa. A poem in 3 cantos on Kṛishṇa's theft of the celestial tree. With a commentary by the author.] पुंगनूरु १८१२ [*Punganur*, 1890.] *obl.* 8°. **14072. ccc. 22.(1.)**

NĀRĀYAṆAPRAPANNA ṢRĪNIVĀSADĀSA. *See* NATHU BHAGAVĀN DHOLKIĀ.

NĀRĀYAṆAPRASĀDA MISRA, *son of Sobhārāma.* *See* TANTRAS. [*Māheṣvaratantra.*] माहेश्वर तंत्रम् *etc.* [Māheṣvaratantra. Edited with Hindi translation by Nārāyaṇaprasāda and Mukundarāma.] [1902.] 12°. **14033. a. 45.(5.)**

NĀRĀYAṆAPRASĀDA MIṢRA and MUKUNDARĀMA MIṢRA, *sons of Ṣobhārāma.* विनयपंचाशिका *etc.* [Vinayapañchāṣikā. Stanzas to be used as forms of complimentary address, *etc.*, at weddings. With Sanskrit gloss and Hindi translations, *etc.*] pp. 68. *Moradabad*, १९५५ [1899.] 8°. **14028. c. 44.(2.)**

—— विज्ञप्तिशतकम् । अर्थात् विवाहविनय पद्यावली *etc.* [Vijñaptiṣataka, or Vivāhavinayapadyāvalī. An amplified edition of the preceding, comprising 100 stanzas, with further matter.] pp. ii. 107. मुंबय्यां १९५८ [*Bombay*, 1902.] 8°. **14028. c. 44.(3.)**

NĀRĀYAṆA SAKHĀRĀMA PANṢE. *See* JAYADEVA, *son of Mahādeva.* Prasanna Râghava . . . Edited with an introduction and notes . . . by Shivaram . . . Paranjpe . . . and Narayan Sakharam Panse. 1894. 8°. **14079. c. 62.**

NĀRĀYAṆA ṢĀSTRĪ, *T. S.* Sriharsha the Dramatist. A dissertation on the age and identity of the author of the Priyadarsika, the Ratnavali, and the Nagananda, [identifying him with Dhāvaka or Bhāsaka,] *etc.* pp. i. 21. *Madras*, [1902.] 8°. **14058. b. 40.(2.)**

Dissertation for the M.A. Degree Examination, 1902.

NĀRĀYAṆA ṢĀSTRĪ, *son of Anantakṛishṇa, of the Zamorin's College, Calicut.* Anandavalleesatakam. Sivavimsati. Bhagavannamabbhajanam. Being adorations, in homely Sanskrit verse, to Bhagavati, Siva and Vishnu, *etc.* (ദെവീസ്തോത്രം ശിവവിംശതിഃ ഭഗവന്നാമകീർത്തനമിതിമം ത്രയം) pp. 40. *Calicut*, 1902. 8°. **14072. ccc. 22.(4.)**

—— नीतिकथामञ्जरी. [Nītikathāmañjarī, or Kathāmañjarī.] Being a collection of [twelve] puranic tales wretten [*sic*] in homely sanskrit for use in High Schools, *etc.* pp. 70. *Pattambi*, 1902. 8°. **14072. ccc. 22.(5.)**

NĀRĀYAṆA ṢĀSTRĪ, *Dēvanaguḍi.* *See* ĀPASTAMBA. — *Dharmasūtra.* ధర్మసూత్రమ్ *etc.* [Dharmasūtra. With commentary. Edited by Dēvanaguḍi and Doḍḍabeli Nārāyaṇa Ṣāstrī.] [1897.] 8°. **14039. b. 24.**

—— *See* PURĀṆAS.—*Skandapurāṇa.* శ్రీకాశీఖండము [Kāṣīkhaṇḍa. Edited by Dēvanaguḍi and Doḍḍabeli Nārāyaṇa Ṣāstrī.] [1899.] 8°. **14016. c. 57.**

NĀRĀYAṆA ṢĀSTRĪ, *Doddabeli.* See ĀPASTAMBA.—*Dharmasūtra.* ಧರ್ಮಸೂತ್ರಮ್ *etc.* [Dharmasūtra. With commentary. Edited by Dēvanagudi and Doddabeli Nārāyaṇa Ṣāstrī.] [1897.] 8°. **14039. b. 24.**

—— See KĀLATATTVAVIVEKAVALLARI. ಶ್ರೀ ... ಸ್ವಪ್ನಮಂಜರಿಯು *etc.* [Svapnamañjari. Edited with Canarese translation by Nārāyaṇa.] [1896.] 8°. **14053. ccc. 10.**

—— See PURĀṆAS.—*Skandapurāṇa.* ಶ್ರೀ ಕಾಶೀಖಂಡ॥ [Kāṣīkhaṇḍa. Edited by Dēvanagudi and Doddabeli Nārāyaṇa Ṣāstrī.] [1899.] 8°. **14016. c. 57.**

NĀRĀYAṆA ṢĀSTRĪ, *Rādhāmaṅgalam Vaidyanātha*, also called VĀSUDEVA. ॥ ॐ प्लवगषष्टिः *etc.* [Plavagashashṭi. A poem of 68 stanzas, setting forth religious and philosophic doctrines in an allegory typifying the heart as an ape.] pp. 32. *Coleroon*, 1904. 16°. **14076. a. 16.(6.)**

NĀRĀYAṆA ṢĀSTRĪ, *Ṣvetāraṇyam.* See HARSHADEVA. Rathnavali. With Sanskrit commentary by . . . Narayana Sastriar. 1903. 8°. **14080. c. 45.**

—— See VEṄKAṬANĀTHA VEDĀNTĀCHĀRYA. Hamsasandesa. With Sanskrit commentary, English notes and translation, by . . . Narayana Sastriar, *etc.* 1902. 8°. **14072. cc. 63.**

NĀRĀYAṆA ṢĀSTRĪ GODBOLE. See NĀRĀYAṆA BĀLAKṚISHṆA GODBOLE.

NĀRĀYAṆA ṢĀSTRĪ PAṬAVARDHANA. See GADĀDHARA BHAṬṬĀCHARYA. ॥ व्युत्पत्तिवादः *etc.* [Vyutpattivāda. Edited by Nārāyaṇa.] [1899.] 8°. **14093. b. 27.(2.)**

—— See JÑĀNENDRA SARASVATĪ. वैयाकरणसिद्धान्तकौमुदी . . . तत्त्वबोधिनी *etc.* [Tattvabodhinī. Followed by the Subodhinī. Edited by Nārāyaṇa.] 1897. 8°. **14090. e. 25.**

—— See NĀGEṢA BHAṬṬA. [*Paribhāshenduṣekhara.*] परिभाषेन्दुशेखरः *etc.* [Paribhāshenduṣekhara. With commentary. Edited by Nārāyaṇa.] [1897.] 8°. **14090. d. 33.**

NĀRĀYAṆA ṢĀSTRĪ PURANDARE. See NĀRĀYAṆA VIṬṬHALA PURANDARE.

NĀRĀYAṆA SOMAYĀJĪ, *Kalvakūrtipalli.* శ్రీ ... శ్రీరామోత్సవరత్నాకరము *etc.* [Rāmotsavaratnākara. A compilation treating of the cult of Rāma and Sītā. Comprising (1) Navaratnamālikā, lections from various Purāṇas and the Tattvasaṅgraharāmāyaṇa, upon the Rāmāyaṇa and rituals connected with it; and (2) Navarātrakalpavallī, chapters on the rituals of the cult, compiled from the Ānandarāmāyaṇa of the Ṣatakoṭi-rāmacharita, Purāṇas, and cognate works.] pp. 330, ii. iv. చెన్నపురి ౧౮౯౮ [*Madras*, 1898.] 8°. **14028. d. 66.**

NĀRĀYAṆĀṢRAMA, *disciple of Nṛisimhāṣrama.* See NṚISIṂHĀṢRAMA, *disciple of Jagannāthāṣrama.* अथ सटीकभेदधिक्कारः *etc.* [Bhedadhikkāra. With the commentary Bhedadhikkārasatkriyā of Nārāyaṇāṣrama.] [1891.] *obl.* 4°. **14048. f. 22.**

NĀRĀYAṆA SUDARṢANA, *Bālasarasvatī.* See SHAKSPERE (W.). Vasantikaswapnam, *etc.* [Edited with English introduction by Nārāyaṇa Sudarṣana.] 1892. 8°. **14080. c. 34.**

—— Kalividhunana. A Sanscrit drama in ten acts [on the story of Kali and Damayantī,] by Pundit Bhattasree Balasaraswathi C. R. Narayana Sastree. (कलिविधूननम्) pp. viii. 141. *Kumbhakonam*, 1891. 8°. **14079. b. 37.(2.)**

NĀRĀYAṆASVĀMI AIYAR, *K.* See YOGAVĀSISHṬHARĀMĀYAṆA. A translation of Yoga-Vâsishṭa Laghu . . . by K. Narayanswami Aiyer. 1896. 8°. **14048. cc. 5.**

NĀRĀYAṆASVĀMI AIYAR, *M.* See ĀGAMAS. [*Mṛigendrāgama.*] The Mrigendra Agama. [Edited with translation by Nārāyaṇasvāmi Aiyar.] 1900-1901. 4°. [*Siddhanta Deepika.*] **14170. fff. 4.(vol. 4.)**

NĀRĀYAṆA TĪRTHA, *Paramahaṃsa Parivrājakāchārya.* ஸ்ரீ க்ருஷ்ணலீலாதரங்கிணீ *etc.* [Kṛishṇalīlātaraṅgiṇī. A series of devotional verses on the sports of Kṛishṇa, intermixed with short prose passages. Edited by G. Nṛisiṃha Bhāgavata.] pp. 134, ii. சென்னை [*Madras*,] 1901. 8°. **14072. ccc. 30.**

NĀRĀYAṆA TĪRTHA, *disciple of Rāmagovinda.* See ĪṢVARA KṚISHṆA. Sáṅkhya Káriká. With [a translation of] . . . Náráyaṇa's gloss [called Sāṅkhyachandrikā]. 1898. 8°. [*Sáṅkhya Philosophy.*] **14048. b. 34.(fasc. 1.)**

NĀRĀYAṆA TĪRTHA, *disciple of Śivarāma Tīrtha, and son of Nīlakaṇṭha.* **भाट्टभाषाप्रकाशः** *etc.* [Bhāṭṭabhāshāprakāṣa. A treatise on the terminology of the Mīmāṃsāsūtra. Edited with preface by Svāmī Bhāgavatāchārya.] pp. ii. 61. **काश्याम्** १९०० [*Benares*, 1900.] 8°. **14004. a. 4.(2.)**

Forms part of no. 26 *of the* Chowkhambâ Sanskrit Series.

NĀRĀYAṆA VIDYĀVINODA ĀCHĀRYA. *See* BHAṬṬI. ভট্টিকাব্যম্ *etc.* [Bhaṭṭikāvya. With Vidyāvinoda's gloss, following the Saṅkshiptasāra grammar, *etc.*] [1902, *etc.*] 8°. **14070. dd. 24.**

—— *See* BHAṬṬI. ভট্টিকাব্যম্ *etc.* [Bhaṭṭikāvya. Sargas i.-v., with commentaries of Vidyāvinoda, *etc.*] [1895-1896.] 8°. **14076. d. 49.**

NĀRĀYAṆA VIṬṬHALA PURANDARE, *Vaidya. See* DHANVANTARI. **राजनिघण्टुसहितो धन्वन्तरीयनिघण्टुः** *etc.* (The Râjanighanta and the Dhanvantari-nighanta . . . Edited [with indices] by . . . Náráyaṇa Shastri Purandare.) [1896.] 8°. **14003. ccc. (no. 33.)**

NARENDRAKṚISHṆA ŚIROMAṆI. **ধর্ম্ম-জীবন** *etc.* [Dharmajīvana. A treatise on the religious life. In 2 parts, the first, entitled Nityakṛityaprakaraṇa, being a compendium in Bengali of rules for the practice of religion, copiously illustrated from Sanskrit texts, and the second, styled Stavakavachaprakaraṇa, a collection of Sanskrit hymns and metrical incantations from Purāṇas, Tantras, and other sources. With an appendix containing various *dhyānas, praṇāmas*, and incantations for the worship of Śiva and Pārvatī.] pp. ii. viii. 312. **কলিকাতা** ১৩০৬ [*Calcutta*, 1899.] 12°. **14028. bb. 2.**

NARENDRANĀTHA DATTA. *See* VIVEKĀNANDA.

NARINDA, *Ū, of Pupphārāma, Thabyu-zeik.* သဒ္ဒါဒိနဝိနိစ္ဆယပ္ပကာသနီကျမ်း [Saddhadānādivinichchhayappakāsanī. Burmese homilies on charity and other virtues, illustrated from Pali texts.] pp. 99. ရန်ကုန် ၁၂၅၅ [*Rangoon*, 1893.] 8°. **14300. d. 17.(6.)**

NARMADĀŚAṄKARA BHAṬṬA. *See* GOVINDA ŚĀSTRĪ, *Bhāradvāja.* **लघुजटाजूटः** . . . Laghu Jatajoota, *etc.* [Edited by Kṛishṇa and Narmadāśaṅkara.] 1899. 8°. **14092. b. 45.(1.)**

NARMADĀŚAṄKARA DĀMODARA ŚĀSTRĪ, *of Bhaunagar. See* HEMACHANDRA, *disciple of Devachandra.* **अभिधानचिन्तामणिः** *etc.* [Abhidhānachintāmaṇi, *etc.* Edited by Narmadāśaṅkara.] [1900.] 12°. **14090. b. 46.**

NAROTTAMADĀSA, *the Bengali Poet.* **শ্রীশ্রীপ্রেমভক্তিচন্দ্রিকা** *etc.* [Premabhaktichandrikā. A Bengali Vaishṇava poem. Edited by Rāmadayālu Ghosha, with Sanskrit commentary by Viśvanātha Chakravartī and Bengali notes by Rādhikānātha Gosvāmī.] pp. 4, 161. **কলিকাতা** [*Calcutta*, 1896.] 12°. **14123. e. 20.**

NAROTTAMA ṬHĀKURA. *See* NAROTTAMADĀSA, *the Bengali Poet.*

NASARVĀNJĪ, *P. S., of Guntur.* శ్రీ . . . శ్రీరామజననము. [Rāmajanana. A Vaishṇava devotional work, comprising stanzas in Sanskrit, Hindi, and Telugu, with Telugu exposition. Second edition.] pp. ii. iii. 99. గుంటూరు యేలూరు [*Guntur, Ellore* printed,] 1901. 8°. **14175. a. 3.(10.)**

NAṢĪR al-DĪN (MUḤAMMAD ibn MUḤAMMAD), *al-Ṭūsī. See* EUCLID. The Rekhâgaṇita, or Geometry in Sanskrit. Composed [*i.e.* translated from the Arabic version of Naṣīr al-Dīn] by Samrâḍ Jagannâtha, *etc.* 1901-1902. 8°. **14053. ccc. 36.**

NAṬEŚA ŚĀSTRĪ, *Saṅgēndi Mahāliṅgam. See* BĀṆA. Harshacharita . . . Translated . . . by . . . Natesa Sastri, *etc.* 1901. 12°. **14060. b. 16.(2.)**

—— *See* SADĀŚIVA BRAHMENDRA. Ātmavidyāvilāsa, *etc.* [Edited with English translation by Naṭeśa.] 1899. 8°. [*The Brahmavâdin.*] **14048. g. 1.(vol. 4.)**

—— —— The Ātmavidyā Vilāsa . . . [Edited with biography and translation] by . . . Natesa Sastriar. New edition. 1901. 8°. **14048. bb. 42.(4.)**

—— A Review of Sakuntala of Kalidasa. By Pandit S. M. Natesa Sastri. pp. i. i. 74. *Madras*, 1897. 8°. **14079. b. 41.**

NATHU BHAGAVĀN DHOLKIĀ. *See* AMARAJĪ HARIŚAṄKARA TRAVĀṚĪ and NATHU BHAGAVĀN DHOLKIĀ. ॥ प्रपन्न शिक्षामृत *etc.* [Prapannaṣikshāmṛita.] [1897.] 12°. **14028. bb. 9.**

NATHURĀM, *of Girnar.* *See* PATAÑJALI.—*Philosophical Works.* श्रीपातंजलयोगदर्शन *etc.* [Pātañjalayogadarṣana. Being the Yogasūtra with the Padabodhinī and the gloss Rahasyadīpikā of Nathurām, comprising Gujarati translations and explanations.] [1901.] 12°. **14048. b. 40.**

NAVADVĪPACHANDRA VIDYĀRATNA, *Gosvāmī.* শ্রীগৌরাঙ্গ-মঙ্গল-সঙ্গীত লীলা-রস-তত্ত্ব-সার-সংগ্রহ *etc.* [Gaurāṅgamaṅgalasaṅgīta - līlārasatattvasārasaṅgraha. A compilation of religious writings of the Chaitanya sect, comprising Bengali lyrics with supplements from the Sanskrit literature of the school. Third edition.] কলিকাতা ১৩০৮ [*Calcutta,* 1902.] 12°. **14123. e. 30.**

In progress.

—— বৈষ্ণবাচারদর্পণ *etc.* [Vaishṇavāchāradarpaṇa, or Vaishṇavasarvasva. An anthological summary of Vaishṇava doctrine of the Chaitanya school, in Bengali and Sanskrit, mostly in verse.] pp. ii. 68. কলিকাতা ১২৬৭ [*Calcutta,* 1860.] 8°. **14123. f. 5.(2.)**

—— বৈষ্ণবাচারদর্পণ। বৈষ্ণবসর্ব্বস্ব *etc.* [Vaishṇavāchāradarpaṇa. A new and much enlarged edition.] pt. i. কলিকাতা ১৮০২ [*Calcutta,* 1880.] 8°. **14123. f. 27.**

—— [Third edition.] pt. i. কলিকাতা ১৮২৩ [*Calcutta,* 1901.] 8°. **14123. f. 56.**

NAVARĀTRA. अथ सर्मंवनवरात्रपद्धतिः सोद्धाराकथासहिता प्रार° [Navarātrapaddhati. A ritual of the Navarātra festival to Durgā held from the 1st to the 9th of Āṣvina. Preceded by the Uddhārākathā, an account of the festival, from the Devībhāgavatapurāṇa iii.] ff. i. 11. कल्याण-मुम्बई १९५५ [*Kalyan,* 1898.] *obl.* 12°. **14028. dd. 5.(2.)**

NAVASMARAṆA. अथ नवस्मरण. [Navasmaraṇa. Nine Jain devotional poems in Sanskrit and Prakrit, *scil.* the Navakāra, Uvasaggahara of Bhadrabāhu, Santikarastotra of Munisundara, Tijayapahutta of Abhayadeva, Bhayahara or Namiūṇa of Mānatuṅga, Ajitaṣānti of Nandisheṇa, Bhaktāmara of Mānatuṅga, Kalyāṇamandira of Siddhasena Divākara, and Bṛihachchhānti. With Gujarati translations.] *See* PRATIKRAMAṆASŪTRA. श्री पंचप्रतिक्रमण सूत्र *etc.* [Pañcha-pratikramaṇasūtra.] pp. 115-186. [1897.] 12°. **14100. a. 20.**

—— नव स्मरण तथा ग्रहशांतिस्तव अने मंत्राधिराजस्तोत्र *etc.* [Navasmaraṇa. Followed by the Grahaṣānti, to the planets, and the Mantrādhirājastotra, to Pārṣvanātha. Edited by Hīrāchand Kakalbhāī.] pp. 126, ii. अमदावाद १९०० [*Ahmadabad,* 1900.] 16°. **14100. a. 24.**

—— अथ श्रीनव स्मरणानि *etc.* [Navasmaraṇa.] *See* JAINASTOTRARATNĀKARA. जैनस्तोत्ररत्नाकरः *etc.* [Jainastotraratnākara.] pp. 1-71. [1901.] 16°. **14100. a. 26.**

—— નવ . . . બૃહન્નસ્મરણ° [Navasmaraṇa. Another collection, comprising the Navakāra, Ajitaṣāntistava, Vīrastava of Pādalipta, Uvasaggahara, Bhayahara, Jīrakāpallī-Pārṣvastava of Merutuṅga, Ṣakrastava, Vīra Gaṇī's Laghvajitaṣāntistava, and Jayaṣekhara Sūri's Bṛihadajitaṣāntistava.] *See* GHELĀBHĀI LĪLĀDHARA. જૈન વિવેક વાણી *etc.* [Jainavivekavāṇī.] pp. 58-73. [1888.] 8°. **14144. g. 26.**

NAVATATTVA. ॥ अथ श्री नवतत्त्व° [Navatattva. A Prakrit poem of 60 stanzas on the 9 principles of Jain philosophy.] *See* SĀMĀYIKASŪTRA. સામાયકસૂત્ર *etc.* [Sāmāyikasūtra.] pp. 74-83. [1900.] 16°. **14100. a. 25.**

This work is not the Navatattva of Devagupta (Jinachandra Gaṇi). It is the Navatattva in common use. A MS. of it in the possession of the British Museum, comprising 50 *verses, states in the colophon of the commentary that these verses were chiefly compiled from the Siddhāntas (Āvaṣyakaniryukti and Āchārāṅgavṛitti), with some original additions, by Maṇiratna (Maṇirayaṇa) Sūri,* satīrthya *of Somapra[bha?] Sūri of the Tapā-gachchha, while the text says that Maṇirayaṇa compiled, abridged, and wrote the work* (Catalogue of Gujarati MSS. in the B.M., *pp.* 10 f.).

—— ॥ नवतत्त्व *etc.* [Navatattva. A recension in 79 stanzas. With Gujarati translation.] *See* HEMAṢAṄKARA LAKSHMĪṢAṄKARA VARDHAMĀNKAR. प्रकरण माला *etc.* [Prakaraṇamālā.] pp. 13-32. [1901.] 8°. **14100. d. 11.**

NAVĪNACHANDRA DĀSA. *See* KSHEMENDRA. Legends and Miracles of Buddha . . . Part 1. Translated from the Avadan Kalpalata . . . by Nobin Chandra Das. 1895. 8°. **14076. c. 64.**

—— A Note on the Ancient Geography of Asia, compiled from Válmiki-Rámáyana . . . By

Nobin Chandra Das. pp. i. viii. 77. *Calcutta*, 1896. 8°. **14003. b. 19.(vol. 4.)**

Issued as a supplement to the Journal of the Buddhist Text Society.

—— [Another copy.] **14058. b. 40.(1.)**

—— A Note on the Antiquity of the Ramayana. By Nobin Chandra Das. pp. 14. *Calcutta*, 1899. 8°. **14058. cc. 3.**

NAVĪNACHANDRA RĀYA, *Bābū*. लघुव्याकरण ... Laghu Vyakarana. The elements of Sanskrit grammar, by Babu Navina Chandra Rai ... with additions and explanations in English by Pandit Tulsi Ram. Fourteenth edition. pp. vi. 132. *Lahore*, 1899. 8°. **14093. b. 41.(2.)**

NAVĪNACHANDRA VIDYĀRATNA. *See* BHAṬṬI. Bhatti ... Cantos i, ii, iii, iv, v. Text with notes by ... Nobin Ch. Vidyaratna ... With English and Bengali translations and ... questions with ... answers. [1894.] 8°. **14070. c. 57.(1.)**

—— *See* KĀLIDĀSA.—*Abhijñānaśakuntala*. अभिज्ञानशकुन्तलम् *etc.* (Kalidasa's Abhijnana Sakuntalam. Edited with an introduction, glossary, English and Bengali translations, various readings, & & &. [*sic*] and the commentary Sarala by ... Nabin Chandra Vidyaratna, *etc.*) [1901.] 8°. **14080. c. 41.**

—— *See* KĀLIDĀSA.—*Meghadūta*. Kalidasa's Meghadutam [I. 1-38]. Containing ... Mallinatha's commentary ... translations ... notes ... by ... Nabin Chandra Vidyaratna. [1901.] 8°. **14085. c. 49.(1.)**

—— *See* KĀLIDĀSA.—*Kumārasambhava*. Kumarasambhabam ... Cantos I, II, III, IV, V, VI, VII ... with notes by ... Nobin Ch. Vidyaratna ... English and Bengali translations and ... questions with ... answers. [1894.] 12°. **14070. c. 57.(2.)**

—— *See* KĀLIDĀSA.—*Raghuvaṃśa*. Raghubamsam. Cantos I-VI. Containing prose version, paraphrase ... Sanjivani ... Bengali and English translations ... notes ... &c. &c. &c. ... Edited by ... Nabin Chandra Vidyaratna. 1901. 8°. **14085. c. 50.**

NAVĪNACHANDRA VIDYĀRATNA (*continued*). *See* MĀGHA. Magha's Shishupal badham. [Sarga i.] Containing an introduction ... paraphrase ... Mallinatha's Sarbankasa ... translations ... notes ... &c. &c. ... by ... Nabin Chandra Vidyaratna. [1901.] 8°. **14085. c. 49.(2.)**

NAWĀB-KHĀN-KHĀNĀN. अथ खेटकौतुक अर्थात् नवाबखानखानाकाज्योतिष *etc.* [Kheṭakautuka, or Nawāb-Khān-Khānā-kā jyotisha. A treatise on astrology, written in Sanskrit saturated with Persian technical terms. With Hindi translation and footnotes.] pt. 1. pp. 75. लखनऊ १८९९ [*Lucknow*, 1899.] 12°. **14053. b. 38.**

—— खेटकौतुकम् *etc.* [Kheṭakautuka. With a Hindi translation.] pp. 44. बंबई १९५८ [*Bombay*, 1902.] 8°. **14053. c. 68.(2.)**

This edition, though seeming to be complete, is almost identical with the preceding, and contains nothing more.

NĀYĀDHAMMAKAHĀ. *See* JÑĀTĀDHARMAKATHĀ.

NAZARI (ORESTE). *See* HITOPADEŚA. Lo Hitopadeça ... tradotto ... da O. Nazari. 1896. 8°. **14072. cc. 49.(2.)**

NEIL (ROBERT ALEXANDER). *See* SUTTAPIṬAKA.—*Khuddakanikāya*. [*Jātaka*.] The Jātaka, *etc.* (Vol. iii., translated by H. T. Francis ... and R. A. Neil.) 1895, *etc.* 8°. **14098. dd. 8.**

NEMCHAND. *See* NEMICHANDRA.

NEMICHANDRA, also called DEVENDRA GAṆĪ. *See* DEVENDRA GAṆĪ.

NEMICHANDRA BHAṆḌĀRĪ. उपदेशसिद्धान्तरत्नमाला *etc.* [Upadeśasiddhāntaratnamālā. A Prakrit poem in 161 stanzas, championing the Digambara Jain church against the unorthodox Śvetāmbaras, Raktāmbaras, *etc.* With a Hindi translation and commentary by Pannālāl of Sujangarh and Marathi translation and commentary by Jayachandra Sītārāma Śrāvaṇe.] pp. 80. नागपुर १८९८ [*Nagpur*, 1898.] 8°. **14100. b. 4.**

NEMICHANDRA NĀRĀYAṆA CHAVḌE. जैन धर्मामृत सार *etc.* [Jainadharmāmṛitasāra. A manual of the doctrines of Digambara Jains. Vol. I, comprising lists of the objects of Jain worship and study, verses upon them in Sanskrit and Prakrit, and explanations thereof, instructions, and verses in Hindi and Marathi, compiled by Nemichandra

Chavḍe. Vol. II, containing a Marathi catechetical exposition of the creed, illustrated from Sanskrit texts, by Nemichandra Sītārāma Bhāgavatakāra, with a Hindi version by Pannālāl of Sujangarh, and a Marathi guide to the ritual of laymen by Nemichandra Sītārāma.] 2 vols. पुणें नागपुर १८९४-१८९९ [*Poona, Nagpur,* 1894-1899.] 8°. **14137. d. 20.**

—— श्री सम्मेदशिखरजी विधान संगीत व संस्कृत पूजन *etc.* [Sammedaṣikharajī-vidhānasaṅgīta. Marathi lyrics celebrating the Sammedaṣikhara (or Sametṣikhar) at Hazaribagh, a spot held sacred by the Jains. Followed by Sammedaṣikharavidhānapūjana, Sanskrit poems on the same topic by Gaṅgādāsa disciple of Dharmachandra; with a few Sanskrit and Marathi hymns, *etc.*, appended.] pp. 62. नागपूर [*Nagpur,* 1900.] 12°. **14100. a. 22.**

NEMICHANDRA SĪTĀRĀMA BHĀGAVATAKĀRA. *See* NEMICHANDRA NĀRĀYAṆA CHAVḌE. जैन धर्मामृत सार *etc.* [Jainadharmāmṛitasāra. Vol. II, by Nemichandra Bhāgavatakāra.] [1894-1899.] 8°. **14137. d. 20.**

NEUMANN (KARL EUGEN). *See* SUTTAPIṬAKA.—*Selections.* Buddhistische Anthologie ... übersetzt von Dr. K. E. Neumann. 1892. 8°. **14098. c. 58.**

—— *See* SUTTAPIṬAKA. — *Khuddakanikāya.* [*Dhammapada.*] Der Wahrheitpfad . . . in den Versmaassen des Originals uebersetzt von K. E. Neumann. 1893. 8°. **14098. c. 61.**

—— *See* SUTTAPIṬAKA.—*Khuddakanikāya.* [*Theragāthā.*] Die Lieder der Mönche und Nonnen Gotamo Buddho's, aus den Theragāthā und Therīgāthā . . . übersetzt von K. E. Neumann. 1899. 8°. **14098. dd. 16.**

—— *See* SUTTAPIṬAKA.—*Majjhimanikāya.* Die Reden Gotamo Buddho's aus der Mittleren Sammlung . . . uebersetzt von K. E. Neumann. 1896, *etc.* 8°. **14098. dd. 13.**

—— [Another copy.] **4504. h.**

NGĀ SAUNG TWÈ. ငါးဆောင်တွဲ [Ngā saung twè. Comprising the Maṅgalasutta, Bābira-jayamaṅgalagāthā and Ajjhatta-j°, Ratanapañjara, and Namakāra. With Burmese versions, *etc.*] pp. 54. ရန်ကုန် ၁၂၅၂ [*Rangoon,* 1890.] 8°. **14098. ccc. 11.(1.)**

NIGAMĀNTAMAHĀDEṢIKA. *See* VEṄKAṬANĀTHA VEDĀNTĀCHĀRYA, called KAVITĀRKIKASIṂHA.

NĪLĀGĪTĀ. నీళాగీతా *etc.* [Nīlāgītā. A poem in 30 *pāṣurams*, relating to the cult of the river-goddess Āṇḍāl or Godādevī, translated from a Tamil *tiru-pāvai* hymn into Sanskrit by Govardhanam Raṅgāchārya. Followed by Raṅgarājaprābodhakī, a hymn to Raṅganātha in 10 *pāṣurams,* also from the Tamil. Edited by B. Veṅkaṭāchārya.] pp. 32. బెంగుళూరు ౧౮౯౮ [*Bangalore,* 1898.] 12°. **14076. a. 22.(2.)**

NĪLAKAMALA DEVA. *See* NĪLAKAMALA VIDYĀNIDHI BHAṬṬĀCHĀRYA.

NĪLAKAMALA VIDYĀNIDHI BHAṬṬĀCHĀRYA. *See* JĪMŪTAVĀHANA. জীমূতবাহনকৃত-দায়ভাগঃ *etc.* [Dāyabhāga. With commentary and Bengali translation. Edited by Nīlakamala.] [1898.] 8°. **14038. c. 49.**

—— *See* RAGHUNANDANA BHAṬṬĀCHĀRYA. উদ্বাহতত্ত্বং *etc.* [Udvāhatattva. With commentary. Edited with Bengali translation by Nīlakamala.] [1896.] 8°. **14033. bb. 42.**

—— *See* RĀMAṢAṄKARA DEVA. বৃহৎ-জাতকচন্দ্রিকা *etc.* [Bṛihaj-jātakachandrikā. Edited with Bengali translation by Nīlakamala.] [1892.] 8°. **14053. c. 63.**

—— *See* ṢRĪNIVĀSA ĀCHĀRYA, *Astrologer.* দীপিকা *etc.* [Ṣuddhidīpikā. With Bengali translation by Nīlakamala.] [1901.] 8°. **14053. ccc. 23.**

—— জ্যোতিষতত্ত্ববারিধিঃ *etc.* [Jyotishatattvavāridhi. A manual of astrology, compiled from Sanskrit texts, with notes, commentary, and Bengali translations of the text. Edited by Akshayakumāra Siddhāntaratna.] pp. ii. xii. 568. কলিকাতা ১৩০০ [*Calcutta,* 1894.] 8°. **14053. ccc. 1.**

NĪLAKAṆṬHA, *of Rājamaṅgalam.* മാതംഗലീലാ *etc.* [Mātaṅgalīlā. A metrical treatise on elephant-keeping. With Malayalam translation called Sārārthadīpikā by Pālōḷi Chōyi-vaidyar.] pp. i. i. 88. കോഴിക്കോട [*Calicut,*] 1904. 8°. **14053. ccc. 40.(2.)**

Said to be an epitome of Pālakāpya's work.

NĪLAKAṆṬHA, *son of Ananta, Jyotirvid. See* JAIMINI.—*Jyotishasūtra.* জৈমিনিসূত্রম্ *etc.* [Jaiminisūtra. With the commentary Subodhinī of Nīlakaṇṭha.] [1884.] 8°. **14053. dd. 6.**

NĪLAKAṆṬHA, *son of Govinda*. *See* MAHĀBHĀRATA.—*Entire Work*. মহাভারতম্ *etc.* [Mahābhārata. With the commentary Bhāratabhāvadīpa of Nīlakaṇṭha.] [1897, *etc.*] 8°. **14065. d. 38.**

—— *See* MAHĀBHĀRATA.—*Anuśāsanaparva*. Śiva Sahasranâma Stotra, with . . . Nīlakantha's commentary. English translation, *etc.* 1902. 8°. **14016. dd. 1.**

—— *See* MAHĀBHĀRATA.—*Śāntiparva*. మోక్ష ధర్మము *etc.* [Mokshadharma. With commentary of Nīlakaṇṭha.] 1887, *etc.* 8°. **14065. bbb. 8.**

—— भारतभावदीपः *etc.* [Bhāratabhāvadīpa. Nīlakaṇṭha's commentary on the Mahābhārata. Edited by Aghoranātha Vandyopādhyāya.] कलिकाता १८२१ [*Calcutta*, 1900, *etc.*] 8°. **14068. b. 18.**

In progress.

NĪLAKAṆṬHA, *son of Raṅganātha, Śaiva*. टीकाकारस्य उपोद्घात. [The preface of Nīlakaṇṭha's commentary Tilaka upon the Devībhāgavata.] pp. 18. [1902.] *See* PURĀṆAS.—*Devībhāgavatapurāṇa*. श्रीदेवीभागवत. [Devībhāgavata.] [1902, *etc.*] 8°. **14016. dd. 8.**

NĪLAKAṆṬHA DĪKSHITA, *son of Nārāyaṇa*. कलिविडम्बनम् । [Kaliviḍambana. 102 stanzas on the Kali age.] pp. 12. [1888.] *See* PERIODICAL PUBLICATIONS.—*Bombay*. ग्रन्थरत्नमाला *etc.* (Granth Ratna Málá, *etc.*) Vol. II, no. 2. 1887-[1892.] 8°. **14096. c. 8.(vol. 2.)**

—— नीलकंठदीक्षितकृतं कलिविडंबनं [Kaliviḍambana.] 1888. *See* LAGHUKĀVYĀNI. लघुकाव्यानि . . . Miscellaneous Poetical Pieces, *etc.* pp.231-238. 1888. [*Kāvyetihāsasaṅgraha, Vol. X, no.* 10, 12.] **14072. d. 37.(vol. 10.)**

NĪLAKAṆṬHA MAJUMDĀR. বিবাহ ও নারীধর্ম *etc.* [Vivāha o nārīdharma. A Bengali treatise on marriage and the relation of woman thereunder, illustrated from Sanskrit texts.] pp. iv. ii. 306. কলিকাতা [*Calcutta*, 1901.] 12°. **14125. e. 43.**

NĪLAKAṆṬHA MĪMĀṂSAKABHAṬṬA, *son of Śaṅkara*. *See* ĀDINĀRĀYAṆA PĀTRO. The Hindu Law. Annotated and illustrated by Sanskrit texts[, viz. the writings of Nīlakaṇṭha and others,] *etc.* 1899. 8°. **14039. c. 17.**

NĪLAKAṆṬHA MĪMĀṂSAKABHAṬṬA, *son of Śaṅkara (continued)*. स्वप्नाध्याय *etc.* [Svapnādhyāya. A tract on oneiromancy, forming the last 2 sections of the Āchāramayūkha. With Hindi version.] pp. 17. मुरादाबाद १८९९ [*Moradabad*, 1899.] 12°. **14053. b. 17.(7.)**

NĪLAKAṆṬHA MUNI, *disciple of Bāla Muni*. The Advîtha Párijátha of Nīlakandha Yemin. [Advaitapārijāta, a philosophical poem in 232 stanzas. Followed by 2 hymns, called Harishaḍratna and Śivapañcharatna, by the same author.] Published [with footnotes] by R. Shankar Wariyer. pp.30. *Bombay*, 1901. 16°. **14048. a. 14.(2.)**

In an appended stanza the writer names as his patron Janārdana of Madura.

NĪLAKAṆṬHA ŚARMĀ, *son of Viśveśvaranātha, of Aminabad, Lucknow*. *See* RĀMA, *son of Ananta*. मुहूर्तचिन्तामणिः *etc.* [Muhūrtachintāmaṇi. With Hindi translation and notes by Nīlakaṇṭha.] [1901.] 8°. **14053. ccc. 21.(1.)**

—— बृहज्ज्योतिस्सार सटीक *etc.* [Bṛihaj-jyotissāra. A compendium of astrology. With Hindi translation.] pp. i. x. 314. *Lucknow*, 1902. 8°. **14053. dd. 4.(1.)**

NĪLAKAṆṬHA ŚARMĀ, *Punnacheri-nambi*. *See* NĀRĀYAṆA BHAṬṬA. सुभद्राहरण॰ [Subhadrāharaṇa. Edited with glosses and notes by Nīlakaṇṭha, *etc.*] [1897.] 8°. **14072. cc. 60.(3.)**

—— *See* PURĀṆAS.—*Skandapurāṇa*. कोलापुरक्षेत्रमाहात्म्यं [Kolāpurakshetramāhātmya. Edited by Nīlakaṇṭha.] [1899.] 8°. **14016. c. 56.(2.)**

—— *See* ŚAṄKARA PĀRAŚAVA. उदयचरित्रम् *etc.* [Udayacharitra. Edited by Nīlakaṇṭha.] [1903.] 8°. **14072. c. 52.(2.)**

—— ॥ श्रीः ॥ ९९१ कोळत्वयवैकुम्भमासश्रविज्ञानस्वयावतीर्णघोषपुरमहाराज्ञी-चरित्रम् *etc.* [Ghoshapuramahārājñīcharitra. A biography of the Princess Cheruññāṭṭi Devi, mother of Prince Mānavikrama of Calicut. Followed by verses upon her death, by the latter and divers other poets.] pp. 68. पट्टाम्बि १९०२ [*Pattambi*, 1902.] 8°. **14072. d. 45.(3.)**

—— ईहापुरार्यास्तवः *etc.* [Īhāpurāryāstava. A hymn in 115 stanzas to Devī-Īhāpureśvarī.] pp. 40. पट्टांपि १९०० [*Pattambi*, 1900.] 16°. **14028. bb. 11.(10.)**

NĪLAKAṆṬHA ŚARMĀ, *Punnacheri-nambi* (*continued*). மண்டநம் [Maṇḍana, or Śṛiṅgāramañjarīm°. Studies in style, relative to the Śṛiṅgāramañjarī of Mānavikrama.] *See* MĀNAVIKRAMA, *Rājakumāra*. ஸ்ரீசாநவிக்ரமகவிராஜகுமாரேண ... ஆதூா: ஸேஹ்ருத்ஸா: *etc.* [Essays and poems.] [1890.] 8°. **14072. d. 35.**

—— த்ருதீயஸஹ்ருதயஸமாகம: *etc.* [Tṛitīya-sahṛidayasamāgama. A collection of stanzas composed by divers poets at the Sahṛidayasamāgama or third Congress of Wits held under the presidency of Rājakumāra Mānavikrama at Calicut in 1897. Edited by Nīlakaṇṭha and Vāsudeva.] pp. i. 66. பட்டாம்பி [*Pattambi*,] 1899. 8°. **14070. dd. 9.(2.)**

—— तुरीयसहृदयसमागमः *etc.* [Turīya-sahṛidayasamāgama. Stanzas composed at the fourth Congress of Wits held under the presidency of Mānavikrama at Calicut in 1900. Edited by Nīlakaṇṭha and Vāsudeva.] pp. iv. 72. पट्टाम्बि १९०० [*Pattambi*, 1900.] 8°. **14072. d. 45.(1.)**

NĪLAKAṆṬHA ŚIVĀCHĀRYA. *See* ŚRĪKAṆṬHA ŚIVĀCHĀRYA.

NĪLAMAṆI VIDYĀLAṄKĀRA BHAṬṬĀCHĀRYA. উদ্ভট কবিতা-কৌমুদী *etc.* [Udbhaṭakavitākaumudī. Select Sanskrit verses, with Bengali translation and additional matter.] pt. 1. pp. ii. 70, ii. কলিকাতা ১২৯৭ [*Calcutta*, 1890.] 8°. **14085. c. 43.**

NIMBĀDITYA. *See* NIMBĀRKA.

NIMBĀRKA, also known as NIYAMĀNANDA. *See* MAṄGALADĀSA. निम्बार्क स्तोत्रम् *etc.* [Nimbārkastotra. Stanzas in adoration of Nimbārka.] [1901.] *obl.* 12°. **14033. a. 19.(6.)**

—— श्रीभगवन्नियमानन्दविरचित । वेदान्तकामधेनु *etc.* [Vedāntakāmadhenu, or Daṣaślokī. Ten stanzas by Nimbārka, expounding his theory of Vaishṇava Vedānta. Edited with a Hindi commentary styled Sārārthadarṣikā by Kiṣoradāsa of Brindaban.] pp. 31. श्रीवृन्दावन १९५९ [*Brindaban*, 1903.] 8°. **14049. a. 7.(2.)**

NIRBHAYARĀMA BHAṬṬA. ॥ तत्र व्रतोत्सवपर्वादिनिर्णयः ॥ [Vratotsavaparvādinirṇaya. A tract on the dates of the festivals kept by the sect of Vallabhāchārya.] *See* GOVARDHANADĀSA LAKSHMĪDĀSA. बृहत्स्तोत्रसरित्सागर *etc.* [Bṛihat-stotrasaritsāgara.] Vol. ii. [1892.] 12°. **14033. a. 27.(vol. 2.)**

NIRVĀṆAKĀṆḌA. निर्वाणकाण्ड भाषा और प्राकृत दोनों [Nirvāṇakāṇḍa. A Jain Prakrit poem of 27 stanzas, on the release from life of the Jain saints, *etc.* Preceded by a Hindi metrical version.] pp. 15. लखनऊ १९०१ [*Lucknow*, 1901.] 12°. **14100. a. 21.(4.)**

NIRVĀṆASVARŪPA SŪRI. *See* SVARŪPA SŪRI.

NIṢCHALA DĀSA. ॥ श्रीविचारसागर . . . तथा . . . श्रीवृत्तिरत्नावलि *etc.* [Vichārasāgara. A Hindi work on Vedānta, annotated by Pītāmbara Purushottama. Followed by Vṛittiratnāvali, an abstract of Pītāmbara's Hindi commentary on Niṣchala Dāsa's Vṛittiprabhākara, and the 10th *prakaraṇa* of Sāyaṇa's Pañchadaṣī with the commentary of Rāmakṛishṇa and Hindi notes by Pītāmbara. Edited with preface by Ṡāliḣ Muḣammad. Fourth edition.] pp. xii. xxxiv. 378, 673-690; 1 *plate*. मुंबई १९०० [*Bombay*, 1900.] 8°. **14154. ff. 1.**

NĪTIPRAKĀṢIKĀ. नीतिप्रकाशिका Nītiprakāśikā. [A treatise on polity, with especial reference to the military art.] Edited [with introduction] by Gustav Oppert. pp. i. 83. *Madras*, 1882. 8°. **14038. c. 28.(2.)**

The work is ascribed to Vaiṣampāyana.

NĪTISĀRA. നീതിസാരപുസ്തകം [Nītisāra. 100 stanzas on moral topics. With a Malayalam translation.] pp. 42, *lith.* കൊച്ചിയിൽ ൧൦൩൮ [*Cochin*, 1863.] 8°. **14072. b. 26.(1.)**

NITYABODHA BHAṬṬĀCHĀRYA, *son of Jīvānanda Vidyāsāgara*. *See* NARAHARI. राजनिघण्टुः *etc.* (Rajanighantu . . . Edited . . . with . . . modifications and notes . . . by Ashu Bodha . . . and Nitya Bodha, *etc.*) [1899.] 8°. **14043. cc. 15.**

NITYAKARMA. *See* BODHĀNANDA GIRI. ಸರ್ವ ಶಾಸ್ತ್ರ ಸಾರಸಂಗ್ರಹ [Sarvaṣāstrasārasaṅgraha.] [1900.] 4°. **14154. gg. 3.**

—— —— [Second edition.] [1902.] 4°. **14154. gg. 5.**

NITYAKARMA (*continued*). *See* CHATURTHĪLĀLA, *Vaidya.* नित्यकर्मप्रयोगमाला *etc.* [Nityakarmaprayogamālā.] [1898.] 12°. **14028. b. 91.**

—— *See* DIVĀKARA DĀJĪ SĀDHLE. ॥ अथ कृत्यदिवाकरः *etc.* [Kṛityadivākara.] [1899.] *obl.* 8°. **14028. dd. 2.(2.)**

—— *See* GOVINDĀNANDA KAVIKAṄKAṆA BHAṬṬĀCHĀRYA. Varṣa Kriyā Kaumudī. [1902.] 8°. [*Bibliotheca Indica.*] **14002. a. (vol. 149.)**

—— *See* HARICHARAṆA MAJUMDĀR. পুরোহিত-দর্পণ *etc.* [Purohitadarpaṇa.] [1899.] 8°. **14028. d. 72.**

—— *See* JĪVANĀCHĀRYA VALLABHA. ॥ शुक्ल यजुर्वेदीय ॥ ॥ वैष्णवद्विजाह्निकम् *etc.* [Vaishṇavadvijāhnika.] [1901.] 8°. **14154. ee. 12.**

—— *See* NĀGARARĀMA ŚARMĀ. कर्म्मदर्पणम् *etc.* [Karmadarpaṇa.] [1899.] 8°. **14028. d. 56.(3.)**

—— *See* NARENDRAKṚISHṆA ŚIROMAṆI. ধর্ম্ম-জীবন *etc.* [Dharmajīvana.] [1899.] 12°. **14028. bb. 2.**

—— *See* RĀMADATTA, *son of Bhavadeva.* वार्षिकव्रतपद्धतिः *etc.* [Vārshikavratapaddhati.] [1899.] *obl.* 4°. **14033. c. 42.**

—— *See* RĀMAKṚISHṆA PAṆḌITA, *Writer on Dharma.* ನಿತ್ಯಕರ್ಮ ಚಂದ್ರಿಕೆ *etc.* [Nityakarmachandrike.] [1901, *etc.*] 8°. **14033. aa. 33.**

—— [For the Sandhyāvandana or Sandhyāvidhi:] *See* SANDHYĀVANDANA.

—— *See* VĀSUDEVA BHAṬṬĀCHĀRYA. ஆஹ்நிகாம்ருதம் [Āhnikāmṛita.] 1900. 8°. [*Paramātmikopanishad.*] **14033. bbb. 13.**

—— *See* VIDYĀKARA VĀJAPEYĪ. नित्याचारपद्धतिः। Nityācāra-paddhatiḥ, *etc.* 1901, *etc.* 8°. [*Bibliotheca Indica.*] **14002. a. (vol. 151.)**

—— *See* VIHĀRILĀLA, *Kāśmīrī.* यजुर्वेदीयनित्यकर्म्मपद्धतिः *etc.* [Yajurvedīya-nityakarmapaddhati.] [1900.] 8°. **14033. aa. 16.**

—— *See* VIPINACHANDRA KĀVYARATNA. আর্য্যাহ্নিকাচার কৌমুদী *etc.* [Āryāhnikāchārakaumudī.] [1901.] 8°. **14123. f. 49.(3.)**

NITYAKARMA (*continued*). ஆஹ்நிகம் ஸ்ராத்தப்ரயோகமு *etc.* [Āhnika. The daily ritual of the Vaḍagalai Vaishṇavas. Followed by a Śrāddhaprayoga, or ritual for *śrāddhas*, of the same sect. Edited by Tirukuḍandai Deśika.] pp. 128. காஞ்சீ [*Conjevaram,*] 1893. 12°. **14028. b. 82.(3.)**

—— নিত্য কর্ম্মানুষ্ঠান পদ্ধতি *etc.* [Nityakarmānushṭhānapaddhati. A manual of daily ritual, with Bengali rubrics, interpretations, footnotes, *etc.* Followed by a compendium of rules for conduct, called Karmalochana, and an excursus on Tantric worship.] pp. x. ii. 408. কলিকাতা ১৩০৫ [*Calcutta,* 1898.] 8°. **14028. bb. 7.**

—— ॥ अथ काण्वनित्यविधिः प्रारभ्यते ॥ [Kāṇvanityavidhi. The encyclical ritual according to the usage of the Kāṇvas of the White Yajurveda.] ff. 55. मोहमय्यां १८२० [*Bombay,* 1898.] *obl.* 8°. **14028. d. 59.(10.)**

—— யஜுர்வேதாஹ்நிகம் ॥ यजुर्वेदाह्निकम् *etc.* [Yajurvedāhnika. A manual of daily religious rites for Taittirīya Yajurvedīs.] pp. i. 70. சென்னபட்டணம் [*Madras,*] 1899. 12°. **14028. b. 108.**

—— The Nityakarmaprakáshiká. The daily routine of the Aryas. By Pandita Kulanidhi Sharma of Nepal . . . Corrected and enlarged by Pandita Murali Dhara Jhá. (नित्यकर्मप्रकाशिका) pp. i. iv. 81. *Benares,* 1902. 8°. **14033. bbb. 15.(2.)**

—— नित्यकर्मविधिः *etc.* [Nityakarmavidhi. Encyclical rites. Compiled by Nityānanda Śāstrī.] pp. 46. १९५८ [*Bombay,* 1902.] 12°. **14033. a. 45.(4.)**

—— আহ্নিককৃত্যম্। বিশুদ্ধ-নিত্যকর্ম *etc.* [Āhnikakṛitya. Encyclical rites. Edited with Bengali introduction, translation, and notes by Śyāmācharaṇa Kaviratna. Fifth edition.] pp. 154. কলিকাতা ১৩০৮ [*Calcutta,* 1902.] 12°. **14033. a. 49**

—— پتری ترپن الخ [Pitṛitarpaṇa. A ritual of daily worship due to the gods, sages, and ancestors, comprising Sanskrit *mantras* with their transliteration into the Persian script and

Urdu rubrics and notes. Compiled by Harasukha Rāya.] pp. 40, *lith.* امرتسر ۱۹۰۰ [*Amritsar*, 1900.] 16°. **14028. a. 27.(2.)**

—— सामवेदीय पञ्चयज्ञ *etc.* [Sāmavedīya-pañcha-yajña. The Sāmavedī ritual for the "Five Sacrifices." Preceded by the Sandhyāvidhi. The *mantras* according to Gobhila's Sūtra, with Hindi rubrics.] pp. 31. कानपुर १९०२ [*Cawnpore*, 1902.] 16°. **14028. a. 31.**

NITYĀNANDA MUNI, *disciple of Sahajānanda.* See SAHAJĀNANDA SVĀMĪ. शिक्षापत्री. [Śikshāpatrī. With Gujarati *ṭīkā* by Nityānanda.] [1888.] 12°. [*Roz-pāṭha.*] **14144. c. 3.**

NITYĀNANDA PANTA. *See* JAIMINI.—*Mīmāṃsā-sūtra.* जैमिनिसूत्रवृत्तिः *etc.* [Mīmāṃsāsūtra. With commentary by Rāmeṣvara. Edited by Nityānanda.] 1899. 8°. [*The Pandit.*] **14096. d. 6. (vol. 17-21.)**

NITYĀNANDA SARASVATĪ. वेदान्तग्रन्थपञ्चकम् *etc.* [Vedāntagranthapañchaka. Five Vedānta tracts, of which the first four are attributed to Ṣankara, viz. Vākyasudhā, with commentary; the commentary Vedāntasiddhāntadīpikā upon the Hastāmalakastotra, together with the latter text; Nirvāṇapañchaka, with the *vivṛiti* of Nityānanda Sarasvatī; Manīshāpañchaka, with *ṭīkā* of Bālagopālendra; and Brahmavidāṣīrvādapaddhati, ascribed to Sāyaṇa. Edited by Nityānanda Sarasvatī.] pp. 120. बम्बई १८९३ [*Bombay*, 1891.] 12°. **14048. b. 15.(2.)**

NITYĀNANDA ṢĀSTRĪ, *son of Mādhavakāka, Kaṣmīrī.* *See* NITYAKARMA. नित्यकर्मविधिः *etc.* [Nityakarmavidhi. Compiled by Nityānanda.] [1902.] 12°. **14033. a. 45.(4.)**

NITYĀNANDĀṢRAMA, *disciple of Purushottamāṣrama.* *See* UPANISHADS.—*Separate Upanishads.* बृहदारण्यकोपनिषन्मिताक्षरा *etc.* [Bṛihadāraṇyakopanishad. With the commentary Mitāksharā of Nityānandāṣrama.] [1896.] 8°. **14003. ccc. (no. 31.)**

NITYANĀTHA YOGEṢVARA. [For editions of the Kāmaratna sometimes ascribed to this author:] *See* NĀGA BHAṬṬA.

NITYĀNUSANDHĀNA. अथ नित्यानुसन्धान सङ्ग्रहः प्रारभ्यते [Nityānusandhānasangraha. A breviary of devotions for Rāmānujī Vaishṇavas, consisting chiefly of professions of faith in the heads of the sect in their order of succession.] pp. 31. [*Bettia*, 1892.] *obl.* 16°. **14028. b. 79.**

NIYAMĀNANDA. *See* NIMBĀRKA.

NIYOGANIRṆAYA. नियोग-निर्णय *etc.* [Niyoga-nirṇaya. A digest of texts from Smṛiti, Epic, and Puranic literature on the second marriage of widows, with Hindi translation, notes, *etc.*] pp. 59. मेरठ १९५६ [*Meerut*, 1899.] 12°. **14058. a. 14.(2.)**

NOBIN CHANDRA. *See* NAVĪNACHANDRA.

NṚIHARI. *See* NARAHARI.

NṚISIṂHA BHĀGAVATA, *Ghṛitasthānam.* *See* NĀRĀYAṆA TĪRTHA. ஸ்ரீக்ருஷ்ணலீலாதரங்கிணீ *etc.* [Kṛishṇalīlātaranginī. Edited by Nṛisiṃha.] 1901. 8°. **14072. ccc. 30.**

—— *See* VEṄKAṬEṢĀRYA, *Ṣrīdhara.* ஸ்ரீதரஸ்துதிமணிமாலா *etc.* [Ṣrīdharastutimaṇimālā. Edited by Nṛisiṃha.] 1895. 8°. **14076. c. 71.**

NṚISIṂHA BHĀRATĪ, *Pontiff of Sringeri.* *Begin.* ஸ்ரீமதோ ஸ்ரீஜகத்குரு ஸ்வாமிகளவர்கள் . . . ஆஜ்ஞா ஸ்ரீசங்கராசார்ய [Pastoral letters on the religious and legal relations of the brahmans holding the Shaṇṇavatī *agrahāram* to the Sringeri monastery, *etc.*, the first portion being a Sanskrit letter addressed to them in 1854 by Nṛisiṃha, and the remainder partly in Sanskrit and partly in Tamil.] pp. 20. ரக்தாக்ஷி [1865.] 16°. **14058. a. 5.(1.)**

NṚISIṂHĀCHĀRYA SVĀMĪ, *Muḍumba.* जयसिंहाश्वमेधीयम् नाम नाटकम् [Jayasiṃhāṣvamedhīya. A historical drama in 7 acts, composed for the festivities held by Raja Veṅkaṭa Jaggā Rāya on the occasion of the Durbar at Delhi celebrating the coronation of King Edward VII.] pp. 75. वैशाखपट्टण० [*Vizagapatam*,] 1902. 8°. **14080. d. 22.(2.)**

Printed on blue-gray paper.

NṚISIṂHA DAIVAJÑA, *Rājñī - Mahāgnichit.* చిత్సూర్యాలోకనాటకము *etc.* [Chitsūryāloka. An allegorical drama, in 5 acts. Preceded by a short metrical account of the author's family.] pp. 39. *Vizianagram,* 1894. 8°. **14079. b. 42.**

NṚISIṂHA DEVA ṢARMĀ, *of Sialkot. See* ṢAṄKARA ĀCHĀRYA.—*Philosophical Poems, etc.* विवेकचूडामणि: *etc.* [Vivekachūḍāmaṇi. With Hindi commentary. Edited by Nṛisiṃha Deva.] [1902.] 8°. **14049. a. 6.**

NṚISIṂHALĀLAJĪ MAHĀRĀJA, *Gosvāmī. See* VALLABHĀCHĀRYA. अौन्तःकरणप्रबोधको । टीका *etc.* [Antaḥkaraṇaprabodha. With Braj commentary by Nṛisiṃhalālajī.] [1900.] 8°. **14028. d. 35.(4.)**

NṚISIṂHA MIṢRA, *Vajapeyī.* ପାର୍ବଣ ଶ୍ରାଦ୍ଧକାରିକା *etc.* [Pārvaṇaṣrāddhakārikā. Memorial verses on the periodical rites of the *ṣrāddha,* with Oriya translation and notes. Compiled from the work of Nṛisiṃha and edited by Rāmachandra Chatushpāṭhī and Rudranārāyaṇa Shaḍaṅgī.] pp. 30. *Balasore,* 1900. 12°. **14028. b. 61.(6.)**

NṚISIṂHARĀMA MUKHOPĀDHYĀYA. साहित्यरत्नाकर: *etc.* [Sāhityaratnākara. Four excerpts selected as models of style for beginners, viz. (1) the introduction and book i. of the Hitopadeṣa ; (2) extracts from the Rāmāyaṇa, Ayodhyākāṇḍa xii.-xiv., xvii.-xx. ; (3) Hariṣchandropākhyāna, from the Mārkaṇḍeyapurāṇa ; (4) Dhruvopākhyāna, from the Vishṇupurāṇa. Edited with notes by Nṛisiṃharāma. Second edition.] pp. ii. i. 76. कलिकाता [*Calcutta,*] 1898. 12°. **14065. b. 18.**

NṚISIṂHA SARASVATĪ, *disciple of Krishṇānanda. See* SADĀNANDA YOGĪNDRA. The Vedântasâra . . . with the commentaries[, called respectively Subodhinī and Vidvanmanorañjanī,] of Nṛisiṃhasarasvatî and Râmatîrtha, *etc.* 1894. 8°. **14048. dd. 15.**

—— *See* SADĀNANDA YOGĪNDRA. সটীক . . . বেদান্তসার *etc.* [Vedāntasāra. With commentary of Nṛisiṃha.] [1903.] 12°. **14048. b. 41.**

NṚISIṂHA SARASVATĪ TĪRTHA. ವೇದಾನ್ತಡಿಣ್ಡಿಮಃ *etc.* [Vedāntaḍiṇḍima. A tract on monist philosophy in 91 stanzas. Edited by Ellambhaṭṭa Sitārāma Ṣastrī.] pp. 8. ಬೆಂಗಳೂರು ೧೮೯೭ [*Bangalore,* 1897.] 8°. **14048. cc. 9.(2.)**

NṚISIṂHA ṢARMĀ, *Brahmachārī. See* PARĀṢARA. [*Smṛiti.*] श्रीपराशरसंहिता *etc.* [Parāṣarasaṃhitā. With Gujarati translation by Nṛisiṃha.] [1899.] 8°. **14038. c. 48.**

NṚISIṂHA ṢĀSTRĪ, *Kānkānphallī, disciple of Tātārya. See* TRIVIKRAMA DEVA. ప్రాకృతశబ్దప్రదీపిక [Prākṛitaṣabdapradīpikā. Trivikrama's aphorisms, with Nṛisiṃha's commentary.] [1890.] 8°. [*Sambhurahasya.*] **14053. ccc. 31.**

—— *See* TRIVIKRAMA DEVA. प्राकृतशब्दप्रदीपिका । [Prākṛitaṣabdapradīpikā. With commentary by Nṛisiṃha.] 1895, *etc.* 8°. [*Grandha Pradarsani.*] **14003. c. 2.(9.)**

NṚISIṂHĀṢRAMA, *disciple of Jagannāthāṣrama. See* PADMAPĀDA. The Pañchapâdikâ, *etc.* (Part II. The Pañchapâdikâvivaraṇa . . . With extracts from the . . . Bhâvaprakâśikâ [of Nṛisiṃhāṣrama,] *etc.*) 1891-1892. 8°. **14048. dd. 3.(vol. 2.)**

—— अथ सटीकभेदधिक्कारः प्रारभ्यते ॥ [Bhedadhikkāra. A Vedantic refutation of the Nyāya psychology. With the commentary Bhedadhikkārasatkriyā of Nārāyaṇāṣrama.] ff. 65. बनारस [*Benares,* 1891.] *obl.* 4°. **14048. f. 22.**

NṚITYAGOPĀLA KAVIRATNA. दर्पशातनम् *etc.* [Darpaṣātana. A drama in five acts, founded on the story of Paraṣurāma.] pp. 86. कलिकाता [*Calcutta,* 1893.] 8°. **14079. c. 57.(3.)**

—— रामावदानम् *etc.* [Rāmāvadāna. A drama in five acts, on the legend of Rāma.] pp. 66. कलिकाता° १८९२ [*Calcutta,* 1892.] 8°. **14079. c. 57.(2.)**

NUWWĀB-KHĀN-KHĀNĀN. *See* NAWĀB-KHĀN-KHĀNĀN.

NYĀYABINDU. The Nyayabindutika of Dharmottaracharya[, a commentary on the Nyāyabindu, a short handbook of Buddhist logic] : to which is added the Nyayabindu. Edited by Peter Peterson. (न्यायबिन्दुटीका ।) pp. ix. 134. 1889. *See* ACADEMIES, *etc.*—Calcutta.—*Asiatic Society of Bengal.* Bibliotheca Indica. New Series. [Vol. 128.] 1848, *etc.* 8°. **14002. a.(vol. 128.)**

The Nyāyabindu is probably the work of Dharmakīrti.

NYĀYAVĀCHASPATI. *See* RUDRA NYĀYAVĀCHASPATI.

NYĀYAVĀGĪṢA, *son of Vidyānidhi.* *See* RĀMACHANDRA NYĀYAVĀGĪṢA.

O . . . L . . . SARMA. *See* ṢARMĀ (O. L.).

OBHĀSĀLAṄKĀRĀBHIDDHAJA, known as MYITKWE HSAYA. *See* KACHCHĀYANA.—*Kachchāyanappakaraṇa.* သဒ္ဒါကြီးဂဏ္ဌိကျမ်း *etc.* [Saddā-kyī-gaṇṭhi. Followed by the Saddā-lûn, containing the aphorisms with Obhāsālaṅkāra's Burmese commentary.] 1900. 8°. **14098. dd. 21.**

ODAYADEVA. *See* VĀDĪBHASIṂHA SŪRI.

OERTEL (HANNS). *See* BRĀHMAṆAS.—*Talavakārabrāhmaṇa.* The Jāiminīya or Talavakāra Upaniṣad Brāhmaṇa: text, translation, and notes. By H. Oertel. 1894. 8°. [*Journal of the American Oriental Society.*] **Ac. 8824.(vol. 16.)**

—— *See* BRĀHMAṆAS. — *Talavakārabrāhmaṇa.* Extracts from the Jāiminīya-Brāhmaṇa and Upanishad-Brāhmaṇa . . . [Edited and translated] by Dr. H. Oertel. 1893. 8°. [*Journal of the American Oriental Society.*] **Ac. 8824.(vol. 15.)**

—— Contributions from the Jāiminīya Brāhmaṇa to the history of the Brāhmaṇa literature, *etc.* 1897-1898. *See* ACADEMIES, *etc.*—Boston, *Mass.*—*American Oriental Society.* Journal, *etc.* Vols. xviii.-xix. 1849, *etc.* 8°. **Ac. 8824.(vol. 18, 19.)**

OLCOTT (HENRY STEELE). *See* SUTTAPIṬAKA.—*Selections.* අවවාදරත්නසංග්‍රහව *etc.* [Avavādaratnasaṅgrahava. The "Golden Rules of Buddhism," compiled by H. S. Olcott.] 1891. 12°. **14098. a. 32.(3.)**

—— *See* SUTTAPIṬAKA.—*Selections.* The Golden Rules of Buddhism . . . By H. S. Olcott. [In English.] 1902. 12°. **14098. a. 32.(4.)**

OLDENBERG (HERMANN). *See* VEDAS.—Ṛigveda.—*Selections of Hymns and Verses.* Vedic Hymns, *etc.* (Translated by H. Oldenberg. Part ii., *etc.*) 1897. 8°. [*Sacred Books of the East.*] **2003. b. (vol. 46.)**

OLDENBURG (SERGYEI). Буддійскій Сборникъ „Гирлянда Джатакъ" и Замѣтки о Джатакахъ. pp. 59. Санктпетербургъ, 1892. 8°. **4504. h. 15.**

—— Dr. Serge D'Oldenburg "On the Buddhist Jātakas." [Translated] by H. Wenzel. (A detailed account of the Jātaka Mālā, then comparative tables of the Jātaka Mālā and the Cariyapīṭaka, and an account of . . . the *Sutasoma* Jātaka . . . in the Bhadrakalpāvadāna.) 1893. *See* ACADEMIES, *etc.*—London.—*Royal Asiatic Society of Great Britain and Ireland.* The Journal . . . 1893. pp. 301-356. 1834, *etc.* 8°. **Ac. 8820/3 & 2098. a, b.**

OMAN (JOHN CAMPBELL). Struggles in the Dawn. The stories of the great Indian epics, the Ramayana and Mahabharata, *etc.* pp. vi. 270. *Lahore,* 1893. 8°. **11824. ccc. 43.**

—— The Great Indian Epics. The stories of the Ramayana and the Mahabharata [in an English epitome,] *etc.* pp. vi. i. 231; 5 *plates. London, Edinburgh* [printed], 1894. 8°. **011850. g. 39.**

—— [Second edition.] pp. x. i. 256; 5 *plates. London,* 1899. 8°. **2504. k. 18.**

Forms part of Bohn's Standard Library.

O-MI-TO-KING. *See* SUKHĀVATĪVYŪHA.

OPPERT (GUSTAV). *See* NĪTIPRAKĀṢIKĀ. नीतिप्रकाशिका Nītiprakāśikā. Edited [with introduction] by G. Oppert. 1882. 8°. **14038. c. 28.(2.)**

—— *See* ṢĀKAṬĀYANA. प्रक्रियासंग्रहसहितं शाकटायनव्याकरणम्. The Grammar of Śākaṭāyana, with the . . . commentary of Abhayacandrasūri. Published . . . by G. Oppert. 1892. 8°. **14093. b. 30.**

—— *See* YĀDAVAPRAKĀṢA. वैजयन्ती The Vaijayantī . . . edited by G. Oppert. 1893. 8°. **14093. b. 32.**

ORIENTAL TRANSLATION FUND. *See* ACADEMIES, *etc.*—*London.*

OXFORD ANECDOTA. Anecdota Oxoniensia . . . Aryan Series. *Oxford,* 1881, *etc.* 4°. **12204. f. 8.**

In progress. Works that have recently appeared in this series are to be found under the headings:—

Vol. 1, Pt. 7. Aṣvaghosha.
„ 1, „ 8. Āpastamba.—*Gṛihyasūtra.*

OZÁ (G. U.). *See* GAURĪŚAṄKARA UDAYAŚAṄKARA OJHĀ.

PĀDAPADMA. *See* PADMAPĀDA.

PĀDHYE (HAṆMANTA KRISHṆA). *See* HAṆMANTA KRISHṆA ŚĀSTRĪ PĀDHYE.

PAḌIKAMAṆA-SŪTRA. *See* PRATIKRAMAṆASŪTRA.

PADMAGUPTA, also called **PARIMALA.** The Navasâhasâṅka Charita of Padmagupta alias Parimala, [a heroic poem written about A.D. 1010 in honour of the Paramāra King Sindhurāja of Malwa.] Part I. Containing the preface, the text with various readings, and an index to the ślôkas. Edited by Pandit Vâmana Shâstrî Islâmpurkar. (नवसाहसाङ्कचरितम् ।) *Bombay*, 1895, *etc.* 8°. **14070. dd. 4.**

In progress. Forms no. liii. *of the* Bombay Sanskrit Series.

PADMANĀBHADATTA. সুপদ্মব্যাকরণম্ *etc.* [Supadmavyākaraṇa. A work on Sanskrit grammar, based on Pāṇini. With a gloss by Trailokyanātha Kāvyatīrtha Vidyānidhi. Second edition.] pp. ii. 435. কলিকাতা ১৩০৭ [*Calcutta*, 1901.] 8°. **14090. c. 43.**

—— Supadma Vivaran Panjika. [A gloss upon the Supadma grammar.] Edited [*i.e.* composed] by Mahamahopadhyaya Padmanava Dutt. Commented and published by Pandit Trailokya Nath Bhattacharya, Bidyanidhi Kabyatirtha. সুপদ্মবিবরণপাঞ্জিকা *etc.* pp. ii. 321. কলিকাতা [*Calcutta*, 1903.] 8°. **14092. b. 45.(2.)**

—— उणादिवृत्तिः [Uṇādivṛitti. Aphorisms, with commentary, upon the *uṇādi* affixes, in 2 *pādas*.] 1897-1898. *See* PERIODICAL PUBLICATIONS.—*Calcutta.* विद्योदयः *etc.* [Vidyodaya.] Vol. xxvi—xxvii. 1874, *etc.* 8°. **14096. cc. (vol. 26, 27.)**

PADMANANDĪ DEVA. एकत्वसप्ततिः [Ekatvasaptati. Verses on Jain philosophy.] [1893-1894.] *See* PADMARĀJA PAṆḌITA, *son of Brahmasūri.* काव्याम्बुधि *etc.* [Kāvyāmbudhi.] pts. 1-6. [1893-1896.] 8°. **14028. c. 64.**

Not completed.

PADMAPĀDA, *son of Vimala,* also called SANANDANA. The Pañchapâdikâ of Padmapâda. [A commentary on Śaṅkara's Śārīrakabhāshya I. i. 1-4.] Edited by Râmaśâstrî Bhâgavatâchârya. (Part II. The Pañchapâdikâvivaraṇa [or commentary on the Pañchapādikā,] of Prakâśâtman. With extracts from the [supercommentaries] Tattvadîpana [of Akhaṇḍānanda] and Bhâvaprakâśikâ [of Nṛisiṃhāśrama,] *etc.*) (पञ्चपादिका ।) 2 vols. *Benares*, 1891-1892. 8°. **14048. dd. 3.(vol. 2.)**

Forms vol. 2 *of the* Vizianagram Sanskrit Series.

—— The Pañcapādikā . . . Translated by Arthur Venis. 1901, *etc.* *See* PERIODICAL PUBLICATIONS.—*Benares.* The Pandit, *etc.* New Series. Vol. XXIII, *etc.* 1896, *etc.* 8°. **14096. d. 6.(vol. 23, etc.)**

In progress? This translation was originally destined for publication in the Vizianagram Sanskrit Series.

—— *See* AKHAṆḌĀNANDA, *disciple of Akhaṇḍānubhūti.* तत्त्वदीपनम् . . . Tattvadîpana, a commentary on Panchapádikávivaraṇa, *etc.* 1901, *etc.* 8°. **14049. a. 3.**

—— *See* RĀMĀNANDA SARASVATĪ, *disciple of Govindānanda.* विवरणोपन्यासः . . . Vivaraṇopanyâsa, *etc.* 1901. 8°. **14048. cc. 37.**

PADMARĀJA PAṆḌITA, *son of Brahmasūri.* *See* AKALAṄKA KAVI. ಅಕಲಂಕಾಷ್ಟಕ *etc.* [Akalaṅkāshṭaka. Edited with Canarese commentary by Padmarāja.] [1893.] 8°. **14100. b. 3.(2.)**

—— *See* GUṆABHADRA ĀCHĀRYA. ಪಾರ್ಶ್ವನಾಥಸ್ವಾಮಿ ಪುರಾಣಂ *etc.* [Pārṣvanāthasvāmipurāṇa. Edited with Canarese version by Padmarāja.] [1893.] 8°. **14100. b. 3.(1.)**

—— *See* JINASENA ĀCHĀRYA. ಶ್ರೀ . . . ಮಹಾಪುರಾಣಂ *etc.* [Mahāpurāṇa. Edited with Canarese commentary by Padmarāja.] [1896, *etc.*] 4°. **14100. e. 6.**

—— *See* KRIYĀPUSTAKA. ಕ್ರಿಯಾಪುಸ್ತಕ *etc.* [Kriyāpustaka. Edited by Padmarāja.] [1896.] 8°. **14100. b. 3.(5.)**

—— *See* SOMAPRABHA ĀCHĀRYA. ಸೂಕ್ತಿ ಮುಕ್ತಾವಲಿ *etc.* [Sūktimuktāvali. Edited with Canarese glosses and paraphrases by Padmarāja.] [1892.] 8°. **14028. d. 47.**

—— *See* UDAYARĀGA-DEVARAPADA. ಉದಯರಾಗ-ದೇವರಪದ *etc.* [Udayarāga-devarapada. Edited by Padmarāja.] [1894.] 8°. **14100. b. 3.(3.)**

PADMARĀJA PAṆḌITA, *son of Brahmasūri (continued).* The Budhajana Manoranjani. ಬುಧಜನ-ಮನೋರಂಜನೀ. [A collection of Sanskrit and Canarese writings bearing on the Jain religion.] pts. 1-15. ಬೆಂಗಳೂರು ೧೮೯೦-೧೮೯೪ [*Bangalore,* 1890-1894.] 8°.

14096. c. 11.

—— काव्याम्बुधिः *etc.* [Kāvyāmbudhi. A magazine for the publication of works of Jain Sanskrit literature. Edited by Padmarāja.] pts. 1-7. *Bangalore,* १८९३-१८९६ [1893-1896.] 8°.

14028. c. 64.

No further numbers have been registered.

—— ಮಹಿಸೂರು ಶಾಂತೀಶ್ವರ ಪ್ರತಿಷ್ಠಾ ನಾಟಕವು *etc.* [Mahisūru-ṣāntīṣvara-pratishṭhā-nātaka. A play in Sanskrit and Canarese on the consecration of the image of the Jain *tīrthaṅkara* Ṣāntīṣvara at Mysore in 1897.] pp. 20. ಬೆಂಗಳೂರು ೧೮೯೭ [*Bangalore,* 1897.] 8°.

14100. b. 3.(6.)

—— ಶ್ರೀಮನ್ಮಹಾರಾಜಾಧಿರಾಜ ಶ್ರೀ ಕೃಷ್ಣರಾಜ ಒಡೆಯರವರ ಸೌ॥ ವಾನದ ಪ್ರತಾಪಕುಮಾರೀ ಬಾಯಿ ಮಹಾದೇವಿಯವರ ಪರಿಣಯವು *etc.* [Srīman-mahārājādhirāja - ṣrīkrishṇarājavaḍeyaravara - saubhāgyavatī-vānada-pratāpakumārībāyi-mahādeviyavara-pariṇayavu. A Sanskrit poem, with Canarese translation, upon the wedding of the Maharaja of Mysore with the Princess Pratāpakumārī Bāi, and containing an account of the kings and kingdom of Mysore.] pp. ii. 24. ಚಾಮರಾಜ ನಗರ ೧೯೦೦ [*Mysore,* 1900.] 8°. **14076. c. 76.**

PADMAVIJAYA GAṆĪ, *disciple of Uttamavijaya. See* GAUTAMA, *the Gaṇadhara.* जय . . . गौतमकुलक *etc.* [Gautamakulaka. With Gujarati interpretation and commentary by Padmavijaya.] 1891. 8°. [*Jainakathāratnakoṣa.*] **14144. gg. 1.(vol. 6.)**

PAĬNNĀ. *See* PRAKĪRṆAKA.

PAKSHADHARA, *Logician. See* JAYADEVA MIṢRA.

PAKSHILASVĀMĪ. *See* VĀTSYĀYANA, called PAKSHILASVĀMĪ.

PĀLAKĀPYA. हस्त्यायुर्वेदः *etc.* (The Hastyâyurvéda by Pâlakâpya Muni. [A work on the medical treatment of elephants, in 4 *sthānas.*] Edited by Paṇḍita Ṣivadatta of Jeypore.) pp. ii. ix. 717. पुण्याख्यपत्तने १८९४ [*Poona,* 1894.] 8°.

14003. ccc. (no. 26.)

Forms no. 26 of the Ānandâṣrama Sanskrit Series. *The English title is taken from the cover.*

PĀLĀRĀM, *Munshi, son of Sarmukh Rāi. See* VIṢVAKARMĀ. विश्वकर्म्मा प्रकाश शास्त्रम् *etc.* [Viṣvakarmaprakāṣa. With a Hindi translation made for Pālārām, and hence conjointly with the text styled Pālārām-vilāsa.] [1896.] 8°.

14053. ccc. 7.

PĀLI-NĀMA-VARANEGILLA. පාළි නාමවරනැගිල්ල . . . ආඛ්‍යාතවරනැගිල්ල *etc.* (Kaccayana Namika Rupamala [or Pāli-nāma-varanegilla,] and Akhyata Rupamala. Treatises on Pali Declensions and Conjugations. Edited with notes and . . . translation [in Sinhalese] by the Venerable Sri Dharmarama.) pp. i. 62, i. *Kelani,* 1895. 8°.

14098. c. 42.(2.)

PALI TEXT SOCIETY. *See* ACADEMIES, *etc.—London.*

PALLIPATANA. బల్లిపతనము. బల్లిపలుకు. [Pallipatana. 78 stanzas on the omens implied in the fall of the house-lizard. With Telugu paraphrase, and a Telugu appendix on the omens in the lizard's cry, by Chilakapāṭi Veṅkaṭarāmānuja.] pp. 31. చెన్నపురి [*Madras,*] 1898. 16°.

14053. a. 12.(2.)

PAÑCHADAṢĪMANTRA. ॥ श्रीविद्या दीपिका *etc.* [Ṣrīvidyādīpikā. A commentary, ascribed to Agastya, upon the Pañchadaṣīmantra or mystic formula of the Ṣrīvidyā school.] *See* PURĀṆAS.—*Brahmāṇḍapurāṇa.* [*Lalitātriṣatī.*] Triṡatī, *etc.* pp. 111-117. 1902. 12°.

14033. a. 45.(1.)

PAÑCHĀNANA RĀYA CHAUDHURĪ. *See* PRĀṆAHARI YOGAVIṢĀRADA. কামশাস্ত্র *etc.* [Kāmaṣāstra. With Bengali translation by Pañchānana.] [1901.] 12°.

14053. b. 40.

PAÑCHĀNANA TARKARATNA BHAṬṬĀCHĀRYA, *of Bhatpallī. See* PURĀṆAS.—*Brihan-nāradīya-purāṇa.* बृहन्नारदीयपुराणम् *etc.* [Bṛihan-nāradīya-purāṇa. Edited with Bengali translation by Pañchānana.] [1895.] 12°.

14016. b. 19.

PAÑCHĀNANA TARKARATNA BHAṬṬĀCHĀRYA, *of Bhatpalli* (*continued*). *See* PURĀṆAS.—*Padmapurāṇa.* পদ্মপুরাণম্ *etc.* [Pātālakhaṇḍa. With Bengali translation. Edited by Pañchānana.] [1903.] 8°. **14018. b. 20.**

—— *See* PURĀṆAS.—*Skandapurāṇa.* উৎকলখণ্ডম্ *etc.* [Utkalakhaṇḍa. Edited with Bengali translation by Pañchānana.] [1902.] 8°. **14016. dd. 5.**

—— *See* VĀLMĪKI.—Rāmāyaṇa.—*Entire Text.* রামায়ণম্। *etc.* [Rāmāyaṇa. With Bengali translation. Edited by Pañchānana.] [1904.] 8°. **14068. c. 18.**

PĀÑCHARĀTRA. *See* YĀMUNA ĀCHĀRYA. आगमप्रामाण्यम् . . . Āgamaprāmāṇyam. [A dissertation on the authority of the Pāñcharātra,] *etc.* 1900. 8°. [*The Pandit.*] **14096. d. 6.(vol. 22.)**

—— गायत्रीकवच [Gāyatrīkavacha. A tract on the mystic formula based on the *gāyatrī*, extracted from the Vasishṭhasaṃhitā of the Pāñcharātra.] pp. 14, *lith.* अमृतसर [*Amritsar*, 1902.] *obl.* 12°. **14028. b. 73.(5.)**

—— శ్రీపాంచరాత్రే దేవాలయప్రతిష్ఠాద్యుత్సవాంత కల్పప్రతిపాదికా కపింజల సంహితా *etc.* [Kapiñjalasaṃhitā. One of the 108 *saṃhitās* of the Pāñcharātra, in 32 *adhyāyas*, treating of the rituals for consecrations and other festival observances of the Southern Vaishṇavas. Edited by K. Rāghavāchārya and Dh. Gopālāchārya, with Telugu preface by T. Subba Rāu.] pp. ii. 86, iii. *Cuddapah*, ౧౮౯౬ [1896.] 8°. **14028. d. 59.(5.)**

—— శ్రీమతి పాఞ్చరాత్రే . . . పాద్మతన్త్రమ్ [Pādmatantra. A section of the Pāñcharātra, on Vaishṇava doctrine and ritual, in 33 *adhyāyas.*] pp. 649. మైసూరు [*Mysore*, 18]91. 8°. **14028. d. 44.**

Apparently identical with the Padmasaṃhitā known to form part of the Pāñcharātra.

—— శ్రీపాఞ్చరాత్రే . . . భరద్వాజసంహితాన్తర్గతా ప్రపత్తిప్రపన్నవృత్తిస్వరూపనిరూపికా అష్టాధ్యాయీ *etc.* [Prapattiprapannavṛittisvarūpa. Eight *adhyāyas* on the stage of devotion called *prapatti*, extracted from the Bharadvājasaṃhitā of the Pāñcharātra. With the commentary Ṣrutārthadīpikā of Jagannātha Āchārya, and an introduction by M. Ch. Periyasvāmi Tirumalāchārya. Edited by the latter and M. Ā. Aiyanaiyaṅgār.] pp. xiv. iv. ii. xl. 104, 133, iv. మైసూరు ౧౮౯౪ [*Mysore*, 1894.] 8°. **14028. d. 62.**

The last 4 adhyāyas *belong to the Pariṣishṭa of this Saṃhitā.*

—— শ্রীরাধিকা সহস্র নাম *etc.* [Rādhikāsahasranāma. The thousand names of Rādhikā, extracted from the Nārada-pāñcharātra, V. v.-vi. Edited by Chandraṣekhara Baṛuwā.] pp. i. 30, i. গুৱাহাটী ১৮৭৯ [*Gauhati*, 1879.] 12°. **14028. c. 76.(1.)**

—— ஸ்ரீப்ரச்நஸம்ஹிதா *etc.* [Ṣrīpraṣnasaṃhitā. A compendium of Pāñcharātra religious rituals and philosophical doctrines, in 54 chapters, purporting to be revealed by Vāsudeva to Ṣrī.. Edited by G. Rāmasvāmī Bhaṭṭāchārya.] pp. ii. 188, 152. கும்பகோணம் ॥ [*Kumbakonam,*] 1904. 8°. **14033. bbb. 22.**

This work is mentioned in the Kapiñjalasaṃhitā I. 17 *in the list of canonical Pāñcharātra texts.*

—— పాఞ్చరాత్రమ్ . . . శ్రీవిష్ణుతిలకాఖ్యోయం గ్రన్థః *etc.* [Vishṇutilaka, or Vishṇusiddhāntatilaka. A Pāñcharātra *saṃhitā*, in 8 chapters, upon religious and social principles and practice. Edited by Kondamūr Kōyal Iyyuṇṇi Rāghavāchārya.] pp. xvi. 231. *Bangalore*, 1896. 8°. **14028. d. 63.**

The name Vishṇusiddhāntatilaka *is that given in the Kapiñjalasaṃhitā* I. 16.

PAÑCHATANTRA. A Popular Edition of the First (Second and Third, Fourth and Fifth) Tantra of Vishnuśarman. Containing a full glossary [or rather, glossarial notes, in English,] and a literal translation of the verses occurring in the text. By Mahadeva Shivarâma Âpte. *Poona*, 1893-1894. 12°. **14070. b. 21.**

—— The Pañchatantraka of Vishṇuśarman. Edited by Kâśînâth Pâṇdurang Parab. (पञ्चतन्त्रकम्।) pp. 239. *Bombay*, 1896. 8°. **14070. c. 59.**

—— Pancha Tantra, by Vishnu Sarma. With a [Hindi] commentary [or rather, paraphrase, styled Nītisarvasva] by Pandit Jwala Prasad Misra. (पंचतन्त्रम्) pp. xii. 514. *Bombay*, 1898. 8°. **14070. c. 62.**

—— Das Pañcatantram. Textus ornatior. Eine altindische Märchensammlung, zum ersten Male übersetzt von Richard Schmidt. *Leipzig*, 1901. 8°. **14070. dd. 17.**

—— Pañcatantra. Arische levenswijsheid uit het oude Indië. Novellen, vertellingen, fabelen uit het Sanskrit vertaald door H. G. van der Waals. pp. iii. 151, iv. 132, 123. *Leiden*, 1895. 8°. **14070. c. 54.**

—— Le Novelle Indiane di Visnusarma, Panciatantra. Tradotte . . . da Italo Pizzi. pp. viii. 232. *Torino*, 1896. 8°. **14072. d. 17.(2.)**

—— De Ældste Indiske Æventyr og Fabler eller Fembogen; et uddrag af Visnusarmans Pantjatantra, oversat efter grundteksten af Harald Rasmussen. pp. xxiii. 246. *København*, 1893. 8°. **14070. c. 51.**

—— *See* HERTEL (J.). Kritische Bemerkungen zu Kosegartens Pañcatantra, *etc.* 1902. 8°. [*Zeitschrift der Deutschen Morgenlaendischen Gesellschaft.*] **Ac. 8815/2.(vol. 56.)**

—— *See* SVĀMI ŞĀSTRĪ, *P.K.*, and KĀMEŞVARA AIYAR, *B.V.* Matriculation Examination, 1891. The Sanskrit Text Examiner [upon Pañchatantra I. 6-13 and Mahābhārata, Vanaparva, xxiii.-xxxii.], *etc.* 1891. 12°. **14072. b. 18.**

—— Notes on Panchatantra [I. 6-13. With a translation of the stanzas, *etc.*] pp. 7, 10. *See* MAHĀBHĀRATA.—*Vanaparva.* University of Madras. Matriculation . . . 1891, *etc.* 1891. 8°. **14060. c. 30.(2.)**

—— *See* KIŞORĪMOHANA VIDYĀNIDHI. वैयाकरण-नीतिकौमुदी *etc.* [Vaiyākaraṇa-nītikaumudī. Tales, with verses from the Pañchatantra, *etc.*] [1898.] 12°. **14085. b. 43.**

—— Provesika [*i.e.* texts for the Entrance Examination of the Calcutta University]. Translated into English by Lalit Mohan Sarkar. Part i. Prose section [*scil.* Pañchatantra V. i.-x. and II. v.] pp. 24. *Calcutta*, 1890. 12°. **14070. b. 19.**

—— Der Auszug aus dem Pañcatantra in Kshemendra's Bṛihatkathâmañjarî, *etc.* 1892. 8°. *See* KSHEMENDRA. **14072. d. 41.**

—— अथ-संस्कृतसागर *etc.* [Saṃskṛitasāgara. 22 apologues, with a Hindi version by Rāmasvarūpa Şukla. Edited by Dāmodara Şāstrī.] pp. 74. मुरादाबाद० [*Moradabad*, 1899.] 8°. **14070. c. 63.(2.)**

—— पञ्चतन्त्रम् [Grammatical analyses of fables from the Pañchatantra. With English and Hindi translations.] *See* ACADEMIES, *etc.*—Allahabad.—*University of Allahabad.* संस्कृत-शिक्षा-विवृतिः . . . Sanskrit-Siksha-Vivriti, *etc.* pp. 65-269. 1899. 12°. **14085. b. 39.(2.)**

—— पञ्चतन्त्रम् *etc.* [Pañchatantra, I. xiv.-xxii.] *See* ACADEMIES, *etc.* — Madras. — *University of Madras.* The Sanskrit Text for the Matriculation Examination . . . December 1900. pp. 1-30. 1899. 8°. **14060. c. 30.(3.)**

PAṆḌAVA, *Mahāthera.* *See* KACHCHĀYANA.—*Balāvatāra.* ဗာလာဝတာရ *etc.* [Bālāvatāra. With commentary. Edited by Paṇḍava.] [1900.] 8°. **14098. ccc. 27.(2.)**

PAṆḌAVĀLAṄKĀRA, known as SAGU HSAYA. *See* PAÑÑĀLAṄKĀRA, *of Maṅgalārāma.* နာမမာလာ *etc.* [Nāmamālā. Edited by Paṇḍavālaṅkāra.] 1895. 8°. **14098. ccc. 17.(1.)**

—— *See* SUTTAPIṬAKA.—*Saṃyuttanikāya.* ဒေဝမနုဿစိတ္တပရိဝတ္တဝိဝါဒဝိနိစ္ဆယ [Devamanussachittaparivattavivādavinichchhaya. Being the Daḷhadhammadhanuggahasutta, *etc.*, with Burmese commentary by Paṇḍavālaṅkāra.] 1900. 8°. [*Abidhammā-ngā-saung-twè-kyan.*] **14300. e. 14.**

PAṆḌAVAṂSA, *of the Ichchhāsaya-hkyaung-dhammapāla Kyaung, Sagaing.* ဒုလ္လဘသင်္ဂြိုဟ်ကျမ်း *etc.* [Dullabha-thingyoh-kyan. A compilation of dicta, from Pali texts, upon the birth of a Buddha, birth as a man, and other topics of Buddhist religion. With Burmese introductions, commentaries, *etc.*] pp. xii. 331. မန္တလေး ၁၂၆၁ [*Mandalay*, 1899.] 8°. **14300. d. 21.(2.)**

PANDIT (S. P.). *See* Ṣankara Pāṇḍuranga Paṇḍit.

PAṆḌITADDHAJA, known as Maingkaing Hsaya. တိပိဋကဝိနိစ္ဆယကျမ်း *etc.* [Tipiṭakavinichchhaya-kyan. A collection of works by Paṇḍitaddhaja, comprising (1) responses to questions on points of religion, *etc.*, and (2) divers other tracts—viz. Pumbhāvadīpanī, on gender, Diṭṭhibhedavibhāvanī, on heresies, Vesārajjādidīpaka, on the Buddha's four subjects of confidence *etc.*, and Vikālabhojanangādivinichchhaya, on eating at wrong times—all in Burmese, illustrated from Pali texts; with (3) various short and popular Pali texts with Burmese versions and commentaries, including the Mūlāya-paṭikassana-kammavāchā, Velāmasutta from the Anguttaranikāya, and Sīhaḷasandesakathā, a correspondence with Ceylon, *etc.*] 2 vols. မန္တလေး [*Mandalay*,] 1900-1901. 8°. **14302. i. 19.**

PAṆḌITADDHAJA SĪLĀLAṄKĀRA, *of Mabe.* သဒ္ဒါပုဒ်စိပ် ။ အကျယ်ကျမ်း *etc.* [Saddā-pôk-sit-akyay. A Burmese supercommentary on Kachchāyana's grammar, by Paṇḍitaddhaja, based on Ñāṇābhidhammālaṅkāra's commentary Mukhamattadīpanī-pôk-sit on the Mukhamattadīpanī. With 3 additional Burmese tracts by the same. Edited by Tissa and Janinda.] pp. xii. 500, iii. မန္တလေး ရန်ကုန် ၁၂၅၈ [*Mandalay, Rangoon* printed, 1896.] 8°. **14302. i. 15.**

PAṆḌITARĀJA. *See* Jagannātha Paṇḍitarāja.

PAṆḌITASARVASVA. ପଣ୍ଡିତସର୍ବସ୍ବ *etc.* [Paṇḍitasarvasva. A work on Hindu law. Edited, with an Oriya translation, by Mahendra Deva, Maharaja of Athmallik.] pp. 372, 8. *Cuttack*, 1897. 8°. **14038. d. 36.**

This is perhaps the Paṇḍitasarvasva ascribed to Halāyudha.

PĀṆINI.

Ashṭādhyāyī.

अथ शब्दानुशासनम् [Ashṭādhyāyī. Edited with Sanskrit notes and Hindi translation by Jvālādatta Ṣarmā. Sūtra I. i. 1-30.] [1889.] *See* Jvālādatta Ṣarmā, *of Moradabad.* ॥ विद्यामार्तण्ड *etc.* [Vidyāmārtaṇḍa.] Vol. i. 1, *etc.* [1889.] 8°. **14096. c. 9.**

—— [A new edition of the preceding.] [1900, *etc.*] *See* Jvālādatta Ṣarmā, *of Moradabad.* विद्यामार्तण्ड *etc.* [Vidyāmārtaṇḍa.] Vol. i. 1, *etc.* 1900, *etc.* 8°. **14096. c. 9*.**

In progress?

॥ अथ अष्टाध्यायीसूत्रपाठ॰ [Ashṭādhyāyī. The *sūtras.*] ff. 32. *See* Vedas.—*Appendix.* ॥ अथ . . . षडङ्ग॰ [Shaḍanga.] pt. 5. [1892.] 8°. **14007. c. 27.**

अथ पाणिनीयाष्टकम् . . . The Panini's Grammatical Aphorisms. Edited by Bhimsen Shurma, *etc.* pp. iv. 72. *Allahabad*, 1892. 8°. **14093. b. 35.(2.)**

The Râvaṇârjunîya of Bhatta Bhîma. [A poem composed so as to illustrate the bulk of Pāṇini's Aphorisms i. 2—vi. 1, vi. 3—vii. 4, viii. 2—4, and with these Aphorisms included.] Edited by . . . Paṇḍit Śivadatta . . . and Kâshînâth Pâṇdurang Parab. 1900. 8°. *See* Bhīma, *Bhaṭṭa.* **14072. ccc. 12.(no. 68.)**

अष्टाध्यायी भाषाटीकासहित *etc.* [Ashṭādhyāyī. With a Hindi paraphrase, entitled Chandrakāntā, by Vrajaratna Bhaṭṭāchārya.] pp. vi. 284. बम्बई १९५८ [*Bombay*, 1901.] 8°. **14090. d. 34.**

সিদ্ধান্তসন্দীপনী *etc.* [Siddhāntasandīpanī. A rearrangement of the Aphorisms, with a Bengali commentary, by Vasantakumāra Rāya. Part 3, containing the sections on *kāraka* and *samāsa.*] pp. 179. কলিকাতা ১৩০৮ [*Calcutta*, 1901.] 12°. **14092. a. 17.(3.)**

See Lakshmājī Paṇḍit, *Lingam.* A Lecture on Religion, by the light of the Ashstádhyáyí [*sic*], *etc.* 1890. 8°. **4503. c. 24.(7.)**

See Nandikeṣvara. శ్రీ . . . శ్రీమదాదిసూత్రకా-శికా *etc.* [Nandikeṣvara-kāṣikā, or Ādisūtrakāṣikā. 27 stanzas, with a *vritti*, mystically interpreting the Ṣivasūtra or aphorisms on the alphabet which are prefixed to Pāṇini's grammar. With the commentary ascribed to Upamanyu.] [1902.] 12°. **14033. a. 26.(3.)**

[For the Supadma grammar :] *See* PADMANĀBHADATTA.

[For editions of the Nāmadhātuvṛitti :] *See* SĀYAṆA ĀCHĀRYA.—*Works on Grammar.*

See VIPRARĀJENDRA, *son of Manyudatta.* शब्दामृतसूचीपत्रम् *etc.* [Ṣabdāmrita-sūchīpatra. A key to the Ṣabdāmṛita. With commentaries.] [1890.] 8°. **14092. b. 41.**

KĀṢIKĀ.

काशिका . . . Kashika. A Commentary on Parbnis Grammeratieal aphorisrus [*sic*]. [Begun] by Pandit Jayaditya [and completed by Vāmana Āchārya;] with commentaries added by Pandit Bhagwatprasad Tripathi, *etc.* 2 pts. pp. i. 489, 576. *Benares,* 1890. 8°. **14090. bb. 7.**

भाष्यसङ्गमनी *etc.* [Bhāshyasaṅgamanī. Being the aphorisms of the Mahābhāshya, the text of the Kāṣikā in exposition of the aphorisms of Pāṇini quoted therein, and commentary by Gauragovinda Rāya.] [1903, *etc.*] 8°. *See* PATAÑJALI.—*Grammatical Works.* **14090. bb. 22.**

The Ashṭádhyáyí of Páṇini. Translated into English by Śrísá Chandra Vasu. [Being a translation of the Ashṭādhyāyī with a paraphrase of considerable portions of the Kāṣikā Vṛitti.] 8 pts. *Allahabad,* 1891-1898. 8°. **14093. d. 18.**

Zwei Kapitel der Kāçikā. Übersetzt und mit einer Einleitung versehen von Bruno Liebich. pp. xl. 80. *Breslau,* 1892. 8°. **14093. b. 34.**

MAHĀBHĀSHYA.

[For the Mahābhāshya and works based thereon :] *See* PATAÑJALI.—*Grammatical Works.*

MITĀKSHARĀ.

मिताक्षरा नाम पाणिनीयलघुवृत्तिः *etc.* (The Mitakshara. A commentary on Panini's grammatical aphorisms. By Pandit Annambhatta . . . Edited by Pandit S. P. S. Jagannadhasvami Ayyavaralugaru.) Vol. I, pt. i. pp. 177. *Vizagapatam,* 1895. 8°. **14090. bb. 11.**

Re-issued and continued in the Grandha Pradarsani, *no.* 15. *The English title is from the cover.*

मिताक्षरा नाम पाणिनीयलघुवृत्तिः ॥ [Mitāksharā. Being the aphorisms of Pāṇini with a commentary by Annam Bhaṭṭa.] 1896, *etc.* *See* VEṄKAṬARAṄGANĀTHA SVĀMĪ, *Paravastu.* Grandha Pradarsani, *etc.* [No. 15.] 1895, *etc.* 8°. **14003. c. 2.(15.)**

Incomplete. Re-issued and continued in the Benares Sanskrit Series (no. lxxvi., *etc.*).

PRAKRIYĀKAUMUDĪ.

प्रक्रियाकौमुदी। [Prakriyākaumudī. Aphorisms of Pāṇini with brief commentary by Rāmachandra Āchārya.] 1895, *etc.* *See* VEṄKAṬARAṄGANĀTHA SVĀMĪ, *Paravastu.* Grandha Pradarsani, *etc.* [No. 10.] 1895, *etc.* 8°. **14003. c. 2.(10.)**

Incomplete, breaking off at the end of the Sandhiprakaraṇa.

ପ୍ରକ୍ରିୟାକୌମୁଦୀ . . . Prakriya Kaumudy. By Rama Chandra Acharya. With a commentary entitled the "Bimala" and an Oriya translation by Pandit Purusottam Tarkalankar, and with notes by Pandit Ramachandra Mishra. *Cuttack,* 1902, *etc.* 8°. **14090. bb. 19.**

In progress.

SIDDHĀNTAKAUMUDĪ.

Balamanorama sahitha. Sidhantha Kowmuthi. "ஸித்தாந்தகௌமுதீ" . . . "பாலமநோரமா" . . . ஸஹிதா *etc.* [Siddhāntakaumudī, with the commentary Bālamanoramā of Vāsudeva Dīkshita.] 2 vols. pp. 1116. *Tiruvadi,* நடுக்காவேரி॥ [*Nadukkaveri*], 1889-1901. 8°. **14092. b. 46.**

सिद्धान्तकौमुदी . . . . . Siddhanta Kaumudi . . . . With a commentary entitled the "Tattwabodhini" by Jnanendra Saraswati. And with a Bengali translation. Edited . . . by Kaviraj Binod Lal Sen. 2 vols. *Calcutta,* ১৮১২-১৮১৪ [1890-1892.] 8°. **14090. d. 29.**

The Siddhânta-kaumudî with the Tattvabodhinî commentary of Jnânendra Sarasvati and the Subodhinî commentary of Jayakrishna. [To which are appended the Uṇādisūtra, Ṣikshā, Gaṇapāṭha, Dhātupāṭha, and Liṅgānuṣāsana.] Edited by Dinkar Keshava Shâstri Gâdgil and Vâsudev Lakshmana Shâstri Pansikar. (सिद्धान्तकौमुदी . . .

पाणिनीयव्याकरणसूत्रवृत्तिः) pp. i. i. 672, liv. i. *Bombay,* 1899. 4°. **14092. c. 18.**

मध्यसिद्धान्तकौमुदी *etc.* [Madhyasiddhāntakaumudī, or Madhyakaumudī. An abridgment of the Siddhāntakaumudī, by Varadarāja. With notes by Bālakṛishṇa Gaṇeṣa Yogī. Followed by the Liṅgānuṣāsana with Varadarāja's *vṛitti, etc.* Edited by Jīvarāma Lallurām Raikvāl.] pp. ii. 317, vi. मोहमय्यां १८९५ [*Bombay,* 1895.] 12°. **14090. b. 41.**

मध्यकौमुदी . . . The Madhya Kaumudi by Varada Raja. [Followed by the Liṅgānuṣāsanasūtravṛitti, by the same author.] Edited by Pandit Ganesh Dutt, Shastri. Second edition. pp. ii. 301. *Lahore,* 1899. 12°. **14092. a. 22.**

See Bhaṭṭojī Dīkshita. मनोरमा *etc.* [Manoramā, or Prauḍhamanoramā. A commentary on the Siddhāntakaumudī. With the supercommentary of Hari Dīkshita.] [1900.] 8°. **14093. d. 22.**

See Indradatta Upādhyāya. फक्किकाप्रकाशः *etc.* [Phakkikāprakāṣa. A commentary on the Siddhāntakaumudī.] [1897.] 8°. **14090. c. 38.(4.)**

See Jayakrishṇa, *son of Raghunātha.* अथ सुबोधिनी *etc.* [Subodhinī. A commentary upon the sections on accent and Vedic forms in the Siddhānta-kaumudī.] 1897. 8°. [*Tattvabodhinī.*] **14090. e. 25.**

See Jñānendra Sarasvatī. वैयाकरणसिद्धान्तकौमुदीव्याख्या तत्त्वबोधिनी *etc.* [Tattvabodhinī. A commentary on the Siddhāntakaumudī.] 1897. 8°. **14090. e. 25.**

See Nageṣa Bhaṭṭa. [*Ṣabdenduṣekhara.*] ॥ लघुशब्देन्दुशेखरः *etc.* [Laghu-ṣabdenduṣekhara. An abridged commentary on the Siddhāntakaumudī.] 1901, *etc.* 8°. **14090. bb. 20.**

Appendix.

[*Dhātupāṭha.*] माधवीया धातुवृत्तिः. The Dhátuvritti of Mádhavácharya. [Being the Dhātupāṭha with Sāyaṇa's commentary. Followed by Sāyaṇa's Nāmadhātuvṛitti.] . . . Edited by A. Mahádeva Śástri (and . . . K. Rangácharya). 4 vols. 1894-1903. *See* Mysore. — *Government of Mysore.* Government Oriental Library Series. Bibliotheca Sanskrita, *etc.* No. 3, 23, 24, 31. 1893, *etc.* 8°. **14004. b. 3.**

—— माधवीया धातुवृत्तिः । नामधातुवृत्तिश्च *etc.* [Dhātu-vṛitti. Followed by the Nāmadhātuvṛitti. Edited by Dāmodara Ṣāstrī Sahasrabuddhi.] pp. iii. xxix. 394, 358, ii. 66. काश्यां १८९७ [*Benares,* 1897.] 8°. **14093. b. 39.**

A reprint from the Pandit.

—— अथ धातुपाठः [Dhātupāṭha.] *See* above, Siddhāntakaumudī. The Siddhânta-kaumudî, *etc.* pp. 661-671. 1899. 4°. **14092. c. 18.**

—— [For editions of the Dhātukāvya, a poem illustrating the usage of verbal roots according to Bhīmasena's Dhātupāṭha :] *See* Nārāyaṇa Bhaṭṭa, *Kerala.*

[*Gaṇapāṭha.*] अथ गणपाठः [Gaṇapāṭha.] *See* above, Siddhāntakaumudī. The Siddhânta-kaumudî, *etc.* pp. 643-660. 1899. 4°. **14092. c. 18.**

[*Liṅgānuṣāsana.*] लिङ्गानुशासनम् *etc.* [Liṅgānuṣā-sana. Edited with Bengali notes by Mukunda-dayālu Vasu.] pp. 30. কোচবিহার ১৩০১ [*Kuch Behar,* 1894.] 12°. **14090. b. 43.(2.)**

—— लिङ्गानुशासनम् । [Liṅgānuṣāsana. In the *vṛitti* of Varadarāja.] *See* above, Siddhānta-kaumudī. मध्यसिद्धान्तकौमुदी *etc.* [Madhyasiddhānta-kaumudī.] pp. 315-317. [1895.] 12°. **14090. b. 41.**

—— लिङ्गानुशासनम् [Liṅgānuṣāsana, in the form ascribed to Bhaṭṭojī. With Varadarāja's *vṛitti.*] *See* above, Siddhāntakaumudī. मध्यकौमुदी . . . The Madhya Kaumudi, *etc.* pp. 295-301. 1899. 12°. **14092. a. 22.**

—— अथ लिङ्गानुशासनम् [Liṅgānuṣāsana. In the forms ascribed both to Bhaṭṭojī and to Paṇini.] *See* above, Siddhāntakaumudī. The Siddhânta-kaumudî, *etc.* pp. 636-640, 671-672. 1899. 4°. **14092. c. 18.**

[*Ṣikshā.*] ॥ अथ शिक्षा° [Ṣikshā.] ff. 4. *See* VEDĀS.—*Appendix.* ॥ अथ . . . षडङ्ग° [Shaḍaṅga.] pt. 1. [1892.] *obl.* 8°. **14007. c. 27.**

—— पाणिनीयशिक्षा ॥ [Ṣikshā. Followed by a commentary on the same, styled Ṣikshāprakāṣa, in which the Ṣikshā is ascribed to Piṅgala.] *See* YUGALAKIṢORA VYĀSA PĀṬHAKA. श्रीमद्याज्ञवल्क्यादि . . . शिक्षासङ्ग्रहः . . . A collection of Śikshás, *etc.* pp. 378-393. 1893. 8°. **14093. b. 31.**

—— अथ शिक्षा [Ṣikshā.] *See* above, SIDDHĀNTA-KAUMUDĪ. The Siddhânta-kaumudî, *etc.* pp. 641-642. 1899. 4°. **14092. c. 18.**

PAÑÑĀBHISIRI SADDHAMMADDHAJA, *of the Vajirārāma.* ဒွတ္တိံသာကာရဒီပကကျမ်း [Dvattiṃsākāradīpaka. A Burmese work upon the text Aṅguttaranikāya I. xxi. 1, and treating of the constituents of the body and their foulness.] pp. ii. 104. *Rangoon,* 1881. 8°.
14300. d. 20.(1.)

PAÑÑAGGA. Sugata Vidatthividhana. A description of the size of Lord Buddha's body [and of several of his personal effects] by the Venerable (Paññā Agga or) Prawaraiswaryalankarna Sangharaja . . . With a [Sinhalese] paraphrase [and a preface in English and Sinhalese] by the Rev. C. A. Seelakkhandha. (සුගතවිදත්ථිවිධානය) pp. ii. ii. 51, i. *Ambalangoda,* 1894. 8°.
14098. c. 68.(2.)

Pp. 17-25 *are wanting.*

PANNĀLĀL, *Bāklīwāl, of Sujangarh.* *See* NEMICHANDRA BHANḌĀRĪ. उपदेशसिद्धान्तरत्नमाला *etc.* [Upadeṣasiddhāntaratnamālā. With Hindi translation and commentary by Pannālāl.] [1898.] 8°.
14100. b. 4.

—— *See* NEMICHANDRA NĀRĀYAṆA CHAVḌE. जैनधर्मामृत सार *etc.* [Jainadharmāmṛitasāra. Vol. II, with Hindi version by Pannālāl.] [1894-1899.] 8°. **14137. d. 20.**

—— *See* SAMANTABHADRA SVĀMĪ. रत्नकरण्डश्रावकाचार *etc.* [Ratnakaraṇḍa-ṣrāvakāchāra. Edited with analysis and Hindi translation and notes by Pannālāl.] [1898.] 12°. **14028. b. 84.(1.)**

PAÑÑĀLAṄKĀRA, *of Maṅgalārāma Kyaung, Maungdaung.* *See* MOGGALLĀNA. အဘိဓာနက္ခရာ-ဝလိ *etc.* [Abhidhānakkharāvalī. A compilation by Paññālaṅkāra, comprising an index to the Abhidhānappadīpikā, lists, *etc.*] 1896. 8°.
14098. ccc. 25.

—— နာမမာလာကျမ်း *etc.* [Nāmamālā. A Burmese treatise on the Pali noun-systems, with extracts from Pali works. Followed by Kachchāyana's Nāmakappa and a number of aphorisms from Aggavaṃsa's Saddanīti. Edited by Paṇḍavālaṅkāra.] pp. ii. v. 268. မန္တလေး [*Mandalay,*] 1895. 8°. **14098. ccc. 17.(1.)**

Claims to be based upon the Saddanīti, Rūpasiddhi, Chūlanirutti, Niruttipiṭaka, Bālāvatāra, Sīhalanāmamālā, &c.

PAÑÑĀLAṄKĀRA, *Mahādhammarājādhirājaguru.* သင်္ခေပဂရုဘဏ္ဍဝိနိစ္ဆယကျမ်း *etc.* [Saṅkhepagarubhaṇḍavinichchhaya, Vitthāra-g°., and Vichitra-g°. Three treatises on clerical discipline, the third being in 55 Pali stanzas with Burmese *nissaya,* the others in Burmese with Pali quotations.] *See* VINAYAPIṬAKA.—*Appendix.* ဝိနယ-သမူဟဝိနိစ္ဆယကျမ်း *etc.* [Vinayasamūhavinichchhaya-kyan.] Vol. I, pp. 1-70. 1899, *etc.* 8°.
14300. e. 15.

PAÑÑĀMOLI TISSA, *Toṭagamuvē.* *See* ANURUDDHA. Abhidharmarthasaṅgraha sanna . . . Edited by . . . T. Pannamoli Tissa, *etc.* 1897. 8°.
14098. ccc. 6.

—— *See* MOGGALLĀNA. Sinhalese Translation of Abhidhanapradipika . . . Edited by . . . Pannamolitissa, *etc.* 1895. 8°. **14098. ccc. 1.**

PAÑÑĀRAṂSI THERA, *of Thaye-khetta.* ဥပါ-သကဝိနိစ္ဆယ [Upāsakavinichchhaya. A collection of Pali quotations, with Burmese translation and commentary, on the religious duties of laymen.] pp. 344. ၁၂၄၄ [*Rangoon,* 1882.] 8°.
14300. e. 3.

PAÑÑĀRATANA, *of Vijayārāma-vihāra.* *See* SUTTAPIṬAKA.—*Majjhimanikāya.* මජ්ඣිමනිකායො *etc.* [Majjhimanikāya. Edited by Saraṇaṅkara and Paññāratana.] 1895. 8°. **14098. dd. 11.**

PAÑÑASĀMI. Sāsanavaṃsa (a history of Buddhism). Edited [with introductory dissertation, *etc.*,] by Mabel Bode. 1897. 8°. *See* ACADEMIES, *etc.*—London.—*Pali Text Society.* PAÑÑASĀMI. **14098. b. 37.**

PAÑÑĀSĀRA, *of Kosgoda.* *See* JINAVAṂSA PAÑÑĀSĀRA.

PAÑÑĀSEKHARA, *Kōdāgoḍa.* *See* ÑĀṆAKITTI. අභිධම්ම සම්මොහවිනොදනිඅත්ථයොජනා *etc.* (The Abhidhamma Sammohavinodani Atthayojana . . . Edited by . . . Pannasekhara Thera.) [1893.] 8°. **14098. dd. 5.(2.)**

—— බුද්ධපටිපත්තිදීපනිය . . . Buddha Patipattidipaniya. Or Buddhist Service. Second edition. pp. ii. 43. [*Galle,*] 1893. 16°. **14098. a. 26.**

PAÑÑĀSIHA, *Mahāsaddhammasāmi.* ဆပ္ပစ္စယဒီပက [Chhappachchayadīpaka. A commentary on the Vuttodaya.] *See* SAṄGHARAKKHITA. ဝုတ္တောဒယသန်းကျမ်း *etc.* [Vuttodaya.] pp. 51-173. [1899.] 8°. **14098. ccc. 27.(3.)**

PAÑÑĀSIHA SĀSANĀLAṄKĀRA, *of Mahākhemikārāma.* *See* VINAYAPIṬAKA. ပိဋကတ်ကျမ်း *etc.* [Vinayapiṭaka. Vol. vii., the Parivāra, with interpretation by Paññāsiha.] 1903-1904. 8°. **14099. aa. 7.**

PANSE (N. S.). *See* NĀRĀYAṆA SAKHĀRĀMA PANṢE.

PANSIKAR (V. L.). *See* VĀSUDEVA LAKSHMAṆA ṢĀSTRĪ PAṆṢĪKAR.

PANTULU (M. B.) *See* BUCHCHAIYA PANTULU.

PARAB (K. P.). *See* KĀṢĪNĀTHA PĀṆḌURAṄGA PARAB.

PARAHITARAKSHITA. *See* NĀGĀRJUNA. Études et Textes Tantriques. Pañcakrama [with the gloss of Parahitarakshita] *etc.* 1896. 8°. **Ac. 2647/3. (fasc. 16.)**

PĀRALIṄGA PRABHU AIYĀ. *See* PARAMARAHASYA. ॥ अथ श्री परमरहस्य० [Paramarahasya. With paraphrase in Marathi. Edited by Pāraliṅga Aiyā.] [1887.] *obl.* 4°. **14048. e. 24.**

PĀRALIṄGA PRABHU AIYĀ (*continued*). वीरशैवान्वय मूलतत्व प्रकाश *etc.* [Vīraṣaivānvayamūlatattvaprakāṣa. Extracts compiled from Āgamik works, bearing upon the origins and practices of the Vīraṣaiva or Liṅgāyat sect. With a Marathi translation.] pp. ii. 46. बार्शी [*Barsi,* 1893.] 12°. **14033. a. 29.**

PARAMĀNANDA, *Pandit, of Narnaul.* *See* DHANAṂJAYA, *Jain writer.* विषापहार *etc.* [Vishāpahāra. With a rendering in Hindi verse by Paramānanda.] [1900.] 12°. **14100. a. 21.(2.)**

PARAMĀNANDA, *Svāmī, of Peshawar.* पितापुत्रधर्मप्रकाश *etc.* [Pitāputradharmaprakāṣa. A Hindi lecture on parental and filial love, with an anthology of Sanskrit verses.] pp. 102. काशी १९५८ [*Benares,* 1901.] 8°. **14156. d. 21.**

PARAMĀNANDA, *J. N.* *See* ṢAṄKARA ĀCHĀRYA.—*Doubtful and Supposititious Works.* Charapatapanjari [*sic*] . . . translated by Mr. J. N. Parmanand. 1901. 8°. [*Compendium of the Raja Yoga Philosophy.*] **14048. bb. 53.**

PARAMARAHASYA. ॥ अथ श्री परमरहस्य० [Paramarahasya. A metrical work in 17 *adhyāyas* on the Vīraṣaiva doctrines. With an expanded metrical paraphrase in Marathi. Edited by Pāraliṅga Prabhu Aiyā.] 17 pts. बार्शी १८०९ [*Barsi,* 1887.] *obl.* 4°. **14048. e. 24.**

The Marathi work is dated 1522 Samvat.

PARAMEṢVARA DĪKSHITA, *of Chidambaram.* *See* PURĀṆAS.—*Skandapurāṇa.* ஸ்ரீசமீவநக்ஷேத்ரமாஹாத்ம்யம் *etc.* [Ṣamīvanakshetramāhātmya. Edited by Parameṣvara.] [1899.] 12°. **14016. a. 29.**

PARAMEṢVARA JHĀ, *of Tarauni.* *See* GADASIṂHA. ऊष्मविवेक: *etc.* [Ūshmaviveka. With commentary by Parameṣvara.] [1890.] 8°. **14093. b. 17.(2.)**

—— *See* ṢRĀDDHA. एकोद्दिष्ट पद्धती *etc.* [Ekoddishṭapaddhati. With notes by Parameṣvara.] [1898.] *obl.* 4°. **14028. e. 33.(2.)**

—— *See* VĪREṢVARA ṬHAKKURA. छन्दोगानांविवाहादिसंस्कारपद्धति: *etc.* [Chhandogānāṃ Vivāhādisaṃskārapaddhati, *etc.* Edited with notes by Parameṣvara.] [1902.] *obl.* 4°. **14033. c. 31.(3.)**

PARAMEṢVARA JHĀ, *of Tarauni* (*continued*). **मिथिलेशप्रशस्तिः** *etc.* [Mithileṣapraṣasti. An account of the late Maharaja of Darbhangah, Lakshmīṣvarasiṃha, and the accession of the present chief, Rameṣvarasiṃha.] pp. 14. **दरभङ्गा १८९९** [*Darbhangah*, 1899.] 12°. **14058. a. 17.**

PARANJPYE (K. B.). *See* KEṢAVA BĀLAKṚISHṆA PARĀÑJPYE.

PARANJPE (S. M.). *See* ṢIVARĀMA MAHĀDEVA PARĀÑJPYE.

PARĀṢARA. [*Horā.*] [For the Uḍudāyapradīpa, also called Bāla-pārāṣarya or Laghu-pārāṣarī, purporting to be founded upon the Pārāṣarī Horā ascribed to Parāṣara :] *See* UḌUDĀYAPRADĪPA.

—— [*Ṣikshā.*] **अथ . . . पाराशरी शिक्षा** *etc.* [Pārāṣarī Ṣikshā. 160 stanzas of the Mādhyandina school on Vedic phonetics, claiming the authority of Parāṣara.] *See* YUGALAKIṢORA VYĀSA PĀṬHAKA. **श्रीमद्याज्ञवल्क्यादि . . . शिक्षासङ्ग्रहः** . . . A collection of Śikshás, *etc.* pp. 52-71. 1893. 8°. **14093. b. 31.**

—— [*Smṛiti.*] ପରାଶର-ସଂହିତା *etc.* [Parāṣarasaṃhitā. With an Oriya translation by Rāmachandra, Raja of Talcher, from the Bengali version by Jaganmohana Tarkālaṅkāra.] pp. i. iv. iii. 121. *Cuttack*, 1887. 8°. **14038. c. 44.(1.)**

—— —— ಪರಾಶರಮಾಧವೀಯ ಧರ್ಮಶಾಸ್ತ್ರವು *etc.* [Parāṣara-mādhavīya-dharmaṣāstra. The text of Parāṣara's Smṛiti with a Canarese translation of the latter and of Sāyaṇa's commentary by Cheñchōḷī Veṅkaṇṇāchārya.] pp. ii. xiv. xvi. ii. 611, 513. ಬೆಂಗಳೂರು ೧೮೯೦ [*Bangalore*, 1890.] 8°. **14038. d. 31.**

—— —— The Parâśara Dharma Saṃhitâ or Parâśara Smṛiti, with the commentary of Sâyaṇa Mâdhavâchârya. Edited with various readings, critical notes, an index, appendices, *etc.*, by Paṇḍit Vâman Śâstri Islâmapurkar. (**पराशरधर्मसंहिता अथवा पराशरस्मृतिः**) *Bombay*, 1893, *etc.* 8°. **14039. a. 15.**

In progress. Forms nos. xlvii., xlviii., lix., *etc.*, *of the* Bombay Sanskrit Series.

—— —— **श्रीपराशरसंहिता** અથવા પારાશર-ધર્મશાસ્ત્ર. [Parāṣarasaṃhitā. With a Gujarati translation called Maṅgalā by Brahmachārī Nṛisiṃha Ṣarmā. Edited by Kahānjī Dharmasiṃha.] pp. i. i. i. vii. 117, i. મુંબઈ : ૧૮૯૯ [*Bombay*, 1899.] 8°. **14038. c. 48.(2.)**

—— —— সানুবাদ পরাশরসংহিতা *etc.* [Parāṣarasaṃhitā. Edited with Bengali translation by Kālīprasanna Vidyāratna.] pp. ii. ii. v. 100. কলিকাতা ১৩১০ [*Calcutta*, 1903.] 8°. **14039. b. 15.(3.)**

—— —— பராசரஸ்ம்ருதி *etc.* [Parāṣarasaṃhitā. The Sanskrit text in both Grantham and Tamil characters. Edited with Tamil translation by Āḍūr Īchambāḍi Deṣikāchārya.] pp. 2, viii. 80, 68. சென்னை [*Madras*,] 1902. 8°. **14039. b. 30.**

—— *See* SĀYAṆA ĀCHĀRYA.—*Works on Smṛiti.* శ్రీ . . . వ్యవహారకాండః *etc.* [Mādhavīya - vyavahārakāṇḍa. Sāyaṇa's commentary upon the Vyavahārakāṇḍa of the Parāṣarasaṃhitā.] [1898.] 8°. **14039. c. 16.**

PARĀṢARA BHAṬṬA, *son of Ṣrīvatsāṅka Kūrattāṛvān*, also called RAṄGANĀTHA. *See* MAHĀBHĀRATA.—*Anuṣāsanaparva.* **भगवद्गुणदर्पणाख्यभाष्य** . . . **श्रीविष्णोर्नामसहस्रम्** *etc.* [Vishṇusahasranāma. With Parāṣara Bhaṭṭa's commentary Bhagavadguṇadarpaṇa.] [1894.] 8°. **14065. e. 27.**

—— அஷ்டஶ்லோகீ [Ashṭaṣlokī. A Vaishṇava religious poem in 8 stanzas. With Tamil version, analysis, and commentary.] *See* VARADĀCHĀRYA, *Vātsya*, called NAḌĀḌŪR AMMĀḶ. ப்ரபன்னபாரிஜாதம் *etc.* [Prapannapārijāta.] pp. 128-147. [1895.] 8°. **14028. d. 55.**

PĀRASKARA. *See* BHĪMASENA ṢARMĀ. **अथ स्मार्तकर्मपद्धतिः** *etc.* [Smārtakarmapaddhati. Liturgies on the basis of Pāraskara's Gṛihyasūtra.] [1900.] 8°. **14033. c. 45.(2.)**

—— *See* BHĪMASENA ṢARMĀ. **अथ-उपनयनपद्धतिः** *etc.* [Upanayanapaddhati. Directions for investiture with the sacred cord, *etc.*, on the basis of Pāraskara's Gṛihyasūtra.] [1900.] 8°. **14033. c. 45.(1.)**

—— *See* HARIVALLABHA ṢARMĀ. **संस्कारमार्तण्डः** *etc.* [Saṃskāramārtaṇḍa. Adapted from the Gṛihyasūtra of Pāraskara, *etc.*] [1901.] 8°. **14033. bbb. 10.(1.)**

PĀRASKARA (*continued*). पारस्करगृह्यसूत्रम् *etc.* [Pāraskaragṛihyasūtra, or Kātīyagṛihyas°. With 4 commentaries, viz. Karka Upādhyāya's Gṛihyabhāshya; Jayarāma's Sajjanavallabhā; Harihara's *vyākhyā*, with his Prayogapaddhati; and Gadādhara Dīkshita's Gṛihyasūtrabhāshya. Followed by the Pariśishṭakaṇḍikā and other ritual tracts ascribed to Kātyāyana, with commentaries and *prayogas* by Kāmadeva Dīkshita, Harihara, Karka, and Gadādhara. With introduction by Gaṇeṣadatta Tripāṭhī. Edited by Devanātha Ṣarmā and Bālamukunda Bhaṭṭa Gaṇurkar.] pp. xvi. xliii. 639. काश्यां १९५२ [*Benares*, 1896.] 4°.
14010. f. 10.

PARAṢURĀMA NĀRĀYAṆA PĀTANKAR. *See* KĀLIDĀSA.—*Abhijñānaṣakuntala.* The Abhijnâna-ŝakuntala . . . The purer Devanagari text. Edited with . . . translation, various readings, a preface . . . notes and . . . appendices. By P. N. Patankar. 1902. 8°.
14080. d. 26.

PARIMALA. *See* PADMAGUPTA, also called PARIMALA.

PARITTA.

BURMESE EDITIONS.

မဟာပရိတ်မှန်းကြီး [Mahā-payeik-hmûn-kyī. The Paritta, with Burmese paraphrase. Preceded and followed by divers Buddhist lections, chiefly short Pali texts with Burmese translations and commentaries.] pp. 168. ရန်ကုန် ၁၂၅၉ [*Rangoon*, 1897.] 8°.
14098. ccc. 41.

မဟာပရိတ်တော်ကြီး ပါဠိ *etc.* [Mahāparitta, including the Machchhaparitta. Edited by the Sein-pan-goṇ-ôk Hsaya.] pp. 31. မန္တလေး [*Mandalay*,] 1898. 12°.
14098. a. 33.

ဓာရဏပရိတ်တော် *etc.* [Dhāraṇaparitta, or Avadhāraṇap°. With Burmese version, *etc.*] *See* ĀSABHA, *Ū.* အာဇီဝဋ္ဌမကာဒိသီလ။ဝိနိစ္ဆယ ကျမ်း။ [Ājīvaṭṭhamakādisīlavinichchhaya.] pp. 98-106. [1900.] 8°.
14300. d. 4.(3.)

[For Burmese collections of Pali-Burmese texts including editions of the Paritta, see under the following headings:]

HSAY SAUNG TWÈ.
JAYAMAṄGALAGĀTHĀ.
SĀDHUNARADHAMMA-SĀ-TAN.
TA-HSÈ-HNIT SAUNG TWÈ.
TA-HSÈ-THÔN SAUNG TWÈ.

SINHALESE EDITIONS.

මහපිරිත්පොත. [Mahāparitta, in Sinhalese Maha-pirit-pota. A revised edition.] pp. 60, ii. [*Colombo*,] 1891. 8°.
14098. d. 42.(2.)

පිරුවානාපොත්වහන්සේ චතුභාණවාර පාලි *etc.* [Piruvānā-pot-vahansē.] pp. 158. [*Colombo*,] 1891. 8°.
14098. c. 70.

—— [Another edition.] pp. 115, 44. [*Colombo*,] 1891. 8°.
14098. ccc. 7.

PARIVĀRA. *See* VINAYAPIṬAKA.

PĀRTHASĀRATHI AIYAṄGĀR. *See* LOKĀCHĀRYA PILLAI. Tattva-traya . . . translated by Srí-Párthasárathy Aiyangar. 1900. 8°.
14170. ee. 17.

PĀRTHASĀRATHI DĀSA. *See* PĀRTHASĀRATHI AIYAṄGĀR.

PĀRTHASĀRATHI MIṢRA. *See* JAIMINI.—*Mīmāṃsāsūtra.* मीमांसाश्लोकवार्तिकम् *etc.* (The Mîmânsâ-śloka-vârtika . . . With the commentary called Nyâyaratnâkara by Pârtha Sârathi Miśra, *etc.*) 1898-1899. 8°.
14004. a. 3.

—— *See* JAIMINI.—*Mīmāṃsāsūtra.* Çlokavārtika. Translated . . . with extracts from the commentaries of . . . Pārthasārathi Miṣra, *etc.* 1900, *etc.* 8°. [*Bibliotheca Indica.*]
14002. a. (vol. 146.)

—— न्यायरत्नमाला *etc.* (Nyâyaratnamâlâ. [A summary of the Tantravārttika.] By Pandit Śri Partha Śarthi Misra. Edited by Mahâmahopâdhyâya Pandit Gangadhar Shastri.) pp. i. i. ii. 212. काश्याम् १९०० [*Benares*, 1900.] 8°.
14004. a. 7.

Forms nos. 28-29 *of the* Chowkhambâ Sanskrit Series. *The English title is taken from the wrapper.*

PATAÑJALI. [*Life.*] *See* RĀMABHADRA DĪKSHITA. The Patañjali-charita, *etc.* 1895. 8°. [*Kâvyamâlâ.*] **14072. ccc. 12.(no. 51.)**

GRAMMATICAL WORKS.

The Vyâkaraṇa-mahâbhâshya . . . Edited by F. Kielhorn . . . Second edition revised. *Bombay*, 1892, *etc.* 8°. **14090. d. 28.**

In progress.

See NĀGEṢA BHAṬṬA. [*Mahābhāshyapradīpoddyota.*] Mahābhāṣya Pradīpoddyota[, a commentary on Kaiyyaṭa's commentary to the Mahābhāshya] *etc.* 1901, *etc.* 8°. [*Bibliotheca Indica.*] **14002. a. (vol. 140.)**

भाष्यसङ्गमनी तत्त्वसङ्कलनीसहिता । [Bhāshyasaṅgamanī. Being the aphorisms of the Mahābhāshya, the text of the Kāṣikā in exposition of the aphorisms of Pāṇini quoted therein, and a commentary by Gauragovinda Rāya; together with a supercommentary by the latter, styled Tattvasaṅkalanī.] (Samanvaya Series.) कलिकाता० १८२५ [*Calcutta*, 1903, *etc.*] 8°. **14090. bb. 22.**

In progress. The publication of this work began originally in the Ṣrutaprakāṣa *and* Ṣabdaprakāṣa, *Calcutta* 1886.

PHILOSOPHICAL WORKS.

योगदर्शनम् *etc.* [Yogadarṣana. Being the Yoga-sūtra with the *bhāshya* ascribed to Bādarāyaṇa or Vyāsa, the supercommentary of Vāchaspati Miṣra called Yogatattvavaiṣāradī, and a gloss by the editor, Bālarāma Udāsīna.] pp. i. 320. कलिकाता १९४७ [*Calcutta*, 1890.] 8°. **14048. dd. 6.**

পাতঞ্জলদর্শনম্ । [Pātañjaladarṣana. Comprising the Aphorisms, the *bhāshya* ascribed to Vyāsa, the *vṛitti* of Bhojarāja styled Rājamārtaṇḍa, the *ṭīkā* of Vāchaspati Miṣra, and the *ṭīkā* Yogamaṇiprabhā of Rāmānanda Sarasvatī, with occasional Bengali translations and notes.] [1891, *etc.*] *See* PERIODICAL PUBLICATIONS.—*Calcutta.* অরুণোদয় *etc.* [Aruṇodaya.] Pt. i., no. 25. [1890, *etc.*] 4°. **14133. g. 16.(pt. i., no. 25.)**

Imperfect, extending only to I. xxxii.

Patañjalasûtrâṇi. With the scholium of Vyâsa and the commentary of Vâchaspati [and as an appendix the text of the Aphorisms alone]. Edited by Râjârâm Shâstrî Bodas. (पातञ्जलसूत्राणि ।) pp. v. 230, ii. *Bombay*, 1892. 8°. **14048. dd. 10.**

Forms vol. xlvi. *of the* Bombay Sanskrit Series.

యోగసారము [Yogasāra. The Yoga Aphorisms, with Telugu version by Ṣrīnivāsa Jagannātha Svāmī.] 1892-1893. 12°. *See* PERIODICAL PUBLICATIONS.—*Vizagapatam.* సకలవిద్యాభివర్ధని *etc.* [Sakalavidyābhivardhanī.] Vol. 1, pt. i.-x. 1892-1897. 12° & 8°. **14174. g. 38.(vol. 1.)**

Not completed.

पातञ्जलदर्शनप्रकाश *etc.* [Pātañjaladarṣanaprakāṣa. Being the Aphorisms with a Hindi translation and commentary by Bālarāma Udāsīna. Preceded by commendatory verses by divers authors. Edited with Hindi annotations by Ātmasvarūpa Udāsīna.] pp. ix. xi. 16, 10, 16, 406, 10; 2 *plates.* *Bankipure*, १८९७ [1897.] 8°. **14048. d. 59.**

पातञ्जलयोगशास्त्राचाअभिप्राय *etc.* [Pātañjala-yoga-ṣāstrā-chā Abhiprāya. The Aphorisms with Marathi translation and commentary by Nānābhāī Sadānandajī Reḷe.] pp. viii. 162; 4 *plates.* मुंबईंत १८९७ [*Bombay*, 1897.] 8°. **14048. dd. 31.(1.)**

पातञ्जलयोगशास्त्रम् *etc.* [Yogaṣāstra. The Aphorisms, with the *bhāshya* ascribed to Vyāsa and a Marathi translation of the whole by Nānābhāī Sadānandajī Reḷe.] pp. ii. iv. 194. मुम्बय्याम् १८९७ [*Bombay*, 1897.] 8°. **14048. dd. 31.(2.)**

পাতঞ্জল দর্শন *etc.* [Pātañjaladarṣana. The Aphorisms with a brief commentary, the *bhāshya* ascribed to Vyāsa, and Bengali translations thereof and Bengali commentary. Compiled and edited by Pūrṇachandra Vedāntachuñchu.] pp. viii. 349, i. কলিকাতা ১৮৯৮ [*Calcutta*, 1898.] 8°. **14048. cc. 23.**

योगदर्शनम् *etc.* [Yogadarṣana. The Yoga Aphorisms. Edited by Rāmasvarūpa Ṣarmā of Moradabad.] pp. 11. १८९८ [*Moradabad*, 1898.] 8°. **14048. cc. 21.(3.)**

The Aphorisms of Patanjali. With the commentaries of Vyas, Vachaspati, and Bhoja, and

Bhasha translation. Edited by Munishwar Sharma, *etc.* pt. i. pp. 60. *Jagraon, Agra* [printed, 1899.] 8°. **14048. c. 75.(2.)**

This forms part of vol. 3 of a series entitled "M. K. Granth Mala, a collection of Sanskrit writings." Apparently no more has been registered. This fascicule contains nothing of Bhoja's commentary or of the Hindi translation. It was intended that these should appear in later fascicules.

श्रीपातंजलयोगदर्शन *etc.* [Pātañjalayogadarṣana. Being the Yogasūtra with the commentary Padabodhinī, and the gloss Rahasyadīpikā of Nathurām, comprising Gujarati translations and explanations of the aphorisms.] pp. xxx. 651. અમદાવાદ ૧૯૦૧ [*Ahmadabad*, 1901.] 12°. **14048. b. 40.**

The Yoga-sutra of Patanjali. Translation, with introduction, appendix, and notes based upon several authentic commentaries. By Manilal Nabhubhai Dvivedi, *etc.* pp. ii. viii. 99, vii. *Bombay*, [1890 ?] 8°. **14048. cc. 33.**

—— [A reprint of the preceding.] *Bombay*, [1904 ?] 8°. **14049. b. 22.**

Patanjali's Yoga Aphorisms [in English, with commentary by Svāmī Vivekānanda]. *See* VIVEKĀNANDA, *Svāmī*. Yoga Philosophy, *etc.* pp. 95-234. 1896. 8°. **4503. b. 22.**

—— —— pp. 81-194. 1897. 8°. **14048. cc. 2.(1.)**

Patanjali's Yoga Aphorisms [in English, with commentary by Svāmī Vivekānanda]. *See* VIVEKĀNANDA, *Svāmī*. Vedânta Philosophy, *etc.* pp. 95-228. 1897. 8°. **4503. b. 31.**

Raja-Yoga, or Conquering the internal Nature, [*scil.* the Aphorisms in English with introduction and commentary] by the Swami Vivekananda. pp. i. ii. 159. *Calcutta*, 1901. 8°. **14048. bb. 54.**

See KĀLĪVARA VEDĀNTAVĀGĪṢA. হিন্দুশাস্ত্র *etc.* [Shaḍdarṣana. A Bengali exposition of the six systems.] [1895.] 8°. [*Hindu-ṣāstra.*] **14085. c. 45.(vol. 1.)**

See VIJÑĀNABHIKSHU. An English Translation, with Sanskrit Text, of the Yogasara-sangraha, *etc.* 1894. 12°. **14048. b. 26.**

Yoga Sastra: the Yoga Sutras of Patanjali examined; with a notice of Swami Vivekananda's Yoga Philosophy. pp. ii. 69; 1 *plate*. 1897. *See* EAST. The Sacred Books of the East Described and Examined. Hindu Series. Vol. II, pt. 4. 1895, *etc.* 8°. **14010. cc. 9.(vol. 2.)**

PATANKAR (P. N.). *See* PARAṢURĀMA NĀRĀYAṆA PĀTANKAR.

PATHAK (K. B.). *See* KĀṢĪNĀTHA BĀPŪ PĀṬHAKA.

PĀṬIMOKKHA. *See* VINAYAPIṬAKA.

PAṬISAMBHIDĀMAGGA. *See* SUTTAPIṬAKA.

PAṬṬĀBHIRĀMA DĪKSHITA, *D. Uḍāli.* *See* VEDĀNTASAÑJÑĀPRAKARAṆA. వేదాంతసంజ్ఞాప్రకరణమ్ *etc.* [Vedāntasañjñāprakaraṇa. Edited by Paṭṭābhirāma.] [1890.] 8°. **14048. bb. 42.(1.)**

PAṬṬĀBHIRĀMA ṢĀSTRĪ, *of Bangalore.* ಶ್ರೀ ಋಷ್ಯಶೃಂಗೋಪಾಖ್ಯಾನವು *etc.* [Ṛishyasṛingopākhyāna. The tale of Ṛishya Ṣṛinga, as recounted in the Skanda and Bhavishyottara Purāṇas, Mahābhārata, Rāmāyaṇa, Adhyātmarāmāyaṇa, and Saṅgraharāmāyaṇa. Compiled and edited with Canarese translation and preface by Paṭṭābhirāma.] pp. viii. 275. ಬೆಂಗಳೂರು ೧೮೯೧ [*Bangalore*, 1891.] 8°. **14016. c. 45.**

PAṬṬHĀNA. *See* ABHIDHAMMAPIṬAKA.

PAVANAVIJAYA. পবনবিজয়স্বরোদয়ঃ। [Pavanavijaya-svarodaya. A treatise on the magical operation of the breath, *etc.*, in 324 vv. With Bengali translation, *etc.*] pp. 35. [1891, *etc.*] *See* PERIODICAL PUBLICATIONS.—*Calcutta.* অরুণোদয় *etc.* [Aruṇodaya.] Pt. i., no. 13. [1890, *etc.*] 4°. **14133. g. 16.(pt. i., no. 13.)**

—— পবন-বিজয় স্বরোদয় শাস্ত্রম্ *etc.* [Pavanavijaya-svarodayaṣāstra, or Bṛihat-svarodayatantra. Another recension of the preceding in 433 verses (36 chapters). With Bengali translation and notes.] pp. 118. *Calcutta*, [1901.] 12°. **14033. a. 41.(4.)**

—— পবনবিজয় স্বরোদয়ঃ *etc.* [Pavanavijaya-svarodaya. A similar treatise in 21 *adhyāyas*. Edited by Kālīprasanna Vidyāratna. Second edition.] pp. ii. 116. কলিকাতা ১২৯৮ [*Calcutta*, 1892.] 12°. **14028. b. 72.(2.)**

PAVOLINI (Paolo Emilio). *See* Ānandadhara, *disciple of Vidyādhara.* The Mādhavânala-kathā . . . with a translation of the Prakrit passages. By Dr. E. P. Pavolini. 1893. 8°. [*Transactions of the Ninth International Congress of Orientalists.*]
Ac. 8806. (Session 9.)

—— *See* Bharaṭakadvātriṃṣikā. Bharaṭakadvātriṃçikā. [Edited by P. E. Pavolini.] 1897. 8°. [*Studi Italiani di Filologia Indo-Iranica.*]
P.P. 4884. da.(vol. 1.)

—— *See* Devendra Gaṇī. Le Novelline Prācrite di Maṇḍiya e di Agaladatta. [An Italian translation by P. E. Pavolini of two stories from commentaries on the Uttarādhyayana.] 1892. 8°.
14100. c. 18.

—— *See* Devendra Gaṇī. La Novella di Brahmadatta. [An Italian translation by P. E. Pavolini of the story from Devendra's commentary on the Uttarādhyayana.] 1892. 8°. [*Giornale della Società Asiatica Italiana.*]
Ac. 8804. (vol. 6.)

—— *See* Kundakunda Āchārya. Il Compendio dei Cinque Elementi . . . [Edited by P. E. Pavolini.] 1901. 8°. [*Giornale della Società Asiatica Italiana.*] **Ac. 8804. (vol. 14.)**

—— *See* Rasavāhinī. Il settimo capitolo della Rasavāhinī. (Rasavāhinī, I, 8-10.) [Edited with translation by P. E. Pavolini.] 1894-1897. [*Giornale della Società Asiatica Italiana.*]
Ac. 8804. (vol. 8, 10.)

—— *See* Ṣaṅkara Āchārya. — *Commentaries.* [*Upanishads.*] La introduzione del commento di Çaṅkara alla Kāṭhakopaniṣad. [With translation and notes] per P. E. Pavolini. 1892. 8°.
14010. dd. 5. (3.)

—— *See* Somaprabha Āchārya. Gli Scritti di Somaprabhācārya. [With translation of his Sindūraprakara. By P. E. Pavolini.] 1898. 8°. [*Studi Italiani di Filologia Indo-Iranica.*]
P.P. 4884. da. (vol. 2.)

—— *See* Vimalachandra Sūri. Una Redazione Pracrita della Praçnottararatnamālā. [Edited with translation by P. E. Pavolini.] 1897-1898. [*Giornale della Società Asiatica Italiana.*]
Ac. 8804. (vol. 11.)

PAYĀ-SHI-HKO. ဘုရားရှိခိုးအမျိုးမျိုး ပုံနှိပ် ။ [Payā-shi-hko. A handbook of Buddhist devotions, consisting of various Pali excerpts, *etc.*, for the most part with Burmese translations.] pp. 64. ရန်ကုန် ၁၂၅၅ [*Rangoon*, 1893.] 8°.
14098. ccc. 16.(2.)

—— [Another edition.] pp. 64. ရန်ကုန် ၁၂၅၇ [*Rangoon*, 1895.] 8°. **14098. ccc. 16.(3).**

PEILE (James Braithwaite). Catalogue of native publications in the Bombay Presidency from 1st January 1865 to 30th June 1867, and of some works omitted in the previous catalogue [of Sir A. Grant]. Prepared under orders of Government by J. B. Peile. pp. 120. *Bombay*, 1869. 8°. **14096. ccc. 6.**

Continued in the form of quarterly lists, in accordance with the Act of 1867.

—— [Another copy.] **752. e. 15.**

PERERA (N. A.). Basaga Sangrahava. භෛෂජ-සංග්‍රහව. [Bheshajasangrahava. A medical treatise, compiled from Sanskrit authorities by N. A. Perera.] pp. 30. *Colombo*, 1892. 8°.
14043. c. 43.(2.)

PERIODICAL PUBLICATIONS.

Allahabad.

आर्यसिद्धान्त [Āryasiddhānta. Vols. 3, 4. Edited by Bhīmasena Ṣarmā. Second edition.] प्रयाग १८९५ [*Allahabad*, 1895.] 8°. **14033. b. 49.**

Bangalore.

Kâvyakalpadrumam. ಕಾವ್ಯಕಲ್ಪದ್ರುಮಮ್ *etc.* [A magazine for the publication of classical poems in Sanskrit and Canarese. Edited by Kommāṇḍūr Ṣrīnivāsa Aiyaṅgār.] Vol. I, pt. 1. *Bangalore*, 1897. 8°. **14076. cc. 1.**

Apparently no more has been published. Portions of Kālidāsa's Kumārasambhava and Meghadūta and of Ṣrīharsha's Naishadha appeared here.

Bellary.

The Astrological Magazine. Edited by B. Suryanarain Row, *etc.* *Bellary, Madras*, 1895, *etc.* 8°. **P.P. 1560. m.**

In progress. Vol. iv. and following volumes have been published at Madras.

PERIODICAL PUBLICATIONS (*continued*).

BENARES.

काशीविद्यासुधानिधिः The Pandit. A monthly publication of the Benares College, devoted to Sanskrit literature. New series. 1876, *etc.* 8°. **14096. d. 6.**

In progress.

BERLIN.

Zeitschrift für vergleichende Litteraturgeschichte . . . Neue Folge. *Berlin, Weimar*, 1887, *etc.* 8°. **P.P. 4748. ma.**

In progress.

BOMBAY.

ग्रन्थरत्नमाला *etc.* (Granth Ratna Málá, a monthly Sanscrit magazine.) Vol. I, no. 1 – Vol. V, no. 8. मुम्बय्याम् [*Bombay,*] 1887-[1892.] 8°. **14096. c. 8.**

The Indian Antiquary. A journal of oriental research in archaeology, history, literature, languages, philosophy, religion, folklore, *etc.* Edited by J. Burgess. (Vol. xiii., edited by J. Burgess and A. Führer; vol. xiv.-xvii., edited by J. F. Fleet and R. C. Temple; vol. xviii., edited by J. F. Fleet, R. C. Temple and W. Crooke; vol. xix.-xx., edited by J. F. Fleet and R. C. Temple; vol. xxi. *etc.* by R. C. Temple.) *Bombay*, 1872, *etc.* 4°. **14096. e.**

In progress.

See INDIA.—*Archaeological Survey.* Epigraphia Indica, *etc.* (Vol. iii., *etc.*, published . . . as a supplement to the "Indian Antiquary.") 1892, *etc.* Fol. & 4°. **1710. b. 13, 14.**

श्रीपुष्टिमार्गप्रकाश: *etc.* [Pushṭimārgaprakāṣa. An organ of the Pushṭimārga or Hedonist Vaishṇava school of Vallabhāchārya, in Gujarati and Sanskrit.] મુંબઈ ૧૮૧૫ [*Bombay*, 1893, *etc.*] 8°. **14150. c. 15.**

In progress?

The Theosophist. A monthly journal devoted to Oriental philosophy, art, literature, and occultism, embracing mesmerism, spiritualism and other secret sciences. Conducted by H. P. Blavatsky, *etc.* (Vol. x., *etc.* Conducted by H. S. Olcott.) *Bombay, Madras*, 1879, *etc.* Fol. & 8°. **P.P. 636. cm.**

In progress. Vol. 16 ff. have been published at Madras.

CALCUTTA.

অরুণোদয় *etc.* [Aruṇodaya. A Bengali monthly magazine chiefly devoted to astrology and magic, in which are published divers Sanskrit texts bearing on these subjects, with Bengali translations. Edited by Rasikamohana Chaṭṭopādhyāya.] Vol. I-V. iii. কলিকাতা ১২৯৭ [*Calcutta*, 1890, *etc.*] 4°. **14133. g. 16.**

No numbers have been registered since 1897.

The Oriental. A monthly journal devoted to the resuscitation of Indian literature. *Calcutta*, 1898, *etc.* 8°. **Ac. 8825. b.**

In progress.

उषा वैदिकपत्रिका। [Ushā. A journal of Vedic (chiefly Sāmavedic) and kindred studies, usually issued monthly, and containing Sanskrit texts with commentaries, reviews, and other articles in Sanskrit and Bengali. Compiled and edited by Satyavrata Sāmaṣramī.] Vol. I-II. viii. *Calcutta*, १८११ [1889]-1893. 8°. **14010. c. 43.**

The texts published in this series which have already been registered in Professor Bendall's Catalogue are to be found in the latter under the headings:—

Āpisali.
Brāhmaṇas.—*Mantrabrāhmaṇa.*
Madhusūdana, *Guru.*
Vedas.—*Sāmaveda.*

विद्योदयः *etc.* [Vidyodaya. A magazine of literature.] कलिकाता [*Calcutta,*] 1874, *etc.* 8°. **14096. cc.**

In progress.

CHIDAMBARAM.

ப்ரஹ்மவித்யா *etc.* [Brahmavidyā. A monthly journal of literature, in Sanskrit and Tamil.] சிதம்பரம் கஅஅசு [*Chidambaram*, 1886, *etc.*] 4°. **14096. dd. 3.**

In progress?

COLOMBO.

The Buddhist. The English organ of the Southern Buddhist Church. Edited by C. W. Leadbeater, vol. 1. (By A. E. Buultjens, vol. 2. By L. C. Wijesinha, vol. 3, 4, no. 1-26. By A. E. Buultjens, vol. 4, no. 27, *etc.* By C. Jinarājadāsa, vol. 11, no. 7-12. By D. B. Jayatilaka, vol. 10, *etc.*) *Colombo*, 1888, *etc.* 8°. **P.P. 636. cn.**

In progress.

FLORENCE.

Studi Italiani di Filologia Indo-Iranica. Diretti da Francesco L. Pullé. *Firenze*, 1897, *etc.* 8°. **P.P. 4884. da.**

In progress.

KUMBAKONAM.

The Sanskrit Journal. Issued every month. Edited by R. Krishnamachariar . . . and B. V. Kamesvara Aiyar, *etc.* *Kumbhakonam, Pudukota*, 1896, *etc.* 8°. **14096. ccc. 1.**

In progress. From 1897 published at Pudukottai, but still printed at Kumbakonam.

LONDON.

The Babylonian & Oriental Record: a Monthly Magazine of the Antiquities of the East. Editorial Committee: Prof. T. de Lacouperie, T. G. Pinches, and W. C. Capper. *London*, 1886, *etc.* 8°. **P.P. 3780.**

In progress.

LOUVAIN.

Le Muséon. Revue internationale publiée par la Société des Lettres et des Sciences. (Le Muséon. Études philologiques, historiques, et religieuses. . . . Nouvelle série. 1900.) *Louvain*, 1881, *etc.* 8°. **P.P. 4453.**

In progress.

MADRAS.

The Astrological Magazine, *etc.* *See* above, BELLARY. **P.P. 1560. m.**

The Brahmavâdin. A fortnightly religious and philosophical journal. *Madras*, 1895, *etc.* 4° & 8°. **14048. g. 1.**

In progress. From Vol. V. i. *onwards the issue has been monthly. The quarto size was abandoned after Vol. II.*

The Light of Truth, or Siddhanta Deepika. A monthly journal [chiefly in English,] devoted to religion, philosophy, literature, science, &c. [Edited by J. M. Nāgaratnam Piḷḷai.] *Madras*, 1897, *etc.* 4°. **14170. fff. 4.**

In progress.

PERIODICAL PUBLICATIONS (*continued*).

MADRAS (*continued*).

The Somaravi. An occasional (A quarterly) publication on Hindu philosophy [in Tamil and English, illustrated from Sanskrit texts]. Edited . . . by C. E. Srinivasaragavacharriar . . . *சோம-ரவி etc.* Vol. I. i.-v. *Madras*, 1895-1896. 4°. **14170. ccc. 1.**

The Theosophist, *etc.* *See* above, BOMBAY. **P.P. 636. cm.**

The Vaishnavite . . . A monthly journal devoted to the Visishtadwaita philosophy, Hindu morality, and piety. *Madras*, 1898, *etc.* 8°. **759. d. 7.**

In progress.

MYSORE.

ವೀರಶೈವಮತಪ್ರಕಾಶಿಕೆ [Vīraṣaivamataprakāṣikā. A monthly journal for the publication of texts and treatises in Sanskrit and Canarese bearing on the tenets of the Vīraṣaiva or Lingāyat sect.] Vol. I-IV. vi. ಮೈಸೂರು ೧೮೯೨-೧೮೯೫ [*Mysore*, 1892-1895.] 8°. **14028. d. 39.**

The chief Sanskrit texts published are catalogued under the headings:

Basavapurāṇa. Ṣaṅkara Ārādhya.

PALERMO.

Archivio per lo Studio delle Tradizioni Popolari. Rivista trimestrale diretta da G. Pitrè e S. Salomone-Marino. *Palermo, Torino*, 1882, *etc.* 8°. **P.P. 4168. d.**

In progress.

PARIS.

Revue de Linguistique et de Philologie Comparée, *etc.* *Paris*, 1867, *etc.* 8°. **P.P. 4964. d.**

In progress.

Revue de l'Histoire des Religions, *etc.* *Paris, Saint-Quentin* [printed], 1880, *etc.* 8°. **P.P. 37. cc.**

In progress. Forms part of the Annales du Musée Guimet.

POONA.

काव्येतिहास-संग्रह [Kāvyetihāsasaṅgraha. A monthly serial for the publication of early Marathi and of Sanskrit poetical and historical works.] 11 vols. पुणे १८७८-१८८८ [*Poona*, 1878-1888.] 8°. **14072. d. 37.**

The Kavi. कवि. [A monthly magazine for the publication of classical poetry.] Vol. I. i.-ix. पुणे १८९५ [*Poona*, 1895.] 8°. **14070. c. 56.**

Apparently no more has been published. The works commenced are the Kumārasambhava, Meghadūta, and Raghuvaṃśa of Kālidāsa.

PUDUKOTTAI.

The Sanskrit Journal, *etc.* *See* above, KUMBAKONAM. **14096. ccc. 1.**

VIZAGAPATAM.

సకలవిద్యాభివర్ధని *etc.* [Sakalavidyābhivardhanī. A magazine for the publication of scientific and philosophical works in Sanskrit and Telugu.] Vol. I-IV. vi. *Vizagapatam*, 1892-1897. 12° & 8°. **14174. g. 38.**

PERIYASVĀMI TIRUMALĀCHĀRYA, *Maṇḍayam Chakravarti.* *See* GARAḶAPURĪŚA ŚĀSTRĪ. చమ్పూరామాయణ ॥ [Champūrāmāyaṇa. Yuddhakāṇḍa, edited with a commentary called Madhumañjarī by Periyasvāmi.] [1891.] 8°. **14072. cc. 52.**

—— *See* PĀÑCHARĀTRA. శ్రీ ... అప్పాధ్యాయా *etc.* [Prapattiprapannavṛittisvarūpa. With introduction by Periyasvāmi. Edited by the latter, *etc.*] [1894.] 8°. **14028. d. 62.**

PERIYAVĀCHĀN PIḶḶAI, called KṚISHṆA SŪRI. *See* VĀLMĪKI. — Rāmāyaṇa. — *Abridgments and Selections.* இந்த தனிஸ்லோகம் *etc.* [Taniślokam. Stanzas from the Rāmāyaṇa, with Tamil glosses and commentary by Periyavāchān Piḷḷai expounding Viśishṭādvaita doctrine.] [1899, *etc.*] 8°. **14065. bbb. 6.**

—— —— తనిశ్లోకమ్ *etc.* [Tani-ślokam. Another edition, containing the glosses in Telugu.] [1899, *etc.*] 8°. **14065. bbb. 7.**

—— *See* VĀLMĪKI. — Rāmāyaṇa. — *Portions.* அபயப்ரதாநஸாரம் *etc.* [Abhayapradānasāra. Being VI. xvii.-xix. 1-9 and 23, with exposition in Tamil by Periyavāchān Piḷḷai.] [1891.] 8°. **14060. c. 32.(1.)**

PETAVATTHU. *See* SUTTAPIṬAKA.—*Khuddakanikāya.*

PETERSON (PETER). *See* ALWAR.—*Library of the Maharaja of Alwar.* Catalogue of the Sanskrit Manuscripts . . . By P. Peterson. 1892. 4°. **14096. dd. 4.**

—— *See* BHAUNAGAR.—*Archæological Department.* A Collection of . . . Inscriptions, *etc.* [With a preface by P. Peterson.] [1895?] 4°. **14058. d. 6.**

—— *See* DAṆḌĪ. ॥ दशकुमारचरितं . . . The Daśakumâracharita, *etc.* (Part II. [Books iv.-viii.] Edited . . . by P. Peterson.) 1873-1891. 8°. **14076. c. 45.**

—— *See* KALHAṆA. The Râjataraṅgiṇî, *etc.* (Vol. III. Containing the supplements . . . of Jonarâja, Srîvara and Prâjyabhaṭṭa. Edited by P. Peterson.) 1892-1896. 8°. **14058. b. 27.**

—— *See* NYĀYABINDU. The Nyayabindutika . . . Edited by P. Peterson. 1889. 8°. [*Bibliotheca Indica.*] **14002. a. (vol. 128.)**

—— *See* SIDDHARSHI. उपमितिभवप्रपंचा कथा . . . The Upamitibhavaprapancha Katha . . . (Originally) edited by (the late) P. Peterson (and continued by . . . H. Jacobi). 1899, *etc.* 8°. [*Bibliotheca Indica.*] **14002. a. (vol. 144.)**

—— *See* VEDAS.—Ṛigveda.—*Selections of Hymns and Verses.* Handbook to the study of the Rigveda, by P. Peterson, *etc.* 1890-1892. 8°. **14010. c. 50.**

—— *See* VEDAS.—Ṛigveda.—*Selections of Hymns and Verses.* Hymns from the Rigveda, edited with Sayana's commentary, notes, and a translation by P. Peterson. Second edition. 1898. 8°. **14007. cc. 26.**

—— *See* VEDAS.—Ṛigveda.—*Selections of Hymns and Verses.* A Second Selection of Hymns . . . Edited, with Sâyaṇa's commentary and notes, by P. Peterson. 1899. 8°. **14010. cc. 11.**

—— A fourth report of operations in search of Sanskrit MSS. in the Bombay Circle, April

1886–March 1892, *etc.* pp. cxlii. 177, 58. *Bombay,* 1894. 8°. **14096. cc. 3.**

Forms the extra number (no. xlix.A) *of the Journal of the Bombay Branch of the Royal Asiatic Society, vol.* xviii.

—— A fifth report of operations in search of Sanscrit MSS. in the Bombay Circle. April 1892–March 1895, *etc.* pp. i. lxxxviii. 317. *Bombay,* 1896. 8°. **14096. cc. 3.**

—— A sixth report of operations in search of Sanscrit MSS. in the Bombay Circle. April 1895–March 1898, *etc.* pp. xxviii. 144. *Bombay,* 1899. 8°. **14096. cc. 3.**

PHILLIPS (MAURICE). The Teaching of the Vedas. What light does it throw on the origin and development of religion? pp. viii. 240. *London, Aberdeen* [printed], 1895. 8°. **4503. aaa. 12.**

PIḶḶAI LOKĀCHĀRYA. *See* LOKĀCHĀRYA PIḶḶAI.

PIṄGALA ĀCHĀRYA. [For the Pāṇinīyaṣikshā sometimes ascribed to Piṅgala:] *See* PĀṆINI.—*Appendix.* [*Ṣikshā.*]

—— ॥ अथ छन्द° [Chhandaḥsūtra.] ff. 6. *See* VEDAS.—*Appendix.* ॥ अथ . . . षडङ्ग° [Shaḍaṅga.] pt. 4. [1892.] *obl.* 8°. **14007. c. 27.**

—— The Prâkṛita-piṅgala-sûtras. With the commentary [Piṅgalapradīpa] of Lakshmînâtha Bhaṭṭa. Edited by Paṇdit Śivadatta . . . and Kâśînâth Pâṇdurang Parab. (प्राकृतपिङ्गलसूत्राणि ।) pp. i. x. 239. 1894. *See* DURGĀPRASĀDA, *son of Vrajalāla,* and KĀṢĪNĀTHA PĀṆḌURAṄGA PARAB. Kâvyâmâlâ. [No.] 41. 1886, *etc.* 8°. **14072. ccc. 12.(no. 41.)**

—— Prákrita-paiṅgalam. With the commentaries of Viśwanátha-Pañchánana, Vanśídhara, Krishṇa and Yádavendra. Edited, and supplemented with a complete index and glossary of all Prákrita words in the text, by Chandra Mohana Ghosha. (प्राकृतपैङ्गलं) pp. viii. xiii. 702. 1902. *See* ACADEMIES, *etc.*—Calcutta.—*Asiatic Society of Bengal.* Bibliotheca Indica. New Series. [Vol. 148.] 1848, *etc.* 8°. **14002. a. (vol. 148.)**

—— प्राकृतं पिङ्गलच्छन्दःशास्त्रम् । [Prākṛitachchhandaḥṣāstra. With the commentary Rahasyākhyāyinī of Maheṣachandra Chūḍāmaṇi.] 1900, *etc.* *See* PERIODICAL PUBLICATIONS.—*Calcutta.* विद्योदयः *etc.* [Vidyodaya.] Vol. xxix., *etc.* **14096. cc. (vol. 29, etc.)**

PINGLE, *Bhavánráv A.* *See* BHAVĀNRĀU PINGLE.

PISCHEL (RICHARD). *See* HEMACHANDRA, *disciple of Devachandra.* Materialien zur Kenntnis des Apabhraṃśa . . . Von R. Pischel. 1902. 4°. [*Abhandlungen der Koeniglichen Gesellschaft der Wissenschaften zu Goettingen.*] **14093. d. 23.**

—— *See* TRIPIṬAKA. Bruchstücke des Sanskritkanons der Buddhisten . . . Von R. Pischel. 1904. 8°. **14070. ee. 1.**

PIṬAKAS, *Three.* [For the Pali Canon:] *See* ABHIDHAMMAPIṬAKA, SUTTAPIṬAKA, and VINAYAPIṬAKA.

—— [For the Sanskrit Canon:] *See* TRIPIṬAKA.

PĪTĀMBARA GOVINDARĀMA BHAṬṬA, *of Sanand.* ॥ द्विजस्त्रीणामाह्निकम् ॥ श्री द्विजस्त्रिओनुं आह्निक *etc.* [Dvijastrīṇām Āhnika. A manual of daily religious duties for women of the Brahman, Kshatriya, and Vaiṣya castes, comprising Sanskrit texts with Gujarati explanations, rubrics, *etc.* Compiled, with Gujarati introduction, by Pītāmbara Bhaṭṭa. Third edition.] pp. 30, i. 128. અમદાવાદ ૧૮૯૯ [*Ahmadabad,* 1899.] 12°. **14028. b. 107.**

PĪTĀMBARA NYĀYARATNA. *See* VOPADEVA. मुग्धबोधः *etc.* (Mugdhabodha, *etc.*) [Edited by Pītāmbara.] [1901.] 12°. **14092. a. 25.**

PĪTĀMBARA PURUSHOTTAMA, *disciple of Bāpū Sarasvatī.* *See* SĀYAṆA ĀCHĀRYA. — *Works on Philosophy, etc.* श्रीपंचदशी सटीका सभाषा ॥ [Pañchadaṣī. With Pītāmbara's Hindi commentary called Tattvaprakāṣikā. Followed by Gajendramoksha, with notes by Pītāmbara.] [1897.] 8°. **14048. e. 25.**

—— *See* SĀYAṆA ĀCHĀRYA.—*Works on Philosophy, etc.* ॥ श्रीपंचदशी *etc.* [Pañchadaṣī. Prakaraṇa x. With Hindi notes by Pītāmbara.] [1900.] 8°. [*Vichārasāgara.*] **14154. ff. 1.**

PĪTĀMBARA PURUSHOTTAMA, *disciple of Bāpū Sarasvatī (continued)*. *See* UPANISHADS.—*Separate Upanishads.* श्रीबृहदारण्यकोपनिषत् *etc.* [Bṛihadāraṇyakopanishad. Edited with a Hindi translation, a Hindi commentary, and notes by Pītāmbara. Preceded by a short metrical account of certain Upanishads, entitled Ṣrutishaḍliṅgasaṅgraha, with Hindi translation, also by the latter.] [1892.] 8°. **14007. c. 24.**

PITṚIMEDHA. *See* BHĀRADVĀJA. భారద్వాజసూత్రము *etc.* [Bhāradvājasūtra. 45 aphorisms from a Pitṛimedhasūtra.] 1897. 8°. **14028. d. 59.(7.)**

—— *See* CALAND (W.). ॥ पितृमेधसूत्राणि ॥ The Pitṛmedhasūtras of Baudhāyana, Hiraṇyakeśin, Gautama, *etc.* 1896. 8°. [*Deutsche Morgenlaendische Gesellschaft: Abhandlungen.*] **753. f. 18.**

—— అనాహితాగ్నిపైతృమేధిక ప్రయోగ *etc.* [Anāhitāgni-paitṛimedhikaprayoga. A manual for the performance of the *pitṛimedha* rites for the souls of deceased laymen, based upon and illustrated from the Vājasaneyisaṃhitā and literature derived thence. With a Telugu *kriyāpaddhati* or guide.] చెన్నపురము [*Madras*,] 1897, *etc.* 8°. **14028. d. 70.**

In progress?

PITṚITARPAṆA. *See* NITYAKARMA.

PIZZI (ITALO). *See* PAÑCHATANTRA. Le Novelle Indiane di Visnusarma . . . Tradotte . . . da I. Pizzi. 1896. 8°. **14072. d. 17.(2.)**

PLEYTE (C. M.). *See* LALITAVISTARA. Die Buddhalegende in den Skulpturen des Tempels von Bôrô-Budur [elucidated by a summary of the Lalitavistara] von C. M. Pleyte. 1901. 4°. **14070. f. 7.**

PO. *See* HPO.

POHL (EMIL). *See* ṢŪDRAKA. Vasantasena. Drama . . . mit freier Benutzung der Dichtung des . . . Sudraka, von E. Pohl. [Adapted from the version of L. Fritze.] 1893. 8°. **14079. b. 40.**

—— *See* ṢŪDRAKA. Vasantasena . . . efter . . . Pohls tyska bearbetning, *etc.* 1894. 12°. **11755. dd.**

POORNA. *See* DEVĪPRASĀDA, *Rāi*, called PŪRṆA.

POTAYA, *son of Ṣiṅganna, of Kakimrani.* ప్రసఙ్గరత్నావళి [Prasaṅgaratnāvalī. Miscellaneous stanzas, with Telugu translations.] 1893-1897. 12°. *See* PERIODICAL PUBLICATIONS.—*Vizagapatam.* సకలవిద్యాభివర్ధని *etc.* [Sakalavidyābhivardhanī.] Vol. I, pt. viii.—Vol. II, pt. ix., Vol. IV, pt. ii., iii. 1892-1897. 12° & 8°. **14174. g. 38.**

Dated in a chronogram 1388 *Ṣaka. Incomplete.*

POUSSIN (L. DE LA VALLÉE). *See* LA VALLÉE POUSSIN (L. DE).

PRABHĀCHANDRA ĀCHĀRYA. जैनकथाद्वाविंशतिः [Jainakathādvāviṃṣati. Twenty-two stories, extracted from Prabhāchandra's commentary on Samantabhadra's Ratnakaraṇḍa.] pp. 36. मुंबय्यां १९५३ [*Bombay*, 1897.] 12°. **14100. a. 16.**

PRABHĀCHANDRA DEVA, *disciple of Ratnakīrti.* *See* SAMĀDHIṢATAKA. श्री . . . श्रीसमाधिशतकं *etc.* (The Samâdhi-śataka . . . with commentary by Prabhâchandra, *etc.*) 1895. 12°. **14048. b. 29.**

PRABHENDU. [For the Samādhiṣataka sometimes attributed to Prabhendu:] *See* SAMĀDHIṢATAKA.

PRABHUDATTA MIṢRA, *Ādigauḍa.* *See* ṢAUNAKA. महर्षिशौनकप्रणीतम् ऋक्प्रातिशाख्यम् । . . . Śaunaka's Prátiśákhya . . . with the commentary of Uvvaṭa. Edited . . . by . . . Yugalakiśora Vyâsa . . . and . . . Prabhudatta Śarmâ. 1903. 8°. **14090. c. 40.**

PRABHUDAYĀLU, *Mu'āfīdār and 'Ilāḳedār of Terhi, Banda.* समीक्षाकर *etc.* [Samīkshākara. Select Aphorisms from the Vaiṣeshika, Sāṅkhya, and Vedānta systems, with a commentary designed to reconcile the apparent discrepancies of the philosophical schools, by Prabhudayālu. With Hindi paraphrases, notes, *etc.*] pp. 79. मेरठ [१८]९८ [*Meerut*, 1898.] 8°. **14048. e. 22.(2.)**

This work is eighth in a series of publications of similar character by the same author.

PRABHURĀMA JĪVANARĀMA VAIDYA. *See* ṢĀRṄGADHARA, *son of Dāmodara.* Sârangdhara Saṃhitâ. Edited by Prabhurám, *etc.* 1891. 16°. **14043. b. 12.**

PRAJÑĀKARAMATI ṢRĪJÑĀNA. *See* ṢĀNTIDEVA. Bodhicaryāvatāre Prajñāpāramitāparicchedaḥ. [With commentary of Prajñākaramati.] 1898. 4°. [*Bouddhisme: Études et Matériaux.*]
14028. e. 32.

PRAJÑĀKARA MIṢRA, *son of Vidyākara. See* KĀLIDĀSA, *Pseud., author of the Nalodaya.* नलोदयः । [Nalodaya. With the commentary Subodhinī of Prajñākara.] [1895.] 8°. [*Granthāvalī of Kālidāsa.*]
14070. d. 34.(vol. 2.)

—— *See* KĀLIDĀSA, *Pseud., author of the Nalodaya.* नलोदय° [Nalodaya. With Prajñākara's Subodhinī.] [1899.] 8°.
14070. dd. 11.

—— *See* KĀLIDĀSA, *Pseud., author of the Nalodaya.* ॥ नलोदय° [Nalodaya. With Prajñākara's Subodhinī.] [1902.] 8°.
14076. d. 54.

PRAJÑĀKARA ṢRĪJÑĀNA. *See* PRAJÑĀKARAMATI ṢRĪJÑĀNA.

PRAJÑĀPĀRAMITĀ. The Larger Pragñâ-pâramitâ-hridaya-sûtra. (The Smaller Pragñâ-pâramitâ-hridaya-sûtra.) [Translated by F. Max Müller.] 1894. *See* MUELLER (F. M.). The Sacred Books of the East, *etc.* Vol. xlix., pt. 2. 1879, *etc.* 8°.
2003. b. (vol. 49.)

—— The Eleventh Chapter. On the Evolution of the Works of Māra. (Ashṭa Sahasrikā, Chapter xviii. The Evolution of Çunyata. [Translated] by Paṇḍit Hara Prasad Çāstri.) 1894. *See* ACADEMIES, *etc.*—Calcutta.—*Buddhist Text Society of India.* Journal, *etc.* Vol. II., pt. ii., iii. 1893, *etc.* 8°.
14003. b. 19.(vol. 2.)

PRĀJYA BHAṬṬA. चतुर्थी राजतरङ्गिणी । [Chaturthī Rājataraṅgiṇī. The third supplement to Kalhaṇa's history.] 1896. *See* KALHAṆA. The Râjataraṅgiṇî, *etc.* Vol. iii., pp. 321-406. 1892-1896. 8°.
14058. b. 27.

—— Kings of Kashmira: being a translation of the Sanskrita works of ... Prājyabhaṭṭa ... by Jogesh Chunder Dutt. *See* KALHAṆA. Kings of Káshmíra, *etc.* Vol. iii. 1879-1898. 12°.
14070. b. 13.

PRAKĀṢĀNANDA PURĪ. *See* BRAHMĀNANDA TĪRTHA, *son of Ṣaṅkara.* तार्किकमोहप्रकाशः *etc.* [Tārkikamohaprakāṣa. With Hindi version by Prakāṣānanda. Followed by Dayānandamohaprakāṣa, likewise with Hindi version.] [1892.] 8°.
14048. dd. 8.

PRAKĀṢĀNUBHAVA. *See* PRAKĀṢĀTMĀ, *disciple of Ānandānubhava.*

PRAKĀṢĀTMĀ, *disciple of Ānandānubhava,* also called PRAKĀṢĀNUBHAVA. *See* AKHAṆḌĀNANDA, *disciple of Akhaṇḍānubhūti.* तत्त्वदीपनम् ... Tattvadîpana, a commentary on Panchapádikávivaraṇa, [Prakāṣātmā's commentary on Padmapāda's Pañchapādikā,] *etc.* 1901, *etc.* 8°.
14049. a. 3.

—— *See* PADMAPĀDA. The Pañchapâdikâ, *etc.* (Part II. The Panchapâdikâvivaraṇa, *etc.*) 1891-1892. 8°.
14048. dd. 3.(vol. 2.)

—— *See* RĀMĀNANDA SARASVATĪ, *disciple of Govindānanda.* विवरणोपन्यासः ... Vivaraṇopanyâsa, *etc.* 1901. 8°.
14048. cc. 37.

PRAKĪRṆAKA. ॥ अथ दशपयन्ना मूल सूत्र प्रारंभः ॥ [Dasa-païnnā, or Daṣa-prakīrṇaka. The 3rd section of the Ṣvetāmbara Jain Canon, following the Upāṅgas, and comprising 10 *prakīrṇakas,* viz. Taṃḍulaveyāliya (Taṇḍulavaikālika), Deviṃdathao (Devendrastava), Gaṇivijjā (Gaṇividyā), Chaüsaraṇa (Chatuḥṣaraṇa), Saṃthāra (Saṃstāra), Āürapachchakkhāṇa (Āturapratyākhyāna), Bhattaparinnā (Bhaktaparijñā), Chaṃdavijjā (Chandravidyā), Mahāpachchakkhāṇa, and Maraṇavibhatti (°vibhakti).] ff. 73. बनारस १८८६ [*Benares,* 1886.] *obl.* 4°.
14100. f. 12.

—— चउसरण तथा आउरपच्चक्खाण पयन्नानुं भाषांतर गुणस्थानक्रमारोह अने ... तत्त्वार्थसूत्रसहित [Chaüsaraṇa-païnna and Āürapachchakkhāṇa-païnna. The first and second *païnnas,* ascribed to Vīrabhadra the disciple of Mahāvīra, each word having the Sanskrit equivalent printed above it and the Gujarati translation below it, with a Gujarati commentary on each verse. Followed by Ratnaṣekhara's Guṇasthānakramāroha and Umāsvāti's Tattvārthasūtra, and preceded by a Gujarati introduction.] ff. viii. 33, 44, 6, 10. राजनगरे १९५७ [*Rajnagar, Ahmadabad,* 1902.] *obl.* 8°.
14100. c. 24.

PRAMADĀDĀSA MITRA, *Bahādur, Rāi. See* MAHĀBHĀRATA. — Bhagavadgītā. — *English.* The

Bhagavad Gîtâ . . . Translated by Pramadâdâsa Mitra. 1896. 16°. **14060. a. 15.**

—— *See* UTPALA DEVĀCHĀRYA. शिवस्तोत्रावली . . . Sivastotrâvalî . . . with the commentary of Kshemarâja. Edited by . . . Pramadâdâsa Mittra, *etc.* 1902-1903. 8°. **14004. a. 15.**

PRAMATHANĀTHA TARKABHŪSHAṆA, *Professor at Calcutta Sanskrit College. See* BHĀSKARA, *son of Mudgala.* अर्थसंग्रहः *etc.* [Arthasaṅgraha. Edited with a commentary styled Amalā by Pramathanātha.] [1899.] 8°. **14048. c. 79.(3.)**

—— *See* GAṄGEṢA UPĀDHYĀYA. व्याप्ति-पञ्चकम् *etc.* [Vyāptipañchaka. With a commentary called Rahasyavivṛiti by Pramathanātha.] [1897.] 8°. **14048. cc. 21.(1.)**

PRĀṆAHARI YOGAVIṢĀRADA. কামশাস্ত্র বা মোহিনীতন্ত্র *etc.* [Kāmaṣāstra, or Mohinītantra. A treatise on erotics and magic in connexion therewith, in 4 parts. Preceded by verses on the Daṣamahāvidyā of Devī, *etc.* With a Bengali translation by Pañchānana Rāya Chaudhurī.] pp. xiv. 188. কলিকাতা ১৩০৭ [*Calcutta*, 1901.] 12°. **14053. b. 40.**

PRĀṆAJĪVANA HARIHARA, *Ṣāstrī.* માનવ ધર્મ-માલા. મનુષ્યનું કર્તવ્ય [Mānavadharmamālā. An anthology of moral and religious stanzas and excerpts, chiefly from the Manusmṛiti. With Gujarati translation.] pp. xxvii. 371. મુંબઈ ૧૯૦૩ [*Bombay*, 1903.] 12°. **14072. b. 29.**

PRAPHULLACHANDRA RĀYA. A History of Hindu Chemistry [in English,] from the earliest times to the middle of the sixteenth century A.D., with Sanskrit texts, variants, translation and illustrations, *etc.* *Calcutta, London*, 1902, *etc.* 8°. **14053. dd. 1.**

In progress.

PRASAṄGĀBHARAṆA. प्रसंगाभरणम् । [Prasaṅgābharaṇa. Miscellaneous stanzas.] pp. 30. [1891.] *See* PERIODICAL PUBLICATIONS.—*Bombay.* ग्रन्थरत्नमाला *etc.* (Granth Ratna Málá, *etc.*) Vol. IV, no. 10, 11. 1887-[1892.] 8°. **14096. c. 8. (vol. 4.)**

PRASANNA BĀI, *daughter of Raṇachhoḍalāla Prāṇaṣaṅkara. See* SADĀNANDA YOGĪNDRA. वेदान्तसार *etc.* [Vedāntasāra. With Gujarati paraphrase and commentary by Prasanna Bāi.] [1899.] 12°. **14048. a. 25.**

PRASANNAKUMĀRA ṢĀSTRĪ BHAṬṬĀCHĀRYA. *See* KṚISHṆĀNANDA VĀGĪṢA BHAṬṬĀCHĀRYA. বৃহৎ তন্ত্রসার *etc.* [Bṛihat-tantrasāra. With Bengali translation by Prasannakumāra.] [1896.] 4°. **14033. c. 39.**

—— *See* UPANISHADS.—*Small Collections.* উপনিষদাবলী *etc.* [Upanishadāvalī. Edited with Bengali translations by Prasannakumāra.] [1896.] 12°. **14010. b. 12.**

—— যোগাম্বুধি *etc.* [Yogāmbudhi. A collection of 6 treatises on Yoga, viz. Gheraṇḍasaṃhitā, Ṣivasaṃhitā, Shaṭchakranirūpaṇa, Ashṭāvakrasaṃhitā, Yogiyājñavalkya, and Brahmasaṃhitā. Edited with Bengali translations by Prasannakumāra.] 6 pts. কলিকাতা ১৩০৩ [*Calcutta*, 1896.] 16°. **14048. a. 19.**

Each work has a separate pagination.

PRASANNAKUMĀRA SENA, *of Konnagar. See* GOTAMA. The Naya [*sic*] Philosophy . . . edited by P. C. Sen. [1896.] 8°. **14048. c. 36.(2.)**

—— A Digest of Rulings on Hindu Law. pp. 16. *Konnagar*, [1896.] 8°. **14039. b. 14.(2.)**

A supplement to the author's "Summary of Hindu Law."

PRASANNAKUMĀRA VIDYĀRATNA, *Smārtachūḍāmaṇi.* শ্রীগৌরাঙ্গ-তত্ত্ব সহ শ্রীগৌরাঙ্গ-চরিত *etc.* [Gaurāṅgacharita. A biography of Chaitanya. Preceded by Gaurāṅgatattva, an account of his doctrine. In Bengali, illustrated from Sanskrit texts.] pp. 270. কলিকাতা [*Calcutta*, 1899.] 8°. **14127. bb. 13.**

PRAṢASTAPĀDA. The Bhâshya of Praśastapâda [upon the Vaiṣeshika Aphorisms], together with the [commentary upon it entitled] Nyâyakandalî of Śrîdhara. Edited by Vindhyeśvarîprasâda Dvivedin. (प्रशस्तपादभाष्यम् ।) pp. xxiv. xxx. i. ix. ii. 331. *Benares*, 1895. 8°. **14048. dd. 3.(vol. 4.)**

Forms vol. 4 of the Vizianagram Sanskrit Series.

PRĀTAHSMARAṆA. ప్రాతఃస్మరణము తాత్పర్యసహితము *etc.* [Prātaḥsmaraṇa. The morning offices, with Telugu translation.] (Vaksudha Series No. II.) pp. 70. *Madras*, ౧౯౦౧ [1901.] *obl.* 16°. **14028. a. 27.(5.)**

PRATĀPARUDRA DEVA, *Raja of Orissa.* See ĀDINĀRĀYAṆA PĀTRO. The Hindu Law. Annotated and illustrated by Sanskrit texts[, viz. the writings of Pratāparudra and others,] *etc.* 1899. 8°. **14039. c. 17.**

—— The Hindu Law of Inheritance, according to the Sarasvatí-vilása : translated from the original Sanskrit, by . . . Thomas Foulkes. [With the Sanskrit text appended.] (सरस्वतीविलासे व्यवहारकाण्डे दायभागः) pp. xxviii. 194, i. 162. *London*, 1881. 8°. **14039. a. 16.**

PRATĀPASIṂHA, *Shāh Bahādur, Maharaja of Nepal.* Puraścharyarṇava. [An encyclopædia of ritual.] Compiled by H.H. the Maharaja Pratapa Sinha Shah Bahadur of Nepaul. Part i. (Part ii., *etc.*) . . . Edited by Shri Pandita Murali Dhara Jha. (पुरश्चर्यार्णवः) *Benares*, 1901, *etc.* 8°.

In progress. **14033. bbb. 14.**

PRAṬIKRAMAṆASŪTRA. લોકાગચ્છીય શ્રાવકસ્ય સાર્થ પંચ પ્રતિક્રમણસૂત્ર *etc.* [Pañcha-pratikramaṇasūtra. The *sāmāyika* and *paḍikamaṇa* rituals, according to the Lokāgachchhīya sect of the Ṣvetāmbaras, with annotations *etc.* in Gujarati and an appendix of Gujarati hymns. Edited by Kalyāṇchandjī Jaichandjī. Second edition.] pp. vi. 236, *lith.* મોહમયી ૧૯૩૯ [*Bombay*, 1883.] 8°. **14144. g. 18.**

—— અથ . . . પ્રતિક્રમણ° [Pratikramaṇasūtra. With notes *etc.* in Gujarati.] *See* GHELĀBHĀĪ LĪLĀDHARA. જૈન વિવેક વાણી *etc.* [Jainavivekavāṇī.] pt. i., pp. 8-75. [1888.] 8°. **14144. g. 26.**

—— *Begin.* ॥ श्रीनवकारमंत्र *etc.* [Sāmāyikasūtra and Pratikramaṇasūtra. With rubrics, commentaries, *etc.*, in the Marwari dialect of Gujarati.] *See* TILOK ṚISHJĪ. अथ ज्ञानप्रदीपक° [Jñānapradīpaka.] ff. 1-37. [1890.] *obl.* 8°. **14144. g. 37.**

—— श्री पंचप्रतिक्रमण सूत्र . अर्थ सहित [Pañchapratikramaṇasūtra. Comprising the Sāmāyikasūtra, Chaityavandana, Pratikramaṇa, Navasmaraṇa, and Ratnākara-pachīsī, with Gujarati translations, explanations, rubrics, *etc.*, and a series of Gujarati hymns. Second edition.] pp. xvi. 438; 3 *plates.* अमदावाद १८९७ [*Ahmadabad*, 1897.] 12°. **14100. a. 20.**

—— [Another copy.] **14144. f. 31.**

—— सामायक तथा पडिकमणा की पोथी अर्थ सहित [Pratikramaṇasūtra. Preceded by the Sāmāyikasūtra. With rubrics, notes, and translations in the Marwari dialect of Hindi.] pp. 128, *lith.* दिल्ली १९५४ [*Delhi*, 1898.] *obl.* 8°. **14100. c. 22.**

—— શ્રી પડિક્કમણા સૂત્ર *etc.* [Pratikramaṇasūtra. With Gujarati version, notes, *etc.*] pp. 48. વઢવાણ અમદાવાદ [*Wadhwan, Ahmadabad* printed, 1900.] 12°. **14100. a. 23.**

—— પ્રતિક્રમણ સૂત્રના અર્થ [Pratikramaṇasūtra. With Gujarati glosses. Edited by Hīrāchand Kakalbhāī.] pp. iv. 124. અમદાવાદ ૧૯૦૩ [*Ahmadabad*, 1903.] 16°. **14100. a. 31.**

—— अथ . . . वंदित्तासूत्र अथवा प्रतिक्रमण सूत्र *etc.* [Ṣrāddhapratikramaṇasūtra, or Ṣrāvakapr°., here also styled Vanditta-sūtra. A metrical version of the lay Confessional, in 50 Prakrit stanzas. With a Gujarati translation of Ratnaṣekhara Sūri's Sanskrit commentary and other explanatory matter.] 1890. *See* BHĪMASIṂHA MĀṆAKA. जैनकथारत्नकोष *etc.* [Jainakathāratnakoṣa.] Vol. iv., pp. 1-459. [1890-1893.] 8°. **14144. gg. 1.(vol. 4.)**

—— [For the Vandittā-sūtra, as included in the *paḍikamaṇa* ritual :] *See* above.

—— [For the Sāmāyikasūtra published as a separate ritual :] *See* SĀMĀYIKASŪTRA.

PRAVARAIṢVARYĀLAṄKARAṆA. *See* PAÑÑAGGA.

PRAVARASENA. The Setubandha [or Rāvaṇavadha] of Pravarasena. [With the commentary Rāmasetupradīpa of Rāmadāsa Bhūpati.] Edited by Paṇḍit Śivadatta . . . and Kâśînâth Pâṇdurang Parab. (सेतुबन्धम्।) pp. v. 497. 1895. *See* DURGĀPRASĀDA, *son of Vrajalāla*, and KĀṢINĀTHA PĀṆḌURAṄGA PARAB. Kâvyamâlâ. [No.] 47. 1886, *etc.* 8°. **14072. ccc. 12.(no. 47.)**

PRAYĀGAJĪ ṬHĀKARSĪ. श्रीप्रमाणसहस्री *etc.* [Pramāṇasahasrī. 1000 extracts on topics of religion and philosophy, with Gujarati translation and commentaries. With portrait and obituary account of the compiler. Second edition.] pp. xvii. 82, 229, 13. મુંબઈ ૧૮૯૦ [*Bombay*, 1890.] 8°. **14085. d. 29.**

PREMACHANDRA TARKAVĀGĪṢA. *See* JÑĀNACHANDRA CHAUDHURĪ. সমস্যাকল্পলতা *etc.* [Samasyākalpalatā. Impromptu verses by Premachandra and others.] [1900.] 8°. **14079. c. 72.**

—— প্রেমচন্দ্র তর্কবাগীশের রচিত কবিতা। [Kavitā. Selections from the poetical works of Premachandra.] *See* RĀMĀKSHAYA CHAṬṬOPĀDHYĀYA. প্রেমচন্দ্র তর্কবাগীশের জীবনচরিত *etc.* [Premachandra Tarkavāgiṣer Jivanacharita o Kavitāvalī.] pp. 129-183. [1901.] 12°. **14127. aa. 16.**

PREM SHAMSHER, *Thāpā Kshatriya. See* TATTVABODHA. तत्त्वबोध: *etc.* [Tattvabodha. With translation in Nepali by Prem Shamsher.] [1891.] 12°. **14048. b. 23.(3.)**

PRETAMAÑJARĪ. प्रेतमञ्जरी [Pretamañjarī. A manual of funeral rites. Edited by Ṣikharanātha Suvedī.] काश्याम् [*Benares*, 1902, *etc.*] *obl.* 12°. *In progress.* **14028. bb. 4.(3.)**

PṚITHUYAṢAS, *son of Varāhamihira.* षट्पञ्चाशिका *etc.* [Shaṭpañchāṣikā. With the Hindi paraphrase by Badarinātha.] pp. 40. लखनऊ १९०१ [*Lucknow*, 1901.] 8°. **14053. ccc. 21.(2.)**

PṚITHVĪDHARA, *Courtier of Rāmasiṃha Deva of Mithila. See* ṢŪDRAKA. The Mṛichchhakaṭika . . . Containing . . . a vṛitti or vivṛiti by Prithvîdhara, *etc.* 1896, *etc.* 8°. **14079. c. 63.**

—— *See* ṢŪDRAKA. The Mṛichchhakaṭika . . . with the commentary of Pṛithvîdhara, *etc.* 1900. 8°. **14079. c. 60.(2.)**

PRIYĀDĀSA ĀCHĀRYA, *Gosvāmī.* सुसिद्धान्तोत्तम: *etc.* [Susiddhāntottama. An exposition of Vaishṇava doctrine. With commentary by the author.] pp. 516, viii. ii. xiv. प्रयागे १९५८ [*Allahabad*, 1901.] 12°. **14033. a. 48.**

PRIYATAMADHARMA-SABHĀ. *See* HARIVALLABHA ṢARMĀ. संस्कारमार्तण्ड: *etc.* [Saṃskāramārtaṇḍa. Rules for rites of the Priyatamadharma-Sabhā of Shikarpur.] [1901.] 8°. **14033. bbb. 10.(1.)**

PROME HSAYA. ဗြဟ္မဝိဟာရသင်္ဂဟကျမ်း *etc.* [Brahmavihārasaṅgaha. A compendium of dicta on the condition of *brahmavihāra*, compiled from Pali literature, with Burmese commentaries, *etc.*, by a Prome Hsaya. Followed by the Chatudhamma-dīpanī, a Burmese tract on the terms *khandha, āyatana, dhātu,* and *sachcha*, by the same author; and the Vipassanā-shuhbway-akyin, a Burmese lectionary by Ālokābhivara.] pp. 34. *Moulmein*, 1882. 8°. **14300. d. 9.(2.)**

PRUSSIA. Verzeichniss der Handschriften im Preussischen Staate. I. Hannover. 3. Göttingen 3. (Sanskrit-Handschriften [in the Universitäts-Bibliothek of Göttingen]. Beschrieben von . . . Franz Kielhorn.) pp. viii. 551, 244. *Berlin, Göttingen* [printed], 1894. 8°. **011901. g.**

PUGGALAPAÑÑATTI. *See* ABHIDHAMMAPIṬAKA.

PULLÈ (FRANCESCO LORENZO). *See* PERIODICAL PUBLICATIONS.—*Florence.* Studi Italiani di Filologia Indo-Iranica. Diretti da F. L. Pullé. 1897, *etc.* 8°. **P.P. 4884. da.**

—— *See* RĀJAṢEKHARA. Antarakathāsaṃgrahaḥ Ǵainīyaḥ. [Edited by F. L. Pullé.] 1897, *etc.* 8°. [*Studi Italiani di Filologia Indo-Iranica.*] **P.P. 4884. da. (vol. 1.)**

—— Catalogo dei Manoscritti Ǵiainici della Biblioteca Nazionale Centrale di Firenze, *etc.* (Parte I. Siddhānta.) nos. 1-4. pp. 40. *Firenze*, 1894, *etc.* 8°. **14096. dd. 2.**
No more published.

PUÑÑĀNANDA, *Kollupiṭiyē. See* SUTTAPIṬAKA.—*Majjhimanikāya.* Sælasuttra Sannaya, *etc.* [Edited by Puññānanda.] [1896.] 8°. **14098. d. 45.(3.)**

PURĀṆAS.

SELECTIONS.

See GOVARDHANADĀSA LAKSHMĪDĀSA. बृहत्स्तोत्रसरित्सागर *etc.* [Bṛihat-stotrasaritsāgara. A collection of religious poems, compiled from Puranic literature, *etc.*] [1892.] 12°. **14033. a. 27.**

See LAKSHMĪNṚISIṂHA ṢĀSTRĪ, *Challā-nāgaliṅga.* పురాణోక్తకర్మప్రకాశిక *etc.* [Purāṇoktakarmaprakāṣika. Rules for divers rites, compiled from Purāṇas, *etc.*] [1899.] 8°. **14028. c. 79.**

PURĀṆAS (*continued*).

SELECTIONS (*continued*).

See NĀRĀYAṆA SOMAYĀJĪ, *Kalvakūrtipalli*. శ్రీ ... శ్రీరామోత్సవరత్నాకరః *etc.* [Rāmotsavaratnākara. Comprising lections from various Purāṇas, *etc.*] [1898.] 8°. **14028. d. 66.**

হিন্দুশাস্ত্র ... অষ্টাদশ পুরাণ। [Ashṭādaṣa-purāṇa. Selections from the 18 Purāṇas, with Bengali translations and prefaces. Compiled by Āṣutosha Ṣāstrī and Hṛishīkeṣa Ṣāstrī.] pp. i. 325. [1897.] *See* RAMEṢACHANDRA DATTA. হিন্দুশাস্ত্র *etc.* [Hinduṣāstra.] Pt. ix. [1895-1897.] 8°. **14085. c. 45.(vol. 2.)**

अथ जयंतीसहितं षड्विंशत्येकादशीमाहात्म्यं प्रा० [Ekādaṣīmāhātmya. Being the lections for each of the 26 Ekādaṣī festivals, extracted from various Purāṇas. Preceded by an Ekādaṣīnirṇaya, and followed by the Rāmanavamīvratamāhātmya from the Skandapurāṇa, the Nṛisiṃhajayantīkathā from the Nṛisiṃhapurāna, and the Kṛishṇajanmāshṭamīkathā and Vāmanajayantīkathā from the Bhavishyottarapurāṇa. With Gujarati translations of all but the first.] ff. 189. मुंबई [*Bombay*, 1899.] *obl.* 8°. **14016. d. 55.**

॥ अथ एकादशीमाहात्म्य भाषाटीकाप्रारंभः ॥ [Ekādaṣīmāhātmya. A somewhat different recension. With a Nepali translation by Harihara Ṣarmā.] ff. 270. बनारस [*Benares*, 1903.] *obl.* 8°. **14016. dd. 11.**

This recension agrees with that of the Bombay editions of 1858 *and* 1863.

कैवल्यरत्नम् *etc.* [Kaivalyaratna. An exposition of monism, compiled from the Upapurāṇas, *etc.*, by Vāsudevajñāna Muni. Reprinted from "The Pandit" (new series, vols. v.-vi.), and edited by Rāma Ṣāstrī Mānavallī.] pp. ii. xxiii. 120. काश्याम् १९०१ [*Benares*, 1901.] 8°. **14016. d. 57.**

శ్రీలక్ష్మీనృసింహ సహస్ర నామస్తోత్రమ్. (శ్రీరామస॥ శ్రీగోపికాగీతా॥) [Lakshmīnṛisiṃhasahasranāma, from the Nṛisiṃhapurāṇa; Rāmasahasranāma, from the Ṣivapurāṇa; and Gopikāgītā, *i.e.* Bhāgavatapurāṇa X. xxxi. 1-19.] *See* SAHASRANĀMASTABAKA. శ్రీసహస్రనామస్తబకమ్ [Sahasranāmastabaka.] pp. 33-106, 385-9. [1902.] *obl.* 16°. **14033. a. 52.**

PURĀṆAS (*continued*).

SELECTIONS (*continued*).

॥ शाकद्वीपीय कुलभास्करः *etc.* [Ṣākadvīpīya-kulabhāskara. A work, composed chiefly of Puranic extracts, upon the origins of the Ṣākadvīpīya Brahmans. Compiled by Kāṣīnātha Pāṭhaka.] pp. 33. गयायां १९५८ [*Gaya*, 1901.] 8°. **14058. b. 45.**

శ్రీవేఙ్కటాచలమాహాత్మ్యగ్రంథః *etc.* [Veṅkaṭāchalamāhātmyagrantha. A series of excerpts from the Purāṇas, *etc.*, on the legends of the Tirupati hill sacred to Vishṇu. Followed by a list of 108 sacred names of the god from the Varāhapurāṇa, and another list of 1000 names from the Brahmāṇḍapurāṇa. Compiled by Rāmakiṣoradāsa, and edited by Tekkuḷūru Ṣrīnivāsa Raṅgāchārya.] 15 pts. 4 *plates*. చెన్నపురి ౧౮౯౬ [*Madras*, 1896.] 8°. **14016. c. 50.**

The following works are quoted:—Ādityapurāṇa, Bhavishyottarap°., Brahmap°., Brahmāṇḍap°., Garuḍapurāṇa, Harivaṃṣa, Mārkaṇḍeyap°., Padmap°., Skandap°., Vāmanap°., Varāhap°.

శ్రీవేంకటేశ్వర మాహాత్మ్యసారసంగ్రహమ్ *etc.* [Veṅkaṭeṣvaramāhātmyasārasaṅgraha. A collection of hymns and other religious poems bearing on the cult of Vishṇu-Veṅkaṭeṣvara at Tirupati.] pp. iii. 126; 1 *plate*. చెన్నపురి [*Madras*, 1895.] 12°. **14028. b. 100.**

ĀDIPURĀṆA.

আদিপুরাণ *etc.* [Ādipurāṇa. An *upapurāṇa* in 29 *adhyāyas*. With a Bengali translation.] 2 pts. pp. 182, 254. *Calcutta*, 1891. 8°. **14016. c. 47.**

AGNIPURĀṆA.

अग्निपुराणम् *etc.* [Agnipurāṇa, or Āgneyapurāṇa. An encyclopædia of mythology, religious doctrine, ritual, science, and art, in 383 *adhyāyas*.] pp. xix. 484. पुण्याख्यपत्तने १९०० [*Poona*, 1900.] 8°. **14003. ccc. (no. 41.)**

Forms no. 41 *of the* Ānandāṣrama Sanskrit Series.

अथाग्नेयमहापुराणं प्रारभ्यते [Āgneyapurāṇa.] ff. ix. 209; 1 *plate*. *Bombay*, १९५८ [1902.] *obl.* Fol. **14018. e. 4.**

PURĀṆAS (*continued*).

AGNIPURĀṆA (*continued*).

A prose English translation of Agni Puranam. Edited and published by Manmatha Nath Dutt, *etc.* 2 vols. pp. vii. xviii. 1346. 1903-1904. *See* MANMATHANĀTHA DATTA. The Wealth of India, *etc.* Vol. viii. 1892, *etc.* 8°.

14085. d. 32.(vol. 8.)

प्रायश्चित्तनिर्णयः *etc.* [Prāyaṣchittanirṇaya. Seven chapters on expiations, forming *adhyāyas* 168-174 of this Purāṇa.] pp. 35. मुम्बय्यां १९५८ [*Bombay,* 1902.] 12°.

14033. a. 45.(2.)

अथ श्री राजगृह माहात्म्यम् [Rājagṛihamāhātmya. An exposition of the sanctity of Rajagriha in Patna. With Hindi version.] pp. 148. प्रयाग १८९८ [*Allahabad,* 1898.] *obl.* 12°.

14016. b. 21.(2.)

Apparently not in the printed edition.

अथ श्रीराजगृह माहात्म्यम्। *etc.* [Rājagṛihamāhātmya. With a Hindi translation by Ballī Miṣra. Second edition.] pp. 111. पटना [*Patna,*] 1904. *obl.* 12°.

14016. b. 23.(3.)

अथ शकुनमञ्जरी *etc.* [Ṣakunamañjarī. Three chapters on augury, forming *adhyāyas* 230-232 of this Purāṇa.] pp. 15. मुम्बय्यां १९५८ [*Bombay,* 1902.] 12°.

14033. a. 45.(3.)

BHĀGAVATAPURĀṆA.

॥ अथ श्रीमद्भागवतप्रारंभः ॥ [Bhāgavatapurāṇa. Preceded by the Bhāgavatamāhātmya. With a translation into Gujarati prose.] 14 pts. मुंबई [*Bombay,* 1891.] *obl.* Fol.

14018. c. 30.

अथ प्राकृत श्रीमद्भागवतार्थदर्शन *etc.* [Bhāgavatārthadarṣana. Being the Bhāgavatapurāṇa, with a Marathi interpretation and commentary founded upon that of Ṣrīdhara Svāmī. Skandhas 1-5.] 5 pts. मुंबई १८१४ [*Bombay,* 1892.] 8°.

14016. e. 40.

Begin. श्रीमद्भागवतसुबोधिन्यां प्रथमस्कंधप्रारंभः [Bhāgavatapurāṇa. With the commentary Subodhinī of Vallabhāchārya.] [1893, *etc.*] *See* PERIODICAL PUBLICATIONS. — *Bombay.* श्रीपुष्टिमार्गप्रकाशः *etc.* [Pushṭimārgaprakāṣa.] Vol. I, pt. 2 ff. [1893, *etc.*] 8°.

14150. c. 15.

In progress?

PURĀṆAS (*continued*).

BHĀGAVATAPURĀṆA (*continued*).

શ્રીભાગવત સુબોધિનીજીનું ગુજરાતી ભાષાંતર [Bhāgavatapurāṇa. With a Gujarati translation of the Subodhinī of Vallabhāchārya.] [1893, *etc.*] *See* PERIODICAL PUBLICATIONS.—*Bombay.* श्रीपुष्टिमार्गप्रकाशः *etc.* [Pushṭimārgaprakāṣa.] Vol. I, pt. 2 ff. [1893, *etc.*] 8°.

14150. c. 15.

॥ श्रीभागवतं भक्तमनोरञ्जनीटीकोपेतं प्रारभ्यते ॥ [Bhāgavatapurāṇa. With the commentary Bhaktamanorañjanī or Bhaktarañjanī of Bhagavatprasāda Āchārya, expounding the doctrines of the Svāminārāyaṇī sect. Edited with introduction, biography of Sahajānanda, and annotations by Vihārilāla Āchārya.] 13 pts. मुम्बापुर्यां वेदपबाङ्कचन्द्रे [*Bombay,* 1897.] *obl.* Fol.

14018. cc. 2.

॥ अथ गूर्जरभाषासमन्वितं श्रीमद्भागवतं प्रारभ्यते ॥ [Bhāgavatapurāṇa. Preceded by the Bhāgavatamāhātmya from the Padmapurāṇa. With Gujarati translation and commentary by Ichchhārāma Sūryarāma Deṣāi.] 13 pts. मुंबई १८९९ [*Bombay,* 1899.] *obl.* Fol.

14016. f. 14.

॥ श्रीमद्भागवतसंहिता *etc.* [Bhāgavatapurāṇa. Preceded by the Bhāgavatamāhātmya. With a Gujarati translation by Giridharalāla Amṛitalāla Nyāyā.] 14 pts. अमदावाद १८९९ [*Ahmadabad,* 1899.] *obl:* 4°.

14016. f. 13.

अथ श्रीमद्भागवतं पद्यभाषानंदाबुनिधियुतम् [Bhāgavatapurāṇa. With a metrical Hindi paraphrase, entitled Ānandāmbunidhi, by Maharaja Raghurājasiṃhajū Deva.] 12 pts. मुम्बय्यां १९५६-१९५७ [*Bombay,* 1899-1900.] *obl.* Fol.

14018. cc. 3.

अथ अन्वितार्थप्रकाशिकाख्यव्याख्यासहिते ॥ ॥ श्रीमद्भागवते प्रथमस्कन्धः ॥ ॥ प्रारभ्यते (द्वितीय° *etc.*) [Bhāgavatapurāṇa. With the commentary Anvitārthaprakāṣikā of Gaṅgāsahāya Ṣarmā, and with the Bhāgavatamāhātmya *etc.* prefixed.] 12 pts. *Kalyan,* [1901.] *obl.* Fol.

14018. e. 3.

श्रीवेदव्यासेन प्रणीतं श्रीमद्भागवतम् [Bhāgavatapurāṇa. Edited with Hindi preface and translation called Kīrtivardhinī by Rāmasvarūpa Ṣarmā.] 2 vols. pp. viii. vi. 928, viii. 2071; 16 *plates.* मुरादाबाद° १९५८ [*Moradabad,* 1901.] 8°.

14018. a. 2.

PURĀṆAS (*continued*).

BHĀGAVATAPURĀṆA (*continued*).

A prose English translation of Srimadbhagabatam . . . Edited . . . by Manmatha Nath Dutt. 12 pts. 1895-1896. *See* MANMATHANĀTHA DATTA. The Wealth of India, *etc.* Vol. ii., iii. 1892, *etc.* 8°. **14085. d. 32.(vol. 2, 3.)**

[A reprint of the preceding edition, bks. i.-v.] 5 pts. *Calcutta*, 1896. 8°. **14016. dd. 7.**

Le Bhâgavata Purâṇa ou histoire poétique de Krĭchṇa. Traduit et publié par E. Burnouf. (Tome 4, par M. Hauvette-Besnault. Tome 5, par M. Hauvette-Besnault et le R. P. Roussel.) 5 tom. 1840-1898. *See* ACADEMIES, *etc.*—Paris.—*Bibliothèque Nationale.* Collection Orientale, *etc.* 1836, *etc.* Fol. **756. l. 3.**

A study of the Bhagavata Purana, or Esoteric Hinduism. [Being an abridgment of the text with notes, in English,] by Purnendu Narayana Sinha. pp. iii. vi. 436. *Benares*, 1901. 8°. **14016. dd. 4.**

गोपीगीता. (चतुःश्लोकी भागवत, ब्रह्मस्तुति) [Gopīgītā (X. xxxi. 1-19 of this Purāṇa); Chatuḥṣlokī Bhāgavata (II. ix. 32-35); and Brahmastuti (X. xiv. 1-41). With poetical Marathi paraphrases and amplifications by Vāmana.] *See* VĀMANA PAṆḌITA, *the Marathi Poet.* **वामनी ग्रंथ** *etc.* [Vāmanī Grantha.] Vol. 3. pp. 154-160, 361-2, 443-515. [1889-1891.] 8°. **14140. b. 23.(vol. 3.)**

ଭକ୍ତିରତ୍ନାବଳୀ *etc.* [Bhaktiratnāvalī. An anthology of devotional verses from the Bhāgavata, arranged in 13 *virachanas* by Vishṇupurī of Tirhut. With the commentary of Ṣrīdhara Svāmī and a metrical paraphrase in Oriya by Bhīmadāsa. Edited with analyses *etc.* by Gopālavallabha Dāsa.] pp. iii. ix. 338. *Cuttack*, 1900. 12°. **14016. b. 27.**

श्रीमद्गीताप्रपूर्त्तिः । व्याख्यानसहिता । [Gītāprapūrti. A series of extracts compiled from the Bhāgavatapurāṇa so as to form a supplement of the Bhagavadgītā, illustrating and expanding its principles and spirit. With a commentary. By Gauragovinda Rāya.] pp. viii. 413, xxii. **कलिकातायां १८२४** [*Calcutta*, 1902.] 8°. **14016. e. 44.**

PURĀṆAS (*continued*).

BHĀGAVATAPURĀṆA (*continued*).

Légendes Morales de l'Inde, empruntées au Bhagavata Purana et au Mahabharata. Traduites du sanscrit par A. Roussel. (Les littératures populaires de toutes les nations, tome xxxviii.-xxxix.) 2 vols. *Paris*, 1900-1901. 12°. **14065. b. 20.**

॥ **गजेंद्रमोक्ष** *etc.* [Gajendramoksha. An episode forming bk. VIII. i. 30—iv. 26 of the Bhāgavatapurāṇa, with Hindi notes by Pītāmbara.] pp. 24. *See* SĀYAṆA ĀCHĀRYA.—*Works on Philosophy, etc.* **श्रीपंचदशी** *etc.* [Pañchadaṣī.] [1897.] 8°. **14048. e. 25.**

শ্রীকৃষ্ণলীলা। *etc.* [Kṛishṇalīlā. Being bk. X. i.-li. of the Bhāgavata, with glosses, Bengali paraphrases, and additional chapters in Bengali prose and verse upon Vaishṇava doctrine and ritual, including a version of the Bhagavadgītā. Compiled and edited by Ṣyāmalāla Gosvāmī.] pp. 1298. কলিকাতা ১৩১০ [*Calcutta*, 1904.] 8°. **14016. dd. 10.**

ରାସପଞ୍ଚାଧ୍ୟାୟୀ *etc.* [Rāsapañchādhyāyī. Being bk. X. xxix.-xxxiii. of the Bhāgavata, describing the sports of Kṛishṇa with the Gopīs. With a prose Oriya translation by Jayīnārāyaṇa Deva.] pp. 84. *Cuttack*, 1901. 12°. **14016. b. 24.(2.)**

শ্রীমদ্ভাগবতান্তর্গত নবযোগেন্দ্রোপাখ্যান ও উদ্ধবগীতা *etc.* [Navayogendropākhyāna and Uddhavagītā, *i.e.* bk. xi. of the Bhāgavata. With analysis, translation, and commentary in Bengali. Edited by Ṣyāmalāla Gosvāmī.] pp. i. ii. 512. [*Calcutta*, 1900.] 8°. **14018. b. 19.**

ସଚିତ୍ର ଏକାଦଶସ୍କନ୍ଧ *etc.* [Sachitra Ekādaṣa-skandha. Being selections from bk. xi. of the Bhāgavata with the metrical Oriya paraphrase of the whole book by Jagannātha Dāsa. Illustrated with woodcuts.] pp. 218. *Cuttack*, 1901. 12°. **14016. b. 24.(1.)**

See JĪVA GOSVĀMĪ. **षट्सन्दर्भ॰** [Shaṭsandarbha, or Bhāgavatasandarbha. A commentary upon the Bhāgavata, supplementing the work of Ṣrīdhara.] [1899-1901.] 8°. **14016. d. 62.**

PURĀṆAS (*continued*).

BHĀGAVATAPURĀṆA (*continued*).

See MURALĪDHARA RĀYA. Sree Krishna. [An epitome of the *līlās* of Kṛishṇa as narrated in the Mahābhārata and Bhāgavata,] *etc.* 1901. 8°.
4503. df. 5.

See ROUSSEL (A.). Cosmologie Hindoue d'après le Bhâgavata Purâna, *etc.* 1898. 12°.
4503. dd. 10.

See RŪPA GOSVĀMĪ. লঘুভাগবতামৃত *etc.* [Laghubhāgavatāmṛita. An exposition of the doctrine of Chaitanya as set forth in the Bhāgavata.] [1897.] 8°.
14016. c. 58.

See RŪPA GOSVĀMĪ. श्रीलघुभागवतामृतम् । *etc.* [Laghubhāgavatāmṛita.] [1903.] 8°. **14076. d. 55.**

See ṢIVACHANDRA SIDDHĀNTA. শ্রীমদ্ভাগবতবিচারঃ *etc.* [Bhāgavatavichāra. An essay proving the Bhāgavata to be the work of Vyāsa.] [1893.] 8°.
14016. c. 56.(1.)

See VALLABHĀCHĀRYA. श्रीभागवतार्थतत्त्वदीप° *etc.* [Bhāgavatārthatattvadīpanibandha. A metrical summary of the Bhāgavata.] [1893, *etc.*] 8°. [*Pushṭimārgaprakāṣa.*]
14150. c. 15.

BHAVISHYAPURĀṆA.

See ṢIVAPRASĀDA ṢARMĀ, *disciple of Raghunātha.* । चयहानिवंशभूषणम् *etc.* [Chayahānivaṃṣabhūshaṇa. An account, based upon the Bhavishyapurāṇa, of the Chauhan Kshatriyas.] 1903. 8°.
14058. cc. 7.

॥ अथ श्रीभविष्यमहापुराणं प्रारभ्यते ॥ [Bhavishyapurāṇa. Edited by Govinda Paraṣurāma Ṣāstrī Rāverkar.] 4 pts. मुंबय्यां १८१६-१८१९ [*Bombay*, 1896-1897.] *obl.* Fol.
14018. cc. 1.

An interpolated edition ; see the Zeitschrift d. Deutschen Morg. Gesellschaft, Bd. lvii., *p.* 276.

भविष्यत्पुराणांतर्गत प्रभुलिंगलीला. [Prabhuliṅgalīlā. A mythological work embodying doctrines of the Vīraṣaiva sect, in 25 cantos, alleged to form part of the Bhavishyapurāṇa. With Marathi translation by Kṛishṇājī Nārāyaṇa Joṣī. Edited by Mallikārjuna Ṣāstrī.] मुंबई १९०३-१९०४ [*Bombay*, 1903-1904.] 8°.
14016. dd. 9.

Forms nos. 6, 7, and 8 *in the* Vīraṣaiva-liṅgi-brāhmaṇa-dharmagranthamālā *published by Rāu Sāhib Mallappā Basappā Vārad.*

PURĀṆAS (*continued*).

BHAVISHYOTTARAPURĀṆA.

अनन्तकथा । पूजापद्धतिश्च *etc.* [Anantakathā. The legend of the god Ananta, preceded by rules for his cult. Edited by Pañchānana Ṣarmā.] pp. 19. दरभङ्गा १९०१ [*Darbhangah*, 1901.] *obl.* 12°.
14016. b. 26.

॥ अथ . . . महालक्ष्मीव्रतकथा प्रारभ्यते ॥ [Mahālakshmīvratakathā. The legend of the Mahālakshmī festival. With Hindi translation by Gaṇeṣa Kāṣīnātha Kāḷe.] ff. 17. कल्याण-मुंबई १९५६ [*Kalyan*, 1900.] *obl.* 8°.
14016. d. 59.

ऋषिपंचमी व्रत कथा [Ṛishipañchamīvratakathā. The ritual and legend of the Ṛishipañchamī festival. With Gujarati translation by Kalyāṇajī Raṇachhoḍajī Vyāsa.] ff. 34. अमदावाद १९५५ [*Ahmadabad*, 1899.] 12°.
14028. b. 78.(3.)

॥ अथ ऋषिपंचमी व्रत कथा ॥ [Ṛishipañchamīvratakathā. With Gujarati translation by Pūrṇachandra Achaleṣvara Ṣarmā.] ff. 18. अमदावाद १९५५ [*Ahmadabad*, 1899.] *obl.* 8°. **14028. d. 37.(2.)**

ಭವಿಷ್ಯೋತ್ತರಪುರಾಣಾಂತರ್ಗತ ಋಶ್ಯಶೃಂಗೋಪಾಖ್ಯಾನವು. [Ṛishyaṣriṅgopākhyāna. The tale of Ṛishya Ṣriṅga, as recounted in the Tuṅgabhadrākhaṇḍa, *adhyāya* 19. With Canarese translation.] *See* PAṬṬĀBHIRĀMA ṢĀSTRĪ. ಋಶ್ಯಶೃಂಗೋಪಾಖ್ಯಾನವು *etc.* [Ṛishyaṣriṅgopākhyāna.] pp. 157-171. [1891.] 8°.
14016. c. 45.

BRAHMĀṆḌAPURĀṆA.

ব্রহ্মাণ্ড-পুরাণম্ *etc.* [Brahmāṇḍapurāṇa. Edited with Bengali notes and translation by Nagendranātha Vasu.] pts. 1-23. pp. xvi. 728. কলিকাতা ১২৯৮-১৩০১ [*Calcutta*, 1891-1894.] 8°.
14016. c. 46.

No more has been registered.

[*Adhyātmabhāgavata.*] अथ ककारादिकृष्णाष्टोत्तरसहस्रनामस्तोत्रम् । [Kakārādi-kṛishṇāshṭottarasahasranāmastotra. An excerpt of 360 stanzas, forming *adhyāya* 34 in the Ṣrutirahasya of the Adhyātmabhāgavata assigned to this Purāṇa, and containing 1008 names and epithets of Kṛishṇa beginning with the letter *k*. Edited by Govinda Paraṣurāma Rāverkar.] ff. 53. मुंबय्यां १९५७ [*Bombay*, 1901.] *obl.* 12°.
14016. b. 25.

PURĀṆAS (*continued*).

BRAHMĀṆḌAPURĀṆA (*continued*).

[*Adhyātmarāmāyaṇa.*] ॥ अथ अध्यात्मरामायणार्थबोधः प्रारभ्यते *etc.* [Adhyātmarāmāyaṇa. With translation and notes in Marathi.] 7 pts. [*Bombay*, 1892.] *obl.* 8°. **14016. c. 40.**

—— अध्यात्मरामायण सटीक ॥ *etc.* [Adhyātmarāmāyaṇa. With a Hindi paraphrase and commentary by Baijnāthjī of Manpur.] pp. v. 639. लखनऊ १८९४ [*Lucknow*, 1894.] Fol. **14018. c. 33.**

—— অধ্যাত্মরামায়ণম্ *etc.* [Adhyātmarāmāyaṇa. With the commentary Setu of Rāma Varmā. Edited with analyses and Bengali translations and paraphrases by Khagendranātha Ṣāstrī.] কলিকাতা ১৩০৮ [*Calcutta*, 1901, *etc.*] 8°. *In progress.* **14016. d. 61.**

—— শ্রীশ্রীরামগীতা। [Rāmagītā. A Yogic Vaishṇava poem of 62 stanzas, from the Uttarakāṇḍa, *sarga* v., of the Adhyātmarāmāyaṇa. With commentary and Bengali translation.] *See* KĀLĪPRASANNA VIDYĀRATNA BHAṬṬĀCHĀRYA. যোগাঙ্কুর *etc.* [Yogāṅkura.] pp. 97-156. [1894.] 12°. **14048. b. 28.(2.)**

—— रामगीता सटीक [Rāmagītā. With Hindi metrical version and prose paraphrase by Girijāprasāda. Second edition.] pp. 34. लखनऊ १८९८ [*Lucknow*, 1898.] 8°. **14048. dd. 9.(2.)**

—— रामगीतापञ्चरत्न प्रारंभः। [Rāmagītāpañcharatna. Five lections for the worship of Rāma,—(1) Rāmagītā; (2) Rāmasahasranāmastotra, from the Rudrayāmalatantra; (3) Rāmastuti, from the Yuddhakāṇḍa of the Adhyātmarāmāyaṇa; (4) Rāmānusmṛiti, from the Brahmāṇḍapurāṇa, Brahmanāradasaṃvāda; (5) Ṣabarīmoksha, *i.e.* Adhyātmarāmāyaṇa, Araṇyakāṇḍa, *sarga* x. Prefaced by appropriate *mantras, etc.*] ff. 42. [*Bombay*, 1899.] *obl.* 16°. **14028. a. 25.**

[*Ādipuramāhātmya.*] பேரூர் [*sic*] ஸ்தலபுராணம் . . . [illegible] *etc.* [Ādipuramāhātmya, in Tamil Pērūrsthalapurāṇam. The local legends of Perur, from the *uparibhāga* of the Kaumārakhaṇḍa, in 27 *adhyāyas*. Edited by N. Kṛishṇa Ṣāstrī, K. Dorasvāmi Ṣāstrī, and Rāmakṛishṇa Ṣāstrī of Kalpadi.] pp. iv. viii. 195. பலக்காட் ௧௯௦௨ [*Palghat*, 1902.] 8°. **14016. dd. 6.**

PURĀṆAS (*continued*).

[*Lalitāsahasranāma.*] శ్రీలలితారహస్యనామసాహస్రభాష్యం *etc.* [Lalitāsahasranāmastotra, or Lalitārahasyanāmasāhasra. With the commentary Saubhāgyabhāskara of Bhāskararāya Dikshita.] pp. vi. 288. *Karvetnagar*, 1892. 4°. **14016. e. 41.**

—— శ్రీలలితారహస్యనామసాహస్రభాష్యము *etc.* [Lalitārahasyanāmasāhasra. With a commentary in Telugu based upon that of Bhāskararāya, by N. Guruliṅga Ṣāstrī.] pp. 206. చెన్నపట్టణము ౧౯౦౦ [*Madras*, 1900.] 8°. **14016. c. 63.**

—— Lalita Sahasranama, with Bhaskararaya's commentary. Translated into English, [with an introduction,] by R. Anantakrishna Sastri. pp. v. 324. *Madras*, 1899. 8°. **14016. c. 59.**

[*Lalitātriṣatī.*] Triśatî with Śrî Śankrâchârya's Bhâsya [called Triṣatīnāmārthaprakāṣikā. Being Ṣaṅkara's commentary on the 300 names of Lalitā-Devī contained in the Triṣatī or Lalitātriṣatīstotra in the Stotrakhaṇḍa of the Uttarakhaṇḍa of this Purāṇa. Followed by the] Panchadaśî Mantra with Agastya's Bhâshya and Triśatî text[, *scil.* the complete Lalitātriṣatīstotra]. Edited by R. Ananta Krishna Sastry. pp. ii. 134. *Bombay*, 1902. 12°. **14033. a. 45.(1.)**

[*Malaharopākhyāna.*] మలహరోపాఖ్యానమ్ [Malaharopākhyāna. The legend of Malahara. 24 chapters from the Skandabādarāyaṇasaṃvāda in the *uttarabhāga* of this Purāṇa.] pp. i. 41. *Vizagapatam*, 1896. 8°. **14016. c. 29.(3.)**

—— मलहरोपाख्यानम्. [Malaharopākhyāna.] pp. 51. *Vizagapatam*, 1897. 8°. **14016. c. 29.(2.)**

[*Nāsiketopākhyāna.*] Il "Nāsiketopākhyānam" secondo i MSS : "1253" e "916 c" dell' "India Office," preceduto da una notizia sulle "Visioni indiane." [By Ferdinando Belloni-Filippi.] 1902-1904. *See* ACADEMIES, *etc.*—Florence.—*Società Asiatica Italiana.* Giornale, *etc.* Vol. xv.-xvii. 1887, *etc.* 8°. **Ac. 8804. (vol. 15-17.)**

PURĀṆAS (*continued*).

BRAHMĀṆḌAPURĀṆA (*continued*).

[*Rāmānusmṛiti.*] **अथ रामानुस्मृति॰** [Rāmānusmṛiti. An excerpt from the dialogue of Brahma and Nārada.] *See* above, [*Adhyātmarāmāyaṇa.*]

रामगीतापञ्चरत्न प्रा॰ [Rāmagītāpañcharatna.] ff. 35-37. [1899.] *obl.* 16°. **14028. a. 25.**

[*Uttaragītā.*] [For the Uttaragītā, sometimes alleged to form part of this Purāṇa :] *See* UTTARAGĪTĀ.

BRAHMAPURĀṆA.

ब्रह्मपुराणम् *etc.* (The Brahma-purâṇa by Śrîmat Vyâsa, edited by Pandits at the Ânandâśrama.) pp. i. xvii. 595. **पुण्याख्यपत्तने १८९५** [*Poona*, 1895.] 8°. **14003. ccc. (no. 28.)**

Forms no. 28 of the Ânandâśrama Sanskrit Series. *The English title is from the cover.*

ஸ்ரீஹஸ்திகிரிமாஹாத்ம்யம் *etc.* [Hastigirimāhātmya. Eighteen *adhyāyas* from the Bhṛigunāradasaṃvāda, treating of the legends of the Vaishṇava shrine at Hastigiri or Anamalai. With a popular Tamil exposition in the *maṇipravālam* style.] pp. ii. ii. 255. **காஞ்சி** [*Conjevaram*,] 1898. 8°. **14016. c. 51.**

कर्मविपाकसंहिता. नक्षत्रचरणफलदर्शिका *etc.* [Karmavipākasaṃhitā. A treatise in 111 *adhyāyas*, purporting to form part of the Pitṛikalpottara of this Purāṇa, and treating of the knowledge of nativities as conditioned by *karma*, expiations, *etc.* Edited with Hindi translation by Nandalāla Ṣarmā.] pp. ii. iii. 371. **मुम्बयी १९०२** [*Bombay*, 1902.] 8°. **14053. ccc. 42.**

॥ कर्मविपाक संहिता *etc.* [Karmavipākasaṃhitā. With a Nepali translation by Sadāśiva Ṣarmā.] pp. 425. *Benares*, **१९५९** [1902.] 8°.

14053. dd. 3.

BṚIHAN-NĀRADĪYAPURĀṆA.

बृहन्नारदीयपुराणम् *etc.* [Bṛihan-nāradīyapurāṇa. Edited with Bengali translation by Pañchānana Tarkaratna.] pp. 122, 152. **কলিকাতা ১৩০১** [*Calcutta*, 1895.] 12°. **14016. b. 19.**

सार्थ पुरुषोत्तममाहात्म्य॰ [Purushottamamāhātmya. A Vaishṇava excerpt, in 31 chapters. With a Marathi translation.] ff. 69. **पुणे १९०१** [*Poona*, 1901.] *obl.* 8°. **14016. d. 60.**

According to the official Catalogue of Books Printed (1901, III, *p.* 32), *the translator is Bhāskara Nārāyaṇa Goḍbole.*

DEVĪBHĀGAVATAPURĀṆA.

श्रीदेवीभागवत. [Devībhāgavata. With the preface of Nīlakaṇṭha's commentary Tilaka. Skandhas i.-iii., edited with a Marathi translation by Vishṇu Lakshmaṇa Ṣāstrī Purohita. Skandha iv., with Marathi translation, edited by Kāśīnātha Vāmana Lele.] **वाई** [*Ahmadabad*, *Wai*, 1902, *etc.*] 8°. **14016. dd. 8.**

In progress. A separate issue of the work as published in the serial styled Purāṇādarṣa. *Bks.* i.-iii. *seem to have been printed at Ahmadabad and published at Wai*; *Bk.* iv. *is printed and published at Wai. The translator of Bk.* iv. *is not named.*

अथ श्रीदेवीगीता॰ [Devīgītā. 10 chapters forming bk. vii. 31-40.] *See* GOVARDHANADĀSA LAKSHMĪDĀSA.

बृहत्स्तोत्रसरित्सागर *etc.* [Bṛihat-stotrasaritsāgara.] Vol. i., pp. 347-385. [1892.] 12°.

14033. a. 27.(vol. 1.)

सावित्र्युपाख्यान *etc.* [Sāvitryupākhyāna. The legend of Sāvitrī, forming bk. ix. 26-38 of this Purāṇa. With a Hindi translation by Jvālāprasāda Miṣra.] pp. 256. **बंबई १९५८** [*Bombay*, 1902.] 12°.

14016. b. 28.

अथ देवीभागवते . . . नवरात्रार्चनविधिः [Uddhārākathā, or Navarātrārchanavidhi. An account of the Navarātra festival, forming bk. iii. 26-27.] *See* NAVARĀTRA. **अथ सर्वत्रनवरात्रपद्धतिः** *etc.* [Navarātrapaddhati.] ff. 1-8. [1898.] *obl.* 12°.

14028. dd. 5.(2.)

GAṆEṢAPURĀṆA.

अथ . . . गणेशपंचरत्न॰ [Gaṇeṣapañcharatna. Comprising the Gaṇeṣakavacha, Gaṇeṣasahasranāma, and Gaṇeṣagītā from this Purāṇa; Gaṇeṣastavarāja from the Bhavishyottarapurāṇa; and Gaṇeṣahṛidaya from Mudgaleyapurāṇa.] *See* GOVARDHANADĀSA LAKSHMĪDĀSA. **बृहत्स्तोत्रसरित्सागर** *etc.* [Bṛihat-stotrasaritsāgara.] Vol. i., pp. 22-94. [1892.] 12°.

14033. a. 27.(vol. 1.)

PURĀṆAS (*continued*).

GARUḌAPURĀṆA.

(The Garuda Puranam.) 1900, *etc.* See MANMATHANĀTHA DATTA. The Wealth of India, *etc.* Vol. ix. 1892, *etc.* 8°. **14085. d. 32.(vol. 9.)**

In progress. The title is from the wrapper.

[For the Ratnaparīkshā, sometimes alleged to be an extract from this Purāna :] *See* BUDDHA BHAṬṬA.

अथगरुडपुराणंप्रारभ्यते [Sāroddhāra. Comprising 13 chapters from the Pretakalpa of the Garuḍapurāṇa.] pp. 119, *lith.* अमृतसर [*Amritsar*, 1900.] *obl.* 8°. **14016. e. 43.**

Inside the last leaf are printed 15 *stanzas styled* Garuḍapurāṇaśravaṇaphala.

KALKIPURĀṆA.

कल्किपुराण *etc.* (Kalki-purana [in Sanskrit and Hindi]. Translated [with Hindi commentary] by P. Baldew Prasad Mishra of Moradabad.) pp. viii. ii. viii. 356. मुंबई १९५४ [*Bombay*, 1897.] 8°. **14016. d. 52.**

কল্কিপুরাণম্ *etc.* [Kalkipurāṇa. With Bengali translation by Kālīprasanna Vidyāratna.] pp. vi. 247. কলিকাতা ১৩০৬ [*Calcutta*, 1899.] 8°. **14016. d. 36.(2.)**

LIṄGAPURĀṆA.

॥ हरतालिकापूजाकथासटीकप्रारम्भः ॥ [Haratālikāpūjākathā. 75 stanzas on the legend of the Haratālikāpūjā rite, preceded by the appropriate liturgy. With Hindi version by Śyāmamanohara Vaidya.] ff. 12. *Lucknow*, १९०० [1900.] *obl.* 8°. **14033. c. 44.(4.)**

MĀRKAṆḌEYAPURĀṆA.

The Márkandeya Puránam. Translated . . . into English prose by Charu Chandra Mukerjea. pts. 1-3. pp. iv. 192. *Calcutta*, 1893-1894. 8°. **14016. c. 44.**

A prose English translation of Markandeya Puranam. Edited . . . by Manmatha Nath Datt. pp. iv. 502. 1896. *See* MANMATHANĀTHA DATTA. The Wealth of India, *etc.* Vol. v. 1892, *etc.* 8°. **14085. d. 32.(vol. 5.)**

PURĀṆAS (*continued*).

MĀRKAṆḌEYAPURĀṆA (*continued*).

A prose English translation of Markandeya Purana . . . Edited . . . by Manmatha Nath Datt, *etc.* pp. iv. vi. 502. *Calcutta*, 1897. 8°. **14016. d. 58.**

A reprint of the preceding edition.

[*Devīmāhātmya.*] ॥ अथ दुर्गासप्तशती *etc.* [Devīmāhātmya, also called Durgāpāṭha, Durgāsaptaśatī, or Chaṇḍī. Preceded by *prayogas* of the Kātyāyanītantra, the Śatachaṇḍīvidhi, Devīkavacha, Argalāstotra, Kīlakastotra, Navārṇavidhi, and Rātrisūkta ; and followed by the Devīsūkta and the lections styled Prādhānikarahasya, Vaikṛitikarahasya, and Mūrtirahasya.] ff. 19, 15, 6, 4, 197 ; 8 *plates.* काश्यां १९५५ [*Benares*, 1898.] *obl.* 12°. **14016. b. 22.**

—— अथ दुर्गापाठ प्रारम्भः [Durgāpāṭha. Preceded by the Devīkavacha, Argalāstotra, Kīlakastotra, Navārṇavidhi, Rātrisūkta, *dhyānas*, and *nyāsas.*] *Allahabad*, १८९९ [1899.] *obl.* 12°. **14016. a. 28.**

—— ॥ अथ सप्तशती प्रारम्भः ॥ [Saptaśatī. Preceded by divers rituals appropriate to its study, with the Argalāstotra, Kīlakast°., and Rātrisūktas ; and followed by the Devīsūkta, the Prādhānikarahasya, Vaikṛitikar°., and Mūrtir°., and the Śatachaṇḍīvidhi.] ff. i. 171. *Lucknow*, 1899. *obl.* 12°. **14028. bb. 3.**

—— శ్రీదుర్గాసప్తశతీస్తవరత్నమ్ *etc.* [Durgāsaptaśatīstavaratna. Comprising the Devīmāhātmya, preceded by the Navārṇamantra, Argalāstotra, Kīlakast°., Kavachast°., Chaṇḍīhṛidayast°., Chaṇḍīdhvajast°., Mālāmantrast°., Pārāyaṇamahāsaṅkalpa, *etc.*, and followed by the Prādhānikarahasya, Vaikṛitikar°., and Mūrtir°., the Sarasvatīsūkta, Lakshmīs°., and Kālīs°., the Saṃhārajapakrama, Brahmaśāpavimochana, Vāchanakrama, Aparādhakshamāpaṇastotra, Kāmyaprayogavidhi, Sampuṭīkrama, Śatachaṇḍīvidhi, *etc.*] pp. 99. చెన్నపురి ౧౮౯౯ [*Madras*, 1899.] *obl.* 8°. **14016. d. 56.**

—— ಶ್ರೀಶ್ರೀಚಂಡೀ *etc.* [Chaṇḍī. Preceded by rules for reading, *dhyānas*, the Argalāstotra, Kīlakast°.,

PURĀṆAS (*continued*).

Kavachast°., Devīsūkta, and appropriate *saṅkalpas*; and accompanied by a commentary entitled Tattvaprakāṣikā by Gopālachandra Chakravartī and a Bengali version, *etc.* Edited by Kālīpada Vidyāratna.] pp. iv. xviii. 488. কলিকাতা [*Calcutta*, 1900.] 16°.

14028. a. 29.

——— ॥ अथदुर्गासप्तशती ॥ [Durgāsaptaṣatī. Preceded by the appropriate rituals, the Argalāstotra, Kīlakast°., Vedic and Tantric Rātrisūkta, *etc.*; and followed by the Vedic and Tantric Devīsūkta and the Rahasyas.] ff. i. 169. *Lucknow*, 1900. *obl.* 12°.

14028. bb. 8.

[*Hariṣchandropākhyāna.*] मार्कण्डेय-पुराणम् । हरिश्चन्द्रोपाख्यानम् । [Harischandropākhyāna. With notes.] *See* NṚISIṂHARĀMA MUKHOPĀDHYĀYA. साहित्य-रत्नाकरः [Sāhityaratnākara.] pp. 54-70. 1898. 12°.

14065. b. 18.

MATSYAPURĀṆA.

मत्स्यपुराण सटीक *etc.* [Matsyapurāṇa. With a Hindi translation by Vasatirāma of Beri. Edited by Vasatirāma and Kālīcharaṇa of Agra.] pp. viii. 979. लखनऊ १८९२ [*Lucknow*, 1892.] 4°.

14018. c. 31.

कथा गणेशचतुर्थी की *etc.* [Gaṇeṣachaturthīkathā. The legend of the Gaṇeṣachaturthī holiday.] pp. 8, *lith.* अमृतसर १९५८ [*Amritsar*, 1902.] *obl.* 12°.

14016. b. 23.(2.)

NĀRADAPURĀṆA.

ഹരിഭക്തിസുധോദയഃ *etc.* [Haribhaktisudhodaya. An exposition of the Vaishṇava doctrine of devotion, in 20 *adhyāyas*. With the commentary of Ṣrīdhara Svāmī. Edited by Goshṭhīpuram Harihara Ṣāstrī, Vishṇupuram Rāmachandra Ṣāstrī, and Hālāsyanātha Ṣāstrī.] pp. ii. 289. കുംഭഘോണ ॥ [*Kumbakonam*,] 1892. 8°.

14016. c. 48.

[For the Bṛihan-nāradīyapurāṇa, as distinct from the Nāradopapurāṇa :] *See* above, BṚIHAN-NĀRADĪYAPURĀṆA.

PURĀṆAS (*continued*).

PADMAPURĀṆA.

पद्मपुराणम् *etc.* (The Padmapurâṇa, edited from several Mss. by . . . Rao Saheb Vishwanáth Nárâyaṇa Maṇdlic.) 4 vols. pp. 1919, v. x. vii. पुण्याख्यपत्तने १८९३-१८९४ [*Poona*, 1893-1894.] 8°.

14003. ccc.

Issued as an 'Extra Number' of the Ānandāṣrama Sanskrit Series. *The English title is from the cover of vols.* 2 *and* 3.

॥ अथ श्रीपाद्मं महापुराणं प्रारभ्यते ॥ [Padmapurāṇa.] 7 pts. मुंबई १८९५ [*Bombay*, 1895.] *obl.* Fol.

14018. dd. 5.

श्रीगौडप्रकाश *etc.* [Gauḍaprakāṣa. An excerpt, purporting to be from the Pātālakhaṇḍa, on the settlement in Gujarat of Gauḍa Brahmans from Malwa in the reign of Vijayasiṃha Siddharāja, their *gotras*, *pravaras*, *etc.*, with Gujarati translation. Followed by tabular lists of these divisions, and prefaced by two legends of the settlement of the Gauḍas. Edited and translated by Daulatrām Nārāyaṇa Chhāṇīkar.] pp. ii. iii. ii. 41, x. i. ii. वडोदरा अमदावाद [*Baroda*, *Ahmadabad*, 1899.] 8°.

14058. b. 39.

കാർത്തികമാഹാത്മ്യം *etc.* [Kārttikamāhātmya, or Kṛittikām°. 30 chapters (Uttarakhaṇḍa xc. ff.) on the legend of the Kṛittikās or Pleiades and the month Kārttika. Edited by Veṅkaṭāchala Ṣāstrī of Kalpadi.] pp. viii. 66. ശ്രീശുദ്ധാനന്ദപക്ഷാ ॥ വിജയം ॥ [*Palghat*, 1898.] 8°.

14016. c. 60.

Begin. శ్రీమాఘమాహాత్మ్యసారమ్. [Māghamāhātmyasāra. Comprising Māghasnānaphalaprabhāva, an excerpt from the Māghamāhātmya (Uttarakhaṇḍa ccxxxix.) on the religious efficacy of bathing in the Mahāmāgham festival at Kumbakonam, with a Tamil and an abridged Telugu version, and 10 Sanskrit stanzas on the divinity of Kumbakonam, *etc.* Compiled by Kṛishṇanjī Dave.] pp. 18. *Madras*, 1897. 12°.

No title-page. **14016. b. 20.**

পদ্মপুরাণম্। পাতালখণ্ডম্। অনুবাদ সমেতম্ *etc.* [Pātālakhaṇḍa. With a Bengali translation by

PURĀṆAS (*continued*).

Jagannātha Vidyārṇava, Vīreṣanātha Kāvyatīrtha, and others. Edited by Pañchānana Tarkaratna.] pp. i. iii. 743. কলিকাতা ১৩১০ [*Calcutta*, 1903.] 8°. **14018. b. 20.**

A different recension from that of the Bombay editions, containing only 72 *adhyāyas.*

॥ पुष्कर माहात्म्य भाषा टीका ॥ [Pushkaramāhātmya. Twenty *adhyāyas*, purporting to be from this Purāṇa, on the legends of Pushkar. With a Hindi prose translation by Ṣivaprasāda Mākhanlāl.] pp. 170. अजमेर १९५४ [*Ajmere*, 1898.] *obl.* 8°. **14016. d. 51.**

Different from the passage in the Srishṭikhaṇḍa xix.

সচিত্র রতিশাস্ত্র *etc.* [Ratiṣāstra. A treatise on the Ars Amoris, purporting to be compiled from this Purāṇa. Edited and translated into Bengali by Maṇīndralāla Ghosha. Third edition.] pp. 135; 11 *plates*. কলিকাতা ১৩০৮ [*Calcutta*, 1901.] 12°. **14053. b. 42.**

॥ अथ श्रीरेणुकासहस्रनामस्तोत्रप्रारंभः ॥ [Reṇukāsahasranāmastotra. 1000 names of Reṇukā, purporting to be from the Māyopākhyāna in this Purāṇa.] ff. 11. १८२२ [*Bombay*, 1900.] *obl.* 12°. **14016. b. 23.(1.)**

अथ शिवगीता *etc.* [Ṣivagītā. An excerpt in 16 *adhyāyas*, purporting to be from the Uttarakhaṇḍa, on the doctrines of the Ṣaiva Vedānta.] *See* GOVARDHANADĀSA LAKSHMĪDĀSA. बृहत्स्तोत्रसरित्सागर *etc.* [Bṛihat-stotrasaritsāgara.] Vol. i., pp. 221-282. [1892.] 12°. **14033. a. 27.(vol. 1.)**

Sivageetha . . . శివగీత *etc.* [Ṣivagītā. In 20 *adhyāyas*. Edited with Telugu version by N. Veṅkaṭasubbā Ṣāstrī.] pp. 130; 11 *plates*. చెన్నపట్టణము [*Madras*,] 1897. 8°. **14016. c. 55.**

পদ্মপুরাণম্। উত্তরখণ্ডম্ *etc.* [Uttarakhaṇḍa. Edited with Bengali translation by Rāmanārāyaṇa Vidyāratna.] মুর্শিদাবাদ ১৩০৫ [*Murshidabad*, 1899, *etc.*] 4°. **14016. e. 45.**

In progress?

বৃন্দাবন প্রাপ্ত্যুপায় *etc.* [Vṛindāvanaprāptyupāya. Comprising an excerpt purporting to form the Pātālakhaṇḍa xcix.-cviii. and a metrical Bengali paraphrase of the same, esoterically setting forth the stories of Krishṇa's amours and cognate legends, by Viṣvambhara Pāni.] pp. i. ii. 244. কলিকাতা ১৩০৬ [*Calcutta*, 1900.] 8°. **14076. c. 75.(1.)**

Quite different from the editions of the Pātālakhaṇḍa.

[For editions of the Bhāgavatamāhātmya (Uttarakhaṇḍa clxxxix.) published together with the Bhāgavatapurāṇa:] *See* above, BHĀGAVATAPURĀṆA.

PARĀṢARAPURĀṆA.

శ్రీ . . . శ్రీమద్రామాయణమాహాత్మ్యం॥ [Rāmāyaṇamāhātmya. Ten *adhyāyas* on the subject of the Rāmāyaṇa.] *See* VĀLMĪKI. — Rāmāyaṇa. — *Entire Text.* శ్రీమద్రామాయణమ్ *etc.* [Rāmāyaṇa.] pp. xxiv.-lv. [1897.] 8°. **14065. d. 37.**

ṢIVAPURĀṆA.

శ్రీకాళహస్తిస్థలమాహాత్మ్యగ్రంథః [Kālahastisthalamāhātmya. An accouut, in 90 *adhyāyas*, of the local legends and cult of the Ṣaiva shrine at Kalahasti, in a dialogue between Romaṣa and Bharadvāja, purporting to form part of the Ṣivarahasyasaṅgraha in this Purāṇa. Edited by Chēṭṭūr Veṅkaṭasubrahmaṇya Ṣāstrī.] pp. ii. xii. vi. 903, xiv. *Venkatagiri*, ౧౮౯౩ [1893.] 8°. **14016. c. 41.**

SKANDAPURĀṆA.

अर्बुदमाहात्म्यसारः *etc.* [Arbudamāhātmyasāra. Verses on the sanctity of Mount Abu. Abridged from the Skandapurāṇa by Sadāṣiva Ṣaṅkara Ṣāstrī. With Hindi translation, notes, and a map.] pp. 72. मुम्बयाम् १९५० [*Bombay*, 1894.] 8°. **14016. c. 42.(3.)**

அர்த்தகிரி மாஹாத்மியம் Ardhagiri Mâhâtmya of Kâśî Khanda of the Skânda Purana. [Twelve chapters on the local legends of Trichengode. Followed by the Ardhanārīṣvarasahasranāma, 1000 names of the androgynous presiding deity.] Edited by R. Anantakrishna Sastri. pp. iv. 105. *Madras*, 1902. 8°. **14016. dd. 2.**

PURĀṆAS (*continued*).

SKANDAPURĀṆA (*continued*).

श्रीभूतपुरीमाहात्म्य *etc.* [Bhūtapurīmāhātmya. Four *adhyāyas* on the sanctity and legends of the town of Bhutapuri.] pp. 50. कल्याण-मुंबई १८१५ [*Kalyan*, 1893.] 8°. **14016. c. 42.(2.)**

ഉ.ഉ.6...ബില്വാഷ്ടോത്തരശതകം [Bilvāshṭottaraṣataka. An excerpt from the Ṣiva-rahasya, treating of the sanctity of the *bilva* or Aegle Marmelos sacred to Ṣiva.] pp. 15. നടുക്കാവേരി [*Nadukkaveri*,] 1901. 16°. **14028. bb. 11.(1.)**

श्रीगङ्गासहस्रनामावली *etc.* [Gaṅgāsahasranāmāvalī. 1000 epithets of the goddess Gaṅgā, from the Kāṣikhaṇḍa. Edited by Rāmakrishṇa Ṣāstrī Thatte.] pp. 69. श्रीकाश्यां १९५५ [*Benares*, 1899.] *obl.* 32°. **14016. a. 26.**

శ్రీకాశీఖండము అయం గ్రంథః *etc.* [Kāṣī-khaṇḍa. In 2 parts and 100 *adhyāyas*. Edited by Dēvanaguḍi Nārāyaṇa Ṣāstrī and Doḍḍabeli Nārāyaṇa Ṣāstrī.] pp. vi. 711. బెంగళూరు॥ ౧౮౯౯ [*Bangalore*, 1899.] 8°. **14016. c. 57.**

کاشی کہنڈ [Kāṣīkhaṇḍa. An abridged Persian translation, by Paṭnī Mal, with many excerpts from the Sanskrit text.] pp. 289, *lith.* [*Lucknow*, 1865?] 8°. **Pers. 236.**

इदंपुस्तकं ... श्रीकाश्यपक्षेत्रस्य माहात्म्यम् ॥ ॥ काचाकुरुचिपुराणम् *etc.* (Kâsyapakshetramâhâtmyam. The Purana of Kachankuruchi [a sacred place near Kollangode, in Bidar. Forming 29 *adhyāyas* in the Bhūgola-khaṇḍa of this Purāṇa.] Edited by Ganapathi Sastri of Panganad.) pp. 56. *Kumbakonam*, 1903. 8°. **14016. dd. 2.(3.)**

The English title is from the wrapper.

कोलापुरक्षेत्रमाहात्म्यं *etc.* [Kolāpurakshetramāhātmya, or Mūkāmbikāpurāṇa. Being 22 *adhyāyas* from the Sahyādrikhaṇḍa, pt. ii., on the local legends of Kolhapur, and especially those of the goddess Mūkāmbikā. Edited with footnotes and introduction by Punnacheri-nambi Nīlakaṇṭha Ṣarmā.] pp. iv. 135. पट्टम्पि १८९९ [*Pattambi*, 1899.] 8°. **14016. c. 56.(2.)**

PURĀṆAS (*continued*).

SKANDAPURĀṆA (*continued*).

ஸ்ரீ ... நாககிரிமாஹாத்ம்யம் நாக புராணத்தும் ... ஸ்ரீஞானஸம்பந்த ஸ்வாமி சரித்ரமும் *etc.* (நாககிரி மாஹாத்மியம்) [Nāgagirimāhātmya. 16 chapters on the sacred legends of the Nāgagiri, or Anamalai, at Trichengode. Followed by Jñāna-sambandhacharitra, a history of the Ṣaiva saint Ñānasambandhar, by Mahādeva Ṣāstri, and Ardhanārīṣvarāshṭottaranāmāvali, a metrical list of 108 names of the androgynous manifestation of Ṣiva-Pārvatī at Trichengode.] pp. 69, i. சென்னை [*Madras*,] 1903. 8°. **14016. dd. 2.(2.)**

The Tamil title is from the wrapper.

ಸ್ಕಾಂದಪುರಾಣದೊಳಗಣ ನಾಗರ ಖಂಡ. [Nāgara-khaṇḍa. Twelve *adhyāyas* on Brahmanic cosmology and ceremony in connexion with the genealogies and family rites of Viṣvakarmā Brahmans.] *See* below, VASISHṬHAPURĀṆA. ಗೋತ್ರ-ಖಂಡವು *etc.* [Gotrakhaṇḍa.] pp. 43-114. 1897. 8°. **14016. c. 52.**

Nepal Mâhâtmya[, in 30 *adhyāyas*] from [the Himavatkhaṇḍa of the] Skanda Purâna. Edited by Sri Paṇḍita Murali Dhara Jha. (नेपालमाहात्म्यम्।) pp. iii. 180. *Benares*, 1901. 8°. **14016. dd. 3.**

ਨਿੰਦਤ ਭ੍ਰਸ਼ਟਾਚਾਰ ਅਰਥਾਤ ਤਮਾਲ ਨਿਖੇਧਃ *etc.* [Nindita-bhrashṭāchāra, or Tamālanishedha. 26 stanzas, purporting to be from the 52nd *adhyāya* of the Mathurākhaṇḍa, upon the sin of smoking tobacco and its penalties. With Panjabi translation and an appendix of Panjabi verses by Anūp Singh.] pp. 40. ਅੰਮ੍ਰਿਤਸਰ [*Amritsar*, 1902.] 12°. **14033. a. 33.(4.)**

ਨਿੰਦਤ ਭ੍ਰਸ਼ਟਾਚਾਰ *etc.* [Nindita-bhrashṭāchāra, or Tamāladoshanirūpaṇa. The same text as the preceding, with Panjabi translation and appended matter in Panjabi prose and verse by Bhāī Mohan Singh Vaidya.] pp. 56. ਅੰਮ੍ਰਿਤਸਰ ੧੯੦੨ [*Amritsar*, 1902.] 12°. **14033. a. 33.(5.)**

പ്രണവകല്പഃ *etc.* [Praṇavakalpa. An excerpt from the Mantraprastāva of the Vaishṇavasaṃhitā, upon the mystic syllable *Om* and the ceremonies connected with it, followed by tables of the

PURĀṆAS (*continued*).

1000, 108, and 16 names for it and a ritual from the Prapañchasārasaṅgraha of Gīrvāṇendra Sarasvatī. Edited by Gopāla Śāstrī.] pp. 56. கும்பகோணம் ॥ [*Kumbakonam,*] 1902. 8°. **14033. b. 55.(2.)**

ಸಟೀಕಾ ಶ್ರೀಋಷ್ಯಶೃಂಗೋಪಾಖ್ಯಾನವು. [Ṛishyaśṛiṅgopākhyāna. The tale of Ṛishya Śṛiṅga, as recounted in 11 *adhyāyas* of the Tuṅgabhadrākhaṇḍa. With Canarese translation.] *See* PAṬṬĀBHIRĀMA ŚĀSTRĪ. ಶ್ರೀಋಷ್ಯಶೃಂಗೋಪಾಖ್ಯಾನವು *etc.* [Ṛishyaśṛiṅgopākhyāna.] pp. 1-156. [1891.] 8°. **14016. c. 45.**

ஸ்ரீஸமீவநக்ஷேத்ரமாஹாத்ம்யம் *etc.* [Śamīvanakshetramāhātmya. 12 *adhyāyas* from the Sanatkumārasaṃhitā, on the local legends of Śamīvana or Kovilur district. Edited by Paramesvara Dīkshita.] pp. 50. சிதம்பரம் ॥ விகாரி [*Chidambaram,* 1899.] 12°. **14016. a. 29.**

অথ সত্য নারায়ণ ব্রত *etc.* [Satyanārāyaṇavratakathā. The legend of the god Satyanārāyaṇa and his worship, in 5 chapters, from the Revākhaṇḍa.] *See* RASIKACHANDRA VASU. রত্নোদ্ধার *etc.* [Ratnoddhāra.]. pp. 61-74. [1899.] 12°. **14028. b. 66.(4.)**

॥ अथ सत्यनारायण कथा ॥ [Satyanārāyaṇakathā. With the preliminary rituals. With Gujarati translation, and a Gujarati *ārti* appended.] ff. 57. अमदावाद १८९९ [*Ahmadabad,* 1899.] *obl.* 8°. **14016. c. 61.(2.)**

(Satya-narayana, or God is Truth.) [Translated with notes by Rāmakṛishṇa Mādhavarāu Chonkar.] pp. 37, 32. [*Bombay,* 1897.] 32°. **14016. a. 25.**
No title-page.

ஸிவதத்வஸுதாநிதி: *etc.* [Śivatattvasudhānidhi. 10 *adhyāyas* from the Malayāchalakhaṇḍa of the Sanatkumārasaṃhitā, on Śaiva doctrine. With the commentary Chintāmaṇi of Śrīnivāsa Dīkshita.] pp. 152. [*Chidambaram,*] 1898. 8°. **14016. d. 53.**

சிவதத்துவசுதாநிதி *etc.* [Śivatattvasudhānidhi. With a Tamil version of Śrīnivāsa Dīkshita's commentary Chintāmaṇi.] pp. 191. சிதம்பரம் [*Chidambaram,*] 1898. 8°. **14016. d. 54.**

PURĀṆAS (*continued*).

SKANDAPURĀṆA (*continued*).

ಸೋಮವಂಶಾರ್ಯಕ್ಷತ್ರಿಯ ಪುರಾಣವು *etc.* [Somavaṃśāryakshatriyapurāṇa. Being *adhyāyas* 85-96 in the Varṇavivaraṇakhaṇḍa of the Sanatkumārasaṃhitā, descriptive of Brahmanic cosmology and policy, the Solar and Lunar dynasties, and myths and morals chiefly relating to the latter. With Canarese translation.] pp. iv. 170. ಬೆಂಗಳೂರು ೧೮೯೫ [*Bangalore,* 1895.] 8°. **14016. c. 53.**

श्रीमाळपुराण અથવા स्कंदपुराण माहेनुं श्रीमाळमहात्म्य *etc.* [Śrīmālamāhātmya, or Śrīmālapurāṇa. The legend of Śrīmāla as contained in the Brāhmyavibhāga, *parichchheda* iii. With Gujarati translation, preface, and appendices, *etc.*, by Jaṭāśaṅkara Līlādhara and Keśavajī Viśvanātha.] pp. x. 684. અમદાવાદ ૧૮૯૯ [*Ahmadabad,* 1899.] 8°. **14016. c. 62.**

श्रीसुदाममहात्म्य *etc.* [Sudāmamāhātmya. An account of the religious claims of the Kedārakuṇḍa and river Aśmāvatī, excerpted from the Prahlādasaṃhitā. Followed by a life of the Vaishṇava saint Sudāmā and a hymn to Śiva, in Gujarati, and the Chatuḥślokī Bhāgavata and Saptaślokī Gītā. Edited with Gujarati paraphrases of the Sanskrit and annotations by Motīchand Kapurchand Gāndhī.] pp. x. 116; 1 *plate.* મુંબઈ ૧૮૯૮ [*Bombay,* 1898.] 16°. **14016. a. 30.**

సుజ్ఞానదీపము - గురుగీతలు *etc.* [Sujñānadīpa, or Gurugītā. Four *adhyāyas* in the Uttarakhaṇḍa, upon the Advaita teachers. Followed by the Gurvashṭaka and Bhrāntirahitaśloka, short popular religious poems. With Telugu glosses and translation to each verse by Phīlkhānā Śaṅkara Rāu, and a Telugu poem called Gurusevāpaddhati.] pp. ii. 152. మద్రాసు ౧౮౯౮ [*Madras,* 1898.] 8°. **14016. c. 54.**

ஸூதஸம்ஹிதா *etc.* [Sūtasaṃhitā. With the commentary Tātparyadīpikā of Sāyaṇa.] pp. 492. சிதம்பரம் ॥ நந்தந ॥ [*Chidambaram,* 1892.] 4°. **14016. e. 42.**

सूतसंहिता। श्रीमाधवाचार्यप्रणीततात्पर्यदीपिकाव्याख्यासमेता *etc.* (The Sûtasamhitá. With the commentary of . . .

PURĀṆAS (*continued*).

Mádhavácházrya. Edited [with indices to the stanzas] by Pandit Vàsudeva Śástri Paṇaśíkara.) 3 vols. pp. i. xxix. 1061, lvii. पुस्तकाख्यपत्तने १८९३ [*Poona*, 1893.] 8°. **14003. ccc. (no. 25.)**

Forms no. 25 *of the* Ānandāṣrama Sanskrit Series. *The English title is taken from the cover.*

উৎকলখণ্ডম্ *etc.* [Utkalakhaṇḍa. The section of this Purāṇa treating of the legends *etc.* of Orissa. Edited with Bengali translation by Pañchānana Tarkaratna.] pp. ii. ii. 305. কলিকাতা ১৩০৯ [*Calcutta*, 1902.] 8°. **14016. dd. 5.**

॥ अथ भाषाटीकोपेतं वैशाखमाहात्म्य प्रारम्भः ॥ [Vaiṣākhamāhātmya. 25 *adhyāyas* on the legends and cults associated with the month Vaiṣākha. With Hindi translation.] ff. 152; 1 *plate.* मुंबय्यां १९५७ [*Bombay*, 1901.] *obl.* 4°. **14016. f. 15.(2.)**

ஸ்ரீசுக ஷூாஉபாராணாஂதகஂதஂ வடாரண்ய-மாஹாத்ம்யஂ *etc.* (வடாரண்யமான்மியம.) [Vaṭāraṇyamāhātmya. 11 *adhyāyas* from the Kshetravaibhavavistāra, Uparibhāga, on the legends of the Vaṭāraṇya or Ālangāḍu. Followed by a Tamil version by Rāmasvāmi Aiyar of Enaṅguḍi.] pp. 112, 66. நடுக்காவேரி [*Nadukkaveri*,] 1898. 16°. **14016. a. 27.**

ವಿನಾಯಕವ್ರತಕಥಾ *etc.* [Vināyakavratakathā. An account of the cult of Vināyaka, purporting to be from the Skandapurāṇa, with appropriate ritual. With Canarese translation.] pp. 22. ಬೆಂಗಳೂರು ೧೮೯೦ [*Bangalore*, 1890.] 8°. **14028. d. 58.(1.)**

వినాయకవ్రతకల్పము [Vināyakavratakalpa. With Telugu translation, *etc.*] pp. 12. *Cocanada*, 1899. 12°. **14028. b. 61.(3.)**

Different from the preceding work. Printed on yellow paper.

శ్రీ . . . వీరశైవధర్మనిర్ణయె . . . శతితతమో-ధ్యాయః [Vīraṣaivadharmanirṇaya. An exposition of the principles of the Vīraṣaiva-Advaita school, from the Ṣaṅkarasaṃhitā, *adhyāyas* 180-185.] *See* ṢIVĀDVAITAPAÑCHAKA. శివాద్వైతపంచక *etc.* [Ṣivādvaitapañchaka.] pp. 2-39. [1897.] 8°. **14048. cc. 8.(4.)**

PURĀṆAS (*continued*).

SKANDAPURĀṆA (*continued*).

[For the Gurugītā, also called Sujñānadīpa:] *See* above.

[For the Bhagavadgītāmāhātmya (Uttarakhaṇḍa xiii.) as prefixed to the text of the Bhagavadgītā:] *See* MAHĀBHĀRATA.—*Bhagavadgītā.*

[For the Rāmāyaṇamāhātmya in the Uttarakhaṇḍa of this Purāṇa, which is sometimes prefixed to the Rāmāyaṇa:] *See* VĀLMĪKI.—*Rāmāyaṇa.*

VĀMANAPURĀṆA.

॥ अथ वामनपुराणं भाषाटीकासमेतं प्रारभ्यते ॥ [Vāmanapurāṇa. Edited with a Hindi translation by Ṣyāmasundaralāla Tripāṭhī of Bans Bareilly.] ff. iii. 273; 1 *plate.* *Bombay*, १९६० [1904.] Fol. **14018. c. 34.**

॥ अथ वामनपुराणं प्रारभ्यते ॥ [Vāmanapurāṇa. Edited by Ṣyāmasundaralāla Tripāṭhī.] ff. iv. 102; 1 *plate.* मुंबई १९६० [*Bombay*, 1904.] Fol. **14018. c. 35.**

VARĀHAPURĀṆA.

अथ श्रीमद्वाराहमहापुराणं प्रारभ्यते । [Varāhapurāṇa. With an index by Jīvanarāma Kālidāsa Goṇḍlekar.] ff. ix. 197; 2 *plates.* *Bombay*, १९५९ [1903.] Fol. **14016. f. 16.**

दुर्गाकवच् । अर्गला कीलक् सहित *etc.* [Durgākavacha, or Devīkavacha. A magic ritual of Devī. Followed by the Argalāstotra from the Mārkaṇḍeyapurāṇa, the Durgākīlakastotra, and the Durgānavārṇa. Edited with Nepali translation by Pandit Viṣvanātha Ṣarmā.] pp. 66; 6 *plates.* काशी १९०३ [*Benares*, 1903.] 8°. **14016. dd 12.**

[For editions of the Bhagavadgītā containing as preface the Bhagavadgītāmāhātmya from this Purāṇa:] *See* MAHĀBHĀRATA.—*Bhagavadgītā.*

[For editions of the Devīmāhātmya containing also the Devīkavacha from this Purāṇa:] *See* above, MĀRKAṆḌEYAPURĀṆA. [*Devīmāhātmya.*]

PURĀṆAS (*continued*).

VASISHṬHAPURĀṆA.

ಗೋತ್ರಖಂಡವೂ, ಸ್ಕಾಂದಪುರಾಣಾಂತರ್ಗತ ನಾಗರಖಂಡವೂ *etc.* [Gotrakhaṇḍa. Being *khaṇḍa* iii. *adhyāya* 6 f., descriptive of Viṣvakarmā and the Brahman races claiming descent from him; with short hymns, Canarese explanations and notes on the genealogies of the Viṣvakarmā Brahmans and on the rites connected with them, *etc.* Followed by the Nāgarakhaṇḍa of the Skandapurāṇa, on Brahmanic cosmology and ceremony in the same reference; with an appendix of quotations from various Purāṇas and the Mahābhārata. Compiled by Subbaṇṇāchārya son of Hiraṇṇaiyan.] pp. 120. *Bangalore*, 1897. 8°.
14016. c. 52.

VISHṆUPURĀṆA.

A prose English translation of Vishnupuranam, based on Professor H. H. Wilson's translation, *etc.* 1894. pp. i. xii. 464. *See* MANMATHANĀTHA DATTA. The Wealth of India, *etc.* Vol. i. 1892, *etc.* 8°. **14085. d. 32.(vol. 1.)**

A prose English translation of Vishnupuranam . . . Edited . . . by Manmatha Nath Dutt. pp. i. xii. 464. 1896. 8°. **14016. d. 31.**

A reprint of the preceding edition.

The Vishnu Purana: an abridgment is given, *verbatim*, from the English translation of H. H. Wilson . . . with an examination of the book in the light of the present day. pp. viii. 80. 1895. *See* EAST. The Sacred Books of the East Described and Examined. Hindu Series. Vol. III, pt. 3. 1895, *etc.* 8°. **14010. cc. 9.(vol. 3.)**

See DHĪRENDRANĀTHA PĀLA. Srikrishna; his life and teachings. [An English study, based on the Mahābhārata and Vishṇupurāṇa,] *etc.* 1901. 8°.
10606. c. 39.

विष्णु-पुराणम् । ध्रुवोपाख्यानम् । [Dhruvopākhyāna. With notes.] *See* NṚISIṂHARĀMA MUKHOPĀDHYĀYA. साहित्य-रत्नाकरः *etc.* [Sāhityaratnākara.] pp. 71-76. 1898. 12°. **14065. b. 18.**

PURĀṆAS (*continued*).

VISHṆUPURĀṆA (*continued*).

यमगीता *etc.* [Yamagītā. 39 stanzas on the legend of Yama, purporting to be from this Purāṇa. Edited with a translation into easy Gorkhali by Raṅganātha Rimol.] pp. 24. *Benares*, 1889. 8°. **14016. c. 42.(1.)**

APPENDIX.

See PURUSHOTTAMA ṢARMĀ, *son of Ṣārṅgadhara.* स्थलप्रकाशः *etc.* [Sthalaprakāṣa. A work based on the Purāṇas and giving an account of places of pilgrimage and of the origins of the Udīchya Brahmans.] [1898.] 8°. **14058. b. 38.**

See RUDRADATTA ṢARMĀ. पुराण परीक्षा *etc.* [Purāṇaparīkshā. A proof that the Purāṇas are uncanonical and modern.] [1898.] 12°.
14154. cc. 5.

See WRIGHTSON (R.). An introductory treatise on Sanscrit Hagiographa . . . Part II.—The Veda and Puranas, *etc.* 1859. 12°. **4506. de. 16.**

PŪRṆA. *See* DEVĪPRASĀDA, *Rāi.*

PŪRṆACHANDRA ACHALEṢVARA ṢARMĀ. *See* PURĀṆAS.—*Bhavishyottarapurāṇa.* ॥ अथ ऋषिपंचमी व्रत कथा ॥ [Ṛishipañchamīvratakathā. With Gujarati translation by Pūrṇachandra.] [1899.] *obl.* 8°. **14028. d. 37.(2.)**

—— *See* YOGAVĀSISHṬHARĀMĀYAṆA. योगवासिष्ठ *etc.* [Yogavāsishṭharāmāyaṇa. Sections i. and ii. Edited with Gujarati version by Pūrṇachandra.] [1900.] 16°. **14048. a. 27.**

PŪRṆACHANDRA ṢARMĀ, *of Rajnagar.* *See* HARSHAKĪRTI SŪRI. श्रीयोगचिन्तामणि *etc.* [Yogachintāmaṇi. With Gujarati version by Pūrṇachandra.] [1898.] 8°. **14053. ccc. 20.**

PŪRṆACHANDRA VEDĀNTACHUÑCHU SĀṄKHYABHŪSHAṆA, *of Berhampur.* *See* ĪṢVARA KṚISHṆA. সাংখ্যতত্ত্ব-কৌমুদী *etc.* [Sāṅkhyatattvakaumudī. With Sanskrit grammatical explanations and Bengali translations and notes by the editor, Pūrṇachandra.] [1901.] 8°.
14048. dd. 34.(1.)

PŪRṆACHANDRA VEDĀNTACHUÑCHU SĀṄKHYABHŪSHAṆA, *of Berhampur (continued). See* PATAÑJALI. — *Philosophical Works.* পাতঞ্জল দর্শন *etc.* [Pātañjaladarṣana. The Aphorisms with commentary, *bhāshya*, and Bengali translations, *etc.* Compiled and edited by Pūrṇachandra.] [1898.] 8°. **14048. cc. 23.**

PŪRṆAKALAṢA GAṆĪ, *disciple of Jineṣvara. See* HEMACHANDRA, *disciple of Devachandra.* The Kumârapâlacharita . . . with a commentary by Pûrṇakalaṡagaṇi, *etc.* 1900. 8°. **14100. c. 23.**

PŪRṆĀNANDA. *See* UPANISHADS.—*Separate Upanishads.* কৈবল্যোপনিষৎ *etc.* [Kaivalyopanishad. With Bengali translation by Pūrṇānanda.] [1870?] 12°. **14010. b. 8.(1.)**

PŪRṆĀNANDA, *Brahmanishṭha Brahmachārī, of Lunawara. See* UPANISHADS.—*Separate Upanishads.* श्री निरालम्बोपनिषत् *etc.* [Nirālambopanishad. With Gujarati translation by Pūrṇānanda.] [1898.] *obl.* 12°. **14010. b. 3.(2.)**

PŪRṆĀNANDAGIRI, *Paramahaṃsa. See* PŪRṆĀNANDA GOSVĀMĪ.

PŪRṆĀNANDA GOSVĀMĪ, *disciple of Brahmānanda.* ষট্চক্র-নিরূপণং। [Shaṭchakranirūpaṇa, or Shaṭchakrabheda. A Yogic tract of 57 stanzas on the action of the Ṣakti or cosmic energy in the 6 centres of the microcosm. With commentary and Bengali translation.] *See* KĀLĪPRASANNA VIDYĀRATNA BHAṬṬĀCHĀRYA. যোগাঙ্কুর *etc.* [Yogāṅkura.] pp. 1-84. [1894.] 12°. **14048. b. 28.(2.)**

—— ষট্চক্র-নিরূপণম্। [Shaṭchakranirūpaṇa. With Bengali translation.] pp. 60. *See* PRASANNAKUMĀRA ṢĀSTRĪ BHAṬṬĀCHĀRYA. যোগাম্বুধি *etc.* [Yogāmbudhi.] [1896.] 16°. **14048. a. 19.**

—— षट्चक्र *etc.* [Shaṭchakra. With a Hindi version.] pp. 38. कानपुर १८९९ [*Cawnpore,* 1899.] 8°. **14028. c. 85.(7.)**

The pages are numbered 46—83.

—— श्री . . . षट्चक्रनिरूपणचित्रम्। . . . Shatchakra Niroopan Chittra. [Being the Shaṭchakranirūpaṇa with illustrative plates and] with [Sanskrit] Bhashya and Bhasha, [*i.e.* Hindi version,] containing the pictures of the different Nerves and Plexuses of the human body with their full description showing the easiest method how to practise Pranayam by the mental suspension of breath through meditation only. By Shri Swami Hansa Swaroop. pp. 28; 10 *plates.* *Muzaffurpur,* [1903.] 4°. **14033. d. 25.**

—— श्यामारहस्यम् *etc.* [Ṣyāmārahasya. A ritual of Ṣyāmā-worship in 15 *parichchhedas*, partly original and partly compiled from the Tantras. Edited by Jīvānanda Vidyāsāgara. Second edition.] pp. 208. कलिकाता १८९६ [*Calcutta,* 1896.] 8°. **14033. aa. 6.(2.)**

The author enumerates as sources the Vīratantra, Phetkāriṇit°., Kālikākulasarvasva. Kālit°., Yāmalat°., Kulachūḍāmaṇit°, Kumārit°., Kulārṇavat°., Kālikalpa, Bhairavat°., Kālikākulasadbhāva, and Uttarat°.

—— श्यामारहस्यतन्त्र *etc.* [Ṣyāmārahasya. With Hindi version by Hariṣaṅkara Ṣāstrī.] pp. i. 338. *Moradabad,* १८९९ [1899.] 8°. **14033. c. 41.**

PŪRṆENDU NĀRĀYAṆA SIṂHA. *See* PURĀṆAS.—*Bhāgavatapurāṇa.* A study of the Bhagavata Purana . . . by Purnendu . . . Sinha. 1901. 8°. **14016. dd. 4.**

PURUSHOTTAMA, *son of Pītāmbara.* ॥ अथ द्रव्यशुद्धिः ॥ [Dravyaṣuddhi. A treatise on formal cleanness, according to the school of Vallabhāchārya.] *See* GOVARDHANADĀSA LAKSHMĪDĀSA. बृहत्स्तोत्रसरित्सागर *etc.* [Bṛihat-stotrasaritsāgara.] Vol. ii. [1892.] 12°. **14033. a. 27.(vol. 2.)**

PURUSHOTTAMA, *son of Vishṇu.* The Vishṇubhaktikalpalatâ of Purushottama. [A cycle of religious poems.] With the commentary of Mahîdhara. Edited by . . . Paṇdit Durgâprasâd and Kâśinâth Pâṇdurang Parab. (विष्णुभक्तिकल्पलता।) pp. i. i. 86, i. 1892. *See* DURGĀPRASĀDA, *son of Vrajalāla,* and KĀṢĪNĀTHA PĀṆḌURAṄGA PARAB. Kâvyamâlâ. [No.] 31. 1886, *etc.* 8°. **14072. ccc. 12.(no. 31.)**

PURUSHOTTAMA BHAṬṬA, *son of Lakshmīnātha.* नीतिमनोरमा . . . Niti-manorma. [A short work on morals, in verse and prose.] By Purusottam Bhatt. pp. 55. काशी १८८९ [*Benares,* 1889.] 8°. **14076. b. 25.(3.)**

PURUSHOTTAMA DEVA, *Grammarian.* The Trikâṇḍaśesha, the Hârâvalî, the Ekâksharakosha, and the Dvirûpakosha of Purushottamadeva.

Edited by Paṇḍit Durgâprasâd, Kâśinâth Pâṇdurang Parab and Paṇḍit Śivadatta. (त्रिकाण्डशेष-हारावली-एकाक्षरकोश-द्विरूपकोशाः) pp. i. 38, 12, 3, 4, i. ii. 1889. *See* DURGĀPRASĀDA, *son of Vrajalála*, and others. The Abhidhâna-sangraha, *etc.* No. 2-5. 1889, *etc.* 8°. **14090. e. 20.(no. 2-5.)**

—— অথ দ্বিরূপকোষঃ । [Dvirūpakoṣa. A list of Sanskrit words of two different forms of spelling, extracted from Purushottama's Dvirūpakoṣa.] *See* GOPĪRAMAṆA TARKARATNA. কোষচন্দ্রিকা । [Koṣachandrikā.] pp. 58-60. [1893.] 12°. **14090. b. 44.(1.)**

—— द्विरूपकोशः ॥ [Dvirūpakoṣa.] 1895-1896. *See* VEṄKAṬARAṄGANĀTHA SVĀMĪ. Grandha Pradarsani, *etc.* [No. 5.] 1895, *etc.* 8°. **14003. c. 2.(5.)**

Here ascribed to Śrīharsha. The appended lexicon is unfinished.

—— একাক্ষরকোষ । [Ekāksharakoṣa. With a Bengali translation.] *See* GOPĪRAMAṆA TARKARATNA. কোষচন্দ্রিকা *etc.* [Koṣachandrikā.] pp. 25-37. [1893.] 12°. **14090. b. 44.(1.)**

—— लघुरत्नकोषः । [Laghu-ratnakoṣa. A vocabulary in 60 stanzas ascribed to Purushottama Deva.] pp. 5. *See* GADASIṂHA. ऊष्मविवेकः *etc.* [Ūshmaviveka.] [1890.] 8°. **14093. b. 17.(2.)**

PURUSHOTTAMA GAṆESA GHĀRPURE. *See* SOMANĀTHA, *son of Mudgala.* रागविबोधः *etc.* [Rāgavibodha. Edited by Purushottama.] [1894.] 8°. **14053. cc. 67.**

PURUSHOTTAMAJĪ, *Gosvāmī.* तुलसीमालाधारणवादः *etc.* [Tulasīmālādhāraṇavāda. A tract on the wearing of the *tulsī* or basil-plant by Vaishṇavas. With a Braj-bhāshā translation by Ratnagopāla Bhaṭṭa, and a Gujarati version.] pp. 30. मुंबई १९५८ [*Bombay*, 1902.] 8°. **14028. d. 69.**

PURUSHOTTAMA MISRA, *of Cuttack.* *See* PURUSHOTTAMA TARKĀLAṄKĀRA.

PURUSHOTTAMA ŚARMĀ, *son of Śārṅgadhara.* श्रीस्थल प्रकाशः किंवा उदीच्य प्रकाशः [Sthalaprakāṣa, also called Udīchyaprakāṣa and Purāṇasārasaṅgraha. A work in 41 *adhyāyas* or *marīchis* based upon the Purāṇas and giving an account of the chief places of pilgrimage visited by Hindus and of the origins and history of the Udīchya Brahmans from the time of Raja Mūladeva. Edited with Gujarati translation by Amṛitarāma Karuṇāśaṅkara Ṭhākura, and supplemented by a Gujarati treatise on the modern history of Udīchya Brahmans by Prāṇagovinda Rājārāma Ṭhākura.] pp. xii. 336, ii. 104. અમદાવાદ ૧૯૫૪ [*Ahmadabad*, 1898.] 8°. **14058. b. 38.**

PURUSHOTTAMA TARKĀLAṄKĀRA. *See* PĀṆINI. —*Prakriyākaumudī.* ପ୍ରକ୍ରିୟାକୌମୁଦୀ . . . Prakriya Kaumudy . . . With a commentary entitled the "Bimala" and an Oriya translation by . . . Purusottam Tarkalankar, *etc.* 1902, *etc.* 8°. **14090. bb. 19.**

PURUSHOTTAMA VIDYĀVĀGĪṢA BHAṬṬĀCHĀRYA. প্রয়োগরত্নমালা ব্যাকরণম্ । সমগ্রম্ *etc.* [Prayogaratnamālā. A metrical grammar. With the commentary Prabhāprakāṣikā of Jayakṛishṇa son of Vidyānanda on the *samāsa* and *ākhyāta* sections, the Pañjikā of Jīveṣvara on the *taddhita*, and the Kṛitpradīpikā of Mahendra on the *kṛit*. Edited with a second commentary upon the whole work, styled Gūḍhaprakāṣikā, by Siddhanātha Vidyāvāgīṣa. Followed by Purushottama's Paribhāshāsūtra and Kārikāvalī.] pp. i. ii. iii. i. i. iii. iv. iv. vii. vi. vi. 1548, 32. কোচবিহার ১৮১২-১৮১৫ [*Kuch Bihar*, 1890-1893.] 4°. **14090. e. 22.**

The Prayogaratnamālā was composed in Śaka 1490 in the reign of Nara-Nārāyaṇa of Kuch Bihar (A.D. 1534–84), *who had brought Purushottama into his country. Jayakrishṇa in his introductory stanzas pays his respects to Prāṇa-Nārāyaṇa* (A.D. 1627–66), *who is perhaps the Prāṇa-Nārāyaṇa in eulogy of whom Jagannātha Paṇḍitarāja composed his "Prāṇābharaṇa."*

PUSHKARA ŚARMĀ, *of Mirganj.* ब्राह्मणादर्श *etc.* [Brāhmaṇādarṣa. A treatise on Brahman *gotras*, showing the Veda, *pravara*, *ṣākhā*, and *sūtra* of each.] pp. 18. गया १९५३ [*Gaya*, 1896.] 8°. **14028. d. 57.(1.)**

PUSHPADANTA. अथ शिवमहिम्नःस्तोत्रम् [Mahimnaḥstotra, or Ṣivamahimastotra. Followed by Upamanyu's Ṣivastotra.] pp. 6. मथुरायां [*Muttra*, 1892.] *obl.* 12°. **14033. a. 19.(2.)**

—— शिवमहिम्नस्तोत्रम् । व्याख्योपेतम् । [Ṣivamahimastotra. With commentary.] pp. 32. [1892.] *See* PERIODICAL PUBLICATIONS.—*Bombay.* ग्रन्थरत्नमाला *etc.* (Granth Ratna Málá, *etc.*) Vol. V, no. 7, 8. 1887-[1892.] 8°. **14096. c. 8.(vol. 5.)**

PYAW, *Ū*, *of Taungdwin.* *See* Ñāṇābhidhammālaṅkāra.

R . . . K . . . KAVIBHŪSHAṆA. *See* Kavibhūshaṇa (R. K.).

R . . . N . . . SAMĀDDĀR. *See* Samāddār (R. N.).

RABHASANANDĪ. ষট্‌কারকম্। [Shaṭkāraka. A tract in 14 verses on the usage of cases. With a prose commentary.] *See* Ramānātha Rāi. শব্দরত্নম্ *etc.* [Ṣabdaratna.] pp. 57-77. [1893.] 8°. **14093. b. 36.(1.)**

RĀDHĀKĀNTA DEVA, *Raja.* শব্দকল্পদ্রুমঃ . . . সংস্কৃতমহাকোষ *etc.* [Ṣabdakalpadruma. Edited by Kṛishṇagopāla Bhakta. Third edition.] কলিকাতা ১৩১০ [*Calcutta*, 1903, *etc.*] 4°. **14092. cc. 2.**

In progress.

RĀDHĀKṚISHṆA MIṢRA. *See* Ambikādatta. द्रव्यस्तोत्रम् *etc.* [Dravyastotra. With Hindi translation by Rādhākṛishṇa.] [1893.] 16°. **14072. b. 4.(4.)**

RĀDHĀKṚISHṆA ṢARMĀ. *See* Ṣaṅkara Āchārya. —*Doubtful and Supposititious Works.* गोविन्दाष्टकम् *etc.* [Govindāshṭaka, or Charpaṭapañjarī. With Hindi version by Rādhākṛishṇa.] [1901.] 12°. **14028. bb. 5.(1.)**

RĀDHĀKṚISHṆA ṢĀSTRĪ, *of Pudukottai.* ॥ नीतिदशप्रबन्धी . . . The Nitidasaprabandhi. [Ten Sanskrit ethical poems, for the most part translated from the Tamil by Rādhākṛishṇa, viz. (1) Mandāramālā, *i.e.* the Āttiṣūdi of Avvaiyār; (2) Ṣamyākamālā, *i.e.* Avvaiyār's Konṟaivendan; (3) Bālanīti, by Rādhākṛishṇa Ṣāstrī; (4) Vāgullāsa, *i.e.* Avvaiyār's Vākkuṇḍām or Mūdurai; (5) Nityupākhyāna, by Rādhākṛishṇa Ṣāstrī; (6) Jayaṣaktikara, *i.e.* the Veṯṯivēṟkai of Ativīra Rāma Pāṇḍiyan; (7) Tattvapadavī, *i.e.* Avvaiyār's Nalvaṟi; (8) Sanmārgadarpaṇa, *i.e.* Ṣivaprakāṣa's Nanneṟi; (9) Nītipañchāṣat, by Rādhākṛishṇa Ṣāstrī; (10) Nītimārgapradīpikā, *i.e.* the Nītineṟiviḷakkam of Kumaragurupara.] Edited by Radhakrishna Sastriar. 10 pts. *Kumbakonam*, 1894. 8°. **14085. c. 46.**

RĀDHĀMOHANA GOSVĀMĪ BHAṬṬĀCHĀRYA. *See* Gotama. न्यायसूत्रविवरणम्। [Nyāyasūtra. With the Nyāyasūtravivaraṇa of Rādhāmohana.] 1901, *etc.* 8°. [*The Pandit.*] **14096. d. 6.(vol. 23, etc.)**

RĀDHĀMOHANA GOSVĀMĪ BHAṬṬĀCHĀRYA (*continued*). *See* Raghunandana Bhaṭṭāchārya. মলমাসতত্ত্বম্ *etc.* [Malamāsatattva. With commentaries of Rādhāmohana, *etc.*] [1900.] 8°. **14033. bbb. 5.**

—— *See* Raghunandana Bhaṭṭāchārya. প্রায়শ্চিত্ততত্ত্বম্ *etc.* [Prāyaṣchittatattva. With commentary of Rādhāmohana.] [1903.] 8°. **14033. bbb. 20.(1.)**

RĀDHĀNĀTHA, *Rāi, Rāi Bahādur, Inspector of Schools.* *See* Kālidāsa.—*Selections.* कालिदास-सूक्तयः Kalidas's Apothegms [*sic*]. [Selected, with English and Bengali paraphrases,] by Rai Radhanath . . . Bengal edition. [1903.] 12°. **14085. b. 23.(2.)**

—— —— Indian edition. [1903.] 12°. **14085. b. 23.(3.)**

RĀDHIKĀPRASĀDA ṢARMĀ. বৈষ্ণবসদ্ধর্ম্মভাস্করঃ। [Vaishṇavasaddharmabhāskara. A religious tract of the Vaishṇava sect. First *prakāṣa.*] pp. 7. রাণাঘাট [*Ranaghat*, 1892.] 12°. **14028. b. 82.(2.)**

RĀGHAVA ĀCHĀRYA, *Astrologer.* *See* Ṣrīnivāsa Āchārya, *Astrologer.* দীপিকা *etc.* [Ṣuddhidīpikā. With commentaries of Rāghava, *etc.*] [1901.] 8°. **14053. ccc. 23.**

RĀGHAVA BHAṬṬA, *Rhetorician.* *See* Kālidāsa.—*Abhijñānaṣakuntala.* The Abhijñánaśakuntala . . . With the commentary styled 'Arthadyotanika of Rághavabhatta, *etc.* 1898. 8°. **14080. c. 37.**

RĀGHAVĀCHĀRYA, *Kaḷattūri.* *See* Bhāradvāja. భారద్వాజ . . . శిక్ష ॥ [Bhāradvājaṣikshā. With the commentary Rāghavīya of Rāghavāchārya.] 1893. 8°. **14092. a. 27.**

RĀGHAVĀCHĀRYA, *Koṇḍamūr Kōyal Iyuṇṇi.* *See* Pāñcharātra. శ్రీ . . . కపింజల సంహితా *etc.* [Kapiñjalasaṃhitā. Edited by Rāghavāchārya, *etc.*] [1896.] 8°. **14028. d. 59.(5.)**

—— *See* Pāñcharātra. పాఞ్చరాత్రమ్ *etc.* [Vishṇutilaka. Edited by Rāghavāchārya.] 1896. 8°. **14028. d. 63.**

RĀGHAVAJĪ KARṢANJĪ. *See* Vallabhāchārya. श्रीमद्वल्लभाचार्यजी विरचित षोडश ग्रंथ० [Shoḍaṣa-grantha. Edited with analysis and Gujarati translations *etc.* by Rāghavajī.] [1899.] 8°. **14033. aa. 25.**

RĀGHAVĀNANDA, *Astronomer.* দিনচন্দ্রিকামতে পঞ্চাঙ্গসাধন। অর্থাৎ পঞ্জিকাগণনা। [Pañchāṅga-sādhana, or Pañjikāgaṇanā. A treatise on the calculation of the calendar, comprising Rāghavānanda's Dinachandrikā with Bengali version, notes, *etc.*] pp. 22. [1890, *etc.*] *See* PERIODICAL PUBLICATIONS.—*Calcutta.* অরুণোদয় *etc.* [Aruṇodaya.] Pt. i., no. 3. [1890, *etc.*] 4°.

14133. g. 16.(pt. i., no. 3.)

RĀGHAVĀRYA, *son of Pāṭṭarārya.* *See* VEṄKAṬĀRYA YAJVĀ. ലക്ഷ്മീസഹസ്രം *etc.* [Lakshmīsahasra. With the commentary Gūḍhārthavivaraṇa of Rāghavārya.] [1892.] 8°.

14028. d. 49.

RĀGHAVENDRA GURU. *See* KṚISHṆĀCHĀRYA, *Sārvabhauma.* अथ श्रीराघवेंद्रगुरोस्तारहार: *etc.* [Rāghavendratārahāra and Rāghavendraprārthanāvalī. Poems in praise of Rāghavendra.] [1892.] *obl.* 16°.

14028. b. 80.(1.)

RĀGHAVENDRA RĀU, C. *See* MAHĀBHĀRATA.—*Vanaparva.* University of Madras . . . Notes on the Mahabharata [and Pañchatantra,] with English translation, by C. Raghavendra Rao . . . and Kundalagiriyachar. 1891. 8°.

14060. c. 30.(2.)

RĀGHAVENDRA SAKHĀJĪ, *Gosvāmī.* साकेताधीशयुगलरहस्यस्तोत्रम् *etc.* [Sāketādhīṣayugalarahasyastotra. A hymn of 12 stanzas to Rāma as king of Ayodhyā. With Hindi translation by Pandit Sītārāmaṣaraṇa.] pp. 16. कानपुर [*Cawnpore*, 1901.] *obl.* 12°.

14033. a. 19.(5.)

RAGHUDEVA SARASVATĪ, *son of Viṣveṣvara.* मैथिलवर-पण्डितराजरघुदेवसरस्वतीविरचिता बिरुदावली *etc.* [Birudāvalī. A series of model poetical panegyrics. Edited with a commentary styled Vibudharājirañjinī by Chakradhara Jhā of Sagarpur.] pp. iii. 113. काश्यां १९६० [*Benares*, 1904.] 8°.

14076. d. 57.

RAGHUNANDANA BHAṬṬĀCHĀRYA, *son of Harihara.* स्मृतितत्त्वस्य प्रथमो भाग: (द्वितीयोभाग:) [Smṛitattva. A digest of religious law. Terminated by the ritual of Durgā styled Ṣāradīyā Mahāpūjāpaddhati. Edited by Jīvānanda Vidyāsāgara. Second edition.] 2 vols. कलिकाता १८९५ [*Calcutta*, 1895.] 8°.

14033. aa. 9.

RAGHUNANDANA BHAṬṬĀCHĀRYA, *son of Harihara (continued).*

—— *See* ṢIVANĀTHA VIDYĀVĀCHASPATI. স্মৃতিবিচারসারকৌমুদী *etc.* [Smṛitivichārasārakaumudī. Disquisitions on points in the writings of Raghunandana.] [1897.] 8°.

14033. bb. 45.(1.)

—— মহামহোপাধ্যায় স্মার্ত্ত শ্রীরঘুনন্দন ভট্টাচার্য্য-বিরচিত তিথ্যুদ্বাহতত্ত্বয়োঃ। আক্ষেপ-সমাধানম্ *etc.* [Ākshepasamādhāna. An interpretation by Ānandachandra Bhaṭṭāchārya Vidyābhūshaṇa of crucial passages in Raghunandana's Tithitattva and Udvāhatattva, with the text of those passages.] pp. i. 85. ঢাকা ১২৯৯ [*Dacca*, 1893.] 12°.

14033. a. 31.

The work seems complete, although the wrapper-titlepage bears the note prathamakhaṇḍam.

—— মলমাসতত্ত্বম্ *etc.* [Malamāsatattva. The 6th section of the Smṛitittattva, treating of the observances connected with intercalary months. With the commentaries of Kāṣirāma Vāchaspati and Rādhāmohana Gosvāmī. Edited by Chaṇḍīcharaṇa Smṛitibhūshaṇa. Second edition.] pp. iv. 402. কলিকাতা ১৩০৬ [*Calcutta*, 1900.] 8°.

14033. bbb. 5.

—— প্রায়শ্চিত্ততত্ত্বম্ *etc.* [Prāyaṣchittatattva. The 4th section of the Smṛitittattva, on lustration. With commentary of Rādhāmohana Gosvāmī. Edited by Chaṇḍīcharana Smṛitibhūshaṇa.] pp. ii. 226. কলিকাতা ১৩১০ [*Calcutta*, 1903.] 8°.

14033. bbb. 20.(1.)

—— তিথিতত্ত্বম্ *etc.* [Tithitattva. The first section of the Smṛitittattva, on the religious calendar. With the commentary of Kāṣirāma Vāchaspati. Edited with annotations by Chaṇḍīcharaṇa Smṛitibhūshaṇa. Second edition.] pp. vi. 460. কলিকাতা ১৩০৮ [*Calcutta*, 1901.] 8°.

14033. bb. 45.(3.)

—— উদ্বাহতত্ত্বং *etc.* [Udvāhatattva. The 9th section of the Smṛitittattva, treating of marriage. With the commentary of Kāṣirāma Vāchaspati. Edited with a Bengali translation of the text by Nīlakamala Vidyānidhi.] pp. ii. 140. কলিকাতা ১৩০২ [*Calcutta*, 1896.] 8°. **14033. bb. 42.**

—— উদ্বাহতত্ত্বম্। দেবপ্রতিষ্ঠাতত্ত্বম্ *etc.* [Udvāhatattva. With the commentary of Kāṣirāma.

Followed by the Devapratishṭhātattva (pt. 17 of the Smṛititattva) and a ritual for reconsecrations. Edited by Chaṇḍīcharaṇa Smṛitibhūshaṇa. Second edition.] pp. 80, 12, 2. কলিকাতা ১৩০৮ [*Calcutta*, 1902.] 8°. **14033. bb. 45.(4.)**

RAGHUNĀTHA, *son of Devakīnandana, Gosvāmī.* गोस्वामीश्रीरघुनाथजीकृतग्रंथाः ॥ [Miscellaneous religious writings in verse on the doctrine of Vallabhāchārya.] pp. 32. *See* GOVARDHANADĀSA LAKSHMĪDĀSA. बृहत्स्तोत्रसरित्सागर *etc.* [Bṛihat-stotra-saritsāgara.] Vol. ii. [1892.] 12°. **14033. a. 27.(vol. 2.)**

RAGHUNĀTHA, *son of Vināyaka, Nāgara. See* SĀRASVATASŪTRA. लघुभाष्यम् *etc.* [Sārasvatasūtra. With the commentary Laghu-bhāshya of Raghunātha.] [1901.] 8°. **14093. b. 44.**

RAGHUNĀTHA DAIVAJÑA, *son of Nṛisiṃha.* मुहूर्तमाला *etc.* [Muhūrtamālā. A metrical work, in nine chapters, on astrologically auspicious moments. With the commentary Saundaryabodhinī by Maheśvara Rāmachandra Sukhṭhaṇkar. Edited by Rāmachandra Vāmana Karaṇḍe.] pp. ii. 15, 218. मुंबयी १८१४ [*Bombay*, 1892.] 8°. **14053. c. 62.**

RAGHUNĀTHADĀSA GOSVĀMĪ. সটীক . . . শ্রীস্তবপুষ্পাঞ্জলিঃ *etc.* [Stavapushpāñjali. A series of Vaishṇava lyrics compiled from the Stavamālā of Rūpa Gosvāmī and Raghunāthadāsa's Stavāvali. With commentary, *etc.*] [1902.] 8°. *See* RŪPA GOSVĀMĪ. **14072. ccc. 34.**

RAGHUNĀTHAPRASĀDA SUKALA, *son of Sītārāma.* అనుపానతరంగిణి *etc.* [Anupānataraṅgiṇī. A metrical treatise on Materia Medica. With Telugu translation by Puvvāḍa Rāmachandra Rāu.] pp. iii. 79; 1 *plate.* *Madras*, ౧౮౯౫ [1895.] 8°. **14043. c. 46.**

—— వాజీకరకల్పద్రుమము *etc.* [Vājīkarakalpadruma. A treatise on aphrodisiacs. With Telugu translation by S. Subbarāmaiya.] pp. iii. 73. *Madras*, ౧౯౦౧ [1901.] 8°. **14043. cc. 18.**

RAGHUNĀTHA RĀMAKṚISHṆA BHĀGAVATA. *See* VIṬHOBĀ AṆṆĀ. विठोबा अण्णाकृत पदसमूह *etc.* [Padasamūha. Edited by Raghunātha.] [1890.] 8°. **14140. b.**

RAGHUNĀTHA ŚARMĀ, *Tāntrika. See* ĀGAMASĀRA. अथ महामारी कल्पः *etc.* [Mahāmārīkalpa. With Hindi translation by Raghunātha.] [1901.] 8°. **14033. b. 42.(4.)**

RAGHUNĀTHA ŚĀSTRĪ PARVATE. *See* GAṄGEŚA UPĀDHYĀYA. హేత్వాభాససామాన్యనిరుక్తిః *etc.* [Hetvābhāsasāmānyanirukti. Followed by Gadādhara's Gādādharī and Raghunātha's gloss Nyāyaratna upon Gadādhara.] [1893.] 8°. **14048. dd. 14.**

RAGHUNĀTHA ŚIROMAṆI. *See* GAṄGEŚA UPĀDHYĀYA. The Tattva-chintámaṇi, *etc.* (Part IV, Çabda-khaṇḍa . . . with the Ākhyātavāda and the Naṇvāda of . . . Raghunātha, *etc.*) 1888-1901. 8°. [*Bibliotheca Indica.*] **14002. a. (vol. 98.)**

—— *See* GAṄGEŚA UPĀDHYĀYA. హేత్వాభాససామాన్యనిరుక్తి *etc.* [Hetvābhāsasāmānyanirukti. With the Dīdhiti of Raghunātha, Gadādhara's commentary upon the latter, *etc.*] [1893.] 8°. **14048. dd. 14.**

—— *See* GAṄGEŚA UPĀDHYĀYA. केवलान्वयि अनुमानम् *etc.* [Kevalānvayyanumāna. With Raghunātha's Śiromaṇi, *etc.*] [1897.] 8°. **14048. bb. 45.(4.)**

—— *See* GAṄGEŚA UPĀDHYĀYA. పక్షత *etc.* [Pakshatā. With Raghunātha's Dīdhiti. Followed by Gadādhara's Gādādharī upon the latter.] [1890.] 8°. **14048. e. 19.**

—— *See* GAṄGEŚA UPĀDHYĀYA. पक्षता *etc.* [Pakshatā. With the Śiromaṇi of Raghunātha, *etc.*] [1897.] 8°. **14048. bb. 45.(5.)**

—— *See* GAṄGEŚA UPĀDHYĀYA. The Pramanyavadaha [*sic*] by . . . Gadadara . . . with Thathva Chinthamani by Gangasopadyaya and Didhithi by Raghunadha . . . Vol. 1. 1901. 8°. [*Śāstramuktāvalī.*] **14049. a. 1.(no. 4.)**

—— *See* GAṄGEŚA UPĀDHYĀYA. A Collection of Sadharana, Asadharana, Anupasamhari, and Virodha, Grandhas. By . . . Gadadhara Bhattacharya. With [the corresponding passages from the] Mani and Didhithi of Gangesopadhyaya and Raghunatha, *etc.* 1900. 8°. [*Nyāyaratnāvalī.*] **14048. e. 31.(2.)**

RAGHUNĀTHA ŚIROMAṆI (*continued*). See GAṄGEŚA UPĀDHYĀYA. सत्प्रतिपक्ष° [Satpratipakshagrantha. The section on *satpratipaksha*, with the corresponding portions of the Dīdhiti and Gādādharī.] 1901. 8°. [*Nyāyaratnāvalī.*] **14048. e. 31.(3.)**

—— *See* GAṄGEŚA UPĀDHYĀYA. Savyabhichara Samanyaniruktbi. By . . . Gadadhara Bhattacharya. With [the corresponding passages from the] Mani and Didhithi of Gangesopadhyaya and Raghunatha, *etc.* 1900. 8°. [*Nyāyaratnāvalī.*] **14048. e. 31.(1.)**

—— *See* GAṄGEŚA UPĀDHYĀYA. సిద్ధాంతలక్షణమ్ *etc.* [Siddhāntalakshaṇa. With Raghunātha's Dīdhiti and Gadādhara's Gādādharī.] [1893.] 8°. **14048. dd. 13.**

—— *See* GAṄGEŚA UPĀDHYĀYA. सिद्धान्तलक्षणम् *etc.* (Siddhantalakshana . . . With the commentaries of Raghunatha Siromani, and Mathuranatha Tarkabagisha, *etc.*) [1896.] 8°. **14048. c. 79.(1.)**

—— *See* GAṄGEŚA UPĀDHYĀYA. व्याप्तिपञ्चकम् *etc.* [Vyāptipañchaka. With an extract from Raghunātha's commentary Śiromaṇi, *etc.*] [1896.] 8°. **14048. e. 28.**

—— *See* UDAYANA ĀCHĀRYA. आत्मतत्त्वविवेकः *etc.* [Ātmatattvaviveka, or Bauddhadhikkāra. With portions of the gloss of Mathurānātha, the exposition styled Bauddhadhikkāradīdhiti by Raghunātha, *etc.*] [1900, *etc.*] 8°. **14048. dd. 28.**

—— Avachedakata Nirukthi. [An excerpt from the Gādādharī.] By . . . Gadadhara Bhattacharya. With Didhithi of Raghunadha Siromani, *etc.* (अवच्छेदकतानिरुक्तिः ॥) pp. 57. 1901. *See* ANANTĀCHĀRYA, *Prativādibhayaṅkara.* शास्त्रमुक्तावली The Sasthramukthâvalî, *etc.* No. 11. 1899, *etc.* 8°. **14049. a. 1.(no. 11.)**

—— व्यागदीशीव्यधिकरणधर्म्मावच्छिन्नाभावः [Vyadhikaraṇadharmāvachchhinnābhāva. Being the section from Raghunātha's commentary upon the chapter of that name in the Vyāptivāda of Gaṅgeśa's Anumānakhaṇḍa. With Jagadīśa's supercommentary Chaturdaśalakshaṇī.] ff. 40, *lith.* बनारस १८८९ [*Benares*, 1889.] *obl.* 4°. **14048. f. 21.**

RAGHUNĀTHA TEMPLE LIBRARY, *of Jammu.* *See* JAMMU.—*Raghunātha Temple Library.*

RAGHUNĀTHA VARMĀ, *Udāsīna, son of Gulābrāi and disciple of Rāmadayālu.* लौकिकन्यायसंग्रहः . . . Laukikanyāyasaṁgraha. [A treatise on the popular instances applied as examples in philosophy.] . . . Edited by Mahāmahopādhyāya Gaṅgādhara Śāstrī. pp. ii. ii. viii. 166. 1902. *See* PERIODICAL PUBLICATIONS.—*Benares.* The Pandit, *etc.* New Series. Vol. XXIII-XXIV. 1876, *etc.* 8°. **14096. d. 6.(vol. 23, 24.)**

—— [A reprint of the preceding.] pp. ii. ii. viii. 166. काश्याम् १९०२ [*Benares*, 1902.] 8°. **14049. b. 8.**

RAGHURĀJASIṂHAJŪ DEVA, *Maharaja.* *See* PURĀṆAS.—*Bhāgavatapurāṇa.* अथ श्रीमद्भागवते *etc.* [Bhāgavatapurāṇa. With metrical Hindi paraphrase by Raghurājasiṃhajū Deva.] [1899-1900.] *obl.* Fol. **14018. cc. 3.**

RAGHUVAṂŚA ŚARMĀ, *of Sumerpur.* *See* MANU, *son of Lakshmaṇa.* वैद्यकसर्वस्वम् *etc.* [Vaidyakasarvasva. With Hindi translation. Edited by Raghuvaṃśa.] [1896.] 12°. **14043. b. 9.(2.)**

—— *See* RĀMA, *Physician.* वैद्यकसारशंकर ग्रंथः *etc.* [Vaidyakasāraśaṅkara. With Hindi translation. Edited by Raghuvaṃśa.] [1896.] 12°. **14043. b. 9.(3.)**

RAGHUVĪRA DĪKSHITA, *son of Viṭṭhala.* *See* ŚAṄKARA BHAṬṬA, *son of Nīlakaṇṭha.* ॥ अथ . . . कुंडार्कः *etc.* [Kuṇḍārka. With the commentary Kuṇḍārkamarīchimālā by Raghuvīra.] [1893.] *obl.* 8°. **14028. dd. 5.(1.)**

RĀICHAND MOTĪLĀL, *Rector of the Dharmottejaka-Pāṭhaśālā, Borsad.* श्री जैनधर्मतत्त्वसंग्रह *etc.* [Jainadharmatattvasaṅgraha. A manual of the doctrine of Digambara Jains, comprising selected Sanskrit verses with Gujarati translations, expositions, and religious poems.] pp. 64. અમદાવાદ ૧૮૯૯ [*Ahmadabad*, 1899.] 12°. **14100. b. 5.**

RĀICHAND NĀGAR. *See* JAYADEVA, *son of Bhojadeva.* गीतगुविन्दादरस *etc.* [Gītagovindādarṣa. Being the Gītagovinda with an imitation in Hindi verse by Rāichand.] [1858.] 8°. **14076. c. 73.(1.)**

RĀJAÇEKHARA. *See* RĀJAŚEKHARA.

RĀJĀDHIRĀJASIṂHA, *King of Ceylon.* Rājādhirājasinha's Poem, the Asadrisajātakaya. Edited, with . . . notes &c., [and the prose text of the Jātaka in Pali and Sinhalese prefixed,] by . . . F. W. De Silva . . . and J. D. Kannangera . . . අසදිස ජාතකය. pp. xi. ii. i. 43, vii. ii. *Galle*, 1889. 8°. **14165. i. 18.**

RĀJAGOPĀLĀCHĀRYA, *T.* *See* ACADEMIES, *etc.*—Madras.—*University of Madras.* The F.A. Sanskrit Text 1899, with . . . notes, translation, paraphrase &c. by T. Rajagopalachariar. [1898.] 8°. **14079. b. 34.(4.)**

RĀJAKṚISHṆA CHAṬṬOPĀDHYĀYA. निसर्गाभिनयम् . . . Nisargábhinayam. A Sanskrit poetry-book, [*i.e.* a collection of short original poems,] *etc.* pp. 48. *Calcutta*, 1890. 12°. **14072. b. 17.(2.)**

RĀJAKUMĀRA SENA GUPTA KAVIRATNA, *Kavirāja.* *See* RĀJAVALLABHA. রাজবল্লভীয়-দ্রব্যগুণঃ *etc.* [Rājavallabhīya-dravyaguṇa. Edited with Bengali translation by Rājakumāra Sena Gupta.] [1891.] 8°. **14043. c. 42.(1.)**

RAJANĪKĀNTA GUPTA. जयदेवचरित *etc.* [Jayadevacharita. A biography of the poet Jayadeva, translated from the Bengali into Hindi by Sarayūprasāda Miṣra. With an appendix containing portions of Dhoyī's Pavanadūta.] pp. 80. पटना १९०१ [*Patna*, 1901.] 8°. **14156. g. 75.**

RĀJARĀJA VARMĀ, *A. R.*, *Kōyi-tamburān*, called BĀLA KAVI. ഗൈർവാണീവിജയഃ [Gairvāṇīvijaya. An allegorical play in one act on the foundation of Sanskrit schools in Travancore.] pp. 12. பாலக்காடு [*Palghat*,] 1890. 8°. **14079. c. 48.(2.)**

Published as a supplement to the Vijñānachintāmaṇi.

—— श्री . . . विटविभावरी *etc.* [Viṭavibhāvarī, or Rādhāmādhava. A poem in 4 *yāmas* on the sports of Vāsudeva. With a commentary called Chandrikā by M. Udaya Varmā.] pp. 41. १८९४ [*Pattambi*, 1894.] 8°. **14072. c. 52.(1.)**

RĀJARĀJEṢVARA-ṢAṄKARĀṢRAMASVĀMĪ. *See* ṢAṄKARA, *Āchārya-Svāmi, Pontiff of Dwarka.*

RĀJĀRĀMA, *Pandit, of the Dayānanda Anglo-Vedic College, Lahore.* *See* ĀRYA SAMĀJ. आर्य्य सन्ध्या पद्धति *etc.* [Āryasandhyāpaddhati. Daily prayers, with Hindi introductions, rules, translations, *etc.*, by Rājārāma and Chhajjū Singh.] [1897.] 12°. **14028. b. 96.(1.)**

—— ॥ उपदेश सप्तक *etc.* [Upadeṣasaptaka. A series of quotations, under 7 heads, bearing upon moral and religious duties, with a Hindi translation and commentary setting forth the doctrines of the Ārya Samāj.] pp. 155. लाहौर १९५९ [*Lahore*, 1902.] 12°. **14085. b. 46.**

Forms no. 1 *of the* Dharmagranthāvali.

RĀJĀRĀMA GAṆEṢA BOḌAS, *Mahāmahopādhyāya.* *See* PATAÑJALI.—*Philosophical Works.* Patañjalasûtrâṇi. With the scholium of Vyâsa and the commentary of Vâchaspati. Edited by Râjârâm Shâstrî Bodas. 1892. 8°. **14048. dd. 10.**

—— *See* UPANISHADS. — *Separate Upanishads.* ईशावास्योपनिषत्° ((1) Shri Ísávásyopanishad with . . . (2) the Bháshya of . . . Uatabhattácharya . . . (6) The Bhashyás of . . . Anantácharya. And (7) Ánandabhattopádhyáya. Edited by . . . Rájárama Ŝastrí, *etc.*) [1888.] 8°. **14003. ccc. (no. 5.)**

—— Veda-prâmânya-chandrikâ. A treatise on the authority of the Vedas, by the late . . . Râjârâm Shâstri Bodas, *etc.* (वेदप्रामाण्यचन्द्रिका ।) pp. iii. 80. *Bombay*, 1902. 8°. **14007. c. 9.(3.)**

RĀJĀRĀMA RĀMAKṚISHṆA BHĀGAVATA. *See* UPANISHADS.—*Small Collections.* An attempt to interpret in Marāthī the Eleven Upanishads. With preface, translation and notes in English . . . by Râjârâma . . . Bhâgavata. 1898, *etc.* 8°. **14010. cc. 10.**

RĀJĀRĀMA ṢĀSTRĪ, *Mahāmahopādhyāya.* *See* RĀJĀRĀMA GAṆEṢA BOḌAS.

RĀJAṢEKHARA, *of Maladhārī-gachchha.* Antarakathāsaṃgrahaḥ Gainīyaḥ. [A collection of stories attributed to Rājaṣekhara. Edited by F. L. Pullé.] 1897, *etc.* *See* PERIODICAL PUBLICATIONS.—*Florence.* Studi Italiani di Filologia Indo-Iranica, *etc.* Vol. I, *etc.* 1897, *etc.* 8°. **P.P. 4884. da.(vol. 1, etc.)**

In progress.

RĀJAṢEKHARA, *son of Durduka.* Rāja-çekhara's Karpūra-mañjarī. A drama by the Indian poet Rājaçekhara . . . Critically edited in the original Prākrit, with a glossarial index, and an essay on the life and writings of the poet, by Sten Konow . . . and translated into English with notes by Charles Rockwell Lanman. pp. xxvi. 289. 1901. *See* Academies, *etc.*—Cambridge, *Mass.*—*Harvard University.* Harvard Oriental Series, *etc.* Vol. iv. 1891, *etc.* 8°. **14003. l. 3.(vol. 4.)**

—— [Another copy.] **14080. e. 6.**

RĀJASUNDARA (J. S.), *Ārachchi.* *See* Sāyanna. Prayogasamuchchaya . . . With a new Sinhalese paraphrace [*sic*] by J. S. Rajasundara, *etc.* [1895.] 8°. **14043. c. 43.(3.)**

RĀJAVALLABHA. রাজবল্লভীয়-দ্রব্যগুণঃ *etc.* [Rājavallabhīya-dravyaguṇa, also called Dravyaguṇa, Rājavallabhanighaṇṭu, or Rājavallabha. A metrical treatise on Materia Medica, in 6 *parichchhedas*, ascribed to a legendary Rājavallabha, and redacted by Nārāyaṇadāsa Kavirāja. Edited with a Bengali translation by Rājakumāra Sena Gupta Kaviratna.] pp. ii. 160. কলিকাতা ১২৯৮ [*Calcutta*, 1891.] 8°. **14043. c. 42.(1.)**

—— राजवल्लभनिघण्टुः *etc.* [Rājavallabhanighaṇṭu. Edited with a Hindi translation styled Dravyachandrikā by Ṣālagrāma Vaiṣya.] pp. vi. xvi. 212. कल्याण-मुंबई १९५२ [*Kalyan*, 1896.] 8°. **14043. cc. 7.**

—— দ্রব্যগুণঃ *etc.* [Dravyaguṇa. Edited with a Bengali translation by Rājendranātha Sena Kaviratna.] কলিকাতা ১৯৫৮ [*Calcutta*, 1901.] 12°. **14043. b. 14.(3.)**

RĀJENDRALĀLA MITRA. *See* Ṣaunaka. Bṛihaddevatá . . . Edited by . . . Rájendralála Mitra. 1893. 8°. [*Bibliotheca Indica.*] **14002. a. (vol. 127.)**

—— *See* Upanishads.—*Small Collections.* Selections from the Upanishads. Translated into English. [With a part of the Chhāndogya Upanishad, translated by Rājendralāla.] With notes, *etc.* 1895. 8°. [*Sacred Books of the East Described and Examined.*] **14010. cc. 9.(vol. 2.)**

—— Notices of Sanskrit MSS. . . . published under orders of the Government of Bengal. (Vol. X, by Haraprasád Shástri.) 10 vols. *Calcutta*, 1871-1892. 8°. **14096. cc.**

The second series of these Notices, *by Haraprasāda Sāstrī, is catalogued under the name of the latter.*

RĀJENDRANĀTHA SENA KAVIRATNA. *See* Rājavallabha. দ্রব্যগুণঃ *etc.* [Dravyaguṇa. Edited with Bengali translation by Rājendranātha Sena.] [1901.] 12°. **14043. b. 14.(3.)**

RĀKHĀLDĀS NYĀYARATNA. *See* Haridāsa Ṣāstrī. तत्त्वसारविचारः . . . Tattvasára Vichára. An examination of . . . Rákháldás Nyáyaratna's Tattvasára, *etc.* 1891. 8°. **14048. bb. 51.(3.)**

—— शक्तिवाद-रहस्य-प्रकाशः [Ṣaktivādarahasyaprakāṣa. A dissertation on semasiology, in exposition of Gadādhara's Ṣaktivāda.] pp. 48. वाराणस्यां १९५३ [*Benares*, 1896.] 8°. **14048. bb. 50.(2.)**

RĀKHĀLDĀS VIDYĀRATNA. A Manual of Sanskrit Composition and Translation [in Sanskrit, Bengali, and English,] *etc.* pp. iv. 105. *Howrah*, 1891. 12°. **14092. a. 13.(2.)**

—— A Manual of Sanskrit Composition and Translation, through the medium of English . . . New edition. pp. 107. *Calcutta*, 1895. 12°. **14092. a. 16.**

—— अनुवादभानु [Anuvādabhānu.] A manual of Sanscrit composition. By Rekhal Dass, Vidyaratana. Hindi translation [of the rules] by Pandit Krishna Datta. pp. ii. 148, viii. *Lahore*, 1902. 12°. **14160. a. 43.**

RĀMA, *Munshī, of Jalandhar.* آریہ سنگیت مالا [Āryasaṅgītamālā. A collection of Hindi hymns for the liturgies of the Ārya Samāj. Followed by select Vedic *mantras* of benediction, with Hindi translation.] pp. 8, 144, 31, 24, *lith.* جلندھر ۱۹۵۷ [*Jalandhar*, 1900.] 12°. **14154. cc. 7.**

RĀMA, *Physician.* वैद्यकसारशंकर ग्रंथ *etc.* [Vaidyakasāraṣaṅkara. A concise treatise on Hindu pathology, with a Hindi translation by Vasatirāma son of Ṣālagrāma. Edited by Raghuvaṃsa Ṣarmā.] pp. vi. 70. मुंबई १९५३ [*Bombay*, 1896.] 12°. **14043. b. 9.(3.)**

RĀMA, *son of Ananta, Astrologer.* मुहूर्तचिन्तामणिः *etc.* [Muhūrtachintāmaṇi. A manual of astrology, in 14 chapters. With Hindi translation by Vanamālī Chaturvedī. Edited by Sītārāma Ṣrīkṛishṇa Jāṃbbekar.] pp. ii. vii. 196. मुंबा° १९०२ [*Bombay*, 1902.] 8°. **14053. cc. 69.**

RĀMA, *son of Ananta, Astrologer* (*continued*). मुहूर्तचिन्तामणिः *etc.* [Muhūrtachintāmaṇi. With Hindi translation and notes by Nīlakaṇṭha son of Viśveśvaranātha.] pp. xvii. 258. लक्ष्मणपुरे १९५७ [*Lucknow*, 1901.] 8°. **14053. ccc. 21.(1.)**

—— [Another copy.] **14053. ccc. 44.**

RĀMABHADRA DĪKSHITA, *Kaṇḍaramāṇikkam, son of Yajñarāma.* ஜாநகீபரிணய-நாடகம் *etc.* [Jānakīpariṇaya. A drama in 7 acts on the marriage of Rāma and Sītā. Edited by A. Rāmānujāchārya.] pp. 168. *Madras*, 1892. 8°. **14079. c. 59.**

—— The Patañjali-charita of Râmabhadra Dikshit. [A poetical account of Patañjali, in 8 *sargas*.] Edited by Paṇḍit Śivadatta . . . and Kâśînâth Pâṇḍurang Parab. (पतञ्जलिचरितम् ।) pp. 57. 1895. *See* DURGĀPRASĀDA, *son of Vrajalāla*, and KĀŚĪNĀTHA PĀṆḌURAṄGA PARAB. Kâvyamâlâ. [No.] 51. 1886, *etc.* 8°. **14072. ccc. 12.(no. 51.)**

—— ஸ்ரீ . . . பதஞ்ஜலிவிஜயமஹாகாவ்ய-ப்ராரம்ப: [Patañjalivijaya, *i.e.* Patañjali-charita.] pp. 24. 1901-1902. *See* PERIODICAL PUBLICATIONS. — *Chidambaram.* ப்ரஹ்மவித்யா *etc.* [Brahmavidyā.] Vol. xv., no. 1-6. 1886, *etc.* 4°. **14096. dd. 3. (vol. 15.)**

—— The Śṛingâratilaka Bhâṇa of Râmabhadra Díkshita. [A comedy.] Edited by Paṇḍit Śivadatta . . . and Kâśînâth Pâṇḍurang Parab. [With a biography of the poet and an account of contemporary writers by T. S. Kuppūsvāmi Śāstrī.] (शृङ्गारतिलकम् ।) pp. ii. xxiv. 58. 1894. *See* DURGĀPRASĀDA, *son of Vrajalāla*, and KĀŚĪNĀTHA PĀṆḌURAṄGA PARAB. Kâvyamâlâ. [No.] 44. 1886, *etc.* 8°. **14072. ccc. 12.(no. 44.)**

RĀMA BRAHMENDRA. జగద్గురుపరంపరానామ-మాలా *etc.* [Jagadguruparamparānāmamālā. A list, in 20 stanzas, of the Pontiffs succeeding Śaṅkara in the Kāmakoṭi *pīṭha* of the Śāradā *maṭha* at Conjevaram.] *See* MAṬHĀMNĀYA. శ్రీమ-ఠామ్నాయః *etc.* [Maṭhāmnāya, *etc.*] pp. 9-10. 1894. 8°. **14048. bb. 42.(3.)**

RĀMA BRAHMENDRA (*continued*). ॥ अथ जगद्गुरुपरम्परानाममाला ॥ [Jagadguruparamparānāmamālā.] *See* SVĀMINĀTHA ŚRAUTĪ, *Brahmadeśam*. ॥ वेदान्तपञ्चप्रकरणी *etc.* [Vedāntapañchaprakaraṇī.] [1895.] 8°. **14048. bb. 51.(5.)**

—— அத ஜகத்குருபரம்பராநாமமாலா [Jagadguruparamparānāmamālā.] *See* SADĀŚIVA BRAHMENDRA. புண்யஶ்லோகமஞ்ஜரீ *etc.* [Puṇyaślokamañjarī.] pp. 33-34. [1895.] 8°. **14048. bb. 42.(2.)**

RĀMACHANDRA, *Raja of Talcher.* *See* PARĀŚARA. [*Smriti.*] ପରାଶର-ସଂହିତା *etc.* [Parāśarasaṃhitā. With Oriya translation by Rāmachandra.] 1887. 8°. **14038. c. 44.(1.)**

RĀMACHANDRA, *Korāḍa.* శృంగారసుధార్ణవః . . . Srungara Sudarnava. [A dramatic monologue of the *bhāṇa* class, descriptive of scenes in the streets of Bhadrāchalam.] By Korada Ramachendra. Edited by K. D. Nagaswaram. pp. i. 65. *Masulipatam*, 1899. 8°. **14079. c. 54.(2.)**

RĀMACHANDRA, *Veḷḷāla.* శ్రీ . . . శ్రీకృష్ణవిజయ-వ్యాయోగః . . . లంబోదరప్రహసనం *etc.* [Kṛishṇavijaya. A drama of the *vyāyoga* type on the legend of Krishṇa and Rukmiṇī. Followed by Kālidāsa-Veṅkaṭeśvara's Lambodaraprahasana.] pp. 25, 30. మహీశూర ॥ ౧౮౯౦ [*Mysore*, 1890.] 8°. **14080. d. 22.(1.)**

—— సరసకవికులానందనంనామభాణః *etc.* [Sarasakavikulānandana. A drama of the *bhāṇa* type. Edited by Siṅgam Bhaṭṭa of Mysore.] pp. 67, iii. మహీసుర ॥ ౧౮౯౪ [*Mysore*, 1894.] 8°. **14079. c. 68.**

RĀMACHANDRA, *son of Janārdana.* राधाविनोदः । [Rādhāvinoda. An artificial poem in 19 stanzas. With the commentary Prakāśa of Nārāyaṇa Bhaṭṭa.] pp. 16. [1890.] *See* PERIODICAL PUBLICATIONS.—*Bombay.* ग्रन्थरत्नमाला *etc.* (Granth Ratna Málá, *etc.*) Vol. IV, no. 2. 1887-[1892.] 8°. **14096. c. 8.(vol. 4.)**

—— राधाविनोद° [Rādhāvinoda. With commentary of Nārāyaṇa.] pp. 13. *See* JAYADEVA, *son of Bhojadeva.* श्रीगीतगोविंद° [Gītagovinda.] pp. 174-186. [1891.] 8°. **14072. d. 42.**

RĀMACHANDRA, *son of Siddheṣvara.* *See* UPANISHADS.—*Separate Upanishads.* ईशावास्योपनिषत्° *etc.* ((1) Shri Ísávásyopanishad with . . . (3) The Rahasya of . . . Brahmánanda. (4) The Rahasya Vivriti by Ramachandra Pandita, *etc.*) [1888.] 8°. **14003. ccc. (no. 5.)**

—— *See* UPANISHADS.—*Separate Upanishads.* The Îśavâsyopanishad. Translated . . . with . . . notes from the Tikas of . . . Ramchandra, *etc.* 1896. 8°. **14010. cc. 6.**

—— *Begin.* अथ वेदपरिभाषासूत्रशिक्षां व्याख्यास्यामः ॥ [Vedaparibhāshāsūtraṣikshā. A skeleton of the *padas* of the White Yajurveda in the Mādhyandina school, giving the catchwords and mnemonic signs indicating the chief characteristics of the text. Followed by the Vedaparibhāshākārikāṣikshā, in explanation thereof, by the same author.] *See* YUGALAKISORA VYĀSA PĀṬHAKA. ओमथाशब्दमादि . . . शिक्षासङ्ग्रहः . . . A collection of Śikshás, *etc.* pp. 306-326. 1893. 8°. **14093. b. 31.**

RĀMACHANDRA ĀCHĀRYA, *son of Krishna.* *See* PĀṆINI. — *Prakriyākaumudī.* प्रक्रियाकौमुदी । [Prakriyākaumudī. Aphorisms of Pāṇini with commentary by Rāmachandra.] 1895, *etc.* 8°. [*Grandha Pradarsani.*] **14003. c. 2. (10.)**

—— *See* PĀṆINI.— *Prakriyākaumudī.* ପ୍ରକ୍ରିୟା-କୌମୁଦୀ . . . Prakriya Kaumudy . . . With a commentary . . . and an Oriya translation by . . . Purusottam Tarkalankar, *etc.* 1902, *etc.* 8°. **14090. bb. 19.**

RĀMACHANDRA BHĀRATĪ, called BAUDDHĀGAMACHAKRAVARTĪ. Bhakti Sataka. One hundred ślokas on reverence and love. Translated by Pandit Hara Prasád Śástri. [With the Sanskrit text appended.] (भक्तिशतकम् ।) 1893. *See* ACADEMIES, *etc.*—Calcutta.—*Buddhist Text Society of India.* Journal, *etc.* Vol. I, pt. ii., pp. 21-43. 1893, *etc.* 8°. **14003. b. 19.(vol. 1.)**

—— भक्तिशतकम् ॥ Bhakti-shatakam, *etc.* [Edited with introduction and Sanskrit commentary by Sīlakkhandha Thera.] pp. iv. 49. 1896. *See* ACADEMIES, *etc.*—Calcutta.—*Buddhist Text Society of India.* Buddhist Texts, *etc.* 1894, *etc.* 8°. **14004. c. (vol. 1, no. 2.)**

RĀMACHANDRA BHĀRATĪ, called BAUDDHĀGAMACHAKRAVARTĪ (*continued*). वृत्तमालाख्या । By Rámachandra Kavibhárati. [Vṛittamālākhyā. 52 Sanskrit stanzas illustrative of divers metres. Edited by Sīlakkhandha Thera.] 1894. *See* ACADEMIES, *etc.*—Calcutta.—*Buddhist Text Society of India.* Journal, *etc.* Vol. II, pt. i. 1893, *etc.* 8°. **14003. b. 19.(vol. 2.)**

Imperfect, breaking off in v. 45.

RĀMACHANDRA BUDHENDRA. *See* BHOJARĀJA. The Champû-Râmâyaṇa . . . With the commentary [Mañjūshikā] of Râmachandra, *etc.* 1898. 8°. **14070. dd. 5.**

—— *See* BHOJARĀJA. The Kishkindhakanda . . . with an extract from the commentary of Ramachandra, *etc.* 1898. 8°. **14076. b. 36.(2.)**

RĀMACHANDRA CHATUSHPĀṬHĪ, *Vājapeyī.* *See* NṚISIṂHA MIṢRA. ପାର୍ବଣ ଶ୍ରାଦ୍ଧକାରିକା *etc.* [Pārvaṇaṣrāddhakārikā. Compiled and edited by Rāmachandra and Rudranārāyaṇa.] 1900. 12°. **14028. b. 61.(6.)**

RĀMACHANDRA CHATUSHPĀṬHĪ and RUDRANĀRĀYAṆA SHADAṄGĪ. ଶ୍ରାଦ୍ଧବ୍ୟବସ୍ଥା ଓ ପ୍ରୟୋଗ *etc.* [Ṣrāddhavyavasthā o Prayoga. A treatise on the principles and practice of the *ṣrāddha* rites.] pp. 66. *Balasore,* 1899. 12°. **14028. b. 61.(5.)**

RĀMACHANDRA DĪNĀNĀTHA ṢĀSTRĪ, *of Ahmadabad.* *See* HARIBHADRA SŪRI. ॥ श्रीधर्मबिन्दु ॥ *etc.* [Dharmabindu. With Gujarati translation of text and commentary by Rāmachandra.] [1894.] *obl.* 4°. **14100. f. 13.**

—— *See* KRISHṆADATTA, *disciple of Gopālānanda Svāmī.* ॥ एकत्वखण्डनारम्भः ॥ [Ekatvakhaṇḍana. Edited by Rāmachandra.] [1892.] *obl.* 8°. **14028. d. 50.(3.)**

—— *See* MERUTUṄGA ĀCHĀRYA. प्रबन्धचिन्तामणिः *etc.* [Prabandhachintāmaṇi. Edited by Rāmachandra.] [1888.] 8°. **14058. b. 31.**

—— *See* SOMAPRABHA ĀCHĀRYA. शृंगार वैराग्य तरंगिणी *etc.* [Sṛiṅgāravairāgyataraṅgiṇī. With Gujarati translation and commentary by Rāmachandra.] [1891.] *obl.* 8°. **14072. c. 51.**

RĀMACHANDRA GAṄGĀDHARA ŚĀSTRĪ. *See* ŚAṄKARA, *Āchārya-Svāmī, Pontiff of Dwarka.* ॥ त्रिदण्डिमतविभेदिनी *etc.* [Tridaṇḍimatavibhedinī. With introduction by Rāmachandra.] [1899.] 8°.
14048. e. 33.

RĀMACHANDRA GHOSHA VIDYĀVINODA. *See* CHĀṆAKYA. [*Shorter Recension.*] Morals of Cháṇakya. Rendered into English verse by Rámchandra Ghosh, *etc.* 1891. 12°.
14072. b. 10.(3.)

RĀMACHANDRA KAVIBHĀRATĪ. *See* RĀMACHANDRA BHĀRATĪ.

RĀMACHANDRA MIŚRA. *See* PĀṆINI.—*Prakriyā-kaumudī.* ପ୍ରକ୍ରିୟାକୌମୁଦୀ . . . Prakriya Kaumudy . . . With . . . notes by . . . Ramachandra Mishra. 1902, *etc.* 8°.
14090. bb. 19.

RĀMACHANDRA NANDA. *See* VIVĀHAPADDHATI. ବିବାହପଦ୍ଧତି *etc.* [Vivāhapaddhati. Edited by Rāmachandra.] 1900. 12°.
14028. b. 78.(5.)

RĀMACHANDRA NYĀYAVĀGĪŚA, *son of Vidyānidhi.* কাব্যচন্দ্রিকা Kabyachandrica. A rhetorical book with notes by Annada Charan Tarka Churamony, *etc.* pp. 36. কুমিল্লা ১২৯২ [*Comillah,* 1885.] 12°.
14053. b. 29.

—— কাব্যচন্দ্রিকা *etc.* [Kāvyachandrikā. With a commentary entitled Subodhinī by Jagadbandhu Tarkavāgīśa. Edited by Rohiṇīkānta Vidyābhūshaṇa.] pp. 38. ঢাকা ১৩০৩ [*Dacca,* 1896.] 8°.
14053. c. 65.

RĀMACHANDRA PAṆḌITA, *Commentator on Upanishads.* *See* RĀMACHANDRA, *son of Siddheśvara.*

RĀMACHANDRA RĀU, *Puvvāḍa.* *See* RAGHUNĀTHAPRASĀDA SUKALA. అనుపానతరంగిణి *etc.* [Anupānataraṅgiṇī. With Telugu translation by Rāmachandra Rāu.] [1895.] 8°. **14043. c. 46.**

—— *See* VĀGBHAṬA, *son of Siṃhagupta.* బాహటం॥ [Ashṭāṅgahṛidaya, or Bāhaṭa. Part ii. Edited with Telugu translation by Rāmachandra Rāu.] 1898. 4°. **14043. ddd. 1.**

RĀMACHANDRA ŚARMĀ, *Astronomer.* দিনকৌমুদীমতে পঞ্চাঙ্গসাধন অর্থাৎ পঞ্জিকাগণনা। [Pañchāṅgasādhana, or Pañjikāgaṇanā. A treatise on the making of the calendar, comprising Rāmachandra's Dinakaumudī, with tables, *etc.*] [1891, *etc.*] *See* PERIODICAL PUBLICATIONS. — *Calcutta.* অরুণোদয় *etc.* [Aruṇodaya.] Pt. i., no. 7. [1890, *etc.*] 4°. **14133. g. 16.(pt. i., no. 7.)**

Contains only pp. 1-34.

—— দিনকৌমুদী *etc.* [Dinakaumudī. Edited with Bengali translation by Viśvambhara Jyotishārṇava.] pt. i. pp. x. 37. কলিকাতা ফরিদপুর ১৮২০ [*Faridpur, Calcutta* printed, 1898.] 12°.
14053. b. 31.(3.)

RĀMACHANDRA ŚĀSTRĪ, *of Lahore.* *See* NĀGARARĀMA ŚARMĀ, *son of Śivalāla.* कर्मदर्पणम् *etc.* [Karmadarpaṇa. Edited by Rāmachandra.] [1899.] 8°. **14028. d. 56.(3.)**

RĀMACHANDRA ŚĀSTRĪ, *Mahārājapuram.* *See* VAIDYANĀTHA DĪKSHITA. ஸ்ம்ருதி-முக்தாபல ... *etc.* [Smṛitimuktāphala. Vol. v., with Tamil translation by Rāmachandra.] 1898, *etc.* 4°. **14039. c. 15.(vol. 5.)**

RĀMACHANDRA ŚĀSTRĪ, *Vishṇupuram.* *See* PURĀṆAS.—*Nāradapurāṇa.* ஹரிபக்திஸுதோதய: *etc.* [Haribhaktisudhodaya. With commentary of Śrīdhara Svāmī. Edited by Rāmachandra and others.] 1892. 8°. **14016. c. 48.**

RĀMACHANDRA ŚĀSTRĪ, *Mūñjūrpaṭṭu, son of Kuppā Śāstri.* *See* UPANISHADS. — *General Collections.* அஷ்டோத்தரசதோபநிஷத: *etc.* [Ashṭottaraśatopanishadaḥ. Edited by Veṅkaṭakṛishṇa and Rāmachandra.] 1896. 8°.
14010. cc. 8.

RĀMACHANDRĀŚRAMA. *See* RĀMĀŚRAMA ĀCHĀRYA.

RĀMACHANDRA TARKĀLAṄKĀRA. *See* ŚĀTĀTAPA. শাতাতপীয়-কর্মবিপাকঃ *etc.* [Śātātapīya-karmavipāka. With Bengali translation by Rāmachandra.] [1902.] 8°. **14033. aa. 28.(3.)**

RĀMACHANDRA TĪRTHA, *disciple of Vāsudeva Sarasvatī.* *See* UPANISHADS.—*Selections.* மஹாவாக்யரத்நாவலி: [Mahāvākyaratnāvali. Compiled by Rāmachandra.] 1896. 8°. [*Ashṭottaraśatopanishadaḥ.*]
14010. cc. 8.

RĀMACHANDRA TĪRTHA, *disciple of Vāsudeva Sarasvatī (continued)*. *See* UPANISHADS.—*Selections.* अथ महावाक्यरत्नावलि *etc.* [Mahāvākyaratnāvali.] [1903.] 12°. **14010. b. 25.**

RĀMACHANDRA ṬOLAR. *See* RĀMACHANDRA CHATUSHPĀṬHĪ.

RĀMACHANDRA VĀMANA KARAṆḌE. *See* RAGHUNĀTHA DAIVAJÑA, *son of Nṛisiṃha.* मुहूर्तमाला *etc.* [Muhūrtamālā. With commentary. Edited by Rāmachandra.] [1892.] 8°. **14053. c. 62.**

RĀMA DAIVAJÑA. *See* RĀMA, *son of Ananta.*

RĀMADĀSA BHŪPATI, *Raja of Boṇli, Jaipur.* *See* PRAVARASENA. The Setubandha of Pravarasena. [With the commentary Rāmasetupradīpa of Rāmadāsa,] *etc.* 1895. 8°. [*Kāvyamālā.*] **14072. ccc. 12.(no. 47.)**

RĀMADĀSA DĪKSHITA. *See* KṚISHṆA MIṢRA, *Dramatist.* प्रबोधचन्द्रोदयम् *etc.* [Prabodhachandrodaya. With the gloss Prakāṣa by Rāmadāsa.] [1898.] 8°. **14080. c. 39.**

RĀMADATTA, *son of Bhavadeva, Jyotirvid.* वार्षिकव्रतपद्धति: *etc.* [Vārshikavratapaddhati. A manual of rites of the year.] pp. 543, xv. नैनीताल १८९९ [*Naini Tal,* 1899.] *obl.* 4°. **14033. c. 42.**

RĀMADATTA, *son of Wazīr-chand.* *See* RĀMADAYĀLU, *Jyotirvid.* ॥ अथ ... संकेतनिधि: *etc.* [Saṅketanidhi. With commentary by Rāmadatta.] [1894.] *obl.* 4°. **14053. e. 30.**

RĀMADATTA ṬHAKKURA, *son of Gaṇeṣvara.* *End.* इति ... वाजसनेयिनांविवाहादिपद्धति: समाप्ता ॥ [Vājasaneyināṃ Vivābādi-saṃskārapaddhati. A treatise on the lustrations of marriage, *etc.*, for Vājasaneyīs. With notes by Parameṣvara Jhā.] pp. 104. *See* VĪREṢVARA ṬHAKKURA. छन्दोगानांविवाहादिसंस्कारपद्धति: *etc.* [Chhandogānāṃ Vivāhādi-saṃskārapaddhati, *etc.*] [1902.] *obl.* 4°. **14033. c. 31.(3.)**

RĀMADAYĀLU, *Jyotirvid, of Amritsar.* ॥ अथ सटीक: संकेतनिधि: प्रारभ्यते ॥ [Saṅketanidhi. A metrical treatise on astrology in 9 *saṅketas*, commenced by Ghāsīrām son of Wazīr-chand, and completed by the latter's younger brother Rāmadayālu. With a commentary by Rāmadatta son of Wazīr-chand.] ff. 113. मुम्बयी १९५१ [*Bombay,* 1894.] *obl.* 4°. **14053. e. 30.**

RĀMADAYĀLU GHOSHA. *See* NAROTTAMADĀSA, *the Bengali Poet.* শ্রীশ্রীপ্রেমভক্তিচন্দ্রিকা *etc.* [Premabhaktichandrikā. Edited by Rāmadayālu.] [1896.] 12°. **14123. e. 20.**

RĀMADAYĀLU KAVI, *son of Devadatta.* अथ वृत्तचन्द्रिकाप्रारंभ: ॥ [Vṛittachandrikā. A treatise on Sanskrit prosody, in 3 *prakāṣas.*] ff. 27. १८९९ [*Bombay,* 1899.] *obl.* 12°. **14053. a. 13.(2.)**

RĀMADAYĀLU MAJUMDĀR. শ্রীবিচার চন্দ্রোদয় ... পঞ্চদেবতা ধ্যান ও স্তোত্র *etc.* [Vichārachandrodaya. A Bengali exposition, in catechetical form, of the Vedānta system, preceded by a selection of Sanskrit Vedantic hymns by Ṣaṅkara and others. Followed by the Vedāntastotrāvalī, Sanskrit hymns, chiefly by Ṣaṅkara, and Pañchadevatādhyāna and Pañchadevatāstava, Sanskrit hymns and mystic meditations upon the five deities, ascribed to Ṣaṅkara and others.] pp. xvi. iii. 266. কলিকাতা ১৩০৮ [*Calcutta,* 1901.] 12°. **14123. e. 22.**

RĀMADĪNA SIṂHA, *Mahārājakumāra.* *See* GRIERSON (G. A.). Curiosities of Indian Literature ... Edited ... by ... Ramadina Sinha. 1895. 12°. **14085. b. 45.(1.)**

RĀMAGOPĀLA ṢARMĀ, and others. परमारवंशान्तर्गत श्रीमदुमट राज्यका इतिहास *etc.* [Ūmaṭ-rājya-kā Itihāsa, or Umaṭ-vaṃṣya-rāja-vṛittāntavarṇana. A poem of 351 stanzas, describing the principality of Narsinghgarh and its history, down to the present ruler, Mahtāb-singh. With Hindi prose paraphrase.] *See* YAMUNĀDĀSA ṢĀṆḌILYA. महताबदिवाकर *etc.* [Mahtāb-divākara.] pp. 509-560. [1895.] 8°. **14154. c. 20.**

RĀMAKARṆA, *son of Baladeva.* *See* MURĀRIDĀNA. ॥ यशवन्तयशोभूषण० [Yaṣavantayaṣobhūshaṇa. Edited by Rāmakarṇa.] [1897.] 4°. **14156. ff. 1.**

—— *See* MURĀRIDĀNA. ॥ यशवन्तयशोभूषण० [Yaṣavantayaṣobhūshaṇa. Edited by Rāmakarṇa.] [1901.] 4°. **14053. g. 17.**

RĀMAKIṢORADĀSA, *Vairāgī.* *See* PURĀṆAS.—*Selections.* శ్రీ వేఙ్కటాచలమాహాత్మ్యగ్రంథః *etc.* [Veṅkaṭāchalamāhātmyagrantha. Compiled by Rāmakiṣoradāsa.] [1896.] 8°. **14016. c. 50.**

RĀMAKṚISHṆA, *Daivajña.* प्रश्नचण्डेश्वरः *etc.* [Praṣna-chaṇḍeṣvara. An astrological treatise, with a commentary styled Vishṇupadī and a Hindi paraphrase by Vishṇudatta Vaidika.] pp. i. 103. मुम्बय्यां १८१६ [*Bombay*, 1894.] 8°. **14053. d. 51.**

RĀMAKṚISHṆA, *disciple of Sāyaṇa.* *See* SĀYAṆA ĀCHĀRYA.—*Works on Philosophy, etc.* ॥ श्रीपंचदशी *etc.* [Pañchadaṣī. With Rāmakṛishṇa's commentary.] [1897.] 8°. **14048. e. 25.**

—— *See* SĀYAṆA ĀCHĀRYA.—*Works on Philosophy, etc.* ॥ श्रीपंचदशी *etc.* [Pañchadaṣī. Prakaraṇa x. With Rāmakṛishṇa's commentary.] [1900.] 8°. [*Vichārasāgara.*] **14154. ff. 1.**

RĀMAKṚISHṆA BHAṬṬĀCHĀRYA, *son of Gopālakṛishṇa, of Karupur.* *See* VAIDYANĀTHA DĪKSHITA. ஸ்ம்ருதிமுக்தாபலே ப்ரயோக: . . . காண்ட: *etc.* [Smṛitimuktāphala. Vol. ii., with Tamil translation by Rāmakṛishṇa.] 1898, *etc.* 4°. **14039. c. 15.(vol. 2.)**

—— *See* VIKHANAS. ஸ்ரீவைகாநஸஸூத்ரப்ரயோகே ப்ரயோகஸம்புடிகா *etc.* [Vaikhānasasūtraprayoga. Edited by Nārāyaṇa and Rāmakṛishṇa.] [1897.] 12°. **14028. b. 86.**

RĀMAKṚISHṆA GOPĀLA BHĀṆḌĀRKAR. *See* BĀLĀJĪ HARI PHĀṬAK. A Guide to the Study of Dr. Bhandarkar's First Book of Sanskrit. 1898. 12°. **14085. b. 41.(2.)**

—— *See* JAYAKṚISHṆA GAṄGĀDĀSA BHAKTA. Guide to [Bhāṇḍārkar's] Sanskrit Second Book. Part I, *etc.* [1900.] 12°. **14085. b. 36.(2.)**

—— *See* LAKSHMĪNĀRĀYAṆA ṢĀSTRĪ, *Bhāgavata.* संक्षिप्तरामचरितम् *etc.* [Saṅkshipta-rāmacharita. Part ii., illustrating the rules in the first 15 lessons of Bhāṇḍārkar's Second Book of Sanskrit.] [1900.] 8°. **14072. cc. 61.**

—— A Note on the Age of Marriage and its Consummation, according to Hindu religious Law, *etc.* [In English, illustrated from Sanskrit texts.] pp. 53. *Poona*, 1891. 12°. **14038. b. 11.**

Pp. 24—32 are wanting.

RĀMAKṚISHṆA GOPĀLA BHĀṆḌĀRKAR (*continued*). Lists of Sanskrit Manuscripts in Private Libraries in the Bombay Presidency. Compiled under the superintendence of R. G. Bhandarkar . . . Part I. pp. 167. *Bombay*, 1893. 8°. **14096. c. 12.**

RĀMAKṚISHṆA MĀDHAVARĀU CHONKAR. *See* PURĀṆAS. — *Skandapurāṇa.* (Satya-narayana, or God is Truth.) [Translated with notes by Rāmakṛishṇa Chonkar.] [1897.] 32°. **14016. a. 25.**

RĀMAKṚISHṆA PAṆḌITA, *Writer on Dharma.* ನಿತ್ಯಕರ್ಮ ಚಂದ್ರಿಕೆ ಎಂಬ . . . ಬ್ರಾಹ್ಮಣಸಮುದಾ-ಚಾರ ಪದ್ಧತಿಯು *etc.* [Nityakarmachandrike. A metrical handbook of the regular rites incumbent on Brahmans. With Canarese version by Kammarḍi Subrāya Ṣāstri. Edited by Jammaṭige Nāga Bhaṭṭa.] ಬೆಂಗಳೂರು ೧೯೦೧ [*Bangalore*, 1901, *etc.*] 8°. **14033. aa. 33.**

In progress.

RĀMAKṚISHṆA PARAMAHAṂSA. The Sayings of Sri Ramakrishna Paramahamsa . . . With a prefatory note by Dewan Bahadur, Justice, S. Subhramania Aiyer. pp. i. 68. *Madras*, 1898. 8°. **14048. cc. 22.**

Forms no. 7 of the Brahmavadin *Series.*

RĀMAKṚISHṆA ṢĀSTRĪ, *son of Trivikramanārāyaṇa (Pichchu-ṣāstri), of Kalpadi.* *See* ĀPASTAMBA. —*Gṛihyasūtra.* ஆபஸ்தம்ப க்ருஹ்ய ப்ரயோக வ்யாக்யானம் ... *etc.* [Āpastambagṛihyaprayoga. Edited by Īṣvara Yajvā and Rāmakṛishṇa.] [1899.] 8°. **14028. c. 80.**

—— *See* BAUDHĀYANA. போதாயந க்ரு-ஹ்யோக்த . . . ப்ரயோக॥ [Bodhāyanagṛihyokta-jātakarmādi-prayoga. With the *kārikā* of Gopāla. Edited with a gloss on the latter work by Rāmakṛishṇa.] [1900.] 8°. **14038. c. 37.(2.)**

—— *See* BRĀHMAṆAS. — *Taittirīyabrāhmaṇa.* அஶ்வமேத॥ [Aṣvamedha, Āruṇa, and Taittirīyopanishad. Edited by Rāmakṛishṇa.] [1900.] 8°. **14007. cc. 28.**

—— *See* PURĀṆAS.—*Brahmāṇḍapurāṇa.* [*Ādipuramāhātmya.*] பேரூர் [*sic*] ஸ்தலபுராணம் *etc.* [Ādipuramāhātmya. Edited by Rāmakṛishṇa and others.] [1902.] 8°. **14016. dd. 6.**

RĀMAKṚISHṆA ŚĀSTRĪ, *son of Trivikramanārāyaṇa (Pichchu-śāstri), of Kalpadi (continued)*. See SUBRAHMAṆYA, *son of Deveṣa*. ஸ்ரீக்ருஷ்ணார்யாசதகம் *etc*. [Śrikṛishṇāryāṣataka. Edited by Rāmakṛishṇa.] [1899.] 16°. **14028. b. 102.(2.)**

—— *See* VĀLMĪKI.—Rāmāyaṇa.—*Entire Text*. ஸ்ரீ . . . ஸ்ரீமத்ராமாயணம் [Rāmāyaṇa. With commentary. Edited by Rāmakṛishṇa.] [1903, *etc.*] 4°. **14068. c. 17.**

—— *See* VEDAS.—Yajurveda.—*Ātreyisaṃhitā*. உபம் காண்டாநுக்ரமணிகா *etc*. [Kāṇḍānukramaṇikā. With metrical epitome, *etc*. Edited by Rāmakṛishṇa.] [1900.] 8°. **14010. b. 14.(2.)**

—— *See* VEDAS.—Yajurveda.—*Taittirīyasaṃhitā*. ஸைக்ஷ்யவேதீக . . . ஸாஙவனாதநேவ: . . . க்ருஷ்யஜுர்வேதஸம்ஹிதா [Taittirīyasaṃhitā. Edited by Rāmakṛishṇa.] 1902. 8°. **14007. b. 17.**

RĀMAKṚISHṆA ŚĀSTRĪ PAṬAVARDHANA, also called TĀTYĀ ŚĀSTRĪ. *See* BHAṬṬOJĪ DĪKSHITA. शब्दकौस्तुभः . . . Shabdakoustubha . . . Edited . . . by . . . Rama Krishna Shastri, *etc*. 1898, *etc*. 8°. **14004. a. 2.**

—— *See* BHAṬṬOJĪ DĪKSHITA. बृहत् वैयाकरणभूषणं . . . Brihat Vaiyâkaraṇa Bhûshaṇa . . . also Padârtha Dìpikâ . . . Edited by . . . Ráma Krishṇa Śástri, *etc*. 1900. 8°. **14048. cc. 34.**

—— *See* GOPĪNĀTHA DĪKSHITA. संस्काररत्नमाला । Sanskar Ratna Mala . . . Edited . . . by . . . Rama Krishna Shastri, *etc*. 1898, *etc*. 8°. **14004. a. 1.**

—— *See* NĀGEŚA BHAṬṬA. [*Paribhāshenduśekhara*.] परिभाषेन्दुशेखरः *etc*. [Paribhāshenduśekhara. With a commentary entitled Bhūti by Rāmakṛishṇa.] [1897.] 8°. **14090. d. 33.**

—— *See* VIŚVEŚVARA BHAṬṬA. भाट्टचिन्तामणिः . . . Bhâṭṭa Chintâmani . . . Edited by . . . Ráma Krishṇa Śástri, *etc*. [1900, *etc*.] 8°. **14004. a. 6.**

RĀMAKṚISHṆA ŚĀSTRĪ THATTE, *of Benares*. *See* PURĀṆAS.—*Skandapurāṇa*. श्रीगङ्गासहस्रनामावली *etc*. [Gaṅgāsahasranāmāvalī. Edited by Rāmakṛishṇa.] [1899.] *obl*. 32°. **14016. a. 26.**

RĀMĀKSHAYA CHAṬṬOPĀDHYĀYA, *Rāi Bahādur*. ✓ প্রেমচন্দ্র তর্কবাগীশের জীবনচরিত ও কবিতাবলী *etc*. [Premachandra Tarkavāgīṣer Jīvanacharita o Kavitāvalī. A biography of the late Premachandra Tarkavāgīśa, in Bengali, followed by selections from his Sanskrit poems. Third edition.] pp. vi. i. 215; 1 *plate*. কলিকাতা ১৯০১ [*Calcutta*, 1901.] 12°. **14127. aa. 16.**

RĀMALĀLA GAṆĪ. *See* JINAPŪJĀ. श्री जिन पूजा महोदधि *etc*. [Jinapūjāmahodadhi. Edited by Rāmalāla.] [1902.] 8°. **14144. gg. 5.**

RĀMA MIŚRA ŚĀSTRĪ, *Svāmī, of the Sanskrit College, Benares*. *See* JAIMINI.—*Mīmāṃsāsūtra*. संकर्ष-काण्डम् . . . Saṁkarsha Káṇḍa . . . with the commentary . . . of Bháskara, edited with notes by . . . Ráma Miśra Śástrí. [1894.] 8°. [*The Pandit*.] **14096. d. 6.(vol. 14, 15.)**

—— *See* RĀMĀNUJA.—*Original Works*. वेदार्थसंग्रहः . . . Vedártha Saṁgraha. With the gloss . . . by Sudarśanasúri. Edited with a commentary called Snehapúrtti by . . . Ráma Miśra Śástrí. [1894.] 8°. [*The Pandit*.] **14096. d. 6.(vol. 15, 16.)**

—— *See* VEṄKAṬANĀTHA VEDĀNTĀCHĀRYA. न्यायसिद्धाञ्जनम् . . . Nyāyasiddhāñjanam . . . Edited by . . . Ráma Miśra Śástrí. 1901. 8°. [*The Pandit*.] **14096. d. 6.(vol. 23.)**

—— *See* VEṄKAṬANĀTHA VEDĀNTĀCHĀRYA. सर्वार्थसिद्धियुतः तत्त्वमुक्ताकलापः । . . . Tattvamuktákalápa with Sarvárthasiddhi . . . Edited by . . . Ráma Miśra Sástrí. 1900. 8°. [*The Pandit*.] **14096. d. 6.(vol. 18-22.)**

—— *See* YĀMUNA ĀCHĀRYA. आगमप्रामाण्यम् . . . Āgamaprāmāṇyam . . . Edited by . . . Ráma Miśra Śāstrī. 1900. 8°. [*The Pandit*.] **14096. d. 6.(vol. 22.)**

—— *See* YĀMUNA ĀCHĀRYA. सिद्धित्रयम् *etc*. (Siddhitrayam . . . edited by . . . Râma Miśra Shâstrî.) 1900. 8°. **14004. a. 10.**

—— तात्पर्यदीपिकायां स्नेहपूर्तिः । [Snehapūrti. A commentary upon the Tātparyadīpikā or commentary of Sudarṣana Āchārya upon Rāmānuja's Vedārthasaṅgraha.] pp. iv. 202. 1895-1896.

See PERIODICAL PUBLICATIONS. — *Benares.* The Pandit, *etc.* New Series. Vols. XVII-XVIII. 1876, *etc.* 8°. **14096. d. 6.(vol. 17, 18.)**

—— स्नेहपूर्तिपरीक्षा। [Snehapūrtiparīkshā. A dissertation upon the Snehapūrti. Edited by Keșava Ṣāstrī.] pp. 55. 1895-1896. *See* PERIODICAL PUBLICATIONS. — *Benares.* The Pandit, *etc.* New Series. Vol. XVII-XVIII. 1876, *etc.* 8°. **14096. d. 6.(vol. 17, 18.)**

—— तुरीयमीमांसा . . . Turiyamimámsá[, a treatise upon the fundamental Vedic principles underlying Ṣaṅkara's teaching and the religious rank of men of the fourth *āsrama,*] by . . . Ráma Miśra Śástri. pp. ix. viii. i. i. 144. काश्यां १९०१ [*Benares,* 1901.] 8°. **14058. b. 46.**

—— *See* KRISHṆĀNANDA SARASVATĪ, *disciple of Sachchidānanda.* ब्राह्मणसर्वस्व *etc.* [Brāhmaṇasarvasva. A critique of the Turīyamīmāṃsā.] [1902.] 8°. **14039. b. 21.(2.)**

—— उद्वाहसमयमीमांसा [Udvāhasamayamīmāṃsā.] . . . Hindu Marriage according to the Dharmaśāstras, *etc.* [With preface in English and Hindi.] pp. iii. 50. *Banāras,* 1890. 8°. **14039. b. 15.(2.)**

RĀMĀNANDA RĀYA. श्रीजगन्नाथवल्लभनाटकम् *etc.* [Jagannāthavallabhanāṭaka. A drama depicting the loves of Kṛishṇa and Rādhā. With a Hindi translation by Bālakṛishṇa Gosvāmī. Edited by Lakshmaṇa Āchārya.] pp. ii. 108, ii. वृन्दावन° १९५८ [*Brindaban,* 1901.] 8°. **14079. d. 46.**

RĀMĀNANDA SARASVATĪ, *disciple of Govindānanda.* *See* PATAÑJALI. — *Philosophical Works.* পাতঞ্জলদর্শনম্। [Pātañjaladarṣana. Comprising the Aphorisms, the *ṭīkā* Yogamaṇiprabhā of Rāmānanda, *etc.*] [1891, *etc.*] 4°. [*Aruṇodaya.*] **14133. g. 16.(pt. i., no. 25.)**

—— विवरणोपन्यासः . . . सटीका वाक्यसुधा। Vivaraṇopanyâsa, a commentary on Vivaranatâtparya, [consisting of a summary of Prakāṣātmā's Pañchapādikāvivaraṇa,] a treatise on Vedanta philosophy . . . Also Vâkyasudhâ by Śrî Śankarâchârya, with a commentary by Śrî Brahmânanda Bhâratî. Edited by Paṇḍit Dámodara Śástrí Sahasrabuddhe. pp. ii. 152, i. 33. *Benares,* 1901. 8°. **14048. cc. 37.**

Forms nos. 55 *and* 56 *of the* Benares Sanskrit Series.

RĀMĀNANDA SARASVATĪ, *son of Tirumalāchārya, and disciple of Mukundāṣrama.* *See* BĀDARĀYAṆA. బ్రహ్మామృతవర్షిణి *etc.* [Brahmasūtra. With the commentary Brahmāmṛitavarshiṇī or Brahmasūtraguruvṛitti of Rāmānanda, here styled Dharma Bhaṭṭa.] 1900. 8°. **14048. c. 77.**

RĀMANĀRĀYAṆA DĀSA, *of Faizabad.* *See* AGASTYA. ॥ अथ अगस्त्यसंहिता° [Agastyasaṃhitā. Edited by Rāmanārāyaṇa Dāsa.] 1898. *obl.* 8°. **14028. dd. 7.**

—— *See* HANUMATSAṂHITĀ. अथ हनुमत्संहिता° [Hanumatsaṃhitā. Edited by Rāmanārāyaṇa Dāsa *etc.* Followed by Pañchadhā-bhaktirasa, a tract on the religious emotions, by Rāmanārāyaṇa Dāsa.] [1900.] *obl.* 8°. **14033. c. 44.(3.)**

—— *See* UPANISHADS.—*Small Collections.* श्री . . . श्रीरामतापनीयोपनिषद् *etc.* [Rāmatāpanīyopanishad and Rāmopanishad. With Sanskrit gloss called Subodhinī upon the latter by Rāmanārāyaṇa Dāsa.] [1903.] 8°. **14007. b. 11.(2.)**

RĀMANĀRĀYAṆA VIDYĀRATNA. *See* KAVIKARṆAPŪRA. অলঙ্কারকৌস্তুভঃ *etc.* [Alaṅkārakaustubha. Edited with Bengali version by Rāmanārāyaṇa.] [1899.] 8°. **14053. ccc. 25.**

—— *See* KAVIKARṆAPŪRA. শ্রীচৈতন্যচরিতামৃত° [Chaitanyacharitāmṛita. Edited with Bengali translation by Rāmanārāyaṇa.] [1885-1892.] 8°. **14058. b. 28.**

—— *See* PURĀṆAS.—*Padmapurāṇa.* পদ্মপুরাণম্। *etc.* [Uttarakhaṇḍa. Edited with Bengali translation by Rāmanārāyaṇa.] [1899, *etc.*] 4°. **14016. e. 45.**

—— *See* RŪPA GOSVĀMĪ. উজ্জ্বলনীলমণিঃ *etc.* [Ujjvalanīlamaṇi. With commentaries. Edited with Bengali translation by Rāmanārāyaṇa.] [1889.] 8°. **14053. d. 49.**

RAMĀNĀTHA CHAKRAVARTĪ. *See* RAMĀNĀTHA RĀI.

RAMĀNĀTHA RĀI, *son of Vedagarbha Tarkāchārya. See* SARVAVARMĀ.—*Appendix.* গণতত্ত্ব-দীপিকা *etc.* [Gaṇatattvadīpikā. The *dhātupāṭha*, with the commentary Manoramā of Ramānātha.] [1900.] 8°. **14093. b. 20.(3.)**

—— *See* SARVAVARMĀ.—*Appendix.* সটীক কাতন্ত্র-গণমালা *etc.* [Kātantragaṇamālā. The *dhātupāṭha*, with Ramānātha's commentary.] [1903.] 12°. **14092. a. 24.(3.)**

—— শব্দরত্নম্ *etc.* [Ṣabdaratna, or Ṣabdasādhyaprayoga. A treatise on grammatical inflections according to the Kātantra school. Followed by the Shaṭkāraka, a short tract in verse on the usage of cases, by Rabhasanandī, with a commentary. Edited by Bhuvanachandra Siddhāntachūḍāmaṇi. Second edition.] pp. 77. নোয়াখালী ১৮১৫ [*Noakhali*, 1893.] 8°. **14093. b. 36.(1.)**

RAMĀNĀTHA ṢARMĀ, *of Benares. See* TRIPURĀNĀTHA VIDVĀN. शालग्रामपरीक्षा *etc.* [Ṣālagrāmaparīkshā. Edited by Ramānātha.] [1899.] 8°. **14028. c. 78.**

RĀMANĀTHA ṢARMĀ, *son of Govindadatta, Gautama. See* GAṆEṢA, *son of Gopāla.* जातकालंकारः *etc.* [Jātakālaṅkāra. With Hindi translation by Rāmanātha.] [1902.] 8°. **14053. ccc. 41.**

RAMAṆĪRAṄGA. *See* RATIMAÑJARĪ.

RĀMĀNUJA, *Founder of the Sect.*

COMMENTARIES.

See BĀDARĀYAṆA. శ్రీవేదాన్తసారసహితశ్రీభాష్యః *etc.* [Brahmasūtra. With the commentaries of Rāmānuja entitled Vedāntasāra and Vedāntadīpa.] [1890.] 8°. **14048. c. 73.**

See BĀDARĀYAṆA. வேதாந்தஸாரः [Brahmasūtra. With the commentary Vedāntasāra of Rāmānuja.] 1894. 8°. **14048. bb. 48.**

See BĀDARĀYAṆA. The Vedānta-Sūtras with the Śrī-Bhāshya of Rāmānujāchārya. Translated into English, *etc.* 1899. 8°. **14048. cc. 29.**

The Chatussûtrî [*i.e.* Brahmasūtra I. i. 1-4 with commentary] from Shrimat Râmânujâchâryâ's Shribhashya. Edited with a gloss by Pandit Vasudevashastri . Abhyankar. (श्रीभाष्ये चतुःसूत्री.) pp. ii. iv. 231, ix. iii. *Poona,* 1904. 8°. **14049. a. 11.**

See ANANTĀRVĀR, *Maṇḍayam A.*, and NARASIṂHAIYAṄGĀR, *P. T.* वेदान्तवादावली *etc.* [Vedāntavādāvalī. A collection of treatises in exposition of Viṣishṭādvaita-Vedānta and the system of Rāmānuja.] [1898, *etc.*] 8°. **14048. cc. 18.**

See BĀDARĀYAṆA. அதிகரணஸாராவலி *etc.* [Brahmasūtra. With the Adhikaraṇasārāvalī, a metrical epitome of Rāmānuja's Ṣrībhāshya.] [1900-1902.] 8°. **14048. e. 32.**

See RAṄGĀCHĀRYA, *P.T.K.* ॥ भगवद्रामानुजभाष्यानुसारिसिद्धान्तसंग्रहः ॥ [An epitome of the system expounded in Rāmānuja's commentaries on the Brahmasūtra.] [1900.] 8°. [*Brahmasūtra.*] **14048. cc. 30.**

See RAṄGARĀMĀNUJA, *disciple of Tātāchārya.* वेदान्त विषयवाक्यदीपिका *etc.* [Vishayavākyadīpikā. A treatise upon the scriptural passages quoted in the Ṣrībhāshya.] [1899.] 8°. **14048. e. 26.**

See VEṄKAṬANĀTHA VEDĀNTĀCHĀRYA. శ్రీ ... తత్త్వటీకా *etc.* [Tattvaṭīkā. A treatise expounding various passages of the Ṣrībhāshya.] 1904, *etc.* 8°. **14049. b. 24.**

See MAHĀBHĀRATA. — Bhagavadgītā. — *English.* Ṣrī Bhagavad-gītā, with Ṣrī Rāmānujāchārya's Viṣishtādvaita-commentary, *etc.* 1898. 8°. **14048. cc. 26.**

See UPANISHADS.–*Small Collections.* தசோபநிஷத்-த்ராவிடபாஷ்யம் *etc.* [Daṣopanishad-drāviḍabhāshya. Ten Upanishads, with Tamil commentary comprising translations of the commentaries of Rāmānuja, *etc.*] [1897]-1898. 8°. **14010. dd. 14.**

ORIGINAL WORKS.

The Refuge-seeker's Prayer and the Answer of the Lord. Saranâgati-gadya. Being one of ... Râmânuja's Three Prose Pieces, Gadya-traya. [Translated into English.] 1896. *See* PERIODICAL

PUBLICATIONS.—*Madras.* The Brahmavâdin, *etc.* Vol. I, pp. 221-222, 230-231. 1895, *etc.* 4° & 8°. **14048. g. 1.(vol. 1.)**

॥ वेदान्ततत्वसारः *etc.* [Vedāntatattvasāra. With Hindi translation by Mahavīraprasāda Nārāyaṇa Siṃha.] pp. iv. iii. 60. प्रयागे १८८३ [*Allahabad*, 1893.] 8°. **14048. dd. 12.(2.)**

वेदार्थसंग्रहः . . . Vedártha Saṁgraha. With the gloss called Tátparyadípiká by Sudarśanasúri. Edited with a commentary called Snehapúrtti by . . . Ráma Miśra Śástri. pp. iv. ii. vii. 256. [1894.] *See* PERIODICAL PUBLICATIONS.—*Benares.* The Pandit, *etc.* New Series. Vol. XV—XVI. 1876, *etc.* 8°. **14096. d. 6.(vol. 15, 16.)**

Vedartha Sangraha. A discourse on the Upanishads, *etc.* [Selections, translated into English.] 1895-1897. *See* PERIODICAL PUBLICATIONS.—*Madras.* The Brahmavâdin, *etc.* Vol. I, no. ii., iii., v., vii., viii., xi., Vol. II, no. vi., xvi. 1895, *etc.* 4° & 8°. **14048. g. 1.(vol. 1, 2.)**

Ramanuja's Popular Teaching. [Being a translation of and commentary upon the "Eighty-two Aphorisms" ascribed to Rāmānuja.] *See* RAṄGĀCHĀRULU, *M.* Life and Teachings of Ramanuja, *etc.* pp. 41-76. 1895. 8°. **14048. dd. 20.**

RĀMĀNUJĀCHĀRYA, *A., Bhāradvāja.* *See* RĀMABHADRA DĪKSHITA. ஜாநகீபரிணயம் ॥ [Jānakīpariṇaya. Edited by Rāmānujāchārya.] 1892. 8°. **14079. c. 59.**

RĀMĀNUJĀCHĀRYA, *Kandādai Varadārya, Vādhūla.* श्रीमद्वेदपादरामायणम्. वेदपादेश्चित्रितम् *etc.* [Vedapādarāmāyaṇa. A poetical summary of the Rāmāyaṇa of Vālmīki, having the last quarter of every verse composed of quotations from Vedic and other religious works. Edited by Tirumaṅgalam Naḍādūr Narasiṃhāchārya.] pp. 31. *Madras*, 1902. 8°. **14072. b. 31.**

RĀMĀNUJĀCHĀRYA, *Tirumalai Kaṇḍyūru.* *See* MAHĀBHĀRATA.—*Vanaparva.* యక్షప్రశ్నలు *etc.* [Yakshapraṣna. Edited with Telugu paraphrase, *etc.*, by Rāmānujāchārya.] 1901. 8°. **14065. c. 53.**

—— కవిహృదయసర్వస్వము *etc.* [Kavihṛidayasarvasva. An anthology of stanzas on social and moral topics. Compiled with Telugu translations by Rāmānujāchārya.] pt. i. *Madras*, 1901. 8°. **14072. ccc. 31.**

In progress?

RĀMĀNUJĀCHĀRYA AIYAR, *son of Paravastu Ṣrīnivāsa.* *See* JAGANNĀTHA PAṆḌITARĀJA. శ్రీ . . . పండితరాజశతకము *etc.* [Ṣatakas. With some translations into Telugu by Rāmānujāchārya.] 1895. 12°. **14070. b. 22.**

RĀMĀNUJADĀSA, surnamed DOḌḌAYĀCHĀRYA and MAHĀCHĀRYA. *See* VEṄKAṬANĀTHA VEDĀNTĀCHĀRYA. The Sathadushani . . . with [the commentary] Chandamarutha by Thoddaia charia, *etc.* 1901. 8°. [*Ṣāstramuktāvali.*] **14049. a. 1. (no. 5.)**

RĀMAPRASANNA GHOSHA. গৌরচন্দ্রোদয় *etc.* [Gaurachandrodaya. A Bengali anthological work on Chaitanya and his religious teaching, chiefly consisting of Sanskrit quotations with Bengali commentaries, *etc.*] pp. ii. 216, iv. গোবরহাটী বহরমপুর ১৩০৮ [*Gobarhati, Berhampur* printed, 1901.] 8°. **14123. ff. 5.**

RĀMAPRATĀPA ṢARMĀ. *See* KSHAURANIRṆAYA. अथ . . . क्षौरनिर्णयः *etc.* [Gṛihasthānāṃ Kshauranirṇaya. With Hindi translation by Rāmapratāpa.] [1902.] 12°. **14033. a. 33.(3.)**

RĀMARUDRA BHAṬṬA. *See* VIṢVANĀTHA PAÑCHĀNANA BHAṬṬĀCHĀRYA. कारिकावली *etc.* [Kārikāvalī. With the Rāmarudrī Ṭīkā or Dinakarītaraṅgiṇī by Rāmarudra.] [1895.] 8°. **14048. dd. 25.**

—— —— [Another edition.] [1896.] 8°. **14048. dd. 26.**

RĀMAṢAṄKARA DEVA. বৃহৎ-জাতকচন্দ্রিকা *etc.* [Bṛihaj-jātakachandrikā. An astrological work. Edited with additions and a Bengali translation by Nīlakamala Vidyānidhi.] pp. ii. x. i. 408. কলিকাতা ১৮৯৩ [*Calcutta*, 1892.] 8°. **14053. c. 63.**

RĀMAṢAṄKARA RĀYA. *See* MAHĀBHĀRATA.—Bhagavadgītā.—*Sanskrit and Vernaculars.* ଶ୍ରୀମଦ୍-ଭଗବଦ୍ଗୀତା *etc.* [Bhagavadgītā. With Oriya translation by Rāmaṣaṅkara Rāya.] 1898. 8°. **14065. c. 14.(1.)**

RĀMA ṢĀSTRĪ, *Pseud.* ఉపహాసః *etc.* [Upahāsa. A satire in Sanskrit verse and prose on the Karāva caste and on the theories regarding their origin as given in Veligama Sumaṅgala's "Itihāsa."] pp. ii. 13; 1 *plate.* 2439 [*Colombo*, 1895.] 8°.
14058. b. 35.(1.)

RĀMA ṢĀSTRĪ, *Maṇḍikal.* Aryádharmaprakásika. आर्यधर्मप्रकाशिका *etc.* [An outline of Hindu religion and philosophy, for Hindu schools.] pp. vii. 162. महीशूर° १८९० [*Mysore*, 1890.] 8°. **14028. d. 43.**

RĀMA ṢĀSTRĪ, *Rāvāḍi, of Rayadrug.* See ṢAṄKARA ĀCHĀRYA.—*Philosophical Poems, etc.* వివేక చూ-డామణి *etc.* [Vivekachūḍāmaṇi. With Telugu commentaries compiled by Rāma Ṣāstrī.] [1898.] 8°. **14048. c. 72.(2.)**

RĀMA ṢĀSTRĪ BHĀGAVATĀCHĀRYA, *of the Sanskrit College, Benares.* See LOKĀCHĀRYA PIḶḶAI. तत्त्वत्रयम् *etc.* (The Vedânta-tattwatraya . . . with a commentary. Edited by Swâmî Bhâgavatâchâryya.) 1900. 8°. **14004. a. 4.**

—— See NĀRĀYAṆA TĪRTHA, *disciple of Ṣivarāma Tīrtha.* भाट्टभाषाप्रकाशः *etc.* [Bhāṭṭabhāshāprakāṣa. Edited by Bhāgavatāchārya.] [1900.] 8°. **14004. a. 4.(2.)**

—— See PADMAPĀDA. The Pañchapâdikâ . . . Edited by Râmaśâstrî Bhâgavatâchârya. (Part II. The Pañchapâdikâvivaraṇa, *etc.*) 1891-1892. 8°. **14048. dd. 3.(vol. 2.)**

RĀMA ṢĀSTRĪ MĀNAVALLĪ. See AKHAṆḌĀNANDA, *disciple of Akhaṇḍānubhūti.* तत्त्वदीपनम् . . . Tattvadîpana . . . Edited by Râma Śâstrî Tailanga. 1901, *etc.* 8°. **14049. a. 3.**

—— See ANANTADEVA, *son of Āpadeva.* सिद्धान्ततत्त्वं *etc.* [Siddhāntatattva. Edited by Rāma Ṣāstrī.] 1900. 8°. [*The Pandit.*] **14096. d. 6.(vol. 22.)**

—— See APYAYA DĪKSHITA. चित्रमीमांसा *etc.* [Chitramīmāṃsā. Edited by Rāma Ṣāstrī.] 1891. 8°. [*The Pandit.*] **14096. d. 6.(vol. 13.)**

—— See APYAYA DĪKSHITA. अथ वृत्तिवार्त्तिकम् । [Vṛittivārttika. Edited by Rāma Ṣāstrī.] 1890. 8°. [*The Pandit.*] **14096. d. 6.(vol. 12.)**

—— See BĀDARĀYAṆA. The Vedântakalpataru . . . Edited by Râmaśâstrî Tailaṅga. 1895-1897. 8°. **14048. dd. 3.(vol. 11.)**

RĀMA ṢĀSTRĪ MĀNAVALLĪ (*continued*). See BĀDARĀYAṆA. The Vedântakalpataruparimala . . . Edited by Râmaśâstrî Tailaṅga. 1895-1898. 8°. **14048. dd. 3.(vol. 12.)**

—— See BĀDARĀYAṆA. The Vivaraṇaprameyasaṃgraha . . . Edited by Râmaśâstrî Tailaṅga. 1893. 8°. **14048. dd. 3.(vol. 5.)**

—— See JAIMINI.—*Mīmāṃsāsūtra.* मीमांसाश्लोकवार्तिकम् *etc.* (The Mîmânsâ-śloka-vârtika . . . With the commentary . . . by Pârtha Sârathi Miśra. Edited by Râma Śâstrî Tailaṅga.) 1898-1899. 8°. **14004. a. 3.**

—— See PURĀṆAS.—*Selections.* कैवल्यरत्नम् *etc.* [Kaivalyaratna. Edited by Rāma Ṣāstrī.] [1901.] 8°. **14016. d. 57.**

—— See ṢIVĀDITYA MIṢRA. The Saptapadârthî . . . Together with . . . the Mitabhâshiṇî . . . Edited by Râmaśâstrî Tailaṅga. 1893. 8°. **14048. dd. 3.(vol. 6.)**

—— See SUREṢVARA ĀCHĀRYA. नैष्कर्म्यसिद्धिनाम वेदान्तप्रकरणम् . . . Naishkarmyasiddhi . . . with a commentary . . . Edited & annotated by . . . Ráma Śástrí Mánavallí. 1890, *etc.* 8°. **14048. dd. 7.**

—— See VARARUCHI. प्राकृतप्रकाशः . . . Prakrita Prakasha . . . Rivised [*sic*] by . . . Rama Shastri Tailanga. 1899. 8°. **14093. b. 27.(3.)**

RĀMA ṢĀSTRĪ TAILAṄGA. See RĀMA ṢĀSTRĪ MĀNAVALLĪ.

RĀMĀṢRAMA ĀCHĀRYA. See SĀRASVATASŪTRA. सिद्धान्तचन्द्रिकोत्तरार्द्धः *etc.* [Sārasvatasūtra. With the commentary Siddhāntachandrikā of Rāmāṣrama. Part ii. With Hindi commentary based on the Subodhinī of Sadānanda.] [1900.] 4°. **14092. c. 20.**

RĀMASUBRAHMAṆYA ṢĀSTRĪ, *Tiruviṣalūr.* सर्वमतसंग्रहविलासः *etc.* [Sarvamatasaṅgrahavilāsa. A summary of the various Hindu creeds.] pp. viii. 128, xxiii. *Madras*, 1900. 12°. **14048. b. 39.**

RĀMA SUDHĪVARA, *Chāvali, son of Nṛisiṃha.* అలంకారముక్తావళి *etc.* [Alaṅkāramuktāvalī. A treatise on the ornamentation of style.] pp. vii. 66; 1 *plate.* *Vizagapatam*, 1897. 8°. **14053. ccc. 12.**

RĀMA SUDHĪVARA, *Chāvali, son of Nrisiṃha* (*continued*). అలంకారముక్తావళి *etc.* [Alaṅkāramuktāvalī. With the commentary Ratnaṣobhākara of Krishṇa Sūri.] pp. vi. 200, vi. *Vizagapatam*, 1898. 8°. **14053. ccc. 24.**

RĀMASVĀMI AIYAR, *of Enaṅgudi.* See PURĀṆAS.—*Skandapurāṇa.* ஸ்ரீ . . . வடாரண்யமாஹாத்ம்யம் *etc.* [Vaṭāraṇyamāhātmya. Followed by a Tamil version by Rāmasvāmi.] 1898. 16°. **14016. a. 27.**

RĀMASVĀMĪ BHAṬṬĀCHĀRYA, also called GOPĀLASVĀMĪ. *See* PĀÑCHARĀTRA. ஸ்ரீப்ரச்னஸம்ஹிதா *etc.* [Ṣrīpraṣnasaṃhitā. Edited by Rāmasvāmī.] 1904. 8°. **14033. bbb. 22.**

RĀMASVĀMI NĀYUḌU, *Kāñchipuram.* *See* MAHĀBHĀRATA. — Bhagavadgītā. —*Sanskrit and Vernaculars.* ஸ்ரீபகவத்கீதை *etc.* [Bhagavadgītā. Edited and translated by Ṣrīnivāsa and Rāmasvāmi.] [1899.] 16°. **14065. b. 19.**

RĀMASVĀMI RĀJU, *P.V.* श्रीमद्राजाङ्गलमहोद्यानादेशः *etc.* (Srimat Rajangala Mahodyanam.—An account [in mythological form] of the origin and rise of the Angala (British) Empire, on Earth in Samskrita verse . . . with Angala Translation.) pts. i.-iii. pp. 96. *Kumbhakonam*, 1894. 4°. **14076. f. 10.**

—— श्रीमत्पण्डितराजतरङ्गिणी । Sreemat Pandita Rajatarangini. A brief account of the life and character of Pandit Iswara Chandra Vidyasagara, being a portion of Sreemat Rajangala Mahodyanam, which is an account of the origin and rise of the British empire, in Sanskrit verse, *etc.* pp. ii. 11. *Calcutta*, 1893. 4°. **14076. f. 11.**

RĀMASVĀMĪ ṢĀSTRĪ, *Brahmaṣrī.* *See* VAIDYANĀTHA DĪKSHITA. ஸ்ம்ருதி-முக்தாபலே ப்ரத: . . . காண்ட: *etc.* [Smṛitimuktāphala. Vol. i., with Tamil translation by Rāmasvāmī.] 1898, *etc.* 4°. **14039. c. 15.(vol. 1.)**

RĀMASVĀMĪ ṢĀSTRĪ, *Guṇḍu.* అయ్. సీతా-కల్యాణచంపూప్రబంధః *etc.* [Sītākalyāṇa. A *champū*, or poetical work in prose and verse, upon the nuptials of Sītā, in 3 *ullāsas.*] pp. i. 72. *Cocanada*, ౧౯౦౩ [1903.] 8°. **14072. cc. 65.**

RĀMASVARŪPA ṢARMĀ, *son of Bholānāth, of Moradabad*, called ṚISHIKUMĀRA. *See* BĀDARĀYAṆA. वेदान्तदर्शनम् *etc.* [Vedāntadarṣana. Edited by Rāmasvarūpa.] [1898.] 8°. **14048. cc. 21.(6.)**

—— *See* GAṆAPATI, *son of Rāvala Hariṣaṅkara.* मुहूर्त्त गणपति *etc.* [Muhūrtagaṇapati. Edited with Hindi version by Rāmasvarūpa.] [1898.] 8°. **14053. d. 57.**

—— *See* KAPILA. ॥ सांख्यदर्शनम् *etc.* [Sāṅkhyadarṣana. Edited by Rāmasvarūpa.] [1897.] 8°. **14048. cc. 21.(4.)**

—— *See* MAHĀBHĀRATA.—Bhagavadgītā.—*Sanskrit and Vernaculars.* भगवद्गीता [Bhagavadgītā. Edited with Hindi translation by Rāmasvarūpa.] [1897.] 8°. **14065. c. 49.**

—— *See* MANU.—*Dharmaṣāstra.* मनुस्मृति *etc.* [Manusmṛiti. With a Hindi translation by Rāmasvarūpa.] [1902.] 8°. **14039. c. 19.**

—— *See* PATAÑJALI. — *Philosophical Works.* योगदर्शनम् *etc.* [Yogadarṣana. Edited by Rāmasvarūpa.] [1898.] 8°. **14048. cc. 21.(3.)**

—— *See* PURĀṆAS.—*Bhāgavatapurāṇa.* श्री . . . श्रीमद्भागवतम् [Bhāgavatapurāṇa. Edited with Hindi translation by Rāmasvarūpa.] [1901.] 8°. **14018. a. 2.**

—— *See* ṢAṄKARA ĀCHĀRYA. — *Doubtful and Supposititious Works.* श्री . . . प्रबोधसुधाकर *etc.* [Prabodhasudhākara. With Hindi translation by Rāmasvarūpa.] [1901.] 8°. **14049. b. 5.**

—— *See* UTTARAGĪTĀ. उत्तरगीता *etc.* [Uttaragītā. With Hindi version by Rāmasvarūpa.] [1900.] 12°. **14065. b. 24.**

—— *See* VEDAS. — Yajurveda. — *Vājasaneyisaṃhitā.* शुक्लयजुर्वेद *etc.* [Vājasaneyisaṃhitā. Edited with Sanskrit glosses, analyses, and a Hindi commentary by Rāmasvarūpa.] 1899, *etc.* 8°. **14007. b. 15.**

RĀMASVARŪPA ṢUKLA, *son of Gaṇeṣaprasāda.* *See* PAÑCHATANTRA. अथ-संस्कृतसागर *etc.* [Saṃskṛitasāgara. With Hindi version by Rāmasvarūpa.] [1899.] 8°. **14070. c. 63.(2.)**

RĀMA TARKAVĀGĪṢA. *See* VOPADEVA. मुग्धबोध *etc.* [Mugdhabodha. With commentaries of Rāma, *etc.*] [1891.] 8°. **14092. b. 44.**

RĀMA TARKAVĀGĪŚA (*continued*). *See* VOPADEVA. মুগ্ধবোধং *etc.* [Mugdhabodha. With Durgādāsa's commentary as far as the end of the *kṛidantādhyāya* and Rāma's commentary thence to the end.] [1894.] 8°. **14090. e. 24.**

RĀMATĪRTHA YATI, *disciple of Kṛishṇatīrtha. See* SADĀNANDA YOGĪNDRA. The Vedântasâra . . . with the commentaries[, called respectively Subodhinī and Vidvanmanorañjanī,] of Nṛisiṁhasarasvatî and Râmatîrtha, *etc.* 1894. 8°. **14048. dd. 15.**

—— *See* ŚAṄKARA ĀCHĀRYA.—*Two or More Works.* Śrí-Śankarácharya's Miscellaneous Works, *etc.* [Vol. III, Upadeṣasahasrī, with Rāmatīrtha's commentaries Upadeṣārthavibhāga and Padayojanikā.] 1898-1899. 8°. [*Mysore Government Oriental Library Series: Bibliotheca Sanskrita.*] **14004. b. 10.(vol. 3.)**

—— *See* SUREṢVARA ĀCHĀRYA. मानसोल्लासो *etc.* [Mānasollāsa. With the commentary of Rāmatīrtha entitled Mānasollāsavṛittānta.] 1895. 8°. [*Mysore Government Oriental Library Series: Bibliotheca Sanskrita.*] **14004. b. 5.**

RĀMATOSHAṆA VIDYĀLAṄKĀRA. प्राणतोषिणी *etc.* [Prāṇatoshiṇī. A compendium of Tantric rituals. Third edition.] pp. xxix. 1097. कलिकाता १८९८ [*Calcutta,* 1898.] 8°. **14033. aa. 3.**

RĀMAVALLABHĀ ṢARAṆA, *of Faizabad. See* HANUMATSAṂHITĀ. अथ श्रीहनुमत्संहिता *etc.* [Hanumatsaṃhitā. Edited by Rāmanārāyaṇa Dāsa and Rāmavallabhā Ṣaraṇa.] [1900.] *obl.* 8°. **14033. c. 44.(3.)**

RĀMA VĀRIYAR, *of Trichur. See* AMARASIṂHA. അമരകോശം *etc.* [Amarakoṣa. Edited with Malayalam interpretation by Rāma Vāriyar.] [1891.] 8°. **14090. bb. 8.**

—— *See* VĀGBHAṬA, *son of Siṃhagupta.* അഷ്ടാംഗഹൃദയം *etc.* [Ashṭāṅgahṛidaya. With Malayalam paraphrase by Rāma Vāriyar.] [1891-1892.] 8°. **14043. c. 41.**

RĀMA VARMĀ, *son of Himmat Varmā. See* PURĀṆAS.—*Brahmāṇḍapurāṇa.* [*Adhyātmarāmāyaṇa.*] অধ্যাত্মরামায়ণম্ *etc.* [Adhyātmarāmāyaṇa. With the commentary Setu of Rāma Varmā.] [1901, *etc.*] 8°. **14016. d. 61.**

RĀMA VARMĀ, *Yuvarāja of Vañchi.* The Rukmiṇīpariṇaya of Râmavarman. [A mythological drama in 5 acts.] Edited by Paṇdit Śivadatta . . . and Kâśînâth Pâṇdurang Parab. (रुक्मिणीपरिणयम् ।) pp. 52. 1894. *See* DURGĀPRASĀDA, *son of Vrajalāla,* and KĀŚĪNĀTHA PĀṆḌURAṄGA PARAB. Kâvyamâlâ. [No.] 40. 1886, *etc.* 8°. **14072. ccc. 12.(no. 40.)**

Vañchi (i.e. the Tamil Vañjai) *is the modern Karur.*

RĀMAVILĀSA and VRAJAVILĀSA, *of Singha, Shahjahanpur.* नित्यकर्म *etc.* [Nityakarma. A manual of the daily rites of the Ārya Samāj. With Hindi rubrics, *etc.*] pp. 22. मेरठ [१८]९९ [*Meerut,* 1899.] 12°. **14028. b. 81.(3.)**

RĀMĀYAṆASAMPRADĀYA. శ్రీమద్రామాయణసంప్రదాయార్థసంగ్రహః [Rāmāyaṇasampradāyārthasaṅgraha. A treatise on the religious and historical significance of the Rāmāyaṇa.] *See* VĀLMĪKI.—Rāmāyaṇa.—*Entire Text.* శ్రీమద్రామాయణమ్ *etc.* [Rāmāyaṇa.] pp. vii.-xxiv. [1897.] 8°. **14065. d. 37.**

RĀMENDRASUNDARA TRIVEDĪ. *See* VAṂṢĪVADANA ṢARMĀ. পুণ্ডরীককুলকীর্ত্তিপঞ্জিকা *etc.* [Puṇḍarīkakulakīrttipañjikā. Edited with Bengali translation and appendices by Rāmendrasundara.] [1901.] 8°. **14058. b. 47.**

RAMEṢACHANDRA, *Bhikshu, of Chittagong.* বৌদ্ধালঙ্কার *etc.* [Bauddhālaṅkāra. A lectionary of short Pali texts on Buddhist religion. With translations and explanations in Bengali.] pt. i. pp. ii. 34. চট্টগ্রাম ২৪৩৪ [*Chittagong,* 1891.] 12°. **14098. a. 22.(2.)**

RAMEṢACHANDRA DATTA. *See* MAHĀBHĀRATA.—*Appendix.* Maha-Bharata . . . Condensed into English verse by Romesh Dutt, *etc.* 1899. 8°. **14065. c. 45.**

—— *See* VĀLMĪKI. — Rāmāyaṇa. — *Appendix.* Ramayana . . . Condensed into English verse by Romesh Dutt, *etc.* 1900. 8°. **14065. c. 47.**

—— Lays of Ancient India. Selections from Indian [*i.e.* Sanskrit and Pali] poetry rendered into English verse by Romesh Chunder Dutt. pp. xv. 224. *London,* 1894. 8°. **2318. h. 9.**

Forms part of Trübner's Oriental Series.

RAMEṢACHANDRA DATTA (*continued*). हिन्दूशास्त्र *etc.* [Hindu-śāstra. Selections from Sanskrit literature with Bengali translations, edited with prefaces by Rameṣachandra Datta. Pt. i., selections from the Vedas, Pt. ii. from the Upanishads, *etc.*, and Pt. iii. from Āṣvalāyana's Ṣrautasūtra and Gṛihyasūtra, Gobhila's Gṛihyasūtra, and Gautama's Dharmasūtra, edited and translated by Rameṣachandra Datta and Satyavrata Sāmaṣramī. Pt. iv., extracts from Manu and other Dharmaṣāstras, compiled by Kṛishṇakamala Bhaṭṭāchārya. Pt. v., extracts from the texts of the six philosophical schools, with expositions, compiled by Kālīvara Vedāntavāgīṣa. Pt. vi., a Bengali summary of the Rāmāyaṇa. Pt. vii., selections from the Mahābhārata, compiled by Dāmodara Vidyānanda. Pt. viii., the Bhagavadgītā, with Bengali translation by Baṅkimchandra Chaṭṭopādhyāya and Dāmodara. Pt. ix., extracts from the 18 Purāṇas, compiled by Āṣutosha Ṣāstrī and Hṛishīkeṣa Ṣāstrī.] 2 vols. কলিকাতা ১৩০২-১৩০৩ [*Calcutta*, 1895-1897.] 8°. **14085. c. 45.**

RĀMEṢVARA BHAṬṬA, *son of Bālamukunda, of Agra.* See AGNIVEṢA. अञ्जननिदानम् *etc.* [Āñjananidāna. Edited with a Hindi translation styled Prabodhinī and notes by Rāmeṣvara.] [1898.] 8°. **14043. c. 45.(1.)**

—— See GAṆEṢA, *son of Keṣava.* ग्रहलाघवम् *etc.* (Grahalaghava . . . Corrected by Pt. Rameshwar Bhatt.) 1899. 8°. **14053. ccc. 26.**

—— See HARSHADEVA. रत्नावली *etc.* (The Ratnávalí . . . Edited with Hindi translation by . . . Rámeshwar Bhatt.) 1895. 8°. **14080. c. 35.**

RĀMEṢVARĀNANDA ṢARMĀ, *Yogī.* See ṢIVAKUMĀRA ṢĀSTRĪ, *Mahāmahopādhyāya.* श्रीरामेश्वरानन्दयशोभूषणं *etc.* [Rāmeṣvarānanda-yaṣobhūshaṇa. Panegyrics addressed to Rāmeṣvarānanda.] [1902.] 8°. **14058. cc. 4.**

RĀMEṢVARA ṢIVAYOGĪ, *disciple of Sadāṣiva Brahmendra.* See BHĀSKARA, *son of Mudgala.* ॥ अर्थसङ्ग्रहः *etc.* [Arthasaṅgraha. With the commentary Kaumudī of Rāmeṣvara.] [1897.] 8°. **14048. cc. 20.**

—— See JAIMINI.—*Mīmāṃsāsūtra.* जैमिनिसूत्रवृत्तिः *etc.* [Mīmāṃsāsūtra. With the commentary Subodhinī by Rāmeṣvara.] 1899. 8°. [*The Pandit.*] **14096. d. 6.(vol. 17-21.)**

RĀMEṢVARA SŪRI, *Mīmāṃsaka.* See RĀMEṢVARA ṢIVAYOGĪ.

RĀMUṆṆI VAIDYAR, *Māḍāvil.* See KALYĀṆASAUGANDHIKA. വടക്കൻ കല്യാണസൌഗന്ധികം *etc.* [Vaḍakkan Kalyāṇasaugandhikaṃ. Edited, with Malayalam glossary, *etc.*, by Rāmuṇṇi Vaidyar.] 1895. 8°. **14072. cc. 60.(2.)**

RAṆACHHODAJĪ UDDHAVAJĪ ṢĀSTRĪ. See MAHĀBHĀRATA.—*Abridgments and Selections.* श्रीमद्भगवद्गीता पञ्चरत्न *etc.* [Pañcharatna. Followed by the Īṣa, Kena, Muṇḍaka, and Aitareya Upanishads. Edited with Gujarati translations and commentaries by Raṇachhoḍajī.] [1896.] 8°. **14060. d. 15.**

—— See UPANISHADS.—*Small Collections.* ईश केन मुण्डक अने ऐतरेयोपनिषद् *etc.* [Īṣa, Kena, Muṇḍaka, and Aitareya Upanishads. Edited with Gujarati translations and commentaries by Raṇachhoḍajī.] [1896.] 8°. **14010. dd. 10.(1.)**

RĀṆARAṄGAMALLA. See BHOJARĀJA.

RAṆASIṂHA (WILLIAM PERERA). See ANNAM BHAṬṬA. The Tarka Sangraha . . . Edited with a Sinhalese translation . . . by W. P. Ranesinghe, *etc.* 1880. 8°. **14048. dd. 22.**

RANESINGHE. See RAṆASIṂHA.

RAṄGĀCHĀRULU, *M.* Life and Teachings of Ramanuja, or The Spirit of Visistadwitism, *etc.* [Including a translation of and commentary upon the "Eighty-two Aphorisms" ascribed to Rāmānuja.] pp. ix. 93. *Madras*, 1895. 8°. **14048. dd. 20.**

RAṄGĀCHĀRYA, *S., of Srirangam.* See BHAVABHŪTI. The Mahâvîracharita . . . With the commentary of Vîrarâghava. Edited by . . . S. Rangachariar, *etc.* 1892. 8°. **14080. c. 32.**

—— See KĀLIDĀSA.—*Raghuvaṃṣa.* F. A. Examination of 1892. The Complete Sanskrit Text with . . . Sanskrit commentary . . . English notes, and . . . translation, by S. Rangachariar . . . and V. Srinivasa Aiyar. 1891. 8°. **14076. c. 59.**

RAṄGĀCHĀRYA, *Govardhanam.* See NĪLĀGĪTĀ. నీలాగీత *etc.* [Nīlāgītā. Translated into Sanskrit by Raṅgāchārya.] [1898.] 12°. **14076. a. 22.(2.)**

RAṄGĀCHĀRYA, *Malūr.* See BĀDARĀYAṆA. The Vedānta-Sūtras with the Śrī-Bhāshya ... Translated ... by M. Raṅgāchārya, *etc.* 1899. 8°. **14048. cc. 29.**

—— See MADRAS.—*Government Oriental Manuscripts Library.* A Descriptive Catalogue ... By ... Seshagiri Sastri (and M. Rangacharya), *etc.* 1901, *etc.* 8°. **14096. ccc. 4.**

RAṄGĀCHĀRYA, *Mușurpākkam Kaḍāmbi.* See VĀLMĪKI. — Rāmāyaṇa. — *Portions.* ஸ்ரீ ... ஸுந்தரகாண்டம் *etc.* [Sundarakāṇḍa. Edited with Tamil translation by Raṅgāchārya.] [1902.] 8°. **14065. bbb. 9.**

RAṄGĀCHĀRYA, *Paṇḍitaratna Tarkatīrtha Kastūri.* See GAṄGEŚA UPĀDHYĀYA. పక్షత *etc.* [Pakshatā. Edited by Raṅgāchārya.] 1890. 8°. **14048. e. 19.**

—— See JAIMINI.—*Gṛihyasūtra.* ॥ जैमिनिगृह्यसूत्रम् *etc.* [Jaiminigṛihyasūtra. With commentary of Śrīnivāsa. Edited by Raṅgāchārya.] 1898. 8°. **14028. c. 74.**

—— See MYSORE. — *Government of Mysore.* Government Oriental Library Series. Bibliotheca Sanskrita ... Edited by A. Mahádeva Śástri (and ... K. Rangácharya). 1893, *etc.* 8°. **14004. b.**

—— శ్రీ ... వాధూల ప్రవర నిర్ణయః॥ [Vādhūlapravaranirṇaya. A treatise on the genealogy of the Vādhūla tribe of Brahmans. Composed by order of the Mahādeșika of the Parakāla Saṃsthān at Mysore, as an epistle, and preceded by a summary in 8 stanzas by the latter.] pp. 15. కంచి [*Conjevaram*,] 1900. 8°. **14058. b. 32.(3.)**

RAṄGĀCHĀRYA, *Paravastu.* See JAGANNĀTHA PAṆḌITARĀJA. శ్రీ ... పండితరాట్ శతకశ్లోకములు [Paṇḍitarātșatakaşloka. Edited by Raṅgāchārya.] [1899.] 12°. **14070. b. 28.**

RAṄGĀCHĀRYA, *Tekkuḷūru Śrīnivāsa.* See ŚRĪNIVĀSA RAṄGĀCHĀRYA, *Tekkuḷūru.*

RAṄGĀCHĀRYA SVĀMĪ, *of Venkatagiri.* कुदृष्टिध्वान्तमार्तण्डः । तत्र प्रथमो मयूखः (२।३।४। मयूखाः ।) [Kudṛishṭidhvāntamārtaṇḍa. A reply to criticisms upon the Viṣishṭādvaita system of Rāmānuja.] 2 vols. मुंबापुर्यां १९५६ [*Bombay*, 1900.] 8°. **14048. bb. 41.**
In progress?

RANGANADHASWAMY AYYAVARALUGARU, *S.P.V.* See VEṄKAṬARAṄGANĀTHA SVĀMĪ, *Paravastu.*

RAṄGANĀTHA, *son of Bālakṛishṇa.* See KĀLIDĀSA. —*Vikramorvaşīya.* The Vikramorvaśīyam ... with English notes, containing extracts from two commentaries, [*scil.* of Kāṭayavema and Raṅganātha,] *etc.* 1901. 8°. **14080. c. 42.**

RAṄGANĀTHA, *son of Ballāla.* See SŪRYASIDDHĀNTA. सूर्यसिद्धान्त *etc.* [Sūryasiddhānta. The Madhyādhikāra, with Raṅganātha's gloss Gūḍhārthaprakāşaka.] [1890, *etc.*] 4°. [*Aruṇodaya.*] **14133. g. 16.(pt. i., no. 5.)**

RAṄGANĀTHA, *son of Vatsāṅka.* See PARĀŚARA BHAṬṬA.

RAṄGANĀTHĀCHĀRYA, *Paravastu Veṅkaṭa.* See VEṄKAṬARAṄGANĀTHA ĀCHĀRYA.

RAṄGANĀTHĀCHĀRYA, *Śrīpuram Naḍādūr.* See VEṄKAṬANĀTHA VEDĀNTĀCHĀRYA. వేదాన్తాచార్యవిజయః॥ [Vedāntāchāryavijaya. Edited by Raṅganāthāchārya.] [1892.] 8°. **14048. dd. 17.**

RAṄGANĀTHA RIMOL. See PURĀṆAS.—*Vishṇupurāṇa.* यमगीता *etc.* [Yamagītā. Edited with a translation into Gorkhali by Raṅganātha.] 1889. 8°. **14016. c. 42.(1.)**

RAṄGANĀTHA SAKHĀRĀMA LĀḶE, *of Kikwi.* आरोग्यसिंधु . शुक्रसंहिता किंवा कामशास्त्र *etc.* [Ārogyasindhu, also termed Şukrasaṃhitā and Kāmaşāstra. A treatise on sexual disorders, with Marathi translation and notes, *etc.* Edited by Gaṇeṣa Raṅganātha Lāḷe.] pp. iii. 131. पुणें १९०० [*Poona*, 1900.] 8°. **14043. cc. 14.**

—— विषमंजरी *etc.* [Vishamañjarī. A compilation on toxicology, chiefly in Sanskrit aphorisms with Marathi translations, notes, *etc.*] pp. ii. 85. पुणें १९०० [*Poona*, 1900.] 8°. **14043. c. 45.(3.)**

RAṄGANĀTHASVĀMĪ, *Paravastu Veṅkaṭa.* See VEṄKAṬARAṄGANĀTHA SVĀMĪ.

RAṄGARĀJĀCHĀRYA, *Vātsya Naḍādūr, Mahāmahopādhyāya. See* VEṄKAṬANĀTHA VEDĀNTĀCHĀRYA. श्रीः . . . हंससन्देशः० (Hamsa Sandesa . . . With . . . [Sanskrit] commentary [called Haṃsasandeśaprakāśa by Raṅgarājāchārya], *etc.*) 1903. 12°. **14060. b. 19.**

RAṄGARĀMĀNUJA, *disciple of Tātāchārya. See* SANDHYĀVANDANA. யஜுர்வேத ஸந்த்யாவந்தநம் *etc.* [Sandhyāvandana. Followed by the Purushasūkta, Śrīsūkta, *etc.* With extracts, in a Tamil translation, from the commentaries of Raṅgarāmānuja and others.] 1901. 8°. **14033. aa. 27.**

—— वेदान्त विषयवाक्यदीपिका *etc.* [Vishayavākyadīpikā. A treatise upon the scriptural passages quoted in the Śrībhāshya of Rāmānuja. With footnotes by Lakshmaṇadāsa, disciple of Lakshmaṇa Āchārya, of Brindaban.] pp. i. 375. मुंबय्यां १९५५ [*Bombay*, 1899.] 8°. **14048. e. 26.**

The title-page ascribes the annotations to Lakshmaṇa Āchārya.

RAṄGAYĀRYA, *Tiruppattūr, son of Rāmasvāmī.* సంబంధాసంబంధవివేచనము *etc.* [Sambandhāsambandhavivechana. A compilation of passages from various authorities on the relations of family and caste in reference to marriage.] pp. ii. 52. పుంగనూరు ౧౮౯౧ [*Punganur*, 1891.] *obl.* 8°. **14039. b. 21.(1.)**

RASAMAYA SIDDHA, *son of Ṭīkamlāl, of Delhi. See* LĀḌILĪ CHANDRA. सिद्धिसाधन *etc.* [Brahmastava. With a Hindi prose translation and commentary, styled Siddhisādhana, by Rasamaya Siddha.] [1890.] 8°. **14048. e. 22.(1.)**

RASAVĀHINĪ. Rasavāhinī. Buddhistiske Legender. Paa Dansk i Udvalg [of six stories] med Indledning, af Dines Andersen. (Studier fra Sprog- og Oldtidsforskning, utgivne af det Philologisk-historiske Samfund. Nr. 6.) pp. 32, ii. *Kjøbenhavn*, 1891. 8°. **Ac. 9877/2. (vol. 1, no. 6.)**

—— Il settimo capitolo della Rasavāhinī. (Rasavāhinī, I. 8-10.) [Edited with translation by P. E. Pavolini.] 1894, 1896-1897. *See* ACADEMIES, *etc.*—Florence.—*Società Asiatica Italiana.* Giornale, *etc.* Vols. viii., pp. 179-186, x., pp. 175-198. 1887, *etc.* 8°. **Ac 8804. (vol. 8, 10.)**

RĀSHṬRAPĀLAPARIPṚICHCHHĀ. राष्ट्रपालपरिपृच्छा। Rāṣṭrapālaparipṛcchā. Sūtra du Mahāyāna. Publié par L. Finot. pp. xvi. ii. 69. 1901. *See* ACADEMIES, *etc.*—St. Petersburg.—*Academia Scientiarum Imperialis.* Bibliotheca Buddhica. Vol. ii. 1897, *etc.* 8°. **14003. dd. 2.**

RASIKACHANDRA VASU, *of Barisal.* রত্নোদ্ধার *etc.* [Ratnoddhāra. Comprising a Bengali poem on the legend and cult of the god Satyanārāyaṇa, and the Satyanārāyaṇavratakathā from the Skandapurāṇa, with Bengali appendix.] pp. 83. বরিশাল ১৩০৬ [*Barisal*, 1899.] 12°. **14028. b. 66.(4.)**

RASIKACHANDRA VIDYĀRATNA. *See* DURGASIṂHA, *Commentator on the Kātantra.* কলাপ-ব্যাকরণম্ . . . চতুষ্টয়টীকা *etc.* [Chatushṭayaṭīkā. Ch. II. i.-iii. Edited by Rasikachandra.] 1893. 8°. **14090. bb. 13.(1.)**

—— *See* SUSHEṆA, *Kavirāja.* কলাপ-ব্যাকরণম্ . . . চতুষ্টয়কবিরাজঃ *etc.* [Chatushṭayakavirāja. Ch. II. Edited by Rasikachandra.] 1894. 8°. **14090. bb. 13.(3.)**

—— *See* TRILOCHANADĀSA. কলাপ-ব্যাকরণম্ . . . চতুষ্টয়পঞ্জী *etc.* [Chatushṭayapañjī. Ch. II. Edited by Rasikachandra.] 1893. 8°. **14090. bb. 13.(2.)**

RASIKALĀLA GUPTA, *Kavirāja. See* MĀDHAVA, *son of Indukara.* Nidana . . . An English translation, with Sanskrit passages, by . . . Russick Lal Gupta. 1892. 8°. **14043. cc. 6.**

—— *See* ŚAṄKARA SENA. Science of Sphygmica . . . an English translation with Sanskrit passages by . . . Russick Láll Gupta. 1891. 12°. **14043. b. 11.**

RASIKAMOHANA CHAṬṬOPĀDHYĀYA. *See* JAIMINI.—*Jyotishasūtra.* জৈমিনিসূত্রম্ *etc.* [Jaiminisūtra. With commentary of Nīlakaṇṭha. Edited by Rasikamohana.] [1884.] 8°. **14053. dd. 6.**

—— *See* PERIODICAL PUBLICATIONS.—*Calcutta.* অরুণোদয় *etc.* [Aruṇodaya. Edited by Rasikamohana.] [1890, *etc.*] 4°. **14133. g. 16.**

—— *See* TANTRAS. [*Collections.*] বিবিধ-মূল-তন্ত্র। [Vividha-mūla-tantra. Edited by Rasikamohana.] [1903, *etc.*] 8°. **14033. c. 48.**

RASIKAMOHANA CHAṬṬOPĀDHYĀYA (*continued*). লুপ্তগুপ্ত শাস্ত্রের সূচীপত্র *etc.* [Lupta-gupta-śāstrer Sūchīpatra. Index to the astrological and Tantric publications, both Sanskrit and Bengali, of Rasikamohana. With a Bengali and English preface.] pt. i. pp. vi. xl. 176. কলিকাতা ১৩০২ [*Calcutta*, 1894.] 8°. **14033. bbb. 2.**

RĀŚIKOŚA. অথ রাশিকোষ। [Rāśikośa. A vocabulary of synonyms for the signs of the zodiac. With Bengali translation.] *See* GOPĪRAMAṆA TARKARATNA. কোষচন্দ্রিকা *etc.* [Kośachandrikā.] pp. 38-39. [1893.] 12°. **14090. b. 44.(1.)**

RASMUSSEN (HARALD). *See* PAÑCHATANTRA. De Ældste Indiske Æventyr og Fabler . . . oversat . . . af H. Rasmussen. 1893. 8°. **14070. c. 51.**

RATANAJOTI, *Giridhara.* *See* BUDDHAGHOSA. [*Papañchasūdanī.*] පපඤ්චසූදනී *etc.* [Papañchasūdanī. Edited by Ratanajoti.] 1898. 8°. **14098. ccc. 8.**

—— *See* SUTTAPIṬAKA.—*Majjhimanikāya.* Angulimala Suttraya, *etc.* [With interpretation *etc.* in Sinhalese. Edited by Ratanajoti.] 1891. 8°. **14098. c. 53.(3.)**

RATANAPĀLA, *Gammullē.* *See* SUTTAPIṬAKA.—*Khuddakanikāya.* [*Vimānavatthu.*] විමානවත්‍ථු *etc.* [Vimānavatthu. With paraphrastic Sinhalese commentary by Ratanapāla.] 1890. 8°. **14098. c. 63.(1.)**

RATANAPAÑJARA. [For Burmese collections of Burmese-Pali texts including editions of the devotional Pali poem called Ratanapañjara or Ratanā-shwe-hkyaing, with its Burmese translation, see under the following headings :]

HKYAUK SAUNG TWÈ.
HSAY SAUNG TWÈ.
JAYAMAṄGALAGĀTHĀ.
KO SAUNG TWÈ.
NGĀ SAUNG TWÈ.
TA-HSÈ-HNIT SAUNG TWÈ.
TA-HSÈ-THÔN SAUNG TWÈ.

RATIMAÑJARĪ. রতিমঞ্জরী বা রমণীরঙ্গ *etc.* [Ratimañjarī, or Ramaṇīraṅga. A poetical manual of the Art of Love, based upon the works of Jayadeva and Kavikarṇapūra and the Smaradīpikā. With a Bengali version, chiefly in verse. Edited by Kālīprasanna Vidyāratna.] pp. i. iv. 88. কলিকাতা ১৩০৮ [*Calcutta*, 1901.] 12°. **14053. b. 41.(1.)**

RATIŚĀSTRA. রতি-শাস্ত্র *etc.* [Ratiśāstra. An Ars Amoris in 17 cantos. With Bengali translation by Kālīprasanna Vidyāratna. Second edition.] pp. ii. 176 ; 7 *plates.* কলিকাতা ১৩০১ [*Calcutta*, 1895.] 12°. **14053. b. 28.**

RATNACHANDRA GAṆĪ, *disciple of Śāntichandra.* *See* SAMYAKTVASAPTATIKĀ. अथ संयक्त्वसित्तरी *etc.* [Samyaktvasaptatikā. With Gujarati commentary by Ratnachandra.] [1890.] 8°. [*Jainakathāratnakoṣa.*] **14144. gg. 1.(vol. 3.)**

RATNAGOPĀLA BHAṬṬA, *of Benares.* *See* PURUSHOTTAMAJĪ, *Gosvāmī.* तुलसीमालाधारणवादः *etc.* [Tulasīmālādhāraṇavāda. With Braj-bhāshā translation by Ratnagopāla.] [1902.] 8°. **14028. d. 69.**

RATNAKAṆṬHA, *Rājānaka, son of Śaṅkarakaṇṭha.* *See* JAGADDHARA, *grandson of Gauradhara.* The Stutikusumâñjali . . . With the commentary [Laghupañchikā] of . . . Ratnakaṇṭha, *etc.* 1891. 8°. [*Kâvyamâlâ.*] **14072. ccc. 12.(no. 23.)**

—— *See* VĀSUDEVA, *disciple of Bhārata Guru.* The Yudhishṭhiravijaya . . . With the commentary of . . . Ratnakaṇṭha, *etc.* 1897. 8°. [*Kâvyamâlâ.*] **14072. ccc. 12.(no. 60.)**

RATNĀKARA, *Rājānaka, son of Amṛitabhānu.* The Haravijaya of Râjânaka Ratnâkara. [A mythological poem in 50 cantos.] With the commentary of Râjânaka Alaka. Edited by Paṇdit Durgâprasâd and Kâśinâth Pâṇdurang Parab. [With an index of the verses by G. A. Jacob.] (हरविजयम् ।) pp. ii. iv. 708, lviii. 1890. *See* DURGĀPRASĀDA, *son of Vrajalāla,* and KĀŚINĀTHA PĀṆDURAṄGA PARAB. Kâvyamâlâ. [No.] 22. 1886, *etc.* 8°. **14072. ccc. 12.(no. 22.)**

RATNĀKARA DĪKSHITA, *Samrāṭ Pauṇḍarīkayājī, son of Deva Bhaṭṭa.* जयसिंहकल्पद्रुमः । सफलव्रतकल्पमहीरुहः धर्मशास्त्रग्रन्थः *etc.* [Jayasiṃhakalpadruma, or °kalpadrumoddyota, or Vratakalpadruma. A treatise on the celebration of festivals, in 19 *stabakas*, composed by order of the Maharaja Jaisingh of Jaipur. Edited by Harinārāyaṇa Śarmā.] pp. xx. 912 ; 1 *plate.* मुम्बय्यां १९५९ [*Bombay*, 1903.] 8°. **14033. c. 47.**

RATNĀKARA SŪRI. अथ रत्नाकर पचीशी. [Ratnākara-pachīsī. 25 Jain devotional stanzas. With Gujarati gloss.] See PRATIKRAMAṆASŪTRA. अथ पंचप्रतिक्रमण सूत्र etc. [Pañcha-pratikramaṇasūtra.] pp. 202-208. [1897.] 12°. **14100. a. 20.**

RATNAM AIYAR, *T.R.* See BĀṆA. The Parvati Parinaya ... With Sanskrit commentary, English notes & translation by T. R. Ratnam Aiyar. 1898. 8°. **14079. b. 34.(3.)**

—— See BHAVABHŪTI. The Mahâvîracharita ... With ... commentary ... Edited by T. R. Ratnam Aiyar, *etc.* 1892. 8°. **14080. c. 32.**

—— See BHAVABHŪTI. The Uttara-Râmacharita ... With ... commentary ... Edited by T. R. Ratnam Aiyar ... and Kâśînâth ... Parab. 1899. 8°. **14080. c. 40.**

—— See KĀLIDĀSA.—*Abhijñānaśakuntala.* A Literal English Translation of Abhijnana Sakuntala ... by T. R. Ratnam Aiyar. 1896. 8°. **14079. b. 23.(2.)**

—— See KĀLIDĀSA.—*Mālavikāgnimitra.* Malavikagnimitra ... translated ... By T. R. Ratnam Aiyer. 1891. 8°. **14079. c. 58.**

RATNAMĀLĀ. रत्नमाला । [Ratnamālā. The first *avadāna.*] 1894. See ACADEMIES, *etc.*—Calcutta.—*Buddhist Text Society of India.* Journal, *etc.* Vol. I, pt. iv. 1893, *etc.* 8°. **14003. b. 19.(vol. 1.)**

See Rājendralāla Mitra, Nepalese Buddhist Literature, *p.* 197 f.

—— [A separate issue of the same.] **14004. c. (vol. 1, no. 7.)**

—— The Merchant's Wife. Translated from the ... Ratnamálá by ... Mahendra Lal Das. 1894. See ACADEMIES, *etc.*—Calcutta.—*Buddhist Text Society of India.* Journal, *etc.* Vol. II, pt. iii. 1893, *etc.* 8°. **14003. b. 19.(vol. 2.)**

RATNAMĀNA, *of Kathmandu.* मू [*leg.* भू] शरच्चन्द्र १९५१ स्थीये ... पञ्चाङ्गम् [Almanack for Samv. 1951. Compiled by Ratnamāna.] [1893.] *obl.* 16°. See EPHEMERIDES. **14096. a. 3.**

RATNAPARĪKSHĀ. Navaratnaparîkṣâ[, or Ratnaparīkshā. A tract in 183 stanzas on the lapidary art, sometimes alleged to form part of Nārāyaṇa Paṇḍita's Smṛitisāroddhāra. With French translation.] See FINOT (L.). Les Lapidaires Indiens, *etc.* pp. 141-178. 1896. 8°. **Ac. 8929.(fasc. 111.)**

—— [For the works of this title ascribed to Agastya :] See AGASTYA.

RATNAŚEKHARA SŪRI, *disciple of Hematilaka, of the Bṛihad-gachchha.* ॥ गुणस्थानक्रमारोहः ॥ [Guṇasthānakramāroha. A Jain poem in 137 stanzas describing the stages in the soul's progress.] ff. 6. See PRAKĪRṆAKA. चउसरण तथा आउरपच्चक्खाण पयन्ना° [Chaüsaraṇa-païnna, *etc.*] [1902.] *obl.* 8°. **14100. c. 24.**

RATNAŚEKHARA SŪRI, *disciple of Munisundara, of the Tapā-gachchha.* See PRATIKRAMAṆASŪTRA. अथ ... वंदित्तासूत्र *etc.* [Śrāddhapratikramaṇasūtra. With Gujarati translation of Ratnaśekhara's Sanskrit commentary.] [1890.] 8°. [*Jainakathāratnakoṣa.*] **14144. gg. 1.(vol. 4.)**

—— श्राद्धविधि तथा ... विधिकौमुदी नामनी टीकानुं भाषांतर *etc.* [Śrāddhavidhi. A metrical compendium, in 17 Prakrit *gāthās,* of Jain religious duties. With the [Śrāddha-]vidhikaumudī, a commentary by the same author, translated into Gujarati by Dāmodara Govindāchārya.] pp. xiv. 492. अमदावाद १८९९ [*Ahmudabad,* 1899.] 8°. **14100. e. 8.**

The praśasti at the end gives the date of composition as 1506 *Samv.*

—— શ્રી શ્રાદ્ધવિધિ પ્રકરણ *etc.* [Śrāddhavidhi. With a Gujarati translation of the Kaumudī by the editor, Chīmanlāl Sākalchand Mārphatīyā.] pp. iv. viii. iv. 520, iv. મુંબઈ ૧૮૯૯ [*Bombay,* 1899.] 8°. **14100. d. 7.**

RATNAVĒLU MUDALIYĀR, *Ikkāḍu.* பஸ்ம மஹாத்மியம் *etc.* [Bhasmamāhātmya. An anthology of passages bearing upon the ashes or burnt cow-dung with which Śaivas smear themselves. With Tamil translation.] pp. 42. சென்னை [*Madras,*] 1902. 8°. **14033. b. 55.(3.)**

RATNEŚVARA, *courtier of Rāmasiṃha Deva.* See BHOJARĀJA. सरस्वतीकण्ठाभरणम् *etc.* [Sarasvatīkaṇṭhābharaṇa. With Ratneśvara's commentary, entitled Darpaṇa, upon Sections i.-iii.] [1894.] 8°. **14053. cc. 68.**

RĀUJĪ RĀMACHANDRA KĀḶE. Exhaustive Notes on Bana's Harshacharita. Chapters i, ii & iii (iv), *etc.* 2 pts. *Bombay*, 1892-1894. 12°. **14076. b. 30.**

RAVIDATTA ŚĀSTRĪ, *son of Śivasahāya, of Beri.* *See* Kāśīnātha Upādhyāya. धर्मसिंधु *etc.* [Dharmasindhu. With Hindi translation by Ravidatta.] [1892.] 8°. **14033. bb. 39.**

—— भैषज्यरत्नावली *etc.* [Bhaishajyaratnāvalī. A work on therapeutics, compiled from Sanskrit sources, with a Hindi translation.] pp. i. xviii. 882. लखनऊ १८९३ [*Lucknow*, 1893.] 4°. **14043. f. 3.**

REGNAUD (Paul). *See* Bharata Muni. Bhāratīya-Nāṭya-Cāstram[*sic*]... Précédée d'une préface de M. P. Regnaud, *etc.* 1898, *etc.* 8°. **Ac. 365. (fasc. xl.)**

—— *See* Bharata Muni. La Métrique de Bharata ... suivi d'une interprétation française par M. P. Regnaud. 1881. 4°. [*Annales du Musée Guimet.*] **7704. h. 21. (tom. 2.)**

—— *See* Subhāshita. Stances Sanskrites Inédites, *etc.* [Edited with translation by P. Regnaud.] 1883-1885. 8°. **Ac. 8922. (année 1, 3.)**

—— *See* Vedas.—Ṛigveda.—*Entire Text.* Le Rig-véda. Texte et traduction ... Par P. Regnaud. 1900, *etc.* 4°. **14007. d. 22.**

—— *See* Vedas.—Ṛigveda.—*Selections of Hymns and Verses.* Études Védiques, *etc.* [By P. Regnaud.] 1890. 8°. [*Revue de l'Histoire des Religions.*] **P.P. 37. cc. (tom. 21, 22.)**

—— Le Rig-véda et les Origines de la Mythologie Indo-européenne, *etc.* 1892, *etc.* *See* Academies, *etc.*—Paris.—*Musée Guimet.* Annales ... Bibliothèque d'Études. Tom. i. 1892, *etc.* 8°. **7704. i. (tom. 1.)**

In progress.

—— Comment naissent les mythes. Les sources védiques du Petit Poucet. La légende hindoue du déluge.—Purūravas et Urvaçī. Avec ... un appendice sur l'état actuel de l'exégèse védique, *etc.* pp. xx. 249. *Paris, Lyon* [printed], 1897. 12°. **4503. dd. 13.**

Forms part of the Bibliothèque de Philosophie Contemporaine. *The wrapper bears the date* 1898.

—— Études Védiques et Post-védiques. I. L'énigme védique et les énigmes de l'hymne I, 164 du Rig-Véda. — Texte et traduction. II. La Katha-Upanisad.—Texte et traduction ... par Paul Regnaud. (Annales de l'Université de Lyon, fasc. xxxviii.) pp. viii. 217. *Paris, Lyon*, 1898. 8°. **Ac. 365. (fasc. xxxviii.)**

REVĀDHARA UPRETĪ. *See* Gumānī Panta. गुमानी नीति *etc.* [Gumānī-nīti. Edited with Hindi translation by Revādhara.] 1894. 8°. **14076. d. 51.**

REVAṆA, *Siddha, son of Vīranārādhya.* శైవసిద్ధాంతశిఖామణి [Śaivasiddhāntaśikhāmaṇi. An exposition of the creed of the Vīraśaiva sect, in 20 *parichchhedas.* With the *ṭīkā* of Vṛisheṣvara.] *See* Śivādvaitapañchaka. శివాద్వైతపంచక *etc.* [Śivādvaitapañchaka.] pp. 99-174. [1897.] 8°. **14048. cc. 8.(4.)**

RHYS DAVIDS (C. F.). *See* Davids (C. F. Rhys).

RHYS DAVIDS (T. W.). *See* Davids (T. W. Rhys).

RICE (Benjamin Lewis). *See* Bhaṭṭākalaṅka Deva. Bhaṭṭâkalaṅka Dêva's Karṇâṭaka Śabdânuśâsanam; with its vṛitti ... and vyâkhyâ ... Edited [with an account of Canarese literature and translation of each aphorism] by B. L. Rice. 1890. 4°. **14176. k. 7.**

—— *See* Mysore. Epigraphia Carnataca ... Published ... by B. L. Rice. 1886, *etc.* 4°. **14058. c. 8.**

—— *See* Nāga Varmā. Nâga Varmmâ's Karṇâṭaka Bhâshâ-Bhûshaṇa ... Edited, with an introduction [and translation of the aphorisms], by L. Rice. 1884. 8°. **14176. k. 9.**

RIDDING (Caroline Mary). *See* Bāṇa. The Kādambarī ... Translated ... by C. M. Ridding. 1896. 8°. [*Oriental Translation Fund.*] **14003. bb. (ser. 2, vol. 7.)**

ROER (HANS HEINRICH EDUARD). *See* UPANISHADS.—*Small Collections.* Selections ... translated into English [by H. Roer, *etc.*]. With notes, *etc.* 1895. 8°. [*Sacred Books of the East Described and Examined.*] **14010. cc. 9.(vol. 2.)**

ROHIṆĪKĀNTA VIDYĀBHŪSHAṆA. *See* RĀMACHANDRA NYĀYAVĀGĪṢA. কাব্যচন্দ্রিকা *etc.* [Kāvyachandrikā. With commentary. Edited by Rohiṇīkānta.] [1896.] 8°. **14053. c. 65.**

ROHIṆĪNANDANA SARKĀR. *See* KĀLIDĀSA.—*Collected Works.* মহাকবি কালিদাসের গ্রন্থাবলী *etc.* [Granthāvalī. Comprising Kumārasambhava, with commentary of Rohiṇīnandana on viii.-xvii., *etc.*] [1895.] 8°. **14070. d. 34.(vol. 2.)**

ROMESH CHUNDER DUTT. *See* RAMEṢACHANDRA DATTA.

ROOT (E. D.). Sakya Buddha: a versified, annotated narrative of his life and teachings; with an excursus, containing citations from the Dhammapada, or Buddhist Canon, *etc.* pp. viii. 171. *New York,* 1880. 8°. **4503. b. 35.**

ROUSE (WILLIAM HENRY DENHAM). *See* SUTTAPIṬAKA.—*Khuddakanikāya.* [*Jātaka.*] The Jātaka, *etc.* (Vol. ii., iv., translated by W. H. D. Rouse.) 1895, *etc.* 8°. **14098. dd. 8.(vol. 2, 4.)**

ROUSSEL (ALFRED). *See* PURĀṆAS.—*Bhāgavatapurāṇa.* Le Bhâgavata Purâṇa ... Traduit ... par E. Burnouf. (Tome 5, par M. Hauvette-Besnault et le R. P. Roussel.) 1840-1898. Fol. [*Collection Orientale.*] **756. l. 3.**

—— *See* PURĀṆAS.—*Bhāgavatapurāṇa.* Légendes Morales de l'Inde ... Traduites ... par A. Roussel. 1900-1901. 12°. **14065. b. 20.**

—— *See* VĀLMĪKI.—Rāmāyaṇa.—*Entire Text.* Le Râmâyana ... Traduit ... par A. Roussel, *etc.* 1903, *etc.* 4°. **14068. c. 15.**

—— De la Prière chez les Hindous. [Select devotional poems, translated from the Bṛihatstotraratnākara by A. Roussel.] 1889-1890. *See* PERIODICAL PUBLICATIONS.—*Louvain.* Le Muséon, *etc.* Tom. VIII, IX. 1881, *etc.* 8°. **P.P. 4453. (tom. 8, 9.)**

ROUSSEL (ALFRED) (*continued*). Cosmologie Hindoue d'après le Bhâgavata Purâna, *etc.* pp. 399, i. *Paris, Arcis-sur-Aube* [printed], 1898. 12°. **4503. dd. 10.**

ROZ-PĀṬHA. रोजपाठ [Roz-pāṭha. Daily prayers, hymns, and lections of the Svāmī-Nārāyaṇī sect, in Gujarati, including also the Ṣikshāpatrī of Sahajānanda with the Gujarati *ṭīkā* of Nityānanda.] pp. vi. 416. अमदावाद १९४४ [*Ahmadabad,* 1888.] 12°. **14144. c. 3.**

RUCHAKA. *See* RUYYAKA.

RUCHIRĀMA SAHNI, *of Government College, Lahore.* *See* DAYĀNANDA SARASVATĪ SVĀMĪ. The Niyoga Doctrine of the Arya Samaj ... With some remarks by Ruchi Ram Sahni. 1897. 12°. **14033. a. 33.(1.)**

RUDRADATTA ṢARMĀ. पुराण परीक्षा *etc.* [Purāṇaparīkshā. A proof that the Purāṇas are uncanonical and modern. In Hindi, with Sanskrit quotations.] pp. 66. दीनापुर १९५५ [*Dinapur,* 1898.] 12°. **14154. cc. 5.**

RUDRADHARA MAHOPĀDHYĀYA, *brother of Haladhara, son of Lakshmīdhara.* वर्षकृत्यम् । *etc.* [Varshakṛitya. A manual for the holy days of the year. Edited with supplements by Jagaddhara Ṣarmā Mīmāṃsaka of Gangauli.] pp. xiii. 228. काश्यां १८२५ [*Benares,* 1903.] 8°. **14033. bbb. 24.**

RUDRANĀRĀYAṆA SHAḌAṄGĪ. *See* NṚISIṂHA MIṢRA, *Vājapeyī.* ପାର୍ବଣ ଶ୍ରାଦ୍ଧକାରିକା *etc.* [Pārvaṇaṣrāddhakārikā. Compiled and edited by Rāmachandra and Rudranārāyaṇa.] 1900. 12°. **14028. b. 61.(6.)**

—— *See* RĀMACHANDRA CHATUSHPĀṬHĪ and RUDRANĀRĀYAṆA SHAḌAṄGĪ. ଶ୍ରାଦ୍ଧବ୍ୟବସ୍ଥା ଓ ପ୍ରୟୋଗ *etc.* [Ṣrāddhavyavasthā o Prayoga.] 1899. 12°. **14028. b. 61.(5.)**

RUDRA NYĀYAVĀCHASPATI, *son of Vidyāvilāsa.* *See* BHAVĀNANDA SIDDHĀNTAVĀGĪṢA. কারকচক্রম্ *etc.* [Kārakachakra. With the commentaries of Rudra called Raudrī, *etc.*] [1900.] 8°. **14090. bb. 15.(1.)**

RUDRĀSHṬĀDHYĀYĪ. *See* VEDAS.—Yajurveda.—*Vājasaneyisaṃhitā.*

RUDRA TARKAVĀGĪŚA. *See* RUDRA NYĀYA-VĀCHASPATI.

RUDRĪ. [For the Rudrī, Rudrajapa, or Śatarudriya of the Yajurveda according to both the Taittirīya and Vājasaneyī schools :] *See* VEDAS.—*Yajurveda.*

—— [For the Rudrī of the Sāmaveda :] *See* VEDAS.—*Sāmaveda.*

RŪPADEVA GOSVĀMĪ. *See* RŪPA GOSVĀMĪ.

RŪPA GOSVĀMĪ. চাটুপুষ্পাঞ্জলিঃ। (মুকুন্দমুক্তাবলী।) [Chāṭupushpāñjali and Mukundamuktāvalī. Two Vaishṇava devotional poems.] *See* VIHĀRILĀLA PĀIN. ভবসিন্ধু-তরণী। [Bhavasindhutaraṇī.] pp. 92-94, 123-129. [1902.] 8°. **14033. bbb. 17.**

—— ହଂସଦୂତ *etc.* [Haṃsadūta. A Vaishṇava poem on the legend of Rādhā and Kṛishṇa, in imitation of the Meghadūta. With metrical translation in Oriya by Kapileśvara Vidyābhūshaṇa.] pp. 33. *Cuttack,* 1894. 12°. **14070. b. 24.**

The present recension contains 100 *verses only; the last verse corresponds to v.* 99 *of the edition in Haeberlin's Anthology, which contains* 142 *in all.*

—— হংসদূতম্ *etc.* [Haṃsadūta. With Bengali translation.] pp. 46. কলিকাতা ১৩০৫ [*Calcutta,* 1898.] 12°. **14060. b. 17.**

Forms part iii. *of the series* Vaishṇava-Granthâvalī, *and contains* 101 *vv.*

—— লঘুভাগবতামৃত *etc.* [Laghu-bhāgavatāmṛita. An exposition of the Vaishṇava doctrine of Chaitanya as set forth in the Bhāgavata and cognate works, and consisting of two parts styled Kṛishṇāmṛita and Bhaktāmṛita. With a Sanskrit commentary by Baladeva Vidyābhūshaṇa, and Bengali translation and notes by Madanagopāla Gosvāmī. Edited by Balaichānd Gosvāmī and Atulakṛishṇa Gosvāmī.] pp. viii. xxxii. ii. 184, 97. কলিকাতা ১৩০৪ [*Calcutta,* 1897.] 8°. **14016. c. 58.**

—— श्रीलघुभागवतामृतम्। सटिप्पण-भाषानुवाद और तात्पर्य *etc.* [Laghu-bhāgavatāmṛita. With the Sanskrit commentary of Baladeva Vidyābhūshaṇa, and a Hindi translation and gloss by Baladevaprasāda Miśra. Edited by Jvālāprasāda Miśra.] pp. xvi. 272. बंबई १९५९ [*Bombay,* 1903.] 8°. **14076. d. 55.**

—— সটীক ও সানুবাদ শ্রীস্তবপুষ্পাঞ্জলিঃ *etc.* [Stavapushpāñjali. A series of Vaishṇava devotional lyrics of the Chaitanya sect, compiled from the Stavamālā of Rūpa Gosvāmī, as arranged by Jīva Gosvāmī, and from Raghunāthadāsa Gosvāmī's Stavāvali. With commentary and Bengali translation. Edited by Baṭudāsa Gosvāmī.] pp. ii. ii. 538. বৃন্দাবন ১৯৫৮ [*Brindaban,* 1902.] 8°. **14072. ccc. 34.**

—— উজ্জ্বলনীলমণিঃ *etc.* [Ujjvalanīlamaṇi. A work on the art of Poetics, especially as applied to the legend of Kṛishṇa. With the commentary called Lochanarochanī by Jīva Gosvāmī and that called Ānandachandrikā by Viśvanātha Chakravartī. Edited with a Bengali translation by Rāmanārāyaṇa Vidyāratna. Second edition.] pp. i. i. ii. x. 992. মুর্শিদাবাদ ১২৯৫ [*Murshidabad,* 1889.] 8°. **14053. d. 49.**

RŪṚMALL ŚARMĀ, *of Khetri.* अजितप्रकाशपंचांगम् *etc.* [Ajitaprakāśa-pañchāṅga. Compiled by Rūṛmall.] [1897.] *obl.* 8°. *See* EPHEMERIDES. **14096. b. 11.**

RUSSICK LAL GUPTA. *See* RASIKALĀLA GUPTA.

RUYYAKA, *Rājānaka, son of Tilaka.* The Alankârasarvasva of Râjânaka Ruyyaka. [A treatise on the art of poetry.] With the commentary [Alaṅkāravimarśini] of Jayaratha. Edited by . . . Paṇdit Durgâprasâd and Kâśînâth Pâṇdurang Parab. (अलंकारसर्वस्वम्।) pp. ii. 205, iv. i. 1893. *See* DURGĀPRASĀDA, *son of Vrajalāla,* and KĀŚĪNĀTHA PĀṆḌURAṄGA PARAB. Kâvyamâlâ. [No.] 35. 1886, *etc.* 8°. **14072. ccc. 12.(no. 35.)**

In Aufrecht's Catalogus Catalogorum *the commentary is assigned to Jayadratha, brother of Jayaratha.*

S. A. *See* A., (S.).

ŚABARASVĀMĪ, *Mīmāṃsaka.* [For editions of Kumārila's commentary upon Śabarasvāmī's Mīmāṃsāsūtrabhāshya :] *See* JAIMINI.—*Mīmāṃsāsūtra.*

ṢABARASVĀMĪ, *son of Dīptasvāmi.* *See* HARSHAVARDHANA, *son of Śrīvardhana.* ॥ अथ . . . लिङ्गानुशासनम् ॥ [Liṅgānuṣāsana. With extracts from Ṣabarasvāmī's commentary.] 1890. 8°. [*Die Indischen Genuslehren.*] **14093. d. 19.**

SABBATHIER (P.). *See* ĀṢVALĀYANA. Études de Liturgie Védique. L'Agnishṭoma, d'après le Çrauta-Sûtra d'Âçvalâyana [Chapter V], par M. P. Sabbathier. 1890. 8°. [*Journal Asiatique.*] **Ac. 8808. (Ser. viii., tom. 15.)**

ṢABDARŪPĀVALI. एकाक्षरकोशसमेता शब्दरूपावलिः [Ṣabdarūpāvali. Examples of the Sanskrit declensions and conjugations. Followed by the Ekāksharī-koṣa.] pp. 49. *Benares,* 1890. 12°. **14090. b. 38.(2.)**

ṢABDASAṄGRAHA. अथ शब्दसंग्रह ॥ [Ṣabdasaṅgraha. A Hindi glossary of Sanskrit words.] *See* KOṢAṢABDĀRTHASAṄGRAHA. कोष शब्दार्थसंग्रह *etc.* [Koṣaṣabdārthasaṅgraha.] pp. 293-368. [1899.] 8°. **14160. c. 40.**

SACHCHIDĀNANDA ARAṆYA, *Svāmī, of Kāpilāṣrama, Hugli.* *See* HARIHARĀNANDA. ॐ . . . सांख्यतत्त्वालोकः *etc.* [Sāṅkhyatattvāloka. Edited with Bengali translation, notes, and appendices by Sachchidānanda.] [1903.] 8°. **14049. b. 14.**

SACHCHIDĀNANDA YOGĪ. *See* ṢIVAṢAṄKARA PAṆḌYĀJĪ.

SADĀNANDA GAṆĪ. *See* SĀRASVATASŪTRA. सिद्धान्तचन्द्रिकोत्तरार्द्धः *etc.* [Sārasvatasūtra. With the Siddhāntachandrikā of Rāmāṣrama. Part II. With a Hindi commentary based on the Subodhinī of Sadānanda.] [1900.] 4°. **14092. c. 20.**

SADĀNANDA YOGĪNDRA. ॥ वेदान्तसार भाषाटीका । (Bedantsar. Rendered into hindi.) [Being the Vedāntasāra, with a Hindi commentary by Mādhavānanda Bhārati.] pp. 104, *lith.* *Benares,* 1889. 8°. **14154. e. 27.(3.)**

Described as a first edition on the wrapper, and as second edition on the title-page. The English title is from the wrapper.

—— वेदांतसार *etc.* [Vedāntasāra. With a Sanskrit commentary. Edited with a Marathi introduction and paraphrase of text and commentary by Veṅkaṭarāu Rāmachandra.] pp. ii. 30, 135. पुणे १८९१ [*Poona,* 1891.] 8°. **14048. c. 74.**

—— అద్వైతవేదాంతసారః [Advaitavedāntasāra, *i.e.* the Vedāntasāra. With Telugu translation by Ṣrīnivāsa Jagannātha Svāmī.] pp. 69. 1893-1894. *See* PERIODICAL PUBLICATIONS.—*Vizagapatam.* సకలవిద్యాభివర్ధని *etc.* [Sakalavidyābhivardhanī.] Vol. I, pt. ix.–Vol. II, pt. ix. 1892-1897. 12° & 8°. **14174. g. 38.(vol. 1, 2.)**

—— The Vedântasâra . . . together with the commentaries [, called respectively Subodhinī and Vidvanmanorañjanī,] of Nṛisiṁhasarasvatî and Râmatîrtha. Edited with notes and indices by Colonel G. A. Jacob. pp. xi. 215. *Bombay,* 1894. 8°. **14048. dd. 15.**

—— বেদান্তসারঃ। [Vedāntasāra. With Bengali translation.] [1895.] *See* RAMEṢACHANDRA DATTA. হিন্দুশাস্ত্র *etc.* [Hindu-ṣāstra.] Pt. v., pp. 153-205. [1895-1897.] 8°. **14085. c. 45.(vol. 1.)**

—— वेदान्तसार *etc.* [Vedāntasāra. With Gujarati paraphrase and commentary by Prasanna Bāi.] pp. iii. 112. અમદાવાદ ૧૮૯૯ [*Ahmadabad,* 1899.] 12°. **14048. a. 25.**

—— সটীক সানুবাদ বেদান্ত-সার *etc.* [Vedāntasāra. With the commentary Subodhinī of Nṛisiṁha Sarasvatī, and a Bengali translation by Kālīvara Vedāntavāgīṣa. Edited by Hīrālāl Ḍhol. Third edition.] pp. iv. 80, 53. কলিকাতা ১৩০৯ [*Calcutta,* 1903.] 12°. **14048. b. 41.**

Forms section 3 of the series Vidyākalpadruma, *and part 2 of the series* Ṣaṅkaradarṣana.

—— The Vedanta-sara: translated by Dr. J. R. Ballantyne . . . With an introduction, notes, and an examination of its contents. pp. iv. 129. 1898. *See* EAST. The Sacred Books of the East Described and Examined. Hindu Series. Vol. II, pt. 3. 1895, *etc.* 8°. **14010. cc. 9.(vol. 2.)**

—— Vedánt Sára of Sadánanda Swámi. Translated by Mr. W. Ward. *See* ṢAṄKARA ĀCHĀRYA.—*Two or More Works.* A Compendium of the Raja Yoga Philosophy, *etc.* pp. 83-102. 1901. 8°. **14048. bb. 53.**

SADĀṢIVA, called YUVARĀJA KAVI, *of Koṭiliṅgapuram, Malabar.* अथ . . . सादाशिवी° (मुररिपुस्तोत्रम् *etc.*) [Sādāṣivī or Sphuṭaṣlokaprakaraṇa, Muraripustotra, Hetvābhāsodāharaṇaṣlokāḥ, Sudhānandalaharīstotra, Tripuradahanacharita, *etc.* Miscellaneous short poems.] 1881-1882. *See* LAGHUKĀVYĀNI. लघुकाव्यानि . . . Miscellaneous Poetical Pieces, *etc.* pp. 1-25. 1888. 8°. [*Kāvyetihāsasaṅgraha*, Vol. 4-5.] **14072. d. 37.(vol. 4, 5.)**

—— The Rasasadana Bhâṇa of Yuvarâja. [A dramatic monologue.] Edited by Paṇdit Śivadatta and Kâśînâth Pâṇdurang Parab. (रससदनभाणः ।) pp. 65. 1893. *See* DURGĀPRASĀDA, *son of Vrajalāla*, and KĀṢĪNĀTHA PĀṆḌURAṄGA PARAB. Kâvyamâlâ. [No.] 37. 1886, *etc.* 8°. **14072. ccc. 12.(no. 37.)**

SADĀṢIVA ĀCHĀRYA DĪKSHITA, *son of Ṣiromaṇi.* *See* HEMĀDRI. The . . . Dánakhanda . . . Revised and enlarged by . . . Sadáshíva Áchárya, *etc.* 1902, *etc.* 8°. **14033. bbb. 16.**

—— आचार्यवंशावली । *etc.* [Āchāryavaṃṣāvalī. A history, in prose and verse, of the author's family in Nepal, and a biography of his father Ṣiromaṇi.] pp. ii. vii. iii. 79; 2 *plates.* काश्याम् १९५९ [*Benares*, 1903.] 8°. **14058. b. 50.**

SADĀṢIVABHAṬṬA SAKHAMBHAṬṬA VAIṢAMPĀYANA. *See* SADĀṢIVA SAKHĀRĀMA VAIṢAMPĀYANA.

SADĀṢIVA BHĪMARĀU BHĀGAVATA. *See* KĀLIDĀSA. — *Mālavikāgnimitra.* The Mâlavikâgnimitram . . . Edited with . . . English notes by Sadâsiv . . . Bhâgwat, *etc.* 1897. 8°. **14079. c. 66.**

SADĀṢIVA BODHENDRA. *See* SADĀṢIVA BRAHMENDRA.

SADĀṢIVA BRAHMENDRA, *disciple of Paramaṣivendra.* जगद्गुरुरत्नमालास्तवः । (बोधार्या°, गीति रत्नमाला, आत्मविद्याविलासः *etc.*) [Jagadgururatnamālāstava, or Gururatnamālikā. 87 stanzas on the pontiffs of the Ṣāradā monastery at Conjevaram, with the commentary Sushumā of Ātmabodhendra. Preceded by Bodhāryā, a Vedantic poem in 158 stanzas, also by Sadāṣiva, and followed by other religious-philosophic poems by him, viz. Gītiratnamālā (6 lyrics), Ātmavidyāvilāsa (64 stanzas), Ṣivamānasikapūjā (30 stanzas), and Saparyāparyāyastava (27 stanzas), with a biography of Sadāṣiva.] *See* SVĀMINĀTHA ṢRAUTĪ. ॥ वेदान्तपञ्चप्रकरणी *etc.* [Vedāntapañchaprakaraṇī.] [1895.] 8°. **14048. bb. 51.(5.)**

—— శ్రీ . . . అద్వైతతారావళి [Advaitatārāvali. A philosophical poem in 28 stanzas.] *See* LAKSHMĪDHARA. శ్రీ . . . అద్వైతమకరన్ద॥ [Advaitamakaranda.] pp. 22-24. 1891. 8°. **14048. bb. 39.(4.)**

—— Ātmavidyāvilāsa of Sadāsiva Brahma. [Edited with English translation by S. M. Naṭeṣa Ṣāstrī.] 1899. *See* PERIODICAL PUBLICATIONS.—*Madras.* The Brahmavâdin. Vol. IV, pp. 761-779. 1895, *etc.* 8°. **14048. g. 1.(vol. 4.)**

—— The Ātmavidyā Vilāsa . . . [Edited with a biography of Sadāṣiva and translation] by Pandit S. M. Natesa Sastriar. New edition. pp. viii. 8, 9. *Madras*, 1901. 8°. **14048. bb. 42.(4.)**

—— போதாயாப்யாஹம் வேதாந்தகுருகணம் *etc.* [Bodhāryā. In 160 stanzas. Followed by the Gaṅgādharāshṭaka, a hymn to Ṣiva, by Sudarṣana Āchārya. Edited by Ṣrīnivāsāchārya.] pp. 22. சிதம்பரம் [*Chidambaram*,] 1888. 12°. **14048. b. 38.(2.)**

The Bodhāryā is here ascribed to Ṣaṅkara.

—— புண்யஸ்லோகமஞ்சரி *etc.* [Puṇyaṣlokamañjarī. Epitaphs on the pontiffs of the Kāmakoṭi *pīṭha* founded by Ṣaṅkara at Conjevaram, from Ṣaṅkara to Aruṇagiri Chandrachūḍendra; with biographical notes. Followed by a supplement to the same, by Ātmabodhendra; Mahādevendra Sarasvatī's Jagadguruparamparāstuti and Rāma Brahmendra's Jagadguruparamparānāmamālā, commemorating the pontifical successors of Ṣaṅkara; and the Āmnāyavistara from the Maṭhāmnāyasetu, ascribed to Ṣaṅkara, on clerical discipline.] pp. 38. கும்பகோணம் ॥ கலிகள [*Kumbakonam*, 1895.] 8°. **14048. bb. 42.(2.)**

The Puṇyaṣlokamañjarī is wrongly ascribed on the title-page to Ṣaṅkara.

SADĀṢIVA DĪKSHITA, *of Alsur.* ఆగమికశివపూజా-విధి *etc.* [Āgamikaṣivapūjāvidhi. A Ṣaiva liturgy based on the Ṣaiva Āgamas. Followed by the Āgamasāratriṣatī Nāmāvalī, 300 names of Ṣiva; Devyashṭottaraṣatanāmāvalī, 108 names of Devī; a mystic ritual based on the Pādmatantra and Kāraṇāgama; Ṣivadarṣanapaddhati; Aparādhastotra and Devīpañcharatnast.°, ascribed to Ṣaṅkara; and the Subrahmaṇyastotra of Gopāla Krishṇa. Compiled by Sadāṣiva, and edited by Viṣveṣvara Ṣāstrī and Lokanātha Kavi.] pp. iii. ii. 120. బెంగళూరు ౧౮౯౩ [*Bangalore*, 1893.] 12°. **14028. b. 85.**

SADĀṢIVA MIṢRA. ଚନ୍ଦନଚମ୍ପୂ କାବ୍ୟଂ [Chandana-champū. A composition in prose and verse describing the festival called Chandanayātrā.] pp. 22. *Cuttack*, 1900. 12°. **14079. a. 8.(4.)**

SADĀṢIVA MIṢRA, *of Puri. See* GADĀDHARA RĀJAGURU. Gadādhara Paddhatau Kālasāra ... Edited by Sadāçiva Miçra of Puri. 1900, *etc.* 8°. [*Bibliotheca Indica.*] **14002. a. (vol. 147.)**

SADĀṢIVA SAKHĀRĀMA VAIṢAMPĀYANA. अथ सदाशिव प्रसाद प्रारंभः [Sadāṣivaprasāda. A Ṣaiva liturgy.] ff. ii. i. iii. 93. [*Poona*, 1900.] *obl.* 12°. **14033. a. 40.**

SADĀṢIVA ṢAṄKARA ṢĀSTRĪ. *See* PURĀṆAS.—*Skandapurāṇa.* अर्बुदमाहात्म्यसारः *etc.* [Arbuda-māhātmyasāra. Abridged from the Skandapurāṇa by Sadāṣiva.] [1894.] 8°. **14016. c. 42.(3.)**

SADĀṢIVA ṢARMĀ, *Pandit. See* PURĀṆAS.—*Brahmapurāṇa.* ॥ कर्मविपाक संहिता *etc.* [Karma-vipākasaṃhitā. With Nepali translation by Sadāṣiva.] [1902.] 8°. **14053. dd. 3.**

SADĀSUKHA, *Terah-panthī, of Jaipur. See* SAMANTABHADRA SVĀMĪ. श्रीरत्नकरंडश्रावकाचार [Ratna-karaṇḍa-ṣrāvakāchāra. With Hindi translation and commentary by Sadāsukha.] [1897.] *obl.* 4°. **14100. e. 7.**

—— *See* UMĀSVĀTI. ॥ अथ तत्वार्थसूत्र° [Tattvārtha-sūtra. With Hindi commentary by Sadāsukha.] [1896.] *obl.* 8°. **14100. d. 9.**

SADĀSUKHA DĀSA. *See* SADĀSUKHA, *Terah-panthī.*

SADĀSUKHA LĀLA. *See* KOṢARATNĀKARA. कोशरत्नाकर *etc.* [Koṣaratnākara. Edited by Sadāsukha Lāla.] [1876.] 8°. **14160. c. 37.**

SADĀTEJA, *disciple of Saddhammañāṇa.* (ဝစ္စဝါ-စကသဋီကာ) [Vachchavāchaka. A Pali metrical tract on orthoepy, in 59 stanzas. With a *ṭīkā* or *vaṇṇanā* by Saddhammanandi.] *See* SADDHAMMASIRI. သဒ္ဒတ္ထဘေဒစိန္တာ *etc.* [Saddatthabheda-chintā, *etc.*] pp. 129-164. [1897.] 8°. **14098. ccc. 17.(2.)**

—— ဝစ္စဝါစကပါဠိ။ [Vachchavāchaka.] *See* SADDĀ-NGAY. သဒ္ဒါငယ် *etc.* [Saddā-ngay.] pp. 99-103. [1898.] 8°. **14098. ccc. 23.(1.)**

—— —— pp. 100-104. [1899.] 8°. **14098. ccc. 24.(1.)**

—— ဝစ္စဝါဋီကာ *etc.* [Vachchavāchaka. With Burmese commentary by Tipiṭakālaṅkāra Siriddhaja.] [1898.] *See* SADDĀ-NGAY. သဒ္ဒါငယ် *etc.* [Saddā-ngay.] Vol. i., pp. 152-165. [1898-1900.] 8°. **14098. ccc. 22.**

SADDABINDU. သဒ္ဒဗိန္ဒုပါဠိ။ [Saddabindu. A Pali tract summarising Kachchāyana's grammar.] *See* SADDĀ-NGAY. သဒ္ဒါငယ် *etc.* [Saddā-ngay.] pp. 47-48. [1898.] 8°. **14098. ccc. 23.(1.)**

Ascribed in the Gandhavaṃsa and Sāsanavaṃsa to Kyaswā (king of Pagan, who succeeded in 1234 *A.D.).*

—— —— pp. 47-48. [1899.] 8°. **14098. ccc. 24.(1.)**

—— သဒ္ဒဗိန္ဒု *etc.* [Saddabindu. With Burmese translation.] [1898.] *See* SADDĀ-NGAY. သဒ္ဒါငယ် *etc.* [Saddā-ngay.] Vol. iii., pp. 140-149. [1898-1900.] 8°. **14098. ccc. 22.**

SADDĀ-NGAY. သဒ္ဒါငယ် *etc.* [Saddā-ngay. A collection of Pali grammatical works based on Kachchāyana, with Burmese commentaries. Vol. i., comprising (1) Saddhammasiri's Saddattha-bhedachintā, on orthoepy, (2) Dhammānanda's Kachchāyanasāra, (3) Sadāteja's Vachchavāchaka, on orthoepy, (4) Saddhammañāṇa's Vibhattyattha, on inflexion. Vol. ii., comprising (5) Saṅgharakkhita's Sambandhachintā, on syntactical relation, (6) Dhammānanda's Kachchāyanabheda, on grammatical terminology, (7) Ariyavaṃsa's Ganthābharaṇa, on particles, *etc.* Vol. iii., comprising

(8) Nāgita's Saddasāratthajālinī, on the principles of grammar and stylistic, (9) Saddhammaguru's Saddavutti, on the classification of nouns, (10) Saddabindu, a summary of Kachchāyana. Vol. iv., comprising (11) Dhammasenāpati's Kārikā, (12) Vijitāvī's Vāchakopadesa. Vol. v., comprising (13) a Burmese *nissaya* on Saddhammakitti's Ekakkharakosa, a vocabulary of monosyllabic roots, (14) Jambuddhaja's Rūpabhedappakāsanī, a tract on the discrimination between similar terms.] 5 vols. ရန်ကုန် ၁၂၆၀ – ၁၂၆၂ [*Rangoon*, 1898-1900.] 8°. **14098. ccc. 22.**

—— သဒ္ဒါငယ် *etc.* [Saddā-ngay. Containing the Saddatthabhedachintā, Kachchāyanasāra, Ekakkharakosa, Saddavutti, Saddabindu, Saddasāratthajālinī, Sambandhachintā, Vibhattyattha, Vachchavāchaka, and Ganthābharaṇa, the Ganthaṭṭhi of Maṅgala Thera, and the Vāchakopadesa, Kachchāyanabheda, and Kārikā, in the Pali text only.] pp. ii. 191. ရန်ကုန် ၁၂၆၀ [*Rangoon*, 1898.] 8°. **14098. ccc. 23.(1.)**

—— [Second edition.] pp. ii. 191. ရန်ကုန် ၁၂၆၁ [*Rangoon*, 1899.] 8°. **14098. ccc. 24.(1.)**

SADDHAMMAGURU, *Mahāthera*. သဒ္ဒဝုတ္တိပါဌ်။ [Saddavutti. A Pali tract on the systems of nouns.] *See* SADDĀ-NGAY. သဒ္ဒါငယ် *etc.* [Saddā-ngay.] pp. 40-46. [1898.] 8°. **14098. ccc. 23.(1.)**

—— —— pp. 40-46. [1899.] 8°. **14098. ccc. 24.(1.)**

—— သဒ္ဒဝုတ္တိ *etc.* [Saddavutti. With Burmese translation.] [1898.] *See* SADDĀ-NGAY. သဒ္ဒါငယ် *etc.* [Saddā-ngay.] Vol. iii., pp. 111-139. [1898-1900.] 8°. **14098. ccc. 22.**

SADDHAMMAKITTI, *Mahāthera*. ဧကက္ခရကောသပါဌ်။ [Ekakkharakosa. A Pali dictionary of monosyllabic roots, based upon Sanskrit lexica.] *See* SADDĀ-NGAY. သဒ္ဒါငယ် *etc.* [Saddā-ngay.] pp. 31-39. [1898.] 8°. **14098. ccc. 23.(1.)**

—— —— pp. 31-39. [1899.] 8°. **14098. ccc. 24.(1.)**

SADDHAMMAKITTI, *Mahāthera* (*continued*). ဧကက္ခရကောသနိဿျ။ [Ekakkharakosa. With a Burmese *nissaya* by a Hsaya of the Weyanbongyaw Kyaung, Ratanāsikha, Konbaung.] [1900.] *See* SADDĀ-NGAY. သဒ္ဒါငယ် *etc.* [Saddā-ngay.] Vol. v., pp. 1-139. [1898-1900.] 8°. **14098. ccc. 22.**

SADDHAMMĀLAṄKĀRA. *See* KACHCHĀYANA. — *Chūlanirutti.* අභිනව චූලනිරුත්ති *etc.* [Abhinavachūlanirutti. A new recension of the Chūlanirutti, compiled by Saddhammālaṅkāra.] 1896. 12°. **14098. a. 7.(3.)**

SADDHAMMAÑĀṆA. ဝိဘတျတ္ထပါဌ်။ [Vibhattyattha. A Pali tract on inflexion.] *See* SADDĀ-NGAY. သဒ္ဒါငယ် *etc.* [Saddā-ngay.] pp. 96-98. [1898.] 8°. **14098. ccc. 23.(1.)**

—— —— pp. 97-99. [1899.] 8°. **14098. ccc. 23.(1.)**

—— ဝိဘတျတ္ထ *etc.* [Vibhattyattha. With Burmese translation by Tipiṭakālaṅkāra Siriddhaja.] [1898.] *See* SADDĀ-NGAY. သဒ္ဒါငယ် *etc.* [Saddā-ngay.] Vol. i., pp. 166-180. [1898-1900.] 8°. **14098. ccc. 22.**

SADDHAMMANANDI THERA, *of the Khemāvatāra Vihāra.* *See* SADĀTEJA. (ဝစ္စဝါစကသင်္ဂဟ) [Vachchavāchaka. With a *ṭīkā* or *vaṇṇanā* by Saddhammanandi.] [1897.] 8°. [*Saddatthabheda-chintā.*] **14098. ccc. 17.(2.)**

SADDHAMMASIRI. သဒ္ဒတ္ထဘေဒစိန္တာ *etc.* [Saddatthabhedachintā. A Pali tract on orthoepy, with a *dīpanī* or gloss by a Mahāthera of the Shwe-gudi Kyaung. Followed by the Vachchavāchaka of Sadāteja, with *ṭīkā* of Saddhammanandi; the Ganthābharaṇa of Ariyavaṃsa, with *ṭīkā* of Jāgara; the Chhandomañjarī of Visuddhāchāra, with Burmese *nissaya* and *alaṅkāra*; a Burmese *nissaya* on the Saddatthabhedachintā; and the Nām-gôṇ-thit, a Burmese work on the classes of nouns.] pp. 381, iv. ပက္ကလေး ၁၂၅၉ [*Mandalay*, 1897.] 8°. **14098. ccc. 17.(2.)**

The colophon asserts that the gloss to the Saddatthabhedachintā was written in Sakkaraj 724 = A.D. 1362.

SADDHAMMASIRI (*continued*). သဒ္ဒတ္ထဘေဒစိန္တာပါဠိ॥ [Saddatthabhedachintā.] *See* SADDĀ-NGAY. သဒ္ဒါငယ် *etc.* [Saddā-ngay.] pp. 1-25. [1898.] 8°. **14098. ccc. 23.(1.)**

—— —— pp. 1-25. [1899.] 8°. **14098. ccc. 24.(1.)**

—— သဒ္ဒတ္ထဘေဒစိန္တာ *etc.* [Saddatthabheda-chintā. With the Burmese commentary of Tipiṭa-kālaṅkāra Siriddhaja.] [1898.] *See* SADDĀ-NGAY. သဒ္ဒါငယ် *etc.* [Sadda-ngay.] Vol. i., pp. 1-117. [1898-1900.] 8°. **14098. ccc. 22.**

—— သဒ္ဒတ္ထဘေဒစိန္တာ *etc.* [Saddatthabheda-chintā. Followed by the Kachchāyanasāra, Vutto-daya, and Abhidhānappadīpikā.] pp. 118, viii. မန္တလေး [*Mandalay,*] 1903. 8°. **14099. bb. 2.**

SADDHĀNANDA, *of Kosgoda.* *See* SUTTAPIṬAKA.—*Khuddakanikāya.* [*Petavatthu.*] පේතවත්ථු *etc.* [Petavatthu. With commentary by Paññāsāra. Edited by Saddhānanda.] 1893-1896. 8°. **14098. c. 63.(2.)**

SĀDHANA. Deux Collections Sanscrites et Tibétaines de Sādhanas. [By F. W. Thomas.] 1903. *See* PERIODICAL PUBLICATIONS. — *Louvain.* Le Muséon, *etc.* Nouvelle Série. Vol. IV, pp. 1-42. 1881, *etc.* 8°. **P.P. 4453. (nouvelle sér., vol. 4.)**

SĀDHUNARADHAMMA-SĀ-TAN. သာဓုနရဓမ္မစာတန်း [Sādhunaradhamma-sā-tan. A lectionary of divers Pali *suttas* and other selections from the canonical writings with Burmese commentaries. Edited by Ū Kesinda.] pp. 99. ရန်ကုန် ၁၂၅၉ [*Rangoon,* 1897.] 8°. **14098. ccc. 26.(4.)**

SĀGARA, *Ū, of Pattamya-cheti.* *See* VINAYA-PIṬAKA. [*Mahāvagga.*] အာဒိတ္တပရိယာယသုတ် *etc.* [Ādittapariyāyasutta. With Burmese translation by Sāgara. Followed by the Dvattiṃsā-kāra-kammaṭṭhāna, compiled by Sāgara.] 1898. 8°. **14098. ccc. 26.(6.)**

SĀGARADDHAJA, *of Weyan-hbôn-thā Kyaung,* known as SINDE HSAYA. *See* VINAYAPIṬAKA. ဝိနည်း॥ *etc.* [Vinayapiṭaka. Vol. i., ii., the Mahāvagga, with interpretation by Sāgaraddhaja.] 1903-1904. 8°. **14099. aa. 1, 2.**

SAHAJĀNANDA SVĀMĪ, also called SVĀMĪ NĀRĀYAṆA. *See* PURĀṆAS.—*Bhāgavatapurāṇa.* ॥ श्रीभागवतं *etc.* [Bhāgavatapurāṇa. With commentary expounding the doctrines of the Svāminārāyaṇī sect, biography of Sahajānanda, *etc.*] [1897.] *obl.* Fol. **14018. cc. 2.**

—— शिक्षापत्री. [Ṣikshāpatrī. A poem on Vaishṇava ethics and religion, in 212 stanzas. With Gujarati *ṭīkā* by Nityānanda Muni.] *See* ROZ-PĀṬHA. रोजपाठ [Roz-pāṭha.] pp. 275-386. [1888.] 12°. **14144. c. 3.**

—— *See* DAYĀNANDA SARASVATĪ SVĀMĪ. शिक्षापत्रीध्वान्तनिवारणः *etc.* [Ṣikshāpattrīdhvāntanivāraṇa. A polemic against Sahajānanda.] [1900.] 12°. **14028. c. 25.(2.)**

SAHASRANĀMASTABAKA. శ్రీసహస్రనామస్తబకమ్. [Sahasranāmastabaka. A series of Vaishṇava hymns containing each 1000 names of a deity—viz., the Vishṇusahasranāma from the Mahābhārata; Lakshmīnṛisiṃhas°. from Nṛisiṃhapurāṇa; Rāmas°. from Ṣivapurāṇa; Gopālas°. from Sammohanatantra; Hayagrīvas°.; Kṛishṇas°. from Vishṇudharmottara; and Lakshmīs°. from Sanatkumārasaṃhitā; together with the Mukundamālā, Gopikāgītā, Stotraratna, and other lists of names, *mantras,* and hymns.] pp. iii. 420. చెన్నపురాన్గమ్ ౧౯౦౨ [*Madras,* 1902.] *obl.* 16°. **14033. a. 52.**

SĀHIBAHĀDURĀṢRITA. *See* MAHEṢA ṢARMĀ, *of Srinagar.*

ṢAILAJĀNANDA OJHĀ. *Begin.* भगवान-गुणविभूषण-राजभक्तिपरायण-भारतजनगण-समीपे सादरमावेदनम् । [A short poem on the Jubilee of Queen Victoria's reign, with English and Bengali translations.] pp. 3. [*Calcutta?* 1887?] 8°. **14076. cc. 2.(1.)**

SAINT JOHN (RICHARD FLEMING SAINT ANDREW). *See* SUTTAPIṬAKA. — *Khuddakanikāya.* [*Jātaka.*] Bhūridatta Jātaka. [Translated from the Burmese.] By R. . . . St. John. 1892. 8°. [*Journal of the Royal Asiatic Society.*] **Ac. 8820/3 & 2098. a, b.**

ṢĀKAṬĀYANA. प्रक्रियासंग्रहसहितं शाकटायनव्याकरणम्. The Grammar of Śākaṭāyana, with the Prakriyā-saṅgraha commentary of Abhayacandrasūri. Published for the first time by Gustav Oppert. Vol. i. pp. xiv. clx. 387. *Madras*, 1892. 8°. **14093. b. 30.**

In progress? This volume contains the Sūtrapāṭha.

—— ॥ अथ ... लिङ्गानुशासनम् ॥ [Liṅgānuṣāsana. With German translation and extracts from Yakshavarmā's commentary Chintāmaṇi, *etc.*] *See* FRANKE (R. O.). Die Indischen Genuslehren, *etc.* pp. 65-82. 1890. 8°. **14093. d. 19.**

The commentator styles himself in the colophon of MSS. Yakshavarmā; *but in the introduction to the commentary upon Bhaṭṭākalaṅka's Karṇāṭakaṣabdānuṣāsana he is called* Gaṅgeṣa.

ṢAKTIDHARA SUKULA, *son of Balabhadra. See* SĀRASVATASŪTRA. सारस्वत *etc.* [Sārasvatavyākaraṇa. With Hindi commentary by Umādatta and Ṣaktidhara.] [1891.] 8°. **14090. bb. 6.**

—— *See* SĀRASVATASŪTRA. सिद्धान्तचन्द्रिकोत्तरार्द्धः *etc.* [Sārasvatasūtra. With the Siddhāntachandrikā. Edited by Ṣaktidhara.] [1900.] 4°. **14092. c. 20.**

—— *See* VĀLMĪKI.—Rāmāyaṇa.—*Entire Text.* ॥ अथ ... रामायणम् ॥ [Rāmāyaṇa. Preceded by an index and Hindi preface by Ṣaktidhara.] [1902.] Fol. **14068. d. 11.**

—— *See* VIṢVAKARMĀ. विश्वकर्मा प्रकाश शास्त्रम् *etc.* [Viṣvakarmaprakāṣa. With Hindi translation by Ṣaktidhara.] [1896.] 8°. **14053. ccc. 7.**

ṢĀLAGRĀMA MIṢRA, *son of Anantarāma, of Ajmere. See* GOTAMA. न्यायतत्वबोधिनी ... Nyayatatwa Bodhini [, *i.e.* the Nyāyasūtra with a Hindi commentary founded on that of Vātsyāyana] by Misra Shaligram Shastree. [1894.] 8°. **14048. dd. 12.(3.)**

ṢĀLAGRĀMA ṢUKLA, *son of Nārāyaṇadāsa.* अन्त्येष्टिकर्मसमुच्चय [Antyeshṭikarmasamuchchaya. A digest of rules for funeral rites and *ṣrāddhas*, in 11 *prakaraṇas*.] 8 pts., *lith.* मुरादाबाद १८९५ [*Moradabad*, 1895.] *obl.* 8°. **14028. dd. 1.**

The title-page, as well as the colophon of the 11*th chapter, ascribes the authorship to Nārāyaṇadāsa, son of Ṣālagrāma.*

ṢĀLAGRĀMA VAIṢYA, *of Moradabad. See* KĀMAKAUTŪHALA. कामकौतूहल *etc.* [Kāmakautūhala. With Hindi translation by Ṣālagrāma.] [1902.] 8°. **14043. cc. 19.(2.)**

—— *See* RĀJAVALLABHA. राजवल्लभनिघण्टुः *etc.* [Rājavallabhanighaṇṭu. Edited with a Hindi translation by Ṣālagrāma.] [1896.] 8°. **14043. cc. 7.**

—— *See* TRIMALLA BHAṬṬA, *son of Vallabha.* द्रव्यगुणशतक *etc.* [Dravyaguṇaṣataka. With Hindi translation by Ṣālagrāma.] [1897.] 12°. **14043. b. 13.**

—— *See* VOPADEVA, *son of Keṣava.* वोपदेववैद्यकशतक *etc.* [Vopadeva-vaidyakaṣataka. With Hindi translation by Ṣālagrāma.] [1896.] 8°. **14043. c. 42.(2.)**

ṢĀLIGRĀMA. *See* ṢĀLAGRĀMA.

ŚĀLIḤ MUḤAMMAD, *Sharīf. See* NIṢCHALA DĀSA. ॥ श्रीविचारसागर *etc.* [Vichārasāgara, *etc.* Edited by Śāliḥ Muḥammad.] [1900.] 8°. **14154. ff. 1.**

—— *See* SĀYAṆA ĀCHĀRYA.—*Works on Philosophy, etc.* ॥ श्रीपंचदशी *etc.* [Pañchadaṣī. With commentary. Edited by Śāliḥ Muḥammad.] [1897.] 8°. **14048. e. 25.**

SĀMA BHAGAVĀN. *See* ṢYĀMA BHAGAVĀN, *Sādhu.*

SAMĀDDĀR (R. N.). Mahatma Dayananda Sarasvati. [A biography based in part on Dayānanda's autobiography.] pp. iii. 44. *Calcutta*, [1898.] 16°. **14058. a. 5.(3.)**

SAMĀDHIRĀJASŪTRA. समाधिराजसूत्रम् । Samādhirāja-sūtram. [A North-Buddhist sacred text, in prose and verse.] For the first time edited by Rai Çarat Chandra Dās . . . and Pandit Harimohan Vidyābhūshaṇ. 1896, *etc.* *See* ACADEMIES, *etc.*—Calcutta.—*Buddhist Text Society of India.* Buddhist Texts, *etc.* 1894, *etc.* 8°. **14004. c. (vol. 2, no. 2.)**

In progress?

SAMĀDHIṢATAKA. श्रीप्रभेन्दुविरचितं श्रीसमाधिशतकं *etc.* (The Samâdhi-śataka of Prabhendu, [a Jain philosophical poem in 105 stanzas,] with commentary by Prabhâchandra[, in Sanskrit. Followed by the Samâdhiṣataka] translated into English, with notes, by Manilal N. Dvivedi.) pp. 105, ii. ii. 26, i. *Ahmedabad*, 1895. 12°. **14048. b. 29.**

Prabhendu, the alleged author, is apparently but a ghost of the commentator Prabhāchandra. The latter calls our author Pūjyapāda, *and this suggests that he is no other than Devanandi, who composed a still surviving Samādhiṣataka. A verse at the end of the commentary calls him also* Prabhendu-prabhu, *but perhaps is spurious. A Prabhāchandra, disciple of Ratnakīrti, is known to have written a commentary on a* ṣāstra *of Pūjyapāda, which is probably the present work (see Peterson, 2nd Report, p. 165; 4th Report, p.* lxxxi.*; 5th Report, p.* 317*; 6th Report, p.* xii.*).*

—— ॥ अथ समाधि शतक ॥ [Samādhiṣataka. With Gujarati translation.] *See* HEMAṢAṄKARA LAKSHMĪṢAṄKARA VARDHAMĀNKAR. प्रकरण माला *etc.* [Prakaraṇamālā.] pp. 192-216. [1901.] 8°. **14100. d. 11.**

SAMANTABHADRA. ॥ आर्यसमन्तभद्रचर्याप्रणिधानराज-नामविहरतिस्म ॥ ༄། །ཨཱརྱ་ས་མ་ནྟ་བྷ་དྲ་ཙརྻཱ་པྲ་ཎི་དྷཱ་ན་རཱ་ཛ་ནཱ་མ་བི་ཧ་ར་ཏི་སྨ། ། ༄། །འཕགས་པ་བཟང་པོ་སྤྱོད་པའི་སྨོན་ལམ་གྱི་རྒྱལ་པོ་ཞེས་བྱ་བ་བཞུགས་སོ། ། [Ārya-samantabhadra-charyā-praṇidhānarāja, in Tibetan 'Phags pa bzang po spyod pai smon lam gyi rgyal po. Devotions to the Bodhisattva Samantabhadra, in Sanskrit and Tibetan.] ff. 19. [*Peking?*] *n.d.* *obl.* Fol. **Tib. 62.(2.)**

The Sanskrit text is given in both Lantsa and Tibetan script.

SAMANTABHADRA SVĀMĪ. रत्नकरंडश्रावकाचार अथवा . . . रत्नकरंड उपासकाध्ययन *etc.* [Ratnakaraṇḍaṣrāvakāchāra, or Ratnakaraṇḍa-upāsakādhyayana. A poem of the Digambara Jain school, in 150 stanzas, on the duties of layman. Edited with Marathi and Hindi translations by Hīrāchand Nemchand.] pp. xvi. 176. मुंबईत १८९५ [*Bombay*, 1895.] 16°. **14028. b. 74.**

The editor states that this work was written in Samvat 125.

—— श्रीरत्नकरंड श्रावकाचार [Ratnakaraṇḍa-ṣrāvakāchāra. With a Hindi translation and copious commentary by Sadāsukha of Jaipur.] ff. 376. देवबन्द कानपुर १८९७ [*Deoband, Cawnpore* printed, 1897.] *obl.* 4°. **14100. e. 7.**

—— रत्नकरण्डश्रावकाचार *etc.* [Ratnakaraṇḍa-ṣrāvakāchāra. Edited with a Sanskrit analysis and Hindi prose translation and notes by Pannālāl of Sujangarh.] pp. 58. नागपुर १८९८ [*Nagpur*, 1898.] 12°. **14028. b. 84.(1.)**

SAMANTABHADRA SVĀMĪ (*continued*).

—— *See* PRABHĀCHANDRA ĀCHĀRYA. जैनकथा-द्वाविंशतिः [Jainakathādvāvimṣati. Twenty-two stories, extracted from Prabhāchandra's commentary on Samantabhadra's Ratnakaraṇḍa.] [1897.] 12°. **14100. a. 16.**

SAMANTAPĀSĀDIKA THERA. ဝစနတ္ထ–ဇော–တိက–ဋီကာ [Vachanatthajotika-ṭīkā. A commentary on the Vuttodaya.] *See* SAṄGHARAKKHITA. ဝုတ္တောဒယသန်းကျမ်း *etc.* [Vuttodaya.] pp. 8-50. [1899.] 8°. **14098. ccc. 27.(3.)**

SAMARASEKHARA (W. A.). *See* SUTTAPIṬAKA.—*Entire Text.* Buddhist Pali Texts . . . Vol. 1 (2, *etc.*) . . . Sinhalese translation by W. A. Samarasekera. [1903, *etc.*] 8°. **14099. bbb. 1.**

SAMATHAVIPASSANĀ. သမထဝိပဿနာသညာ ၇ပါး ကမ္မဋ္ဌာန်း [Samathavipassanāsaññā-satta-kammaṭṭhāna. A Pali anthology bearing upon the religious exercises producing the perceptions leading to spiritual quietude and insight, compiled from the Piṭakas, *etc.* With Burmese translations.] pp. 64. *Moulmein*, 1877. 16°. **14098. a. 34.**

SĀMĀYIKASŪTRA. [For this ritual as included in that of *paḍikammaṇa*:] *See* PRATIKRAMAṆASŪTRA.

—— अथ सामायक सूत्र. अर्थ सहित. [Sāmāyikasūtra. With the Chaityavandana, Gujarati translations, rubrics, *etc.*] *See* KEṢAVALĀLA ṢIVARĀMA. जैनबालज्ञानसुबोध *etc.* [Jaina-bālajñānasubodha.] [1888.] 12°. **14144. f. 30.(2.)**

—— सामायक सूत्र. अर्थ सहित. [Sāmāyikasūtra. With Gujarati translation and rubrics.] *See* JAINAKĀVYAPRAKĀṢA. જૈનકાવ્યપ્રકાશ *etc.* [Jainakāvyaprakāṣa.] pp. 1-32. [1894.] 16°. **14144. c. 9.**

—— —— *See* JAINAKĀVYAPRAKĀṢA. जैन काव्यप्रकाश *etc.* [Jainakāvyaprakāṣa.] pp. 1-32. [1894.] 16°. **14144. c. 10.**

—— સામાયકસૂત્ર *etc.* [Sāmāyikasūtra. With Gujarati translations, notes, prayers, and other matter bearing on the Jain religion.] pp. viii.

160. અમદાવાદ ૧૯૦૦ [*Ahmadabad,* 1900.] 16°. **14100. a. 25.**

The Prakrit is printed in the Gujarati script.

SĀMBAṢIVA GHANAPĀṬHĪ, *Mañjakuḍi.* *See* BRĀHMAṆAS.—*Taittirīyabrāhmaṇa.* தைத்திரீய-யப்ராஹ்மணே ப்ரபாடகஃ *etc.* [Taittirīyabrāhmaṇa. Edited by Vaidyanātha and Sāmbaṣiva.] 1900, *etc.* 8°. **14007. cc. 30.**

ṢAMBHU MIṢRA. क्रमकारिकाशिक्षा ॥ [Kramakārikāṣikshā. A tract of the Mādhyandina school in 93 stanzas, on the rules of sequence for the recitation of the White Yajurveda.] *See* YUGALAKIṢORA VYĀSA PĀṬHAKA. श्रीमद्याज्ञवल्क्यादि . . . शिक्षासङ्ग्रहः . . . A collection of Śikshás, *etc.* pp. 369-377. 1893. 8°. **14093. b. 31.**

ṢAMBHURAHASYA. శ్రీశంభురహస్యాఖ్యపురాణాంతర్గతం కవికావ్యాదిప్రశంసాపరమధ్యాయచతుష్టయం *etc.* [Kavikāvyādipraṣaṃsā, four *adhyāyas* from the so-called Ṣambhurahasya-purāṇa in exposition of poetry and commendation of Prakrit, *etc.* Followed by the Prākṛitaṣabdapradīpikā, Trivikrama's aphorisms of Prakrit grammar with the commentary of Kāukānphallī Nṛisiṃha Ṣāstrī, and the Rāghavayādavīya, an artificial poem by Veṅkaṭārya Yajvā, with the author's commentary. Edited by Pandit Tātāchārya.] pp. 84, 42. మహీశూరు॥ ౧౮౯౦ [*Mysore,* 1890.] 8°. **14053. ccc. 31.**

A sheet (pp. 5-12 of the last work) is missing.

SAMRÂḌ JAGANNÂTHA. *See* JAGANNĀTHA, *Samrāṭ.*

SĀMUDRIKA. သာမုဒ္ဒိကလက္ခဏာ *etc.* [Sāmudrikalakkhaṇa. A Pali version of the Sāmudrika, with Burmese version by Y̲an Hnin.] *See* HITOPADEṢA. ဟိတောပဒေသ *etc.* [Hitopadeṣa.] pp. 29-59. [1882.] 8°. **14098. ccc. 19.(1.)**

A version that is apparently abridged and considerably diverges from the Ceylon manual, as well as from the Northern version.

—— বৃহৎসামুদ্রিক *etc.* [Sāmudrika, or Bṛihat-s°. Enlarged from several sources and edited with Bengali translation by Kālīprasanna Vidyāratna.] pp. 160. কলিকাতা ১২৯৯ [*Calcutta,* 1892.] 8°. **14053. cc. 66.**

SĀMUDRIKA (*continued*). সানুবাদ বৃহৎ সামুদ্রিক *etc.* [Bṛihat-sāmudrika. With Bengali introduction, translation, and notes. Edited by Harinārāyaṇa Jyotīratna.] pp. ii. 152. *Calcutta,* [1902.] 8°. **14053. ccc. 4.(4).**

SAMYAKTVASAPTATIKĀ. अथ . . . सम्यक्त्वसित्तरी *etc.* [Samyaktvasaptatikā, or Sammattasittarī. A Prakrit poem in 70 verses on the Jain theory of *samyaktva* or the state of grace. With Gujarati commentary by Ratnachandra Gaṇī.] 1890. *See* BHĪMASIṂHA MĀṆAKA. जैनकथारत्नकोष *etc.* [Jainakathāratnakoṣa.] Vol. III, pp. 114-385. [1890-1893.] 8°. **14144. gg. 1.(vol. 3.)**

The commentary was composed Samv. 1676.

SAṂYUTTANIKĀYA. *See* SUTTAPIṬAKA.

SANANDANA. *See* PADMAPĀDA, *son of Vimala.*

SANĀTANA GOSVĀMĪ. वैष्णवसङ्गीतिकानि । [Vaishṇavasaṅgītikāni. Vaishṇava devotional songs.] 1895. *See* PERIODICAL PUBLICATIONS.—*Calcutta.* विद्योदयः *etc.* [Vidyodaya.] Vol. xxiv. 1874, *etc.* 8°. **14096. cc. (vol. 24.)**

SANATKUMĀRA. ಗೃಹವಾಸ್ತುದರ್ಪಣ. [Gṛihavāstudarpaṇa. A treatise on the rites proper for the building of houses, ascribed to the sage Sanatkumāra. Edited with a Canarese paraphrase by Ṣrīnivāsapuram Lokanātha Kavi.] pp. iv. 98. ಬೆಂಗಳೂರು [*Bangalore,*] 1894. 8°. **14053. ccc. 17.**

SANATKUMĀRASAṂHITĀ. ॥ श्रीरामस्तवराज ॥ भावप्रकाशिका टीका सहित *etc.* [Rāmastavarāja. 99 verses in adoration of Rāma. With a Hindi commentary called Bhāvaprakāṣikā by Sītārāmaṣaraṇa.] pp. 186, vi. *Moradabad,* 1901. 8°. **14028. c. 66.(2.)**

SANDHYĀVANDANA. अथर्व वेदनो वेदोक्त त्रिकाळी संध्या. [Trikālī Sandhyā. According to the ritual of the Atharvaveda. With Gujarati rubrics.] pp. 8. અમદાવાદ ૧૮૯૧ [*Ahmadabad,* 1891.] 12°. **14028. b. 81.(2.)**

—— ॥ श्री ऋग्वेदोक्त त्रिकाल संध्या *etc.* [Trikālasandhyā. The sunrise, noon, and sunset prayers of the Ṛigveda. With a Gujarati explanation of the rites connected with them and their mystic significance.] pp. 36. अमदावाद १९५३ [*Ahmadabad,* 1897.] 16°. **14010. b. 13.**

SANDHYĀVANDANA (*continued*). ஆரியர் சந்தியாவந்தநம் *etc.* [Āryar-sandhyāvandanam. The Sanskrit text in Tamil characters, with Tamil version and notes by S. P. Narasimmalu Nāyuḍu.] pp. 8. *Coimbatore,* 1898. 8°. **14170. e. 47.(8.)**

—— The Sandhyavandanam of Rig, Yajus, and Sâma Vedins. With a literal translation, an explanatory paraphrase & commentary in English. By B. V. Kamesvara Aiyar. pp. 132. *Madras,* 1898. 12°. **14028. b. 97.(2.)**

Reprinted from the Sanskrit Journal, *vol.* 1.

—— **सन्ध्याभाष्यसमुच्चयः** *etc.* [Sandhyābhāshyasamuchchaya. A collection of commentaries upon the *sandhyā* prayers, including (1) Khaṇḍarāja Dīkshita's Bahvṛichasandhyāmantrārthadīpikā, with his gloss Prabhā; (2) Bahvṛichasandhyāpaddhatibhāshya, an exposition of the same ritual; (3) Madhvāchārya's Bahvṛichasandhyāmantravṛitti; (4) Kṛishṇa Paṇḍita's Taittirīyasandhyābhāshya; (5) Bhaṭṭojī Dīkshita's Taittirīyasandhyābhāshya; (6) Sāyaṇa's Taittirīyasandhyābhāshya. Edited by Kāṣīnātha Ṣāstrī Āgāṣe.] pp. i. 33, 26, 24, 66, 8, 8, 18. **पुण्याख्यपत्तन° १८९९** [*Poona,* 1899.] 8°. **14003. ccc. (no. 40.)**

Forms no. 40 *of the* Ānandāṣrama Sanskrit Series.

—— **अथ सन्ध्याविधिः** *etc.* [Sandhyāvidhi. Compiled with a Hindi version by Vaidyanātha Ṣāstrī.] pp. 14. *See* VAIDYANĀTHA ṢĀSTRĪ TIVĀṚĪ, *of Jalalabad,* AND OTHERS. [Miscellaneous tracts.] No. 20. [1899.] 12°. **14033. a. 37.**

—— సంధ్యావందన పరిషేచన యజ్ఞోపవీత-ధారణ మంత్రములు [Sandhyāvandana-parishechana-yajñopavītadhāraṇa-mantra. The text of the Sandhyāvandana and of the prayers said on sprinkling water before meals and putting on the cord. With Telugu notes, rubrics, *etc.*] pp. 12. *Madras,* 1899. 12°. **14028. b. 61.(4.)**

—— **त्रिवर्णकर्मपद्धतिः** *etc.* [Trivarṇakarmapaddhati. A ritual for use at the *sandhyās* by the three castes, comprising (1) *sandhyāniyamas,* (2) the *sandhyāprayoga,* and (3) Gaṅgāsthitinirṇaya, a proof of the permanence of the Ganges. Edited with Hindi version, rubrics, and notes by Harivallabha Kṛishṇavallabha.] **मुरादाबाद १९५६** [*Moradabad,* 1899.] 12°. **14028. bb. 4.(2.)**

SANDHYĀVANDANA (*continued*). **त्रिकाल संध्या** *etc.* [Trikālasandhyā. The Sandhyāvandana according to the Yajurveda. Edited with Gujarati preface by Amathārāma Lilādhara Vyāsa. Second edition.] pp. 11. **अमदावाद १९००** [*Ahmadabad,* 1900.] 12°. **14028. b. 104.(2.)**

—— **अथ वाजसनेयी प्रातःसन्ध्या प्रारभ्यते ।** [Vājasaneyī Prātaḥsandhyā. The morning prayers of the Vājasaneyī school.] ff. 9. **काश्यां १९५६** [*Benares,* 1900.] *obl.* 12°. **14028. b. 102.(3.)**

—— **सन्ध्यादर्पणः** *etc.* [Sandhyādarpaṇa. Being the Sandhyāvandana for the Mādhyandina school, with citations of authorities, Hindi translations, notes in Hindi and Sanskrit, and the text of the Sandhyāvandana for the other Brahman schools and non-Brahman castes. Compiled by Devīdatta Joṣī.] pp. xviii. 296, xiii. vi. **प्रयागनगरे १९०१** [*Allahabad,* 1901.] 4°. **14033. bbb. 11.**

—— யஜுர்வேத ஸந்த்யாவந்தநம் ஸாமவேத ஸந்த்யாவந்தநம் புருஷ . . . ஸ்ரீ . . . பூ . . . நீளா . . . நாராயணஸூக்தம் *etc.* [Sandhyāvandana, according to the Yajurvedī and Sāmavedī schools. Followed by the Purushasūkta, Ṣrīsūkta, Bhūsūkta, Nīlāsūkta, and Nārāyaṇasūkta. With extracts, in a Tamil translation, from the commentaries of Raṅgarāmānuja, Sāyaṇa, Ānandatīrtha, Vaidyanātha Dīkshita, Bhaṭṭa Bhāskara, Kṛishṇa Paṇḍita, and others. Edited and translated by Ṣyāmadeṣika Ṣrīṣaila Tātāchārya.] pp. 104, 38. சென்னை [*Madras,*] 1901. 8°. **14033. aa. 27.**

—— **अथ शुक्ल यजुर्वेदीय तर्पणसहित सन्ध्या** [Ṣukla-yajurvedīya-sandhyā. The ritual for the schools of the White Yajurveda. Followed by the ritual for the *tarpaṇa.*] ff. 17. *Benares,* [1901.] *obl.* 12°. **14033. a. 19.(3.)**

त्रिकुटीविलासस्य प्रथमभागात्मकः बृहत्सन्ध्याविधिः । [Bṛihat-sandhyāvidhi, or Vaidika-bṛihat-sandhyā. A compendium of *sandhyā* ritual by Svāmī Haṃsasvarūpa, forming part 1 of his Trikuṭīvilāsa. Comprising the formulae and appropriate texts with Hindi translations, notes, *etc.*] pp. v. 208, iv. **मुज़फ्फ़रपुर° १९५९** [*Muzaffarpur,* 1902.] 12°. **14033. a. 51.**

SANDHYĀVANDANA (*continued*).

—— *See* GOPĀLĀCHĀRLU, *S. E.* Sandhyâvandana, *etc.* 1893. 12°. **4505. de. 2.(7.)**

—— —— [Second edition.] 1902. 12°. **14028. b. 104.(3.)**

[For the Sandhyāvandana as contained in editions of the whole or parts of the daily ritual :] *See* NITYAKARMA.

ŚĀṆḌILYA. Nârada Sûtra. An enquiry into Love, Bhakti-jijnâsâ. Translated . . . with an independent commentary by E. T. Sturdy. pp. 68. *London, Aberdeen* [printed], 1896. 8°. **14028. c. 68.**

Forms no. 1 *of* "*Indian Ideals.*"

—— Religion of Love, or Hundred Aphorisms of Sandilya. Translated from the Sanskrit, with original texts, English translation and an independent commentary in English, by Jadunath Mozoomdar. pp. xv. 53. *Jessore*, 1898. 12°. **14028. b. 92.**

SĀNDRĀNANDA ĀCHĀRYA. *See* UPANISHADS.—*Separate Upanishads.* কৃষ্ণ-যজুর্ব্বেদীয়-উপনিষদঃ *etc.* [Taittirīyopanishad. Edited with Bengali translation and notes by Sāndrānanda.] [1896.] 8°. **14010. cc. 3.(2.)**

SAṄGAMEŚVARA ŚĀSTRĪ, *Gummalūri.* పంచలక్షణ్యుపరి సంగమేశ్వరీయాభిధానేయమభినవా-టిప్పణీ *etc.* [Saṅgameśvarīya. A commentary upon Mathurānātha Tarkavāgīśa's commentary to the Pañchalakshaṇī of Gaṅgeśa.] pp. ii. 70. బెజవాడ [*Bezvada*, 1896.] 12°. **14048. b. 33.(1.)**

SAṄGHĀNANDA, *Kaṁburugamuvē.* පදවීති හාරානිසංසය සහ තත්කාලප්‍රතිපදාව *etc.* [Padavītihārānisaṃsaya. A collection of Pali stanzas for Buddhist worship, with explanations and instructions in Sinhalese. Edited by Mahagoḍa Ñāṇissara.] pp. 48. කොළඹ 2437 [*Colombo*, 1894.] 12°. **14098. a. 29.(1.)**

SAṄGHARAKKHITA. ဏွာဒိမောဂ္ဂလာန်ပါဌ်-နိဿျ *etc.* [Ṇvādi-moggallāna. A Pali treatise on gender, based on the grammar of Moggallāna. With a Burmese *nissaya* by Sīlavilāsa.] pp. xxv. 125. ရန်ကုန် ၁၂၆၂ [*Rangoon*, 1900.] 8°. **14098. ccc. 29.(3.)**

—— သမ္ဗန္ဓစိန္တာ *etc.* [Sambandhachintā. A Pali treatise on syntactical relation. With a Burmese *nissaya* by Medhiyaddhaja.] [1898.] *See* SADDĀ-NGAY. သဒ္ဒါငယ် *etc.* [Saddā-ngay.] Vol. ii., pp. 1-82. [1898-1900.] 8°. **14098. ccc. 22.**

The author is said in the Gandhavaṃsa (§ ii.) *to have been* vuttodayakāro nāmāchariyo, *not* Saṅgharakkhita.

—— သမ္ဗန္ဓစိန္တာ *etc.* [Sambandhachintā.] *See* SADDĀ-NGAY. သဒ္ဒါငယ် *etc.* [Saddā-ngay.] pp. 81-95. [1898.] 8°. **14098. ccc. 23.(1.)**

—— —— pp. 82-96. [1899.] 8°. **14098. ccc. 24.(1.)**

—— အလင်္ကာနိဿျ *etc.* [Subodhālaṅkāra, or Alaṅkāra, in Burmese called Aliṅkā. A work on the art of poetry. With Burmese paraphrase by the Yaw-myo-sā Atwin-wûn.] pp. 363. ရန်ကုန် ၁၂၆၁ [*Rangoon*, 1899.] 8°. **14302. i. 16.**

—— အလင်္ကာ ပါဌ် *etc.* [Subodhālaṅkāra. Followed by the Vuttodaya, known in Burmese as the Hsan.] *See* MOGGALLĀNA. အဘိဓာန် *etc.* [Abhidhānappadīpikā.] pp. 93-123. [1898.] 8°. **14098. ccc. 23.(2.)**

—— —— pp. 93-123. [1899.] 8°. **14098. ccc. 24.(2.)**

—— ဆန္ဒသာရတ္ထိပ္ပါယပကာသနီကျမ်း *etc.* [Vuttodaya. Preceded by Chhandasārādhippāyappakāsanī, a Burmese commentary by Ñāṇindābhi Kaviddhaja. Second edition.] pp. ii. 64. မန္တလေး [*Mandalay*,] 1897. 8°. **14098. ccc. 27.(1.)**

The Gandhavaṃsa (§ ii.) *ascribes the Vuttodaya to a* vuttodayakāro nāmāchariyo, *distinct from* Saṅgharakkhita.

—— ဝုတ္တောဒယသန်း ကျမ်း *etc.* [Vuttodaya. With a commentary, styled Vachanatthajotika, by Samantapāsādika Thera, and another, entitled

Chhappachchayadīpaka, by Paññāsīha Mahāsaddhammasāmi.] pp. 173. ပစ္စလေး ၁၂၆၁ [*Mandalay*, 1899.] 8°. **14098. ccc. 27.(3.)**

—— ဆန်း နိဿျ *etc.* [Chhandonissaya, in Burmese Hsan-neikthaya. Being the Vuttodaya in Pali, with Burmese word-for-word translation and commentary by Chakkindābhisiri. Followed by the Hsan-linkā, *i.e.* Chhandālaṅkāra, a Burmese poem by the latter on the subject of the Vuttodaya.] pp. 122. ရန်ကုန် ၁၂၆၂ [*Rangoon*, 1900.] 8°. **14098. c. 74.**

—— ဝုတ္တောဒယဆန်းပါဠိ။ [Vuttodaya.] *See* SADDHAMMASIRI. သဒ္ဒတ္ထဘေဒစိန္တာ *etc.* [Saddatthabhedachintā, *etc.*] pp. 33-39. 1903. 8°. **14099. bb. 2.**

SAN HTÛN AUNG, *Maung.* *See* ZIN-PYU-MYA-SHIN. ကိုးဆောင်ချုပ်ဓမ္မသတ် *etc.* [Ko-saung-hkyôk-dhammathat. Section viii. Edited, with Burmese translations, by San Htûn Aung and Kyaw Zan Ū.] [1894.] 8°. **14098. ccc. 20.**

ṢANIPŪJĀPADDHATI. শ্রীশ্রীশনিপূজাপদ্ধতি ও পাঁচালী *etc.* [Ṣanipūjāpaddhati. A brief ritual of the worship of the planet-god Ṣani or Saturn as prescribed in the Skandapurāṇa. Followed by Ṣanipāñchālī, a Bengali poem on the legend and cult of Ṣani.] pp. 25. *Calcutta*, [1901.] *obl.* 8°. **14028. dd. 10.(2.)**

ṢAṄKARA, *Āchārya-Svāmī, Pontiff of Dwarka.* ॥ त्रिदण्डिमतविभेदिनी *etc.* [Tridaṇḍimatavibhedinī. A polemic against the schools of Rāmānuja and other sects of Vedānta. With an introduction by Rāmachandra Gaṅgādhara Ṣāstrī.] Vol. i. pp. ii. iii. 191, 14. वाराणस्यां १९५६ [*Benares*, 1899.] 8°. **14048. e. 33.**

—— ॥ विमर्शः ॥ [Vimarṣa. A treatise on the nature of time and *māyā*, the incarnations culminating in the birth of Ṣaṅkara, history of the latter with lists of his apostolic successors, and divers other topics of philosophy and religion. With a biographical preface by Vishṇu Ṣāstrī.] pp. iv. 89. वाराणस्यां १९५५ [*Benares*, 1898.] 8°. **14048. cc. 21.(2.)**

ṢAṄKARA ĀCHĀRYA.

TWO OR MORE WORKS.

शंकराचार्य पंचरत्न *etc.* [Ṣaṅkarāchārya-pañcharatna. Being the Vivekachūḍāmaṇi, Aparokshānubhūti, Svātmanirūpaṇa, Ātmabodha, and Vākyavṛitti. Edited with a Gujarati translation by Jayarāma Raghunātha.] 5 pts. *Bombay*, १९४८ [1892.] 12°. **14098. b. 24.**

Śrí-Śankarácbárya's Miscellaneous Works . . . श्रीशङ्करभगवत्पादीयप्रकरणग्रन्थावलिः [Vol. I, the commentaries on the Vishṇusahasranāma and Sanatsujātīya with the original text; Vol. II, Aparokshānubhūti and Ṣataṣlokī, with commentaries ascribed respectively to Sāyaṇa and Ānandagiri, and Haristuti and Daṣaṣlokī with the commentaries of Svayamprakāṣa and Madhusūdana respectively, called Haritattvamuktāvalī and Siddhāntabindu; Vol. III, Upadeṣasahasrī, with Rāmatīrtha's commentaries called Upadeṣārthavibhāga and Padayojanikā; Vol. IV, Ātmabodha, Vivekachūḍāmaṇi, Vākyavṛitti, Svātmanirūpaṇa, Yogatārāvalī, and Sarvavedāntasiddhāntasārasaṅgraha.] . . . Edited by A. Mahádeva Śástri . . . and Panditaratnam K. Rangáchárya. 1898-1899. *See* MYSORE.—*Government of Mysore.* Government Oriental Library Series. Bibliotheca Sanskrita, *etc.* Nos. 19-22. 1893, *etc.* 8°. **14004. b. 10.**

A Compendium of the Raja Yoga Philosophy, comprising the principal treatises of Shrimat Shankaracharya and other renowned authors [*scil.* the Aparokshānubhūti and Vākyasudhā, in Sanskrit, with translation by Maṇilāla Dvivedī; Ātmaviveka and Vivekachūḍāmaṇi, translated by Mohinīmohana Chaṭṭopādhyāya; Ātmabodha, translated by B. Narasiṃhaiyā; Sadānanda's Vedāntasāra, translated by W. Ward; and the Charpaṭapañjarī, translated by J. N. Paramānanda. Second edition.] pp. i. i. 161. *Bombay*, 1901. 8°. **14048. bb. 53.**

Âtmânâtma-viveka, or Discrimination of Spirit and Not-Spirit . . . and Âtmabodha . . . Translated . . . by Mohini M. Chatterjee [and B. Narasiṃhaiyā respectively]. pp. 66. *Bombay*, [1904.] 16°. **14048. a. 30.**

Reprinted from the "Compendium of Raja Yoga Philosophy."

শঙ্করাচার্য্যের গ্রন্থমালা *etc.* [Ṣaṅkarāchāryer Granthamālā. Comprising the Ātmabodha, Aparokshānubhūti, and Vākyavṛitti, together with 49 of the philosophical and religious poems generally ascribed to Ṣaṅkara. With Bengali translations by Kālīprasanna Vidyāratna. Second edition.] pp. iii. 208. কলিকাতা ১৩০৯ [*Calcutta*, 1903.] 8°. **14033. aa. 30.**

SELECTIONS.

See MAṆILĀLA NABHUBHĀĪ DVIVEDĪ. The Imitation of Śankara. Being . . . texts bearing on the Advaita [from Ṣaṅkara's works, *etc.*, with English translation,] *etc.* 1895. 8°. **14048. cc. 1.**

COMMENTARIES.

[*Bhagavadgītā.*] *See* MAHĀBHĀRATA. — Bhagavadgītā.—*Sanskrit.* श्रीमद्भगवद्गीता . . . The Bhagavad-gítá, with the commentary of Śrí Śankarácharya, *etc.* 1895. 8°. [*Mysore Government Oriental Library Series : Bibliotheca Sanskrita.*] **14004. b. 6.**

—— *See* MAHĀBHĀRATA.—Bhagavadgītā.—*Sanskrit.* श्रीमद्भगवद्गीता *etc.* (Shrîmat Bhagavadgîta with the Bháshya by . . . Śankarácharya, *etc.*) 1897. 8°. **14003. ccc. (no. 34.)**

—— *See* MAHĀBHĀRATA. — Bhagavadgītā. — *English.* The Bhagavad-gîtâ, with the commentary of Shrî Shankarâchârya, *etc.* 1897. 8°. **14048. cc. 25.**

—— *See* MAHĀBHĀRATA.—Bhagavadgītā.—*Sanskrit and English.* The Bhagabat Gita with [English translation of] the commentary by Shri Shankaracharya, *etc.* 1902. 8°. **14065. c. 52.**

[*Brahmasūtra.*] *See* BĀDARĀYAṆA. The Vedânta-Sûtras with the commentary by Saṅkarâkârya. Translated by G. Thibaut. 1890-1896. 8°. [*Sacred Books of the East.*] **2003. b. (vol. 34, 38.)**

—— *See* AKHAṆḌĀNANDA, *disciple of Akhaṇḍānubhūti.* तत्त्वदीपनम् . . . Tattvadîpana, a commentary on Panchapádikávivaraṇa, [Prakāṣātmā's commentary on Padmapāda's Pañchapādikā, the latter being a commentary upon Ṣaṅkara's Bhāshya I. i. 1-4] *etc.* 1901, *etc.* 8°. **14049. a. 3.**

ṢAṄKARA ĀCHĀRYA (*continued*).

—— *See* BĀDARĀYAṆA. ॥ ब्रह्मविद्याभरणम् *etc.* [Brahmasūtra. With the commentary of Advaitānanda upon Ṣaṅkara's *bhāshya.*] 1894. 8°. [*Advaitamañjarī.*] **14048. e. 23.**

—— *See* BĀDARĀYAṆA. The Vedânta-kalpataru of Amalânanda. [Comprising the Brahmasūtra with the supercommentary of Amalānanda upon the Bhāmatī in elucidation of Ṣaṅkara's Ṣārīrakabhāshya,] *etc.* 1895-1897. 8°. **14048. dd. 3.(vol. 11.)**

—— *See* BĀDARĀYAṆA. The Vedânta-kalpataruparimala of Appayadîkshita, *etc.* 1895-1898. 8°. **14048. dd. 3.(vol. 12.)**

—— *See* BĀDARĀYAṆA. బ్రహ్మసూత్రదీపిక *etc.* [Brahmasūtra. With commentary based on that of Ṣaṅkara.] [1897.] 8°. **14048. cc. 8.(3.)**

—— *See* PADMAPĀDA. The Pañchapâdikâ . . . [A commentary on Ṣaṅkara's Ṣārīrakabhāshya I. i. 1-4] *etc.* (Part II. The Pañchapâdikâvivaraṇa, *etc.*) 1891-1892. 8°. **14048. dd. 3.(vol. 2.)**

—— *See* PADMAPĀDA. The Pañcapādikā . . . Translated by A. Venis. 1901, *etc.* 8°. [*The Pandit.*] **14096. d. 6.(vol. 23, etc.)**

—— *See* RĀMĀNANDA SARASVATĪ, *disciple of Govindānanda.* विवरणोपन्यासः . . . Vivaraṇopanyasa . . . [a summary of Prakāṣātmā's Pañchapādikāvivaraṇa,] *etc.* 1901. 8°. **14048. cc. 37.**

—— *See* SUDARṢANA ĀCHĀRYA, *Panjābī.* ॥ श्रीः . . . The Adwaita Chandrika. A work on Vedanta philosophy of Shankar, *etc.* 1901. 8°. **14048. dd. 16.(1.)**

[*Lalitātriṣatī.*] *See* PURĀṆAS.—*Brahmāṇḍapurāṇa.* [*Lalitātriṣatī.*] Triśatî with . . . Śankrâchârya's Bhâsya [called Triṣatīnāmārthaprakāṣikā,] *etc.* 1902. 12°. **14033. a. 45.(1.)**

[*Sanatsujātīya.*] *See* MAHĀBHĀRATA. — *Udyogaparva.* सनत्सुजातीय॰ [Sanatsujātīya. With commentary of Ṣaṅkara.] 1898. 8°. [*Mysore Government Oriental Library Series : Bibliotheca Sanskrita.*] **14004. b. 10.(vol. 1.)**

ṢAṄKARA ĀCHĀRYA (*continued*).

COMMENTARIES (*continued*).

[*Upanishads.*] *See* UPANISHADS. — *Small Collections.* Selections from the Upanishads. Translated into English. With notes from Sankara Acharya, *etc.* 1895. 8°. [*Sacred Books of the East Described and Examined.*] **14010. cc. 9.(vol. 2.)**

—— *See* UPANISHADS.—*Small Collections.* उपनिषदावली *etc.* [Upanishadāvalī. Ten Upanishads, including the Muṇḍakop.° and Kaṭhop.°, with the commentaries of Ṣaṅkara.] [1896.] 12°. **14010. b. 12.**

—— *See* UPANISHADS.—*Small Collections.* தசோபநிஷத்த்ராவிடபாஷ்யம் *etc.* [Daṣopanishaddrāviḍabhāshya. Ten Upanishads, with a Tamil commentary comprising translations of the commentary of Ṣaṅkara, *etc.*, with the Kārikā of Gauḍapāda and Ṣaṅkara's commentary thereupon in Tamil.] [1897]-1898. 8°. **14010. dd. 14.**

—— *See* UPANISHADS.—*Small Collections.* The Isa, Kena & Mundaka Upanishads [in Sanskrit and English] and Sri Sankara's commentary [in English], *etc.* (Vol. II, The Katha and Prasna Upanishads, *etc.* Vol. III, IV, The Chhândogya Upanishad, *etc.* Vol. V, The Aitareya and Taittiriya Upanishads, *etc.*) 1898, *etc.* 12°. **14010. b. 20.**

—— *See* UPANISHADS.—*Small Collections.* Amritabindu and Kaivalya Upanishads. With commentaries [in English, compiled from the works of Ṣaṅkara and others]. Translated . . . by A. Mahadeva Sastri. 1898. 12°. **14010. b. 19.**

—— *See* UPANISHADS.—*Selections.* ॥ अथ शान्तिपाठः ॥ [Ṣāntipāṭha. With commentaries of Ṣaṅkara.] 1892. 8°. [*Ushā.*] **14010. c. 43.(vol. 2.)**

—— Aitareyopanishad. Sankara's Introduction [in English]. 1898. *See* PERIODICAL PUBLICATIONS.—*Madras.* The Brahmavâdin, *etc.* Vol. III, pp. 480-488. 1895, *etc.* 8°. **14048. g. 1.(vol.3.)**

—— *See* SUREṢVARA ĀCHĀRYA. बृहदारण्यकोपनिषद्भाष्यवार्त्तिकम् *etc.* (Bṛihadáraṇyakopanishadbháshyavártika ... [A commentary upon the Bṛihadāraṇyakopanishad as expounded by Ṣaṅkara,] *etc.*) [1892-1894.] 8°. **14003. ccc.(no. 16.)**

—— Translation of [passages from] Sankara's commentary on the Chandogya Upanishad. 1898. *See* PERIODICAL PUBLICATIONS.—*Madras.* The Brahmavâdin, *etc.* Vol. III, pp. 440-451. 1895, *etc.* 8°. **14048. g. 1.(vol. 3.)**

—— *See* UPANISHADS.—*Separate Upanishads.* ईशावास्योपनिषत्° ((1) Shri Ísávásyopanishad with the Bháshya of . . . Śankarácbárya and Commentary by . . . Ánandadnyána, *etc.*) [1888.] 8°. **14003. ccc. (no. 5.)**

—— *See* UPANISHADS.—*Separate Upanishads.* ईशोपनिषत् *etc.* (Isa-Upanishad. With the Bhasyas of Baladeva Vidyabhushana, Sri Sankaracharyya, *etc.*) 1895. 8°. **14010. cc. 3.(1.)**

—— *See* UPANISHADS.—*Separate Upanishads.* The Ísavâsyopanishad. Translated . . . with the commentaries of Sri Sankaracharya and Sri Anantacharya, *etc.* 1896. 8°. **14010. cc. 6.**

—— La introduzione del commento di Çaṅkara alla Kāṭhakopaniṣad. [With translation and notes] per P. E. Pavolini. pp. 7. *Roma,* 1892. 8°. **14010. dd. 5.(3.)**

Extracted from the Rendiconti *of the Reale Accademia dei Lincei, session of Feb.* 21, 1892.

—— *See* UPANISHADS.—*Separate Upanishads.* केनोपनिषत्° (The Kenopanishat with the Pada and Vákya Bháshyás of . . . Śankarácbárya and commentary of . . . Ánandadnyána, *etc.*) [1888.] 8°. **14003. ccc. (no. 6.)**

—— Translation of [passages from] Sankara's commentary on Kena Upanishad. 1897. *See* PERIODICAL PUBLICATIONS.—*Madras.* The Brahmavâdin, *etc.* Vol. III, pp. 99-103, 182-185. 1895, *etc.* 8°. **14048. g. 1.(vol. 3.)**

—— *See* UPANISHADS.—*Separate Upanishads.* The Mândûkyopanishad. With . . the Bhâshya

ṢAṄKARA ĀCHĀRYA (*continued*).

COMMENTARIES (*continued*).

of Śankara. Translated into English, *etc.* 1894. 8°. **14007. cc. 24.**

—— *See* UPANISHADS.—*Separate Upanishads.* **मुण्डकोपनिषत्°** [Muṇḍakopanishad. With the commentary of Ṣaṅkara, the gloss of Ānandagiri, *etc.*] [1889.] 8°. **14003. ccc. (no. 9.)**

—— Translation of [passages from] Sankara's commentary on the Mundaka Upanishad. 1898. *See* PERIODICAL PUBLICATIONS.—*Madras.* The Brahmavâdin, *etc.* Vol. III, pp. 360-365. 1895, *etc.* 8°. **14048. g. 1.(vol. 3.)**

—— *See* UPANISHADS.—*Separate Upanishads.* **नृसिंहपूर्वोत्तरतापनीयोपनिषत्** *etc.* [Nṛisiṃhatāpanīyopanishad. Parts i. and ii., the former with the commentary of Ṣaṅkara.] [1895.] 8°. **14003. ccc. (no. 30.)**

—— *See* UPANISHADS.—*Separate Upanishads.* **प्रश्नोपनिषत्°** (Śri Praśnopanishad with the Bháshya of . . . Śankarácharya and its commentary by . . . Ánandajnyána, *etc.*) [1889.] 8°. **14003. ccc. (no. 8.)**

—— [Translation of Ṣaṅkara's commentary on] Prasnopanishad vi. 3. 1897. *See* PERIODICAL PUBLICATIONS.—*Madras.* The Brahmavâdin, *etc.* Vol. III, pp. 57-62. 1895, *etc.* 8°. **14048. g. 1.(vol. 3.)**

—— Brahmánandavalli of Taittariya Upanishad. [Selections] translated from Sankara's commentary. 1897. *See* PERIODICAL PUBLICATIONS.—*Madras.* The Brahmavâdin, *etc.* Vol. II, no. 25, 26. 1895, *etc.* 4°. **14048. g. 1.(vol. 2.)**

[*Vishṇusahasranāma.*] *See* MAHĀBHĀRATA.—*Anuṣāsanaparva.* **श्रीविष्णुसहस्रनाम°** [Vishṇusahasranāma. With commentary of Ṣaṅkara.] 1898. 8°. [*Mysore Government Oriental Library Series: Bibliotheca Sanskrita.*] **14004. b. 10.(vol. 1.)**

—— *See* MAHĀBHĀRATA.—*Anuṣāsanaparva.* The Vishnu Sahasranama, with Sri Sankaracharya's commentary, translated into English, *etc.* 1901. 8°. **14048. bb. 52.**

ṢAṄKARA ĀCHĀRYA (*continued*).

PHILOSOPHICAL POEMS, ETC.

शंकराचार्य-पंचरत्न *etc.* [Ṣaṅkarāchārya-pañcharatna. Being the Vivekachūḍāmaṇi, Aparokshānubhūti, Svātmanirūpaṇa, Ātmabodha, and Vākyavṛitti. With Gujarati translation.] [1892.] 12°. *See* above, TWO OR MORE WORKS. **14098. b. 24.**

अपरोक्षानुभूतिः (दशश्लोकी *etc.*) [Aparokshānubhūti, with the commentary ascribed to Sāyaṇa; Daṣaṣlokī, with that of Madhusūdana; Upadeṣasahasrī, with that of Rāmatīrtha; and the Ātmabodha, Vivekachūḍāmaṇi, Vākyavṛitti, and Svātmanirūpaṇa.] *See* above, TWO OR MORE WORKS. Śrí-Śankarácharya's Miscellaneous Works, *etc.* Vol. II-IV. 1898-1899. 8°. [*Mysore Government Oriental Library Series: Bibliotheca Sanskrita.*] **14004. b. 10.(vol. 2-4.)**

—— A Compendium of the Raja Yoga Philosophy . . . [*scil.* the Aparokshānubhūti and Vākyasudhā, with translation by Maṇilāla Dvivedī; Ātmaviveka and Vivekachūḍāmaṇi, translated by Mohinīmohana Chaṭṭopādhyāya; Ātmabodha, translated by B. Narasiṃhaiyā, *etc.*] 1901. 8°. *See* above, TWO OR MORE WORKS. **14048. bb. 53.**

अपरोक्षानुभूति. [Aparokshānubhūti. With the Marathi *samaṣlokī* version of Vāmana.] [1891.] *See* VĀMANA PAṆḌITA, *the Marathi Poet.* **वामनी ग्रंथ** *etc.* [Vāmanī Grantha.] Vol. 4, pp. 179-200. [1889-1891.] 8°. **14140. b. 23.(vol. 4.)**

श्रीमच्छंकराचार्यप्रणीता अपरोक्षानुभूतिः *etc.* [Aparokshānubhūti. Edited with Maṛathi translation and commentary by Vishṇu Vāmana Bāpaṭ, calling himself Āchāryabhakta Vishṇu.] pp. ii. 123. **मुंबई १८२५** [*Bombay,* 1903.] 12°. **14048. b. 44.**

Aparokshanubhuti, *etc.* [Translated into English.] 1901. *See* PERIODICAL PUBLICATIONS.—*Madras.* The Brahmavâdin, *etc.* Vol. VI, no. 5. 1895, *etc.* 8°. **14048. g. 1.(vol. 6.)**

Unfinished.

ಶ್ರೀ . . . ಆತ್ಮಬೋಧಾ ಪ್ರಕರಣಂ [*sic*] *etc.* [Ātmabodha. With Canarese translation and com-

ŚAṄKARA ĀCHĀRYA (*continued*).

PHILOSOPHICAL POEMS, ETC. (*continued*).

mentary by Vedānta Veṅkaṭa Subbaiya.] pp. 2, 52. ಬೆಂಗಳೂರು [*Bangalore,*] 1902. 12°.
14048. b. 16.(3.)

The Awakening to the Self. Translated from the Sanskrit of Shankara the Master by Charles Johnston. pp. 31. *New York*, 1897. *obl.* 12°.
14048. a. 18.

Atma Bodha, or Knowledge of Spirit. [Translated into English.] *See* SĪTĀNĀTHA DATTA. Sankaracharya, *etc.* pp. 49-62. 1897. 12°.
14048. a. 22.

Atmabodha, or the Perception of Self. Translated . . . by . . . N. Dhole. 1899. *See* PERIODICAL PUBLICATIONS.—*Calcutta.* The Oriental, *etc.* Vol. I, no. 9-10. 1898, *etc.* 8°.
Ac. 8825. b. (vol. 1.)

Atma Bodha. Or Knowledge of the Self ... [Translated] by Chunilal C. Bohra. 1901. *See* PERIODICAL PUBLICATIONS.—*Madras.* The Brahmavâdin, *etc.* Vol. VI, no. 7-8. 1895, *etc.* 8°.
14048. g. 1.(vol. 6.)

Atma Bodha. Selbsterkenntnis . . . Übersetzt von Franz Hartmann. pp. iii. 19. *Leipzig, Meerane* [printed, 1895.] 8°. **14048. bb. 9.(3.)**

অজ্ঞানবোধিনী। হরিতত্ত্বমুক্তাবলী *etc.* [Ajñānabodhinī, also called Adhyātmopadeśavidhi: A commentary, ascribed to Śaṅkara, on his Ātmabodha. Followed by the Harim-īdestuti.] pp. 28, 8. কলিকাতা ১২৮১ [*Calcutta*, 1874.] 8°. **14048. bb. 45.(1.)**

అయం సిద్ధాంతబిందుః *etc.* [Daśaślokī. With the commentary Siddhāntabindu or Siddhāntatattvab°. of Madhusūdana Sarasvatī upon it. Followed by the Hastāmalakaśloka.] pp. 36. చెన్నపరి॥ ౧౮౯౨ [*Madras*, 1892.] 8°.
14048. cc. 9.(1.)

॥ सिद्धान्तबिन्दुः *etc.* [Daśaślokī. With the commentary Siddhāntabindu of Madhusūdana Sarasvatī and the supercommentary Nyāyaratnāvalī or Ratnāvalī of Brahmānanda Sarasvatī.] pp. i. iv. 212. 1893. *See* HARIHARA ŚĀSTRĪ, *Goshṭhīpuram*, and others. ॥ अद्वैतमञ्जरी *etc.* [Advaitamañjarī.] 1892-1895. 8°. **14048. e. 23.**

See SUREŚVARA ĀCHĀRYA. पञ्चीकरणवार्त्तिकम् । [Pañchīkaraṇavārttika. A metrical paraphrase of Śaṅkara's Pañchīkaraṇaprakriyā.] 1891. 8°. [*Vidyodaya.*] **14096. cc. (vol. 20.)**

See SUREŚVARA ĀCHĀRYA. मानसोल्लासो *etc.* [Mānasollāsa. Followed by Pañchīkaraṇavārttika.] 1895. 8°. [*Mysore Government Oriental Library Series: Bibliotheca Sanskrita.*]

——— Svatmanirupanam . . . translated into English by J. Harihara Aiyar. 1900-1901. *See* PERIODICAL PUBLICATIONS.—*Madras.* The Brahmavâdin, *etc.* Vol. VI, no. 1-4. 1895, *etc.* 8°.
14048. g. 1.(vol. 6.)

अथ वाक्यसुधाप्रारम्भः [Vākyasudhā. With commentary.] *See* NITYĀNANDA SARASVATĪ. वेदान्तग्रन्थपञ्चकम् *etc.* [Vedāntagranthapañchaka.] pp. 1-47. [1891.] 12°. **14048. b. 15.(2.)**

श्री . . . वाक्यसुधा *etc.* [Vākyasudhā. With commentary of Brahmānanda Bhāratī.] pp. i. 33. *See* RĀMĀNANDA SARASVATĪ, *disciple of Govindānanda.* विवरणोपन्यासः . . . Vivaraṇopanyâsa, *etc.* 1901. 8°. **14048. cc. 37.**

దృగ్దృశ్యవివేకము *etc.* [Vākyasudhā, here called Dṛigdṛiśyaviveka. With a commentary in Telugu, based upon the Vākyasudhāvyākhyā of Brahmānanda Bhāratī, by Aparokshānubhavī Vakulābharaṇa Paradeśī.] pp. iv. 84. చెన్నపట్టణము [*Madras,*] 1901. 8°. **14048. bb. 55.**

The poem is here ascribed to Vidyāranya.

ദൃഗ്ദൃശ്യവിവേകഃ പ്രകരണം. ടീകാദ്വയസമലംകൃതം ഭാഷാനുവാദസഹിതം ച. [Vākyasudhā, or Dṛigdṛiśyaviveka. With two commentaries. Edited with a Malayalam translation by

ṢAṄKARA ĀCHĀRYA (*continued*).

PHILOSOPHICAL POEMS, ETC. (*continued*).

E. P. Subrahmaṇya Ṣāstrī.] pp. i. i. 65. *Palghat*, 1903. 8°. **14049. a. 7.(3.)**

Vakya Vritti . . . [Translated] by Chunilal C. Bohra. 1901. *See* PERIODICAL PUBLICATIONS.—*Madras*. The Brahmavâdin, *etc.* Vol. VI, no. 12, pp. 751-760. 1895, *etc.* 8°. **14048. g. 1.(vol. 6.)**

వివేకచూడామణి *etc.* [Vivekachūḍāmaṇi. With Telugu glosses and commentaries compiled by Rāvāḍi Rāma Ṣāstrī. Edited by R. Trivikrama Ṣāstrī.] pp. 225. బళ్లారి పట్టణం [*Bellary*, 1898.] 8°. **14048. c. 72.(2.)**

॥ अथ सुबोधिनीव्याख्ययासहितविवेकचूडामणिप्रारम्भः ॥ [Vivekachūḍāmaṇi. With the commentary Subodhinī of Harināmadatta Miṣra.] ff. iii. 102. काश्यां १९५८ [*Benares*, 1901.] *obl.* 4°. **14048. e. 36.**

विवेकचूडामणिः *etc.* [Vivekachūḍāmaṇi. With Hindi commentary, styled Advaitāmṛitabodhinī, and verbal analysis by Aravindānanda Yati. Edited with footnotes by Nṛisiṃha Deva Ṣarmā.] pp. xii. 746. लवपुरे १९०२ [*Lahore*, 1902.] 8°. **14049. a. 6.**

Das Palladium der Weisheit. Viveka Chudamani . . . Aus dem Sanskrit übersetzt von Mohini Chatterji. pp. i. 98. *Leipzig, Meerane* [printed, 1895.] 8°. **14048. bb. 9.(4.)**

DOUBTFUL AND SUPPOSITITIOUS WORKS.

See RĀMADAYĀLU MAJUMDĀR. শ্রীবিচার চন্দ্রোদয় *etc.* [Vichārachandrodaya. A Bengali exposition of the Vedānta, preceded by a selection of Vedantic hymns by Ṣaṅkara and others. Followed by the Vedāntastotrāvalī, hymns chiefly by Ṣaṅkara, and Pañchadevatādhyāna and Pañchadevatāstava, hymns and meditations upon the five deities, ascribed to Ṣaṅkara and others.] [1901.] 12°. **14123. e. 22.**

मोहमुद्गरः। (যতিপঞ্চক ও সাধনপঞ্চক।) [Mohamudgara, Yatipañchaka, and Sādhanapañchaka. With Bengali metrical translation.] *See* TĀRAKUMĀRA KAVIRATNA. পঞ্চামৃত *etc.* [Pañchāmṛita.] pp. 11-29. [1892.] 12°. **14028. b. 73.(1.)**

ṢAṄKARA ĀCHĀRYA (*continued*).

DOUBTFUL AND SUPPOSITITIOUS WORKS (*continued*).

అపరాధస్తోత్రం (దేవీపంచరత్న॥) [Aparādhastotra and Devīpañcharatnastotra.] *See* SADĀṢIVA DĪKSHITA, *of Alsur*. ఆగమికశివపూజావిధిః *etc.* [Āgamikaṣivapūjāvidhi.] pp. 112-116, 119-120. [1893.] 12°. **14028. b. 85.**

अथ श्रीमच्छङ्कराचार्यै कृत प्रश्नोत्तराणि ॥ (अथ साधनपंचको निरूप्यते ॥) [Praṣnottarī and Sādhanapañchaka. With Hindi version.] pp. 5, 2. *See* SUKHĀNANDA TRIPĀṬHĪ, *Prājña*. ॥ ब्रह्म विलासं *etc.* [Brahmavilāsa.] [1894.] 8°. **14048. dd. 32.(1.)**

Saundaryalahari of Śrí Śankaráchárya with Lakshmídhara's commentary, Bhávanopanishad with Bháskararája's commentary, and Deví-panchastaví [comprising the Laghustuti, Charchāstava, Ghaṭastava, Ambāstava, and Sakalajananīstotra]. Edited [with introduction] by A. Mahádeva Śástri . . . and Panditaratnam K. Rangácharya. (सौन्दर्यलहरी . . . भावनोपनिषत् . . . देवी-पञ्चस्तवी च.) pp. xiii. iv. 253, 27, ii. 1896. *See* MYSORE.—*Government of Mysore*. Government Oriental Library Series. Bibliotheca Sanskrita. No. 11. 1893, *etc.* 8°. **14004. b. 8.**

The name Ānandalaharī *is usually given only to vv.* 1-41 *of the first of these works; the remaining* 59 vv. *of it, or (as here) the whole* 100, *are styled* Saundaryalaharī.

शतश्लोकी *etc.* (हरिस्तुतिः, योगतारावली *etc.*) [Ṣataṣlokī, with commentary ascribed to Ānandagiri; Haristuti, with the commentary of Svayamprakāṣa; Yogatārāvalī; and Sarvavedāntasiddhāntasārasaṅgraha.] *See* above, TWO OR MORE WORKS. Śri-Śankaráchárya's Miscellaneous Works, *etc.* Vol. II, IV. 1898-1899. 8°. [*Mysore Government Oriental Library Series: Bibliotheca Sanskrita.*] **14004. b. 10.(vol. 2, 4.)**

మణిత్రయి *etc.* [Maṇitrayī. Three Vaishṇava poems ascribed to Ṣaṅkara and his disciples, viz. Lakshmīnṛisiṃhastotra, Govindadvādaṣamañjarikāst.° or Bhajagovinda, and Govindachaturdaṣamañjarikāst.° With Telugu introduction, word-for-word translations, and commentaries by K. Tiruveṅkaṭāchārya.] pp. 202. *Madras*, 1899. 16°. **14028. a. 28.**

ŚAṄKARA ĀCHĀRYA (*continued*).

DOUBTFUL AND SUPPOSITITIOUS WORKS (*continued*).

Lord Shankar's Song [, viz. the Bhajagovinda in 16 stanzas, followed by two other poems ascribed to Śaṅkara, in Sanskrit and English]. *See* UPANISHADS.—*Separate Upanishads.* An English translation of the Prashnopanishat, *etc.* pp. 36-47. 1899. 12°. **14048. a. 20.(2.)**

শঙ্করাচার্য্যের গ্রন্থমালা *etc.* [Śaṅkarāchāryer Granthamālā. Comprising the Ātmabodha, Aparokshānubhūti, and Vākyavṛitti, together with 49 of the philosophical and religious poems generally ascribed to Śaṅkara. With Bengali translations by Kālīprasanna Vidyāratna.] [1903.] 8°. *See* above, TWO OR MORE WORKS. **14033. aa. 30.**

अम्बाष्टकम् [Ambāshṭaka. With commentary.] pp. 12. [1889.] *See* PERIODICAL PUBLICATIONS.—*Bombay.* **ग्रन्थरत्नमाला** *etc.* (Granth Ratna Málá, *etc.*) Vol. II, no. 8. 1887-[1892.] 8°. **14096. c. 8.(vol. 2.)**

[For texts of the Āmnāyavistara, purporting to be extracted from the Maṭhāmnāyasetu ascribed to Śaṅkara :] *See* below.

শ্রী অন্নপূর্ণার ধ্যান [Annapūrṇāstotra. With a lithographed picture of the temple of the goddess at Benares.] pp. 4; 1 *folding plate.* **काशी** [*Benares,* 1891.] 12°. **14003. e. 2.(20.)**

Dwadasa Manjari of Sreemath Sankaracharya, [also called Bhajagovinda and Charpaṭapañjarī, in the recension of 12 stanzas,] rendered into English verse by O. L. Sarma. [With the Sanskrit text.] pp. 11. *Madanapalle,* 1893. 16°. **14010. a. 4.**

శ్రీగోవిన్దద్వాదశమఞ్జరికాస్తోత్రమ్. [Govindadvādaśamañjarikā. A recension of the Charpaṭapañjarī in 12 stanzas.] *See* above. మణిత్రయి *etc.* [Maṇitrayī.] pp. 100-142. 1899. 16°. **14028. a. 28.**

गोविन्दाष्टकम् । चर्पटपञ्जरी *etc.* [Govindāshṭaka, or Charpaṭapañjarī, in a recension comprising 17 stanzas. With Hindi version by Rādhākṛishṇa Śarmā. Followed by two Hindi hymns to Hari and Kālī.] pp. 13. **मुम्बई १९५७** [*Bombay,* 1901.] 12°. **14028. bb. 5.(1.)**

अथ चर्पटपञ्जरिकास्तोत्र० [Charpaṭapañjarikā. In 16 stanzas.] ff. 7. **रावलपिंडी** [*Rawal Pindi,* 1902.] *obl.* 12°. **14028. b. 73.(6.)**

Charapatapanjari [*sic*] . . . translated by Mr. J. N. Parmanand. *See* above, TWO OR MORE WORKS. A Compendium of the Raja Yoga Philosophy, *etc.* pp. 160-161. 1901. 8°. **14048. bb. 53.**

दक्षिणामूर्तिस्तोत्रम् . . . The Dakshiṇámúrti-stotra of Sri Sankaracharya, with commentaries [entitled respectively Mānasollāsa, Tattvasudhā, and Mānasollāsavṛittānta] by Sureśvaráchárya, Svayamprakáśa & Rámatírtha. [Followed by the poem called Pañchīkaraṇavārttika by Sureṣvara.] Edited by A. Mahádeva Śástri . . . and Panditaratnam K. Rangáchárya. pp. iv. v. 170, vii. 4. 1895. *See* MYSORE. — *Government of Mysore.* Government Oriental Library Series. Bibliotheca Sanskrita. No. 6. 1893, *etc.* 8°. **14004. b. 5.**

The Vedânta Doctrine of Śri Sankarâchârya. [Comprising Śaṅkara's Dakshiṇāmūrtistotra with Sureṣvara's Mānasollāsa, the Praṇavavārttika of the latter, and the Dakshiṇāmūrtyupanishad, translated into English and annotated, with preface and introduction,] by A. Mahâdeva Śâstri. [To which is appended the Sanskrit text of the Dakshiṇāmūrtyupanishad and Dakshiṇāmūrtistotra.] pp. lxxv. 170. *Madras,* 1899. 12°. **14048. b. 36.**

Forms part of the Vedic Religion *Series,* Minor Upanishads, Vol. II.

The Dakshinamurti Stotra, *etc.* [With English metrical translation by S. Veṅkaṭaramaṇan.] 1901. *See* PERIODICAL PUBLICATIONS. — *Madras.* The Light of Truth, or Siddhanta Deepika, *etc.* Vol. IV, no. 10, pp. 217-218. 1897, *etc.* 4°. **14170. fff. 4.(vol. 4.)**

ஶ்ரீதக்ஷிணாமூர்த்யஷ்டகம் [Dakshiṇāmūrtistotra, or °ashṭaka.] *See* VEDAPĀDASTAVA. ஶ்ரீ . . . வேதபாதஸ்தவம் [Vedapādastava.] pp. 27-31. 1903. 16°. **14033. a. 47.(2.)**

ṢAṄKARA ĀCHĀRYA (*continued*).

DOUBTFUL AND SUPPOSITITIOUS WORKS (*continued*).

ଦାରିଦ୍ର୍ୟଭଞ୍ଜନାଷ୍ଟକ [Dāridryabhañjanāshṭaka.] *See* KṚITTIVĀSAS. ବାଲୁଙ୍କେଶ୍ୱରଙ୍କ ଜଣାଣ *etc.* [Bāluṅkeṣvaraṅka Janān.] pp. 10-12. 1901. 16°. **14028. a. 19.(4.)**

This poem is also styled Dāridryaduḥkhabhañjana°, and in the Bṛihat-stotraratnākara °dahanastotra.

శ్రీగోవిన్దచతుర్దశమఞ్జరికాస్తోత్రమ్. [Govindachaturdaṣamañjarikā.] *See* above. మణిత్రయి *etc.* [Maṇitrayī.] pp. 143-200. 1899. 16°. **14028. a. 28.**

হরিতত্ত্বমুক্তাবলী। [Harim-īḍe-stuti, here called Haritattvamuktāvalī, the title usually given to Svayamprakāṣa's commentary.] pp. 8. *See* above, PHILOSOPHICAL POEMS, ETC. অজ্ঞানবোধিনী *etc.* [Ajñānabodhinī.] pt. 2. [1874.] 8°. **14048. bb. 45.(1.)**

॥ श्री हरिमीडे स्तोत्रम् *etc.* [Harim-īḍe-stuti. With a Gujarati commentary by Chidghanānanda, entitled Amṛitadhārā.] pp. i. i. 92. मुंबई [*Bombay*, 1897.] 12°. **14033. a. 32.**

Hymns in Praise of Hari, *etc.* [Harim-īḍe-stotra, in English.] 1902. *See* PERIODICAL PUBLICATIONS.—*Madras.* The Brahmavâdin, *etc.* Vol. VII, no. 2, pp. 198-206. 1895, *etc.* 8°. **14048. g. 1.(vol. 7.)**

ஸ்ரீ ஶங்கராசார்யக்ருத ஜ்ஞானப்ரதீபிகா. [Jñānapradīpikā. A tract of 40 stanzas on Vedānta. With a note on the life of Ṣaṅkara, by Mānavikrama.] *See* MĀNAVIKRAMA KAVI. ஸ்ரீ மாநவிக்ரமகவிராஜகாராகரோணம் ... க்ருதா: ஸைந்ருஷீகா: *etc.* [Essays and poems.] [1890.] 8°. **14072. d. 35.**

శ్రీలక్ష్మీనృసింహస్తోత్రమ్. [Lakshmīnṛisiṃhastotra, or Lakshmīnṛisiṃhakarāvalambast°.] *See* above. మణిత్రయి *etc.* [Maṇitrayī.] pp. 1-99. 1899. 16°. **14028. a. 28.**

लक्ष्मीनृसिंहस्तोत्रम् *etc.* [Lakshmīnṛisiṃhastotra. With a Hindi translation by Govindasiṃha of Benares.] pp. 11. कल्याण-मुंबई १९५७ [*Kalyan*, 1901.] 12°. **14028. b. 93.(6.)**

अथ मनीषापंचकम्. [Manīshāpañchaka. With the *ṭīkā* of Bālagopālendra.] *See* NITYĀNANDA SARASVATĪ.

ṢAṄKARA ĀCHĀRYA (*continued*).

DOUBTFUL AND SUPPOSITITIOUS WORKS (*continued*).

वेदान्तग्रन्थपञ्चकम् *etc.* [Vedāntagranthapañchaka.] pp. 93-112. [1891.] 8°. **14048. b. 15.(2.)**

श्री . . . मठाम्नायः *etc.* [Maṭhāmnāya, or Maṭhāmnāyasetu. A short work in verse ascribed to Ṣaṅkara, and giving the rules of the religious colleges said to have been founded by him. Edited with a preface in Marathi by Dājī Nāgeṣa Dharmādhikārī.] pp. xi. 23. मुंबय्यां १८१४ [*Bombay*, 1892.] 16°. **14048. a. 9.(3.)**

మఠామ్నాయసేతుః [Maṭhāmnāyasetu. A portion, styled Āmnāyavistara, in another recension.] *See* MAṬHĀMNĀYA. శ్రీమఠామ్నాయః *etc.* [Maṭhāmnāya, *etc.*] pp. 11-16. 1894. 8°. **14048. bb. 42.(3.)**

ஆம்நாய . . . விஸ்தாரவிவேக:॥ [Āmnāyavistara.] *See* SADĀṢIVA BRAHMENDRA. புண்யஶ்லோகமஞ்ஜரீ *etc.* [Puṇyaṣlokamañjarī.] pp. 34-38. [1895.] 8°. **14048. bb. 42.(2.)**

The Moha-mudgara . . . With its translation into English and Hindustani verse by Dína Nátha Deva. pp. i. 8. *Calcutta,* 1896. 8°. **14048. dd. 32.(2.)**

Moha-mudgara of Sreemuṭ Sankaracharya. [With English translation.] 1899. *See* PERIODICAL PUBLICATIONS.—*Calcutta.* The Oriental, *etc.* Vol. II, pt. i., pp. 4-6. 1898, *etc.* 8°. **Ac. 8825. b.(vol. 2.)**

ம்ருத்யுஞ்ஜயமாநஸிகபூஜாஸ்தோத்ரம் ॥ [Mṛityuṃjayamānasikapūjāstotra.] *See* APYAYA DĪKSHITA. ஸ்ரீவரதராஜஸ்தவ: *etc.* [Varadarājastava.] pp. 20-27. [1897.] 12°. **14076. a. 19.**

अथ निर्वाणपंचकम् [Nirvāṇapañchaka. With the *vivṛiti* of Nityānanda Sarasvatī.] *See* NITYĀNANDA SARASVATĪ. वेदान्तग्रन्थपञ्चकम् *etc.* [Vedāntagranthapañchaka.] pp. 79-92. [1891.] 12°. **14048. b. 15.(2.)**

Parmarthasara . . . Translated [into English] . . . by N. D[hol]. 1899. *See* PERIODICAL PUBLICATIONS.—*Calcutta.* The Oriental, *etc.* Vol. I, no. 11-12. 1898, *etc.* 8°. **Ac. 8825. b.(vol. 1.)**

ŚAṄKARA ĀCHĀRYA (*continued*).

DOUBTFUL AND SUPPOSITITIOUS WORKS (*continued*).

श्री . . . प्रबोधसुधाकर वेदान्त ग्रन्थ *etc.* [Prabodhasudhākara. A poem in 254 stanzas on Vaishṇava monism. With a Hindi translation by Rāmasvarūpa Ṣarmā.] pp. 83. **मुरादाबाद १९५८** [*Moradabad*, 1901.] 8°. **14049. b. 5.**

संयमिनामनामालिका ॥ [Saṃyaminānamamālikā. A list of the names of Ṛishis, in 17 stanzas, ascribed to Ṣaṅkara.] 1896. *See* VEṄKAṬARAṄGANĀTHA SVĀMĪ. Grandha Pradarsani, *etc.* [No. 12.] 1895, *etc.* 8°. **14003. c. 2.(12.)**

Le Bouddhisme d'après les sources brahmaniques. I. Sarvadarçanasaṁgraha . . . II. Sarvasiddhāntasaṁgraha[, sections iii.-vii., edited by] F. W. Thomas et L. de la Vallée Poussin. 1902. 8°. *See* SĀYAṆA ĀCHĀRYA.—*Works on Philosophy, etc.* **14048. e. 35.**

शतश्लोकीत्यपरनामा वेदान्तकेसरी . . . सटीकः *etc.* [Ṣataṣlokī, or Vedāntakesarī. A century of Vedantic verses. With the commentary of Ānandagiri.] Edited by Janārdana Bāḷājī Moḍak.] [1885-1886.] *See* PERIODICAL PUBLICATIONS.—*Poona.* **काव्येतिहास-संग्रह** [Kāvyetihāsasaṅgraha.] Vol. viii., no. 5-12, ix., no. 9. [1878-1888.] 8°. **14072. d. 37.(vol. 8, 9.)**

శ్రీ . . . శ్రీసౌందర్యలహరి *etc.* [Saundaryalaharī. With the commentary Lakshmīdharā of Lakshmīdhara Deṣika.] pp. 145. కార్వేటినగరు [*Karvaitnagar*,] 1892. 8°. **14028. c. 67.**

আনন্দলহরী-স্তোত্রম্ [Ānandalaharī, or more properly Saundaryalaharī.] pp. 20. *See* JÑĀNĀNANDA DEVA. **सिद्धान्तदर्शन** *etc.* [Siddhāntadarṣana.] [1898.] 12°. **14048. b. 33.(5.)**

The Ānandalaharī, *often confused with the* Saundaryalaharī, *consists of vv.* 1-41 *of the latter.*

સૌંદર્ય લેહેરી તથા આહ્નિકનાં ગાયનો [Saundaryalaharī. With Gujarati prose translation and metrical paraphrase, and preceded by a series of Gujarati hymns for the daily ritual of worshippers of Jagadambā Devī.] pp. i. 72. અમદાવાદ ૧૮૯૯ [*Ahmadabad*, 1899.] 8°. **14048. cc. 9.(4.)**

Ānanda Lahari [*i.e.* Saundaryalaharī 1-41]. With [introduction in English,] yantras and commentaries [based chiefly on the Saubhāgyavardhini of Kaivalyāṣrama, and the commentaries of Lakshmīdhara, Achyutānanda, Ḍiṇḍima, *etc.*] Translated into English by R. Anantakrishna Sastri. Second edition. pp. ii. 88. *Palghat*, 1899. 12°. **14048. b. 35.**

षट्पदमञ्जरी *etc.* [Shaṭpadamañjarī. Being the Shaṭpadī, a hymn to Vishṇu, with a commentary by Ṣaṅkarānanda Tīrtha.] pp. 35. [1889.] *See* PERIODICAL PUBLICATIONS.—*Bombay.* **ग्रन्थरत्नमाला** *etc.* (Granth Ratna Málá, *etc.*) Vol. III, no. 5. 1887-[1892.] 8°. **14096. c. 8.(vol. 3.)**

ஸ்ரீ . . . ஶிவாநந்தலஹரீ. ப்ரதிபதவ்யாக்யானஸஹிதா *etc.* [Ṣivānandalaharī. A century of Ṣaiva verses. With word-for-word interpretations and paraphrases in Tamil. Edited by Lakshmīnārāyaṇapuram Mṛityuṃjaya Ṣāstrī and Veṅkaṭasvāmi Aiyar of Mysore.] pp. i. 122, iv. *Madras*, 1904. 12°. **14048. b. 48.**

Revised by Muddu Ṣāstri of Madras, according to the verses appended.

శ్రీశివసువర్ణమాలాస్తుతిః [Ṣivasuvarṇamālāstuti.] *See* VEṄKAṬARATNA ṢARMĀ, *Kokkoṇḍa.* (భగవన్నామసంకీర్తన రత్నావళి. [Bhagavannāmasaṅkīrtanaratnāvalī,] *etc.*) pp. 33-34. 1886. 8°. **14003. c.**

ஶ்ரீஸுப்ரஹ்மண்யபுஜங்கஸ்தோத்ரம் *etc.* [Subrahmaṇya-bhujaṅgastotra. A hymn of 33 stanzas in the *bhujaṅgaprayāta* metre. Edited with grammatical notes in Sanskrit and with Tamil interpretation and commentary by Mēlmaṅgalam M. N. Subrahmaṇya Ṣāstrī.] pp. viii. 105. நடுக்காவேரி [*Nadukkaveri*,] 1902. 16°. **14028. a. 30.**

The wrapper bears a corresponding title in Tamil.

ṢAṄKARA ĀCHĀRYA (*continued*).

DOUBTFUL AND SUPPOSITITIOUS WORKS (*continued*).

Śankara's Veda-vedánta-sara. Text and translation by A. W. Smart. 1896. *See* PERIODICAL PUBLICATIONS.—*Madras*. The Brahmavâḍin, *etc.* Vol. I, pp. 209, 210. 1895, *etc.* 4°.
14048. g. 1.(vol. 1.)

योगतारावलि [Yogatārāvalī. 29 stanzas on Rājayoga philosophy. With Marathi prose translation.] pp. 2, 6. १८१७ [*Bombay*, 1896.] 8°.
14048. cc. 9.(3.)
This poem is sometimes ascribed to Nandikeṣvara.

[For the Amaruṣataka :] *See* AMARU.

[For the Hastāmalakastotra and its commentary:] *See* HASTĀMALAKA ĀCHĀRYA.

[For the Sannyāsagrahaṇapaddhati :] *See* SANNYĀSAGRAHAṆA.

[For hymns *etc.* ascribed to Ṣaṅkara which are included in the Bṛihat-stotraratnākara :] *See* STOTRARATNĀKARA.

[For the Vajrasūchyupanishad :] *See* UPANISHADS.

[For the Rājayogabhāshya or commentary on the Maṇḍalabrāhmaṇopanishad :] *See* UPANISHADS. — *Separate Upanishads.*

APPENDIX.

See GURUNĀTHA VEṄKAṬEṢA KITTŪR. श्रीशंकरविजयचूर्णिका *etc.* [Ṣaṅkaravijayachūrṇikā. Comprising chronology of Ṣaṅkara's life; Maṭhetivṛitta and Sampradāyachatushṭaya, poems enumerating the *maṭhs* founded by him, *etc.*] [1899.] 8°.
14058. b. 41.

See KRISHṆALĀLA GOVINDARĀMA DEVĀṢRAYĪ. શ્રીમચ્છંકરાચાર્યનો સમય *etc.* [Ṣaṅkarāchārya-no Samaya. A Gujarati dissertation on the chronology of Ṣaṅkara's life.] [1898.] 8°. **14146. gg. 4.**

See RĀMA MIṢRA ṢĀSTRĪ. तुरीयमीमांसा ... Turíyamimáṁsá [, a treatise upon the fundamental Vedic principles underlying Ṣaṅkara's teaching,] *etc.* [1901.] 8°. **14058. b. 46.**

ṢAṄKARA ĀCHĀRYA (*continued*).

APPENDIX (*continued*).

See ṢAṄKARA, *Āchārya-Svāmī, Pontiff of Dwarka.* ॥ विमर्शः ॥ [Vimarṣa. A treatise on the incarnations culminating in Ṣaṅkara, history of the latter, *etc.*] [1898.] 8°. **14048. cc. 21.(2.)**

See ṢAṄKARADĀSA, *P.K.* Sankara, or A brief sketch of Sankara Acharyar's history, *etc.* 1897. 16°.
14028. b. 95.

[For editions of Sāyaṇa's Ṣaṅkaradigvijaya :] *See* SĀYAṆA ĀCHĀRYA.—*Works on Philosophy, etc.*

See SĪTĀNĀTHA DATTA. Sankaracharya. His life and teachings, *etc.* 1897. 12°. **14048. a. 22.**

ṢAṄKARA ĀCHĀRYA, styled ABHINAVA-ṢAṄKARĀCHĀRYA. *See* VEDAS. — Yajurveda. — *Taittirīya-saṃhitā.* ஶத... ருத்ர-த்ரிஶதீ. [Ṣatarudrīya. With commentary by Abhinava-Ṣaṅkarāchārya.] 1903. *obl.* 16°. **14010. a. 8.**

ṢAṄKARA ĀRĀDHYA, *Pramathakavi.* ಸಟೀಕ ಬಸವೇಶವಿಜಯಂ *etc.* [Basaveṣavijaya. A poem in 43 *adhyāyas* on the Vīraṣaiva saint Basava. With Canarese paraphrase.] pp. 761. [1892-1894.] *See* PERIODICAL PUBLICATIONS. — *Mysore.* ವೀರಶೈವಮತಪ್ರಕಾಶಿಕೆ [Vīraṣaivamataprakāṣikā.] Vol. I-III. [1892-1895.] 8°.
14028. d. 39. (vol. 1-3.)

ṢAṄKARA BHAṬṬA, *son of Nārāyaṇa.* ॥ मीमांसाबालप्रकाशः ॥ जैमिनीयद्वादशाध्यायार्थ-संग्रहः *etc.* (Mimânsâbâlaprakâsha, [a commentary on Jaimini's Mīmāṃsāsūtra,] by Ŝree Bhaṭṭa Shankar. Edited by Paṇḍit Mukunda Shâstri.) pp. ii. iii. 183. *Benares*, 1902. 8°. **14004. a. 16.**
Forms nos. 58 *and* 59 *of the* Chowkhambâ Sanskrit Series. *The English title is from the wrapper.*

ṢAṄKARA BHAṬṬA, *son of Nīlakaṇṭha.* ॥ अथ सटीकः कुंडार्कः प्रारभ्यते ॥ [Kuṇḍārka. A tract on the modes of making sacrificial trenches. With the commentary Kuṇḍārkamarīchimālā of Raghuvīra Dīkshita. Edited by Yadurāma Ṣukla.] ff. 17, *lith.* मुंबय्यां १८१४ [*Bombay*, 1893.] *obl.* 8°.
14028. dd. 5.(1.)

ṢAṄKARA DĀJĪ ṢĀSTRĪ PADE. *See* CHARAKA. सार्थ श्रीचरक संहिता. Shree Charaka Sanhita. With translation & . . . notes in Marathi. A quarterly journal. [Edited by Ṣaṅkara Pade.] [1897-1898.] 8°. **14043. cc. 8.**

ṢAṄKARADĀSA, *P.K.* Sankara, or A brief sketch of Sankara Acharyar's history, [in English,] by a Devotee. (Sankara Vilas Series.) pp. v. 35. *Madura,* 1897. 16°. **14028. b. 95.**

ṢAṄKARAIYA DEVĀṄGA, *Yajamāna,* also called ṢIVAṢAṄKARA YOGĪ. *See* ĀGAMAS. [*Siddhāgama.*] ದೇವಲಬ್ರಹ್ಮಬೋಧಕ . . . ಮೂಲಸ್ತಂಭನ *etc.* [Devalabrahmabodhaka-vedokta-mūlastambhana. Edited with Canarese translations and commentaries by Ṣaṅkaraiya.] [1898.] 8°. **14058. b. 37.**

ṢAṄKARA KAVI, *of Mithila.* *See* ṢAṄKHADHARA.

ṢAṄKARALĀLA, *Ṣrotriya, of Bijnaur.* वर्णव्यवस्था *etc.* [Varṇavyavasthā. An anthology from scriptural and other literature bearing upon caste duties. Compiled with a Hindi commentary by Ṣaṅkaralāla.] pp. 33. *Meerut,* [१८]९९ [1899.] 8°. **14058. cc. 1.**

ṢAṄKARALĀLA, *son of Lālā Bhojadeva.* *See* GORAKSHANĀTHA. कामशास्त्र *etc.* [Kāmaṣāstra. Edited with Hindi version by Ṣaṅkaralāla.] [1899.] 8°. **14053. d. 61.**

ṢAṄKARALĀLA, *son of Māheṣvara.* श्रीमच्चंद्रप्रभाचरितम् *etc.* [Chandraprabhācharita, or Chandraprabhābhyudaya. An episode from the author's romance styled Pārvatīpariṇaya.] pp. ii. iii. iv. 164. संवद्वसुवेदनंदेंदु° [*Morvi ?* 1891.] 12°. **14070. b. 26.**

ṢAṄKARALĀLA VARMĀ. संस्कृत वाक्यभानु ॥ [Saṃskṛitavākyabhānu.] A light to Sanskrit conversation. [Being English-Sanskrit phrases and sentences] by Shankara Lala Varma. pp. i. 46. *Lahore,* 1896. 8°. **14093. b. 38.**

ṢAṄKARA MIṢRA, *son of Dineṣvara.* *See* JAYADEVA, *son of Bhojadeva.* The Gita-govinda . . . With the commentaries Rasikapriya of King Kumbha and Rasamanjari of . . . Shankara Mishra, *etc.* 1899. 8°. **14070. dd. 3.**

ṢAṄKARĀNANDA, *disciple of Ānandātmā.* *See* UPANISHADS.—*General Collections.* उपनिषदां समुच्चयः *etc.* (Thirty two Upanisads. With Dîpikâs by . . . Shankarânanda, *etc.*) [1895.] 8°. **14003. ccc. (no. 29.)**

—— *See* UPANISHADS.—*Small Collections.* উপনিষদাবলী *etc.* [Upanishadāvalī. Ten Upanishads, including the Kaivalyop°. with the commentaries of Ṣaṅkarānanda and Nārāyaṇa.] [1896.] 12°. **14010. b. 12.**

—— *See* UPANISHADS.—*Small Collections.* Amritabindu and Kaivalya Upanishads. With commentaries [in English, compiled from the works of Ṣaṅkarānanda and others,] *etc.* 1898. 12°. **14010. b. 19.**

—— *See* UPANISHADS. — *Separate Upanishads.* ईशावास्योपनिषत्° ((1) Shri Ísávásyopanishad with . . . (5) The Dípika by . . . Śankaránanda, *etc.*) [1888.] 8°. **14003. ccc. (no. 5.)**

—— *See* UPANISHADS. — *Separate Upanishads.* The Íśavâsyopanishad. Translated . . . with . . . notes from the Tikas of . . . Sankarananda, *etc.* [1896.] 8°. **14010. cc. 6.**

—— *See* UPANISHADS. — *Separate Upanishads.* केनोपनिषत्° (The Kenopanishad . . . And the Dípikás of the same by . . . Śankaránanda and Náráyaṇa, *etc.*) [1888.] 8°. **14003. ccc. (no. 6.)**

—— *See* UPANISHADS. — *Separate Upanishads.* प्रश्नोपनिषत्° (Śri Praśnopanishad with . . . Dipiká of the same by . . . Śankaránanda, *etc.*) [1889.] 8°. **14003. ccc. (no. 8.)**

ṢAṄKARĀNANDA AVADHŪTA, *disciple of Prakāṣānanda.* *See* NĀNAK. श्रीमद्गुरुनानकगीता *etc.* [Nānakagītā. With Hindi version by Ṣaṅkarānanda.] [1901.] 8°. **14049. b. 4.**

—— *See* NĀNAK. अथ निराकारमीमांसादर्शनम् *etc.* [Nirākāramīmāṃsādarṣana. With Hindi translation of Keṣavānanda's *bhāshya* by Ṣaṅkarānanda.] [1903.] 8°. **14049. bb. 3.**

ṢAṄKARĀNANDA TĪRTHA, *disciple of Ṣivanārāyaṇānanda.* *See* ṢAṄKARA ĀCHĀRYA. —*Doubtful and Supposititious Works.* षट्पदमञ्जरी *etc.* [Shaṭpadamañjarī. Being the Shaṭpadī with commentary by Ṣaṅkarānanda.] [1889.] 8°. [*Granthamālā.*] **14096. c. 8.(vol. 3.)**

ṢAṄKARANĀTHA, *Pandit, of Bhawanipur.* The Classification of Caste according to the Vedas and the Dhurma Shastras. Written by order of the Calcutta Arya Samaj by Pundit Shunker Nath. pp. 56. *Bhowanipore,* 1901. 16°. **4503. d. 3.**

—— The Vedas as the Revelation. Written by order of the Calcutta Arya Samaj by Pundit Shunker Nath. pp. 81. *Bhowanipore,* 1901. 16°. **4503. d. 4.**

ṢAṄKARA PĀṆḌURAṄGA PAṆḌIT. *See* HEMACHANDRA, *disciple of Devachandra.* The Kumârapâlacharita . . . Edited by Shaṅkar . . . Paṇḍit. 1900. 8°. **14100. c. 23.**

—— *See* KĀLIDĀSA.—*Mālavikāgnimitra.* The Mâlavikâgnimitra . . . With the commentary of Kâṭayavema. Edited . . . by Shankar . . . Pandit. 1889. 8°. **14080. c. 31.**

—— *See* KĀLIDĀSA. — *Vikramorvaṣīya.* The Vikramorvaśîyam . . . Edited with English notes . . . by Shankar . . . Paṇḍit, *etc.* 1901. 8°. **14080. c. 42.**

—— *See* VEDAS.—*Atharvaveda.* Atharvaveda-samhitâ. With the commentary of Sâyaṇâchârya. Edited by Shankar . . . Pandit. 1895-1898. 4°. **14010. ee. 1.**

ṢAṄKARA PĀRAṢAVA. उदयचरित्रम् . . . गद्यपद्योभयात्मकं *etc.* [Udayacharitra. A composition in verse and prose, in panegyric of the Maharaja Udayavarmā. Edited, with biography of the author, by Punnacheri Nīlakaṇṭha Ṣarmā.] pp. 36. पट्टाम्बि १९०३ [*Pattambi,* 1903.] 8°. **14072. c. 52.(2.)**

ṢAṄKARA RĀMACHANDRA HATVAḶNE. *See* VARARUCHI. साथे प्राकृत प्रकाश *etc.* [Prākṛitaprakāṣa. Edited with Marathi commentary by Ṣaṅkara Hatvaḷne.] [1900.] 12°. **14092. a. 26.**

ṢAṄKARA RĀU, *Philkhānā.* *See* PURĀṆAS.—*Skandapurāṇa.* సుజ్ఞానదీపము-సురుగీతలు *etc.* [Sujñānadīpa, *etc.* With Telugu glosses and translation by Ṣaṅkara Rāu.] [1898.] 8°. **14016. c. 54.**

ṢAṄKARA ṢĀSTRĪ, *V., of Madras Christian College.* Subantaprakasa. A treatise on the declension of Sanskrit Nouns, *etc.* pp. i. ii. 140. *Madras,* 1898. 12°. **14090. b. 45.(4.)**

ṢAṄKARA SENA. Science of Sphygmica, or Sage Kanád on Pulse, an English translation with Sanskrit passages [*i.e.*, a selection from the text of Ṣaṅkara's Nāḍīprakāṣa with an explanatory paraphrase] by Kăviráj Russick Láll Gupta. pp. xi. 105. *Calcutta,* 1891. 12°. **14043. b. 11.**

ṢAṄKARĀṢRAMASVĀMĪ. *See* ṢAṄKARA, *Āchārya-Svāmī, Pontiff of Dwarka.*

ṢAṄKARASUBRAHMAṆYA SŪRI, *of Koduvayur.* തടാതകാപരിണയം നാമ കാവ്യം *etc.* [Taṭātakāpariṇaya. A romantic poem in 8 cantos upon a theme of local legendary history. With commentary styled Prakāṣikā by Anantanārāyaṇa Ṣāstrī of Kudalur.] pp. i. 247, vi. *Palghat,* 1903. 8°. **14070. dd. 29.**

ṢAṄKARA TRYAMBAKA SAPTARSHI. *See* SĀYAṆA ĀCHĀRYA.—*Works on Philosophy, etc.* श्रीहरिगीता *etc.* [Pañchadaṣī. With Marathi commentary, styled Harigītā, by Harihara Rāya. Edited by Ṣaṅkara Saptarshi.] [1902, *etc.*] 8°. **14049. b. 1.**

ṢAṄKARA VĀRIYAR, *R.* *See* NĪLAKAṆṬHA MUNI, *disciple of Bāla Muni.* The Advîtha Párijátha . . . Published by R. Shankar Wariyer. 1901. 16°. **14048. a. 14.(2.)**

ṢAṄKHADHARA. कविकर्पटिका *etc.* [Kavikarpaṭikā. A short *Gradus ad Parnassum,* or help to poetical composition, here attributed to Ṣaṅkara of Mithila.] pp. 19. *Durbhangah,* 1892. 8°. **14053. c. 58.(3.)**

For the identification with the author of the Laṭakamelaka, compare Aufrecht, Catal. Catalogorum, *and Peterson, Third Report, p.* 21.

SAṄKHĀRABHĀJANĪ. သင်္ခါရဘာဇနီကျမ်း *etc.* [Saṅkhārabhājanī. A Burmese-Pali philosophical treatise. Followed by the Kammaṭṭhān-amyomyo, Pali lists of religious and philosophical terms, with Burmese commentaries, *etc.*] pp. 88. ရန်ကုန် ၁၂၅၆ [*Rangoon,* 1894.] 8°. **14300. d. 22.(8.)**

—— [Another copy.] **14300. d. 19.(5.)**

SANNYĀSAGRAHAṆA. अथ संन्यासग्रहणपद्धति प्रारम्भः [Sannyāsagrahaṇapaddhati. Rules for the ceremonies to be observed on entering the order of *sannyāsī,* ascribed to Ṣaṅkara. Comprising

the Sannyāsaprārthanāvidhi, or preliminary rules, and the Saptasūtra-sannyāsapaddhati.] ff. 35. अयोध्या १९५६ [*Ajodhya*, 1900.] *obl.* 8°.
14033. c. 44.(2.)

Imperfect ; ff. 31, 32 *are missing.*

ṢĀNTANAVA. [For editions of the Phiṭsūtra included in those of the Siddhāntakaumudī :] *See* PĀṆINI.—*Siddhāntakaumudī.*

ṢĀNTIDEVA. बोधिचर्यावतारम् । [Bodhicharyāvatāra. A poem in 10 *parichchhedas* on Buddhist doctrine.] pp. 32. 1894. *See* ACADEMIES, *etc.*—Calcutta. — *Buddhist Text Society of India.* Journal, *etc.* Vol. II, pt. i., ii. 1893, *etc.* 8°.
14003. b. 19.(vol. 2.)

—— [A separate issue of the same.] *See* ACADEMIES, *etc.*—*Calcutta.*—*Buddhist Text Society of India.* Buddhist Texts, *etc.* 1894, *etc.* 8°.
14004. c. (vol. 1, no. 6.)

—— Bodhicaryāvatāre Prajñāpāramitāparicchedaḥ. [Being Book ix. of the Bodhicharyāvatāra. With the commentary of Prajñākaramati Ṣrījñāna.] *See* LA VALLÉE POUSSIN (L. DE). Bouddhisme. Études et Matériaux, *etc.* pp. 233-388. 1898. 4°.
14028. e. 32.

—— [Another copy.] **Ac. 985/6. (tom. 55.)**

—— Bodhicaryâvatâra (Bodhisattvacaryāvatāra) . . . Chapitres i. ii. iii. iv. (v.) et x. Texte et traduction [with introduction, by L. de la Vallée Poussin]. 1891-1896. *See* PERIODICAL PUBLICATIONS.—*Louvain.* Le Muséon, *etc.* Tome XI, XV. 1881, *etc.* 8°. **P.P. 4453. (tom. 11, 15.)**

The text has not been published in this Journal.

—— Çikshāsamuccaya. A compendium of Buddhistic teaching, compiled by Çāntideva, chiefly from earlier Mahāyāna-sūtras. Edited by Cecil Bendall. pp. vii. ii. i. vi. xlvii. 419; 1 *plate.* (1897-) 1902. *See* ACADEMIES, *etc.*—St. Petersburg.—*Academia Scientiarum Imperialis.* Bibliotheca Buddhica. Vol. i. 1897, *etc.* 8°.
14003. dd. 1.

ṢĀNTIMUKURA. ശാന്തി-മുകുരഃ *etc.* [Ṣāntimukura. A digest of lustral rites. Part 1, or Navagrahasamuchchayaṣānti, on the rites relating to the planets. Edited by Chokkanāthapuram Ṣrīnivāsa Ṣāstrī.] pp. 32. കുംഭഘോണ॥ [*Kumbakonam,*] 1901. 16°. **14033. a. 47.(1.)**

ṢĀNTIPRABHA. *See* ṢĀNTIDEVA.

ṢĀNTIPRAKĀṢA. अथ शान्तिप्रकाशान्तर्गत-विनायकशान्तिः । [Vināyakaṣānti. A ritual for the propitiation of Vināyaka or Gaṇeṣa, taken from the Ṣāntiprakāṣa.] pp. 21, iii. मुंबई १९५६ [*Bombay*, 1900.] 12°.
14028. b. 81.(4.)

ṢĀNTI SŪRI. ॥ अथ श्री जीवविचार° [Jīvavichāra, in Prakrit called Jīvaviyāro. A Prakrit poem in 50 stanzas on the Jain psychology.] *See* SĀMĀYIKASŪTRA. સામાયિકસૂત્ર *etc.* [Sāmāyikasūtra.] pp. 67-74. [1900.] 16°. **14100. a. 25.**

—— ॥ जीवविचार *etc.* [Jīvavichāra. In 51 stanzas. With Gujarati translation.] *See* HEMAṢAṄKARA LAKSHMĪṢAṄKARA VARDHAMĀNKAR. प्रकरण माला *etc.* [Prakaraṇamālā.] pp. 1-13. [1901.] 8°.
14100. d. 11.

ṢĀNTI SŪRI, *disciple of Sarvadeva and Abhayadeva.* Le Novelline Prācrite di Maṇḍiya e di Agaladatta. [An Italian translation by P. E. Pavolini of two stories taken from the commentaries on the Uttarādhyayana composed respectively by Devendra and Ṣānti Sūri.] 1892. 8°. *See* DEVENDRA GAṆĪ. **14100. c. 18.**

SAPTARSHI. *See* NARAHARI BHAṬṬA.

SAPTAṢLOKĪ-RĀMĀYAṆA. सप्तश्लोकीरामायण प्रा° [Saptaṣlokī-rāmāyaṇa. A summary of the Rāmāyaṇa in 7 stanzas, ascribed to the Seven Ṛishis.] ff. 4. खेरवाडी [*Kherwadi*, 1901.] *obl.* 16°.
14028. a. 19.(7.)

ṢARACHCHANDRA CHAKRAVARTĪ. ধ্যানমালা *etc.* [Dhyānamālā. A lectionary for mystic meditations upon divers deities, together with the appropriate forms of address and the formulæ termed *bījamantra* and *gāyatrī*. Compiled by Ṣarachchandra Chakravartī.] pp. iv. 106, ii. কলিকাতা ১৩০৭ [*Calcutta*, 1900.] 12°.
14028. b. 66.(5.)

ṢARACHCHANDRA DĀSA, *Rāi Bahādur.* *See* ACADEMIES, *etc.*—Calcutta.—*Buddhist Text Society of India.* Journal . . . Edited by Śarat Ćandra Dás. 1893, *etc.* 8°. **14003. b. 19.**

ṢARACHCHANDRA DĀSA, *Rāi Bahādur (continued).* See KARUṆĀPUṆḌARĪKA. करुणा-पुण्डरीकम् । Karuṇā-puṇḍarīkam . . . edited by . . . Çarat Chandra Dās, *etc.* 1898. 8°. [*Buddhist Texts.*] **14004. c. (vol. 1, no. 3.)**

—— See NĀGĀRJUNA. माध्यमिकावृत्ति । Mádhyamiká Vṛitti . . . edited by . . . Çarat Chandra Dás, *etc.* 1894-1897. 8°. [*Buddhist Texts.*] **14004. c. (vol. 1, no. 1.)**

—— See SAMĀDHIRĀJASŪTRA. समाधिराजसूत्रम् । Samādhirāja-sūtram . . . edited by . . . Çarat Chandra Dās, *etc.* 1896, *etc.* 8°. [*Buddhist Texts.*] **14004. c. (vol. 2, no. 2.)**

—— See SUTTAPIṬAKA. — *Khuddakanikāya.* [*Dhammapada.*] धम्मपदं । Dhammapadam . . . edited by . . . Çarat Chandra Dās, *etc.* 1899. 8°. [*Buddhist Texts.*] **14004. c. (vol. 1, no. 4.)**

—— See SUVARṆAPRABHĀ. सुवर्णप्रभा । Suvarṇa Prabhā . . . edited by . . . Çarat Chandra Dās, *etc.* 1898, *etc.* 8°. [*Buddhist Texts.*] **14004. c. (vol. 2, no. 3.)**

ṢARACHCHANDRA MUKHOPĀDHYĀYA. See ASHṬĀVAKRA. The Astabakra Sanhita. [Translated.] Edited by S. C. Mukhopadhaya. 1902. 8°. **P.P. 656. ba. (vol. x., no. 7.)**

—— See MAHĀBHĀRATA.—*Entire Work.* The Mahabharata . . . Translated . . . with esoteric commentary. Edited by S. C. Mukhopadhaya. 1899, *etc.* 8°. **14065. e. 28.**

——See MAHĀBHĀRATA.–Bhagavadgītā.–*Sanskrit and English.* The Bhagabat Gita . . . Edited by S. C. Mukhopadhaya. 1902. 8°. **14065. c. 52.**

—— The Imitation of Sreekrishna. Quotations [in English] from the Hindu Religious Literature for each day in the year. Compiled by S. C. Mukhopadhaya. pp. xiv. 80. *Calcutta,* 1894. 16°. **14065. a. 7.**

ṢARACHCHANDRA ṢĀSTRĪ. See KARUṆĀPUṆḌARĪKA. करुणा-पुण्डरीकम् । Karuṇā-puṇḍarīkam . . . edited by . . . Çarat Chandra Dās . . . and . . . Çarat Chandra Çāstrī. 1898. 8°. [*Buddhist Texts.*] **14004. c. (vol. 1, no. 3.)**

—— See NĀGĀRJUNA. माध्यमिकावृत्ति । Mádhyamiká Vṛitti . . . edited by . . . Çarat Chandra Dás . . . Harimohan Vidyabhushaṇa (and . . . Çarat Chandra Çāstrī). 1894-1897. 8°. [*Buddhist Texts.*] **14004. c. (vol. 1, no. 1.)**

—— See SUVARṆAPRABHĀ. सुवर्णप्रभा । Suvarṇa Prabhā . . . edited by . . . Çarat Chandra Dās . . . and . . . Çarat Chandra Çāstrī. 1898, *etc.* 8°. [*Buddhist Texts.*] **14004. c. (vol. 2, no. 3.)**

ṢARACHCHANDRA TARKACHŪḌĀMAṆI. See SĀRASVATASŪTRA. सूत्रमाला। *etc.* [Sūtramālā. Comprising the Sārasvatasūtra and the commentary Praveṣikā of Ṣarachchandra.] [1894.] 12°. **14090. b. 42.**

SĀRADĀCHARAṆA SENA KAVIRATNA. See MĀDHAVA, *son of Indukara.* नदीक-निदान *etc.* [Nidāna. With the Vyākhyāmadhukoṣa. Edited by Sāradācharaṇa Sena.] [1901.] 8°. **14043. c. 44.**

SARAṆA. သရဏာဒိဆက္ကကဏ္ဍဒီပနီကျမ်း [Saraṇādichhakkakaṇḍadīpaṇī. A treatise on the Three Refuges of Buddhism, comprising (1) sections on the Refuges, in Burmese, (2) panegyrics on the same, in Pali, with Burmese paraphrases, (3) the Vipassanāñānatantī-sā-tan of Ukkaṃvaṃsamālā, likewise in Pali and Burmese, (4) the Nettihāradīpaṇī-kyan, a Burmese tract based on the Nettippakaraṇa.] pp. iii. 114. ရန်ကုန် ၁၂၆၁ [*Rangoon,* 1899.] 8°. **14300. d. 28.(5.)**

SARAṆAṄKARA, *Bentara.* See SUTTAPIṬAKA.—*Majjhimanikāya.* මජ්ඣිමනිකායො *etc.* [Majjhimanikāya. Edited by Saraṇaṅkara and Paññāratana.] 1895. 8°. **14098. dd. 11.**

SARAṆAṄKARA, *Velivita.* See ABHISAMBODHI-ALAṄKĀRA. අභිසම්බොධි අලඞ්කාරය *etc.* [Abhisambodhi-alaṅkāra. A poem with Sinhalese interpretation, both traditionally ascribed to Saraṇaṅkara.] 1897. 8°. **14098. ccc. 2.**

SĀRANĀTHA ṢARMĀ, *disciple of Gaṇapati Ṣāstrī.* ஆசாரயோக்தி விபூஷணம் *etc.* [Āchāryoktivibhūshaṇa. A tract, in 150 stanzas, on the sectarian marks of Smārta Brahmans.] pp. ii. 24. நடுக்காவேரி அச்சுக்கூடம் [*Nadukkaveri,* 1896.] 8°. **14028. d. 59.(4.)**

SĀRASVATĀBHIDHĀNA. সারস্বতাভিধান। [Sārasvatābhidhāna. A vocabulary of synonyms. With Bengali translation.] *See* GOPĪRAMAṆA TARKARATNA. কোষচন্দ্রিকা *etc.* [Koṣachandrikā.] pp. 21-24. [1893.] 12°. **14090. b. 44.(1.)**

SĀRASVATASŪTRA. श्रीसारस्वतपूर्वार्द्धः *etc.* (उत्तरार्द्धः) [Sārasvatavyākaraṇa. Comprising the Sārasvatasūtra with the Sarasvatīprakriyā or exposition by Anubhūtisvarūpa. Together with a gloss by Lokeṣvara Ṣukla.] 2 pts. pp. 51, 53. लक्ष्मणपुरे १९४७-अब्दवेदांकभू [*Lucknow*, 1890-1892.] 8°. **14093. d. 17.**

—— सारस्वत सटीक *etc.* [Sārasvatavyākaraṇa. With a copious Hindi commentary by Umādatta Tripāṭhī and Ṣaktidhara Sukula.] pt. i. pp. vii. 572. लखनऊ १८९१ [*Lucknow*, 1891.] 8°. **14090. bb. 6.**

—— सारस्वतं व्याकरणम् *etc.* (Saraswata Vyakaranam . . . A Sanskrit grammar [comprising the Sārasvatasūtra with the exposition] by Anubhuti Swarupacharya. With the commentary of Chandrakirti Suri. Edited . . . by Pandit Jibananda Vidyasagara . . . Second edition.) Vol. ii. pp. i. 388. कलिकाता १८९३ [*Calcutta*, 1893.] 8°. **14093. b. 43.**

The English title is from the wrapper.

—— सारस्वतं व्याकरणम् *etc.* [Sārasvatavyākaraṇa. Being the Sārasvatasūtra as conveyed and expounded in the commentary of Anubhūtisvarūpa.] pp. ii. 146. मुम्बय्यां १९५२ [*Bombay*, 1896.] 8°. **14090. c. 39.**

—— ॥ सारस्वतं व्याकरणम् *etc.* [Sārasvatavyākaraṇa. Being the Sārasvatasūtra with a Gujarati version by Vaidyanātha Motīrāmjī of the Sarasvatīprakriyā.] pt. i. pp. iv. 240. લીંબડી ૧૯૫૫ [*Limri*, 1899.] 12°. **14092. a. 20.**

—— सारस्वतं व्याकरणम् *etc.* (The Saraswata Vyakarana. A Sanskrit grammar by Anubbuti Swarupacharya. With the commentary [Sārasvataprasāda] of Vasudeva Bhatta. Part i. Edited . . . by Pandit-kulapati Shri Jibananda Vidyasagara. . . . Second edition.) pp. 231. कलिकाता १९०१ [*Calcutta*, 1901.] 8°. **14090. bb. 15.(2.)**

English title taken from wrapper.

—— সূত্রমালা। অর্থাৎ বৃহৎ সারস্বতীয় সূত্রাবলী *etc.* [Sūtramālā, or Bṛihat-sārasvatīyasūtrāvalī. Comprising the Sārasvatasūtra and the commentary Praveṣika of Ṣarachchandra Tarkachūḍāmaṇi. Edited with Bengali preface by Dhanamjaya Deva Varmā.] pt. i. কুমিল্লা ১৩০৮ [*Comillah*, 1894.] 12°. **14090. b. 42.**

Extends to the end of the Taddhitādhyāya. Apparently the second half has not been published. The editor in his preface points out that the Sārasvatavyākaraṇa has come down in three forms. Anubhūtisvarūpa first arranged and commented upon the Aphorisms in his treatise, which is sometimes styled Laghvākhya. *Mayūbhūtisvarūpa and Rāmāṣrama also wrote treatises based on the latter; and moreover Rāmāṣrama composed the Siddhāntachandrikā, for which he drew upon the Mahābhāshya, and which he "caused to be read" to Bhānuji Dikshita. The work of Mayūbhūtisvarūpa and Rāmāṣrama forms the Bṛihat-sārasvata, on which the present commentary is founded.*

—— सिद्धान्तचन्द्रिकोत्तरार्द्धः *etc.* [Sārasvatasūtra. With the commentary Siddhāntachandrikā of Rāmāṣrama Āchārya. Part ii., comprising a Dhātupāṭha and a list of the Aphorisms, both alphabetically arranged; a table of *kridanta* stems, styled Kṛidantabhūshaṇakoṣa; and the latter half of the Aphorisms with the Siddhāntachandrikā, from the Parasmaipadaprakriyā to the end. With a Hindi commentary by Chandramauli Ṣarmā, based on the Subodhinī of Sadānanda Gaṇī. Edited, annotated, and tabulated by Ṣaktidhara Sukula.] pt. ii. pp. ii. i. cxxxii. 764. लक्ष्मणपुरे १९०० [*Lucknow*, 1900.] 4°. **14092. c. 20.**

—— लघुभाष्यम् *etc.* [Sārasvatasūtra. With the commentary Laghu-bhāshya of Raghunātha son of Vināyaka, and as an appendix the Sūtra alone. Edited by Vaṃṣīdhara of Nabha.] pp. ii. 460. मुम्बय्यां १८२२ [*Bombay*, 1901.] 8°. **14093. b. 44.**

SARASVATĪNIGHAṆṬU. සරස්වතී නිඝණ්ටුව [Sarasvatīnighaṇṭu. A dictionary of Materia Medica. With notes in Sinhalese.] pp. ii. 75. *Colombo*, 1884. 8°. **14043. d. 44.(2.)**

A reprint of the edition published at the Lankabhinava-Vishruta Press, Colombo, in 1865.

SARASVATĪṢESHA ṢĀSTRĪ, *of Venkatagiri.* *See* ṢIṄGA BHŪPĀLA. రసార్ణవసుధాకరః [Rasārṇavasudhākara. Edited by Sarasvatīṣesha.] [1895.] 8°. **14053. ccc. 13.**

ŚARAT ĆANDRA. *See* ṢARACHCHANDRA.

ṢARATKUMĀRA SENA. *See* KĀLIDĀSA.—*Suppositititious Works.* কালিদাসের কবিতা *etc.* [Kālidāser

Kavitā. Compiled and edited with Bengali translation and biography of the poet by Ṣaratkumāra Sena.] [1901.] 12°. **14076. b. 26.(2.)**

SARAYŪPRASĀDA MIṢRA, *of Allahabad.* See Ṣārṅgadhara, *son of Dāmodara.* शान्तरसनिर्देशः *etc.* [Ṣāntarasanirdeṣa. Edited by Sarayūprasāda.] [1897.] 12°. **14070. b. 29.**

—— *See* Ṣivaṣarma Sūri. वासुदेवरसानन्दः *etc.* [Vāsudevarasānanda. Edited by Sarayūprasāda.] [1897.] 12°. **14028. c. 76.(2.)**

SARAYŪPRASĀDA VĀJAPEYĪ, *of Gaurilakha.* *See* Lakshmīnārāyaṇa Ṣarmā, *of Benares.* मदनमुखचपेटिका *etc.* [Madanamukhachapeṭikā. With Hindi translation by Sarayūprasāda.] [1894.] 12°. **14076. b. 34.**

SĀRIPUTTA SAṄGHARĀJA. *See* Anuruddha. Abhidharmarthasangraha sanna. Compiled by Sri Sariputra, *etc.* 1897. 8°. **14098. ccc. 6.**

SARKÁR (Golápchandra). *See* Gulāb-chandra Sarkār.

ṢARMĀ (O. L.). *See* Ṣaṅkara Āchārya.—*Doubtful and Supposititious Works.* Dwadasa Manjari . . . rendered into English verse by O. L. Sarma. 1893. 16°. **14010. a. 4.**

SARNĒLIS, *B. L.* *See* Jīvanātha, *son of Ṣambhunātha.* භාවකුතුහලය *etc.* [Bhāvakutūhala. Edited with Sinhalese gloss and notes by B. L. Sarnēlis.] 1897. 8°. **14053. ccc. 4.**

ṢĀRṄGADEVA, *Nihṣaṅka, son of Soḍhala.* সঙ্গীতরত্নাকর । [Saṅgītaratnākara. A treatise on music. With Ṣiṅga Bhūpāla's commentary.] pp. 47. [1891, *etc.*] *See* Periodical Publications.—*Calcutta.* অরুণোদয় *etc.* [Aruṇodaya.] Pt. i., no. 17. [1890, *etc.*] 4°. **14133. g. 16.(pt. i., no. 17.)**

—— संगीतरत्नाकरः *etc.* (The Sangîta Ratnâkara . . . by Śrî Niśśanka Śarngadeva, with its commentary [called Kalānidhi] by Chatura Kallinâtha and seven very useful appendices containing Swaraprastâr, &c. Edited by Pandit Mangesh Rámkrishṇa Telang.) 2 vols. pp. v. i. 1000. पुण्याख्यपत्तने १८१६-१८१९ [*Poona*, 1896-1897.] 8°. **14003. ccc. (no. 35.)**

Forms no. 35 of the Ānandāṣrama Sanskrit Series. *The English title is that given on the cover of vol. 2.*

ṢĀRṄGADHARA, *son of Dāmodara.* शान्तरसनिर्देशः *etc.* [Ṣāntarasanirdeṣa. Comprising the sections of the Paddhati or anthology from the Vairāgyākhyānaparichchheda to the Videhamuktikathanap°. With notes by Ādityarāma Bhaṭṭāchārya. Edited by Sarayūprasāda Miṣra.] pp. 86. प्रयागे १९५४ [*Allahabad*, 1897.] 12°. **14070. b. 29.**

—— Śârangdhara Saṁhitâ. [A work on medicine.] Edited by Prabhurám Jivanrám Vaidya. (शार्ङ्गधरसंहिता) pp. iv. clv. 351. *Bombay*, 1891. 16°. **14043. b. 12.**

ṢĀRṄGADHARA, *Logician.* *See* Ṣeshaṣārṅgadhara.

SARVĀNANDA SŪRI, *disciple of Dhanaprabha Sūri.* જગડૂ ચરિત *etc.* [Jagaḍūcharita. A poem in 7 *sargas* on the fortunes of the Jain merchant Jagaḍū. With an introduction, translation, and appendices, in Gujarati, by Maganlāl Dalpatrām Khakkhar.] pp. 214, iv. મુંબઈ ૧૮૯૬ [*Bombay*, 1896.] 12°. **14100. b. 9.**

Jagaḍū, or Jhagṛū, was a pious Ṣrīmālī who gained great honour by his generosity in a famine in Samvat 1315.

SARVAVARMĀ. कातन्त्रव्याकरणम् *etc.* [Kātantra. With the commentary Kātantrarūpamāla of Bhāvasena. Edited by Jīvarāma Lallurām Raikvāl.] pp. ii. 222, ii. मुम्बय्यां १९५२ [*Bombay*, 1895.] 8°. **14090. bb. 9.**

The text of the sūtras differs considerably from that edited by Dr. Eggeling. The last aphorism (809) corresponds to IV. v. 81 *of his text.*

—— কলাপসূত্রম্ *etc.* [Kalāpasūtra, or Kātantra. With the Ṣikshāsūtra, Paribhāshās.°, and Balābalas°. Edited by Gurunātha Vidyānidhi.] pp. i. 64. কলিকাতা ১৩০৮ [*Calcutta*, 1901.] 12°. **14092. a. 24.(2.)**

—— [Select Aphorisms of the Kātantra, with portions of Durgasiṃha's *vritti.*] *See* Ṣaurīndramohana Ṭhākura. গান্ধর্ব-কলাপ-ব্যাকরণম্ *etc.* [Gāndharva-kalāpa-vyākaraṇa.] [1902, *etc.*] 8°. **14053. dd. 2.**

—— কলাপ-ব্যাকরণম্ *etc.* [Kalāpavyākaraṇa. Section i., with Durgasiṃha's *vritti*, and notes and a Bengali translation by Chandrakānta Nyāyālaṅkāra. Third edition.] pp. ii. i. i. i. 38. ঢাকা ১৮১০ [*Dacca*, 1889.] 8°. **14090. c. 36.**

—— [Fourth edition.] pp. 47. ঢাকা ১৮১৭ [*Dacca*, 1895.] 12°. **14090. b. 45.(3.)**

SARVAVARMĀ (*continued*). কলাপ-ব্যাকরণম্ . . . সন্ধিবৃত্তিঃ *etc.* [Kalāpavyākaraṇa. Section i., with the commentary of Durgasiṃha. Edited with Bengali annotations by Anukūla Chandra Gupta Kāvyatīrtha. Fourth edition.] pp. 29, iii. ঢাকা ১৮৯৫ [*Dacca*, 1895.] 8°. **14090. bb. 13.(4.)**

—— কলাপ-ব্যাকরণম্ *etc.* [Kalāpavyākaraṇa. Section i., with commentary of Durgasiṃha, and a Bengali translation of the whole and notes by Mahendranātha Bhaṭṭāchārya. Fifth edition.] pp. 28. ঢাকা ১৩০৬ [*Dacca*, 1900.] 8°. **14090. b. 32.(2.)**

—— *See* DURGASIṂHA. কলাপ-ব্যাকরণম্ . . . চতুষ্টয়টীকা *etc.* [Chatushṭayaṭīkā, or Kātantravṛittiṭīkā. Chapter II, *pādas* i.-iii.] 1893. 8°. **14090. bb. 13.(1.)**

—— *See* DURGASIṂHA. নমস্কারবিবেকঃ *etc.* [Namaskāraviveka. Comprising the introductory stanza of Durgasiṃha's Kātantravṛitti and Trilochanadāsa's Pañjikā and Susheṇa's Kalāpachandra thereupon.] [1900.] 12°. **14092. a. 24.(1.)**

—— *See* SUSHEṆA. আখ্যাত-কবিরাজঃ *etc.* [Ākhyātakavirāja. Being §§ 1, 2 of the chapter on *ākhyāta* in Susheṇa's Kalāpachandra, commenting upon the Kātantra iii. 1, 2.] [1895.] 8°. **14093. b. 36.(2.)**

—— *See* SUSHEṆA. কলাপ-ব্যাকরণম্ . . . চতুষ্টয়-কবিরাজঃ *etc.* [Chatushṭayakavirāja. Chapter II.] 1894. 8°. **14090. bb. 13.(3.)**

—— *See* TRILOCHANADĀSA. কলাপ-ব্যাকরণম্ . . . চতুষ্টয়পঞ্জী *etc.* [Chatushṭayapañjī. Chapter II.] 1893. 8°. **14090. bb. 13.(2.)**

APPENDIX.

—— *See* CHAṄGADĀSA. The Sambandhopadesa, *etc.* [A tract forming a supplement to the Kātantra.] 1896. 12°. **14092. a. 10.(2.)**

—— গণতত্ত্ব-দীপিকা *etc.* [Gaṇatattvadīpikā. The *dhātupāṭha* or list of roots according to the Kālāpa school, with the commentary Manoramā of Ramānātha. With Halāyudha's Kavirahasya appended. Edited by Hṛishīkeṣa Vidyāratna and Mahendranātha Bhaṭṭāchārya.] pp. vi. 264. ঢাকা ১৩০৬ [*Dacca*, 1900.] 8°. **14093. b. 20.(3.)**

SARVAVARMĀ [APPENDIX.] (*continued*). সটীক কাতন্ত্র-গণমালা *etc.* [Kātantragaṇamālā. The Kālāpa *dhātupāṭha*, with Ramānātha's commentary Manoramā. Followed by the Daṣabalakārikā. Edited by Gurunātha Vidyānidhi.] pp. ii. xxxii. 243, 8. কলিকাতা ১৩১০ [*Calcutta*, 1903.] 12°. **14092. a. 24.(3.)**

SARVEṢVARA ĀCHĀRYA. *See* ṢRĪNIVĀSA ĀCHĀRYA, *Astrologer.* ଶ୍ରୀଶ୍ରୀନିବାସଦୀପିକା *etc.* [Ṣrīnivāsadīpikā. Edited by Sarveṣvara.] 1900. 12°. **14053. a. 5.(2.)**

—— *See* VIKRAMĀRKACHARITRA. ବତିଶସିଂହାସନ *etc.* [Batriṣ Siṃhāsana. An Oriya version, by Sarveṣvara.] 1900. 12°. **14121. f. 19.(4.)**

SARVEṢVARA SĀRVABHAUMA. *See* GOTAMA. ন্যায়-দর্শন *etc.* [Nyāyadarṣana. With Bengali interpretation by Sarveṣvara.] [1894, *etc.*] 8°. **14048. dd. 21.**

ṢAṢADHARA, *grandson of Rudrasiṃha, and Courtier of Amarasiṃha.* *See* KAVIRĀJA PAṆḌITA. The Râghavapâṇḍavîya . . . With the commentary [Rāghavapāṇḍavīyaprakāṣa] of Saṡadhara, *etc.* 1897. 8°. [*Kâvyamâlâ.*] **14072. ccc. 12. (no. 62.)**

ṢAṢIBHŪSHAṆA CHAKRAVARTĪ. *See* ṢIVACHANDRA SIDDHĀNTA. শ্রীমদ্ভাগবতবিচারঃ *etc.* [Bhāgavatavichāra. Edited by Ṣaṣibhūshaṇa.] [1893.] 8°. **14016. c. 56.(1.)**

ṢAṢIBHŪSHAṆA MITRA MUSTAUPHĪ. *See* KĀṢĪDĀSA MUSTAUPHĪ. শান্তিগীতা *etc.* [Ṣāntigītā. With Bengali commentary by Ṣaṣibhūshaṇa.] 1897. 8°. **14076. b. 41.**

ŚÂSTRI (R. A.). *See* ANANTAKṚISHṆA ṢĀSTRĪ, *R.*

ṢĀSTRĪ PĀNCH KAKKĀ. शास्त्री पांच कक्का अने बाराखडी [Ṣāstrī Pānch Kakkā. The Māgadhī or Jain variety of the Nāgarī alphabet and numerals, with their Gujarati equivalents.] pp. 16, *lith.* अमदावाद १८९४ [*Ahmadabad*, 1894.] 12°. **14100. a. 12.(2.)**

ṢATAKOṬI-RĀMACHARITA. *See* NĀRĀYAṆA SOMAYĀJĪ. శ్రీ . . . శ్రీరామోత్సవరత్నాకరః *etc.* [Rāmotsavaratnākara. Comprising chapters compiled from the Ānandarāmāyaṇa, *etc.*] [1898.] 8°. **14028. d. 66.**

—— ॥ अथ श्रीमदानंदरामायणप्रारंभः ॥ [Ānandarāmāyaṇa. An epic-puranic poem in 9 cantos, upon the legend and cult of Rāma, forming part of the Ṣatakoṭi-rāmacharita. Edited by Vāsudeva Bāḷā Aināpure.] 9 pts. मुम्बय्यां १८२४ [*Bombay*, 1903.] Fol. **14018. c. 32.**

—— [Another copy.] **14018. c. 36.**

ṢATĀNANDA, *son of Ṣaṅkara.* ভাস্বত্যুদাহরণম্ । [Bhāsvatyudāharaṇa. An astronomical tract, with the commentary Bhāsvatīvivaraṇa of Mādhava Miṣra. With Bengali appendices.] pp. 24, 28. [1891, *etc.*] *See* PERIODICAL PUBLICATIONS.—*Calcutta.* অরুণোদয় *etc.* [Aruṇodaya.] Pt. i., no. 19. [1890, *etc.*] 4°.
14133. g. 16. (pt. i., no. 19.)

SATARA-PĀRĀJIKĀ-VINIṢCHAYA. සතරපාරාජිකා විනිශ්චය *etc.* [Satara-pārājikā-viniṣchaya. A Pali compilation on the four *pārājikā* or sins entailing expulsion from the Buddhist clergy. With Sinhalese paraphrase appended. Followed by the Heraṇa-sika, Dinachariyāva, and Satara-saṃvarasīlaya, short Sinhalese tracts on clerical discipline.] pp. 19, iii. කොළඹ [*Colombo*,] 1897. 8°. **14098. ccc. 3.(1.)**

SATARĀ-PARIVEṆA-UPATAPASSI. වෘත්තමාලය ශෙන්මෙපොත *etc.* [Vṛittamālā, or Vuttamālā-sandesasataka. A century of stanzas illustrating Pali metres. With Sinhalese interpretation.] pp. 32. [*Colombo*,] 1895. 8°. **14098. c. 42.(3.)**

—— [Another edition, with a different title-page.] pp. 32. *Colombo*, 1896. 8°.
14098. b. 20.(2.)

ṢĀTĀTAPA. শাতাতপীয়-কর্ম্মবিপাকঃ *etc.* [Ṣātātapīya-karmavipāka. A tract on sins and their expiations. With Bengali translation by Rāmachandra Tarkālaṅkāra. Edited by Kālīpada Vidyāratna.] pp. ii. 43. কলিকাতা ১৩০৯ [*Calcutta*, 1902.] 8°. **14033. aa. 28.(3.)**

ṢAṬHAKOPĀCHĀRYA, *Iyyuṇṇi, son of Jagannāthāchārya. See* VEṄKAṬĀCHĀRYA, *son of Govindāchārya.* చాత్తాదశ్రీవైష్ణవద్విజషోడశకర్మాణి *etc.* [Chāttāda-ṣrīvaishṇava-dvija-shoḍaṣakarmāṇi. Edited by Ṣaṭhakopāchārya.] [1902.] 8°. **14170. ee. 47.**

ṢAṬHAKOPĀCHĀRYA, *Mohanūr Kandāḍai. See* BHOJARĀJA. Champû Râmâyaṇa. Bâlakâṇḍa. With . . . commentary, English translation and . . . notes by . . . M. C. Satakopachariar. [1896.] 8°. **14076. c. 67.(1.)**

—— ॥ निरोष्ठ्यरामायणसंग्रहः ॥ ॥ निरोष्ठ्यदण्डकसहितः *etc.* [Niroshṭhyarāmāyaṇasaṅgraha. A poetical summary of the Rāmāyaṇa, composed without labial vowels or consonants; to which is added a Niroshṭhyadaṇḍaka.] pp. 24. *Kumbakonam*, 1901. 8°. **14072. cc. 62.(2.)**

ṢAṬHAKOPA YATI, *Ādivan, of Ahobilam.* వాసంతికాపరిణయము ॥ [Vāsantikāpariṇaya. A mythological play in 5 acts.] *See* BHAVABHŪTI. ఉత్తరరామచరిత్ర ॥ [Uttararāmacharita, *etc.*] pp. 229-284. [1892.] 8°. **14080. d. 23.**

SATĪṢACHANDRA ĀCHĀRYA, *Vidyābhūshaṇa. See* SATĪṢACHANDRA VIDYĀBHŪSHAṆA.

SATĪṢACHANDRA VANDYOPĀDHYĀYA. Sáṅkhya Philosophy, by Satish Chandra Banerji . . . Fasciculus I. Sáṅkhya Káriká with Gauḍapáda's scholia and Náráyaṇa's gloss. pp. lvi. 300; 1 *plate. Calcutta*, 1898. 12°. **14048. b. 34.**
In progress?

SATĪṢACHANDRA VIDYĀBHŪSHAṆA. *See* ACADEMIES, *etc.*—Calcutta.—*Mahābodhi Society.* Kaccayana's Pali Grammar. Edited . . . and translated into English by Satis Chandra Acharyya, Vidyabhusana. 1901. 12°. **14098. a. 39.**

—— *See* NĀGĀRJUNA. The Mādhyamika School . . . By . . . Satīç Chandra Vidyā Bhushan, *etc.* 1895-1898. 8°. [*Journal of the Buddhist Text Society of India.*] **14003. b. 19. (vol. 3-6.)**

SATSAṄGIJĪVANA. धर्मामृत *etc.* [Dharmāmṛita. An account of the religious principles of the Svāmī-Nārāyaṇa sect, forming ch. 1-6 in *prakaraṇa* iv. of the Satsaṅgijīvana. With a Gujarati translation by Ṣukānanda Muni.] pp. ii. ii. 142. राजकोट अमदावाद १९०२ [*Rajkot, Ahmadabad*, 1902.] 12°. **14033. a. 50.**

SATYACHARAṆA RĀYA. *See* DAYĀNANDA SARASVATĪ SVĀMĪ. पञ्च महायज्ञविधिः *etc.* [Pañchamahāyajñavidhi. With Bengali introduction and translations by Satyacharaṇa.] [1898.] 16°.
14028. a. 26.

SATYĀNANDA AGNIHOTRĪ. पतिव्रतादर्पण *etc.* [Pativratādarpaṇa. An anthology from the Mahābhārata and other poems, illustrative of the virtues of the ideal wife. With Hindi notes and paraphrases.] pp. 63. लाहौर १९५५ [*Lahore*, 1899.] 16°. **14076. a. 24.**

Forms no. 3 *of the* Jātiya-ṣiksha *Series.*

—— ऋषि-वाक्य संग्रह *etc.* [Ṛishivākyasangraha. An anthology of moral verses and apophthegms, with Hindi versions.] pp. 24. लाहौर १९५८ [*Lahore*, 1901.] 12°. **14085. b. 31.(2.)**

Forms no. 6 *of the* Jātiya-ṣiksha *Series.*

SATYĀNANDA MUHAMMAD. *See* UPANISHADS.—*Separate Upanishads.* ईशोपनामकवाजसनेयोपनिषद *etc.* [Īṣopanishad. With Hindi verse-translation by Satyānanda.] [1890.] 8°. **14010. c. 52.(2.)**

SATYĀSHĀDHA. *See* HIRAṆYAKEṢĪ.

SATYAVRATA SĀMAṢRAMĪ BHAṬṬĀCHĀRYA. *See* BRĀHMAṆAS.—*Aitareyabrāhmaṇa.* The Aitareya Bráhmaṇa . . . with the commentary of Sáyaṇa . . . Edited by . . . Satyavrata Sámaśramí. 1895, *etc.* 8°. [*Bibliotheca Indica.*] **14002. a. (vol. 134.)**

—— *See* BRĀHMAṆAS. — *Ṣatapathabrāhmaṇa.* ॥ शतपथब्राह्मणम् . . . The Çatapatha Brāhmaṇa . . . with the commentary of Sāyaṇa . . . Edited by . . . Satyavrata Sāmaçramī. 1900, *etc.* 8°. [*Bibliotheca Indica.*] **14002. a. (vol. 145.)**

—— *See* PERIODICAL PUBLICATIONS. — *Calcutta.* उषा *etc.* [Ushā. Compiled and edited by Satyavrata Sāmaṣramī.] [1889]-1893. 8°. **14010. c. 43.**

—— *See* RAMEṢACHANDRA DATTA. हिन्दूशास्त्र *etc.* [Hindu-ṣāstra. Pt. i., ii., and iii., edited and translated by Rameṣachandra Datta and Satyavrata Sāmaṣramī.] [1895-1897.] 8°. **14085. c. 45.(vol. 1.)**

—— *See* VEDAS. — Yajurveda. — *Taittirīyasaṃhitā.* The Sanhitá of the Black Yajur Veda, with the commentary of Mádhava, *etc.* (Vol. vi., edited by . . . Satyavrata Sámaśramí.) 1854-1899. 8°. [*Bibliotheca Indica.*] **14002. a. (vol. 26.)**

—— *See* YĀSKA. The Nirukta. With commentaries. Edited by . . . Satyavrata Sámaśramí. 1882-1891. 8°. [*Bibliotheca Indica.*] **14002. a. (vol. 89.)**

—— ॥ त्रयीपरिचयः *etc.* [Trayīparichaya. Vedic studies.] pt. i. pp. 130. 1893. *See* PERIODICAL PUBLICATIONS.—*Calcutta.* उषा *etc.* [Ushā.] Vol. II, no. vii.-viii. [1889]-1893. 8°. **14010. c. 43.(vol. 2.)**

—— ॥ त्रयीसङ्ग्रहः *etc.* [Trayīsangraha. A digest of the matter of the Vedas, chiefly in the form of excerpts from them and their Brāhmaṇas, *etc.*] pp. 230. 1892-1893. *See* PERIODICAL PUBLICATIONS.—*Calcutta.* उषा *etc.* [Ushā.] Vol. II, no. iii.-viii. [1889]-1893. 8°. **14010. c. 43.(vol. 2.)**

ṢAUDDHODANI. The Alankâraśekhara of Keśavamiśra[, comprising the Alaṅkārasūtra or aphorisms of Rhetoric ascribed to Ṣauddhodani with the commentary of Keṣava made at the direction of Māṇikyachandra, Raja of Kot Kangra]. Edited by Paṇḍit Śivadatta . . . and Kâśînâth Pâṇdurang Parab. (अलंकारशेखरः ।) pp. 84. 1895. *See* DURGĀPRASĀDA, *son of Vrajalāla*, and KĀṢĪNĀTHA PĀṆḌURAṄGA PARAB. Kâvyamâlâ. [No.] 50. 1886, *etc.* 8°. **14072. ccc. 12.(no. 50.)**

SAUER (WILHELM). *See* MAHĀBHĀRATA.—*Vanaparva.* Mahabhárata und Wate . . . von W. Sauer[, comprising translations from the Vanaparva with corresponding Germanic legends]. 1893. 4°. **11840. m. 39.(6.)**

ṢAUNAKA. [For the Charaṇavyūha ascribed to Ṣaunaka :] *See* CHARAṆAVYŪHA.

—— Bṛihad-devatá, or An Index to the Gods of the Rigveda . . . To which have been added Arshánukramaṇí Chhandonukramaṇí and Anuvákánukramaṇí in the form of appendices. Edited by . . . Rájá Rájendralála Mitra. (बृहद्देवता ।) pp. 333. 1893. *See* ACADEMIES, *etc.*—Calcutta.—*Asiatic Society of Bengal.* Bibliotheca Indica. New Series. [Vol. 127.] 1848, *etc.* 8°. **14002. a. (vol. 127.)**

—— महर्षिशौनकप्रणीतम् ऋक्प्रातिशाख्यम् । . . . . Śaunaka's Prátiśákhya of the Rigveda, with the commentary of Uvvaṭa. Edited and annotated by the late Paṇḍit Yugalakiśora Vyâsa . . . and his esteemed pupil Paṇḍit Prabhudatta Śarmâ. pp. 399, ii. *Benares*, 1903. 8°. **14090. c. 40.**

Forms no. 48, 59, 64, *and* 79 *of the Benares Sanskrit Series.*

ṢAURĪNDRAMOHANA ṬHĀKURA, *Sir.* *See* NĀRĀYAṆA BHAṬṬA, called MṚIGARĀJALAKSHMĀ. Stanzas from Veṇi Samhára Nátaka, set to music by Raja Sir Sourindro Mohun Tagore. 1893. 8°. **14080. c. 17.(2.)**

—— The seven principal musical notes of the Hindus, with their presiding deities, [being a series of poems in the metres appropriate to these notes, with their musical setting in European notation and English translation,] composed in celebration of the birth-day of . . . the Empress of India, by . . . Sir Sourindro Mohun Tagore, *etc.* (Indian Music's Address to Empress Victoria.) pp. 51. *Calcutta,* 1892. 4°. **14053. e. 25.(2.)**

—— A Benedictory Song [in Sanskrit and English,] composed, set to music and sung on the occasion of the presence of . . . Sir Alexander Mackenzie . . . and Lady Mackenzie, at an Indian musical party, held at the Horocoomar Bhavan, Pathuriaghata Rajbati, *etc.* (कल्याणगानम् . . . Kalyáṇagánam : or A Benedictory Song.) pp. 16. *Calcutta,* 1896. 8°. **14070. c. 64.**

With European musical notation.

—— Śrímad-Victoria-Máhátmyam. The Greatness of the Empress Victoria : a Sanskrit poem, set to music, with an English translation and sixty-three illustrations, descriptive of sixty years of Her Majesty's sovereignty. Composed for the sixtieth anniversary of the imperial reign by Rája Sir Sourindro Mohun Tagore. pp. i. iii. 300. *London,* [1898.] 4°. **14076. e. 4.**

—— Abhra, or A few notes on Talc, compiled and translated into English from various Sanskrit works, by Raja Sir Sourindro Mohun Tagore. pp. 28. *Calcutta,* 1899. 8°. **14053. ccc. 29.**

—— গান্ধর্ব্ব-কলাপ-ব্যাকরণম্ *etc.* [Gāndharva-kalāpa-vyākaraṇa. A grammar of musical science, in the form of aphorisms and commentary, following the method of the Kātantra, and accompanied by the appropriate Aphorisms of the latter with portions of Durgasiṃha's *vṛitti.*] কলিকাতা ১৮২৪ [*Calcutta,* 1902, *etc.*] 8°.

In progress? **14053. dd. 2.**

—— The Coronation : being a compilation [in English] of the procedure as laid down in the Hindu classical works, with [translations of Sanskrit] stanzas [illustrating the 6 *rāgas* and 36 *rāgiṇis,* together with their Sanskrit text and musical setting, and descriptions of their mythological embodiments,] specially addressed to his Most Gracious Majesty the Emperor of India : by his Imperial Majesty's devoted and loyal subject Raja Sir Sourindra Mohun Tagore. pp. 200. *Calcutta,* 1903. 12°. **14053. ccc. 46.**

SAVĀILĀL CHHOṬĀLĀL VORĀ. શબ્દ ચિંતામણિ *etc.* [Ṣabdachintāmaṇi. A Sanskrit-Gujarati lexicon.] pp. ii. vii. iv. xix. 1408 ; 1 *plate.* વડોદરા અમદાવાદ ૧૯૦૦ [*Baroda, Ahmudabad,* 1900.] 8°. **14150. b. 36.**

SĀYAṆA ĀCHĀRYA.

WORKS ON ṢRUTI.

[*Āraṇyakas.*] *See* ĀRAṆYAKAS.—*Aitareyāraṇyaka.* ऐतरेयारण्यकम् *etc.* [Aitareyāraṇyaka. With the commentary Vedārthaprakāṣa of Sāyaṇa.] [1898.] 8°. **14003. ccc. (no. 38.)**

—— *See* ĀRAṆYAKAS.—*Taittirīyāraṇyaka.* तैत्तिरीयारण्यकम् *etc.* [Taittirīyāraṇyaka. With Sāyaṇa's commentary.] [1897-1898.] 8°. **14003. ccc. (no. 36.)**

—— *See* ĀRAṆYAKAS.—*Taittirīyāraṇyaka.* சுபர்ணமந்த்ரம் *etc.* [Trisuparṇamantra. With commentary of Sāyaṇa.] [18]96. 16°. **14028. b. 80.(2.)**

—— *See* ĀRAṆYAKAS.—*Taittirīyāraṇyaka.* त्रिसुपर्ण *etc.* [Trisuparṇamantra. With commentary of Sāyaṇa.] [1900.] 8°. **14028. d. 35.(2.)**

[*Brāhmaṇas.*] *See* BRĀHMAṆAS. — *Aitareyabrāhmaṇa.* The Aitareya Bráhmaṇa . . . with the commentary of Sáyaṇa, *etc.* 1895, *etc.* 8°. [*Bibliotheca Indica.*] **14002. a. (vol. 134.)**

—— *See* BRĀHMAṆAS.—*Aitareyabrāhmaṇa.* ऐतरेयब्राह्मणम् *etc.* (The Aitaréya Bráhmaṇam, with the Bháshya of . . . Sáyaṇáchárya, *etc.*) [1896.] 8°. **14003. ccc. (no. 32.)**

—— *See* BRĀHMAṆAS.—*Ārsheyabrāhmaṇa.* ॥ आर्षेयब्राह्मणम् *etc.* [Ārsheyabrāhmaṇa. With commentary of Sāyaṇa.] 1891-1892. 8°. [*Ushā.*] **14010. c. 43.(vol. 1, 2.)**

—— *See* BRĀHMAṆAS. — *Ṣhaḍviṃṣabrāhmaṇa.* Das Ṣaḍviṃçabrāhmaṇa. Mit Proben aus Sāyaṇas Kommentar, *etc.* 1894. 8°. **14010. dd. 4.**

SĀYAṆA ĀCHĀRYA (*continued*).

Works on Śruti. [*Brāhmaṇas.*] (*continued*).

—— See Brāhmaṇas.—*Taittirīyabrāhmaṇa.* **तैत्तिरीयब्राह्मणम्** *etc.* [Taittirīyabrāhmaṇa. With commentary of Sāyaṇa.] [1898.] 8°.
14003. ccc. (no. 37.)

—— See Brāhmaṇas.—*Vaṃśabrāhmaṇa.* **॥ वंशब्राह्मणम्** *etc.* [Vaṃśabrāhmaṇa. With Sāyaṇa's commentary.] 1892. 8°. [*Ushā.*]
14010. c. 43.(vol. 2.)

[*Upanishads.*] See Upanishads.—*Selections.* **॥ अथ शान्तिपाठः ॥** [Śāntipāṭha. With commentaries of Sāyaṇa.] 1892. 8°. [*Ushā.*] **14010. c. 43.(vol. 2.)**

—— See Upanishads.—*Separate Upanishads.* **नृसिंहपूर्वोत्तरतापनीयोपनिषत्** *etc.* [Nṛisiṃhatāpanīyopanishad. Parts i. and ii., the latter with the commentary of Sāyaṇa.] [1895.] 8°.
14003. ccc. (no. 30.)

—— See Upanishads.—*Separate Upanishads.* ఓ ... తైత్తిరీయ *etc.* [Taittirīyopanishad. The Śikshāvallī, Ānandavallī, and Bhṛiguvallī. With Sāyaṇa's commentary.] 1904. 8°. **14007. b. 20.**

—— See Upanishads.—*Separate Upanishads.* The Taittirîya Upanishad, with the commentaries of ... Sâyana ... Translated into English, *etc.* 1903. 8°. **14007. b. 23.**

—— Extracts from Vedántic commentaries. Translated from Vidyâranya's Taittirîyaupanishad-Dipîkâ [*sic*] [by S. Sitārāma Śāstrī]. 1897. *See* Periodical Publications.—*Madras.* The Brahmavâdin, *etc.* Vol. II, no. 11-17. 1895, *etc.* 4°.
14048. g. 1.(vol. 2.)

[*Vedas.*] See Sandhyāvandana. **सन्ध्याभाष्यसमुच्चयः** *etc.* [Sandhyābhāshyasamuchchaya. A collection of commentaries upon the *sandhyā* prayers, including Sāyaṇa's Taittirīyasandhyābhāshya.] [1899.] 8°.
14003. ccc. (no. 40.)

—— See Sandhyāvandana. யஜுர்வேத ஸந்த்யாவந்தநம் *etc.* [Sandhyāvandana. Followed by the Purushasūkta, Śrīsūkta, Bhūsūkta, *etc.* With extracts, in a Tamil translation, from the commentaries of Sāyaṇa and others.] 1901. 8°.
14033. aa. 27.

SĀYAṆA ĀCHĀRYA (*continued*).

Works on Śruti. [*Vedas.*] (*continued*).

—— See Vedas.—*Atharvaveda.* Atharvaveda-samhitâ. With the commentary of Sâyaṇâchârya, *etc.* 1895-1898. 4°. **14010. ee. 1.**

—— See Vedas.—Ṛigveda.—*Selections of Hymns and Verses.* Handbook to the study of the Rigveda ... Part I. Introductory. (Sayana's Preface to his commentary . . . the commentary itself on the first three hymns and a translation into English of the Preface.) (Part II. The seventh Mandala, *etc.*) 1890-1892. 8°. **14010. c. 50.**

—— See Vedas.—Ṛigveda.—*Selections of Hymns and Verses.* Hymns from the Rigveda ... with Sayana's commentary, *etc.* 1898. 8°. **14007. cc. 26.**

—— See Vedas.—Ṛigveda.—*Selections of Hymns and Verses.* A Second Selection of Hymns from the Ṛigveda . . . with Sâyaṇa's commentary, *etc.* 1899. 8°. **14010. cc. 11.**

—— See Vedas.—Ṛigveda.—*Selections of Hymns and Verses.* **ऋग्वसूक्तसंग्रहः** *etc.* (Hymns from the Ṛigveda [Book i.] . . . with Sáyana's commentary, *etc.*) 1903. 8°. **14007. b. 19.**

—— **ঋগ্বেদভাষ্যোপদ্ঘাতপ্রকরণ** [*sic*] *etc.* [Ṛigvedabhāshyopodghāta. The introduction to Sāyaṇa's commentary on the Ṛigveda. With Bengali translation and notes.] pp. i. 65, 112. যশোহর ১৮২৩ [*Jessore,* 1901.] 12°. **14007. b. 16.**

—— See Vedas.—*Sāmaveda.* **सामवेद॰** *etc.* (Samavedasanhita. Whith [*sic*] the commentary of Sayanacharya, *etc.*) [1892.] 8°. **14007. b. 9.**

—— See Vedas.—Yajurveda.—*Taittirīyasaṃhitā.* **तैत्तिरीयसंहिता** ... The Taittiriya Saṃhitá ... with the commentary of Bhaṭṭabháskaramiśra [supplemented in parts of *kāṇḍa* v. 7 and vii. 4-5 by the commentary of Sāyaṇa], *etc.* 1894, *etc.* 8°. [*Mysore Government Oriental Library Series: Bibliotheca Sanskrita.*] **14004. b. 4.(vol. 9, 12.)**

—— See Vedas.—Yajurveda.—*Taittirīyasaṃhitā.* **कृष्णयजुर्वेदीयतैत्तिरीयसंहिता** *etc.* [Taittirīyasaṃhitā. With commentary of Sāyaṇa.] [1900, *etc.*] 8°.
14003. ccc. (no. 42.)

SĀYAṆA ĀCHĀRYA (*continued*).

WORKS ON SMṚITI.

See PARĀṢARA. [*Smṛiti.*] ಪರಾಶರಮಾಧವೀಯ ಧರ್ಮಶಾಸ್ತ್ರವು *etc.* [Parāṣara-mādhavīya-dharma-ṣāstra. With a Canarese translation of Sāyaṇa's commentary.] [1890.] 8°. **14038. d. 31.**

See PARĀṢARA. [*Smṛiti.*] The Parâśara Dharma Saṃhitâ ... with the commentary of Sâyaṇa, *etc.* 1893, *etc.* 8°. **14039. a. 15.**

శ్రీ ... శ్రీమాధవపండితైః పరాశరస్మృతి రాజ-ధర్మవ్యాఖ్యానావసరే ప్రణీతోఽయం వ్యవహారకాండః *etc.* [Mādhavīya-vyavahārakāṇḍa. Sāyaṇa's commentary upon the Vyavahārakāṇḍa of the Parāṣarasaṃhitā. Edited by Ṣāttanūru Kalyāṇasundara Ṣāstrī.] pp. ii. 192. చెన్నపురి ౧౮౯౮ [*Madras*, 1898.] **14039. c. 16.**

WORKS ON THE PURĀṆAS.

See PURĀṆAS.—*Skandapurāṇa.* ஸூதஸம்ஹிதா *etc.* [Sūtasaṃhitā. With the commentary Tātparyadīpikā of Sāyaṇa.] [1892.] 4°. **14016. e. 42.**

See PURĀṆAS. — *Skandapurāṇa.* सूतसंहिता *etc.* (The Sûtasamhitá. With the commentary of ... Mádhaváchárya, *etc.*) [1893.] 8°. **14003. ccc. (no. 25.)**

WORKS ON PHILOSOPHY, ETC.

See BĀDARĀYAṆA. The Vivaraṇaprameyasaṃgraha[, an exposition of Vedānta in the form of a commentary upon the Brahmasūtra, I. i. 1-4, ascribed to the authorship] of Mâdhavâchârya, *etc.* 1893. 8°. **14048. dd. 3.(vol. 5.)**

See JAIMINI.—*Mīmāṃsāsūtra.* जैमिनीयन्यायमाला *etc.* (Jaiminîyanyâyamâlâ or Pûrvamîmânsâdhikarananyâyamâlâ by Srí Mâdhavâchârya. With his own commentary, *etc.*) [1892.] 8°. **14003. ccc. (no. 24.)**

—— *See* ṢAṄKARA ĀCHĀRYA.—*Two or More Works.* Śri-Śankaráchárya's Miscellaneous Works, *etc.* [Vol. II, Aparokshānubhūti, with commentaries ascribed to Sāyaṇa, *etc.*] 1898-1899. 8°. [*Mysore Government Oriental Library Series: Bibliotheca Sanskrita.*] **14004. b. 10.(vol. 2.)**

SĀYAṆA ĀCHĀRYA (*continued*).

WORKS ON PHILOSOPHY, ETC. (*continued*).

अथ ब्रह्मविदाशीर्वादपद्धतिः [Brahmavidāṣīrvādapaddhati. A tract on Vedānta, ascribed to Sāyaṇa.] *See* NITYĀNANDA SARASVATĪ. वेदान्तग्रन्थपञ्चकम् *etc.* [Vedāntagranthapañchaka.] pp. 113-120. [1891.] 12°. **14048. b. 15.(2.)**

The Jivanmuktiviveka, or The path to liberation in this life. By Swâmi Śri Vidyâraṇyasarswati. Rendered into English by Manilal N. Dvivedi. pp. xii. i. 195. *Bombay*, 1897. 8°. **14048. cc. 6.**

శ్రీ ... శ్రీవేదాంతపంచదశీ॥ [Pañchadaṣī. With an interpretation and commentary in Telugu by Lakshmīnārāyaṇa Ṣāstrī.] 3 pts. చెన్నపురి [*Madras*,] 1895-1898. 8°. **14048. dd. 24.**

॥ श्रीपंचदशी सटीका सभाषा *etc.* [Pañchadaṣī. With Rāmakṛishṇa's Sanskrit commentary, and Pītāmbara Purushottama's Hindi commentary called Tattvaprakāṣikā. Followed by the Gajendramoksha, with notes by Pītāmbara, and preceded by Hindi prefaces and indices. Edited by Ṣāliḥ Muḥammad. Second edition.] pp. x. lviii. 937, 24; 1 *plate.* मुंबई १८९१ [*Bombay*, 1897.] 8°. **14048. e. 25.**

The Panchadaśhî. A treatise on Vedânta philosophy by Vidyâranya Swâmi. With Chandrakânta Vivaran and author's life [in Gujarati]. Translated into Gujarati by Ichchârâm Suryarâm Desâi [with introduction, index, and the Sanskrit text]. (પંચદશી) pp. xiv. v. 745, xii. *Bombay*, 1900. 4°. **14048. e. 34.**

श्रीहरिगीता . हरिहररायकृत पंचदशीवर ओवीबद्ध टीका *etc.* [Pañchadaṣī. With a Marathi commentary in Ovī verse, styled Harigītā, by Harihara Rāya. Edited by Ṣaṅkara Tryambaka Saptarshi.] मुंबई [*Bombay*, 1902, *etc.*] 8°. **14049. b. 1.**

In progress?

श्रीमद्विद्यारण्यमुनिप्रणीता पंचदशी *etc.* [Pañchadaṣī. Edited with a Marathi translation and commentary by Vishṇu Vāmana Ṣāstrī Bāpaṭ.] मुंबई १९०४ [*Bombay*, 1904, *etc.*] 12°. **14048. b. 46.**

In progress.

SĀYAṆA ĀCHĀRYA (*continued*).

WORKS ON PHILOSOPHY, ETC. (*continued*).

A Handbook of Hindu Pantheism. The Panchadasi of Sreemut Vidyaranya Swami. Translated with copious annotations by Nandalal Dhole. Second edition. 2 vols. *Calcutta*, 1899-1900. 8°. **14048. cc. 32.**

Forms part of "Dhole's Vedanta Series."

॥ श्रीपंचदशी ॥ ॥ अथ नाटकदीपः ॥ ॥ दशमप्रकरणम् ॥ १० ॥ [Pañchadaṣī. Prakaraṇa x., styled Nāṭakadīpa. With Rāmakrishṇa's commentary, and Hindi notes by Pitāmbara Purushottama.] *See* NIṢCHALA DĀSA. ॥ श्रीविचारसागर *etc.* [Vichārasāgara.] pp. 673-690. [1900.] 8°. **14154. ff. 1.**

Merely a reprint from the edition of the whole work by the same editor.

శ్రీశంకరవిజయము *etc.* [Ṣaṅkaravijaya. With the commentary Ṣaṅkaravijayaḍiṇḍima of Dhanapati Sūri.] pp. xv. 480. బెంగుళూరు ౧౮౯౪ [*Bangalore*, 1894.] 8°. **14048. cc. 11.**

ಶಂಕರವಿಜಯವು *etc.* [Ṣaṅkaravijaya, or Ṣaṅkaradigvijaya. Edited with a Canarese translation and commentary entitled Vāgvṛitti by Dakshiṇāmūrti Ṣāstrī.] pt. 1-5. ಬೆಂಗಳೂರು ೧೮೯೮ [*Bangalore*, 1898.] 8°. **14070. dd. 15.**

Apparently no more has been published.

The Saṅkshepaśaṁkarajaya of Mâdhavâchârya, with Gujarâtî translation. Edited with notes and criticised [*sic*] essay on the date of Śaṁkarâchârya by Kṛishṇalâla Govindarâma Devâśrayî. (સંક્ષેપશંકરજય) pp. i. iv. 14, 88, 34, 19, 412; 1 *plate*. *Bombay*, 1899. 8°. **14048. cc. 35.**

Le Bouddhisme d'après les sources brahmaniques. I. Sarvadarçanasaṁgraha [, pp. 7-27 of the Calcutta edition of 1858, translated with notes by] L. de la Vallée Poussin. II. Sarvasiddhāntasaṁgraha [, sections iii.-vii., edited by] F. W. Thomas et L. de la Vallée Poussin. pp. 96. *Louvain*, 1902. 8°. **14048. e. 35.**

Extrait du Muséon.

WORKS ON GRAMMAR.

See PĀṆINI.—*Appendix*. [*Dhātupāṭha*.] माधवीया धातुवृत्तिः. The Dhátuvṛitti . . . [Being the Dhātupāṭha with Sāyaṇa's commentary. Followed by Sāyaṇa's Nāmadhātuvṛitti], *etc.* 1894-1903. 8°. [*Mysore Government Oriental Library Series: Bibliotheca Sanskrita.*] **14004. b. 3.**

SĀYAṆA ĀCHĀRYA (*continued*).

WORKS ON GRAMMAR (*continued*).

See PĀṆINI.—*Appendix*. [*Dhātupāṭha*.] माधवीया धातुवृत्तिः *etc.* [Dhātuvṛitti. Followed by the Nāmadhātuvṛitti.] [1897.] 8°. **14093. b. 39.**

॥ अथ माधवीया नामधातुवृत्तिः ॥ [Nāmadhātuvṛitti. Edited by Dāmodara Ṣāstrī Sahasrabuddhi.] 1897. *See* PERIODICAL PUBLICATIONS.—*Benares*. The Pandit, *etc.* New Series. Vol. XIX. 1876, *etc.* 8°. **14096. d. 6. (vol. 19.)**

SĀYANNA. Prayogasamuchchaya, or A treatise on pharmacology, accepted commonly as a part of [Sāyanna's] Bhaisajya Kalpa. With a new Sinhalese paraphrace [*sic*] by J. S. Rajasundara Arachchy, *etc.* (ප්‍රයොගසමුච්චය) pp. iv. 96. *Colombo*, 2438 [1895]. 8°. **14043. c. 43. (3.)**

ṢAYYĀDĀNAPADDHATI. शय्यादानपद्धति [Ṣayyādānapaddhati. Rules for giving couches with furniture to Brahmans.] pp. 16. लाहौर [*Lahore*, 1901.] 12°. **14028. b. 93. (5.)**

ṢAYYAṀBHAVA, *the Yugapradhāna*. The Daśavaikālika-sūtra by Śayyambhava [, the third *mūlasūtra* in the Canon of the Ṣvetāmbara Jains,] and the Daśavaikālika-niryukti by Bhadrabāhu. Published in Roman characters [by E. Leumann] . . . with a German introduction, containing . . . a summary of . . . niryukti verses 222-297 . . . a list of all the tales . . . in Haribhadra's Bṛhadvṛtti . . . a list of parallel passages to the niryukti . . . a translation of the first three Adhyayanas of the sūtra . . . a shorted [*sic*] translation of most of the tales given in full by Haribhadra. Abstract [*i.e.* extract] from vol. xlvi. of the Journal of the German Oriental Society. pp. 581-663. [*Leipzig*, 1892.] 8°. **14100. c. 17. (2.)**

—— अथ श्री दशवैकालिक *etc.* [Daṣavaikālika, sections i.-iv.] *See* SŪTRAKṚIDAṄGA. महावीरस्तुति *etc.* [Mahāvīrastuti.] pp. 65-82. [1892.] 12°. **14100. a. 14.**

SCERBO (FRANCESCO). Radici Sanscrite. [An alphabetical dictionary of roots, with references to the Dhātupāṭha.] pp. xvi. 85. *Firenze*, 1892. 8°. **12907. ee. 46.**

SCHACK (ADOLF FRIEDRICH VON), *Count*. See KĀLIDĀSA. — *Raghuvaṃṣa*. Raghuvansa ... In deutscher Nachbildung von ... Graf von Schack. 1890. 8°. **12205. e. 12.(no. 3.)**

SCHERMAN (LUCIAN). Materialien zur Geschichte der Indischen Visionslitteratur, *etc.* pp. v. 161. *Leipzig*, 1892. 8°. **4504. h. 12.**

SCHIEFNER (ANTON). *See* MAHĀVYUTPATTI. Buddhistische Triglotte ... mit einem kurzen Vorwort versehen von A. Schiefner. 1859. *obl.* Fol. **761. l.**

SCHMIDT (RICHARD). *See* PAÑCHATANTRA. Das Pañcatantram. Textus ornatior ... Übersetzt von R. Schmidt. 1901. 8°. **14070. dd. 17.**

—— *See* ṢRĪVARA. Das Kathākāutukam ... verglichen mit Dschāmī's Jusuf und Zuleikha ... Von R. Schmidt. 1893. 8°. **14070. d. 33.(1.)**

—— *See* ṢRĪVARA. Śrīvara's Kathākāutukam ... Sanskrit und Deutsch, von R. Schmidt. 1898. 8°. **14070. dd. 1.**

—— *See* ṢUKASAPTATI. Specimen der Dinālāpanikāçukasaptati. Von Dr. R. Schmidt. 1891-1892. 8°. [*Zeitschrift der Deutschen Morgenlaendischen Gesellschaft.*] **Ac. 8815/2. (Bd. 45, 46.)**

—— *See* ṢUKASAPTATI. Die Çukasaptati. Textus simplicior. Herausgegeben von R. Schmidt. 1893. 8°. [*Deutsche Morgenlaendische Gesellschaft: Abhandlungen.*] **753. f. 18.**

—— *See* ṢUKASAPTATI. Die Çukasaptati. Textus simplicior ... übersetzt von R. Schmidt. 1894. 8°. **14072. ccc. 23.**

—— *See* ṢUKASAPTATI. Der Textus Ornatior der Çukasaptati ... von R. Schmidt. 1896. 8°. **14070. d. 33.(2.)**

—— *See* ṢUKASAPTATI. Der Textus Ornatior der Śukasaptati ... herausgegeben von R. Schmidt. 1898. 4°. **14070. e. 19.**

—— *See* ṢUKASAPTATI. Die Śukasaptati. Textus ornatior ... uebersetzt von R. Schmidt. 1899. 8°. **14070. dd. 10.**

SCHMIDT (RICHARD) (*continued*). *See* ṢUKASAPTATI. Der Textus Simplicior der Śukasaptati in der Recension der Handschrift A, *etc.* 1900-1901. 8°. [*Zeitschrift der Deutschen Morgenlaendischen Gesellschaft.*] **Ac. 8815/2.(vol. 54, 55.)**

—— *See* VĀTSYĀYANA, called MALLANĀGA. Das Kāmasūtram ... Nebst dem ... Commentare ... des Yaçōdhara ... übersetzt ... von R. Schmidt. 1897. 8°. **14053. d. 50.**

—— Anmerkungen zu dem Textus Simplicior der Śukasaptati, *etc.* 1894. *See* ACADEMIES, *etc.* — Germany. — *Deutsche Morgenlaendische Gesellschaft.* Zeitschrift, *etc.* Bd. 48, no. 4. 1846, *etc.* 8°. **Ac. 8815/2.(Bd. 48.)**

—— Altindische Schelmenbücher. *Lotus-Verlag, Leipzig*, [1903, *etc.*] 8°. **14070. g.**

In progress. Works published in this series are separately catalogued under the headings:
Kshemendra. Dāmodaragupta.

SCHMILINSKY (GUSTAV). *See* KĀLIDĀSA.—*Abhijñānaṣakuntala.* Sakuntala ... Frei bearbeitet von G. Schmilinsky. 1900. 8°. **14079. b. 40.(2.)**

SCHOEBEL (CHARLES). Le Râmâyana, au point de vue religieux, philosophique et moral, *etc.* pp. 233, i. 1888. *See* ACADEMIES, *etc.*—Paris.—*Musée Guimet.* Annales, *etc.* Tome xiii. 1880, *etc.* 4°. **7704. h. 21.(tom. 13.)**

SCHROEDER (LEOPOLD VON). *See* SUTTAPIṬAKA.—*Khuddakanikāya.* [*Dhammapada.*] Worte der Wahrheit — Dhammapadam ... in deutscher Uebersetzung ... von L. von Schroeder. 1892. 12°. **14098. a. 25.**

—— *See* VEDAS. — Yajurveda. — *Kāṭhaka.* ॥ काठकम् ॥ Kāṭhakam ... Herausgeben von L. von Schroeder. 1900, *etc.* 8°. **14007. dd. 2.**

—— Das Kāṭhaka, seine Handschriften, seine Accentuation und seine Beziehung zu den indischen Lexicographen und Grammatikern, *etc.* 1895. *See* ACADEMIES, *etc.*—Germany.—*Deutsche Morgenlaendische Gesellschaft.* Zeitschrift, *etc.* Bd. 49, no. 1. 1846, *etc.* 8°. **Ac. 8815/2.(Bd. 49.)**

Die Tübinger Kaṭha-Handschriften und ihre Beziehung zum Taittirîya-Âraṇyaka. Von L. von Schroeder. Herausgegeben mit einem Nachtrage

von G. Bühler. 1897. *See* ACADEMIES, *etc.*—Vienna.—*Kaiserliche Akademie der Wissenschaften.* Sitzungsberichte, *etc.* Band 137. 1849, *etc.* 8°.
Ac. 810/6. (Bd. 137.)

SCHTSCHERBATSKOI. *See* SHCHERBATSKY.

SEELAKKHANDHA THERA. *See* SĪLAKKHANDHA THERA.

SEJJAMBHAVA. *See* ṢAYYAMBHAVA.

SEN (P. C.). *See* PRASANNAKUMĀRA SENA.

SENART (ÉMILE). *See* SUTTAPIṬAKA.—*Khuddakanikāya.* [*Dhammapada.*] Le Manuscrit Kharoṣṭhī du Dhammapada. Les fragments Dutreuil de Rhins, par M. É. Senart. 1898. 8°.
Ac. 8808. (Ser. ix., tom. 12.)

ṢESHĀCHALAM NĀYUḌU, *Koṇḍa.* *See* CHAKRA KAVI. చిత్రప్రశ్నోత్తర రత్నావళి *etc.* [Chitraprasnottararatnāvali. Edited with Telugu commentaries and paraphrases by Ṣeshāchalam.] [1899.] 8°. **14072. cc. 55.(2.)**

ṢESHĀCHĀRLU, *G.* *See* ṢESHĀCHĀRYA, *Gaṭṭupalli.*

ṢESHĀCHĀRYA, *Gaṭṭupalli.* *See* VĀLMĪKI. — Rāmāyaṇa.—*Entire Text.* శ్రీ . . . రామాయణము [Rāmāyaṇa. Edited with Telugu translation by Ṣeshāchārya.] 1902, *etc.* 12°. **14065. b. 26.**

—— *See* VĀLMĪKI. — Rāmāyaṇa. — *Abridgments and Selections.* వాల్మీకిరత్నములు *etc.* [Vālmīkiratna. Compiled with Telugu paraphrases and notes by Ṣeshāchārya.] 1901. 12°.
14065. b. 25.

ṢESHĀCHĀRYA RAṄGĀCHĀRYA, *of Srirangam.* श्री रंगनाथोत्सवविवरणम् *etc.* [Raṅganāthotsavavivaraṇa. Prayers and hymns for the festivals of Raṅganātha at Srirangam, with detailed rules for the ritual in Hindi.] pp. ii. 44. कुम्भघोण° [*Kumbakonam,*] 1897. 8°. **14028. d. 56.(2.)**

ṢESHĀDRI AIYAR, *Ṣ.*, called DRAVIḌA. *See* HITOPADEṢA. English Translation of Hitopadesha, by B. T. Dravid, alias Sheshadri Iyar. 1896. 8°.
14070. c. 58.

—— *See* KĀLIDĀSA. — *Mālavikāgnimitra.* The Mâlavikâgnimitra . . . With the commentary of Kátayavêma . . . edited with critical notes and translation . . . by Ṣ. Ṣêshâdri Ayyar. 1896. 8°.
14080. c. 36.

—— *See* NĀRĀYAṆA BHAṬṬA, called MṚIGARĀJALAKSHMĀ. The Venisamhâra . . . Edited [with introduction and notes in English] by B. T. Dravid . . . and S. T. Dravid. 1896. 8°.
14079. c. 65.(1.)

ṢESHAGIRI ṢĀSTRĪ, *M.* *See* MADRAS.—*Government Oriental Manuscripts Library.* A Descriptive Catalogue . . . By . . . Seshagiri Sastri, *etc.* 1901, *etc.* 8°. **14096. ccc. 4.**

—— Report on a Search for Sanskrit and Tamil Manuscripts for the year 1896-97 (1893-94) . . . Prepared under the orders of the Govt. of Madras. 2 vols. *Madras,* 1898-1899. 8°.
14096. ccc. 2.

ṢESHAṢĀRṄGADHARA. *See* UDAYANA ĀCHĀRYA. The Lakṣaṇāvalī . . . with the commentary Nyāyamuktāvalī of Çeṣaçārṉgadhara, *etc.* 1900. 8°. [*The Pandit.*] **14096. d. 6.(vol. 21-22.)**

SETUBANDHA. *See* PRAVARASENA.

SHĀH-BAHĀDUR-ĀṢRITA. *See* MAHEṢA ṢARMĀ, *of Srinagar.*

SHĀH-JAHĀN BEGAM, *Ra'īsah of Bhopal.* خزانة اللغات [Khizānat al-lughāt. A dictionary of select terms in Hindustani, Persian, Arabic, Sanskrit, English, and Turkish. Compiled by order of Shāh-jahān Begam.] 2 vols., *lith.* بهوپال ۱۳۰۳ [*Bhopal,* 1886-1887.] Fol. **14117. e. 29.**

The English and Sanskrit are given in Arabic characters as well.

SHAKSPERE (WILLIAM). Vasantikaswapnam, an adaptation of Shakespeare's Midsummer-Night's Dream. A Sanskrit drama in five acts, by R. Krishnamachari. [Edited with an English introduction by Bālasarasvatī Nārāyaṇa Sudarṣana.] (वासन्तिकस्वप्नम्). pp. ii. xv. 69, i. *Kumbhakonam,* 1892. 8°. **14080. c. 34.**

SHANKARA. *See* ṢAṄKARA.

SHAṆMUKHASUNDARA MUDALIYĀR, *K.* *See* ĀGAMAS. ஸ்ரீமத் ஸகலாகமஸார ஸங்க்ரஹம் *etc.* [Sakalāgamasārasaṅgraha. Edited by Shaṇmukhasundara.] [1900.] 8°. **14033. aa. 11.**

SHAṆMUKHASUNDARA MUDALIYĀR, *K.* (*continued*). See ĀGAMAS. [*Kāraṇāgama.*] ஸ்ரீமத் . . . காரணாகமம் *etc.* [Kāraṇāgama. Edited by Shaṇmukhasundara.] [1900-1902.] 8°.
14033. aa. 8.

SHAṆṆAVATĪ. See NṚISIṂHA BHĀRATĪ. *Begin.* ശ്രീംഗേരി ശ്രീജഗദ്ഗുരു ... *etc.* [Pastoral letters on the relations of the brahmans holding the Shaṇṇavatī *agrahāram* to the Sringeri monastery.] [1865.] 16°.
14058. a. 5.(1.)

SHCHERBATSKY (THEDOR IPPOLITOVICH). See HARI KAVI, *son of Nārāyaṇa Sūri.* Über das Haihayendracarita des Harikavi. [Comprising cantos i. and ii., edited with German translation, notes, and introduction] von Th. von Schtscherbatskoi. 1900. 8°.
Ac. 1125/3.(classe hist.-phil., vol. iv., no. 9.)

SHINGON. 眞言諸經常用集 [Shingon Shokiō Jōyōshiu. The ordinary *sūtras* of the Shingon sect, comprising Buddhist *dhāraṇīs, etc.*, in Sanskrit, with transliteration into Japanese characters and a Chinese translation by Daikōchi.] [*Miako,* 1851.] 8°.
16007. a. 5.

SHIN-KYIN-WUT. ရှင့်ကျင့်ဝတ် *etc.* [Shin-kyin-wut. An anthology of short Pali texts, with Burmese versions, for the use of neophytes.] pp. 48. ရန်ကုန် ၁၂၅၄ [*Rangoon,* 1892.] 8°.
14098. ccc. 16.(1.)

—— ရှင်ကျင့်ဝတ်သစ် *etc.* [Shin-kyin-wut. The same work, in a slightly different recension.] pp. 35. ပန္တံလေး [*Mandalay,* 1900.] 8°.
14098. c. 32.(4.)

SHISHIR KUMAR GHOSE. See ṢIṢIRAKUMĀRA GHOSHA.

SHIUGEN. 修驗常用集 [Shiugen Jōyōshiu. The ordinary *sūtras* of the Shiugen sect, including some Buddhist *dhāraṇīs, etc.*, in Sanskrit, with Japanese transliteration.] 2 maki. *n.d.* 8°.
16006. a. 7.

SHIVARAM. See ṢIVARĀMA.

SHODAṢASLOKĪ ṢIKSHĀ. अथ षोडशश्लोकी शिक्षा *etc.* [Shoḍaṣaṣlokī Ṣikshā. 16 stanzas of the Mādhyandina school on Vedic phonetics.] See YUGALAKIṢORA VYĀSA PĀṬHAKA. श्रीमद्याज्ञवल्क्यादि . . . शिक्षासङ्ग्रहः . . . A collection of Ṣikshás, *etc.* pp. 164-165. 1893. 8°.
14093. b. 31.

SHRINATHA. See ṢRĪNĀTHA.

SHRIVARA. See ṢRĪVARA.

SHUKA. See ṢUKA.

SHUNKER NATH. See ṢAṄKARANĀTHA.

SHWE THĀ Ū. See SUTTAPIṬAKA.—*Dīghanikāya.* ဂိဟိဝိနယ *etc.* [Gihivinaya. Edited by Shwe Thā Ū.] [1894.] 8°.
14098. ccc. 21.

ṢIDDAPPĀCHĀRI. See MŪLASTAMBHAPURĀṆA. ಮೂಲಸ್ತಂಭಪುರಾಣವು *etc.* [Mūlastambhapurāṇa. With Canarese translation by Gaṇṭyappāchāri and Ṣiddappāchāri.] 1893. 8°.
14028. c. 63.

SIDDHANĀTHA, *Astrologer.* ఆరూఢరత్నసిద్ధాంజనమ్ *etc.* [Ārūḍharatnasiddhāñjana. A metrical treatise on astrology. With Telugu translation by Piṅgala Veṅkaṭarāma Joṣi.] pp. ii. 44. చెన్నపురి ౧౮౯౫ [*Madras,* 1895.] 8°.
14053. c. 67.

SIDDHANĀTHA VIDYĀVĀGĪṢA. See PURUSHOTTAMA VIDYĀVĀGĪṢA BHAṬṬĀCHĀRYA. প্রয়োগরত্নমালা *etc.* [Prayogaratnamālā. Edited with a commentary, styled Gūḍhaprakāṣikā, by Siddhanātha.] [1890-1893.] 4°.
14090. e. 22.

SIDDHARSHI. उपमितिभवप्रपञ्चा कथा । सिद्धर्षिप्रणीता । The Upamitibhavaprapancha Katha of Siddharshi. [A series of Jain stories in prose, interspersed with poetry.] (Originally) edited by (the late) Peter Peterson (and continued by . . . Hermann Jacobi). 1899, *etc.* See ACADEMIES, *etc.*—Calcutta.—*Asiatic Society of Bengal.* Bibliotheca Indica. New Series. [Vol. 144.] 1848, *etc.* 8°.
14002. a. (vol. 144.)

In progress. The title is from the wrappers.

—— Sacram Memoriam . . . Friderici Guilelmi III Universitatis Fridericiae Guilelmiae Rhenanae conditoris . . . indicit Adolfus . . . Kamphausen . . . Inest Upamitabhavaprapancae Kathae specimen, ab Hermanno Georgio Iacobi editum. pp. 24. *Bonnac,* [1891.] 8°.
14070. e. 16.(2.)

SIDDHARSHI (*continued*). La Upamitabhavaprapañcā Kathā di Siddharṣi. La novella allegorica della vita umana. I-II. [Translated by Ambrogio Ballini.] 1904, *etc.* *See* ACADEMIES, *etc.* — Florence. — *Società Asiatica Italiana.* Giornale, *etc.* Vol. xvii., *etc.* 1887, *etc.* 8°.
Ac. 8804. (vol. 17, etc.)
In progress.

SIDDHASENA DIVĀKARA. कल्याणमन्दिरस्तोत्रम् । [Kalyāṇamandirastotra. A Jain hymn of 44 stanzas.] *See* JAINASTOTRASAṄGRAHA. जैनस्तोत्रसंग्रहः *etc.* [Jainastotrasaṅgraha.] pp. 14-23. [1890.] 12°.
14100. a. 13.

—— सार्थ कल्याणमंदिरस्तोत्र *etc.* [Kalyāṇamandirastotra. With a translation and notes in Marathi.] pp. iii. 32. मुंबई १८९१ [*Bombay*, 1891.] 12°.
14028. b. 69.(2.)

—— कल्याणमंदिर स्तोत्र *etc.* [Kalyāṇamandirastotra. Edited with prose translation, metrical version, notes, and biography of the poet in Gujarati by Harajīvana Rāichand Shāh. Second edition.] pp. xii. 44. अमदावाद १९०१ [*Ahmadabad*, 1901.] 12°.
14100. b. 11.

—— कल्याणमन्दिरस्तोत्रम् । [Kalyāṇamandirastotra.] *See* JAINANITYAPĀṬHA. अथ जैननित्यपाठसंग्रहः [Jainanityapāṭhasaṅgraha.] pp. 66-82. [1901.] *obl.* 16°.
14100. a. 27.

—— [For the editions of the Kalyāṇamandirastotra included in the collection styled Navasmaraṇa :] *See* NAVASMARAṆA.

—— श्री ... श्रीवर्द्धमान द्वात्रिंशिका *etc.* [Vardhamānadvātriṃśikā. A Jain devotional poem of 32 stanzas. With commentary by Udayasāgara, and Gujarati translation of the text and commentary.] pp. ii. 60. અમદાવાદ ૧૯૦૩ [*Ahmadabad*, 1903.] 12°.
14100. a. 21.(4.)

SIDDHASENA SŪRI. *See* JINABHADRA GAṆĪ. Jinabhadra's Jitakalpa, mit Auszügen aus Siddhasena's Cûrṇi, *etc.* 1892. 8°.
14100. d. 2.

SIEG (EMIL). *See* BHĀRADVĀJA. Bhâradvâjaçîkshâ. Cum versione latina, excerptis ex commentario, adnotationibus ... edidit E. Sieg. 1892. 8°.
14093. d. 16.

—— Die Sagenstoffe des Ṛgveda und die indische Itihâsatradition, *etc.* *Stuttgart*, 1902, *etc.* 8°.
14007. cc. 31.
In progress.

ṢIHLAṆA MIṢRA. The Çántiçatakam : or A Hundred Verses on Tranquillity. Translated and edited ... by Mohendranath Chatterjee, with notes and original text. pp. i. iv. 55, 24. *Calcutta*, 1896. 12°.
14070. b. 25.

—— शान्तिशतक-श्लोक-रत्नमाला *etc.* [Śāntiṣatakaṣlokaratnamālā. With a rearrangement of the words and a Hindi translation by Musaddī-rām Ṣarmā.] pp. 54. अजमेर० [*Ajmere*, 1904.] 8°.
14070. c. 63.(3.)
Contains only 74 stanzas.

ṢIKHARANĀTHA SUVEDĪ, *Kavi.* *See* PRETAMAÑJARĪ. प्रेतमञ्जरी [Pretamañjarī. Edited by Ṣikharanātha.] [1902, *etc.*] *obl.* 12°.
14028. bb. 4.(3.)

—— थरगोत्रप्रवरावलि *etc.* [Tharagotrapravarāvali. Tables and descriptions of the *pravaras* of the Thar families, in Sanskrit and Nepali.] pp. ii. 56 ; 1 *plate.* श्रीकाशी १९५९ [*Benares*, 1903.] 12°.
14058. a. 8.(4.)

SĪLĀCHĀRA, *of Zayit, Ācharìya of Thet-ngay-gyin Kyaung.* *See* NĀGITA. သဒ္ဒသာရတ္ထဇာလိနီ *etc.* [Saddasāratthajālinī. With Burmese commentary by Sīlāchāra.] [1898.] 8°. [*Saddāngay.*]
14098. ccc. 22.

SĪLAKKHANDHA THERA, *C.A.*, *of Dodanduwa.* *See* ANURUDDHA. Anuruddha S'ataka ... With a commentary by ... Seelakkhandha Thēra. 1899. 8°. [*Buddhist Texts.*] **14004. c. (vol. 1, no. 5.)**

—— *See* BUDDHAGHOSA. [*Visuddhimagga.*] विसुद्धिमग्गो । Visuddhi Maggo ... Edited by ... Seelakkhanda Thera. 1896, *etc.* 8°. [*Buddhist Texts.*]
14004. c. (vol. 2, no. 1.)

—— *See* PAÑÑAGGA. Sugata Vidatthividhana ... With a [Sinhalese] paraphrase [and preface] by ... Seelakkhandha. 1894. 8°.
14098. c. 68.(2.)

—— *See* RĀMACHANDRA BHĀRATĪ. भक्तिशतकम् ॥ Bhakti-shatakam, *etc.* [Edited with Sanskrit commentary by Sīlakkhandha.] 1896. 8°. [*Buddhist Texts.*] **14004. c. (vol. 1, no. 2.)**

—— *See* RĀMACHANDRA BHĀRATĪ. वृत्तमालाख्या *etc.* [Vṛittamālākhyā. Edited by Sīlakkhandha.]

2 T

1894. 8°. [*Journal of the Buddhist Text Society of India.*] **14003. b. 19.(vol. 2.)**

—— *See* SUTTAPIṬAKA. — *Khuddakanikāya.* [*Dhammapada.*] धम्मपदं। Dhammapadam . . . edited by . . . Çarat Chandra Dās . . . and . . . Seelakkhandha Thera. 1899. 8°. [*Buddhist Texts.*] **14004. c. (vol. 1, no. 4.)**

SĪLĀNANDA, *Telvattē.* *See* SUTTAPIṬAKA.—*Khuddakanikāya.* [*Vimānavatthu.*] විමානවත්ථු *etc.* [Vimānavatthu. With commentary by Ratanapāla. Edited by Silānanda.] 1890. 8°. **14098. c. 63.(1.)**

SĪLAVILĀSA, *Thera.* *See* SAṄGHARAKKHITA. ဍွာ-ဒိမောဂ္ဂလာန်ပါဠိနိဿယ *etc.* [Nvādi-moggallāna. With Burmese *nissaya* by Silavilāsa.] [1900.] 8°. **14098. ccc. 29.(3.)**

ṢILHAṆA. *See* ṢIHLAṆA MIṢRA.

SIṂHA BHŪPĀLA. *See* ṢIṄGA BHŪPĀLA.

SIṂHADEVA GAṆĪ. *See* VĀGBHAṬA, *son of Soma.* The Vâgbhatâlaṃkâra . . . With the commentary of Siṃhadevagaṇi, *etc.* 1895. 8°. [*Kâvyamâlâ.*] **14072. ccc. 12.(no. 48.)**

SIMON (RICHARD). *See* AMARU. Das Amaruçataka . . . mit einer Einleitung und Auszügen aus den Commentatoren versehen, von R. Simon. 1893. 8°. **14072. d. 43.**

—— Quellen zur indischen Musik, *etc.* 1902, *etc.* *See* ACADEMIES, *etc.*—Germany.—*Deutsche Morgenlaendische Gesellschaft.* Zeitschrift, *etc.* Bd. 56, *etc.* 1846, *etc.* 8°. **Ac. 8815/2.(vol. 56, etc.)**
In progress?

ṢIṄGA BHŪPĀLA, *Sarvajña, Raja of Venkatagiri.* *See* ṢĀRṄGADEVA, *Nihṣaṅka, son of Soḍhala.* सङ्गीतरत्नाकर। [Saṅgītaratnākara. With Ṣiṅga Bhūpāla's commentary.] [1891, *etc.*] 4°. [*Aruṇodaya.*] **14133. g. 16.(pt. i., no. 17.)**

—— రసార్ణవ సుధాకరం నాట్యాలంకారశాస్త్రమ్ *etc.* [Rasārṇavasudhākara. A treatise, in 3 *vilāsas,* on the aesthetic and stylistic principles of the drama. Edited by Sarasvatīṣesha Ṣāstrī.] pp. i. 234, viii. వెంకటగిరి నగరమ్ [*Venkatagiri,* 1895.] 8°. **14053. ccc. 13.**
On this work and its author see Seshagiri Sastri's "Report" (1896-97), *no.* 1, *pp.* 7 ff.

ṢIṄGAM BHAṬṬA, *of Mysore.* *See* RĀMACHANDRA, *Vellāla.* సరసకవికులానందనం *etc.* [Sarasakavikulānandana. Edited by Ṣiṅgam Bhaṭṭa.] [1894.] 8°. **14079. c. 68.**

SIṄGARĀJU KĀNŪ ṢĀSTRI. *See* DHANVANTARI. ధన్వంతరినిఘంటువు *etc.* [Dhanvantarinighaṇṭu. Edited with Telugu interpretation by Siṅgarāju Kānū and Veṅkaṭappā Rāu.] [1892.] 8°. **14043. c. 40.**

SINHA (P. N.). *See* PŪRṆENDU NĀRĀYAṆA SIṂHA.

SIRISADDHAMMAKITTI. *See* SADDHAMMAKITTI.

ṢIROMAṆI DĪKSHITA, *Āchārya, of Nepal.* *See* SADĀṢIVA ĀCHĀRYA DĪKSHITA. आचार्यवंशावली। *etc.* [Āchāryavaṃṣāvalī. A biography of Ṣiromaṇi.] [1903.] 8°. **14058. b. 50.**

ṢIṢIRAKUMĀRA GHOSHA. Lord Gauranga; or Salvation for all. [A biography of Chaitanya in English] by Shishir Kumar Ghose. 2 vols. *Calcutta,* 1897-1898. 8°. **4506. df.**

ṢĪTALACHANDRA VEDĀNTABHŪSHAṆA. वेदान्तविजयम् *etc.* [Vedāntavijaya. An exposition of Vedānta philosophy.] pp. i. 79. कलिकाता १८९३ [*Calcutta,* 1892.] 8°. **14048. bb. 51.(4.)**

SĪTĀNĀTHA DATTA. Sankaracharya. His life and teachings. [With] a translation of Atmabodha, *etc.* pp. i. i. 72. *Calcutta,* 1897. 12°. **14048. a. 22.**

—— —— Third edition. pp. i. i. 72. *Calcutta,* 1899. 12°. **14048. a. 28.**

SĪTĀRĀMA AIYAR, *C. Subbarāma.* *See* KĀLIDĀSA. —*Ritusaṃhāra.* The Ritusanhara . . . with notes and English translation, by C. S. Sitaram Ayyar. 1897. 8°. **14070. c. 60.**

SĪTĀRĀMAṢARAṆA, *Pandit, of Cawnpore.* *See* RĀGHAVENDRA SAKHĀJĪ. साकेताधीशयुगलरहस्यस्तोत्रम् *etc.* [Sāketādhīṣayugalarahasyastotra. With Hindi translation by Sītārāmaṣaraṇa.] [1901.] *obl.* 12°. **14033. a. 19.(5.)**

—— *See* SANATKUMĀRASAṂHITĀ. ॥ श्रीरामस्तवराज *etc.* [Rāmastavarāja. With a Hindi commentary called Bhāvaprakāṣikā by Sītārāmaṣaraṇa.] 1901. 8°. **14028. c. 66.(2.)**

SĪTĀRĀMA ṢARMĀ, *son of Bālamukunda.* तीर्थनिन्दकमुखचपेटिका *etc.* [Tīrthanindakamukhachapeṭikā. A polemical tract asserting the sanctity of holy places, in answer to Bhīmasena Ṣarmā's tract styled Tīrthavishaya, in which the latter asserts the contrary in a polemic against Sītārāma's preceptor Rājārāma Ṣāstrī. With Hindi translation.] pt. i. pp. 44. कानपुर १८१३ [*Cawnpore*, 1891.] 8°. **14033. bb. 40.**

SĪTĀRĀMA ṢĀSTRĪ, *S. See* SĀYAṆA ĀCHĀRYA.—*Works on Ṣruti.* [*Upanishads.*] Extracts from Vedántic commentaries. Translated from Vidyâranya's Taittirîyaupanishad-Dipikâ [*sic*] [by Sītārāma]. 1897. 4°. [*Brahmavâdin.*] **14048. g. 1.(vol. 2.)**

—— *See* UPANISHADS.—*Small Collections.* The Isa, Kena & Mundaka Upanishads and Sri Sankara's commentary, translated by S. Sitarama Sastri . . . First volume. (Vol. II, The Katha and Prasna Upanishads . . . translated by S. Sitarama Sastri. Vol. V, The Aitareya & Taittiriya Upanishads . . . translated by S. Sitarama Sastri.) 1898, *etc.* 12°. **14010. b. 20.**

—— *See* YĀJÑAVALKYA. [*Dharmaṣāstra.*] The Inheritance Chapter of Yájnavalkya with Visvarúpa's commentary. Translated . . . by S. Sitarama Sastri, *etc.* 1900. 8°. **14038. d. 22.(2.)**

SĪTĀRĀMA ṢĀSTRĪ, *Ellambhatta. See* NṚISIṂHA SARASVATĪ TĪRTHA. ವೇದಾಂತಡಿಂಡಿಮಃ *etc.* [Vedāntaḍiṇḍima. Edited by Sītārāma.] [1897.] 8°. **14048. cc. 9.(2.)**

SĪTĀRĀMA ṢRĪKṚISHṆA JĀMBHEKAR. *See* BHARTṚIHARI. अथ भर्तृहरिशतकम् *etc.* [Bhartṛihariṣataka. With Sanskrit commentary and Hindi paraphrases. Edited by Sitārāma.] [1902.] 8°. **14076. d. 53.**

—— *See* RĀMA, *son of Ananta.* मुहूर्तचिन्तामणिः *etc.* [Muhūrtachintāmaṇi. With Hindi translation. Edited by Sītārāma.] [1902.] 8°. **14053. cc. 69.**

SĪTĀṢARAṆA, *of Cawnpore. See* SĪTĀRĀMAṢARAṆA.

ṢITIKAṆṬHA BHAṬṬA. *See* JAIMINI.—*Mīmāṃsāsūtra.* जैमिनिसूत्रवृत्तिः *etc.* [Mīmāṃsāsūtra. With the commentary Subodhinī, sometimes ascribed to Ṣitikaṇṭha.] [1899.] 8°. [*The Pandit.*] **14096. d. 6.**

ṢIVABASAIYA, *Kāṭāpuri.* ಆದಿ ವೀರಮಾಹೇಶ್ವರ ಮೂಲ ಪೀಠಿಕೆ *etc.* [Ādivīramāheṣvaramūlapīṭhikā. A compilation from Āgamik works on the origins, divisions, and principles of the Lingāyat sect.] pp. 26. ಧಾರವಾಡ ೧೮೯೧ [*Dharwar*, 1891.] 12°. **14058. a. 8.(1.)**

ṢIVACHANDRA GUI. *See* ACADEMIES, *etc.*—Calcutta.—*Calcutta Sanskrit College.* A Descriptive Catalogue of Sanskrit Manuscripts in the Library of the Calcutta Sanskrit College . . . by Hṛishikeśa Śástri . . . and Śiva Chandra Gui. 1892, *etc.* 8°. **14096. cc. 10.**

—— *See* UDAYANA ĀCHĀRYA. कुसुमाञ्जलिः। [Kusumāñjali. With commentary by Ṣivachandra.] 1891, *etc.* 8°. [*Vidyodaya.*] **14096. cc. (vol. 20, etc.)**

ṢIVACHANDRA SIDDHĀNTA, *Mahāmahopādhyāya.* শ্রীমদ্ভাগবতবিচারঃ *etc.* [Bhāgavatavichāra. An essay proving the Bhāgavatapurāṇa to be the work of Vyāsa. Edited with a Bengali preface by Ṣaṣibhūshaṇa Chakravartī.] pp. iv. 11. কলিকাতা ১৮১৪ [*Calcutta*, 1893.] 8°. **14016. c. 56.(1.)**

ṢIVADĀSA. *See* VETĀLAPAÑCHAVIṂṢATI. Vetālapańcavimçatikā, *etc.* [Translated into Italian from Ṣivadāsa's recension.] 1897, *etc.* 8°. [*Studi Italiani di Filologia Indo-Iranica.*] **P.P. 4884. da. (vol. 1, etc.)**

ṢIVADĀSA SENA. *See* CHAKRAPĀṆIDATTA. চক্রদত্তঃ *etc.* [Chakradatta. With the commentary Tattvachandrikā of Ṣivadāsa.] [1900.] 8°. **14043. cc. 17.**

—— *See* CHAKRAPĀṆIDATTA. द्रव्यगुणः *etc.* [Dravyaguṇa. With commentary of Ṣivadāsa.] [1897.] 8°. **14043. c. 37.(2.)**

ṢIVADATTA, *son of Badarīnātha, Dādhīcha Pandit, of Jaipur. See* BĀDARĀYAṆA. वैयासिकन्यायमाला *etc.* (Vaiyásikanyáyamálá . . . Edited by . . . S'ivadatta.) 1891. 8°. **14003. ccc. (no. 23.)**

—— *See* DURGĀPRASĀDA, *son of Vrajalāla*, and KĀṢĪNĀTHA PĀṆḌURAṄGA PARAB. Kâvyamâlâ . . . Edited by . . . Durgâprasâda [and after his death, from no. 36 onward, by Ṣivadatta] and Kâshînâtha Pâṇduranga Paraba. 1886, *etc.* 8°. **14072. ccc. 11, 12.**

—— *See* DURGĀPRASĀDA, *son of Vrajalāla*, and KĀṢĪNĀTHA PĀṆḌURAṄGA PARAB. The Prâchîna-

lekha-mâlâ . . . Edited by . . . Durgâprasâd (Vol. II, by . . . Śivadatta) . . . and Kâśînâth Pâṇḍurang Parab. 1892, *etc.* 8°. [*Kâvyamâlâ.*]
14072. ccc. 12.(no. 34, 64.)

—— *See* DURGĀPRASĀDA, *son of Vrajalāla,* and others. The Abhidhâna-sangraha . . . Edited by . . . Durgâprasâd, Kâśînâth Pâṇḍurang Parab and . . . Śivadatta. 1889- . 8°. **14090. e. 20.**

—— *See* JAIMINI. — *Mīmāṃsāsūtra.* जैमिनीयन्यायमाला *etc.* (Jaiminîyanyâyamâlâ . . . by Śrî Mâdhavâchârya. With his own commentary and Jaiminî's Sûtràs . . . Edited by . . . Sivadatta.) [1892.] 8°. **14003. ccc. (no. 24.)**

—— *See* PĀLAKĀPYA. हस्त्यायुर्वेदः *etc.* (The Hastyâyurvéda . . . Edited by . . . Śivadatta, *etc.*) [1894.] 8°. **14003. ccc. (no. 26.)**

—— *See* ŚRĪHARSHA, *son of Hīra Paṇḍita.* Śriharsha's Naishadhîyacharita, with the commentary . . . of Nârâyaṇa. Edited with . . . notes by . . . Śivadatta. 1894. 8°. **14070. d. 35.**

ŚIVADATTA SIṂHA VARMĀ. । अथविष्णुभक्तिप्रमोदः । [Vishṇubhaktipramoda. A treatise on the cult of Vishṇu. Compiled by Śivadatta Siṃha, assisted by Jagannātha Tripāṭhī.] pp. 116 ; 1 *plate.* बनारस १९४६ [*Benares,* 1890.] 8°. **14028. c. 62.(2.)**

ŚIVADATTA UPĀDHYĀYA. अथ ज्योतिषसार *etc.* [Jyotishasāra. A manual of astrology. With a Nepali version by Viśvarāja Harihara Sarmā.] pp. v. 205. *Benares,* [1902.] 8°. **14053. dd. 4.(2.)**

ŚIVĀDITYA MIŚRA. सप्तपदार्थी . . . Çivādityi Saptapadārthī. Primum edidit prolegomena interpretationem latinam explanationes et exempla adiecit Augustus Winter. pp. xi. 22, 28. *Lipsiae, Bonn* [printed], 1893. 8°. **14048. dd. 2.**

—— The Saptapadârthî, [a manual] of the Vaiśeshika system, of Śivâditya. Together with its commentary the Mitabhâshiṇî of Mâdhava Sarasvatî. Edited by Râmaśâstrî Tailaṅga. pp. vii. i. vii. 81. *Benares,* 1893. 8°.
14048. dd. 3.(vol. 6.)

Forms vol. 6 *of the* Vizianagram Sanskrit Series. *The editor states that in one MS. the work is ascribed in the colophon to Vyoma Śivāchārya.*

—— Die Saptapadārthī des Śivāditya. [Translated into German] von A. Winter. 1899. *See* ACADEMIES, *etc.* — Germany. — *Deutsche Morgenlaendische Gesellschaft.* Zeitschrift, *etc.* Bd. 53, no. 2. 1846, *etc.* 8°. **Ac. 8815/2.(Bd. 53.)**

ŚIVĀDVAITAPAÑCHAKA. శివాద్వైతపంచక *etc.* [Śivâdvaitapañchaka. Five tracts of the Vīraśaiva sect of the Śaiva-Advaita school,—viz. ch. 180-185 of the Śivashaṇmukhasaṃvāda in the Śaṅkarasaṃhitā of the Skandapurāṇa; Śivānubhavasūtra, 8 chapters, from the Vātūlāgama; Viśeshārthaprakāśikā, 5 chapters; Revaṇa's Śaivasiddhāntaśikhāmaṇi, 20 chapters; and Vātūlāgama, ch. 1-10 of the Sahasragranthasaṃhitā. Edited by M. Mallikārjuna Śāstrī.] pp. ii. 212. ఏలూరు నగరే [*Ellore,* 1897.] 8°.
14048. cc. 8.(4.)

ŚIVAKUMĀRA MIŚRA. যতীন্দ্র-জীবন-চরিতম্ *etc.* [Yatīndrajīvanacharita. A poem on the history of Bhāskarānanda Sarasvatī, with other panegyrical poems appended. With a Bengali translation by Sureśvara Nārāyaṇa Deva.] pp. v. 89. *Calcutta,* ১২৯৯ [1892.] 8°. **14058. b. 26.(2.)**

ŚIVAKUMĀRA ŚĀSTRĪ, *Mahāmahopādhyāya,* **and others.** श्रीरामेश्वरानन्दयशोभूषणं *etc.* [Rāmeśvarānandayaśobhūshaṇa. A series of panegyrics in Sanskrit, Hindi, and Gujarati, addressed to Rāmeśvarānanda Śarmā.] pp. 14. मुम्बय्यां १९५८ [*Bombay,* 1902.] 8°. **14058. cc. 4.**

SĪVALI-GĀTHĀ. ရှင်သီဝလိဂါထာ [Shin-Sīvali-gāthā. A Pali poem in praise of Sīvali Thera.] *See* JAYANTĀBHIVAṂSA. သဒ္ဓမ္မပါလမေဓနီ *etc.* [Saddhammapālamedhanī.] pp. 66-67. [1872.] 8°. **14300. d. 28.(1.)**

—— ရှင်သီဝလိဂါထာ [Shin-Sīvali-gāthā.] *See* PAYĀ-SHI-HKO. ဘုရားရှိခိုး *etc.* [Payā-shi-hko.] pp. 56-58. [1893.] 8°. **14098. ccc. 16.(2.)**

ŚIVĀLIKHITA. සිවාලිඛිතය *etc.* [Śivālikhita. A short astrological treatise in verse, with translation and other matter in Sinhalese. Third edition.] pp. vii. 71. කොළඹ [*Colombo,*] 1890. 16°. **14053. a. 12.(1.)**

ŚIVĀNANDA KARMANDI, *of Kalahasti. See* UPANISHADS. — *Separate Upanishads.* भस्मजाबालोपनिषत् *etc.* [Bhasmajābālopanishad. With commentary of Śivānanda.] [1893.] 8°. **14010. cc. 4.**

ṢIVANĀRĀYAṆA ṢIROMAṆI. *See* VOPADEVA. Kavikalpadruma ... With the commentaries ... of Durgadas Vidyabagis. Edited ... by ... Sivanarayan Siromani, *etc.* 1897. 8°.
14090. c. 38.(2.)

ṢIVANĀTHA VIDYĀVĀCHASPATI. *See* HARSHADEVA. रत्नावली *etc.* [Ratnāvalī. With commentary, entitled Vidyotanī, by Ṣivanātha.] [1900.] 8°.
14079. c. 65.(2.)

—— স্মৃতিবিচারসারকৌমুদী *etc.* [Smṛitivichārasārakaumudī. Disquisitions on points in the writings of Raghunandana.] pp. ii. 67. কলিকাতা ১৮১৯ [*Calcutta*, 1897.] 8°. **14033. bb. 45.(1.)**

ṢIVAPAÑCHĀYATANAPŪJĀ. ॥ अथ शिवपंचायतनपूजाप्रयोगप्रारंभः ॥ [Ṣivapañchāyatanapūjāprayoga. A handbook for the rite of that name, extending over the ceremonies of *pūjā*, *brahmayajñatarpaṇa*, *gotrapravara*, and *vaiṣvadeva*, with an *ārti* appended. Edited by Nārāyaṇaṣaṅkara Viṣvanātha Guvintī.] ff. 26. १८५६ [*Bombay*, 1900.] *obl.* 12°. **14028. b. 102.(4.)**

ṢIVAPRAKĀṢA DEṢIKA, *Turaimaṅgalam.* ॥ सन्मार्गदर्पणम् ... The Sanmargadarpanam. [A Sanskrit version of the] Nanneri [*i.e.* நன்னெறி] of Sivaprakasa Swami. Translated ... by Radhakrishna Sastriar. pp. 10. *See* RADHĀKṚISHṆA ṢĀSTRĪ, *of Pudukottai.* नीतिदशप्रबन्धी ... The Nitidasaprabandhi, *etc.* No. 8. 1894. 8°. **14085. c. 46.**

ṢIVAPRAKĀṢA POTADĀR, *son of Harasahāya Mal.* सुजनप्रकाश *etc.* [Sujanaprakāṣa. Comprising collections of (1) devotional poems, in Hindi; (2) stanzas and poems on divination and astrology, in Hindi and in Sanskrit with Hindi translation; and (3) medical recipes, *etc.*, in the same languages.] pp. viii. 104. कल्याण-मुंबई १८२१ [*Kalyan*, 1900.] 8°. **14053. cc. 62.(2.)**

ṢIVAPRASĀDA, *Brahma-bhaṭṭa, son of Nārāyaṇa Rāya.* ब्रह्मभट्ट प्रदीप *etc.* [Brahmabhaṭṭapradīpa. A poem on the Brahma-bhaṭṭa caste, in Sanskrit and Hindi, with Hindi prose translation.] pp. 7, 31. कानपुर [*Cawnpore*, 1890.] 8°.
14048. cc. 8.(1.)

ṢIVAPRASĀDA MĀKHANLĀL, *of Pushkar. See* PURĀṆAS.—*Padmapurāṇa.* पुष्कर माहात्म्य° [Pushkaramāhātmya. With Hindi translation by Ṣivaprasāda.] [1898.] *obl.* 8°. **14016. d. 51.**

ṢIVAPRASĀDA ṢARMĀ, *disciple of Raghunātha, of Birpur, Ghazipur.* । चयहानिवंशभूषणम् । अर्थात् चौहान क्षत्रियों की वंशावली *etc.* [Chayahānivaṃṣabhūshaṇa, or Chauhān Kshatriyoṇ kī Vaṃṣāvalī. An account in 428 verses, based upon the Bhavishyapurāṇa, of the ancient history of the Chauhān Kshatriyas, with especial reference to the Loniyā caste. With preface by Lakshmīnārāyaṇa son of Kālikādatta, and Hindi translation of the verses.] pp. viii. ii. 148. प्रयाग १९०३ [*Allahabad*, 1903.] 8°. **14058. cc. 7.**

The title is spelt Chaihāniv°. *in the body of the book.*

ṢIVARĀMAKṚISHṆA ṢĀSTRĪ, *Ādhanakoṭṭai.* ப்ரயோகசிந்தாமணி: *etc.* [Prayogachintāmaṇi. A manual of domestic ritual according to the school of Āpastamba. Edited with a commentary called Kalpavallī and a *kārikā* or metrical epitome styled Gṛihyakalparatna by the author's son, Ā. Svāminātha Ṣāstrī.] pp. viii. 207. கும்பகோணம் ॥ [*Kumbakonam*,] 1901. 8°. **14033. aa. 22.**

ṢIVARĀMA MAHĀDEVA PARĀÑJPYE. *See* JAYADEVA, *son of Mahādeva.* Prasanna Râghava ... Edited with an introduction and notes ... by Shivaram ... Paranjpe and Narayan ... Panse. 1894. 8°. **14079. c. 62.**

—— *See* KEṢAVA MIṢRA, *Logician.* The Tarkabhâshâ ... with the commentary of Govardhana. Edited with an introduction and notes ... by Shivaram ... Paranjape. 1894. 8°.
14048. dd. 18.

ṢIVARĀMA PĀṆḌE, *Vaidya.* एडवर्ड राज्याभिषेक ... Edward Rajyabhishek. A Sanskrit-Hindi poem on the coronation of his Majesty the King-Emperor, Edward VII, by Pandit Shivaram Pande. pp. iii. 5. प्रयाग [*Allahabad*, 1902.] 12°.
14072. b. 27.(1.)

—— राज्याभिषेक दरबार ... Rajya bhishek. Sanskrit-Hindi verses in honour of the Delhi Coronation Darbar of His Majesty the King-Emperor Edwrd [*sic*] vii. ... To be recited by the boys of the Allahabad Orphonage [*sic*] on the Darbar day. pp. iv. 12. प्रयाग [*Allahabad*, 1903.] 12°. **14072. b. 27.(2.)**

ṢIVARĀMA RĀUJĪ KHOPAKAR. *See* JAYADEVA, *son of Mahādeva.* Prasanna-raghava . . . With . . . English notes . . . by Shivarama . . . Khopakar. 1894. 8°. **14080. d. 24.**

ṢIVARĀMA ṢĀSTRĪ, *Iñjikollai, of Kumbakonam.* *See* VEDAS. — Yajurveda. — *Vājasaneyisaṃhitā.* வாஜஸநேயஸம்ஹிதா ... பாஷ்யார்த்தஸங்க்ரஹஸஹிதா *etc.* [Vājasaneyisaṃhitā. With a brief commentary, styled Bhāshyārthasaṅgraha, by Ṣivarāma.] 1901, *etc.* 8°. **14007. cc. 29.**

ṢIVARĀMA TĀNBĀ DUBE. *See* MOROPANTA. The Râmâyaṇs of Moropant . . . Edited . . . by the editors of the 'Kâvyasangraha' (Vâmana Dâjî Oka . . . and Śivarâma . . . Dube.) 1891-1896. 8°. **14140. aa. 2.**

ṢIVASAṂHITĀ. শিবসংহিতা। [Ṣivasaṃhitā. A treatise on Yoga. With Bengali translation.] pp. 47. [1891, *etc.*] *See* PERIODICAL PUBLICATIONS. — *Calcutta.* অরুণোদয় *etc.* [Aruṇodaya.] Pt. i., no. 22. [1890, *etc.*] 4°. **14133. g. 16.(pt. i., no. 22.)**

Sometimes said to belong to the Skandapurāṇa.

—— শিবসংহিতা। [Ṣivasaṃhitā. With Bengali version.] pp. 297. *See* PRASANNAKUMĀRA ṢĀSTRĪ BHAṬṬĀCHĀRYA. যোগাম্বুধি *etc.* [Yogâmbudhi.] [1896.] 16°. **14048. a. 19.**

—— The Esoteric Science and Philosophy of the Tantras. Shiva Sanhita, translated [with an introduction] by Srischandra Basu. New edition. pp. lviii. 61. *Calcutta,* 1893. 8°. **14028. d. 52.**

—— Practical Yoga Philosophy, or Siva-sanhita, in English . . . [Translated] with copious explanatory notes by B. N. Banerjee. pp. vii. 116. *Calcutta,* 1894. 12°. **14048. b. 28.(1.)**

ṢIVAṢAṄKARA PAṆḌYĀJĪ, *R.* The Hindu Excelsior Series. Edited by R. Sivasankara Pandiah. 1885, *etc.* 12° & 8°. **14003. c.**

Works published in this series which are not registered in Prof. Bendall's Catalogue may be found under the following headings:—

Mahābhārata.—*Bhagavadgītā.*
Ṣivaṣaṅkara Paṇḍyā.
Vālmiki.—*Rāmāyaṇa.*
Veṅkaṭaratna Ṣarmā.

—— Upâkhyâna Ratnâvalî : Aryan Anecdotes : containing excellent moral and religious anecdotes in English, from ancient Aryan books [viz. the Epics and Purāṇas]. Edited [*i.e.* translated] by R. Sivasankara Pandiyaji. pp. xii. 60. *Madras,* 1890. 12°. **14003. c.**

No. xii. *of the editor's* Hindu Excelsior Series.

—— Introductory Text-book of Hindu Ethics and Theology : [a compilation of Sanskrit texts with dissertations thereon in English] by R. Sivasankara Pandiyaji. pp. iv. 180. *Madras,* 1892. 12°. **14003. c.**

No. xiii. *of the editor's* Hindu Excelsior Series.

—— Arya Dharma Bodhini. Aryan Religious Instructor. Containing the essence of Aryan morality and religion expressed in simple Sanskrit stanzas with Telugu translations. By . . . R. Sivasankara Pandiyaji. pp. 24. *Madras,* 1897. 12°. **14003. c.**

No. xiv. *of the* Hindu Excelsior Series.

ṢIVAṢAṄKARA ṢARMĀ, *Kāvyatīrtha, Maithila.* *See* UPANISHADS.—*Separate Upanishads.* (छान्दोग्योपनिषद्भाष्य) [Chhāndogyopanishad. With *pada*-analysis, Sanskrit commentary, and Hindi translation and paraphrase by Ṣivaṣaṅkara.] [1904, *etc.*] 8°. **14007. f. 5.**

—— —— [1905, *etc.*] 8°. **14007. f. 6.**

ṢIVAṢAṄKARA ṢĀSTRĪ, *Kastūri, of Rajamahendri.* గులాంఖాదరుచరిత్రము *etc.* [Ghulām-Kādir-charitra. A poem on the life and work of Ghulām Kādir, a conciliator of Islam and Hinduism. With Telugu version.] pp. i. 49. రాజమహేంద్రవరము [*Rajamahendri,* 1900.] 8°. **14058. b. 44.**

ṢIVAṢAṄKARA YOGĪ. *See* ṢAṄKARAIYA DEVĀṄGA.

ṢIVAṢARMA SŪRI, *son of Makaranda.* वासुदेवरसानन्दः *etc.* [Vāsudevarasānanda. An anthological and expository work on the attributes of Vishṇu. Edited by Sarayūprasāda Miṣra.] pp. 203, vi. प्रयागे १९५४ [*Allahabad,* 1897.] 12°. **14028. c. 76.(2.)**

ṢIVASVARODAYA. శివస్వరోదయము *etc.* [Ṣivasvarodaya. A treatise upon divination from the breath, *etc.*, in 395 stanzas. Edited with Telugu translation by N. Guruliṅga Ṣāstrī.] pp. 68. చెన్నపట్టణము ౧౯౦౧ [*Madras,* 1901.] 8°. **14033. aa. 28.(2.)**

ṢIVATĀṆḌAVA. अथ ताण्डव प्रतिबिम्ब अर्थात् शिवतांडव स्तोत्र *etc.* [Ṣivatāṇḍavastotra, or Tāṇḍavapratibimba. A Ṣaiva hymn in 15 stanzas. With Hindi metrical version and notes by Muralīdhara of Bhagalpur.] pp. 9. *Bhagalpur,* 1900. 12°. **14028. b. 66.(2.)**

Ascribed to Rāvana.

—— अथ शिवताण्डवस्तोत्रं *etc.* [Ṣivatāṇḍavastotra. Followed by a Ṣivanāmāvalyashṭaka.] ff. 15. मुंबई [*Bombay,* 1902.] *obl.* 16°. **14028. a. 27.(4.)**

—— शिवताण्डवम् सटीकम् ॥ [Ṣivatāṇḍavastotra. With commentary called Ṣivatāṇḍavachandrikā by Lakshmīnārāyaṇa Ṣarmā.] *See* LAKSHMĪNĀRĀYAṆA ṢARMĀ, *disciple of Thākuradatta.* कवीन्द्रलक्ष्मीनारायणजीका जीवनचरित्र *etc.* [Kavīndra-Lakshmīnārāyaṇa-jī-kā Jīvanacharitra.] pp. 15-26. [1902.] 8°. **14072. d. 46.**

SLATER (THOMAS EBENEZER). Studies in the Upanishads, *etc.* pp. 76. *Madras,* 1897. 8°. **14016. c. 49.**

SMART (ALEXANDER WILLIAM). *See* ṢANKARA ĀCHĀRYA.—*Doubtful and Supposititious Works.* Śankara's Veda-vedánta-sara. Text and Translation by A. W. Smart. 1896. 4°. [*Brahmavādin.*] **14048. g. 1.(vol. 1.)**

SNYDER (EDMUND NATHANIEL). Der Commentar und die Textüberlieferung des Mahāvaṃsa. Inaugural-Dissertation . . . von Edmund N. Snyder. pp. 51. *Berlin,* 1891. 8°. **14098. d. 22.(2.)**

ṢOBHĀKARA BHAṬṬA. *See* NĀRADA. [*Ṣikshā.*] सटीका नारदीशिक्षा ॥ [Nāradaṣikshā. With commentary by Ṣobhākara.] 1893. 8°. [*Ṣikshāsaṅgraha.*] **14093. b. 31.**

ṢOBHANA MUNI, *Jain Poet.* शोभनस्तवनावली *etc.* [Ṣobhanastavanāvalī. Hymns by Ṣobhana and others.] [1897.] 12°. *See* ḌĀHYĀBHĀI FATHCHAND and MOTĪLĀL MAHĀSUKHBHĀI. **14100. a. 17.**

SOCIETÀ ASIATICA ITALIANA. *See* ACADEMIES, *etc.*—*Florence.*

SOHIRĀ. *See* SOHIROBĀNĀTH ĀMBIYE.

SOHIROBĀNĀTH ĀMBIYE. The Poems of Sohirobânâtha Âmbiye, a renowned sage of Bândém. 1. Siddhânta Samhitâ. [A philosophical Sanskrit poem, with metrical Marathi paraphrase.] . . . Edited . . . by Vâmana Dâjî Oka. (पारमार्थिक कवितासंग्रह.) *Bombay,* 1896, *etc.* 8°. **14140. aa. 12.**

In progress. Forms no. 22 etc. of the Kāvyasangraha.

SOLĀKĀRAṆAPŪJĀ. अथ सोलाकारण पूजाप्रारंभः [Solākāraṇapūjā. A Sanskrit and Prakrit ritual of the Digambara Jains, enumerating the 16 causes of salvation.] *See* DAṢALAKSHAṆĪ. दशलक्षण्यादि पूजनसंग्रह *etc.* [Daṣalakshaṇyādi-pūjanasaṅgraha.] ff. 46-65. [1899.] *obl.* 8°. **14100. b. 7.**

SOL-SVAPNA. सोल सपना प्रारंभ [Sol-svapna. A Jain legend in Prakrit. With supralinear Gujarati translation.] pp. 22, *lith.* मुंबइ [*Bombay,* 1894.] *obl.* 8°. **14100. d. 6.**

SOMĀBHĀĪ MAṄGALADĀSA. ॥ श्री कोट्यर्क भक्तिप्रदीप *etc.* [Koṭyarkabhaktipradīpa. A handbook of devotions to the deity Koṭyarka, for the use of the Kharait sect of Vaishṇavas. Comprising Sanskrit texts with Gujarati translations, commentaries, *etc.*] pp. 36; 1 *plate.* અમદાવાદ ૧૯૦૧ [*Ahmadabad,* 1901.] 12°. **14028. b. 73.(3.)**

SOMADEVA, *son of Rāma.* Bunte Geschichten vom Himalaja. Novellen, Schwänke und Märchen [from the Kathāsaritsāgara] . . . deutsch von Johannes Hertel. pp. xxi. 186. *München, Altenburg* [printed], 1903. 8°. **14070. dd. 25.**

SOMADEVA, *Courtier of Vigraharāja Deva.* Sanskrit Plays, partly preserved as inscriptions at Ajmere. [Comprising a large part of Somadeva's Lalitavigraharājanāṭaka, a drama in honour of the author's patron Vigraharāja, and of Vigraharāja's Harakelināṭaka. Edited] by . . . F. Kielhorn. 1891. *See* PERIODICAL PUBLICATIONS.—*Bombay.* The Indian Antiquary, *etc.* Vol. xx., pp. 201-212. 1872, *etc.* 4°. **14096. e. (vol. 20.)**

—— Bruchstücke des Lalita-vigraharâja Nâṭaka. Von F. Kielhorn. 1893. *See* ACADEMIES, *etc.*—Goettingen.—*Academia Georgia Augusta.* Nachrichten . . . Aus dem Jahre 1893. pp. 552-570. [1845, *etc.*] 8°. **2097. a.**

—— Bruchstücke indischer Schauspiele in Inschriften zu Ajmere [viz., of the Lalitavigraharājanāṭaka and Harakelināṭaka]. Von F. Kielhorn. pp. vi. 30; 4 *plates.* *See* ACADEMIES, *etc.*—Goettingen.—*Koenigliche Gesellschaft der Wissenschaften.* Festschrift, *etc.* pt. 2. 1901. 4°. **Ac. 670.**

SOMADEVA SŪRI, *disciple of Nemideva*. The Yaśastilaka of Somadeva Sûri. [A Jain romantic poem.] With the commentary of Śrutadeva [*i.e.* Şrutasāgara] Sûri. . . . Edited by . . . Paṇḍit Śivadatta . . . and Kâshînâth Pâṇḍurang Parab. (यशस्तिलकम् ।) 2 pts. pp. 621, 419. 1901-1903. *See* DURGĀPRASĀDA, *son of Vrajalāla*, and KĀŞĪNĀTHA PĀṆḌURAṄGA PARAB. Kâvyamâlâ. [No.] 70. 1886, *etc.* 8°. **14072. ccc. 12. (no. 70.)**

SOMANĀTHA, *son of Mudgala*. रागविबोधः *etc.* [Rāgavibodha. A treatise on music, in 5 *vivekas*. With the author's commentary. Edited by Purushottama Gaṇeşa Ghārpure.] 5 pts. पुण्याख्यपत्तने १८१७ [*Poona*, 1894.] 8°. **14053. cc. 67.**

The first part was published by the editor in 1889 in the Saṅgītamīmāṃsaka, and here appears in its second edition.

SOMAPRABHA ĀCHĀRYA. अथ . . . सिंदूरप्रकरः *etc.* [Sindūraprakara, or Sūktimuktāvali. A Sanskrit poem in 100 stanzas setting forth the Jain doctrines. With a Sanskrit commentary by Harshakīrti Sūri, a Gujarati *bālāvabodha*, and a Gujarati metrical version by Banārasī Dāsa.] 1890. *See* BHĪMASIṂHA MĀṆAKA. जैनकथारत्नकोष *etc.* [Jainakathāratnakoşa.] Vol. I, pp. 1-184. [1890-1893.] 8°. **14144. gg. 1. (vol. 1.)**

—— ಸೂಕ್ತಿ ಮುಕ್ತಾವಲಿ *etc.* [Sūktimuktāvali. In 98 stanzas. Edited with Canarese glosses and paraphrases by Padmarāja Paṇḍita.] pp. 86. ಬೆಂಗಳೂರು ೧೮೯೨ [*Bangalore*, 1892.] 8°. **14028. d. 47.**

—— Gli Scritti di Somaprabhâćârya. [With a translation of his Sindūraprakara. By P. E. Pavolini.] 1898. *See* PERIODICAL PUBLICATIONS. —*Florence*. Studi Italiani di Filologia Indo-Iranica, *etc.* Vol. ii., pp. 33-72. 1897, *etc.* 8°. **P.P. 4884. da. (vol. 2.)**

—— शृंगार वैराग्य तरंगिणी *etc.* [Şriṅgāravairāgyataraṅgiṇī. Jain ethical verses. With a Gujarati translation and commentary by Rāmachandra Dīnānātha founded on the Sanskrit commentary of Nandalāla.] pp. i. 31. અમદાવાદ ૧૮૯૧ [*Ahmadabad*, 1891.] *obl.* 8°. **14072. c. 51.**

SOMEŞVARA BHAṬṬA, *son of Mādhava*. *See* JAIMINI. — *Mīmāṃsāsūtra*. न्यायसुधा . . . Nyâyasudhâ, [also called Rāṇaka and Sarvopakāriṇī,] a commentary on Tantravârtika. By . . . Sômeshwara, *etc.* 1901, *etc.* 8°. **14004. a. 14.**

SOMEŞVARA DEVA, *son of Kumāra, Purohita to Bhīmadeva of Aṇahillapattana*. The Surathotsava of Someśvaradeva. [A mythological romance in verse, in 15 cantos.] Edited by . . . Paṇḍit Śivadatta . . . and Kâśînâth Pâṇḍurang Parab. (सुरथोत्सवम् ।) pp. xvi. 111. 1902. *See* DURGĀPRASĀDA, *son of Vrajalāla*, and KĀŞĪNĀTHA PĀṆḌURAṄGA PARAB. Kâvyamâlâ. [No.] 73. 1886, *etc.* 8°. **14072. ccc. 12. (no. 73.)**

SÖRENSEN (S.). An Index to the Names in the Mahabharata, with short explanations and a concordance to the Bombay and Calcutta editions and P. C. Roy's translation. *London, Hertford* [printed], 1904, *etc.* 4°. **14065. f. 5.**

In progress.

SOUKHAVATI-VYOUHA-SOUTRA. *See* SUKHĀVATĪVYŪHA.

SOURINDRO MOHUN TAGORE. *See* ŞAURĪNDRAMOHANA ṬHĀKURA.

SPEIJER (J. S.). *See* SPEYER (J. S.).

SPEYER (JACOB SAMUEL). *See* ĀRYA ŞŪRA. Jâtakamalâ . . . Translated . . . by J. S. Speyer. 1893. 8°. [*Bijdragen tot de Taal-, Land- en Volkenkunde van Nederlandsch-Indië.*] **Ac. 7519. (5de volgr., 8ste deel.)**

—— *See* ĀRYA ŞŪRA. The *Gâtakamâlâ* . . . Translated . . . by J. S. Speyer. 1895. 8°. [*Sacred Books of the Buddhists.*] **14003. ccc. (vol. 1.)**

ŞRĀDDHA. *See* ĀBDIKĀRĀDHANAVIDHI. ಅಬ್ದಿಕಾರಾಧನವಿಧಿಃ *etc.* [Ābdikārādhanavidhi. A manual for rites in honour of the dead.] 1897. 8°. **14028. d. 59. (6.)**

—— *See* BHĪMASENA ŞARMĀ. शास्त्रार्थ आगरा *etc.* [Şāstrārtha Āgrā. A correspondence on *şrāddhas*.] [1901.] 8°. **14033. bbb. 10. (3.)**

—— *See* BHŪDHARA CHAṬṬOPĀDHYĀYA. धर्मानुष्ठान *etc.* [Dharmānushṭhāna. A manual for *saṃskāras*, *şrāddhas, etc.*] [1896.] 12°. **14028. bb. 1.**

ṢRĀDDHA (*continued*). *See* CALAND (W.). Ueber Totenverehrung, *etc.* 1888. 8°. [*Koninklijke Akademie van Wetenschappen te Amsterdam: Verhandelingen.*] **Ac. 944/3. (Deel 17.)**

—— *See* CALAND (W.). Altindischer Ahnencult, *etc.* 1893. 8°. **4503. ee. 29.**

—— *See* CHATURTHILĀLA. अथ अन्त्येष्टि श्राद्ध प्रकाशः *etc.* [Antyeshṭiṣrāddhaprakāṣa.] [1898.] *obl.* 8°. **14028. dd. 2. (1.)**

—— *See* DIVĀKARA DĀJĪ SĀDHLE. ॥ अथ कृत्यदिवाकरः *etc.* [Kṛityadivākara.] [1899.] *obl.* 8°. **14028. dd. 2. (2.)**

—— *See* KĀTYĀYANA. परिशिष्टकण्डिका [Pariṣishṭakaṇḍikā, *etc.* Followed by the Ṣrāddhasūtra, with Karka's *vyākhyā* and the *bhāshya* and Ṣrāddhasūtrapaddhati of Gadādhara Dīkshita, *etc.*] [1896.] 4°. [*Pāraskaragṛihyasūtra.*] **14010. f. 10.**

—— *See* NĀGARARĀMA ṢARMĀ. कर्म्मदर्पणम् *etc.* [Karmadarpaṇa.] [1899.] 8°. **14028. d. 56. (3.)**

—— *See* NṚISIṂHA MIṢRA. ପାର୍ବଣ ଶ୍ରାଦ୍ଧକାରିକା *etc.* [Pārvaṇaṣrāddhakārikā.] 1900. 12°. **14028. b. 61. (6.)**

—— *See* RĀMACHANDRA CHATUSHPĀṬHĪ and RUDRANĀRĀYAṆA SHAḌAṄGĪ. ଶ୍ରାଦ୍ଧବ୍ୟବସ୍ଥା *etc.* [Ṣrāddhavyavasthā o Prayoga.] 1899. 12°. **14028. b. 61. (5.)**

—— *See* ṢĀLAGRĀMA ṢUKLA. अन्त्येष्टिकर्मसमुच्चय [Antyeshṭikarmasamuchchaya.] [1895.] *obl.* 8°. **14028. dd. 1.**

—— ॥ अथापात्रिकपार्वणश्राद्धप्रयोगः ॥ [Apātrikapārvaṇa-ṣrāddhaprayoga. A manual for the performance of the *apātrika ṣrāddha* to the spirits of the 3 preceding generations.] ff. 9. कल्याण मुंबई १८१५ [*Kalyan*, 1893.] *obl.* 8°. **14033. c. 31. (2.)**

—— ஶ்ராத்தப்ரயோகஃ [Ṣrāddhaprayoga. The ritual of the Vaḍagalai Vaishṇavas.] *See* NITYAKARMA. ஆஹ்னிகம் *etc.* [Āhnika.] pp. 92-128. 1893. 12°. **14028. b. 82. (3.)**

—— अ... पार्वणं श्राद्धम् *etc.* [Apātrika-pārvaṇa-ṣrāddha. A tract on *ṣrāddhas* held at the conjunction of sun and moon, according to the Mādhyandina school of the Vājasaneyisaṃhitā. Edited with a commentary styled Jyeshṭhānandī by Chaturthilāla of Ratnagarh.] pp. iv. 116, *lith.* मुंबय्यां १८१६ [*Bombay*, 1895.] 12°. **14010. b. 15.**

—— एकोद्दिष्ट पद्धती *etc.* [Ekoddishṭapaddhati. A ritual for *ṣrāddhas* of single ancestors, according to the schools of the Chhandogas and Vājasaneyīs. With notes by Parameṣvara Jhā. Second edition.] pp. 24. दरभङ्गा १८१९ [*Darbhangah*, 1898.] *obl.* 4°. **14028. e. 33. (2.)**

—— अथ पार्वणश्राद्धपद्धति प्रारम्भः ॥ [Pārvaṇa-ṣrāddhapaddhati. A ritual for *ṣrāddhas* at the new and full moon.] ff. 16. *Lucknow*, 1899. *obl.* 8°. **14033. c. 44. (1.)**

—— गयापद्धति *etc.* [Gayāpaddhati. Rules for *ṣrāddha* rites at Gaya. Compiled with Hindi rubrics and notes by Tārāchandra Bhaṭṭāchārya.] pp. 35. *Benares*, १९५८ [1901.] 8°. **14033. aa. 5. (4.)**

SREENIVASA. *See* ṢRĪNIVĀSA.

ṢRĪCHANDANA, *Piṇḍika.* *See* JAYADEVA, *son of Bhojadeva.* ବସନ୍ତରାସ *etc.* [Vasantarāsa. Being the Gītagovinda with paraphrases *etc.* in Oriya verse by Ṣrīchandana.] 1902. 8°. **14070. dd. 21. (2.)**

ṢRĪDEVA. *See* ANANTADEVA, *son of Nāgadeva.*

ṢRĪDHARA, *son of Baladeva.* *See* PRAṢASTAPĀDA. The Bhâshya of Praśastapâda, together with the Nyâyakandalî of Śrîdhara, *etc.* 1895. 8°. **14048. dd. 3. (vol. 4.)**

ṢRĪDHARA RĀMAKṚISHṆA BHĀṆḌĀRKAR. (Report of the preliminary tour . . . through Central India, the Central Provinces and Rajputana in connection with the search for Sanskrit manuscripts.) pp. 21. *Bombay*, 1904. 4°. *No title-page.* **14096. f. 7. (2.)**

ṢRĪDHARA SVĀMĪ. *See* MAHĀBHĀRATA.—Bhagavadgītā.—*Sanskrit and Vernaculars.* শ্রীমদ্ভগবদ্গীতা *etc.* [Bhagavadgītā. With Ṣrīdhara's commentary.] [1895.] 16°. **14065. b. 15.**

—— *See* MAHĀBHĀRATA. — Bhagavadgītā. — *Sanskrit.* श्रीमद्भगवद्गीता *etc.* [Bhagavadgītā. With the Subodhinī of Ṣrīdhara.] [1901.] 8°. **14003. ccc. (no. 45.)**

ṢRĪDHARA SVĀMĪ (*continued*). *See* PURĀṆAS.—*Bhāgavatapurāṇa.* ଭକ୍ତିରତ୍ନାବଳୀ *etc.* [Bhaktiratnāvalī. With commentary of Ṣrīdhara.] 1900. 12°. **14016. b. 27.**

—— *See* PURĀṆAS.—*Nāradapurāṇa.* ஹரிபக்தி-ஸுதோதய: *etc.* [Haribhaktisudhodaya. With commentary of Ṣrīdhara.] 1892. 8°. **14016. c. 48.**

ṢRĪDHARA VEṄKAṬEṢĀRYA. *See* VEṄKAṬEṢĀRYA, *Ṣrīdhara.*

ṢRĪHARSHA, *Dramatist.* *See* HARSHADEVA.

ṢRĪHARSHA, *son of Hīra Paṇḍita.* [For the Dvirūpakoṣa sometimes ascribed to Ṣrīharsha:] *See* PURUSHOTTAMADEVA.

—— Śrîharsha's Naishadhîyacharita, with the commentary Naishadhîyaprakâśa of Nârâyaṇa. Edited with [biography and] critical and exegetical notes by Pandit Śivadatta. (नैषधीयचरितम् ।) pp. xviii. iv. 1043, xx. *Bombay,* 1894. 8°. **14070. d. 35.**

—— Nîshadha Charita. [Cantos x.-xii.] With the commentary, Nishada Prakasa of Narayanabhatta. With an introduction and notes, critical and explanatory, by P. K. Kalyanarama Sastri. (B.A. Degree Examination, 1903.) pp. iv. 148, 80. *Madras,* 1903. 8°. **14072. ccc. 36.**

The title is from the cover.

ṢRĪJÑĀNA, *Prajñākara.* *See* PRAJÑĀKARAMATI ṢRĪJÑĀNA.

ṢRĪKĀNTA MIṢRA, *Maithila, of Benares.* ॥ साम्बकमलानन्दकुलरत्नं ॥ नाम काव्यम् *etc.* [Sāmbakamalānandakularatna. A historical poem in 15 *sargas,* in panegyric of Prince Kamalānanda Siṃha of Srinagar and of his family.] pp. i. iii. 208, iii.; 2 *plates.* काश्याम् १९५८ [*Benares,* 1901.] 4°. **14058. cc. 5.**

ṢRĪKAṆṬHADATTA, *Vaidya.* *See* MĀDHAVA, *son of Indukara.* सटीक-निदान *etc.* [Nidāna. With the commentary Vyākhyāmadhukoṣa by Ṣrīkaṇṭhadatta (from the Prameha-madhumeha-piḍakā-nidāna to the end).] [1901.] 8°. **14043. c. 44.**

—— *See* VṚINDA. वृन्दमाधव° (The Vṛindamâdhava ... with its commentary 'Kusumávali' [commenced] by Śrî kanthadutta [and completed by Nārāyaṇa son of Bhābhalla,] *etc.*) [1894.] 8°. **14003. ccc. (no. 27.)**

ṢRĪKAṆṬHA KAVI, *Elandūr, son of Rāma Dīkshita.* అభినవకాదమ్బరీచమ్పూప్రబన్ధః [Abhinavakādambarī. A *champū* on the story of Bāṇa's Kādambarī. In 6 *āṣvāsas,* with a preface summarising the plot. Edited by Chakravarti Aiyaṅgār.] pp. 18, 101. మహీశూర ॥ ౧౮౯౨ [*Mysore,* 1892.] 8°. **14076. c. 72.**

ṢRĪKAṆṬHA ṢĀSTRĪ, *Sāggera.* *See* AMARU. శృంగారామరుకకావ్యమ్ *etc.* [Ṣṛiṅgārāmarukakāvya. With commentary, *etc.* Edited by Ṣrīkaṇṭha.] 1898. 8°. **14076. c. 69.**

—— *See* BALLĀLA. శ్రీభోజచరిత్రం *etc.* [Bhojacharitra. Edited by Ṣrīkaṇṭha.] 1898. 8°. **14076. c. 70.**

—— శ్రీకంఠశాస్త్రిణావిరచితా ... ధాతురూపప్రకాశికావిజయతేతమామ్. [Dhāturūpaprakāṣikā. A treatise on the roots of the Sanskrit tongue. Edited by Chakravarti Aiyaṅgār.] pp. xxiv. 914, xlviii. మహీశూర ॥ ౧౮౯౮ [*Mysore,* 1898.] 8°. **14090. c. 41.**

ṢRĪKĀṆṬHA ṢIVĀCHĀRYA, also called NĪLAKAṆṬHA, *disciple of Ṣvetāchārya.* *See* BĀDARĀYAṆA. విశిష్టాద్వైత ... భాష్యం *etc.* [Brahmasūtra. With the Ṣaiva-Viṣishṭādvaita commentary, commonly styled Ṣrīkaṇṭhabhāshya or Ṣaivabhāshya, of Ṣrīkaṇṭha.] [1890.] 8°. **14048. e. 20.**

—— *See* BĀDARĀYAṆA. ப்ரஹ்மஸூத்ர-ஸ்ரீகண்டஶிவாசார்ய-பாஷ்யம் *etc.* [Brahmasūtra. With the exposition of Ṣrīkaṇṭha.] [1899.] 8°. **14048. c. 72.(3.)**

—— *See* BĀDARĀYAṆA. The Vedánta-sútras with Śrikantha-bháshya. [Translated into English.] 1897, *etc.* 4°. [*Siddhanta Deepika.*] **14170. fff. 4.(vol. 1- .)**

ṢRĪKṚISHṆA KAVI. *See* KṚISHṆA ṢARMĀ, *disciple of Vāsudeva.*

ṢRĪKṚISHṆALĀLĀ. *See* KṚISHṆALĀLĀ.

ṢRĪKṚISHṆA VIDYĀVĀGĪṢA. *See* KṚISHṆĀNANDA VĀGĪṢA BHAṬṬĀCHĀRYA.

ṢRĪNĀTHA VEDĀNTAVĀGĪṢA BHAṬṬĀCHĀRYA. *See* JAGADĪṢVARA BHAṬṬĀCHĀRYA, *Dramatist.* हास्यार्णवप्रहसनम् *etc.* (Hasyarnaba . . . Edited [with a commentary] . . . by . . . Shrinatha Vedantabagisha.) [1896.] 8°. **14079. c. 53.(2.)**

ṢRĪNIVĀSA ĀCHĀRYA, *Astrologer.* ଶ୍ରୀନିବାସଦୀପିକା *etc.* [Ṣrīnivāsadīpikā, or Ṣuddhidīpikā. An astrological poem, with Oriya paraphrase and commentary by Bhuvaneṣvara Kavichandra. Edited by Sarveṣvara Āchārya.] pp. xiv. 265. *Cuttack,* 1900. 12°. **14053. a. 5.(2.)**

—— দীপিকা বা শুদ্ধিদীপিকা *etc.* [Ṣuddhidīpikā. With the commentaries of Govindānanda Kavikaṅkaṇa and Rāghava Āchārya, and a Bengali translation by Nilakamala Vidyānidhi. Edited by Gurunātha Vidyānidhi Kāvyatīrtha.] pp. ii. viii. 472. কলিকাতা ১৩০৮ [*Calcutta,* 1901.] 8°. **14053. ccc. 23.**

—— শুদ্ধিদীপিকা *etc.* [Ṣuddhidīpikā. With the commentary of Govindānanda. Edited with a Bengali translation of the text by Chaṇḍīcharaṇa Smṛitibhūshaṇa. Second edition.] pp. xi. 293. কলিকাতা ১৩০৮ [*Calcutta,* 1901.] 8°. **14053. ccc. 33.**

ṢRĪNIVĀSA ADHVARĪ, *Mīmāṃsaka. See* JAIMINI.—*Gṛihyasūtra.* ॥ जैमिनिगृह्यसूत्रम् *etc.* [Jaiminisūtra. With the commentary Subodhinī of Ṣrīnivāsa.] 1898. 8°. **14028. c. 74.**

ṢRĪNIVĀSA AIYAṄGĀR. *See* SVĀTMĀRĀMA. हठयोगप्रदीपिका *etc.* (The Hatha-yoga Pradîpikâ . . . Translated by Shrinivâs Iyângâr, *etc.*) 1893. 12°. **14048. b. 30.**

ṢRĪNIVĀSA AIYAṄGĀR, *Kommaṇḍūr. See* PERIODICAL PUBLICATIONS.—*Bangalore.* Kâvyakalpadrumam, *etc.* [Edited by Ṣrīnivāsa Aiyaṅgār.] 1897. 8°. **14076. cc. 1.**

ṢRĪNIVĀSA AIYAṄGĀR, *Maṇḍayam B., of Chikballapur High School, formerly Translator to the Education Department of Mysore.* The Aryan Prayer-book, in Sanskrit, with an English translation. परब्रह्मस्तुतिः [Parabrahmastuti. A series of devotional extracts from the Upanishads, Epics, *etc.*] Compiled by M. B. Srinivasaiengar . . . Tentative edition. pp. iv. 64. *Bombay,* 1902. 16°. **14028. bb. 12.**

ṢRĪNIVĀSA AIYAṄGĀR, *Mēlukōṭe. See* VĀDIBHASIṂHA SŪRI. ಕ್ಷತ್ರಚೂಡಾಮಣಿಕಾವ್ಯವು *etc.* [Kshatrachūḍāmaṇi. With Canarese translation and commentary by Ṣrinivāsa Aiyaṅgār.] 1900. 8°. **14100. b. 8.**

ṢRĪNIVĀSA AIYAR, *V., of Trichinopoli. See* KĀLIDĀSA.—*Raghuvaṃṣa.* F. A. Examination of 1892. The Complete Sanskrit Text with . . . Sanskrit commentary . . . English notes, and . . . translation, by S. Rangachariar . . . and V. Srinivasa Aiyar. 1891. 8°. **14076. c. 59.**

ṢRĪNIVĀSA APPAN-AIYAṄGĀR, *Vaittamānidi Mudumbai. See* VĀLMĪKI.—Rāmāyaṇa.—*Portions.* அபயப்ரதாநஸாரம் *etc.* [Abhayapradānasāra. Edited by Ṣrīnivāsa.] [1891.] 8°. **14060. c. 32.(1.)**

ṢRĪNIVĀSĀCHĀRYA, *disciple of Vaidyeṣvara. See* SADĀSIVA BRAHMENDRA. போதார்யா ॥ [Bodhāryā, *etc.* Edited by Ṣrīnivāsāchārya.] 1888. 12°. **14048. b. 38.(2.)**

ṢRĪNIVĀSĀCHĀRYA, *K.N., of Conjeveram. See* VEṄKAṬANĀTHA VEDĀNTĀCHĀRYA. సఙ్కల్పసూర్యోదయః *etc.* [Saṅkalpasūryodaya. With commentary. Edited by Ṣrīnivāsāchārya.] [1904.] 8°. **14079. c. 73.**

ṢRĪNIVĀSĀCHĀRYA, *Kōyil Īyuṇṇi, Bhāradvāja. See* VEṄKAṬANĀTHA VEDĀNTĀCHĀRYA. సఙ్కల్పసూర్యోదయః *etc.* [Saṅkalpasūryodaya. With a commentary called Prabhāvalī by Ṣrīnivāsāchārya.] [1904.] 8°. **14079. c. 73.**

ṢRĪNIVĀSĀCHĀRYA, *Lakshmīpuram. See* GAṄGEṢA UPĀDHYĀYA. గాధాధరీయము సిద్ధాన్తలక్షణమ్ *etc.* [Siddhāntalakshaṇa. Edited by Ṣrīnivāsāchārya.] [1893.] 8°. **14048. dd. 13.**

ṢRĪNIVĀSĀCHĀRYA, *Mahābhāshyam, son of Govindāchārya.* ஐயம் யதீந்த்ரமததீபிகா *etc.* [Yatīndramatadīpikā. An exposition of the Viṣishṭādvaita system.] pp. 76. அணிக்காரஞ்சத்ரம் [*Anikkaranchattram,* 18]98. 12°. **14048. b. 33.(4.)**

ṢRĪNIVĀSĀCHĀRYA, *Nedumaram V. R.* See ĀRUḌHAṢĀSTRA. ஞானப்ரதீபிகை *etc.* [Ārūdhaṣāstra. With Tamil commentary by Ṣrīnivāsāchārya and Sorṇaṣāstri.] [1899.] 8°. **14053. ccc. 27.**

ṢRĪNIVĀSA DĪKSHITA, *K.*, *Vedāntadeṣika, Parasamaya-pañchānana-pāñchajanya, son of Rāmasvāmī.* See BĀDARĀYAṆA. లక్ష్మీవిశిష్టాద్వైతభాష్య॥ [Brahmasūtra. With the Lakshmīviṣishṭādvaitabhāshya, a commentary of the Vaikhānasa-Viṣishṭādvaita school by Ṣrīnivāsa, and the super-commentary Nigamachūḍādarpaṇa by Sundararāja.] 1896. 8°. **14048. dd. 29.(2.)**

—— See BĀDARĀYAṆA. ലക്ഷ്മീവിശിഷ്ടാ-ദ്വൈതഭാഷ്യം *etc.* [Brahmasūtra. Sūtra i., with Ṣrīnivāsa's Lakshmīviṣishṭādvaitabhāshya and the Nigamachūḍādarpaṇa of Sundararāja.] 1896. 8°. **14048. dd. 29.(1.)**

—— See HIRAṆYAKEṢĪ. ഗൃഹ്യസൂത്രം [Gṛihyasūtra. Edited by Ṣrīnivāsa.] 1901. 12°. **14038. b. 10.(1.)**

—— See KAMALĀKARA BHAṬṬA. ശൂദ്രകമലാകരഃ॥ [Ṣūdrakamalākara. Edited with a commentary called Ṣūdrasarvasva and Tamil translation by Ṣrīnivāsa.] 1901, *etc.* 4°. [*Brahmavidyā.*] **14096. dd. 3.(vol. 15, etc.)**

—— See PURĀṆAS. — *Skandapurāṇa.* ശിവതത്ത്വസുധാനിധിഃ *etc.* [Ṣivatattvasudhānidhi. With the commentary Chintāmaṇi of Ṣrīnivāsa.] 1898. 8°. **14016. d. 53.**

—— See PURĀṆAS. — *Skandapurāṇa.* சிவதத்துவசுதாநிதி *etc.* [Ṣivatattvasudhānidhi. With a Tamil version of Ṣrīnivāsa's commentary.] 1898. 8°. **14016. d. 54.**

—— See UPANISHADS. — *General Collections.* ഉപനിഷദ്വിദ്യാ *etc.* [Upanishadvidyā. A collection of Upanishads with Tamil translations, commentaries, *etc.* Compiled and edited by Ṣrīnivāsa.] 1898, *etc.* 8°. **14010. cc. 13.**

—— See UPANISHADS. — *Separate Upanishads.* శ్రీగాణపతచరణోపహారః॥ [Gaṇapatyupanishad. With commentary Gāṇapatacharaṇopahāra by Ṣrīnivāsa.] 1901. 8°. **14010. c. 35.(3.)**

ṢRĪNIVĀSA DĪKSHITA, *K.*, *Vedāntadeṣika (continued).* [Another edition of the preceding, in the Grantham character.] 1901. 8°. **14007. b. 4.(2.)**

—— See UPANISHADS. — *Separate Upanishads.* ஜாபாலோபநிடத। [Jābālopanishad. Followed by the commentary of Ṣrīnivāsa, in Tamil.] 1900. 8°. **14007. b. 12.(2.)**

—— See UPANISHADS. — *Separate Upanishads.* വജ്രസൂച്യോപനിഷദ്ഭാഷ്യം *etc.* [Vajrasūchyopanishad. With commentary by Ṣrīnivāsa.] 1893. 8°. **14007. b. 4.(1.)**

—— —— [Second edition.] 1900. 8°. **14007. b. 12.(3.)**

—— See UPANISHADS. — *Modern and Fictitious Upanishads.* ശ്രീ... പാരമാത്മികോപനിഷദ്ഭാഷ്യം *etc.* [Pāramātmikopanishad. With commentary by Ṣrīnivāsa.] 1900. 8°. **14033. bbb. 13.**

—— See VAIDYANĀTHA DĪKSHITA. സ്മൃതിമുക്താഫലെ പ്രഭാഃ... കാണ്ഡഃ *etc.* [Smṛitimuktāphala. With the commentary Prabhā of Ṣrīnivāsa.] 1898, *etc.* 4°. **14039. c. 15.**

—— ஆரண்யகாநுபவசதகம் *etc.* [Āraṇyakānubhavaṣataka. A century of verses on life in a hermitage.] pp. 28. சிதம்பரம்॥ விகாரி [*Chidambaram*, 1899.] 16°. **14076. a. 16.(2.)**

—— உ சித்தப்ரபோதநசதகம் *etc.* [Chittaprabodhanaṣataka. A century of verses addressed to the intelligence.] pp. 24. நடுக்காவேரீ॥ [*Nadukkaveri,*] 1901. 16°. **14028. bb. 11.(2.)**

—— தீநதேவநசதகம் *etc.* [Dīnadevanaṣataka. A century of elegies.] pp. 24. ஸ்ரீ நடுக்காவேரீ [*Nadukkaveri*, 1901.] 16°. **14072. a. 1.(4.)**

—— உ குருராஜசதகம் *etc.* [Gururājaṣataka. A hymn in 103 verses to Ṣiva as teacher.] pp. 24. நடுக்காவேரீ॥ [*Nadukkaveri,*] 1901. 16°. **14028. bb. 11.(3.)**

—— ஸ்ரீஹேதிராஜஸ்தவசதகம் *etc.* [Hetirājastavaṣataka. A hymn of 102 verses to Ṣiva-Hetirāja.] pp. 31. நடுக்காவேரீ॥ [*Nadukkaveri,*] 1901. 16°. **14028. bb. 11.(4.)**

ṢRĪNIVĀSA DĪKSHITA, *K.*, *Vedāntadeṣika* (*continued*). ஹிரண்யகேஶிமஹிமஸங்க்ரஹ: etc. [Hiraṇyakeṣimahimasaṅgraha. A short poetical account of the lawgiver Hiraṇyakeṣī. With a commentary styled Hiraṇyakeṣimahimaprakāṣa by the author.] pp. 24. நடுக்காவேரி [*Nadukkaveri*,] 1901. 16°. **14072. a. 1.(3.)**

—— கலிபரிதேவநஶதகம் etc. [Kaliparidevanaṣataka. One hundred stanzas on the Iron Age.] pp. 23. சிதம்பரம் விகாரி [*Chidambaram*, 1899.] 16°. **14076. a. 16.(3.)**

—— ப்ரணதார்த்திஹரமுஹூர்த்தஶதகம் etc. [Praṇatārtiharamuhūrtaṣataka. A century of verses addressed to Ṣiva-Praṇatārtihara.] pp. 20. நடுக்காவேரி [*Nadukkaveri*,] 1901. 16°. **14072. a. 1.(2.)**

—— இது ஸிம்ஹபுரி ப்ரஸந்நாஞ்ஜநேயஶதகம் etc. [Prasannāñjaneyaṣataka. A century of stanzas in various metres, addressed to the monkey-god Hanumān as worshipped at Sholinghar.] pp. 24. நடுக்காவேரி [*Nadukkaveri*,] 1901. 16°. **14028. bb. 11.(5.)**

—— శ్రీ సింహపురి ప్రసన్నాంజనేయశతకం etc. [Prasannāñjaneyaṣataka.] pp. 17. నెల్లూరు [*Nellore*,] 1901. 8°. **14028. d. 28.(4.)**

—— இது ப்ராதஸ்ஸ்மரணஶதகம் etc. [Prātaḥsmaraṇaṣataka. A century of devotional Ṣaiva verses.] pp. 24. நடுக்காவேரி [*Nadukkaveri*,] 1901. 16°. **14028. bb. 11.(6.)**

—— இதம் ... ஶாரதாப்ராக்ருதஸுமமஞ்ஜரீஶதகம் etc. [Ṣāradāprākṛitasumamañjarīṣataka. A series of 100 Prakrit stanzas composed on the occasion of the Ṣāradānavarātra festival at the Sringeri *math* and addressed to the tutelary goddess Ṣāradā. With Sanskrit translation.] pp. 36. நடுக்காவேரி [*Nadukkaveri*,] 1901. 16°. **14028. bb. 11.(7.)**

—— ஶ்ரீஶிவகுருஸௌந்தர்யஸாகரஸ்தவஸாஹஸ்ரிகா etc. [Ṣivagurusaundaryasāgarastavasāhasrikā. A series of devotional verses composed for the occasion of the Ṣivarātri of the *ṣarvari* year (January 1901).] pp. iv. xi. 126, 1; 1 *plate*. நடுக்காவேரி [*Nadukkaveri*,] 1901. 8°. **14072. ccc. 29.**

ṢRĪNIVĀSA DĪKSHITA, *K.*, *Vedāntadeṣika* (*continued*). இயம் ... ஶிவபஞ்சசிஹ்நஹரிசந்தநாக்ய: ப்ரபந்த: etc. [Ṣivapañchachihnaharichandana. A poem, in 7 *pañchakas*, on the five tokens of the Ṣaiva devotee. With a commentary by the author, called Kusumodgama. Edited by Rāmanātha Ṣāstrī.] pp. ii. 64, ii. நடுக்காவேரி சார்வரி [*Nadukkaveri*, 1900.] 8°. **14033. bb. 45.(2.)**

—— இது ஶிவதாண்டவஸ்தவஶதகம் etc. [Ṣivatāṇḍavastavaṣataka. A hymn in 10 decads and 106 stanzas, on the dance of Ṣiva.] pp. 26. நடுக்காவேரி [*Nadukkaveri*,] 1901. 16°. **14028. bb. 11.(8.)**

—— இது ஸ்வர்ணாகர்ஷணபைரவஶதகம் etc. [Svarṇākarshaṇabhairavaṣataka. A hymn of 102 stanzas to Ṣiva-Kālabhairava as dispenser of prosperity.] pp. 26. நடுக்காவேரி [*Nadukkaveri*,] 1901. 16°. **14028. bb. 11.(9.)**

—— శ్రీ ... కృత్యయోర్భిన్నదేశత్వాదితి శ్లోకస్య తాత్పర్యనిర్ణయః etc. [An essay in verse and prose upon the interpretation of stanza 51 (beginning *kṛityayor bhinnadeṣatvād*) in act ii. of the Abhijñānaṣakuntala.] pp. 7. నడుకావేరి ౧౯౦౨ [*Nadukkaveri*, 1902.] 16°. **14076. a. 16.(5.)**

ṢRĪNIVĀSA DĪKSHITA, *Ṣrīṣaila*. The Siddanthachinthamani. A work on Vedanta philosophy. By Sreenivasa Charya, *etc.* (सिद्धान्त चिन्तामणिः ।) pp. 76. 1902. *See* ANANTĀCHĀRYA, *Prativādibhayaṅkara*. शास्त्रमुक्तावली. The Ŝasthramukthâvalî, *etc.* No. 13. 1899, *etc.* 8°. **14049. a. 1.(no. 13.)**

ṢRĪNIVĀSA GOPĀLĀCHĀRYA, *Ṣarukkai Lāḍapuram*. *See* HARSHADEVA. இதம் ... நாகாநந்தம் etc. [Nāgānanda. Edited by Ṣrīnivāsa.] [1897.] 8°. **14079. d. 44.**

ṢRĪNIVĀSA GOVINDA BHĀNAP. *See* HARSHADEVA. नागानन्द etc. (The Nâgânandam ... Edited with ... Sanskrit and English notes by Shrînivâs ... Bhânap.) 1892. 8°. **14080. c. 33.**

ṢRĪNIVĀSA JAGANNĀTHA SVĀMĪ, *Paravastu*. *See* JAGANNĀTHA SVĀMĪ, *Paravastu Ṣrīnivāsa*.

ṢRĪNIVĀSA KAVI, styled GARUḌAVĀHANA. दिव्यसूरिचरितम्॥ [Divyasūricharita. A poetical account of the leaders of the Rāmānuja sect.] 1895, *etc.* *See* VEṄKAṬARAṄGANĀTHA SVĀMĪ, *Paravastu.* Grandha Pradarsani, *etc.* [No. 7.] 1895, *etc.* 8°. **14003. c. 2.(7.)**

Incomplete, breaking off at viii. 45.

ṢRĪNIVĀSA MAKHĪ. *See* ṢRĪNIVĀSA DĪKSHITA.

SRINIVASA RAGAVACHARRIAR, *C.E.* *See* ṢRĪNIVĀSA RĀGHAVĀCHĀRYA, *K.I.*

ṢRĪNIVĀSA RĀGHAVĀCHĀRYA, *K.I.* *See* PERIODICAL PUBLICATIONS.—*Madras.* The Somaravi . . . Edited . . . by C. E. Srinivasaragavacharriar, *etc.* 1895-1896. 4°. **14170. ccc. 1.**

ṢRĪNIVĀSA RĀGHAVĀCHĀRYA, *Paraṇḍalam Aragar-tirumalai Māḍabhūshi.* *See* VĀLMĪKI.—Rāmāyaṇa.—*Entire Text.* ஸ்ரீராமாயணம் *etc.* [Rāmāyaṇa. Edited with introductions, glosses, and paraphrases in Tamil by Ṣrīnivāsa.] 1897, *etc.* 4°. **14068. c. 14.**

ṢRĪNIVĀSA RAṄGĀCHĀRYA, *Tekkulūru.* *See* PURĀṆAS. — *Selections.* శ్రీవెఙ్కటాచలమాహాత్మ్యగ్రంథః *etc.* [Veṅkaṭāchalamāhātmyagrantha. Edited by Ṣrīnivāsa.] [1896.] 8°. **14016. c. 50.**

ṢRĪNIVĀSA ṢĀSTRĪ, *K., of Brahmavidyā Press, Chidambaram.* *See* ṢRĪNIVĀSA DĪKSHITA.

ṢRĪNIVĀSA TĀTĀCHĀRYA, *Addaṅgi-tirumalai, son of Kalyāṇa Tātāchārya.* *See* BĀDARĀYAṆA. లక్ష్మీవిశిష్టాద్వైతభాష్య॥ [Brahmasūtra. With Lakshmīvisishṭādvaitabhāshya and Nigamachūḍādarpaṇa. Edited by Ṣrīnivāsa.] 1896. 8°. **14048. dd. 29.(2.)**

—— *See* BĀDARĀYAṆA. லக்ஷ்மீவிஶிஷ்டாத்வைதபாஷ்யம் *etc.* [Brahmasūtra. Sūtra i., with Lakshmīvisishṭādvaitabhāshya and Nigamachūḍādarpaṇa. Edited by Ṣrīnivāsa.] 1896. 8°. **14048. dd. 29.(1.)**

ṢRĪNIVĀSA TĀTĀCHĀRYA, *Koṭi-kanyādāna, of Srirangam.* विष्णु तत्व प्रकाश *etc.* [Vishṇutattvaprakāṣa. A metrical exposition of the Vaishṇava system of the Rāmānuja school. With a Gujarati translation.] pp. vi. 188. अमदावाद १८९८ [*Ahmadabad,* 1891.] 8°. **14028. d. 45.**

Originally an answer to the attacks made on the Vaishṇava churches by Lakshmaṇagiri in 1863.

ṢRĪNIVĀSA TĀTĀCHĀRYA SVĀMĪ, *Addaṅgi-tirumalai Lakshminṛisiṃha,* called KALYĀṆA. *See* MAHĀBHĀRATA. — Bhagavadgītā. — *Sanskrit and Vernaculars.* ஸ்ரீபகவத்கீதை *etc.* [Bhagavadgītā. Edited and translated by Ṣrīnivāsa and Rāmasvāmi.] [1899.] 16°. **14065. b. 19.**

—— *See* UPANISHADS.—*Small Collections.* தசோபநிஷத்த்ராவிடபாஷ்யம் *etc.* [Daṣopanishaddrāviḍabhāshya. With Tamil commentary. Compiled and edited by Ṣrīnivāsa.] [1897]-1898. 8°. **14010. dd. 14.**

ṢRĪNIVĀSA TRYAMBAKA DRAVIḌA. *See* NĀRĀYAṆA BHAṬṬA, called MṚIGARĀJALAKSHMĀ. The Venisamhâra . . . Edited [with introduction and notes in English] by B. T. Dravid . . . and S. T. Dravid. 1896. 8°. **14079. c. 65.(1.)**

ṢRĪPATI BHAṬṬA, *son of Nāgadeva.* श्रीपतिपद्धतिः [Ṣrīpatipaddhati, or Jātakapaddhati. A manual of horoscopy in 8 *adhyāyas.* With English translation.] 1903. *See* VAIDYANĀTHA, *son of Veṅkaṭādri.* जातकपारिजातः [Jātakapārijāta,] *etc.* 1903, *etc.* 8°. **14053. ccc. 48.**

ṢRĪRĀMULU PANTULU, *Dāsu.* వైశ్యధర్మదీపిక. (The Vaisyadharmadipica. An exposition of the religious duties of the Vaisyas.) [Comprising Sanskrit extracts with Telugu expositions, *etc.*] pp. 7, viii. 182. ఏలూరు [*Ellore,*] 1893. 8°. **14174. b. 42.**

The English title is from the cover.

ṢRĪRAṄGĀCHĀRYA, *Ṣrīṣailānantapurusha, of Ṣrīpadapuram.* *See* BĀDARĀYAṆA. Karyadhi karana vada . . . [Comprising the Aphorisms IV. iii. 6-15, with commentary] by . . . Sreeranga chariar, *etc.* 1901. 8°. [*Ṣāstramuktāvalī.*] **14049. a. 1.(no. 7.)**

—— నిర్ణయసుధాసముద్రే ఉపాకర్మనిర్ణయో నామ ప్రథమః కల్లోలః *etc.* [Upākarmanirṇaya, or Upākarmādinirṇayakallola. A treatise in 6 *taraṅgas* on the rules for the performance of the Vedic *upākarma* or formal commencement of study, forming the first *kallola* in the author's Nirṇayasudhāsamudra. Followed by a hymn styled Ujjvala-Veṅkaṭanāthastotra, in 11 stanzas.] pp. xvii. xix. 309, 5. ꠰ [*Conjevaram,*] 1902. 8°. **14033. aa. 26.**

ṢRĪRAṄGĀRYA. *See* ṢRĪRAṄGĀCHĀRYA.

ṢRĪṢACHANDRA CHAKRAVARTĪ, *of Dacca College.* *See* HARSHADEVA. The Ratnavali . . . Edited with English and Bengali translations, a Sanskrit commentary, and Anglo-Sanskrit notes by Sris Chandra Chakravarti, *etc.* 1902. 12°. **14080. b. 12.**

ṢRĪṢACHANDRA VASU. *See* GHERAṆḌA. The Gheranda Sanhita . . . Translated . . . by Sris Chandra Vasu. 1895. 12°. **14028. b. 75.**

—— *See* PĀṆINI.—*Kāṣikā.* The Ashṭádhyáyí . . . Translated . . . by Śríśa Chandra Vasu. 1891-1898. 8°. **14093. d. 18.**

—— *See* ṢIVASAṂHITĀ. The Esoteric Science . . . Shiva Sanhita, translated by Srischandra Basu. 1893. 8°. **14028. d. 52.**

—— *See* UPANISHADS. — *Separate Upanishads.* The Îśavâsyopanishad. Translated into English, with the commentaries of Sri Sankaracharya and Sri Anantacharya, and notes . . . By Srisa Chandra Vasu. 1896. 8°. **14010. cc. 6.**

—— *See* UPANISHADS.—*Separate Upanishads.* Isavasya Upanishad. With . . . anvaya, vritti, word meaning, translation, notes and index by Sris Chandra Vasu . . . and M. A. C. Thirlwall. 1902. 12°. **14007. b. 13.(2.)**

ṢRĪṢAILA TĀTAYĀCHĀRYA. *See* VEṄKAṬANĀTHA VEDĀNTĀCHĀRYA. సఙ్కల్పసూర్యోదయః *etc.* [Saṅkalpasūryodaya. With a commentary by Ṣrīnivāsāchārya, completed in act x. by a commentary called Prabhāprasādinī by Ṣrīṣaila.] [1904.] 8°. **14079. c. 73.**

SRIS CHANDRA. *See* ṢRĪṢACHANDRA.

ṢRĪṢVARA VIDYĀLAṄKĀRA BHAṬṬĀCHĀRYA, *of Kakina.* Vijayini-kávyam. A Sanskrit epic poem in twelve cantos [upon the life and times of Queen Victoria,] by Sriswar Vidyalankar . . . Edited with occasional notes by Kokileswar Bhattacharyya Vidyaratna. pp. iv. vi. 282, ii. ; 1 *plate.* *Calcutta,* 1902. 8°. **14058. b. 48.**

—— Dilli-mahotsava-kavyam. A Sanskrit poem on the Delhi-Durbar, in six cantos . . . Edited with elucidative notes [chiefly in English] . . . by Kokilesvar Bhattacharyya Vidyaratna. (दिल्लीमहोत्सव-काव्यम्) pp. ii. iv. i. 166 ; 4 *plates.* *Calcutta,* 1903. 8°. **14076. d. 56.**

ṢRĪVALLABHAN. *See* UṆṆIKIḌĀVA TAMBURĀN.

ṢRĪVARA, *disciple of Jonarāja.* Śrīvara's Kathākāutukam. Die Geschichte von Joseph in persisch-indischen Gewande. Sanskrit und Deutsch, von Richard Schmidt. pp. x. 210. *Kiel, Bonn* [printed], 1898. 8°. **14070. dd. 1.**

—— The Kathâkautuka of Śrîvara. Edited by . . . Paṇḍit Śivadatta . . . and Kâśînâth Pâṇdurang Parab. (कथाकौतुकम् ।) pp. iii. 103. 1901. *See* DURGĀPRASĀDA, *son of Vrajalāla,* and KĀṢĪNĀTHA PĀṆḌURAṄGA PARAB. Kâvyamâlâ. [No.] 72. 1886, *etc.* 8°. **14072. ccc. 12.(no. 72.)**

—— Das Kathākāutukam des Çrīvara, verglichen mit Dschāmi's Jusuf und Zuleikha[, its prototype]. Nebst Textproben. Von Richard Schmidt. pp. 46. *Kiel, Bonn* [printed], 1893. 8°. **14070. d. 33.(1.)**

—— तृतीया राजतरङ्गिणी । [Tṛitīyā Rājataraṅgiṇī. The second supplement to Kalhaṇa's history.] 1896. *See* KALHAṆA. The Râjataraṅgiṇî, *etc.* Vol. iii., pp. 117-319. 1892-1896. 8°. **14058. b. 27.**

—— Kings of Kashmira : being a translation of the Sanskrita works of . . . Shrîvara . . . by Jogesh Chunder Dutt. *See* KALHAṆA. Kings of Káshmíra, *etc.* Vol. iii. 1879-1898. 12°. **14070. b. 13.**

ṢRĪVATSĀṄKA, *son of Devīmanīshī.* ஸ்ரீகூரேஶ்வரஸூநுஶ்ரீவத்ஸாங்க விரசித ஸப்தலக்ஷணம் etc. [Saptalakshaṇa. A treatise on the phonetic peculiarities of the Taittirīya-saṃhitā, in 6 *prakaraṇas,* styled Ṣamānapr°.,

Vilaṅghyapr°., Naparapr°., Taparapr°., Avarṇipr°., Aniṅgyapr°. Edited with a commentary by Muḷḷanguḍi A. Vaidyanātha Ṣāstrī.] pp. 122. கும்பகோணம் [*Kumbakonam*,] 1899. 8°.
14092. b. 43.

ŚRUTADEVA. *See* ṢRUTASĀGARA.

ṢRUTAKĪRTI TRAIVIDYA. *See* DHANAṂJAYA, *son of Vasudeva.*

ṢRUTASĀGARA SŪRI. *See* SOMADEVA SŪRI. The Yaśastilaka . . . With the commentary of Śrutadeva [*i.e.* Ṣrutasāgara] Sûri, *etc.* 1901-1903. 8°. [*Kâvyamâlâ.*] **14072. ccc. 12.(no. 70.)**

STEFANI (ED. LUIGI DE). *See* MADIRĀVATĪKATHĀNAKA. La Novellina . . . di Madirāvatī. [Edited with translation by E. L. de Stefani.] 1900. 8°. [*Giornale della Società Asiatica Italiana.*]
Ac. 8804. (vol. 13.)

STEIN (MARC AUREL). *See* JAMMU.—*Raghunātha Temple Library.* Catalogue of the Sanskrit Manuscripts . . . by M. A. Stein. 1894. 4°.
14096. f. 8.

—— *See* KALHAṆA. Kalhaṇa's Râjataraṅgiṇî . . . Edited by M. A. Stein, *etc.* 1892. 4°.
14058. d. 4.

—— *See* KALHAṆA. Kalhaṇa's Rājataraṅgiṇī, . . . Translated, with an introduction, commentary, and appendices, by M. A. Stein. 1900. 4°.
14058. c. 9.

STEINTHAL (PAUL). *See* JÑĀTĀDHARMAKATHĀ. Specimen der Nâyâdhammakahâ . . . von P. Steinthal. 1881. 8°. **14100. c. 17.(1.)**

—— *See* SUTTAPIṬAKA.—*Khuddakanikāya.* [*Jātaka.*] Aus den Geschichten früherer Existenzen Buddhas . . . Übersetzt von P. Steinthal. 1893, *etc.* 8°. [*Zeitschrift fur Vergleichende Litteraturgeschichte.*] **P.P. 4748. ma. (Bd. 6, ff.)**

STENZLER (ADOLF FRIEDRICH). Metrische Sammlungen aus Stenzler's Nachlass. Veröffentlicht von Dr. Kühnau. 1890. *See* ACADEMIES, *etc.*—Germany.—*Deutsche Morgenlaendische Gesellschaft.* Zeitschrift, *etc.* Bd. 44, no. 1. 1846, *etc.* 8°.
Ac. 8815/2. (Bd. 44.)

STEVENSON (JAMES HENRY). *See* TOLMAN (H. C.) and STEVENSON (J. H.). The Vanderbilt Oriental Series, *etc.* 1900, *etc.* 12°. **14003. m.**

STOTRARATNĀKARA. बृहत्स्तोत्ररत्नाकरः *etc.* [Bṛihatstotraratnākara. A collection of 151 hymns and religious-philosophical poems.] pp. vi. 415; 8 *plates.* मुंबय्यां १८१४ [*Bombay*, 1892.] 12°.
14028. b. 77.

—— [A new edition, containing 181 hymns.] pp. xii. 536. मुंबय्यां १८२३ [*Bombay*, 1901.] 16°.
14028. bb. 10.

—— De la Prière chez les Hindous. [Select devotional poems, translated from the Bṛihatstotraratnākara by A. Roussel.] 1889-1890. 8°. *See* ROUSSEL (A.). [*Muséon.*]
P.P. 4453. (tom. 8, 9.)

STOTRASAṄGRAHA. (ಸ್ತೋತ್ರ ಸಂಗ್ರಹ) [Stotrasaṅgraha. Jain hymns in Sanskrit and Prakrit in praise of the *tīrthaṅkaras* and Jain doctrine.] p. 24. ಬೆಂಗಳೂರು ೧೮೯೬ [*Bangalore*, 1896.] 8°.
No title-page. **14100. b. 3.(4.)**

STREHLY (G.). *See* MANU. — *Dharmaṣāstra.* Mânava Dharma Çâstra. Les Lois de Manou. Traduites . . . par G. Strehly. 1893. 8°. [*Annales du Musée Guimet : Bibliothèque d'Études.*]
7704. i. (tom. 2.)

STRONG (DAWSONNE MELANCHTHON). *See* SUTTAPIṬAKA.—*Khuddakanikāya.* [*Udāna.*] The Udāna . . . Translated . . . by . . . D. M. Strong. 1902. 8°. **14098. ccc. 36.**

—— The Doctrine of the Perfect One, or The Law of Piety. Compiled [from Pali texts] by . . . D. M. Strong. pp. 19. *London*, 1902. 8°.
4506. df. 15.(3.)

STRONG (SANDFORD ARTHUR). *See* ACADEMIES, *etc.* — London. — *Pali Text Society.* UPATISSA. The Mahā-bodhi-vaṁsa. Edited by S. A. Strong. 1891. 8°. **14098. b. 29.(2.)**

STUDI ITALIANI DI FILOLOGIA INDO-IRANICA. *See* PERIODICAL PUBLICATIONS.—*Florence.*

STURDY (ED. T.). *See* [Addenda] NĀRADA. [*Sūtra.*] Nârada Sûtra . . . Translated . . . with an independent commentary by E. T. Sturdy. 1896. 8°. **14028. c. 68.**

SUBASIMHA (D. J.). *See* SUTTAPIṬAKA.—*Selections.* අවවාදරත්නසංග්‍රහව *etc.* [Avavādaratnasaṅgrahava. Translated into Sinhalese by D. J. Subasimha.] 1891. 12°. **14098. a. 32.(3.)**

—— *See* SUTTAPIṬAKA. — *Selections.* Sutra Sangraha. [Translated by D. J. Subasimha.] 1894. 8°. [*The Buddhist.*] **P.P. 636. cn.(vol. 6.)**

SUBBAIYA PANTULU, *Kākarla.* *See* VEṄKAṬAVARADADĀSA, *Paidiganṭamu*, and SUBBAIYA PANTULU, *Kākarla.* శ్రీతారకనామత్రయము *etc.* [Tārakanāmatraya.] 1900. 8°. **14033. bbb. 9.**

SUBBAṆṆĀCHĀRYA, *son of Hiraṇṇaiyan.* *See* PURĀṆAS.—*Vasishṭhapurāṇa.* గోత్రఖండప్రా *etc.* [Gotrakhaṇḍa, *etc.* Compiled by Subbaṇṇāchārya.] 1897. 8°. **14016. c. 52.**

SUBBARĀMAIYA, *Siḍugu.* *See* RAGHUNĀTHAPRASĀDA SUKALA. వాజీకరకల్పద్రుమము *etc.* [Vājikarakalpadruma. With Telugu translation by Subbarāmaiya.] [1901.] 8°. **14043. cc. 18.**

SUBBARÂYÂRYA, *Koralla.* *See* UḌUDĀYAPRADĪPA. Ándhra Párásaryamu . . . with . . . introduction, by K. Subbaráyárya, *etc.* 1898. 12°.
14053. b. 31.(4.)

SUBHĀSHITA. Stances Sanskrites Inédites, d'après un manuscrit de la Bibliothèque Universitaire de Lyon. [Edited with translation by Paul Regnaud.] (Annuaire de la Faculté des Lettres de Lyon. Première année, fascicule ii. Troisième année, fascicule ii.) 1883-1885. 8°.
Ac. 8922.(année 1, 3.)

The editor states that the MS. bears only the corrupt title atha subhāshita(savaskṛita)ṣloka[ḥ].

SUBHĀSHITASAṄGRAHA. Subhāṣita-saṃgraha. (An anthology of extracts from Buddhist works compiled by an unknown author, to illustrate the doctrines of scholastic and of mystic . . . Buddhism. Edited by Cecil Bendall.) pp. 100. *Louvain,* 1905. 8°. **14070. ee. 2.**

Extrait du "Muséon," Nouvelle Série, iv.-v.

—— —— *See* PERIODICAL PUBLICATIONS. — *Louvain.* Le Muséon, *etc.* Nouvelle Série. Vol. IV, V. 1881, *etc.* 8°.
P.P. 4453. (nouvelle sér., vol. 4, 5.)

SUBHAṢĪLA GAṆĪ, *disciple of Lakshmīsāgara.* Pañcaçatī-prabodhasambandhaḥ, o Le Cinquecento Novelle Antiche di Çubhaçīla-Gaṇi. Edite e tradotte per cura di Ambrogio Ballini. 1904, *etc.* *See* PERIODICAL PUBLICATIONS. — *Florence.* Studi Italiani di Filologia Indo-Iranica, *etc.* Vol. vi., *etc.* 1897, *etc.* 8°. **P.P. 4884. da.(vol. 6, etc.)**

In progress.

SUBHAṬA. The Dûtângada of Subhata. [A drama on the story of Rāma and Rāvaṇa.] Edited by Paṇdit Durgâprasâd and Kâśînâth Pâṇdurang Parab. (दूताङ्गदम् ।) pp. 15. 1891. *See* DURGĀPRASĀDA, *son of Vrajalāla,* and KĀŚĪNĀTHA PĀṆḌURAṄGA PARAB. Kâvyamâlâ. [No.] 28. 1886, *etc.* 8°. **14072. ccc. 12.(no. 28.)**

SUBHŪTI, *Vaskaḍuvē.* A Complete Index to the Abhidhánappadípiká [in Pali], with explanatory and grammatical notes [in Pali, Pali-Sinhalese glossary, and English index]. By W. Subhúti Mahá Théra. (අභිධානප්පදීපිකා සූචි) pp. xxxiv. 520, viii. *Colombo,* 1893. 8°.
14098. c. 62.

—— The Siam Standard Paritta. Cularaja Paritta, Maharaja Paritta, &c. Adapted for religious rites in Siam for different occasions. Compiled by . . . W. Subhuti . . . assisted by . . . P. C. Jinavarawansa. (චූලරාජ පිරිත සහ මහාරාජ පිරිත.) pp. xi. 28; 4 *plates.* *Colombo,* 1897. 8°. **14098. b. 22.**

SUBRAHMAṆYA, *son of Deveṣa Ṣāstrī of Mailattur, disciple of Krishṇa Paṇḍita.* ஸ்ரீக்ருஷ்ணார்யா-ஸதகம் *etc.* [Ṣrīkṛishṇāryāṣataka. A century of *āryā* verses upon Kṛishṇa. Edited by Rāmakṛishṇa Ṣāstrī of Kalpadi.] pp. 24. பாலக்காடு [*Palghat,* 1899.] 16°. **14028. b. 102.(2.)**

On the last page of the wrapper is a short commendatory poem.

SUBRAHMAṆYAM, *Chevali.* *See* SUBRAHMAṆYA ṢĀSTRĪ, *Chevali.*

SUBRAHMAṆYA ṢARMĀ, *Ṣēḍambi.* *See* BĀDARĀYAṆA. అథ శ్రీబ్రహ్మసూత్రభాష్యం *etc.* [Brahmasūtra. With commentary of Ānandatīrtha. Edited by Subrahmaṇya.] [1898.] *obl.* 12°.
14048. b. 33.(3.)

SUBRAHMAṆYA ṢĀSTRĪ, *of Jodhpur*. *See* MURĀRIDĀNA. ॥ यशवन्तयशोभूषण॰ [Yaṣavantayaṣobhūshaṇa. Translated into Sanskrit by Subrahmaṇya.] [1901.] 4°. **14053. g. 17.**

SUBRAHMAṆYA ṢĀSTRĪ, *E. P., of Elappalli, Palghat*. *See* ṢAṄKARA ĀCHĀRYA.—*Philosophical Poems, etc.* വാക്യസുധാ etc. [Vākyasudhā. Edited with Malayalam translation by Subrahmaṇya.] 1903. 8°. **14049. a. 7.(3.)**

—— *See* YOGAVĀSISHṬHARĀMĀYAṆA. ലഘുയോഗവാസിഷ്ഠ സാരം *etc.* [Laghu-yogavāsishṭhasāra. With Malayalam translation by Subrahmaṇya.] [1903.] 8°. **14049. b. 17.(2.)**

SUBRAHMAṆYA ṢĀSTRĪ, *K., of Udayār-pāḷayam*. க்ருஷ்ணயஜுர்வேத தைத்திரீய ஸம்ஹிதா ப்ராஹ்மணாரண்யக காடக பஞ்சாசதனுக்ரமணிகா *etc.* [Pañchāṣadanukramaṇikā. An index of catchwords for the Taittirīyasaṃhitā, its Brāhmaṇa, Āraṇyaka, and Kāṭhaka.] pp. 93, viii. நடுக்காவேரி ஹேமலம்ப [*Nadukkaveri*, 1897.] 12°. **14028. b. 78.(2.)**

SUBRAHMAṆYA ṢĀSTRĪ, *S., of K. H. School, Tanjore*. *See* ACADEMIES, *etc.*—Madras.—*University of Madras*. B. A. Degree Examination 1901. The Sanskrit text with . . . commentary . . . introductions and . . . notes. Part i. By Subrahmanya Sastri . . . and P. S. Sundaram Ayyar, *etc.* 1900. 8°. **14072. c. 50.(2.)**

—— *See* VĀDĪBHASIṂHA SŪRI. The Gadyachintâmani . . . [Edited with preface] by T. S. Kuppuswami Sastri . . . and S. Subrahmanya Sastri. 1902. 8°. **14070. dd. 23.**

SUBRAHMAṆYA ṢĀSTRĪ, *V., of Bangalore*. *See* VAIDYANĀTHA, *son of Veṅkaṭādri*. जातकपारिजातः [Jātakapārijāta] . . . With . . . translation. And श्रीपतिपद्धतिः [Ṣrīpatipaddhati] . . . With . . . translation, notes and examples. By V. Subrahmanya Sastri. 1903, *etc.* 8°. **14053. ccc. 48.**

SUBRAHMAṆYA ṢĀSTRĪ, *Chevali, of Vizagapatam*. *See* JAYADEVA, *son of Mahādeva*. The Andhra Chandraloka of Adidamu Soorakavi, with the Sanskrit Chandraloka of Appayya Deekshita. Edited . . . by . . . Subrahmanyam. 1898. 8°. **14053. c. 66.**

SUBRAHMAṆYA ṢĀSTRĪ, *Chevali, of Vizagapatam (continued)*. ఆశౌచసారము [Āṣauchasāra. A Telugu treatise on formal uncleanness. With an appendix of extracts from Sanskrit authorities.] pp. iv. ii. 40. *Vizagapatam*, 1898. 8°. **14028. d. 24.(2.)**

—— Exercises in Sanskrit Translation . . . a collection of the papers in Sanskrit [*i.e.* for translation from English into Sanskrit] set at the Matriculation Examination of the Madras University from 1872 to 1895. Edited [with translation into Sanskrit] . . . by Ch. Subrahmanyam. pp. ii. 52. *Vizagapatam*, 1896. 12°. **14092. a. 17.(1.)**

SUBRAHMAṆYA ṢĀSTRĪ, *Mēlmaṅgalam M. N.* *See* ṢAṄKARA ĀCHĀRYA.—*Doubtful and Supposititious Works*. ஸ்ரீஸுப்ரஹ்மண்யபுஜங்கஸ்தோத்ரம் *etc.* [Subrahmaṇya-bhujaṅgastotra. Edited with grammatical notes in Sanskrit and with Tamil interpretation and commentary by Subrahmaṇya.] 1902. 16°. **14028. a. 30.**

SUBRAHMAṆYA ṢĀSTRĪ, *Ṣennimalai*. *See* VAIDYANĀTHA DĪKSHITA. ஸ்ம்ருதிமுக்தாபலெ ப்ரயச்ச . . . காண்ட: *etc.* [Smṛitimuktāphala. Vol. iii. and iv., with Tamil translation by Subrahmaṇya.] 1898, *etc.* 4°. **14039. c. 15.(vol. 3, 4.)**

SUBRĀYA ṢĀSTRI, *Kammarḍi*. *See* RĀMAKṚISHṆA PAṆḌITA, *Writer on Dharma*. ನಿತ್ಯಕರ್ಮ ಚಂದ್ರಿಕೆ *etc.* [Nityakarmachandrike. With Canarese version by Subrāya.] [1901, *etc.*] 8°. **14033. aa. 33.**

SUCHARITA MIṢRA. *See* JAIMINI. — *Mīmāṃsāsūtra*. Çlokavārtika. Translated . . . with extracts from the commentaries of Sucarīta [*sic*] Miçra, the Kāçikā, *etc.* 1900, *etc.* 8°. [*Bibliotheca Indica.*] **14002. a.(vol. 146.)**

SUDARṢANA ĀCHĀRYA, *Panjābī*. ॥ श्रीः . . . अद्वैतचन्द्रिका The Adwaita Chandrika. A work on Vedanta philosophy of Shankar, compiled by Pandit Sudarshanacharya Punjabi. [Followed by 8 stanzas to Ṣiva.] pp. iii. 47, i. *Benares*, 1901. 8°. **14048. dd. 16.(1.)**

SUDARṢANA ĀCHĀRYA, *son of Vāgvijaya*, called ṢRUTAPRAKĀṢIKĀCHĀRYA. *See* ĀPASTAMBA.—*Gṛihyasūtra*. आपस्तम्बगृह्यसूत्रम् . . . The Ápastamba-Gṛihya-Sútra, with the commentary [Tātparyadarṣana or

Gṛihyatātparyadarṣana] of Sudarśanáchárya, *etc.* 1893. 8°. [*Mysore Government Oriental Library Series: Bibliotheca Sanskrita.*] **14004. b. 1.**

—— *See* RĀMĀNUJA.—*Original Works.* वेदार्थसंग्रहः . . . Vedártha Saṅgraha. With the gloss called Tátparyadípiká by Sudarśanasúri, *etc.* [1894.] 8°. [*The Pandit.*] **14096. d. 6.(vol. 15, 16.)**

—— *See* RĀMA MIṢRA ṢĀSTRĪ. तात्पर्यदीपिकायां स्नेहपूर्तिः । [Snehapūrti. A commentary upon the Tātparyadīpikā or commentary of Sudarṣana upon Rāmānuja's Vedārthasaṅgraha.] 1895-1896. 8°. [*The Pandit.*] **14096. d. 6.(vol. 17, 18.)**

—— *See* RĀMA MIṢRA ṢĀSTRĪ. स्नेहपूर्तिपरीक्षा। [Snehapūrtiparikshā. A dissertation upon the Snehapūrti.] 1895-1896. 8°. [*The Pandit.*] **14096. d. 6.(vol. 17, 18.)**

SUDARṢANA ĀCHĀRYA, *Ṣāmbhavaṣikhāmaṇi*, also called HARADATTA. ஸ்ரீஹாக்ஷ—கூ சாசூதஷ்கம் etc. [Gaṅgādharāshṭaka. A Vedantic hymn to Ṣiva.] *See* SADĀṢIVA BRAHMENDRA. வொயாயா [Bodhāryā.] pp. 20-22. 1888. 12°. **14048. b. 38.(2.)**

The colophon gives the two names of the author, which suggest his identity with the Haradatta-Sudarṣana who wrote the Padamañjarī, on whom see Seshagiri Sastri's "Report," No. 2 (1893-94), pp. 13 ff.

SUDARṢANĀCHĀRYA, *Pañchanadīya.* *See* SUDARṢANA ĀCHĀRYA, *Panjābī.*

SUDARṢANA NANDA, *of Sutahat, Cuttack.* *See* CHĀṆAKYA. [*Shorter Recension.*] ଚାଣକ୍ୟଶ୍ଳୋକ *etc.* [Chāṇakyaṣloka. With Oriya metrical version by Sudarṣana.] 1901. 12°. **14076. b. 26.(4.)**

SUDARṢANĀRYA, *Commentator on Āpastamba.* *See* SUDARṢANA ĀCHĀRYA, *son of Vāgvijaya.*

SUDARṢANASAṂHITĀ. हनुमत कवच, प्रत्यंगिरास्तोत्रम् *etc.* [Hanumatkavacha. A formulary for the invocation of Hanumān, extracted from the Sudarṣanasaṃhitā. Followed by the Pratyaṅgirāstotra of Chaṇḍeṣvara Ṣūlapāṇi. Edited by Gaṅgādhara Ṣāstrī Draviḍa.] pp. 9, 14. काशी १८७१ [*Benares,* 1897.] 8°. **14033. aa. 5.(1.)**

SUDARŚANASÚRI. *See* SUDARṢANA ĀCHĀRYA, *son of Vāgvijaya.*

SUDARṢANENDRA SARASVATĪ. *See* MAHĀDEVENDRA SARASVATĪ.

SUDASSANA VARADHAMMASĀMI, known as SANKYAUNG HSAYA. *See* VINAYAPIṬAKA. ဝိနည်း *etc.* [Vinayapiṭaka. Vol. v., vi., the Chūlavagga, with interpretation by Sudassana.] 1903-1904. 8°. **14099. aa. 5, 6.**

SUDHĀKARA DVIVEDĪ, *Mahāmahopādhyāya.* *See* BRAHMADEVA. करणप्रकाशः *etc.* (Karaṇaprakâśa . . . [Edited] with a commentary and theory of numbers . . . by . . . Sudhâkara Dvivadî.) [1899.] 8°. **14004. a. 5.**

—— *See* BRAHMAGUPTA. ब्राह्मस्फुटसिद्धान्तो . . . Brāhmasphuṭasiddhānta and Dhyānagrahopadeṣādhyāya . . . Edited with . . . commentary by . . . Sudhākara Dvivedin. 1902. 8°. [*The Pandit.*] **14096. d. 6.(vol. 23, 24.)**

—— *See* EUCLID. रेखागणितस्यैकादशद्वादशाध्यायौ *etc.* [Rekhāgaṇita. A translation of the propositions of Euclid's Elements, by Sudhākara Dvivedī. Books xi.-xii. With commentary.] [1891.] 8°. **14053. d. 53.**

—— *See* VARĀHAMIHIRA. The Bṛihat Saṃhitâ . . . With the commentary of Bhaṭṭotpala. Edited by . . . Sudhákara Dvivedi. 1895-1897. 8°. **14048. dd. 3.(vol. 10.)**

—— दिग्मीमांसा . . . Digmimámsá, or The East Point and the Age of the Veda, *etc.* pp. i. 48. 1899. *See* PERIODICAL PUBLICATIONS.—*Benares.* The Pandit, *etc.* New Series. Vol. XXI. 1876, *etc.* 8°. **14096. d. 6.(vol. 21.)**

—— गणकतरङ्गिणी . . . Gaṇaka Taraṅgiṇi, or Lives of Hindú Astronomers, *etc.* pp. 134, i. i. vii. 1892. *See* PERIODICAL PUBLICATIONS.—*Benares.* The Pandit, *etc.* New Series. Vol. XIV. 1876, *etc.* 8°. **14096. d. 6.(vol. 14.)**

—— श्रीसंवत् १९४७ . . . तिथिपत्रं *etc.* [Almanack for 1890. Compiled by Sudhākara Dvivedī.] [1889.] *obl.* 8°. *See* EPHEMERIDES. **14096. b. 10.(1.)**

SŪDRAKA. The Mṛichchhakaṭika, or Toy Cart. A prakaraṇa, by King Śûdraka. Vol. I. Containing two commentaries, (1) the Suvarṇâlaṁkaraṇa of Lalla Dîkshita, and (2) a vṛitti or vivṛiti by Prithvîdhara; and (3) various readings Edited by Nârâyaṇa Bâlakṛishṇa Godabole. (सच मृच्छकटिकं) *Bombay*, 1896, *etc.* 8°. **14079. c. 63.**

In progress? Forms no. lii. *of the* Bombay Sanskrit Series.

—— The Mṛichchhakaṭika of Śûdraka, with the commentary of Pṛithvîdhara. Edited by Kâshinâth Pâṇḍurang Parab. (श्रीशूद्रककविविरचितं मृच्छकटिकम् ।) pp. 294, vi. *Bombay*, 1900. 8°. **14079. c. 60.(2.)**

—— The Mrichchhakati, or The Toy-Cart. A drama. Translated . . . by H. H. Wilson. pp. xi. 200. 1901. *See* Wilson (H. H.). Hindu Dramatic Works, *etc.* 1901. 12°. **14080. b. 13.**

—— Vasantasenâ, oder Das irdene Wägelchen. Ein altindisches, dem König Çûdraka zugeschriebenes Schauspiel. Frei wiedergegeben von Michael Haberlandt. pp. xx. 214. *Leipzig*, 1893. 16°. **14079. a. 9.**

Forms part of the Kleine Ausgabe Liebeskind.

—— [Another copy.] **11746. a. 2.**

—— Vasantasena. Drama in fünf Akten, mit freier Benutzung der Dichtung des . . . Sudraka, von Emil Pohl. [Adapted from the version of L. Fritze.] pp. 128. *Stuttgart*, 1893. 8°. **14079. b. 40.**

—— Vasantasena. Indiskt drama i 5 akter af Konung Sudrâka [*sic*]. Fritt efter Emil Pohls tyska bearbetning af Frans Hedberg. pp. 119. *Stockholm*, 1894. 12°. **11755. dd.**

No. 247 *of the* Svenska Teatern.

SUGATAPĀLA, *Varāpiṭiyē*. *See* Suttapiṭaka.—*Selections*. Sútra Saṅgraha. Edited by . . . Sugatapála, *etc.* 1890-1895. 8°. **14098. dd. 6.**

—— *See* Suttapiṭaka. — *Selections*. සුත්‍ත සඞ්ගහට්ඨකථා *etc.* [Suttasaṅgahaṭṭhakathā. Edited by Sugatapāla.] [1897.] 8°. **14098. dd. 15.**

SUJĀTĀBHISIRIDDHAJA, known as Moda Hsaya, *of Laykaing*. ဝိနယသာရရာသိကျမ်း *etc.* [Vinayasārarāsi. 6 essays in Pali and Burmese on divers points of ecclesiastical discipline, entitled Sambhogavinichchhaya-sā-tan, Vinichchhayarāsi-kyan, Gāmasīmāvinichchhaya, Vissāsagāhav°., Uchchāsayanav°., and Kappav°.] pp. vi. 644, iii. ပြည်လေး [*Mandalay*,] 1900. 8°. **14098. ccc. 31.**

Pp. 289-296 *are missing.*

ṢUKA. शुकविरचितम् . . . निर्वाणाष्टकम् [Nirvāṇāshṭaka. 8 stanzas on the vanity of this world, ascribed to Ṣuka. With a commentary by Gaṅgādharendra Sarasvatī.] pp. 12. [1889.] *See* Periodical Publications.—*Bombay*. ग्रन्थरत्नमाला *etc.* (Granth Ratna Málá, *etc.*) Vol. II, no. 7. 1887-[1892.] 8°. **14096. c. 8.(vol. 2.)**

ṢUKA, *son of Buddhyāṣraya*. Kings of Kashmira: being a translation of the Sanskrita works of . . . Shuka, by Jogesh Chunder Dutt. *See* Kalhaṇa. Kings of Káshmira, *etc.* Vol. iii. 1879-1898. 12°. **14070. b. 13.**

ṢUKĀCHĀRYA, *Bhāgavatarāddhāntam*, *Vātsya*. *See* Bādarāyaṇa. శ్రీశుకభాష్యమ్ *etc.* [Brahmasūtra. With commentary of Ṣukāchārya.] [1892.] 8°. **14048. c. 76.**

ṢUKADEVA. बृहज्ज्योतिषसार . . . Vrihaj-jyotiṣsar, [a manual of astrology,] with Hindi translation. pp. xii. 332. *Benares*, 1897. 8°. **14053. d. 52.**

ṢUKĀNANDA MUNI. *See* Satsaṅgijīvana. धर्मामृत *etc.* [Dharmāmṛita. With Gujarati translation by Ṣukānanda.] [1902.] 12°. **14033. a. 50.**

ṢUKARAMBHĀSAṂVĀDA. Dialogue de Çuka et de Rambha sur l'amour et la science suprême. [Ṣriṅgārajñānanirṇaya.] Publié [with French translation] par J.-M. Grandjean. 1887. *See* Academies, *etc.*—Paris.—*Musée Guimet.* Annales, *etc.* Tom. x., pp. 477-499. 1880, *etc.* 4°. **7704. h. 21.(tom. 10.)**

—— రమ్భాశుకసంవాదః [Ṣukarambhāsaṃvāda. With Telugu translation.] *See* Rāmānujāchārya, *Tirumalai Kandyūru*. కవిహృదయసర్వస్వము *etc.* [Kavihṛidayasarvasva.] pt. 1, pp. 146-156. 1901. 8°. **14072. ccc. 31.**

ṢUKASAPTATI. Die Çukasaptati. Textus simplicior. Herausgegeben von Richard Schmidt. pp. x. 212, i. 1893. *See* Academies, *etc.*—Germany.—*Deutsche Morgenlaendische Gesellschaft.* Abhandlungen, *etc.* Bd. 10, No. 1. 1859, *etc.* 8°. **753. f. 18.**

ŞUKASAPTATI (*continued*). Der Textus Simplicior der Śukasaptati in der Recension der Handschrift A. Von Richard Schmidt. 1900-1901. *See* ACADEMIES, *etc.*—Germany.—*Deutsche Morgenlaendische Gesellschaft.* Zeitschrift, *etc.* Bd. 54, 55. 1846, *etc.* 8°. **Ac. 8815/2. (vol. 54, 55.)**

—— Die Çukasaptati. Textus simplicior. Aus dem Sanskrit übersetzt von Richard Schmidt. pp. i. 102. *Kiel, Bonn* [printed], 1894. 8°. **14072. ccc. 23.**

—— *See* SCHMIDT (R.). Anmerkungen zu dem Textus Simplicior der Śukasaptati, *etc.* 1894. 8°. [*Zeitschrift der Deutschen Morgenlaendischen Gesellschaft.*] **Ac. 8815/2. (Bd. 48.)**

—— Der Textus Ornatior der Śukasaptati. Kritisch herausgegeben von Richard Schmidt. pp. 100. *München*, 1898. 4°. **14070. e. 19.**

From the Abhandlungen der königl. bayerischen Akademie der Wissenschaften, 1 *Cl.*, xxi. *Bd.*, ii. *Abtheil.*

—— Die Śukasaptati. Textus Ornatior. Aus dem Sanskrit uebersetzt von Richard Schmidt. pp. iv. 149. *Stuttgart*, 1899. 8°. **14070. dd. 10.**

—— Der Textus Ornatior der Çukasaptati. [An abstract, with specimens of the text.] Ein Beitrag zur Märchenkunde, von Richard Schmidt. pp. vi. 70, i. *Stuttgart*, 1896. 8°. **14070. d. 33. (2.)**

—— Specimen der Dinālāpanikāçukasaptati. Von Dr. Richard Schmidt. 1891-1892. *See* ACADEMIES, *etc.*—Germany.—*Deutsche Morgenlaendische Gesellschaft.* Zeitschrift, *etc.* Bd. 45, 46. 1846, *etc.* 8°. **Ac. 8815/2. (Bd. 45, 46.)**

SUKHĀNANDANĀTHA, *Brahmāvadhūta.* शब्दार्थचिन्तामणिः *etc.* [Şabdārthachintāmaṇi. A thesaurus and lexicon of the Sanskrit language.] 4 vols. अग्रपुरे राजधान्युदयपुरे १९२१-१९४२ [*Agra, Udaipur*, 1864-1885.] 4°. **14092. cc. 1.**

The first two volumes were published at Agra in 1864, *under private patronage. The remainder was printed under the patronage of the Maharana of Mewar at Udaipur in* 1883-5.

SUKHĀNANDA TRIPĀṬHĪ, *Prājña, son of Durgāprasāda.* ॥ ब्रह्म विलासं *etc.* [Brahmavilāsa. A Vedantic poem of 378 stanzas in Sanskrit and Hindi. Followed by the Praşnottarī and Sādhanapañchaka ascribed to Şaṅkara, with Hindi translations by Sukhānanda.] pp. 63, 5, 2. *Delhi*, १८९४ [1894.] 8°. **14048. dd. 32. (1.)**

SUKHĀVATĪVYŪHA. 梵漢阿彌陀經 [Bonkan Amida Kiō, *i.e.* the Sukhāvatīvyūha or Amitābhasūtra. The Sanskrit text, with transliteration into Japanese characters and a Chinese version by Jōmei Sōjō.] [1773.] 8°. **16010. a. 13.**

—— Textes Sanscrits découverts au Japon. Lecture faite devant la "Royal Asiatic Society of Great Britain and Ireland" par M. F. Max Müller . . . Traduit par M. de Milloué, *etc.* [With special reference to the Sukhāvatīvyūha, and with a translation and the original Sanskrit text of the latter in the Japanese recension.] 1881. *See* ACADEMIES, *etc.* — Paris. — *Musée Guimet.* Annales, *etc.* Tom. ii., pp. 1-37. 1880, *etc.* 4°. **7704. h. 21. (tom. 2.)**

—— O-mi-to-king, ou Soukhavati-vyouhasoutra. D'après la version chinoise de Koumarajiva. Traduit du chinois par MM. Imaïzoumi et Yamata. [Followed by a facsimile of the Sanskrit text as preserved in a Chinese MS.] 1881. *See* ACADEMIES, *etc.*—Paris.—*Musée Guimet.* Annales, *etc.* Tom. ii., pp. 38-64. 1880, *etc.* 4°. **7704. h. 21. (tom. 2.)**

—— The Larger Sukhâvatî-vyûha. (The Smaller Sukhâvatî-vyûha.) [Translated with notes *etc.* by F. Max Müller.] 1894. *See* MUELLER (F. M.). The Sacred Books of the East, *etc.* Vol. xlix., pt. 2. 1879, *etc.* 8°. **2003. b. (vol. 49.)**

SUKUMĀRA PIḶḶAI, *Karayamveṭṭattu.* ലക്ഷണാസ്വയംവരം *etc.* [Lakshaṇāsvayaṃvara. A lyrical drama, in Sanskrit and Malayalam verse, upon the union of Duryodhana's daughter Lakshaṇā with Sāmba.] pp. ii. i. 26. ൧൮൭൫ [*Tangacheri*, 1899.] 8°. **14072. d. 45. (2.)**

ŞŪLAPĀṆI, *Sāhuṛiyān, Mahāmahopādhyāya.* प्रायश्चित्तविवेकः *etc.* [Prāyaşchittaviveka. Being that part of Şūlapāṇi's Smṛitiviveka which treats of expiatory rituals. With the commentary, entitled Tattvārthakaumudī, of Govindānanda Kavikaṅkaṇa. Edited by Jīvānanda Vidyāsāgara. Second edition.] pp. iv. 544. कलिकातायां १८९३ [*Calcutta*, 1893.] 8°. **14028. c. 81.**

ŚŪLAPĀṆI, *Sāhuṛiyān, Mahāmahopādhyāya (continued).* প্রায়শ্চিত্তবিবেকঃ *etc.* [Prāyaṣchittaviveka. With Govindānanda's commentary. Edited with Bengali notes by Chaṇḍīcharaṇa Smṛitibhūshaṇa. Third edition.] pp. viii. 520. কলিকাতা ১৩১০ [*Calcutta,* 1903.] 8°. **14033. aa. 31.**

SUMANA, *Ū,* called MYINMU HSAYA. မြင်းမူ တရားစာလက်သစ် [Myinmū-tayā-sā-let-thit. A Burmese anthological work on Buddhist doctrine, in Pali and Burmese.] pp. 142. ရန်ကုန် ၁၂၅၃ [*Rangoon,* 1891.] 8°. **14300. d. 22.(3.)**

—— သုစိတြဒေသနာ ... မြင်းမူလက်သစ်တရားစာ [Suchitradesanā Myinmū-let-thit-tayā-sā. Burmese homilies, illustrated by Pali texts. Second edition.] pp. v. 200. ရန်ကုန် ၁၂၅၅ [*Rangoon,* 1893.] 8°. **14300. d. 22.(4.)**

—— [Another edition.] pp. 200. ရန်ကုန် ၁၂၆၁ [*Rangoon,* 1900.] 8°. **14300. d. 32.(5.)**

SUMAṄGALA, *Doḍampahala.* See VAGĒGODA THERA. Ākhyāta Pada. Edited by . . . Sumangala. 1889. 8°. **14165. k. 17.(2.)**

SUMAṄGALA, *Hikkaḍuvē.* See KACHCHĀYANA.—*Bālāvatāra.* Bálávatára . . . With a commentary, by . . . Sumangala. 1892. 8°. **14098. c. 60.**

—— See KACHCHĀYANA.—*Bālāvatāra.* ဗာလာဝတာရဋီကာပါဌ် *etc.* [Bālāvatāra. With commentary of Sumaṅgala.] [1900.] 8°. **14098. ccc. 27.(2.)**

SUMAṄGALA, *Medagama.* See KACHCHĀYANA.—*Rūpasiddhi.* මහාරූපසිද්ධි *etc.* [Rūpasiddhi. Edited by Sumaṅgala and Dhammaratana.] 1891-1897. 8°. **14098. d. 39.**

SUMAṄGALASĀMI. ဋီကာကျော်ပါဌ်။ [Ṭīkā-kyaw̱, or Abhidhammatthavibhāvanī. A work in elucidation of Anuruddha's Abhidhammatthasaṅgaha.] pp. 174. ရန်ကုန် ၁၂၅၉ [*Rangoon,* 1898.] 8°. **14098. ccc. 14.**

—— ဋီကာကျော် *etc.* [Ṭīkā-kyaw̱. Parts i.-iii. (§§ 1-156). With Burmese *nissaya* by Janindābhisiri of Sinde.] See ANURUDDHA. ဋီကာကျော် *etc.* [Abhidhammatthasaṅgaha, *etc.*] [1898.] 8°. **14098. ccc. 15.**

—— (ဋီကာကျော်နိဿယ) [Ṭīkā-kyaw̱-nissaya. Being sect. ii.-iv. of the Ṭīkā-kyaw̱ with Burmese *nissaya* by Janindābhisiri.] pp. iv. 432. [*Rangoon,* 1891.] 8°. **14098. ccc. 34.**
No title-page.

—— ဋီကာကျော်နိသျသစ်။ [Ṭīkā-kyaw̱. With Burmese *nissaya* by Ū Kelāsa.] pp. ii. 504. မန္တလေး [*Mandalay,*] 1903. 8°. **14099. b. 2.**

—— See ĀDICHCHAVAṂSA. ဋီကာကျော်ဂဏ္ဌိကျမ်း *etc.* [Ṭīkā-kyaw̱-ganṭhi-kyan. A Burmese dissertation upon the Ṭīkā-kyaw̱.] [1901.] 8°. **14300. d. 35.**

SUMAṄGALASĀMI, *Maṇiddhaja.* ဥပသမ္ပဒါဒီပနီပါဌ် *etc.* [Upasampadādīpanī. 47 Pali stanzas on the subject of priestly ordination, with a Burmese *nissaya.* Followed by Duruttadīpanī, a Burmese treatise on the wrong reading of sacred books, illustrated from Pali texts.] See VINAYAPIṬAKA.—*Appendix.* ဝိနယသမူဟဝိနိစ္ဆယကျမ်း *etc.* [Vinayasamūhavinichchhaya-kyan.] Vol. I, pp. 412-476. 1899, *etc.* 8°. **14300. e. 15.**

SUMATIHARSHA GAṆĪ. See BHĀSKARA ĀCHĀRYA. करणकुतूहलम् *etc.* [Karaṇakutūhala. With the commentary Gaṇakakumudakaumudī of Sumatiharsha.] [1902.] 8°. **14053. ccc. 34.**

SUMATI-NĀGIL-CHARITRA. सुमति नागिल चरित्र तथा संजतासंजत अने गछकुगछनो अधिकार. [Sumati-Nāgil-charitra. A series of compositions consisting of select texts from Jain Sanskrit and Prakrit works with paraphrases, *etc.*, in Gujarati verse, treating of the story of Sumati and of Jain religious duties.] pp. viii. 155. अमदावाद १९३३ [*Ahmadabad,* 1876.] 8°. **14144. g. 21.**

SUMATIVIJAYA. See KĀLIDĀSA.—*Raghuvaṃṣa.* The Raghuvanśa . . . with full extracts . . . from the commentaries of . . . Sumativijaya, *etc.* 1897. 8°. **14072. c. 53.**

SUMEDHAṄKARA, *Bēruvala.* See DHAMMASIRI. Kudusika . . . With paraphrase by . . . Medhankara. Revised by . . . Sumedhankara, *etc.* 1894. 8°. **14098. d. 43.**

SUNDARA. *See* VIDYĀSUNDARA.

SUNDARA, *of Vijitārāma, Thanlan Cheti.* မဏိမေဓဇောတကကျမ်း *etc.* [Maṇimedhajotakakyan. A Burmese treatise on Buddhist psychology, based upon the Abhidhammatthasaṅgaha, and illustrated from Pali texts.] pp. ii. 200. *Moulmein,* 1882. 8°. **14300. d. 17.(2.)**

SUNDARADEVA ŞARMĀ, *Paṇḍyā.* See CHAKRADHARA, *son of Vāmana.* ॥ यंत्र चिन्तामणि *etc.* [Yantrachintāmaṇi. Edited with Hindi and Sanskrit commentaries, *etc.*, by Sundaradeva.] [1898.] 8°. **14053. c. 56.(4.)**

SUNDARALĀLA MIŞRA, *Dādhīcha, disciple of Rājārāma.* ॥ दाधीचदर्पणः ॥ ग्रन्थः *etc.* [Dādhīchadarpaṇa. A handbook of the religious duties of Dādhīcha Brahmans, with Hindi translation.] pp. ii. ii. 59. कानपुर० १९०३ [*Cawnpore,* 1903.] 8°. **14058. b. 45.(2.)**

SUNDARAM AIYAR, *N., of Shencottah.* Subhashita Ratnamala, or A Garland of the Gems of Sanskrit Poetry. Being an anthology consisting of about 3000 slokas under numerous subjects, alphabetically and metrically arranged, *etc.* (ஸுபாஷிதரத்நமாலா) pp. i. ii. 263. *Tiruvadi,* 1894. 8°. **14076. c. 68.**

SUNDARAM AIYAR, *P. S.* See ACADEMIES, *etc.*—Madras.—*University of Madras.* B.A. Degree Examination 1901. The Sanskrit Text with . . . commentary . . . introductions and . . . notes. Part I. By Subrahmanya Sastri . . . and P. S. Sundaram Ayyar, *etc.* 1900. 8°. **14072. c. 50.(2.)**

SUNDARARĀJA ĀCHĀRYA, *Naḍādūr Varadāchārya, of Srirangam.* See BĀDARĀYAṆA. அதிகரணஸாராவலீ *etc.* [Brahmasūtra. With the Adhikaraṇasārāvalī and a commentary, styled Sahṛidayahṛidayaprakāşikā, by Sundararāja.] [1900-1902.] 8°. **14048. e. 32.**

SUNDARARĀJA BHAṬṬĀCHĀRYA, *Elattūr Varadarāja.* See BĀDARĀYAṆA. లక్ష్మీవిశిష్టాద్వైతభాష్య॥ *etc.* [Brahmasūtra. With the Lakshmīvişishṭādvaitabhāshya of Şrīnivāsa Dīkshita and the supercommentary Nigamachūḍādarpaṇa by Sundararāja.] 1896. 8°. **14048. dd. 29.(2.)**

—— See BĀDARĀYAṆA. லக்ஷ்மீவிசிஷ்டா-த்வைதபாஷ்யம் *etc.* [Brahmasūtra. Sūtra i., or Jijñāsādhikaraṇa, with Şrīnivāsa Dīkshita's Lakshmīvişishṭādvaitabhāshya and the Nigamachūḍādarpaṇa of Sundararāja.] 1896. 8°. **14048. dd. 29.(1.)**

—— See KEŞAVA KAVI, *Vedādhinātha Bhaṭṭāchārya.* ஸ்ரீகோதாபரிணய சம்பூ-காவ்யம் *etc.* [Godāpariṇaya. With the commentary Sumanorañjanī of Sundararāja.] 1896. 8°. **14070. dd. 9.(1.)**

—— See UPANISHADS.—*Modern and Fictitious Upanishads.* ஸ்ரீ . . . பாரமாத்மிகோபநி-ஷத்பாஷ்யம் *etc.* [Pāramātmikopanishad. With commentary by Şrīnivāsa Dīkshita and supercommentary styled Chandrikā by Sundararāja.] 1900. 8°. **14033. bbb. 13.**

—— Snusha Vijayam. A drama in one act, *etc.* (ஸ்நுஷாவிஜயாக்யம் ரூபகம்) pp. 39. *Tinnevelly,* 1890. 12°. **14079. a. 8.(1.)**

SUNDARARĀJAM AIYAR, *R.* See DEVATĪRTHA SVĀMĪ. Udásina Sádhu Stotra. [Translated by Sundararājam Aiyar.] 1898. 8°. [*The Theosophist.*] **P.P. 636. cm.(vol. 19.)**

SUNDARARĀJA ŞARMĀ, *D.* வ்யாஸ வாத்ஸ்யாயந மகர்ஷிகள் அருளிச்செய்த பார்யாதருமம் *etc.* (Vyasa and Vatsyayana's Bharyadharmam. [Comprising 37 aphorisms of Vātsyāyana's Kāmasūtra on wifely duty and the dialogue of Satyabhāmā and Draupadī from the Vanaparva of the Mahābhārata. Edited] with a Tamil commentary [and glosses], and a Tamil version of [portions of] Kalidasa's Abhijnanasakuntala . . . by D. Sundararaja Sarma, with an [English] introduction by K. Sundararama Aiyer . . . New edition.) pp. i. i. ii. xviii. 197, i. சென்னை [*Madras,*] 1901. 12°. **14085. b. 44.**

The English title is taken from the wrapper.

SUNDARARĀMA AIYAR, *K.* *See* SUNDARARĀJA ŚARMĀ, *D.* வ்யாஸ வாத்ஸ்யாயந . . . பார்யா-தருமம் *etc.* (Vyasa and Vatsyayana's Bharyadharmam . . . with an [English] introduction by K. Sundararama Aiyer, *etc.*) 1901. 12°. **14085. b. 44.**

SUNDARĀRYA. *See* SUNDARAM AIYAR.

ŚŪRA, *Ārya.* *See* ĀRYA ŚŪRA.

SŪRAIYA, *Gorti, of Nedunur.* *See* UPANISHADS.—*Separate Upanishads.* శ్రీ . . . తైత్తిరీయోపనిషత్ ॥ [Taittirīyopanishad. With Sāyaṇa's commentary. Edited by Sūraiya.] 1904. 8°. **14007. b. 20.**

SURENDRACHANDRA BAKHSHĪ. নারায়ণী স্নান *etc.* [Nārāyaṇī-snāna. A Bengali tract, illustrated from Sanskrit texts, on the legends and rites connected with the custom of bathing in the Karatoya at Mahasthan and Siladvip, Bogra District, Bengal, on the lunar conjunction called Nārāyaṇīyoga.] pp. 9. বগুড়া ১৩০৬ [*Bogra*, 1899.] 12°. **14028. b. 66.(3.)**

SURENDRALĀLA GOSVĀMĪ, *Tarkatīrtha Bhaṭṭāchārya.* *See* GOTAMA. न्यायसूत्रविवरणम् । [Nyāyasūtra. With commentary of Rādhāmohana. Edited by Surendralāla.] 1901, *etc.* 8°. [*The Pandit.*] **14096. d. 6.(vol. 23, etc.)**

—— *See* INDRADATTA UPĀDHYĀYA. फक्किकाप्रकाशः *etc.* [Phakkikāprakāṣa. Edited by Surendralāla.] [1897.] 8°. **14090. c. 38.(4.)**

—— *See* KEṢAVA MIṢRA, *Logician.* तर्कभाषा . . . The Tarkabhāṣā . . . With the commentary . . . of Viçwakarman. Edited by Surendralāla, *etc.* 1901. 8°. [*The Pandit.*] **14096. d. 6.(vol. 22, 23.)**

—— *See* UDAYANA ĀCHĀRYA. The Lakṣaṇāvalī . . . with the commentary Nyāyamuktāvalī of Çeṣaçārṅgadhara. Edited by Surendralāla, *etc.* 1900. 8°. **14096. d. 6.(vol. 21, 22.)**

SURENDRANĀTHA GOSVĀMĪ. আর্য্য-ধাত্রীবিদ্যা *etc.* [Āryadhātrīvidyā. A Bengali treatise on midwifery, with copious quotations from Sanskrit and English authorities.] pt. i. pp. i. i. 72. কুমারখালী ১৩০৬ [*Kumarkhali*, 1900.] 8°. **14043. cc. 11.**

In progress?

SUREṢVARA ĀCHĀRYA. *See* JACOB (G. A.). अनुक्रमणिका [Index to Sureṣvara's Taittirīyopanishadbhāshyavārttika.] [1893 ?] 8°. **14003. ccc. (no. 13, pt. 2.)**

—— [For the Svārājyasiddhi, sometimes ascribed to Sureṣvara :] *See* SVĀRĀJYASIDDHI.

—— *See* UPANISHADS.—*Separate Upanishads.* The Taittirîya Upanishad, with the commentaries of . . . Sureśvarâchârya . . . Translated into English, *etc.* 1903. 8°. **14007. b. 23.**

—— बृहदारण्यकोपनिषद्भाष्यवार्तिकम् *etc.* (Bṛihadáraṇyakopanishadbháshyavártika by . . . Suréśwarácharya. [A metrical commentary upon the Bṛihadāraṇyakopanishad as expounded by Ṣaṅkara.] With its commentary by . . . Ânandajnána[, styled Ṣāstraprakāṣikā,] and an index of all the verses in the work. Edited by Pandit Káśinâtha Śástri Ágáśe.) 3 vols. pp. i. xviii. 2075, cxxiv. ii. *Poona*, १८१२ [1892]-1894. 8°. **14003. ccc. (no. 16.)**

Forms no. 16 *of the* Ānandāṣrama Sanskrit Series. *The English title is from the cover of vol.* 3.

—— मानसोल्लासो नाम दक्षिणामूर्तिस्तोत्रवार्तिकम् *etc.* [Mānasollāsa. A metrical *vārttika* upon the Dakshiṇāmūrtistotra. With the commentary of Rāmatīrtha entitled Mānasollāsavṛittānta. Followed by Sureṣvara's Pañchīkaraṇavārttika, in 64 stanzas, summarising Ṣaṅkara's Pañchīkaraṇaprakriyā.] 1895. *See* MYSORE.—*Government of Mysore.* Government Oriental Library Series. Bibliotheca Sanskrita. No. 6, pp. 25-170, 1-7. 1893, *etc.* 8°. **14004. b. 5.**

—— नैष्कर्म्यसिद्धिर्नाम वेदान्तप्रकरणम् ... Naishkarmyasiddhi. A treatise on Vedánta . . . with a commentary called Chandriká by Jńánottama Miśra. Edited & annotated by Paṇḍit Ráma Śástrí Mánavallí. *Benares*, 1890, *etc.* 8°. **14048. dd. 7.**

In progress? Forming nos. 38, 41, 43, *of the* Benares Sanskrit Series.

—— पञ्चीकरणवार्त्तिकम् । [Pañchīkaraṇavārttika. A metrical paraphrase of Ṣaṅkara's Pañchīkaraṇaprakriyā. With the commentary Pañchīkaraṇavārttikābharaṇa.] 1891. *See* PERIODICAL PUBLICATIONS.—*Calcutta.* विद्योदयः *etc.* [Vidyodaya.] Vol. xx., pt. 5-12. 1874, *etc.* 8°. **14096. cc. (vol. 20.)**

SURESVARA ĀCHĀRYA (*continued*). Sureśvarácharya's Pranava-vártika. Translated into English [by A. Mahādeva Śāstrī]. *See* ŚAṄKARA ĀCHĀRYA.—*Doubtful and Supposititious Works.* The Vedânta Doctrine of Śrî Sankarâchârya, *etc.* pp. 141-149. 1899. 12°.
14048. b. 36.

—— The Sambandhavārtika, *etc.* [Translated by S. Veṅkaṭaramaṇan.] 1901, *etc.* *See* PERIODICAL PUBLICATIONS.—*Benares.* The Pandit, *etc.* New Series. Vol. XXIII, *etc.* 1876, *etc.* 8°.
14096. d. 6.(vol. 23, etc.)
In progress.

SURESVARA NĀRĀYAṆA DEVA. *See* ŚIVAKUMĀRA MIŚRA. যতীন্দ্র-জীবন-চরিতম্ *etc.* [Yatīndrajīvanacharita. With Bengali translation by Sureśvara.] 1892. 8°.
14058. b. 26.(2.)

SŪRYABALIRĀMA CHAUBE. *See* JAYADEVA, *son of Mahādeva.* चन्द्रालोकालङ्कार० [Chandrāloka. With commentary by Sūryabalirāma.] [1895.] 8°.
14053. c. 64.

SURYANARAIN ROW. *See* SŪRYANĀRĀYAṆA RĀU.

SŪRYANĀRĀYAṆA PANTULU, *V.* The Law of Adoption. As laid down in the Sastras and interpreted by Courts. pp. i. iii. xx. v. xxii. 340. *Narasapur*, 1903. 8°.
5319. b. 29.

SŪRYANĀRĀYAṆA RĀU, *Beṅgalūr.* *See* PERIODICAL PUBLICATIONS.—*Bellary.* The Astrological Magazine. Edited by B. Suryanarain Row, *etc.* 1895, *etc.* 8°.
P.P. 1560. m.

—— *See* VEṄKAṬEŚA DAIVAJÑA. सर्वार्थचिन्तामणि. Sarwarthachintamani, with ... translation ... notes and illustrations, by B. Suryanarain Row. 1899. 8°.
14053. d. 58.

—— *See* YAJÑANĀRĀYAṆA VEṄKAṬEŚVARĀRYA. Jatakachundrika ... translation, with ... notes and illustrations in English, by B. Suryanarain Row. 1898. 8°.
14053. ccc. 4.(2.)

—— —— [Another edition.] 1900. 8°.
14053. cc. 21.(3.)

SŪRYANĀRĀYAṆA ŚĀSTRĪ, *Daṇḍiguṇṭa.* *See* AMARASIṂHA. నామలింగానుశాసనము *etc.* [Nāmaliṅgānuśāsana. With analyses, introductions, and notes in Telugu. Edited by Sūryanārāyaṇa.] 1899. 8°.
14090. bb. 14.

SŪRYANĀRĀYAṆA SIDDHĀNTĪ, *of Lucknow.* *See* ḌHUṆḌHIRĀJA. जातकाभरण *etc.* [Jātakābharaṇa. With Hindi version by Sūryanārāyaṇa.] [1900.] 8°.
14053. ccc. 32.

—— पत्रा श्रीसंवत् १९५३ *etc.* [Almanack for Samvat 1953. Compiled by Sūryanārāyaṇa.] [1896.] *obl.* 8°. *See* EPHEMERIDES.
14096. b. 10.(2.)

SŪRYANĀRĀYAṆA VISHAYĪ. *See* BHARTṚIHARI. ନୀତିଶତକ ସୂର୍ଯ୍ୟନାରାୟଣ ଟୀକା *etc.* [Nītiśataka. With Oriya commentary by Sūryanārāyaṇa.] 1896. 8°.
14072. cc. 14.(2.)

SŪRYASIDDHĀNTA. সূর্য্যসিদ্ধান্ত। মধ্যাধিকারঃ। [Sūryasiddhānta. The Madhyādhikāra, with Raṅganātha's gloss Gūḍhārthaprakāśaka and a Bengali version of the stanzas.] [1890, *etc.*] *See* PERIODICAL PUBLICATIONS.—*Calcutta.* অরুণোদয় *etc.* [Aruṇodaya.] Pt. i., no. 5. [1890, *etc.*] 4°.
14133. g. 16.(pt. i., no. 5.)
Imperfect, breaking off at ii. 7. *An appendix, styled* Sūryasiddhānta-udāharaṇa, *follows.*

—— सूर्यसिद्धान्त अर्थात् खगोलविद्या का अतिप्राचीन सर्वमान्य आर्षग्रन्थ ... Surya Siddhanta. An ancient astronomy of India. Compiled about 2165000 years ago and translated into Hindi and published [with the original Sanskrit text and an introduction] by Udaya Narain Singh. pp. xv. 149, 128. *Biddoopur, Meerut* [printed], १९६० [1903.] 8°.
14053. dd. 8.

SUSHEṆA, *Kavirāja.* কলাপচন্দ্রঃ [The introduction to the Kalāpachandra, treating of the introductory stanza of Durgasiṃha's Kātantravṛitti.] *See* DURGASIṂHA. নমস্কারবিবেকঃ *etc.* [Namaskāraviveka.] pp. 29-70. [1900.] 12°.
14092. a. 24.(1.)

—— আখ্যাত-কবিরাজঃ *etc.* [Ākhyātakavirāja. Being §§ 1, 2 of the chapter on *ākhyāta* in Susheṇa's Kalāpachandra, commenting upon the Kātantra iii. 1, 2. Edited by Mādhavachandra Tarkachūḍāmaṇi.] pp. 90. ঢাকা ১৩০১ [*Dacca*, 1895.] 8°.
14093. b. 36.(2.)
A reprint of the edition of 1890.

—— কলাপ-ব্যাকরণম্ ... চতুষ্টয়কবিরাজঃ *etc.* [Chatushṭayakavirāja, or Kalāpachandra. A commentary on the Kātantra. Chapter II. Edited by Rasikachandra Vidyāratna.] pp. 138. *Dacca*, 1894. 8°.
14090. bb. 13.(3.)

SUŞRUTA. श्रीसुश्रुताचार्येण विरचिता सुश्रुतसंहिता . . . Sushrut Sanhita. Taught by Dhanwaniari [*sic*] and composed by his disciple Sushrutacharya. With the Hindi commentary of Shri Krishna Lal. pp. xc. 1340; 40 *plates*. *Muttra*, 1895. 8°. **14043. dd. 2.**

The outer title-page bears the date 1896.

—— সুশ্রুত-সংহিতা *etc.* [Suşrutasaṃhitā. With the commentary Nibandha of Ḍallaṇa. Edited with a Bengali translation by Kālīprasanna Kaviṣekhara.] 2 vols. pp. ii. c. 1802. কলিকাতা ১৮৯৮ [*Calcutta*, 1898.] 8°. **14043. dd. 8.**

—— सुश्रुतसंहिता । The Suçruta-saṁhitā . . . Translated from the original Sanskrit by Dr. A. F. R. Hoernle. 1897, *etc.* *See* ACADEMIES, *etc.*—Calcutta.—*Asiatic Society of Bengal.* Bibliotheca Indica. New Series. [Vol. 139.] 1848, *etc.* 8°. **14002. a. (vol. 139.)**

In progress.

—— *See* ḌALLAṆA MIŞRA. निबन्धसंग्रहाख्या सुश्रुतसंहिताया व्याख्या *etc.* (Nibandhasaṅgraha. A commentary on the Sushrutasanhita, *etc.*) 1891. 8°. **14043. d. 48.**

—— Susruta Sutra-sthana. 1st part. Translated [verbally into Sinhalese] under the instruction of . . . M. Nanissara . . . by S. A. Fernando. [With the Sanskrit text.] (සුශ්‍රුතසූත්‍රස්ථානය.) pp. 80. *Colombo*, 1896. 8°. **14043. e. 32.**

—— Nidanasthana of the Susrita [*sic*]. Translated [in a Sinhalese *sannaya*, appended to the complete Sanskrit text,] and edited by H. D. Abhayawardhane Appuhamy, *etc.* (නිදානස්ථානය.) pp. ii. 92. *Colombo*, 1891. 8°. **14043. e. 25.**

Uniform with a similar edition of the Sarīrasthāna *issued from the same press.*

SŪTRAKṚIDAÑGA. Sûtrakritânga. [The second *aṅga* of the Jain scriptures. Translated from the Prakrit, with notes, *etc.*, by H. Jacobi.] 1895. *See* MUELLER (F. M.). The Sacred Books of the East, *etc.* Vol. xlv., pp. 233-435. 1879, *etc.* 8°. **2003. b. (vol. 45.)**

The name of this Aṅga (in Prakrit Sūyagaḍaṅga) *is in Sanskrit* Sūtrakṛidaṅga, *in which form it appears in Umāsvāti's Tattvārthasūtrabhāshya and other authorities.*

—— महावीरस्तुति विगेरे *etc.* [Mahāvīrastuti (*scil.* i. 6 of this Aṅga), also styled Vīrastuti and Puchchhissuṇaṃ. With Gujarati interpretation and notes. Preceded by a Gujarati life of Mahāvīra. Followed by the Daşavaikālikasūtra i.-iv., and Uttarādhyayana iii.-iv., *etc.* Edited by Kachrābhāī Gopāladāsa.] pp. xvi. 88. अमदावाद १८९२ [*Ahmadabad*, 1892.] 12°. **14100. a. 14.**

—— શ્રી મહાવીર સ્તુતિ *etc.* [Mahāvīrastuti. Followed by the Chhūṭakagāthās and some Gujarati verses.] pp. i. 16. સુરત ૧૮૯૩ [*Surat*, 1893.] 12°. **14144. c. 8.(2.)**

—— પુચ્છિસ્સુણં (वीरस्तुति, આર્દ્રકુમારના અધ્યયનનો . . . કથા) [Mahāvīrastuti. Followed by *srutaskandha* II. vi., styled Ārdrakumārādhyayana or Adda-ajjh°. With Gujarati translations and notes.] *See* JAINAJÑĀNAPRAKĀṢA. जैन ज्ञान प्रकाश *etc.* [Jainajñānaprakāṣa.] pt. i., pp. 1-53. [1898.] 12°. **14100. a. 19.**

SUTTANIPĀTA. *See* SUTTAPIṬAKA.—*Khuddakanikāya.*

SUTTAPIṬAKA.

ENTIRE TEXT.

สุตฺตนฺตปิฏก *etc.* [Suttapiṭaka, or Suttantapiṭaka. Comprising the Dīghanikāya, Majjhimanikāya, Saṃyuttanikāya, Aṅguttaranikāya, and the Khuddakapāṭha, Dhammapada, Udāna, Itivuttaka, Suttanipāta, Mahāniddesa, Chūlaniddesa, and Paṭisambhidāmagga of the Khuddakanikāya.] 20 vols. ๑๑๓ [*Bangkok*, 1894.] 8°. **14098. cc. 9-28.**

Forms part of the King of Siam's edition of the Tipiṭaka.

Buddhist Pali Texts. With a translation into Sinhalese. Edited under the direction of W. Arthur De Silva . . . Vol. 1 (2, *etc.*). Digha Nikaya, [in Pali, with] Sinhalese translation by W. A. Samarasekera. (සිංහල සන්නය සහිත පාලි ත්‍රිපිටක ධර්ම. දීඝනිකාය) *Colombo*, *London*, 2447, *etc.* [1903, *etc.*] 8°. **14099. bbb.**

In progress.

သုတ္တန်ပိဋကတ်။ . . . သုတ်သီလက္ခန်ပါဠိတော်နိဿယ။ [Suttapiṭaka. Vols. i.-iv., the Dīghanikāya, with the Burmese interpretation of Ariyālaṅkāra of Neyin. Edited by Hsaya Hbi, Hsaya Ko Aung Min, and Hsaya Ko Kyaw.] ရန်ကုန် [*Rangoon*,] 1904, *etc.* 8°. **14099. aa. 8.**

In progress.

SUTTAPIṬAKA (*continued*).

ENTIRE TEXT (*continued*).

See PAṆḌITADDHAJA, known as MAING-KAING HSAYA. တိပိဋကဝိနိစ္ဆယကျမ်း *etc.* [Tipiṭakavinichchhaya-kyan.] 1900-1901. 8°. **14302. i. 19.**

SELECTIONS.

[For the stanzas selected from the Suttapiṭaka which are comprised in the Paritta :] *See* PARITTA.

See SĀDHUNARADHAMMA-SĀ-TAN. သာဓုနရဓမ္မသာ-တမ်း [Sādhunaradhamma-sā-tan. A lectionary of *suttas, etc.*, with Burmese commentaries.] [1897.] 8°. **14098. ccc. 26.(4.)**

See WARD (E.). Light from the East. Being selections from the teachings of the Buddha[, chiefly the Suttapiṭaka] *etc.* 1901. 12°. **4506. a. 7.**

See WARREN (H. C.). Buddhism in Translations, *etc.* [Being select passages translated from the Suttapiṭaka, *etc.*] 1896. 8°. [*Harvard Oriental Series.*] **14003. l. 3. (vol. 3.)**

See WINDISCH (W. O. E.). Māra und Buddha, *etc.* [Illustrated by extracts and translations from the Suttapiṭaka, *etc.*] 1895. 4°. **759. e. 1.**

අවවාදරත්න සඞ්ගහව *etc.* [Avavādaratna-saṅgrahava. The "Golden Rules of Buddhism," compiled by H. S. Olcott from the Suttapiṭaka. Translated into Sinhalese and published with the original Pali stanzas by D. J. Subasiṃha.] pp. 26. [*Colombo,*] 1891. 12°. **14098. a. 32.(3.)**

The Golden Rules of Buddhism. Compiled from the Bana books. By Henry S. Olcott. [In an English translation.] Third and revised edition. pp. ii. 22. *Madras*, 1902. 12°. **14098. a. 32.(4.)**

Buddhistische Anthologie. Texte aus dem Pāli-Kanon, zum ersten Mal übersetzt von Dr. Karl Eugen Neumann. pp. xxviii. 236, i. *Leiden*, 1892. 8°. **14098. c. 58.**

Sútra Saŋgraha. [Suttasaṅgaha. An ancient collection of 85 *suttas* from the Suttapiṭaka.]

SELECTIONS (*continued*).

Edited [with glosses] by Revd. Warápiṭiyé Sugatapála, *etc.* (සුත්තසඞ්ගහො) pp. iii. i. 148, ii. *Kelaniya*, 1890-1895. 8°. **14098. dd. 6.**

සුත්තසඞ්ගහට්ඨකථා *etc.* [Suttasaṅgahaṭṭhakathā. A Pali commentary on the Suttasaṅgaha. Edited by Varāpiṭiyē Sugatapāla.] pt. i. pp. 80. 2441 [*Colombo*, 1897.] 8°. **14098. dd. 15.**

Sutra Sangraha. [Being portions of the Suttasaṅgaha, translated by D. J. Subasiṃha.] 1894. *See* PERIODICAL PUBLICATIONS. — *Colombo.* The Buddhist, *etc.* Vol. vi., no. 31-50. 1888, *etc.* 8°. **P.P. 636. cn. (vol. 6.)**

သုတ်ကမ္မဋ္ဌာန်းအမျိုးမျိုး [Thôk-kammaṭṭhān-amyo-myo. A collection of thirteen *suttas* and other excerpts from the Suttapiṭaka, with Burmese version and commentary by the Hnegyo Pongyi. Followed by the Sikkhāpadavinichchhaya-anuttānapadappakāsanī, a Burmese tract elucidating difficulties in the Sikkhāpadavinichchhaya, by the same writer.] pp. 92. ရန်ကုန် ၁၂၆၀ [*Rangoon*, 1898.] 8°. **14098. ccc. 26.(5.)**

AṄGUTTARANIKĀYA.

The Aṅguttara-Nikāya. Part III. Edited by Prof. E. Hardy. Pañcaka-nipāta, and Chakka-nipāta. (Part IV . . . Sattaka-nipāta, Aṭṭhaka-nipāta, and Navaka-nipāta. Part V . . . Dasaka-nipāta, and Ekādasaka-nipāta.) 1896-1900. 8°. *See* ACADEMIES, *etc.*—London.—*Pali Text Society.* SUTTAPIṬAKA. **14098. b. 27.**

අඞ්ගුත්තර නිකායො *etc.* (Anguttara Nikaya. Collated and revised by H. Devamitta Thera, *etc.*) pt. i. pp. 80. *Colombo*, 2436 [1893.] 8°. **14098. d. 41.**

Anguttara-Nikaya. Translated [to the end of I. i.] . . . by L. C. Wijesinha, Mudaliyar. (Translated [from I. ii. onward] . . . by Mudaliyar E. R. Gooneratna.) 1891, 1896, *etc.* *See* PERIODICAL PUBLICATIONS.—*Colombo.* The Buddhist, *etc.* Vol. iii., no. 19, Vol. viii., nos. 30-52, *etc.* 1888, *etc.* 8°. **P.P. 636. cn. (vol. 3, 8, etc.)**

Unfinished.

Aṅguttaranikāya (*continued*).

See Buddhaghosa. [*Manorathapūraṇī.*] මනොරථපූරණී *etc.* [Manorathapūraṇī. The commentary on the Aṅguttaranikāya.] 1893-1896. 8°. **14098. c. 64.**

දානුප්පත්තිසූත්‍රය *etc.* [Dānuppattisutta (*i.e.* Nipāta VIII, Dānavagga, § 35). Edited with a Sinhalese interpretation by Suvaṇṇajotyāsabha.] pp. 7, i. කොළඹ [*Colombo,*] 1892. 8°. **14098. c. 53.(4.)**

කාලකාරාම සූත්‍රය [Kālakārāmasutta (*i.e.* Nipāta IV, Uruvelavagga, § 24). With a Sinhalese commentary.] pp. i. 54, i. *Colombo,* 1889. 8°. **14098. c. 53.(2.)**

කාලාමසූත්‍රය *etc.* [Kālāmasutta (*i.e.* Nipāta III, Mahāvagga, § 65). Followed by a Sinhalese commentary.] pp. 29, ii. මහනුවර [*Kandy,*] 1893. 8°. **14098. c. 53.(5.)**

කම්මනිදානසූත්‍රය *etc.* [Karmanidānasūtraya (*i.e.* Kammanidānasutta, or Nipāta III, Devadūtavāgga, § 33). Followed by Buddhaghosa's commentary, from his Manorathapūraṇī, and by a word-for-word interpretation in Sinhalese.] pp. 20, i. *Colombo,* 1897. 8°. **14098. c. 73.(6.)**

The Maithunasaṇyoga Sutraya [*i.e.* Methunasaṃyogasutta, or Nipāta VII, Mahāyaññavagga, § 47]. With [Sinhalese] paraphrase by Rev. T. Nanawimala Tissa . . . මෛථුනසංයොග සූත්‍රය *etc.* pp. 16. කොළඹ 2440 [*Colombo,* 1897.] 8°. **14098. c. 72.(4.)**

මල්ලිකොවාද සූත්‍රය *etc.* [Mallikovādasutta (*i.e.* Nipāta IV, Mahāvagga, § 197). Preceded by the Namaskāra-gāthās, with other religious verses, and introductions in Sinhalese, and followed by a Sinhalese interpretation and other illustrative matter.] pp. 40. [*Colombo,*] 1894. 8°. **14098. d. 45.(1.)**

Imperfect at the end.

Praptakarma Sutra [*i.e.* the Pattakammasutta, or Nipāta IV, Pattakammavagga, § 61] . . . ප්‍රාප්තකම්මසූත්‍රය *etc.* [With the Pali Aṭṭhakathā and a Sinhalese interpretation and commentary.] pp. 46, i. [*Colombo,*] 1893. 8°. **14098. c. 53.(6.)**

Aṅguttaranikāya (*continued*).

සප්පුරිසදාන සූත්‍රය *etc.* [Sappurisadānasutta (Nipāta V, Tikaṇḍakivagga, § 148). Followed by a Sinhalese word-for-word translation, paraphrases, *etc.*] pp. i. 20. කොළඹ [*Colombo,*] 1897. 8°. **14098. c. 73.(8.)**

සප්තාර්‍යධනසූත්‍ර සත්තරිය *etc.* [Saptāryadhanasūtra, or Sattāriyadhanasutta (Nipāta VII, Dhanavagga, § i. 6). Followed by a Sinhalese word-for-word translation.] pp. 24. කොළඹ [*Colombo,*] 1896. 8°. **14098. ccc. 4.(2.)**

Wrongly paginated, the numbers running 1-8 *and* 17-24, *though nothing is missing.*

සප්තසූර්‍යොද්ගමනසූත්‍රය *etc.* [Saptasūryodgamanasūtra, or Sattasūriyuggamanasutta (Nipāta VII, Mahāvagga, § 62). Followed by a word-for-word Sinhalese interpretation, and a Sinhalese discourse, styled Lokavināsaya, on the end of the present and the beginning of the next world. Second edition.] pp. 56. පෑලියගොඩ [*Peliyagoda,*] 1898. 8°. **14098. ccc. 4.(4.)**

සරභ සූත්‍රය *etc.* [Sarabhasutta (Nipāta III, Mahāvagga, § 64). Followed by Buddhaghosa's commentary from the Manorathapūraṇī and by a Sinhalese word-for-word interpretation and a translation.] pp. 21, i. කොළඹ [*Colombo,*] 1897. 8°. **14098. c. 73.(7.)**

වෙලාමසූත්‍රය *etc.* [Velāmasutta (Nipāta IX, Sīhanādavagga, § 20). Followed by a Sinhalese word-for-word interpretation.] pp. 16. *Colombo,* 1892. 8°. **14098. ccc. 4.(1.)**

ဝေလာမသုတ် *etc.* [Velāmasutta. With Burmese version and commentary.] *See* Paṇḍitaddhaja, known as Maingkaing Hsaya. တိပိဋကဝိနိစ္ဆယကျမ်း *etc.* [Tipiṭakavinichchhayakyan.] Vol. II, pp. 309-324. 1900-1901. 8°. **14302. i. 19.**

ව්‍යාඝ්‍රපද්‍යසූත්‍රය *etc.* [Vyāghrapadyasūtra, or Byagghapajjasutta (*i.e.* Nipāta VIII, Sa-ādhānavagga, § 54). With a Sinhalese interpretation.] pp. 17. [*Peliyagoda,*] 1893. 8°. **14098. ccc. 2.(2.)**

AṄGUTTARANIKĀYA (*continued*).

See PAÑÑĀBHISIRI SADDHAMMADDHAJA. ဒွတ္တိံသာကာရဒီပကကျမ်း [Dvattiṃsākāradīpaka. A Burmese work upon the text Aṅguttaranikāya I. xxi. 1.] 1881. 8°. **14300. d. 20.(1.)**

DĪGHANIKĀYA.

Dialogues of the Buddha. [Comprising the Brahmajāla, Sāmaññaphala, Ambaṭṭha, Soṇadaṇḍa, Kūṭadanta, Mahāli, Jāliya, Kassapa-sihanāda, Poṭṭhapāda, Subha, Kevaddha, Lohichcha, and Tevijja Suttas.] Translated from the Pâli by T. W. Rhys Davids. pp. xxiv. 334. 1899. *See* MUELLER (F. M.). The Sacred Books of the Buddhists, *etc.* Vol. ii. 1895, *etc.* 8°. **14003. ccc. (vol. 2.)**

Chakkawatti Sihanada Sutta. [Forming iii. (Pāṭikavagga 3) of this Nikāya.] With a Singhalese praphrase [*sic*] . . . චක්කවත්ති සිංහනාද සූත්‍රය. pp. xv. 61. *Colombo*, 1895. 8°. **14098. c. 69.(8.)**

ဒသုတ္တရသုတ်ပါဠိတော်နိဿယ [Dasuttarasutta (*scil.* Pāṭikavagga 11). With Burmese paraphrase by Ū Guṇinda.] pp. 155, i. ရန်ကုန် ၁၂၅၇ [*Rangoon*, 1895.] 8°. **14098. ccc. 9.(3.)**

ဂိဟိဝိနယကျမ်း *etc.* [Gihivinaya, or Sigālovādasutta (Pāṭikavagga 8). With Burmese paraphrase. Edited by Shwe Thā Ū.] pp. i. i. iii. 45. စစ်တွေ ၁၂၅၆ [*Akyab*, 1894.] 8°. **14098. ccc. 21.(1.)**

මහාසමයසූත්‍රය *etc.* [Mahāsamayasutta (*i.e.* ii. 7, or Mahāvagga 7, of this Nikāya). With a Sinhalese *udāna-kathā* or introduction, interpretation, *etc.*] pp. iv. 28, i. [*Colombo*,] 1891. 8°. **14098. c. 69.(2.)**

මහාසමයසූත්‍රය ආදී සූත්‍රහත *etc.* [Mahāsamayasutta. Followed by 6 *suttas* of the Suttanipāta. With Sinhalese interpretations, *etc.*] pp. ii. 70. කොළඹ [*Colombo*,] 1895. 8°. **14098. d. 45.(2.)**

මහාසතිපට්ඨානසූත්‍රය. [Mahāsatipaṭṭhānasutta (*scil.* Mahāvagga 9).] *See* DE ALWIS GUṆATILAKA

DĪGHANIKĀYA (*continued*).

(*Don* A.). බෞද්ධප්‍රතිපත්තිදීපනිය *etc.* [Bauddhapratipattidīpaniya.] pp. 23-59. 1890. 12°. **14165. a. 58.(5.)**

—— —— 1895. 12°. **14098. a. 29.(2.)**

—— —— 1897. 12°. **14098. a. 29.(3.)**

Satipattana [*sic*] Sutta. Sermon on the Four Earnest Meditations. [With translation and notes by A. E. Buultjens.] 1893. *See* PERIODICAL PUBLICATIONS. — *Colombo*. The Buddhist, *etc.* Vol. v., no. 32-41. 1888, *etc.* 8°. **P.P. 636. cn. (vol. 5.)**

မဟာသတိပဋ္ဌာနသုတ်ပါဠိအနက် *etc.* [Mahāsatipaṭṭhānasutta. With Burmese commentary by Chakkindābhisiri. Followed by (1) the Chaturārakkhadhamma, a series of Pali stanzas on the observance of the four principles of *buddhānussati*, *mettā*°., *asubhā*°., and *maraṇā*°., with commentary and Burmese translation by Chakkindābhisiri; (2) the Ovāda-mettā-sā, a Burmese dissertation by the Shwegyin Hsaya on the *kammaṭṭhānas*, *etc.*; and (3) the Ngā-yan-min-payeik or Machchharājaparitta, *i.e.* the Chariyāpiṭaka III. x., with Burmese preface.] pp. 161. ရန်ကုန် ၁၂၅၇ [*Rangoon*, 1895.] 8°. **14098. ccc. 9.(2.)**

See BUDDHAGHOSA. [*Sumaṅgalavilāsinī.*] Buddhagosha's [*sic*] Commentary on the Maha Satipaṭṭhana Sutta. 1894. 8°. [*The Buddhist.*] **P.P. 636. cn. (vol. 6.)**

KHUDDAKANIKĀYA.

[**Chariyāpiṭaka.**] စရိယာပိဋကတ် *etc.* [Chariyāpiṭaka. With a Burmese exegetical commentary by Kaviñāṇaddhaja.] pp. ii. iii. 240. မန္တလေး [*Mandalay*,] 1899. 8°. **14098. c. 29.(2.)**

—— ငါးရံ့မင်းပရိတ် *etc.* [Ngā-yan-min-payeik, or Machchharājaparitta (*i.e.* the Chariyāpiṭaka III. x.). With a Burmese preface styled Ngā-yan-min-payeik-ī atthuppatti.] *See* above,

KHUDDAKANIKĀYA. [*Chariyāpiṭaka.*] (*cont.*)

DĪGHANIKĀYA. မဟာသတိပဋ္ဌာနသုတ် *etc.* [Mahāsatipaṭṭhānasutta.] pp. 156-161. [1895.] 8°. **14098. ccc. 9.(2.)**

—— မစ္ဆပရိတ္တံ [Machchhaparitta.] *See* PARITTA. —*Burmese Editions.* မဟာပရိတ် *etc.* [Mahāparitta.] pp. 29-31. 1898. 12°. **14098. a. 33.**

[Dhammapada.] ධම්මපදං . . . The Dhammapada, or Principles of Morality. Revised by Rev. H. Dewamitta. pp. ii. 29. *Colombo*, 2429 [1886.] 8°. **14098. d. 44.**

—— धम्मपदं। Dhammapadam. [With the commentary of Buddhaghosa.] For the first time edited by Rai Çarat Chandra Dās . . . and Rev. Seelakkhandha Thera. pp. 114. 1899. *See* ACADEMIES, *etc.*—Calcutta.—*Buddhist Text Society of India.* Buddhist Texts, *etc.* 1894, *etc.* 8°. **14004. c. (vol. 1, no. 4.)**

The first part of this edition, down to the end of the Bālavagga, appeared in the Journal of the Buddhist Text Society.

—— The Dhammapada. Being a collection of moral verses in Pāli. Edited a second time with a literal Latin translation and notes for the use of Pāli students. By V. Fausbøll. pp. xvi. 94. *London, Copenhagen* [printed], 1900. 8°. **14098. b. 23.**

—— ধম্মপদ। অর্থাৎ ধম্মপদ নামক পালি গ্রন্থের মূল, অন্বয়, সংস্কৃত ব্যাখ্যা ও বঙ্গানুবাদ *etc.* [Dhammapada. The Pali text in Bengali characters, edited with *anvaya*, Sanskrit paraphrase, and Bengali version by Chāruchandra Vasu.] pp. ii. xii. 237. কলিকাতা ১৯০৪ [*Calcutta*, 1904.] 12°. **14098. a. 43.**

—— Le Manuscrit Kharoṣṭhī du Dhammapada. Les fragments Dutreuil de Rhins, par M. Émile Senart. 1898. *See* ACADEMIES, *etc.* — Paris.—*Société Asiatique.* Journal Asiatique, *etc.* Ser. ix., tom. 12. pp. 193-308. 1822, *etc.* 8°. **Ac. 8808. (Ser. ix., tom. 12.)**

—— Dhammapada: being Footprints in the Way of Life, the system of ethic law bequeathed by Gautama Buddha. [A translation of the Dhammapada founded upon that of Max Müller.] . . . Together with . . . extracts . . . reflections

KHUDDAKANIKĀYA. [*Dhammapada.*] (*cont.*)

and observations, spiritual and philosophical, by J. P. C(ooke). pp. 32, 16, iv. *Boston*, [*Mass.*, 1890.] 8°. **4503. bb. 23.(4.)**

—— Worte der Wahrheit—Dhammapadam—Eine zum Buddhistischen Canon gehörige Spruchsammlung, in deutscher [metrical] Uebersetzung, herausgegeben von Leopold von Schroeder. pp. xxii. 150. *Leipzig*, 1892. 12°. **14098. a. 25.**

—— Der Wahrheitpfad. Ein buddhistisches Denkmal . . . in den Versmaassen des Originals uebersetzt von Karl Eugen Neumann. pp. viii. 182. *Leipzig*, 1893. 8°. **14098. c. 61.**

—— The Dhammapada. A collection of verses. Being one of the canonical books of the Buddhists. Translated from Pâli by F. Max Müller. (The Sutta-nipâta . . . Translated from Pâli by V. Fausböll.) Second edition. pp. lxiii. 100, xvii. 212. 1898. *See* MUELLER (F. M.). The Sacred Books of the East, *etc.* Vol. x. 1879, *etc.* 8°. **2003. a. (vol. 10.)**

—— Hymns of the Faith. Dhammapada. Being an ancient anthology preserved in the Short Collection of the sacred scriptures of the Buddhists. Translated from the Pâli by Albert J. Edmunds. pp. xiii. 109. *London*, [*Chicago* printed], 1902. 8°. **14098. c. 74.**

—— *See* BUDDHAGHOSA. [*Manorathapūraṇī.*] The story of the merchant Ghosaka . . . [as given in the Manorathapūraṇī and the Dhammapadaṭṭhakathā], *etc.* 1898. 8°. [*Journal of the Royal Asiatic Society.*] **Ac. 8820/3 & 2098. a, b.**

—— Excursus [containing extracts from Max Müller's translation of the Dhammapada]. *See* ROOT (E. D.). Sakya Buddha, *etc.* pp. 143-171. 1880. 8°. **4503. b. 35.**

[Jātaka.] The Jātaka together with its commentary: being tales of the anterior births of Gotama Buddha . . . Edited . . . by V. Fausbøll, *etc.* (Vol. vii. Index to the Jātaka and its commentary, containing a complete index of proper names and titles, together with a list of

KHUDDAKANIKĀYA. [*Jātaka.*] (*cont.*)

the introductory Gāthās and an index of parallel verses. By Dines Andersen. [With a *post-scriptum* by V. Fausbøll.]) 7 vols. *London*, 1877-1897. 8°. **14098. d. 23.**

—— The Jātaka, or Stories of the Buddha's Former Births. Translated from the Pāli by various hands, under the editorship of Professor E. B. Cowell. Vol. i., translated by Robert Chalmers. (Vol. ii., translated by W. H. D. Rouse. Vol. iii., translated by H. T. Francis ... and R. A. Neil. Vol. iv., translated by W. H. D. Rouse.) *Cambridge*, 1895, *etc.* 8°. **14098. dd. 8.**

In progress.

—— *See* GILMORE (D. C.). A Brief Vocabulary to ... Jatakas I-XL, *etc.* 1895. 12°. **14098. a. 27.**

—— Nine Jatakas. Pali text with vocabulary by Levi H. Elwell. pp. i. i. 120. *Boston* [*Mass.*], *Amherst* [printed], 1886. 16°. **14098. a. 24.**

—— Aus den Geschichten früherer Existenzen Buddhas ... Übersetzt von Paul Steinthal. 1893, *etc.* *See* PERIODICAL PUBLICATIONS.—*Berlin.* Zeitschrift für vergleichende Litteraturgeschichte, *etc.* 1887, *etc.* 8°. **P.P. 4748. ma. (Bd. 6, ff.)**

In progress.

—— Two Jātakas: Temiya and Mahājanaka. For class use. Based upon Burmese MSS. Edited by James Gray. pp. 87. *Calcutta*, 1903. 12°. **14098. a. 42.**

—— අසදිස ජාතකං [Asadisajātaka.] *See* RĀJĀDHIRĀJASIṂHA. Rājādhirājasinha's Poem, the Asadrisajātakaya, *etc.* 1889. 8°. **14165. i. 18.**

—— Bhūridatta Jātaka. [Translated from the Burmese version, with the *gāthās* in the original Pali.] By R. F. St. Andrew St. John. 1892. *See* ACADEMIES, *etc.* — London. — *Royal Asiatic Society of Great Britain and Ireland.* The Journal ... 1892. pp. 77-139. 1834, *etc.* 8°. **Ac. 8820/3 & 2098. a, b.**

—— Mahājanakajātakaṁ, or the Buddhistic story of King Mahājanaka. Based on Burmese manuscripts of Buddhaghosa's commentary on the "Jātakaṁ." Edited by James Gray ... With English translation. pp. 47. *Rangoon, Calcutta* [printed], 1901. 12°. **14098. a. 40.**

The English translation was published separately, and is not in this volume.

—— Mahājanakajātakaṁ. Translation [by James Gray]. pp. 52. [*Rangoon,*] *Calcutta* [printed,] 1901. 12°. **14098. a. 4.(3.)**

—— သမဏဘဒြကထာဂါထာ [Samaṇa-bhadrakathā-gāthā. Eight stanzas from the Soṇa-jātaka (Nipāta lx.), with Burmese interpretation by Javana Mahāthera.] *See* MINGUN-ALAY HSAYA. ပဉ္စစတ္တာလီသပုစ္ဆာ *etc.* [Pañchachattālīsa-puchchāvisajjanā.] [1892.] 8°. **14300. d. 19.(4.)**

—— Temiyajātakaṁ or The Buddhistic Story of Prince Temiya. Based on Burmese manuscripts of Buddhaghosa's commentary on the "Jātakaṁ." Edited by James Gray. pp. 38. *Rangoon, Calcutta* [printed], 1900. 12°. **14098. a. 38.**

—— Temiyajātakaṁ. Translation [by James Gray]. pp. 43. [*Rangoon,*] *Calcutta* [printed,] 1900. 12°. **14098. a. 4.(2.)**

[**Petavatthu.**] ප්‍රෙතවස්තු ප්‍රකරණය *etc.* [Petavatthu, or Pretavastuprakaraṇaya. With Sinhalese commentary by Jinavaṃsa Paññāsāra. Edited by Saddhānanda of Kosgoda.] pt. 1, 3, 5. කොළඹ [*Colombo,*] 1893-1896. 8°. **14098. c. 63.(2.)**

—— *See* ACADEMIES, *etc.*—London.—*Pali Text Society.* DHAMMAPĀLA. Dhammapāla's Paramattha-dīpanī, Part III. Being the commentary on the Petavatthu, *etc.* 1894. 8°. **14098. b. 35.**

[**Suttanipāta.**] සුත්තනිපාතො *etc.* [Suttanipāta. With the commentary Paramatthajotikā of Buddhaghosa. Edited by Valāṇē Dhammānanda.] pt. 1. pp. 80. කොලම්බ [*Colombo,*] 1897. 8°. **14098. ccc. 5.**

Extends to the middle of the Khaggavisāṇasutta.

—— The Sutta-nipâta ... Translated from Pâli [with an introduction] by V. Fausböll. Second

KHUDDAKANIKĀYA. [*Suttanipāta.*] (*cont.*)

edition. pp. xvii. 212. 1898. *See* MUELLER (F. M.). The Sacred Books of the East, *etc.* Vol. x., pt. 2. 1879, *etc.* 8°. **2003. a. (vol. 10.)**

—— Die Reden Gotamo Buddho's aus der Sammlung der Bruchstücke Suttanipāto des Pāli-Kanons, übersetzt von Karl Eugen Neumann. pp. xii. 410. *Leipzig,* 1905. 8°. **14098. dd. 29.**

—— සම්මා පරිබ්බාජනීය සූත්‍රය. (කලහ විවාද සූත්‍රය *etc.*) [Sammāparibbājanīyasutta, Kalahavivādas°., Chūḷavyūhas°., Mahāvyūhas°., Tuvaṭakas°., and Purābhedas°. With Sinhalese interpretations.] *See* above, DĪGHANIKĀYA. මහාසමයසූත්‍රය *etc.* [Mahāsamayasutta, *etc.*] pp. 28-68. 1895. 8°. **14098. d. 45.(2.)**

—— ආලවකසූත්‍රය *etc.* [Ālavakasutta (Suttanipāta I. 10). Followed by a Sinhalese word-for-word translation. Second edition.] pp. iii. 60. *Colombo,* 1897. 8°. **14098. c. 73.(4.)**

—— චුන්දසූත්‍රය [Chundasutta (Suttanipāta I. 5). With a Sinhalese word-for-word translation.] pp. 6. කොළඹ [*Colombo,*] 1896. 8°. **14098. c. 72.(6.)**

—— ධම්මිකසූත්‍රය *etc.* [Dhammikasutta (Suttanipāta II. 14). Followed by Buddhaghosa's *aṭṭhakathā* and a Sinhalese interpretation.] pp. 25. කොළඹ [*Colombo,*] 1895. 8°. **14098. c. 69.(5.)**

—— කසීභාරද්වාජ සූත්‍රය *etc.* [Kasībhāradvājasutta (Suttanipāta I. 4). Followed by a Sinhalese word-for-word gloss and a translation.] pp. ii. 25. කොළඹ [*Colombo,*] 1896. 8°. **14098. c. 72.(5.)**

—— ကာယဝိစ္ဆိန္ဒနိကသုတ်ပါဠိတော်။ [Kāyavichchhindanikasutta, *i.e.* Vijayasutta (I. xi.). With Burmese interpretation by Chakkindābhisiri.] *See* VINANDĀSABHA. သီလဝိသောဓနီကျမ်း။ *etc.* [Sīlavisodhanī.] pp. 174-228. [1905.] 8°. **14099. b. 5.**

—— මහාමඞ්ගලසූත්‍රය *etc.* [Mahāmaṅgalasutta (Suttanipāta II. 4). With an ancient

KHUDDAKANIKĀYA. [*Suttanipāta.*] (*cont.*)

Sinhalese commentary. Edited by Hōkandara Devānanda.] pp. iv. 74, iv. [*Colombo,*] 1894. 8°. **14098. d. 42.(3.)**

—— မင်္ဂလသုတ်ဋီကာနှင့်...ငါးဌာနအဓိကရဏာသကကျမ်းခြောက်ပုစ္ဆာဝိသဇ္ဇနာ *etc.* [Mahāmaṅgalasutta. With Burmese commentary. Followed by Burmese Questions and Answers by Ū Āsabha, together with Rulings by the Maungdaung Hsaya, *etc.*] pp. 72. ရန်ကုန် ၁၂၅၆ [*Rangoon,* 1894.] 8°. **14300. d. 22.(7.)**

—— —— [Another edition.] pp. 72. ရန်ကုန် ၁၂၅၉ [*Rangoon,* 1897.] 8°. **14300. d. 19.(8.)**

—— [For Burmese collections of Burmese-Pali texts including the Mahāmaṅgalasutta with its Burmese translation, see under the following headings :]

HKYAUK SAUNG TWÈ.

HSAY SAUNG TWÈ.

KO SAUNG TWÈ.

NGĀ SAUNG TWÈ.

TA-HSÈ-HNIT SAUNG TWÈ.

TA-HSÈ-THÔN SAUNG TWÈ.

—— ပဓာနသုတ်ပါဠိ. [Padhānasutta (Suttanipāta III. 2). With Burmese version by Ñāṇālaṅkāra.] *See* TILOKA. အရိယာမဂ္ဂဒီပနီကျမ်း *etc.* [Ariyamaggadīpanī.] pp. 301-333. [1899.] 8°. **14300. d. 28.(4.)**

—— ရာဟုလသုတ် [Rāhulasutta (Suttanipāta II. 11). With Burmese interpretation.] *See* JAYANTĀBHIVAṂSA. သဒ္ဓမ္မပါလမေဓာနီ *etc.* [Saddhammapālamedhanī.] pp. 39-45. [1872.] 8°. **14300. d. 28.(1.)**

—— ရာဟုလသုတ် [Rāhulasutta. With Burmese interpretation.] *See* PAYĀ-SHI-HKO. ဘုရားရှိခိုး *etc.* [Payā-shi-hko.] pp. 40-47. [1893.] 8°. **14098. ccc. 16.(2.)**

—— —— [1895.] 8°. **14098. ccc. 16.(3.)**

KHUDDAKANIKĀYA. [*Theragāthā.*]

[Theragāthā.] Die Lieder der Mönche und Nonnen Gotamo Buddho's, aus den Theragāthā und Therīgāthā, zum ersten Mal übersetzt von Karl Eugen Neumann. pp. viii. 392. *Berlin, Leipzig* [printed], 1899. 8°. **14098. dd. 16.**

—— သမဏပဋိရူပ *etc.* [Samaṇapaṭirūpa. Nine stanzas from Nipāta x. of the Theragāthā, with Burmese interpretation by Javana Mahāthera.] *See* MINGUN-ALAY HSAYA. ပဉ္စစတ္တာလီသပုစ္ဆာ *etc.* [Pañchachattālīsa-puchchhāvisajjanā.] [1892.] 8°. **14300. d. 19.(4.)**

[Therīgāthā.] Die Lieder der Mönche und Nonnen Gotamo Buddho's, aus den Theragāthā und Therīgāthā . . . übersetzt von Karl Eugen Neumann. 1899. 8°. *See* above, [*Theragāthā.*] **14098. dd. 16.**

—— *See* ACADEMIES, *etc.* — London. — *Pali Text Society.* DHAMMAPĀLA. Paramattha Dīpanī . . . Part V. The commentary on the Therīgāthā, *etc.* 1893. 8°. **14098. b. 35.**

[Udāna.] The Udāna, or The Solemn Utterances of the Buddha. Translated from the Pali by . . . D. M. Strong. pp. i. viii. 129. *London,* 1902. 8°. **14098. ccc. 36.**

[Vimānavatthu.] විමානවත්ථුප්‍රකරණය *etc.* [Vimānavatthu. With a paraphrastic Sinhalese commentary by Gammullē Ratanapāla. Edited by Telvattē Sīlānanda.] pt. 1-3. pp. 48. [*Colombo,*] 1890. 8°. **14098. c. 63.(1.)**

—— *See* ACADEMIES, *etc.* — London. — *Pali Text Society.* DHAMMAPĀLA. Dhammapāla's Paramattha-dīpanī, Part IV. Being the commentary on the Vimāna-vatthu, *etc.* 1901. 8°. **14098. b. 35.**

MAJJHIMANIKĀYA.

The Majjhima-Nikāya. Edited by Robert Chalmers. Vol. II. (Vol. III . . . With indices . . . by Mabel Bode.) 1896-1902. 8°. *See* ACADEMIES, *etc.*—London.—*Pali Text Society.* SUTTAPIṬAKA. **14098. b. 25.**

MAJJHIMANIKĀYA (*continued*).

මජ්ඣිමනිකායො *etc.* [Majjhimanikāya. Edited by Saraṇaṅkara and Paññāratana.] pt. 1. pp. i. 80. [*Colombo,*] 1895. 8°. **14098. dd. 11.**

Die Reden Gotamo Buddho's aus der Mittleren Sammlung Majjhimanikāyo des Pāli-Kanons. Zum ersten Mal uebersetzt von Karl Eugen Neumann. 3 vols. *Leipzig,* 1896-1902. 8°. **14098. dd. 13.**

—— [Another copy.] **4504. h.**

See BUDDHAGHOSA. [*Papañchasūdanī.*] පපඤ්චසූදනී *etc.* [Papañchasūdanī. Being the commentary on the Majjhimanikāya.] 1898. 8°. **14098. ccc. 8.**

The Nativity of the Buddha. [Being the text of the Achchhariyabbhutasutta, *i.e.* I. iii. (Uparipaṇṇāsa, Suññatāvagga), § 3.] By Robert Chalmers. 1895. *See* ACADEMIES, *etc.*—London.—*Royal Asiatic Society of Great Britain and Ireland.* The Journal . . . 1895. pp. 751-771. 1834, *etc.* 8°. **Ac. 8820/3 & 2098. a, b.**

අච්ඡරියබ්භුතසූත්‍රය *etc.* [Achchhariyabbhutasutta. Followed by Buddhaghosa's commentary and a Sinhalese word-for-word translation.] pp. ii. 43. කොළඹ [*Colombo,*] 1897. 8°. **14098. ccc. 4.(3.)**

Angulimala Suttraya [*i.e.* II. iv. (Majjhimapaṇṇāsa, Rājavagga), §6]. අඞ්ගුලිමාල සූත්‍රය *etc.* [With an interpretation and the legend of Aṅgulimāla Thera, in Sinhalese. Edited by Giridhara Ratanajoti.] pp. 28, 7, i. [*Colombo,*] 1891. 8°. **14098. c. 53.(3.)**

බාලපණ්ඩිතසූත්‍රය *etc.* [Bālapaṇḍitasutta, *i.e.* III. iii. (Uparipaṇṇāsa, Suññatāvagga), § 9, of this Nikāya. With a Sinhalese interpretation.] pp. 48, ii. [*Colombo,*] 1893. 8°. **14098. c. 53.(7.)**

බ්‍රහ්මායුසූත්‍රය *etc.* [Brahmāyusutta (*i.e.* Majjhimapaṇṇāsaka, Brāhmaṇavagga 1). With Sinhalese word-for-word interpretation.] pp. ii. 73. [*Colombo,*] 1896. 8°. **14098. c. 72.(1.)**

Chetokhila Sutraya . . . චෙතොඛිල සූත්‍රය. [Comprising the Chetokhilasutta (*i.e.* Mūlapaṇṇāsaka, Sīhanādavagga 6), followed by a Sinhalese word-for-word translation and Buddhaghosa's commentary.] pp. 26. කොළඹ [*Colombo,*] 1897. 8°. **14098. c. 73.(1.)**

MAJJHIMANIKĀYA (*continued*).

Chachakka Suttaraya . . . ඡඡක්කසූත්‍රය *etc.* [Comprising the Chhachhakkasutta (*i.e.* Uparipaṇṇāsaka, Saḷāyatanavagga 6), with Buddhaghosa's commentary and a Sinhalese word-for-word translation.] pp. ii. 34. බ්‍රැඩියාවත්තේ [*Brendiyavatta,*] 1896. 8°. **14098. c. 72.(3.)**

චූලපුණ්ණමාසූත්‍රය *etc.* [Chūlapuṇṇamāsutta, or III. i. (Uparipaṇṇāsa, Devadahavagga), § 10. With a Sinhalese interpretation.] pp. 15. කොළඹ [*Colombo,*] 1893. 8°. **14098. c. 53.(8.)**

චුල්ලවෙදල්ල සූත්‍රය *etc.* [Chullavedallasutta (*i.e.* Mūlapaṇṇāsaka, Chūḷayamakavagga 4). Edited with a Sinhalese word-for-word gloss and a translation by Leṇadora Dhammarakkhita.] pp. 32. කොළඹ 2440 [*Colombo,* 1897.] 8°. **14098. c. 73.(2.)**

ඝටිකාර සූත්‍රය *etc.* [Ghaṭīkārasutta (*i.e.* Majjhimapaṇṇāsaka, Rājavagga 1). Followed by a Sinhalese word-for-word translation.] pp. 28, i. [*Colombo,*] 1897. 8°. **14098. c. 73.(3.)**

The Madhura Sutta concerning Caste. [II. iv. (Majjhimapaṇṇāsa, Rājavagga), § 4. With an extract from the Papañchasūdanī and translation.] By Robert Chalmers. 1894. *See* ACADEMIES, *etc.*—London.—*Royal Asiatic Society of Great Britain and Ireland.* The Journal . . . 1894. pp. 341-366. **Ac. 8820/3 & 2098. a, b.**

The Raṭṭhapāla Sutta. [III. iv. (Majjhimapaṇṇāsa, Rājavagga), § 2. With translation.] By Walter Lupton. 1894. *See* ACADEMIES, *etc.*—London.—*Royal Asiatic Society of Great Britain and Ireland.* The Journal . . . 1894. pp. 769-806. 1834, *etc.* 8°. **Ac. 8820/3 & 2098. a, b.**

Sankharuppatti Sutraya. සඞ්ඛාරුප්පත්ති සූත්‍රය *etc.* [Comprising the Saṅkhāruppattisutta (*i.e.* Uparipaṇṇāsaka, Anupadavagga 10) with Buddhaghosa's commentary and a Sinhalese word-for-word translation appended.] pp. 29. *Colombo,* 1896. 8°. **14098. c. 72.(2.)**

Sælasuttra Sannaya. සෙලසූත්‍ර සන්නය *etc.* [Selasutta (*i.e.* Majjhimapaṇṇāsaka, Brāhmaṇavagga 2). Preceded by a Sinhalese paraphrase and followed by a Sinhalese *sannaya.* Edited by Kollupiṭiyē Puññānanda.] pp. i. vii. i. 36. 2439 [*Colombo,* 1896.] 8°. **14098. d. 45.(3.)**

වම්මීකසූත්‍රය *etc.* [Vammīkasutta, or I. iii. (Mūlapaṇṇāsa, Opammavagga), § 3. Followed by a Sinhalese interpretation.] pp. 16. [*Colombo,*] 1893. 8°. **14098. c. 69.(4.)**

Weranjasutraya . . . වෙරඤ්ජසූත්‍රය *etc.* [Verañjasutta, or I. v. (Mūlapaṇṇāsa, Chūlayamakavagga), § 2. Followed by a Sinhalese interpretation. Edited by Māgammana Medhānanda.] pp. 28. *Brandiyawatte,* 1893. 8°. **14098. c. 69.(3.)**

SAṂYUTTANIKĀYA.

ပူတော်။ . . . ဗောဇ္ဈင်သုတ်ပါဠိအနက် *etc.* [Mahākassapa-bojjhaṅgasutta, Mahāmoggallāna-bojjhaṅgasutta, and Mahāchunda-bojjhaṅgasutta. Being nos. 14-16 (Gilānavagga 4-6) of the Bojjhaṅgasaṃyutta (sect. xlvi. of this Nikāya, or bk. ii. of the Mahāvagga). With Burmese interpretation. Followed by an appendix in Burmese and the Abhiṇhasutta with Burmese version.] pp. 45. မန္တလေး [*Mandalay,*] 1904. 12°. **14098. a. 37.(2.)**

အနမတဂ္ဂသုတ်ပါဠိတော်။ [Anamataggasutta (II, Nidānavagga, bk. iv.). With Burmese interpretation by Chakkindābhisiri.] *See* VINANDĀSABHA. သီလဝိသောဓနီကျမ်း။ *etc.* [Sīlavisodhanī.] pp. 229-277. [1905.] 8°. **14099. b. 5.**

ခန္ဓဝဂ္ဂသံယုတ်ပါဠိတော်နိက်လာသောအနတ္တ-လက္ခဏာသုတ် *etc.* [Anattalakkhaṇasutta, also styled Pañchas°., from the Upāyavagga in the Khandhasaṃyutta of the Khandhavagga. Followed by a word-for-word Burmese translation.] ff. 8, *lith.* *obl.* Fol. **14098. a. 36.**

Without date or place of publication.

ආශිවිෂොපම සූත්‍රය *etc.* [Āṣīrvishopamasūtra, or Āsīvisasutta (Saḷāyatanavagga, xxiii. § 1). With an interpretation and old amplified version in Sinhalese.] pp. ii. 33, i. *Colombo,* 1891. 8°. **14098. c. 69.(7.)**

SAṂYUTTANIKĀYA (*continued*).

ဒေဝမနုဿစိတ္တပရိဝတ္တဝိဝါဒဝိနိစ္ဆယ [Devamanussachittaparivattavivādavinichchhaya. Comprising the Daḷhadhammadhanuggahasutta (*i.e.* Nidānavagga, Opammasaṃyutta ix.), illustrated from other Pali works and furnished with Burmese commentary by the Sagu Hsaya Paṇḍavālaṅkāra.] *See* ABHIDHAMMAPIṬAKA.—*Dhammasaṅgaṇi.* အဘိဓမ္မာငါးစောင်တွဲကျမ်း *etc.* [Abhidhammā-ngā-saung-twè-kyan.] pp. 382-413. 1900. 8°.
14300. e. 14.

ဓမ္မစကြာပ္ပဝတ္တနသုတ် [Dhammachakkappavattanasutta (*i.e.* Mahāvagga, xii. 2). Preceded and followed by short excerpts from the Piṭakas on the cardinal doctrines of Buddhism. With Burmese *nissayas*.] pp. ii. 61. မန္တလေး [*Mandalay*, 1901.] 8°. **14098. c. 32.(2.)**

පබ්බතූපම සූත්‍රය *etc.* [Pabbatūpamasutta (*i.e.* Sagāthavagga, Kosalasaṃyutta 5). Followed by Buddhaghosa's commentary and a Sinhalese word-for-word translation.] pp. 12. කොළඹ [*Colombo*,] 1897. 8°. **14098. c. 73.(5.)**

තමෝතමපරායණ සූත්‍රය *etc.* [Tamotamaparāyaṇasutta, or Puggalasutta. Forming I. iii. (Sagāthavagga, Kosalasaṃyutta) of the Saṃyuttanikāya, *vagga* 3, § 1. With a word-for-word Sinhalese gloss.] pp. 15. [*Peliyagoda*,] 1897. 8°. **14098. ccc. 4.(5.)**

SUVAṆṆAJOTYĀSABHA, *Uḍugampala.* *See* SUTTAPIṬAKA.—*Aṅguttaranikāya.* දානුප්පත්ති සූත්‍රය *etc.* [Dānuppattisutta. Edited with Sinhalese interpretation by Suvaṇṇajotyāsabha.] 1892. 8°.
14098. c. 53.(4.)

SUVARṆAPRABHĀ. सुवर्णप्रभा । Suvarṇa Prabhā. [A series of stories and homilies, in prose and verse, treating of the ethics and philosophy of Northern Buddhism.] For the first time edited by Rai Çarat Chandra Dās . . . and Paṇḍit Çarat Chandra Çāstrī. 1898, *etc.* *See* ACADEMIES, *etc.*— Calcutta.—*Buddhist Text Society of India.* Buddhist Texts, *etc.* 1894, *etc.* 8°.
14004. c. (vol. 2, no. 3.)

SUVARṆAVAṆIK. Vyavasthá Patra, or recorded opinion that the Suvarnavaniks are Vaisya's &c. of five of the most leading pandits in Bengal. (सुवर्णवणिग्विषयिका व्यवस्था ।) pp. 20. *Calcutta*, [1902.] 12°. **14058. a. 8.(3.)**

SŪYAGAḌAṄGA. *See* SŪTRAKṚIDAṄGA.

SVĀMĪ MIŚRA ŚĀSTRĪ. *See* RĀMA MIŚRA SĀSTRĪ.

SVĀMĪ NĀRĀYAṆA. *See* SAHAJĀNANDA SVĀMĪ.

SVĀMINĀTHA ŚĀSTRĪ, *Ādhanakoṭṭai.* *See* ŚIVARĀMAKṚISHṆA ŚĀSTRĪ, *Ā.* ப்ரயோகசிந்தாமணி: *etc.* [Prayogachintāmaṇi. Edited with a commentary called Kalpavallī and a *kārikā* styled Gṛihyakalparatna by Svāminātha.] 1901. 8°.
14033. aa. 22.

SVĀMINĀTHA ŚRAUTĪ, *Brahmadeśam.* ॥ वेदान्तपञ्चप्रकरणी *etc.* [Vedāntapañchaprakaraṇī. Poems of the Advaita-vedānta school—viz. Bodhāryā, by Sadāśiva Brahmendra; Jagadgururatnamālāstava or Gururatnamālikā, by the same, with the commentary Sushumā of Ātmabodhendra; Gītiratnamālā, religious lyrics, by the same; Jagadguruparamparāstava, by Mahādevendra Sarasvatī; Jagadguruparamparānāmamālā, by Rāma Brahmendra; a biography of Sadāśiva, based on old records, by the editor; and Ātmavidyāvilāsa, Śivamānasikapūjā, and Saparyāparyāyastava, by Sadāśiva. Edited by Svāminātha.] pp. 92, 33. कुम्भघोण° १८९५ [*Kumbakonam*, 1895.] 8°.
14048. bb. 51.(5.)

SVĀMI ŚĀSTRĪ, *P.K.*, **and KĀMEŚVARA AIYAR,** *B.V.* Matriculation Examination, 1891. The Sanskrit Text Examiner [upon the texts Pañchatantra I. 6-13 and Mahābhārata, Vanaparva, xxiii.-xxxii.], containing exhaustive questions with answers . . . the *vigraha* of important compounds, and an analysis of the subject-matter of the Bharata portion, *etc.* pp. 62, ii. *Tiruvadi*, 1891. 12°. **14072. b. 18.**

SVAPNĀDHYĀYA. ସ୍ୱପ୍ନାଧ୍ୟାୟ *etc.* [Svapnādhyāya. 52 stanzas on oneiromancy. Edited with Oriya metrical version by Kapileśvara Vidyābhūshaṇa.] pp. 9. *Cuttack*, 1880. 12°. **14053. b. 17.(3.)**

SVĀRĀJYASIDDHI. ॥ स्वाराज्यसिद्धौ प्रारम्भः etc. [Svārājyasiddhi. An anonymous Vedantic treatise in verse. With a commentary, called Kaivalyakalpadruma, by Gaṅgādhara Sarasvatī. Edited by Amaradāsa.] 3 pts., *lith.* काशी १९४७ [*Benares*, 1891.] *obl.* Fol. **14048. ee. 2.**

—— स्वाराज्यसिद्धिः etc. [Svārājyasiddhi. With the commentary Kaivalyakalpadruma of Bhāskarānanda Sarasvatī.] pp. ii. 238; 1 *plate.* काशी १९५३ [*Benares*, 1896.] 8°. **14048. dd. 27.**

In the preface the work is ascribed to Sureśvara.

SVARĀSHṬAKA. अथ स्वराष्टकशिक्षा ॥ [Svarāshṭakaśikshā. A tract of the Mādhyandina school on Vedic phonetics.] *See* YUGALAKIŚORA VYĀSA PĀṬHAKA. श्रीमद्याज्ञवल्क्यादि . . . शिक्षासंग्रहः . . . A collection of Śikshás, *etc.* pp. 362-368. 1893. 8°. **14093. b. 31.**

SVARODAYAŚĀSTRA. *See* PAVANAVIJAYA.

SVARŪPA SŪRI, *Udāsina*, also called NIRVĀṆASVARŪPA. *See* NĀNAK. अथ निराकारमीमांसादर्शनम् *etc.* [Nirākāramīmāṃsādarśana. With an exposition by Keśavānanda, a supercommentary styled Svarūpadīpikā by Svarūpa Sūri, *etc.*] [1903.] 8°. **14049. bb. 3.**

SVĀTMĀRĀMA. হঠযোগপ্রদীপিকা। [Haṭhayogapradīpika. With the commentary Jyotsnā by Brahmānanda, and a Bengali translation.] pp. 84, ii. [1891, *etc.*] *See* PERIODICAL PUBLICATIONS.—*Calcutta.* অরুণোদয় *etc.* [Aruṇodaya.] Pt. i., no. 21. [1890, *etc.*] 4°. **14133. g. 16.(pt. i., no. 21.)**

—— हठयोगप्रदीपिका *etc.* (The Hatha-yoga Pradipika of Swâtmârâm Swâmi. Translated by Shrinivâs Iyângâr ... with the original text and its commentary [by Brahmānanda,] *etc.*) pp. 203, x. 106. *Bombay*, 1893. 12°. **14048. b. 30.**

—— ஹடயோகப்பிரதீபிகை *etc.* [Haṭhayogapradīpikā. Edited with a Tamil translation and commentary styled Tattvapradīpikā by V. Kuppusvāmi Rāju.] pp. vi. iv. ii. 272. திருவையாறு தாருகி [*Trivadi*, 1897.] 8°. **14048. cc. 16.**

—— శ్రీస్వాత్మారామయోగీంద్రవిరచిత హఠయోగప్రదీపిక తాత్పర్యసహితము *etc.* [Haṭhayogapradīpikā. With Telugu translation and commentary by Ō. V. Dorasāmaiya, together with a Telugu essay on Rājayoga by the same and 26 plates illustrating the postures of the Yoga.] pp. 4, 11, 5, 2, i. 228, 2, 20; 26 *plates.* చెన్నపురి [*Madras*,] 1903. 8°. **14049. b. 23.**

—— Svâtmârâma's Haṭhayogapradîpikâ, die Leuchte des Haṭhayoga ... übersetzt und als Inaugural-Dissertation ... vorgelegt von Hermann Walter. pp. i. i. xxxiv. 52. *München*, 1893. 8°. **14048. c. 75.(1.)**

SVAYAMBHŪPURĀṆA. The Vṛihat Svayambhú Puráṇam[, a poetical Buddhist hagiology]. Containing the traditions of the Svayambhú Kshetra in Nepal. Edited by Paṇḍit Haraprasád Sástrí. 1894-1900. *See* ACADEMIES, *etc.* — Calcutta. — *Asiatic Society of Bengal.* Bibliotheca Indica. New Series. [Vol. 133.] 1848, *etc.* 8°. **14002. a. (vol. 133.)**

—— Svayambhūpurāṇa [in the 12-chapter recension]. Dixième chapitre. [Edited] par L. de la Vallée Poussin. (Université de Gand. Recueil de travaux publiés par la faculté de philosophie et lettres. 9° fascicule.) pp. 19. *Gand*, 1893. 8°. **Ac. 2647/3.(fasc. 9.)**

—— Maṇicūḍāvadāna, as related in the fourth chapter of the Svayambhūpurāṇa ... [An epitome, in French.] By Louis de la Vallée Poussin. 1894. *See* ACADEMIES, *etc.* — London. — *Royal Asiatic Society of Great Britain and Ireland.* The Journal ... 1894. pp. 297-319. 1834, *etc.* 8°. **Ac. 8820/3 & 2098. a, b.**

SVAYAMPRAKĀŚA YATI. *See* LAKSHMĪDHARA. శ్రీ... అద్వైతమకరన్దః॥ [Advaitamakaranda. With the commentary Rasābhivyakti of Svayamprakāśa.] 1891. 8°. **14048. bb. 39.(4.)**

—— *See* ŚAṄKARA ĀCHĀRYA.—*Two or More Works.* Śri-Śankaráchárya's Miscellaneous Works, *etc.* [Vol. II, Haristuti, with the commentaries of Svayamprakāśa called Haritattvamuktāvalī, *etc.*] 1898-1899. 8°. [*Mysore Government Oriental Library Series: Bibliotheca Sanskrita.*] **14004. b. 10.(vol. 2.)**

—— *See* ŚAṄKARA ĀCHĀRYA. — *Doubtful and Supposititious Works.* दक्षिणामूर्तिस्तोत्रम् . . . The Dakshiṇámúrti-stotra . . . with commentaries [entitled respectively Mānasollāsa, Tattvasudhā, and Mānasollāsavṛittānta] by Sureśvarāchārya, Svayamprákása & Rámatírtha, *etc.* 1895. 8°. [*Mysore Government Oriental Library Series: Bibliotheca Sanskrita.*] **14004. b. 5.**

SWAMI VIVEKANANDA. *See* VIVEKĀNANDA, *Svāmī.*

ṢYĀMA BHAGAVĀN, *Sādhu, Brahmanishṭha Svāmī.* सामस्वानुभूत्यादर्शः . . . तथा आत्मविशेषणात्ममालिका [Sāmasvānubhūtyādarṣa and Ātmaviṣeshaṇamālikā. Two poems, in Hindi and Sanskrit respectively, expounding the author's system of Vaishṇava monism. With annotations in the same languages, and prefatory Sanskrit poems called Gurvashṭaka by Jñānānanda Yati and Dakshiṇāmūrtipañchaka by Ṣyāma.] pp. ii. 96. १८५६ [*Bombay,* 1900.] 12°. **14028. b. 81.(5.)**

ṢYĀMĀCHARAṆA KAVIRATNA. *See* NITYAKARMA. আহ্নিককৃত্যম্ *etc.* [Āhnikakṛitya. Edited with Bengali introduction, translation, *etc.*, by Ṣyāmācharaṇa.] [1902.] 12°. **14033. a. 49.**

—— *See* VOPADEVA. মুগ্ধবোধং *etc.* [Mugdhabodha. Edited with notes by Ṣyāmācharaṇa.] [1904.] 12°. **14092. a. 28.(4.)**

ṢYĀMALĀLA, *son of Baladeva, of Bans Bareilly.* स्त्रीजातकम् *etc.* [Strijātaka. A metrical treatise on the physiognomic and astrological modes of divining the qualities of women. With a Hindi translation, styled Ṣyāmasundarī, by the author.] pp. xxiv. 268. मुम्बय्यां १९५८ [*Bombay,* 1902.] 8°. **14053. ccc. 37.**

ṢYĀMALĀLA GOSVĀMĪ, *Siddhāntavāchaspati. See* BĀDARĀYAṆA. বেদান্তদর্শন *etc.* [Vedāntadarṣana. Being the Brahmasūtra with the Govindabhāshya, a Bengali translation by Ṣyāmalāla of the *bhāshya, etc.*] 1894. 8°. **14048. dd. 23.**

—— *See* BALADEVA VIDYĀBHŪSHAṆA. সিদ্ধান্তরত্নম্ *etc.* [Siddhāntaratna. With commentary. Edited, with Bengali translation, by Ṣyāmalāla.] [1897.] 8°. **14048. cc. 24.**

—— *See* JĪVA GOSVĀMĪ. ষট্‌সন্দর্ভ॰ [Shaṭsandarbha. Edited by Ṣyāmalāla.] [1899-1901.] 8°. **14016. d. 62.**

—— *See* PURĀṆAS. — *Bhāgavatapurāṇa.* শ্রীকৃষ্ণলীলা। *etc.* [Kṛishṇalīlā. Compiled and edited by Ṣyāmalāla.] [1904.] 8°. **14016. dd. 10.**

ṢYĀMALĀLA GOSVĀMĪ, *Siddhāntavāchaspati (continued). See* PURĀṆAS.—*Bhāgavatapurāṇa.* শ্রী . . . নবযোগেন্দ্রোপাখ্যান *etc.* [Navayogendropākhyāna and Uddhavagītā. With translation *etc.* in Bengali. Edited by Ṣyāmalāla.] [1900.] 8°. **14018. b. 19.**

—— *See* UPANISHADS. — *Separate Upanishads.* ईशोपनिषत् *etc.* (Isa-Upanishad. With the Bhasyas of Baladeva . . . Sankaracharyya and the Tika of Anandagiri . . . With Bengali translation and commentary. Edited by Sri Syamalala . . . With an English translation and commentary.) 1895. 8°. **14010. cc. 3.(1.)**

ṢYĀMAMANOHARA VAIDYA. *See* PURĀṆAS.—*Liṅgapurāṇa.* ॥ हरतालिकापूजाकथा॰ [Haratālikāpūjākathā. With Hindi version by Ṣyāmamanohara.] [1900.] *obl.* 8°. **14033. c. 44.(4.)**

ṢYĀMASUNDARALĀLA TRIPĀṬHĪ, *of Moradabad. See* TANTRAS. [*Siddhaṣaṅkaratantra.*] सिद्धशङ्करतन्त्रम् *etc.* [Siddhaṣaṅkaratantra. With Hindi version by Ṣyāmasundaralāla and Kanhaiyālāl.] [1899.] 8°. **14033. bbb. 6.**

—— *See* VĀMAMĀRGA. वाममार्गे भैरवीचक्र [Vāmamārga. Edited with Hindi version by Ṣyāmasundaralāla.] 1899. 12°. **14033. a. 38.**

ṢYĀMASUNDARALĀLA TRIPĀṬHĪ, *son of Baṅkelāl, of Bans Bareilly. See* NĀGA BHAṬṬA. ॥ सिद्ध डाकिनी . . . तन्त्र *etc.* [Kāmaratna. With Hindi translation by Ṣyāmasundara.] [1897.] 12°. **14028. b. 71.(5.)**

—— *See* PURĀṆAS.—*Vāmanapurāṇa.* ॥ अथ वामनपुराणं *etc.* [Vāmanapurāṇa. Edited with Hindi translation by Ṣyāmasundaralāla.] [1904.] Fol. **14018. c. 34.**

—— *See* PURĀṆAS.—*Vāmanapurāṇa.* ॥ अथ वामनपुराणं *etc.* [Vāmanapurāṇa. Edited by Ṣyāmasundaralāla.] [1904.] Fol. **14018. c. 35.**

—— ज्योतिषतत्त्वसुधार्णवः ज्योतिषग्रन्थः *etc.* [Jyotishatattvasudhārṇava. A manual of astrology, compiled from various sources, with Hindi translation.] pp. vi. ii. xvi. 487. मुम्बय्यां १९५९ [*Bombay,* 1903.] 8°. **14053. dd. 5.**

ṢYĀMASUNDARA ṢARMĀ, *son of Baṅkelāl. See* ṢYĀMASUNDARALĀLA TRIPĀṬHĪ.

TACHCHU - ṢĀSTRAM. മനുഷ്യാലയചന്ദ്രിക എന്നപേരായ തച്ചുശാസ്ത്രം *etc.* [Manushyālayachandrikā, or Tachchu-ṣāstram. A primer of architecture, in 65 stanzas, with Malayalam translation and notes.] pp. 38. പാലക്കാട നഗരം ॥ [*Palghat*, 1893.] 8°. **14053. ccc. 14.**

TAGORE (S. M.), *Sir*. *See* ṢAURĪNDRAMOHANA ṬHĀKURA, *Sir*.

TA-HSÈ-HNIT SAUNG TWÈ. တဆဲ့နှစ်ဆောင်တွဲ [Ta-hsè-hnit saung twè. Comprising the Maṅgala-sutta, Jayamaṅgalagāthās, Ratanapañjara, Namakāra, Lokanīti, and Paritta, in Pali, with Burmese interpretation, *etc.*; Payeik-kyī-vatthu, Burmese homilies on the Paritta; three Burmese grammatical tracts; and analyses and glosses of certain Pali words.] pp. 282. ရန်ကုန် ၁၂၆၁ [*Rangoon*, 1899.] 8°. **14098. ccc. 39.**

TA-HSÈ-THÔN SAUNG TWÈ. တဆဲ့သုံးဆောင်တွဲ [Ta-hsè-thôn saung twè. Comprising the Maṅgala-sutta, Jayamaṅgalagāthās, Ratanapañjara, Namakāra, Lokanīti, and Paritta, with Burmese interpretation; five Burmese tracts on grammatical and religious topics; and analyses and glosses of certain Pali words.] pp. 314. ရန်ကုန် ၁၂၆၂ [*Rangoon*, 1900.] 8°. **14098. ccc. 40.**

—— [Another issue of the same texts, with some further matter appended.] pp. 292. ရန်ကုန် ၁၂၆၆ [*Rangoon*, 1905.] 8°. **14049. bb. 4.**

TAKAKUSU (JUNJIRŌ). *See* AMITĀYURDHYĀNA-SŪTRA. Amitâyur-Dhyâna-Sûtra, *etc.* [Translated by J. Takakusu.] 1894. 8°. [*Sacred Books of the East.*] **2003. b. (vol. 49.)**

—— A Pāli Chrestomathy. With notes and glossary giving Sanskrit and Chinese equivalents. By J. Takakusu. pp. xciv. vi. 272. *Tokyo*, 1900. 8°. **14098. ccc. 33.**

TAMMANĀCHĀRYA, *Gonnabattula*. *See* VARĀHANARASIṂHĀCHĀRYA. శ్రీ ... శ్రీమద్విశ్వకర్మాన్వయప్రదీపికా ॥ [Viṣvakarmānvayapradīpikā. With Telugu translation by Tammanāchārya.] [1902.] 8°. **14058. b. 42.**

TANTRAS. [*Collections.*] বিবিধ-মূল-তন্ত্র। [Vividha-mūla-tantra. A collection of Tantras. Edited by Rasikamohana Chaṭṭopādhyāya.] কলিকাতা ১৩০৯ [*Calcutta*, 1903, *etc.*] 8°. **14033. c. 48.**

In progress.

—— [*Selections.*] *Begin.* ॥ श्रीगणेशाय नमः ॥ ॥ श्रीमद्वगलामुखी एकादशमहारत्न ॥ [Vagalāmukhyekādaṣamahāratna. A Tantrik ritual for the goddess Vagalāmukhī, professedly compiled from the Rudrayāmala, Siddheṣvara, and Viṣvasāroddhāra Tantras, *etc.*] [*Benares*, 1900.] *obl.* 16°. **14033. a. 39.**

Imperfect: the leaves after fol. 145 are missing.

—— [*Bhūtaḍāmaratantra.*] ভূতডামরঃ। [Bhūtaḍāmaratantra. With Bengali version.] pp. 40. [1891.] *See* PERIODICAL PUBLICATIONS.—*Calcutta.* অরুণোদয় *etc.* [Aruṇodaya.] Pt. i., no. 12. 1890, *etc.* 4°. **14133. g. 16.(pt. i., no. 12.)**

—— —— भूत डामर तन्त्र *etc.* [Bhūtaḍāmaratantra.] pp. ii. 162. मेरट १८९५ [*Meerut*, 1895.] 8°. **14033. bbb. 3.**

—— —— বৃহদ্ভূতডামরঃ। [Bṛihad-bhūtaḍāmaratantra.] pp. 20. [1893, *etc.*] *See* PERIODICAL PUBLICATIONS.—*Calcutta.* অরুণোদয় *etc.* [Aruṇodaya.] Pt. i., no. 26. [1890, *etc.*] 4°. **14133. g. 16.(pt. i., no. 26.)**

—— [*Brahmayāmalatantra.*] कबीरशतक सटीक *etc.* [Kabīr-ṣataka. A century of verses from the Pātālakhaṇḍa, on the significance of the name and attributes of Kabīr. With Hindi metrical paraphrase by Akhai-rām.] pp. 66. बनारस १९५८ [*Benares*, 1901.] 8°. **14033. bbb. 15.(1.)**

—— [*Ḍāmaratantra.*] कार्तवीर्यकवचम् [Kārtavīryārjunakavacha. Preceded by *nyāsas* and *dhyānas*. Edited by Gaṅgādhara Ṣāstrī Draviḍa.] pp. 31. काशी १८९७ [*Benares*, 1897.] 8°. **14033. aa. 5.(3.)**

—— —— (डामरतन्त्रम्) [Kārtavīryārjunakavacha. With Hindi paraphrase by Hariṣaṅkara Ṣāstrī and Lālamaṇi Ṣāstrī.] pp. 38. [*Moradabad*, 1898.] 8°. **14033. bbb. 4.(1.)**

No title-page.

—— [*Dattātreyatantra.*] दत्तात्रेयतन्त्रम् [Dattātreyatantra.] *See* INDRAJĀLAVIDYĀSAṄGRAHA. इन्द्रजालविद्यासंग्रहः *etc.* (Indrajalavidyasangraha.) pp. 135–182. [1891.] 8°. **14033. aa. 7.**

TANTRAS. [*Dattātreyatantra.*] (*continued*). দত্তাত্রেয়ঃ। [Dattātreyatantra. With Bengali translation.] pp. 28. [1891, *etc.*] *See* PERIODICAL PUBLICATIONS.—*Calcutta.* অরুণোদয় *etc.* [Aruṇodaya.] Pt. i., no. 14. [1890, *etc.*] 4°.
14133. g. 16.(pt. i., no. 14.)

—— —— दत्तात्रेयतंत्रम् *etc.* [Dattātreyatantra Edited with Hindi translation by Jvālāprasāda Miśra of Garhi Khiri.] pp. ii. 115. मुंबय्यां १९५९ [*Bombay*, 1902.] 12°. **14033. aa. 29.**

—— [*Gaurīkāñjalikātantra.*] অথ গৌরীকাঞ্চলিকা। [Gaurīkāñjalikā. With a Bengali translation and an appendix containing additional matter.] pp. 66. [1893, *etc.*] *See* PERIODICAL PUBLICATIONS.—*Calcutta.* অরুণোদয় *etc.* [Aruṇodaya.] Pt. i., no. 30. [1890, *etc.*] 4°.
14133. g. 16.(pt. i., no. 30.)

—— [*Gāyatrītantra.*] गायत्रीतन्त्रं *etc.* [Gāyatrītantra. A tantra treating of the cult of the Gāyatrī, in 5 *paṭalas.*] pp. 59. *Benares*, 1897. 8°.
14033. aa. 5.(2.)

—— —— శ్రీగాయత్రీతంత్రము *etc.* [Gāyatrītantra. Edited with Telugu translation by N. Guruliṅga Śāstrī.] pp. 122. చెన్నపురి ౧౯౦౧ [*Madras*, 1901.] 8°. **14033. aa. 28.(1.)**

—— [*Jñānasaṅkalinītantra.*] জ্ঞানসঙ্কলিনীতন্ত্রম্ [Jñānasaṅkalinītantra. With a Bengali translation.] pp. 8. [1891, *etc.*] *See* PERIODICAL PUBLICATIONS.—*Calcutta.* অরুণোদয় *etc.* [Aruṇodaya.] Pt. i., no. 20. [1890, *etc.*] 4°.
14133. g. 16.(pt. i., no. 20.)

—— —— ज्ञानसङ्कलिनीतन्त्रम् *etc.* [Jñānasaṅkalinītantra.] pp. 15. कलिकाता १८९२ [*Calcutta*, 1892.] 8°.
14033. aa. 1.(1.)

—— —— জ্ঞান-সঙ্কলিনী তন্ত্রম্ *etc.* [Jñānasaṅkalinītantra. With Bengali translation by Vaishṇavacharaṇa Basāk. Third edition.] pp. 31. কলিকাতা [*Calcutta*, 1901.] 12°. **14033. a. 41.(3.)**

—— [*Kālītantra.*] कालीतन्त्र। [Kālītantra. With Hindi translation by Kanhaiyālāl Miśra.] pp. 199. *Moradabad*, १९०२ [1902.] 8°. **14033. bbb. 15.(3.)**

—— [*Kātyāyanītantra.*] अथ प्रयोगाः *etc.* [*Prayogas* of the Kātyāyanītantra for the ritual of Durgā.] *See* PURĀṆAS.—*Mārkaṇḍeyapurāṇa.* [*Devīmāhātmya.*] ॥ अथ दुर्गासप्तशती *etc.* [Devīmāhātmya.] ff. 1-7. [1898.] *obl.* 12°. **14016. b. 22.**

—— [*Kriyoḍḍīśatantra.*] ক্রিয়োড্ডীশঃ। [Kriyoḍḍīśa. A manual of magic in 22 *paṭalas.* Followed by the Pichchhilātantra, *paṭalas* v.-ix.] pp. 14. [1893, *etc.*] *See* PERIODICAL PUBLICATIONS.—*Calcutta.* অরুণোদয় *etc.* [Arunodaya.] Pt. i., no. 28. [1890, *etc.*] 4°. **14133. g. 16.(pt. i., no. 28.)**

—— [*Kulārṇavatantra.*] कुलार्णवतन्त्रम् *etc.* [Kulārṇavatantra. A manual of the rites and doctrines of the Kaulika sect of Śāktas. Edited by Jīvānanda Vidyāsāgara.] pp. 159. कलिकाता १८९७ [*Calcutta*, 1897.] 8°.
14028. c. 71.

—— [*Kumāratantra.*] குமாரதந்த்ரம். [Kumāratantra.] pp. xvi. 260. சென்னை க்ரோதி [*Madras*, 1904.] 8°. **14033. aa. 37.**

—— [*Mahānirvāṇatantra.*] মহানির্ব্বাণতন্ত্রম্ *etc.* [Mahānirvāṇatantra. With Bengali translation.] pp. 994. কলিকাতা ১৩০৩ [*Calcutta*, 1896.] 16°.
14033. a. 30.

Identical in all but size and arrangement with the 8vo. Calcutta edition of 1888.

—— —— মহানির্ব্বাণ তন্ত্র *etc.* [Mahānirvāṇatantra. With Bengali translation by Gopāladāsa Mukhopādhyāya.] pp. 223, 232. কলিকাতা ১৩০৭ [*Calcutta*, 1901.] 8°. **14033. aa. 17.**

—— —— A prose English translation of Mahanirvana Tantram, *etc.* pp. ii. x. xxxii. 315, xxx. 1900. *See* MANMATHANĀTHA DATTA. The Wealth of India, *etc.* Vol. vii. 1892, *etc.* 8°.
14085. d. 32. (vol. 7.)

—— —— A prose English translation of Mahanirvana Tantram. Edited . . . by Manmatha Nath Dutt. pp. ii. x. xxxii. 315, xxx. *Calcutta*, 1900. 8°. **14033. bbb. 8.**
A reprint of the preceding edition.

—— —— Mahanirvana-tantram. Compiled by Sreeman Maheshwar Bhagwat. Purva Kandam. Corrected by Pundit Jwala Prasad Misra . . . Translated [into Hindi, with the original text,] by P. Baldeo Prasad Misra of Moradabad. (महानिर्वाणतन्त्रम्।) pp. xvi. 548. *Bombay*, 1896. 8°.
14033. aa. 2.

TANTRAS (*continued*). [*Māheṣvaratantra.*] माहेश्वर तंत्रम् *etc.* [Māheṣvaratantra. Edited with a Hindi translation by Nārāyaṇaprasāda Miṣra and Mukundarāma Miṣra.] pp. iv. 52. मोहमय्यां १९५९ [*Bombay*, 1902.] 12°. **14033. a. 45.(5.)**

—— [*Pratyaṅgirātantra.*] ॥ प्रत्यंगिरातंत्र ॥ [Pratyaṅgirātantra.] pp. 40. *Lucknow*, १९०१ [1901.] 12°. **14028. bb. 5.(2.)**

—— [*Rudrayāmalatantra.*] बीजप्रश्नावली *etc.* [Bījapraṣnāvalī. An excerpt from the Rudrayāmala, teaching the mystic powers of the letters. With Hindi version by Vaidyanātha Ṣāstrī.] pp. 12. *See* VAIDYANĀTHA ṢĀSTRĪ TIVĀṚĪ, *of Jalalabad*, and others. [Miscellaneous tracts.] No. 17. [1899.] 12°. **14033. a. 37.**

—— —— *End.* इति . . . श्रीसहस्रनामस्तोत्रं *etc.* [Rāmasahasranāmastotra. One thousand names of Rāma.] *See* PURĀṆAS.—*Brahmāṇḍapurāṇa.* [*Adhyātmarāmāyaṇa.*] रामगीतापञ्चरत्न प्रा° [Rāmagītāpañcharatna.] ff. 12-32. [1899.] *obl.* 16°. **14028. a. 25.**

—— —— अथ बगलामुखीस्तोत्रं *etc.* [Vagalāmukhīstotra. A hymn in 17 stanzas, with *nyāsas* and *dhyānas.*] ff. 17. कल्याण-मुंबई [*Kalyan*, 1901.] 16°. **14028. a. 19.(5.)**

—— [*Ṣābaratantra.*] শাবরঃ। [Ṣābara. Excerpts from the Gorakshasiddhiharaṇa in the Dattātreyasiddhisopāna and from other parts of the Ṣābaratantra or Siddhaṣābarat°.] pp. 17. [1893, *etc.*] *See* PERIODICAL PUBLICATIONS.—*Calcutta.* অরুণোদয় *etc.* [Aruṇodaya.] Pt. i., no. 29. [1890, *etc.*] 4°. **14133. g. 16.(pt. i., no. 29.)**

—— [*Sammohanatantra.*] ॥ अथ श्रीगर्गसंहितामाहात्म्यम् ॥ [Gargasaṃhitāmāhātmya. A panegyric on the Gargasaṃhitā, comprising 4 *adhyāyas* from this Tantra.] *See* GARGA. ॥ अथ श्रीमद्गर्गसंहिता *etc.* [Gargasaṃhitā.] [1898.] *obl.* 4°. **14028. e. 34.**

—— [*Sarvavijayitantra.*] सर्वविजयीतन्त्र *etc.* [Sarvavijayitantra. A Tantra treating of the medicinal properties of herbs, divers charms, *etc.* With Hindi version by Baladevaprasāda Miṣra.] pp. ii. 48. मुरादाबाद [*Moradabad*, 1898.] 12°. **14033. a. 35.(3.)**

TANTRAS (*continued*). [*Siddhaṣaṅkaratantra.*] सिद्धशङ्करतंत्रम् *etc.* [Siddhasaṅkaratantra. A treatise, ascribed to Vyāsa, on the magical way to salvation, in 10 *paṭalas.* With Hindi version by Ṣyāmasundaralāla Tripāṭhī and Kanhaiyālāl of Moradabad.] pp. ii. 75. मुरादाबाद १९५६ [*Moradabad*, 1899.] 8°. **14033. bbb. 6.**

—— [*Uḍḍāmeṣvaratantra.*] *See* above, [*Ḍāmaratantra.*]

—— [*Uḍḍīṣatantra.*] উড্ডীশঃ। [Uḍḍīṣatantra.] pp. 29. [1891, *etc.*] *See* PERIODICAL PUBLICATIONS.—*Calcutta.* অরুণোদয় [Aruṇodaya.] Pt. i., no. 23. [1890, *etc.*] 4°. **14133. g. 16.(pt. i., no. 23.)**

—— —— उड्डीशतंत्र [Uḍḍīṣatantra.] pp. 51. *Lucknow*, 1897. 16°. **14028. b. 90.**

—— —— ॥ उड्डीस तन्त्र *etc.* [Uḍḍīṣatantra. With a Hindi preface and translation by Baladevaprasāda Miṣra.] pp. xvi. 231. *Moradabad*, कानपुर [*Cawnpore* printed], 1898. 12°. **14033. a. 35.(2.)**

—— [*Viṣvasāratantra.*] গুরুগীতা *etc.* [Gurugītāstotra. With Bengali translation and rules for the ritual. Second edition.] pp. 36. শ্রীরামপুর ১৯০১ [*sic*] [*Serampur*, 1892.] 8°. **14028. b. 72.(1.)**

—— [*Yoginītantra.*] সানুবাদ যোগিনীতন্ত্রম্ *etc.* [Yoginītantra. With Bengali version. Edited by Kālīmohana Bhaṭṭāchārya. Third edition.] pp. 286. কলিকাতা ১৩০১ [*Calcutta*, 1894.] 8°. **14033. aa. 12.**

—— —— योगिनीतन्त्रम् *etc.* (Yoginitantra. Edited ... by ... Jibananda Vidyasagara ... Second edition.) pp. 236. *Calcutta*, 1897. 8°. **14033. aa. 6.(4.)**

English title taken from the cover.

—— —— ॥ श्रीः ॥ देवादिदेव महादेवजीप्रणीत योगिनीतन्त्र *etc.* [Yoginītantra. Edited with Hindi translation by Kanhaiyālāl Miṣra.] pp. iii. x. iii. 516. बम्बई १९६० [*Bombay*, 1903.] 8°. **14033. aa. 34.**

APPENDIX.

—— *See* BHAVAṢAṄKARA TANTRAVIṢĀRADA. সর্বসিদ্ধিপ্রদায়িনী মহাশক্তি তন্ত্র *etc.* [Mahāṣaktitantra.] [1901.] 12°. **14033. a. 10.(2.)**

—— *See* BRAHMĀNANDAGIRI TĪRTHA. तारारहस्यम् *etc.* [Tārārahasya.] [1896.] 8°. **14033. aa. 6.(3.)**

TANTRAS. [APPENDIX.] (*continued*). *See* GOVARDHANADĀSA LAKSHMĪDĀSA. बृहत्स्तोत्रसरित्सागर *etc.* [Bṛihat-stotrasaritsāgara.] [1892.] 12°. **14033. a. 27.**

—— *See* GURUNĀTHA VIDYĀNIDHI. নিত্য তন্ত্রম্ *etc.* [Nityatantra.] 1891. 8°. **14028. c. 65.**

—— *See* KĀLIKĀNANDA AVADHŪTA. गंधोत्तमानिर्णय: [Gandhottamānirṇaya.] [1900.] 8°. **14033. aa. 13.**

—— *See* KĀLĪPRASANNA VIDYĀRATNA BHAṬṬĀCHĀRYA. নিত্যতন্ত্রম্ *etc.* [Nityatantra.] 1900. 8°. **14033. aa. 18.**

—— *See* KṚIKALĀSADĪPIKĀ. বিবিধসাধন। কৃকলাসদীপিকা। [Kṛikalāsadīpikā.] [1893, *etc.*] 4°. [*Aruṇodaya.*] **14133. g. 16.(pt. i., no. 31.)**

—— *See* KRISHṆĀNANDA VĀGĪŚA BHAṬṬĀCHĀRYA. বৃহৎ তন্ত্রসার *etc.* [Bṛihat-tantrasāra.] [1896.] 4°. **14033. c. 39.**

—— [For editions of the Kāmaratnatantra :] *See* NĀGA BHAṬṬA.

—— *See* PERIODICAL PUBLICATIONS.—*Calcutta.* অরুণোদয় *etc.* [Aruṇodaya.] [1890, *etc.*] 4°. **14133. g. 16.**

—— *See* PŪRṆĀNANDA GOSVĀMĪ. श्यामारहस्यम् *etc.* [Śyāmārahasya.] [1896.] 8°. **14033. aa. 6.(2.)**

—— *See* PŪRṆĀNANDA GOSVĀMĪ. श्यामारहस्य° [Śyāmārahasya.] [1899.] 8°. **14033. c. 41.**

—— *See* SUDARŚANASAṂHITĀ. हनुमत कवच *etc.* [Hanumatkavacha.] [1897.] 8°. **14033. aa. 5.(1.)**

—— জপরহস্য। [Japarahasya. Rules for Tantric prayers, compiled from divers Tantras, *etc.*] pp. 10. *See* PERIODICAL PUBLICATIONS.—*Calcutta.* অরুণোদয় *etc.* [Aruṇodaya.] Pt. i., no. 8. [1890, *etc.*] 4°. **14133. g. 16.(pt. i., no. 8.)**

TĀRĀCHANDRA BHAṬṬĀCHĀRYA. *See* ŚRĀDDHA. गयापद्धति *etc.* [Gayāpaddhati. Compiled with Hindi rubrics *etc.* by Tārāchandra.] [1901.] 8°. **14033. aa. 5.(4.)**

TĀRAKANĀTHA DĀSA GUPTA. *See* NARAHARI DĀSA GUPTA. দুর্গাপূজা-পদ্ধতি *etc.* [Durgāpūjāpaddhati. Edited by Tārakanātha.] [1901.] 8°. **14033. bb. 42.(2.)**

TĀRĀKUMĀRA KAVIRATNA. कृष्णभक्तिरसामृतम् . . . কৃষ্ণভক্তিরসামৃত *etc.* [Krishṇabhaktirasāmṛita. A religious poem treating of the cult of Krishna. With Bengali metrical version and notes.] pp. iii. 154, 5. *Calcutta*, ১২৯৯ [1892.] 8°. **14028. c. 66.(1.)**

—— [Second edition.] pp. iv. 2, 152. *Calcutta*, ১৩০৬ [1900.] 8°. **14076. c. 75.(2.)**

—— পঞ্চামৃত *etc.* [Pañchāmṛita. Five religious poems—viz. the Gaṅgāshṭaka, Mohamudgara, Yatipañchaka, Sādhanapañchaka, and Bhaktagītā—compiled with Bengali verse-translations and notes by Tārākumāra. Second edition.] pp. ii. 67. কলিকাতা ১২৯৯ [*Calcutta*, 1892.] 12°. **14028. b. 73.(1.)**

TĀRĀNĀTHA TARKAVĀCHASPATI BHAṬṬĀCHARYA. तुलादानादिपद्धति : *etc.* [Tulādānādipaddhati. A treatise on the penitential rites involving largesses equal to the donor's weight, *etc.* Edited by Jīvānanda Vidyāsāgara. Second edition.] pt. i. pp. viii. 331. कलिकाता १८९६ [*Calcutta*, 1896.] 8°. **14028. c. 82.**

TĀRĀPADA KĀVYATĪRTHA. *See* BHAṬṬI. ভট্টিকাব্যম্ *etc.* [Bhaṭṭikāvya. Sargas i.-v., with Bengali translation by Tārāpada.] [1895-1896.] 8°. **14076. d. 49.**

TĀRĀPADA NYĀYARATNA. কারক চন্দ্রিকা *etc.* [Kārakachandrikā. A metrical explanation of the principles of the Sanskrit noun-system, with foot-notes.] pp. 28. কলিকাতা ১৩০৯ [*Calcutta*, 1902.] 8°. **14090. c. 44.**

TĀRIṆĪŚAṄKARA VIDYĀRATNA. जरासन्धवधम् *etc.* [Jarāsandhavadha. A poem in 10 cantos on the fall of King Jarāsandha of Magadha. With footnotes.] pp. iv. 65. कलिकाता १८२१ [*Calcutta*, 1900.] 8°. **14076. c. 73.(3.)**

TARKATĪRTHA RĀMĀNUJĀCHĀRYA. *See* VĀLMĪKI. — Rāmāyaṇa. — *Portions.* ஸ்ரீ . . . சுந்தரகாண்டம் *etc.* [Sundarakāṇḍa. With Tamil paraphrase. Edited by Tarkatīrtha.] 1901. 12°. **14060. b. 18.**

TĀTĀCHĀRYA, *Pandit, of Mysore.* *See* ŚAMBHURAHASYA. శ్రీశంభురహస్య॥ [Kavikāvyādipraśaṃsā. Edited by Tātāchārya.] [1890.] 8°. **14053. ccc. 31.**

TĀTĀCHĀRYA, *Kāñchipuram Syāmadeṣika Srīṣaila.* See SANDHYĀVANDANA. யஜுர்வேத ... ஸந்த்யாவந்தனம் *etc.* [Sandhyāvandana, *etc.* With extracts, in a Tamil translation, from commentaries. Edited and translated by Tātāchārya.] 1901. 8°. **14033. aa. 27.**

TATTVABODHA. तत्त्वबोध: *etc.* [Tattvabodha. With a translation in Nepali by Prem Shamsher.] pp. 59. १९४८ [*Benares*, 1891.] 12°. **14048. b. 23.(3.)**

—— Tattwa Bodha, Daseinserkenntnis, von Sankaracharya. Aus dem Sanskrit übersetzt von F. Hartmann. pp. vi. 55. *Leipzig, Meerane* [printed, 1895.] 8°. **14048. bb. 9.(2.)**

TATTVASĀRĀYAṆA. *See* GURUJÑĀNAVĀSISHṬHA.

TĀTYĀ ṢĀSTRĪ PAṬAVARDHANA. *See* RĀMAKṚISHṆA ṢĀSTRĪ PAṬAVARDHANA.

TAUNGDWINGYI HSAYA. ဂန္ထရာသီကျမ်း *etc.* [Gantharāsī-kyan. A compendium of Pali dicta on the 12 forms of *kamma* and their effects, with Burmese commentaries. Followed by two Burmese tracts.] pp. 202. ပန္တလေး [*Mandalay,*] 1899. 8°. **14300. d. 22.(12.)**

—— သုတဝန္ဒနာဘုရားရှိခိုး *etc.* [Sutavandanā-payā-shi-hko. A series of Pali devotional stanzas, each with a reference to a special point of doctrine, and accompanied by a Burmese commentary. Edited by Hsaya Thaing.] pp. 114. ရန်ကုန် ၁၂၆၀ [*Rangoon*, 1899.] 8°. **14098. ccc. 16.(4.)**

TAWNEY (CHARLES HENRY). *See* GREAT BRITAIN AND IRELAND.—*India Office.*—*Library.* Catalogue of Two Collections of Sanskrit Manuscripts . . . in the India Office Library. Compiled by C. H. Tawney . . . and F. W. Thomas. 1903. 8°. **14096. ccc. 8.**

—— *See* KĀLIDĀSA.—*Mālavikāgnimitra.* The Malavikágnimitra . . . translated . . . by C. H. Tawney. 1891. 12°. **14080. b. 9.(1.)**

—— *See* KATHĀKOṢA. The Katháko̧ça . . . Translated . . . by C. H. Tawney, *etc.* 1895. 8°. [*Oriental Translation Fund.*] **14003. bb. (ser. 2, vol. 2.)**

TAWNEY (CHARLES HENRY) (*continued*). *See* MERUTUṄGA ĀCHĀRYA. The Prabandhacintāmaṇi . . . Translated . . . by C. H. Tawney. 1901. 8°. [*Bibliotheca Indica.*] **14002. a. (vol. 143.)**

TAW SEIN KO. *See* DHAMMACHETĪ. The Kalyānī Inscriptions . . . Text and translation [by Taw Sein Ko]. 1892. 8°. **14098. dd. 9.**

—— *See* DHAMMACHETĪ. A Preliminary Study of the Kalyani Inscriptions . . . [including the text and translation] by Taw Sein-Ko. 1893. 4°. **14098. dd. 17.**

—— Some Remarks on the Kalyani inscriptions, *etc.* [With an appendix containing the text of the inscriptions in Burmese characters.] pp. 19. 58. *Bombay*, 1894. 8°. **14098. dd. 24.**

The "Remarks" are reprinted from the Indian Antiquary.

TAYLOR (ARNOLD C.). *See* ACADEMIES, *etc.*—London.—*Pali Text Society.* ABHIDHAMMAPIṬAKA. Kathāvatthu. Edited by A. C. Taylor. 1894-1897. 8°. **14098. b. 32.(2.)**

TEJAṢCHANDRA VIDYĀNANDA. *See* KĀLIDĀSA. —*Collected Works.* মহাকবি কালিদাসের গ্রন্থাবলী *etc.* [Granthāvalī. Comprising the Abhijñānaṣakuntala and Vikramorvaṣīya, with gloss by Tejaṣchandra, *etc.*] [1895.] 8. **14070. d. 34.(vol. 4.)**

TELANG (K. T.). *See* KĀṢĪNĀTHA TRYAMBAKA TELANG.

TELANG (M. R.). *See* MAṄGEṢA RĀMAKṚISHṆA TELANG.

TELAWKA. *See* TILOKA.

TEMPLE (RICHARD CARNAC). *See* PERIODICAL PUBLICATIONS.—*Bombay.* The Indian Antiquary, *etc.* (Vol. xiv.—xx., edited by J. F. Fleet and R. C. Temple, *etc.*; vol. xxi. *etc.* by R. C. Temple). 1872, *etc.* 4°. **14096. e.**

TETMATHE-UMINHLAIN PONGYI. ဒါနဖလုပ္ပတ္တိကျမ်း *etc.* [Dānaphaluppatti-kyan. Homilies on the fruits of charity as determining after-births. In Burmese, illustrated from Pali texts.] pp. iv. 200. ရန်ကုန် ၁၂၅၃ [*Rangoon*, 1891.] 8°. **14300. d. 25.(6.)**

TEZA (EMILIO). *See* BHARTṚIHARI. Un Centinaio di Sentenze Morali di Bhartrhari. Versione rimata di E. Teza. 1897. 8°. **14070. dd. 13.(2.)**

THA DO OUNG. *See* THA TO AUNG.

ṬHĀKURADĀSA, *the Marathi Poet.* ठाकूरदास बावांचे उपलब्ध ग्रंथ. [Ṭhākuradāsa-Bāvāṅchen Upalabdha Grantha. The works of Ṭhākuradāsa, including a metrical version of the Bhagavadgītā with the original Sanskrit text.] pp. iv. i. 146. मुंबई १८९७ [*Bombay,* 1897.] 8°. **14140. b. 28.**

ṬHĀKURADĀSA GUPTA. Swârthândha-prakâshikâ. स्वार्थान्धप्रकाशिका ॥ [A Hindi polemic against the pretensions of Brahmans, illustrated from Sanskrit texts.] pp. 7, 110. काशी १९०२ [*Benares,* 1902.] 12°. **14154. d. 30.**

ṬHĀKURAPRASĀDA, *Vedāntāchārya.* *See* YOGAVĀSISHṬHARĀMĀYAṆA. योगवासिष्ठ महारामायणम् *etc.* [Yogavāsishṭharāmāyaṇa. With Hindi version by Ṭhākuraprasāda.] [1900, *etc.*] 8°. **14048. e. 29.**

THA TO AUNG. A Grammar of the Pali Language after Kaccâyana, by Tha Do Oung . . . Vol. I. Containing Sandhi, Nâma and Kâraka, and Samâsa. (Vol. II. Containing Taddhita, Kita, Uṇâdi, Âkhyâta, Upasagga and Nipâta particles. Vol. III, being a dictionary of Pali word-roots. Vol. IV, Chandam &c.) *Akyab,* 1899-1902. 8°. **14098. dd. 18.**

THEISTIC TEXTS. ब्राह्मधर्म्म-प्रतिपादक-श्लोकसंग्रहः *etc.* (A Compilation of Theistic Texts from the Hindu, Buddhist, Shikh, Jewish, Christian, Mahomedan, Parsee, and Chinese Scriptures. ব্রাহ্মধর্মপ্রতিপাদক শ্লোকসংগ্রহ) [With Bengali version. Fifth edition.] pp. 224. *Calcutta,* 1904. 12°. **14072. b. 33.**

THERAGĀTHĀ. *See* SUTTAPIṬAKA. — *Khuddakanikāya.*

THIBAUT (GEORGE). *See* BĀDARĀYAṆA. The Vedânta-Sûtras with the commentary by *Sañkarâkârya.* Translated [with introduction] by G. Thibaut. 1890-1896. 8°. [*Sacred Books of the East.*] **2003. b. (vol. 34, 38.)**

THIRLWALL (M. A. C.). *See* UPANISHADS.—*Separate Upanishads.* Isavasya Upanishad. With . . . anvaya, vritti, word meaning, translation, notes and index by Sris Chandra Vasu . . . and M. A. C. Thirlwall. 1902. 12°. **14007. b. 13.(2.)**

THOMAS (FREDERICK WILLIAM). *See* BĀṆA. The Harṣa-carita . . . Translated by E. B. Cowell . . . and F. W. Thomas. 1897. 8°. [*Oriental Translation Fund.*] **14003. bb. (ser. 2, vol. 8.)**

—— *See* GREAT BRITAIN AND IRELAND.—*India Office.—Library.* Catalogue of Two Collections of Sanskrit Manuscripts . . . in the India Office Library. Compiled by C. H. Tawney . . . and F. W. Thomas. 1903. 8°. **14096. ccc. 8.**

—— *See* SĀDHANA. Deux Collections . . . de Sādhanas. 1903. 8°. [*Muséon.*] **P.P. 4453. (nouvelle sér., vol. 4.)**

—— *See* SĀYAṆA ĀCHĀRYA.—*Works on Philosophy, etc.* Le Bouddhisme d'après les sources brahmaniques . . . II. Sarvasiddhāntasaṁgraha[, edited by] F. W. Thomas et L. de la Vallée Poussin. 1902. 8°. **14048. e. 35.**

—— The Jānakīharaṇa of Kumāradāsa, *etc.* 1901. *See* ACADEMIES, *etc.* — London. — *Royal Asiatic Society of Great Britain and Ireland.* The Journal . . . 1901. pp. 253-280. 1834, *etc.* 8°. **Ac. 8820/3 & 2098. a, b.**

THORSTEINSON (STEINGRIM). *See* MAHĀBHĀRATA. —*Vanaparva.* Nal og Damajanti. . . . Í íslenzkri þýðingu eptir S. Thorsteinson. 1895. 12°. **14065. b. 16.**

THŪPAVAṀSA. ථූපවංශය *etc.* [Thūpavaṃsa. An account of the teaching of Buddha and the temples built over his relics. Translated into Pali by Vāchissara or Vāgīṣvara, from the Sinhalese original by an author styling himself Sakalavidyāchakravarti Parākrama of Ceylon. Edited by Baddēgama Dhammaratana.] pp. i. 82, i. පෑලියගොඩ [*Peliyagoda,*] 1896. 8°. **14098. d. 44.(2.)**

TILAK (B. G.). *See* BĀLA GAṄGĀDHARA TILAKA.

TILBE (H. H.). Pāli First Lessons, *etc.* pp. x. i. 124. *Rangoon,* 1902. 12°. **12906. de. 25.**

Forms part of the Student's Pali Series.

TILOKA, *Shin.* No. 1. The Small Hand Book of Buddhist Religion of Buddha Thāthana Noggaha School, from I, to III, Standards. [Comprising a series of well-known short texts, chiefly Pali with Burmese translation.] Compiled by Shin Télawka . . . ဗုဒ္ဓသာသနာနုဂ္ဂဟ-ကျောင်းသုံး ဝါအုပ် *etc.* pp. x. 93. မန္တလေး [*Mandalay,*] 1901. 12°. **14300. c. 7.**

TILOKA, *Ū, of Maṇijoti Kyaung, Mandalay.* ဝေါကိဏ္ဏတ္ထဒီပနီ *etc.* [Vokiṇṇatthadīpanī. Burmese homilies on the Buddhist conceptions of life and morals, with Pali anthology.] pp. 63. မန္တလေး ၁၂၆၁ [*Mandalay,* 1899.] 8°. **14300. d. 32.(3.)**

TILOKA, *Ū, of Kyaikto.* အရိယာမဂ္ဂဒီပနီကျမ်း *etc.* [Ariyamaggadīpanī. A Burmese treatise on the godly life, illustrated from Pali texts, by Tiloka. Followed by the Padhānasutta of the Suttanipāta, with Burmese commentary by Ñāṇālaṅkāra Mahāthera of Môn-ywa.] pp. vii. ii. 336. ရန်ကုန် ၁၂၆၁ [*Rangoon,* 1899.] 8°. **14300. d. 28.(4.)**

TILOK ṚISHJĪ, *Mahārāja.* अथ ज्ञानप्रदीपकप्रारंभः । [Jñānapradīpaka. A collection of Jain works, comprising the Pratikramaṇasūtra with explanations in the Marwari dialect of Gujarati followed by devotional writings, hymns, *etc.*, in the latter tongue.] ff. iii. 197. मुंबई १८९० [*Bombay,* 1890.] *obl.* 8°. **14144. g. 37.**

TIN, *Ū, of Maulmain.* See ANURUDDHA. သရူပတ္ထဒီပနီကျမ်း ။ [Sarūpatthadīpanī. A summary of the Saṅgaha, by Ū Tin.] 1883. 8°. **14300. d. 4.(5.)**

TINKAṚI SMṚITIRATNA, *of Sibpur.* জ্ঞানতত্ত্ব নিরূপণম্ *etc.* [Jñānatattvanirūpaṇa. An anthology of texts treating of the conditions of knowledge. Compiled and edited with a Bengali translation by Tinkaṛi Smṛitiratna.] pt. i. pp. 146. কলিকাতা ১৩০৬ [*Calcutta,* 1899.] 12°. **14048. b. 38.(3.)**

TIPIṬAKA. [For the Pali Canon :] *See* ABHIDHAMMAPIṬAKA, SUTTAPIṬAKA, and VINAYAPIṬAKA.

TIPIṬAKĀLAṄKĀRA SIRIDDHAJA, called BAGAYA HSAYA. *See* ABHIDHAMMAPIṬAKA. — *Dhammasaṅgaṇi.* မာတိကာ *etc.* [The *mātikā* of the Dhammasaṅgaṇi and the Dhātukathā, with Burmese exegeses by Tipiṭakālaṅkāra, followed by two treatises of the same author, viz. Yamaik-gaṇṭhi and Vithi-let-yo-hmat-pôn.] [1900.] 8°. **14098. dd. 23.**

—— *See* ANURUDDHA. အဘိဓမ္မတ္ထသင်္ဂြိုဟ် *etc.* [Abhidhammatthasaṅgaha. Followed by a Burmese *nissaya* by Tipiṭakālaṅkāra.] [1890.] 8°. **14098. ccc. 10.(1.)**

—— *See* ANURUDDHA. အဘိဓမ္မတ္ထသင်္ဂြိုဟ် *etc.* [Abhidhammatthasaṅgaha. With the *nissaya* of the Bagaya Hsaya.] [1898.] 8°. **14098. ccc. 10.(2.)**

—— —— [Another edition.] [1899.] 8°. **14098. ccc. 10.(3.)**

—— *See* ANURUDDHA. အဘိဓမ္မတ္ထသင်္ဂြိုဟ် ချုပ် *etc.* [Abhidhammatthasaṅgaha. Followed by a Burmese *nissaya* abridged from that of Tipiṭakālaṅkāra.] [1901.] 8°. **14098. ccc. 35.**

—— *See* ARIYAVAṂSA. ဂန္ထာဘရဏ *etc.* [Ganthābharaṇa. With Burmese commentary by Tipiṭakālaṅkāra.] [1898.] 8°. [*Saddā-ngay.*] **14098. ccc. 22.**

—— *See* BUDDHAGHOSA. [*Sammohavinodanī.*] ဝိဘင်း . . . အဖွင့် *etc.* [Sammohavinodanī. In the recension of Tipiṭakālaṅkāra.] [1901.] 8°. **14098. dd. 25.**

—— *See* DHAMMĀNANDA ĀCHARIYA. ကစ္စာယနဘေဒ *etc.* [Kachchāyanabheda. With Burmese commentary by Tipiṭakālaṅkāra.] [1898.] 8°. [*Saddā-ngay.*] **14098. ccc. 22.**

—— *See* DHAMMĀNANDA ĀCHARIYA. ကစ္စာယနသာရ *etc.* [Kachchāyanasāra. With Burmese commentary of Tipiṭakālaṅkāra.] [1898.] 8°. [*Saddā-ngay.*] **14098. ccc. 22.**

—— *See* KACHCHĀYANA. — *Kachchāyanappakaraṇa.* ပါးကရာပ္ပ။သဒ္ဒါကြီး *etc.* [Bā-ka-yā-mū Saddā-kyī. The aphorisms of Kachchāyana with Burmese commentary by Tipiṭakālaṅkāra.] [1898.] 8°. **14098. ccc. 12.(1.)**

—— *See* SADĀTEJA. ဝစ္စဝါစက *etc.* [Vachchavāchaka. With Burmese commentary by Tipiṭakālaṅkāra.] [1898.] 8°. [*Saddā-ngay.*] **14098. ccc. 22.**

—— *See* SADDHAMMAÑĀṆA. ဝိဘတျတ္ထ *etc.* [Vibhattyattha. With Burmese translation by Tipiṭakālaṅkāra.] [1898.] 8°. [*Saddā-ngay.*] **14098. ccc. 22.**

—— *See* SADDHAMMASIRI. သဒ္ဒတ္ထဘေဒစိန္တာ *etc.* [Saddatthabhedachintā. With Burmese commentary of Tipiṭakālaṅkāra.] [1898.] 8°. [*Saddā-ngay.*] **14098. ccc. 22.**

TIPPABHŪPĀLA, *Gopendra. See* VĀMANA ĀCHĀRYA. काव्यालङ्कारकामधेनुः [Kāvyālaṅkāravṛitti. With the commentary Kāvyālaṅkārakāmadhenu of Tippabhūpāla.] 1895, *etc.* 8°. [*Grandha Pradarsani.*] **14003. c. 2.(3.)**

TĪRTHAVANDANĀSTOTRA. ॥ तीर्थवन्दना स्तोत्र ॥ [Tīrthavandanāstotra. A hymn on the Jain shrines, in 10 stanzas.]. *See* DYĀNATI RĀYA. समाधिमरण *etc.* [Samādhimaraṇa.] pp. 7-11. [1901.] 12°. **14100. a. 21.(3.)**

TIRUKUḌANDAI DEṢIKA, *of Kumbakonam. See* NITYAKARMA. ஆஹ்நிகம் *etc.* [Āhnika. Edited by Tirukuḍandai Deṣika.] 1893. 12°. **14028. b. 82.(3.)**

TIRUNĀRĀYAṆA PERUMĀḶ SVĀMI. *See* KṚISHṆAIYAṄGĀR. ವಜ್ರಮುಕುಟೀಮಹೋತ್ಸವವರ್ಣನ *etc.* [Vajramukuṭīmahotsavavarṇana. Edited by Tirunārāyaṇa.] [1900.] 16°. **14076. a. 16.(4.)**

TIRUVEṄGAḌĀCHĀRYA. *See* TIRUVEṄKAṬĀCHĀRYA.

TIRUVEṄKAṬĀCHĀRYA, *Komāṇḍūr. See* ṢAṄKARA ĀCHĀRYA.—*Doubtful and Supposititious Works.* మణిత్రయి *etc.* [Maṇitrayī. With Telugu translations and commentaries by Tiruveṅkaṭāchārya.] 1899. 16°. **14028. a. 28.**

TISSA, *Ū, of Myinwunmin Kyaung, Mandalay. See* ABHIDHAMMAPIṬAKA.—*Dhammasaṅgaṇi.* မာတိကာ *etc.* [The *mātikā* of the Dhammasaṅgaṇi and the Dhātukathā, *etc.* Edited by Tissa and Janinda.] [1900.] 8°. **14098. dd. 23.**

—— *See* JĀGARĀBHIDDHAJA. အဘိဓမ္မတ္ထသင်္ဂဟဂဏ္ဌိသစ် *etc.* [Abhidhammatthasaṅgaha-gaṇṭhithit, *etc.* Edited by Tissa and Janinda.] [1898.] 8°. **14300. e. 4.**

—— —— [Another edition.] [1901.] 8°. **14300. e. 18.**

—— *See* PAṆḌITADDHAJA SĪLĀLAṄKĀRA. သဒ္ဒါပုဒ်စစ်၊ အကျယ် *etc.* [Saddā - pôk - sit - akyay. Edited by Tissa and Janinda.] [1896.] 8°. **14302. i. 15.**

TISSA, *Ū,* **and JANINDA,** *Ū.* သမူဟနိယမဒီပနီကျမ်း *etc.* [Samūhaniyamadīpanī. A collection of Burmese *niyamas* on Pali grammar with dissertations thereon, and including also Nyāt-aya-kauk, the introductory stanzas of Vimalabuddhi's Mukhamattadīpanī with a copious Burmese commentary.] pp. ii. 802, iv. ပဋ္ဌလေး ၁၂၅၉ [*Mandalay,* 1898.] 8°. **14302. i. 17.**

TOLMAN (HERBERT CUSHING) **and STEVENSON** (JAMES HENRY). The Vanderbilt Oriental Series. Edited by H. C. Tolman and J. H. Stevenson. *New York, Cincinnati, Chicago,* 1900, *etc.* 12°. **14003. m.**
In progress.

TOTĀRĀM VARMĀ. स्त्री धर्मबोधिनी . . . Stri Dharm Bodhini. [A Hindi treatise on the duties of woman, based upon and illustrated by texts from Sanskrit religious and legendary literature.] By Babu Tota Ram. Second edition. pp. ii. 115. *Aligarh,* 1899. 8°. **14156. d. 18.**

TRAILOKYAMOHANA GUHA NIYOGĪ. गीतभारतम्। भिक्टोरिया स्मृतिसंरक्षकं काव्यमन्दिरम्। Geet Bharatam. The Lays of India. The Memorial Poem-Temple of Empress Victoria, *etc.* [Being Sanskrit lyrics in 21 cantos, with English translation.] pp. 8, 15, 117; 2 *plates.* *Calcutta,* 1902. 8°. **14072. cc. 63.(2.)**

TRAILOKYANĀTHA BHAṬṬĀCHĀRYA, *Kāvyatīrtha Vidyānidhi.* See PADMANĀBHADATTA. সুপদ্মব্যাকরণম্ etc. [Supadmavyākaraṇa. With gloss by Trailokyanātha.] [1901.] 8°. **14090. c. 43.**

—— See PADMANĀBHADATTA. Supadma Vivaran Panjika ... Commented and published by ... Trailokya Nath Bhattacharya, *etc.* [1903.] 8°. **14092. b. 45.(2.)**

TRILOCHANADĀSA, *Grammarian.* See DURGASIṂHA. নমস্কারবিবেকঃ *etc.* [Namaskāraviveka. Comprising the introductory stanza of Durgasiṃha's Kātantravṛitti and Trilochanadāsa's Pañjikā thereupon.] [1900.] 12°. **14092. a. 24.(1.)**

—— কলাপ-ব্যাকরণম্ ... চতুষ্টয়পঞ্জী *etc.* [Chatushṭayapañjī, or Kātantravṛittipañjikā. A commentary on Durgasiṃha's Kātantravṛitti. Chapter ii. Edited by Rasikachandra Vidyāratna.] pp. 84. *Dacca,* 1893. 8°. **14090. bb. 13.(2.)**

—— আখ্যাতপঞ্জী। *etc.* [Ākhyātapañjī. The commentary on the section upon the verbs in Durgasiṃha's *vṛitti* upon the Kātantra. Edited by Mādhavachandra Tarkachūḍāmaṇi. Third edition.] pp. 140. ঢাকা ১৮৯৫ [*Dacca,* 1895.] 8°. **14090. bb. 13.(5.)**

TRIMALLA BHAṬṬA, *son of Vallabha.* शतश्लोकी निघण्टुः *etc.* [Śataślokī. A work on medicaments. With a Hindi translation by Krishṇalāla.] pp. ii. 38. मुंबई १९५१ [*Bombay,* 1894.] 8°. **14043. e. 28.**

This is the work published in 1869 *under the title* Pathyāpathya.

—— द्रव्यगुणशतक *etc.* [Dravyaguṇaśataka, or Śataślokī. With a Hindi translation by Śālagrāma Vaiśya.] pp. viii. 73. बंबई १९५३ [*Bombay,* 1897.] 12°. **14043. b. 13.**

TRIPIṬAKA. [For the texts of the Pali Canon :] *See* ABHIDHAMMAPIṬAKA, SUTTAPIṬAKA, and VINAYAPIṬAKA.

—— Bruchstücke (Neue Bruchstücke) des Sanskritkanons der Buddhisten aus Idykutšari, Chinesisch-Turkestān. Von R. Pischel. (Sitzungsberichte der Königlich Preussischen Akademie der Wissenschaften ... 1904. xxv., xxxix. ... Sonderabdruck.) 2 pts. *Berlin,* 1904. 8°. **14070. ee. 1.**

TRIPURĀNĀTHA VIDVĀN, *of Nepal.* शालग्रामपरीक्षा *etc.* [Śālagrāmaparikshā. An anthological work treating of the god or sacred symbol Saligram, his *lakshaṇas* and cult. Edited with preface *etc.* by Ramānātha Śarmā.] pp. iv. x. v. iv. 266. काश्याम् १९५५ [*Benares,* 1899.] 8°. **14028. c. 78.**

TRIPURĀRI, *son of Parvatanātha.* See BHAVABHŪTI. The Mâlatîmâdhava ... With the commentaries of Tripurâri [on Acts i.-vii.,] *etc.* 1892. 8°. **14079. c. 61.**

TRIVEDÎ (K. P.). *See* KAMALĀŚAṄKARA PRĀṆAŚAṄKARA TRIVEDĪ.

TRIVIKRAMA, *Poet.* कुवलयाश्वविलासः। [Kuvalayāśvavilāsa. A *champū* in 6 *ullāsas.*] pp. 118. [1890-1891.] *See* PERIODICAL PUBLICATIONS.—*Bombay.* ग्रन्थरत्नमाला *etc.* (Granth Ratna Málá, *etc.*) Vol. IV, no. 2-7. 1887-[1892.] 8°. **14096. c. 8.(vol. 4.)**

—— त्रिविक्रमकृतं व्याजोक्तिशतकं. [Vyājoktiśataka. A century of enigmatic verses.] 1888. *See* LAGHUKĀVYĀNĪ. लघुकाव्यानि ... Miscellaneous Poetical Pieces, *etc.* pp. 158-170. 1888. [*Kāvyetihāsasaṅgraha, Vol.* X, *no.* 5.] **14072. d. 37.(vol. 10.)**

TRIVIKRAMA DEVA. प्राकृतमणिदीपः ॥ [Prākṛitamaṇidīpa. Being the aphorisms of Trivikrama on Prakrit grammar, with short notes ascribed to Apyaya Dikshita.] 1895, *etc.* *See* VEṄKAṬARAṄGANĀTHA SVĀMĪ. Grandha Pradarsani, *etc.* [No. 8.] 1895, *etc.* 8°. **14003. c. 2.(8.)**

Incomplete, breaking off at I. iv. 99.

—— प्राकृतशब्दानुशासनम् ॥ [Prākṛitaśabdānuśāsana, also termed Trivikrama[vyākaraṇa]vṛitti. Aphorisms of Prakrit grammar, with commentary.] 1895, *etc.* *See* VEṄKAṬARAṄGANĀTHA SVĀMĪ. Grandha Pradarsani, *etc.* [No. 1.] 1895, *etc.* 8°. **14003. c. 2.(1.)**

This edition contains only adhyāya I.

—— ప్రాకృతశబ్దప్రదీపికా [Prākṛitaśabdapradīpikā. Trivikrama's aphorisms of Prakrit grammar with Kānkānphallī Nṛisiṃha Śāstrī's commentary.] *See* ŚAMBHURAHASYA. శ్రీశంభురహస్య ॥ [Kavikāvyādipraśaṃsā, *etc.*] pp. 20-84. [1890.] 8°. **14053. ccc. 31.**

TRIVIKRAMA DEVA (*continued*). प्राकृतशब्दप्रदीपिका। [Prākṛitaṣabdapradīpikā. Select aphorisms of Trivikrama, with a commentary by Kānkānphalli Nṛisiṃha Ṣāstrī.] 1895, *etc.* *See* VEṄKAṬARAṄGANĀTHA SVĀMĪ. Grandha Pradarsani, *etc.* [No. 9.] 1895, *etc.* 8°. **14003. c. 2.(9.)**
Incomplete.

TRIVIKRAMA MANĪSHĪ. *See* TRIVIKRAMA ṢĀSTRĪ, *Rāyadurgam.*

TRIVIKRAMA ṢĀSTRĪ, *Rāyadurgam, son of Bālamukunda.* *See* ṢAṄKARA ĀCHĀRYA.—*Philosophical Poems, etc.* వివేక చూడామణి *etc.* [Vivekachūḍāmaṇi. Edited by Trivikrama.] [1898.] 8°. **14048. c. 72.(2.)**

—— కావ్యప్రయోగరత్నావలి *etc.* [Kāvyaprayogaratnāvalī. 157 stanzas illustrating correct grammatical usages, with a commentary styled Sumanomanovinodinī.] pp. x. 125, ii. బళ్ళారి [*Bellary,*] 1897. 8°. **14090. c. 38.(3.)**

TRYAMBAKA GURUNĀTHA KĀḶE. *See* ĀGAMAS. [*Sūkshmāgama.*] सूक्ष्मागम *etc.* [Sūkshmāgama. With Marathi translation by Tryambaka Kāḷe.] [1901.] 8°. **14033. aa. 20.**

TUEBINGEN, *University of.* *See* ACADEMIES, *etc.*—Tuebingen.—*Eberhard-Karls-Universitaet.*

TUKĀRĀM TĀTYĀ. *See* MAHĀBHĀRATA.—Bhagavadgītā.—*Sanskrit and Vernaculars.* ज्ञानेश्वरी *etc.* [Bhagavadgītā. With the Jñāneṣvarī. Edited with glosses in Marathi by Tukārām Tātyā.] [1897.] 12°. **14060. b. 15.**

TULASĪPŪJĀ. अथ तुलसीपूजा प्रारंभः। [Tulasīpūjā. A ritual of the sacred basil plant.] ff. 8. मुंबई [*Bombay,* 1899.] *obl.* 16°. **14028. a. 27.(1.)**

TULASĪRĀMA, *Pandit.* *See* NAVĪNACHANDRA RĀYA. लघुव्याकरण . . . Laghu Vyakarana . . . with additions and explanations in English by Pandit Tulsi Ram. 1899. 8°. **14093. b. 41.(2.)**

TULASĪRĀMA, *Seṭh, of Moradabad,* **and others.** शास्त्रार्थ पत्र [Ṣāstrārthapatra. A religious controversy carried on by letters between Pandits of the Dharma Sabhā of Moradabad and the Ārya Samāj of Chandausi, chiefly in Sanskrit, with Hindi translations.] pp. 27. कानपुर [*Cawnpore,* 1896.] 8°. **14028. d. 67.**

TULASĪRĀMA ṢARMĀ, *of Kuchesar.* शास्त्रार्थ खुर्जा *etc.* [Ṣāstrārtha Khurjā. A report, in Hindi, of a controversy between members of the Ārya Samāj and the Dharmasabhā in Khurja as to the sanction of idolatry said to be conveyed in certain Vedic texts here quoted.] pp. 30. प्रयाग १९४९ [*Allahabad,* 1890.] 8°. **14154. c. 16.(2.)**

—— [Second edition.] pp. 38. प्रयाग १९५० [*Allahabad,* 1894.] 8°. **14154. c. 16.(3.)**

TULASĪRĀMA SVĀMĪ, *of Meerut.* *See* UPANISHADS.—*Separate Upanishads.* श्वेताश्वतरोपनिषद् *etc.* [Ṣvetāṣvataropanishad. With Sanskrit and Hindi commentary by Tulasīrāma.] [1897.] 8°. **14010. dd. 10.(2.)**

—— *See* VEDAS.—*Sāmaveda.* सामवेदभाष्यम् *etc.* (The Samvedbhashyam . . . With the commentary in Sanskrit and Hindi by Tulsi Ram Swami.) [1898, *etc.*] 8°. **14007. dd. 1.**

—— भास्करप्रकाश अर्थात् दयानन्दतिमिरभास्कर का उत्तर *etc.* (The Bhaskarprakasha. Or, Reply to Dayanand-timir-bhaskar[, Jvālāprasāda Miṣra's polemic against Dayānanda's Satyārthaprakāṣa. In Hindi, with numerous extracts from Sanskrit texts].) pp. iv. ii. 334, 92. *Meerut,* 1899. 8°. **14154. ee. 13.(1.)**

TURRINI (GIUSEPPE). *See* KĀLIDĀSA.—*Raghuvaṃṣa.* Il Laménto dél Ré Àgia sópra Indumatî . . . Côi Comménti di Mallinâta. Recàto . . . a comúne volgàre pér cúra di G. Turrini. 1899, *etc.* 4°. **14070. e. 20.**

—— *See* VEDAS.—Ṛigveda.—*Selections of Hymns and Verses.* Raccòlta dégli ínni dél Vèda . . . pér cúra di G. Turrini, *etc.* 1899, *etc.* 4°. **14010. ee. 4.**

TŪSĪ. *See* NAṢĪR al-DĪN (MUḤAMMAD ibn MUḤAMMAD).

TWET-HKAUNG HSAYA. ကမ္မဋ္ဌာန်းသံပေါက် အမျိုးမျိုး [Kammaṭṭhān-thanpauk-amyo-myo. A manual of the *kammaṭṭhānas,* comprising Pali lists of their subjects with Burmese translations and commentaries. Together with the Gôṇ-taw or 9 virtues of the Buddha, Dhamma, and Saṅgha, and the Mettā-po, with Burmese versions, *etc.*] pp. 24. ၇၃၆၅ ၁၂၅၅ [*Rangoon*, 1893.] 8°. **14300. d. 22.(6.)**

TYĀGARĀJA DĪKSHITA, *Mahāmahopādhyāya, of Mannargudi.* See YAJÑEŚA ŚARMĀ. ॥ श्रीत्यागराजविजयः ॥ *etc.* [Tyāgarājavijaya. A biographical panegyric upon Tyāgarāja.] [1904.] 12°. **14058. a. 19.**

—— ஸ்ரீத்யாகராஜஸ்தவ: *etc.* [Tyāgarājastava. A series of Ṣaiva hymns. With the author's commentary. Edited by Goshṭhīpuram Harihara Ṣāstrī.] pp. 141. கும்பகோணம் ॥ கஅகச [*Kumbakonam*, 1894.] 8°. **14028. d. 58.(2.)**

—— விபூதிருத்ராக்ஷதாரண நிருபணம் *etc.* [Vibhūtirudrākshadhāraṇanirūpaṇa. A treatise on the Ṣaiva practice of smearing the body with burnt cow-dung and wearing rosaries of *elæocarpus* berries. Translated from Tyāgarāja's Sanskrit work called Durjanoktinirāsa into Tamil by Eṭṭayapuram Veṅkaṭāchala Dīkshita, but with the quotations in the original Sanskrit. With notes by Virudai Ṣivañāna Yogi.] pp. vi. 130, iii. சென்னை [*Madras*,] 1901. 12°. **14170. d. 85.(1.)**

UATA. See UVAṬA.

UDAKAṢĀNTI. ఉదకశాంతివిధిః *etc.* [Udakaṣāntividhi. A manual, compiled from Vedic texts, for the performance of the lustratory rite called *udakaṣānti* as prescribed, according to tradition, by Baudhāyana. Edited by B. Veṅkaṭanārāyaṇa of Maddagiri.] pp. 44, v. బెంగళూరు ౧౯౦౦ [*Bangalore*, 1900.] 8°. **14028. d. 35.(3.)**

UDĀNA. See SUTTAPIṬAKA.—*Khuddakanikāya.*

UDAYACHANDRA DATTA. The Materia Medica of the Hindus, by Udoy Chand Dutt . . . With a glossary of Indian plants by George King . . . With additions and alterations by Kaviraj Binod Lall Sen and Kaviraj Athutosh [*sic*] Sen. Second edition. pp. xx. 355. *Calcutta*, 1900. 8°. **14043. c. 48.**

UDAYANA ĀCHĀRYA. See GOTAMA. The Nyâyasûtras with . . . extracts from the Nyâyavârttika and the Tâtparyaṭîkâ[, the Nyāyavārttikatātparyapariṣuddhi of Udayana,] *etc.* 1896. 8°. **14048. dd. 3.(vol. 9.)**

—— आत्मतत्त्वविवेकः *etc.* [Ātmatattvaviveka, or Bauddhadhikkāra. A treatise combating the views of the Buddhists as to the metaphysical Self. With portions of the gloss Bauddhadhikkārarahasya of Mathurānātha Tarkavāgīṣa, the exposition styled Bauddhadhikkāradīdhiti by Raghunātha Ṣiromaṇi, and portions of the gloss upon the latter by Gadādhara. Edited with a preface and a gloss upon Mathurānātha's commentary by Yadunātha Sārvabhauma.] नवद्वीपात् कलिकाता १८२२ [*Nadia, Calcutta* printed, 1900, *etc.*] 8°. **14048. dd. 28.**

In progress? The book is styled Bauddhadhikāra *in the preface; and this mistake is found elsewhere.*

—— कुसुमाञ्जलिः । [Kusumāñjali. Principles of the Nyāya. With commentary by Ṣivachandra Gui.] 1891, *etc.* See PERIODICAL PUBLICATIONS.—*Calcutta.* विद्योदयः *etc.* [Vidyodaya.] Vol. xx., *etc.* 1874, *etc.* 8°. **14096. cc. (vol. 20, etc.)**

—— लक्षणावली *etc.* [Lakshaṇāvalī. A tract on the definitions of the six Vaiṣeshika categories. Edited by Vindhyeṣvarīprasāda Dube.] pp. 13. *Benares*, 1897. 8°. **14048. bb. 20.(2.)**

Published as a supplement to no. 50 *of the* Benares Sanskrit Series.

—— The Lakṣaṇāvalī of Udayanācārya. With the commentary Nyāyamuktāvalī of Çeṣaçārṅgadhara. Edited by Surendralāla Gosvāmin. [With bibliographical notice by A. Venis.] pp. 72, v. ii. 1900. See PERIODICAL PUBLICATIONS.—*Benares.* The Pandit, *etc.* New Series. Vol. XXI-XXII. 1876, *etc.* 8°. **14096. d. 6.(vol. 21, 22.)**

—— ॥ लक्षणावली *etc.* [Lakshaṇāvalī. With the commentary Lakshaṇāvalīprakāṣa of Viṣvanātha Pañchānana. Edited by Lokanātha Upādhyāya.] pp. ii. xviii. 195. काश्याम् १८२२ [*Benares*, 1901.] 8°. **14049. a. 4.(3.)**

UDAYA NĀRĀYAṆA SIṂHA, *of Biddupur.* See SŪRYASIDDHĀNTA. सूर्यसिद्धान्त . . . Surya Siddhanta . . . translated into Hindi . . . by Udaya Narain Singh. [1903.] 8°. **14053. dd. 8.**

UDAYARĀGA-DEVARAPADA. ಉದಯರಾಗದೇವರಪದದ ಮೊದಲನೆಪುಸ್ತಕ *etc.* [Udayarāga-devarapada. Jain hymns, in Sanskrit and Canarese. Edited by Padmarāja Paṇḍita.] pt. i. pp. 10. ಬೆಂಗಳೂರು ೧೮೯೪ [*Bangalore*, 1894.] 8°. **14100. b. 3.(3.)**

UDAYASĀGARA, *disciple of Vidyāsāgara, of Chāndrakula, Vidhipaksha-gachchha.* *See* SIDDHASENA DIVĀKARA. श्री ... श्रीवर्द्धमानद्वात्रिंशिका *etc.* [Vardhamānadvātriṃṣikā. With commentary by Udayasāgara.] [1903.] 12°. **14100. a. 21.(4.)**

UDAYASAUBHĀGYA GAṆĪ. *See* HEMACHANDRA, *disciple of Devachandra.* Materialien zur Kenntnis des Apabhraṃśa, *etc.* [Comprising the examples in Hemachandra's grammar with the translation of Udayasaubhāgya, *etc.*] 1902. 4°. [*Abhandlungen der Koeniglichen Gesellschaft der Wissenschaften zu Goettingen.*] **Ac. 670.(Bd. 5, no. 4.)**

UDAYA VARMĀ, *Raja of Mavelikara.* *See* AMARU. Amaruka Satakum . . . With introduction and notes by Udaya Varma. 1893. 8°. **14072. cc. 56.**

—— *See* RĀJARĀJA VARMĀ. श्री ... विटविभावरी *etc.* [Viṭavibhāvarī. With a commentary called Chandrikā by Udaya Varmā.] [1894.] 8°. **14072. c. 52.(1.)**

UDBHAṬA. Alaṅkārasārasaṅgraha. [A summary of Rhetoric, in 6 chapters. Edited by G. A. Jacob.] 1897. *See* JACOB (G. A.). Notes on Alaṅkāra Literature, *etc.* 1897-1898. [*Journal of the Royal Asiatic Society.*] **Ac. 8820/3 & 2098. a, b.**

UDDYOTAKARA, *Pāṣupatāchārya, Bhāradvāja.* *See* GOTAMA. The Nyâyasûtras with Vâtsyâyana's Bhâshya and extracts from the Nyâyavârttika [of Uddyotakara], *etc.* 1896. 8°. **14048. dd. 3.(vol. 9.)**

—— *See* VĀCHASPATI MIṢRA. [*Nyāyavārttikatātparyaṭīkā.*] The Nyâyavârttikatâtparyaṭîkâ of Vâchaspati, *etc.* [A commentary upon Uddyotakara's commentary Nyāyavārttika on the Nyāyasūtra.] 1898. 8°. **14048. dd. 3.(vol. 13.)**

UDOY CHAND DUTT. *See* UDAYACHANDRA DATTA.

UḌUDĀYAPRADĪPA. උඩුදායප්‍රදීපය හෙවත් ලඝුපාරාශරිය *etc.* [Uḍudāyapradīpa, or Laghupārāṣarī. A treatise on astrology, purporting to be founded on the Pārāṣarī Horā of Parāṣara. With a Sinhalese interpretation by D. Fernando, Tambi-Appu Gurunnânse.] pp. ii. 13. [*Colombo,*] 1888. 8°. **14053. cc. 63.(3.)**

—— Ándhra Párásaryamu, Telugu commentary of Bála Párásaryamu [*i.e.* the text, with Telugu commentary, of the Uḍudāyapradīpa], being an elementary treatise on astrology, with an elaborate introduction, by Koraḷḷa Subbaráyárya ... బాలపారాశర్య వ్యాఖ్యానము, ఆంధ్రపారాశర్యము. pp. vi. 87. *Madras,* 1898. 12°. **14053. b. 31.(4.)**

UKKAṂVAṂSAMĀLĀ, *Mahāthera.* ဝိပဿနာဉာဏတန္တိသာတန်း [Vipassanāñāṇatantī-sātan. A compendium of Pali dicta for aspirants to the tenfold spiritual insight, with Burmese translation and commentary.] pp. 29. *Rangoon,* ၁၂၄၃ [1881.] 8°. **14300. d. 22.(2.)**

—— ဝိပဿနာကမ္မဋ္ဌာန် *etc.* [Vipassanāñāṇatantī-sā-tan, here called Vipassanā-kammaṭṭhān.] *See* SARAṆA. သရဏာဒိဆက္ကကဏ္ဍဒီပဏီကျမ်း [Saraṇādichhakkakaṇḍadīpaṇī.] pp. 74-99. [1899.] 8°. **14300. d. 28.(5.)**

ULWAR. *See* ALWAR.

UMĀDATTA TRIPĀṬHĪ, *of Farukhabad.* *See* SĀRASVATASŪTRA. सारस्वत *etc.* [Sārasvatavyākaraṇa. With Hindi commentary by Umādatta and Ṣaktidhara.] [1891.] 8°. **14090. bb. 6.**

—— कूटपद्यव्याख्या *etc.* [Kūṭapadyavyākhyā. An anthology of 16 stanzas with a commentary by Umādatta. Followed by Ayodhyāprasāda's Ṣivastotra or Ṣambhust°. with the commentary Bhaktamanorañjanī of Umādatta; a stanza on the influence of the teacher, by Narasiṃhadatta, with a commentary styled Yājñī by Yajñadatta; and a stanza addressed to Vishṇu, by Yajñadatta, with a commentary called Nārasiṃhī by Narasiṃhadatta.] pp. ii. 103. कल्याण-मुंबई १९५६ [*Kalyan,* 1899.] 12°. **14072. b. 24.**

UMĀSVĀTI. ॥ अथ तत्वार्थसूत्रटीकाप्रारंभः ॥ [Tattvārthasūtra, also called Tattvārthādhigama and Daṣasūtrī. An aphoristic summary of Jain doctrine, in 10 *adhyāyas*. With a Hindi commentary by Sadāsukha of Jaipur.] ff. 66. मुंबई १८९६ [*Bombay*, 1896.] *obl.* 8°. **14100. d. 9.**

—— तत्वार्थ सूत्र *etc.* [Tattvārthasūtra. Edited by Nāthūrām Lamechū.] pp. 44. लखनऊ [*Lucknow*, 1897.] 12°. **14100. a. 15.(2.)**

—— श्रीतत्वार्थसूत्रम्. मूल [Tattvārthasūtra.] ff. 23. मुरादाबाद १९५४ [*Moradabad*, 1897.] *obl.* 12°. **14100. a. 15.(3.)**

—— तत्वार्थसूत्राणि [Tattvārthasūtra.] pp. 32. लाहौर १९०० [*Lahore*, 1900.] 12°. **14100. a. 6.(2.)**

Forms no. 34 in the Jain Religious Tracts Series, *published by Bābū Jñānachandra.*

—— तत्वार्थसूत्रम् । [Tattvārthasūtra.] *See* JAINANITYAPĀṬHA. अथ जैननित्यपाठसंग्रहः [Jainanityapāṭhasaṅgraha.] pp. 119-160. [1901.] *obl.* 16°. **14100. a. 27.**

—— ॥ श्रीतत्वार्थसूत्रम् ॥ [Tattvārthasūtra.] ff. 10. *See* PRAKĪRṆAKA. चउसरण तथा आउरपच्चक्खाण पयन्ना° [Chaüsaraṇa-païnna, *etc.*] [1902.] *obl.* 8°. **14100. c. 24.**

—— अथ . . . तत्वार्थसूत्रः ॥ [Tattvārthasūtra.] pp. 43. लखनऊ १९०१ [*Lucknow*, 1901.] *obl.* 12°. **14100. a. 6.(4.)**

—— अथ तत्वार्थसूत्रादि ॥ नित्यपाठक्रिया ॥ [Tattvārthasūtra. Followed by Jinasena's Jinasahasranāma and Mahāchandrajī's Hindi metrical version of the Sāmāyika.] 3 pts. लखनऊ १९०१ [*Lucknow*, 1901.] *obl.* 16°. **14100. a. 28.**

The title is taken from the cover.

UMEṢACHANDRA BHAṬṬĀCHĀRYA SMṚITIRATNA. গৌড়াদ্য দ্রাবিড় বৈদিকশ্রেণী ব্রাহ্মণ-কুলপরিচায়ক প্রশ্নোত্তরমালা *etc.* [Praṣnottaramālā. An account, in catechetical form, of the origin, functions, and history of the Gauḍ, Drāviḍ, and Vaidik Brahmans. In Bengali, illustrated from Sanskrit texts.] pp. 39. *Calcutta*, 1900. 8°. **14058. a. 8.(2.)**

UMEṢACHANDRA GUPTA KAVIRATNA, *Kavirāja.* Vaidyakaśabdasindhu, or A comprehensive lexicon of Hindu medical terms and names of drugs with their synonyms in Latin, Sanskrit, Hindi, Telugu, Bengali, &c., with copious references to, and quotations from, standard works, *etc.* (वैद्यकशब्दसिन्धुः) pp. xxxiv. iv. 1112. *Calcutta*, 1894. 8°. **14043. e. 30.**

UMRĀO SINGH, *Ṭhākura, of Moradabad.* अघमर्षणद्विजराज *etc.* [Aghamarshaṇa-dvijarāja. An anthology of passages bearing upon the modes of expiation of sin, with Hindi commentary.] pp. 58, ii. मुरादाबाद १९५९ [*Moradabad*, 1903.] 8°. **14033. bbb. 25.**

UṆĀDISŪTRA. উণাদিসূত্রম্ । [Uṇādisūtra. Selections, with a commentary in Sanskrit and Bengali by Mukundadayālu Vasu.] pp. 10. কোচবিহার ১৩০০ [*Kuch Behar*, 1893.] 12°. **14092. a. 17.(2.)**

—— [For the Uṇādi Aphorisms of the Saupadma school :] *See* PADMANĀBHADATTA.

—— [For editions of the Uṇādisūtra included in the Siddhāntakaumudī :] *See* PĀṆINI. — *Siddhāntakaumudī.*

UṆṆIKIḌĀVA TAMBURĀN, *Maṅgaḍa Kōvilagatta,* also called ṢRĪVALLABHAN. ഭാനുകോപവിജയം കഥകളി *etc.* [Bhānukopavijaya. A poetic narrative, alternately told in Sanskrit stanzas and Malayalam verse and prose, of the legend of Padmāsura's attempted rape of Indrāṇī.] pp. 44. പട്ടാമ്പി [*Pattambi*,] 1896. 16°. **14076. a. 16.(7.)**

—— പത്മാസുരോത്ഭവം കഥകളി *etc.* [Padmāsurodbhava. The story of the birth of Padmāsura, son of Kaṣyapa, told in Sanskrit verses alternating with Malayalam.] pp. 46. പട്ടാമ്പി [*Pattambi*,] 1896. 16°. **14072. a. 1.**

UPAGRANTHASŪTRA. ॥ उपग्रन्थसूत्रम् ॥ [Upagranthasūtra. A tract on expiatory rites forming a *pariṡishṭa* to the Sāmavedī Kalpasūtra.] 1892. *See* PERIODICAL PUBLICATIONS.—*Calcutta.* उषा *etc.* [Ushā.] Vol. II, no. i. [1889]-1893. 8°. **14010. c. 43.(vol. 2.)**

Imperfect, breaking off at the end of the 5th section of prapāṭhaka 3.

UPĀKARMA. யஜுர்வேதோபாகர்மம் *etc.* [Yajurvedopākarma. A treatise on the rites connected with the periodic renewal of the study of the Yajurveda.] pp. 16. கல்பாதி ॥ ஶார்வரி ॥ [*Kalpadi*, 1900.] 16°. **14010. a. 5.(2.)**

UPAMANYU, *Maharshi, son of Vyāghrapāda.* See NANDIKEṢVARA. శ్రీ . . . శ్రీమత్తాంగదిసూత్రకాశికా *etc.* [Nandikeṣvara-kāṣikā. With the commentary Tattvavimarṣinī ascribed to Upamanyu.] [1902.] 12°. **14033. a. 26.(3.)**

UPANISHADS.

GENERAL COLLECTIONS.

॥ अथ दशोपनिषच्छान्तिसमेता अष्टोत्तरशतमुपनिषदः प्रारभ्यन्ते ॥ [108 Upanishads. Followed by a Ṣāntipāṭha.] ff. 868, iii. मोहमय्यां १८१७ [*Bombay*, 1895.] *obl.* 8°. **14007. b. 6.**

Contains the Adhyātma (*or* Pāramārthikādhyātma), Advayatāraka, Aitareya, Akshamālikā, Akshi, Amṛitabindu (*or* Brahmabindu), Amṛitanāda, Annapūrṇā, Āruṇika (Āruṇeyi *or* Gūḍhāruṇika), Atharvaṣikhā, Atharvaṣiras, Ātmā, Ātma[pra]bodha, Avadhūta, Avyakta, Bahvṛicha, Bhasmajābāla, Bhāvanā, Bhikshuka, Brahma, Brahmavidyā, Bṛihadāraṇyaka (or Brāhmaṇa), Bṛihajjābāla, Bṛihannārāyaṇa (or Mahānārāyaṇa, *from* Taittirīyāraṇyaka), Chhāndogya, Dakshiṇāmūrti, Darṣana (*or* Jābāladarṣana), Dattātreya, Devī, Dhyānabindu, Ekākshara, Gaṇapati (*or* G°.-atharvaṣirsha), Garbha, Gāruḍa, Gopālatāpani, Haṃsa, Hayagriva, Iṣāvāsya, Jābāla, Jābāli, Kaivalya, Kālāgnirudra, Kalisantāraṇa, Kaṭha[rudra], Kaṭha[valli], Kaushītaki-brāhmaṇa, Kena (*or* Talavakāra), Kṛishṇa, Kshurikā, Kuṇḍikā, Mahā, Mahāvākya, Maitrāyaṇi (*or* Maitri), Maitreyi, Maṇḍalabrāhmaṇa, Māṇḍūkya, Mantrikā (or Chūlikā), Mudgala, Muktikā, Muṇḍaka, Nādabindu, Nāradaparivrājaka, Nārāyaṇa, Nirālamba, Nirvāṇa, Nṛisiṃhatāpani, Paiṅgala, Pañchabrahma, Parabrahma, Paramahaṃsa, Paramahaṃsaparivrājaka, Pāṣupata-brahma, Prāṇāgnihotra, Praṣna, Rāmarahasya, Rāmatāpanī, Rudrahṛidaya, Rudrākshajābāla, Ṣāṇḍilya, Sannyāsa, Ṣarabha, Sarasvatīrahasya, Ṣārīraka, Sarva[sāra] (or Sarvopanishatsāra), Ṣāṭyāyanīya, Saubhāgyalakshmi, Sāvitrī, Sītā, Skanda, Subāla, Ṣukarahasya, Sūrya, Ṣvetāṣvatara, Taittirīya, Tārasāra, Tejobindu, Tripādvibhūti-mahānārāyaṇa, Tripura, Tripurātāpinī, Triṣikhibrāhmaṇa, Turīyātītāvadhūta, Vajrasūchikā, Varāha, Vāsudeva, Yājñavalkya, Yogachūḍāmaṇi, Yogakuṇḍali, Yogaṣikhā, *and* Yogatattva *Upanishads.*

उपनिषदां समुच्चयः *etc.* (Thirty two Upanishads. With Dîpikâs by . . . Nârâyaṇa and Shankarânanda. Edited by Pandits at the Ánandâśrama.) pp. xi. 608. पुण्याख्यपत्तने १८९५ [*Poona*, 1895.] 8°. **14003. ccc. (no. 29.)**

Forms no. 29 *of the* Ānandāṣrama Sanskrit Series. *The English title is from the cover.*

The Upanishads in this volume are:— Atharvaṣikhā, Atharvaṣiras, Amṛitanāda, Amṛitabindu, or Brahmabindu (with two commentaries), Ātmā, Āruṇeyi, Kaivalya, Kaushītaki, Kshurikā, Garbha, Gopālatāpanī, Chūlikā, Jābāla, Tejobindu, Dhyānabindu, Nādabindu, Nīlarudra, Paramahaṃsa, Piṇḍa, Prāṇāgnihotra, Brahma, Brahmavidyā, Maitri (*another recension*), Yogatattva, Yogaṣikhā, Rāmatāpanī, Sannyāsa, Sarva, Haṃsa (*another*).

அஷ்டோத்தரஶதோபநிஷத: *etc.* [Ashṭottaraṣatopanishadaḥ. 108 Upanishads. Followed by the Rudranamaka and Rudrachamaka; Nārāyaṇīyā-yājñikyupanishad (*i.e.* Bṛihannārāyaṇa, from Taittirīyāraṇyaka); Purushasūkta; Ṣrīsūkta; Pañchaṣānti; Ābrahman; Mahāvākyaratnāvali; and Brahmasūtra. Edited by K. Veṅkaṭakṛishṇa Ṣāstrī and Mūñjūrpaṭṭu Rāmachandra Ṣāstrī.] pp. iii. 890. చెన్నపురి [*Madras*,] 1896. 8°. **14010. cc. 8.**

Contains the Upanishads in the Bombay edition of 1895.

The Twenty-eight Upanishads, Îsha & others. [Edited] by Vâsudev Laxmaṇ Shâstrî Phaṇsîkar. (अष्टाविंशत्युपनिषदः ।) pp. i. ii. 372. *Bombay*, 1904. 16°. **14010. a. 9.**

Contains the Īṣa, Kena, Kaṭha, Praṣna, Muṇḍaka, Māṇḍūkya, Taittirīya, Aitareya, Chhāndogya, Bṛihadāraṇyaka, Ṣvetāṣvatara, Kaivalya, Jābāla, Garbha, Nārāyaṇātharvaṇa (i.e. *that commonly known as* Nārāyaṇa), Nārāyaṇa (i.e. Bṛihannārāyaṇa, *from* Taittirīyāraṇyaka), Bṛihajjābāla, Kaushītaki, Sūrya, Kṛishṇa, Hayagriva, Dattātreya, Rudrāksha-jābāla, Mahāvākya, Kalisantāraṇa, Jābāli, Bahvṛicha, and Muktikā.

உபநிஷத்ஸ்த்ரா. உபநிஷத்வித்யா *etc.* [Upanishadvidyā. A collection of Upanishads with Tamil translations, commentaries, *etc.* Compiled and edited by Ṣrīnivāsa Dīkshita.] நடுக்காவேரி [*Nadukkaveri*,] 1898, *etc.* 8°. **14010. cc. 13.**

In progress?

Sechzig Upanishad's des Veda, aus dem Sanskrit übersetzt und mit Einleitungen und Anmerkungen versehen von Dr. Paul Deussen. pp. xxv. 920. *Leipzig*, 1897. 8°. **14010. dd. 8.**

Contains the Aitareya, Kaushītaki, Chhāndogya, Kena, Taittirīya, Mahānārāyaṇa (*from* Taittirīyāraṇyaka), Kaṭha, Ṣvetāṣvatara, Maitrāyaṇi, Bṛihadāraṇyaka, Īṣa, Muṇḍaka, Praṣna, Māṇḍūkya, Garbha, Prāṇāgnihotra, Piṇḍa, Ātmā, Sarva, Gāruḍa, Brahmavidyā, Kshurikā, Chūlikā, Nādabindu, Brahmabindu (*i.e.* Amṛitabindu), Amṛitabindu (*i.e.* Amṛitanāda), Dhyānabindu, Tejobindu, Yogaṣikhā, Yogatattva, Haṃsa, Brahma, Sannyāsa, Āruṇeyi, Kaṭhaṣruti, Paramahaṃsa, Jābāla, Āṣrama, Atharvaṣiras, Atharvaṣikhā, Nīlarudra, Kālāgnirudra, Kaivalya, Mahā, Nārāyaṇa, Ātmabodha, Nṛisiṃhatāpani, *and* Rāmatāpanī, *with ten others translated from Anquetil Duperron's* Oupnek'hat.

SMALL COLLECTIONS.

[*Two or More Upanishads.*]

ईशादिदशोपनिषत्संग्रहः *etc.* [Īṣa, Kena, Kaṭha, Praṣna, Muṇḍaka, Māṇḍūkya, Taittirīya, Aitareya, Chhāndogya, Bṛihadāraṇyaka, and Ṣvetāṣvatara Upanishads.] 11 pts. मुम्बापुर्यां १९४३ [*Bombay*, 1886.] 12°. **14010. b. 9.**

SMALL COLLECTIONS (*continued*).

Herr Böhtlingk legte drei kritisch gesichtete und übersetzte Upanishad[, viz. the Kaṭha, Aitareya, and Praṣna,] mit erklärenden Anmerkungen vor. 1890. *See* ACADEMIES, *etc.* — Leipsic. — *Koeniglich Sacchsische Gesellschaft der Wissenschaften.* Berichte, *etc.* Bd. 42. pp. 127-197. 1848, *etc.* 8°. **Ac. 700/2. (Bd. 42.)**

उपनिषत्संग्रहः [Upanishatsaṅgraha. Comprising, of this series, the Brihannārāyaṇa; the 5th *prapāṭhaka* of the Chhāndogya; the Ṣikshāvallī of the Taittirīya; and pt. 1 of the Bṛihadāraṇyaka Upanishad. Edited with Sanskrit glosses and Marathi paraphrases, notes, and introductions by Veṅkaṭarāu Rāmachandra.] पुण्याख्यपत्तने १८१२ [*Poona*, 1890, *etc.*] 8°. **14010. c. 51.**

In progress.

ईश . . . माण्डूक्याभिधाः षण्मूलोपनिषदः [Īṣa, Kena, Kaṭha, Praṣna, Muṇḍaka, and Māṇḍūkya Upanishads. Edited by Bhīmasena Ṣarmā.] ff. 48. प्रयाग १८९२ [*Allahabad*, 1892.] *obl.* 16°. **14010. a. 3.**

Selections from the Upanishads. Translated into English. [Comprising the Kaṭha, Īṣa, Ṣvetāṣvatara, and part of the Bṛihadāraṇyaka Upanishads, translated by H. H. E. Roer. With a part of the Chhāndogya Upanishad, translated by Rājendralāla Mitra.] With notes from Sankara Acharya and others. pp. viii. 106. 1895. *See* EAST. The Sacred Books of the East Described and Examined. Hindu Series. Vol. II, pt. 1. 1895, *etc.* 8°. **14010. cc. 9. (vol. 2.)**

উপনিষদাবলী *etc.* [Upanishadāvalī. Ten Upanishads, including (1) the Muktikopanishad; (2) the Garbhop°., Brahmop°., Sarvop°., Brahmabindūp°. (Amṛitabindūp°.), Rāmop°. or Rāmarahasyop°., and Nādabindūp°., with the commentaries of Nārāyaṇa; (3) the Kaivalyop°., with the commentaries of Ṣaṅkarānanda and Nārāyaṇa; and (4) the Muṇḍakop°. and Kaṭhop°., with the commentaries of Ṣaṅkara. Edited with Bengali translations by Prasannakumāra Ṣāstrī.] pp. 184. কলিকাতা ১৩০২ [*Calcutta*, 1896.] 12°. **14010. b. 12.**

Begin. वाजसनेयसंहितोपनिषद्. [Īṣa, Kena, Muṇḍaka, and Aitareya Upanishads. With Gujarati translations and commentaries by Raṇachhoḍajī Uddhavajī Ṣāstrī.] pp. 103. *See* MAHĀBHĀRATA.—*Abridgments and Selections.* श्रीमद्भगवद्गीता पञ्चरत्न *etc.* [Pañcharatna, *etc.*] [1896.] 8°. **14060. d. 15.**

ईश केन मुण्डक अने ऐतरेयोपनिषद् *etc.* [Īṣa, Kena, Muṇḍaka, and Aitareya Upanishads. Edited with Gujarati translations and commentaries by Raṇachhoḍajī Uddhavajī Ṣāstrī. Second edition.] pp. 103. मुंबई १८९६ [*Bombay*, 1896.] 8°. **14010. dd. 10. (1.)**

A separate publication of the latter part of the edition of the Pañcharatna published by this editor.

The Upanishads. Translated . . . with a preamble and arguments by G. R. S. Mead . . . and Jagadîsha Chandra Chaṭṭopâdhyâya, *etc.* Vols. 1, 2. *London*, 1896. *obl.* 8°. **14007. b. 5.**

In progress?

Ishopanishat. (Mandukyopanishat, Mundakopanishat.) [With English translations and expositions according to the doctrines of the Ârya Samâj.] *See* GURUDATTA VIDYĀRTHĪ. Works, *etc.* pp. 109-157. 1897. 8°. **14010. dd. 11.**

—— —— pp. 107-167. 1902. 8°. **759. c. 20.**

అధ్యాత్మోపనిషత్తు ఆత్మోపనిషత్తు *etc.* [Adhyātmopanishad and Ātmopanishad. With Telugu glosses and paraphrases by Ēlēṣvarapu Veṅkaṭappaiya Ṣāstri.] pp. 30, 17. *Madras*, 1897. 8°. **14010. dd. 13.**

தசோபநிஷத்த்ராவிடபாஷ்யம் *etc.* [Daṣopanishad-drāviḍabhāshya. Ten Upanishads,—viz. the Īṣāvāsya, Kena, Kaṭha, Praṣna, Muṇḍaka, Māṇḍūkya, Aitareya, Bṛihadāraṇyaka, Chāndogya, and Taittirīya—with a Tamil commentary comprising word-for-word interpretations of the text and translations of the commentaries of Ṣaṅkara and Rāmānuja, together with the Kārikās of Gauḍapāda in Sanskrit and Ṣaṅkara's commentary thereupon in Tamil. Compiled and edited by A. Ṣrīnivāsa Tātāchārya Svāmī.] 6 pts. சென்னை நகரம் [*Madras*, 1897]-1898. 8°. **14010. dd. 14.**

The text of each verse is printed in both Grantham and Telugu character.

SMALL COLLECTIONS (*continued*).

[illegible] . . . பஞ்சதசோபநிஷத் *etc.* [Pañchadaṣopanishadaḥ. Fifteen Upanishads, *scil.* the Kaivalya, Nārāyaṇa, Amṛitabindu (Brahmabindu), Maitrāyaṇi, Maitreyi, Sarvasāra, Nirālamba, Ātmabodha, Nāradaparivrājaka, Skanda, Paiṅgala, Ṣārīraka, Varāha, Kalisantāraṇa, and Muktikā. Edited with Tamil introduction, notes, and translation by Villavarambal Kuppusvāmi Aiyar.] pp. ii. x. iv. ii. 449, ix. சென்னபட்டணம் ஹெவிளம்பி [*Madras*, 1898.] 8°. **14010. cc. 12.**

॥ ईशावास्योपनिषत् *etc.* [Īṣāvāsya, Kena, and part of the Māṇḍūkya Upanishads. With Canarese translation and commentary.] *See* KRISHṆĀCHĀRYA, *T. R.* ॥ कन्नडभाषान्तरमाला *etc.* [Kannaḍabhāshāntaramālā.] pt. 1. [1898.] 8°. **14007. b. 14.**

Amritabindu [*i.q.* Brahmabindu] and Kaivalya Upanishads [in Sanskrit, together with the Ṣāntipātha and extracts from Gauḍapāda's Kārikās]. With commentaries [in English, compiled from the works of Ṣaṅkara Āchārya, Ṣaṅkarānanda, and Nārāyaṇa]. Translated into English by A. Mahadeva Sastri. pp. xxiv. 16, 94. *Madras*, 1898. 12°. **14010. b. 19.**

Forms Vol. I of the Vedic Religion Series, Minor Upanishads.

The Isa, Kena & Mundaka Upanishads [in Sanskrit and English] and Sri Sankara's commentary [in English], translated by S. Sitarama Sastri . . . First volume. (Vol. II, The Katha and Prasna Upanishads . . . translated by S. Sitarama Sastri. Vol. III, IV, The Chhándogya Upanishad and Sri Sankara's commentary, translated by Gangánath Jhá. Vol. V, The Aitareya & Taittiriya Upanishads . . . translated by S. Sitarama Sastri.) *Madras*, 1898, *etc.* 12°. **14010. b. 20.**

In progress.

An attempt to interpret in Marâthî the Eleven Upanishads. With preface, translation and notes in English . . . by Râjârâma Râmakṛishṇa Bhâgavata. (उपनिषदांची मीमांसा) *Bombay*, 1898, *etc.* 8°. **14010. cc. 10.**

In progress.

अथारुणेयोपनिषद् *etc.* (परमहंसोपनिषद् *etc.*) [Āruṇeyi, Paramahaṃsa, Yogatattva, Yogaṣikhā, Brahmavidyā, Ātmā, Piṇḍa, Nādabindu, Brahmabindu, Sarvasāra, Garbha, and Kaivalya Upanishads. With Hindi versions by Vaidyanātha Ṣāstrī and Kanhaiyālāl Ṣarmā.] *See* VAIDYANĀTHA ṢĀSTRĪ TIVĀRĪ, *of Jalalabad*, and others. [Miscellaneous tracts.] Nos. 40-51. [1899.] 12°. **14033. a. 37.**

Several of these Upanishads are merely excerpts from the original texts.

Begin. ఓమ్. శ్రీశాన్తానన్దసరస్వతీస్వామిచర్చర-ణారవిన్దాభ్యాంనమోనమః *etc.* [Kaivalya, Nārāyaṇa, Taittirīya, and Nārāyaṇīyā-yājñikī Upanishads. Preceded by the Gurustotra, Parabrahmāshṭottaraṣatanāmāvali, and Mantrapushpa, and followed by the Purushasūkta, Ṣrīsūkta, and Bhūsūkta.] pp. 206. *Madras*, 1899. 32°. **14010. a. 6.**

उपनिषत्प्रसादः नवमदशमोपनिषदो मृद्वी टीका *etc.* [Upanishatprasāda. The Chhāndogya and Bṛihadāraṇyaka Upanishads, with a brief commentary by Bhāskarānanda Sarasvatī.] pp. ii. ii. 618; 1 *plate.* काश्यां १९५६ [*Benares*, 1899.] 8°. **14010. dd. 15.**

The Telugu Upanishads, Isa- Kena- Katha- Prasna- Munda & Mandukya. [Translated] by Mahamahopadhyaya Sri Paravastu Venkata Ranganathacharya Aryavaraguru. With original Sanskrit texts. Part I. (Taittireeya and Purushasoocta . . . Part II.) (ఆంధ్రోపనిషత్తులు.) *Vizagapatam*, 1899, *etc.* 8°. **14007. b. 11.(1.)**

In progress? The English title is taken from the wrapper.

(దశోపనిషదః) [Daṣopanishadaḥ. The Aitareya, Taittirīya, Īṣa, Kena (here called Sāmavedīyatalavakāra), Kaṭha, Muṇḍaka (here called Ātharvaṇa), Māṇḍūkya, Praṣna (here called Shaṭpraṣna), Bṛihadāraṇyaka, and Chhāndogya Upanishads. Preceded by the Madhvāshṭottarastotra from the Pāñcharātra.] pp. 342. చెన్నపురాయమ్ ౧౯౦౧ [*Madras*, 1901.] *obl.* 12°. **14010. b. 22.**

No title-page.

ईशादिदशोपनिषदः *etc.* [Īṣādi-daṣopanishadaḥ. The Īṣa, Kena, Kaṭha, Praṣna, Muṇḍaka, Māṇḍūkya,

SMALL COLLECTIONS (*continued*).

Taittirīya, Aitareya, Chhāndogya, and Bṛihadāraṇyaka Upanishads.] pp. 325. अजमेर° १९६० [*Ajmere*, 1903.] 12°. **14010. b. 24.**

श्री ... श्रीरामतापनीयोपनिषद् ... श्रीरामोपनिषच्च [Rāmatāpanīyopanishad and Rāmopanishad. With a Hindi commentary upon the former by Visvesvara Dāsa and a Sanskrit gloss called Subodhinī upon the latter by Rāmanārāyaṇa Dāsa.] pp. ii. 120, 12. *Moradabad*, [1903.] 8°. **14007. b. 11.(2.)**

SELECTIONS.

From the Upanishads. [Selections from the Kaṭha, Prasna, and Chhāndogya. Translated] by Charles Johnston. pp. x. 55. *Dublin*, 1896. 12°. **14010. b. 10.**

॥ अथ शान्तिपाठः ॥ [Ṣāntipāṭha. A series of prayers to be said on reading the 10 great Upanishads, compiled chiefly from the Taittirīya, Bṛihadāraṇyaka, Nṛisiṃhatāpanī, and Ṣvetāṣvatara Upanishads, and in part from Āraṇyakas. With the commentaries of Ṣaṅkara and Sāyaṇa, and a Bengali translation by Hārāṇachandra Vandyopādhyāya.] pp. 24. 1892. *See* PERIODICAL PUBLICATIONS.—*Calcutta*. उषा *etc.* [Ushā.] Vol. II, no. iv. [1889]-1893. 8°. **14010. c. 43.(vol. 2.)**

॥ अथ ... शान्तयः ॥ [Ṣāntipāṭha.] *See* above, *General Collections*. ॥ अथ ... अष्टोत्तरशतमुपनिषदः *etc.* [108 Upanishads.] ff. 866-868. [1895.] *obl.* 8°. **14007. b. 6.**

Passages from the Upanishads. [Rendered into English verse.] *See* RAMEṢACHANDRA DATTA. Lays of Ancient India, *etc.* pp. 53-82. 1894. 8°. **2318. h. 9.**

হিন্দুশাস্ত্র ... ব্রাহ্মণ, আরণ্যক ও উপনিষদ্। [Selections from the Upanishads. Edited with Bengali translation and preface on the Brāhmaṇa literature by Rameṣachandra Datta and Satyavrata Sāmaṣramī.] pp. i. 117. [1895.] *See* RAMEṢACHANDRA DATTA. হিন্দুশাস্ত্র *etc.* [Hindu-ṣāstra.] Part ii. [1895-1897.] **14085. c. 45.(vol. 1.)**

மஹாவாக்யரத்நாவளி: [Mahāvākyaratnāvali. A collection of extracts from the 108 Upanishads.

SELECTIONS (*continued*).

Compiled by Rāmachandra Tīrtha, disciple of Vāsudeva Sarasvatī.] *See* above, *General Collections*. அஷ்டோத்தரஶதோபநிஷத: *etc.* [Ashṭottaraṣatopanishadaḥ.] pp. 835-868. 1896. 8°. **14010. cc. 8.**

अथ महावाक्यरत्नावलि सर्वोपनिषन्महावाक्यानां संग्रहरूपा *etc.* [Mahāvākyaratnāvali. Edited by Mukunda Jhā.] pp. 53. मुरादाबाद १९०३ [*Moradabad*, 1903.] 12°. **14010. b. 25.**

Differs in its introductory matter from other copies.

మహావాక్యరత్నావళి *etc.* [Mahāvākyaratnāvali. With grammatical analyses and a Telugu commentary called Suprabhā by Pulugurti Nṛisiṃhāmātya. Edited by Gurudanti Veṅkaṭāchala Ṣarmā.] pp. i. 356. చెన్నపురి [*Madras*,] 1904. 8°. **14007. b. 25.**

இந்து பைபில் என்னும் ஆரியர் சத்திய வேதம் *etc.* (The Hindu Holy Bible, containing the Old Testament: or [selections from the] Upanishaths [printed in Tamil characters, with English translation and Tamil introductions, translation, commentary, *etc.*]. Compiled by S. P. Narasimmalu Nayudu.) pp. viii. 24, ii. 272. *Coimbatore*, 1898. 8°. **14170. ee. 15.**

The English title is from the cover.

वेदान्तसमन्वयः व्याख्यानान्वितः। [Vedāntasamanvaya. A digest of Upanishadic passages, with a Vedantic commentary harmonising the interpretations of the various schools, by Gauragovinda Rāya.] (Samanvaya Series.) कलिकातायां १८२५ [*Calcutta*, 1903, *etc.*] 8°. **14049. bb. 2.**

In progress.

Brahmopasanam [a lectionary of the Brāhma Samāj, consisting of extracts from the older Upanishads with Telugu translations and commentaries,] is respectfully dedicated to the esteemed and venerable Chandra Sekhara Brahmananda Swami, Pradhana Acharya of the Bangalore Brahma Samaj, by . . . P. R. Rangiah Naidu. pp. 59. *Madras*, 1904. 16°. **14010. a. 10.**

Some Sayings from the Upanishads. Done into English with notes by L. D. Barnett. pp. 59. *London, Leyden* [printed], 1905. 8°. **14007. b. 24.**

SELECTIONS (*continued*).

See MAṆILĀLA NABHUBHĀĪ DVIVEDĪ. The Imitation of Śankara. Being ... texts bearing on the Advaita [from the Upanishads, *etc.*, with English translation,] *etc.* 1895. 8°. **14048. cc. 1.**

See ṢRĪNIVĀSA AIYAṄGĀR, *M.B.* The Aryan Prayer-book, in Sanskrit, with an English translation ... [A series of devotional extracts from the Upanishads,] *etc.* 1902. 16°. **14028. bb. 12.**

SEPARATE UPANISHADS.

अथ-ऋग्वेदीयैतरेयोपनिषद्भाष्यम् *etc.* [Aitareyopanishad. With commentary in Sanskrit and Hindi by Bhīmasena Ṣarmā.] pp. iv. 99. इटावा [१८]९७ [*Etawah*, 1897.] 8°. **14010. cc. 7.(1.)**

—— [Second edition.] pp. iv. 100. इटावा १९०० [*Etawah*, 1900.] 8°. **14010. cc. 3.(3.)**

ऐतरेयोपनिषद् *etc.* [Aitareyopanishad. Edited with analyses and Hindi glossaries to each verse by Ẓālim Singh, assisted by Gaṅgādatta and Rāmadatta Joshī.] pp. ii. 48. लखनऊ १९०० [*Lucknow*, 1900.] 8°. **14007. dd. 3.(4.)**

See ṢAṄKARA ĀCHĀRYA.—*Commentaries.* [*Upanishads.*] Aitareyopanishad. Sankara's Introduction [in English]. 1898. 8°. [*The Brahmavâdin.*] **14048. g. 1.(vol. 3.)**

भस्मजाबालोपनिषत् *etc.* [Bhasmajābālopanishad. With the commentary of Ṣivānanda Karmandi.] pp. iv. 77. श्रीकाश्यन्त० विश्वावसु [*Benares*, 1893.] 8°. **14010. cc. 4.**

भावनोपनिषत् *etc.* [Bhāvanopanishad. With the commentary of Bhāskararāya.] 1896. *See* MYSORE.—*Government of Mysore.* Government Oriental Library Series. Bibliotheca Sanskrita. No. 11, pp. 231-253. 1893, *etc.* 8°. **14004. b. 8.**

Il primo capitolo della Brahma-Upanishad, coll' annessovi commento di Nârâyaṇa, tradotto e criticamente discusso dal Dr. Carlo Formichi. pp. vii. 15. *Kiel, Lipsia* [printed], 1897. 4°. **14010. ee. 2.**

श्रीबृहदारण्यकोपनिषत् *etc.* [Bṛihadāraṇyakopanishad. Edited with a Hindi translation, a Hindi commentary founded on the works of Ṣaṅkara and

SEPARATE UPANISHADS (*continued*).

Ānandagiri, and notes by Pītāmbara Purushottama. Preceded by a short metrical account of certain Upanishads, entitled Ṣrutishaḍliṅgasaṅgraha, with a Hindi translation, also by the latter.] 3 vols. pp. xx. liv. 2453, ii. मुंबई १८९२ [*Bombay*, 1892.] 8°. **14007. c. 24.**

बृहदारण्यकोपनिषन्मिताक्षरा *etc.* [Bṛihadāraṇyakopanishad. With the commentary Mitāksharā of Nityānandāṣrama. Edited by Kāṣīnātha Bāla Ṣāstrī Āgāṣe.] pp. i. 271. पुण्याख्यपत्तने १८९६ [*Poona*, 1896.] 8°. **14003. ccc. (no. 31.)**

Forms no. 31 *of the* Ānandāṣrama Sanskrit Series.

L'Upanishad du Grand Aranyaka, Brihadâranyakopanishad [according to the Mādhyandina recension]. Traduite ... par A.-Ferdinand Herold. pp. 159. *Paris, Saint-Amand* [printed], 1894. 8°. **14007. c. 23.**

See SUREṢVARA ĀCHĀRYA. बृहदारण्यकोपनिषद्भाष्यवार्तिकम् *etc.* (Bṛihadáraṇyakopanishad-bháshyavártika ... [A metrical commentary upon the Bṛihadāraṇyakopanishad as expounded by Ṣaṅkara] *etc.*) [1892]-1894. 8°. **14003. ccc. (no. 16.)**

Chhandogya Upanishad. [With analyses and Telugu word-for-word version and commentary.] Edited by M. B. Pantulu. ఛాన్దోగ్యోపనిషత్ *etc.* pp. vi. 520. *Madras*, 1899. 8°. **14010. dd. 16.**

Forming the supplement to the Hindu Reformer *of Madras, no.* xi.

(छान्दोग्योपनिषद्भाष्य) [Chhāndogyopanishad. With *pada*-analysis, Sanskrit commentary setting forth doctrines of the Ārya Samāj, and Hindi translation of text and paraphrase of commentary, by Ṣivaṣaṅkara Ṣarmā.] अजमेर १९०४ [*Ajmere*, 1904, *etc.*] 8°. **14007. f. 5.**

In progress.

छान्दोग्योपनिषद् भाष्यम् *etc.* [Chhāndogyopanishad. Another edition of the preceding.] अजमेर० १९६१ [*Ajmere*, 1905.] 8°. **14007. f. 6.**

In progress.

See LITTLE (C. E.). A Grammatical Index to the Chāndogya-upaniṣad, *etc.* [1900?] 12°. **14003. m. 2.**

SEPARATE UPANISHADS (*continued*).

See ṢAṄKARA ĀCHĀRYA.—*Commentaries.* [*Upanishads.*] Translation of [passages from] Sankara's commentary on the Chandogya Upanishad. 1898. 8°. [*The Brahmavádin.*] **14048. g. 1.(vol. 3.)**

Dakshinámúrti = Upanishad. Translated into English, with notes [and an appendix containing the Sanskrit text]. *See* ṢAṄKARA ĀCHĀRYA.—*Doubtful and Supposititious Works.* The Vedânta Doctrine of Śrí Sankarâchârya, *etc.* pp. 153-167. 1899. 12°. **14048. b. 36.**

శ్రీగాణపతచరణోపహారాభిధం శ్రీగణపత్యుపనిష-ద్వ్యాఖ్యానం *etc.* [Gaṇapatyupanishad, or Gaṇapatyatharvaṣīrsha. With a commentary styled Gāṇapatacharaṇopahāra by Ṣrīnivāsa Dikshita.] pp. 12. శ్రీమన్నడుక్కావేరి [*Nadukkaveri,*] 1901. 8°. **14010. c. 35.(3.)**

ஸ்ரீ கணபதி சரணோபஹாரம் ॥ [Another edition, in the Grantham character.] pp. 14. ஸ்ரீ நடுக்காவேரி [*Nadukkaveri,*] 1901. 8°. **14007. b. 4.(2.)**

अथ श्री वेदान्तर्गत-गोपालतापनीउपनिषत् *etc.* [Gopālatāpanyupanishad. With a gloss. Edited with a Hindi translation by Kanhaiyālāl Ṣarmā of Moradabad.] pp. ii. 68, ii. मुरादाबाद १९५५ [*Moradabad,* 1898.] 8°. **14010. c. 51.(4.)**

Gopala Tapani Upanishad. Part i. [Translated, with extracts from the commentaries of Nārāyaṇa Tīrtha, Viṣveṣvara Paṇḍita, and Apyaya Dīkshita, by R. Anantakṛishṇa Ṣāstrī.] 1899. *See* PERIODICAL PUBLICATIONS.—*Bombay.* The Theosophist, *etc.* Vol. XX, no. iv, v. 1879, *etc.* 8°. **P.P. 636. cm. (vol. 20.)**

ईशावास्योपनिषत्सटीकशाङ्करभाष्योपेता *etc.* ((1) Shri Íśávásyopanishad with the Bháshya of . . . Śankaráchárya and Commentary by . . . Ánandadnyána. Edited by . . . Bāḷa Śástri Agáśe. (2) The Bháshya of . . . Uatabhattácharya. Edited by . . . Rájárama Śástrí. (3) The Rahasya of . . . Brahmánanda. (4) The Rahasya Vivriti by Ramachandra Pandita. (5) The Dípika by . . . Śankaránanda. Edited by Pandits at the Ánandásrama. (6) The Bhashyás of . . . Anantácharya. And (7) Ánandabhattopádhyáya. Edited by . . . Rájárama Sâstrí.) 7 pts. पुण्याख्यपत्तने १८१० [*Poona,* 1888.] 8°. **14003. ccc. (no. 5.)**

Forms no. 5 *of the* Ānandāṣrama Sanskrit Series. *The English title is taken from the cover.*

ईशोपनामकवाजसनेयोपनिषद् *etc.* [Īṣopanishad, or Vājasaneyopanishad. With a Hindi verse-translation by Satyānanda Muhammad. Followed by several verses in Sanskrit and Hindi.] pp. 12. लखनऊ १८९० [*Lucknow,* 1890.] 8°. **14010. c. 52.(2.)**

वाजसनेयोपनिषद्भाष्यम् ॥ ईशावास्योपनाममूलकम् . . . Vajasaneyopnishat [*i.e.* Īṣopanishad]. With [Sanskrit and Hindi] commentary of Bhimsen Sharma. Second edition. pp. 42. *Allahabad,* 1892. 8°. **14007. c. 26.(1.)**

Isa Upanishad, or The last chapter of the Sukla Yajur Veda, with text, easy Sanskrit notes, English and Bengali translation . . . ঈশা উপনিষদ্ *etc.* pp. ii. 18. *See* YADUNĀTHA MAJUMDĀR. The Indian Sage, *etc.* pt. i. 1893. 12°. **14048. a. 20.(1.)**

ईशोपनिषत् *etc.* (Isa-Upanishad. With the Bhasyas of Baladeva Vidyabhushana, Sri Sankaracharyya and the Tika of Anandagiri &c. &c. &c. With Bengali translation and commentary. Edited by Sri Syamalala Gosvami, Siddhanta Vachaspati. With an English translation and commentary.) pp. ii. 52, i. 6. *Calcutta,* 1895. 8°. **14010. cc. 3.(1.)**

The Íśavâsyopanishad. Translated into English, with the commentaries of Sri Sankaracharya and Sri Anantacharya, and notes from the Tikas of Anandagiri, Uvatacharya, Sankarananda, Ramchandra Pandit and Anandabhatta. By Srisa Chandra Vasu. pp. vi. 68. *Bombay,* 1896. 8°. **14010. cc. 6.**

Isavasyopanishad [in Telugu and Tamil characters]. With [Tamil glosses and] commentaries [by] Sreemat Paramahamsa Bala Subrahmania Brahma Swamy. (ஈசாவாஸ்யோபநிஷத்-டீகா) pp. i. 106. சென்னை [*Madras,* 1899.] 8°. **14010. b. 21.**

Forms no. 1 *of the* Bala Brahman Series.

SEPARATE UPANISHADS (*continued*).

ایش اوپنشد کا اُردو ترجمہ الخ [Īṣopanishad. With an Urdu translation and commentary based on the teachings of the Ārya Samāj by Kṛipārāma of Bulandshahr.] pp. 32, *lith.* مُرادابان [*Moradabad*, 1899.] 8°. **14007. dd. 5.**

वाजसनेयोपनिषद् *etc.* [Īṣopanishad, or Vājasaneyopanishad. With Hindi translation and exposition by Badarīdatta Ṣarmā, preacher of the Ārya Samāj.] pp. 18. **मेरठ १९५८** [*Meerut*, 1901.] 8°. **14007. b. 4.(3.)**

Isavasya Upanishad. With the Sanskrit text, anvaya, vritti, word meaning, translation, notes and index by Sris Chandra Vasu . . . and M. A. C. Thirlwall. (Vedanta Series.) pp. xxi. 32, 9. *Allahabad*, 1902. 12°. **14007. b. 13.(2.)**

ஜாபாலோபநிடதத்தின் பொழிப்புரையும் விசேடவுரையும் *etc.* [Jābālopanishad. Followed by the commentary of Ṣrīnivāsa Dīkshita, in Tamil. Edited by Ṣivānandasāgara Yogīṣvara. Second edition.] pp. 88, vii. நடுக்காவேரி [*Nadukkaveri*,] 1900. 8°. **14007. b. 12.(2.)**

কৈবল্যোপনিষৎ *etc.* [Kaivalyopanishad. With a Bengali translation by Pūrṇānanda.] pp. 8. কলিকাতা [*Calcutta*, 1870?] 12°. **14010. b. 8.(1.)**

Kaivalyopanishad. [Translated by R. Anantakṛishṇa Ṣāstrī. With appended notes, also in English.] 1899. *See* PERIODICAL PUBLICATIONS.—*Madras*. The Light of Truth, *etc.* Vol. II, no. 9, pp. 201-208. 1897, *etc.* 4°. **14170. fff. 4.(vol. 2.)**

अथ कठोपनिषद्भाष्यम् *etc.* [Kaṭhopanishad, or Kaṭhavallī. With Sanskrit and Hindi commentary by Bhīmasena Ṣarmā. Second edition.] pp. 220. **प्रयाग १८९३** [*Allahabad*, 1893.] 8°. **14007. c. 26.(3.)**

Kaṭha-Upanišad. [Text,] traduction et commentaire. *See* REGNAUD (P.). Études Védiques et Post-Védiques, *etc.* pp. 57-167. 1898. 8°. **Ac. 365. (fasc. xxxviii.)**

कठोपनिषद् *etc.* [Kaṭhopanishad. With Hindi translation and exposition by Badarīdatta Ṣarmā, preacher of the Ārya Samāj. Edited by Tulasīrāma Svāmī.] pp. 96. **मेरठ १९६०** [*Meerut*, 1903.] 12°. **14007. b. 4.(5.)**

SEPARATE UPANISHADS (*continued*).

Kâthaka-upanishad. Öfversatt från sanskrit af Andrea Butenschön. [With preface by K. F. Johansson.] pp. 62, i. *Stockholm*, 1902. 8°. **14007. b. 27.**

La Kâ*th*aka-upanisad, tradotto in italiano e preceduta da una notizia sul panteismo indiano [by Ferdinando Belloni-Filippi]. pp. x. 150. *Pisa*, 1905. 8°. **14007. b. 26.**

See ṢAṄKARA ĀCHĀRYA.—*Commentaries. [Upanishads.]* La introduzione del commento di Çaṅkara alla Kāṭhakopaniṣad, *etc.* 1892. 8°. **14010. dd. 5.(3.)**

केनोपनिषत्पदटीकाशाङ्करपदभाष्यवाक्यभाष्योपेता *etc.* (The Kenopanishad with the Pada and Vákya Bháshyás of . . . Śankarácharya and Commentary of . . . Ánandadnyána. Edited by . . . Bála Sástri Agáśe. And the Dípikás of the same by . . . Śankaránanda and Náráyaṇa. Edited by Pandits at the Ánandáśrama.) 3 pts. **पुण्याख्यपत्तने १८१०** [*Poona*, 1888.] 8°. **14003. ccc. (no. 6.)**

Forms no. 6 of the Ānandāṣrama Sanskrit Series. *The English title is taken from the cover.*

सामवेदीय तलवकारोपनिषत् केनोपनिषत् *etc.* [Kena or Talavakāra Upanishad. With commentary in Sanskrit and Hindi by Bhīmasena Ṣarmā. Second edition.] pp. 56. **प्रयाग १८९३** [*Allahabad*, 1893.] 8°. **14007. c. 26.(2.)**

An English translation of the Kena Upanishat with [Sanskrit text and English] exposition by Durga Prasad. pp. 34. *Lahore*, 1898. 12°. **14010. b. 8.(3.)**

கேநோபநிஷத்தீபிகை *etc.* [Kenopanishad. With the commentary Kenopanishaddīpikā of Bālasubrahmaṇya Brahmasvāmī, in Tamil.] pp. 207. சென்னை [*Madras*,] 1900. 12°. **14007. b. 13.(1.)**

The Sanskrit verses are printed in the Grantham character, with transliteration into Tamil letters.

కేనోపనిషద్దీపిక *etc.* [Kenopanishad. With the commentary Kenopanishaddīpikā of Bālasubrahmaṇya Brahmasvāmī, in Telugu.] pp. ii. 124. చెన్నపురి ౧౯౦౦ [*Madras*, 1900.] 8°. **14007. b. 12.(1.)**

SEPARATE UPANISHADS (*continued*).

तलवकारोपनिषद् *etc.* [Kenopanishad. With Hindi translation and exposition by Badarīdatta Ṣarmā, preacher of the Ārya Samāj.] pp. 32. मेरठ १९५८ [*Meerut*, 1901.] 8°. **14007. b. 4.(4.)**

See ṢAṄKARA ĀCHĀRYA.—*Commentaries.* [*Upanishads.*] Translation of [passages from] Sankara's commentary on Kena Upanishad. 1897. 8°. [*The Brahmavâdin.*] **14048. g. 1.(vol. 3.)**

অথর্ব্ববেদীয় – ক্ষুরিকোপনিষৎ। [Kshurikopanishad. With Bengali paraphrase.] *See* KĀLĪPRASANNA VIDYĀRATNA BHAṬṬĀCHĀRYA. যোগাঙ্কুর *etc.* [Yogāṅkura.] pp. 85-96. [1894.] 12°. **14048. b. 28.(2.)**

మహోపనిషత్తు *etc.* [Mahopanishad. With Telugu glosses and paraphrases by Ēlēṣvarapu Veṅkaṭappaiya Ṣāstri.] pp. 175. *Madras*, 1899. 8°. **14010. dd. 5.(4.)**

मण्डलब्राह्मणोपनिषत् राजयोगभाष्यसहिता. The Maṇḍala-bráhmaṇopanishad, [a Yogic tractate belonging to the White Yajurveda,] with a commentary [styled Rājayogabhāshya, and vulgarly ascribed to Ṣaṅkara]. Edited by A. Mahádeva Śástri ... and Panditaratnam K. Rangácharya. pp. viii. 36, iv. 1896. *See* MYSORE.—*Government of Mysore.* Government Oriental Library Series. Bibliotheca Sanskrita, *etc.* No. 10. 1893, *etc.* 8°. **14004. b. 7.**

Different from the Upanishad described by Rajendralal Mitra, Notices of Sanskrit MSS., *no.* 682. *The commentary is ascribed in some MSS. to a pupil of Sadānanda Avadhūta.*

—— [Another edition.] 1899. 8°. **14010. cc. 14.**

Râja Yoga Bhâshya. Translated from original MSS. of the Adyar Library by Pandit R. Ananthakrishna Sastryar. pp. 27. *Madras*, 1896. 8°. **14048. c. 70.(2.)**

Reprinted from The Theosophist.

माण्डूक्योपनिषत् *etc.* (Bhasha [*i.e.* Hindi] Translation of Pandit Guru Datta, M.A.'s English translation and exposition of Mandukyopanishat, [with the Sanskrit text,] by Atma Ram.) pp. 80. *Lahore*, 1891. 12°. **14010. b. 8.**

SEPARATE UPANISHADS (*continued*).

अथ माण्डूक्योपनिषद्भाष्यम् *etc.* [Māṇḍūkyopanishad. With commentary in Sanskrit and Hindi by Bhīmasena Ṣarmā. Second edition.] pp. 24, 38. प्रयाग १८९४ [*Allahabad*, 1894.] 8°. **14007. c. 26.(4.)**

The Vedic Philosophy, or An Exposition of the Sacred and Mysterious Monosyllable ओम् Aum. The Mândukya Upanishad ... with English translation and [English] commentary and an introduction by Har Nârâyana. pp. ii. i. xliii. 128. *Bombay*, 1895. 8°. **14010. cc. 2.**

The Mandukyopanishat. Being the exposition of Om ... Translated and expounded by Pandit Guru Datta Vidyarthi. Chicago edition. pp. 34. *Lahore*, 1893. 8°. **14010. dd. 5.(1.)**

The Mândûkyopanishad. With Gaudapâda's Kârikâs and the Bhâshya of Śankara. Translated into English [with introduction] by Manilal N. Dvivedi. pp. i. xlvi. 137, v. *Bombay*, 1894. 8°. **14007. cc. 24.**

See GAUḌAPĀDA ĀCHĀRYA. গৌড়পাদীয় আগম *etc.* [Āgamaṣāstra, or Māṇḍūkyopanishatkārikāḥ.] [1890.] 8°. **14010. c. 52.(4.)**

मुण्डकोपनिषत्सटीकशाङ्करभाष्योपेता *etc.* [Muṇḍakopanishad. With the commentary of Ṣaṅkara, the gloss of Ānandagiri, and the Dīpikā of Nārāyaṇa.] pp. ii. 47, 13. पुण्याख्यपत्तने १८१० [*Poona*, 1889.] 8°. **14003. ccc. (no. 9.)**

Forms no. 9 *of the* Ānandāṣrama Sanskrit Series.

अथ मुण्डकोपनिषद्भाष्यम् *etc.* [Muṇḍakopanishad. With commentary in Sanskrit and Hindi by Bhīmasena Ṣarmā. Second edition.] pp. 154. प्रयाग १८९४ [*Allahabad*, 1894.] 8°. **14007. c. 26.(5.)**

मुण्डकोपनिषद् *etc.* [Muṇḍakopanishad. Edited with analyses and Hindi glossaries to each verse by Ẓālim Singh, assisted by Gaṅgādatta and Rāmadatta Joshī.] pp. ii. 82. लखनऊ १९०० [*Lucknow*, 1900.] 8°. **14007. dd. 3.(2.)**

See ṢAṄKARA ĀCHĀRYA.—*Commentaries.* [*Upanishads.*] Translation of [passages from] Sankara's commentary on the Mundaka Upanishad. 1898. 8°. [*The Brahmavâdin.*] **14048. g. 1.(vol. 3.)**

SEPARATE UPANISHADS (*continued*).

श्री निरालम्बोपनिषत् *etc.* [Nirālambopanishad. With a Gujarati translation by Brahmachārī Pūrṇānanda.] pp. 39. लुणावाडा १९५४ [*Lunawara*, 1898.] *obl.* 12°. **14010. b. 3.(2.)**

नृसिंहपूर्वोत्तरतापनीयोपनिषत् *etc.* [Nṛisiṃhatāpanīyopanishad. Parts i. and ii., the former with the commentary of Ṣaṅkara, the latter with the commentary of Sāyaṇa.] pp. i. 158. पुण्याख्यपत्तने १८९५ [*Poona*, 1895.] 8°. **14003. ccc. (no. 30.)**

Forms no. 30 *of the* Ānandāṣrama Sanskrit Series.

प्रश्नोपनिषत्सटीकशाङ्करभाष्योपेता *etc.* (Śri Praśnopanishad with the Bháshya of ... Śankarácharya and its commentary by ... Ánandajnyána, also Dípiká of the same by ... Śankaránanda. Edited by Pandits at the Ánandáśrama.) pp. ii. 71, 24. पुण्याख्यपत्तने १८९० [*Poona*, 1889.] 8°. **14003. ccc. (no. 8.)**

Forms no. 8 *of the* Ānandāṣrama Sanskrit Series. *The English title is taken from the cover.*

अथ प्रश्नोपनिषद्भाष्यम् *etc.* [Praṣnopanishad. With commentary in Sanskrit and Hindi by Bhīmasena Ṣarmā. Second edition.] pp. 148. प्रयाग १८९४ [*Allahabad*, 1894.] 8°. **14007. c. 26.(6.)**

प्रश्नोपनिषद् *etc.* [Praṣnopanishad. Edited with analyses and Hindi glossaries to each verse by Ẓālim Singh, assisted by Gaṅgādatta and Rāmadatta Joshī.] pp. ii. 88. लखनऊ १९०० [*Lucknow*, 1900.] 8°. **14007. dd. 3.(1.)**

An English translation of the Prashnopanishat. Containing six questions of life and death. With Sanscrit text. By Durgaprasad, *etc.* [Followed by the Charpaṭapañjarī and 2 other hymns ascribed to Ṣaṅkara, in Sanskrit and English, and 2 religious poems in Hindi.] pp. 50. *Lahore*, 1899. 12°. **14048. a. 20.(2.)**

See ṢAṄKARA ĀCHĀRYA.—*Commentaries.* [*Upanishads.*] [Translation of Ṣaṅkara's commentary on] Prasnopanishad vi. 3. 1897. 8°. [*The Brahmavádin.*] **14048. g. 1.(vol. 3.)**

अथ-कृष्णयजुर्वेदीयश्वेताश्वतरोपनिषद्-भाष्यम् ... Shwetashwataropanishat with [Sanskrit and Hindi] commentary of Bhimsen sharma. pp. iii. 208. *Etawah*, 1897. 8°. **14010. cc. 7.(2.)**

SEPARATE UPANISHADS (*continued*).

श्वेताश्वतरोपनिषद् *etc.* [Ṣvetāṣvataropanishad. With a Sanskrit and Hindi commentary by Tulasīrāma Svāmī.] pp. 112. मेरठ १८९७ [*Meerut*, 1897.] 8°. **14010. dd. 10.(2.)**

अथ तैत्तिरीयोपनिषद्भाष्यम् *etc.* [Taittirīyopanishad. The Ṣikshāvallī, Ānandav°., and Bhṛiguv°. With commentary in Sanskrit and Hindi by Bhīmasena Ṣarmā. Second edition.] pp. 180. प्रयाग [१८]९५ [*Allahabad*, 1895.] 8°. **14007. c. 26.(7.)**

কৃষ্ণ-যজুর্ব্বেদীয়-উপনিষদঃ ... ভৃগূপনিষৎ, শিক্ষোপনিষৎ, ব্রহ্মবিদোপনিষৎ, এবং নারায়ণোপনিষৎ *etc.* [Taittirīyopanishad. In its 4 divisions, here styled respectively Bhṛigūpanishad, Ṣikshop°., Brahmavidop°. [*sic*], and Nārāyaṇop°. (*i.e.* Bṛihannārāyaṇop°. of the Taittirīyāraṇyaka). Edited with Bengali translation and notes by Sāndrānanda Āchārya.] 4 pts. কলিকাতা ১৩০৩ [*Calcutta*, 1896.] 8°. **14010. cc. 3.(2.)**

तैत्तिरीयोपनिषत्. [Taittirīyopanishad. With Bhāskara Miṣra's commentary.] 1896, *etc.* *See* VEṄKAṬARAṄGANĀTHA SVĀMĪ. Grandha Pradarsani, *etc.* [No. 11.] 1895, *etc.* 8°. **14003. c. 2.(11.)**

Incomplete.

தைத்திரீயோபநிஷத் *etc.* [Taittirīyopanishad. The 4 sections.] pp. 34. *See* BRĀHMAṆAS.—*Taittirīyabrāhmaṇa.* அஶ்வமேதம் ॥ [Aṣvamedha, *etc.*] [1900.] 8°. **14007. cc. 28.**

तैत्तिरीयोपनिषद् *etc.* [Taittirīyopanishad. The Ṣikshāvallī, Ānandav°., and Bhṛiguv°. Edited with analyses and Hindi glossaries to each *anuvāka* by Ẓālim Singh, assisted by Gaṅgādatta and Rāmadatta Joshī.] pp. i. 126. लखनऊ १९०० [*Lucknow*, 1900.] 8°. **14007. dd. 3.(3.)**

ತೈತ್ತಿರೀಯೋಪನಿಷತ್ *etc.* [Taittirīyopanishad. Edited with Canarese translation, notes, and introductions by R. S. Veṅkaṭakṛishṇaiya.] ಬೆಂಗಳೂರು [*Bangalore*,] 1901, *etc.* 12°. **14010. b. 23.**

In progress.

தைத்திரீயோபநிஷத் ॥ [Taittirīyopanishad. The 4 sections. Edited by Muḷḷaṅguḍi Vaidyanātha Ṣāstrī.] pp. 54. கும்பகோணம் ॥ [*Kumbakonam*,] 1903. 8°. **14007. f. 2.**

SEPARATE UPANISHADS (*continued*).

தைத்திரீயோபநிஷத் ॥ த்ராவிடபாட-க்ரமவதீ ॥ [Taittirīyopanishad. In the "Dravidian" recension, comprising the Ṣikshāvallī and Nārāyaṇav°. Edited by Muḷḷaṅguḍi Vaidyanātha Ṣāstrī.] pp. 44. கும்பகோணம் ॥ [*Kumbakonam,*] 1903. 8°. **14007. f. 3.**

The Taittirîya Upanishad, with the commentaries of *S*ankarâchârya, Sure*s*varâchârya and Sâya*n*a . . . Translated into English by A. Mahadeva Sastri. [With the Sanskrit text of the Upanishad.] (Vedic Religion.) pp. xxiv. 791. *Mysore,* 1903. 8°. **14007. b. 23.**

శ్రీ . . . శ్రీ విద్యారణ్య మునిభిః విరచితేన బృహద్వివరణేనోపేతా తైత్తిరీయోపనిషది, శీక్షావల్లీ-ఆనందవల్లీ-భృగువల్లీ. [Taittirīyopanishad. The Ṣikshāvallī, Ānandavallī, and Bhṛiguvallī. With Sāyaṇa's commentary. Edited by Gorti Sūraiya.] pp. 107, iii. 170, iv. 35, ii. చెన్నపురాగ్రం [*Madras,*] 1904. 8°. **14007. b. 20.**

See SAṄKARA ĀCHĀRYA.—*Commentaries.* [*Upanishads.*] Brahmánandavalli of Taittariya Upanishad. [Selections] translated from Sankara's commentary. 1897. 4°. [*The Brahmavâdin.*] **14048. g. 1.(vol. 2.)**

வஜ்ரஸூச்யுபநிஷத்பாஷ்யம் [*sic*] *etc.* [Vajrasūchyupanishad. With commentary by Ṣrīnivāsa Dīkshita.] pp. 38. [*Chidambaram,*] 1893. 8°. **14007. b. 4.(1.)**

This Upanishad is popularly attributed to Ṣaṅkara.

—— [Second edition.] pp. 32. நடுக்காவேரி [*Nadukkaveri,*] 1900. 8°. **14007. b. 12.(3.)**

MODERN AND FICTITIOUS UPANISHADS.

பில்வோபநிஷத்ப்ராரம்ப: [Bilvopanishad.] *See* ĀRAṆYAKAS. — *Taittirīyāraṇyaka.* அத த்ரிஸுபர்ணமந்த்ர: *etc.* [Trisuparṇamantra.] pp. 16-20. [18]96. 16°. **14028. b. 80.(2.)**

ಅಥ ದೇವಲೋಪನಿಷತ್ [Devalopanishad and Devāṅgasaptāvatāranirṇaya-vedasāropanishad. Two tracts on the divinity of Devala. With Canarese translations.] *See* ĀGAMAS. [*Siddhāgama.*]

MODERN AND FICTITIOUS UPANISHADS (*continued*).

ದೇವಲಬ್ರಹ್ಮಬೋಧಕ ... ವೇದೋಕ್ತ ಮೂಲಸ್ತಂಭನ *etc.* [Devalabrahmabodhaka-vedokta-mūlastambhana.] pp. 81-100. [1898.] 8°. **14058. b. 37.**

गायत्र्युपनिषत् [Gāyatryupanishad. A tract on the mystic powers of the *gāyatrī* prayer.] pp. 16, *lith.* अमृतसर [*Amritsar,* 1902.] *obl.* 12°. **14028. b. 73.(4.)**

कालिकोपनिषत् *etc.* [Kālikopanishad. A tract on the mystic worship of Dakshiṇa-Kālī, purporting to be excerpted from the Saubhāgyakāṇḍa of the Atharvaveda. With Hindi version by Munnālāl.] pp. 9. कानपुर १८९९ [*Cawnpore,* 1899.] 8°. **14028. c. 85.(5.)**

मृत्युलांगूलउपनिषद *etc.* [Mṛityulāṅgūlopanishad. With a Hindi version. Second edition.] pp. 8, *lith.* स्यालकोट १९०० [*Sialkot,* 1900.] 12°. **14028. b. 62.(2.)**

This Tantric incantation has been published in the Indian Antiquary, II. 266, *by Mr. Burnell, and ibid.* XVI. 287 *by Col. Jacob.*

मृत्युलांगूल तथा सूर्य्योपनिषद् । *etc.* [Mṛityulāṅgūlopanishad and Sūryopanishad. Edited with some Hindi notes and verses by Bodhānanda Giri.] pp. 8. लाहौर १९०४ [*Lahore,* 1904.] 12°. **14010. b. 3.(3.)**

ஶ்ரீ...ஶ்ரீபாரமாத்மிகோபநிஷத்பாஷ்யம்... சந்த்ரிகாஸஹிதம் [Pāramātmikopanishad. A Vaishṇava Upanishad in 11 *anuvākas.* With a commentary according to the Vaikhānasa school by K. Ṣrīnivāsa Dīkshita and a supercommentary styled Chandrikā by Sundararāja Bhaṭṭāchārya. Followed by Āhnikāmṛita, a manual for the daily rites according to the Vaikhānasa school, by Vāsudeva Bhaṭṭāchārya.] pp. 164, i. 123, ii. கும்பகோணம் [*Kumbakonam,*] 1900. 8°. **14033. bbb. 13.**

APPENDIX.

See DALAPATI RĀYA. The Sacred Books of India. No. I. The Upanishads. Vol. First. An introduction to their study, *etc.* 1897. 12°. **14010. b. 18.**

See GURUJÑĀNAVĀSISHṬHA. గురుజ్ఞానవాసిష్ఠే జ్ఞానకాండః *etc.* [Gurujñānavāsishṭha. An ex-

APPENDIX (*continued*).

position of Anubhavādvaita theory and practice, including discussions on the Upanishads.] [1882]-1897. 4°. **14048. e. 8.**

See SLATER (T. E.). Studies in the Upanishads, *etc.* 1897. 8°. **14016. c. 49.**

The Theosophy of the Upanishads. Part i. Self and Not Self. pp. 203. *London, Aberdeen* [printed], 1896. 8°. **4503. b. 42.**

UPĀSAKACHARIYĀ. ဥပါသကစရိယကျမ်း [Upāsakachariyā. A lectionary of short Pali texts upon the cardinal doctrines of Buddhism, with Burmese word-for-word translations, *etc.*] pp. 44. ၁၂၅၅ [*Rangoon*, 1893.] 8°. **14098. ccc. 3.(2.)**

UPĀSAKADAŚĀḤ. उपासक दशा प्रारंभ [Upāsakadaśāḥ, in Prakrit Uvāsagadasāo. The seventh *aṅga* of the Jains. With Gujarati supralinear translation.] pp. 124, *lith.* [*Bombay*, 1895.] *obl.* 8°. **14100. d. 3.**

No printed title-page. The title is written by hand.

UPATISSA. The Mahā-bodhi-vaṁsa. Edited by S. Arthur Strong. 1891. 8°. *See* ACADEMIES, *etc.*—London.—*Pali Text Society.* UPATISSA. **14098. b. 29.(2.)**

UPENDRAMOHANA GOSVĀMĪ NYĀYARATNA. তত্ত্বকল্পতরুঃ *etc.* [Tattvakalpataru. A metrical dissertation on Vedānta philosophy from the Chaitanya-Vaishṇava standpoint, in 26 *śākhās.*] pp. i. 198. কলিকাতা ১৯১৮ [*Calcutta*, 1891.] 8°. **14028. c. 69.**

UPENDRANĀTHA CHAKRAVARTĪ. *See* KRAMADĪŚVARA. সংক্ষিপ্তসার॰ [Saṅkshiptasāravyākaraṇa. Abridged and edited, with Bengali translation, by Upendranātha.] 1891. 8°. **14090. c. 38.**

UPENDRANĀTHA SENA GUPTA. *See* CHAKRAPĀṆIDATTA. চক্রদত্তঃ *etc.* [Chakradatta. Edited by Devendranātha and Upendranātha.] [1900.] 8°. **14043. cc. 17.**

UŚANAS. *See* VEDAS.—Atharvaveda.—*Pariśishṭa.* The Auçanasādbhutāni, *etc.* 1893. 8°. [*Journal of the American Oriental Society.*] **Ac. 8824. (vol. 15.)**

UTPALA, *Bhaṭṭa.* *See* VARĀHAMIHIRA. बृहज्जातकम् *etc.* [Bṛihaj-jātaka. With Utpala's commentary.] [1893.] 4°. **14133. g. 16.(pt. i., no. 1.)**

—— *See* VARĀHAMIHIRA. The Bṛihat Saṁhitâ . . . With the commentary [Saṁhitâvivṛiti] of Bhaṭṭotpala, *etc.* 1895-1897. 8°. **14048. dd. 3.(vol. 10.)**

UTPALA DEVĀCHĀRYA, *Vandya.* *See* KALLAṬA. The Spandapradîpikâ of Utpalâchârya, a commentary on the Spandakârikâ, *etc.* 1898. 8°. **14048. dd. 3.(vol. 14.)**

—— शिवस्तोत्रावली . . . Sivastotrâvalî, [a series of hymns to Śiva,] . . . with the commentary of Kshemarâja. Edited by the late Rai Pramadâdâsa Mittra Bahâdur . . . and his son Śrî Kâlîcharaṇa Mittra. pp. i. 163. *Benares*, 1902-1903. 8°. **14004. a. 15.**

Forms nos. 51 *and* 63 *of the* Chowkhambâ Sanskrit Series. *The title is from the wrapper.*

UTTARADHARMA. *See* DHARMOTTARA ĀCHĀRYA.

UTTARĀDHYAYANA. Uttarâdhyayana. [The 8th division of the Aṅgabāhya in the canon of the Digambara Jains. Translated from the Prakrit, with notes, *etc.*, by H. Jacobi.] 1895. *See* MUELLER (F. M.). The Sacred Books of the East, *etc.* Vol. xlv., pp. 1-232. 1879, *etc.* 8°. **2003. b. (vol. 45.)**

—— उत्तराध्ययन सूत्रनुं पहेलुं अध्ययन. [Uttarādhyayana. The first *adhikāra*, or Vinayādhyayana (Viṇayajjh°.) With Gujarati translations and notes.] *See* JAINAJÑĀNAPRAKĀŚA. जैन ज्ञान प्रकाश *etc.* [Jainajñānaprakāṣa.] pt. 1, pp. 54-89. [1898.] 12°. **14100. a. 19.**

UTTARAGĪTĀ. उत्तरगीता *etc.* [Uttaragītā. Three chapters on Yogic philosophy, forming a sequel to the Bhagavadgītā, and alleged to be derived from the Bhīshmaparva or Aśvamedhaparva of the Mahābhārata, or from the Brahmāṇḍapurāṇa, *etc.* With a Hindi version by Rāmasvarūpa son of Bholānāth.] pp. 56. कानपुर १९०० [*Cawnpore*, 1900.] 12°. **14065. b. 24.**

—— உத்தரகீதை *etc.* [Uttaragītā. With a Tamil paraphrase and notes, based upon the commentary

of Gauḍapāda, by V. Kuppusvāmi Rāju.] pp. ii. 61. தஞ்சை சோபகிருது [Tanjore, 1903.] 12°. **14048. a. 29.(3.)**
Forms no. 1 *of the series* Gitai-kottu.

—— The Uttara Gita: being the initiation of Arjuna by Shri Krishna into Yoga and Dnyana. Translated by D.[*sic*] K. Laheri. pp. i. 50. *Bombay*, [1893.] 16°. **14016. a. 24.(1.)**

—— [Another edition.] pp. 49. *Bombay*, 1902. 16°. **14016. a. 24.(2.)**

UVĀSAGADASĀO. *See* UPĀSAKADAŚĀḤ.

UVAṬA. *See* ŚAUNAKA. महर्षिशौनकप्रणीतम् ऋक्प्रातिशाख्यम् । . . . Śaunaka's Prátiśákhya . . . with the commentary of Uvvaṭa, *etc.* 1903. 8°. **14090. c. 40.**

—— *See* UPANISHADS.—*Separate Upanishads.* ईशावास्योपनिषत्० ((1) Shri Īsávásyopanishad with . . . (2) The Bháshya of . . . Uatabhattácharya, *etc.*) [1888.] 8°. **14003. ccc. (no. 5.)**

—— *See* UPANISHADS.—*Separate Upanishads.* The Īsavâsyopanishad. Translated . . . with . . . notes from the Tikas of . . . Uvatacharya, *etc.* 1896. 8°. **14010. cc. 6.**

UYYOJANĪDĪPAṆĪ. ဥယျောဇနီဒီပဏီ [Uyyojanīdīpaṇī. Moral and philosophical stanzas in Pali, with Burmese version.] *See* CHANDIMĀ, *Thāvara*, called KYĀ-KOY. ဆက္ကပဉှာကျမ်း *etc.* [Chhakkapañhā-kyan, *etc.*] pp. 340-352. 1898. 8°. **14300. d. 19.(9.)**

VĀCHASPATI. *See* RUDRA NYĀYAVĀCHASPATI.

VĀCHASPATI MISRA, *disciple of Mārtaṇḍatilaka.* [*Bhāmatī.*] *See* BĀDARĀYAṆA. The Vedântakalpataru of Amalânanda. [Comprising the Brahmasūtra with the supercommentary of Amalānanda upon the Bhāmatī of Vāchaspati,] *etc.* 1895-1897. 8°. **14048. dd. 3.(vol. 11.)**

—— [*Nyāyavārttikatātparyaṭīkā.*] *See* GOTAMA. The Nyâyasûtras with . . . extracts from the Nyâyavârttika and the Tâtparyaṭîkâ [of Vāchaspati,] *etc.* 1896. 8°. **14048. dd. 3.(vol. 9.)**

—— —— The Nyâyavârttikatâtparyaṭîkâ of Vâchaspati Miśra. [A commentary upon Uddyotakara's commentary Nyāyavārttika on the Nyāyasūtra.] Edited by Mahâmahopâdhyâya Gaṅgâdhara Śâstrî Tailaṅga. (न्यायवार्त्तिकतात्पर्यटीका) pp. ii. x. ii. 513. *Benares*, 1898. 8°. **14048. dd. 3.(vol. 13.)**
Forms no. 15=*vol.* 15 *of the* Vizianagram Sanskrit Series.

—— [*Sāṅkhyatattvakaumudī.*] *See* ĪŚVARA KṚISHṆA. সাংখ্যতত্ত্ব-কৌমুদী *etc.* [Sāṅkhyatattvakaumudī. Comprising the Sāṅkhyakārikā and the commentary of Vāchaspati.] [1901.] 8°. **14048. dd. 34.(1.)**

—— —— *See* ĪŚVARA KṚISHṆA. Der Mondschein der Sâṃkhya-Wahrheit, Vâcaspatimiçra's Sâṃkhya-tattva-kaumudî in deutscher Uebersetzung . . . von R. Garbe. 1892. 4°. [*Abhandlungen der Bayerischen Akademie der Wissenschaften.*] **Ac. 713/6. (vol. 19.)**

—— —— *See* ĪŚVARA KṚISHṆA. An English Translation, with the Sanskrit Text, of the [Sāṅkhyakārikā with the commentary] Tattvakaumudî . . . of Vâchaspati, *etc.* 1896. 8°. **14048. cc. 3.**

—— [*Tattvabindu.*] तत्त्वबिन्दुः । [Tattvabindu. A Vedantic treatise. Edited by Gaṅgādhara Śāstrī.] pp. 34. 1892. *See* PERIODICAL PUBLICATIONS.—*Benares.* The Pandit, *etc.* New Series. Vol. XIV. 1876, *etc.* 8°. **14096. d. 6.(vol. 14.)**

—— [*Yogatattvavaiśāradī.*] *See* PATAÑJALI.—*Philosophical Works.* योगदर्शनम् *etc.* [Yogadarśana. Being the Yogasūtra with the *bhāshya*, the supercommentary of Vāchaspati called Yogatattvavaiśāradī, *etc.*] [1890.] 8°. **14048. dd. 6.**

—— —— *See* PATAÑJALI.—*Philosophical Works.* পাতঞ্জলদর্শনম্। [Pātañjaladarśana. Comprising the Aphorisms, the *ṭīkā* of Vāchaspati, *etc.*] [1891, *etc.*] 4°. [*Aruṇodaya.*] **14133. g. 16.(pt. i., no. 25.)**

—— —— *See* PATAÑJALI.—*Philosophical Works.* Patañjalasûtrâṇi. With . . . the commentary of Vâchaspati, *etc.* 1892. 8°. **14048. dd. 10.**

—— —— *See* PATAÑJALI.—*Philosophical Works.* The Aphorisms of Patanjali. With the commentaries of . . . Vachaspati, *etc.* [1899.] 8°. **14048. c. 75.(2.)**

VĀCHISSARA MAHĀTHERA. *See* THŪPAVAṂSA. ථූපවංසො *etc.* [Thūpavaṃsa. Translated into Pali by Vāchissara, from the Sinhalese original.] 1896. 8°. **14098. d. 44.(2.)**

VĀDĪBHASIṂHA SŪRI, *disciple of Pushpasena*, previously known as ODAYADEVA. The Gadyachintâmani of Vâdîbhasimha. [A Jain romance, on the legend of Jīvandhara or Jīvaka, in 11 *lambas*. Edited with Sanskrit preface] by T. S. Kuppuswami Sastri . . . and S. Subrahmanya Sastri. (Sarasvativilasa Series No. 1.) pp. vii. 169, i. *Madras*, 1902. 8°. **14070. dd. 23.**

—— **क्षत्रचूडामणि°** [Kshatrachūḍāmaṇi. A romance on the legend of Jīvandhara, in 11 *lambas*.] [1893-1896.] *See* PADMARĀJA PAṆḌITA. **काव्याम्बुधिः** *etc.* [Kāvyāmbudhi.] pts. 1-7. [1893-1896.] 8°. **14028. c. 64.**

Not completed.

—— ಕ್ಷತ್ರಚೂಡಾಮಣಿಕಾವ್ಯವು *etc.* [Kshatrachūḍāmaṇi. With a Canarese translation and commentary by M. Ṣrīnivāsa Aiyaṅgār.] pp. 468. ಬೆಂಗಳೂರು [*Bangalore*,] 1900. 8°. **14100. b. 8.**

—— The Kshattrachudamani of Vadibhasimha. With critical and explanatory notes [in Sanskrit] by T. S. Kuppuswami Sastriyar. (Sarasvativilasa Series No. iii.) pp. 143. *Tanjore*, 1903. 8°. **14070. dd. 30.**

VĀDIRĀJA, *Jain Poet.* **एकीभावस्तोत्रम् ।** [Ekībhāvastotra. A hymn in 26 stanzas.] *See* JAINASTOTRASAṄGRAHA. **जैनस्तोत्रसंग्रहः** *etc.* [Jainastotrasaṅgraha.] pp. 24-29. [1890.] 12°. **14100. a. 13.**

—— **एकीभावस्तोत्रम् ।** [Ekībhāvastotra.] *See* JAINANITYAPĀṬHA. **अथ जैननित्यपाठसंग्रहः** [Jainanityapāṭhasaṅgraha.] pp. 83-94. [1901.] *obl.* 16°. **14100. a. 27.**

VĀDIRĀJA TĪRTHA. *See* MAHĀBHĀRATA.—*Entire Work.* **॥ महाभारतम्** *etc.* [Mahābhārata. With the commentary Lakshālaṅkāra of Vādirāja.] [1898, *etc.*] 4°. **14065. f. 4.**

VĀGBHAṬA, *son of Nemikumāra, Jain Rhetorician.* The Kâvyânuśâsana of Vâgbhatta. With his own gloss [styled Alaṅkāratilaka]. Edited by Paṇdit Sivadatta . . . and Kâśînâth Pâṇdurang Parab. (**काव्यानुशासनम् ।**) pp. i. 68. 1894. *See* DURGĀPRASĀDA, *son of Vrajalāla*, and KĀṢĪNĀTHA PĀṆḌURAṄGA PARAB. Kâvyamâlâ. [No.] 43. 1886, *etc.* 8°. **14072. ccc. 12.(no. 43.)**

VĀGBHAṬA, *son of Siṃhagupta.* അഷ്ടാംഗഹൃദയം *etc.* [Ashṭāṅgahṛidaya. A manual of medicine. With a Malayalam paraphrase by K. Rāma Vāriyar.] pts. 1,2,4-6. ത്രിശ്ശിവപെരൂർ [illegible]—[illegible] [*Trichur*, 1891-1892.] 8°. **14043. c. 41.**

—— Ashtanga Hridaya . . . Translated into Sinhalese [with the original text and Sinhalese commentary] by W. B. de Alwis . . . Revised by M. Nanissara, *etc.* (අෂ්ටාංග හෘදය සංහිතාව) pt. i. pp. 80. *Colombo*, 1893. 8°. **14043. d. 45.**

—— వాహటమనునామాంతరముగల అష్టాంగ-హృదయము *etc.* [Ashṭāṅgahṛidaya, or Bāhaṭa. Part ii., comprising the Chikitsāsthāna, Kalpasth°., and Uttarasth°. Edited with a Telugu translation by Puvvāḍa Rāmachandra Rāu.] pp. vi. xxxviii. 664; 1 *plate*. *Madras*, 1898. 4°. **14043. ddd. 1.**

—— **अष्टाङ्गहृदय-उत्तरस्थानम्** *etc.* [Ashṭāṅgahṛidaya. The Uttarasthāna, or bk. vi., with indices and a Gujarati translation by Chhoṭālāl Narbherām Bhaṭṭa.] pp. iii. xxiv. 614. **अमदावाद १९०१** [*Ahmadabad*, 1901.] 8°. **14043. cc. 22.**

VĀGBHAṬA, *son of Soma, Jain Rhetorician.* **अलंकारशास्त्रम् ।** [Alaṅkāraṣāstra. With the commentary of Jinavardhana.] pp. 104. [1889-1890.] *See* PERIODICAL PUBLICATIONS.—*Bombay.* **ग्रन्थरत्नमाला** *etc.* (Granth Ratna Málá, *etc.*) Vol. III, no. 3-7. 1887-[1892.] 8°. **14096. c. 8.(vol. 3.)**

—— The Vâgbhatâlaṃkâra of Vâgbhata. With the commentary of Siṃhadevagaṇi. Edited by Paṇḍit Śivadatta . . . and Kâśînâth Pâṇdurang Parab. (**वाग्भटालंकारः ।**) pp. 68. 1895. *See* DURGĀPRASĀDA, *son of Vrajalāla*, and KĀṢĪNĀTHA PĀṆḌURAṄGA PARAB. Kâvyamâlâ. [No.] 48. 1886, *etc.* 8°. **14072. ccc. 12.(no. 48.)**

—— The Neminirvâṇa of Vâgbhaṭa. [A poem in 15 *sargas* on the worldly and spiritual experiences of Nemi.] Edited by Paṇḍita Śivadatta . . . and Kâśînâth Pâṇdurang Parab. (**नेमिनिर्वाणम् ।**) pp. 85, xiii. 1896. *See* DURGĀPRASĀDA, *son of Vrajalāla*, and KĀṢĪNĀTHA PĀṆḌURAṄGA PARAB. Kâvyamâlâ. [No.] 56. 1886, *etc.* 8°. **14072. ccc. 12.(no. 56.)**

The author of this work is either the same as the Vāgbhaṭa of the Alaṅkāra, or is older than he.

VAGĒGOḌA THERA. Ākhyáta Pada. [Pali rules for the conjugation of Pali verbs, with explanations in Pali and Sinhalese.] Edited by Dodampahala Sumangala, *etc.* (ආඛ්‍යාතපදය.) pp. ii. 55. *Colombo,* 1889. 8°. **14165. k. 17.(2.)**

VĀGĪṢVARA MAHĀSTHAVIRA. *See* VĀCHISSARA MAHĀTHERA.

VAIDYA (C. V.). *See* CHINTĀMAṆI VINĀYAKA VAIDYA.

VAIDYAKAKOṢA. अथ वैद्यककोश° [Vaidyakakoṣa. A Hindi glossary of Sanskrit medical terms.] *See* KOṢAṢABDĀRTHASAṄGRAHA. कोष शब्दार्थसंग्रह *etc.* [Koṣaṣabdārthasaṅgraha.] pp. 241-292. [1899.] 8°. **14160. c. 40.**

VAIDYAKASĀRA. వైద్యకసారః *etc.* [Vaidyakasāra. A treatise on medicine. With Telugu commentary.] 1892-1895. 12°. *See* PERIODICAL PUBLICATIONS.—*Vizagapatam.* సకలవిద్యాభివర్ధని *etc.* [Sakalavidyābhivardhanī.] Vol. I, pt. i.—Vol. II, pt. x. 1892-1897. 12° & 8°. **14174. g. 38.**

Not completed.

VAIDYANĀTHA, *son of Rāma Bhaṭṭa,* surnamed TATSAT. *See* MAMMAṬA ĀCHĀRYA. The Kâvyapradîpa . . . with the commentary [Prabhā] of Vaidyanâtha, *etc.* 1891. 8°. [*Kâvyamâlâ.*] **14072. ccc. 12.(no. 24.)**

VAIDYANĀTHA, *son of Veṅkaṭādri, Bhāradvāja.* జాతకపారిజాతము *etc.* [Jātakapārijāta. A metrical manual of horoscopy. With Telugu version by N. Guruliṅga Ṣāstrī.] pp. viii. 440. చెన్నపురి ౧౮౯౭ [*Madras,* 1897.] 8°. **14053. ccc. 9.**

—— जातकपारिजात: [Jātakapārijāta,] the first two adhyayas (adhyayas 3-6, 7-10, *etc.*). With an English translation. And श्रीपतिपद्धति: [Ṣrīpatipaddhati,] adhyayas 1-4 (5-8). With an English translation, notes and examples. By V. Subrahmanya Sastri. *Bombay,* 1903, *etc.* 8°. **14053. ccc. 48.**

In progress.

VAIDYANĀTHA AIYAR, *T. V.* *See* ACADEMIES, *etc.*—Madras.—*University of Madras.* Complete Sanskrit Text for the F. A. Examination, 1901. With full notes, translation . . . &c., by T. V. Vaidyanatha Aiyar. 1900. 8°. **14072. ccc. 24.(2.)**

VAIDYANĀTHA DĪKSHITA, *Kaṇḍaramāṇikkam.* *See* SANDHYĀVANDANA. யஜுர்வேத . . . ஸந்த்யாவந்தநம் *etc.* [Sandhyāvandana, *etc.* With extracts, in a Tamil translation, from the commentaries of Vaidyanātha and others.] 1901. 8°. **14033. aa. 27.**

—— ஸ்ம்ருதிமுக்தாபலே ப்ரதம: வர்ணாஶ்ரமதர்மகாண்ட: *etc.* (த்விதீய: ஆஹ்நிககாண்ட:, த்ருதீய: ஆஶௌசகாண்ட:, சதுர்த்த: ஶ்ராத்தகாண்டே பூர்வபாக:, பஞ்சம: திதிநிர்ணயகாண்ட:) [Smṛitimuktāphala. A digest of ceremonial law and tradition. With the commentary Prabhā of Ṣrīnivāsa Dīkshita. Vol. i., or Varṇāṣramadharmakāṇḍa, on the forms of caste-life, with Tamil translation by Rāmasvāmī Ṣāstrī. Vol. ii., or Āhnikakāṇḍa, on the encyclic rituals, with Tamil translation by Rāmakṛishṇa Bhaṭṭāchārya. Vol. iii., or Āṣauchakāṇḍa, on formal uncleanness, and Vol. iv., or Part i. of the Ṣrāddhakāṇḍa, on *ṣrāddha* rites, with Tamil translation by Ṣ. Subrahmaṇya Ṣāstrī. Vol. v., or Tithinirṇayakāṇḍa, on determination of the calendar, with Tamil translation by M. Rāmachandra Ṣāstrī.] சிதம்பரம் ॥ நடுக்காவேரி [*Chidambaram, Nadukkaveri,*] 1898, *etc.* 4°. **14039. c. 15.**

In progress.

—— காலநிரூபணாக்ய திதிநிர்ணயகாண்ட: ॥ *etc.* [Kālanirūpaṇa, *i.e.* the Tithinirṇayakāṇḍa of the Smṛitimuktāphala. Edited by Muḷḷaṅguḍi A. Vaidyanātha Ṣāstrī.] pp. iv. 60. கும்பகோணம் ॥ [*Kumbakonam,*] 1904. 8°. **14033. aa. 36.**

VAIDYANĀTHA MOTĪRĀMJĪ, *Bhaṭṭa.* *See* SĀRASVATASŪTRA. ॥ सारस्वत *etc.* [Sārasvatavyākaraṇa. Being the Sārasvatasūtra with Gujarati version by Vaidyanātha of the Sarasvatīprakriyā.] [1899.] 12°. **14092. a. 20.**

VAIDYANĀTHA ṢĀSTRĪ, *Muḷḷaṅguḍi A.* *See* BRĀHMAṆAS.—*Taittirīyabrāhmaṇa.* தைத்திரீயயஜுர்ப்ராஹ்மணே ப்ரதமாஷ்டகம் *etc.* [Taittirīyabrāhmaṇa. Edited by Vaidyanātha and Sāmbaṣiva.] 1900, *etc.* 8°. **14007. cc. 30.**

VAIDYANĀTHA ṢĀSTRĪ, *Mullaṅguḍi A.* (*continued*). *See* ṢRĪVATSĀṄKA, *son of Devīmanīshī.* ஸ்ரீ ... ஸப்தலக்ஷணீ *etc.* [Saptalakshaṇa. Edited with commentary by Vaidyanātha.] 1899. 8°. **14092. b. 43.**

—— *See* UPANISHADS.—*Separate Upanishads.* தைத்திரீயோபநிஷத் ॥ [Taittirīyopanishad. Edited by Vaidyanātha.] 1903. 8°. **14007. f. 2.**

—— *See* UPANISHADS.—*Separate Upanishads.* தைத்திரீயோபநிஷத் ॥ *etc.* [Taittirīyopanishad. Edited by Vaidyanātha.] 1903. 8°. **14007. f. 3.**

—— *See* VAIDYANĀTHA DĪKSHITA. காலநிரூபண ॥ [Kālanirūpaṇa. Edited by Vaidyanātha.] 1904. 8°. **14033. aa. 36.**

—— *See* VEDAS.—Yajurveda.—*Taittirīyasaṃhitā.* ஸ்ரீக்ருஷ்ணயஜுஸ்ஸம்ஹிதா ॥ [Kṛishṇayajussaṃhitā-padasaraṇī. The Pada text, with notes by the editor, Vaidyanātha.] 1898-1900. 8°. **14007. f. 1.**

—— *See* VEDAS.—Yajurveda.—*Taittirīyasaṃhitā.* ஷட்விம்ஶதிஸூத்ரம் *etc.* [Shaḍviṃṣatisūtra. Edited by Vaidyanātha.] [1899.] 16°. **14010. a. 5.(1.)**

—— *See* VEDAS.—Yajurveda.—*Taittirīyasaṃhitā.* [*Prātiṣākhya.*] தைத்திரீயப்ராதிஶாக்யம் *etc.* [Taittirīyaprātiṣākhya. With the Tribhāshyaratna. Edited by Vaidyanātha.] 1900. 12°. **14007. b. 10.**

—— *See* VEDAS.—Yajurveda.—*Taittirīyasaṃhitā.* [*Prātiṣākhya.*] தைத்திரீயப்ராதிஶாக்யம் *etc.* [Taittirīyaprātiṣākhya. With commentary of Gārgya Gopāla. Edited by Vaidyanātha.] 1901. 8°. **14090. e. 26.**

VAIDYANĀTHA ṢĀSTRĪ, *son of Nārāyaṇa, of Moradabad.* *See* VIṢVANĀTHA PAÑCHĀNANA BHAṬṬĀCHĀRYA. न्यायसिद्धान्तमुक्तावली *etc.* [Kārikāvalī. The Pratyakshakhaṇḍa, with the Nyāyasiddhāntamuktāvalī. Edited with Hindi translation, commentary, *etc.*, by Vaidyanātha.] [1901.] 8°. **14049. b. 7.**

—— चौदहरत्न. अर्थात् १२५ पुस्तकों का समूह॥ [Chaudah Ratna. A collection of 125 short writings and excerpts from writings, in prose and verse, both Sanskrit and Hindi, bearing upon religious and mystic rituals, philosophy and theosophy, divination, legend and history, arts, *etc.* Second edition.] pp. 586. मुरादाबाद १९०२ [*Moradabad*, 1902.] 12°. **14033. a. 54.**

VAIDYANĀTHA ṢĀSTRĪ TIVĀRĪ, *of Jalalabad,* **and others.** [Miscellaneous tracts, chiefly Sanskrit texts with Hindi versions, treating of religious and Tantric rites, funeral ceremonies, astrology, philosophy, aesthetics, medicine, *etc.*, the most important being Bījapraṣnāvalī, an excerpt from the Rudrayāmalatantra, a Sandhyāvidhi, and twelve Upanishads. Translated for the most part by Vaidyanātha Ṣāstrī and Kanhaiyālāl Ṣarmā, and in a few cases by Baladevaprasāda Miṣra and Jayantīprasāda Upādhyāya.] मुरादाबाद [*Moradabad*, 1899.] 12°. **14033. a. 37.**

Each of these tracts (of which there are 100) has a title-page and pagination of its own.

VAIDYANĀTHA VYĀSA, *of Benares.* गणेशपरिणयं नाम नाटकम् *etc.* [Gaṇeṣapariṇaya. A mythological play in 7 acts, composed for the prize annually offered at the Siddhi-Vināyaka-pūjā festival of Mithila by Raja Bābū Janeṣvara Siṃha. With preface by Gaṅgānātha Ṣarmā.] pp. i. i. 51; 1 *plate.* प्रयागे १९०४ [*Allahabad*, 1904.] 12°. **14079. b. 44.**

VAIRĀGYAṢATAKA. ॥ श्री वैराग्य शतकम् ॥ [Vairāgyaṣataka. A century of Jain Prakrit verses on suppression of the passions. With Gujarati translation.] *See* HEMAṢAṄKARA LAKSHMĪṢAṄKARA VARDHAMĀNKAR. प्रकरण माला *etc.* [Prakaraṇamālā.] pp. 114-136. [1901.] 8°. **14100. d. 11.**

VAISHṆAVACHARAṆA BASĀK. *See* KĀLIDĀSA.—*Supposititious Works.* কালিদাসের কবিতা *etc.* [Kālidāser Kavitā. Compiled and edited by Vaishṇavacharaṇa Basāk.] [1897.] 12°. **14127. aa. 14.(1.)**

—— *See* TANTRAS. [*Jñānasaṅkalinītantra.*] জ্ঞানসঙ্কলিনী তন্ত্রম্ *etc.* [Jñānasaṅkalinītantra. With Bengali translation by Vaishṇavacharaṇa.] [1901.] 12°. **14033. a. 41.(3.)**

VAISHṆAVAS. শ্রীশ্রীসনাতন-বৈষ্ণব-ব্রত-দিন ও উৎসব সময়প্রভৃতির নির্ণয় পুস্তক। [Sanātanavaishṇavavratadina o utsavasamayaprabhṛitir nirṇayapustaka.

A treatise on the dates of the ancient festivals of the Eastern Vaishṇavas, in Bengali, illustrated from Sanskrit texts.] কালকাতা ১৩০৭ [*Calcutta*, 1900.] 8°. **14123. ff. 4.**

In progress.

VAIṢVADEVAPADDHATI. ବୈଶ୍ୱଦେବପଦ୍ଧତି *etc.* [Vaiṣvadevapaddhati. A manual of the *vaiṣvadeva* rite. Edited by Sarveṣvara Āchārya.] pp. 4. *Cuttack*, 1902. 16°. **14028. b. 106.(3.)**

VAITARAṆĪDĀNA. वैतरणी दान पद्धतिः ॥ [Vaitaraṇīdānapaddhati. Rules for the gift of a cow to enable departed souls to pass the infernal river Vaitaraṇī. Edited by Dunīchand Ṣarmā.] pp. 45, *lith.* अमृतसर १९५९ [*Amritsar*, 1903.] *obl.* 12°. **14033. a. 28.(2.)**

VAJRACHCHHEDIKĀ. Vajracchedikâ Prajñâpâramitâ. Traduite du texte sanscrit avec comparaison des versions chinoise et mandchoue, par M. C. de Harlez. 1891. *See* ACADEMIES, *etc.*—Paris.—*Société Asiatique.* Journal Asiatique, *etc.* Ser. viii., tom. 18. pp. 440-509. 1822, *etc.* 8°. **Ac. 8808. (Ser. viii., tom. 18.)**

—— The Va*g*ra*kkh*edikâ. [Translated with notes, *etc.*, by F. Max Müller.] 1894. *See* MUELLER (F. M.). The Sacred Books of the East, *etc.* Vol. xlix., pt. 2. 1879, *etc.* 8°. **2003. b. (vol. 49.)**

VAKULĀBHARAṆA PARADEṢĪ, *Aparokshānubhavī.* *See* ṢAṄKARA ĀCHĀRYA.—*Philosophical Poems, etc.* వాక్యసుధావేకము *etc.* [Vākyasudhā. With commentary in Telugu by Vakulābharaṇa.] 1901. 8°. **14048. bb. 55.**

—— శుకబ్రహ్మకైవల్యము అను శ్రీశుకమహర్షిచరిత్ర *etc.* [Ṣukabrahmakaivalya, or Ṣukamaharshicharitra. A narrative of the legends connected with the mythical sage Ṣuka and exposition of the Vedantic doctrines ascribed to him. In Telugu, illustrated from Sanskrit texts.] pp. ii. 140. చెన్నపట్టణం [*Madras*,] 1899. 8°. **14174. gg. 4.**

VALLABHA BHAṬṬA. अलङ्कारकौमुदी *etc.* [Alaṅkārakaumudī. Explanations and illustrations of the terms of rhetoric.] pp. 11. [1889.] *See* PERIODICAL PUBLICATIONS.—*Bombay.* ग्रन्थरत्नमाला *etc.* (Granth Ratna Málá, *etc.*) Vol. II, no. 11. 1887-[1892.] 8°. **14096. c. 8.(vol. 2.)**

VALLABHĀCHĀRYA, called MAHĀPRABHUJĪ. *See* PURĀṆAS.—*Bhāgavatapurāṇa.* *Begin.* श्रीमद्भागवतसुबोधिन्यां प्रथमस्कंधप्रारंभः [Bhāgavatapurāṇa. With the commentary Subodhinī of Vallabhāchārya.] [1893, *etc.*] 8°. [*Pushṭimārgaprakāṣa.*] **14150. c. 15.**

—— ષોડશ ગ્રંથ *etc.* [Shoḍaṣa-grantha. 16 religious-philosophical poems, viz. Yamunāshṭaka, Bālabodha, Siddhāntamuktāvalī, Pushṭipravāhamaryādābheda, Siddhāntarahasya, Navaratnastotra, Antaḥkaraṇaprabodha, Vivekadhairyāṣraya, Kṛishṇāṣraya, Chatuḥṣlokī, Bhaktivardhinī, Jalabheda, Pañchapadyāni, Sannyāsanirṇaya, Nirodhalakshaṇa, and Sevāphala. Edited with Gujarati translations and explanations by Mādhavajī Gopālajī Vaidya.] pp. 97. મુંબઇ ૧૮૯૬ [*Bombay*, 1896.] 8°. **14028. c. 70.**

—— श्रीमद्वल्लभाचार्यजी विरचित षोडश ग्रंथोनुं पदच्छेद *etc.* [Shoḍaṣa-grantha. Edited with analysis and Gujarati translations and annotations by Rāghavajī Karṣanjī. Preceded by a Gujarati preface by Nathu Nānājī and Tribhuvanadāsa Yādavajī, and Gujarati hymns.] pp. viii. vi. 328, vii. मुंबई १८९९ [*Bombay*, 1899.] 8°. **14033. aa. 25.**

—— तत्र महाप्रभुजीकृतग्रंथाः । [Purushottamasahasranāma, Tattvadīpanibandha (*i.e.* pt. 1 of the Tattvārthadīpa), Trividhalīlānāmāvalī, and other minor poems on religious topics.] pp. 148. *See* GOVARDHANADĀSA LAKSHMĪDASA. बृहत्स्तोत्रसरित्सागर *etc.* [Bṛihat-stotrasaritsāgara.] Vol. ii. [1892.] 12°. **14033. a. 27.(vol. 2.)**

—— श्रीतत्त्वार्थदीपः । . . . निबन्ध इति प्रसिद्धः *etc.* [Tattvārthadīpa, or Nibandha. A metrical summary by Vallabhāchārya of his philosophical and religious doctrine, in 3 parts, pt. 1 summarising the Bhagavadgītā, pt. 2 giving rules on various points, and pt. 3 epitomising the Bhāgavatapurāṇa. With the author's commentary Tattvārthadīpaprakāṣa on pts. 1, 2, and the first half of 3, and followed by the beginnings of supercommentaries by Kalyāṇarāya and Gaṭṭūlāl. Edited by Nandakiṣora Ṣāstrī son of Rameṣa.] pp. viii. 393, 22; 2 *plates.* मोहमय्याम् १९०४ [*Bombay*, 1904.] 8°. **14049. bb. 5.**

VALLABHĀCHĀRYA, called MAHĀPRABHUJĪ (*continued*). श्रीभागवतार्थतत्त्वदीपनिबंधे प्रथमस्कन्धप्रारंभः (द्वितीयस्कन्धनिबन्धः, तृतीयस्क० *etc.*) [Bhāgavatārthatattvadīpanibandha. Pt. 3 of the Tattvārthadīpa.] [1893, *etc.*] *See* PERIODICAL PUBLICATIONS.—*Bombay.* श्रीपुष्टिमार्गप्रकाशः *etc.* [Pushṭimārgaprakāṣa.] Vol. I, pt. i., Vol. VI, pt. viii., *etc.* [1893, *etc.*] 8°. *In progress.* **14150. c. 15.**

—— श्रीअंतःकरणप्रबोधकी । टीका *etc.* [Antaḥkaraṇaprabodha. A devotional tract in 10 stanzas. With Braj commentary by Gosvāmī Nṛisiṃhalālajī Mahārāja.] pp. 11. १८२२ [*Bombay*, 1900.] 8°. **14028. d. 35.(4.)**

VALLABHA DEVA, *son of Ānanda Deva.* *See* KĀLIDĀSA.—*Raghuvaṃṣa.* The Raghuvanśa . . . with full extracts . . . from the commentaries of . . . Vallabha, *etc.* 1897. 8°. **14072. c. 53.**

VALLABHARĀMA KALYĀṆAJĪ ṢUKLA, *of Bulsar.* *See* VEDAS.—Yajurveda.—*Vājasaneyisaṃhitā.* ॥ अथ वाजसनेयसंहिता० [Vājasaneyisaṃhitā. Edited by Vallabharāma.] [1893-1894.] *obl.* 8°. **14010. cc. 5.**

VALLÉE POUSSIN (L. DE LA). *See* LA VALLÉE POUSSIN (L. DE).

VĀLMĪKI.

RĀMĀYAṆA.

Entire Text.

శ్రీమద్రామాయణమ్ *etc.* [Rāmāyaṇa. Preceded by the Rāmāyaṇapārāyaṇakrama, a tract on the study of the poem; Rāmāyaṇasampradāyārthasaṅgraha, a treatise on its religious and historical significance; Rāmāyaṇamāhātmya, from the Parāṣaropapurāṇa; Rāmachandrapaṭṭābhishekaprayoga, a guide to the ceremony styled *rāmapaṭṭābhisheka*; Rāmāshṭottaraṣatanāma, 108 names of Rāma; and Gāyatrīrāmāyaṇa, an acrostic on the Gāyatrī, compiled from the Rāmāyaṇa.] pp. lx. 892; 4 *plates.* చెన్నపుర్యామ్ ౧౮౯౭ [*Madras*, 1897.] 8°. **14065. d. 37.**

This edition does not include the Uttarakāṇḍa.

ஸ்ரீராமாயணம் *etc.* [Rāmāyaṇa. Edited with introductions, glosses, and paraphrases in Tamil by P. A. M. Ṣrīnivāsa Rāghavāchārya.] சென்னை [*Madras*,] 1897, *etc.* 4°. **14068. c. 14.**

In progress. The volume containing the Sundarakāṇḍa is in the second edition, and differs from the other volumes by being of smaller size and containing no transcription of the text in Telugu characters.

RĀMĀYAṆA.—*Entire Text (continued).*

॥ अथश्रीमद्वाल्मीकीयरामायणम् ॥ [Rāmāyaṇa. With a Hindi translation by Maheṣadatta Sukula of Dhanauli. Preceded by an index and Hindi preface by Ṣaktidhara Sukula and the Rāmāyaṇamāhātmya from the Skandapurāṇa with Hindi translation.] pp. 54, 58, 35, 250, 502, 265, 268, 314, 634, 434; 9 *plates.* लखनऊ १९०२ [*Lucknow*, 1902.] Fol. **14068. d. 11.**

శ్రీవాల్మీకిరామాయణమునందలి బాలకాండము *etc.* (అయోధ్యాకాండము, అరణ్యకాండము *etc.*) [Rāmāyaṇa. Preceded by the Gāyatrīrāmāyaṇa, ritual rules for reading the text according to the Vaishṇava and Smārta schools, *etc.* Edited with Telugu translation by Gaṭṭupalli Ṣeshāchārya.] చెన్నపురి [*Madras*,] 1902, *etc.* 12°. **14065. b. 26.**

In progress.

ஶ்ரீ... ஶ்ரீமத்ராமாயணவ்யாக்யாஸர்வார்த்தஸாரஃ *etc.* [Rāmāyaṇa. With the commentary Sarvārthasāra of Veṅkateṣvara Yajvā. Edited by Rāmakṛishṇa Ṣāstrī of Kalpadi.] கல்பாத்தி [illegible] [*Kulpadi*, 1903, *etc.*] 4°. **14068. c. 17.**

In progress.

রামায়ণম্ । *etc.* [Rāmāyaṇa. With Bengali translation. Edited by Pañchānana Tarkaratna. Third edition.] pp. i. ix. 1469. কলিকাতা ১৩১১ [*Calcutta*, 1904.] 8°. **14068. c. 18.**

The Ramayana. Translated into English prose . . . Edited . . . by Manmatha Nath Dutt. 7 vols. pp. viii. 1933. *Calcutta*, 1892-1894. 8°. **14065. bbb. 3.**

A reprint of the issue of 1889-91.

Le Râmâyana de Vâlmîki. Traduit en français par Alfred Roussel, *etc.* (Bibliothèque Orientale. Tome vi., vii., *etc.*) *Paris, Saint-Amand* [printed], 1903, *etc.* 4°. **14068. c. 15.**

In progress.

Abridgments and Selections.

संक्षिप्तवाल्मीकिरामायणम् । [Saṅkshipta-vālmīki-rāmāyaṇa. An abridgment of the Rāmāyaṇa, with glosses, by Chintāmaṇi Vināyaka Vaidya.] pp. ii. 348, v. x. कल्याण मुंबई १९०२ [*Kalyan*, 1902.] 8°. **14065. c. 55.**

RĀMĀYAṆA.—*Abridgments and Selections* (*continued*).

Selections from Ramayana. रामायण संग्रह: Compiled by Jai Chandra, *etc.* pp. 104, iv. *Lahore*, 1893. 8°. **14060. c. 32.(2.)**

Forms no. 3 of the Dayanand Anglo-Vedic College Sanskrit Series.

The Light of India; or Sita. Complied [*sic*] [chiefly from R. T. H. Griffith's translation of the Rāmāyaṇa] by Narayana Hemchandra. pp. viii. 327. *Ahmedabad*, [1895.] 16°. **14065. a. 8.**

Ramayana Niti Ratnavali. Moral gems from the Ramayana. Containig [*sic*] the most excellent Sanskrit moral stanzas selected from Valmiki Ramayana with English translations and explanations [*sic*]. Edited by ... R. Sivasankara Pandiyaji. Second edition. pp. xxiv. 17. *Madras*, 1897. 12°. **14003. c.**

Forms no. 6 of the editor's Hindu Excelsior Series.

இந்த தனிஶ்லோகம் *etc.* [Tani-ṣlokam. Select stanzas from the Rāmāyaṇa, with Tamil glosses and commentary by Periyavāchān Piḷḷai expounding Viṣishṭādvaita doctrine.] சென்னப்பட்டணம் ௧௮௯௯ [*Madras*, 1899, *etc.*] 8°. **14065. bbb. 6.**

In progress.

ఈ తనిశ్లోకమ్ *etc.* [Tani-ṣlokam. Another edition of the preceding, containing the glosses in Telugu, the whole being printed in the Telugu script.] చెన్నపట్టణము ౧౮౯౯ [*Madras*, 1899, *etc.*] 8°. *In progress.* **14065. bbb. 7.**

వాల్మీకిరత్నములు *etc.* [Vālmīkiratna. Compiled with Telugu paraphrases and notes by Gaṭṭupalli Ṣeshāchārya.] (Gems from Valmiki.) pp. xvi. 582; 1 *plate*. చెన్నపురి [*Madras*,] 1901. 12°. **14065. b. 25.**

ஸ்ரீமத்வால்மீகிராமாயணாந்தர்கத: ஸுந்தரகாண்ட: [Sundarakāṇḍa. Preceded by introductory devotional verses, *etc.*, the Saṅksheparāmāyaṇa (Bālakāṇḍa, ch. 1), Gāyatrīrāmāyaṇa, Rāmamūrter Avatāraghaṭṭa (Bālakāṇḍa, ch. 17 of the Bombay edition, 18 of the 1897 Madras edition), and Sītāvivāhaghaṭṭa (Bālakāṇḍa, ch. 73); and followed by the Ādityahṛidayastotra (Yuddhakāṇḍa, ch. 106 of the Bombay edition, 107 of the 1897 Madras edition) and Rāmamūrter Paṭṭābhishekaghaṭṭa (Yuddhakāṇḍa, ch. 131).] pp. 391. கும்பகோண ॥ [*Kumbakonam*,] 1903. *obl.* 16°. **14065. a. 9.**

RĀMĀYAṆA (*continued*).

Portions.

ఆంధ్రటీకాతాత్పర్యసహిత శ్రీరామాయణమ్. బాలకాండము. [Bālakāṇḍa. With Telugu gloss and commentaries, based on those of Govindarāja and Maheṣvara Tīrtha, *etc.*] pt. i.-v. చెన్నపురి ౧౮౯౮ [*Madras*, 1898.] 8°. **14060. d. 16.**

Apparently no more has been published.

(The Ramayan.) [Bālakāṇḍa i.-ii., in Griffith's metrical version. Followed by the Raghuvaṃṣa xiv. 26—xv. 73, translated by the same.] pp. 25. *Bombay*, [1891.] 12°. **14076. b. 24.(4.)**

Without title-page or acknowledgment of sources.

रामायणम् *etc.* [Bālakāṇḍa, i.-xi.] *See* ACADEMIES, *etc.*—Madras.—*University of Madras.* The Sanskrit Text for the Matriculation Examination ... December 1900. pp. 31-66. 1899. 8°. **14060. c. 30.(3.)**

ಶ್ರೀಮದ್ರಾಮಾಯಣದಲ್ಲಿನ ಋಷ್ಯಶೃಂಗೋಪಾಖ್ಯಾನವು. [Ṛishyaṣṛiṅgopākhyāna. The tale of Ṛishya Ṣṛiṅga, as told in the Bālakāṇḍa, ix.-xvi. With Canarese translation.] *See* PAṬṬĀBHIRĀMA ṢĀSTRĪ. ಶ್ರೀಋಷ್ಯಶೃಂಗೋಪಾಖ್ಯಾನವು *etc.* [Ṛishyaṣṛiṅgopākhyāna.] pp. 209-264. [1891.] 8°. **14016. c. 45.**

वाल्मीकीयरामायणम् । अयोध्या वर्णनम् [Ayodhyāvarṇana. Word-for-word grammatical analyses of the description of Ayodhyā in the Bālakāṇḍa. With English and Hindi translations.] *See* ACADEMIES, *etc.*—Allahabad.—*University of Allahabad.* संस्कृत-शिक्षा-विवृति: ... Sanskrit-Siksha-Vivriti, *etc.* pp. 369-405. 1899. 12°. **14085. b. 39.(2.)**

रामायणम् *etc.* [Rāmāyaṇa. A series of abridged extracts from the Ayodhyākāṇḍa, xii.-xiv., xvii.-xx. With notes.] *See* NṚISIṂHARĀMA MUKHOPĀDHYĀYA. साहित्य-रत्नाकर: *etc.* [Sāhityaratnākara.] pp. 19-53. 1898. 12°. **14065. b. 18.**

ஸ்ரீவால்மீகி ராமாயணம். சுந்தரகாண்டம் *etc.* [Sundarakāṇḍa. With Tamil paraphrase by Tenmaḍam Veṅkaṭanarasiṃhāchārya. Edited by Tarkatīrtha Rāmānujāchārya.] pp. xiv. 770; 8 *plates*. சென்னை [*Madras*,] 1901. 12°. **14060. b. 18.**

RĀMĀYAṆA.—*Portions (continued).*

ஸ்ரீவால்மீகிராமாயண ஸுந்தரகாண்டம் *etc.* [Sundarakāṇḍa. Edited with a Tamil translation by Musuṟpākkam Kaḍāmbi Raṅgāchārya.] pp. ix. 182, 233. சென்னை பலவு [*Madras*, 1902.] 8°.
14065. bbb. 9.

அபயப்ரதாநஸாரம் *etc.* [Abhayapradānasāra. Being VI. (Yuddhakāṇḍa) xvii.-xix. 1-9 and 23, with an exposition in Tamil by Periyavāchān Piḷḷai according to the Tengaḷai-Vaishṇava school. Edited by Śrīnivāsa Appan-Aiyaṅgār.] pp. 78. சென்னைப்பட்டணம் கர [*Madras*, 1891.] 8°.
14060. c. 32.(1.)

The text is given in Telugu and Tamil characters.

Appendix.

[For the Gāyatrīrāmāyaṇa, an acrostic of 25 stanzas compiled from the Rāmāyaṇa, of which the initial letters spell the Gāyatrī, and which is sometimes prefixed to editions of the Rāmāyana :] *See* above.

See AGNIVEṢA. श्रीमद्रामायणम् । [Ṣataṣlokī-rāmāyaṇa, or Rāmāyaṇasāra. A poetical epitome of the Rāmāyaṇa.] [1890.] 8°. [*Grantharatnamālā.*]
14096. c. 8. (vol. 3.)

See AGNIVEṢA. समयनिरूपणरामायण *etc.* [Samayanirūpaṇa-rāmāyaṇa. Excerpts from the Rāmāyaṇasāra.] [1900.] 12°.
14065. b. 21.

See APYAYA DĪKSHITA. सविवरणम् श्रीरामायण . . . सारसंग्रहस्तोत्र *etc.* [Rāmāyaṇasārasaṅgrahastotra and Bhāratasārasaṅgrahastotra. Two hymns enunciating the supremacy of Ṣiva as the essence of the Rāmāyaṇa and Mahābhārata.] [1895.] 8°.
14028. d. 54.

See HAAFNER (J.). Proeve van Indische Dichtkunde volgens den Ramaijon, *etc.* 1823. 8°.
14065. c. 48.

See JACOBI (H. G.). Das Râmâyaṇa. Geschichte und Inhalt, nebst Concordanz der gedruckten Recensionen, *etc.* 1893. 8°.
14065. d. 35.

See JACOBI (H. G.). Ein Beitrag zur Rāmāyanakritik, *etc.* 1897. 8°. [*Zeitschrift der Deutschen Morgenlaendischen Gesellschaft.*]
Ac. 8815/2.(vol. 51.)

RĀMĀYAṆA.—*Appendix (continued).*

See NĀRĀYAṆA SOMAYĀJĪ, *Kalvakūrtipalli.* శ్రీ . . . శ్రీరామోత్సవరత్నాకరః *etc.* [Rāmotsavaratnākara. Comprising lections upon the Rāmāyaṇa and rituals connected with it, *etc.*] [1898.] 8°.
14028. d. 66.

See NAVĪNACHANDRA DĀSA. A Note on the Ancient Geography of Asia, compiled from Válmiki-Rámáyana, *etc.* 1896. 8°.
14003. b. 19.(vol. 4.)

See OMAN (J. C.). Struggles in the Dawn. The stories of . . . the Ramayana and Mahabharata, *etc.* 1893. 8°.
11824. ccc. 43.

See OMAN (J. C.). The Great Indian Epics. The stories of the Ramayana and the Mahabharata, *etc.* 1894. 8°.
011850. g. 39.

—— —— [Second edition.] 1899. 8°.
2504. k 18.

See RĀMĀNUJĀCHĀRYA, *Kandāḍai Varadārya.* श्रीमद्वेदपादरामायणम् *etc.* [Vedapādarāmāyaṇa. A poetical summary of the Rāmāyaṇa, having the last quarter of every verse composed of quotations from Vedic and other religious works.] 1902. 8°.
14072. b. 31.

See ṢAṬHAKOPĀCHĀRYA, *M. K.* ॥ निरोष्ठ्यरामायणसंग्रहः *etc.* [Niroshṭhyarāmāyaṇasaṅgraha. A poetical summary of the Rāmāyaṇa, composed without labial vowels or consonants.] 1901. 8°.
14072. cc. 62.(2.)

See SCHOEBEL (C.). Le Râmâyana, au point de vue religieux, philosophique et moral, *etc.* 1888. 4°. [*Annales du Musée Guimet.*]
7704. h. 21.(tom. 13.)

See VĪRARĀGHAVA TĀTĀCHĀRYA. శ్రీరామచన్ద్రోదయః [Rāmachandrodaya. A treatise on the Rāmāyaṇa.] [1891.] 8°.
14072. ccc. 32.

The Ramayana of Valmiki. An English abridgment, with introduction, notes, and review. pp. xiv. 153; 1 *plate.* 1896. *See* EAST. The Sacred Books of the East Described and Examined. Hindu Series. Vol. III, pt. 1. 1895, *etc.* 8°.
14010. cc. 9.(vol. 3.)

RĀMĀYAṆA.—*Appendix (continued)*.

Ramayana. The Epic of Rama, Prince of India. Condensed into English verse by Romesh Dutt ... Illustrations designed from Indian sources by E. Stuart Hardy. pp. 194. *London*, 1900. 8°. **14065. c. 47.**

Rama & the Monkeys. Adapted for children from the Ramayana by Geraldine Hodgson. Illustrated, *etc.* pp. xiii. 104; 7 *plates*. *London, Edinburgh* [printed], 1903. 12°. **012200. e. 8.(no. 13.)**

Forms part of the Temple Classics for Young People.

YOGAVĀSISHṬHARĀMĀYAṆA.

[For this work, popularly ascribed to Vālmīki:] *See* YOGAVĀSISHṬHARĀMĀYAṆA.

VĀMAMĀRGA. वाममार्ग भैरवीचक्र [Vāmamārga, or Bhairavīchakra. A handbook for the performance of the mystic orgies of the 'left-handed' Śāktas. Edited with a Hindi version by Śyāmasundaralāla Tripāṭhī.] pp. 48. *Moradabad*, 1899. 12°. **14033. a. 38.**

VĀMANA ĀCHĀRYA. *See* PĀṆINI. — *Kāśikā*. काशिका ... Kashika ... [Begun] by Pandit Jayaditya [and completed by Vāmana,] *etc.* 1890. 8°. **14090. bb. 7.**

—— *See* PĀṆINI.—*Kāśikā*. The Ashṭádhyáyí ... Translated into English, *etc.* [Being a translation of the Ashṭādhyāyī with a paraphrase of portions of the Kāśikā.] 1891-1898. 8°. **14093. d. 18.**

—— *See* PATAÑJALI. — *Grammatical Works*. भाष्यसङ्गमनी *etc.* [Bhāshyasaṅgamanī. Being the aphorisms of the Mahābhāshya, the text of the Kāśikā, and a commentary.] [1903, *etc.*] 8°. **14090. bb. 22.**

—— काव्यालङ्कारकामधेनुः ॥ [Kāvyālaṅkāravṛitti. Aphorisms and expositions of style. With the commentary Kāvyālaṅkārakāmadhenu of Gopendra Tippabhūpāla.] 1895, *etc.* *See* VEṄKAṬARAṄGANĀTHA SVĀMĪ. Grandha Pradarsani, *etc.* [No. 3.] 1895, *etc.* 8°. **14003. c. 2.(3.)**

Incomplete, breaking off at III. 17.

VĀMANA BHAṬṬA BĀṆA. The Śringârabhûshaṇa of Vâmana-bhatta-bâṇa. [A dramatic composition of the *bhāṇa* type.] Edited by Paṇḍit Śivadatta ... and Kâśînâth Pâṇdurang Parab. (शृङ्गारभूषणम् ।) pp. 19. 1896. *See* DURGĀPRASĀDA, *son of Vrajalāla*, and KĀŚINĀTHA PĀṆḌURAṄGA PARAB. Kâvyamâlâ. [No.] 58. 1886, *etc.* 8°. **14072. ccc. 12.(no. 58.)**

—— शृङ्गारभूषणभाणः ... Sringarabhooshanabhana, *etc.* pp. i. 28. 1897. *See* VEṄKAṬARAṄGANĀTHA SVĀMĪ. Grandha Pradarsani, *etc.* [No. 16.] 1895, *etc.* 8°. **14003. c. 2.(16.)**

VĀMANA DĀJĪ OK. *See* MAHĀBHĀRATA.—Bhagavadgītā.—*Sanskrit and Vernaculars*. The Yathârthadîpikâ ... Edited ... by Vâman ... Oka. 1896, *etc.* 8°. **14140. aa. 16.**

—— *See* MOROPANTA. The Miscellaneous Poems of Moropanta ... Edited ... by Vâman ... Oka. 1896, *etc.* 8°. **14140. aa. 17.**

—— *See* MOROPANTA. The Râmâyaṇs of Moropant ... Edited ... by the editors of the 'Kâvyasangraha' (Vâmana ... Oka, *etc.*). 1891-1896. 8°. **14140. aa. 2.**

—— *See* SOHIROBĀNĀTH ĀMBIYE. The Poems of Sohirobânâtha ... Edited ... by Vâmana ... Oka. 1896, *etc.* 8°. **14140. aa. 12.**

—— *See* VĀMANA PAṆḌITA, *the Marathi Poet*. The Poems of Vâmana ... Edited ... by Vâmana ... Oka. 1894-1901. 8°. **14140. aa. 5.**

VĀMANA PAṆḌITA, *the Marathi Poet*. The Yathârthadîpikâ, *etc.* 1896, *etc.* 8°. *See* MAHĀBHĀRATA.—Bhagavadgītā.—*Sanskrit and Vernaculars*. **14140. aa. 16.**

—— वामनी ग्रंथ *etc.* [Vāmanī Grantha. The Marathi poems of Vāmana, together with the Sanskrit texts upon which some are based, and two Sanskrit poems by Vāmana, viz. the Anubhūtileśa (with Marathi metrical version by Sāmrājya Vāmana) and Siddhântavijaya.] 4 vols. मुंबईंत १८८९-१८९१ [*Bombay*, 1889-1891.] 8°. **14140. b. 23.**

—— The Poems of Vâmana Paṇdita, the great Marâthî poet of the Mahârâshtra. [Including in vol. 3 the Sanskrit poems, viz. the Siddhānta-vijaya and Anubhūtileṣa.] . . . Edited . . . by Vâmana Dâjî Oka. (कवितासंग्रह.) 3 vols. *Bombay*, 1894-1901. 8°. **14140. aa. 5.**

Forms nos. 8, 19, *and* 33 *of the* Kâvyasangraha.

VĀMANA ṢĀSTRĪ ISLĀMPURKAR. *See* Arisiṃha. काव्यकल्पलता *etc.* [Kāvyakalpalatā. With commentary of Amarachandra. Translated into Marathi by Vāmana Ṣāstrī.] [1891.] 8°. **14140. b. 24.**

—— *See* Kallaṭa. The Spandapradîpikâ . . . Edited by . . . Vâman . . . Islâmpurkar, *etc.* 1898. 8°. **14048. dd. 3.(vol. 14.)**

—— *See* Padmagupta. The Navasâhasâṅka Charita . . . Edited by . . . Vâmana . . . Islâmpurkar. 1895, *etc.* 8°. **14070. dd. 4.**

—— *See* Parāṣara. [*Smṛiti.*] The Parâśara Dharma Saṃhitâ . . . with the commentary of Sâyaṇa . . . Edited . . . by . . . Vâman . . . Islâmapurkar. 1893, *etc.* 8°. **14039. a. 15.**

VĀMANA ṢIVARĀMA ĀPṬE. *See* Kālidāsa.—*Mālavikāgnimitra.* The Mâlavikâgnimitram . . . with . . . English translation chiefly collected from the notes given in class by the late Mr. V. S. Apte, *etc.* 1897. 8°. **14079. c. 66.**

—— Kusumamala, or A Collection of Choice Extracts . . . No. I. . . . 2nd edition . . . revised by M. S. Apte. pp. ii. ii. 86, 35. *Poona*, 1894. 12°. **14085. c. 44.**

—— Kusumamâlâ . . . No. II. Designed for students preparing for the Matriculation Examination. With explanatory notes . . . Fourth edition. Revised . . . by M. S. Apte. pp. iv. 196, 54. *Poona*, 1902. 8°. **14085. c. 51.**

—— The Student's Hand-book of Progressive Exercises. Part I (Part II) . . . Fifth edition . . . revised by M. S. Apte. 2 pts. *Poona*, 1894-1899. 12°. **14092. a. 14.**

VAMṢĪDHARA, *Pandit.* *See* Garga. ॥ अथ श्रीगर्गसंहिता *etc.* [Gargasaṃhitā. With Hindi translation by Vaṃṣīdhara.] [1898.] *obl.* 4°. **14028. e. 34.**

VAMṢĪDHARA, *of Nabha.* *See* Sārasvatasūtra. लघुभाष्यम् *etc.* [Sārasvatasūtra. With the Laghubhāshya of Raghunātha. Edited by Vaṃṣīdhara.] [1901.] 8°. **14093. b. 44.**

VAMṢĪDHARA, *son of Krishṇadeva.* *See* Piṅgala Āchārya. Prákrita-paiṅgalam. With the commentaries of . . . Vanśidhara, *etc.* 1902. 8°. [*Bibliotheca Indica.*] **14002. a. (vol. 148.)**

VAMṢĪDHARA MISRA. वैद्यमनउत्सव: । [Vaidyamanaütsava. A metrical handbook of medical practice, in 7 chapters.] pp. 48, iii. [1890.] *See* Periodical Publications.—*Bombay.* ग्रन्थरत्नमाला *etc.* (Granth Ratna Málá, *etc.*) Vol. IV, no. 3-5. 1887-[1892.] 8°. **14096. c. 8.(vol. 4.)**

VAMṢĪVADANA ṢARMĀ. পুণ্ডরীককুলকীর্ত্তিপঞ্জিকা ফতেসিংহ জমিদারীর ইতিবৃত্ত [Puṇḍarīkakulakīrtti-pañjikā. A poem in 5 chapters narrating the history of the Puṇḍarika family or zamindars of Fatehsingh from its settlement to about 200 years ago. Edited with Bengali translation and appendices on the subsequent history of the family, *etc.*, by Rāmendrasundara Trivedī.] pp. ii. 88; 10 *plates.* *Calcutta*, ১৩০৭ [1901.] 8°. **14058. b. 47.**

VANAMĀLĪ CHATURVEDĪ, *son of Bhānurāma.* *See* Rāma, *son of Ananta.* मुहूर्तचिन्तामणि: *etc.* [Muhūrtachintāmaṇi. With Hindi translation by Vanamālī.] [1902.] 8°. **14053. cc. 69.**

—— *See* Yavanajātaka. यवनजातक *etc.* [Yavanajātaka. With Hindi translation by Vanamālī.] [1901.] 8°. **14053. ccc. 4.(3.)**

VANDERBILT ORIENTAL SERIES. *See* Tolman (H. C.) and Stevenson (J. H.).

VAṄGASENA, *son of Gadādhara.* चिकित्सासारसंग्रह: *etc.* (Chikitsasarasangraha. A treatise on Hindu medicine by Banga Sena. Edited . . . by Pandit Jibananda Vidyasagara . . . Second edition.) pp. ii. 1030. *Calcutta*, 1893. 8°. **14043. cc. 9.**

The English title is from the wrapper.

—— ॥ श्री: ॥ अखिलवैद्यकग्रन्थानां शिरोभूषण: श्रीमद्विप्रवर्यगदाधरतनयवङ्गसेनविदुषा विरचित: वङ्गसेन: *etc.* [Vaṅgasena, or Chikitsāsārasaṅgraha. With a Hindi translation by Lālā Ṣālagrāma Vaiṣya of Moradabad, completed by Ṣaṅkaralāla son of Bhojadeva, and with a Hindi preface by Ṣaṅkaralāla and his brother Hariṣaṅkara.] pp. xvi. xxxvi. 1096; 1 *plate.* *Bombay*, १९६१ [1905.] 4°. **14043. ddd. 2**

VARADĀCHĀRYA, *Tirumaṅgalam Naḍādūr.* See VARADĀCHĀRYA, *Mīmāṃsāvallabha Vātsya.* வரதேசிகவைபவப்ரகாசிகா etc. [Varadadeṣikavaibhavaprakāṣikā, *etc.* Edited with prefaces in Tamil and Sanskrit by N. Varadāchārya, *etc.*] 1897. 8°. **14076. d. 50.**

VARADĀCHĀRYA, *Mīmāṃsāvallabha Vātsya, son of Vīrarāghava.* வரதேசிகவைபவப்ரகாசிகா வரதேசிகாப்யுதயநாடக ஸகாவ்ய ... ஸமவதாராதநஸங்க்ரஹ: ஸுதர்ஸநஸ்தோத்ரஞ்ச etc. [Varadadeṣikavaibhavaprakāṣikā, a short work in prose and verse, Varadadeṣikābhyudaya, a poem in 8 *sargas*, and Varadadeṣikaprabhāvadīpa, a poem of 325 stanzas, with various smaller poems in commemoration and worship of the Vaishṇava teacher Varadāchārya or Naḍādūr Ammāḷ. With Bhagavadārādhanasaṅgraha and Sudarṣanastotra, 2 short religious poems by the latter, *etc.* Edited with prefaces in Tamil and Sanskrit by Naḍādūr Varadāchārya and Naḍādūr Narasiṃhāchārya.] pp. viii. 172. சென்னபட்ணம் ॥ [*Madras,*] 1897. 8°. **14076. d. 50.**

VARADĀCHĀRYA, *Vātsya*, called NAḌĀDŪR AMMĀḶ, *son of Devarāja.* See VARADĀCHĀRYA, *Mīmāṃsāvallabha Vātsya.* வரதேசிகவைபவப்ரகாசிகா etc. [Varadadeṣikavaibhavaprakāṣikā, Varadadeṣikābhyudaya, Varadadeṣikaprabhāvadīpa, *etc.*, in commemoration of Naḍādūr Ammāḷ. With Bhagavadārādhanasaṅgraha and Sudarṣanastotra, 2 religious poems by the latter, *etc.*] 1897. 8°. **14076. d. 50.**

—— ப்ரபன்னபாரிஜாதம் *etc.* [Prapannapārijāta. A poem on the religious system of Viṣishṭādvaita Vaishṇavas, in 10 *paddhatis.* Followed by Paratvādipañchakastuti and Paramārthastuti, short poems of like nature, also by Varadāchārya; Parāṣara Bhaṭṭa's Ashṭaṣlokī; Yāmuna Āchārya's Chatuḥṣlokī; and a life of Varadāchārya, in Tamil prose. Edited with Tamil interpretations and commentary, *etc.*, by Ahobilāchārya.] pp. ii. 160, v. சென்னை நகரம் [*Madras,* 1895.] 8°. **14028. d. 55.**

The Sanskrit stanzas are printed in both Grantham and Telugu character.

—— Prapannapārijāta. The Refugee's Pârijâta. [In English.] 1899-1900. *See* PERIODICAL PUBLICATIONS.—*Madras.* The Brahmavâdin. Vol. V, no. i.-vi. 1895, *etc.* 8°. **14048. g. 1.(vol. 5.)**

—— The Thathva Nirnaya. Visishtadwaita philosophy [proving the identity of Nārāyaṇa with Para-Brahma]. By Sri Varadacharya, *etc.* (तत्त्वनिर्णयः ॥) pp. 23. 1902. *See* ANANTĀCHĀRYA, *Prativādibhayaṅkara.* शास्त्रमुक्तावली The Ŝasthramukthâvalî, *etc.* No. 12. 1899, *etc.* 8°. **14049. a. 1.(no. 12.)**

VARADĀCHĀRYA, *son of Ghaṭikāṣata Sudarṣanāchārya*, also called AMMĀḶ ĀCHĀRYA. யதிராஜவிஜயநாம நாடகம் ॥ வேதாந்தவிலாஸாபரநாமதேயம் *etc.* [Yatirājavijaya, or Vedāntavilāsa. An allegorical drama in 6 acts, setting forth the teachings and triumphs of Rāmānuja as its hero. Edited by Koṭikannikādānaṃ Vīrarāghava Tātāchārya.] pp. 62. கும்பகோணம் ॥ ௧௯௦௨ [*Kumbakonam,* 1902.] 8°. **14080. d. 22.(3.)**

Pp. 57-60 are wanting.

Burnell (Tanjore Catalogue, p. 1716) quotes an introductory stanza not found in this edition, and wrongly calls the play "recent." The author's grandfather Varadāchārya was grandson of Sudarṣuna, the nephew of Rāmānuja.

VARADĀCHĀRYA SŪRI, *Kuṣika, son of Varada Guru, son of Varada Deṣika.* See MAHĀBHĀRATA.—*Anuṣāsanaparva.* भगवद्गुणदर्पणाख्यभाष्य-निर्वचन ... श्रीविष्णोर्नामसहस्रम् *etc.* [Vishṇusahasranāma. With Parāṣara Bhaṭṭa's commentary Bhagavadguṇadarpaṇa, the grammatical supercommentary Bhagavannāmasahasranirvachana or Vishṇun.° by Varadāchārya, *etc.*] [1894.] 8°. **14065. e. 27.**

VARADA DEṢIKA, *Vātsya.* See VARADĀCHĀRYA, *Vātsya*, called NAḌĀDŪR AMMĀḶ.

VARADĀKĀNTA LAHIRĪ. See UTTARAGĪTĀ. The Uttara Gita . . . Translated by D.[*sic*] K. Laheri. [1893.] 16°. **14016. a. 24.(1.)**

—— —— [Another edition.] 1902. 16°. **14016. a. 24.(2.)**

VARADARĀJA, *Logician.* तार्किकरक्षा *etc.* (The Tārkikarakṣā[, a defence of the Nyāya and Vaiṣeshika systems of philosophy,] and Sārasaṃgraha [, a commentary thereon,] of Varadarāja. With the glosses Niṣkaṇṭakā of Mallinātha Kolācala and Laghudīpikā of Jñānapūrṇa.) [With English introduction and notes by A. Venis. Edited by

Vindhyeṣvarīprasāda Dube.] pp. xxxiii. viii. ii. v. vi. vi. 364. 1903. *See* PERIODICAL PUBLICATIONS.—*Benares.* The Pandit, *etc.* New Series. Vol. XXI-XXIV. 1876, *etc.* 8°.

14096. d. 6.(vol. 21-24.)

This author is styled Varajid Varadarāja *by Burnell* (*Tanjore Catal.*, *p.* 119*b*).

—— [A separate issue of the above, reprinted from the "Pandit."] pp. xxxiii. viii. ii. v. vi. vi. 364. वाराणस्याम् १९०३ [*Benares*, 1903.] 8°.

14049. a. 8.

VARADARĀJA, *Chaṭaviṭikanṭa.* *See* PĀṆINI.—*Siddhāntakaumudī.* मध्यसिद्धान्तकौमुदी *etc.* [Madhyasiddhāntakaumudī. An abridgment of the Siddhāntakaumudī, by Varadarāja.] [1895.] 12°.

14090. b. 41.

—— *See* PĀṆINI.—*Siddhāntakaumudī.* मध्यकौमुदी . . . The Madhya Kaumudi by Varada Raja, *etc.* [Followed by the Liṅgānuṣāsanasūtravṛitti.] 1899. 12°.

14092. a. 22.

VARADARĀJA AIYAṄGĀR, *M. Bhīma.* *See* BĀDARĀYAṆA. The Vedānta-Sūtras with the Śri-Bhāshya . . . Translated . . . by M. Raṅgāchārya and M. B. Varadarāja Aiyangār. 1899. 8°.

14048. cc. 29.

VARADĀRYA, *Kuṣika, son of Varada Guru.* *See* VARADĀCHĀRYA SŪRI.

VARĀHAMIHIRA. বৃহজ্জাতকম্ *etc.* [Bṛihaj-jātaka. With Utpala's commentary, and a Bengali commentary.] pp. 156. [1893.] *See* PERIODICAL PUBLICATIONS.—*Calcutta.* অরুণোদয় *etc.* [Aruṇodaya.] Pt. i., no. 1. [1890, *etc.*] 4°.

14133. g. 16.(pt. i., no. 1.)

—— වෘහජ්ජාතකය *etc.* (Brihatjataka of Varahamihira. Translated into Sinhalese[, with the original Sanskrit text,] by A. J. Wikkramasinha.) pt. ii. pp. iv. 18-92. *Colombo*, 1896. 8°.

14053. ccc. 3.(1.)

—— ஸ்ரீ . . . உபாத்யாயீநாமகஹோரா-வ்யாக்யா *etc.* [Bṛihaj-jātaka. With Govinda Somayājī's commentary Daṣādhyāyī upon chapters i.-x. Edited by V. Veṅkaṭāchala Ṣāstrī of Kalpadi.] pp. 256. *Palghat,* கொள்ளாயி [1905.] 8°.

14053. ccc. 51.

Chapters xi. *ff. are divided so as to form only* 16 adhyāyas. *The* 16*th* adhyāya *of the northern texts is omitted.*

VARĀHAMIHIRA (*continued*). ഹോരാശാസ്ത്രം. ഭാഷാവ്യാഖ്യാനം *etc.* [Horāṣāstra. Being the Bṛihaj-jātaka, *adhyāyas* i.-v. Edited with a Malayalam translation and commentary by K. Rāma Vāriyar.] pp. i. ii. 4, 332. തൃശ്ശിവപേരൂർ ൧൦൬൫ [*Trichur*, 1890.] 8°.

14053. ccc. 52.

—— বৃহৎসংহিতা । [Bṛihat-saṃhitā. With Bengali translation.] pp. 232. [1890, *etc.*] *See* PERIODICAL PUBLICATIONS.—*Calcutta.* অরুণোদয় *etc.* [Aruṇodaya.] Pt. i., no. 4. [1890, *etc.*] 4°.

14133. g. 16.(pt. i., no. 4.)

—— The Bṛihat Saṃhitâ by Varâhamihira. With the commentary [Saṃhitâvivṛiti] of Bhaṭṭotpala. Edited by Mahámahopádhyáya Sudhákara Dvivedí. (बृहत्संहिता) 2 vols. pp. ii. iii. ii. i. vii. 1263, vii. ii. viii. ii. i. vi. *Benares*, 1895-1897. 8°.

14048. dd. 3.(vol. 10.)

Forms vol. 10 *of the* Vizianagram Sanskrit Series.

—— Bṛhatsaṃhitâ . . . Adhyâyas lxxx.-lxxxiii. [Treating of the lapidary art. With French translation.] *See* FINOT (L.). Les Lapidaires Indiens, *etc.* pp. 59-75. 1896. 8°.

Ac. 8929.(fasc. 111.)

VARĀHANARASIṂHĀCHĀRYA, *Gonnabattula.* శ్రీ . . . శ్రుత్యాది సారసంగ్రహాఖ్య శ్రీమద్విశ్వకర్మాన్వయప్రదీపికాఖ్యేయమాఖ్యాయికా *etc.* [Viṣvakarmānvayapradīpikā, or Ṣrutyādisārasaṅgraha. A metrical summary of cosmogonic, religious, and other legends relating to the deity Viṣvakarmā and the families bearing that name. With Telugu translation by Tāmmanāchārya.] pp. iv. 199. వైశాఖపురాగ్రం [*Vizagapatam*, 1902.] 8°.

14058. b. 42.

VARAMUNI SVĀMĪ. *See* MAṆAVĀLA MĀMUNI.

VARARUCHI. [For the Ṣrutabodha ascribed to Vararuchi:] *See* KĀLIDĀSA.—*Supposititious Works.*

—— ॥ अथ . . . लिङ्गविशेषविधिः ॥ [Liṅgaviṣeshavidhi.] *See* FRANKE (R. O.). Die Indischen Genuslehren, *etc.* pp. 118-134. 1890. 8°.

14093. d. 19.

—— सार्थ प्राकृत प्रकाश *etc.* [Prākṛitaprakāṣa. Aphorisms of Prakrit grammar, in 12 *parichchhedas.* Edited with Marathi introduction and commentary by Ṣaṅkara Rāmachandra Hatvaḷne.] pp. vi. xviii. 111. पुणे १९०० [*Poona*, 1900.] 12°. **14092. a. 26.**

—— प्राकृतप्रकाशः . . . Prakrita Prakasha, [or rather, the commentary thereon, styled Prākṛitamanoramā,] by Pandita Bhamaha, with the sutras of Vararuchi [properly styled Prākṛitaprakāṣa]. Rivised [*sic*] by Pandit Rama Shastri Tailanga. pp. 42. *Benares*, 1899. 8°. **14093. b. 27.(3.)**

VARASADDHAMMAKITTI. *See* SADDHAMMAKITTI.

VARASAMBODHI, Ū. ရေဇကြိုးတရားစာ *etc.* [Ye-za-gyoh-tayā-sā. A collection of Burmese homilies, with Pali texts, for occasions when offerings are made.] pp. 161. ရန်ကုန် ၁၂၅၅ [*Rangoon*, 1893.] 8°. **14300. d. 22.(5.)**

VARASĀMI, Ū. လက္ခဏာဒိဘေဒကျမ်း [Lakkhaṇādibheda. A Burmese anthological work on the philosophical concepts of *lakkhaṇa*, *rasa*, *pachchupaṭṭhāna*, and *padaṭṭhāna*, illustrated from the Pali.] pp. 84. ရန်ကုန် ၁၂၅၃ [*Rangoon*, 1891.] 8°. **14300. d. 20.(3.)**

VARDHAMĀNA, *disciple of Govinda.* गणरत्नमहोदधिः *etc.* [Gaṇaratnamahodadhi. Edited by Bhīmasena Ṣarmā.] pp. ii. iii. 251, lxviii. प्रयाग १८९४ [*Allahabad*, 1894.] 8°. **14090. d. 30.**

VASANTAKUMĀRA BHAṬṬĀCHĀRYA, *Kāvyatīrtha Vidyāratna.* माइकेलचरितम् . . . Life of Micheal [*sic*] Madhushudana Datta [in Sanskrit verse] . . . by Basanta Kumar . . . Bhattacharjya, *etc.* pt. i. pp. ii. 44. कलिकाता [*Calcutta*,] 1890. 12°. **14058. a. 7.**

VASANTAKUMĀRA RĀYA. *See* PĀṆINI.—*Ashṭādhyāyī.* सिद्धान्तसन्दीपनी *etc.* [Siddhāntasandīpanī. A rearrangement of the Aphorisms, with Bengali commentary, by Vasantakumāra Rāya.] [1901.] 12°. **14092. a. 17.(3.)**

VASATIRĀMA, *son of Ṣālagrāma, of Beri. See* MANU, *son of Lakshmaṇa.* वैद्यकसर्वस्वम् *etc.* [Vaidyakasarvasva. With Hindi translation by Vasatirāma.] [1896.] 12°. **14043. b. 9.(2.)**

—— *See* PURĀṆAS.—*Matsyapurāṇa.* मत्स्यपुराण *etc.* [Matsyapurāṇa. With Hindi translation by Vasatirāma.] [1892.] 4°. **14018. c. 31.**

VASATIRĀMA, *son of Ṣālagrāma, of Beri (continued). See* RĀMA, *Physician.* वैद्यकसारशंकर ग्रंथ *etc.* [Vaidyakasāraṣaṅkara. With Hindi translation by Vasatirāma.] [1896.] 12°. **14043. b. 9.(3.)**

VĀSAVA, Ū, *of Akauk-wûn.* စေတီယင်္ဂဏဒီပကကျမ်း *etc.* [Chetiyaṅgaṇadīpaka-kyan. A Burmese treatise on the sanctity of Buddhist temples, illustrated by quotations from Pali texts.] pp. 48. မန္တလေး ၁၂၆၀ [*Mandalay*, 1898.] 8°. **14300. d. 26.(7.)**

VASISHṬHA. धनुर्वेदसंहिता *etc.* [Vāsishṭhī Dhanurvedasaṃhitā. A treatise on archery and cognate military sciences, ascribed to Vasishṭha. With a Hindi translation attributed on the title-page to Haradayālu Svāmī and in the colophon to Rāmarakshapāla, and with diagrams.] pp. ii. 108. मुंबई १९५८ [*Bombay*, 1902.] 8°. **14053. ccc. 35.**

—— ॥ अथ वासिष्ठीहवनपद्धतिप्रा° [Vāsishṭhī Havanapaddhati. A ritual for oblations, ascribed to Vasishṭha.] ff. 38. *Lucknow*, 1900. *obl.* 8°. **14033. b. 33.(3.)**

—— ॥ अथ वाशिष्ठीहवनपद्धतिः प्रारम्भः ॥ [Vāsishṭhī Havanapaddhati.] pp. 86. *Bara Banki*, [1902.] *obl.* 8°. **14028. dd. 13.**

—— अथ वासिष्ठी शिक्षा *etc.* [Vāsishṭhī Ṣikshā. A list of catchwords of the divisions of the Ṛigveda and Yajurveda, *etc.*, claiming the authority of Vasishṭha, and belonging to the Mādhyandina school.] *See* YUGALAKIṢORA VYĀSA PĀṬHAKA. श्रीमद्याज्ञवल्क्यादि . . . शिक्षासङ्ग्रहः . . . A collection of Śikshás, *etc.* pp. 36-45. 1893. 8°. **14093. b. 31.**

VĀSISHṬHARĀMĀYAṆA. *See* YOGAVĀSISHṬHARĀMĀYAṆA.

VASU (SRIS CHANDRA). *See* ṢRĪṢACHANDRA VASU.

VĀSUDEVA, *disciple of Bhārata Guru.* The Yudhishṭhiravijaya of Vâsudeva. [A heroic poem of 8 *āṣvāsas*, in *yamaka* style.] With the commentary of Râjânaka Ratnakaṇṭha. Edited by . . . Paṇdit Śivadatta . . . and Kâśinâth Pându-rang Parab. (युधिष्ठिरविजयम् ।) pp. ii. 220, xv. i. 1897. *See* DURGĀPRASĀDA, *son of Vrajalāla*, and KĀṢĪNĀTHA PĀṆḌURAṄGA PARAB. Kâvyamâlâ. [No.] 60. 1886, *etc.* 8°. **14072. ccc. 12.(no. 60.)**

VĀSUDEVA, *Rādhāmaṅgalam Vaidyanātha.* See NĀRĀYAṆA ŚĀSTRĪ, *Rādhāmaṅgalam V.*

VĀSUDEVA ADHVARĪ. See VĀSUDEVA DĪKSHITA.

VĀSUDEVA BĀḶĀ AINĀPURE. See ŚATAKOṬI-RĀMACHARITA. ॥ अथ आनंदरामायण० [Ānanda-rāmāyaṇa. Edited by Vāsudeva Ainăpure.] [1903.] Fol. **14018. c. 32.**

VĀSUDEVA BHAṬṬA, *Grammarian.* See SĀRA-SVATASŪTRA. सारस्वतं व्याकरणम् *etc.* (The Saraswata Vyakarana ... With the commentary [Sārasvata-prasāda] of Vasudeva Bhatta, *etc.*) [1901.] 8°. **14090. bb. 15.(2.)**

VĀSUDEVA BHAṬṬĀCHĀRYA, *son of Raṅganātha.* ஆஹ்நிகாம்ருதம் [Āhnikāmṛita. A treatise on the daily ritual of Vaishṇavas of the Vaikhānasa school, based upon the Vaikhānasasūtra, *etc.* With commentary by the author's son, Nārā-yaṇa.] pp. 123, ii. See UPANISHADS.—*Modern and Fictitious Upanishads.* பாரமாத்மிகோபநி-ஷத்ப்ரப்ருதி *etc.* [Pāramātmikopanishad, *etc.*] 1900. 8°. **14033. bbb. 13.**

VĀSUDEVĀCHĀRYA, *S., of Wesleyan College, Madras.* See BHALLAṬA. The Bhallata Satakam ... With Sanskrit commentary and translation. By S. Vasudeva Chariyar. 1898. 8°. **14070. dd. 12.**

—— See BHOJARĀJA. The Kishkindhakanda ... Edited, with English notes & translation, by S. Vasudevachariar. 1898. 8°. **14076. b. 36.(2.)**

VĀSUDEVA DĪKSHITA, *Grammarian.* See PĀṆINI. —*Siddhāntakaumudī.* Balamanorama sahitha. Sidhantha Kowmuthi, *etc.* [Siddhāntakaumudī, with the commentary Bālamanoramā of Vāsudeva.] 1889-1901. 8°. **14092. b. 46.**

VĀSUDEVAJÑĀNA MUNI. See PURĀṆAS.—*Selections.* कैवल्यरत्नम् *etc.* [Kaivalyaratna. An exposition of monism, compiled by Vāsudevajñāna.] [1901.] 8°. **14016. d. 57.**

VĀSUDEVA LAKSHMAṆA PAṆṢĪKAR. See JAYA-DEVA, *son of Bhojadeva.* The Gita-govinda ... With ... commentaries ... Edited ... by Mangesh ... Telang and Wasudev ... Pansikar. 1899. 8°. **14070. dd. 3.**

VĀSUDEVA LAKSHMAṆA PAṆṢĪKAR (*continued*). See KṚISHṆA MIŚRA, *Dramatist.* प्रबोधचन्द्रोदयम् *etc.* [Prabodhachandrodaya. With commentary, *etc.* Edited by Vāsudeva Paṇṣīkar.] [1898.] 8°. **14080. c. 39.**

—— See PĀṆINI. — *Siddhāntakaumudī.* The Siddhânta-kaumudî with ... commentary ... Edited by Dinkar ... Gâdgil and Vâsudev ... Pansikar. 1899. 4°. **14092. c. 18.**

—— See PURĀṆAS.—*Skandapurāṇa.* सूतसंहिता *etc.* (The Sûtasamhitá. With the commentary of ... Mádhavácharya. Edited by ... Vâsudeva Śaśtri Paṇaśikara.) [1893.] 8°. **14003. ccc. (no. 25.)**

—— See UPANISHADS.—*General Collections.* The Twenty-eight Upanishads ... [Edited] by Vâsu-dev ... Phaṇsîkar. 1904. 16°. **14010. a. 9.**

VĀSUDEVA ŞARMĀ, *V.* See NĀRĀYAṆA BHAṬṬA. सुभद्राहरणचम्पूकाव्यम् *etc.* [Subhadrāharaṇa. Edited by Nīlakaṇṭha and Vāsudeva Şarmā.] [1897.] 8°. **14072. cc. 60.(3.)**

—— See NĪLAKAṆṬHA ŞARMĀ, *Punnacheri-nambi.* த்ருதீயஸஹ்ருதயஸமாகம: *etc.* [Tṛitīya-sahṛidayasamāgama. Edited by Nīlakaṇṭha and Vāsudeva.] 1899. 8°. **14070. dd. 9.(2.)**

—— —— तुरीयसहृदयसमागमः *etc.* [Turīya-sahṛi-dayasamāgama. Edited by Nilakaṇṭha and Vāsu-deva.] [1900.] 8°. **14072. d. 45.(1.)**

VĀSUDEVA ŞĀSTRĪ, *Brahmaşrī.* See APYAYA DĪKSHITA. பஞ்சரத்நஸ்துதிஸ்தோத்ரா *etc.* [Pañ-charatnastuti. Edited by Vāsudeva.] [1897.] 8°. **14028. d. 59.(8.)**

VĀSUDEVA ŞĀSTRĪ ABHYAṄKAR. See RĀMĀ-NUJA.—*Commentaries.* The Chatussûtrî ... Edited with a gloss by ... Vasudevashastri Abhyankar. 1904. 8°. **14049. a. 11.**

VĀSUDEVA YATI, *Paramahaṃsa Parivrājakā-chārya.* வாஸுதேவமநநம்: ... வாசுதேவமனனமென்கிற கிரந்தம் *etc.* [Vāsu-devamanana. A Vedantic treatise. With a Tamil version by V. Kuppusvāmi Aiyar.] pp. i. i. 195, i. சென்னை ஜய [*Madras*, 1895.] 8°. **14048. dd. 19.**

VĀTSYA MĪMĀṂSĀVALLABHA VARADĀCHĀRYA. *See* VARADĀCHĀRYA, *Mīmāṃsāvallabha Vātsya.*

VĀTSYA VARADĀCHĀRYA. *See* VARADĀCHĀRYA, *Vātsya,* called NAḌĀDŪR AMMĀḶ.

VĀTSYĀYANA, called MALLANĀGA. Das Kāmasūtram des Vātsyāyana. Die indische Ars Amatoria. Nebst dem vollständigen Commentare Jayamangalā des Yaçōdhara. Aus dem Sanskrit übersetzt und herausgegeben von Richard Schmidt. pp. v. 478. *Leipzig,* 1897. 8°. **14053. d. 50.**

—— வாத்ஸ்யாயநஸூத்திரம். [Vātsyāyanasūtra. 37 aphorisms on wifely duty, consisting chiefly of the Kāmasūtra IV. i. With Tamil glosses and commentary.] *See* SUNDARARĀJA ṢARMĀ, *D.* வ்யாஸ வாத்ஸ்யாயந . . . பார்யாதருமம் *etc.* (Vyasa and Vatsyayana's Bharyadharmam, *etc.*) pp. 1-95. 1901. 12°. **14085. b. 44.**

VĀTSYĀYANA, called PAKSHILASVĀMĪ. *See* GOTAMA. The Nyâyasûtras with Vâtsyâyana's Bhâshya [called Nyāyabhāshya], *etc.* 1896. 8°. **14048. dd. 3.(vol. 9.)**

VEDĀNTĀCHĀRYA. *See* VEṄKAṬANĀTHA VEDĀNTĀCHĀRYA.

VEDĀNTADEṢIKA. *See* VEṄKAṬANĀTHA VEDĀNTĀCHĀRYA.

VEDĀNTASAÑJÑĀPRAKARAṆA. వేదాంతసంజ్ఞాప్రకరణమ్ *etc.* [Vedāntasañjñāprakaraṇa. A glossary of technical terms in the Vedānta philosophy. Edited by Paṭṭābhirāma Dīkshita.] pp. 30. చెన్నపురి ౧౮౯౦ [*Madras,* 1890.] 8°. **14048. bb. 42.(1.)**

The text appears to correspond with that of the work described in Rajendralal Mitra's 'Notices' (*no.* 1485), *which is also styled* Vedāntasañjñānirūpaṇa *and* Sañjñāprakaraṇa.

VEDAPĀDASTAVA. ശ്രീജൈ . . . വെദപാദ-സ്തവാഖ്യം സ്തവരാജഃ [Vedapādastava. A Ṣaiva hymn, put into the mouth of Jaimini, and popularly ascribed to him. Followed by Ṣaṅkara's Dakshiṇāmūrtyashṭaka.] pp. 31. *Palghaut,* 1903. 16°. **14033. a. 47.(2.)**

VEDAS.

SELECTIONS.

See JAMBHA. जंभसंहिता *etc.* [Jambhasaṃhitā. An anthological work from Vedic and other sources.] [1899.] 8°. **14028. dd. 8.**

See SATYAVRATA SĀMAṢRAMĪ BHAṬṬĀCHĀRYA. ॥ त्रयी-सङ्ग्रहः *etc.* [Trayīsaṅgraha. A digest of the matter of the Vedas, chiefly in the form of excerpts from them and their Brāhmaṇas, *etc.*] 1892-1893. 8°. **14010. c. 43.(vol. 2.)**

हिन्दूशास्त्र . . . বেদ সংহিতা। [Vedasaṃhitā. Selections from the Atharvaveda, Ṛigveda, and Vājasaneyisaṃhitā. Edited with Bengali translations and preface by Rameṣachandra Datta and Satyavrata Sāmaṣramī.] pp. i. 107. [1895.] *See* RAMEṢACHANDRA DATTA. हिन्दूशास्त्र *etc.* [Hinduṣāstra.] Pt. i. [1895-1897.] 8°. **14085. c. 45.(vol. 1.)**

ऋग्वेदादिभाष्यभूमिका *etc.* [Ṛigvedādibhāshyabhūmikā. A compilation by Dayānanda Sarasvatī from the Vedic hymns, with Sanskrit and Hindi commentaries. Second edition.] pp. ii. 394, iii. अजमेर १९४९ [*Ajmere,* 1893.] 8°. **14010. dd. 12.**

अथ स्वस्ति वाचनम् [Svastivāchana. Select *mantras* of benediction, with Hindi translation.] pp. 31, 24. *See* RĀMA, *Munshī.* آریه سنگیت مالا الخ [Āryasaṅgītamālā.] [1900.] 12°. **14154. cc. 7.**

अथ बृहन्मंत्रसंहिता *etc.* [Bṛihan-mantrasaṃhitā. A collection of divers Vedic hymns and formulæ for ritual purposes.] pt. i. ff. 104. बसरूर १८२२ [*Basrur,* 1900.] *obl.* 8°. **14028. c. 83.**

हवनमन्त्राः *etc.* [Havanamantrāḥ. Select Vedic verses, for the rites of worship, prayer for blessing, and lustration.] pp. 12. मुरादाबाद १९०१ [*Moradabad,* 1901.] 8°. **14010. c. 33.(2.)**

ATHARVAVEDA.

Atharvavedasaṃhitâ. With the commentary of Sâyaṇâchârya. Edited by Shankar Pândurang Pandit. 4 vols. *Bombay,* 1895-1898. 4°. **14010. ee. 1.**

ATHARVAVEDA (*continued*).

॥ अथर्ववेदसंहिता *etc.* [Atharvaveda. In the Saṃhitā text.] pp. 298. अजमेर १९५७ [*Ajmere*, 1900.] 8°. **14010. cc. 16.(2.)**

The Kashmirian Atharvaveda, School of the Pāippalādas. Reproduced by chromophotography from the manuscript in the University Library at Tübingen. Edited under the auspices of the Johns Hopkins University in Baltimore and of the Royal Eberhard-Karls-University in Tübingen, Württemberg, by Maurice Bloomfield ... and Richard Garbe, *etc.* 3 pts. *Baltimore, Stuttgart* [printed], 1901. Fol. **14010. e. 15.**

The Hymns of the Atharva-veda. Translated with a popular commentary by Ralph T. H. Griffith. 2 vols. 1895-1896. *See* PERIODICAL PUBLICATIONS.—*Benares*. The Pandit, *etc.* New Series. Vol. XV-XIX (supplement). 1876, *etc.* 8°. **14096. d. 6.(vol. 15-19, supplement.)**

—— [A separate issue of the preceding publication.] 2 vols. *Benares*, 1895-1896. 8°. **14010. dd. 7.**

Hymns of the Atharva-Veda, together with extracts from the ritual books and the commentaries. Translated [with introduction, *etc.*,] by Maurice Bloomfield. pp. lxxiv. 716. 1897. *See* MUELLER (F. M.). The Sacred Books of the East, *etc.* Vol. xlii. 1879, *etc.* 8°. **2003. b. (vol. 42.)**

Atharva-véda. Traduction et commentaire. Le Livre VII (VIII et IX; X, XI, et XII; XIII) de l'Atharva-Véda. Traduit et commenté par Victor Henry. *Paris, Chalon-sur-Saone* [printed], 1891-1896. 8°. **14010. c. 53.**

The Atharva-veda Described; with a classified selection of hymns [in the version of R. T. H. Griffith], explanatory notes and review. pp. 68. 1897. *See* EAST. The Sacred Books of the East Described and Examined. Hindu Series. Vol. I, pt. 2. 1895, *etc.* 8°. **14010. cc. 9.(vol. 1.)**

Pariśishṭa.

आसुरीकल्पः *etc.* [Āsurīkalpa. A short manual of magic in an apparently corrupt version of semi-prose form. With Hindi version by Vrajaratna Bhaṭṭāchārya.] pp. 12. *Hardwar, Moradabad* [printed], १९५६ [1899.] 8°. **14033. aa. 1.(3.)**

ATHARVAVEDA—*Pariśishṭa* (*continued*).

The Auçanasādbhutāni, [a tract on portents,] text & translation. By James Taft Hatfield. 1893. *See* ACADEMIES, *etc.*—Boston, *Mass.*—*American Oriental Society*. Journal, *etc.* Vol. xv., pp. 207-220. 1849, *etc.* 8°. **Ac. 8824. (vol. 15.)**

Appendix.

See HENRY (V.). La Magie dans l'Inde Antique. [With special reference to the Atharvaveda.] 1904. 12°. **08631. f. 35.**

[For versions of the Sandhyāvandana according to the schools of this Veda:] *See* SANDHYĀVANDANA.

See UPANISHADS.—*Modern and Fictitious Upanishads.* कालिकोपनिषत् *etc.* [Kālikopanishad. Purporting to be excerpted from the Saubhāgyakāṇḍa of the Atharvaveda.] [1899.] 8°. **14028. c. 85.(5.)**

See YUGALAKIŚORA VYĀSA PĀṬHAKA. श्रीमद्याज्ञवल्क्यादि ... शिक्षासङ्ग्रहः ... A collection of Śikshás, *etc.* [including the Māṇḍūkī Śikshā of the Atharva.] 1893. 8°. **14093. b. 31**

RIGVEDA.

Entire Text.

॥ ऋग्वेदभाष्यम् *etc.* [Ṛigveda. In the Saṃhitā and Pada texts, with commentaries grammatical and paraphrastic, in Sanskrit and Hindi, by Dayānanda Sarasvatī.] प्रयाग अजमेर १९३९-१९५६ [*Allahabad*, 1882-1895, *Ajmere*, 1899.] 8°. **14010. cc. 15.**

A reprint of the earlier edition, so far as it goes. The present edition ends with the 7th maṇḍala. *In progress?*

॥ ऋग्वेदसंहिता *etc.* [Ṛigveda. In the Saṃhitā text.] pp. 658. अजमेर १९५७ [*Ajmere*, 1900.] 8°. **14010. cc. 16.(1.)**

The Hymns of the Rigveda. Translated with a popular commentary by Ralph T. H. Griffith. Second edition. 2 vols. *Benares*, 1896-1897. 8°. **14007. b. 7.**

Ṛigveda—*Entire Text (continued).*

Le Rig-véda. Text et traduction. Neuvième maṇḍala. Le culte védique du soma. Par Paul Regnaud. *Paris, Chalon-sur-Saone* [printed], 1900, *etc.* 4°. **14007. d. 22.**

In progress?

Selections of Hymns and Verses.

[Two or More.]

Handbook to the study of the Rigveda, by P. Peterson. Part I. Introductory. (Sayana's Preface to his commentary ... the commentary itself on the first three hymns [with the text] and a translation into English of the Preface.) (Part II. The seventh Mandala, *etc.*) 2 pts. *Bombay*, 1890-1892. 8°. **14010. c. 50.**

Forms nos. xli. *and* xliii. *of the* Bombay Sanskrit Series.

Hymns from the Rigveda, edited with Sayana's commentary, notes, and a translation by Peter Peterson. Second edition. pp. viii. 293. *Bombay*, 1898. 8°. **14007. cc. 26.**

Forms no. xxxvi. *of the* Bombay Sanskrit Series.

Hymns from the Ṛigveda, edited with Sâyaṇa's commentary, notes, and a translation, by Peter Peterson ... Revised and enlarged by S. R. Bhandarkar. Third edition. pp. xiii. 329. *Bombay*, 1905. 8°. **14007. g. 1.**

Forms no. xxxvi. *of the* Bombay Sanskrit Series.

A Second Selection of Hymns from the Ṛigveda. Edited, with Sâyana's commentary and notes, by Peter Peterson. pp. i. 287. *Bombay*, 1899. 8°. **14010. cc. 11.**

Forms no. lviii. *of the* Bombay Sanskrit Series.

Raccòlta dégli ínni dél Vèda recàti di sàṁskṛito a comúne volgàre pér cúra di Giusèppe Turrini ... Il Ṛigvèda spiegàto cól Ṛigvèda. *Bologna*, 1899, *etc.* 4°. **14010. ee. 4.**

In progress.

ऋक्सूक्तसंग्रहः ॥ श्रीसायणभाष्यसहितः *etc.* (Hymns from the Rigveda [Book i.]. Prescribed for the Honours in Sanskrit Examination of the Panjab University. Edited with Sáyana's commentary,

Ṛigveda—*Selections (continued).*

bhúmiká, rules on accent, etc., by Pandit Hirá-nanda Múlarája Shástri.) pp. iii. iv. 299. *Lahore*, 1903. 8°. **14007. b. 19.**

The English title is taken from the wrapper.

പുരുഷസൂക്തം॥ (ശ്രീസൂക്തം॥) [Purusha-sūkta (x. 90) and Ṣrīsūkta (a *khila* to v. 87).] *See* Upanishads.—*General Collections.* അഷ്ടോത്തരശതോപനിഷദഃ *etc.* [Ashṭottaraṣatopanishadaḥ.] pp. 824-827. 1896. 8°. **14010. cc. 8.**

తైత్తిరీయారణ్యకే—బ్రహ్మమేధే పురుషసూక్తమ్. (శ్రీసూక్తమ్.) [Purushasūkta and Ṣrīsūkta.] *See* Upanishads.—*Small Collections. Begin.* ఓమ్ శ్రీశాన్తానన్దసరస్వతీ ... నమః *etc.* [Kaivalya Upanishad, *etc.*] pp. 186-203. 1899. 32°. **14010. a. 6.**

अथ श्रीसूक्तसह माध्यंदिनशाखीय पुरुषसूक्तप्रारम्भः । [Purushasūkta. Arranged for reading according to the rules of the Mādhyandina *ṣākhā*. Followed by the Ṣrīsūkta, with *dhyānas, etc.*] ff. 14. **मुंबई १९५८** [*Bombay*, 1901.] *obl.* 12°. **14028. b. 93.(4.)**

புருஷஸூக்தம். (ஶ்ரீஸூக்தம்.) [Purushasūkta and Ṣrīsūkta. With Tamil interpretation and extracts, in a Tamil translation, from the commentaries of Sāyaṇa, Ānandatīrtha, and the Viṣishṭādvaita school.] *See* Sandhyāvandana. யஜுர்வேத ... ஸந்த்யாவந்தநம் *etc.* [Sandhyāvandana, *etc.*] 1901. 8°. **14033. aa. 27.**

അഥ പുരുഷസൂക്തം (ശ്രീസൂക്തം) [Purushasūkta and Ṣrīsūkta.] *See below,* Yajurveda.—*Taittirīyasaṃhitā.* ശ്രീരുദ്രപ്രശ്നഃ *etc.* [Rudrapraṣna.] pp. 34-48. 1901. 16°. **14010. a. 7.**

सहस्रशीर्षा के मन्त्र तथा अन्य वेद मन्त्र [Sahasraṣīrshā-mantra, *i.e.* the Purushasūkta. Preceded by Ṛigveda I. i. With Hindi version of the former.] pp. 31. **लाहौर** [*Lahore*, 1901.] 16°. **14028. a. 19.(8.)**

RIGVEDA—*Selections (continued).*

Études Védiques. Traduction d'un hymne à l'Aurore, I. 123 du Rig-veda. (L'hymne III. 1 du Rig-véda.) [By Paul Regnaud.] 1890. *See* PERIODICAL PUBLICATIONS. — *Paris.* Revue de l'Histoire des Religions, *etc.* Tome xxi.—xxii. 1880, *etc.* 8°. **P.P. 37. cc. (tom. 21, 22.)**

Vedic Hymns. Translated [with introductions, notes, *etc.*] by F. Max Müller. Part i. Hymns to the Maruts, Rudra, Vâyu, and Vâta. (Vedic Hymns. Translated by Hermann Oldenberg. Part ii. Hymns to Agni.) 2 vols. 1891-1897. *See* MUELLER (F. M.). The Sacred Books of the East, *etc.* Vol. xxxii., xlvi. 1879, *etc.* 8°. **2003. b. (vol. 32, 46.)**

Quarante Hymnes du Rig-véda, traduits et commentés par Abel Bergaigne. (Publiés par V. Henry.) 1892-1894. *See* ACADEMIES, *etc.*—Paris.—*Société de Linguistique de Paris.* Mémoires, *etc.* Tom. 8. 1868, *etc.* 8°. **Ac. 9810. (tom. 8.)**

Vedic Hymns. [Fourteen hymns, translated into English verse.] *See* RAMEṢACHANDRA DATTA. Lays of Ancient India, *etc.* pp. 1-52. 1894. 8°. **2318. h. 9.**

An Account of the Vedas; with numerous extracts from the Rig-veda [in R. T. H. Griffith's version]. Second edition. pp. vi. 154. 1897. *See* EAST. The Sacred Books of the East Described and Examined. Hindu Series. Vol. I, pt. 1. 1895, *etc.* 8°. **14010. cc. 9. (vol. 1.)**

Single Hymns and Verses.

Vedic Texts. [Select verses from the Ṛigveda with an English exposition in which an attempt is made to construe the texts as conveying modern scientific doctrine, in accordance with the principles of Dayānanda Sarasvatī. By Gurudatta Vidyārthī.] No. 1, 2. *Lahore,* 1888. 8°. **14007. d. 20.**

The tracts in this series are—No. 1. "The Atmosphere" (based on Ṛigveda I. ii. 1); No. 2. "The Composition of Water" (based on I. ii. 7).

RIGVEDA—*Single Hymns and Verses (continued).*

—— [Another edition.] No. 1, 3. *Lucknow,* 1894. 12°. **14010. b. 16.**

*Comprising No. 1. "The Atmosphere"; No. 3. "*गृहस्थ*. Being a scientific exposition of Mantras Nos. 1, 2 & 3 of the xxx Sukta of the Rigveda, bearing on the subject of household" [i.e. on Rigv. I. l. 1-13].*

Vedic Texts. [A reprint, comprising "The Atmosphere," "Composition of Water," and "Grihastha."] *See* GURUDATTA VIDYĀRTHĪ. Works of . . . Guru Datta Vidyarthi, *etc.* pp. 158-168. 1897. 8°. **14010. dd. 11.**

—— —— pp. 169-183. 1902. 8°. **759. c. 20.**

Vedic Texts. [A new series, by Pandit Gaṅgāprasāda.] No. 1, 2. *Lakhimpur, Moradabad,* 1896-1897. 8°. **14010. dd. 9.**

The tracts in this series are—No. 1. "The Constitution of Human Society" (on Ṛigv. X. xc. 12); No. 2. "Septenary Composition of Solar Light" (on I. l. 8-9)

L'Énigme du Rigveda et les Énigmes de l'Hymne i. 164. (Texte et traduction.) *See* REGNAUD (P.). Études Védiques, *etc.* pp. 1-55. 1898. 8°. **Ac. 365. (fasc. xxxviii.)**

The Srisuktha Bhashyam, *etc.* [Ṣrīsūkta (a *khila* to v. 87), with a Viṣishṭādvaita commentary.] (श्रीसूक्त भाष्यम्) pp. ii. 9. 1899. *See* ANANTĀCHĀRYA, *Prativādibhayaṅkara.* शास्त्रमुक्तावली The Ŝasthramukthâvalî, *etc.* No. 1. 1899, *etc.* 8°. **14049. a. 1. (no. 1.)**

An Essay on the Vrishâkapi Hymn of the Rigveda [viz. Hymn x. 86. With a translation of the text]. By Narâyan Aiyangâr. pp. 38. *Madras,* 1899. 8°. **14010. c. 35.(2.)**

The Purusha Sukta [*i.e.* Hymn x. 90, in Sanskrit.] Translated and explained by B. V. Kamesvara Aiyar. pp. 102. *Madras,* 1898. 12°. **14028. b. 97.(1.)**

Reprinted from the Sanskrit Journal, *vol.* 2.

Purusha Suktha Bhashyam. [The Purushasūkta with a commentary] by P. B. Anantha chariar, *etc.* (पुरुषसूक्तभाष्यम् ।) pp. ii. ii. 92. 1901. *See*

Ṛigveda—*Single Hymns and Verses* (*continued*).

Anantāchārya, *Prativādibhayaṅkara.* शास्त्रमुक्तावली The Ŝasthramukthâvalî, *etc.* No. 9. 1899, *etc.* 8°.
14048. a. 1.(no. 9.)

ఆంధ్రపురుషసూక్తము. [Purushasūkta. In Telugu and Sanskrit.] pp. 6. 1902. *See* Upanishads. — *Small Collections.* The Telugu Upanishads, *etc.* Part ii. 1899, *etc.* 8°.
14007. b. 11.

Mudgala, ou l'Hymne du Marteau [x. 102]. Suite d'énigmes védiques. Par M. V. Henry. 1895. *See* Academies, *etc.* — Paris. — *Société Asiatique.* Journal Asiatique, *etc.* Ser. ix., tom. 6. pp. 516-548. 1822, *etc.* 8°.
Ac. 8808.(Ser. ix., tom. 6.)

[For editions of the Devīsūkta (x. 125) and Rātrisūkta (x. 127) published together with the Devīmāhātmya :] *See* Purāṇas. — *Mārkaṇḍeya-purāṇa.* [*Devīmāhātmya.*]

Prātiṣākhya.

See Ṣaunaka. महर्षिशौनकप्रणीतम् ऋक्प्रातिशाख्यम् । . . . Śaunaka's Prátiśákhya of the Rigveda, with the commentary of Uvvaṭa, *etc.* 1903. 8°.
14090. c. 40.

Appendix.

See Dāhavidhi. अथ ॥ ऋग्वेदस्य दाहविधिः *etc.* [Ṛigvedasya Dāhavidhi. The ritual for burning the dead, according to the Ṛigveda.] [1899.] *obl.* 12°.
14033. a. 42.

See Durgāprasāda, *Editor of the "Harbinger."* The First (Second, Third, Fourth) Vedic Reader, *etc.* 1894-1895. 12°.
14010. b. 11.

See Guérinot (A.). De Rhetorica Vedica, *etc.* 1900. 8°.
011852. h. 23.

See Guérinot (A.). Recherches sur l'origine de l'idée de Dieu d'après le Rig-veda, *etc.* 1900. 8°.
Ac. 365.(nouvelle série II, fasc. iii.)

See Henry (V.). La Magie dans l'Inde Antique. [With special reference to the Ṛigveda.] 1904. 12°.
08631. f. 35.

Ṛigveda—*Appendix* (*continued*).

See Hirzel (A.). Der Rigveda und seine Sprache, *etc.* 1895. 8°.
012901. i. 2.(11.)

[For the Pāṇinīyaṣikshā belonging to this Veda :] *See* Pāṇini.—*Appendix.* [*Ṣikshā.*]

See Regnaud (P.). Le Rig-veda et les Origines de la Mythologie Indo-européenne, *etc.* 1892, *etc.* 8°. [*Annales du Musée Guimet: Bibliothèque d'Études.*]
7704. i. (tom. 1.)

See Regnaud (P.). Comment naissent les mythes. Les sources védiques du Petit Poucet, *etc.* 1897. 12°.
4503. dd. 13.

[For versions of the Sandhyāvandana according to the schools of this Veda :] *See* Sandhyāvandana.

See Ṣaunaka. Bṛihad-devatá, or An Index to the Gods of the Rigveda . . . To which have been added Arsbánukramaṇí Chhandonukramaṇí and Anuvákánukramaṇí, *etc.* 1893. 8°. [*Bibliotheca Indica.*]
14002. a. (vol. 127.)

See Sāyaṇa Āchārya.—*Works on Ṣruti.* [*Vedas.*] ঋগ্বেদভাষ্যোপদ্ঘাতপ্রকরণ [*sic*] *etc.* [Ṛigvedabhāshyopodghāta. The introduction to Sāyaṇa's commentary on the Ṛigveda.] [1901.] 12°.
14007. b. 16.

See Sieg (E.). Die Sagenstoffe des Ṛgveda und die indische Itihâsatradition, *etc.* 1902, *etc.* 8°.
14007. cc. 31.

SĀMAVEDA.

सामपदसंहिता । अर्थतः सामवेदीयार्चिकग्रन्थानां पदपाठः *etc.* [Sāmaveda. In the Padasaṃhitā, according to the Kauthumī *ṣākhā.* Edited by Satyavrata Sāmaṣramī.] pp. 234. [1889-1891.] *See* Periodical Publications.—*Calcutta.* उषा *etc.* [Ushā.] Vol. I, no. v.-xi. [1889]-1893. 8°.
14010. c. 43.(vol. 1.)

श्रीसामवेदस्य संहिता *etc.* (सामवेदस्य ब्रह्मभाष्यम्) [Sāmaveda. Edited with an interpretation and commentary in Hindi, styled Brahmabhāshya, by Jvālāprasāda Ṣarmā.] 2 pts. pp. 436, 508, ix. ii., *lith.* आगरा १८९०-१८९१ [*Agra*, 1890-1891.] 8°.
14010. d. 30.

SĀMAVEDA (*continued*).

सामवेदसंहितायाः प्रथमोभागः (द्वितीयोभागः) *etc.* (Samavedasanhita. Whith [*sic*] the commentary of Sayanaacharya. Edited and published by Pandit Jibananda Vidyasagara . . . Second edition.) 2 pts. pp. xxvii. 1-329, 361-1030. *Calcutta*, 1892. 8°. **14007. b. 9.**

The English title is taken from the wrapper. The text of the Pūrvārchika, as in Benfey's edition, ends with the 9th daśati *of Prap.* vi.; *but the lacuna of 32 pp. in the pagination suggests that it was intended to add after this the 5* prapāṭhakas *found in this place, e.g. in the Ajmere edition.*

सामवेदभाष्यम् *etc.* (The Samvedbhashyam. A monthly eddition [*sic*] of Sam Ved Sanhita. With the commentary in Sanskrit and Hindi by Tulsi Ram Swami.) मेरठ [१८]९८ [*Meerut*, 1898, *etc.*] 8°. **14007. dd. 1.**

In progress?

॥ सामवेदसंहिता *etc.* [Sāmaveda. In the Saṃhitā text.] pp. 120. अजमेर १९५७ [*Ajmere*, 1900.] 8°. **14010. cc. 16.(3.)**

The Hymns of the Sâmaveda. Translated with a popular commentary by Ralph T. H. Griffith. pp. v. i. 338, xxxviii. *Benares*, 1893. 8°. **14010. dd. 3.**

॥ अथाग्निष्टोमसामानि ॥ [Agnishṭomasāmāni. With commentary by the editor.] pp. 16. 1892. *See* PERIODICAL PUBLICATIONS.—*Calcutta.* उषा *etc.* [Ushā.] Vol. II, no. vi. [1889]-1893. 8°. **14010. c. 43.(vol. 2.)**

॥ अथ आशीस्सामानि *etc.* [Āṣīs-sāmāni. As used in domestic rites by the Kauthumas, with their Brāhmaṇa texts.] pp. 28. 1892. *See* PERIODICAL PUBLICATIONS.—*Calcutta.* उषा *etc.* [Ushā.] Vol. II, no. iv.-vi. [1889]-1893. 8°. **14010. c. 43.(vol. 2.)**

॥ अथ ब्रह्मयज्ञपाठः ॥ [Brahmayajñapāṭha. In the version of the Kauthumas, and with the Arishṭavarga appended.] pp. 35. 1892. *See* PERIODICAL PUBLICATIONS.—*Calcutta.* उषा *etc.* [Usha.] Vol. II, no. iii. [1889]-1893. 8°. **14010. c. 43.(vol. 2.)**

தஶராத்ரஸாமாநி ஊஹகாநே உஸாந-த்ராஷ்டகோஷயம் த்ருஷு: *etc.* [Daṣarātra. Being

SĀMAVEDA (*continued*).

the Ūhagāna I. i.-VI. i. In the Kauthuma recension. Edited by Lakshmaṇa Ṣrautī.] pp. 134. [illegible] சுபகிருது [*Tiruvadi*, 1902.] 8°. **14007. b. 18.**

شامگی رودهری [*sic*] सामगायन रुद्री [Sāmagāyanarudrī. *Mantras* for the Rudrajapa of Sāmavedīs, with musical accentuation.] pp. 15, *lith.* अमृतसर [*Amritsar*, 1890.] 8°. **14010. b. 14.(1.)**

॥ अथ संहितासप्तकम् ॥ [Saṃhitāsaptaka. Seven *saṃhitās* of *sāmāni*, with appropriate Brāhmaṇa texts.] pp. 30. 1892. *See* PERIODICAL PUBLICATIONS.—*Calcutta.* उषा *etc.* [Ushā.] Vol. II, no. ii. [1889]-1893. 8°. **14010. c. 43.(vol. 2.)**

॥ अथ सप्तदश महासामानि ॥ [Saptadaṣa Mahāsāmāni. Seventeen *sāmāni*, with appropriate texts from the Brāhmaṇa.] pp. 16. 1892. *See* PERIODICAL PUBLICATIONS. — *Calcutta.* उषा *etc.* [Ushā.] Vol. II, no. ii. [1889]-1893. 8°. **14010. c. 43. (vol. 2.)**

See DĀHAVIDHI. अथ ॥ सामवेदस्य दाहविधिः *etc.* [Sāmavedasya Dāhavidhi. The ritual for burning the dead, according to the Sāmaveda.] [1898.] *obl.* 12°. **14033. a. 43.**

See NITYAKARMA. सामवेदीय पञ्चयज्ञ *etc.* [Sāmavedīya-pañchayajña.] [1902.] 16°. **14028. a. 31.**

See PERIODICAL PUBLICATIONS.—*Calcutta.* उषा *etc.* [Ushā. A journal of Vedic (chiefly Sāmavedic) and other studies.] [1889]-1893. 8°. **14010. c. 43. (vol. 2.)**

[For versions of the Sandhyāvandana according to the schools of this Veda :] *See* SANDHYĀVANDANA.

See VĪREṢVARA ṬHAKKURA. छन्दोगानां . . . पद्धतिः *etc.* [Chhandogānāṃ Vivāhādi-saṃskārapaddhati. A treatise on the lustrations of marriage *etc.* for Sāmavedīs.] [1902.] *obl.* 4°. **14033. c. 31.(3.)**

SĀMAVEDA (*continued*).

See YUGALAKIṢORA VYĀSA PĀṬHAKA. श्रीमच्छाण्डिल्यादि . . . शिक्षासङ्ग्रहः . . . A collection of Śikshás . . . [including the Nāradī, Gautamī, and Lomaṣī Ṣikshās of the Sàmaveda,] *etc.* 1893. 8°.

14093. b. 31.

YAJURVEDA.

ĀTREYISAṂHITĀ.

काण्डानुक्रमणिका [Kāṇḍānukramaṇikā. An index to the subject-matter of this Saṃhitā and its Brāhmaṇa, with a metrical epitome.] pp. 10. 1894. *See* MYSORE. — *Government of Mysore.* Government Oriental Library Series. Bibliotheca Sanskrita, *etc.* No. 4. 1893, *etc.* 8°.

14004. b. 4. (no. 4.)

[illegible] *etc.* [Kāṇḍānukramaṇikā. With metrical epitome. Together with a commentary by Kṛishṇa Ṣarmā of Karuppatur. Edited by Rāmakṛishṇa Ṣāstrī of Kalpadi.] pp. 22. [illegible] [*Palghat,* 1900.] 8°.

14010. b. 14.(2.)

KĀṬHAKA.

See SCHROEDER (L. VON). Das Kāṭhaka, seine Handschriften, seine Accentuation und seine Beziehungen zu den indischen Lexicographen und Grammatikern, *etc.* 1895. 8°. [*Zeitschrift der Deutschen Morgenlaendischen Gesellschaft.*]

Ac. 8815/2. (Bd. 49.)

See SCHROEDER (L. VON). Die Tübinger Kaṭha-Handschriften, *etc.* 1897. 8°. [*Sitzungsberichte der Kaiserlichen Akademie der Wissenschaften, Wien.*]

Ac. 810/6. (Bd. 137.)

॥ काठकम् ॥ Kâṭhakam. Die Saṃhitâ der Kaṭha-Çâkhâ. Herausgegeben von Leopold von Schroeder. *Leipzig,* 1900, *etc.* 8°.

14007. dd. 2.

In progress.

TAITTIRĪYASAṂHITĀ.

The Sanhitá of the Black Yajur Veda, with the commentary of Mádhava Áchárya. Edited (vol. i., ii.) by Dr. E. Roer and E. B. Cowell, M.A. (Vol. vi., edited by Paṇḍit Satyavrata Sámaśramí.) 6 vols. 1854-1899. *See* ACADEMIES, *etc.* — Calcutta. — *Asiatic Society of Bengal.* Bibliotheca Indica, *etc.* [Vol. 26.] 1848, *etc.* 8°.

14002. a. (vol. 26.)

तैत्तिरीयसंहिता . . . The Taittiríya Saṃhitá of the Black . . . Yajur-Veda [in the Saṃhitā and Pada text], with the commentary of Bhaṭṭabháskaramiśra [styled Jñānayajña; and supplemented in the first volume by the Kāṇḍānukramaṇikā and in parts of *kāṇḍa* v. 7 and vii. 4-5 by the commentary of Sāyaṇa]. . . . Edited by A. Mahádeva Śástri . . . and Panditaratnam K. Rangácharya. 1894, *etc.* *See* MYSORE.—*Government of Mysore.* Government Oriental Library Series. Bibliotheca Sanskrita, *etc.* No. 4, 5, 9, 12-14, 16-18, *etc.* 1893, *etc.* 8°. **14004. b. 4.**

In progress.

कृष्णयजुर्वेदीयतैत्तिरीयसंहिता *etc.* [Taittirīyasaṃhitā. In the Saṃhitā and Pada texts. With the commentary of Sāyaṇa. Edited by Kāṣīnātha Ṣāstrī Āgāṣe.] पुण्याख्यपत्तने १९०० [*Poona,* 1900, *etc.*] 8°.

14003. ccc. (no. 42.)

In progress. Forms no. 42 *of the* Ānandāṣrama Sanskrit Series.

[illegible] *etc.* [Taittirīyasaṃhitā. Edited with notes by Rāmakṛishṇa Ṣāstrī of Kalpadi.] 5 pts. *Palghat,* 1902. 8°.

14007. b. 17.

[illegible] *etc.*) [Kṛishṇayajussaṃhitā-padasaraṇī. The Pada text of the Saṃhitā, with notes by the editor, Muḷḷaṅguḍi Vaidyanātha Ṣāstrī.] 7 pts. [illegible] ॥ [*Kumbakonam,*] 1898-1900. 8°.

14007. f. 1.

The Mantrapāṭha, or The Prayer Book of the Āpastambins. Edited . . . with the commentary of Haradatta and translated by M. Winternitz, *etc.* 1897. 4°. *See* ĀPASTAMBA.—*Gṛihyasūtra.*

12204. f. 8. (vol. 1, pt. 8.)

[illegible] [Rudranamaka, or Rudrapraṣna (Taitt.-s. IV. v.); Rudrachamaka (T.-s. IV. vii. 1f.); and

YAJURVEDA—*Taittirīyasaṃhitā (continued).*

Ābrahman (T.-s. VII. v. 18, Taittirīyabrāhmaṇa III. viii. 13, T.-s. IV. v. 3, and T.-br. III. ix. 5.)] *See* UPANISHADS.—*General Collections.* அஷ்டோத்தரஶதோபநிஷத: *etc.* [Ashṭottaraṣatopanishadaḥ.] pp. 793-802, 831-834. 1896. 8°. **14010. cc. 8.**

ஶ்ரீருத்ரப்ரஶ்ந: ॥ ருத்ரகவசம் ... ஶ்ரீஸூக்த பூஸூக்த ஸஹித: *etc.* [Rudraprasna, or Rudranamaka; Rudrachamaka; Purushasūkta; Ṣrīsūkta; Bhūsūkta (Taitt.-s. I. v. 3, 1-2); Durgāsūkta (Taitt.-Āraṇyaka, X. i. 64ff.); and Rudrakavacha.] pp. 55. கும்பகோண ॥ [*Kumbakonam,*] 1901. 16°. **14010. a. 7.**

ருத்ர ... ஶ்ரீஶதருத்ரீய ... *etc.* [Ṣatarudrīya (*i.e.* Taitt.-s. IV. v. 1-11). With commentary by Abhinava-ṣaṅkarāchārya. Edited by P. Gaṇapati Ṣāstrī.] pp. 111, 257, iv. கும்பகோண ॥ [*Kumbakonam,*] 1903. *obl.* 16°. **14010. a. 8.**

See NITYAKARMA. யஜுர்வேதாஹ்நிகம் *etc.* [Yajurvedāhnika.] 1899. 12°. **14028. b. 108.**

[For versions of the Sandhyāvandana according to the schools of this Veda:] *See* SANDHYĀVANDANA.

See ṢRĪVATSAṄKA. ஶ்ரீ ... ஸப்தலக்ஷணம் *etc.* [Saptalakshaṇa. A treatise on the phonetic peculiarities of the Taittirīyasaṃhitā.] 1899. 8°. **14092. b. 43.**

See SUBRAHMAṆYA ṢĀSTRĪ, *K.* க்ருஷ்ணயஜுஸ்ஸம்ஹிதா ... பஞ்சாஶதநுக்ரமணிகா *etc.* [Pañchāṣadanukramaṇikā. An index of catch-words for the Taittirīyasaṃhitā, *etc.*] [1897.] 12°. **14028. b. 78.(2.)**

See UPĀKARMA. யஜுர்வேதோபாகர்ம *etc.* [Yajurvedopākarma. A treatise on the rites connected with the renewal of the study of the Yajurveda.] [1900.] 16°. **14010. a. 5.(2.)**

See VEṄKAṬĀCHALA ṢARMĀ, *A. N.* ஸ்வராவதாநம் ॥ [Svarāvadhāna. A treatise on the accentuation of the Taittirīyasaṃhitā.] 1901. 8°. **14010. c. 32.(2.)**

YAJURVEDA—*Taittirīyasaṃhitā (continued).*

ஷட்விம்ஶதிஸூத்ரம் *etc.* [Shaḍviṃṣatisūtra. Lists of catchwords and forms in the Saṃhitā of importance for purposes of recitation and grammatical study. Edited by M. A. Vaidyanātha Ṣāstrī.] pp. 24. கும்பகோண ॥ ௧௮௯௯ [*Kumbakonam,* 1899.] 16°. **14010. a. 5.(1.)**

[*Prātiṣākhya.*] ப்ராதிஶாக்ய ... ப்ராதிசாக்கியம். [Prātiṣākhya. Edited by Lakshmaṇāchārya Ghanapāṭhī and Sundara Ghanapāṭhī.] pp. 40. பத்துநகர ॥ [*Trivadi,*] 1891. 16°. **14010. a. 2.**

—— தைத்திரீயப்ராதிஶாக்யம் த்ரிபாஷ்யரத்நவ்யாக்யாஸஹிதம் *etc.* [Taittirīyaprātiṣākhya. With the commentary Tribhāshyaratna. In 24 *adhyāyas.* Edited by M. A. Vaidyanātha Ṣāstrī.] pp. ii. 198. கும்பகோண ॥ [*Kumbakonam,*] 1900. 12°. **14007. b. 10.**

—— ఇదంపాఖలు త్రిభాష్యరత్నంనాము ప్రాతిశాఖ్య [*sic*] వివరణమ్ [Prātiṣākhya. Ch. 1-12, with the commentary Tribhāshyaratna.] pp. 62. శ్రీమచ్చెన్నపురి [*Madras,*] 1904. 8°. **14007. b. 21.**

—— தைத்திரீயப்ராதிஶாக்யம் *etc.* [Taittirīyaprātiṣākhya. With the commentary Vaidikābharaṇa of Gārgya Gopāla Miṣra. Edited by Muḷḷaṅguḍi Vaidyanātha Ṣāstrī.] pp. i. 164. கும்பகோண ॥ [*Kumbakonam,*] 1901. 8°. **14090. e. 26.**

—— *See* LUEDERS (H.). Die Vyâsa-Çikshâ, besonders in ihrem Verhältnis zum Taittirîya-Prâtiçâkhya, *etc.* 1895. 8°. **011840. m. 55.**

VĀJASANEYISAṂHITĀ.

श्रीशुक्लयजुर्वेदे माध्यन्दिनीया वाजसनेयसंहिता *etc.* [Vājasaneyisaṃhitā. Edited with introduction and a commentary styled Vedārthapradīpa or Giridharabhāshya in Hindi by Giriprasāda Varmā.] pp. 1182, vi. xxi., *lith.* विश्वामित्रपुरी १९३० [*Biswan,* 1874.] 4°. **14010. f. 9.**

YAJURVEDA—*Vājasaneyisaṃhitā (continued).*

॥ अथ वाजसनेयसंहितापदप्रारम्भः ॥ [Vājasaneyisaṃhitā. In the Pada text. Edited by Vallabharāma Ṣukla.] ff. 168, 105. मोहमय्यां १८१४-१८१५ [*Bombay*, 1893-1894.] *obl.* 8°. **14010. cc. 5.**

॥ यजुर्वेदसंहिता *etc.* [Vājasaneyisaṃhitā. In the Saṃhitā text.] pp. 159. अजमेर १९५६ [*Ajmere*, 1899.] 8°. **14010. cc. 16.(4.)**

शुक्लयजुर्वेद *etc.* [Vājasaneyisaṃhitā. According to the Mādhyandina school. Edited with Sanskrit glosses, analyses, and a Hindi commentary, based on those of Uvaṭa, Mahīdhara, *etc.*, by Rāmasvarūpa Ṣarmā of Moradabad.] *Moradabad*, 1899, *etc.* 8°. **14007. b. 15.**

In progress?

வாஜஸநேயஸம்ஹிதா காண்வீ ஶ்ரீமச்சுக்லயஜுர்வேதஸம்ஹிதா *etc.* [Vājasaneyisaṃhitā. In the Kāṇva recension, with a brief commentary, styled Bhāshyārthasaṅgraha, by Iñjikollai Ṣivarāma Ṣāstrī. Edited by Kāṣīchintāmaṇi Bhaṭṭa.] கும்பகோணம் ॥ [*Kumbakonam*,] 1901, *etc.* 8°. **14007. cc. 29.**

In progress.

वाजसनेयिश्रीशुक्लयजुर्वेदसंहिता । माध्यन्दिनीयशाखापाठसमेता *etc.* [Vājasaneyisaṃhitā. In the Mādhyandina recension. With literal interpretation and commentary in Hindi styled Miṣrabhāshya, and as an appendix the Yājñavalkya-ṣikshā, with Hindi interpretation, the Anuvākasūtrādhyāya, and the Sarvānukramaṇī, together with additional dissertations by the editor and translator, Jvālāprasāda Miṣra.] 2 vols. pp. xii. 1408, 9. मुम्बय्यां १९५९ [*Bombay*, 1903.] 8°. **14007. f. 4.**

॥ अथ शुक्लयजुर्वेदीय वाजसनेयि ॥ ॥ संहितायाः पदपाठस्य पूर्वार्द्ध ॥ प्रारम्भः ॥ [Vājasaneyisaṃhitā. In the Pada text. Part I, comprising *adhyāyas* i.-xx.] ff. 235. बनारस १९५० [*Benares*, 1894.] *obl.* 8°. **14007. d. 19.**

The Texts of the White Yajurveda. Translated with a popular commentary by Ralph T. H. Griffith. pp. xx. 344, i. *Benares*, 1899. 8°. **14007. b. 8.**

॥ अथ रुद्री भाषाटीका प्रारम्भः ॥ (शुक्ल यजुर्वेदीय षडङ्ग रुद्राष्टाध्यायी) [Rudrajapa, also called Rudrī or Rudrāshṭādhyāyī. Lections for the cult of Ṣiva-Rudra according to the school of the White Yajurveda. In 10 chapters, comprising respectively (1) miscellaneous extracts, (2) Vāj.-s. xxxi. 1-22, (3) xvii. 33-49, (4) xxxiii. 30-43, (5) xvi. 1-66, (6) iii. 56-63, (7) xxxix. 7-13, (8) xviii. 1-29, (9) xxxvi. 1-24, and (10) miscellaneous verses. With Hindi translation and preface by Baladevaprasāda Miṣra.] ff. 47. काशी [*Benares*,] 1897. *obl.* 8°. **14028. dd. 3.(1.)**

॥ श्रीरुद्राभिषेकानुष्ठानपद्धतिः *etc.* [Rudrābhishekānushṭhānapaddhati. The same ritual as the preceding, but arranged in 8 chapters, with omission of the 10th. With a commentary. Preceded by lustratory rituals, Mahānyāsa, Pañchavaktrapūjā, *etc.*, and followed by an *ārti* and the Mantrapushpāñjali. Edited with Gujarati introduction and notes by Bhagulāl Bhāuṣaṅkar Bhaṭṭa.] pp. ix. 3, 13, 12, 13, 3, 107, 9, i. v. राजनगरे १९५५ [*Rajnagar*, 1899.] 8°. **14028. c. 69.(2.)**

Chapter VI. *contains* Vāj.-s. iii. 56-63, xvii. 31-32, xxxix. 7-13; VII. *contains* xviii. 1-29; VIII. *contains* xxxvi. 1-24.

अथ . . . शुक्लयजुर्वेदीय षडङ्ग रुद्राष्टाध्यायी *etc.* [Rudrāshṭādhyāyī. In 10 chapters. With a Hindi preface and translation by Vrajaratna Bhaṭṭāchārya.] ff. 73. कल्याण-मुंबई [*Kalyan*, 1900.] *obl.* 8°. **14028. dd. 9.**

Arranged like the edition of 1897.

ରୁଦ୍ରାଭିଷେକ *etc.* [Rudrābhisheka, or Ṣatarudra. A ritual, comprising Vāj.-s. xvi., verses 1-66, with other extracts from the same.] pp. 12. *Cuttack*, 1900. 12°. **14028. b. 78.(4.)**

See DĀHAVIDHI. अथ ॥ यजुर्वेदस्य दाहविधिः *etc.* [Yajurvedasya Dāhavidhi. The ritual for burning the dead, according to the Yajurveda.] [1898.] *obl.* 12°. **14033. a. 44.**

See JĪVANĀCHĀRYA VALLABHA, *Gosvāmī.* ॥ शुक्ल यजुर्वेदीय ॥ ॥ वैष्णवद्विजाह्निकम् *etc.* [Vaishṇavadvijāhnika. A manual of encyclical rites according to the Vājasaneyisaṃhitā.] [1901.] 8°. **14154. ee. 12.**

YAJURVEDA—*Vājasaneyisaṃhitā (continued).*

See KĀTYĀYANA. महर्षिकात्यायनप्रणीतम् ... सर्वानुक्रमसूत्रम् ... Kátyáyana's Sarvánukramasutras of the White Yajurveda, with the commentary of Yájñikánantadeva, *etc.* 1893, *etc.* 8°. **14007. c. 25.**

See PITṚIMEDHA. యాజుషానాహితాగ్నిపైతృమేధికప్రయోగః ॥ [Anāhitāgni-paitṛimedhikaprayoga. A manual of *pitṛimedha* rites for laymen, based upon and illustrated from the Vājasaneyisaṃhitā.] 1897, *etc.* 8°. **14028. d. 70.**

See RĀMADATTA ṬHAKKURA. *End.* इति ... वाजसनेयिनां ... पद्धतिः *etc.* [Vājasaneyinām Vivāhādisaṃskārapaddhati. A treatise on the lustrations of marriage *etc.* for Vājasaneyis.] [1902.] *obl.* 4°. [*Chhandogānāṃ Vivāhādi-saṃskārapaddhati.*] **14033. c. 31.(3.)**

[For versions of the Sandhyāvandana according to the schools of this Veda :] *See* SANDHYĀVANDANA.

See VIHĀRILĀLA, *Kāṣmīrī.* यजुर्वेदीयनित्यकर्म्मपद्धतिः *etc.* [Yajurvedīya-nityakarmapaddhati. A manual of religious duties for Yajurvedīs.] [1900.] 8°. **14033. aa. 16.**

See YUGALAKIṢORA VYĀSA PĀṬHAKA. श्रीमद्याज्ञवल्क्यादि ... शिक्षासङ्ग्रहः ... A collection of Śikshás by Yájñavalkya and others, [chiefly of the Mādhyandina school,] *etc.* 1893. 8°. **14093. b. 31.**

APPENDIX.

See BĀLA GAṄGĀDHARA TILAKA. The Orion, or Researches into the antiquity of the Vedas, *etc.* 1893. 12°. **14053. b. 27.**

[For editions of the Satyārthaprakāṣa, in which are enunciated the methods of Vedic exegesis used by the Ārya Samāj :] *See* DAYĀNANDA SARASVATĪ SVĀMĪ.

See CHANDRAKĀNTA TARKĀLAṄKĀRA. कातन्त्रच्छन्दःप्रक्रिया ... Kātantra Cchandah Prakriyā, *etc.* [A treatise on Vedic grammar, according to the Kātantra school.] 1896. 8°. **14090. bb. 10.**

See DURGĀPRASĀDA, *Editor of the "Harbinger."* The First (Second, Third, Fourth) Vedic Reader, *etc.* 1894-1895. 12°. **14010. b. 11.**

APPENDIX (*continued*).

See GURUDATTA VIDYĀRTHĪ. Works of ... Guru Datta Vidyarthi. [Comprising English essays on Vedic subjects, from the standpoint of Dayānanda Sarasvatī's doctrines,] *etc.* 1897. 8°. **14010. dd. 11.**

—— —— [Another edition.] 1902. 8°. **759. c. 20.**

See GURUDATTA VIDYĀRTHĪ. The Terminology of the Vedas and the European Scholars, *etc.* 1899. 8°. **4504. cc. 15.(2.)**

See MADRAS.—*Government Oriental Manuscripts Library.* A Descriptive Catalogue of the Sanskrit Manuscripts of the Government Oriental Manuscripts Library ... Vol. i.—Vedic Literature. 1901. 8°. **14096. ccc. 4.**

See NĀRĀYAṆA AIYAṄGĀR. Essays on Indo-Aryan Mythology, *etc.* 1898-1901. 8°. **14028. c. 72.**

See PERIODICAL PUBLICATIONS.—*Calcutta.* उषा *etc.* [Ushā. A journal of Vedic and kindred studies, *etc.*] [1889]-1893. 8°. **14010. c. 43.**

See PHILLIPS (M.). The Teaching of the Vedas, *etc.* 1895. 8°. **4503. aaa. 12.**

See above, ṚIGVEDA.—*Selections of Hymns and Verses.* An Account of the Vedas; with numerous extracts from the Rig-Veda [in Griffith's version]. 1897. 8°. [*Sacred Books of the East Described and Examined.*] **14010. cc. 9.(vol. 1.)**

See ṢAṄKARANĀTHA, *Pandit.* The Vedas as the Revelation, *etc.* 1901. 16°. **4503. d. 4.**

See SATYAVRATA SĀMAṢRAMĪ BHAṬṬĀCHĀRYA. ॥ त्रयीपरिचयः *etc.* [Trayīparichaya. Vedic studies.] 1893. 8°. [*Ushā.*] **14010. c. 43.(vol. 2.)**

See ṢRĪRAṄGĀCHĀRYA, *Ṣrīṣailānantapurusha.* శ్రీరాయసుధాసముద్రఉపాకర్మనిర్ణయః *etc.* [Upākarmanirṇaya. A treatise on the rules for the Vedic *upākarma*, or commencement of study.] 1902. 8°. **14033. aa. 26.**

See TULASĪRĀMA ṢARMĀ, *of Kuchesar.* शास्त्रार्थ खुर्जा *etc.* [Ṣāstrārtha Khurjā. A report of a con-

APPENDIX (*continued*).

troversy as to the sanction of idolatry said to be conveyed in certain Vedic texts.] [1890.] 8°. **14154. c. 16.(2.)**

—— —— [1894.] 8°. **14154. c. 16.(3.)**

See WRIGHTSON (R.). An introductory treatise on Sanscrit Hagiographa ... Part II.—The Veda, *etc.* 1859. 12°. **4506. de. 16.**

॥ अथ वेदस्य षडङ्ग प्रारम्भः ॥ [Shaḍaṅga. Texts forming specimens of the six *aṅgas* or aids to Vedic study.] 6 pts. मोहमय्यां १८१४ [*Bombay*, 1892.] *obl.* 8°. **14007. c. 27.**

VEDEHA THERA. समन्तकूटवर्णना। By Âćârya Videha. [Samantakūṭavarṇanā. A Buddhist poem upon Adam's Peak. Stanzas 1-113.] 1893. *See* ACADEMIES, *etc.*—Calcutta.—*Buddhist Text Society of India.* Journal, *etc.* Vol. 1, pt. ii., pp. 20-30. 1893, *etc.* 8°. **14003. b. 19.(vol. 1.)**

VĒLU-PILḶAI, *N.* പാചക ചിന്താമണി. Pachaca Chindamony, *etc.* [Pāchakachintāmaṇi. A manual of the culinary art, in Malayalam, illustrated by a series of Sanskrit texts.] pt. i. pp. vi. xiii., 202. തിരുവനന്തപുരത്തു ൧൮൬൭ [*Trivandrum*, 1892.] 8°. **14053. ccc. 8.**

—— പാചകചിന്താമണി ... Pachakachinthamoni. Part i., *etc.* [Second edition.] pp. iii. ii. xv. vi. 228. *Tangacherry*, 1902. 8°. **14053. ccc. 39.**

VEMA BHŪPĀLA, *Vīranārāyaṇa Peddakomaṭi.* *See* AMARU. శృంగారామరుకకావ్యమ్ *etc.* [Ṣriṅgārāmarukakāvya, *i.e.* Amaruṣataka. With the commentary Ṣriṅgāradīpikā of Vema Bhūpāla.] 1898. 8°. **14076. c. 69.**

VEṆĪMĀDHAVA NYĀYARATNA. *See* YĀJÑAVALKYA. [*Gītā.*] যোগিযাজ্ঞবল্ক্যম্ *etc.* [Yogiyājñavalkya. Edited with Bengali translation by Veṇīmādhava.] [1893.] 8°. **14048. bb. 50.(1.)**

VEṆĪNĀTHA VANDYOPĀDHYĀYA. *See* ṢIVASAṂHITĀ. Practical Yoga Philosophy, or Sivasanhita, in English ... [Translated] with ... notes by B. N. Banerjee. 1894. 12°. **14048. b. 28.(1.)**

VENIS (ARTHUR). *See* APYAYA DĪKSHITA. The Siddhāntaleça ... Translated by A. Venis. 1899, *etc.* 8°. [*The Pandit.*] **14096. d. 6.(vol. 21, etc.)**

—— *See* PADMAPĀDA. The Pañcapādikā ... Translated by A. Venis. 1901, *etc.* 8°. [*The Pandit.*] **14096. d. 6.(vol. 23, etc.)**

—— *See* UDAYANA ĀCHĀRYA. The Lakṣaṇāvalī, *etc.* [With bibliographical notice by A. Venis.] 1899-1900. 8°. [*The Pandit.*] **14096. d. 6.(vol. 21-22.)**

—— *See* VARADARĀJA, *Logician.* तार्किकरक्षा *etc.* (The Tārkikarakṣā and Sārasaṃgraha, *etc.*) [With introduction and notes by A. Venis.] 1903. 8°. [*The Pandit.*] **14096. d. 6.(vol. 21-25.)**

—— *See* VIZIANAGRAM SANSKRIT SERIES. The Vizianagram Sanskrit Series. Under the superintendence of A. Venis. 1890-1898. 8°. **14048. dd. 3.**

—— Copper-plate Grant of Vaidyadeva King of Kâmarûpa, *etc.* (Three Copper-plate Grants of Govindachandra of Kanauj.) [Edited and translated by A. Venis.] 2 pts. *See* PERIODICAL PUBLICATIONS.—*Benares.* The Pandit, *etc.* New Series. Vol. XV (supplement). 1876, *etc.* 8°. **14096. d. 6.(vol. 15, supplement.)**

VEṄKAIYA, *Vaṅgala, of Polamur.* *See* ĀPASTAMBA. — *Ṣrautasūtra.* ఆధానపంచకము *etc.* [Ādhānapañchaka. Edited by Veṅkaiya.] 1898. 8°. **14028. d. 65.**

VEṄKAṆṆĀCHĀRYA, *Cheñchōḷi.* *See* PARĀṢARA. [*Smṛiti.*] ಪರಾಶರಮಾಧವೀಯ ಧರ್ಮಶಾಸ್ತ್ರವು *etc.* [Parāṣara-mādhavīya-dharmaṣāstra. The text of Parāṣara's Smṛiti with a Canarese translation of the latter and of Sāyaṇa's commentary by Veṅkaṇṇāchārya.] [1890.] 8°. **14038. d. 31.**

VEṄKANNA KAVI, *Jayanti.* ప్రహ్లాదచంపూప్రబంధః [Prahlādachampūprabandha. A composition on the legend of Prahlāda, in 3 *stabakas.*] pp. ii. 54, ii. *Vizagapatam*, 1899. 8°. **14072. cc. 55.(3.)**

VEṄKAṬĀCHALA DĀSA, *Maidavūl, of Kalahasti.* శ్రీనారదాష్టోత్తరశతస్తోత్రం *etc.* [Nāradāshṭottara-śatastotra. 108 salutations to the saint Nārada under different names, preceded by a metrical list of names.] pp. 6. [*Madras*,] 1900. 32°. **14028. b. 67.(3.)**

VEṄKAṬĀCHALA DĪKSHITA, *Eṭṭayapuram.* See TYĀGARĀJA DĪKSHITA. விபூதிருத்திராக்ஷதாரண நிரூபணம் *etc.* [Vibhūtirudrākshadhāraṇanirūpaṇa. Translated into Tamil by Veṅkaṭāchala.] 1901. 12°. **14170. d. 85.(1)**

VEṄKAṬĀCHALAM PANTULU, *Chavendra.* A lecture on the Christian and Hindu doctrines of Ereation[*sic*] by Ch. Venkatachallam Pantulu Garu. Second edition. pp. 23. *Masulipatam*, 1890. 8°. **4506. c. 29.(1.)**

—— A lecture on the Christian and Hindu doctrines of Providence by Ch. Venkatachalam Pantulu Garu. 2 pts. *Masulipatam*, 1891. 8°. **4506. c. 29.(2.)**

VEṄKAṬĀCHALA ṢARMĀ, *Ādanūr N.*, also called KUPPU ṢĀSTRI. ஸ்வராவதான நிரூபணம் *etc.* [Svarāvadhāna. A treatise on the accentuation of the words of the Taittirīyasaṃhitā.] pp. 24. கும்பகோணம் [*Kumbakonam*,] 1901. 8°. **14010. c. 32.(2.)**

VEṄKAṬĀCHALA ṢARMĀ, *Gurudanti.* See UPANISHADS.—*Selections.* మహావాక్యరత్నావళి *etc.* [Mahāvākyaratnāvali. Edited by Veṅkaṭāchala.] 1904. 8°. **14007. b. 25.**

VEṄKAṬĀCHALA ṢĀSTRĪ, *V., of Kalpadi.* See MUHŪRTAPADAVĪ. സഭാഷാ മുഹൂൎത്തപദവി *etc.* [Muhūrtapadavī. With Malayalam commentary. Edited by Veṅkaṭāchala.] [1897.] 8°. **14053. ccc. 11.**

—— See PURĀṆAS.—*Padmapurāṇa.* கார்த்திகமாஹாத்மியம் *etc.* [Kārttikamāhātmya. Edited by Veṅkaṭāchala.] [1898.] 8°. **14016. c. 60.**

—— See VARĀHAMIHIRA. ப்ரு... உபாத்யாயீ [Brihaj-jātaka. With Govinda's Daṣādhyāyī. Edited by Veṅkaṭāchala.] [1905.] 8°. **14053. ccc. 51.**

VEṄKAṬĀCHALA ṢĀSTRĪ, *Dubbāka.* See MAHĀBHĀRATA. — *Ṣāntiparva.* శ్రీమన్మహాభారతము శాన్తిపర్వము *etc.* [Ṣāntiparva. Edited with interpretations and expositions in Telugu by Veṅkaṭāchala.] [1891-1893.] 8°. **14060. d. 14.**

—— వైశ్యశాఙ్కరియను పురాణోక్తషోడశకర్మ ప్రయోగ ప్రకాశికయందు పూర్వభాగము *etc.* [Vaiṣyaṣāṅkarī. A manual of the sixteen chief duties of the Vaiṣya caste, compiled from the Purāṇas.] pt. 1. pp. iv. xiii. 119. కడప ౧౮౯౧ [*Cuddapah*, 1891.] 8°. **14028. d. 42.**

VEṄKAṬĀCHALA ṢĀSTRĪ, *Kāṣi-Ṣesha.* अब्धिनौयानमीमांसा *etc.* [Abdhinauyānamīmāṃsā. A discussion of the propriety of Hindus visiting Europe and America.] pp. ii. 204; 1 *plate.* मुम्बयी १९५९ [*Bombay*, 1903.] 8°. **14038. c. 50.**

VEṄKAṬĀCHĀRYA, *son of Govindāchārya, son of Nainīchārya.* చాత్తాదశ్రీవైష్ణవద్విజషోడశకర్మాణి *etc.* [Chāttāda-ṣrīvaishṇava-dvijashoḍaṣakarmāṇi. The liturgies for the 16 chief domestic rites of Chāttādu-Ṣrīvaishṇava Brahmans, in Sanskrit, Tamil, and Telugu. Edited by Iyyuṇṇi Ṣaṭhakopāchārya.] pp. xiv. 192. చెన్నపురి ౧౯౦౨ [*Madras*, 1902.] 8°. **14170. ee. 47.**

VEṄKAṬĀCHĀRYA, *Ariṣānaphāla.* See VEṄKAṬĀRYA YAJVĀ.

VEṄKAṬĀCHĀRYA, *B., of Kolar.* See NĪLĀGĪTĀ. నీలాగీత *etc.* [Nīlāgītā. Edited by Veṅkaṭāchārya.] [1898.] 12°. **14076. a. 22.(2.)**

VEṄKAṬĀCHĀRYA, *Gautama, Physician.* Bruhad Vaidya Ratnakaramu. [A manual of the medical art, in Telugu, with the original Sanskrit stanzas,] compiled by Venkatacharya Pandit. బృహద్వైద్యరత్నాకరము *etc.* pp. xvi. 640. చెన్నపురి [*Madras*,] 1902. 8°. **14043. cc. 23.**

VEṄKAṬĀCHĀRYA, *Tūppūl, of Bangalore.* See BĀDARĀYAṆA. శ్రీశుకభాష్యమ్ *etc.* [Brahmasūtra. With commentary of Ṣukāchārya. Edited by Veṅkaṭāchārya.] [1892.] 8°. **14048. c. 76.**

—— See MAHĀBHĀRATA.—Bhagavadgītā.—*Sanskrit and Vernaculars.* ಶ್ರೀಗೀತಾರ್ಥಸಾರವು *etc.*

[Gītārthasāra. The Bhagavadgītā with notes and commentaries, in Canarese, edited by Veṅkaṭāchārya.] 1898-1901. 8°. **14048. cc. 19.**

VEṄKAṬĀCHĀRYA NṚISIṂHĀCHĀRYA, *of Baroda.* *See* JAYADEVA, *son of Mahādeva.* Prasannaraghava . . . With the Sanskrit commentary of Vyanketacharya Upadhye, *etc.* 1894. 8°. **14080. d. 24.**

VEṄKAṬADEṢIKA, *Chandragiri.* ராமாநுஜதயாபாத்ரவ்யாக்யாநம் *etc.* [Rāmānujadayāpātravyākhyāna. A dissertation, in Sanskritised Tamil, upon a Sanskrit stanza of salutation to Veṅkaṭanātha Vedāntāchārya.] pp. 28. காஞ்சீபுரம் [*Conjevaram,* 1883.] 8°. **14028. d. 59.(1.)**

VEṄKAṬĀDHVARĪ, *author of the Ṣrīnivāsachampū.* *See* VEṄKAṬEṢA, *disciple of Nṛisiṃha.*

VEṄKAṬĀDHVARĪ, *author of the Viṣvaguṇādarṣa.* *See* VEṄKAṬĀRYA YAJVĀ, *Ariṣānaphāla.*

VEṄKAṬAKṚISHṆAIYA, *R. S.* *See* UPANISHADS.—*Separate Upanishads.* ತೈತ್ತಿರೀಯೋಪನಿಷತ್ *etc.* [Taittirīyopanishad. Edited with Canarese translation, notes, and introductions by Veṅkaṭakṛishṇaiya.] 1901, *etc.* 12°. **14010. b. 23.**

VEṄKAṬAKṚISHṆA ṢĀSTRĪ, *K.* *See* ĀRAṆYAKAS. — *Taittirīyāraṇyaka.* ஸ்ரீ . . . வேங்கடேசாரண்யஸார *etc.* [Taittirīyāraṇyaka, *etc.* Edited by Veṅkaṭakṛishṇa and Deṣikāchārya.] 1894. 8°. **14010. cc. 1.**

—— *See* UPANISHADS. — *General Collections.* அஷ்டோத்தரஶதோபநிஷத: *etc.* [Ashṭottarașatopanishadaḥ. Edited by Veṅkaṭakṛishṇa and Rāmachandra.] 1896. 8°. **14010. cc. 8.**

VEṄKAṬANARASIṂHĀCHĀRYA, *Tenmaḍam.* *See* VĀLMĪKI.—Rāmāyaṇa.—*Portions.* ஸ்ரீவால்மீகி ராமாயணம். சுந்தரகாண்டம் *etc.* [Sundarakāṇḍa. With Tamil paraphrase by Veṅkaṭanarasiṃhāchārya.] 1901. 12°. **14060. b. 18.**

VEṄKAṬANĀRĀYAṆA, *Belūr, of Maddagiri.* *See* UDAKAṢĀNTI. ఉదకశాంతివిధిః *etc.* [Udakaṣāntividhi. Edited by Veṅkaṭanārāyaṇa.] [1900.] 8°. **14028. d. 35.(3.)**

VEṄKAṬANĀRĀYAṆA RĀYA, *son of Vemulakoṇḍa Konaya.* शशिकला *etc.* [Ṣaṣikalā. A poem in 50 stanzas on the moon, figured in the erotic style. Edited by Kollūr Kāmaṣāstrī.] pp. i. 12. श्रीविजयनगर° [*Vizianagram,*] 1898. 8°. **14076. b. 33.**

VEṄKAṬANĀTHA VEDĀNTĀCHĀRYA, called KAVITĀRKIKASIṂHA. *See* BĀDARĀYAṆA. அதிகரணஸாராவளி *etc.* [Brahmasūtra. With the Adhikaraṇasārāvalī, a metrical epitome of Rāmānuja's Ṣrībhāshya by Veṅkaṭanātha, and a commentary upon the Adhikaraṇasārāvalī by N. Sundararāja.] [1901-1902.] 8°. **14048. e. 32.**

—— *See* YĀMUNA ĀCHĀRYA. Gitartha Sangrha [*sic*] . . . with Gitartha Sangraha Raksha, a comentary [*sic*] of . . . Vadanta Desika, *etc.* 1901. 8°. [*Ṣāstramuktāvalī.*] **14049. a. 1. (no. 10.)**

—— The Dasadeepakanighantu of Sri Vedantacharya Venkatanatha [a metrical treatise on words of ten meanings]. Edited . . . by S. P. V. Ranganathasvamy Ayyavaralugaru. (दशदीपकनिघण्टुः) pp. i. 7. *Vizagapatam,* 1898. 12°. **14092. a. 21.(1.)**

Forms no. 2 of the Koṣamañjari *series.*

—— Hamsasandesa. [A poem on an imaginary message from Rāma to Sītā, in imitation of the Meghadūta.] With Sanskrit commentary, English notes and translation, by Swetaranyam Narayana Sastriar . . . and an Experienced Graduate. (F. A. Examination of 1903.) pp. 2, 43, 42, 18. *Madras,* 1902. 8°. **14072. cc. 63.**

—— श्रीः . . . हंससन्देशाख्यम् महाकाव्यम् . . . हंससन्देश प्रकाशाख्यया व्याख्यया सहितम्. (Hamsa Sandesa . . . With an [English] introduction [by N. V. Deṣikāchārya and G. Kastūriraṅga Aiyaṅgār], [Sanskrit] commentary [called Haṃsasandeṣaprakāṣa, by Vātsya Naḍādūr Raṅgarājāchārya], [English] notes and translation in verse [by Deṣikāchārya and Kastūriraṅga Aiyaṅgār]. Edited by . . . P. Ananda Charlu.) pp. i. iv. i. xxxv. 183, 86, 25. *Madras,* 1903. 12°. **14060. b. 19.**

The English title is from the cover.

—— The Meemamsapaduka, *etc.* [Mīmāṃsāpādukā. A philosophical-religious poem in 173 stanzas.] (मीमांसापादुका।) pp. 31. 1900. *See*

ANANTĀCHĀRYA, *Prativādibhayaṅkara.* शास्त्रमुक्तावली The Ŝasthramukthâvalî, *etc.* No. 3. 1899, *etc.* 8°. **14049. a. 1.(no. 3.)**

—— न्यायसिद्धाञ्जनम् . . . Nyāyasiddhānjanam [a Vedantic treatise in 6 chapters,] by Venkaṭanātha Deśika. Edited by . . . Ráma Miśra Śástri. pp. iv. ii. 183, iii. 1901. *See* PERIODICAL PUBLICATIONS. — *Benares.* The Pandit, *etc.* New Series. Vol. XXIII. 1876, *etc.* 8°. **14096. d. 6.(vol. 23.)**

—— [A reprint of the preceding.] pp. iv. ii. iii. 183. काश्याम् १९०१ [*Benares,* 1901.] 8°. **14049. b. 11.**

—— సఙ్కల్పసూర్యోదయః . . . ప్రభావళీ సమాఖ్యయా వ్యాఖ్యయా సహ *etc.* [Saṅkalpasūryodaya. An allegorical drama in 10 acts. With a commentary called Prabhāvalī by Kōyil Īyuṇṇi Śrīnivāsāchārya, completed in act x. by a commentary called Prabhāprasādinī by Śrīśaila Tātayāchārya. Edited by K. N. Śrīnivāsāchārya.] pt. ii. pp. viii. xi. 393. శ్రీ కాంచ్యాం ౧౯౦౪ [*Conjeveram,* 1904.] 8°. **14079. c. 73.**

Forms no. 4 of the Conjeeveram Oriental Literary Institution Series. *Part* i. *(acts 1-5) is wanting.*

—— The Sathadushani. [A Vedantic controversial treatise] by Sri Vedanta Desika, with [the commentary] Chandamarutha by [Rāmānujadāsa, surnamed] Thoddaia charia . . . Vol. 1 [containing chapters 1-15]. (॥ शतदूषणी ॥) 1901. *See* ANANTĀCHĀRYA, *Prativādibhayaṅkara.* शास्त्रमुक्तावली The Ŝasthramukthâvalî, *etc.* No. 5. 1899, *etc.* 8°. **14049. a. 1.(no. 5.)**

—— सर्वार्थसिद्धियुतः तत्त्वमुक्ताकलापः । . . . Tattvamuktákalápa with [the author's commentary] Sarvárthasiddhi . . . Edited by . . . Ráma Miśra Sástri. pp. 723, v. ii. viii. 1900. *See* PERIODICAL PUBLICATIONS.—*Benares.* The Pandit, *etc.* New Series. Vol. XVIII.-XXII. 1876, *etc.* 8°. **14096. d. 6.(vol. 18-22.)**

—— శ్రీః . . . తత్త్వటీకా . . . శారీరక మీమాంసా భాష్యవ్యాఖ్యా *etc.* [Tattvaṭīkā. A treatise expounding various passages of the Śrībhāshya of Rāmānuja, in verse with prose commentary. Edited by Peruṅgaṭṭūr Ghaṇṭāvatārāchārya.] శ్రీకాంచ్యాం [*Conjevaram,*] 1904, *etc.* 8°. **14049. b. 24.**

In progress. Forms no. 1 *of the series* Śrisūktimāla.

—— వేదాన్తాచార్యవిజయాహ్వయః ఆచార్యచమ్పూః *etc.* [Vedāntāchāryavijaya, or Āchāryachampū. An anonymous *champū* composition describing the triumphs of the Vedāntāchārya, in 6 *stabakas.* Edited by Śrīpuram Naḍādūr Raṅganāthāchārya.] pp. 78, ii. చెన్నపట్టణే నన్దనం [*Madras,* 1892.] 8°. **14048. dd. 17.**

VEṄKAṬANṚISIṂHĀRYA, *T. E. S., of Yadugiri.* *See* KUPPAN AIYAṄGĀR.

VEṄKAṬAPPAIYA ŚĀSTRI, *Ēlēśvarapu, of Narsapur.* *See* UPANISHADS. — *Small Collections.* అధ్యాత్మోపనిషత్తు *etc.* [Adhyātmopanishad and Ātmopanishad. With Telugu glosses and paraphrases by Veṅkaṭappaiya.] 1897. 8°. **14010. dd. 13.**

—— *See* UPANISHADS. — *Separate Upanishads.* మహోపనిషత్తు *etc.* [Mahopanishad. With Telugu glosses and paraphrases by Veṅkaṭappaiya.] 1899. 8°. **14010. dd. 5.(4.)**

VEṄKAṬAPPĀ RĀU, *Piḍugu.* *See* DHANVANTARI. ధన్వంతరినిఘంటువు *etc.* [Dhanvantarinighaṇṭu. Edited with Telugu interpretation by Siṅgarāju Kānū and Veṅkaṭappā Rāu.] [1892.] 8°. **14043. c. 40.**

VEṄKAṬAPRAPANNĀBHI SVĀMĪ, *Rājayogānanda.* *See* MAHĀBHĀRATA.—Bhagavadgītā.—*Sanskrit and Vernaculars.* శ్రీభగవద్గీతార్థబోధిని *etc.* [Bhagavadgītā. With a Telugu paraphrase, styled Bhagavadgītārthabodhini, by Veṅkaṭaprapannābhi Svāmī.] 1901. 12°. **14065. b. 27.**

VEṄKAṬARĀGHAVA ŚARMĀ, *Annavaram, disciple of Rāmasubrahmaṇya.* *See* BĀDARĀYAṆA. బ్రహ్మసూత్రార్థదీపికా *etc.* [Brahmasūtra. With commentary styled Brahmasūtrārthadīpikā. Edited by Veṅkaṭarāghava.] [1897.] 8°. **14048. cc. 8.(3.)**

—— *See* BĀDARĀYAṆA. బ్రహ్మామృతవర్షిణీ *etc.* [Brahmasūtra. With commentary of Rāmānanda. Edited by Veṅkaṭarāghava.] 1900. 8°. **14048. c. 77.**

VEṄKAṬARĀMA, *Kauṇḍinya, of Karuppatur.* See KṚISHṆA ŚARMĀ, *of Karuppatur.*

VEṄKAṬARĀMA JOŚĪ, *Piṅgala, of Madras.* See SIDDHANĀTHA, *Astrologer.* ఆరూఢరత్నసిద్ధాంజనమ్ *etc.* [Ārūḍharatnasiddhāñjana. With Telugu translation by Veṅkaṭarāma.] [1895.] 8°. **14053. c. 67.**

VEṄKAṬARAMAṆAN, *Sillattūr.* See ŚAṄKARA ĀCHĀRYA.—*Doubtful and Supposititious Works.* The Dakshinamurti Stotra, *etc.* [With metrical translation by S. Veṅkaṭaramaṇan.] 1901. 4°. [*Siddhanta Deepika.*] **14170. fff. 4.(vol. 4.)**

—— *See* SUREŚVARA ĀCHĀRYA. The Sambandhavārtika, *etc.* [Translated by Veṅkaṭaramaṇan.] 1901, *etc.* 8°. [*The Pandit.*] **14096. d. 6.(vol. 23, etc.)**

VEṄKAṬARĀMĀNUJA, *Chilakapāṭi.* See PALLĪPATANA. బల్లిపతనము *etc.* [Pallīpatana. With Telugu paraphrase and appendix by Veṅkaṭarāmānuja.] 1898. 16°. **14053. a. 12.(2.)**

VEṄKAṬARĀMĀNUJA SVĀMĪ, *Paravastu, son of Śrīnivāsa Bhaṭṭanāthāchārya.* See JAGANNĀTHA PAṆḌITARĀJA. శ్రీ ... శతకము *etc.* [338 stanzas of the Śatakas. Edited by Veṅkaṭarāmānuja.] 1895. 12°. **14070. b. 22.**

VEṄKAṬARĀMA ŚĀSTRĪ, *S., of Mysore.* See KĀMANDAKI. Kámandakíya Nítisára. With full notes ... translation ... &c. by S. Venkatarama Sastry. 1895. 8°. **14070. c. 55.**

—— कथाशतकम् "Kathasataka." 100 popular stories translated from vernacular originals into simple Sanskrit prose ... and "Sloka Trisati Bharati," 300 slokas from Mahabharata. pp. iv. 169. *Kumbakonam*, 1898. 8°. **14070. c. 63.(1.)**

VEṄKAṬARĀMA ŚĀSTRĪ, *Iṅguva.* See BHĀRADVĀJA. భారద్వాజసూత్రము *etc.* [Bhāradvājasūtra. Edited by Veṅkaṭarāma.] 1897. 8°. **14028. d. 59.(7.)**

VEṄKAṬARĀMA ŚĀSTRĪ, *Nallicheri V. S.* See NĀRĀYAṆA BHAṬṬA, called MṚIGARĀJALAKSHMĀ. வெணீஸம்ஹாரம் [Veṇīsaṃhāra. Edited by Veṅkaṭarāma.] 1902. 8°. **14080. c. 44.**

—— ஆபஸ்தம்பிநாம் உபாகரணப்ரயோக: *etc.* [Āpastambinām Upākaraṇaprayoga. A manual of the *upākaraṇa* rite according to the school of Āpastamba.] pp. 18. நடுக்காவேரி [*Nadukkaveri*, 1901.] 8°. **14039. b. 26.(2.)**

VENKATA RANGACHARYA, *Paravastu.* See VEṄKAṬARAṄGANĀTHA ĀCHĀRYA.

VEṄKAṬARAṄGANĀTHA ĀCHĀRYA, *Paravastu, Mahāmahopādhyāya.* See MAHĀBHĀRATA.—*Śāntiparva.* మోక్షధర్మము *etc.* [Mokshadharma. With the commentary of Nīlakaṇṭha and the Vyāsahṛidaya, and likewise a Telugu translation. Edited by Veṅkaṭaraṅganātha.] 1887, *etc.* 8°. **14065. bbb. 8.**

—— *See* UPANISHADS.—*Small Collections.* The Telugu Upanishads ... [Translated] by ... Venkata Ranganathacharya, *etc.* 1899, *etc.* 8°. **14007. b. 11.(1.)**

—— आङ्गलाधिराज्यस्वागतम् Welcome the English Empire. [Āṅglādhirājya-svāgata. A poem on the British rule, with English prose translation.] pp. 32. 1896. *See* VEṄKAṬARAṄGANĀTHA SVĀMĪ. Grandha Pradarsani, *etc.* [No. 13.] 1895, *etc.* 8°. **14003. c. 2.(13.)**

—— आर्षमतसंग्रहः [Ārshamatasaṅgraha. A brief account of ancient schools of philosophic and religious thought. With Telugu translation.] pp. 12. 1893. *See* PERIODICAL PUBLICATIONS.—*Vizagapatam.* సకలవిద్యాభివర్ధని [Sakalavidyābhivardhanī.] Vol. I, pt. viii. 1892-1897. 12°. **14174. g. 38.**

—— लघुशब्दानुशासनम् ॥ [Laghu-śabdānuśāsana. A treatise on grammar.] 1895, *etc.* *See* VEṄKAṬARAṄGANĀTHA SVĀMĪ. Grandha Pradarsani, *etc.* [No. 2.] 1895, *etc.* 8°. **14003. c. 2.(2.)**

Not completed. It breaks off with the verb-root ghṛiṇ.

—— Laghu Sabdárdhasarvaswa. A Sanscrit encyclopædia by Sri Paravastu Venkata Rangacharya Aryavaraguru ... లఘుశబ్దార్థసర్వస్వమ్ *etc.* *Vizagapatam*, 1877, *etc.* 4°. **14092. c. 19.**

In progress.

—— The Manjula Naishadha. [A drama] by Mahamahopadhyaya Sri Paravastu Venkata Rangacharyulu Ayyavaralugaru, *etc.* (मञ्जुलनैषधम् नाम नाटकम्) pp. 96. 1896. *See* VEṄKAṬARAṄGANĀTHA SVĀMĪ. Grandha Pradarsani, *etc.* [No. 14.] 1895, *etc.* 8°. **14003. c. 2.(14.)**

VEṄKAṬARAṄGANĀTHA SVĀMĪ, *Paravastu.* *See* VEṄKAṬANĀTHA VEDĀNTĀCHĀRYA. The Dasadeepakanighantu . . . Edited . . . by S. P. V. Ranganathasvamy Ayyavaralugaru. 1898. 12°. **14092. a. 21.(1.)**

—— Grandha Pradarsani. A collection of oriantal [*sic*] works edited by S. P. V. Ranganadhaswamy Ayyavaralugaru. *Vizagapatam*, 1895, *etc.* 8°. **14003. c. 2.**

In progress. The issue was suspended from 1898 to 1902. The works published in this series will be found under the headings:—

Agastya.	Trivikrama Deva.
Aruṇagirinātha.	Upanishads.—*Separate Upanishads.*
Pāṇini.	Vāmana Āchārya.
Purushottama Deva.	Vāmana Bhaṭṭa Bāṇa.
Ṣaṅkara Āchārya.	Veṅkaṭaraṅganātha Āchārya.
Ṣrinivāsa Kavi.	

VEṄKAṬARATNA ṢARMĀ, *Kokkoṇḍa.* (భగవన్నామసంకీర్తన రత్నావళి [Bhagavannāmasaṅkīrtanaratnāvalī, or] The Gem-Necklace of Divine Songs. స్తుతిరత్నావళి. [Stutiratnāvalī, or] The Gem-Necklace of Divine Praise.) [Followed by the Suvarṇamālāstuti ascribed to Ṣaṅkara. With English introduction and essay on the esoteric meaning of certain religious symbols by Ṣivaṣaṅkara Paṇḍyājī, and an appendix of quotations proving the unity of the Supreme Being, collected by the same.] pp. viii. 41. *Madras*, 1886. 8°. **14003. c.**

Forms no. 6 of Ṣivaṣaṅkara Paṇḍyājī's Hindu Excelsior Series. *Without title-page.*

VEṄKAṬARĀU RĀMACHANDRA. *See* SADĀNANDA YOGĪNDRA. वेदान्तसार *etc.* [Vedāntasāra. Edited with a Marathi introduction and paraphrase by Veṅkaṭarāu.] [1891.] 8°. **14048. c. 74.**

—— *See* UPANISHADS.—*Small Collections.* उपनिषत्संग्रहः [Upanishatsaṅgraha. Edited with Sanskrit glosses and Marathi paraphrases, notes, and introductions by Veṅkaṭarāu.] [1890, *etc.*] 8°. **14010. c. 51.**

VEṄKAṬĀRYA DĪKSHITA, *son of Raghunātha.* *See* VEṄKAṬĀRYA YAJVĀ.

VEṄKAṬĀRYA YAJVĀ, *Ariṣānaphāla, son of Raghunātha.* லக்ஷ்மீஸஹஸ்ரம் *etc.* [Lakshmīsahasra. A cycle of Vaishṇava poems, in 25 *stabakas.* With the commentary Gūḍhārthavivaraṇa of Rāghavārya.] pp. viii. 647, xii. கும்பகோணம்॥ வா॥ [*Kumbakonam*, 1892.] 8°. **14028. d. 49.**

—— శ్రీ... సవ్యాఖ్యానరాఘవయాదవీయ॥ [Rāghavayādavīya. An artificial poem of the *anuloma-viloma* type, which may be read either as a Rāmāyaṇa or as a Bhārata, with the author's commentary.] pp. 42. *See* ṢAMBHURAHASYA. శ్రీశంభురహస్య॥ [Kavikāvyādipraṣaṃsā, *etc.*] [1890.] 8°. **14053. ccc. 31.**

One sheet is wanting.

—— उत्तररामचरित्रचम्पूः । [Uttararāmacharitra. A *champū* composition on the later history of Rāma, in 2 *sargas*, with annotations.] pp. 72. [1890.] *See* PERIODICAL PUBLICATIONS.—*Bombay.* ग्रन्थरत्नमाला *etc.* (Granth Ratna Málá, *etc.*) Vol. III, no. 7-9. 1887-[1892.] 8°. **14096. c. 8.(vol. 3.)**

Published from a unique MS. from Gwalior, which is apparently imperfect in some passages.

—— The Vishwaguṇâdarsh Champu of Venkatâdhvari. [A poetical itinerary, in *champū* form, descriptive of various regions, especially in Southern India, and of divers characters.] Edited with commentary Padârthchandrikâ by Bâlkrishna Ganesh Yogi. (विश्वगुणादर्शचम्पूः) pp. xiv. 313, ix. *Bombay*, 1899. 8°. **14076. c. 74.**

VEṄKAṬA SĀRVABHAUMA. *See* KĀLIDĀSA, *Pseud.*, [*i.e.* KĀLIDĀSA SĀRVABHAUMA BHAṬṬĀCHĀRYA.] पुष्पबाणविलासः । [Pushpabāṇavilāsa. With commentary of Veṅkaṭa.] [1895.] 8°. [*Kālidāser Granthāvali.*] **14070. d. 34. (vol. 2.)**

—— *See* KĀLIDĀSA, *Pseud.*, [*i.e.* KĀLIDĀSA SĀRVABHAUMA BHAṬṬĀCHĀRYA.] पुष्पबाणविलासम् *etc.* [Pushpabāṇavilāsa. With commentary of Veṅkaṭa.] [1901.] 8°. **14072. cc. 62.(3.)**

VEṄKAṬA ṢĀSTRĪ, *Indrakaṇṭi Gopāla.* ఫలప్రదర్శినినామక గ్రంథ్యం *etc.* [Phalapradarṣinī. A collection of stanzas, partly original, partly compiled from standard astrological works, and treating of the influence of the various positions of the planets. With Telugu paraphrase and commentary.] pp. i. vi. 101. *Vizagapatam*, 1898. 8°. **14053. ccc. 22.**

VEṄKAṬA ṢESHAIYA, *Vetsā.* సంస్కృతాంధ్రనిఘంటుః . . . A Sanskrit-Telugu Dictionary, *etc.* pp. i. ii. i. i. i. 387. *Madras*, 1893. 8°. **14174. n. 26.**

VEṄKAṬASIMHĀDRI JAGAPATI RĀJU, *Rājā Vatsavāya.* మహాయోగానందామృతకల్పవల్లి *etc.* [Mahāyogānandāmṛitakalpavalli. A pharmacopœia, consisting of verses from various sources with Telugu commentary.] pp. xiii. vi. 248, 5. తుని ౧౯౦౨ [*Tuni*, 1902.] 8°.
14043. dd. 10.

VEṄKAṬA SUBBAIYA, *Vedānta.* *See* ŚAṄKARA ĀCHĀRYA. — *Philosophical Poems, etc.* ಶ್ರೀ . . . ಆತ್ಮಬೋಧಾ॥ [Ātmabodha. With Canarese translation and commentary by Veṅkaṭa Subbaiya.] 1902. 12°.
14048. b. 16.(3.)

VEṄKAṬASUBBĀ ŚĀSTRĪ, *Nelaṭūru.* *See* PURĀṆAS. — *Padmapurāṇa.* Sivageetha, *etc.* [Edited with Telugu version by Veṅkaṭasubbā.] 1897. 8°.
14016. c. 55.

VEṄKAṬASUBRAHMAṆYA ŚĀSTRĪ, *Cheṭṭūr.* *See* PURĀṆAS. — *Śivapurāṇa.* శ్రీకాళహస్తిస్థలమాహాత్మ్యము॥ [Kālahastisthalamāhātmya. Edited by Veṅkaṭasubrahmaṇya.] [1893.] 8°.
14016. c. 41.

VEṄKAṬASVĀMI AIYAR, *of Mysore.* *See* ŚAṄKARA ĀCHĀRYA. — *Doubtful and Supposititious Works.* ஸ்ரீ . . . சிவானந்தலஹரீ *etc.* [Śivānandalaharī. With interpretations in Tamil. Edited by Mṛityuṃjaya and Veṅkaṭasvāmi.] 1904. 12°.
14048. b. 48.

VEṄKAṬASVĀMI NĀYUḌU, *Ummadiseṭṭi.* సంగీతవిద్యాదర్పణము *etc.* [Saṅgītavidyādarpaṇa. A manual of music, comprising Sanskrit verses with Telugu explanations and dissertations.] pp. vii. 335. చెన్నపురి [*Madras*,] 1901. 8°.
14174. e. 31.

VEṄKAṬAVARADADĀSA, *Paidigaṇṭamu*, and **SUBBAIYA PANTULU**, *Kākarla.* శ్రీతారకనామత్రయము *etc.* [Tārakanāmatraya. A devotional compilation, comprising 3 series of deities' names—viz. (1) Mahālakshmīsahasranāmāvalīślokāḥ, with a Nāmāvalī of the same; (2) Veṅkaṭeśasahasranāmāvalīślokāḥ, with Nāmāvalī of the same; (3) Āñjaneyasahasranāmāvalīślokāḥ, with Nāmāvalī, a Hanumatkavacha, and a *maṅgala.*] pp. iv. i. 168. చెన్నపురి [*Madras*,] 1900. 8°.
14033. bbb. 9.

VEṄKAṬA YAJVĀ, *Chintalapāṭi.* *See* KĀLĀMṚITA. ಕಾಲಾಮೃತ॥ [Kālāmṛita. With commentary of Veṅkaṭa.] 1891. 8°.
14053. cc. 61.

VEṄKAṬEŚA, *disciple of Nṛisiṃha*, also called VEṄKAṬĀDHVARĪ. The Śrînivâsavilâsa Champu [or Śrīnivāsachampū] of Venkateśa Kavi. [A composition in 5 *uchchhvāsas.*] With the commentary of Dharanîdhara. Edited by ... Paṇdit Durgâprasâd and Kâśînâth Pâṇdurang Parab. (श्रीनिवासविलासचम्पूः ।) pp. 141. 1893. *See* DURGĀPRASĀDA, *son of Vrajalāla*, and KĀŚĪNĀTHA PĀṆḌURAṄGA PARAB. Kâvyamâlâ. [No.] 33. 1886, *etc.* 8°.
14072. ccc. 12.(no. 33.)

VEṄKAṬEŚA DAIVAJÑA, *son of Appayārya.* सर्वार्थचिन्तामणि. Sarwarthachintamani, with original text in Devanagari and English translation, with copious notes and illustrations, by B. Suryanarain Row. Part 1. *Bellary*, 1899. 8°.
14053. d. 58.

VEṄKAṬEŚA PAṆḌITA, *author of the Jātakachandrikā.* *See* YAJÑANĀRĀYAṆA VEṄKAṬEŚVARĀRYA.

VEṄKAṬEŚA RĀMAKṚISHṆA KETKAR. ज्योतिर्गणितम् सकृत्प्रत्याख्योदाहरणकोष्टकादिभिः समलंकृतम् *etc.* [Jyotirgaṇita. A modern treatise on astronomy.] pp. 8, 8, vi. 426, i. i.; 4 *plates.* पुण्याख्यपत्तने १८९८ [*Poona*, 1898.] 8°.
14053. dd. 10.

VEṄKAṬEŚĀRYA, *Śrīdhara.* ஸ்ரீதர ஸ்துதிமணிமாலா *etc.* [Śrīdharastutimaṇimālā. Fourteen religious poems, viz. Achyutāshṭaka, Ākhyāshashṭi, Ārtiharastotra, Dayāśataka, Ḍolānavaratnamālikā, Doshaparihārāshṭaka, Jambunāthāshṭaka, Kṛishṇadvādaśamañjarī, Kulīrāshṭaka, Mātṛibhūtaśataka, Śivabhaktalakshaṇa, Śivabhaktikalpalatikā, Stutipaddhati, and Tārāvalīstotra. Edited by Ghṛitasthānam Nṛisiṃha Bhāgavata.] pp. 80. கும்பகோணம்॥ [*Kumbakonam*,] 1895. 8°.
14076. c. 71.

VEṄKAṬEŚA ŚĀSTRĪ, *S.* *See* KĀLĀMṚITA. ಕಾಲಾಮೃತ॥ [Kālāmṛita. With Canarese paraphrase by Veṅkaṭeśa.] 1891. 8°. **14053. cc. 61.**

VEṄKAṬEŚVARA. *See* KĀLIDĀSA, called VEṄKAṬEŚVARA.

VEṄKAṬEŚVARA YAJVĀ, *Hārīta.* *See* VĀLMĪKI.—Rāmāyaṇa.—*Entire Text.* ஸ்ரீ . . . ஸ்ரீமத்ராமாயணம்॥

[Rāmāyaṇa. With the commentary Sarvārthasāra of Veṅkaṭeṣvara.] [1903, *etc.*] 4°.
14068. c. 17.

VETĀLAPAÑCHAVIṂŚATI. Vetālapañcaviṃçatikā. Il venticinquenovelle d'un lemure. [Translated into Italian from Ṣivadāsa's recension, with critical notes, by V. Bettei.] 1897, *etc.* *See* PERIODICAL PUBLICATIONS.—*Florence.* Studi Italiani di Filologia Indo-Iranica, *etc.* Vol. i., *etc.* 1897, *etc.* 8°. **P.P. 4884. da. (vol. 1, etc.)**

—— Novelle del Vetâla. (Novella I-V.) Tradotte dal sanscrito [by F. G. Fumi.] 1892. *See* PERIODICAL PUBLICATIONS.—*Palermo.* Archivio per lo Studio delle Tradizioni Popolari, *etc.* Vol. XI, pp. 1-28. 1882, *etc.* 8°. **P.P. 4168. d. (vol. 11.)**

—— 6 Novelle Soprannumerarie alla Vetālapancaviçati. [Translated by V. Bettei.] 1894. *See* PERIODICAL PUBLICATIONS.—*Palermo.* Archivio per lo Studio delle Tradizioni Popolari, *etc.* Vol. XIII, pp. 313-325, 537-554. 1882, *etc.* 8°.
P.P. 4168. d.(vol. 13.)

VIBHAṄGA. *See* ABHIDHAMMAPIṬAKA.

VICTORIA, *Queen of Great Britain and Ireland.* *See* BALADEVA SIṂHA, *Raja of Kama.* A Vijayapatra of Digvijainie Victoria, *etc.* 1889. 12°.
14058. a. 15.

—— *See* KERALAVARMĀ. ശ്രീ വിക്ടോറിയാ ചരിതസംഗ്രഹം *etc.* [Victoria-charitasangraha. A brief poetical history of Queen Victoria.] [1889.] 8°. **14076. cc. 2.(2.)**

—— *See* KRISHṆACHANDRA, *of Benares.* Preeti Kusumanjali . . . [Poems] compiled . . . to commemorate the Diamond Jubilee of Her Most Gracious Majesty Victoria, *etc.* 1897. 12°.
14072. b. 27.(3.)

—— *See* KULACHANDRA ṢARMĀ. शोकमहोर्मिः *etc.* [Ṣokamahormi. A dialogue on the death of Queen Victoria.] [1901.] 8°. **14072. ccc. 33.**

—— *See* ṢAILAJĀNANDA OJHĀ. *Begin.* सगयानगुणविभूषया - राजभक्तिपरायया - भारतजनगया - समीपे सादरमावेदनम् । [A poem on the Jubilee, with English and Bengali translations.] [1887 ?] 8°.
14076. cc. 2.(1.)

—— *See* ṢAURĪNDRAMOHANA ṬHĀKURA. The seven principal musical notes of the Hindus . . . composed in celebration of the birth-day of . . . the Empress of India, *etc.* 1892. 4°.
14053. e. 25.(2.)

—— *See* ṢAURĪNDRAMOHANA ṬHĀKURA. Śrimad-Victoria-Máhátmyam. The Greatness of the Empress Victoria: a Sanskrit poem, set to music, with an English translation, *etc.* [1898.] 4°.
14076. e. 4.

—— *See* ṢRĪṢVARA VIDYĀLAṄKĀRA BHAṬṬĀCHĀRYA. Vijayiní-kávyam. A Sanskrit epic poem . . . [upon the life and times of Queen Victoria,] *etc.* 1902. 8°. **14058. b. 48.**

—— *See* TRAILOKYAMOHANA GUHA NIYOGĪ. गीतभारतम् . . . Geet Bharatam . . . The Memorial Poem-Temple of Empress Victoria, *etc.* 1902. 8°.
14072. cc. 63.(2.)

—— *See* YĀDAVEṢVARA TARKARATNA. अश्रुबिन्दुकाव्यम् *etc.* [Aṣrubindukāvya. An elegy on the death of Queen Victoria.] 1901. 12°. **14072. b. 25.**

VIÇWAKARMAN. *See* VIṢVAKARMĀ.

VIDARBHARĀJA. *See* BHOJARĀJA.

VIDEHA. *See* VEDEHA THERA.

VIDYĀBHŪSHAṆA. *See* BALADEVA VIDYĀBHŪSHAṆA.

VIDYĀKARA VĀJAPEYĪ, *son of Ṣambhukara.* नित्याचारपद्धतिः । Nityācāra-paddhatiḥ. [A treatise on *smārta* rites] by Vidyākara Vājapeyi. Edited by Paṇḍita Vinoda Vihāri Bhaṭṭācāryya. 1901, *etc.* *See* ACADEMIES, *etc.*—Calcutta.—*Asiatic Society of Bengal.* Bibliotheca Indica. New Series. [Vol. 151.] 1848, *etc.* 8°. **14002. a. (vol. 151.)**
In progress.

VIDYĀNĀTHA, *Courtier of Pratāparudra.* प्रतापरुद्रकल्याणम् । [Pratāparudrakalyāṇa. A historical drama in 5 acts, in glorification of Pratāparudra of Orangal.] pp. 40. [1891.] *See* PERIODICAL PUBLICATIONS.—*Bombay.* ग्रन्थरत्नमाला *etc.* (Granth Ratna Málá, *etc.*) Vol. V, no. 1, 2. 1887-[1892.] 8°. **14096. c. 8.(vol. 5.)**

VIDYĀPATI ṬHĀKURA, *son of Gaṇapati, of Mithila.* *See* DHĪRASIṂHA DEVA. दुर्गाभक्तितरङ्गिणी

[Durgābhaktitaraṅgiṇī. Composed ostensibly by Dhīrasiṃha Deva, with the assistance of Vidyāpati.] [1900.] 8°. **14033. bbb. 7.**

—— শৈবসর্ব্বস্ব-সার etc. [Śaivasarvasvasāra. An anthology of extracts from the Purāṇas and other religious works bearing on the worship of Śiva. Edited with Bengali translations by Bhāgyavān Vidyālaṅkāra.] pp. 162, v. দ্বারভাঙ্গা ১৩০৪ [*Darbhangah*, 1897.] 8°. **14028. d. 57.(2.)**

VIDYĀPRAKĀŚA. *See* VIDYĀTĪRTHA.

VIDYĀRAṆYA. *See* SĀYAṆA ĀCHĀRYA.

VIDYĀSUNDARA. विद्यासुन्दर-चौरपंचाशिका etc. [Vidyāsundara. A romantic poem, in 54 stanzas, treating of the loves of Vidyā and Sundara. Followed by Bilhaṇa's Chaurapañchāśikā. With a Hindi translation of both poems by Mahīdhara Śarmā of Tibari.] 2 pts. pp. ii. 28, 30. बम्बई १९५१ [*Bombay*, 1894.] 12°. **14070. b. 23.**

VIDYĀTĪRTHA, *Svāmī*, known also as VIDYĀPRAKĀŚA. कान्यकुब्जचिन्तामणि etc. [Kānyakubjachintāmaṇi. A series of stanzas bearing on caste duties, rituals, and ethics, with especial reference to Brahmans, and their history in Kanoj. With tables, lists, *etc.*, of the latter's *kulas*, *gotras*, Vedas, Upavedas, *śākhās*, and *sūtras*, and Hindi commentaries, *etc.*] pp. 98. मुंबई १९५६ [*Bombay*, 1899.] 8°. **14058. b. 35.(2.)**

—— महाराष्ट्रकुलवंशावली etc. [Mahārāshṭrakulavaṃśāvalī. An account in 58 stanzas of the Marathi castes and families. With Hindi notes and paraphrase.] pp. 44. कल्याण-मुंबई १९५५ [*Kalyan*, 1898.] 12°. **14058. a. 14.(1.)**

—— विद्यासदुपदेश etc. [Vidyāsadupadeśa. Three series of stanzas on moral and religious topics, with Hindi versions and commentaries.] pp. 132, ii. कल्याण-मुंबई १९५६ [*Kalyan*, 1900.] 8°. **14085. c. 48.**

VIDYĀVINODA ĀCHĀRYA. *See* NĀRĀYAṆA VIDYĀVINODA ĀCHĀRYA.

VIGGYANA BHIKSHU. *See* VIJÑĀNABHIKSHU.

VIGRAHARĀJA, *Vīsaladeva, Chauhan, king of Śākambharī.* The concluding portion of Vigraharâjadêva's Harakêli-nâṭaka. 1891. *See* PERIODICAL PUBLICATIONS.—*Bombay.* The Indian Antiquary, *etc.* Vol. xx., pp. 210-212. 1872, *etc.* 4°. **14096. e. (vol. 20.)**

—— Harakeli-nāṭaka. [Edited by F. Kielhorn.] *See* ACADEMIES, *etc.*— Goettingen. —*Koenigliche Gesellschaft der Wissenschaften.* Festschrift, *etc.* pt. 2, pp. 16-30. 1901. 4°. **Ac. 670.**

—— [For editions of the drama Lalitavigraharājanāṭaka, in honour of Vigraharāja :] *See* SOMADEVA, *Courtier of Vigraharāja Deva.*

VIHĀRILĀLA, *Kāṣmīrī, of Cuttack.* ଆୟୁର୍ବେଦ ପ୍ରବେଶିକା etc. [Āyurvedapraveṣikā. An Oriya manual of medical practice, including an alphabetically arranged Sanskrit account of the pharmacopœia with Oriya translation, styled Aushadha-prastuta-praṇālī.] pp. x. xlvii. 689. *Cuttack*, 1903. 12°. **14121. c. 15.**

—— यजुर्वेदीयनित्यकर्म्मपद्धतिः etc. [Yajurvedīyanityakarmapaddhati. A manual of daily religious duties for Yajurvedīs, compiled from divers sources, and including texts of various hymns, *etc.*] pp. iii. i. ix. 218. कलिकाता १९०० [*Calcutta*, 1900.] 8°. **14033. aa. 16.**

VIHĀRILĀLA ĀCHĀRYA, *Pontiff of the Svāmī-Nārāyaṇī Sect.* *See* BHAGAVATPRASĀDA ĀCHĀRYA. श्रीसारोपदेशः etc. [Sāropadeśa. With Gujarati translation by Vihārilāla.] [1896.] 12°. **14028. b. 83.**

—— *See* PURĀṆAS.—*Bhāgavatapurāṇa.* ॥ श्रीभागवत etc. [Bhāgavatapurāṇa. With commentary of Bhagavatprasāda. Edited with introduction, biography of Sahajānanda, and annotations by Vihārilāla.] [1897.] *obl.* Fol. **14018. cc. 2.**

VIHĀRILĀLA MITRA. *See* YOGAVĀSISHṬHARĀMĀYAṆA. The Yoga-vásishtha-mahárámáyana . . . Translated . . . by Vihári-lála Mitra.. 1891-1899. 8°. **14049. b. 9.**

VIHĀRILĀLA PĀIN. ভবসিন্ধু-তরণী। [Bhavasindhutaraṇī. A Sanskrit and Bengali anthology, chiefly of poems, for the edification of Vaishṇavas, the Sanskrit portion including Puranic extracts, lists of deities' names, hymns, Rūpa

Gosvāmī's Chāṭupushpāñjali and Mukundamuktāvalī, *etc.*] pp. xiii. 342; 2 *plates*. [*Calcutta*, 1902.] 8°. **14033. bbb. 17.**

VIJAYA, *Ū*, *of Ambavana, Dabein.* ဧကာဒသပုစ္ဆာဝိသဇ္ဇနာ *etc.* [Ekādasapuchchhāvisajjanā. Responses to 11 questions on the various manifestations of *karma* in the cycle of being. Followed by Nānāpuchchhāvisajjanā, a series of responses on miscellaneous topics preceded by 19 Pali stanzas. In Burmese, illustrated from Pali texts. Second edition.] pp. iii. 213. ရန်ကုန် ၁၂၆၁ [*Rangoon*, 1899.] 8°. **14300. d. 10.(4.)**

VIJAYA GAṆĪ, *disciple of Rāmavijaya, of the Tapā Gachchha.* *See* KĀLIDĀSA. — *Raghuvaṃṣa.* The Raghuvanśa . . . with full extracts . . . from the commentaries of . . . Vijayagani, *etc.* 1897. 8°. **14072. c. 53.**

VIJAYALAKSHMĪ SŪRI, *Ānanda-Sūri-Gachchhanāyaka.* उपदेशप्रासाद भाषान्तर *etc.* [Upadeṣaprāsāda. A digest of Jain philosophical and religious doctrine, arranged in 12 *sthambhas* for daily reading, and comprising verses, homilies, and stories. Translated into Gujarati, with the verses retained in the original Sanskrit and Prakrit. Edited by Chīmanlāl Sākaḷchand Marphatīyā.] मुंबई १९०२ [*Bombay*, 1902, *etc.*] 8°. **14100. d. 10.**

In progress.

VIJAYĀNANDA SŪRI, also called ĀTMĀRĀMAJĪ. *See* ĀTMĀRĀMAJĪ ĀNANDAVIJAYAJĪ.

VIJAYARAKSHITA, *Vaidya.* *See* MĀDHAVA. सटीक-निदान *etc.* [Nidāna. With the commentary Vyākhyāmadhukoṣa by Vijayarakshita (as far as the end of the Aṣmarī-nidāna), *etc.*] [1901.] 8°. **14043. c. 44.**

VIJAYASIṂHA (LOUIS CORNEILLE). *See* PERIODICAL PUBLICATIONS.—*Colombo.* The Buddhist . . . Edited by C. W. Leadbeater, vol. 1. (By L. C. Wijesinha, vol. 3, 4, no. 1-26.) 1888, *etc.* 8°. **P.P. 636. cn.**

—— *See* SUTTAPIṬAKA.—*Aṅguttaranikāya.* Anguttara-Nikaya. Translated [to the end of I. i.] . . . by L. C. Wijesinha, *etc.* 1891, *etc.* 8°. **P.P. 636. cn. (vol. 3, 8.)**

VIJITĀVI, *Mahāthera.* ဝါစကောပဒေသပါဠိ။ [Vāchakopadesa. A Pali tract on grammar.] *See* SADDĀ-NGAY. သဒ္ဒါငယ် *etc.* [Saddā-ngay.] pp. 124-141. [1898.] 8°. **14098. ccc. 23.(1.)**

A colophon gives the date as Sakk. 967=1605 A.D.

—— —— pp. 126-144. [1899.] 8°. **14098. ccc. 24.(1.)**

—— ဝါစကောပဒေသ *etc.* [Vāchakopadesa. With Burmese version.] [1899.] *See* SADDĀ-NGAY. သဒ္ဒါငယ် *etc.* [Saddā-ngay.] Vol. iv., pp. 161-231. [1898-1900.] 8°. **14098. ccc. 22.**

VIJÑĀNABHIKSHU. *See* BĀDARĀYAṆA. ब्रह्मसूत्रभाष्यम् *etc.* (Brahma Sutra. With its commentary Viggyanamrita by Sri Viggyana Bhikshu, *etc.*) 1901. 8°. **14004. a. 8.**

—— *See* KAPILA. The Sāṃkhya-pravacana-bhāṣya . . . by Vijñānabhikṣu, *etc.* 1895. 8°. [*Harvard Oriental Series.*] **14003. l. 3.(vol. 2.)**

—— An English Translation, with Sanskrit Text [edited by Vindhyeṣvarīprasāda Dube,] of the Yogasara-sangraha . . . Translated by Ganĝânâtha Jha. (योगसारसंग्रहः ।) 2 pts. *Bombay*, 1894. 12°. **14048. b. 26.**

VIJÑĀNEṢVARA. *See* ĀDINĀRĀYAṆA PĀTRO. The Hindu Law. Annotated and illustrated by Sanskrit texts[, viz. the writings of Vijñāneṣvara and others,] *etc.* 1899. 8°. **14039. c. 17.**

—— *See* YĀJÑAVALKYA. [*Dharmaṣāstra.*] மிதாக்ஷரா ॥ [Yājñavalkyasmṛiti. With Vijñāneṣvara's Mitākusharā.] 1901, *etc.* 4°. [*Brahmavidyā.*] **14096. dd. 3.(vol. 15, etc.)**

—— *See* YĀJÑAVALKYA. [*Dharmaṣāstra.*] Mitákshará. Vyávahára Adhyáy, Part III. [Being Yājñavalkyasmṛiti II. 150 *sqq.* to the end, with the Mitākusharā.] Translated, *etc.* 1892. 8°. **14038. d. 35.**

VIKHANAS. *See* MARĪCHI. అథమరీచిపటలే జ్ఞానకాణ్డప్రారమ్భః [Jñānakāṇḍa of the Vaikhānasa, an exposition of Viṣishṭādvaita theosophy ascribed in its principles to Vikhanas.]

1896. 8°. [*Brahmasūtra: Lakshmīviṣishṭādvaita-bhāshya.*] **14048. dd. 29.(2.)**

—— *See* MARĪCHI. ஜயமரீசிப்ரோக்த ஜ்ஞாநகாண்ட ॥ [Jñānakāṇḍa.] 1896. 8°. [*Brahmasūtra: Lakshmīviṣishṭādvaitabhāshya.*] **14048. dd. 29.(1.)**

—— *See* BLOCH (T.). Über das Gṛhya- und Dharmasūtra der Vaikhānasa. 1896. 8°. **14028. d. 53.**

—— *See* VĀSUDEVA BHAṬṬĀCHĀRYA. ஆஹ்நிகாம்ருதம் [Āhnikāmṛita. A treatise on the daily ritual of Vaishṇavas, based upon the Vaikhānasasūtra, *etc.*] 1900. 8°. [*Pāramātmikopanishad.*] **14033. bbb. 13.**

—— ஶ்ரீவைகாநஸஸூத்ரப்ரயோகே ப்ரயோகஸம்புடிகா *etc.* [Vaikhānasasūtraprayoga. The Gṛihyasūtra of the Vaikhānasas, with commentary. First *sampuṭikā*. Edited by Nārāyaṇa Bhaṭṭāchārya and Rāmakṛishṇa Bhaṭṭāchārya.] pp. iv. 98. நடுக்காவேரி ஹேமலம்ப [*Nadukkaveri*, 1897.] 12°. **14028. b. 86.**

VIKRAMA, *son of Sāṅgaṇa.* नेमिदूतकाव्य *etc.* [Nemidūta, or Nemicharita. A Jain poem of 126 stanzas on the story of Nemi, containing a line of Kālidāsa's Meghadūta interwoven in every stanza. With a Marathi translation by Kṛishṇājī Nārāyaṇa Joṣī.] pp. i. 64. मुंबई १८९२ [*Bombay*, 1892.] 12°. **14028. b. 69.(3.)**

VIKRAMĀRKACHARITA. দ্বাত্রিংশৎ পুত্তলিকা। [Dvātriṃṣat-puttalikā, or Vikramārkacharita. With Bengali translation.] *See* KĀLIDĀSA.—*Collected Works.* মহাকবি কালিদাসের গ্রন্থাবলী *etc.* [Granthāvalī.] [Vol. 2.] pp. 965-1225. [1895.] 8°. **14070. d. 34.(vol. 2.)**

The text follows the recension of the Calcutta edition of 1881.

—— ବତିଶସିଂହାସନ *etc.* [Batriṣ Siṃhāsana. An Oriya version by Sarveṣvara Āchārya of the Vikramārkacharita, with the original Sanskrit stanzas.] pp. 145. *Cuttack*, 1900. 12°. **14121. f. 19.(4.)**

VIKRAMASIṂHA (A. J.). *See* VARĀHAMIHIRA. බෘහජ්ජාතකය *etc.* (Brihatjataka . . . Translated into Sinhalese by A. J. Wikkramasinha.) 1896. 8°. **14053. ccc. 3.(1.)**

VIKRAMASIṂHA (*Don* MARTINO DE ZILVA). Catalogue of the late Professor Fr. Max Müller's Sanskrit Manuscripts. Compiled by Don M. de Z. Wickremasinghe. 1902. *See* ACADEMIES, *etc.*—London.—*Royal Asiatic Society of Great Britain and Ireland.* The Journal . . . 1902. pp. 611-651. 1834, *etc.* 8°. **Ac. 8820/3 & 2098. a, b.**

VIMA BHŪPĀLA. *See* VEMA BHŪPĀLA.

VIMALABUDDHI. *See* PAṆḌITADDHAJA SĪLĀLAṄKĀRA. သဒ္ဒါပုဒ်စိတ်၊အကျယ် *etc.* [Saddā-pôk-sit-akyay. A Burmese supercommentary on Kachchāyana, based upon Ñāṇābhidhammālaṅkāra's commentary on the Mukhamattadīpanī.] [1896.] 8°. **14302. i. 15.**

—— ညာသ်အရကောက် [Nyāt-aya-kauk. Being the introductory stanzas of the commentary, styled Nyāsa or Mukhamattadīpanī, upon Kachchāyana's grammar, with a copious Burmese commentary.] *See* TISSA, *Ū*, and JANINDA, *Ū*. သမူဟနိယမဒီပနီကျမ်း *etc.* [Samūhaniyamadīpanī.] pp. 696-794. [1898.] 8°. **14302. i. 17.**

VIMALACHANDRA SŪRI. Una Redazione Pracrita della Praçnottarararatnamālā. [Edited with translation by P. E. Pavolini.] 1897-1898. *See* ACADEMIES, *etc.* — Florence. — *Società Asiatica Italiana.* Giornale, *etc.* Vol. xi., pp. 153-163. 1887, *etc.* 8°. **Ac. 8804. (vol. 11.)**

VIMALĀCHĀRA, *Mahāthera.* ကထိနဒီပနီပါဠိ (နိဿယ) [Kaṭhinadīpanī. A collection of Pali texts referring to the *kaṭhina* robes of Buddhist friars, followed by a Burmese *nissaya.*] *See* VINAYAPIṬAKA.—*Appendix.* ဝိနယသမူဟဝိနိစ္ဆယကျမ်း *etc.* [Vinayasamūhavinichchhaya-kyan.] Vol. I, pp. 327-376. 1899, *etc.* 8°. **14300. e. 15.**

VIMALADĀSA, *disciple of Anantasena Devasvāmī, of Vīragrāma.* Saptha Bhangee Tharangini. [A treatise on the sevenfold *syādvāda* of the Jain logic] by Vimala Dasa, *etc.* (सप्तभङ्गी तरङ्गिणी ।) pp. i. 52. 1901. *See* ANANTĀCHĀRYA, *Prativādibhayaṅkara.* शास्त्रमुक्तावली The Sasthramukthāvalī, *etc.* No. 8. 1899, *etc.* 8°. **14049. a. 1.(no. 8.)**

VIMALĀLAṄKĀRA KAVIDDHAJA, called MAUNG-DAUNG HSAYA. *See* JAYAMAṄGALAGĀTHĀ. ပြင်-အောင်ခြင်းရှစ်ပါးနိဿျ *etc.* [Apyin-aung-hkyin. With Burmese version by Vimalālaṅkāra. Followed by the Madhurovādakathā, a Burmese homily by the same.] 1893. 8°. **14098. ccc. 26.(2.)**

—— *See* KACHCHĀYANA.—*Kachchāyanappakaraṇa.* သဒ္ဒါရှစ်စောင်သုတ်နက် [Saddā-shit-saung-thôk-net. Edited by Vimalālaṅkāra.] [1897.] 8°. **14098. ccc. 12.(2.)**

—— —— [Third edition.] [1899.] 8°. **14098. ccc. 12.(3.)**

VIMĀNAVATTHU. *See* SUTTAPIṬAKA.—*Khuddakanikāya.*

VINANDĀSABHA, *of Mangyichaung.* သီလဝိ-သောဓနီကျမ်း။ . . . ကာယဝိစ္ဆိန္ဒနိကသုတ်။ [Sīlavisodhanī. A Burmese treatise by Vinandāsabha on the moral duties of Buddhism. Followed by the Kāyavichchhindanikasutta or Vijayasutta and the Anamataggasutta, both with Burmese interpretations by Chakkindābhisiri.] pp. ii. 277. ရန်ကုန် ၁၂၆၆ [*Rangoon*, 1905.] 8°. **14099. b. 5.**

VINĀYAKA NĀRĀYAṆA JYOTIRVID, *Bhaṭṭa.* समासकुसुमावलिः *etc.* [Samāsakusumāvali. A treatise on Sanskrit compound words, in the form of verses with a commentary.] pp. iv. ii. 26. मोहमय्याम् १८९० [*Bombay*, 1890.] 12°. **14090. b. 38.(3.)**

VINĀYAKA SADĀSIVA PAṬAVARDHANA. *See* BHAVABHŪTI. The Uttara Rama Charita . . . with . . . English translation . . . notes . . . vocabulary . . . and an introduction by Vinayak . . . Patvardhan. 1895. 8°. **14080. d. 25.**

VINAYAPIṬAKA. วินยปิฏก *etc.* [Vinayapiṭaka.] 8 vols. ๑๑๒ [*Bangkok*, 1894.] 8°. **14098. cc. 1-8.**

Forms part of the King of Siam's edition of the Tipiṭaka.

—— ဝိနည်းပိဋကတ်။ . . . ဝိနည်းမဟာဝါပါဠိတော်နိဿျသစ်။ *etc.* (ပါရာဇိကက်ပါဠိတော်နိဿျသစ်၊ ပါစိတ်ပါဠိတော်နိဿျသစ်၊ စူဠဝါပါဠိတော်နိဿျသစ်။, *etc.*) [Vinayapiṭaka. The text with Burmese word-for-word interpretation. Vol. i., ii., the Mahāvagga, with interpretation by Sāgaraddhaja; vol. iii., the Pārājika, and vol. iv., the Pāchittiya, with interpretation by Jāgarābhiddhaja; vol. v., vi., the Chullavagga, with interpretation by Sudassana Varadhammasāmi; vol. vii., the Parivāra, with interpretation by Paññāsīha Sāsanālaṅkāra. Edited by Hsaya Hbi, Hsaya Ko Aung Min, and Hsaya Ko Kyaw̱.] 7 vols. ရန်ကုန် [*Rangoon*,] 1903-1904. 8°. **14099. aa. 1-7.**

—— [*Selections.*] *See* WARREN (H. C.). Buddhism in Translations. [Being select passages translated from the Vinayapiṭaka,] *etc.* 1896. 8°. [*Harvard Oriental Series.*] **14003. l. 3.(vol. 3.)**

—— —— ဝိနည်းတရားတော်ကား၊ . . . ကမ္မာ-ကမ္မဝိနိစ္ဆယ။ပါတိမောက္ခုဒ္ဒေသ။တို့နှင့်တကွ။ ဒွေမာတိကာပါဠိတော်။ [Dvemātikā. Being (1) the Bhikkhupāṭimokkha and Bhikkhunīpāṭimokkha; (2) Kammākammavinichchhaya, extracts from the Parivāra XV. i. 1-3, XIX. i. 8-12, VII. i., and other Vinaya texts; and (3) Pāṭimokkhuddesa, Burmese notes on the Pāṭimokkha. Edited by Hsaya Ū Hpy̱e.] pp. 64. ရန်ကုန် ၁၂၆၆ [*Rangoon*, 1904.] 8°. **14099. b. 3.**

—— [*Chullavagga.*] သင်္ဂါယနာတင်ဝိနည်းကျမ်း *etc.* [Saṅgāyanā-tin-wini-kyan. A recital of various ecclesiastical topics of the Dhamma, in catechetic form, derived from the Chullavagga XI, and furnished with a Burmese translation by Hpo Yan. Preceded by the Gôṇ-taw̱-hpwin, or Virtues of the Buddha, Dhamma, and Saṅgha, with Burmese version and commentary by the same.] pp. 70. ရန်ကုန် ၁၂၆၁ [*Rangoon*, 1900.] 8°. **14098. ccc. 26.(8.)**

—— [*Mahāvagga.*] အာဒိတ္တပရိယာယသုတ်။ ဒွတ္တိံသကာယကမ္မဋ္ဌာန်း *etc.* [Ādittapariyāyasutta (Mahāvagga I. xxi.). With Burmese translation by Ū Sāgara. Followed by the Dvattiṃsakāyakammaṭṭhāna, a manual for the practice of *kammaṭṭhānas* by reflection upon the 32 *ākāras*, in Pali and Burmese, compiled by Sāgara.] pp. 39. ပန္တလေး [*Mandalay*,] 1898. 8°. **14098. ccc. 26.(6.)**

—— —— පටිච්චසමුප්පාදය *etc.* [Paṭichcha-samuppādaya. A treatise on the Buddhist doctrine of causation. Comprising the Bodhikathā (*i.e.* Mahāvagga I. i.) with explanatory matter in Sinhalese and illustrations from other canonical writings. Edited by W. A. De Silva.] pp. ii. 70, ii. [*Colombo*,] 1895. 12°. **14098. b. 21.(2.)**

—— —— Patichcha Samuppadaya, *etc.* [Edited by M. Dharmaratna.] pp. ii. 61; 1 *plate*. කොළඹ 2439 [*Colombo*, 1896.] 8°. **14098. d. 45.(4.)**

—— [*Pāṭimokkha.*] ဘိက္ခုပါတိမောက် (ဘိက္ခုနီပါတိမောက်) [Bhikkhupāṭimokkha and Bhikkhunīpāṭimokkha.] *See* WINI-NGAY. ဝိနည်းငယ် လေးစောင် *etc.* [Wini-ngay le saung.] pp. 1-72. [1898.] 8°. **14098. ccc. 9.(4.)**

—— —— ဘိက္ခုပါတိမောက် *etc.* (ဘိက္ခုနီပါတိမောက်) [Bhikkhupāṭimokkha and Bhikkhunīpāṭimokkha.] *See* WINI-NGAY. ဝိနည်းငယ် *etc.* [Wini-ngay le saung.] pp. 1-75. 1903. 8°. **14099. bb. 1.**

—— —— ဘိက္ခုပါတိမောက် *etc.* [Bhikkhupāṭimokkha and Bhikkhunīp°.] *See* above, [*Selections.*] ဝိနည်း ... ဒွေမာတိကာ *etc.* [Dvemātikā.] pp. 1-46. [1904.] 8°. **14099. b. 3.**

—— [*Suttavibhaṅga.*] *See* BUDDHAGHOSA. [*Samantapāsādikā.*] ဘိက္ခုဝိဘင် ... အဋ္ဌကထာ *etc.* [The commentary upon Part 1 of the Suttavibhaṅga, viz. the Pārājika, Saṅghādisesa, Aniyata, and Nissaggiya-pāchittiya.] [1902.] 8°. **14099. aaa. 1.**

—— —— *See* SATARA-PĀRĀJIKĀ-VINIṢCHAYA. සතරපාරාජිකා විනිශ්චය *etc.* [Satara-pārājikā-viniṣchaya. A compilation on the four *pārājikā*, *etc.*] 1897. 8°. **14098. ccc. 3.(1.)**

Appendix.

—— *See* PAṆḌITADDHAJA, known as MAINGKAING HSAYA. တိပိဋကဝိနိစ္ဆယကျမ်း *etc.* [Tipiṭaka-vinichchhaya-kyan.] 1900-1901. 8°. **14302. i. 19.**

—— —— ဝိနယသမူဟဝိနိစ္ဆယကျမ်း *etc.* [Vinayasamūhavinichchhaya-kyan. A collection of treatises upon points of clerical discipline, some in Burmese with illustrative Pali texts, others compiled or composed wholly in Pali. Vol. I, second edition; Vol. II, III, first edition.] ပန္တလေး [*Mandalay*,] 1899, *etc.* 8°. **14300. e. 15.**

In progress. The editor, according to the official List of Books Registered (2nd quarter, 1900), is Ū Nirodha.

The most important Pali works in this collection are to be found under the following headings:—

Vol. I. Paññālaṅkāra.
Vimalāchāra.
Sumaṅgalasāmi.
Kammavāchā.
Vol. II. Suttapiṭaka.

VINAYAVIJAYA GAṆĪ, *disciple of Kīrtivijaya.* *See* HEMACHANDRA, *disciple of Devachandra.* हैमलघुप्रक्रिया° [Haima-laghuprakriyā. An abridgment and rearrangement of the aphorisms of Hemachandra's Śabdānuṣāsana, with commentary, by Vinayavijaya.] [1892.] 12°. **14090. b. 40.**

VINDHYEṢVARĪPRASĀDA DUBE. *See* PRAṢASTAPĀDA. The Bhâshya of Praśastapâda, together with the Nyâyakandalî of Śrîdhara. Edited by Vindhyeśvarîprasâda Dvivedin. 1895. 8°. **14048. dd. 3.(vol. 4.)**

—— *See* UDAYANA ĀCHĀRYA. लक्षणावली *etc.* [Lakshaṇāvalī. Edited by Vindhyeṣvarīprasāda.] 1897. 8°. **14048. bb. 20.(2.)**

—— *See* VARADARĀJA, *Logician.* तार्किकरक्षा *etc.* (The Tārkikarakṣā and Sārasaṃgraha . . . With the glosses . . . of Mallinatha . . . and . . . Jñānapūrṇa.) [Edited by Vindhyeṣvarīprasāda.] 1903. 8°. [*The Pandit.*] **14096. d. 6. (vol. 21-25.)**

—— *See* VIJÑĀNABHIKSHU. An English Translation, with Sanskrit Text [edited by Vindhyeṣvarīprasāda,] of the Yogasara-sangraha, *etc.* 1894. 12°. **14048. b. 26.**

VINDHYEṢVARĪRĀYA ṢARMĀ. *See* Bhartṛihari. An English translation of Bhartrihari's Niti-Shataka, by Vindhyeshwari Roy Sharma. 1897. 8°. **14076. b. 36.(1.)**

VINODALĀLA SENA GUPTA. *See* Bharatasena, *son of Gaurāṅga Mallika.* চন্দ্রপ্রভা *etc.* [Chandraprabhā. Edited by Vinodalāla Sena Gupta.] [1893.] 8°. **14058. b. 29.**

—— *See* Bharatasena, *son of Gaurāṅga Mallika.* রত্নপ্রভা *etc.* [Ratnaprabhā. Edited by Vinodalāla Sena.] [1892.] 8°. **14058. b. 34.**

—— *See* Pāṇini.—*Siddhāntakaumudī.* সিদ্ধান্তকৌমুদী . . . Siddhanta Kaumudi . . . With . . . the "Tattwabodhini" . . . And with a Bengali translation. Edited . . . by Kaviraj Binod Lal Sen. [1890-1892.] 8°. **14090. d. 29.**

—— *See* Udayachandra Datta. The Materia Medica of the Hindus . . . With additions and alterations by Kaviraj Binod Lall Sen, *etc.* 1900. 8°. **14043. c. 48.**

VINODAVIHĀRĪ BHAṬṬĀCHĀRYA. *See* Vidyākara Vājapeyī. नित्याचारपद्धतिः। Nityācāra Paddhatiḥ . . . Edited by . . . Vinoda Vihāri Bhaṭṭācāryya. 1901, *etc.* 8°. [*Bibliotheca Indica.*] **14002. a.(vol. 151.)**

VIPINACHANDRA KĀVYARATNA. আর্য্যাহ্নিকাচার কৌমুদী *etc.* [Āryāhnikāchārakaumudī. An anthological treatise, in Sanskrit and Bengali, upon the daily religious observances of the Hindus. New edition.] pp. xii. ii. iv. 131. কলিকাতা [*Calcutta,* 1901.] 8°. **14123. f. 49.(3.)**

VIPINAVIHĀRĪ GHOSHĀL. মুক্তি এবং তাহার সাধন *etc.* [Mukti evaṃ tāhār sādhana. A Bengali treatise on salvation and the means to its attainment, regarded from a liberal standpoint. Copiously illustrated from Sanskrit texts on religious, philosophical, mystic, and legal subjects. Third edition.] pp. vi. 224. কলিকাতা ১৯০১ [*Calcutta,* 1901.] 8°. **14123. f. 57.**

VIPINAVIHĀRĪ VANDYOPĀDHYĀYA and KULACHANDRA DE DĀSA. হুঁকাপুরাণ মাহাত্ম্য *etc.* [Huṇkāpurāṇamāhātmya. A burlesque of the Paurāṇik style, in six cantos, on *hukā*-smoking. With a Bengali translation.] pp. 11. কলিকাতা ১২৯৮ [*Calcutta,* 1892.] 8°. **14072. b. 21.**

VIPRARĀJENDRA, *son of Manyudatta.* *See* Jayarāma, *disciple of Viprarājendra.* श्रीविप्रराजेन्द्रदिग्विजयः *etc.* [Viprarājendradigvijaya. A poetical account of the successes of Viprarājendra as a teacher.] [1891.] 8°. **14048. dd. 5.(1.)**

—— शब्दामृतसूचीपत्रम् *etc.* [Ṣabdāmṛita-sūchīpatra. A key to the Ṣabdāmṛita. With two commentaries entitled Tattvārthadīpikā and Vyākritāṅkura, both by the same author.] pp. 124. काश्यां १९४७ [*Benares,* 1890.] 8°. **14092. b. 41.**

—— षड्दर्शन *etc.* [Shaḍdarṣana. A metrical review of the chief systems of philosophy, in six chapters, with commentaries and notes by the author.] pp. 97. काश्यां १९४७ [*Benares,* 1890.] 8°. **14048. dd. 5.(2.)**

—— त्रिमणिदीपकम् *etc.* [Trimaṇidīpaka. A rhetorical exposition of the religious and secular objects of life, in three cantos. With a prose commentary called Trimaṇivivṛiti by the author.] pp. 40. काश्यां १९४६ [*Benares,* 1890.] 12°. **14076. b. 25.(2.)**

—— वर्णाश्रमधर्मनिर्णयः [Varṇāṣramadharmanirṇaya. A work in 127 stanzas upon caste-duties. With a commentary called Dharmatattvaikanirṇaya by the author.] pp. 44. काश्यां [*Benares,* 1891.] 8°. **14038. c. 43.(3.)**

VĪRABHADRA, *disciple of the Tīrthaṅkara Mahāvīra.* [For the Païnnas ascribed to this saint :] *See* Prakīrṇaka.

VĪRANANDĪ, *son of Abhayanandī.* The Chandraprabhacharita of Vîranandî. [A Jain poetical romance in 19 *sargas.*] Edited by . . . Paṇdit Durgâprasâd and Kâsînâth Pâṇdurang Parab. (चन्द्रप्रभचरितम्।) pp. iv. 153, i. 1892. *See* Durgāprasāda, *son of Vrajalāla,* and Kāṣīnātha Pāṇḍuraṅga Parab. Kâvyamâlâ. [No.] 30. 1886, *etc.* 8°. **14072. ccc. 12.(no. 30.)**

VĪRANĀRĀYAṆA PEDDAKOMAṬI. *See* VEMA BHŪPĀLA.

VĪRARĀGHAVA, *Vādhūla*, called AṆṆĀPPAṄGĀR. *See* BHAVABHŪTI. The Mahâvîracharita . . . With the commentary [Bhāvapradyotinī] of Vîrarâghava, *etc.* 1892. 8°. **14080. c. 32.**

—— *See* BHAVABHŪTI. ఉత్తరరామచరిత॥ [Uttararāmacharita. With a commentary called Talasparṣinī by Vīrarāghava.] 1891. 8°. **14080. d. 21.**

—— *See* BHAVABHŪTI. ఉత్తరరామచరిత॥ [Uttararāmacharita. With commentary of Vīrarāghava.] [1892.] 8°. **14080. d. 23.**

—— *See* BHAVABHŪTI. The Uttara-Râmacharita . . . With the commentary of Vîrarâghava, *etc.* 1899. 8°. **14080. c. 40.**

VĪRARĀGHAVA TĀTĀCHĀRYA, *of Conjevaram.* శ్రీరామచంద్రోదయః [Rāmachandrodaya. A treatise on the religious, historical, and other aspects of the Rāmāyaṇa.] pt. i. pp. 32. చెన్నపురి ౧౮౯౧ [*Madras*, 1891.] 8°. **14072. ccc. 32.**
Apparently no more published. The work is posthumous.

VĪRARĀGHAVA TĀTĀCHĀRYA, *Koṭikannikādānam.* *See* VARADĀCHĀRYA, *son of Ghaṭikāṣata Sudarṣanāchārya.* யதிராஜவிஜய ॥ [Yatirājavijaya. Edited by Tātāchārya.] [1902.] 8°. **14080. d. 22.(3.)**

VĪRAṢAIVA. ಸಟೀಕ ವೀರಶೈವ ದೀಕ್ಷಾವಿಧಿಯು [Vīraṣaivadīkshāvidhi. A manual of the initiatory rites of the Vīraṣaivas. Edited, with Canarese commentary, by Karibasava Ṣāstri.] pp. iii. vii. 84. *Mysore*, 1897. 8°. **14028. d. 64.**

—— ವೀರಶೈವಕಂಠಾಭರಣನಾಮಕೋಯಂ ಗ್ರಂಥಃ [Vīraṣaivakaṇṭhābharaṇa. Litanies of the Vīraṣaiva sect.] pp. 42. ಮೈಸೂರು ನಂದನ॥ [*Mysore*, 1892.] *obl.* 8°. **14028. d. 59.(3.)**

VĪRAVIJAYA. સ્નાત્ર પૂજા *etc.* [Snātrapūjā. A Jain ritual for bathing the images of the *tīrthaṅkaras*, with hymns in Prakrit and Gujarati.] pp. 32. અમદાવાદ ૧૮૯૭-૯૮ [*Ahmadabad*, 1897-1898.] 12°. **14144. c. 8.(3.)**

VĪREṢANĀTHA KĀVYATĪRTHA. *See* PURĀṆAS.—*Padmapurāṇa.* পদ্মপুরাণম্ *etc.* [Pātālakhaṇḍa. With Bengali translation by Vīreṣanātha and others.] [1903.] 8°. **14018. b. 20.**

—— ব্রতমালা-বিধান। [Vratamālāvidhāna. A treatise upon the observance of Hindu festivals. Compiled from Sanskrit texts, with Bengali explanations, rubrics, *etc.*] pp. iii. v. 532. কলিকাতা ১৩১০ [*Calcutta*, 1903.] 12°. **14033. a. 55.**

VĪREṢVARA KĀVYATĪRTHA. *See* VĪREṢANĀTHA KĀVYATĪRTHA.

VĪREṢVARA ṢĀSTRĪ, *Ārādhya*, styled HUCHCHAVĪRA ṢĀSTRĪ. ವೀರಶೈವಾನ್ವಯಚಂದ್ರಿಕಾ. [Vīraṣaivānvayachandrikā. A metrical account, in 5 chapters, of the origins of the Vīraṣaiva sect and their cult and doctrines, compiled from legendary and devotional literature. With Canarese translation.] pp. v. 181. ಬೆಂಗಳೂರು ೧೮೯೦ [*Bangalore*, 1890.] 8°. **14028. d. 41.**

—— [Another edition.] ಬೆಂಗಳೂರು ೧೮೯೧ [*Bangalore*, 1891.] 8°. **14028. d. 40.**

VĪREṢVARA ṬHAKKURA, *son of Devāditya.* छन्दोगानांविवाहादिसंस्कारपद्धतिः . . . वाजसनेयिनांविवाहादिसंस्कारपद्धतिश्च *etc.* [Chhandogānāṃ Vivāhādi-saṃskārapaddhati. A treatise on the lustrations of marriage *etc.* for Sāmavedīs, by Vīreṣvara. Followed by Vājasaneyināṃ Vivāhādi-saṃskārapaddhati, a like work for Vājasaneyīs, by Rāmadatta Ṭhakkura. Edited with notes by Parameṣvara Jhā.] pp. vi. 156, 104. दरभंगा १८२४ [*Darbhangah*, 1902.] *obl.* 4°. **14033. c. 31.(3.)**

VIṢĀKHADATTA. *See* AḶASIṄGALA ĀCHĀRYA. ಚಾಣಿಕ್ಯ ತಂತ್ರ ಚಮತ್ಕಾರ *etc.* (Chanikya Tantra Chamatcara, *etc.*) [A summary of the Mudrārākshasa.] 1880. 16°. **14076. a. 21.**

VĪSALADEVA VIGRAHARĀJA. *See* VIGRAHARĀJA.

VIṢESHĀRTHAPRAKĀṢIKĀ. విశేషార్థప్రకాశిక [Viṣeshārthaprakāṣikā. A treatise expounding the creed of the Ṣaiva Siddhānta according to the Vīraṣaivas. Adhikaraṇas 1-5.] *See* ṢIVĀDVAITAPAÑCHAKA. శివాద్వైతపంచక *etc.* [Ṣivādvaitapañchaka.] pp. 69-98. [1897.] 8°. **14048. cc. 8.(4.)**

VISHṆU, *Āchāryabhakta.* See VISHṆU VĀMANA BĀPAṬ.

VISHṆUDATTA, *Vaidika, son of Dunichandra, of Kapurthala.* See RĀMAKṚISHṆA, *Daivajña.* प्रश्नचण्डेश्वरः *etc.* [Prasnachaṇḍesvara. With a commentary styled Vishṇupadī and Hindi paraphrase by Vishṇudatta.] [1894.] 8°. **14053. d. 51.**

—— See VIVĀHAPADDHATI. वैवर्त्तिकानां नवरत्नविवाहपद्धतिः *etc.* [Navaratna-vivāhapaddhati. Edited with commentary in Hindi and appendices by Vishṇudatta.] [1892.] 8°. **14033. b. 59.**

—— जादूविद्यासंग्रह भाषा टीका. Jadu Vidya Sangraha. [A compendium of magic, with a Hindi translation.] By P. Bishnu Datt Vaidik, *etc.* Second edition. pp. iv. 208. कपूरथला १८५५ [*Kapurthala*, 1898.] 8°. **14053. ccc. 19.**

VISHṆU LAKSHMAṆA ṢĀSTRĪ PUROHITA. See PURĀṆAS. — *Devībhāgavatapurāṇa.* श्रीदेवीभागवत. [Devībhāgavata. Skandhas i.-iii., edited with Marathi translation by Vishṇu Purohita.] [1902, *etc.*] 8°. **14016. dd. 8.**

VISHṆUPADA MUKHOPĀDHYĀYA. See AMARASIṂHA. পাণ্ডিত্যম্ *etc.* (Panditya. The Imperial Lexicon . . . based on Amarkosh. Edited . . . by Bishnupada Mukhopadhyaya.) 1894. 8°. **14093. b. 37.**

VISHṆUPADA ṢARMĀ. See NANDAGOPĀLA VANDYOPĀDHYĀYA.

VISHṆUPURĪ, *of Tirhut.* See PURĀṆAS.—*Bhāgavatapurāṇa.* ଭକ୍ତିରତ୍ନାବଳୀ *etc.* [Bhaktiratnāvalī. An anthology of verses from the Bhāgavata, arranged in 13 *virachanas* by Vishṇupurī.] 1900. 12°. **14016. b. 27.**

VISHṆUSTAVAMAÑJARI. വിഷ്ണുസ്തവമഞ്ജരി *etc.* [Vishṇustavamañjari. Nine Vaishṇava hymns, including the Bhajagovinda ascribed to Ṣaṅkara Āchārya.] pp. 16. തങ്കച്ചേരി ൧൦൭൭ [*Tangacheri*, 1902.] 12°. **14028. b. 73.(7.)**

VISHṆU VĀMANA BĀPAṬ, calling himself ĀCHĀRYABHAKTA VISHṆU. See ṢAṄKARA ĀCHĀRYA. —*Philosophical Poems, etc.* श्री . . . अपरोक्षानुभूतिः *etc.* [Aparokshānubhūti. Edited with Marathi translation and commentary by Vishṇu Bāpaṭ.] [1903.] 12°. **14048. b. 44.**

—— See SĀYAṆA ĀCHĀRYA.—*Works on Philosophy, etc.* श्री . . . पंचदशी *etc.* [Pañchadaṣī. Edited with Marathi translation and commentary by Vishṇu Bāpaṭ.] [1904, *etc.*] 12°. **14048. b. 46.**

VISHWANÁTH. See VIṢVANĀTHA.

VISUDDHĀCHĀRA THERA, *of Visuddhārāma.* ဆန္ဒောမဉ္ဇရီပါဌ် [Chhandomañjarī. A Pali treatise in 6 *parichchhedas* on metre. Followed by a *nissaya* and *alaṅkāra* on the same, in Burmese.] See SADDHAMMASIRI. သဒ္ဒတ္ထဘေဒစိန္တာ *etc.* [Saddatthabhedachintā.] pp. 209-261. [1897.] 8°. **14098. ccc. 17.(2.)**

—— ဆိဒ္ဒပိဓါနနီကျမ်း *etc.* [Chhiddapidhānanī. A series of Burmese homilies on ethical and metaphysical topics, illustrated from Pali texts.] မန္တလေး ၁၂၆၁ [*Mandalay*, 1899, *etc.*] 8°. **14300. d. 29.**

In progress.

—— ဒါဌာဓါတုဝင်ဂါထာချီးဘုရားရှိခိုး [Dāṭhādhātu-win-gāthā-hkyī-payā-shi-hko. A series of Pali stanzas in adoration of the Buddha, based on the legend of the Dāṭhāvaṃsa, with a Burmese version.] See JĀGARĀBHIDHAJA. ဝိစိတြဝန္ဒနာဘုရားရှိခိုး *etc.* [Vichitravandanā.] pp. 62-96. 1900. 8°. **14098. ccc. 26.(7.)**

—— —— pp. 60-93. [1900.] 8°. **14098. ccc. 21.(2.)**

—— ဓါတွတ္ထသင်္ဂြိုဟ် *etc.* [Dhātvatthasaṅgaha. A metrical vocabulary of Pali roots, with Burmese version. Followed by two Burmese dissertations by the same writer, viz. Kachchāyanappaṇāmakauk, on the introductory stanzas of Kachchāyana's grammar, and Nettibāratthadīpanī-thit, a commentary upon the Nettippakaraṇa; and lastly, by a Burmese work styled Saṅkhepa-that-pôn or That-pôn-thit, on Burmese stylistic.] pp. i. 371, iii. မန္တလေး [*Mandalay*,] 1896. 8°. **14098. ccc. 18.**

VISUDDHĀCHĀRA THERA, *of Visuddhārāma* (*continued*). ධාතුවත්ථසංගහය *etc.* [Dhātvatthasaṅgaha. Edited by Yālagama Dhammālaṅkāra.] pp. ii. 80. කොළඹ [*Colombo*,] 1897. 8°. **14098. a. 31.**

—— ဓါတွတ္ထသင်္ဂြိုဟ်ပါဠိနိဿယ *etc.* [Dhātvatthasaṅgaha. With Burmese translation by the author.] pp. 232. မန္တလေး [*Mandalay*, 1901.] 8°. **14098. ccc. 38.**

—— ဝိသိဋ္ဌဝန္ဒနာဘုရားရှိခိုး [Visiṭṭhavandanā-payā-shi-hko. Devotional stanzas in Pali, with Burmese commentary.] *See* JĀGARĀBHIDDHAJA. ဝိစိတြဝန္ဒနာဘုရားရှိခိုး *etc.* [Vichitravandanā.] pp. 97-117. 1900. 8°. **14098. ccc. 26.(7.)**

—— —— pp. 93-97. 1900. 8°. **14098. ccc. 21.(2.)**

VIṢUDDHĀNANDA SARASVATĪ. यतीन्द्रविशुद्धानन्दोक्ति प्रकाशः *etc.* [Yatīndra-Viṣuddhānandoktiprakāṣa. Thirty-three dicta by Viṣuddhānanda on points mainly concerning the Yoga philosophy. Compiled and furnished with a commentary by Gaurīnātha Ṣarmā. Edited by Vāṇīṣa Jhā Kāvyatīrtha.] pp. 56, i. वाराणस्यां १९४८ [*Benares*, 1891.] 8°. **14048. dd. 9.**

VISUDDHĀRĀMĀCHARIYA. *See* VISUDDHĀCHĀRA THERA.

VIṢVA ĀCHĀRYA. *End.* इति ... पञ्चधाटी स्तोत्रं *etc.* [Pañchadhāṭīstotra. A Vaishṇava hymn of 7 verses.] *See* MAṄGALADĀSA. निम्बार्क स्तोत्रम् *etc.* [Nimbārkastotra.] ff. 2-3. [1901.] *obl.* 12°. **14033. a. 19.(6.)**

VIṢVADEVA ĀCHĀRYA. রাঘব দীপিকা *etc.* [Rāghavadīpikā. A modern poem in nine cantos on the life of a devotee named Rāghava Rāma and his wife Jayadurgā, said to have been an incarnation of Ardhakālī. Edited with a translation and additional matter in Bengali by Durgāmohana Smṛititīrtha.] 2 pts. pp. vi. 26, xvi. 63; 3 *plates.* বারাণস্যাম্ [*Benares*, 1892.] 8°. **14028. d. 48.(2.)**

VIṢVAKARMĀ, *the God.* विश्वकर्म्मा प्रकाश शास्त्रम् *etc.* [Viṣvakarmaprakāṣa. A work on architecture. With a Hindi translation made by Ṣaktidhara Sukula for Munshi Pālārām, and hence conjointly with the text styled Pālārām-vilāsa.] pp. iv. 304. लखनऊ १८९६ [*Lucknow*, 1896.] 8°. **14053. ccc. 7.**

The preface states that the work, first communicated by Brahma to Ṣiva, was thence transmitted successively to Garga, Parāṣara, Bṛihadratha, and Viṣvakarmā.

Pp. 17-24, 113-120, *and* 225-232 *are missing.*

—— ॥ अथ विश्वकर्मप्रकाशो भाषाटीकायुतः प्रारभ्यते ॥ [Viṣvakarmaprakāṣa. With a Hindi translation by Mihirachandra Miṣra.] ff. i. 95. मुंबय्यां १९५२ [*Bombay*, 1896.] *obl.* 4°. **14053. e. 31.**

—— విశ్వకర్మ ప్రకాశిక *etc.* [Viṣvakarmaprakāṣikā or °prakāṣa. With a Telugu translation by N. Guruliṅga Ṣāstrī.] pp. ii. 226. చెన్నపురి [*Madras*, 1896.] 8°. **14053. ccc. 15.**

—— विश्वकर्माज्ञान [Viṣvakarmajñāna. 167 stanzas from a work styled Viṣvakarmajñānabodhakapurāṇa, on the legend of Viṣvakarmā. With Gujarati translation.] *See* KALYĀṆADĀSA BHĀṆĀBHĀĪ GUJJAR. (શિલ્પ સાર સંગ્રહ *etc.*) [Ṣilpasārasaṅgraha.] [1898.] 8°. **14028. dd. 6.**

VIṢVAKARMĀ, *disciple of Viṣvanātha.* *See* KEṢAVA MIṢRA, *Logician.* तर्कभाषा . . . The Tarkabhāṣā . . . With the commentary Nyāyapradipa of Viçwakarman, *etc.* 1901. 8°. [*The Pandit.*] **14096. d. 6.(vol. 22-23.)**

VIṢVAMBHARA JYOTISHĀRṆAVA. *See* RĀMACHANDRA ṢARMĀ, *Astronomer.* দিনকৌমুদী *etc.* [Dinakaumudī. Edited with Bengali translation by Viṣvambhara.] [1898.] 12°. **14053. b. 31.(3.)**

VIṢVAMBHARA PĀNI. *See* PURĀṆAS.—*Padmapurāṇa.* বৃন্দাবন প্রাপ্ত্যুপায় *etc.* [Vṛindāvanaprāptyupāya. Comprising an excerpt and a metrical Bengali paraphrase, by Viṣvambhara.] [1900.] 8°. **14076. c. 75.(1.)**

VIṢVANĀTHA CHAKRAVARTĪ. *See* KAVIKARṆAPŪRA. অলঙ্কারকৌস্তুভঃ *etc.* [Alaṅkārakaustubha. With the commentary Subodhanī of Viṣvanātha.] [1899.] 8°. **14053. ccc. 25.**

—— *See* NAROTTAMADĀSA, *the Bengali Poet.* শ্রীশ্রীপ্রেমভক্তিচন্দ্রিকা *etc.* [Premabhaktichandrikā. With Sanskrit commentary by Viṣvanātha.] [1896.] 12°. **14123. e. 20.**

VIṢVANĀTHA CHAKRAVARTĪ (*continued*). *See* RŪPA GOSVĀMĪ. उज्ज्वलनीलमणिः *etc.* [Ujjvalanīlamaṇi. With the commentary Ānandachandrikā by Viṣvanātha.] [1889.] 8°. **14053. d. 49.**

—— सटीकम् श्रीकृष्णभावनामृत महाकाव्यम् *etc.* [Śrīkrishṇabhāvanāmṛita. A poem in 20 cantos upon the legend of Krishṇa. With an anonymous commentary. Edited by Kṛishṇachandra Bhāgavatabhūshaṇa.] pp. i. ix. 504. श्रीवृन्दावन॰ ४१८ [*Brindaban*, 1904.] 8°. **14070. dd. 31.**

The poem was finished in Ṣaka 1601.

VIṢVANĀTHA KAVI, *nephew of Agastya.* The Saugandhikāharaṇa of Viśvanâthakavi. [A short mythological play, of the *vyāyoga* type.] Edited by . . . Paṇḍit Śivadatta . . . and Kâśînâth Pâṇdurang Parab. (सौगन्धिकाहरणम् ।) pp. 37. 1902. *See* DURGĀPRASĀDA, *son of Vrajalāla*, and KĀṢĪNĀTHA PĀṆḌURAṄGA PARAB. Kâvyamâlâ. [No.] 74. 1886, *etc.* 8°. **14072. ccc. 12.(no. 74.)**

This play is cited by Viṣvanātha Kavirāja in his Sāhityadarpaṇa (VI. 514), *but not as his own work. Our author mentions as his king a Pratāparudra, possibly Pratāparudra Deva Gajapati of Orissa (reigned* A.D. 1503-24).

VIṢVANĀTHA KAVIRĀJA. *See* MOREṢVARA RĀMACHANDRA KĀḶE. The Sâhityasârasangraha . . . based on the works of . . . Vishwanatha, *etc.* 1891. 12°. **14053. a. 13.**

—— साहित्यदर्पणस्य सूचीपत्रम् *etc.* [Sāhityadarpaṇasya Sūchīpatra. An index to the Sāhityadarpaṇa.] pp. 22. कलिकाता १८८६ [*Calcutta*, 1886.] 8°. **14053. ccc. 18.**

VIṢVANĀTHA NĀRĀYAṆA MAṆḌALĪKA, *Rāu Sāhib.* *See* ACADEMIES, *etc.*—Bombay.—*Bombay Branch of the Royal Asiatic Society.* Catalogue of Manuscripts and Books belonging to the Bhau Daji Memorial. Prepared under the superintendence of . . . Vishvanáth Náráyan Mandlik, *etc.* 1882. 8°. **14096. cc. 11.**

—— *See* PURĀṆAS.—*Padmapurāṇa.* पद्मपुराणम् *etc.* (The Padmapurâṇa, edited . . . by . . . Vishwanáth . . . Maṇdlic.) [1893-1894.] 8°. **14003. ccc.**

VIṢVANĀTHA PAÑCHĀNANA BHAṬṬĀCHĀRYA, *Tarkālaṅkāra.* *See* GOTAMA. The Nyâyasûtras with . . . extracts from the Nyâyavârttika . . . [and the Gautamasūtravṛitti, called also Nyāyasūtravṛitti, of Viṣvanātha], *etc.* 1896. 8°. **14048. dd. 3.(vol. 9.)**

—— *See* PIṄGALA ĀCHĀRYA. Prákrita-paiṅgalam. With the commentaries of Viśwanátha-Pañchánana, *etc.* 1902. 8°. [*Bibliotheca Indica.*] **14002. a. (vol. 148.)**

—— *See* UDAYANA ĀCHĀRYA. ॥ लक्षणावली *etc.* [Lakshaṇāvalī. With the commentary Lakshaṇāvalīprakāṣa of Viṣvanātha.] [1901.] 8°. **14049. a. 4.(3.)**

—— कारिकावली *etc.* [Kārikāvalī. A manual of Vaiṣeshika logic. With its commentary Nyāyasiddhāntamuktāvalī and two supercommentaries, viz. the Dinakarī or Muktāvalīprakāṣa commenced by Mahādeva Bhaṭṭa and finished by Dinakara Bhaṭṭa, and the Rāmarudrī Ṭīkā or Dinakaritaraṅgiṇī by Rāmarudra Bhaṭṭa.] pp. 529. काश्यां १९५२ [*Benares*, 1895.] 8°. **14048. dd. 25.**

—— [Another edition. Edited by Govinda Ṣāstrī of Benares.] pp. 521. काश्यां १९५३ [*Benares*, 1896.] 8°. **14048. dd. 26.**

—— भाषापरिच्छेदः *etc.* [Kārikāvalī, or Bhāshāparichchheda. With the commentary Siddhāntamuktāvalī.] pp. iv. 120. मुम्बय्यां १९५६ [*Bombay*, 1900.] 8°. **14048. e. 30.**

—— Kârikâvali by Visvanatha Panchanana. With a new commentary Prajnamanorama by Pandit Durgadatta Sastri . . . कारिकावली . . . प्राज्ञमनोरमाख्यनूतनव्याख्यया सम्भूषिता. pp. 65, 5. लवपुरे १९५९ [*Lahore*, 1902.] 8°. **14049. b. 16.**

—— न्यायसिद्धान्तमुक्तावली प्रत्यक्षखण्ड मिदम् *etc.* [Kārikāvalī. The Pratyakshakhaṇḍa, with the commentary Nyāyasiddhāntamuktāvalī. Edited with Hindi translation of the whole, commentary, and footnotes by Vaidyanātha Ṣāstrī of Moradabad.] pp. iii. 234, ii. मुरादाबाद॰ १९५८ [*Moradabad*, 1901.] 8°. **14049. b. 7.**

—— शक्तिवाद-व्युत्पत्तिवाद-विवृतिः *etc.* [Ṣaktivādavivṛiti, Vyutpattivādavivṛiti, Jyeshṭhatvavādavivṛiti, Lakāravādavivṛiti, and Sādṛiṣyavādavivṛiti. Five essays on dissertations of Gadādhara

Bhaṭṭāchārya. Edited by Sadāṣiva Jhā.] pp. 77. वाराणसेय० १९५७ [*Benares*, 1900.] 8°.
14049. a. 4.(2.)

VIṢVANĀTHA ṢARMĀ, *Nepali Pandit.* See PURĀṆAS.—*Varāhapurāṇa.* दुर्गाकवच। etc. [Durgākavacha, *etc.* Edited with Nepali translation by Viṣvanātha.] [1903.] 8°. **14016. dd. 12.**

VIṢVANĀTHA YAJÑEṢVARA ṢĀSTRĪ. *See* YAJÑEṢVARA ṢĀSTRĪ, *V.*

VIṢVARĀJA HARIHARA ṢARMĀ. *See* ṢIVADATTA UPĀDHYĀYA. अथ ज्योतिषसार etc. [Jyotishasāra. With Nepali version by Viṣvarāja.] [1902.] 8°.
14053. dd. 4.(2.)

VIṢVARŪPA, *Jurist.* *See* YĀJÑAVALKYA. [*Dharmaṣāstra.*] The Inheritance Chapter of Yájñavalkya with Visvarúpa's commentary. Translated into English, *etc.* [With Sanskrit text appended.] 1900. 8°. **14038. d. 22.(2.)**

VIṢVĀSA, *Kavīndra.* *See* NARAHARI DĀSA GUPTA.

VIṢVAVIHĀRĪ ANUJA. *See* YĀJÑAVALKYA. [*Gītā.*] ॥ श्रीयाज्ञवल्क्यसंहितोपनिषत् *etc.* [Yājñavalkyagītā, here styled Yājñavalkyasaṃhitopanishad. Edited with Gujarati translation and preface by Viṣvavihārī.] [1901.] 8°. **14048. cc. 39.**

VIṢVEṢVARA, *Vedantic Commentator.* *See* ASHṬĀVAKRA. अष्टावक्र *etc.* [Ashṭāvakra. With the commentary Adhyātmapradīpikā of Viṣveṣvara.] 1896. 8°. **14048. dd. 32.(3.)**

—— *See* UPANISHADS.—*Separate Upanishads.* Gopala Tapani Upanishad. Part i. [Translated, with extracts from the commentaries of Viṣveṣvara, *etc.*] 1899. 8°. [*The Theosophist.*]
P.P. 636. cm. (vol. 20.)

VIṢVEṢVARA BHAṬṬA, also called GĀGĀ BHAṬṬA. भाट्टचिन्तामणिः . . . Bhâṭṭa Chintâmani of Mahâmahopâdhyâya Sri Gâgâ Bhatta. [A commentary on the Mīmāṃsāsūtra.] Edited by Paṇḍit Ráma Krishṇa Sástri, *etc.* काश्याम् १९०० [*Benares*, 1900, *etc.*] 8°. **14004. a. 6.**

In progress. Forms no. 25, 27, *etc., of the* Chowkhambhâ Sanskrit Series.

VIṢVEṢVARA DĀSA, *of Ajodhya.* *See* UPANISHADS.—*Small Collections.* श्री . . . श्रीरामतापनीयोपनिषद् *etc.* [Rāmatāpanīyopanishad, *etc.* With Hindi commentary by Viṣveṣvara Dāsa.] [1903.] 8°. **14007. b. 11.(2.)**

VIṢVEṢVARANĀTHA CHANDIKA. The First Elements of the Yoga. [With quotations from Sanskrit works.] By B. N. Chandik. pp. 61. *Madras,* 1897. 16°. **14048. a. 21.**

—— The Second or the Last Elements of the Yoga. By Bissessur Nath Chandik. [Prefaced by a life of the author, by Kahān Chand Shaikh.] pp. i. i. v. 129. *Madras,* 1898. 8°. **14048. cc. 27.**

VIṢVEṢVARA PAṆḌITA, *son of Lakshmīdhara.* The Alankâra-kaustubha of Viśveśvara Paṇḍit, [a treatise on style,] with his own gloss. Edited by . . . Paṇḍit Śivadatta . . . and Kâshînâth Pâṇdurang Parab. (अलंकारकौस्तुभम्।) pp. ii. i. 419, viii. viii. 1898. *See* DURGĀPRASĀDA, *son of Vrajalāla,* and KĀṢĪNĀTHA PĀṆḌURAṄGA PARAB. Kâvyamâlâ. [No.] 66. 1886, *etc.* 8°.
14072. ccc. 12. (no. 66.)

VIṢVEṢVARA SUDHĪ. *See* VIṢVEṢVARA BHAṬṬA.

VIṬHOBĀ AṆṆĀ. विठोबा अण्णाकृत पदसमूह *etc.* [Padasamūha. Short poems and dramatic scenes, on religious and legendary topics, in Marathi and Sanskrit. Followed by some Marathi stanzas by divers authors. Edited by Raghunātha Rāmakṛishṇa Bhāgavata. Second edition.] pp. iii. iii. i. 68. मुंबई १८९० [*Bombay,* 1890.] 8°.
14140. b. 26.(4.)

—— विठोबाअण्णाकृता शिवगीतिमाला. (कटावः) [Ṣivagītimālā and Kaṭāva. Religious poems, of 50 and 9 stanzas.] 1888. *See* LAGHUKĀVYĀNI. लघुकाव्यानि . . . Miscellaneous Poetical Pieces, *etc.* pp. 179-184. 1888. 8°. [*Kāvyetihāsasaṅgraha, Vol. X, no.* 6.] **14072. d. 37. (vol. 10.)**

VIṬṬHALA DĪKSHITA, *Gosainjī.* *See* VIṬṬHALEṢVARA, called GOSAINJĪ.

VIṬṬHALANĀTHA, *Gosainjī.* *See* VIṬṬHALEṢVARA, called GOSAINJĪ.

VIṬṬHALA PANTA. *See* VIṬHOBĀ AṆṆĀ.

VIṬṬHALEŚVARA, called GOSAINJĪ. श्रीगुसाइंजी . . . कृतग्रंथाः । [Miscellaneous religious writings in verse on the doctrine of Vallabhāchārya.] pp. 92. *See* GOVARDHANADĀSA LAKSHMĪDĀSA. बृहत्स्तोत्रसरित्सागर *etc.* [Bṛihat-stotrasaritsāgara.] Vol. ii. [1892.] 12°. **14033. a. 27. (vol. 2.)**

The date of this author's birth, Samv. 1572, *is given in an appended horoscope.*

VIVĀHAPADDHATI. वैवर्णिकानां नवरत्नविवाहपद्धतिः *etc.* [Navaratna-vivāhapaddhati. A manual of the rites and circumstances of marriage, in nine *prakaraṇas*. Edited with a commentary in Hindi and appendices by Vishṇudatta Vaidika.] pp. xii. 248. मुंबय्याम् १९४९ [*Bombay*, 1892.] 8°. **14033. b. 59.**

—— ବିବାହପଦ୍ଧତି *etc.* [Vivāhapaddhati. A manual of wedding rites. Edited by Rāmachandra Nanda.] pp. 45. *Cuttack*, 1900. 12°. **14028. b. 78.(5.)**

VIVEKĀNANDA, *Svāmī*, [*i.e.* NARENDRANĀTHA DATTA.] *See* PATAÑJALI. — *Philosophical Works.* Raja-Yoga . . . [*scil.* the Aphorisms in English with introduction and commentary] by the Swami Vivekananda. 1901. 8°. **14048. bb. 54.**

—— Yoga Philosophy. Lectures . . . on Râja Yoga, or Conquering the Internal Nature; also Patanjali's Yoga Aphorisms, with commentaries. pp. x. 234. *London*, 1896. 8°. **4503. b. 22.**

—— —— [Another issue of the same.] pp. ix. 194. *Madras*, 1897. 8°. **14048. cc. 2.(1.)**

—— Vedânta Philosophy. Lectures . . . on Râja Yoga and other subjects [*scil.* Bhaktiyoga, *etc.*]; also Patanjali's Yoga Aphorisms, with commentaries, and glossary of Sanskrit terms. pp. xv. 376; 1 *plate*. *New York, Albany* [printed], 1897. 8°. **4503. b. 31.**

—— Bhakti-Yoga, *etc.* pp. 75. *Madras*, 1896. 8°. **14048. cc. 2.(2.)**

Forms no. 3 *of the* Brahmavâdin Series; *a reprint from the* Brahmavâdin.

VIVIDHA-BOL-RATNĀKARA. विविध बोल रत्नाकर *etc.* [Vividha-bol-ratnākara. An exposition of the theory and practice of the Jain religion, comprised in a series of selected Sanskrit and Prakrit aphorisms, verses, and poems, together with a copious Gujarati commentary, *etc.*] 2 vols. અમદાવાદ ૧૯૪૬ [*Ahmadabad*, 1890.] 16° & 8°. **14144. g. 36.**

VIZIANAGRAM SANSKRIT SERIES. The Vizianagram Sanskrit Series. [A collection of Sanskrit philosophical texts, founded chiefly on MS. material in Benares, and published under the patronage of H. H. the late Maharaja of Vizianagram. Edited] under the superintendence of Arthur Venis. *Benares*, 1890-1898. 8°. **14048. dd. 3.**

This series came to an end in 1898, *in consequence of the death of H. H. the Maharaja. Arrangements were then made to publish in the* Pandit *the translations of the Siddhāntaleśa and Pañchapādikā originally intended for publication in this series.*

Works appearing in this series are to be found under the headings:—

No. 1 = Vol. I. Apyaya Dikshita.
,, 3, 5 = ,, II. Padmapāda.
,, 6 = ,, IV. Praśastapāda.
,, 7 = ,, V. Bādarāyaṇa.
,, 8 = ,, VI. Śivāditya Miśra.
,, 10, 11 = ,, VIII, IX. Gotama.
,, 12 = ,, X. Varāhamihira.
,, 13, 14 = ,, XI, XII. Bādarāyaṇa.
,, 15 = ,, XIII. Vāchaspati Miśra.
,, 16 = ,, XIV. Kallaṭa.

VOPADEVA. *See* HARANĀTHA VIDYĀRATNA. সুগমমুগ্ধবোধ° [Sugama-mugdhabodha. The Mugdhabodha of Vopadeva versified and simplified.] [1891.] 12°. **14092. a. 11.(2.)**

—— मुग्धबोधं व्याकरणम् *etc.* [Mugdhabodha. With the commentaries of Durgādāsa Vidyāvāgīśa and Rāma Tarkavāgīśa. Edited by Jīvānanda Vidyāsāgara.] pp. i. 866. कलिकाता १८९१ [*Calcutta*, 1891.] 8°. **14092. b. 44.**

—— মুগ্ধবোধং ব্যাকরণং *etc.* [Mugdhabodha. With Durgādāsa's commentary as far as the end of the *kṛidantādhyāya* and Rāma Tarkavāgīśa's commentary thence to the end, together with a Bengali paraphrase of each *sūtra*.] pp. xviii. 800. কলিকাতা ১৮৯৪ [*Calcutta*, 1894.] 8°. **14090. e. 24.**

—— বৃহন্মুগ্ধবোধব্যাকরণম্ *etc.* [Bṛihan-mugdhabodhavyākaraṇa. The Mugdhabodha of Vopadeva with additions by Kṛishṇanātha Nyāyapañchānana. Edited with biographical preface in Bengali by the latter.] pp. iv. xii. 468. কলিকাতা ১৮২০ [*Calcutta*, 1898.] 8°. **14093. b. 41.(1.)**

—— মুগ্ধবোধং ব্যাকরণং *etc.* (Mugdhabodha Vyakorna. By Bopadeba Goswamee.) [Edited by

Pītāmbara Nyāyaratna. Third edition.] pp. 154. কলিকাতা ১৩০৮ [*Calcutta*, 1901.] 12°. **14092. a. 25.**

The English title is taken from the wrapper.

—— মুগ্ধবোধং ব্যাকরণম্ *etc.* [Mugdhabodha. Edited with notes by Şyāmācharaṇa Kaviratna.] pp. viii. 276. কলিকাতা ১৮২৬ [*Calcutta*, 1904.] 12°. **14092. a. 28.(4.)**

—— Kavikalpadruma. Or The Dhatupatha of . . . Bopadeva. With the commentaries [called] Dhatudipika of Durgadas Vidyabagis. Edited with additional notes by . . . Sivanarayan Siromani . . . सटीककविकल्पद्रुमः *etc.* pp. iii. 349. *Calcutta*, 1897. 8°. **14090. c. 38.(2.)**

VOPADEVA, *son of Keṣava and disciple of Dhaneṣa.* वोपदेववैद्यकशतक *etc.* [Vopadevavaidyakaṣataka. A collection of medical recipes in verse. With a Hindi translation by Şālagrāma Vaiṣya.] pp. iv. 59. मुंबई १९५३ [*Bombay*, 1896.] 8°. **14043. c. 42.(2.)**

VRAJARATNA BHAṬṬĀCHĀRYA, *of Moradabad.* *See* AGNIVEṢA. समयनिरूपणरामायण *etc.* [Samayanirūpaṇarāmāyaṇa. Edited with Hindi version by Vrajaratna.] [1900.] 12°. **14065. b. 21.**

—— *See* KĀLIDĀSA.—*Ṛitusaṃhāra.* ऋतुसंहारः *etc.* [Ṛitusaṃhāra. With Hindi translation by Vrajaratna.] [1901.] 8°. **14070. dd. 21.(1.)**

—— *See* KAMALĀKARA BHAṬṬA. निर्णयसिन्धु *etc.* [Nirṇayasindhu. Edited with Hindi translation by Vrajaratna.] [1901.] 8°. **14028. dd. 12.**

—— *See* PĀṆINI.—*Ashṭādhyāyī.* अष्टाध्यायी *etc.* [Ashṭādhyāyī. With a Hindi paraphrase, entitled Chandrakāntā, by Vrajaratna.] [1901.] 8°. **14090. d. 34.**

—— *See* VEDAS.—Atharvaveda.—*Pariṣishṭa.* आसुरीकल्पः *etc.* [Āsurīkalpa. With Hindi version by Vrajaratna.] [1899.] 8°. **14033. aa. 1.(3.)**

—— *See* VEDAS.—Yajurveda.—*Vājasaneyisaṃhitā.* अथ . . . रुद्राष्टाध्यायी *etc.* [Rudrāshṭādhyāyī. With Hindi translation by Vrajaratna.] [1900.] *obl.* 8°. **14028. dd. 9.**

VRAJAVILĀSA, *of Singha, Shahjahanpur.* *See* RĀMAVILĀSA and VRAJAVILĀSA. नित्यकर्म *etc.* [Nityakarma.] [1899.] 12°. **14028. b. 81.(3.)**

VRAJENDRANĀTHA ŞĪLA. Comparative Studies in Vaishnavism and Christianity. With an examination of the Mahabharata legend about Narada's pilgrimage to Svetadvipa and an introduction on the historico-comparative method. By Brajendranath Seal. pp. xi. 103. *Calcutta*, 1899. 8°. **14058. cc. 2.**

VṚINDA. वृन्दमाधवापरनामा सिद्धयोगः *etc.* (The Vṛindamâdhava or Siddhiyoga [*sic*] of Vṛindamuni, [a treatise on the *materia medica* and its application, in 82 *adhikāras*,] with its commentary 'Kusumávali' [commenced] by Śrî kanthadutta [and completed by Nārāyaṇa son of Bhābhalla]. Edited by Pandita Hanmanta Śastrî Pâdhyé.) pp. i. x. 665. *Poona*, 1894. 8°. **14003. ccc. (no. 27.)**

Forms no. 27 of the Ānandāṣrama Sanskrit Series. *The English title is from the cover.*

VṚISHEṢVARA, *Siddha, son of Revaṇa.* *See* REVAṆA. శైవసిద్ధాంతశిఖామణి [Şaivasiddhāntaṣikhāmaṇi. With *ṭīkā* of Vṛisheṣvara.] [1897.] 8°. [*Şivādvaitapañchaka.*] **14048. cc. 8.(4.)**

VYĀḌI. ॥ अथ विकृतिवल्ली ॥ [Vikṛitivallī. A treatise on the recitation of the Vedas. Chapter i., or Jaṭāpaṭala, with the commentary Vikṛitikaumudī of Gaṅgādhara Bhaṭṭāchārya.] pp. 16. [1889.] *See* PERIODICAL PUBLICATIONS.—*Calcutta.* उषा *etc.* [Ushā.] Vol. I, no. ii. [1889]-1893. 8°. **14010. c. 43.(vol. 1.)**

VYAṄKAṬA. [For names beginning with this word :] *See* VEṄKAṬA.

VYAṄKAṬEṢA RĀMACHANDRA. *See* VEṄKAṬARĀU RĀMACHANDRA.

VYANKETACHARYE. *See* VEṄKAṬĀCHĀRYA.

VYĀṚI. *See* VYĀḌI.

VYĀSA. *See* LUEDERS (H.). Die Vyâsa-Çikshâ, besonders in ihrem Verhältnis zum Taittirîya-Prâtiçâkhya, *etc.* 1895. 8°. **011840. m. 55.**

—— [For the Brahmasūtra, attributed to Vyāsa :] *See* BĀDARĀYAṆA.

VYĀSA (*continued*). [For the Mahābhārata, ascribed to Vyāsa :] *See* MAHĀBHĀRATA.

—— [For the Yogasūtrabhāshya, ascribed to Vyāsa :] *See* PATAÑJALI.—*Philosophical Works*.

—— [For the Purāṇas, ascribed to Vyāsa :] *See* PURĀṆAS.

—— [For the Siddhaṣaṅkaratantra, sometimes ascribed to Vyāsa :] *See* TANTRAS. [*Siddhaṣaṅkaratantra.*]

WAALS (H. G. VAN DER). *See* PAÑCHATANTRA. Pañcatantra . . . vertaald door H. G. van der Waals. 1895. 8°. **14070. c. 54.**

WALTER (HERMANN). *See* SVĀTMĀRĀMA. Svâtmârâma's Haṭhayogapradîpikâ . . . übersetzt . . . von H. Walter. 1893. 8°. **14048. c. 75.(1.)**

WARD (EDITH). Light from the East. Being selections from the teachings of the Buddha[, chiefly the Suttapiṭaka]. Arranged with an introduction by Edith Ward. With foreword by Annie Besant. (Life and Light Books.) pp. i. xxxi. 50, ii. *London*, 1901. 12°. **4506. a. 7.**

WARD (WILLIAM). *See* SADĀNANDA YOGĪNDRA. Vedánt Sára . . . Translated by Mr. W. Ward. 1901. 8°. [*Compendium of Raja Yoga Philosophy.*] **14048. bb. 53.**

WARREN (HENRY CLARKE). *See* BUDDHAGHOSA. [*Visuddhimagga.*] Table of contents . . . By H. C. Warren. 1893. 8°. [*Journal of the Pali Text Society.*] **14098. b.**

—— Buddhism in Translations. [Being select passages translated from the Suttapiṭaka, Vinayapiṭaka, Visuddhimagga, Milindapañha, *etc.*] By Henry Clarke Warren. pp. xx. 520. 1896. *See* ACADEMIES, *etc.*—Cambridge, *Mass.*—*Harvard University*. Harvard Oriental Series, *etc.* Vol. iii. 1891, *etc.* 8°. **14003. l. 3.(vol. 3.)**

WASUDEV LAXUMAN PANSIKAR. *See* VĀSUDEVA LAKSHMAṆA PAṆṢĪKAR.

WEBER (ALBRECHT). *See* DHANEṢVARA SŪRI. The Śatrunjaya Mâhâtmyam. A contribution to the history of the Jainas by . . . A. Weber. [Being an analysis of the work of Dhaneṣvara,] *etc.* 1901. 4°. [*Indian Antiquary.*] **14096. e. (vol. 30.)**

—— Gurupūjākaumudī. [A collection of 30 essays on Indian philology.] Festgabe zum fünfzigjährigen Doctorjubiläum Albrecht Weber dargebracht von seinen Freunden und Schülern. pp. 128; 1 *plate*. *Leipzig*, 1896. 4°. **11826. k. 22.**

WEBER (J.). *See* HOERNLE (A. F. R.). Facsimile Reproduction of Weber MSS., *etc.* 1902. 4°. **759. k. 1.**

WENZEL (HEINRICH). *See* OLDENBURG (S.). Dr. Serge D'Oldenburg "On the Buddhist Jātakas." [Translated] by H. Wenzel. 1893. 8°. [*Journal of the Royal Asiatic Society.*] **Ac. 8820/3 & 2098. a, b.**

WICKREMASINGHE. *See* VIKRAMASIṂHA.

WIJESINHA (L. C.). *See* VIJAYASIṂHA (L. C.).

WIKKRAMASINHA. *See* VIKRAMASIṂHA.

WILKINS (*Sir* CHARLES). *See* MAHĀBHĀRATA.—Bhagavadgītā.—*English*. The Bhagavad Gita: with an English translation [based on that of Wilkins], *etc.* 1895. 8°. [*Sacred Books of the East Described and Examined.*] **14010. cc. 9.(vol. 2.)**

—— *See* MAHĀBHĀRATA. — Bhagavadgītā. — *English*. The Bhagavad-gita, *etc.* [In the version of Wilkins.] [1902.] 8°. [*Sakuntala.*] **012208. ee. 117.**

WILLIAMS, afterwards **MONIER-WILLIAMS** (*Sir* MONIER). *See* KĀLIDĀSA.— *Abhijñānaṣakuntala.* Śakoontalá . . . Translated . . . by Sir M. Monier-Williams. 1894. 8°. **012207. l. 81.**

WILSON (HORACE HAYMAN). *See* KĀLIDĀSA.—*Collected Works*. Works of Kalidasa . . . 2. Vikramaurvashi [translated by H. H. Wilson]. . . 4. Meghaduta [translated by H. H. Wilson], *etc.* 1901. 12°. **14080. b. 10.**

—— *See* KĀLIDĀSA.—*Meghadūta*. The Meghadúta . . . Translated into English verse, with notes and illustrations, by H. H. Wilson, *etc.* 1901. 8°. **14070. dd. 22.**

—— *See* KĀLIDĀSA.—*Meghadūta.* The Meghaduta, *etc.* [In the version of Wilson.] [1902.] 8°. [*Sakuntala.*] **012208. ee. 117.**

—— *See* PURĀṆAS.—*Vishṇupurāṇa.* A prose English translation of Vishnupuranam, based on Professor H. H. Wilson's translation, *etc.* 1894. 8°. [*Wealth of India.*] **14085. d. 32.(vol. 1.)**

—— *See* PURĀṆAS.—*Vishṇupurāṇa.* The Vishnu Purana: an abridgment . . . from the English translation of H. H. Wilson, *etc.* 1895. 8°. [*Sacred Books of the East Described and Examined.*] **14010. cc. 9.(vol. 3.)**

—— Hindu Dramatic Works. Translated . . . by H. H. Wilson . . . (1) Malati Madhava. (2) Ratnavali. (3) The Mrichchhakati. 3 pts. *Calcutta,* 1901. 12°. **14080. b. 13.**

WINDISCH (WILHELM OSCAR ERNST). Māra und Buddha, *etc.* [Illustrated by extracts and translations from the Suttapiṭaka, Lalitavistara, Buddhacharita, Divyâvadāna, *etc.*] pp. ii. 348. *Leipzig,* 1895. 4°. **759. e. 1.**

Forms no. 4 *in Bd.* xv. *of the* Abhandlungen der Sächsischen Gesellschaft der Wissenschaften (*phil.-hist. Classe*).

WINI-NGAY. ဝိနည်းငယ်လေးစောင်ပါဠိ *etc.* [Wini-ngay le saung. Four Pali works on the Vinaya, viz. the Bhikkhupāṭimokkha, Bhikkhunīpāṭimokkha, Khuddasikkhā, and Mūlasikkhā. Followed by Vinayakosalla, a Burmese tract on clerical discipline.] pp. 148. ရန်ကုန် ၁၂၆၀ [*Rangoon,* 1898.] 8°. **14098. ccc. 9.(4.)**

—— ဝိနည်းငယ်လေးစောင်ပါဠိ *etc.* [Wini-ngay le saung. The same works as in the previous edition, with an additional Burmese chapter called Wini-akyi-hkyôk.] pp. 161. မန္တလေး ၁၂၆၇ [*Mandalay,* 1905.] 8°. **14099. bb. 14.**

—— ဝိနည်းငယ်လေးစောင်ပါဠိ॥ [Wini-ngay le saung. The Pali texts only.] pp. 133, i. မန္တလေး [*Mandalay,*] 1903. 8°. **14099. bb. 1.**

WINTER (AUGUST). *See* ṢIVĀDITYA MIṢRA. सप्तपदार्थी . . . Saptapadārthī . . . edidit prolegomena interpretationem . . . adiecit A. Winter. 1893. 8°. **14048. dd. 2.**

—— *See* ṢIVĀDITYA MIṢRA. Die Saptapadārthī . . . [Translated into German] von A. Winter. 1899. 8°. [*Zeitschrift der Deutschen Morgenlaendischen Gesellschaft.*] **Ac. 8815/2.(Bd. 53.)**

WINTERNITZ (MORIZ). *See* ĀPASTAMBA.—*Gṛihyasūtra.* The Mantrapāṭha . . . Edited . . . with the commentary of Haradatta and translated by M. Winternitz . . . First part. Introduction, Sanskrit text, varietas lectionis, and appendices. 1897. 4°. [*Anecdota Oxoniensia.*] **12204. f. 8.(vol. 1, pt. 8.)**

—— *See* MAHĀBHĀRATA.—*Ādiparva.* On the South-Indian Recension of the Mahabharata. By M. Winternitz. 1898. 4°. [*Indian Antiquary.*] **14096. e. (vol. 27.)**

—— Geschichte der indischen Litteratur, *etc.* (Die Litteraturen des Ostens in Einzeldarstellungen. Band ix.) *Leipzig,* 1905, *etc.* 8°. **011853. f.**

In progress.

WRIGHTSON (RICHARD). An introductory treatise on Sanscrit Hagiographa; or The sacred literature of the Hindus. In two parts: Part I.—The Philosophy of the Hindus. Part II.—The Veda and Puranas, *etc.* pp. xiv. 265. *Dublin,* 1859. 12°. **4506. de. 16.**

WÛT TET SI. ဝတ်တက်စဉ်စာတန်း॥ [Wût tet si sâ-tan. A lectionary, comprising Pali catechisms and short texts on Buddhist doctrine, with Burmese glosses, *etc.*] pp. iv. 56. *Rangoon,* 1882. 8°. **14300. d. 6.(1.)**

YAÇŌDHARA. *See* YAṢODHARA.

YĀDAVAPRAKĀṢA. वैजयन्ती The Vaijayantī. [A Sanskrit lexicon.] . . . For the first time edited [with a Sanskrit-English vocabulary] by Gustav Oppert. pp. x. 895. *Madras,* 1893. 8°. **14093. b. 32.**

YĀDAVENDRA. *See* MAHĀBHĀRATA.—Bhagavadgītā.—*Sanskrit.* श्रीमद्भगवद्गीता *etc.* [Bhagavadgītā. With the commentary Kṛishṇatoshiṇī of Yādavendra.] [1899.] 8°. **14065. c. 51.**

YĀDAVENDRA, surnamed BUDHARĀJENDRA DAṢĀVADHĀNA BHAṬṬĀCHĀRYA. *See* PIṄGALA ĀCHĀRYA. Prákrita-paiṅgalam. With the commentaries of ... Yádavendra, *etc.* 1902. 8°. [*Bibliotheca Indica.*] **14002. a. (vol. 148.)**

YĀDAVEṢVARA TARKARATNA. अश्रुबिन्दुकाव्यम् *etc.* [Aṣrubindukāvya. An elegy on the death of Queen Victoria.] pp. 12. *Calcutta*, 1901. 12°. **14072. b. 25.**

YADUNĀTHA MAJUMDĀR. *See* ṢĀṆḌILYA. Religion of Love, or Hundred Aphorisms of Sandilya. Translated ... with ... commentary in English, by Jadunath Mozoomdar. 1898. 12°. **14028. b. 92.**

—— The Indian Sage. . . [Select works on Hindu philosophy. Edited with notes, and English and Bengali translations] by Jadunath Mozoomdar. *Jessore*, 1893. 12°. **14048. a. 20.(1.)**

Seemingly only the first part of this series has been published, containing the Īṣa Upanishad.

YADUNĀTHA SĀRVABHAUMA, *of Nadia.* *See* UDAYANA ĀCHĀRYA. आत्मतत्त्वविवेकः *etc.* [Ātmatattvaviveka. With portions of the gloss of Mathurānātha, the exposition by Raghunātha, and portions of the gloss upon the latter by Gadādhara. Edited with a preface and gloss upon Mathurānātha's commentary by Yadunātha.] [1900, *etc.*] 8°. **14048. dd. 28.**

YADURĀMA ṢUKLA, *son of Haradatta.* *See* ṢAṄKARA BHAṬṬA, *son of Nīlakaṇṭha* ॥ अथ ... कुंडार्कः *etc.* [Kuṇḍārka. With commentary. Edited by Yadurāma.] [1893.] *obl.* 8°. **14028. dd. 5.(1.)**

YAJÑADATTA TRIPĀṬHĪ, *son of Umādatta.* *See* NARASIṂHADATTA, *disciple of Umādatta.* याज्ञी । [Yājñī. With commentary by Yajñadatta.] [1899.] 12°. [*Kūṭapadyavyākhyā.*] **14072. b. 24.**

—— नारसिंही । [Nārasiṃhī. A stanza by Yajñadatta, capable of being interpreted as an address to Vishṇu, and also in other senses, with a commentary by Narasiṃhadatta.] *See* UMĀDATTA TRIPĀṬHĪ. कूटपद्यव्याख्या *etc.* [Kūṭapadyavyākhyā.] pp. 94-103. [1899.] 12°. **14072. b. 24.**

YAJÑANĀRĀYAṆA VEṄKAṬEṢVARĀRYA. *See* [Addenda] VEṄKAṬEṢVARĀRYA.

YĀJÑAVALKYA. [*Dharmaṣāstra.*] *See* ĀDINĀRĀYAṆA PĀTRO. The Hindu Law. Annotated and illustrated by Sanskrit texts [, *viz.* the writings of Yājñavalkya and others,] *etc.* 1899. 8°. **14039. c. 17.**

—— —— *See* BEAMAN (G. B.). On the Sources of ... Yājñavalkya, *etc.* 1895. 8°. **011850. k. 21.**

—— —— *See* GULĀB-CHANDRA SARKĀR. Hindu Law, *etc.* [With extracts from the law-books of Yājñavalkya and others.] 1897. 8°. **14038. c. 46.**

—— —— *See* KIRSTE (J.). Professor J. Kirstes Collation des Textes der Yâjñavalkyasmṛiti und Analyse der Citate in Aparârkas Commentare, *etc.* 1893. Fol. [*Denkschriften der Kais. Akademie der Wissenschaften zu Wien.*] **Ac. 810/2.(Bd. 42.)**

—— —— संस्कृत याज्ञवल्क्यस्मृतिका भाषानुवाद [Yājñavalkyasmṛiti. With Hindi metrical paraphrase, *etc.*, by Maheṣvar-bakhsh Singh, Raja of Rampur.] pp. iv. 312. [1901.] *See* MAHEṢVAR-BAKHSH SINGH. महेश्वरस्मृति *etc.* [Maheṣvarasmṛiti.] Vol. 2. [1899, *etc.*] 8°. **14039. a. 17.(vol. 2.)**

—— —— ஸ்ரீ காக்ஷ்டாவ்யோ விஜ்ஞாநேஸ்வரீய வ்யாவ்யாஸஹிதா யாஜ்ஞவல்க்ய ஸ்ம்ருதி: [Yājñavalkyasmṛiti. With Vijñāneṣvara's Mitākshara, and a Tamil interpretation.] 1901, *etc.* *See* PERIODICAL PUBLICATIONS.—*Chidambaram.* ப்ரஹ்மவித்யா *etc.* [Brahmavidyā.] Vol. xv., no. 1, *etc.* 1886, *etc.* 4°. **14096. dd. 3.(vol. 15, etc.)**

In progress.

—— —— मिताक्षरा सटीक *etc.* [Yājñavalkyasmṛiti. Text of the Āchārādhyāya and Vyavahārādhyāya, with a Hindi translation and commentary founded on the Mitāksharā by Durgāprasāda Ṣukla.] 2 vols. लखनऊ १८९० [*Lucknow*, 1890.] 4°. **14038. f. 11.**

—— —— Mitákshará. Vyávahára Adhyáy, Part III. [Being Yājñavalkyasmṛiti II. 150 *sqq.* to the end, together with the Mitāksharā of Vijñāneṣvara.] Translated by Girish Chandra Tarkálankár. pp. vi. 136, ix. *Serampore*, 1892. 8°. **14038. d. 35.**

Intended as a continuation of Colebrooke's translation of this chapter, which contained vv. 1-149 only.

—— —— The Inheritance Chapter [or Dāyabhāga] of Yájnavalkya with Visvarúpa's commentary. Translated into English by S. Sitarama Sastri, *etc.* [With Sanskrit text appended.] pp. i. 18, 11. *Madras*, 1900. 8°. **14038. d. 22.(2.)**

—— [*Gītā.*] যোগিযাজ্ঞবল্ক্যম্ *etc.* [Yogiyājñavalkya, or Yājñavalkyagītā. A metrical treatise on the Yoga. Edited with Bengali translation by Veṇīmādhava Nyāyaratna.] pp. i. i. 89. কলিকাতা ১৩০০ [*Calcutta*, 1893.] 8°. **14048. bb. 50.(1.)**

—— —— যোগিযাজ্ঞবল্ক্যম্ । [Yogiyājñavalkya, or Yājñavalkyagītā. With Bengali version.] pp. 128. *See* PRASANNAKUMĀRA ŚĀSTRĪ BHAṬṬĀCHĀRYA. যোগাম্বুধি *etc.* [Yogāmbudhi.] [1896.] 16°. **14048. a. 19.**

—— —— ॥ श्रीयाज्ञवल्क्यसंहितोपनिषत् *etc.* [Yājñavalkyagītā, here styled Yājñavalkyasaṃhitopanishad. Edited with Gujarati translation and preface by Viṣvavihārī Anuja.] pp. xii. 88, i. ii. નડિઆદ અમદાવાદ ૧૯૦૧ [*Nadiad, Ahmadabad* printed, 1901.] 8°. **14048. cc. 39.**

—— [*Śikshās.*] अथ . . . याज्ञवल्क्यकृता . . . शिक्षा *etc.* (अथ मनःस्वारशिक्षा.) [Yājñavalkyaṣikshā and Manaḥsvāraṣikshā. Two tracts of the Mādhyandina school, ascribed to Yājñavalkya, on the phonetics of the White Yajurveda.] *See* YUGALAKIṢORA VYĀSA PĀṬHAKA. श्रीमद्याज्ञवल्क्यादि . . . शिक्षासङ्ग्रहः . . . A collection of Śikshás, *etc.* pp. 1-35, 185-209. 1893. 8°. **14093. b. 31.**

—— —— अथ याज्ञवल्क्यशिक्षा प्रा° [Yājñavalkyaṣikshā. With Hindi interpretation.] *See* VEDAS. — Yajurveda. — *Vājasaneyisaṃhitā.* वाजसनेयि . . . संहिता *etc.* [Vājasaneyisaṃhitā.] Vol. ii. [1903.] 8°. **14007. f. 4.(vol. 2.)**

YAJÑEṢA ṢARMĀ, *son of Nīlakaṇṭha.* ॥ श्रीत्यागराजविजयः ॥ . . . चंपूप्रबन्धः [Tyāgarājavijaya. A biographical panegyric in prose and verse upon the author's grandfather Tyāgarāja Dikshita and his ancestors, including Apyaya Dīkshita.] pp. 162, vii.; 1 *plate.* तञ्जपुरी° १९०४ [*Tanjore*, 1904.] 12°. **14058. a. 19.**

YAJÑEṢVARA ṢĀSTRĪ, *Viṣvanātha.* తపఃప్రకాశిక *etc.* [Tapaḥprakāṣikā. A treatise on religious austerities, with rituals for the worship of Bālā-Tripurasundarī, in Telugu and Sanskrit.] 3 pts. కాకినాడ [*Cocanada*, 18]90. 8°. **14174. b. 60.**

YĀJÑIKADEVA, or YĀJÑIKĀNANTADEVA. *See* ANANTADEVA, *son of Nāgadeva.*

YAJURVIDHĀNA. अथ यजुर्विधान शिक्षा ॥ [Yajurvidhānaṣikshā. A tract of the Mādhyandina school, on the application of the texts of the White Yajurveda to religious and magical uses.] *See* YUGALAKIṢORA VYĀSA PĀṬHAKA. श्रीमद्याज्ञवल्क्यादि . . . शिक्षासङ्ग्रहः . . . A collection of Śikshás, *etc.* pp. 327-361. 1893. 8°. **14093. b. 31.**

YAKSHAVARMĀ, also known as GAṄGEṢA. *See* ṢAKAṬĀYANA. ॥ अथ . . . लिङ्गानुशासनम् ॥ [Liṅgānuṣāsana. With extracts from Yakshavarmā's commentary Chintāmaṇi.] 1890. 8°. [*Die Indischen Genuslehren.*] **14093. d. 19.**

YAMAKA. *See* ABHIDHAMMAPIṬAKA.

YAMATA ( ). *See* SUKHĀVATĪVYŪHA. O-mi-to-king, ou Soukhavati-vyouha-soutra . . . Traduit du chinois par MM. Imaïzoumi et Yamata. 1881. 4°. [*Annales du Musée Guimet.*] **7704. h. 21.(tom. 2.)**

YĀMUNA ĀCHĀRYA, called ĀḶAVANDĀR. *See* MAHĀBHĀRATA. — Bhagavadgītā. — *Sanskrit.* Sri Bhagavad Githa. With Githartha Sangraha, a commentary [purporting to be] by . . . Yamuna charya, *etc.* 1901. 8°. [*Śāstramuktāvalī.*] **14049. a. 1.(no. 6.)**

—— आगमप्रामाण्यम् . . . Āgamaprāmāṇyam. [A dissertation on the authority of the Pāñcharātra and Vaishṇava Tantras.] . . . Edited [with introduction, *etc.*,] by . . . Ráma Miśra Śāstrī. pp. 87, v, ii. i. 1900. *See* PERIODICAL PUBLICATIONS.—*Benares.* The Pandit, *etc.* New Series. Vol. XXII. 1876, *etc.* 8°. **14096. d. 6.(vol. 22.)**

—— சதுஃச்லோகீ [Chatuḥṣlokī. Four stanzas on the goddess Lakshmī. With Tamil version, analysis, and commentary.] *See* VARADĀCHĀRYA, *Vātsya*, called NAḌĀDŪR AMMĀḶ. ப்ரபன்னபாரிஜாதம் *etc.* [Prapannapārijāta.] pp. 148-154. [1895.] 8°. **14028. d. 55.**

—— ஸ்ரீமத்கீதார்த்த ஸங்க்ரஹம் [Gītārthasaṅgraha. An epitome of the Bhagavadgītā.

With Tamil translation.] *See* MAHĀBHĀRATA.—Bhagavadgītā.—*Sanskrit and Vernaculars.* ஸ்ரீ-பகவத்கீதை *etc.* [Bhagavadgītā.] pp. 692-710. [1899.] 16°. **14065. b. 19.**

—— Gitartha Sangrha [*sic*] . . . with Gitartha Sangraha Raksha, a comentary [*sic*] of Sri math Vadanta Desika, *etc.* (**गीतार्थसंग्रह:**) pp. ii. 34. 1901. *See* ANANTĀCHĀRYA, *Prativādibhayaṅkara.* **शास्त्रमुक्तावली** The Ŝasthramukthâvalî, *etc.* No. 10. 1899, *etc.* 8°. **14049. a. 1.(no. 10.)**

—— **सिद्धित्रयम् । वेदान्तप्रकरणम्** *etc.* (Siddhitrayam, a treatise on Vedanta philosophy [of the Viṣishṭādvaita school], by Srî Yâmunâchârya Swâmin, the Paramaguru of Sribhashyacharya Swamin, edited by . . . Râma Misra Shâstrî.) pp. ii. ii. 98. *Benares,* 1900. 8°. **14004. a. 10.**

Forms no. 36 *of the* Chowkhambâ Sanskrit Series. *The English title is from the wrapper.*

—— శ్రీస్తోత్రరత్నమ్. [Stotraratna. A Vaishṇava hymn in 65 stanzas.] *See* SAHASRANĀMASTABAKA. శ్రీసహస్రనామస్తబకమ్. [Sahasranāmastabaka.] pp. 390-406. [1902.] *obl.* 16°. **14033. a. 52.**

—— The Gem of Psalms, *etc.* [An English version of the Stotraratna.] 1899. *See* PERIODICAL PUBLICATIONS.—*Madras.* The Brahmavâdin, *etc.* Vol. IV, pp. 696-705. 1895, *etc.* 8°. **14048. g. 1.(vol. 4.)**

YAMUNĀDĀSA ṢĀṆḌILYA. **महताबदिवाकर** *etc.* [Mahtāb-divākara. A refutation of the doctrines of Dayānanda Sarasvatī, in Hindi, with abundant excerpts from Sanskrit authorities. Preceded by Sanskrit and Hindi verses panegyrising the author's patron, Raja Mahtāb-singh of Narsinghgarh; and followed by Ūmaṭ-vaṃṣya-rājavṛittānta-varṇana, or Ūmaṭ-rājya-kā Itihāsa, a Sanskrit poem upon the history of Narsinghgarh, with Hindi paraphrase, by Rāmagopāla Ṣarmā and others.] pp. ii. iv. 560. **मुम्बई** १९५१ [*Bombay,* 1895.] 8°. **14154. c. 20.**

YAN HNIN, *Hsaya Ū, of Amarapura.* *See* HITOPADEṢA. ဟိတောပဒေသ *etc.* [Hitopadeṣa, viz. the stanzas of Book i. Followed by the Sâmudrika. Edited and translated by Yan Hnin.] [1882.] 8°. **14098. ccc. 19.(1.)**

YAṢAVANTA VĀSUDEVA ĀṬHALYE, *Rāu Bahādur.* *See* ANNAM BHAṬṬA. The Tarka-sangraha . . . with the author's Dîpikâ, & Govardhana's Nyâya-Bodhinî and . . . notes by . . . Yaśavanta . . . Âthalye, *etc.* 1897. 8°. **14048. cc. 7.**

YĀSKA. The Nirukta. With commentaries. Edited by Paṇḍit Satyavrata Sâmaśramî. [Vol. I, text with the commentary Nighaṇṭunirvachana of Devarāja Yajvā. Vol. II-IV, with the Ṛijvarthā of Durga Āchārya, the Pariṣishṭas, essays by the editor, *etc.*] (**निरुक्तम् । निघण्टु:**) 4 vols. 1882-1891. *See* ACADEMIES, *etc.*—Calcutta.—*Asiatic Society of Bengal.* Bibliotheca Indica. New Series. [Vol. 89.] 1848, *etc.* 8°. **14002. a. (vol. 89.)**

—— **॥ अथ निघण्टु॰ (निरुक्त॰)** [Nighaṇṭu and Nirukta.] ff. 14, 78. *See* VEDAS.—*Appendix.* **॥ अथ . . . षडङ्ग॰** [Shaḍaṅga.] pts. 4, 6. [1892.] *obl.* 8°. **14007. c. 27.**

—— **निरुक्तम् ॥ निघण्टु भाष्यम्** *etc.* [Nirukta. Preceded by an alphabetical index of the *pratīkas.*] pp. iii. xix. 152, ii. **अजमेर** १९५० [*Ajmere,* 1893.] 8°. **14090. d. 31.**

—— **वैदिकनिघण्टु** *etc.* [Vaidikanighaṇṭu. The Nighaṇṭu, with notes and indices. Preceded by the Vaidikakoṣa of Bhāskararāya Dikshita, a metrical version of the same.] pp. 32, 73. **मेरठ** [१८]९८ [*Meerut,* 1898.] 12°. **14092. a. 21.(2.)**

YAṢODĀNANDA PRĀMĀṆIKA. *See* HARIMOHANA PRĀMĀṆIKA. কমলাকরুণাবিলাসো নাম গুভাঙ্কঃ *etc.* [Kamalākaruṇāvilāsa. Edited, with notes, by Yaṣodānanda.] [1899.] 8°. **14079. c. 42.(2.)**

YAṢODHARA, *Kāmaṣāstrī.* *See* VĀTSYĀYANA, called MALLANĀGA. Das Kāmasūtram . . . nebst dem . . . Commentare Jayamaṅgalā des Yaçodhara . . . übersetzt . . . von R. Schmidt. 1897. 8°. **14053. d. 50.**

YAṢOVIJAYA. શ્રીજ્ઞાનસાર *etc.* [Jñānasāra. A series of 32 octads of stanzas upon the principles of the Jain creed. With a Gujarati translation and commentary based upon the work of Gambhīravijaya Gaṇī, biography of Yaṣovijaya, and introduction, by Dīpchand Chhaganlāl.] pp. xlv. ii. 220, vi. iii. ૧૯૬૨૧

અમદાવાદ ભાવનગર ૧૮૯૯ [*Baroda, Ahmadabad* printed, *Bhaunagar* published, 1899.] 12°. **14100. b. 6.**

—— Dnyansar of Muni Yashovijaya. Translated into Marâthi from its Gujarâthi translation of Mr. Deepchand Chhaganlal B.A. by Balchand Hirachand. [With the Sanskrit text.] (ज्ञानसारः) pp. i. xlvi. ii. 220, i. *Malegaon*, [1900.] 12°. **14100. b. 10.**

YAVANAJĀTAKA. यवनजातक *etc.* [Yavanajātaka. A treatise on astrology. With Hindi translation by Vanamālī Chaturvedī.] pp. 67. बम्बई १९५८ [*Bombay*, 1901.] 8°. **14053. ccc. 4.(3.)**

YAW-MYO-SĀ ATWIN-WÛN. *See* SAṄGHARAKKHITA. အလင်္ကာရ *etc.* [Subodhālaṅkāra. With Burmese paraphrase by the Yaw-myo-sā Atwin-wûn.] [1899.] 8°. **14302. i. 16.**

YMAÏZOUMI. *See* IMAÏZOUMI.

YOGA. 瑜伽課誦 [Yuga Kwaju, "Yogic Hymns." Including Sanskrit *dhāraṇīs, etc.*, with Japanese transliteration and translation by Kongō Chihō.] 3 maki. [1718.] 8°. **16007. c. 11.**

YOGABĪJA. योगबीजम् *etc.* [Yogabīja. A treatise, in 171 stanzas, on the Yoga 'way of salvation.' With Hindi version by Munnālāl.] pp. 45. कानपुर १९९९ [*Cawnpore*, 1899.] 8°. **14028. c. 85.(6.)**

YOGĀVACHARA. The Yogāvacara's Manual of Indian Mysticism as practised by Buddhists [, in Sinhalese and Pali]. Edited by T. W. Rhys Davids. 1896. 8°. *See* ACADEMIES, *etc.* — London.—*Pali Text Society.* YOGĀVACHARA. **14098. b. 29.(4.)**

YOGAVĀSISHṬHARĀMĀYAṆA. वाशिष्ठमहारामायणम् *etc.* [Yogavāsishṭharāmāyaṇa, or Vāsishṭhamahārāmāyaṇa. An epic poem popularly ascribed to Vālmīki, in which are conveyed doctrines of Yoga and Vedānta. With Ānandabodhendra's commentary Tātparyaprakāṣa. Edited with a Bengali translation and notes by Kālīvara Vedāntavāgīṣa.] কলিকাতা ১৮১৪ [*Calcutta*, 1893, *etc.*] 8°. **14049. a. 2.**

In progress.

—— योगवासिष्ठ महारामायणम् *etc.* [Yogavāsishṭharāmāyaṇa. With a Hindi version by Ṭhākuraprasāda and Hindi preface by Rāi Bahādur Lālā Baijnāth.] मुम्बई १९५७ [*Bombay*, 1900, *etc.*] 8°. **14048. e. 29.**

In progress?

—— The Yoga-vásishtha-mahárámáyana of Válmiki. Translated from the original Sanskrit by Vihári-lála Mitra. 4 vols. *Calcutta*, 1891-1899. 8°. **14049. b. 9.**

—— योगवासिष्ठ . . . वैराग्य अने मुमुक्ष प्रकरणोनुं भूળ *etc.* [Yogavāsishṭharāmāyaṇa. Sections i. and ii. Edited with Gujarati version by Pūrṇachandra Achaleṣvara Ṣarmā.] pp. iii. 837. अमदावाद १९०० [*Ahmadabad*, 1900.] 16°. **14048. a. 27.**

—— A translation of Yoga-Vâsishṭa Laghu—the smaller. [Being an abridgment, ascribed to Abhinanda, of the Yogavāsishṭharāmāyaṇa. Translated] by K. Narayanswami Aiyer. pp. xxiii. 346. *Madras*, 1896. 8°. **14048. cc. 5.**

—— ലഘുയോഗവാസിഷ്ഠ സാരം. സാന്മവാദം *etc.* [Laghu-yogavāsishṭhasāra. An epitome of the Yogavāsishṭha. With Malayalam translation by E. P. Subrahmaṇya Ṣāstrī.] pp. i. i. 56. *Palghat*, [1903.] 8°. **14049. b. 17.(2.)**

This is a text similar to that in the Grantham edition with Mahīdhara's gloss published at Chidambaram in 1889, but contains a little more matter.

YOGENDRA MIṢRA. *See* GOPĀLA BHAṬṬA, *disciple of Prabodhānanda.* ଉପବାସ ତତ୍ତ୍ୱ *etc.* [Upavāsatattva. With explanations in Oriya by Yogendra.] 1898. 12°. **14028. b. 84.(2.)**

YOGEṢACHANDRA DATTA. *See* KALHAṆA. Kings of Káshmíra: being a translation of the . . . Rájataranggini . . . By Jogesh Chunder Dutt. (Vol. iii. Kings of Kashmíra: being a translation of the Sanskrita works of Jonarāja, Shrīvara . . . Prājyabhaṭṭa and Shuka.). 1879-1898. 12°. **14070. b. 13.**

—— Old Relics in Kamrup. [An English essay on the antiquities of Assam, with the text of the inscriptions.] By Jogesh Chunder Dutt. pp. 27. *Calcutta*, [1892.] 12°. **14058. a. 9.**

YOGEṢACHANDRA RĀYA, *of Cuttack College. See* CHANDRAṢEKHARA SIṂHA. Siddhánta-darpaṇa . . . Edited with an introduction by Jogeś Chandra Ráy. 1899. 8°. **14053. ccc. 28.**

YOGĪNDRANĀTHA MUKHOPĀDHYĀYA. *See* MAHĀBHĀRATA. — Bhagavadgītā. — *English.* The Young Men's Gitá . . . Edited by Jogindranath Mukharji. 1900. 12°. **14065. a. 6.(2.)**

YOGĪNDRANĀTHA SENA, *Kavirāja.* The Hindu Medical Writers on the Plague. By Kaviraj Jogindranath Sen. pp. 22. *Calcutta,* [1898?]. 12°. **14043. b. 14.(2.)**

YUGALAKISORA VYĀSA PĀṬHAKA. *See* KĀTYĀYANA. महर्षिकात्यायन . . . सर्वानुक्रमसूत्रम् . . . Kátyáyana's Sarvánukramasutras . . . with the commentary of Yájñikánantadeva. Edited and annotated by . . . Yugalakiśora Páṭhaka. 1893, *etc.* 8°. **14007. c. 25.**

—— *See* ṢAUNAKA. महर्षिशौनकप्रणीतम् ऋक्प्रातिशाख्यम् । . . . Śaunaka's Prátiśákhya . . . with the commentary of Uvvaṭa. Edited and annotated by . . . Yugalakiśora Vyâsa, *etc.* 1903. 8°. **14090. c. 40.**

—— श्रीमद्याज्ञवल्क्यादिमहर्षिप्रणीतः शिक्षासङ्ग्रहः [Sikshāsaṅgraha.] . . . A collection of Śikshás by Yájña-valkya and others, [chiefly of the Mādhyandina school of the White Yajurveda, and also including the Pāṇinīyaśikshā of the Ṛigveda, the Nāradī, Gautamī, and Lomaṣī Ṣikshās of the Sāmaveda, and the Maṇḍūkī Ṣikshā of the Atharva,] with commentaries on some of them. Edited and annotated by . . . Yugalakiśora Vyása. pp. iii. 480. *Benares,* 1893. 8°. **14093. b. 31.**

Forms nos. 35, 40, 42, 44, *and* 46 *of the* Benares Sanskrit Series.

YUGALĀNANYAṢARAṆA, *Svāmī.* सीतारामनामप्रतापप्रकाश *etc.* [Sītārāmanāmapratāpaprakāṣa. A compilation of passages bearing upon the sanctity of the names of Sītā and Rāma. With Hindi translation. Third edition.] pp. 224. लखनऊ १९५८ [*Lucknow,* 1901.] 8°. **14033. bbb. 4.(2.)**

YUVARĀJA KAVI. *See* SADĀṢIVA, called YUVARĀJA KAVI.

ZACHARIAE (THEODOR). *See* HEMACHANDRA, *disciple of Devachandra.* अथ श्रीहेमचन्द्रसूरिप्रणीतोनेकार्थसंग्रहः ॥ . . . The Anekarthasamgraha . . . Edited with extracts from the commentary of Mahendra by T. Zachariæ. 1893. 4°. [*Sources of Sanskrit Lexicography.*] **14090. e. 23.(vol. 1.)**

—— *See* MAṄKHA. अथ श्रीमङ्खकोशष्टीकासारसहितः ॥ The Maṅkhakośa. Edited . . . with extracts from the commentary, and three indexes, by T. Zachariæ. 1897. 4°. [*Sources of Sanskrit Lexicography.*] **14090. e. 23.(vol. 3.)**

—— Epilegomena zu der Ausgabe des Maṅkhakośa. pp. 54. 1899. *See* ACADEMIES, *etc.*—Vienna. — *Kaiserliche Akademie der Wissenschaften.* Sitzungsberichte . . . Philosophische-historische Classe. Band 141. 1849, *etc.* 8°. **Ac. 810/6. (Bd. 141.)**

ẒĀLIM SINGH, *of Akbarpur, Faizabad.* *See* ĪṢVARA KRISHṆA. सांख्यतत्त्वसुबोधिनी *etc.* [Sāṅkhyatattva-subodhinī. Being the Sāṅkhyakārikā, with Hindi glosses and commentary based on that of Gauḍapāda by Ẓālim Singh.] [1899.] 8°. **14048. d. 37.(2.)**

—— *See* MAHĀBHĀRATA.—Bhagavadgītā.—*Sanskrit and Vernaculars.* भगवद्गीता *etc.* [Bhagavadgītā. With grammatical analyses and Hindi interpretations and expositions by Ẓālim Singh.] [1901.] 8°. **14065. c. 54.**

—— *See* UPANISHADS. — *Separate Upanishads.* ऐतरेयोपनिषद् *etc.* [Aitareyopanishad. Edited with analyses and Hindi glossaries to each verse by Ẓālim Singh.] [1900.] 8°. **14007. dd. 3.(4.)**

—— —— मुण्डकोपनिषद् *etc.* [Muṇḍakopanishad. Edited with analyses and Hindi glossaries to each verse by Ẓālim Singh.] [1900.] 8°. **14007. dd. 3.(2.)**

—— —— प्रश्नोपनिषद् *etc.* [Praṣnopanishad. Edited with analyses and Hindi glossaries to each verse by Ẓālim Singh.] [1900.] 8°. **14007. dd. 3.(1.)**

—— —— तैत्तिरीयोपनिषद् *etc.* [Taittirīyopanishad. Edited with analyses and Hindi glossaries to each *anuvāka* by Ẓālim Singh.] [1900.] 8°. **14007. dd. 3.(3.)**

ZALKIKAR, *B.* *See* BHĪMĀCHĀRYA JHAḶKĪKAR.

ZIN-PYU-MYA-SHIN, *King of Toungoo.* ကိုးစောင်ချုပ်ဓမ္မသတ်။အဝဓမ္မသတ်း *etc.* [Ko saung hkyôk dhamma-that, or Navadhammasattha. A Pali digest of 9 law-books. Section viii., treating of the law of inheritance. Edited, with Burmese translations, by Maung San Htûn Aung and Maung Kyaw Zan Ū.] pp.iii.9. ဝဝဲတွေ ၁၂၅၆ [*Akyab,* 1894.] 8°. **14098. ccc. 20.**

ADDENDA.

ABHINAVA-ṢAṄKARĀCHĀRYA. *See* ṢAṄKARA ĀCHĀRYA, styled ABHINAVA-ṢAṄKARĀCHĀRYA.

ACADEMIES, *etc.* — London. — *British Museum.* Catalogue of Sanskrit, Pali, and Prakrit Books in the British Museum acquired during the years 1876-92. By Cecil Bendall. [With preface by Sir Robert K. Douglas.] pp. viii. ii. coll. 624. *London,* 1893. 4°. **Cat. Desk B.**

ACADEMIES, *etc.* — London. — *British Museum.* Catalogue of the Sanskrit Manuscripts in the British Museum. By Cecil Bendall. [With preface by Sir Robert K. Douglas.] pp. vii. 261. *London,* 1902. 4°. **Cat. Desk A.**

ACADEMIES, *etc.*—Madras.—*University of Madras.* *See* KĀLIDĀSA. — *Raghuvaṃṣa.* F. A. Examination of 1892. The Complete Sanskrit Text, *etc.* 1891. 8°. **14076. c. 59.**

ACADEMIES, *etc.*—Madras.—*University of Madras.* *See* MAHĀBHĀRATA. — *Vanaparva.* University of Madras. Matriculation Examination of 1891. Full notes on the Sanskrit text, *etc.* 1891. 8°. **14060. c. 30.(2.)**

ACADEMIES, *etc.*—Madras.—*University of Madras.* *See* SVĀMI ṢĀSTRĪ, *P.K.*, and KĀMEṢVARA AIYAR, *B.V.* Matriculation Examination, 1891. The Sanskrit Text Examiner, *etc.* 1891. 12°. **14072. b. 18.**

AKHAI-RĀM, *disciple of Bhikhārī-dās.* *See* TANTRAS. [*Brahmayāmalatantra.*] **कबीरशतक** *etc.* [Kabīr-ṣataka. With Hindi metrical paraphrase by Akhai-rām.] [1901.] 8°. **14033. bbb. 15.(1.)**

AMMĀḶ ĀCHĀRYA. *See* VARADĀCHĀRYA, *son of Ghaṭikāṣata Sudarṣanāchārya.*

ĀNANDĀCHĀRYA VIDYĀVINODA, *Rāi Bahādur P.* *See* VEṄKAṬANĀTHA VEDĀNTĀCHĀRYA. **श्री:** . . . **हंससन्देशः°** (Hamsa Sandesa . . . Edited by . . . Ananda Charlu.) 1903. 12°. **14060. b. 19.**

ANANTANĀRĀYAṆA ṢĀSTRĪ, *of Kudalur.* *See* ṢAṄKARASUBRAHMAṆYA SŪRI. തടാതകാപരിണയം *etc.* [Taṭātakāpariṇaya. With commentary styled Prakāṣikā by Anantanārāyaṇa.] 1903. 8°. **14070. dd. 29.**

ARIYĀLAṄKĀRA, *of Neyin.* *See* SUTTAPIṬAKA.—*Entire Text.* သုတ္တန်ပိဋကတ် ။ *etc.* [Suttapiṭaka. Vols. i.-iv., the Dīghanikāya, with the Burmese interpretation of Ariyālaṅkāra.] 1904, *etc.* 8°. **14099. aa. 8.**

ARNOLD (*Sir* EDWIN). *See* MAHĀBHĀRATA. — Bhagavadgitā.—*German.* Die Bhagavad Gita . . . In poetischer Form nach Edwin Arnolds Sanskrit-Übersetzung . . . übertragen von F. Hartmann. 1904. 12°. **14060. c. 34.**

BĀDARĀYAṆA. *See* MĀDHAVAMUKUNDACHARAṆA. **परपक्षगिरिवज्र:** *etc.* [Parapakshagirivajra. A polemical exposition of the Brahmasūtra according to the Nimbārka school.] [1902.] 8°. **14049. b. 6.**

BĀDARĀYAṆA. The Chatussûtrî [*i.e.* Brahmasūtra I. i. 1-4 with commentary] from . . . Râmânujâchâryâ's Shribhashya, *etc.* 1904. 8°. *See* RĀMĀNUJA.—*Commentaries.* **14049. a. 11.**

BADARĪDATTA ṢARMĀ. *See* UPANISHADS. — *Separate Upanishads.* **कठोपनिषद्** *etc.* [Kaṭhopanishad. With Hindi translation and exposition by Badarīdatta.] [1903.] 12°. **14007. b. 4.(5.)**

BAIJNĀTHJĪ, *of Dehwa, Manpur.* *See* PURĀṆAS.—*Brahmāṇḍapurāṇa.* [*Adhyātmarāmāyaṇa.*] अध्यात्म-रामायण *etc.* [Adhyātmarāmāyaṇa. With Hindi paraphrase and commentary by Baijnāthjī.] [1894.] Fol. **14018. c. 33.**

BALADEVAPRASĀDA MIṢRA, *son of Sukhānanda, of Moradabad.* *See* RŪPA GOSVĀMĪ. श्रीलघुभाग-वतामृतम् *etc.* [Laghu-bhāgavatāmṛita. With Hindi translation and gloss by Baladevaprasāda.] [1903.] 8°. **14076. d. 55.**

BALADEVA VIDYĀBHŪSHAṆA. *See* JĪVA GOSVĀMĪ. षट्सन्दर्भ॰ [Shaṭsandarbha, or Bhāgavata-sandarbha. With annotations upon the Tattva-sandarbha by Baladeva.] [1899-1901.] 8°. **14016. d. 62.**

BALADEVA VIDYĀBHŪSHAṆA. *See* RŪPA GOSVĀMĪ. श्रीलघुभागवतामृतम् *etc.* [Laghu-bhāgavatāmṛita. With commentary of Baladeva.] [1903.] 8°. **14076. d. 55.**

BĀLA KAVI. *See* RĀJARĀJA VARMĀ.

BALLĪ MIṢRA, *of Patna.* *See* PURĀṆAS.— *Agnipurāṇa.* अथ श्री राजगृह माहात्म्यम् । *etc.* [Rājagṛiha-māhātmya. With Hindi translation by Ballī.] 1904. *obl.* 12°. **14016. b. 23.(3.)**

BALLINI (AMBROGIO). *See* SIDDHARSHI. La Upamitabhavaprapañchā Kathā . . . I-II. [Translated by A. Ballini.] 1904, *etc.* 8°. [*Società Asiatica Italiana : Giornale.*] **Ac. 8804. (vol. 17, etc.)**

BALLINI (AMBROGIO). *See* ṢUBHAṢĪLA GAṆĪ. Pañćaçatī-prabodhasambandhaḥ. . . Edite e tradotte per cura di A. Ballini. 1904, *etc.* 8°. [*Studi Italiani di Filologia Indo-Iranica.*] **P.P. 4884. da.(vol. 6, etc.)**

BĀPAṬ (V. V.). *See* VISHṆU VĀMANA BĀPAṬ.

BARNETT (LIONEL DAVID). *See* UPANISHADS.— *Selections.* Some sayings from the Upanishads. Done into English with notes by L. D. Barnett. 1905. 8°. **14007. b. 24.**

BAṬUDĀSA GOSVĀMĪ. *See* RŪPA GOSVĀMĪ. সটীক . . . শ্রীস্তবপুষ্পাঞ্জলিঃ *etc.* [Stavapushpāñjali. Edited by Baṭudāsa.] [1902.] 8°. **14072. ccc. 34.**

BELLONI-FILIPPI (FERDINANDO). *See* PURĀṆAS.— *Brahmāṇḍapurāṇa.* [*Nāsiketopākhyāna.*] Il "Nāsiketopākhyānam" . . . preceduto da una notizia sulle "Visioni indiane." [By F. Belloni-Filippi.] 1902-1904. 8°. [*Società Asiatica Italiana : Giornale.*] **Ac. 8804. (vol. 15-17.)**

BELLONI-FILIPPI (FERDINANDO). *See* UPANISHADS. — *Separate Upanishads.* La Kâṭhaka-upanisad, tradotto . . . e preceduta da una notizia sul panteismo indiano [by F. Belloni-Filippi]. 1905. 8°. **14007. b. 26.**

BENDALL (CECIL). *See* SUBHĀSHITASAṄGRAHA. Subhāṣita-saṃgraha. (An anthology . . . Edited by C. Bendall.) 1905. 8°. **14070. ee. 2.**

BENDALL (CECIL). Catalogue of Sanskrit, Pali, and Prakrit Books in the British Museum acquired during the years 1876-92. By C. Bendall. 1893. 4°. *See* ACADEMIES, *etc.* — London. — *British Museum.* **Cat. Desk B.**

BENDALL (CECIL). Catalogue of the Sanskrit Manuscripts in the British Museum. By C. Bendall. 1902. 4°. *See* ACADEMIES, *etc.*—London. —*British Museum.* **Cat. Desk A.**

BHĀLACHANDRA ṢAṄKARA DEVASTHALĪ. *See* KĀLIDĀSA.—*Meghadūta.* यक्षसंदेश *etc.* [Yaksha-sandeṣa. Being the Meghadūta with metrical Marathi version by Bhālachandra.] [1902.] 16°. **14076. a. 20.(2.)**

BHANDARKAR (S. R.). *See* ṢRĪDHARA RĀMAKṚISHṆA BHĀṆḌĀRKAR.

BHĀNUBHAṬṬA. *See* HARI KAVI, *son of Nārāyaṇa Sūri.*

BHĀSKARĀNANDA SARASVATĪ, *disciple of Anantarāma.* *See* KĀLIDĀSA, *Pseud., author of the Nalodaya.* ॥ नलोदय॰ [Nalodaya. With Prajñākara's Subodhinī and a gloss by Bhāskarānanda.] [1902.] 8°. **14076. d. 54.**

BHAṬṬOJĪ DĪKSHITA. *See* BHAIRAVA MIṢRA. भैरवी कारकान्ता . . . Karakanta-Bhairavi or commentary . . . on Laghu Shabdaratna, *etc.* 1896. 8°. **14090. d. 32.**

BHĪMASENA ṢARMĀ, *disciple of Dayānanda Sarasvatī*. *See* KĀTYĀYANA. अथ कात्यीयतर्पण॰ [Kātīyatarpaṇaprayoga. Edited with Hindi translations *etc.* by Bhīmasena.] [1902.] *obl.* 12°.
14028. bb. 4.(4.)

BODHĀNANDA GIRI, *of Miani*. *See* UPANISHADS.—*Modern and Fictitious Upanishads*. मृत्युलांगूल *etc.* [Mrityulāṅgūlopanishad and Sūryopanishad. Edited with Hindi notes *etc.* by Bodhānanda Giri.] [1904.] 12°. **14010. b. 3.(3.)**

BOEHTLINGK (OTTO VON). *See* UPANISHADS.—*Small Collections*. Herr Böhtlingk legte drei kritisch gesichtete und übersetzte Upanishad . . . vor. 1890. 8°. [*Koeniglich Saechsische Gesellschaft der Wissenschaften: Berichte*.] **Ac. 700/2.(Bd. 42.)**

BRĀHMAṆAS. *See* LÉVI (S.). La Doctrine du Sacrifice dans les Brâhmaṇas, *etc.* 1898. 8°. **Ac. 8929/7.(vol. 11.)**

BRĀHMA-SAMĀJ. *See* THEISTIC TEXTS. ब्राह्मधर्म्मप्रतिपादक-श्लोकसंग्रहः *etc.* (A Compilation of Theistic Texts, *etc.*) 1904. 12°. **14072. b. 33.**

BRĀHMA-SAMĀJ. *See* UPANISHADS.—*Selections*. Brahmopasanam [a lectionary of the Brāhma Samāj,] *etc.* 1904. 16°. **14010. a. 10.**

BUTENSCHÖN (ANDREA). *See* UPANISHADS.—*Separate Upanishads*. Kâthaka-upanishad. Öfversatt . . . af A. Butenschön. 1902. 8°. **14007. b. 27.**

CHAKRADHARA JHĀ, *son of Ṣatrughna, of Sagarpur*. *See* RAGHUDEVA SARASVATĪ. मैथिल . . . रघुदेव . . . विरचिता विरुदावली *etc.* [Birudāvalī. Edited with a commentary styled Vibudharājirañjinī by Chakradhara.] [1904.] 8°. **14076. d. 57.**

CHAṆḌĪCHARAṆA SMṚITIBHŪSHAṆA. *See* RAGHUNANDANA BHAṬṬĀCHĀRYA. প্রায়শ্চিত্ততত্ত্বম্ *etc.* [Prāyaṣchittatattva. With commentary. Edited by Chaṇḍīcharaṇa.] [1903.] 8°.
14033. bbb. 20.(1.)

CHAṆḌĪCHARAṆA SMṚITIBHŪSHAṆA. *See* ṢŪLAPĀṆI. প্রায়শ্চিত্তবিবেকঃ *etc.* [Prāyaṣchittaviveka. With commentary. Edited with Bengali notes by Chaṇḍīcharaṇa.] [1903.] 8°. **14033. aa. 31.**

CHANDRAṢEKHARA BRAHMĀNANDA SVĀMĪ. *See* UPANISHADS.—*Selections*. Brahmopasanam . . . dedicated to . . . Chandra Sekhara Brahmananda Swami, Pradhana Acharya of the Bangalore Brahma Samaj, *etc.* 1904. 16°. **14010. a. 10.**

CHĀRUCHANDRA VASU. *See* SUTTAPIṬAKA.—*Khuddakanikāya*. [*Dhammapada*.] ধম্মপদ *etc.* [Dhammapada. Edited with *anvaya*, Sanskrit paraphrase, and Bengali version by Chāruchandra Vasu.] [1904.] 12°. **14098. a. 43.**

CHINTĀMAṆI VINĀYAKA VAIDYA. *See* MAHĀBHĀRATA.—*Abridgments and Selections*. Mahabharata. Abridged by C. V. Vaidya. 1902. 8°.
14065. bbb. 11.

CHŌYI-VAIDYAR, *Pālōḷi*. *See* NĪLAKAṆṬHA, *of Rājamaṅgalam*. മാതംഗലീലാ *etc.* [Mātaṅgalīlā. With Malayalam translation by Chōyi-vaidyar.] 1904. 8°. **14053. ccc. 40.(2.)**

COURTILLIER (GASTON). *See* JAYADEVA, *son of Bhojadeva*. Le Gīta-govinda . . . Pastorale . . . Traduite par M. G. Courtillier, *etc.* 1904. 12°.
14070. b. 32.

DARṢANĀNANDA SARASVATĪ, *Svāmī*, *disciple of Anubhavānanda*. *See* KAṆĀDA. وشيشك درشن الخ [Vaiṣeshikadarṣana. With Hindustani translation and commentary by Darṣanānanda.] [1902.] 8°.
14049. b. 18.

DAṢABALA, *Grammarian*. অথ দশ বল কারিকা [Daṣabalakārikā. 39 memorial verses on roots of more than one conjugation.] pp. 8. *See* SARVAVARMĀ.—*Appendix*. সটীক কাতন্ত্র-গণমালা *etc.* [Kātantragaṇamālā.] [1903.] 12°. **14092. a. 24.(3.)**

DASU SRIRAMULU. *See* ṢRĪRĀMULU PANTULU, *Dāsu*.

DEṢIKĀCHĀRYA, *Āḍūr Ichambāḍi*. *See* PARĀṢARA. [*Smṛiti*.] பராசரஸ்ம்ருதி *etc.* [Parāṣarasmṛiti. Edited with Tamil translation by Deṣikāchārya.] 1902. 8°. **14039. b. 30.**

DEṢIKĀCHĀRYA, *Naḍādūr Vedānta*. *See* VEṄKAṬANĀTHA VEDĀNTĀCHĀRYA. श्रीः . . . हंससन्देशः॰ (Hamsa Sandesa . . . With an [English] introduction . . . notes and translation in verse [by Deṣikāchārya and Kastūriraṅga,] *etc.*) 1903. 12°. **14060. b. 19.**

DE SILVA (W. ARTHUR). *See* SUTTAPIṬAKA.—*Entire Text.* Buddhist Pali Texts . . . Edited under the direction of W. A. De Silva, *etc.* [1903, *etc.*] 8°.
14099. bbb.

DHAMMĀNANDA ĀCHARIYA, *of Tha-tôn.* ကစ္စာယနသာရပါဠိ [Kachchāyanasāra.] *See* SADDHAMMASIRI. သဒ္ဒတ္ထဘေဒစိန္တာ *etc.* [Saddatthabhedachintā.] pp. 27-31. 1903. 8°.
14099. bb. 2.

DHAMMASIRI, *Mahāsthavira.* ခုဒ္ဒသိက္ခာပါဠိ॥ [Khuddasikkhā.] *See* WINI-NGAY. ဝိနည်းလေယ် *etc.* [Wini-ngay le saung.] pp. 75-121. 1903. 8°.
14099. bb. 1.

DĪPAVAṂSA. *See* GEIGER (W.). Dīpavaṃsa and Mahāvaṃsa, *etc.* 1901. 8°. **14098. ccc. 28.**

DORASĀMAIYA, *Ōmandūru Vaidyam.* *See* SVĀTMĀRĀMA. శ్రీ . . . హఠయోగప్రదీపిక *etc.* [Haṭhayogapradīpikā. With Telugu translation and commentary by Dorasāmaiya.] 1903. 8°.
14049. b. 23.

DURGĀDATTA ṢĀSTRĪ, *son of Baladeva Purohita.* *See* VIṢVANĀTHA PAÑCHĀNANA BHAṬṬĀCHĀRYA. Kârikâvali . . . With a new commentary Prajnamanorama by . . . Durgadatta, *etc.* [1902.] 8°.
14049. b. 16.

DURGASIṂHA, *Commentator on the Kātantra.* *See* TRILOCHANADĀSA. আখ্যাতপঞ্জী । *etc.* [Ākhyātapañjī. The commentary on the section upon verbs in Durgasiṃha's *vritti.*] [1895.] 8°.
14090. bb. 13.(5.)

EDWARD VII, *King of Great Britain and Ireland.* *See* ṢIVARĀMA PĀṆḌE. राज्याभिषेक दरबार . . . Rajya bhishek . . . verses in honour of the Delhi Coronation Darbar, *etc.* [1903.] 12°. **14072. b. 27.(2.)**

EDWARD VII, *King of Great Britain and Ireland.* *See* ṢRĪṢVARA VIDYĀLAṄKĀRA BHAṬṬĀCHĀRYA. Dillimahotsava-kavyam. A Sanskrit poem on the Delhi-Durbar, *etc.* 1903. 8°. **14076. d. 56.**

GAṆAPATI ṢĀSTRĪ, *Paṇgānāḍ.* *See* PURĀṆAS.—*Skandapurāṇa.* इदङ्किल . . . श्रीकाश्यपक्षेत्रस्य माहात्म्यम् *etc.* (Kâṣyapakshetramâhâtmyam . . . Edited by Ganapathi Sastri, *etc.*) 1903. 8°. **14016. dd. 2.(3.)**

GAṆAPATI ṢĀSTRĪ, *Paṇgānāḍ.* *See* VEDAS.—Yajurveda. — *Taittirīyasaṃhitā.* உடு . . . ஸ்ரீபாஸ்கர-ஸூரியபாஷ்யம். [Ṣatarudrīya. With commentary. Edited by Gaṇapati Ṣāstrī.] 1903. *obl.* 16°.
14010. a. 8.

GAṬṬŪLĀL, *Bhāratamārtaṇḍa Vedāntabhaṭṭāchārya.* *See* VALLABHĀCHĀRYA. श्रीतत्त्वार्थदीपः । *etc.* [Tattvārthadīpa. With the beginnings of supercommentaries by Kalyāṇarāya and Gaṭṭūlāl.] [1904.] 8°. **14049. bb. 5.**

GAURAGOVINDA RĀYA, *Upādhyāya, of the Navavidhāna-maṇḍalī.* *See* PATAÑJALI.—*Grammatical Works.* भाष्यसङ्गमनी *etc.* [Bhāshyasaṅgamanī. Being the aphorisms of the Mahābhāshya, the text of the Kāṣikā, and a commentary by Gauragovinda Rāya; together with a supercommentary by the latter, styled Tattvasaṅkalanī.] [1903, *etc.*] 8°.
14090. bb. 22.

GAURAGOVINDA RĀYA, *Upādhyāya, of the Navavidhāna-maṇḍalī.* *See* UPANISHADS.—*Selections.* वेदान्तसमन्वयः *etc.* [Vedāntasamanvaya. A digest of Upanishadic passages, with a Vedantic commentary harmonising the interpretations of the various schools, by Gauragovinda Rāya.] [1903, *etc.*] 8°. **14049. bb. 2.**

GHAṆṬĀVATĀRĀCHĀRYA, *Peruṅgaṭṭūr.* *See* VEṄKAṬANĀTHA VEDĀNTĀCHĀRYA. శ్రీః . . . తత్త్వటీకా *etc.* [Tattvaṭīkā. Edited by Ghaṇṭāvatārāchārya.] 1904, *etc.* 8°. **14049. b. 24.**

GIRIJĀPRASĀDA, *son of Māṇikchand.* *See* PURĀṆAS.—*Brahmāṇḍapurāṇa.* [*Adhyātmarāmāyaṇa.*] रामगीता *etc.* [Rāmagītā. With Hindi metrical version and prose paraphrase by Girijāprasāda.] [1898.] 8°. **14048. dd. 9.(2.)**

GOVINDA SOMAYĀJĪ, *of Keḷa-nellūr.* *See* VARĀHAMIHIRA. ஸ்ரீ . . . ப்ருஹஜ்ஜாதகம்॥ [Brihaj-jātaka. With Govinda's commentary Daṣādhyāyī upon ch. i.-x.] [1905.] 8°. **14053. ccc. 51.**

HAṂSASVARŪPA, *Svāmī.* *See* PŪRṆĀNANDA GOSVĀMĪ. षट् . . . Shatchakra Niroopan Chittra. [Being the Shaṭchakranirūpaṇa] with Bhashya and Bhasha, containing the pictures of the different Nerves and Plexuses . . . with their full description . . . By . . . Hansa Swaroop. [1903.] 4°.
14033. d. 25.

HARIHARA ŚARMĀ. *See* Purāṇas.—*Selections.* ॥ अथ एकादशीमाहात्म्य° [Ekādaśīmāhātmya. With Nepali translation by Harihara.] [1903.] *obl.* 8°. **14016. dd. 11.**

HBI, *Hsaya.* *See* Suttapiṭaka. — *Entire Text.* သုတ္တန်ပိဋကတ်॥ *etc.* [Suttapiṭaka. Edited by Hbi and others.] 1904, *etc.* 8°. **14099. aa. 8.**

HBI, *Hsaya.* *See* Vinayapiṭaka. ဝိနည်း *etc.* [Vinayapiṭaka. The text with Burmese interpretation. Edited by Hbi, Ko Aung Min, and Ko Kyaw.] 1903-1904. 8°. **14099. aa. 1-7.**

HĪRĀNANDA MŪLARĀJA ŚĀSTRĪ. *See* Vedas.—Ṛigveda.—*Selections of Hymns and Verses.* ऋक्सूक्तसंग्रहः *etc.* (Hymns from the Rigveda . . . Edited with Sáyana's commentary . . . *etc.*, by . . . Hiránanda . . . Shástrí.) 1903. 8°. **14007. b. 19.**

HPYE, *Hsaya Ū.* *See* Vinayapiṭaka. [*Selections*]. ဝိနည်း . . . ဒွေမာတိကာ *etc.* [Dvemātikā. Edited by Ū Hpye.] [1904.] 8°. **14099. b. 3.**

JAGADDHARA ŚARMĀ MĪMĀṂSAKA, *Śrotriyopādhyāya, of Gangauli.* *See* Rudradhara Mahopādhyāya. वर्षकृत्यम् । *etc.* [Varshakṛitya. Edited with supplements by Jagaddhara.] [1903.] 8°. **14033. bbb. 24.**

JĀGARĀBHIDDHAJA, *Saddhammavaṃsa,* known as Shwegyin Hsaya. *See* Vinayapiṭaka. ဝိနည်း *etc.* [Vinayapiṭaka. Vol. iii., the Pārājika, and vol. iv., the Pāchittiya, with interpretation by Jāgarābhiddhaja.] 1903-1904. 8°. **14099. aa. 3, 4.**

JAIMINI. — *Mīmāṃsāsūtra.* *See* Khaṇḍadeva. भाट्टदीपिका । Bhāṭṭa Dīpikā, *etc.* 1899, *etc.* 8°. [*Bibliotheca Indica.*] **14002. a.(vol. 141.)**

JAIMINI.—*Mīmāṃsāsūtra.* *See* Pārthasārathi Miśra. न्यायरत्नमाला *etc.* (Nyâyaratnamâlâ, *etc.*) 1900. 8°. **14004. a. 7.**

JAYĀDITYA, *the Grammarian.* *See* Patañjali.—*Grammatical Works.* भाष्यसङ्गमनी *etc.* [Bhāshyasaṅgamanī. Being the aphorisms of the Mahābhāshya, the text of the Kāśikā, and a commentary.] [1903, *etc.*] 8°. **14090. bb. 22.**

JĪVADEVA GOSVĀMĪ. *See* Jīva Gosvāmī.

KALYĀṆARĀYA. *See* Vallabhāchārya. श्रीतत्त्वार्थदीपः । *etc.* [Tattvārthadīpa. With the beginnings of supercommentaries by Kalyāṇarāya and Gaṭṭūlāl.] [1904.] 8°. **14049. bb. 5.**

KĀŚĪNĀTHA VĀMANA LELE. *See* Purāṇas.—*Devībhāgavatapurāṇa.* श्रीदेवीभागवत. [Devībhāgavata. Skandha iv., with Marathi translation, edited by Kāśīnātha Lele.] [1902, *etc.*] 8°. **14016. dd. 8.**

KASTŪRI RAṄGĀCHĀRYA, *Paṇḍitaratnam.* *See* Raṅgāchārya, *Paṇḍitaratnam Tarkatīrtha Kastūri.*

KELUSKAR (K. A.). *See* Kṛishṇarāu Arjuna Keluskar.

KO AUNG MIN, *Hsaya.* *See* Suttapiṭaka.—*Entire Text.* သုတ္တန်ပိဋကတ်॥ *etc.* [Suttapiṭaka. Edited by Ko Aung Min and others.] 1904, *etc.* 8°. **14099. aa. 8.**

KO KYAW, *Hsaya.* *See* Suttapiṭaka.—*Entire Text.* သုတ္တန်ပိဋကတ်॥ *etc.* [Suttapiṭaka. Edited by Ko Kyaw and others.] 1904, *etc.* 8°. **14099. aa. 8.**

KṚISHṆACHANDRA BHĀGAVATABHŪSHAṆA. *See* Viśvanātha Chakravartī. सटीकम् श्रीकृष्णभावनामृत° [Śrikṛishṇabhāvanāmṛita. Edited by Kṛishṇachandra.] [1904.] 8°. **14070. dd. 31.**

KṚISHṆĀJĪ NĀRĀYAṆA JOŚĪ. *See* Purāṇas.—*Bhavishyapurāṇa.* भविष्यपुराणांतर्गत प्रभुलिंगलीला. [Prabhuliṅgalīlā. With Marathi translation by Kṛishṇājī.] [1903-1904.] 8°. **14016. dd. 9.**

KUMĀRILA BHAṬṬA. *See* Pārthasārathi Miśra. न्यायरत्नमाला *etc.* (Nyâyaratnamâlâ, *etc.*) [1900.] 8°. **14004. a. 7.**

KUPPUSVĀMI RĀJU, *V.* *See* Uttaragītā. உத்தரகீதை *etc.* [Uttaragītā. With Tamil paraphrase and notes by Kuppusvāmi.] [1903.] 12°. **14048. a. 29.(3.)**

KUPPUSVĀMI ŚĀSTRI, *T. S.* *See* Vādībhasiṃha Sūri. The Kshattrachudamani . . . With . . . notes by T. S. Kuppuswami Sastriyar. 1903. 8°. **14070. dd. 30.**

MAHĀBHĀRATA. — BHAGAVADGĪTĀ. — *Appendix.* *See* VALLABHĀCHĀRYA. श्रीतत्त्वार्थदीपः । *etc.* [Tattvārthadīpa. A summary of doctrine, pt. I summarising the Bhagavadgītā.] [1904.] 8°. **14049. bb. 5.**

MAHĀDEVA ŚĀSTRĪ, *Allādi,* known also as MAHĀDEVA AIYAR, *Curator of Mysore Government Oriental Library.* *See* UPANISHADS.—*Separate Upanishads.* The Taittirîya Upanishad, with the commentaries of Sankarâchârya, Suresvarâchârya and Sâyana . . . Translated . . . by A. Mahadeva Sastri. 1903. 8°. **14007. b. 23.**

MOHINĪMOHANA CHATTOPĀDHYĀYA. *See* SAṄKARA ĀCHĀRYA.—*Two or More Works.* Âtmânâtma-viveka . . . Translated . . . by Mohini M. Chatterjee. [1904.] 16°. **14048. a. 30.**

MṚITYUMJAYA ŚĀSTRĪ, *Lakshmīnārāyaṇapuram.* *See* ŚAṄKARA ĀCHĀRYA.—*Doubtful and Supposititious Works.* ஸ்ரீ... ஶிவாநந்தலஹரீ *etc.* [Śivānandalaharī. With interpretations in Tamil. Edited by Mṛityumjaya and Veṅkaṭasvāmi.] 1904. 12°. **14048. b. 48.**

MUKUNDA JHĀ, *of Moradabad.* *See* UPANISHADS.—*Selections.* अथ महावाक्यरत्नावलि° [Mahāvākyaratnāvali. Edited by Mukunda.] [1903.] 12°. **14010. b. 25.**

NANDAKIŚORA ŚĀSTRĪ, *son of Rameśa, of Mathura.* *See* VALLABHĀCHĀRYA. श्रीतत्त्वार्थदीपः । *etc.* [Tattvārthadīpa. With commentary, *etc.* Edited by Nandakiśora.] [1904.] 8°. **14049. bb. 5.**

NĀRADA. [*Sūtra.*] Nârada Sûtra. An enquiry into Love, Bhakti-jijnâsâ. Translated . . . with an independent commentary by E. T. Sturdy. pp. 68. *London, Aberdeen* [printed], 1896. 8°. **14028. c. 68.**

Forms no. 1 *of* "*Indian Ideals.*"

NĀRADA. [*Sūtra.*] ভক্তিসূত্রম্ দেবর্ষি নারদ প্রোক্তম্ *etc.* [Bhaktisūtra, or Nāradasūtra. With Bengali exposition by Śyāmalāla Gosvāmī.] pp. i. 120. কলিকাতা ১৩১১ [*Calcutta,* 1904.] 16°. **14028. bb. 15.**

NARASIṂHAIYĀ, *Basavapatna.* *See* ŚAṄKARA ĀCHĀRYA.—*Two or More Works.* Âtmânâtma-viveka . . . and Âtmabodha . . . Translated by Mohini M. Chatterjee [and B. Narasiṃhaiyā respectively]. [1904.] 16°. **14048. a. 30.**

NĀRĀYAṆA KAVI, *Śrīdhāma-rādhāmaṅgalam.* *See* NĀRĀYAṆA ŚĀSTRĪ, *Rādhāmaṅgalam V.*

NEUMANN (KARL EUGEN). *See* SUTTAPIṬAKA.—*Khuddakanikāya.* [*Suttanipāta.*] Die Reden Gotamo Buddho's aus der Sammlung der Bruchstücke Suttanipāto . . . übersetzt von K. E. Neumann. 1905. 8°. **14098. dd. 29.**

NITYAKARMA. *See* RUDRADHARA MAHOPĀDHYĀYA. वर्षकृत्यम् । *etc.* [Varshakṛitya.] 1903. 8°. **14033. bbb. 24.**

NṚISIṂHĀMĀTYA, *Pulugurti.* *See* UPANISHADS.—*Selections.* మహావాక్యరత్నావళి *etc.* [Mahāvākyaratnāvali. With grammatical analysis and Telugu commentary called Suprabhā by Nṛisiṃhāmātya.] 1904. 8°. **14007. b. 25.**

PARITTA.—*Sinhalese Editions.* The Siam Standard Paritta . . . Compiled by . . . W. Subhuti . . . assisted by . . . P. C. Jinavarawansa. 1897. 8°. *See* SUBHŪTI, *V.* **14098. b. 22.**

PAṬNĪ MAL. *See* PURĀṆAS.—*Skandapurāṇa.* کاشی کهند [Kāśīkhaṇḍa. An abridged Persian translation by Paṭnī Mal.] [1865 ?] 8°. **Pers. 236.**

PETERSON (PETER). *See* VEDAS.—Ṛigveda.—*Selections of Hymns and Verses.* Hymns from the Ṛigveda, edited with Sâyaṇa's commentary, notes, and a translation, by P. Peterson . . . Third edition. 1905. 8°. **14007. g. 1.**

PURĀṆAS.—*Bhāgavatapurāṇa.* *See* VALLABHĀCHĀRYA. श्रीतत्त्वार्थदीपः । *etc.* [Tattvārthadīpa. A summary of doctrine, pt. 3 epitomising the Bhāgavatapurāṇa.] [1904.] 8°. **14049. bb. 5.**

RĀMACHANDRA TĪRTHA, *disciple of Vāsudeva Sarasvatī.* *See* UPANISHADS.—*Selections.* మహావాక్యరత్నావళి *etc.* [Mahāvākyaratnāvali.] 1904. 8°. **14007. b. 25.**

RĀMA VĀRIYAR. *See* VARĀHAMIHIRA. ഹോരാശാസ്ത്രം *etc.* [Horāśāstra. Edited with Malayalam translation and commentary by Rāma Vāriyar.] [1890.] 8°. **14053. ccc. 52.**

RAṄGAIYĀ NĀYUḌU, *P. R.* *See* UPANISHADS.—*Selections.* Brahmopasanam . . . by . . . P. R. Rangiah Naidu. 1904. 16°. **14010. a. 10.**

ṢĀLAGRĀMA VAIṢYA, *of Moradabad.* *See* VAṄGASENA. ॥ श्रीः . . . वङ्गसेनः *etc.* [Vaṅgasena. With Hindi translation by Ṣālagrāma.] [1905.] 4°. **14043. ddd. 2.**

ṢAṄKARA ĀCHĀRYA.—COMMENTARIES. [*Upanishads.*] *See* UPANISHADS.—*Separate Upanishads.* The Taittirîya Upanishad, with the commentaries of Sankarâchârya . . . Translated into English, *etc.* 1903. 8°. **14007. b. 23.**

ṢAṄKARALĀLA, *son of Lālā Bhojadeva.* *See* VAṄGASENA. ॥ श्रीः . . . वङ्गसेनः *etc.* [Vaṅgasena. With Hindi translation by Ṣālagrāma, completed by Ṣaṅkaralāla.] [1905.] 4°. **14043. ddd. 2.**

SARVAVARMĀ. *See* TRILOCHANADĀSA. আখ্যাতপঞ্জী। *etc.* [Ākhyātapañjī.] [1895.] 8°. **14090. bb. 13.(5.)**

SĀYAṆA ĀCHĀRYA.—*Works on Ṣruti.* [*Vedas.*] *See* VEDAS.—Ṛigveda.—*Selections of Hymns and Verses.* Hymns from the Ṛigveda . . . with Sâyaṇa's commentary, *etc.* 1905. 8°. **14007. g. 1.**

SORṆAṢĀSṬRI, *K.*, *of Devakota.* *See* ĀRŪḌHAṢĀSTRA. ஞானப்ரதீபிகை *etc.* [Ārūḍhaṣāstra. With Tamil commentary by Sorṇaṣāstri and Ṣrīnivāsāchārya.] [1899.] 8°. **14053. ccc. 27.**

ṢRĪDHARA RĀMAKṚISHṆA BHĀṆḌĀRKAR. *See* VEDAS. — Ṛigveda. — *Selections of Hymns and Verses.* Hymns from the Ṛigveda . . . Revised and enlarged by S. R. Bhandarkar. 1905. 8°. **14007. g. 1.**

ṢYĀMALĀLA GOSVĀMĪ, *Siddhāntavāchaspati.* *See* [Addenda] NĀRADA. [*Sūtra.*] ভক্তিসূত্রম্ *etc.* [Bhaktisūtra. With Bengali exposition by Ṣyāmalāla.] [1904.] 16°. **14028. bb. 15.**

VARADARĀJA, *Grammarian.* धातुकारिकावलिः । [Dhātukārikāvali. A tract on verbal roots, in 38 stanzas.] 1889. *See* PERIODICAL PUBLICATIONS.—*Bombay.* ग्रन्थरत्नमाला *etc.* (Granth Ratna Málá, *etc.*) Vol. III, no. 4. 1887-[1892.] 8°. **14096. c. 8.(vol. 3.)**

VEṄKAṬEṢVARĀRYA, *son of Yajñanārāyaṇa*, also called VEṄKAṬEṢA. Jatakachundrika, or Moonlight to Astrology. English translation, with [introduction,] original text in Devanagari, and copious notes and illustrations in English, by B. Suryanarain Row. Second edition. *Bellary*, 1898. 8°. **14053. ccc. 4.(2.)**

Imperfect, containing only pp. iii. 1-32.

—— [Another edition.] pp. iv. 80. *Madras*, 1900. 8°. **14053. cc. 21.(3.)**

A reprint of the second edition, with the preface rewritten; published as "second edition, thoroughly revised."

CORRIGENDA.

Col.	Line.	
8	15 from bottom.	For **14003. d. 1.** read **14003. l. 3.**
23	20.	Delete " 1901, *etc.*," and read " pp. i. 786. *Benares*, 1902." Delete "*In progress*" in the footnote.
26	31.	Omit the words " Kāṇḍa 1," *etc.*, and in place of " pp. i. 113 " read " 3 pts. भाष्या [*Benares*, 1901-1904.] 8°."
30	4.	For *P.* read *Panappākam*.
32	20.	For " Harinārāyaṇa " read " Hari Nārāyaṇa. "
35	8.	Omit (1) in the press-mark.
40	7-8 from bottom.	The form *Antakṛita°* is a barbarism. The correct Sanskrit is *Antakṛid-daṣāḥ*.
44	1, 3.	Read **ANUTTARAUPAPĀTIKADAṢĀḤ.**
44	15 from bottom.	In the list given by the editor of the Mantrapāṭha in the Mysore Government Oriental Library Series (Bibliotheca Sanskrita), Mysore 1902, the order of the Sūtras in the Kalpasūtra of the Āpastambīs is—Praṣnas 1-23, Ṣrauta; 24, Paribhāshā-pravarau; 25, Ṣulba; 26-7, Paitṛimedhika; 28, Gṛihya; 29-30, Dharma; 31-2, Mantraprapāṭhakau.
48	1 ff.	The form *Apyaya* is an old error, deriving from the Catalogue of Dr. Haas, for *Appaya*, which accordingly should be read in this and all connected entries.
57	11.	For **14003. d. 1.** read **14003. l. 3.**
65	7-8 from bottom.	For " Annavarōpa " read " Annavaram."
67	5-6.	For " Veṅkaṭarāghava Ṣāstrī " read " Veṅkaṭarāghava Ṣarmā."
72	16.	For " *See* RUDRAJAPA " read " *See* VEDAS.—Yajurveda.—*Vājasaneyisaṃhitā*."
83	14-15 from bottom.	For " *See* RUDRAJAPA " read " *See* VEDAS.—Yajurveda.—*Vājasaneyisaṃhitā*."
84	17.	Delete the press-mark.
91	22.	For " Bhāskarāya " read " Bhāskararāya."
93	4 from bottom.	For " *Benares*, 1898, *etc.*" read " Pādas 1-3. pp. 987. *Benares*, 1898-1899." Delete "*In progress*" in the footnote.
115	7 from bottom.	Read **14099. aaa. 1.**
124	1.	For **CHĀMANLĀL** read **CHĪMANLĀL.** This entry should accordingly be transferred to col. 132.
148	1 f.	The Kachchāyanabheda and Kachchāyanasāra are here attributed to Dhammānanda on the authority of the Gandhavaṃsa (Journ. Pali Text Soc. 1886, p. 74). A common tradition also ascribes them to Yasa or Mahāyasa, of whom nothing appears to be known.
152	12.	After the Chinese title add " in Sanskrit styled Ushṇīshavijaya-dhāraṇī."
153	21.	Read " Patichcha."

Col.	Line.
157	5 from bottom. After "marriage" put a comma, and add "in Sanskrit, with Telugu translation."
160	3-4 of first sub-column. For "Govinda Ṭhakkura, *son of Keṣava*" read "Mammaṭa Āchārya."
162	2. Read मिताक्षरा.
162	16 from bottom. For "*pādas* i.—ii." read "*pādas* i.—iii."
164	16, 18. For **EKĀMBARA** read **EKĀMRA**.
174	1. After **GAṄGĀDHARA SARASVATĪ** add *disciple of Rāmānanda;* and transfer hither the entry under **GAṄGĀDHARENDRA SARASVATĪ** in col. 175. Both these names belong to the same writer.
193	20 from bottom. For **GOVINDĀCHĀRYA,** *A.* read **GOVINDĀCHĀRYA,** *Aḷkoṇḍavilli.*
197	1. After **GRAY** (James) add *continued.*
234	4. Read **IMAÏZUMI** (Yūsaku).
244	3. The correct spelling is doubtless *Kāmādīnava°*.
258	16-20. For "कालविवेकः . . . 1897, *etc.*," read "The Kāla-viveka, a part of Dharmaratna, a treatise on Hindu law and rituals by Jīmūtavāhana. Edited by Paṇḍita Pramathanātha Tarkabhūṣaṇa. (धर्मरत्ने कालविवेकः) pp. xiv. 544, lxxiii. 1905."
272	21,28. Read මහාරූපසිද්ධි.
290	15. Read "Māḍāvil."
298	20 from bottom. For **KĀṢĪCHINTĀMAṆI BHAṬṬA** read **CHINTĀMAṆI BHAṬṬA,** *Kāṣi,* and transfer this title to col. 132.
301	12. For "1891" read "1892."
306	14. For വിക്തോറിയാ read വിക്ടോറിയാ.
308	**KEṢAVĀNANDA SVĀMĪ** the author of the Anubhavānanda Lahari and **KEṢAVĀNANDA SVĀMĪ** the commentator upon Nānak's works are one and the same person. The entry on line 11-17 should accordingly be transferred to follow line 25, and its separate heading struck out.
323	2 from bottom. Read **KUEHNAU** (Richard).
327	8. For *Gotama* read *Gotamya.*
335	2 from bottom. Read "*Challā Nāgaliṅga.*"
337	17. The correct spelling is doubtless *Kāmādīnava°*.
342	9. Omit **Ac. 670.**
349	1 from bottom. Read "from the Mahābhārata and Purāṇas."
353	After the third line insert the footnote: *A new edition of that published in Bombay in* 1881.
354	2-5 from bottom. Read "The Bhagavadgītā, with translations and notes in Persian and Hindi in the Persian character by Lakshmīnārāyaṇa of Agra."
356	6. For "Veṅkaṭaprasannābhi" read "Veṅkaṭaprapannābhi."
359	11-14 from bottom. Transfer this entry to the Anuṣāsanaparva, col. 352, to follow after line 10.
372	12-15. Delete this duplicate entry.
375	10 from bottom. Delete "and Vāsudeva Ṣarmā, *V.*"
410	17-18. Omit these two lines, and see Addenda under **NĀRADA**.
446	1 For "extracted from" read "forming."
512	11, 20 from bottom. The writer catalogued as **PŪRṆACHANDRA ACHALEṢVARA ṢARMĀ** is identical with **PŪRṆACHANDRA ṢARMĀ** whose name immediately follows.
517	4 from bottom. The full title of this author is **RĀDHĀMOHANA VIDYĀVĀCHASPATI GOSVĀMĪ BHAṬṬĀCHĀRYA.**
521	1 from bottom. For **14140. b.** read **14140. b. 26.(4.)**
531	22. After **RĀMACHANDRA ĀCHĀRYA,** *son of Krishṇa,* add *disciple of Gopāla.*
577	4, 5 from bottom. For "Dvattiṃsākārakammaṭṭhāna" read "Dvattiṃsakāyakammaṭṭhāna."
587	9-14. Delete the whole of this entry, which should be catalogued under **NĀRADA**. [*Sūtra.*] See Addenda.
598	14. Add the press-mark **14004. b. 5.**
635	16. Read **SCHMIDT** (J. W. Richard).
636	15. Insert the heading **SCHMIDT** (Richard), *Publisher.*

COL.	LINE.
640	17. For ఆరూఢరత్నసిద్ధాంజనమ్ read ఆరూఢ॥
689	11 from bottom. For *See* YAJÑANĀRĀYAṆA VEṄKAṬEṢVARĀRYA read *See* [Addenda] VEṄKAṬEṢVARĀRYA.
715	5 from bottom. Read **TĀMMANĀCHĀRYA.**
740	5 from bottom. Read °ణజం
750	8-14 from bottom. Correct the entry as follows:—" **छान्दोग्योपनिषद्भाष्यम्** [Chhāndogyopanishad. With *pada*-analysis, Sanskrit commentary setting forth doctrines of the Ārya Samāj, and Hindi translation of text and paraphrase of commentary, by Ṣivaṣaṅkara Ṣarmā.] pp. x. xvi. 889, iv. **अजमेर १९६२** [*Ajmere,* 1905.] 8°."
750	6 from bottom. Read "another edition of part i. of the preceding," and delete the note "*In progress.*"
764	4. For "vol. 15" read "vol. 13."
824	21. For *See* YAJÑANĀRĀYAṆA VEṄKAṬEṢVARĀRYA read *See* [Addenda] VEṄKAṬEṢVARĀRYA.

INDEXES.

The references in this Index are to the names of authors or other headings under which the works are catalogued. Anonymous works catalogued under their titles are designated by the phrase in loco. *Modern works bearing no recognised Sanskrit title are not registered here.*

I. INDEX OF ORIENTAL TITLES.

II. SELECT SUBJECT-INDEX.

The following Index contains a classified list of the most important or interesting works mentioned in the foregoing Index of Titles. Commentaries are excluded, except when they are of especial importance or are either published apart from the original text or give their title to the combined work.

The classification is as follows:—

I. SANSKRIT LITERATURE.

Adages and Proverbs.
Apologues, Ethics, and Polity.
Arts and Sciences.
1. *Architecture.*
2. *Astronomy, Astrology, Geometry, and Mathematics.*
3. *Games.*
4. *Gastronomy.*
5. *Geography.*
6. *Medicine.*
7. *Military Art.*
8. *Mineralogy.*
9. *Music and Dancing.*
10. *Occult Arts, Divination, and Magic.*
11. *Writing.*
12. *Miscellaneous Arts and Sciences.*

Caste and Ethnology.
Drama.
Erotic and Genre Literature.
Fiction.
History.
1. *General Historical Narratives and Materials.*
2. *Biographies, Family Histories, Genealogies, and Succession-lists.*

Law.
Miscellaneous Literature, Bibliography, &c.
Philology.
1. *Grammar.*
2. *Lexicography.*
3. *Phonetics.*

Philosophy and Theology.
1. *Āraṇyakas and Upanishads.*
2. *Advaita Vedānta.*
3. *Viśishṭādvaita Vedānta.*
4. *Pūrva-mīmāṃsā.*
5. *Sāṅkhya.*
6. *Yoga.*
7. *Bhāgavata, Bhakta, Dvaita, Nimbārka, and Pāñcharātra Schools.*
8. *Spanda, Śākta, and Śrīvidyā Schools.*
9. *Nyāya and Vaiśeshika.*
10. *Miscellaneous Schools.*

Poetry.
1. *Religious Poems.*
(i.) *Buddhist.*
(ii.) *Hindu.*
(iii.) *Jain.*
2. *Narrative Poems.*
3. *Ethical Poems and Anthologies.*
4. *Miscellaneous Poems.*
5. *Champū Compositions and Ornate Panegyric Prose.*

Prosody and Metre.
Religion.
1. *Buddhism.*
2. *Christianity.*
3. *Hinduism.*
(i.) *Vedic Saṃhitās and their Literature.*
(ii.) *Ritual Works (Brāhmaṇas and Post-Vedic writings).*
(iii.) *Purāṇas.*
(iv.) *Miscellaneous Religious Works.*
4. *Jainism.*
5. *Sikh Church.*
6. *Theistic Churches (Ārya and Brāhma Samāj).*

Rhetoric (Alaṅkāra).

II. PALI LITERATURE.

Religion and Philosophy.
1. *Canonical Works.*
2. *Non-canonical Works.*

Grammar and Lexicography.
Prosody and Rhetoric.
History.
Law.
Poetry.
Divination.

III. PRAKRIT LITERATURE.

Jain Literature.
1. *Canonical Works.*
2. *Non-canonical Works.*

Other Prakrit Literature.

I. SANSKRIT LITERATURE.

ADAGES AND PROVERBS.

Laukikanyāyāñjali. JACOB (G. A.).
Laukikanyāyasaṅgraha. RAGHUNĀTHA VARMĀ.
Lokoktimuktāvalī [in Kâvyamâlâ (Anthology), 1895]. DURGĀPRASĀDA and KĀŚINĀTHA PĀṆḌURAṄGA PARAB.

APOLOGUES, ETHICS, AND POLITY.

Bhāryādharmam. SUNDARARĀJA ŞARMĀ.
Dharmanītidarpaṇa. JAYADATTA ŞARMĀ.
Hitopadeṣa [*in loco*].
Kámandakíya Nítisára. KĀMANDAKI.
Kusumamâlâ. VĀMANA ŞIVARĀMA ĀPṬE.
Lokadvayopadeṣa. GAṄGĀDATTA.
Mānavadharmamālā. PRĀṆAJĪVANA HARIHARA.
Mitrānurāga. HITOPADEṢA.
Nītikathāmañjarī. NĀRĀYAṆA ŞĀSTRI, *son of Anantakrishṇa.*
Nītimālā. AESOP.
Nītimanoramā. PURUSHOTTAMA BHAṬṬA.
Nītiprakāśikā [*in loco*].
Nītisāra [*in loco*].
——— KĀMANDAKI.
Nītisārasaṅgraha. CHĀṆAKYA.
Pañchatantra[ka]. PAÑCHATANTRA.
Pañchatantrasāra. KSHEMENDRA.
Pātivratyalakshaṇa. DORASĀMAIYA, *O.V.*
Pitāputradharmaprakāṣa. PARAMĀNANDA, *Svāmī.*
Pramāṇasahasrī. PRAYĀGAJĪ ṬHĀKARSĪ.
Provesika. PAÑCHATANTRA.
Saṃskritasāgara. PAÑCHATANTRA.
Strīdharmabodhinī. TOTĀRĀM VARMĀ.
Vaiyākaraṇa-nītikaumudī. KIṢORĪMOHANA VIDYĀNIDHI.
Yathārthaṣāntinirūpaṇa. MUSADDĪ-RĀM ŞARMĀ.
Yathārthasukhāptivarṇana. MUSADDĪ-RĀM ŞARMĀ.

ARTS AND SCIENCES.

1. ARCHITECTURE.

Manushyālayachandrikā. TACHCHU-ŞĀSTRAM.
Pālārām-vilāsa. VIṢVAKARMĀ.
Rājavallabha. MAṆḌANA.
Şilpadīpaka. GAṄGĀDHARA, *Architect.*
Şilpasārasaṅgraha. KALYĀṆADĀSA BHĀṆĀBHĀĪ GUJJAR.
Şilpaṣāstrasārasaṅgraha. KALYĀṆA ŞIVANĀRĀYAṆA.
Tachchu-ṣāstram [*in loco*].
Viṣvakarmaprakāṣa. VIṢVAKARMĀ.

2. ASTRONOMY, ASTROLOGY, GEOMETRY, AND MATHEMATICS.

Ajitaprakāṣa-pañchāṅga. EPHEMERIDES.
Ārūḍharatnasiddhāñjana. SIDDHANĀTHA.
Ārūḍhaṣāstra [*in loco*].
Bāla-pārāṣarya. UḌUDĀYAPRADĪPA.
Bhārgavī Saṃhitā. BHṚIGU.
Bhāsvatyudāharaṇa. ŞATĀNANDA.
Bhāvakutūhala. JĪVANĀTHA.
Bhāvaphalādhyāya. LOMAṢA.
Bhṛigusaṃhitā. BHṚIGU.
Brāhma[sphuṭa]siddhānta. BRAHMAGUPTA.
Bṛihaj-jātaka. VARĀHAMIHIRA.
Bṛihaj-jātakachandrikā. RĀMAṢAṄKARA DEVA.
Bṛihajjyotishārṇava. HARIKṚISHṆA VEṄKAṬARĀMA JYOTIRVID.
Bṛihaj-jyotishasāra. ŞUKADEVA.
Bṛihaj-jyotissāra. NĪLAKAṆṬHA ŞARMĀ, *son of Viṣveṣvaranātha.*
Bṛihat-saṃhitā. VARĀHAMIHIRA.
Chamatkārachintāmaṇi. NĀRĀYAṆA BHAṬṬA, *Astrologer.*
Chaṇḍū-pañchāṅga. EPHEMERIDES.
Daivajñamukhamaṇḍana [*in loco*].
Daṣādhyāyī. [Addenda] GOVINDA SOMAYĀJĪ.
Dhyānagrahopadeṣādhyāya. BRAHMAGUPTA.
Digmīmāṃsā. SUDHĀKARA DVIVEDĪ.
Dinachandrikā. RĀGHAVĀNANDA.
Dinakaumudī. RĀMACHANDRA ŞARMĀ.
Dīpikā. ŞRĪNIVĀSA ĀCHĀRYA.
Gaṇakataraṅgiṇī. SUDHĀKARA DVIVEDĪ.
Golādhyāya. BHĀSKARA ĀCHĀRYA.
Grahagochara. JAYARĀMA, *Astrologer.*
Grahakoṣa [*in loco*].
Grahalāghava. GAṆEṢA, *son of Keṣava.*
Grahaprabodha. NĀGEṢA DAIVAJÑA.
Grahavipra. KEDĀRANĀTHA.
Horāṣāstra. VARĀHAMIHIRA.
Jaiminisūtra. JAIMINI.—*Jyotishasūtra.*
Jātakābharaṇa. ḌHUṆḌHIRĀJA.
Jātakachandrikā. RĀMAṢAṄKARA DEVA.
Jatakachandrika. [Addenda] VEṄKAṬEṢVARĀRYA.
Jātakālaṅkāra. GAṆEṢA, *son of Gopāla.*
Jātakapaddhati. ŞRĪPATI BHAṬṬA.
Jātakapārijāta. VAIDYANĀTHA, *son of Veṅkaṭādri.*
Jñānapradīpikā. ĀRŪḌHAṢĀSTRA.
Jyotiḥṣāstraratna. KṚISHṆA MIṢRA, *Astrologer.*
Jyotirgaṇita. VEṄKAṬEṢA RĀMAKṚISHṆA KETKAR.
Jyotisha. LAGADHA.
Jyotishanavaratna. MIṢRĪLĀLA MIṢRA.
Jyotishasāra. ŞIVADATTA UPĀDHYĀYA.
Jyotishatattvasudhārṇava. ŞYĀMASUNDARALĀLA TRIPĀṬHĪ, *son of Baṅkelāl.*
Jyotishatattvavāridhi. NĪLAKAMALA VIDYĀNIDHI BHAṬṬĀCHĀRYA.
Jyotishatattvavichāra. KANHAIYĀLĀL MIṢRA.
Jyotiṣsar. ŞUKADEVA.
Kālāmṛita [*in loco*].
Karaṇakutūhala. BHĀSKARA ACHĀRYA.
Karaṇaprakāṣa. BRAHMADEVA.
Kaṭapāyā. KĀLIDĀSA.—*Supposititious Works.*

Keṣavajātakapaddhati, or Keṣavī-jātaka. KEṢAVA.
Kheṭakautuka. NAWĀB-KHĀN-KHĀNĀN.
Kṛishṇīya-jyotiḥṣāstraratna. KṚISHṆA MIṢRA, *Astrologer.*
Laghu-pārāṣarī. UḌUDĀYAPRADĪPA.
Laghusaṅgraha. LAKSHMĪNĀRĀYAṆA, *Astrologer.*
Makarandavivaraṇa. DIVĀKARA.
Makarandīya-pañchāṅga. EPHEMERIDES.
Makarandodāharaṇa. DIVĀKARA.
Makarandopapatti. GOKULANĀTHA.
Muhūrtachintāmaṇi. RĀMA, *son of Ananta.*
Muhūrtagaṇapati. GAṆAPATI.
Muhūrtamālā. RAGHUNĀTHA DAIVAJÑA.
Muhūrtamārtaṇḍa. NĀRĀYAṆA BHAṬṬA, *son of Ananta.*
Muhūrtapadavī [*in loco*].
Nāhnidattapañchaviṃṣatikā. NĀHNIDATTA.
Nakshatrakoṣa [*in loco*].
Nawāb-Khān-Khānā-kā jyotisha. NAWĀB-KHĀN-KHĀNĀN.
Pañchāṅga. EPHEMERIDES.
Pañchāṅgasādhana. RĀGHAVĀNANDA.
——— RĀMACHANDRA ṢARMĀ.
Pañjikāgaṇanā. RĀGHAVĀNANDA.
——— RĀMACHANDRA ṢARMĀ.
Pārāṣarya. UḌUDĀYAPRADĪPA.
Phalapradarṣinī. VEṄKAṬA ṢĀSTRĪ, *I.G.*
Praṣnachaṇḍeṣvara. RĀMAKṚISHṆA, *Daivajña.*
Ratnadyota. GAṄGĀRĀMA DVIVEDĪ.
Rekhāgaṇita. EUCLID.
Sajjanavallabha. BHĀNU PAṆḌITA.
Saṅketanidhi. RĀMADAYĀLU, *Jyotirvid.*
Sarvārthachintāmaṇi. VEṄKAṬEṢA DAIVAJÑA.
Sāṭhī. MŪLASAṄKARA JAYĀNANDA.
Shaṭpañchāṣikā. PṚITHUYAṢAS.
Siddhāntadarpaṇa. CHANDRAṢEKHARA SIṂHA.
Siddhāntaṣiromaṇi. BHĀSKARA ĀCHĀRYA.
Ṣivālikhita [*in loco*].
Ṣrīnivāsadīpikā. ṢRĪNIVĀSA ĀCHĀRYA.
Ṣrīpatipaddhati. ṢRĪPATI BHAṬṬA.
Ṣuddhidīpikā. ṢRĪNIVĀSA ĀCHĀRYA.
Sūryasiddhānta [*in loco*].
Tithipattra. EPHEMERIDES.
Uḍudāyapradīpa [*in loco*].
Yantrachintāmaṇi. CHAKRADHARA.
Yavanajātaka [*in loco*].

3. GAMES.

Krīḍākauṣalya. HARIKṚISHṆA VEṄKAṬARĀMA JYOTIRVID.
Tattvanidhi. KṚISHṆARĀJA OḌEYAR.

4. GASTRONOMY.

Pāchakachintāmaṇi. VĒLU-PIḶḶAI, *N.*

5. GEOGRAPHY.

Bhūgola-khagola-varṇana. IṢVARACHANDRA VIDYĀSĀGARA.

6. MEDICINE.

Abhinavanighaṇṭu. DATTARĀMA CHAUBE.
Añjananidāna. AGNIVEṢA.
Anupānataraṅgiṇī. RAGHUNĀTHAPRASĀDA SUKALA.
Ārogyasindhu. RAṄGANĀTHA SAKHĀRĀMA LĀḶE.
Āryadhātrīvidyā. SURENDRANĀTHA GOSVĀMĪ.
Ashṭāṅgahṛidaya. VĀGBHAṬA, *son of Siṃhagupta.*
Aushadha-prastuta-praṇālī. VIHĀRILĀLA, *Kāṣmīrī.*
Aushadhikoṣa. CHAMANRĀI ṢIVAṢAṄKARA.
Aushadhikriyā [*in loco*].
Āyurvedadīpikā. CHAKRAPĀṆIDATTA.
Āyurvedapraveṣikā. VIHĀRILĀLA, *Kāṣmīrī.*
Āyurvedaṣabdārṇava. GAṄGĀPRASĀDA PĀṆḌEYA.
Bāhaṭa. VĀGBHAṬA, *son of Siṃhagupta.*
Bhaisajya Kalpa. SĀYAṆṆA.
Bhaishajyaratnāvalī. GOVINDADĀSA.
——— RAVIDATTA ṢĀSTRĪ.
Bhāvaprakāṣa. BHĀVA MIṢRA.
Bheshajasaṅgrahava. PERERA (N. A.)
Bṛihad-vaidyaratnākara. VEṄKAṬĀCHĀRYA, *Gautama.*
Chakradatta. CHAKRAPĀṆIDATTA.
Charakasaṃhitā. CHARAKA.
Chikitsāsārasaṅgraha. VAṄGASENA.
Dhanvantarinighaṇṭu. DHANVANTARI.
Dravyaguṇa. RĀJAVALLABHA.
Dravyaguṇa[saṅgraha]. CHAKRAPĀṆIDATTA.
Dravyaguṇaṣataka. TRIMALLA BHAṬṬA.
Guḍanigraha-grantha. HEMACHANDRA.
Hastyāyurveda. PĀLAKĀPYA.
Jñānabhaishajyamañjarī. GUMĀNĪ PANTA.
Kāmakutūhala. KANHAIYĀLĀL ṢARMĀ, *son of Jagannātha.*
Kāmakautūhala [*in loco*].
——— RAṄGANĀTHA SAKHĀRĀMA LĀḶE.
Kāmaṣāstra. GORAKSHANĀTHA.
Madanavilāsa. GAṆEṢA RAṄGANĀTHA LĀḶE.
Mādhavanidana. MĀDHAVA.
Mahāyogānandāmṛitakalpavalli. VEṄKAṬASIṂHĀDRI JAGAPATI RĀJU.
Mātaṅgalīlā. NĪLAKAṆṬHA, *of Rājamaṅgalam.*
Mṛityuparikshā. KIṢORĪLĀLA ṢARMĀ.
Nāḍijñāna [*in loco*].
Nāḍīparīkshā. NĀḌĪVIJÑĀNA.
Nāḍīprakāṣa. ṢAṄKARA SENA.
Nāḍivijñāna [*in loco*].
Napuṃsakānandamandāra. KANHAIYĀLĀL ṢARMĀ, *son of Jagannātha.*
Nibandhasaṅgraha. ḌALLAṆA MIṢRA.
Nidāna. MĀDHAVA.
Paribhāshāpradīpa. GOVINDA SENA.
Prayogasamuchchaya. SĀYAṆṆA.
Rājanighaṇṭu. NARAHARI.
Rājavallabha[nighaṇṭu], or Rājavallabhīya-dravyaguṇa. RĀJAVALLABHA.
Rasarājasundara. DATTARĀMA CHAUBE.
Rasendrasārasaṅgraha. GOPĀLAKṚISHṆA.
Ratnaprabhā. KĀLĪPRASANNA KAVIṢEKHARA.
Rogavinischaya. MĀDHAVA.
Sarasvatīnighaṇṭu [*in loco*].
Ṣārṅgadharasaṃhitā. ṢĀRṄGADHARA.
Ṣataṣ'okī. TRIMALLA BHAṬṬA.
Siddhabheshajamaṇimālā. KṚISHṆARĀMA KUNDANARĀMA VYĀSA.
Siddhayoga. VṚINDA.

7. MILITARY ART.

8. MINERALOGY.

9. MUSIC AND DANCING.

10. OCCULT ARTS, DIVINATION, AND MAGIC.

11. WRITING.

12. MISCELLANEOUS ARTS AND SCIENCES.

CASTE AND ETHNOLOGY.

(*See also* LAW, and RELIGION.—3. *Hinduism.*)

DRAMA.

EROTIC AND GENRE LITERATURE.

FICTION.

HISTORY.

1. GENERAL HISTORICAL NARRATIVES AND MATERIALS.

2. BIOGRAPHIES, FAMILY HISTORIES, GENEALOGIES, AND SUCCESSION LISTS.

LAW.

(*See also* CASTE, and RELIGION.—3. *Hinduism.*)

MISCELLANEOUS LITERATURE, BIBLIOGRAPHY, ETC.

PHILOLOGY.

1. GRAMMAR.

2. LEXICOGRAPHY.

3. PHONETICS (Sikshās and Prātiṣākhyas).

PHILOSOPHY AND THEOLOGY.

1. ĀRAṆYAKAS AND UPANISHADS.

Taittirīyāraṇyaka. ĀRAṆYAKAS.
Taittirīya Up°. UPANISHADS.—*General Collections.*
——— ——— *Small Collections.*
——— ——— *Separate Upanishads.*
Taittirīyopanishadbhāshyavārttika. SUREṢVARA ĀCHĀRYA.
Tārasāra Up°. UPANISHADS.—*General Collections.*
Tejobindu Up°. UPANISHADS.—*General Collections.*
Tripurātāpinī Up°. UPANISHADS.—*General Collections.*
Tripura Up°. UPANISHADS.—*General Collections.*
Triṣikhibrāhmaṇa Up°. UPANISHADS.—*General Collections.*
Turīyātītāvadhūta Up°. UPANISHADS.—*General Collections.*
Upanishadān-chī Mīmāṃsā. UPANISHADS.—*Small Collections.*
Upanishadāvalī. UPANISHADS.—*Small Collections.*
Upanishadvidyā. UPANISHADS.—*General Collections.*
Upanishatprasāda. UPANISHADS.—*Small Collections.*
Upanishatsaṅgraha. UPANISHADS.—*Small Collections.*
Vajrasūchi[kā] Up°. UPANISHADS.—*General Collections.*
——— ——— *Separate Upanishads.*
Varāha Up°. UPANISHADS.—*General Collections.*
——— ——— *Small Collections.*
Vāsudeva Up°. UPANISHADS.—*General Collections.*
Yājñavalkya Up°. UPANISHADS.—*General Collections.*
Yogachūḍāmaṇi Up°. UPANISHADS.—*General Collections.*
Yogakuṇḍalī Up°. UPANISHADS.—*General Collections.*
Yogaṣikhā Up°. UPANISHADS.—*General Collections.*
——— ——— *Small Collections.*
Yogatattva Up°. UPANISHADS.—*General Collections.*
——— ——— *Small Collections.*

2. ADVAITA VEDĀNTA.

Adhyātmopadeṣavidhi. ṢAṄKARA ĀCHĀRYA.—*Philosophical Poems, etc.*
Advaitachandrikā. SUDARṢANA ĀCHĀRYA, *Panjābī.*
Advaita[chintā]kaustubha. MAHĀDEVA SARASVATĪ.
Advaitamakaranda. LAKSHMĪDHARA.
Advaitamañjarī. HARIHARA ṢĀSTRĪ, and others.
Advaitānubhūti. GOVINDA.
Advaitapārijāta. NĪLAKAṆṬHA MUNI.
Advaitasāmrājya. KṚISHṆĀNANDA SARASVATĪ, *disciple of Sachchidānanda.*
Advaitasiddhi. MADHUSŪDANA SARASVATĪ.
Advaitatārāvali. SADĀṢIVA BRAHMENDRA.
Āgamaṣāstra. GAUḌAPĀDA ĀCHĀRYA.
Ajñānabodhinī. ṢAṄKARA ĀCHĀRYA.—*Philosophical Poems, etc.*
Akāṣaṣataka. ACHYUTA.
Anubhavānandalaharī. KEṢAVĀNANDA SVĀMĪ.
Anubhūtileṣa. VĀMANA PAṆḌITA, *the Marathi Poet.*
Anubhūtimīmāṃsā, or Anubhūtisūtra. ANUBHŪTIMĪMĀṂSĀ.
Anubhūtivivaraṇa. BHĀSKARĀNANDA SARASVATĪ.
Aparokshānubhūti. ṢAṄKARA ĀCHĀRYA.—*Two or More Works.*
——— ——— *Philosophical Poems, etc.*
Ashṭāvakrasaṃhitā. ASHṬĀVAKRA.
Ātmabodha. ṢAṄKARA ĀCHĀRYA.—*Two or More Works.*
——— ——— *Philosophical Poems, etc.*
Âtmânâtma-viveka. ṢAṄKARA ĀCHĀRYA.—*Two or More Works.*
Ātmavidyāvilāsa. SADĀṢIVA BRAHMENDRA.
Ātmaviṣeshaṇamālikā. ṢYĀMA BHAGAVĀN.
Avadhūtagītā. DATTĀTREYA.
Avadhūtānubhūti. ASHṬĀVAKRA.
Bālabodhinī. APPAYA DĪKSHITA.
Bhāmatī. VĀCHASPATI MIṢRA.
Bhedadhikkāra. NṚISIṂHĀṢRAMA.
Bhedavādatiraskāra. ĀRIYAN, *Pseud.*
Bodhāryā. SADĀṢIVA BRAHMENDRA.
Brahmamīmāṃsā. BĀDARĀYAṆA.
Brahmāmṛitavarshiṇī. RĀMĀNANDA SARASVATĪ, *son of Tirumalāchārya.*
Brahmastava. LĀḌILĪ CHANDRA.
Brahmasūtra. BĀDARĀYAṆA.
Brahmavidāṣīrvādapaddhati. SĀYAṆA ĀCHĀRYA.—*Works on Philosophy, etc.*
Brahmavidyā. PERIODICAL PUBLICATIONS.—*Chidambaram.*
Brahmavidyābharaṇa. ADVAITĀNANDA SARASVATĪ.
Brahmavilāsa. SUKHĀNANDA TRIPĀṬHĪ.
Bṛihadāraṇyakopanishadbhāshyavārtika. SUREṢVARA ĀCHĀRYA.
Daṣaṣlokī. ṢAṄKARA ĀCHĀRYA.—*Two or More Works.*
——— ——— *Philosophical Poems, etc.*
Gītāsāroddhāra. KṚISHṆĀNANDA SARASVATĪ, *disciple of Sachchidānanda.*
Gītiratnamālā. SADĀṢIVA BRAHMENDRA.
Gurujñānavāsishṭha [*in loco*].
Harigītā. HARIHARA RĀYA.
Hastāmalakaṣloka (°stotra). HASTĀMALAKA ĀCHĀRYA.
Jīvachintāmaṇi. APYAYA DĪKSHITA.
Jīvanmuktiviveka. SĀYAṆA ĀCHĀRYA.—*Works on Philosophy, etc.*
Jñānapradīpikā. ṢAṄKARA ĀCHĀRYA.—*Doubtful and Supposititious Works.*
Jñānamaṇiprakāṣa. MAṆIṢAṄKARA MAGANLĀL.
Jñāneṣvarī. JÑĀNADEVA.
Kaivalyagāthā. KṚISHṆĀNANDA SARASVATĪ, *disciple of Sachchidānanda.*
Kaivalyaratna. PURĀṆAS.—*Selections.*
Laghuchandrikā. BRAHMĀNANDA SARASVATĪ, *disciple of Paramānanda.*
Mānasollāsa. SUREṢVARA ĀCHĀRYA.
Māṇḍūkyopanishatkārikāḥ. GAUḌAPĀDA ĀCHĀRYA.
Manīshāpañchaka. ṢAṄKARA ĀCHĀRYA.—*Doubtful and Supposititious Works.*

3. VIŚISHṬĀDVAITA VEDĀNTA.

4. PŪRVA-MĪMĀṂSĀ.

5. SĀṄKHYA.

6. YOGA.

7. BHĀGAVATA, BHAKTA, DVAITA, NIMBĀRKA, AND PĀÑCHARĀTRA SCHOOLS.

8. SPANDA, ṢĀKTA, AND ṢRĪVIDYĀ SCHOOLS.

9. NYĀYA AND VAIṢESHIKA.

10. MISCELLANEOUS SCHOOLS.

POETRY.

1. RELIGIOUS POEMS.

(i.) *Buddhist.*

(ii.) *Hindu.*

2. NARRATIVE POEMS.

(*See also* HISTORY.)

3. ETHICAL POEMS AND ANTHOLOGIES.

Jñānabhaishajyamañjarī. GUMĀNĪ PANTA.
Kālidāsa-sūktayaḥ. KĀLIDĀSA.—*Selections.*
Kavitākoraka. AVINĀŚACHANDRA CHAKRAVARTĪ.
Kāvyasaṅgraha. GUMĀNĪ PANTA.
Lokoktimuktāvali [in Kâvyamâlâ (Anthology), 1895]. DURGĀPRASĀDA and KĀŚĪNĀTHA PĀṆḌURAṄGA PARAB.
Mandāramālā, *i.e.* Āttisūḍi. AVVAIYĀR.
Mugdhopadeśa [in Kâvyamâlâ (Anthology), 1891]. DURGĀPRASĀDA and KĀŚĪNĀTHA PĀṆḌURAṄGA PARAB.
Nītidaśaprabandhī. RĀDHĀKṚISHṆA ŚĀSTRĪ.
Nītimārgapradīpikā, *i.e.* Nītineṟi-viḷakkam. KUMARAGURUPARA.
Nītipañchāśat. RĀDHĀKṚISHṆA ŚĀSTRĪ.
Nītiśataka. BHARTṚIHARI.
Nītyupākhyāna. RĀDHĀKṚISHṆA ŚĀSTRĪ.
Pativratādarpaṇa. SATYĀNANDA AGNIHOTRĪ.
Plavagashashṭi. NĀRĀYAṆA ŚĀSTRĪ, *R. V.*
Ramayana Niti Ratnavali. VĀLMĪKI.—Rāmāyaṇa.—*Abridgments and Selections.*
Ṛishivākyasaṅgraha. SATYĀNANDA AGNIHOTRĪ.
Sabhārañjanaśataka [in Kâvyamâlâ (Anthology), 1887]. DURGĀPRASĀDA and KĀŚĪNĀTHA PĀṆḌURAṄGA PARAB.
Śamyākamālā, *i.e.* Kouṟai-vēndan. AVVAIYĀR.
Sanmārgadarpaṇa, *i.e.* Nanneṟi. ŚIVAPRAKĀŚA DEŚIKA.
Śāntigītā. KĀŚĪDĀSA MUSTAUPHĪ.
Śāntiśataka[ślokaratnamālā]. ŚIHLAṆA MIŚRA.
Śāntivilāsa [in Kâvyamâlâ (Anthology), 1890]. DURGĀPRASĀDA and KĀŚĪNĀTHA PĀṆḌURAṄGA PARAB.
Śatopadeśa. GUMĀNĪ PANTA.
Satpurushalakshaṇa. DORASĀMAIYA, *O. V.*
Sevyasevakopadeśa [in Kâvyamâlâ (Anthology), 1886]. DURGĀPRASĀDA and KĀŚĪNĀTHA PĀṆḌURAṄGA PARAB.
Ślokamālāsaṅgraha. ḌAṆḌĪDHAR ŚARMĀ.
Subhāshita [*in loco*].
Subhāshitanīvi [in Kâvyamâlâ (Anthology), 1891]. DURGĀPRASĀDA and KĀŚĪNĀTHA PĀṆḌURAṄGA PARAB.
Subhāshitaratnamālā. SUNDARAM AIYAR, *N.*
Śukarambhāsaṃvāda [*in loco*].
Sumano'ñjali. ANNADĀCHARAṆA TARKACHŪḌĀMAṆI.
Sundarīsudhāra. GOPĀL-RĀU HARI ŚARMĀ.
Tattvapadavī, *i.e.* Nalvaṛi. AVVAIYĀR.
Trimaṇi-dīpaka. VIPRARĀJENDRA.
Upadeśaśataka [in Kâvyamâlâ (Anthology), 1886]. DURGĀPRASĀDA and KĀŚĪNĀTHA PĀṆḌURAṄGA PARAB.
Upâkhyâna Ratnâvalî. ŚIVAŚAṄKARA PAṆḌYĀJĪ.
Vāgullāsa, *i.e.* Vākkuṇḍām or Mūdurai. AVVAIYĀR.
Vairāgyaśataka [in Kâvyamâlâ (Anthology), 1886]. DURGĀPRASĀDA and KĀŚĪNĀTHA PĀṆḌURAṄGA PARAB.
———— BHARTṚIHARI.
Viduranīti. MAHĀBHĀRATA.—*Udyogaparva.*
Vidyāsadupadeśa. VIDYĀTĪRTHA.
Vijñānaśataka. BHARTṚIHARI.

4. MISCELLANEOUS POEMS.

Agaṇana - guṇa - vibhūshaṇa - rāja - bhaktiparāyaṇa bhāratajanagaṇa-samīpe sādaram Avedanam. ŚAILAJĀNANDA OJHĀ.
Akalaṅka Yoga. KṚIPĀNĀTHA ŚARMA VIŚVĀSA.
Amarukaśataka, or Amaruśataka. AMARU.
Āṅglādhirājya-svāgata. VEṄKAṬARAṄGANĀTHA ĀCHĀRYA.
Anyāpadeśaśataka [in Kâvyamâlâ (Anthology), 1890]. DURGĀPRASĀDA and KĀŚĪNĀTHA PĀṆḌURAṄGA PARAB.
———— [in Kâvyamâlâ (Anthology), 1893]. DURGĀPRASĀDA and KĀŚĪNĀTHA PĀṆḌURAṄGA PARAB.
Anyāpadeśaślokaśataka. GOVINDACHANDRA MAHĀPĀTRA DEVA.
Anyoktimuktālatā [in Kâvyamâlâ (Anthology), 1886]. DURGĀPRASĀDA and KĀŚĪNĀTHA PĀṆḌURAṄGA PARAB.
Anyoktiśataka [in Kâvyamâlâ (Anthology), 1888]. DURGĀPRASĀDA and KĀŚĪNĀTHA PĀṆḌURAṄGA PARAB.
Aśrubindukāvya. YĀDAVEŚVARA TARKARATNA.
Bhāminīvilāsa. JAGANNĀTHA PAṆḌITARĀJA.
Bhāratachandra Rāya Guṇākarer granthasaṅkalana. BHĀRATACHANDRA RĀYA.
Bhāvaśataka [in Kâvyamâlâ (Anthology), 1887]. DURGĀPRASĀDA and KĀŚĪNĀTHA PĀṆḌURAṄGA PARAB.
Bhāvavilāsa [in Kâvyamâlâ (Anthology), 1886]. DURGĀPRASĀDA and KĀŚĪNĀTHA PĀṆḌURAṄGA PARAB.
Bhikshāṭanakāvya [in Kâvyamâlâ (Anthology), 1897]. DURGĀPRASĀDA and KĀŚĪNĀTHA PĀṆḌURAṄGA PARAB.
Budhajana Manoranjanī. PADMARĀJA PAṆḌITA.
Chāṭudhārāchamatkārasāra. CHĀṬUDHĀRĀ.
Chaurapañchāśika, or Chorapañchāśat. BILHAṆA.
Chitrapraśnottararatnāvali. CHAKRA KAVI.
Digvijayinī Victoria. BECHANRĀM, *Pandit.*
Dillīmahotsavakāvya. ŚRĪŚVARA VIDYĀLAṄKĀRA BHAṬṬĀCHĀRYA.
Edward-rājyābhisheka. ŚIVARĀMA PĀṆḌE.
Gītabhārata. TRAILOKYAMOHANA GUHA NIYOGĪ.
Haṃsadūta. RŪPA GOSVĀMĪ.
Haṃsasandeśa. VEṄKAṬANĀTHA VEDĀNTĀCHĀRYA.
Hetvābhāsodāharaṇaślokāḥ. SADĀŚIVA, called YUVARĀJA KAVI.
Huṇkāpurāṇamāhātmya. VIPINAVIHĀRĪ VANDYOPĀDHYĀYA and KULACHANDRA DE DĀSA.
Kākadūta. GAURAGOPĀLA ŚIROMAṆI.
Kaliparidevanaśataka. ŚRĪNIVĀSA DĪKSHITA, *K.*
Kaliviḍambana [in Kâvyamâlâ (Anthology), 1888]. DURGĀPRASĀDA and KĀŚĪNĀTHA PĀṆḌURAṄGA PARAB.
———— NĪLAKAṆṬHA DĪKSHITA.
Kalyāṇagāna. ŚAURĪNDRAMOHANA ṬHĀKURA.
Kavi. PERIODICAL PUBLICATIONS.—*Poona.*
Kavichittapramodaka. GOVINDA ANTARVĀṆĪ.
Kavirākshasīya [*in loco*].

5. CHAMPŪ COMPOSITIONS AND ORNATE PANEGYRIC PROSE.

Abhinavakādambarī. ŚRĪKAṆṬHA KAVI.
Āchāryachampū, or Vedāntāchāryavijaya. VEṄKAṬANĀTHA VEDĀNTĀCHĀRYA.
Ānandavṛindāvanachampū. KAVIKARṆAPŪRA.
Bhāgīrathīchampū. ACHYUTA ŚARMĀ MODAKA.
Bhāratachampū. ANANTA BHAṬṬA, *the Poet.*
Bhojachampū. BHOJARĀJA.
Birudāvalī. RAGHUDEVA SARASVATĪ.
Champūbhārata. MĀNAVEDA.
Champūrāmāyaṇa. BHOJARĀJA.
——— GARAḶAPURĪŚA ŚĀSTRĪ.
Chandanachampū. SADĀŚIVA MIŚRA.
Godāpariṇaya. KEŚAVA KAVI.
Jīvandharachampū. HARIŚCHANDRA, *Jain Poet.*
Kiśorachandrānanda. BALADEVA RATHA KAVISŪRYA.
Kuvalayāśvavilāsa. TRIVIKRAMA.
Prahlādachampū. VEṄKANNA KAVI.
Śambarāsuravijaya. BHADRĀDRIRĀMA ŚĀSTRĪ.
Sītākalyāṇa. RĀMASVĀMĪ ŚĀSTRĪ, *Guṇḍu.*
Śrīkṛishṇarājodaya. GĪTĀCHĀRYA.
Śrīnivāsa[vilāsa]champū. VEṄKAṬEŚA.
Subhadrāharaṇa. NĀRĀYAṆA BHAṬṬA.
Svāhāsudhākara [in Kâvyamâlâ (Anthology), 1887]. DURGĀPRASĀDA and KĀŚĪNĀTHA PĀṆḌURAṄGA PARAB.
Tyāgarājavijaya. YAJÑEŚA ŚARMĀ.
Udayacharitra. ŚAṄKARA PĀRAŚAVA.
Uttararāmacharitrachampū. VEṄKAṬĀRYA YAJVĀ.
Vajramukuṭimahotsavavarṇana. KṚISHṆAIYAṄGĀR.
Viśvaguṇādarśa. VEṄKAṬĀRYA YAJVĀ.

PROSODY AND METRE.

Chhandaḥsārahārāvalī. ĀNANDANĀTHA KAVĪNDRAŚEKHARA.
Chhandonukramaṇī. ŚAUNAKA.
Piṅgalachchhandaḥśāstra, or °sūtra. PIṄGALA ĀCHĀRYA.
Śrutabodha. KĀLIDĀSA.—*Supposititious Works.*
Suvṛittatilaka [in Kâvyamâlâ (Anthology), 1886]. DURGĀPRASĀDA and KĀŚĪNĀTHA PĀṆḌURAṄGA PARAB.
Vāṇībhūshaṇa. DĀMODARA MIŚRA.
Vṛittachandrikā. RĀMADAYĀLU KAVI.

RELIGION.

1. BUDDHISM.

(*See also* POETRY.—1. Religious Poems.—i. *Buddhist.*)

Ādikarmapradīpa. ANUPAMAVAJRA.
Amitābhasūtra. SUKHĀVATĪVYŪHA.
Amitāyur-dhyāna-sūtra [*in loco*].
Anuruddhaśataka. ANURUDDHA.
Bodhi[sattva]caryāvatāra. ŚĀNTIDEVA.
Bodhisattvāvadānakalpalatā. KSHEMENDRA.
Buddhacharita. AŚVAGHOSHA.
Caturāryasatyaparīkṣā. NĀGĀRJUNA.
Çikshāsamuccaya. ŚĀNTIDEVA.
Daibutsu Chōdai Darani. DHĀRAṆĪ.
Daizui-kiu Darani. DHĀRAṆĪ.
Divyāvadāna [*in loco*].
Fuh ting tsun shing ṭ'o lo ne. DHĀRAṆĪ.
Han-Fan Tsih-yao. K'ANG-HE.
Jātakamālā. ĀRYA ŚŪRA.
Jyotishkāvadāna. KSHEMENDRA.
Karuṇāpuṇḍarīka [*in loco*].
Lalitavistara [*in loco*].
Mādhyamikasūtra. NĀGĀRJUNA.
Mahāvyutpatti [*in loco*].
Maṇicūḍāvadāna. SVAYAMBHŪPURĀṆA.
Mañjuśrī-nāmasaṅgīti. MAÑJUŚRĪ.
Nyāyabindu [*in loco*].
Pañcakrama. NĀGĀRJUNA.
Pra*gñâ*-pâramitâ-h*ri*daya-sûtra. PRAJÑĀPĀRAMITĀ.
Prajñāpāramitā [*in loco*].
Rāṣṭrapālaparipṛcchā, or Rāṣṭrapālasūtra. RĀSHṬRAPĀLAPARIPṚICHCHHĀ.
Ratnamālā [*in loco*].
Sādhanas [*in loco*].
Samādhirājasūtra [*in loco*].
Samantabhadra-charyā-praṇidhānarāja. SAMANTABHADRA.
Shingon Shokiō Jōyōshiu. SHINGON.
Shiugen Jōyōshiu. SHIUGEN.
Subhāṣita-saṃgraha. SUBHĀSHITASAṄGRAHA.
Sukhāvatīvyūha [*in loco*].
Suvarṇaprabhā [*in loco*].
Svayambhūpurāṇa [*in loco*].
Tripiṭaka [*in loco*].
Vajracchedikâ Prajñâpâramitâ. VAJRACHCHHEDIKĀ.
Yuga Kwaju. YOGA.

2. CHRISTIANITY.

Christa-dharmanīti. BIBLE.

3. HINDUISM.

(*See also* POETRY.—1. Religious Poems.—ii. *Hindu.*)

(i.) *Vedic Saṃhitās and their Literature.*

Ābrahman. VEDAS. — Yajurveda. — *Taittirīyasaṃhitā.*
Agnishṭomasāmāni. VEDAS.—*Sāmaveda.*
Anuvākānukramaṇī. ŚAUNAKA.
Anuvākasūtrādhyāya. KĀTYĀYANA.
Arshānukramaṇī. ŚAUNAKA.
Ārsheyabrāhmaṇa. BRĀHMAṆAS.
Āśis-sāmāni. VEDAS.—*Sāmaveda.*
Atharvaveda. VEDAS.—*Atharvaveda.*
Ātreyisaṃhitā. VEDAS.—*Yajurveda.*
Avasānanirṇaya. ANANTADEVA, *son of Nāgadeva.*
Bhūsūkta. VEDAS.—Yajurveda.—*Taittirīyasaṃhitā.*

(ii.) *Ritual Works (Brāhmaṇas and Post-Vedic Writings).*

(*See also* LAW.)

(iii.) *Purāṇas.*

(iv.) *Miscellaneous Religious Works.*

(*See also* LAW.)

4. JAINISM.

(*See also* FICTION *and* POETRY.—1. Religious Poems.—(iii.) *Jain.*)

5. SIKH CHURCH.

6. THEISTIC CHURCHES (ĀRYA AND BRĀHMA SAMĀJ).

II. PALI LITERATURE.

2. NON-CANONICAL WORKS.

GRAMMAR AND LEXICOGRAPHY.

PROSODY AND RHETORIC.

HISTORY.

LAW.

POETRY.

DIVINATION.

III. PRAKRIT LITERATURE.

JAIN LITERATURE.

1. CANONICAL WORKS.

2. NON-CANONICAL WORKS.

OTHER PRAKRIT LITERATURE.